WRITING AS REVISION

Second Edition

Beth Alvarado
Barbara Cully
Michael Robinson

Cover art provided by the Kathryn Alvarado.

Printed in the United States of America

10 9 8 7 6

Please visit our web site at www.pearsoncustom.com

ISBN 0-536-66552-4

BA 995316

PEARSON CUSTOM PUBLISHING
75 Arlington Street, Suite 300, Boston, MA 02116
A Pearson Education Company

Acknowledgments for photos and illustrations

1. Cover photo and design. Kathryn Alvarado.
   Details from a cast bronze door on the Cathedral of the Sagrada Familia in Barcelona, Spain.
2. Chapter One: Writing as Re-Vision. Kathryn Alvarado.
   Black and white photograph of a page from the Moss Rose (autograph) Album of Elizabeth Corsa Harris, circa 1854. Coryell family archives.
3. Chapter Two: Rereading Hollywood. Daniel Cardis.
   Mixed media: pencil, marker, digital enhancement.
4. Chapter Three: Rereading Science. Kathryn Alvarado.
   "Limbo," black and white photograph. "Digital Limbo," a digital revision of "Limbo."
5. Chapter Four: Reconsidering Gender and Space. Kathryn Alvarado.
   Black and white photograph of tintype of Harris family children, circa 1870. Coryell family archives.
6. Chapter Five: Rereading Romance. Kathryn Alvarado.
   "Revising Degas," black and white photograph.
7. Chapter Six: Writing the Environment. Kathryn Alvarado.
   Black and white photograph.
8. Chapter Seven: Writing from the Borderlands. Kathryn Alvarado.
   Black and white photograph of San Xavier Mission, Tucson, Arizona.
9. Chapter Eight: Writing as Social Witness. Kathryn Alvarado.
   Mixed media: photograph, paint, gel medium.
10. Chapter Nine: Writing of Witness—Perspectives on the Vietnam War. Daniel Cardis. Digitally highlighted pencil sketch of the Tomb of Tu Doc, near Hue, Vietnam.
11. Chapter Ten: Writing of Witness—Perspectives on September 11, 2001. Daniel Cardis. New York City skyline, mixed media: pencil sketch, collaged paper, paint.

Kathryn Alvarado created, collected, and/or formatted all of the images for *Writing as Re-Vision* as part of an internship for Arizona International College, where she was a Liberal Studies major with an emphasis in photography. In addition to photographing public art for the Tucson Pima Arts Council, she has published one other cover photo and had her work displayed in two exhibits.

Daniel Cardis self-identifies as a redneck, hillbilly mixed media artist from West Virginia. Although he's been known to ride some of the best half pipes in the nation, he currently resides in Incline Village, Nevada where he does custom woodworking to support his snowboarding habit.

Re-vision—the act of looking back, of seeing with fresh eyes, of entering an old text from a new critical direction—is more . . . than a chapter in cultural history: it is an act of survival.

—Adrienne Rich

—toward the end, only revision mattered: to look again, more deeply, harder, clearer, the one redemption granted us to ask.

—Jane Hirshfield

Writing As Revision

Editors: Beth Alvarado, Barbara Cully, and Michael Robinson

Preface to Instructors

Peter Elbow in his essay "The War between Reading and Writing—And How to End It" argues that one of the main difficulties in teaching composition stems from the fact that "reading has dominance over writing in the academic or school culture" (5). For instance, in English classes in high schools, "students spend less than three percent" of their time writing, and in most college courses, "reading is more central than writing" (10). Still, Elbow believes that we can "create a better balance and relationship between reading and writing. To do so," he argues, "we will need to give more emphasis to writing in our teaching and our curricular structures and use writing in more imaginative ways. When we achieve this productive balance, even reading will benefit" (5). Our task, then, is to shift the emphasis from reading towards writing in order to create a balance between the two.

We have designed *Writing as Revision* to facilitate this shift in emphasis. First of all, the various chapter introductions recognize, and encourage students to see, that reading and writing are reciprocal processes—when we read a text we are "writing our own reading" of it; in writing, we are re-reading; we must re-read and re-envision our own texts in order to effectively write them. We want to encourage students to practice this kind of active reading by keeping a writer's journal where they can have a running dialog with the texts. Not only should the writer's journal give them a place where they can begin a close reading of the texts they might analyze for their papers, but it should be a place where they feel free to respond, react, question, agree, disagree—and then inquire into their own responses and the assumptions behind them.

Along with our chapter editors, we have made the selections in these chapters with an eye towards engendering this process of inquiry. Janice Lauer, in her article "Writing as Inquiry: Some Questions for Teachers," (Chapter One) defines inquiry in several ways. First of all, it is "the ability to go beyond the known" and its goal is "the discovery of insight"—to create knowledge rather than to acquire it. She points out that "these views of writing as epistemic suggest that when students raise meaningful questions about incongruities in their own worlds, they gain genuine motivation and direction for writing, and that when students discover new understandings through writing, the writing becomes valuable to them and worth sharing with readers." The question, then, for teachers of writing is how can we create conditions conducive to inquiry, where students become active learners who use reading and writing as tools for discovery?

Drawing on her research in philosophy and psychology, Lauer suggests that the catalyst for inquiry is disequilibrium or "cognitive dissonance," a state which

> springs from the perception of a gap between a current set of beliefs or values and some new experience or idea that seems to violate or confound those beliefs. This clash engenders puzzlement, curiosity, a sense of enigma, sometimes of wonder, a pressure to restore equilibrium. While some people suppress such tension, the inquirer, the learner, strives to resolve it by searching for new understanding, by going beyond the known.

Our first assumption, then, is that if we present students with texts that challenge their assumptions, that present them with a new experience or with a novel way of seeing a familiar topic, we can motivate them to explore the text and their responses to it. Our second assumption is that we are *not* teaching what the text "means." In other words, we are not teaching them to read the text the way that we might read it or in the way that others have read it. This is not a literature class. Rather, we're presenting them with ways to engage with the texts themselves—through writing and therefore through re-reading and re-writing. As Gerald Graff might say, we're introducing students to controversies that texts are inherently a part of. We could say that this book presumes an activist pedagogy, and it does, if our definition of activist is to activate our students to think critically, to re-see, to revise, and even to reaffirm. Our goal, then, is not that students come away from the text changed, but that they come away more aware of complexities and challenged to enter the conversation. The ultimate goal, of course, is that their inquiry will result in writing that clearly articulates their own new understandings.

As you will see from the Table of Contents, many of the chapter titles—"Rereading Science," "Reconsidering Gender and Space"—suggest a cultural studies approach or a "revision process" which Adrienne Rich defines as "the act of looking back, of seeing with fresh eyes, of entering an old text from a new critical direction." Each chapter introduction sets up central concepts that can be used by the instructor as critical lenses students can use to approach the texts; further, these concepts will enable students to see connections among texts and thus facilitate their movement from analysis to synthesis as the course progresses. The concepts are not meant to limit the ways the text might be read, but instead to provide an entry point for reading and writing. In the introductions, the chapter editors also suggest ways that the readings of the chapter interrogate and/or reflect the central theme of the chapter.

Just as we believe that readings that challenge students' assumptions can motivate their process of inquiry, we also believe that teaching a number of short interrelated texts can help balance the reading and writing in the classroom. First of all, this approach can allow students more time for the incubation and exploration of their ideas and give the teacher more time to help them with development and arrangement. According to Lonergan, the process of inquiry is "cumulative and organic" or recursive in nature: "later stages presuppose and build on earlier ones" (as cited in Lauer). For this reason, each of the chapters is meant to constitute a 'course' or a 'unit' of related readings. Further, we have seen in teaching these materials that the chapters themselves create either a thematic or conceptual context for each author's work as well as for the students' own writing.

Along with the fiction and poetry, we have included quite a bit of creative non-fiction in order to facilitate the study of *writing,* not only because it provides students with various models of writing in the "real world"—rhetorical analysis, interpretive analysis, cultural critique, autobiography, and reader response—but also because it provides a cultural site for discussions of a cross-disciplinary nature. Of course, it is also entirely possible for you to choose readings from all or several of the chapters based on your own theme or approach. To facilitate this, we have annotated the entries in the Table of Contents, and provide the following synopsis of each chapter:

Chapter One: Writing as Revision is composed of essays that invite students to think about their relationship to literature and language and, specifically, to reading and writing. We placed these essays in the beginning of the book because they situate students in the course by introducing them to issues they may not have considered before: the connections between language, reading, writing and identity; the idea that whole cultural conversations surround texts; and the premise that writing can be used to explore ideas as well as express them. One or more of these essays could be used to introduce the course, to facilitate a discussion of these issues as they arise in the classroom, or to look back over the readings studied. Each piece also presents provocative ideas and controversies within academic and cultural discourses that invite students to hone their reading strategies and critical perspectives.

Chapter Two: Rereading Hollywood provides students with essays that situate "readings" of "texts" within particular genres or conventions; many of these essays "read" films as a way of "rereading" the cultures that produced them. For instance, some of them look at the ways that films play with genre or extend mythic or literary traditions; many of them examine the ways that films perpetuate or explode stereotypes. Because of this, these essays can be paired thematically with readings from other chapters; they also provide students with excellent models of rhetorical analysis and/or cultural critique. Of course, you may also choose to teach a few films as texts, and these essays will provide your students with the vocabulary they'll need to analyze them.

Chapters Three through Ten are designed to form a core of thematic readings for a course; some of the chapters contain a mix of genres and some concentrate on one or two. Along with our chapter editors, we have made the selections in these chapters specifically to present work by authors who transform and reclaim cultural materials through creative writing, revision, research, and critical analysis. The introductory essay at the beginning of each chapter can provide a theoretical lens through which to view the other readings.

Each of these chapters creates a cultural conversation that the students will be asked to analyze and join—through discussions in the classroom, through their own writing, and through their evaluation of one another's work. For instance, **Chapter Three: Rereading Science** contains a variety of essays, stories, and poems that "reread" our relationships to, and attitudes, about various sciences. **Chapter Four: Reconsidering Gender and Space** contains many canonical as well as contemporary works, all of which ask students to consider the relationships between the spaces they dwell within and the ways that those spaces define, reflect, and question gender. **Chapter Five: Rereading Romance** interrogates cultural ideas about romance and love, and contains a variety of narratives and poems that innovate those ideas. **Chapter Six: Writing the Environment** is composed of essays, fiction, and poems, many about the Southwest, that explore the connections between the environment and the narratives we tell ourselves about nature. **Chapter Seven: Writing from the Borderlands** invites students to go on a literary journey through a variety of texts about this region of the country and then to write about their own journeys.

All of the selections in **Chapters Eight through Ten: Writing of Witness** ask students to consider the ways in which various types of texts—editorials and email letters as well as literary texts—bear witness to our shared social lives and to catastrophic events such as war. **Chapter Eight: Writing as Social Witness** contains essays, stories, and poems about our everyday lives, showing the ways that witness can liberate as well as inform us. **Chapter Nine: Perspectives on the Vietnam War** contains essays, memoir, fiction, and poetry from both Vietnamese and American perspectives. These texts were all written in retrospect; the writers are looking back and bearing witness in order to make sense of horrific events for themselves. **Chapter Ten: Perspectives on September 11** situates students in the center of the current controversy, providing them with a variety of non-fiction texts that both witness and argue. Many of the pieces in this chapter challenge students (and teachers) to step out of their own perspectives and to use writing to inquire, witness, and reflect.

As you read the Table of Contents, you will note that some authors are included in more than one chapter and that in **Chapters Seven, Eight**, and **Nine**, several selections by one author are often included. We have made these selections hoping that these pieces will lend themselves to a discussion of a writer's project. In many of these cases, one author's work contains pieces from more than one genre in order to prompt students to consider how genre may influence a writer's rhetorical decisions.

Finally, the essays in **Chapter One**, the chapter introductions, and many of the essays within chapters are not only worthy of serious study but also provide students with models for their own writing. These essays, especially the chapter introductions, encourage students to look back over the texts they've read during the semester and to claim for themselves what these texts have come to mean within the context of their own lives, to claim their own cultural identities. Many of these essays can be read, or reread, at the end of the course as a "lens" for a reflective essay to bring students full-circle to where they are now encouraged to synthesize what they've learned in order to create their own knowledge and add to the cultural conversation they've been studying.

After all, the primary text in any composition course is the on-going text of the students' writing: students continually write—journal entries, drafts of papers, responses to one another's work—in order to explore and express their ideas about what they've learned and to make connections to their own contexts as readers. It is our hope that *Writing as Revision* will both invite them into the cultural conversation and support us in our efforts to create courses that balance reading and writing. These "fifty-fifty" courses, as Elbow calls them, "are probably the most natural and fruitful place for reading and writing mutually to enhance each other; courses where we go back and forth constantly between reading and writing and neither activity is felt as simply a handmaiden to the other one" (19).

Works Cited

Elbow, Peter. "The War Between Reading and Writing—And How to End It." *Rhetoric Review*. Vol 12, No. 1, Fall 1993. 5–24.

Lauer, Janice M. "Writing as Inquiry: Some Questions for Teachers." *Writing as Revision*. 2nd edition.

Rich, Adrienne. "When We Dead Awaken: Writing as Re-Vision." *Writing as Revision*. 2nd edition.

Acknowledgments

We would like to thank many people for their help in the preparation and revision of this anthology including Dr. Tilly Warnock, Dr. Anne-Marie Hall, and Dr. Larry Evers, who supported the second edition from the beginning, and Dr. Thomas P. Miller and Dr. Rudolph Troike who were instrumental in the creation of the first edition. Of course, we thank our chapter editors, Joanna Hearne, Debra White-Stanley, Amanda Brobbel, Jocelyn White, Damla Isik, Wendy Weise-Smith, Jillian Cantor, Leta McGaffey Sharp, Ute Haker, Sharon Wright-Harris, Deborah Margolis, Patty Malesh, and Josh Carney whose collaborative efforts and insight made for a range of readings otherwise not possible. We'd also like to acknowledge the chapter editors of the first edition, whose work provided a foundation for this edition: Mary Beth Callie, Jonathan Dryden, Alesia Garcia, James Livingston, and Maureen Salzer.

Several other people gave us valuable feedback, among them JoAnne Behling, Erec Toso, Susan Roberts, Frances Sjoberg, and Maggie Golston. We'd also like to thank the many graduate student teachers, teaching advisors, and adjunct lecturers who provided feedback on the first edition and suggested readings for the second. We'd like to thank our editor, Rachel Matus, who always gave us helpful advice and timely responses; our research assistant, Alicia

Alvarado, who spent many hours not only helping with research, typing, and copying, but who also read and gave us feedback on several selections; and our artists, Kathryn Alvarado and Daniel Cardis, who created artwork that reflected or interpreted the themes of each chapter. Finally, many thanks to Emily Chiles and Sharon Wright-Harris for their care in proofreading this book.

Beth Alvarado
Barbara Cully
Michael Robinson
Tucson, April 2002

Contents

Elizabeth

The light that shines from friendship's eye
In its pure native glows of Heaven
Can change life's stormy, wintry sky
To summers mild and quiet Even

2

Can pour a flood of pangless joy
In ev'ry breast by anguish riven
And turn from sorrows sad employ
To the sweet notes of praise to Heaven

3

May friendship pure as this be thine
To cheer the darkest hours of life
And cause the sun of peace to shine
Till earthly storms shall cease their strife

Montgomery June - 1854 L. B.

1

Writing as Re-Vision

Barbara Cully

Whenever we take note of the world in any form, be it by writing something down, typing it into a computer or recording on digital audio, digital video, or film, we create a text to which others may respond. These responses in turn are texts that add to the conversation—the cultural discourse—that is saved and reread and reviewed. All writing and research stem from these simple beginnings in the act of "taking note." For me, the human worth of such note taking is entwined with my memories of my cousin Dirk.

Dirk died at the age of 24 of a rattlesnake bite on Mt. Palomar near San Diego in 1970 when I was fifteen. Dirk left behind a journal on three cassette tapes that document his thoughts about whether to stay in college—whether to live in the city or the wilderness. They record his projections into the future regarding his girlfriend at the time, and some thoughts about conversations he had had with a close male friend while hiking the edges of the Grand Canyon. His tapes include an oral delivery of a paper he wrote on population control for one of his anthropology classes at San Diego State University, and a conversation he had with his grandmother while watching the TV broadcast of the Apollo 12 moon landing in the summer of 1969. I have listened to Dirk's tapes twice, once just as I turned 21, nearing the age he was when he died, and again later at the age of 39. One obvious irony, and oddity, is that Dirk's age has remained the same while I have reached and then surpassed his age. Despite his ability to hold still in death, what I hear in his voice—his ideas and his emotions—has changed with time. A paradox opens here: My cousin is unchanged yet growing younger as I listen to him from my own altering circumstances. Before he was a role model way ahead of me in life, going to college, reading Walt Whitman, studying anthropology, writing poems. Now he resembles more the students I teach, with their uncertainties about the future, their love of both technology and the wilderness, and their unsullied spiritual power. At each review the character of Dirk's record is transformed. What will Dirk's tapes sound like to my nieces and nephews as they approach the age I was when Dirk died? Is there anything in his reflections that will help them grapple with questions they will face when they become Dirk's age at 24?

In her essay "When We Dead Awaken: Writing as Re-Vision," Adrienne Rich defines revision as "the act of looking back, of seeing with fresh eyes, of entering an old text from a new critical direction . . . an act of survival." Like Dirk's tapes, every literary text provides an opportunity to listen anew from various vantage points and contexts. This philosophy of rereading and rewriting provides the overall conceptual framework for this anthology. The book is designed to invite you, as students and initiates, into the process of revision first as readers then, most importantly, as writers. It is designed to help us all—students and teachers, since we will explore these texts together—"see with fresh eyes," and enter texts, both familiar and alien, "from a new critical direction" that is of our own making. The chapters are set up to emphasize that rereading and revision are the keys to this making, that analysis can lead to the writing of new texts for new times and circumstances. At the center of this course is the premise that mastering these reading and research components of the writing process is essential for you as university students. These skills and habits of mind will help you achieve critical literacy, which is one of the primary goals of a composition course.

What we learn from classical rhetoric is that human discourse and the art of persuasion take place in realms of uncertainty where speculation, wonder, and attempts at understanding abound and clash and vie for ascendance. For this reason, my writing students and I have long taken comfort—and many lessons—from Janice Lauer's essay, "Writing as Inquiry," where she offers an alternative to argumentation, rebuttal, and debate. As a departure from and an extension of these modes of thought, she offers a scholarly pursuit of "going beyond the known." She explains that the "cognitive dissonance"—the disconnect between what we think we believe and what we think a text is asking us to believe—is resolved not in coming to final terms but in conducting open-ended research and meditation. Her methods allow us a chance to come into insight and to develop informed perspectives on texts of all kinds—texts about social and scientific conflicts, about the political and personal themes of love and war—the stuff of education and of life.

Gerald Graff, who writes under the title "Disliking Books at an Early Age," confesses that reading and writing assignments in school left him cold and unengaged. That is, until he understood that interpretations could be contested, that any reading of a text was in fact up for grabs, that in fact very few readers agree completely. His moment of insight came when he understood he had permission to read for the controversies and to enter the fray. He found then that he had energy for deciding where he stood and enthusiasm for demanding in forceful prose of his own that others prick up their ears and hear him out. His victory over boredom, his ability (like radar) to locate the dramas of the texts he scans and enters becomes a model for us. He challenges us to be the next ones to read and speak—*from* our generations and *to* the generations—about classic works like Mark Twain's *Huckleberry Finn* but also about headlines depicting suicide bombings in Israel, Israel's invasions of Palestinian homes, and the terrifying "breaking news" still full of ghosts and armed forces in the aftermath of September 11, 2001.

We humans love stories and we love music; that is why we fill the airways with a raucous popular culture that is full of stories, full of song. These manic/tender lyrics and twisting plots allow us to celebrate while we drive and shop, work and eat. They offer us tragicomic dramas that are larger than life. They offer us the glitz and buzz of lovers and heroes that remind us, thankfully, that life on the other hand is larger than us. I think it is for this reason that N. Scott Momaday asserts in his essay "The Man Made of Words" that it is through language that human beings create themselves. He says we become fully human when ideas are embodied in literature in its "broadest sense," by which he means texts of all kinds—songs, stories, poems, memoirs, movies, documentaries, and websites. As a Native American, his training is in knowing, through stories, what it is to be human across time. He states, "Only when he is embodied in an idea, and the idea is realized in language, can man take possession of himself."

Similarly, but out of radically different circumstances, author Amy Tan speaks of coming into personal power and identity through the acquistion of a second language. Her essay "Mother Tongue" narrates the story of her mother's struggle with English as a Chinese immigrant. We see her mother's humiliations in restaurants and her inability to get anyone at her bank to take her seriously. Ultimately, Tan offers us a vision (a revision?) of English for native speakers of it: She asserts that there are many Englishes, not just the familiar English we think we know, and that her Chinese mother is the author—whenever she picks up the phone or opens her mouth—of one of them.

What are the implications of ideas such as these for you? One of our authors in Chapter Eight, Audre Lorde, states plainly that she is a black lesbian feminist speaking in the face of a racist, patriarchal and anti-erotic society. It will be up to you as the student reader-writer to decide what you speak *as* and what you speak *in the face of*. In this, of course, Lorde is encouraging us to think about our content; whereas Tita French Baumlin, in her essay "A Good Crot Is Hard to Find," asks us to free our style, to experiment with language nonlinearly, ungrammatically, and in fragments:

> A crot is an old-fashioned word for "bit" or "fragment." Like a stanza is to poetry. Like a note is to music is a crot to my work. Free your crots. Let them stand alone. Long or short, let your crots be crots. Without connecting tissue. Like this . . . a crot without transition is like a new scent wafted on the breeze of the imagination. (Chapter One)

Baumlin, as the poet Charles Simic once put it, wants our mother tongue to send us out to play.

As you read this book, you will notice that you are being invited into a conversation that started long before you were born and that this conversation relies upon you in order to continue. My advice amid this complex, often challenging atmosphere is simply to take in as much as you can and to respond honestly in ways that imitate the conventional and unconventional strategies—of voice, analysis, story-telling, and research—these author-teachers have demonstrated for you. They are gathered here as at a table to speak to you. Think of it as a dinner party without food? Think of the ideas *as* the food? In any case, you are invited. I hope you arrive hungry with flowers in your hands.

Barbara Cully
Tucson, April 2002

Adrienne Rich

Adrienne Rich (b. 1929) is among the most prominent poets of the century. Her first book of poetry was a Yale Series of Younger Poets selection in 1951, the same year she graduated from Radcliffe College. Rich has since published many volumes of poetry and non-fiction, each formally and thematically distinct. Her work has been translated into eight languages, and she has received several honors and awards, including Guggenheim Fellowships (1952 and 1961), a National Book Award (1974) for Diving into the Wreck, *and a Fund for Human Dignity Award from the National Gay and Lesbian Task Force (1981). In her essay "When We Dead Awaken," we follow Rich on a tour, examining the emerging voice in her poetry as she parallels her experience with the emerging consciousness of women. This essay was first delivered, in slightly different form, as a speech. It was published, in 1976, in its present form.*

When We Dead Awaken: Writing as Re-Vision

The Modern Language Association is both marketplace and funeral parlor for the professional study of Western literature in North America. Like all gatherings of the professions, it has been and remains a "procession of the sons of educated men" (Virginia Woolf): a congeries of old-boys' networks, academicians rehearsing their numb canons in sessions dedicated to the literature of white males, junior scholars under the lash of "publish or perish" delivering papers in the bizarrely lit drawing-rooms of immense hotels: a ritual competition veering between cynicism and desperation.

However, in the interstices of these gentlemanly rites (or, in Mary Daly's words, on the boundaries of this patriarchal space), some feminist scholars, teachers, and graduate students, joined by feminist writers, editors, and publishers, have for a decade been creating more subversive occasions, challenging the sacredness of the gentlemanly canon, sharing the rediscovery of buried works by women, asking women's questions, bringing literary history and criticism back to life in both senses. The Commission on the Status of Women in the Profession was formed in 1969, and held its first public event in 1970. In 1971 the Commission asked Ellen Peck Killoh, Tillie Olsen, Elaine Reuben, and myself, with Elaine

---

Reprinted from *On Lies, Secrets, and Silence: Selected Prose, 1966–1978*, by Adrienne Rich (1979), W.W. Noorton & Company.

Hedges as moderator, to talk on "The Woman Writer in the Twentieth Century." The essay that follows was written for that forum, and later published, along with the other papers from the forum and workshops, in an issue of *College English* edited by Elaine Hedges ("Women Writing and Teaching," vol. 34, no. 1, October 1972.) With a few revisions, mainly updating, it was reprinted in *American Poets* in 1976, edited by William Heyen (New York: Bobbs-Merrill, 1976). That later text is the one published here.

The challenge flung by feminists at the accepted literary canon, at the methods of teaching it, and at the biased and astigmatic view of male "literary scholarship," has not diminished in the decade since the first Women's Forum: it has become broadened and intensified more recently by the challenges of black and lesbian feminists pointing out that feminist literary criticism itself has overlooked or held back from examining the work of black women and lesbians. The dynamic between a political vision and the demand for a fresh vision of literature is clear: without a growing feminist movement, the first inroads of feminist scholarship could not have been made, without the sharpening of a black feminist consciousness, black women's writing would have been left in limbo between misogynist black male critics and white feminists still struggling to unearth a white women's tradition: without an articulate lesbian/feminist movement, lesbian writing would still be lying in that closet where many of us used to sit reading forbidden books "in a bad light."

Much, much more is yet to be done; and university curricula have of course changed very little as a result of all this. What *is* changing is the availability of knowledge, of vital texts, the visible effects on women's lives of seeing, hearing our wordless or negated experience affirmed and pursued further in language.

Ibsen's *When We Dead Awaken* is a play about the use that the male artist and thinker—in the process of creating culture as we know it—has made of women, in his life and in his work; and about a woman's slow struggling awakening to the use to which her life has been put. Bernard Shaw wrote in 1900 of this play:

> [Ibsen] shows us that no degradation ever devised or permitted is as disastrous as this degradation; that through it women can die into luxuries for men and yet can kill them; that men and women are becoming conscious of this; and that what remains to be seen as perhaps the most interesting of all imminent social developments is what will happen "when we dead awaken."[1]

It's exhilarating to be alive in a time of awakening consciousness; it can also be confusing, disorienting, and painful. This awakening of dead or sleeping consciousness has already affected the lives of millions of women, even those who don't know it yet. It is also affecting the lives of men, even those who deny its claims upon them. The argument will go on whether an oppressive economic class system is responsible for the oppressive nature of male/female relations, or whether, in fact, patriarchy—the domination of males—is the original model of oppression on which all others are based. But in the last few years the women's movement has drawn inescapable and illuminating connections between our sexual lives and our political institutions. The sleepwalkers are coming awake, and for the first time this awakening has a collective reality; it is no longer such a lonely thing to open one's eyes.

Re-vision—the act of looking back, of seeing with fresh eyes, of entering an old text from a new critical direction—is for women more than a chapter in cultural history: it is an act of survival. Until we can understand the assumptions in which we are drenched we cannot know ourselves. And this drive to self-knowledge, for women, is more than a search for identity: it is part of our refusal of the self-destructiveness of male-dominated society. A radical critique of literature, feminist in its impulse, would take the work first of all as a clue to how we live, how we have been living, how we have been led to imagine ourselves, how our language has trapped as well as liberated us, how the very act of naming has been till now a male prerogative, and how we can begin to see and name—and therefore live—afresh. A change in the concept of sexual identity is essential if we are not going to see the old political order reassert itself in every new revolution. We need to know the writing of the past, and know it differently than we have ever known it; not to pass on a tradition but to break its hold over us.

For writers, and at this moment for women writers in particular, there is the challenge and promise of a whole new psychic geography to be explored. But there is also a difficult and dangerous walking on the ice, as we try to find language and images for a consciousness we are just coming into, and with little in the past to support us. I want to talk about some aspects of this difficulty and this danger.

Jane Harrison, the great classical anthropologist, wrote in 1914 in a letter to her friend Gilbert Murray:

> By the by, about "Women," it has bothered me often—why do women never want to write poetry about Man as a sex—why is Woman a dream and a terror to man and not the other way around? . . . Is it mere convention and propriety, or something deeper?[2]

I think Jane Harrison's question cuts deep into the myth-making tradition, the romantic tradition; deep into what women and men have been to each other; and deep into the psyche of the woman writer. Thinking about that question, I began thinking of the work of two twentieth-century women poets, Sylvia Plath and Diane Wakoski. It strikes me that in the work of both Man appears as, if not a dream, a fascination and a terror; and that the source of the fascination and the terror is, simply, Man's power—to dominate, tyrannize, choose, or reject the woman. The charisma of Man seems to come purely from his power over her and his control of the world by force, not from anything fertile or life-giving in him. And, in the work of both these poets, it is finally the woman's sense of *herself*—embattled, possessed—that gives the poetry its dynamic charge, its rhythms of struggle, need, will, and female energy. Until recently this female anger and this furious awareness of the Man's power over her were not available materials to the female poet, who tended to write of Love as the source of her suffering, and to view that victimization by Love as an almost inevitable fate. Or, like Marianne Moore and Elizabeth Bishop, she kept sexuality at a measured and chiseled distance in her poems.

One answer to Jane Harrison's question has to be that historically men and women have played very different parts in each others' lives. Where woman has been a luxury for man, and has served as the painter's model and the poet's muse, but also as comforter, nurse, cook, bearer of his seed, secretarial assistant, and copyist of manuscripts, man has played a quite different role for the female artist. Henry James repeats an incident which the writer Prosper Mérimée described, of how, while he was living with George Sand,

> he once opened his eyes, in the raw winter dawn, to see his companion, in a dressing-gown, on her knees before the domestic hearth, a candlestick beside her and a red *madras* round her head, making bravely, with her own hands the fire that was to enable her to sit down betimes to urgent pen and paper. The story represents him as having felt that the spectacle chilled his ardor and tried his taste; her appearance was unfortunate, her occupation an inconsequence, and her industry a reproof—the result of which was a lively irritation and an early rupture.[3]

The specter of this kind of male judgment, along with the misnaming and thwarting of her needs by a culture controlled by males, has created problems for the woman writer: problems of contact with herself, problems of language and style, problems of energy and survival.

In rereading Virginia Woolf's *A Room of One's Own* (1929) for the first time in some years, I was astonished at the sense of effort, of pains taken, of dogged tentativeness, in the tone of that essay. And I recognized that tone. I had heard it often enough, in myself and in other women. It is the tone of a woman almost in touch with her anger, who is determined not to appear angry, who is *willing* herself to be calm, detached, and even charming in a roomful of men where things have been said which are attacks on her very integrity. Virginia Woolf is addressing an audience of women, but she is acutely conscious—as she always was—of being overheard by men: by Morgan and Lytton and Maynard Keynes and for that matter by her father, Leslie Stephen.[4] She drew the language out into an exacerbated thread in her determination to have her own sensibility yet protect it from those masculine presences. Only at rare moments in that essay do you hear the passion in her voice; she was trying to sound as cool as Jane Austen, as Olympian as Shakespeare, because that is the way the men of the culture thought a writer should sound.

No male writer has written primarily or even largely for women, or with the sense of women's criticism as a consideration when he chooses his materials, his theme, his language. But to a lesser or greater extent, every woman writer has written for men even when, like Virginia Woolf, she was supposed to be addressing women. If we have come to the point when this balance might begin to change, when women can stop being haunted, not only by "convention and propriety" but by internalized fears of being and saying themselves, then it is an extraordinary moment for the woman writer—and reader.

I have hesitated to do what I am going to do now, which is to use myself as an illustration. For one thing, it's a lot easier and less dangerous to talk about other women writers. But there is something else. Like Virginia Woolf, I am aware of the women who are not with us here because they are washing the dishes and looking after the children. Nearly fifty years after she spoke, that fact remains largely unchanged. And I am thinking also of women whom she left out of the picture altogether—women who are washing other people's dishes and caring for other people's children, not to mention women who went on the streets last night in order to feed their children. We seem to be special women here, we have liked to think of ourselves as special, and we have known that men would tolerate, even romanticize us as special, as long as our words and actions didn't threaten their privilege of tolerating or rejecting us and our work according to *their* ideas of what a special woman ought to be. An important insight of the radical women's movement has been how divisive and how ultimately destructive is this myth of the special woman, who is also the token woman. Every one of us here in this room has had great luck—we are teachers, writers, academicians; our own gifts could not have been enough, for we all know women whose gifts are buried or aborted. Our struggles can have meaning and our privileges—however precarious under patriarchy—can be justified only if they can help to change the lives of women whose gifts—and whose very being—continue to be thwarted and silenced.

My own luck was being born white and middle-class in a house full of books, with a father who encouraged me to read and write. So for about twenty years I wrote for a particular man, who criticized and praised me and made me feel I was indeed "special." The obverse side of this, of course, was that I tried for a long time to please him, or rather, not to displease him. And then of course there were other men—writers, teachers—the Man, who was not a terror or a dream but a literary master and a master in other ways less easy to acknowledge. And there were all those poems about women, written by men: it seemed to be a given that men wrote poems and women frequently inhabited them. These women were almost always beautiful, but threatened with the loss of beauty, the loss of youth—the fate worse than death. Or, they were beautiful and died young, like Lucy and Lenore. Or, the woman was like Maud Gonne, cruel and disastrously mistaken, and the poem reproached her because she had refused to become a luxury for the poet.

A lot is being said today about the influence that the myths and images of women have on all of us who are products of culture. I think it has been a peculiar confusion to the girl or woman who tries to write because she is peculiarly susceptible to language. She goes to poetry or fiction looking for *her* way of being in the world, since she too has been putting words and images together; she is looking eagerly for guides, maps, possibilities; and over and over in the "words' masculine persuasive force" of literature she comes up against something that negates everything she is about: she meets the image of Woman in books written by men. She finds a terror and a dream, she finds a beautiful pale face, she finds La Belle Dame Sans Merci, she finds Juliet or Tess or Salomé, but precisely what she does not find is that absorbed, drudging, puzzled, sometimes inspired creature, herself, who sits at a desk trying to put words together.

So what does she do? What did I do? I read the older women poets with their peculiar keenness and ambivalence: Sappho, Christina Rossetti, Emily Dickinson, Elinor Wylie, Edna Millay, H. D. I discovered that the woman poet most admired at the time (by men) was Marianne Moore, who was maidenly, elegant, intellectual, discreet. But even in reading these women I was looking in them for the same things I had found in the poetry of men, because I wanted women poets to be the equals of men, and to be equal was still confused with sounding the same.

I know that my style was formed first by male poets: by the men I was reading as an undergraduate—Frost, Dylan Thomas, Donne, Auden, MacNiece, Stevens, Yeats. What I chiefly learned from them was craft.[5] But poems are like dreams: in them you put what you don't know you know. Looking back at poems I wrote before I was twenty-one, I'm startled because beneath the conscious craft are glimpses of the split I even then experienced between the girl who wrote poems, who defined herself in writing poems, and the girl who was to define herself by her relationships with men. "Aunt Jennifer's Tigers" (1951), written while I was a student, looks with deliberate detachment at this split.[6]

> Aunt Jennifer's tigers stride across a screen,
> Bright topaz denizens of a world of green.
> They do not fear the men beneath the tree;
> They pace in sleek chivalric certainty.
>
> Aunt Jennifer's fingers fluttering through her wool
> Find even the ivory needle hard to pull.
> The massive weight of Uncle's wedding band
> Sits heavily upon Aunt Jennifer's hand.
>
> When Aunt is dead, her terrified hands will lie
> Still ringed with ordeals she was mastered by.
> The tigers in the panel that she made
> Will go on striding, proud and unafraid.

In writing this poem, composed and apparently cool as it is, I thought I was creating a portrait of an imaginary woman. But this woman suffers from the opposition of her imagination, worked out in tapestry, and her life-style, "ringed with ordeals she was mastered by." It was important to me that Aunt Jennifer was a person as distinct from myself as possible—distanced by the formalism of the poem, by its objective, observant tone—even by putting the woman in a different generation.

In those years formalism was part of the strategy—like asbestos gloves, it allowed me to handle materials I couldn't pick up bare-handed. A later strategy was to use the persona of a man, as I did in "The Loser" (1958):

> *A man thinks of the woman he once loved: first, after the wedding, and then nearly a decade later.*

I

I kissed you, bride and lost, and went
home from that bourgeois sacrament,
your cheek still tasting cold upon
my lips that gave you benison
with all the swagger that they knew—
as losers somehow learn to do.

Your wedding made my eyes ache; soon
the world would be worse off for one
more golden apple dropped to ground
without the least protesting sound,
and you would windfall lie, and we
forget your shimmer on the tree.

Beauty is always wasted: if
not Mignon's song sung to the deaf,
at all events to the unmoved.
A face like yours cannot be loved
long or seriously enough.
Almost, we seem to hold it off.

II

Well, you are tougher than I thought.
Now when the wash with ice hangs taut
this morning of St. Valentine,
I see you strip the squeaking line,
your body weighed against the load,
and all my groans can do no good.

Because you are still beautiful,
though squared and stiffened by the pull
of what nine windy years have done.
You have three daughters, lost a son.
I see all your intelligence
flung into that unwearied stance.

My envy is of no avail.
I turn my head and wish him well
who chafed your beauty into use
and lives forever in a house
lit by the friction of your mind.
You stagger in against the wind.

I finished college, published my first book by a fluke, as it seemed to me, and broke off a love affair. I took a job, lived alone, went on writing, fell in love. I was young, full of energy, and the book seemed to mean that others agreed I was a poet. Because I was also determined to prove that as a woman poet I could also have what was then defined as a "full" woman's life, I plunged in my early twenties into marriage and had three children before I was thirty. There was nothing overt in the environment to warn me: these were the fifties, and in reaction to the earlier wave of feminism, middle-class women were making careers of domestic perfection, working to send their husbands through professional schools, then retiring to raise large families. People were moving out to the suburbs, technology was going to be the answer to everything, even sex; the family was in its glory. Life was extremely private; women were isolated from each other by the loyalties of marriage. I have a sense that women didn't talk to each other much in the fifties—not about their secret emptinesses, their frustrations. I went on trying to write; my second book and first child appeared in the same month. But by the time that the book came out I was already dissatisfied with those poems, which seemed to me mere exercises for poems I hadn't written. The book was praised, however, for its "gracefulness"; I had a marriage and a child. If there were doubts, if there were periods of null depression or active despairing, these could only mean that I was ungrateful, insatiable, perhaps a monster.

About the time my third child was born, I felt that I had either to consider myself a failed woman and a failed poet, or to try to find some synthesis by which to understand what was happening to me. What frightened me most was the sense of drift, of being pulled along on a current which called itself my destiny, but in which I seemed to be losing touch with whoever I had been, with the girl who had experienced her own will and energy almost ecstatically at times, walking around a city or riding a train at night or typing in a student room. In a poem about my grandmother I wrote (of myself): "A young girl, thought sleeping, is certified dead" ("Halfway"). I was writing very little, partly from fatigue, that female fatigue of suppressed anger and loss of contact with my own being; partly from the discontinuity of female life with its attention to small chores, errands, work that others constantly undo, small children's constant needs. What I did write was unconvincing to me; my anger and frustration were hard to acknowledge in or out of poems because in fact I cared a great deal about my husband and my children. Trying to look back and understand that time I have tried to analyze the real nature of the conflict. Most, if not all, human lives are full of fantasy—passive day-dreaming which need not be acted on. But to write poetry or fiction, or even to think well, is not to fantasize, or to put fantasies on paper. For a poem to coalesce, for a character or an action to take shape, there has to be an imaginative transformation of reality which is in no way passive. And a certain freedom of the mind is needed—freedom to press on, to enter the currents of your thought like a glider pilot, knowing that your motion can be sustained, that the buoyancy of your attention will not be suddenly snatched away. Moreover, if the imagination is to transcend and transform experience it has to question, to challenge, to conceive of alternatives, perhaps to the very life you are living at that moment. You have to be free to play around with the notion that day might be night, love might be hate; nothing can be too sacred for the imagination to turn into its opposite or to call experimentally by another name. For writing is re-naming. Now, to be maternally with small children all day in the old way, to be with a man in the old way of marriage, requires a holding-back, a putting-aside of that imaginative activity, and demands instead a kind of conservatism. I want to make it clear that I am *not* saying that in order to write well, or think well, it is necessary to become unavailable to others, or to become a devouring ego. This has been the myth of the masculine artist and thinker; and I do not accept it. But to be a female human being trying to fulfill traditional female functions in a traditional way *is* in direct conflict with the subversive function of the imagination. The word traditional is important here. There must be ways, and we will be finding out more and more about them, in which the energy of creating and the energy of relation can be united. But in those years I always felt the conflict as a failure of love in myself. I had thought I was choosing a full life: the life available to most men, in which sexuality, work, and parenthood could coexist. But I felt, at twenty-nine, guilt toward the people closest to me, and guilty toward my own being.

I wanted, then, more than anything, the one thing of which there was never enough: time to think, time to write. The fifties and early sixties were years of rapid revelations: the sit-ins and marches in the South, the Bay of Pigs, the early anti-war movement, raised large questions—questions for which the masculine world of the academy around me seemed to have expert and fluent answers. But I needed to think for myself—about pacifism and dissent and violence, about poetry and society, and about my own relationship to all these things. For about ten years I was reading in fierce snatches, scribbling in notebooks, writing poetry in fragments; I was looking desperately for clues, because if there were no clues then I thought I might be insane. I wrote in a notebook about this time:

> Paralyzed by the sense that there exists a mesh of relationships—e.g., between my anger at the children, my sensual life, pacifism, sex (I mean sex in its broadest significance, not merely sexual desire)—an interconnectedness which, if I could see it, make it valid, would give me back myself, make it possible to function lucidly and passionately. Yet I grope in and out among these dark webs.

I think I began at this point to feel that politics was not something "out there" but something "in here" and of the essence of my condition.

In the late fifties I was able to write, for the first time, directly about experiencing myself as a woman. The poem was jotted in fragments during children's naps, brief hours in a library, or at 3:00 A.M. after rising with a wakeful child. I despaired of doing any continuous work at this time. Yet I began to feel that my fragments and scraps had a common consciousness and a common theme, one which I would have been very unwilling to put on paper at an earlier time because I had been taught that poetry should be "universal," which meant, of course, non-female. Until then I had tried very much *not* to identify myself as a female poet. Over two years I wrote a ten-part poem called "Snapshots of a Daughter-in-Law" (1958–1960), in a longer, looser mode than I'd ever trusted myself with before. It was an extraordinary relief to write that poem. It strikes me now as too literary, too dependent on allusion; I hadn't found the courage yet to do without authorities, or even to use the pronoun "I"—the woman in the poem is always "she." One section of it, No. 2, concerns a woman who thinks she is going mad; she is haunted by voices telling her to resist and rebel, voices which she can hear but not obey.

2.

Banging the coffee-pot into the sink
she hears the angels chiding, and looks out
past the raked gardens to the sloppy sky.
Only a week since They said: *Have no patience.*

The next time it was: *Be insatiable.*
Then: *Save yourself; others cannot save.*
Sometimes she's let the tapstream scald her arm,
a match burn to her thumbnail,

or held her hand above the kettle's snout
right in the woolly steam. They are probably angels,
since nothing hurts her anymore, except
each morning's grit blowing into her eyes.

The poem "Orion," written five years later, is a poem of reconnection with a part of myself I had felt I was losing—the active principle, the energetic imagination, the "half-brother" whom I projected, as I had for many years, into the constellation Orion. It's no accident that the words "cold and egotistical" appear in this poem, and they applied to myself.

Far back when I went zig-zagging
through tamarack pastures
you were my genius, you
my cast-iron Viking, my helmed
lion-heart king in prison.
Years later now you're young

my fierce half-brother, staring
down from that simplified west
your breast open, your belt dragged down
by an old-fashioned thing, a sword
the last bravado you won't give over
though it weighs you down as you stride

and the stars in it are dim
and maybe have stopped burning.
But you burn, and I know it;
as I throw back my head to take you in
an old transfusion happens again:
divine astronomy is nothing to it.

Indoors I bruise and blunder,
break faith, leave ill enough
alone, a dead child born in the dark.
Night cracks up over the chimney,
pieces of time, frozen geodes
come showering down in the grate.

A man reaches behind my eyes
and finds them empty
a woman's head turns away
from my head in the mirror
children are dying my death
and eating crumbs of my life.

Pity is not your forte.
Calmly you ache up there
pinned aloft in your crow's nest,
my speechless pirate!
You take it all for granted
and when I look you back

it's with a starlike eye
shooting its cold and egotistical spear
where it can do least damage.
Breathe deep! No hurt, no pardon
out here in the cold with you
you with your back to the wall.

The choice still seemed to be between "love"—womanly, maternal love, altruistic love—a love defined and ruled by the weight of an entire culture; and egotism—a force directed by men into creation, achievement, ambition, often at the expense of others, but justifiably so. For weren't they men, and wasn't that their destiny as womanly, selfless love was ours? We know now that the alternatives are false ones—that the word "love" is itself in need of revision.

There is a companion poem to "Orion," written three years later, in which at last the woman in the poem and the woman writing the poem become the same person. It is called "Planetarium," and it was written after a visit to a real planetarium, where I read an account of the work of Caroline Herschel, the astronomer, who worked with her brother William, but whose name remained obscure as his did not.

Thinking of Caroline Herschel, 1750–1848, astronomer, sister of William; and others

A woman in the shape of a monster
a monster in the shape of a woman
the skies are full of them

a woman "in the snow
among the Clocks and instruments
or measuring the ground with poles"

in her 98 years to discover
8 comets

she whom the moon rules
like us
levitating into the night sky
riding the polished lenses

Galaxies of women, there
doing penance for impetuousness
ribs chilled
in those spaces   of the mind

An eye,
    "virile, precise and absolutely certain"
    from the mad webs of Uranisborg
                                        encountering the NOVA

every impulse of light exploding
from the core
as life flies out of us

    Tycho whispering at last
    "Let me not seem to have lived in vain"

What we see, we see
and seeing is changing

the light that shrivels a mountain
and leaves a man alive

Heartbeat of the pulsar
heart sweating through my body

The radio impulse
pouring in from Taurus

    I am bombarded yet   I stand
I have been standing all my life in the
direct path of a battery of signals
the most accurately transmitted most
untranslateable language in the universe
I am a galactic cloud so deep   so involuted that a light wave could take 15
years to travel through me   And has
taken   I am an instrument in the shape
of a woman trying to translate pulsations
into images   for the relief of the body
and the reconstruction of the mind.

In closing I want to tell you about a dream I had last summer. I dreamed I was asked to read my poetry at a mass women's meeting, but when I began to read, what came out were the lyrics of a blues song. I share this dream with you because it seemed to me to say something about the problems and the future of the woman writer, and probably of women in general. The awakening of consciousness is not like the crossing of a frontier—one step and you are in another country. Much of woman's poetry has been of the nature of the blues song: a cry of pain, of victimization, or a lyric of seduction.[7] And today, much poetry by women—and prose for that matter—is charged with anger. I think we need to go through that anger, and we will betray our reality if we try, as Virginia Woolf was trying, for an objectivity, a detachment, that would make us sound more like Jane Austen or Shakespeare. We know more than Jane Austen or Shakespeare knew: more than Jane Austen because our lives are more complex, more than Shakespeare because we know more about the lives of women—Jane Austen and Virginia Woolf included.

Both the victimization and the anger experienced by women are real, and have real sources, everywhere in the environment, built into society, language, the structures of thought. They will go on being tapped and explored by poets, among others. We can neither deny them, nor will we rest there. A new generation of women poets is already working out of the psychic energy released when women begin to move out towards what the feminist philosopher Mary Daly has described as the "new space" on the boundaries of patriarchy.[8] Women are speaking to and of women in these poems, out of a newly released courage to name, to love each other, to share risk and grief and celebration.

To the eye of a feminist, the work Western male poets are now writing reveals a deep, fatalistic pessimism as to the possibilities of change, whether societal or personal, along with a familiar and threadbare use of women (and nature) as redemptive on the one hand, threatening on the other, and a new tide of phallocentric sadism and overt woman-hating which matches the sexual brutality of recent films. "Political" poetry by men remains stranded amid the struggles for power among male groups; in condemning U.S. imperialism or the Chilean junta the poet can claim to speak for the oppressed while remaining, as male, part of a system of sexual oppression. The enemy is always outside the self, the struggle somewhere else. The mood of isolation, self-pity, and self-imitation that pervades "nonpolitical" poetry suggests that a profound change in masculine consciousness will have to precede any new male poetic—or other—inspiration. The creative energy of patriarchy is fast running out; what remains is its self-generating energy for destruction. As women, we have our work cut out for us.

Notes

1. G. B. Shaw, *The Quintessence of Ibsenism* (New York: Hill & Wang, 1922), p. 139.
2. J. G. Stewart, *Jane Ellen Harrison: A Portrait from Letters* (London: Merlin, 1959), p. 140.
3. Henry James, "Notes on Novelists," in *Selected Literary Criticism of Henry James,* Morris Shapira, ed. (London: Heinemann, 1963), pp. 157–58.
4. A. R., 1978: This intuition of mine was corroborated when, early in 1978 I read the correspondence between Woolf and Dame Ethel Smyth (Henry W. and Albert A. Berg Collection, The New York Public Library, Astor, Lenox and Tilden Foundations); in a letter dated June 8, 1933, Woolf speaks of having kept her own personality out of *A Room of One's Own* lest she not be

taken seriously: ". . . how personal, so will they say, rubbing their hands with glee, women always are; *I even hear them as I write.*" (Italics mine.)

5. A. R., 1978: Yet I spent months, at sixteen, memorizing and writing imitations of Millay's sonnets; and in notebooks of that period I find what are obviously attempts to imitate Dickinson's metrics and verbal compression. I knew H. D. only through anthologized lyrics; her epic poetry was not then available to me.
6. A. R., 1978: Texts of poetry quoted herein can be found in A. R., *Poems Selected and New: 1950–1974* (New York: Norton, 1975).
7. A. R., 1978: When I dreamed that dream, was I wholly ignorant of the tradition of Bessie Smith and other women's blues lyrics which transcended victimization to sing of resistance and independence?
8. Mary Daly, *Beyond God the Father: Towards a Philosophy of Women's Liberation* (Boston: Beacon, 1971), pp. 40–41.

Janice M. Lauer

Janice M. Lauer is a Professor of Rhetoric and the co-author of the book Four Worlds of Writing. *Her essay "Writing as Inquiry: Some Questions for Teachers" demonstrates how her interest in interdisciplinary studies has influenced the way she thinks about and teaches writing. It was first published in February 1982 in* College Composition and Communication, *a journal whose primary audience consists of teachers in Composition and Rhetoric.*

Writing as Inquiry: Some Questions for Teachers

In many colleges and universities, committees are reviewing their core curricula, searching for alternatives to the systems of distribution installed in the sixties.[1] Some institutions have returned to required courses to guarantee a broad exposure to the humanities, social sciences, and natural sciences. Others are beginning to view the goal of liberal education as the development of powers, arts, and skills.[2] Among the powers being considered for this kind of core is that of inquiry, the ability to go beyond the known. Its advocates argue that well-educated persons should be able to add to the world's store of knowledge. Its opponents contend that basic literacy or acquisition of the known has greater priority in a crowded undergraduate curriculum. They further object that including inquiry would require adding or revising courses, because most existing general education courses primarily try to expose students to the known, the best that has been thought and said in a given discipline. But these debates overlook the fact that most core curricula already possess courses with potential for helping students to develop the power of inquiry—the composition courses.

During the last twenty years, a number of theorists have pointed out this potential. Young, Becker, and Pike have shown how the practice of writing can prepare for the discovery of insight.[3] Emig has argued for the uniqueness of writing as a way of learning.[4] Odell has contended that the ability to write sensitively and thoughtfully presupposes the ability to formulate and solve problems.[5] Booth has stressed that the supreme purpose of rhetoric is not to "talk someone else into a preconceived view; rather it must be to engage in mutual inquiry or exploration," "to make each other in symbolic interchange."[6] Flower and Hayes have found that the writer's chief task is to define appropriately the rhetorical problem to be solved rather than simply to arrange ideas in some sort of order.[7] These views of writing as

Reprinted from *College Composition and Communication* 33, no. 1, (1982), by permission of the publisher.

epistemic suggest that when students raise meaningful questions about incongruities in their own worlds, they gain genuine motivation and direction for writing, and that when students discover new understandings through writing, the writing becomes valuable to them and worth sharing with readers.

But if we want to engage students in writing as inquiry, we must understand the nature of inquiry. My purpose, therefore, is to review some studies of the inquiry process by philosophers, psychologists, and rhetoricians, and to identify some questions raised by their work about the goals and methods of teaching composition. I do not intend to answer these questions here for two reasons. We have been inundated with articles and textbooks that thrust upon us answers about how to teach writing but that seldom reveal the underlying assumptions about composition, the questions to which these answers respond. Secondly, the questions that spring from an examination of inquiry admit of no single right answers, but rather can have multiple solutions[8] that instructors themselves can discover for their teaching if they deem the questions compelling.

One of the most thought-provoking studies of inquiry has been made by the philosopher Lonergan, who defines the process of inquiry in terms of its goal, the discovery of insight. He speaks of the act of grasping the unity of data, the act of finding a point of significance, the act of reaching a new understanding of old phenomena. He explains that insight comes as a release to the tension of inquiry; it comes suddenly and unexpectedly; and it is a function not of outside circumstances but of one's inner condition.[9] This description raises several questions about writing. What compels some writers to set out on a quest for insight while others remain content with the known? What creates the tension of inquiry for the writer? What "inner conditions" are conducive to insight?

Piaget contends that the catalyst is disequilibrium, a state in which a person's current ways of thinking or current knowledge cannot accommodate changes or new data within or outside him (or her).[10] Festinger calls it "cognitive dissonance," which springs from the perception of a gap between a current set of beliefs or values and some new experience or idea that seems to violate or confound those beliefs.[11] This clash engenders puzzlement, curiosity, a sense of enigma, sometimes of wonder, a pressure to restore equilibrium. While some people suppress such tension, the inquirer, the learner, strives to resolve it by searching for new understanding, by going beyond the known. Rothenburg, a psychiatrist studying great writers, painters, and scientists, describes this tension another way, reporting that many great breakthroughs stem from what he calls "janusian thinking," a perception of apparent contradiction in which two or more opposites or antitheses are entertained simultaneously as equally valid, operative, or true. He contends that such thinking is conscious.

> Janusian thinking lies at the heart of the most striking creative breakthroughs. Contrary to the romantic notions that creativity grows largely out of inspiration, the primary process thinking of dreams, or some unconscious source, I have found janusian thinking . . . to be a fully conscious, intentional, rational process.[12]

Lonergan agrees that inquiry begins with a conscious effort, an attempt to press beyond feelings of dissonance to careful articulations of what he calls the "known unknown" or to "the anticipation of intelligibility."[13] Young advises a writer to express the "known unknown" in the form of a question in order to guide inquiry. A well-formulated question gives direction because it tells the writer whether to seek a "why" or a "what," for example, and thus points out one avenue for exploration and excludes another.[14]

If inquiry begins with dissonance and well-articulated unknowns, further questions arise. How can we encourage students to become sensitive to the enigmas in their experience? How can we help awaken questioning minds often numbed by an educational system that rewards right answers? What kinds of writing assignments can we set to avoid trapping students in contexts so narrow or artificial that they preclude genuine puzzlement or curiosity? What strategies can we offer to guide students to state unknowns well?

An early study by Wallas characterizes the process of inquiry as undulating between conscious and unconscious activity. Good inquirers deliberately explore questions, guided by heuristic procedures that help them vary their perspectives, scan their memories, and create new associations. This conscious activity prepares the inquirer for incubation, the unconscious mulling from which illumination springs. Of course, although careful conscious exploration is conducive to insight, it does not guarantee it. But, if insight strikes, then an investigator must make a second type of deliberate effort, "verification," to test the insight.[15] Lonergan also identifies two kinds of conscious activity: 1) exploring data presented by the senses, aided by heuristic procedures, and 2) testing for certainty or probability.[16] Young proposes three tests to verify insight: Does it correspond with actual experience? Is it consistent with that fund of reliable information the writer has accumulated over the years? Is it useful in answering the writer's question?[17]

If good inquiry demands conscious exploration and verification, what kinds of heuristic procedures will best guide students in recalling what they already know, in gathering and examining data, and in stimulating their imaginations? What strategies will aid students to test their insights, to evaluate evidence, to criticize their tentative judgments? How can we pace our assignments and set deadlines so as to respect the importance of incubation?

Another feature of the process of inquiry, according to Lonergan, is its cumulative and organic nature: later stages presuppose and build on earlier ones.[18] A good articulation of the "known unknown" directs exploration. A thorough and imaginative exploration prepares for insight. Verification follows the discovery of insight. These phases can also be recursive. Exploration may lead the inquirer to reformulate the initial question or form a new one. Verification may require more exploration. Whatever the order, a reciprocity exists among the acts of inquiry, raising for us other questions about teaching. In what ways can our composition classes encourage students to experience for themselves this interaction: to discover the direction and motivation that well-stated questions provide for research, to realize the guidance that powerful heuristics offer the writer in preparing for insight, to appreciate the importance of incubation for illumination? How can we act as enablers, assisting students during these phases of inquiry, maintaining a delicate balance between abandoning them to the "mystery" of discovery and forcing them into a completely linear, mechanical series of operations? Lonergan points out that sometimes the process ends in "inverse insight," the realization that no understanding is possible at this time.[19] Do we allow for inverse insight, teaching students that risks and mistakes are integral to inquiry, that good investigations which end in inverse insight can become grist for exploratory discourse?

Answers to these questions will create a different pedagogy from that generated by concerns about how to help students avoid fragments or write comparison/contrast papers. This pedagogy will also be more difficult because it faces serious obstacles from outside the classroom. Booth points out an insidious one: the tendency of our culture to value objectivism and to dismiss—as mere belief without value—everything that is not verifiable fact. This attitude polarizes "fact" and value, ignoring probability, the spacious ground between objectivity and faith or feelings.[20] In such a culture, students find no encouragement to tackle the difficult search for unknowns or for good reasons to support probable judgments, even though most of the subjects they investigate inhabit the realm of probability in which Aristotle located rhetoric. A culture which extols certainty[21] rewards instead the mastery of verifiable information marshalled in support of existing judgments.

This cultural obstacle to inquiry is reinforced by two psychological blocks, analyzed by Lonergan: 1) the overdevelopment of common sense: the tendency to brush aside as irrelevant, if not silly, any question whose answer would not make an immediately palpable difference to the inquirer, and 2) the love of darkness, rooted in passions and biases that repress any new understanding that threatens a person's intellectual or emotional citadels.[22] Those afflicted by an overdevelopment of common sense see no point in discovering the significance of their own pasts, in searching for meanings new to them in literature or the other arts, in struggling for more reasonable judgments about public issues, in pursuing new understandings in intellectual fields. Those who love darkness fear the discovery of insight because it disrupts their complacency, racking them with growing pains, and inducing changes.

These powerful psychological and cultural obstacles pose more serious threats to developing writers than lack of syntactic maturity or poor control over conventions. In the face of such blocks, must we abandon any hope of teaching writing as inquiry? Or could not these very problems become catalysts to *our* own inquiry, creating the tension necessary to spark *our* explorations for insights about the teaching of composition itself—as inquiry?

Lonergan maintains that the spirit of inquiry flowers only if we learn how to learn, to find answers for ourselves.[23] The goal for Lonergan is to prepare a person who "intelligently generates and critically evaluates every scientific object, every incautious statement, every rigorously logical resting place that offers prematurely a home for the restless dynamism of human understanding."[24] Would not composition courses with such a goal stimulate students to become both better writers and more liberally educated people?

Notes

1. See Harry Levin's essay on Harvard's efforts, "Core, Canon, Curriculum," *College English,* 43 (April, 1981), 352–362.
2. For some discussions of this view see Paul Dressel, *College and University Curriculum* (Berkeley, CA: McCutchan, 1968); Sidney Hook, Paul Kurtz, and Miro Todorovich, eds. *The Philosophy of the Curriculum* (Buffalo, NY: Prometheus Books, 1975). Other sources are available from the Jossey-Bass Series in Higher Education (San Francisco).
3. Richard E. Young, Alton Becker, and Kenneth Pike, *Rhetoric: Discovery and Change* (New York: Harcourt Brace Jovanovich, 1970).
4. Janet Emig, "Writing as a Mode of Learning," *College Composition and Communication,* 28 (May, 1977), 122–28.
5. Lee Odell, "Piaget, Problem-Solving, and Freshman Composition," *College Composition and Communication,* 24 (February, 1973), 36–42.
6. Wayne Booth, *Modern Dogma and the Rhetoric of Assent* (Chicago: University of Chicago Press, 1974), p. 137.
7. Linda Flower and J. R. Hayes, "Problem-Solving Strategies and the Writing Process," *College English,* 39 (December, 1977), 499–61.
8. For one set of answers see Janice Lauer, Gene Montague, Andrea Lunsford, and Janet Emig, *Four Worlds of Writing* (New York: Harper and Row, 1981).
9. Bernard Lonergan, *Insight: A Study of Human Understanding,* 3rd ed. (New York: Philosophical Library, 1970), pp. 3–6.
10. Jean Piaget, *Six Psychological Studies* (New York: Vintage Press, 1968).
11. Leon Festinger, *A Theory of Cognitive Dissonance* (Stanford, CA: Stanford University Press, 1957).
12. Albert Rothenburg, "Creative Contradictions," *Psychology Today,* 13 (June, 1979), p. 55.
13. Lonergan, pp. 86–102; 390–396.
14. Young, Becker, and Pike, p. 92.
15. G. Wallas, *The Art of Thought* (New York: Harcourt Brace, 1926), 79–107.
16. Lonergan, pp. 272–274.
17. Young, Becker, and Pike, pp. 155–163.
18. Lonergan, p. 275.
19. Lonergan, pp. 19–25.
20. Booth, *passim,* especially chapter 1.
21. For a challenge to certainty see Michael Polanyi, *Personal Knowledge: Toward a Post-Critical Philosophy* (New York: Harper & Row, 1958).
22. Lonergan, pp. 173–206.
23. Lonergan, pp. 173–181.
24. Lonergan, p. 69.

Gerald Graff

Gerald Graff, born in Chicago in 1937, was educated in the public school system. He earned his B.A. from the University of Chicago and his Ph.D. from Stanford. His first books are iconoclastic, attacking the deficiencies of popular theory. Literature Against Itself: Literary Ideas in Modern Society *(1979), Graff's second book, is a rebuttal against structuralism and deconstruction. It is with his third book* Professing Literature: An Institutional History *(1987) that Graff becomes a national figure. In this book he addresses the hostility among professors of literature who stand their ground in contrasting schools of thought. Stacey D'Erasmo of the* Village Voice *notes that "Graff wants to move these struggles [between literary schools of thought] out of the convention and into the classroom." Graff is a co-founder of Teachers for a Democratic Culture, a Center-left coalition of scholars who are organized to combat conservative assault against the universities. The following essay originally appeared in the September/October 1992 issue of* Lingua Franca *and is reprinted in slightly different form in his book,* Beyond the Culture Wars: How Teaching the Conflicts Can Revitalize American Education *(1992). Graff comes to the conclusion that "reading books with comprehension, making arguments, writing papers, and making comments in a class discussion are social activities. They involve entering into a cultural or disciplinary conversation, a process not unlike initiation into a social club."*

Disliking Books at an Early Age

I like to think I have a certain advantage as a teacher of literature because when I was growing up I disliked and feared books. My youthful aversion to books showed a fine impartiality, extending across the whole spectrum of literature, history, philosophy, science, and what was known by then (the late 1940s) as social studies. But had I been forced to choose, I would have singled out literature and history as the reading I disliked most. Science at least had some discernible practical use, and you could have fun solving the problems in the textbooks with their clear-cut answers. Literature and history had no apparent application to my experience, and any boy in my school who had cultivated them—I can't recall one who did—would have marked himself as a sissy.

Reprinted from *Beyond the Culture Wars: How Teaching the Conflicts Can Revitalize American Education*, (1992), W.W. Norton & Company.

As a middle-class Jew growing up in an ethnically mixed Chicago neighborhood, I was already in danger of being beaten up daily by rougher working-class boys. Becoming a bookworm would only have given them a decisive reason for beating me up. Reading and studying were more permissible for girls, but they, too, had to be careful not to get too intellectual, lest they acquire the stigma of being "stuck up."

In *Lives on the Boundary,* a remarkable autobiography of the making of an English teacher, Mike Rose describes how the "pain and confusion" of his working-class youth made "school and knowledge" seem a saving alternative. Rose writes of feeling "freed, as if I were untying fetters," by his encounters with certain college teachers, who helped him recognize that "an engagement with ideas could foster competence and lead me out into the world." Coming at things from my middle-class perspective, however, I took for granted a freedom that school, knowledge, and engagement with ideas seemed only to threaten.

My father, a literate man, was frustrated by my refusal to read anything besides comic books, sports magazines, and the John R. Tunis and Clair Bee sports novels. I recall his once confining me to my room until I finished a book on the voyages of Magellan, but try as I might, I could do no better than stare bleakly at the pages. I could not, as we would later say, "relate to" Magellan or to any of the other books my father brought home—detective stories, tales of war and heroism, adventure stories with adolescent heroes (the Hardy Boys, *Hans Brinker,* or *The Silver Skates*), stories of scientific discovery (Paul de Kruif's *The Microbe Hunters*), books on current events. Nothing worked.

It was understood, however, that boys of my background would go to college and that once there we would get serious and buckle down. For some, "getting serious" meant pre-law, pre-med, or a major in business to prepare for taking over the family business. My family did not own a business, and law and medicine did not interest me, so I drifted by default into the nebulous but conveniently noncommittal territory of the liberal arts. I majored in English.

At this point the fear of being beaten up if I were caught having anything to do with books was replaced by the fear of flunking out of college if I did not learn to deal with them. But though I dutifully did my homework and made good grades (first at the University of Illinois, Chicago branch, then at the University of Chicago, from which I graduated in 1959), I continued to find "serious" reading painfully difficult and alien. My most vivid recollections of college reading are of assigned classics I failed to finish: *The Iliad* (in the Richmond Lattimore translation); *The Autobiography of Benvenuto Cellini,* a major disappointment after the paperback jacket's promise of "a lusty classic of Renaissance ribaldry"; E. M. Forster's *A Passage to India,* sixty agonizing pages of which I managed to slog through before giving up. Even Hemingway, Steinbeck, and Fitzgerald, whose contemporary world was said to be "close to my own experience," left me cold. I saw little there that did resemble my experience.

Even when I had done the assigned reading, I was often tongue-tied and embarrassed when called on. What was unclear to me was what I was supposed to *say* about literary works, and why. Had I been born a decade or two earlier, I might have come to college with the rudiments of a literate vocabulary for talking about culture that some people older than I acquired through family, high school, or church. As it was, "cultured" phrases seemed effete and sterile to me. When I was able to produce the kind of talk that was required in class, the intellectualism of it came out sounding stilted and hollow in my mouth. If *Cliffs Notes* and other such crib sheets for the distressed had yet come into existence, with their ready-to-copy summaries of widely taught literary works, I would have been an excellent customer. (As it was, I did avail myself of the primitive version then in existence called *Masterplots*.)

What first made literature, history, and other intellectual pursuits seem attractive to me was exposure to critical debates. There was no single conversion experience, but a gradual transformation over several years, extending into my first teaching positions, at the University of New Mexico and then Northwestern University. But one of the first sparks I remember was a controversy over *The Adventures of Huckleberry Finn* that arose in a course during my junior year in college. On first attempt, Twain's novel was just another assigned classic that I was too bored to finish. I could see little connection between my Chicago upbringing and Huck's pre-Civil War adventures with a runaway slave on a raft up the Mississippi.

My interest was aroused, however, when our instructor mentioned that the critics had disagreed over the merits of the last part of the novel. He quoted Ernest Hemingway's remark that "if you read [the novel] you must stop where the nigger Jim is stolen by the boys. This is the real end. The rest is cheating." According to this school of thought, the remainder of the book trivializes the quest for Jim's freedom that has motivated the story up to that point. This happens first when Jim becomes an object of Tom Sawyer's slapstick humor, then when it is revealed that unbeknownst to Huck, the reader, and himself, Jim has already been freed by his benevolent owner, so that the risk we have assumed Jim and Huck to be under all along has really been no risk at all.

Like the critics, our class divided over the question: Did Twain's ending vitiate the book's profound critique of racism, as Hemingway's charge of cheating implied? Cheating in my experience up to then was something students did, an unthinkable act for a famous author. It was a revelation to me that famous authors were capable not only of mistakes but of ones that even lowly undergraduates might be able to point out. When I chose to write my term paper on the dispute over the ending, my instructor suggested I look at several critics on the opposing sides—T. S. Eliot and Lionel Trilling, who defended the ending, and Leo Marx, who sided with Hemingway.

Reading the critics was like picking up where the class discussion had left off, and I gained confidence from recognizing that my classmates and I had had thoughts that, however stumbling our expression of them, were not too far from the thoughts of famous published critics. I went back to the novel again and to my surprise found myself rereading it with an excitement I had never felt before with a serious book. Having the controversy over the ending in mind, I now had some issues *to watch out for* as I read, issues that reshaped the way I read the earlier chapters as well as the later ones and focused my attention. And having issues to watch out for made it possible not only to concentrate, as I had not been able to do earlier, but to put myself into the text—to read with a sense of personal engagement that I had not felt before. Reading the novel with the voices of the critics running through my mind, I found myself thinking things that I might say about what I was reading, things that may have belonged partly to the critics but also now belonged to me. It was as if having a stock of things to look for and to say about a literary work had somehow made it possible for me to read one.

One of the critics had argued that what was at issue in the debate over *Huckleberry Finn* was not just the novel's value but its cultural significance: If *Huckleberry Finn* was contradictory or confused in its attitude toward race, then what did that say about the culture that had received the novel as one of its representative cultural documents and had made Twain a folk hero? This critic had also made the intriguing observation—I found out only later that it was a critical commonplace at the time—that judgments about the novel's aesthetic value could not be separated from judgments about its moral substance. I recall taking in both this critic's arguments and the cadence of the phrases in which they were couched; perhaps it would not be so bad after all to become the sort of person who talked about "cultural contradictions" and the "inseparability of form and content." Perhaps even mere literary-critical talk could give you a certain power in the real world. As the possibility dawned on me that reading and intellectual discussion might actually have something to do with my real life, I became less embarrassed about using intellectual formulas.

It was through exposure to such critical reading and discussion over a period of time that I came to catch the literary bug, eventually choosing the vocation of teaching. This was not the way it is supposed to happen. In the standard story of academic vocation that we like to tell ourselves, the germ is first planted by an early experience of literature itself. The future teacher is initially inspired by some primary experience of a great book and only subsequently acquires the secondary, derivative skills of critical discussion. A teacher may be involved in instilling this inspiration, but only a teacher who seemingly effaces himself or herself before the text. Any premature or excessive acquaintance with secondary critical discourse, and certainly with its sectarian debates, is thought to be a corrupting danger, causing one to lose touch with the primary passion for literature.

This is the charge leveled against the current generation of literature teachers, who are said to have become so obsessed with sophisticated critical theories that they have lost the passion they once had for literature itself. They have been seduced by professionalism, drawn away from a healthy absorption in literature to the sickly fascination with analysis and theory and to the selfish advancement of their careers.

This hostility to recent theory would not have been so powerful, however, if it were not overlaid on an older set of resentments that long predate the rise of deconstruction and poststructuralism, resentments at literature's having become an academic "field" to begin with. Today's attacks on literary theory are often really attacks on literary criticism, or at least on criticism of the intensely analytic kind that academics practice, which has always been suspected of coming between readers (and students) and the primary experience of literature itself. This resentment is rooted in anxieties about the increasing self-consciousness of modern life, which often leaves us feeling that we are never quite living but only endlessly talking about it, too often in some abstract professional vocabulary. The anxieties are expressed in our romantic literary tradition, which protests against the urban forms of sophistication that, it is believed, cause us to lose touch with the innocence of childhood and our creative impulses.

To those who have never reconciled themselves to the academicization of literature, the seeming overdevelopment of academic criticism with its obtrusive methodology and its endless disputes among interpretations and theories seems a betrayal not just of literature and the common reader but of the professor's own original passion for literature. In a recent letter to an intellectual journal one writer suggests that we should be concerned less about the oft-lamented common reader whom academic critics have deserted than about "the souls of the academics and literati themselves, who, as a result of social and professional pressures, have lost touch with the inner impulses that drew them to the world of books in the first place." What the writer of this letter cannot imagine is that someone might enter academic literary study because he actually *likes* thinking and talking in an analytical or theoretical way about books and that such a person might see his acceptance of "professional pressures" not as a betrayal of the "inner impulses" that drew him "to the world of books in the first place" but as a way to fulfill those impulses.

The standard story ascribes innocence to the primary experience of literature and sees the secondary experience of professional criticism as corrupting. In my case, however, things had evidently worked the other way around: I had to be corrupted first in order to experience innocence. It was only when I was introduced to a critical debate about *Huckleberry Finn* that my helplessness in the face of the novel abated and I could experience a personal reaction to it. Getting into immediate contact with the text was for me a curiously triangular business; I could not do it directly but needed a conversation of other readers to give me the issues and terms that made it possible to respond.

As I think back on it now, it was as if the critical conversation I needed had up to then been withheld from me, on the ground that it could only interfere with my direct access to literature itself. The assumption was that leaving me alone with literary texts themselves, uncontaminated by the interpretations and theories of professional critics, would enable me to get on the closest possible terms with those texts. But being alone with the texts only left me feeling bored and helpless, since I had no language with which to make them mine. On the one hand, I was being asked to speak a foreign language—literary criticism—while on the other hand, I was being protected from that language, presumably for my own safety.

The moral I draw from this experience is that our ability to read well depends more than we think on our ability to *talk well* about what we read. Our assumptions about what is "primary" and "secondary" in the reading process blind us to what actually goes on. Many literate people learned certain ways of talking about books so long ago that they have forgotten they ever had to learn them. These people therefore fail to understand the reading problems of the struggling students who have still not acquired a critical vocabulary.

The standard story of how we learn to read provides little help in dealing with such problems. Seeing criticism (and critical debate) as a distraction from the "primary" experience of literature itself, the standard story implies that the business of teaching is basically simple: Just put the student in front of a good book, provide teachers who are encouraging and helpful, and the rest presumably will take care of itself. The traditional maxim that sums up this view is that a good book "essentially teaches itself." The great teacher is one who knows how to let the book teach itself. And it is true that in the spell cast by such a teacher, it often *seems* as if the work is itself speaking directly to the student without intervention from the teacher's interpretations and theories. But this spell is an illusion. If books really taught themselves, there would be no reason to attend classes; students could simply stay home and read them on their own.

Nevertheless, the standard story remains seductive. Much of the appeal of Allan Bloom's *The Closing of the American Mind* lies in its eloquent restatement of the standard story, with its reassuringly simple view of reading and teaching: "a liberal education means reading certain generally recognized classic texts, just reading them, letting them dictate what the questions are and the method of approaching them—not forcing them into categories we make up, not treating them as historical products, but trying to read them as their authors wished them to be read." What has gone wrong, Bloom suggests, is that instead of letting the texts themselves dictate the questions we ask about them, a generation of overly professionalized teachers has elevated its own narcissistic interests over those of the author and the students. These teachers, as Bloom puts it, engage in "endless debates about methods—among them Freudian criticism, Marxist criticism, New Criticism, Structuralism and Deconstructionism, and many others, all of which have in common the premise that what Plato or Dante had to say about reality is unimportant."

It sounds so commonsensical that only a desiccated academic could disagree. What could be more obvious than the difference between "just" reading books, as ordinary readers have always done, and imposing theories and isms on books, as methodology-crazed academics do? The question, however, is whether anyone ever "just" reads a book the way Bloom describes. We need go no further than Bloom's own quoted statements to see that he himself does not practice the doctrine he preaches. When Bloom invokes the names of Plato and Dante, he does *not* let these authors dictate the questions that govern his discussion but "forces" them into categories he, Allan Bloom, with his twentieth-century preoccupations, has "made up." After all, what did Plato and Dante know about Freudians, Marxists, cultural relativists, and the other contemporary targets of Bloom's polemic? In using Plato and Dante to attack the intellectual and educational trends of his own time, Bloom is not reading these writers as they wished to be read but is *applying* them to a set of contexts they did not and could not have anticipated. This is not to say that Bloom is unfaithful to Plato's text, only that he does not passively take dictation from Plato's text but actively selects from it for his own purposes—just as he accuses theorists of doing.

The philosopher Richard Rorty has succinctly pointed out the trouble with Bloom's "just read the books" theory. Rorty acknowledges that interpreters are obliged "to give authors a run for their money," respecting "an author's way of talking and thinking, trying to put ourselves in her shoes." He argues, however, that "it is not clear how we can avoid forcing books into 'categories we make up. . . .'" We cannot help reading books, Rorty says, "with questions in mind—not questions dictated by the books—but questions we have previously, if vaguely, formulated." Rorty's point is not that reading is merely subjective but that it is inevitably *selective*. It is not that any reading of Plato is as good as any other but that even the most reliable reading has to select certain aspects of the text to emphasize, and the selection will be conditioned by the contingent situations in which the text is read. I would restate Rorty's point this way: As readers we are necessarily concerned with *both* the questions posed by the text and the questions we bring to it from our own differing interests and cultural backgrounds. Bloom thinks he can choose between "just reading" Plato and Dante and applying a "method" to them as do academic Freudians and Marxists. But Bloom's way of reading, which is influenced by his mentor the philosopher Leo Strauss, is as much a "method" as any other, bringing its special set of interests and principles of selection that are not dictated by Plato or Dante.

In teaching any text, one necessarily teaches an interpretation of it. This seems so obvious as to be hardly worth restating, but what follows from it is not obvious and is resisted violently by many who oppose the spread of theory. It follows that what literature teachers teach is not literature but criticism, or literature as it is filtered through a grid of analysis, interpretation, and theory. "Remarks are not literature," said Gertrude Stein in a now-celebrated observation, and Stein was right: Teachers cannot avoid interposing "remarks" between literature and their students—remarks, we hope, that illuminate the works and help our students take personal possession of them, but remarks nevertheless.

If teachers cannot avoid translating the literature they teach into some critical language or other, neither can students, for criticism is the language students are expected to speak and are punished for not speaking well. Inevitably the students who do well in school and college are those who learn to talk more or less like their teachers, who learn to produce something resembling intellectualspeak.

By what process do we imagine students will learn this language? The assumption seems to be that it will happen by a kind of osmosis, as students internalize the talk that goes on in class until they are able to produce a reasonable facsimile of it. However, as a recent textbook writer, Gordon Harvey, points out, not all students "can make this translation, since it requires that they intuit a whole set of intellectual moves and skills . . . too basic for experienced writers to notice themselves carrying out." The polite fiction that students will learn to make the "intellectual moves" by being in the presence of them for several hours a week is usually just that, a polite fiction.

Again, the problem is that what students are able to say about a text depends not just on the text but on their relation to a critical community of readers, which over time has developed an agenda of problems, issues, and questions with respect to both specific authors and texts and to culture generally. When students are screened from this critical community and its debates, or when they experience only the fragmentary and disconnected versions of it represented by a series of courses, they are likely to either be tongue-tied in the face of the text itself or to respond in a limited personal idiom, like the student who "relates to" Hamlet because he, too, had a mean stepfather.

In short, reading books with comprehension, making arguments, writing papers, and making comments in a class discussion are *social* activities. They involve entering into a cultural or disciplinary conversation, a process not unlike initiation into a social club. We obscure this social dimension when we conceive of education as if it were a process of contemplating important truths, values, and "cultural literacy" information in a vacuum and consequently treat such student tasks as reading assignments, making arguments, writing papers, and entering class discussions as if they were a matter of performing abstract procedures in a social void. Choose a topic that interests you, freshman writers are told; organize your paper logically around a central idea, and remember to support your thesis with specific illustration and evidence. Such advice is usually more paralyzing than helpful because it factors out the social conversation that reading, writing, and arguing must be part of in order to become personally meaningful.

Choosing a topic that interests you or making an effective argument depends on having a sense of what *other people* are saying, of what the state of the discussion is. Before my exposure to the critical debate on *Huckleberry Finn,* I had been trying to generate that discussion out of myself, something I did not know how to do. Exposure to the debate made me less of an outsider, provided me with a social community that gave my reading stimulus and direction. I could now discover what my teachers meant by "enjoying literature" because this had ceased to be a matter of vainly struggling to achieve some mysterious and rarefied experience. Relation to a community made the intimacy of literary experience possible.

N. Scott Momaday

N. Scott Momaday (b. 1934) is a novelist, poet, and painter. He is also a professor of English at the University of Arizona. Momaday was born and raised on the Kiowa Indian Reservation in Oklahoma. He earned his Ph.D. from Stanford University in 1963. Among his books are House Made of Dawn *(1968 Pulitzer Prize Winner),* The Way to Rainy Mountain, The Gourd Dancer, *and* Angle of Geese and Other Poems. *Momaday has been the recipient of many awards including an Academy of American Poets Prize (1962), a Guggenheim Fellowship (1966–67), and a National Institute of Arts and Letters Grant (1970). In Momaday's works, Wallace Stegner has observed that he "has not invented himself. . . . He has let the blood speak, looked for tracks, listened and remembered." In "The Man Made of Words" he combines literary criticism with storytelling in ways that show how these two modes of writing can illuminate each other in combination and dialogue. He states: "Storytelling is imaginative and creative in nature. It is an act by which man strives to realize his capacity for wonder, meaning, and delight. It is also a process in which man invests and preserves himself in the context of ideas."*

The Man Made of Words

I want to try to put several different ideas together this morning. And in the process, I hope to indicate something about the nature of the relationship between language and experience. It seems to me that in a certain sense we are all made of words; that our most essential being consists in language. It is the element in which we think and dream and act, in which we live our daily lives. There is no way in which we can exist apart from the morality of a verbal dimension.

In one of the discussions yesterday the question "What is an American Indian?" was raised.

The answer of course is that an Indian is an idea which a given man has of himself. And it is a moral idea, for it accounts for the way in which he reacts to other men and to the world in general. And that idea, in order to be realized completely, has to be expressed.

I want to say some things then about this moral and verbal dimension in which we live. I want to say something about such things as ecology and storytelling and the imagination. Let me tell you a story:

Reprinted from *The Remembered Earth*, edited by Geary Hobson, (1979), University of New Mexico Press.

One night a strange thing happened. I had written the greater part of *The Way to Rainy Mountain*—all of it, in fact, except the epilogue. I had set down the last of the old Kiowa tales, and I had composed both the historical and the autobiographical commentaries for it. I had the sense of being out of breath, of having said what it was in me to say on that subject. The manuscript lay before me in the bright light. Small, to be sure, but complete, or nearly so. I had written the second of the two poems in which that book is framed. I had uttered the last word, as it were. And yet a whole, penultimate piece was missing. I began once again to write.

During the first hours after midnight on the morning of November 13, 1833, it seemed that the world was coming to an end. Suddenly the stillness of the night was broken; there were brilliant flashes of light in the sky, light of such intensity that people were awakened by it. With the speed and density of a driving rain, stars were falling in the universe. Some were brighter than Venus; one was said to be as large as the moon. I went on to say that that event, the falling of the stars on North America, that explosion of meteors which occurred 137 years ago, is among the earliest entries in the Kiowa calendars. So deeply impressed upon the imagination of the Kiowas is that old phenomenon that it is remembered still; it has become a part of the racial memory.

"The living memory," I wrote, "and the verbal tradition which transcends it, were brought together for me once and for all in the person of Ko-sahn." It seemed eminently right for me to deal, after all, with that old woman. Ko-sahn is among the most venerable people I have ever known. She spoke and sang to me one summer afternoon in Oklahoma. It was like a dream. When I was born she was already old; she was a grown woman when my grandparents came into the world. She sat perfectly still, folded over on herself. It did not seem possible that so many years—a century of years—could be so compacted and distilled. Her voice shuddered, but it did not fail. Her songs were sad. An old whimsy, a delight in language and in remembrance, shone in her one good eye. She conjured up the past, imagining perfectly the long continuity of her being. She imagined the lovely young girl, wild and vital, she had been. She imagined the Sun Dance.

There was an old, old woman. She had something on her back. The boys went out to see. The old woman had a bag full of earth on her back. It was a certain kind of sandy earth. That is what they must have in the lodge. The dancers must dance upon the sandy earth. The old woman held a digging tool in her hand. She turned towards the south and pointed with her lips. It was like a kiss, and she began to sing:

> We have brought the earth.
> Now it is time to play.

As old as I am, I still have the feeling of play. That was the beginning of the Sun Dance.

By this time I was back into the book, caught up completely in the act of writing. I had projected myself—imagined myself—out of the room and out of time. I was there with Ko-sahn in the Oklahoma July. We laughed easily together; I felt that I had known her all of my life—all of hers. I did not want to let her go. But I had come to the end. I set down, almost grudgingly, the last sentences:

It was—all of this and more—a quest, a going forth upon the way of Rainy Mountain. Probably Ko-sahn too is dead now. At times, in the quiet of evening, I think she must have wondered, dreaming, who she was. Was she become in her sleep that old purveyor of the sacred earth, perhaps, that ancient one who, old as she was, still had the feeling of play? And in her mind, at times, did she see the falling stars?

For some time I sat looking down at these words on the page, trying to deal with the emptiness that had come about inside of me. The words did not seem real. I could scarcely believe that they made sense, that they had anything whatsoever to do with meaning. In desperation almost, I went back over the final paragraphs, backwards and forwards, hurriedly. My eyes fell upon the name Ko-sahn. And all at once everything seemed suddenly to refer to that name. The name seemed to humanize the whole complexity of language. All at once, absolutely, I had the sense of the magic of words and of names. Ko-sahn, I said, and I said again KO-SAHN.

Then it was that that ancient, one-eyed woman Ko-sahn stepped out of the language and stood before me on the page. I was amazed. Yet it seemed entirely appropriate that this should happen.

"I was just now writing about you," I replied, stammering. "I thought—forgive me—I thought that perhaps you were . . . that you had . . ."

"No," she said. And she cackled, I thought. And she went on. "You have imagined me well, and so I am. You have imagined that I dream, and so I do. I have seen the falling stars."

"But all of this, this imagining," I protested, "this has taken place—is taking place in my mind. You are not actually here, not here in this room." It occurred to me that I was being extremely rude, but I could not help myself. She seemed to understand.

"Be careful of your pronouncements, grandson," she answered. "You imagine that I am here in this room, do you not? That is worth something. You see, I have existence, whole being, in your imagination. It is but one kind of being, to be sure, but it is perhaps the best of all kinds. If I am not here in this room, grandson, then surely neither are you."

"I think I see what you mean," I said meekly. I felt justly rebuked. "Tell me, grandmother, how old are you?"

"I do not know," she replied. "There are times when I think that I am the oldest woman on earth. You know, the Kiowas came into the world through a hollow log. In my mind's eye I have seen them emerge, one by one, from the mouth of the log. I have seen them so clearly, how they were dressed, how delighted they were to see the world around them. I must have been there. And I must have taken part in that old migration of the Kiowas from the Yellowstone to the Southern Plains, near the Big Horn River, and I have seen the red cliffs of Palo Duro Canyon. I was with those who were camped in the Wichita Mountains when the stars fell."

"You are indeed very old," I said, "and you have seen many things."

"Yes, I imagine that I have," she replied. Then she turned slowly around, nodding once, and receded into the language I had made. And then I imagined I was alone in the room.

Once in his life a man ought to concentrate his mind upon the remembered earth, I believe. He ought to give himself up to a particular landscape in his experience, to look at it from as many angles as he can, to wonder about it, to dwell upon it. He ought to imagine that he touches it with his hands at every season and listens to the sounds that are made upon it. He ought to imagine the creatures that are there and all the faintest motions in the wind. He ought to recollect the glare of noon and all the colors of the dawn and dusk.

The Wichita Mountains rise out of the Southern Plains in a long crooked line that runs from east to west. The mountains are made of red earth, and of rock that is neither red nor blue but some very rare admixture of the two like the feathers of certain birds. They are not so high and mighty as the mountains of the Far West, and they bear a different relationship to the land around them. One does not imagine that they are distinctive in themselves, or indeed that they exist apart from the plain in any sense. If you try to think of them in the abstract they lose the look of mountains. They are preeminently in an expression of the larger landscape, more perfectly organic than one can easily imagine. To behold these mountains from the plain is one thing; to see the plain from the mountains is something else. I have stood on the top of Mt. Scott and seen the earth below, bending out into the whole circle of the sky. The wind runs always close upon the slopes, and there are times when you can hear the rush of it like water in the ravines.

Here is the hub of an old commerce. A hundred years ago the Kiowas and Comanches journeyed outward from the Wichitas in every direction, seeking after mischief and medicine, horses and hostages. Sometimes they went away for years, but they always returned, for the land had got hold of them. It is a consecrated place, and even now there is something of the wilderness about it. There is a game preserve in the hills. Animals graze away in the open meadows or, closer by, keep to the shadows of the groves: antelope and deer, longhorn and buffalo. It was here, the Kiowas say, that the first buffalo came into the world.

The yellow grassy knoll that is called Rainy Mountain lies a short distance to the north and west. There, on the west side, is the ruin of an old school where my grandmother went as a wild girl in a blanket and braids to learn of numbers and of names in English. And there she is buried.

> Most is your name the name of this dark stone.
> Deranged in death, the mind to be inheres
> Forever in the nominal unknown,
> Who listens here and now to hear your name.
> The early sun, red as a hunter's moon,
> Runs in the plain. The mountain burns and shines;
> And silence is the long approach of noon
> Upon the shadow that your name defines—
> And death this cold, black density of stone.

I am interested in the way that a man looks at a given landscape and takes possession of it in his blood and brain. For this happens, I am certain, in the ordinary motion of life. None of us lives apart from the land entirely; such an isolation is unimaginable. We have sooner or later to come to terms with the world around us—and I mean especially the physical world, not only as it is revealed to us immediately through our senses, but also as it is perceived more truly in the long turn of seasons and of years. And we must come to moral terms. There is no alternative, I believe, if we are to realize and maintain our humanity; for our humanity must consist in part in the ethical as well as the practical ideal of preservation. And particularly here and now is that true. We Americans need now more than ever before—and indeed more than we know—to imagine who and what we are with respect to the earth and sky. I am talking about an act of the imagination essentially, and the concept of an American land ethic.

It is no doubt more difficult to imagine in 1970 the landscape of America as it was in, say, 1900. Our whole experience as a nation in this century has been a repudiation of the pastoral ideal which informs so much of the art and literature of the nineteenth century. One effect of the Technological Revolution has been to uproot us from the soil. We have become disoriented, I believe; we have suffered a kind of psychic dislocation of ourselves in time and space. We may be perfectly sure of where we are in relation to the supermarket and the next coffee break, but I doubt that any of us knows where he is in relation to the stars and to the solstices. Our sense of the natural order has become dull and unreliable. Like the wilderness itself, our sphere of instinct has diminished in proportion as we have failed to imagine truly what it is. And yet I believe that it is possible to formulate an ethical idea of the land—a notion of what it is and must be in our daily lives—and I believe moreover that it is absolutely necessary to do so.

It would seem on the surface of things that a land ethic is something that is alien to, or at least dormant in, most Americans. Most of us in general have developed an attitude of indifference toward the land. In terms of my own experience, it is difficult to see how such an attitude could ever have come about.

Ko-sahn could remember where my grandmother was born. "It was just there," she said, pointing to a tree, and the tree was like a hundred others that grew up in the broad depression of the Washita River. I could see nothing to indicate that anyone had ever been there, spoken so much as a word, or touched the tips of his fingers to the tree. But in her memory Ko-sahn could see the child. I think she must have remembered my grandmother's voice, for she seemed for a long moment to listen and to hear. There was a still, heavy heat upon that place; I had the sense that ghosts were gathering there.

And in the racial memory, Ko-sahn had seen the falling stars. For her there was no distinction between the individual and the racial experience, even as there was none between the mythical and the historical. Both were realized for her in the one memory, and that was of the land. This landscape, in which she had lived for a hundred years, was the common denominator of everything that she knew and would ever know—and her knowledge was profound. Her roots ran deep into the earth, and from those depths she drew strength enough to hold still against all the forces of chance and disorder. And she drew there from the sustenance of meaning and of mystery as well. The falling stars were not for Ko-sahn an isolated or accidental phenomenon. She had a great personal investment in that awful commotion of light in the night sky. For it remained to be imagined. She must at last deal with it in words; she must appropriate it to her understanding of the whole universe. And, again, when she spoke of the Sun Dance, it was an essential expression of her relationship to the life of the earth and to the sun and moon.

In Ko-sahn and in her people we have always had the example of a deep, ethical regard for the land. We had better learn from it. Surely that ethic is merely latent in ourselves. It must now be activated, I believe. We Americans must come again to a moral comprehension of the earth and air. We must live according to the principle of a land ethic. The alternative is that we shall not live at all.

Ecology is perhaps the most important subject of our time. I can't think of an issue in which the Indian has more authority or a greater stake. If there is one thing which truly distinguishes him, it is surely his regard of and for the natural world.

But let me get back to the matter of storytelling.

I must have taken part in that old migration of the Kiowas from the Yellowstone to the Southern Plains, for I have seen antelope bounding in the tall grass near the Big Horn River, and I have seen the ghost forests in the Black Hills. Once I saw the red cliffs of Palo Duro Canyon. I was with those who were camped in the Wichita Mountains when the stars fell. "You are very old," I said, "and you have seen many things." "Yes, I imagine that I have," she replied. Then she turned slowly around, nodding once, and receded into the language I had made. And then I imagined that I was alone in the room.

Who is the storyteller? Of whom is the story told? What is there in the darkness to imagine into being? What is there to dream and to relate? What happens when I or anyone exerts the force of language upon the unknown?

These are the questions which interest me most.

If there is any absolute assumption in back of my thoughts tonight, it is this: We are what we imagine. Our very existence consists in our imagination of ourselves. Our best destiny is to imagine, at least, completely, who and what, and *that* we are. The greatest tragedy that can befall us is to go unimagined.

Writing is recorded speech. In order to consider seriously the meaning of language and of literature, we must consider first the meaning of the oral tradition.

By way of suggesting one or two definitions which may be useful to us, let me pose a few basic questions and tentative answers:

(1) What is the oral tradition?

The oral tradition is that process by which the myths, legends, tales, and lore of a people are formulated, communicated, and preserved in language by word of mouth, as opposed to writing. Or, it is a *collection* of such things.

(2) With reference to the matter of oral tradition, what is the relationship between art and reality?

In the context of these remarks, the matter of oral tradition suggests certain particularities of art and reality. Art, for example . . . involves an oral dimension which is based markedly upon such considerations as memorization, intonation, inflection, precision of statement, brevity, rhythm, pace, and dramatic effect. Moreover, myth, legend, and lore, according to our definitions of these terms, imply a separate and distinct order of reality. We are concerned here not so much with an accurate representation of actuality, but with the realization of the imaginative experience.

(3) How are we to conceive of language? What are words?

For our purposes, words are audible sounds, invented by man to communicate his thoughts and feelings. Each word has a conceptual content, however slight; and each word communicates associations of feeling. Language is the means by which words proceed to the formulation of meaning and emotional effect.

(4) What is the nature of storytelling? What are the purposes and possibilities of that act?

Storytelling is imaginative and creative in nature. It is an act by which man strives to realize his capacity for wonder, meaning, and delight. It is also a process in which man invests and preserves himself in the context of ideas. Man tells stories in order to understand his experience, whatever it may be. The possibilities of storytelling are precisely those of understanding the human experience.

(5) What is the relationship between what a man is and what he says—or between what he is, and what he thinks he is?

This relationship is both tenuous and complicated. Generally speaking, man has consummate being in language, and there only. The state of human *being* is an idea, an idea which man has of himself. Only when he is embodied in an idea, and the idea is realized in language, can man take possession of himself. In our particular frame of reference, this is to say that man achieves the fullest realization of his humanity in such an art and product of the imagination as literature—and here I use the term "literature" in its broadest sense. This is admittedly a moral view of the question, but literature is itself a moral view, and it is a view of morality.

Now let us return to the falling stars. And let me apply a new angle of vision to that event—let me proceed this time from a slightly different point of view:

In this winter of 1833 the Kiowas were camped on Elm Fork, a branch of the Red River west of the Wichita Mountains. In the preceding summer they had suffered a massacre at the hands of the Osages, and Tai-me, the sacred Sun Dance Doll and most powerful medicine of the tribe, had been stolen. At no time in the history of their migration from the north, and in the evolution of their plains culture, had the Kiowas been more vulnerable to despair. The loss of Tai-me was a deep psychological wound. In the early cold of November 13 there occurred over North America an explosion of meteors. The Kiowas were awakened by the sterile light of falling stars, and they ran out into the false day and were terrified.

The year the stars fell is, as I have said, among the earliest entries in the Kiowa calendars, and it is permanent in the Kiowa mind. There was symbolic meaning in that November sky. With the coming of natural dawn there began a new and darker age for the Kiowa people; the last culture to evolve on this continent began to decline. Within four years of the falling stars the Kiowas signed their first treaty with the government; within twenty, four major epidemics of smallpox and Asiatic cholera destroyed more than half their number; and within scarcely more than a generation their horses were taken from them and the herds of buffalo were slaughtered and left to waste upon the plains.

Do you see what happens when the imagination is superimposed upon the historical event? It becomes a story. The whole piece becomes more deeply invested with meaning. The terrified Kiowas, when they had regained possession of themselves, did indeed imagine that the falling stars were symbolic of their being and their destiny. They accounted for themselves with reference to that awful memory. They appropriated it, recreated it, fashioned it into an image of themselves—imagined it.

Only by means of that act could they bear what happened to them thereafter. No defeat, no humiliation, no suffering was beyond their power to endure, for none of it was meaningless. They could say to themselves, "yes, it was all meant to be in its turn. The order of the world was broken, it was clear. Even the stars were shaken loose in the night sky." The imagination of meaning was not much, perhaps, but it was all they had, and it was enough to sustain them.

One of my very favorite writers, Isak Dinesen, said this: "All sorrows can be borne if you put them into a story or tell a story about them."

Some three or four years ago, I became interested in the matter of "oral tradition" as that term is used to designate a rich body of preliterate storytelling in and among the indigenous cultures of North America. Specifically, I began to wonder about the way in which myths, legends, and lore evolve into that mature condition of expression which we call "literature." For indeed literature is, I believe, the end-product of an evolutionary process, a stage that is indispensable and perhaps original as well.

I set out to find a traditional material that should be at once oral only, unified and broadly representative of cultural values. And in this undertaking, I had a certain advantage, because I am myself an American Indian, and I have lived many years of my life on the Indian reservations of the southwest. From the time I was first able to comprehend and express myself in language, I heard the stories of the Kiowas, those "coming out" people of the Southern plains from whom I am descended.

Three hundred years ago the Kiowa lived in the mountains of what is now western Montana, near the headwaters of the Yellowstone River. Near the end of the 17th century they began a long migration to the south and east. They passed along the present border between Montana and Wyoming to the Black Hills and proceeded southward along the eastern slopes of the Rockies to the Wichita Mountains in the Southern Plains (Southwestern Oklahoma).

I mention this old journey of the Kiowas because it is in a sense definitive of the tribal mind; it is essential to the way in which the Kiowas think of themselves as a people. The migration was carried on over a course of many generations and many hundreds of miles. When it began, the Kiowas were a desperate and divided people, given up wholly to a day-by-day struggle for survival. When it ended, they were a race of centaurs, a lordly society of warriors and buffalo hunters. Along the way they had acquired horses, a knowledge and possession of the open land, and a sense of destiny. In alliance with the Comanches, they ruled the southern plains for a hundred years.

That migration—and the new golden age to which it led—is closely reflected in Kiowa legend and lore. Several years ago I retraced the route of that migration, and when I came to the end, I interviewed a number of Kiowa elders and obtained from them a remarkable body of history and learning, fact and fiction—all of it in the oral tradition and all of it valuable in its own right and for its own sake.

I compiled a small number of translations from the Kiowa, arranged insofar as it was possible to indicate the chronological and geographical progression of the migration itself. This collection (and it was nothing more than a collection at first) was published under the title *"The Journey of Tai-me"* in a fine edition limited to 100 hand printed copies.

This original collection has just been re-issued, together with illustrations and a commentary, in a trade edition entitled "*The Way to Rainy Mountain.*" The principle of narration which informs this latter work is in a sense elaborate and experimental, and I should like to say one or two things about it. Then, if I may, I should like to illustrate the way in which the principle works, by reading briefly from the text. And finally, I should like to comment in some detail upon one of the tales in particular.

There are three distinct narrative voices in "*The Way to Rainy Mountain*"—the mythical, the historical, and the immediate. Each of the translations is followed by two kinds of commentary; the first is documentary and the second is privately reminiscent. Together, they serve, hopefully, to validate the oral tradition to an extent that might not otherwise be possible. The commentaries are meant to provide a context in which the elements of oral tradition might transcend the categorical limits of prehistory, anonymity, and archaeology in the narrow sense.

All of this is to say that I believe there is a way (first) in which the elements of oral tradition can be shown, dramatically, to exist within the framework of a literary continuance, a deeper and more vital context of language and meaning than that which is generally taken into account; and (secondly) in which those elements can be located, with some precision on an evolutionary scale.

The device of the journey is peculiarly appropriate to such a principle of narration as this. And "*The Way to Rainy Mountain*" is a whole journey, intricate with notion and meaning; and it is made with the whole memory, that experience of the mind which is legendary as well as historical, personal as well as cultural.

Without further qualification, let me turn to the text itself.

The Kiowa tales which are contained in "*The Way to Rainy Mountain*" constitute a kind of literary chronicle. In a sense they are the milestones of that old migration in which the Kiowas journeyed from the Yellowstone to the Washita. They recorded a transformation of the tribal mind, as it encounters for the first time the landscape of the Great Plains; they evoke the sense of search and discovery. Many of the tales are very old, and they have not until now been set down in writing. Among them there is one that stands out in my mind. When I was a child, my father told me the story of the arrowmaker, and he told it to me many times, for I fell in love with it. I have no memory that is older than that of hearing it. This is the way it goes:

If an arrow is well made, it will have tooth marks upon it. That is how you know. The Kiowas made fine arrows and straightened them in their teeth. Then they drew them to the bow to see that they were straight. Once there was a man and his wife. They were alone at night in their tipi. By the light of a fire the man was making arrows. After a while he caught sight of something. There was a small opening in the tipi where two hides had been sewn together. Someone was there on the outside, looking in. The man went on with his work, but he said to his wife, "Someone is standing outside. Do not be afraid. Let us talk easily, as of ordinary things." He took up an arrow and straightened it in his teeth; then, as it was right for him to do, he drew it to the bow and took aim, first in this direction and then in that. And all the while he was talking, as if to his wife. But this is how he spoke: "I know that you are there on the outside, for I can feel your eyes upon me. If you are a Kiowa, you will understand what I am saying, and you will speak your name." But there was no answer, and the man went on in the same way, pointing the arrow all around. At last his aim fell upon the place where his enemy stood, and he let go of the string. The arrow went straight to the enemy's heart.

Heretofore the story of the arrowmaker has been the private possession of a very few, a tenuous link in that most ancient chain of language which we call the oral tradition; tenuous because the tradition itself is so; for as many times as the story has been told, it was always but one generation removed from extinction. But it was held dear, too, on that same account. That is to say, it has been neither more nor less durable than the human voice, and neither more nor less concerned to express the meaning of the human condition. And this brings us to the heart of the matter at hand: The story of the arrowmaker is also a link between language and literature. It is a remarkable act of the mind, a realization of words and the world that is altogether simple and direct, yet nonetheless rare and profound, and it illustrates more clearly than anything else in my own experience, at least, something of the essential character of the imagination—and in particular of that personification which in this instance emerges from it: the man made of words.

It is a fine story, whole, intricately beautiful, precisely realized. It is worth thinking about, for it yields something of value; indeed, it is full of provocation, rich with suggestion and consequent meaning. There is often an inherent danger that we might impose too much of ourselves upon it. It is informed by an integrity that bears examination easily and well, and in the process it seems to appropriate our own reality and experience.

It is significant that the story of the arrowmaker returns in a special way upon itself. It is about language, after all, and it is therefore part and parcel of its own subject; virtually, there is no difference between the telling and that which is told. The point of the story lies, not so much in what the arrowmaker does, but in what he says—and indeed that he says it. The principal fact is that he speaks, and in so doing he places his very life in the balance. It is this aspect of the story which interests me most, for it is here that the language becomes most conscious of itself; we are close to the origin and object of literature, I believe; our sense of the verbal dimension is very keen, and we are aware of something in the nature of language that is at once perilous and compelling. "If you are a Kiowa, you will understand what I am saying, and you will speak your name." Everything is ventured in this simple declaration, which is also a question and a plea. The conditional element with which it begins is remarkably tentative and pathetic; precisely at this moment is the arrowmaker realized completely, and his reality consists in language, and it is poor and precarious. And all of this occurs to him as surely as it does to us. Implicit in that simple occurrence is all of his definition and his destiny, and all of ours. He ventures to speak because he must; language is the repository of his whole knowledge and experience, and it represents the only chance he has for survival. Instinctively, and with great care, he deals in the most honest and basic way with words. "Let us talk easily, as of ordinary things," he says. And of the ominous unknown he asks only the utterance of a name, only the most nominal sign that he is understood, that his words are returned to him on the sheer edge of meaning. But there is no answer, and the arrowmaker knows at once what he has not known before; that his enemy is, and that he has gained an advantage over him. This he knows certainly, and the certainty itself is his advantage, and it is crucial; he makes the most of it. The venture is complete and irrevocable, and it ends in success. The story is meaningful. It is so primarily because it is composed of language, and it is in the nature of language in turn that it proceeds to the formulation of meaning. Moreover, the story of the arrowmaker, as opposed to other stories in general, centers upon this procession of words toward meaning. It seems in fact to turn upon the very idea that language involves the elements of risk and responsibility; and in this it seeks to confirm itself. In a word, it seems to say, everything is a risk. That may be true, and it may also be that the whole of literature rests upon that truth.

The arrowmaker is preeminently the man made of words. He has consummate being in language; it is the world of his origin and of his posterity, and there is no other. But it is a world of definite reality and of infinite possibility. I have come to believe that there is a sense in which the arrowmaker has more nearly perfect being than have other men, by and large, as he imagines himself, whole and vital, going on into the unknown darkness and beyond. And this last aspect of his being is primordial and profound.

And yet the story has it that he is cautious and alone, and we are given to understand that his peril is great and immediate, and that he confronts it in the only way he can. I have no doubt that this is true, and I believe that there are implications which point directly to the determination of our literary experience and which must not be lost upon us. A final word, then, on an essential irony which marks this story and gives peculiar substance to the man made of words. The storyteller is nameless and unlettered. From one point of view we know very little about him, except that he is somehow translated for us in the person of an arrowmaker. But, from another, that is all we need to know. He tells us of his life in language, and of the awful risk involved. It must occur to us that he is one with the arrowmaker and that he has survived, by word of mouth, beyond other men. We said a moment ago that, for the arrowmaker, language represented the only chance of survival. It is worth considering that he survives in our own time, and that he has survived over a period of untold generations.

Amy Tan

Amy Tan was born in Oakland, California in 1952; her par were both born in China. Her father was an engineer who been educated in Beijing and her mother left China in 1949, just before the communist revolution. Tan is best known as a fiction writer. Her first book, The Joy Luck Club, *(1989) was nominated for a National Book Award and was later the basis for the film of the same title. She has since published several other novels, including* The Kitchen God's Wife *(1991),* The Hundred Secret Senses *(1995) and* The Bonesetter's Daughter *(2001). This essay, "Mother Tongue," was chosen for inclusion in* Best American Essays 1991.

Mother Tongue

I am not a scholar of English or literature. I cannot give you much more than personal opinions on the English language and its variations in this country or others.

I am a writer. And by that definition, I am someone who has always loved language. I am fascinated by language in daily life. I spend a great deal of my time thinking about the power of language—the way it can evoke an emotion, a visual image, a complex idea, or a simple truth. Language is the tool of my trade. And I use them all—all the Englishes I grew up with.

Recently, I was made keenly aware of the different Englishes I do use. I was giving a talk to a large group of people, the same talk I had already given to half a dozen other groups. The nature of the talk was about my writing, my life, and my book, *The Joy Luck Club*. The talk was going along well enough, until I remembered one major difference that made the whole talk sound wrong. My mother was in the room. And it was perhaps the first time she had heard me give a lengthy speech, using the kind of English I have never used with her. I was saying things like, "The intersection of memory upon imagination" and "There is an aspect of my fiction that relates to thus-and-thus"—a speech filled with carefully wrought grammatical phrases, burdened, it suddenly seemed to me, with nominalized forms, past perfect tenses, conditional phrases, all the forms of standard English that I had learned in school and through books, the forms of English I did not use at home with my mother.

Just last week, I was walking down the street with my mother, and I again found myself conscious of the English I was using, the English I do use with her. We were talking about the price of new and used furniture and I heard myself say-

---

ing this: "Not waste money that way." My husband was with us as well, and he didn't notice any switch in my English. And then I realized why. It's because over the twenty years we've been together I've often used that same kind of English with him, and sometimes he even uses it with me. It has become our language of intimacy, a different sort of English that relates to family talk, the language I grew up with.

So you'll have some idea of what this family talk I heard sounds like, I'll quote what my mother said during a recent conversation which I videotaped and then transcribed. During this conversation, my mother was talking about a political gangster in Shanghai who had the same last name as her family's, Du, and how the gangster in his early years wanted to be adopted by her family, which was rich by comparison. Later, the gangster became more powerful, far richer than my mother's family, and one day showed up at my mother's wedding to pay his respects. Here's what she said in part:

"Du Yusong having business like fruit stand. Like off the street kind. He is Du like Du Zong—but not Tsung-ming Island people. The local people call putong, the river east side, he belong to that side local people. That man want to ask Du Zong father take him in like become own family. Du Zong father wasn't look down on him, but didn't take seriously, until that man big like become a mafia. Now important person, very hard to inviting him. Chinese way, came only to show respect, don't stay for dinner. Respect for making big celebration, he shows up. Mean gives lots of respect. Chinese custom. Chinese social life that way. If too important won't have to stay too long. He come to my wedding. I didn't see, I heard it. I gone to boy's side, they have YMCA dinner. Chinese age I was nineteen."

You should know that my mother's expressive command of English belies how much she actually understands. She reads the *Forbes* report, listens to *Wall Street Week,* converses daily with her stockbroker, reads all of Shirley MacLaine's books with ease—all kinds of things I can't begin to understand. Yet some of my friends tell me they understand 50 percent of what my mother says. Some say they understand 80 to 90 percent. Some say they understand none of it, as if she were speaking pure Chinese. But to me, my mother's English is perfectly clear, perfectly natural. It's my mother tongue. Her language, as I hear it, is vivid, direct, full of observation and imagery. That was the language that helped shape the way I saw things, expressed things, made sense of the world.

Lately, I've been giving more thought to the kind of English my mother speaks. Like others, I have described it to people as "broken" or "fractured" English. But I wince when I say that. It has always bothered me that I can think of no other way to describe it other than "broken," as if it were damaged and needed to be fixed, as if it lacked a certain wholeness and soundness. I've heard other terms used, "limited English," for example. But they seem just as bad, as if everything is limited, including people's perceptions of the limited English speaker.

I know this for a fact, because when I was growing up, my mother's "limited" English limited *my* perception of her. I was ashamed of her English. I believed that her English reflected the quality of what she had to say. That is, because she expressed them imperfectly her thoughts were imperfect. And I had plenty of empirical evidence to support me: the fact that people in department stores, at banks, and at restaurants did not take her seriously, did not give her good service, pretended not to understand her, or even acted as if they did not hear her.

My mother has long realized the limitations of her English as well. When I was fifteen, she used to have me call people on the phone to pretend I was she. In this guise, I was forced to ask for information or even to complain and yell at people who had been rude to her. One time it was a call to her stockbroker in New York. She had cashed out her small portfolio and it just so happened we were going to go to New York the next week, our very first trip outside California. I had to get on the phone and say in an adolescent voice that was not very convincing, "This is Mrs. Tan."

And my mother was standing in the back whispering loudly, "Why he don't send me check, already two weeks late. So mad he lie to me, losing me money."

And then I said in perfect English, "Yes, I'm getting rather concerned. You had agreed to send the check two weeks ago, but it hasn't arrived."

Then she began to talk more loudly. "What he want, I come to New York tell him front of his boss, you cheating me?" And I was trying to calm her down, make her be quiet, while telling the stockbroker, "I can't tolerate any more excuses. If I don't receive the check immediately, I am going to have to speak to your manager when I'm in New York next week." And sure enough, the following week there we were in front of this astonished stockbroker, and I was sitting there red-faced and quiet, and my mother, the real Mrs. Tan, was shouting at his boss in her impeccable broken English.

We used a similar routine just five days ago, for a situation that was far less humorous. My mother had gone to the hospital for an appointment, to find out about a benign brain tumor a CAT scan had revealed a month ago. She said she had spoken very good English, her best English, no mistakes. Still, she said, the hospital did not apologize when they said they had lost the CAT scan and she had come for nothing. She said they did not seem to have any sympathy when she told them she was anxious to know the exact diagnosis, since her husband and son had both died of brain tumors. She said they would not give her any more information until the next time and she would have to make another appointment for that. So she said she would not leave until the doctor called her daughter. She wouldn't budge. And when the doctor finally called her daughter, me, who spoke in perfect English—lo and behold—we had assurances the CAT scan would be found, promises that a conference call on Monday would be held, and apologies for any suffering my mother had gone through for a most regrettable mistake.

I think my mother's English almost had an effect on limiting my possibilities in life as well. Sociologists and linguists probably will tell you that a person's developing language skills are more influenced by peers. But I do think that the language spoken in the family, especially in immigrant families which are more insular, plays a large role in shaping the language of the child. And I believe that it affected my results on achievement tests, IQ tests, and the SAT. While my English skills were never judged as poor, compared to math, English could not be considered my strong suit. In grade school I did moderately well, getting perhaps B's, sometimes B-pluses, in English and scoring perhaps in the sixtieth or seventieth percentile on achievement tests. But those scores were not good enough to override the opinion that my true abilities lay in math and science, because in those areas I achieved A's and scored in the ninetieth percentile or higher.

This was understandable. Math is precise; there is only one correct answer. Whereas, for me at least, the answers on English tests were always a judgment call, a matter of opinion and personal experience. Those tests were constructed around items like fill-in-the-blank sentence completion, such as "Even though Tom was ______, Mary thought he was _____." And the correct answer always seemed to be the most bland combinations of thoughts, for example, "Even though Tom was shy, Mary thought he was charming," with the grammatical structure "even though" limiting the correct answer to some sort of semantic opposites, so you wouldn't get answers like, "Even though Tom was foolish, Mary thought he was ridiculous." Well, according to my mother, there were very few limitations as to what Tom could have been and what Mary might have thought of him. So I never did well on tests like that.

The same was true with word analogies, pairs of words in which you were supposed to find some sort of logical, semantic relationship—for example, "*Sunset* is to *nightfall* as _____ is to ______." And here you would be presented with a list of four possible pairs, one of which showed the same kind of relationship: *red* is to *stoplight*, *bus* is to *arrival*, *chills* is to *fever*, *yawn* is to *boring*. Well, I could never think that way. I knew what the tests were asking, but I could not block out of my mind the images already created by the first pair, "*sunset* is to *nightfall*"—and I would see a burst of colors against a darkening sky, the moon rising, the lowering of a curtain of stars. And all the other pairs of words—red, bus, stoplight, boring—just threw up a mass of confusing images, making it impossible for me to sort out something as logical as saying: "A sunset precedes nightfall" is the same as "a chill precedes a fever." The only way I would have gotten that answer right would have been to imagine an associative situation, for example, my being disobedient and staying out past sunset, catching a chill at night, which turns into feverish pneumonia as punishment, which indeed did happen to me.

I have been thinking about all this lately, about my mother's English, about achievement tests. Because lately I've been asked, as a writer, why there are not more Asian Americans represented in American literature. Why are there few Asian Americans enrolled in creative writing programs? Why do so many Chinese students go into engineering? Well, these are broad sociological questions I can't begin to answer. But I have noticed in surveys—in fact, just last week—that Asian students, as a whole, always do significantly better on math achievement tests than in English. And this makes me think that there are other Asian-American students whose English spoken in the home might also be described as "broken" or "limited." And perhaps they also have teachers who are steering them away from writing and into math and science, which is what happened to me.

Fortunately, I happen to be rebellious in nature and enjoy the challenge of disproving assumptions made about me. I became an English major my first year in college, after being enrolled as pre-med. I started writing nonfiction as a freelancer the week after I was told by my former boss that writing was my worst skill and I should hone my talents toward account management.

But it wasn't until 1985 that I finally began to write fiction. And at first I wrote using what I thought to be wittily crafted sentences, sentences that would finally prove I had mastery over the English language. Here's an example from the first draft of a story that later made its way into *The Joy Luck Club,* but without this line: "That was my mental quandary in its nascent state." A terrible line, which I can barely pronounce.

Fortunately, for reasons I won't get into today, I later decided I should envision a reader for the stories I would write. And the reader I decided upon was my mother, because these were stories about mothers. So with this reader in mind—and in fact she did read my early drafts—I began to write stories using all the Englishes I grew up with: the English I spoke to my mother, which for lack of a better term might be described as "simple": the English she used with me, which for lack of a better term might be described as "broken"; my translation of her Chinese, which could certainly be described as "watered down"; and what I imagined to be her translation of her Chinese if she could speak in perfect English, her internal language, and for that I sought to preserve the essence, but neither an English nor a Chinese structure. I wanted to capture what language ability tests can never reveal: her intent, her passion, her imagery, the rhythms of her speech, and the nature of her thoughts.

Apart from what any critic had to say about my writing, I knew I had succeeded where it counted when my mother finished reading my book and gave me her verdict: "So easy to read."

Tita French Baumlin

Tita French Baumlin, who has a Ph.D. in English with concentrations in British Renaissance Literature and Rhetoric, teaches at Southwest Missouri State University. She wrote this essay and carried out this class exercise during the spring semester of 1984 when she was doing her graduate work at Texas Christian University.

A Good Crot Is Hard to Find

With a copy of Winston Weathers' "The Grammars of Style: New Options in Composition" (*Freshman English News,* Winter, 1976) firmly in hand, I recently resolved to make a fresh attempt at presenting my second semester freshmen with a new exploratory assignment: write a composition using what Weathers calls "Grammar B." I briefly outlined in class some of the significant features of this new style—sentence fragments and/or long and convoluted sentences, word repetitions, odd orthographic devices, and a total disregard for transition between divisions of material. I also offered the students some brief samples from my file, such as Weathers' essay on William Blake (contained in his article) and some inventive newspaper articles; I even brought out my dog-eared, personal (and precious) copy of *Tristram Shandy*. I suggested some possible topics and most of the students left the room with those unmistakable this-is-going-to-be-easy smiles on their faces: *You mean I'm allowed to write incomplete sentences?*

By noon the following day, however, I began to realize that these students, far from complacent, were now in the early stages of panic, having gone home and contemplated their options. One after another, they left notes in my mailbox, sought me in my office, in the library, in the departmental office, in the hallway, all asking the same question: "What is it that you WANT?" Again and again, I smiled and said, "Relax. Have fun with it. See what happens." But my freshmen would not be moved.

I decided that some additional material from Winston Weathers' textbook, *An Alternate Style* (Rochelle Park, N.J.: Hayden Book Company, Inc., 1980), couldn't hurt. I had also decided earlier that I would write this assignment along with my class, not only to show them that it could be done, but also (and most of all) to give *myself* what I believed this assignment promised the students: a liberation from the conventions that, allowed to reign too long at a time, can stifle the creativity on which most of us have an all too tenuous hold. I had not yet hit upon any particular topic for my paper when I sat down at the typewriter, but thumbing

Reprinted from *Rhetoric Review* 3, January 1995.

through *An Alternate Style* worked its magic on me, and within four hours I had produced the following essay, a piece which I hoped would combine a discussion of the significant features of "Grammar B," examples of suggested techniques, an open letter to my composition class, and my own response to the assignment.

"Just Tell Me What You Want"

You listen. And you smile. Try to act eager. Try to BE EAGER. You go home. Write. TRY to write. Pen the words, pencil the words, type the words, anywayyoucan the words, curse the words you use like steel files to try to scrape your way out of prison. Try to free your soul from the bondage of freshman comp. I and II. Free your mind from the bondage of A*B*C*D*F. Why not an E and a G? An F-sharp? Take an A-flat on your next paper. Or a G.

But you traipse into my office. Streams of freshmen YOU CAN ALWAYS TELL THE FRESHMEN THEY'RE THE ONES WITH THE ffffffur-rrrrowwwwwwwed brows AND ANXIOUS EYES and you

say
Just
tell
me
what
you
want,
Miss
French
and
I
will
do
it
OKAY
??

I don't know what I want. On your blank page.
Because I'm not you.
But. Now that I have your attention. I'll tell you what I want.

CHAPTER 1

What Miss French Wants

I want your smiling face in my classroom every time class meets. I want to know you'll be there to read the crazy pieces I stay up until four a.m. writing for you. I want to know your drafts will be clutched in sweaty hands not because you are afraid of poor grades and punishment but because you are thirsting for the good stuff that only we can give you. Your class. Mates.

I want to never again have to reply to ARE WE DOING ANYTHING IMPORTANT TODAY CAUSE IF WE AREN'T I HAVE TO GO TO***** I HAVE A DOCTOR'S APPOINTMENT***** I HAVE A JOB INTERVIEW *****I HAVE OTHER CLASSES/DEMANDING PROFS/LABS/REHEARSALS / PRACTICES / WORKOUTS / DON'T WORRY IT'S AN EXCUSED ABSENCE . . . Not that I believe my every word is Golden. It's just that you never know when the Magic will strike.

Maybe now.
And if you miss it
It may not come again. Come again?

CHAPTER 2

What MISS FRENCH really WANTS

Magic. Free the P*O*Ws of the mind/little bits of grey matter held hostage by the POWERS THAT BE/i.e., THOSE WHO TELL YOU

Please do not write in this area.
Fill out forms in triplicate.
Press hard you are making five copies.
Office use only.
Past due after
Do not fold, staple, or mutilate.
DO NOT
Do not combine process analysis with compare/contrast.
Do not use 2nd person.
Do NOT use 1st person. On pain of death.
Put your thesis statement

HERE.

/victims of the wars your mommas and daddies didn't even know they served in. Liberate slave labor!!! Let judgment come rolling down like waters and righteousness like a mighty stream of words, a torrent of words, a flood of words, of passion, of electric love like you've never known before, of magic that comes from that part of you that holds on to words like a lifeline in a typhoon.

Do you not know that your native tongue is a gift? beyond compare? That what I write and what you read here

EVEN
HERE

makes us human? makes us mankind? makes us man? kind?

> AND GOD SAID, LET US MAKE MAN IN OUR IMAGE, AFTER OUR LIKENESS: AND LET THEM HAVE DOMINION OVER THE FISH OF THE SEA, AND OVER THE FOWL OF THE AIR,

> AND OVER THE CATTLE, AND OVER ALL THE EARTH, AND OVER EVERY CREEPING THING THAT CREEPETH UPON THE EARTH. SO GOD CREATED MAN IN HIS *OWN* IMAGE, IN THE IMAGE OF GOD CREATED HE HIM.

And, behold. It was very good.

don'tforgetdon'tforgetdon'tforgetdon'tforgetdon'tforgetdon'tforget:

Tricks of the Trade

A. What to play with.

1. *Crots.* A crot is an old-fashioned word for "bit" or "fragment." Like a stanza is to poetry. Like a note is to music is a crot to my work. Free your crots. Let them stand alone. Long or short, let your crots be crots. Without connecting tissue. Like this.

Brevity. In brief, a short crot can be like a proverb. A crot without transition is like a new scent wafted on the breeze of the imagination.

> Dear Students,
>
> Longer crots are quite acceptable, as well. The trick is to present your crots in nearly random sequence or in sequences that finally (at last!) suggest a circular pattern. Impose no other kind of order on your crots than the flow of your mind. Use your crots like good snapshots of the wonderful orderly disorder that is your mind.
>
> Very truly, etc.,

Give Your Crots Titles, If You Like

An effective title sometimes says more than the text you put after it.

2. *The Labyrinthine Sentence and the Sentence Fragment.* Give you two kinds of sentences to play with. The Labyrinthine Sentence is just what it sounds like: a long, involuted sentence like a LABYRINTH that flows along, has nooks and crannies, twists, turns, snips, snags, and oh! that fluidity that sings like water slipping and slurrrrppping down the thirsty, rocky, dry creekbeds of our minds; for instance, if you are speaking of eternity, you may want to mention the height of the bluest distances between mountains (gasp!) or perhaps the deepest part of the rolling, moaning, foaming, pitching, roaring ocean, but if you are talking about a misunderstanding—how did it get this way?—between friends, you may need—how did this ever come to pass?—to intersperse your sentence with (pardon me, while I remember and pause to choose my words carefully) the kinds of pauses that such a story might call for, might actually WANT.

On the other hand.

A fragment. Often a single word. Alone. Or a very short phrase. Very. Suggests a far greater awareness of separation. Fragmentation. Not entanglement. But isolation. It can be emphatic. Pointed. Get the point?

3. *The List.* Basically, there are at least two or three ways to create a list.

> If you want to suggest the illusion that the items you are listing are all there, all present in the mind or in the vision, all at once, then you may want to list them in a paragraph of continuous prose, words, phrases, non-*sense* phrases, crots, blips, blobs, bits, bytes, all in one block.

On the other hand, you may want to suggest a catalog. An orderly picture.

A Set of Words That Bounce Off Each Other

One word	Versus another
And yet here	Can be
Another	Well placed
Beside one	Another
Here	And there

Or you may want to list them all in one short vertical list.

Eternity
Wants
Needs
Kindness
Mankindness

Or a list of short phrases
Like bits you might write on a blackboard
Careless as to length, with
Individual phrases free to be very very long
Or short
You thus may say to your reader
I'm keeping my mouth shut
YOU look at these items
YOU make up your own @/*# mind
Add them up
Evaluate them
In your own reality, for
Your reality is
Different from mine.

4. *The Double Voice.*

I would use this technique to present my material as though I were running two compositions down two sides of the page.

I want to try to suggest that I COULD say this OR that about my subject, and in a way I'd like to say both.

I'm dealing with ambiguous realities.

I'm presenting information and FACTS.

I'm commenting upon the facts in such a way that I can help the reader distinguish between the two roles that I can play when I write, as fact-giver AND/ or as interpreter/commentator.

Straight line double voice *Like this when I have something* is harder *else to say* with a conventional typewriter *in between the phrases* because I don't have access to italics which is *to seem like I'm carrying on* easier *a conversation with myself* to say the least *to indicate confusion, maybe, or mixed emotions.*

5. *Repetitions/Refrains.* Hurry! Hurry! I'm almost finished! You find a key word Faster! Faster! or a key phrase and you repeat it. As D. H. Lawrence does here:

Doom.

Doom! Doom! Doom! Something seems to whisper it in the very dark trees of America. Doom!

Doom of what?

Doom of our white day. We are doomed, doomed. And the doom is in America. The doom of our white day. (Want more? Go see "Herman Melville's *Moby Dick,*" in *Studies in Classic American Literature,* London: Heinemann, 1924, okay?)

6. *Language Variegation: Orthographic Schemes and the Foreign Word.*

You might want to play with word spelling, MISSpellings to you, ma'am, to inject some laughs, or to oPUN the door to playing with language and alternate meanings. You can make up words, like Lewis Carroll's Jabjabjabjabjabber-wocky, for as James Joyce says, "A nod to the nabir is better than a wink to the wabsanti." Such play can signal "fun" and "play" to the reader, help articulate the philosophy and presence of *homo ludens* (thank you, Winston Weathers), or remind your reader how delightfully complex language is. Sometimes the tragic flaw of a piece is that there's no comic relief.

Or you might consider sound effects. Winston Weathers told us about Blake's Tygrrrrrrrr, remember? Or how about someone who is speeeeeeeaking slooooowly? Just be playYAYful, if you know what I mean.

Or how about a foreign phrase? Not necessarily to be high-brow, *per se,* but maybe just to indicate "a deliberate spilling over and outside the boundaries of English" (thanks again, W. W.).

Deo gratias!

I'm almost finished!

B. There is no B in this outline. A polite (?) thumb-to-nose at the ones who say DO NOT have an A without a B in an outline.

I say, Let X equal X (thank you, Laurie Anderson) and let the crots fall where they may. *E pluribus unum.*

This isn't easy. It's taken me HOURS to do this first draft. But I had fun. And I have something to work with now. So that I can try to do justice to this assignment. Justice is not just ice, you know. And a good, crot is hard to find.

Just try to mix these different tricks for different effects. Try not to get stuck in one long list or one long unbroken line of prose, unless, of course, you want to. It's just more fun to try on different hats, *Hütte, chapeaux, cappelli,* as it were. Try them ALL on.

You might like what you see in the mirror when you do.

C'est finis!

What?

É finita!

Hold the phone.

Es ist zu Ende!

er, um

Consummatum est!

Bingo!

theend.

FOOTNOTE: Most of the above information (Just the facts, ma'am) and much of the inspiration was GREATfully absorbed from Winston Weathers, *An Alternate Style* (Rochelle Park, N. J.: Hayden Book Company, Inc., 1980). Only the syntax was changed to protect the innocent.
FOOTNOTE: Keep on your toes. . . .

After distributing copies of this essay and explaining its origin, I discussed my paper with the class. One student remarked that he noticed a union of form and content in the paper; several others responded by saying they thought it was funny, while it got the point across, as well. At least when our class period was over, they seemed to have clearer ideas of directions to take in their own papers. Perhaps the best result of this essay was that the students seemed energized and inspired to find their own ways to explore this assignment, rather than frustrated and daunted with the intimidation that usually accompanies the instructor's presentation of his or her own "model essay." This essay WAS a model of the kind of paper I expected from them, but in serving the primary function of informing the class of possible techniques and "tricks of the trade," this paper doubled as a mere class handout, ordinary, innocuous, and informative. Further, the students' classroom responses indicated that they did not dismiss this essay as just another teacher's attempt to "show off." On the contrary, my own creativity seemed to spark similar creativity in the students, urges which pushed each student to explore his or her own unique topic in increasingly unique ways. Best of all, my paper's "topic" was not one which encouraged imitation and thus it did not produce insurmountable mental blocks when these students went about finding suitable topics.

Our first workshop session surprised me. Not one of the students had picked one of my "suggested topics" for the essay, but rather each and every class member had found a subject that had personal meaning in his or her own life, and the resulting wide range of topics added a new dimension of adventure to our first workshop. Furthermore, even though each paper was highly and uniquely personal, this workshop group offered more constructive criticism and suggestions for improvement than ever before. The major phrase for the day became: "Why don't you play with that section and see what happens?" The critics were eager to suggest a playfulness in revision, as were the recipients playful in their responses.

On a practical level, this workshop might have proceeded more smoothly if I had been able to have several drafts duplicated ahead of time so that we could see the visual effects; instead, the authors here had to explain as they read aloud. Still, these authors didn't seem to mind stopping and explaining what each passage was supposed to accomplish—in fact, they seemed to enjoy hashing out their own reasoning behind the techniques they had chosen, and it occurred to me that this was perhaps the first time that the class as a whole had begun to operate on the overt assumption that any given technique must be a careful, rational choice. It is this discovery that leads me to consider that this exercise might work very well for some instructors if it is strategically placed early in the semester, allowing students to discover the value of rationally planning one's rhetoric and of finding union of form and content, then building upon that discovery throughout the remainder of the semester.

On the other hand, saving this assignment for at least mid-semester has its advantages, because, though wildly liberating, such an exercise is simultaneously frustrating in that it demands both creativity and self-consciousness more overtly than do other types of expository writing; a particular group may have to create a certain level of dynamics before it can attempt this venture. Many students reported that this assignment was the most difficult one they faced all year, simply because it is so difficult to break out of the prisons of traditions: sometimes the slaves find out they don't want to be released! Knowing one another well may have helped us voice our frustrations, fears, and discoveries with greater ease, may have helped us support and nurture the growth that such an assignment demanded among us.

In any case, these authors' final drafts astounded me. Every paper showed playful incorporations of the techniques I had offered them, but, best of all, each essay also showed innovations and discoveries that my model essay had not displayed. One chemistry major wrote about the terrors of chemistry class and, while describing her frustration with a particularly esoteric ion, she constructed word pictures that visually displayed the chemical bond. Another student used a word association technique that allowed him to stop in mid-sentence, taking a different direction based upon an alternate meaning of a pivotal word; the final effect was a kind of zipping from crot to crot with little verbal links, suggesting a deeper theme of the complexities of communication in language. A computer science major wrote an entertaining and informative paper about her relationship with computers; she submitted her final draft typed on discarded computer paper. A very fine paper about the subliminal influence of television on our minds showed the subtle, tempting voice of "*t*v*" as a magical, almost imperceptible whisper that interrupts our every thought; the most humorous essay in this group attempted to translate a polite exchange between professor and student into each participants' *real* thoughts through a quadruple voice technique—a dialogue within a dialogue.

The two best papers in the class were perhaps the most dissimilar. A Mexican-American student wrote a fine and fun essay about the frustrations of trying to write this assignment, but he emphasized the double voice technique and created a delightful interplay between his serious and fearful "English" student-self and his free and easy "Mexican" alter ego: the student-self feared that his usage of his second language would always be inferior, stifling any creativity he might ever muster, while the confident alter ego bounced happily between both languages, offering encouragement to forget about pleasing anybody but himself. The alter ego became an impish voice, tempting the student to let out all his frustrations by skipping this assignment altogether. This "I can't write this paper"/"Forget it; have a cigarette, *amigo*" dialogue resulted in a delightful essay that not only produced a wry and ironic "nonessay," but also underscored the deeper poignant struggles of our classmate in his complex, bilingual world. We laughed, but we were also touched by the vulnerability he shared with us; we all felt that some kind of bridge had been crossed.

The other paper was as serious and moving as its partner was funny and profane, proving that this new style is not necessarily most effective in a comic tone. The essay explored the gradual unfolding of the doom of the Jews in Nazi Germany; each page of the essay displayed a different step in the Nazi philosophy, but the words and statistics, nicely interwoven with German phrases, formed a separate arm of the swastika on each page. By the end of the essay, a final page was produced through reductive photocopying so that the previous arms assembled the insignia just as the final edict for extermination was announced, a chilling and sobering progression from mere inflation on page one to genocide on page five. The paper was well researched and artfully produced, but most meaningful to me was the fact that this student sought me in my office *before* the class due date, personally to place his paper into my hands; it was the first time in nearly two semesters that this particular student had handed in an assignment on time.

The mutual admiration among us was at its greatest peak during this entire assignment, but the levels of frustration and bewilderment were highest here, too. Still, aren't the most exhilarating victories usually the hardest won? I, too, shared the sense of pride in looking at this wide range of excellence in these final products that included my own little essay, because we all knew that this particular accomplishment had been so slow in development. One final commentary is perhaps the best summary of the results of this experiment: "You know, at first I thought this assignment was going to be so easy," one student remarked, "but it was hard, one of the hardest papers I've ever written. It was so *hard* to stop writing regular, boring sentences. I never knew I was so locked into traditions. And I never knew that how I write what I want to say could matter so much to me." This student had clearly encountered and explored the limitations both she and conventional English had previously placed on her creativity. And she, like the rest of us, had learned to explore her own unique writer's self in a way that encouraged her to be different, to be stunning, to have fun with her own words and ideas. The students learned that writing well can be both exhausting and exhilarating, frustrating and rewarding. I learned that an instructor's own enthusiasm and creativity is not only contagious but absolutely intrinsic to our students' discovery of creativity and the fun of composition. And we all learned a truth that is demonstrable in Grammar A as well as in Grammar B or any other: a good crot is hard to find.

2

Rereading Hollywood

Joanna Hearne and Debra White-Stanley

During a recent screening of the 1931 version of *Dracula* in a literature and film class at the University of Arizona, everyone laughed when the enormous wooden doors to Dracula's castle creaked open by themselves to admit Dracula's next victim. The young Englishman ventured timidly into the interior of the Transylvanian castle, and was soon swallowed up by its gothic architecture, shadows, and cobwebs. Everyone in the auditorium just knew that Count Dracula would emerge in a black cape, and greet his visitor: "I bid you welcome."

But *how* do we know what Count Dracula is about to do before he does it? Perhaps our knowledge comes from the way that the encounter between Dracula and his victims has been imagined and re-imagined throughout the history of the horror film. To describe this historical process, film historians use the word "genre" to talk about easily recognizable types of films. Out of countless film genres, we are especially familiar with the horror film, the western, the musical, action-adventure films, romantic comedies, science fiction, mysteries, war films, and melodrama. The word "genre" is French for kind, or type, and is derived from the term "genus" which is used in the biological sciences to classify groups of plants or animals.[1] Filmmakers, reviewers, and audiences easily identify genre films through their distinguishing features, or "conventions."[2] These genre conventions, which include plot points, costumes, characters, settings, themes, and music, also make it more economical for studios to produce genre films over and over again. For instance, when we think of the Western genre, gunfights, saloons, horses, and the open spaces of Arizona's Monument Valley may come to mind. The mystery film may trigger flashbacks of Sherlock Holmes' Victorian cap and cape; the musical, Ginger Rogers in her high heels dancing cheek to cheek with Fred Astaire; the action-adventure film, exploding cars and bare-chested heroics. Science fiction genres often involve spaceships, aliens, and lasers. Genres can be combined: *Blade Runner* is part detective and part science fiction, and *Pocahontas* is a romance, a musical, a Western, and an animated children's story. Although we usually associate "genre films" with studio films, independent films—made by filmmakers outside of major film studios—often combine genres in unexpected or unusual ways. An independent film such as *Happiness* (Todd Solondz, 1998), which premiered at the Cannes Film Festival, uses the conventions of film melodrama to explore child molestation, a subject not often seen in "genre films."

We recognize the most common elements of genre because—whether we have taken film classes or not—we are experienced viewers whose very conception of film has been shaped by genre conventions. Television, movies, books, magazines, cartoons, the internet, and casual conversation have taught each of us how to "see" film and film genres. Our viewing experiences teach us to identify the conventions of particular film genres. Filmmakers and studios depend on this knowledge, and with each new film they appeal to the expectations that they have helped to shape. At the same time, because each of us brings our individual experiences to bear as we view genre films, we can still leave the theater with radically different interpretations of the same film. Our conversations about film, whether in the classroom or with family and friends, often take our common notions about film for granted and focus instead on our contrasting views.

It is helpful, too, to know a little bit about film technique, especially *mise-en-scène,* cinematography, and editing, as you talk about genre conventions. *Mise-en-scène* is a French phrase that comes from live theater and means "staging an action." Applied to cinema, the word refers to everything filmed by the camera and controlled by the director and the film crew—the setting, lighting, props, acting, costumes, etc. Cinematography ("writing in movement") refers to how filming takes place, for example the framing, camera position and movement, duration of the shot, film speed, focus, and color. Editing happens after the filming is complete and refers to the ordering of the film footage, particularly through cutting from one shot to the next. In many ways, editing determines the viewer's experience of time and space in the film (for instance, Quentin Tarantino plays with viewers' experience of time in *Pulp Fiction* by putting the "last" scene first). Specific film techniques, such as lighting and setting, can signal different genres. While comedies are often set indoors with bright lighting, horror films happen at night in dark cemeteries and houses, and Westerns are usually shot on location in spectacular outdoor settings with natural lighting. Some genres are defined by standard approaches to *mise-en-scène,* cinematography, and editing. Action films frequently involve actors doing martial arts *(mise-en-scène)*, lots of camera movement (cinematography), and rapid cutting from shot to shot (editing).

Because genre conventions become so familiar to us—indeed, even clichéd—as they appear and re-appear over time, filmmakers constantly re-invent genres to attract new audiences. Count Dracula and Frankenstein, for example, have been re-imagined as the wisecracking Freddy Krueger of *Nightmare on Elm Street,* the clunky T-800 cyborg from the future in *Terminator,* and the aristocratic lesbian vampire who seduces Susan Sarandon in *The Hunger*. Sometimes genre conventions become clichés, and some directors use this to comic effect by parodying over-used formulas (as Mel Brooks does in *Young Frankenstein* [1974] or Wes Craven in *Scream* [1996]). In the classical Greek world, the very idea of genre, as Thomas Sobchack suggests in his article in this chapter, meant "imitations of prior stories"[3] rather than new expressions of human experience in theatre and literature. As you might expect, American genre films also rely on audiences' familiarity with strict rules or conventions.

Perhaps because of the broad appeal of genre films, recent film criticism has examined the way genre conventions communicate our collective cultural anxieties about problems in American society. Representations of femininity and masculinity, sexuality, race, ethnicity, and socio-economic class can tap into problems of power imbalance and inequality that continue to cause deep social rifts. Our project in this chapter is to re-view films in light of genre conventions, asking ourselves how we might best understand the cultural forces at work in the films and in the genres themselves. For example, film critics have connected the rise of feminist attitudes with the development of strong female heroines, such as Ripley (Sigourney Weaver) in *Aliens* (James Cameron, 1986). Other critics have argued that the science fiction films of the 1950s, which show hydrogen bombs creating Godzilla-like monsters, reflect fears of technology run amok.[4] While stories about vampirism can be traced all the way back to ancient Chinese myth, Bram Stoker's novel *Dracula* (1897) expresses Victorian anxieties about female sexuality. In another transformation, the 1931 film adaptation of *Dracula* depicts the Count as a Machiavellian Continental aristocrat in the period between the two world wars, when the United States feared further entanglement in European affairs.

In this way, genre films offer a window on the way film conventions are shaped by the social forces and beliefs of a specific historical moment. While highlighting conventions used by filmmakers, genre criticism can help audiences understand how cinema has contributed to our own perspectives on history and politics. For instance, students watching John Ford's 1939 film *Stagecoach,* starring John Wayne, might experience boredom, admiration, and sadness during one famous scene in which a lone stagecoach is attacked by a group of Apache Indians in Arizona's Monument Valley. Boredom, because the Indian chase scene is such a familiar convention of the John Wayne Western that it's hard to watch it with fresh eyes. Admiration, because the performers and stunt men in the scene are choreographed so gracefully in combat and death. Sadness and frustration because the film misrepresents Western history. The John Wayne Western preceded our current understanding of that history—limited as it is. At the same time, Westerns express national uneasiness about the way the United States was formed—that despite our democratic constitution, our history includes frontier violence, racial inequality, and land theft.

Because genre films depend on the audience's familiarity with prior films and genre conventions, people experience genre in various ways. Critic Greg Smith argues that filmmakers—especially for genre films such as slasher movies—actually *depend* on their audiences to "read into" the movie to create narrative tension. You know, for example, that Dracula only drinks the blood of his victims at night—so when night falls in a Dracula film, beware! But audiences bring much more to the theater than just their knowledge of genre conventions. For example, both Garry Watson and Sherman Alexie, in their articles in this chapter, investigate the Western genre's representation of heroes. Watson argues that Westerns are really about the way American communities have been founded through violence. The heroic gunfighter in *Shane,* for instance, plays an important role in establishing a peaceful community, and yet is too tainted by violence to join that community. Shane helps to found the community, yet must be sacrificed for the community to succeed. Sherman Alexie focuses on the effect racial stereotypes of Indians (especially when played by white actors) had on him as a child growing up on the Spokane Reservation. Both authors are "re-seeing" the conventions of the Western as they interrogate what makes the Western "work." Watson uses the traditional academic tools of close-reading and theoretical frameworks, while Alexie draws on his own personal background and changing responses over time.

The essays in this chapter help readers to identify the standard conventions of well-known film genres, yet sometimes the whole concept of genre becomes problematic. For instance, as film critic Casey McKittrick asks in his essay in this chapter, how do we classify films that portray the sexual abuse of children? Are the many versions of *Lolita* part road film, part romance, part coming-of-age story? Are films that self-consciously portray pedophilia (such as *American Beauty* and *Happiness*) a newly emergent genre, or is pedophilia a theme extending across various genres? Is genre, in important ways, in the eye of the beholder? Some independent films, and films by directors such as David Lynch, quote multiple genres and movements, yet don't seem to fall squarely into any specific genre. The history of African-American cinema similarly spans across many historical genres, such as early "race films" *(The Scar of Shame)*, Blaxploitation films *(Shaft)*, horror films *(Candyman)*, and the gangster film *(Menace II Society)*.[5] Critic bell hooks argues that African-Americans are stereotypically represented in independent and Hollywood films alike.[6]

Delving into the complexities of genre can help you see and write about film in new ways, and provides a fascinating entrance into writing about film. You might see aspects of a film genre that others don't—or you might be drawn to explore one genre rather than others—because of your upbringing, your gender, your ethnicity, your educational interests, or any number of factors. The readings that follow will help you to explore questions of genre for writing either research or personal reflection papers.

But what is to be gained by studying films or film genres? Studios are very aware of trends in reception, and manipulate those trends for profit. In that sense, films are like any other "product"—food, clothes, or cars—and becoming an informed consumer of film maximizes your ability to understand your viewing habits and choices. If you're like most people, you spend a considerable amount of time watching films—at least one or two a week—and you'll want to understand why you're drawn to certain films and not others. Why are you moved, angered, or entertained by some films and not others? Since genre films often reveal a great deal about the social forces that shape them, becoming an active rather than a passive viewer can empower you by providing otherwise elusive insights into the world around you.

Many people also analyze movies because they love them—we love watching films, talking about films, and reading and writing about films. Far from "ruining" the pleasure of watching films, immersing ourselves in the details only increases our enjoyment. "Analyzing" films (or business trends, or genetic structures, or childhood development) offers the opportunity to immerse yourself in something you love, an activity that enriches rather than sabotages the experience. University life provides a space for asking questions about everyday life that usually go unasked, and the skills that come from asking these questions will remain with you, shaping your professional and personal life and decisions.

Works Cited

Bordwell, David and Kristin Thompson, *Film Art: An Introduction*. Sixth Edition. (New York: The McGraw Hill Companies, Inc., 2001) 94.

Guerrero, Ed. "black violence as cinema: from cheap thrills to historical agonies." *Violence and American Cinema*. Ed., J. David Slocum (New York: Routledge, 2001) 211–215.

hooks, bell. "Seduction and Betrayal," *Writing as Revision* (Needham Heights, MA: Simon & Schuster, 2001) 108–111.

Sobchack, Thomas. "Genre Film: A Classical Experience." *Film Genre Reader II*. Ed. Barry Keith Grant. (Austin: University of Texas Press, 1995) 104.

Notes

1. David Bordwell and Kristin Thompson, *Film Art: An Introduction*. Sixth Edition. (New York: The McGraw Hill Companies, Inc., 2001) 94.
2. Bordwell and Thompson, 96.
3. Thomas Sobchack, "Genre Film: A Classical Experience." *Film Genre Reader II*. Ed. Barry Keith Grant. (Austin: University of Texas Press, 1995) 104.
4. Bordwell and Thompson, 100.
5. Ed Guerrero, "black violence as cinema: from cheap thrills to historical agonies." *Violence and American Cinema*. Ed., J. David Slocum (New York: Routledge, 2001) 211–215.
6. bell hooks, "Seduction and Betrayal," *Writing as Revision* (Needham Heights, MA: Simon & Schuster, 2001) 108–111.

Greg M. Smith

Greg M. Smith teaches in the Communications department at Carlow College in Pittsburgh, PA. He is finishing his dissertation at the University of Wisconsin-Madison on film and emotion. He has published several essays in Cinema Journal, *the journal for the Society for Cinema Studies, and an edited collection entitled* On a Silver Platter: CD-ROMs and the Promise of a New Technology *(1999). This essay, published in* Cinema Journal, *asks teachers and students of film to re-think their ideas about the value of film analysis.* Cinema Journal *is published by the Society for Cinema Studies and is one of the major journals in academic film and television studies.*

"It's Just a Movie": A Teaching Essay for Introductory Media Classes

The question arises almost every semester. My introductory film class and I will be hip deep in analyzing the details of a film and a hand will creep up, usually from the back: "Aren't we reading too much into this? After all, it's just a movie." Taking a deep breath, I launch into a spirited defense of our analytic activity. After five or ten minutes, the student usually has a shell-shocked, what-did-I-do-to-deserve-this look on her face.

I have never been pleased with my spur-of-the-moment justifications of film analysis, which tend to come across as a bit defensive. Worst of all, they do not deal fully with the question, which I believe is very profound. Why are we spending so much time finding new meanings in something as insignificant as a movie? Aren't we just "reading into" the film? The student's question deserves a fuller answer, or, rather, it deserves several answers. As a way of finding those answers, this essay extends the dialogue started by that series of brave, inquiring students in my classes.

Leaving Nothing to Chance.

"All right, do you really think that every little thing in the film is there for a reason?"

Lots of things in our everyday world are there by accident. If I trip over a stone, causing me to bump into someone, the encounter is probably not part of a higher design. Random occurrences happen all the time, with no enormous significance. There is a temptation to treat a film in a similar manner, as if everything occurs by chance. Nothing could be further from the truth.

Reprinted from *Cinema Journal*, Fall 2001.

A Hollywood film is one of the most highly scrutinized, carefully constructed, least random works imaginable. Of course, we know this, having seen *Entertainment Tonight*. We all know that it takes thousands of people to create a blockbuster movie: directors, actors, grips, and gaffers. We know that producing a film is a highly coordinated effort by dedicated professionals, but to most people it is a bit of a mystery what all these people do. When we start watching a film, we are encouraged to forget about all that mysterious collective labor. A Hollywood film usually asks us to get caught up in the story, in the world that has been created, so that we are not aware of the behind-the-scenes effort. We tend to forget the thousands of minute decisions that consciously construct the artificial world that has been created.

When I put on a shirt in the morning, I do so with very little thought (as my students will tell you). By contrast, a movie character's shirt is chosen by a professional whose job it is to think about the shirt this character would wear. Similar decisions are made for props, sound, cuts, and so on. Filmmakers work hard to exclude the random from their fictional worlds. Sets are built so that the filmmaker can have absolute control over the environment. Crews spend a great deal of time and expense between shots adjusting the lighting so that each shot will look as polished as possible. When filmmakers do want something to appear random, they carefully choreograph it. For instance, extras who are merely walking by the main characters are told where to go and what to do to appear "natural."

"But what about directors who do not sanitize the film set, who try to let bits of the real world into their films (from the Italian neorealists to Kevin Smith, director of Clerks *[1994])? What about actors like Dustin Hoffman and Robin Williams who like to improvise? What about documentary filmmakers who do not script what happens in front of the camera? Don't these directors and actors let a little bit of chance creep into film?"* Not really. These strategies may allow some chance occurrences to make it into the raw footage. However, the filmmaker and the editor watch the collected footage over and over, deciding which portions of which takes they will assemble into the final cut of a movie. They do so with the same scrutiny that was applied to the actual filming. Even if something occurred on film without their planning for it, they make a conscious choice whether to include that chance occurrence. What was chance in the filming becomes choice in editing.

"Come on, do film professionals from editors to set designers really *spend all that time scrutinizing such details?"* Think of it this way: A Hollywood blockbuster may cost up to $200 million. If you were to make something that costs that much, wouldn't you scrutinize every tiny detail? Even a "low-budget" movie can cost $10 million or so. With so much money riding on a film, there needs to be enormous scrutiny, and this extends to all levels. Of course this process, like all human effort, is fallible; mistakes sometimes creep in (for example, extras in a film set in ancient Rome may be seen wearing wristwatches). All too often, beginning film scholars have a tendency to assume that odd moments in a film are mistakes, when the opposite is more likely to be true. Nothing in a final film is there unless scores of professionals have carefully examined it. You can trust that if something is in a film, it is there for a reason.

A Movie Is Not a Telegram.

"Okay, so the director really cares about the details. But do you think your interpretation is what she really meant to say?"

In high school English classes, you may have been taught to look for the meaning of a literary work, a single sentence that summarizes what the author was trying to convey. So you might have boiled Shakespeare's *Macbeth* down to a single sentence that reveals the moral lesson of the play (perhaps "Greed for power corrupts people"). Similarly, one can reduce a film to its message, which makes the game of interpretation fairly simple. All we have to do is figure out what the author/director was trying to say.

Some filmmakers scoff at the idea that their movies contain messages. Hollywood producer Samuel Goldwyn, for example, is alleged to have said, "If I wanted to send a message, I would've called Western Union." What is at issue here is the conception of what communication is. The traditional understanding of speech considers a sender trying to relay a message to a receiver (often called the S-M-R model). A sender has a clear intention of what she wants to get across to the receiver, but she may not present her message particularly clearly. The receiver tries to understand the message, but she may misunderstand the sender for a variety of reasons. By comparing the sender's intention with the receiver's understanding, one can discover how effective the communication was. For example, if a receiver gets a telegram asking for bail money and then starts collecting the necessary cash, then a successful instance of communication has taken place.

It is tempting to conceptualize a film as communicating a message in a similar way. To find out if a film is effective, one can compare the filmmaker's intentions with our interpretations and see if we "got" it. If a viewer did not receive the message, then perhaps the film is poorly made or perhaps the viewer is not very savvy.

Films, plays, and novels, however, are not telegrams; they are infinitely more complicated. One of the first traps that the budding critic should avoid is thinking that a film can be understood as having a single message that we either "get" or don't get. To think this way is to treat a film like a telegram. The cinema is a richer form of communication than can be conceptualized as sender-message-receiver.

"Okay, so perhaps the filmmaker isn't just sending a single message. Maybe she's sending several messages. If we can figure out what those messages are, then we've got it, yes?"

First of all, there is a thorny question of who the film's "author" is. Unlike a book, hundreds of people put their work into a major film. If all of them are trying to convey meaning, do we have to consider all of their combined intentions? Or if some people's contributions are more important than others (screenwriter, actors, director, cinematographer, producer), then can we understand a film as the sum total of their intentions?

Let's make it easy on ourselves. Assume that the author/filmmaker of a movie is the person who is in charge of coordinating all the decisions in the shooting process: the director. If we can figure out what the director intends, then we've got it, right? If we could interview Hitchcock and gain an understanding of what was going through his mind when he made *Vertigo* (1958), we would have a pretty solid hold on the film, yes?

But can we reduce the film to what the director consciously intended? At times we all express the beliefs, attitudes, and assumptions of our times without necessarily being conscious of doing so. Did Hitchcock fully understand his attitude toward blonde women, or was he propagating a widely held belief? Sometimes the ideology of our day speaks through us with little awareness on our part. In addition, we can unconsciously express personal issues as well as social attitudes. Many believe that the unconscious seeks to express painful things that we have repressed and buried within ourselves. These tensions can emerge in our everyday lives through dreams, Freudian slips, and artwork. Perhaps Hitchcock was unconsciously working through an obsession with cool, aloof women in ways that he did not even understand when he made *Vertigo*. Since human beings cannot be reduced to their conscious thoughts, films should not be reduced to the director's conscious intentions.

"Okay, so if we get a sense of what the director's conscious intentions are, what ideological beliefs she gained from her socialization, and what her unconscious issues are (admittedly a difficult process), then we've arrived at a well-grounded, comprehensive description of what the film is trying to communicate, right?" We have, if we stay within the sender-message-receiver model. But let's step outside that paradigm. Why should we limit the viewer to arriving at only those meanings that come directly from the sender/filmmaker? If I get meaning out of a film and apply it to my life, why should I have to check with the filmmaker to see if it's the right meaning? In other words, why should the filmmaker have more authority over my interpretation of the film than I do?

"Because she's the filmmaker. It's her movie," you may reply. I would respond, "You are the audience. It is your movie, too." If you let go of the notion that the filmmaker is trying to convey a message, then the activity of viewers is to interpret the film according to their lives, their experiences, their tastes—not the filmmaker's. That activity is just as valid as the filmmaker's. The meaning of a movie does not lie solely within the film itself but in the interaction of the film and the audience.

As we learn more and more about how audiences interpret movies, we discover the striking range of interpretations people make. If we consider those "readings" to be somehow less valid than the filmmaker's, then we lose much of the complexity of how movies work, make meaning, and provide pleasure in our society.

"Reading Into" Films.

"But those audiences are just reading things into the movie, right?"

Let's think about what "reading into" a movie is. "That's simple," you might reply. "It's when an audience puts things into the movie that aren't there." That certainly seems straightforward enough. But is it?

Picture yourself watching a horror film in which a group of teenagers are staying at a spooky cabin deep in the woods. It is midnight. A couple sneaks off to a back bedroom and has sex. The attractive young woman then gets up, decides that she is going to take a shower, and says that she will be right back.

You know that this woman will be toast in a matter of minutes.

But how do you know? There is nothing in the film itself that says this woman will die. The same incident (romantic rural location, sexy couple) could take place in a romantic film, and the shower would not raise any hackles. No, the knowledge of her imminent death comes from you, the experienced horror film viewer. You have "read into" the scene.

Like the characters in *Scream* (1996), you know that horror films operate according to a set of rules or conventions that have been established by previous films in the genre. The filmmaker depends on you to know these conventions. She knows that by sending the woman to the shower, she can create tension in the audience ("No! Don't go, you crazy girl!"). The filmmaker can toy with the audience, delaying the inevitable, because she knows that we expect the girl to be slashed. It is our job as audience members to read into the scene; filmmakers count on that.

Movies rely on the audience to supply information that is only hinted at in the film, like the shower convention in horror films. This "reading into" occurs even at the simplest levels of filmmaking. When we see a shot of someone getting into a car and driving away, followed by a shot of the car pulling into another driveway, we understand that the driver drove from one place to another. We understand this without the film actually showing us the drive. If we were limited to what was explicitly laid out in the film, if we did not read into it, then we would not be able to make basic sense out of the movie. There is really no choice of whether to read into a film or not; audiences always do.

This is not to say that you can read a movie in any way you want. Certain pieces of information are established beyond dispute. If you do not think that *Raiders of the Lost Ark* (1981) is about an explorer/archaeologist looking for the Ark of the Covenant, then you have missed something. If you believe that it is about Arctic beekeeping, you are doing a remarkably perverse bit of reading.

Between a pedestrian reading (the driving example, which some would call an inference or expectation) and the ludicrous kind (*Raiders* as about Arctic beekeeping), a wide range of readings are possible. You may find some of them too much of a stretch. What I would ask is that you remain open to the possibility that some of these readings may be interesting. Do not close down your mind simply because an interpretation involves "reading into" a movie, because all film viewings involve this active process. Instead, look at the movie with an open mind and see if there is evidence to support a particular interpretation. If someone says that *Raiders* is really about finding God, Freudian revenge on the father, or Ronald Reagan, see if there is corroborating material.[1] Based on the film, decide if there is a case to be made for one of those interpretations.

Just a Movie.

"Okay, maybe I see the value of coming up with new interpretations of Hamlet *or* Citizen Kane, *but* Raiders? *Or* Evil Dead 2 *(1987)? Come on. Aren't you taking all this a bit too seriously? After all, it's just a movie."*

You would not say, "Why are you analyzing *Hamlet*? After all, it's just Shakespeare." Why is it okay to analyze Shakespeare and not *Evil Dead 2*? The answer has as much to do with the social status of these works as it does with the works themselves.

There was a time when the study of Shakespeare would have been questionable as being not serious enough. At first, scholars in the West did not think that anything written in English was as worthy of study as the classics written in Greek. Homer, Sophocles, and Aristotle were the serious writers whose works were taught in school, not Shakespeare's plays or Dickens's novels. Lawrence Levine has traced how the status of Shakespeare's work has changed in America, from rather lowbrow in vaudeville productions to its current highbrow status.[2] Dickens's novels, now clearly considered classics, were serialized in newspapers as pulp fiction. In their day, to argue that Dickens's work should be taught in schools would have seemed almost scandalous. Such trash obviously could not withstand the scrutiny applied to great works like Homer's *Odyssey,* or so it seemed.

Instead of relying purely on our society's understanding of what artworks are good enough to be taken seriously, we should instead look to the artworks themselves. If we look for rich interpretations of a work, we may find them, or we may not. The point is not to dismiss the process outright simply because it is "just a movie." The proof is in the pudding, as the old saying goes. If your analysis produces insightful, well-grounded interpretations of a film, then it is definitely fruitful for analyzing, even if it is titled *Evil Dead 2.*

No one will argue that all media works are equally rich for analysis. Probably *Hamlet* is a more complex text than *Evil Dead 2*. But that should not lead us to neglect a text that is "just a movie." You should take insight where you can get it. And even if a film is not particularly complex, it can still provide hints about the society that produced it. Events do not have to be overtly complicated to yield knowledge.

For example, Robert Darnton analyzes a particularly unpromising-sounding phenomenon: a mock trial and execution of some cats by the apprentices and journeymen in a Parisian printing shop in the 1730s.[3] What could this bizarre, sadistic, and unusual ritual possibly tell us about eighteenth-century French society? Reading closely, Darnton shows how this odd ceremony reveals much about the relationship between workers and bosses, the sexual and class structures of the society, and the tradition of a craft. His essay demonstrates that even slight cultural artifacts bear the imprint of the society that made them. Examining a film can give us clues about the meanings and assumptions shared by the members of a culture. If a mock trial of cats can reveal social interrelationships, then an uncomplicated film that does not appear to warrant much aesthetic scrutiny can be examined for its social insights. All cultural products carry cultural meaning.

Ruining the Movie.

Part of the resistance to applying analytic tools to a film like *Evil Dead 2* is the belief that such analysis will kill the pleasure of watching the movie. After all, movies are intended to be "mere entertainment." We have already dealt with the question of the filmmaker's intention, so let's not deal further with whether we should be limited to the filmmaker's conception of the film as "mere entertainment." Instead, let's deal with the fear that analyzing a film will destroy the simple pleasure of watching it.

Sometimes it seems that the surest way to ruin a good book is to have to read it for a class. English classes are supposed to make you read things that you would not normally pick up yourself. They force you to read Chaucer or James Joyce, and the hope is that in the process of analyzing these works you'll gain insight into your life. But that is very different from reading Michael Crichton or John Grisham. In the latter case, reading is an escape. If we start thinking too hard about airport novels or mainstream films, doesn't it ruin them?

When people learn that I study the media for a living, they frequently ask, "Are you ever able to just sit back and enjoy a movie, or are you always analyzing it?" The question never rings true because it is phrased as either/or. For me, it is not a matter of substituting cerebral analysis for visceral pleasure; I experience both simultaneously. I can still root for the good guy while admiring a film's editing and thinking about the plot's social ramifications. Similarly, after taking media studies classes, students should be able to add the pleasures of analysis to the pleasures of moviegoing.

I realize that as you are taking an introductory film analysis class, there may not seem to be much pleasure in analysis. It probably seems more like tedious, difficult work. At first, it may seem that you are losing the pleasurable experience of the movie as you dissect it, but as you get better at film analysis, you will be able to recombine those activities. The end result, I believe, is a richer kind of pleasure. I believe that I respond more fully to movies than I did before I started analyzing them. I now feel joy at a well-composed shot, a tautly constructed narrative structure, and an innovative social commentary, as well as the simpler pleasure of finding out whodunit. The outcome we hope for in a film analysis class is not to ruin film watching but to increase the complexity of enjoyment.

"Why do that? Why tinker with the simple pleasure of watching a movie?" This question goes to the foundation of what education is. The basic faith underlying education is that an examined life is better, richer, and fuller than an unexamined life. How do we really know that self-examination is better than the bliss of simple ignorance? Like most statements of faith, there is no way to prove it. But by being in a college classroom, you have allied yourself with those of us who believe that if you do not examine the forces in your life, you will become subject to them. You can go through life merely responding to movies, but if you are an educated person, you will also think about them, about what they mean, and how they are constructed. In so doing, you may experience pleasures and insights that you could not have obtained any other way. This is the promise of the educated life in reading, in living, and in watching movies.

Notes

Thanks to David Bordwell, Henry Jenkins, and Pamela Wilson for their helpful comments on an earlier version of this essay.

1. The idea that Indiana Jones is an avatar of Ronald Reagan is found in Frank P. Tomasulo, "Mr. Jones Goes to Washington: Myth and Religion in *Raiders of the Lost Ark,*" *Quarterly Review of Film Studies* 7, no. 4 (fall 1982): 331–40.
2. Lawrence Levine, *Highbrow/Lowbrow: The Emergence of a Cultural Hierarchy in America* (Cambridge: Harvard University Press, 1990).
3. Robert Darnton, "Workers Revolt: The Great Cat Massacre of the Rue Saint-Séverin," in *The Great Cat Massacre and Other Episodes in French Cultural History* (New York: Random House, 1985), 9–72.

Thomas Sobchack

Thomas Sobchack is currently the Director of Graduate Study for Film and Theatre at the University of Utah, where he has also been an English Professor. He received his Ph.D. from City University of New York. He is the co-author (with Vivian Sobchack) of An Introduction to Film *(1980) and (with Tim Bywater) of* Introduction to Film Criticism *(1989). His articles have appeared in such journals as* Literature/Film Quarterly *and* Journal of Popular Film and Television *and in several anthologies. He is also the film critic for Morning Edition on KUER-FM, the local NPR affiliate. Professor Sobchack's article, published in the useful anthology* Film Genre Reader II *(Austin: University of Texas Press, 1995), argues that the origins of many contemporary film genres, such as the horror film and the musical, can be found in ancient modes of storytelling.*

Genre Film: A Classical Experience

In *An Illustrated Glossary of Film Terms,* Harry M. Geduld and Ronald Gottesman define *genre* as a "category, kind, or form of film distinguished by subject matter, theme, or techniques."[1] They list more than seventy-five genres of film, both fiction and nonfiction. There are categories within categories and categories which overlap and are not mutually exclusive. In light of the difficulty of accurately defining the individual genres, I would rather sidestep the problem by considering the fictional genre film as a single category that includes all that is commonly held to be genre film—i.e., the western, the horror film, the musical, the science fiction film, the swashbuckler—in order to show that all of these films have a common origin and basic form. Bound by a strict set of conventions, tacitly agreed upon by filmmaker and audience, the genre film provides the experience of an ordered world and is an essentially classical structure predicated upon the principles of the classical world view in general and indebted to the *Poetics* of Aristotle in particular; in the genre film the plot is fixed, the characters defined, the ending satisfyingly predictable.

Because the genre film is not realistic, because it is so blatantly dramatic, it has been condescendingly treated by many critics for its failure to be relevant to contemporary issues, philosophies, and aesthetics. Yet the truth of the matter is that

---

Reprinted from *Film Genre Reader II*, (1995), edited by Barry Keith Grant, University of Texas Press.

the genre film lives up to the guiding principle of its classical origins: "there is nothing new under the sun," and truth with a capital T is to be found in imitating the past. The contemporary and the particular are inimical to the prevailing idea in classical thought that knowledge is found in the general conclusions that have stood the test of time. Thus originality, unique subject matter, and a resemblance to actual life are denigrated as values, while conformity, adherence to previous models, and a preoccupation with stylistic and formal matters are held to be the criteria for artistic excellence.

The subject matter of a genre film is a story. It is not about something that matters outside the film, even if it inadvertently tells us something about the time and place of its creation. Its sole justification for existence is to make concrete and perceivable the configurations inherent in its ideal form. That the various genres have changed or gone through cycles of popularity does not alter the fact that the basic underlying coordinates of a genre are maintained time after time. From *The Great Train Robbery* (Edwin S. Porter, 1902) to *The Cowboys* (Mark Rydell, 1972) or *True Grit* (Henry Hathaway, 1968), the western has maintained a consistency of basic content; the motifs, plots, settings, and characters remain the same. What is true of the western is also true of the adventure film, the fantasy film, the crime film, and the musical, or any fictional genre one can identify. Any particular film of any definable group is only recognizable as part of that group if it is, in fact, an imitation of that which came before. It is only because we have seen other films that strongly resemble the particular film at hand that we can say it is a horror film or a thriller or a swashbuckler. Consciously or unconsciously, both the genre filmmaker and the genre audiences are aware of the prior films and the way in which each of these concrete examples is an attempt to embody once again the essence of a well-known story.

This use of well-known stories is clearly a classical practice. Homer, the Greek dramatists, Racine, Pope, Samuel Johnson, and all the other great figures of the classical and neoclassical periods used prior sources for their stories. The formative principle behind the creation of classical art has always been the known and the familiar. The Greeks knew the stories of the gods and the Trojan War in the same way we know about hoodlums and gangsters and G-men and the taming of the frontier and the never-ceasing struggle of the light of reason and the cross with the powers of darkness, not through first-hand experience but through the media. For them it was tales told around the hearth and the yearly ritual of plays; for us it is the newspapers, television, and the movies themselves.

The body of stories is, to use Balazs's terms, the "material" out of which the "content" of a genre film can be made. And it is a strictly delimited area: other films may have the whole of life experience to choose from, but the genre film must be made from certain well-known and immediately recognizable plots—plots usually dealing with melodramatic incidents in which obvious villains and heroes portray the basic conflict of good versus evil. No matter how complicated the plot of a genre film may be, we always know who the good guys and the bad guys are; we always know whom to identify with and for just how long. Sam Spade may be considered by real-life standards to be a man of dubious moral character, but in the world of *The Maltese Falcon* (John Huston, 1941) he is clearly the hero akin to Odysseus threading his way through the obstacles of a hostile universe, using lies and deceit if necessary to complete his task.

Aristotle used the word *mimesis* to describe what a play is about. Supposedly it means imitation. Aristotle goes on to say that a plot is an imitation of a human action, and there are those who see in this definition the prescription for a kind of literal realism, holding the mirror up to life. But Greek drama, from which Aristotle drew his conclusions, was never that at all. Very few people in fifth-century Athens killed their fathers and slept with their mothers. The story of Oedipus, no matter how rife with Freudian implications for us today, was after all simply a story, albeit a kind of horror tale of its time, as were most of the stories upon which Greek writing was based. In practical terms Greek writings are imitations of prior stories, redone, reshaped, given dramatic form or epic form as the case may be, but nevertheless imitations of fictions.

Genre films operate on the same principle. They are made in imitation not of life but of other films. True, there must be the first instance in a series or cycle, yet most cases of the first examples of various film genres can be traced to literary sources, primarily pulp literature. Even the gangster films of the thirties derive not from life itself but from newspaper stories; the musical film, from the musical stage. And once the initial film is made, it has entered the pool of common knowledge known by filmmaker and film audience alike. Imitations and descendants—the long line of "sons of," "brides of," and "the return of"—begin.

One of the paradoxes of a classical approach to form is aptly demonstrated in the genre film's unrelenting pursuit of imitation. Classical theory insists upon the primacy of the original. It is that which must be imitated, and the basic and fundamental elements must not be changed. Therefore, to avoid an exact duplicate, subsequent imitations can merely embroider and decorate, which in most cases destroys the elegance and simplicity of the original design. The Doric column came first, simple, balanced, proportioned, direct. As the years passed, the Doric gave way to the Ionic, and the Ionic to the Corinthian, the last column so cluttered and intricate that it diluted the original idea. Classical painting and architecture gave way to the rococo and the baroque. The decorations increase; the power and the purity of the original are somehow dissipated.

We can see the same process at work in the genre film, and it explains why so often the original version or the "classic" version seems so much better than any of its followers. The original Draculas, silent and sound, *Little Caesar* (Mervyn LeRoy, 1930) and *The Public Enemy* (William Wellman, 1931), *The Iron Horse* (John Ford, 1924) and *The Covered Wagon* (James Cruze, 1923), Busby Berkeley musicals, *The Maltese Falcon*—not only were they progenitors of their kind and therefore to be venerated as examples from the Golden Age, but seen today they have a sparseness and an economy of means that put most of the recent remakes to shame. Christopher Lee cannot compare to Bela Lugosi, and full-color blood cannot make up for the spectral mysteriousness of F. W. Murnau's *Nosferatu* (1922).

A genre film, no matter how baroque it may become, however, still differs fundamentally from other films by virtue of its reliance on preordained forms, known plots, recognizable characters, and obvious iconographies; it is still capable of creating the classical experience because of this insistence on the familiar. It is what we expect in a genre film and what we get. Other fiction films are not genre films precisely because they do the opposite; they go out of their way to be original, unique, and novel. They appear more realistic, more true to life. Their characters are more highly individualized, their actions physically and psychologically more believable, and the events of the plot, employing random events and inconsequential details, well within the realm of possibility.

There are grey areas, of course—films that seem to be closer to genre than others depending on the total effect of the film, the way in which the realistic elements are emphasized or deemphasized, the way in which generic elements are used or abused. Yet for most films the issue is more clear-cut. The ideas and attitudes informing genre films are diametrically opposed to the other kind of fiction film. Although there is a detective (the reporter) and a mystery (what's Rosebud?), it would be difficult to make a case for *Citizen Kane* (Orson Welles, 1941) as a detective or mystery genre film. Though it has certain generic elements, they are not prominent, nor are they the sole justification for the creation of the film. On the other hand, Sherlock Holmes films, the Thin Man series, Charlie Chan movies, and others exist primarily to flesh out the idea of the detective story on film. They exist as variations on the motif of sleuthing. "Who dun it?" is the primary question raised and answered by these movies. No matter how rich a gold mine of interpretation one may find in *The Maltese Falcon,* for example, the basic question dealt with is still "Who dun it?" and not "Who am I?" or "What is the discrepancy between what a man appears to be and what he really is?" This is not to say that something of the latter question is not raised by Sam Spade's character, but certainly the film does not invite the general audience to take the question seriously, even if critics do.

One of the most important characteristics of the classical complex is a concern with form. Genre films, as suggested, are invariably more involved with formal matters both in content and in style, since they begin in imitation of other formal objects and not in imitation of life. In keeping with this notion, the form of a genre film will display a profound respect for Aristotelian dramatic values. There is always a definite sense of beginning, middle, and end, of closure, and of a frame. The film begins with "Once upon a time . . ." and ends only after all the strings have been neatly tied, all major conflicts resolved. It is a closed world. There is little room in the genre film for ambiguity anywhere—in characters, plots, or iconography. But even when seeming ambiguities arise in the course of a film, they must be either deemphasized or taken care of by the end of the film.

The most important single aspect of the genre film that gives it this compact sense of shape is the plot. It's what happens that is most important, not why. Incident crowding on incident, reversal after reversal, all strung out like beads on a string (or a rosary), to be counted one after another until the final shoot-out, the burning of the castle, the destruction of the fiend, the payment of the mortgage on the Big Top, or the return of the spacecraft to earth. Inherent and implicit in the beginning of any genre plot is the end; the elements presented in the exposition at the beginning are all clearly involved with the inevitable conclusion. Nothing extraneous to the plot can be introduced at random, somewhere in the middle. The best genre films always seem shorter than they really are. The classical virtue of economy of means may have been forced upon the genre film because of its usually low production budget, but it has maximized this possible defect. Only those scenes that advance the plot are permitted. Only that dialogue which will keep things moving is allowed. The adage attributed apocryphally to Hitchcock, that you should never use dialogue when you can show it in pictures, is often reversed in the genre film—even in Hitchcock's films. Whenever it takes too long to show it, say it instead. Do anything and everything to keep the plot moving, to create the sense of gathering momentum, of inevitable causality.

To further speed comprehension of the plot, genre films employ visual codes, called iconographies, in order to eliminate the need for excessive verbal or pictorial exposition. Strictly speaking, beyond the use of masks, there is nothing in Greek drama comparable to the iconography of the genre film, for as Aristotle pointed out, "spectacle"—what we see—is the least important element of a play, while it is obviously a primary aspect of film. A more appropriate analogy can be found in the Greek narrative art—the epic poems. Homer is an exceptionally visual poet, particularly when he is describing the armor and weapons of his heroes in *The Iliad; The Odyssey,* too, pictorializes costumes, metamorphoses, monsters, and settings in a way that brings to mind the vividness of the modern equivalent—the genre film.

Iconography consists of certain photographed objects, costumes, and places composing the visible surface of a genre film that creates economically the context and milieu, the field of action on which the plot will unravel itself. Over a period of use in many films, these visual elements have become encrusted with shared meanings, so that dialogue and camera can concentrate on revealing the twists and turns of the plot. Iconography, like familiar plot situations and stereotypical characters, provides a shorthand of mutually recognizable communications that neither filmmaker nor audience need ponder: the jungle is treacherous, the castle that towers darkly over the village is sinister, the flat horizon of the desert is unyielding. Capes and evening clothes create threatening figures unless they are in a musical; laboratories with bubbling liquids are occupied by men tampering with things no human being should.

Like the epithet—a descriptive, characterizing tag line in the epic poems (the "wine-dark sea," the "bronze-shot arrows," the "cunning Odysseus")—the icons of genre films serve to remind the viewer of the internal consistency and familiarity of the characters and places in the film. These places and characters do not change in the course of a film, and very little from film to film. The visual appearance of a western town in one film is just about the same as in other films. The landscape in a sci-fi picture can be depended upon. The world of the musical is always a glittering unreality poised somewhere between our doughty old world and heaven, whether it is set backstage at the Broadway Theater or high in the Swiss Alps.

As indicated above, characterization in a genre film often uses the shorthand of iconography. We know a person by what he wears as opposed to what he says and does. And once known, the character cannot change except in the most limited ways. Curiously enough, the Greek word for *character* as applied to human beings was the same as that applied to a letter of the alphabet. That is, the root word means the "stamp" that imprints the letter on the paper, or the stamp that imprints the character onto the person. Right up until the end of the classical era—and the neoclassical—in the eighteenth century, the prevailing opinion was that human character was imprinted at birth and that it did not develop or change. Though the subsequent revolutions of thought in the nineteenth and twentieth centuries have all but wiped out this idea, the genre film continues to employ this extremely classical concept.

Frequently generalized and known by their vocation, genre characters are conveyed through iconographical means—costumes, tools, settings, and so on. The man who wears a star, whether he is a figure in the crowd or a major character, has a limited range of responses to situations. The same is the case with men who wear lab coats, carry sawed-off shotguns, or drink their whiskey straight. These men are their functions in the plot. Revealed to us through costume, dialogue, or physiognomy, they remind us of other sheriffs, private eyes, and mad scientists from other movies we've seen. Typecasting in the genre film is a bonus, not a debit. It is just one more way of establishing character quickly and efficiently. John Wayne is the character type John Wayne, his face no more expressive than the painted masks used in ancient times by the Greeks. Other performers like Bela Lugosi, Peter Lorre, and Vincent Price are instantly "knowable" as genre figures.

In addition to establishing character with speed and directness, the use of less individualized characters sets up the basis for the existence of Aristotelian catharsis by allowing for an increase in empathy by the audience. Being so much their exteriors, genre characters allow us to easily assume their roles. The fact that we know that they are not realistic, not part of our real world, lets us slip into their trench coats or boots with ease. We can identify so strongly and safely with their roles that we leave the theater walking a little bow-legged or pulling up the collar of a nonexistent trench coat to ward off the wind. Genre characters, because they are so unrealistic and without depth, because they are so consistent and unwavering in their purpose, because they are never forced to come to terms with themselves—they have no "self" in one sense—invite identification with the role or type; that identification releases us from the ordinary and mundane realism of our own lives. We can say, "I wish I were like him"—so tough, so hard-boiled, so ruthless, so lucky, so pure, so wonderfully one-dimensional, so bent on destruction or revenge, or on saving the world that eating and sleeping and other everyday occurrences and responsibilities can never interfere. While we may all live quiet lives of desperation, genre characters do not. We are all Walter Mittys, and for a few short hours we can be lifted out of our inconsequential existences into a world of heroic action.

This difference in level between our world and the world of the genre film I would regard as fulfilling Aristotle's dictum that the characters of drama be elevated. Genre characters are certainly far superior to us in what they can do; they may be limited as ordinary human beings, but they are unlimited as far as action. They can do what we would like to be able to do. They can pinpoint the evil in their lives as resident in a monster or a villain, and they can go out and triumph over it. We, on the other hand, are in a muddle. We know things aren't quite right, but we are not sure if it is a conspiracy among corporations, the world situation, politicians, our neighbors down the street, our boss, our spouse; but whatever it is, we can't call it out of the saloon for a shoot-out or round up the villagers and hunt it down. Genre characters inhabit a world that is better than ours, a world in which problems can be solved directly, emotionally, in action. It is in a sense an ideal plane, a utopia, as far removed from our world as was the world of kings and nobles and Olympian gods from the lives of the Athenians who attended the plays and heard the epics.

That we desire to witness such worlds and to experience classical catharsis is demonstrated by the current phenomenal attendance at martial arts films, the newest of film genres; it would be impossible to count the number of people who partake of such experiences through the older genres as offered on their television screens, both in reruns of theatrical films and the made-for-TV variety. The emotional involvement and subsequent release that Aristotle called catharsis is an obviously desired tonic in our postromantic modern world. Critics, sociologists, psychologists, and politicians may argue over the social impact of literature and films that depict violent action—are they only a reflection of the times or are they a cause of the violence in our culture?—but Aristotle's position is quite clear: there is a social benefit, a point at which art and the good of the community come together. If spectators identify strongly with the figures of the drama, feeling pity and fear as drawn out by the activities going on before their eyes and ears, then, when properly concluded, given the appropriate ending, these emotions are dissipated, leaving viewers in a state of calm, a state of stasis in which they can think rationally and clearly. Properly conceived and executed, the genre film can produce this effect.

The cathartic potentials of the genre film can also be seen as a way in which the tension of cultural and social paradoxes inherent in a human experience can be resolved. Freud in *Civilization and Its Discontents* and Nietzsche in *The Birth of Tragedy* and *The Death of Tragedy* discuss the issue at length. Nietzsche identifies the two poles of human behavior as the Apollonian and the Dionysian. The Apollonian is the urge to individuate the self from others and the Dionysian is the urge to submerge the self into a group, mob, clan, family, or chorus.

Since the conflict between the individual and the group, between self-realization and communal conformity, between the anxiety and loneliness engendered by the freeing of the self and the security of passive identification with the crowd, is so all-pervasive an element of human life, it is not surprising to find this tension between individual needs and community needs metaphorically represented in genre films, not only in gangster films, as Warshow has suggested, or in western films, as Cawelti has stated, but in all genre films. This tension, being so universal, may appear in other films as well, but because of the classical nature of the genre film, the resolution of the tension between these two poles will always be in favor of the community. The human being is after all a social animal. Thus, in classical thought, anything that can relieve or diffuse conflicting emotions and purge them from the individual can only be seen as a social good. Group values must be continually reinforced in the individual; in the old days religion did the job, but in post-Reformation times the burden has moved elsewhere. Patriotic nationalism and world communism have sought to pick up the standard in real life, but the only twentieth-century art that has consistently reenacted the ritual of reaffirmation of group values has been the genre film. Simply enough, it is the form of the genre film, its repetitive quality, its familiarity, and violent plotting that has made this work. During the course of a genre film we can vicariously play out our desire for individuation by identifying with the protagonist free from the anxiety of group censure. Personal fears of actually acting out our fantasies of sex and power are eliminated because we know it is only a movie. There are no penalties to pay, as there are in real life, for being either hero or villain. A short survey of several plot structures found in various genres will serve to show how genre plots are the key to the dispersal of the tension between individual and group.

In the war film, for example, the most popular plot involves a group of men, individuals thrown together from disparate backgrounds, who must be welded together to become a well-oiled fighting machine. During the course of the film, the rough edges of the ornery and the cantankerous, the nonjoiners, the loners, like John Garfield in Hawks's *Air Force* (1943), must be smoothed down to make them fit. They must all hang together or all hang separately. The emphasis is on the team. And, of course, for the war film the end goal of the fighting is always the even larger group, the nation. Or peace in the world, to protect us all from some peculiarly successful individuals—Hitler or Hirohito or the kaiser. The hero's primary function is to mold the group and personally oppose the idea of individualism whenever it rears its head in its own cause and not that of the group effort. What better metaphor than the coward—the man interested only in saving his own skin, who somehow or other must be forced into changing his attitude or else destroyed before he infects the rest of the group. The hero, not just in the war film but in all genre films, is always in the service of the group, of law and order, of stability, of survival, not of himself but of the organization or the institution, no matter how individual his activities, while a villain could be defined as a man who ruthlessly looks after his own needs first and who works for and will sacrifice himself for no one or nothing but himself.

In the swashbuckler, the Errol Flynn character must restore the true social order, and though he may appear to be an outlaw now (which allows him to do all sorts of antisocial actions like killing and robbing), by the end of the film his crimes against the crown have been pardoned since they were all done in a good cause. He kneels to his liege lord and marries the girl (marriage traditionally having connotations of responsibility to the social order).

The police or detective film follows the same general pattern. The cops can do violent antisocial acts (acts which all of us would like to do) with impunity, for they are fulfilling their primary function to catch the guilty party and restore order. At first glance the private-eye film doesn't seem to fit this pattern, but it does. Sam Spade and the police are really on the same side, protecting the mindless masses (who seldom play a central role in the films) from evil. True, the police may be corrupt or stupid or slow to figure things out, yet the end goal is the same. The ideal of commitment to square dealing and presumably to a community of square dealers is demonstrated in the moral integrity of the private eye who can't be bought. Hence we may understand that in the particular social order shown, the police may be stupid or even corrupt, but that there is somewhere a moral order of community and group benefit as opposed to personal and material benefit, an ideal vindicated by the private eye's sending to prison the girl he's fallen in love with.

Horror films and monster films need no elaboration on this point, nor do science fiction films. Though the latter may leave us slightly wondering if the community shown in the film will survive in the future, there is the implicit assertion that there is no survival without the group. Science, that corporate analytical endeavor, will save us if anything can—not any individual. Westerns are also clearly involved with the eventual triumph of the forces of civilization, law and order, even as they are tinged with melancholy for the loss of individual freedom.

The musical will often end with a wedding or the promise of one as the boy and girl come together after overcoming all obstacles—a perfect example of a socially regenerative action, as Northrop Frye has pointed out in his discussion of New Comedy in *The Anatomy of Criticism*. In those musicals in which a star is born, in which it seems as though an individual is rising to the heights of individual achievement, it usually turns out that the star must go on despite personal tragedy, again emphasizing the group—the Broadway show, the production, standing as a metaphor for society.

Any brief rundown of basic plots should serve to demonstrate that the catharsis engendered in genre films is a basic element of their structure. The internal tension between the opposing impulses of personal individuation and submission to the group, which normally is held in check by the real pressures of everyday living, is released in the course of a genre film as the audience vicariously lives out its individual dreams of glory or terror, as it identifies with the stereotyped characters of fantasy life. But in the end those impulses to antisocial behavior (acts of individuation no matter how innocuous or permissible are still tinged with an element of the antisocial) are siphoned off as we accept the inevitable justice of the social order: the group is always right, and we know in our hearts that it is wrong to think otherwise.

In recent years it has become the fashion for some directors to use the elements of the genre film—the plots, characters, and iconographies—to create an antigenre film. That is, they will use everything according to the normal pattern, but simply change the ending so as not to satisfy the audience's expectations of a conventional group-oriented conclusion. If the detective finally gives in and takes the money and the girl, if the crook gets away with it, if an individual solves his problems so as to enhance his position vis-à-vis the world, that is, to increase the distance between his values and the values of the group—then the film has turned its back on the idea of genre. It violates the basic principle of the genre film: the restoration of the social order. Instead of justifying the status quo, these films intend the opposite. They suggest that individuals can succeed in individual schemes, that separation from the group can be had without consequences. In this sense they are not classical but romantic in their tenor.

The genre film is a structure that embodies the idea of form and the strict adherence to form that is opposed to experimentation, novelty, or tampering with the given order of things. The genre film, like all classical art, is basically conservative, both aesthetically and politically. To embody a radical tenor or romantic temper in a classical form is to violate that form at its heart. One can parody the conventions, one can work against the conventions, one can use the conventions with great subtlety and irony. To hold up individual ideals as superior to group ideals, however, changes the whole frame of reference. When a seeming genre film merely changes the ending in a final reversal, catharsis is restricted. The audience is unprepared by what has come before. There is no release of tensions, since the inevitable conclusion for which the audience has come and which would send them back into the real world smiling has not taken place. Rather than stasis, such endings produce agitation, discomfort, a vague anxiety. The guilt of having identified with the scoundrel or hero is never dissipated and viewers must bear the responsibility for their individual desires all alone.

In *Charlie Varrick* (Don Siegel, 1973), an otherwise conventional caper movie, the title character gets away with a million dollars scot-free at the end, which denies the audience the opportunity of saying, "That's the way it is. Nobody gets away with fighting against the mob or syndicate." His escape from just punishment for daring to wrest something of value from the Olympians of today, the banks, the corporations, the Mafia, makes him a Prometheus figure who doesn't get caught. It induces in the audience a kind of irrational radicalism as opposed to a reasonable conformism: "If he can do it, then maybe I, too, can fight the system, the institutions, and win." This is not what ordinary people—fated to a life in society in which they are relatively powerless to change the course of things—like to comfort themselves with and not what a true genre film provides.

For the time that genre characters play out their lives upon the screen we can safely identify with them, confident that the group will assert its overwhelming force in the end—like the chorus in a Greek play, always having the last word, reminding us that "That's the way it is. If you reach beyond your grasp, you will fall." We need not feel guilty; our surrogates will take the blame. We will switch allegiance by the end and become a member of the chorus. Our split personality is no longer split. Crime doesn't pay. True love wins out. The monster is destroyed. The forces of evil and darkness are vanquished by faith and reason. All is for the best in this best of all possible worlds. We have achieved the stasis that Aristotle mentions as the product of catharsis—a quiet calm. This is not to say that this feeling lasts long after we leave the theater, but at least we have been internally refreshed by our brief sojourn in a realm of cosmos, not chaos. If nothing else, the genre film is a paradigm of ritual and order.

The genre film is a classical mode in which imitation not of life but of conventions is of paramount importance. Just as in the classical dramas of Greece, the stories are well known. Though there may be some charm in the particular arrangement of formula variables in the most current example of a genre, the audience seeks the solid and familiar referrents of that genre, expecting and usually receiving a large measure of the known as opposed to the novel. Elevated and removed from everyday life, freed from the straitjacket of mere representationalism, genre films are pure emotional articulation, fictional constructs of the imagination, growing essentially out of group interests and values. Character takes a second place to plot, in agreement with Aristotle's descriptions of drama. And it is this emphasis on the plot that makes genre films the most cinematic of all films, for it is what happens in them, what actions take place before our eyes that are most important. They move; they are the movies.

Note

1. Harry M. Geduld and Ronald Gottesman, *An Illustrated Glossary of Film Terms* (New York: Holt, Rinehart and Winston, 1973), p. 73.

Garry Watson

Garry Watson received his Ph.D. from the University of Sussex, England. He teaches English and American literature at the University of Alberta, Canada. In addition to his essays on the literature and cinema of the American West, Watson has also written about the literature of Henry James, Joseph Conrad, George Eliot and D. H. Lawrence. His scholarship is rooted in the academic tradition and draws from literary and cultural theorists. This article appeared in the film journal CineAction! *and offers an interpretation of the Western using the theories of René Girard.*

The Western: The Genre that Engenders the Nation

> The Western, with its historical setting, its thematic emphasis on the establishment of law and order, and its resolution of the conflict between civilization and savagery on the frontier, is a kind of foundation ritual.
>
> —John Cawelti (73)

I agree that the western is indeed a kind of foundation ritual but I think we will be better able to build on this insight once we realize that the conflict to which Cawelti refers—between civilization and savagery—is part of a larger crisis in legitimation that is best understood as being essentially sacrificial in nature. As I understand it, the western is the genre that typically dramatizes a sacrificial crisis, the violent resolution of which founds or refounds a community or nation.

So what exactly is a sacrificial crisis? I take the idea from René Girard, who defines it—in his book *Violence and the Sacred*—as being, in the last analysis, "a crisis of distinctions" (49). Such a crisis affects the entire cultural order and it coincides with the disappearance of the absolutely crucial difference "between impure violence and purifying violence." What makes this particular distinction so important is the fact that, when it has been effaced, "purification is no longer possible and impure, reciprocal violence spreads throughout the community." In other words, "the distinction between the pure and the impure" is *the* "sacrificial distinction" *par excellence* and it "cannot be obliterated without obliterating all other differences as well" (Girard 49). But at the same time, the moment of complete social breakdown—when

---

Reprinted from *Cineaction*, June 1998, by permission of the publisher and author.

all the differences are obliterated and violent reciprocity or a state of lawlessness has spread throughout the whole community—is also the moment that can "trigger the mechanism of generative unanimity," thus enabling the violence to focus on a surrogate victim whose murder—so long, at least, as the victim is not seen (accurately) as a merely arbitrary scapegoat—can restore "a social system based on multiple and sharply pronounced differences" (188).[1]

Now whatever else it is about, it would be difficult to deny that the western is indeed centrally concerned—and in a somewhat ritualistic manner—with the foundation of community. Think, for example, of such US flag-flying celebrations of the 4th of July as the dance of the homesteaders in *Shane* or the rifle-shooting contest in *Winchester 73*. Or how about the dedication of the first church of Tombstone in *My Darling Clementine*? Or the model town Vienna shows her lover in *Johnny Guitar*? Or the Mormons in pursuit of the promised land in *Wagonmaster*? Or the lesson in civics—with citations from the Declaration of Independence—given by Ransom Stoddard in *The Man Who Shot Liberty Valance*? Or the group that gradually gathers around Josey in *The Outlaw Josey Wales*? Obviously there is no shortage of examples that can help us to see what the western has in common with a Fourth of July ceremony. But on the other hand, what principally distinguishes it from the latter is the fact that it is the *kind* of ritual or ceremony that contains within itself an explanation—in the form of its staging a dramatic conflict that in some respects resembles Girard's sacrificial crisis—as to how the founding took place.

If the western "reaffirms the act of foundation" (Cawelti 73), it does so by identifying that act with the violence produced in the culminating moment when the hero stands firm and risks his life in a deadly shoot-out with the enemy. In a nutshell, the message the western insists on, over and over again, is that it is not, as Ranse would have it, "education," but rather the willingness of someone like Tom Doniphon to stand up to and then shoot someone like Liberty Valance that constitutes—in the words Ranse has written on the blackboard in *The Man Who Shot Liberty Valance*—"the basis of law and order." And also, therefore, the basis of the community in the process of emerging.

I am not suggesting that the Girardian model of the successfully resolved sacrificial crisis fits in every detail. For one thing the mechanism of generative unanimity is seldom triggered in the western and when it *is* its range is restricted—as we shall see later, in the case of *The Wild Bunch*—to that of the tightly-knit group (the group of professionals studied by Will Wright in his *Sixguns and Society* [1975]). The mob-like unanimity of the men led by Emma Small in *Johnny Guitar* is much more the kind of thing Girard has in mind, but it doesn't turn out to be generative. Yet the western does typically end up by staging an act of violence—or, to be more specific, a killing—that founds or restores a community on the basis of the various differences it simultaneously reconstitutes. In fact, it would scarcely be an exaggeration to say that almost the whole point of the western is to be found in the way in which it reenforces—or makes more sharply pronounced—certain differences.

But what about the difference between the pure and the impure? As I've already noted, this is clearly the key sacrificial distinction and yet, at first glance, the western might seem to have little interest in it. But the fact that the terms themselves—purity and impurity—are seldom used is deceptive. Consider, for example, what—after the concluding gun-fight—is most familiar. Many westerns begin with a shot of a wild landscape out of which a figure on horseback can be perceived gradually emerging and coming towards us. There are many exceptions and countless variations but this is one of the basic patterns. What does it mean? Often, I would argue, it is best understood with reference to the situation Girard describes as "the Warrior's Return" (42). Since he is "still tainted with the slaughter of war," a "special sort of impurity clings to the warrior returning to his homeland" and there is the real risk of his "carrying the seed of violence into the very heart of his city" (41). Since the western hero is not usually a soldier, however (even though most westerns are significantly set in the decades following the Civil War), it may be more appropriate for us to think here of the figure on horseback we see coming out of the distance in *Shane,* rather than in *The Searchers*.

Shane

Though we never get to know very much about Shane's past, we do learn that he was once a gunfighter and this makes us realise—at least, in retrospect—that there is some doubt when we first encounter this stranger as to how he will behave. He may not be a warrior but he does carry the seed of violence within him and so the question is whether or not it will turn out to be a purifying violence.

"Any phenomenon linked to impure violence is capable," in Girard's view, "of being inverted and rendered beneficent"—even if, as he insists, "this can take place only within the immutable and rigorous framework of ritual practice" (58). My suggestion, then, is that the early scenes in which Shane is taken in by Joe and Marian Starrett and their son Joey—particularly the scenes in which he shares dinner with them and then works with Joe to remove the stump Joe has been trying on his own to remove for two years—function as purification rituals. And that Shane *needs* purifying or "decontaminating" (41) is made plain by just how trigger-happy he is—not only when the sound of Joey loading his gun with blanks makes him go for *his* gun out in the yard (an incident that occurs before it has been established that he is going to be a friend of Starrett rather than of Ryker) but also, and even more strikingly, when he is startled at the dinner table by the noise of a farm animal outside. There is a similar moment in *Johnny Guitar* when the former gunfighter responds to Turkey's attempt at demonstrating his manhood by going temporarily berserk. And one might also reflect in this context on Ethan Edwards and of the possibility of explaining his failure or refusal to enter into the family circle at the end of *The Searchers* in terms of his being still too contaminated by impure violence to do so—even if, on another level, he is of course notoriously committed to racial purity.

If we think of its effect on Dallas, the Doc and the Ringo Kid especially, then we might want to see the scene in which Lucy Mallory gives birth in *Stagecoach* as another example of a purification ritual. But then, images of purity (like the innocent look on young James Earp's face as his older brothers leave him to go into Tombstone in *My Darling Clementine*) and of impurity (like the one we don't literally see but are asked to imagine, of father and son blocking the well in *The Tall*

T) are plentiful in westerns, and it's not just a matter of individual images, or even of individual scenes. There is a sense in which entire westerns can be described as purification rituals. As quickly becomes apparent when we think of *Rio Bravo,* first of the image of impurity in the opening scene—when Dude gets down on his knees to retrieve a silver dollar from a spittoon—and then of that movie's ending—with Dude cleaned up and triumphant and singing about the river rolling along as he walks down the street with Stumpy (and the latter delightedly picks up Feathers' tights, which Chance has tossed out of the hotel window up above).

But if a sacrificial crisis is one involving the threatened loss of distinctions, then I now need to point to two things: (i) a western in which distinctions are under threat and (ii) some evidence of *other* distinctions in addition to the one we've been focussing on so far. No doubt the most obvious example is that of the conflict between the cattle ranchers and the homesteaders (or small ranchers, or townsfolk) that we find cropping up in such different westerns as *The Man Who Shot Liberty Valance, Johnny Guitar, Rio Bravo, The Ballad of Little Jo* and—most famously, no doubt—in *Shane.* So let's zero in on the latter, on the scene in which Ryker and his men are waiting at Starrett's place to greet the Starretts and Shane on their return from the Fourth of July festivities. Ryker (the cattle rancher) has come to offer Starrett (the homesteader) a job and here is the ensuing exchange:

> STARRETT: You've made things pretty hard for us Ryker—and us in the right all the time.
>
> RYKER: Right? *You* in the right? Look Starrett, when I come to this country you weren't much older than your boy here. We had rough times, me and the other men that are mostly dead now. I got a bad shoulder yet from a Cheyenne arrowhead. We made this country. Found it and we made it. With blood and empty bellies. The cattle we brought in were hazed off by Indians and rustlers. It didn't bother you much anymore because we handled them. We made a safe range out of this. Some of us died doing it. We made it. And then people moved in and never had a raw hide like in the old days. Fence off my range and fence me off from water. Some of 'em like you plough ditches and take out irrigation and water. And so the creek turns dry sometimes. I've got to move my stock because of it. And you say we have no right to the range. The men that did the work and ran the risks have no right? I take you for a fair man Starrett.

As the white-bearded, patriarchal Ryker delivers this speech, his dignity is enhanced and his already-strong case strengthened further by Stevens's decision to photograph him from below, his upper body on horseback silhouetted against the grandeur of the night sky. It's true, as Starrett goes on to say, that Ryker "didn't *find* this country. There was," as Starrett tells him, "trappers here and Indian traders long before you showed up. And they tamed this country more than you did." But Ryker has not exactly denied this. And when Starrett continues by chastising Ryker for "talk[ing] about rights"—"You think you've got the right to say that nobody else has any. Well, that ain't the way the government looks at it"—he seems to have forgotten that *he* was the one to bring this subject up, not Ryker.

So all in all, if the question is Who is morally in the right? the answer—on the basis of this exchange—is not obvious. While we are left in no doubt elsewhere in the film that Ryker, the cattle rancher, is the bad guy and Starrett, the homesteader, the good guy, here, at least, the key distinction—between who is in the right, who in the wrong—is up for grabs. We oughtn't to be too surprised, therefore, to find the two sides each trying to brand the other with the charge of impurity. As, for example, when Chris first tries to provoke a fight with Shane in Grafton's store. "I thought," he remarks (after becoming aware of the presence of homesteaders buying goods in the room next to the saloon area), "I smelled pigs." "Will," he appeals to the bartender, "let's keep the smell of pigs out from where we're drinking." And then, after Shane has entered the saloon and Chris has thrown his drink over him ("have some of this and smell like a man"), one of Chris's friends comments that he has just "fumigated a sodbuster." Predictably, then, when Ryker insults both Shane and Marian by insinuating that there is something sexual between them ("Pretty wife Starrett has"), Shane responds by calling him—in clear if not necessarily conscious imitation of the language in which he has earlier been insulted by Chris—a "dirty, stinking old man." And, in a similar vein, when the conflict escalates later on, we find Stark Wilson forcing Torrey to go for his gun by calling him "Southern trash."

The fact that Torrey dies face down in thick mud is also significant in this context and it might well remind us of young James Earp lying dead in a puddle of rain (in *My Darling Clementine*) or of Angel being dragged through the dirt and dust (in *The Wild Bunch*).[2] The point, however, is that in each of these cases an outrage has been perpetrated. Innocence has been besmirched and degraded and we cry out in indignation, demanding that those who have committed these foul deeds get their just deserts. As Wilson and Ryker eventually get theirs, for example. But why does Shane also have to die? Or does he? Why the uncertainty? And why does Shane have to leave at the end?

According to Girard, communities grow "out of the body of an original victim" (306), a victim who was first regarded by its murderers as accursed but who is later regarded by the community grateful for the peace his death has brought to them as being beneficent. For Girard, this transformation over time of a scapegoated victim into a god is what explains the ambiguous (accursed/beneficent) nature of the sacred. And I would suggest that it provides us with the best answers we are likely to find to the two main questions—Why does the hero leave? Why does he have to die?—we are left with at the end of *Shane*.

Having become too "dirty" or impure to stay, Shane needs to disappear into the wilderness so that he can be cleansed or purified. I'm thinking here of the point Shane is making when he explains to Joey at the end that there is "no living with a killing," "there's no going back," if only because "right or wrong, it's a brand, and a brand sticks." What is this "brand" if not the sort of stigma or taint of impurity that risks sticking not only to the one who carries it but also to those with whom he (or she) comes into contact?

The reason Shane has to die is so that the community being born can be felt to grow out of *him,* or *his* body, rather than—as is of course the case in many westerns—out of his (the hero's) killing of a victim we don't care about. Of course, by no means all western heroes do die but it may be that the films made about those who do—*Shane, The Man Who Shot Liberty Valance, The Wild Bunch* and *The Ballad of Little Jo,* to name just four of them—have a special resonance. But why the uncertainty as to whether or not Shane is actually going to die? By leaving as he does, Shane makes it easier for us to believe that perhaps, against all odds, he *didn't* die, that perhaps, in some sense, he lives on. As we are clearly meant to feel he does, if only in the form of the community his death has given birth to.

When Shane rides off at the end and Joey calls out after him, the latter's words—"Shane" and "Come back"—echo. And it seems to me that when Shane's name fills the valley it creates the effect of a kind of generative unanimity, of an emerging community of little Joeys, all of whom speak with one voice and are formed in the image of its founder. If we recall Shane's last words of advice to Joey—that he return home to grow up "strong and straight," to tell his mother there are no more guns in the valley and to take care of both his parents—we then realize that this community of sons has been entrusted with the task of protecting the wider community of families. If we ask, furthermore, how the protecting is going to get done, the answer, presumably, given the nature of the founding figure, is with guns. So that a double and contradictory message is being conveyed: the two-tiered community in the process of being born is both peaceful and, simultaneously (in Richard Slotkin's phrase), a Gunfighter Nation.

The point, however, that is unequivocally made by the ending of *Shane* is that the gunfighters destined to protect *this* nation will be on the side of the straight and clean rather than the crooked and dirty. We are left in no doubt but that they will be devoted to the defence of civilization or law and order, and to the defeat of savagery or lawlessness. All of which obviously makes them very different from the gunfighters we encounter in *The Wild Bunch* and raises the question as to how the ideas we've been exploring apply to what is surely the greatest of all western movies.

The Wild Bunch

If, as Paul Seydor claims in his extraordinarily rich and helpful essay on Peckinpah's masterpiece, the conventional western can largely be characterized in terms of its insistence on providing "an overlay of good versus evil that is somehow supposed to legitimate the appetite for violence that it whets" (188), then perhaps the first thing that needs to be said about *The Wild Bunch* is how unconventional it is. Not only does it fail to provide this specific kind of "overlay" (with, for example, the fight between the Bunch and the Mapachistas taking place without reference to the Villistas, who might admittedly be thought to embody goodness); the distinction between good and evil virtually dissolves during the astonishing opening sequence in which soldiers are really outlaws in disguise, the law is represented by scavenging bounty hunters, innocent-looking children torture a scorpion with killer ants and we find ourselves wondering if we are not entering into a similar universe to the one Gloucester unforgettably evokes when he claims, at the opening of the fourth act of *King Lear,* that our relationship "to th' gods" is like that of "flies to wanton boys . . . / They kill us for their sport."

It's true that when Peckinpah himself professes to find it "strange"—in view of the fact that he "was trying to tell a simple story about bad men in changing times"—that we "feel a great sense of loss when these killers reach the end of the line (qtd. by Seydor 136), he is himself implicitly invoking (rather than challenging) the related distinction between good and bad. And the first words Pike utters—"If they move, kill 'em"—as he and his men enter the railroad office are clearly those of a man prepared to kill in as ruthless and cold-blooded a manner as seems to him necessary. Indeed, only minutes later, he proves as much when he violently shoves a frightened railroad official out into the street to draw some of the gunfire intended by the hidden bounty-hunters for the bunch, thus allowing the latter the opportunity to take advantage of the momentary confusion when, seconds later, they are in the thick of the fray themselves. These are obviously the words and actions of a man who will let nothing get in the way of what he wants. Nevertheless, while few of us would, in other circumstances, have any hesitation in calling such a man bad or evil, in *these* circumstances the terms don't seem to apply. Not, at any rate, as we ordinarily understand them.

Why is this? Partly because it is the obnoxious Harrigan who represents and enforces the law—with the help of the kind of men whom their leader, the ex-member of the bunch, Thornton, aptly describes later on as "gutter trash"—while Christianity is embodied in the first laughable and then (as they get caught in the crossfire) pathetic South Texas Temperance Union. But mainly because we are being implicitly asked to judge Pike and his men by a different set of criteria, those we associate with the tradition of the epic. It is a matter of the sort of warrior virtues Alasdair MacIntyre describes in his book *After Virtue* (1981), as, for example, in those heroic societies celebrated by Homer, rather than the kind we find in Aristotle or the Bible.

In other words, even though Pike and his men are not *really* soldiers or warriors, Peckinpah's film implicitly asks us to treat them as if they were. Which is disturbing, to say the least. So that while, for example, we can't help noticing how viciously Crazy Lee behaves towards the three hostages he is left to guard—and how the river in the hymn ("Yes, we'll gather at the river") he forces them to sing (in a nightmarish reminder of the very different uses that hymn is put to in Ford's films) has become a river of blood—the emphasis falls *not so much* on this (or on the presumably obscene words he speaks into the ear of the woman hostage) as on his bravery and (to adapt what Dutch says about Angel later on) his willingness, for the benefit of the group, to play "his string right out to the end." After (or along with) courage, loyalty to the group is probably the virtue that counts most, as Pike reminds Lyle and Tector when (having earlier shown their inclination to treat Angel as a second-class group member) they turn on Sykes:

> You're not getting rid of anybody. We're going to stick together, just like it used to be. When you side with a man you stay with him and if you can't do that you're like some animal. You're finished. *We're* finished!

This furnishes one of the main criteria by which Pike implicitly asks to be judged and by which, on a number of occasions, the film does judge him. As, for example, when he is forced to realize, moments after he has come out with this articulation of his code, that he himself has forgotten all about Sykes's grandson,

Crazy Lee, and, in effect, abandoned him to his death. Or, again, in the flashback that shows how he managed to escape when (his, at that time, comrade) Thornton got caught. On these two occasions Pike is found wanting where—as we are surely meant to feel that his decision, in the aftermath of the opening robbery, to execute his blinded comrade is necessary to the survival of the rest of the group. Which doesn't make it any the less disturbing. But think, for an example taken from a very different work, first of the King's reaction to the "bloody" Captain's account of Macbeth's bravery—as "he unseamed [the rebel Macdonwald] from the nave to th' chops/And fixed his head upon our battlements" (*Macbeth* 1.ii.1, 22–23)—at the beginning of Shakespeare's tragedy: "O valiant cousin! worthy gentleman!" (1.ii.24). And then, after Macbeth's own head has been cut off, of the new King's description of him as a "butcher" (V.viii. 69) at the end. Behaviour that can seem admirable in war can seem monstrous out of it. And if, as I am arguing, we are indeed intended to judge Pike and his men by the standards of wartime—even when they are behaving as outlaws—this means that we must be ready to see Pike's willingness to perform this act of execution as being both monstrous *and* admirable at the same time.

As Girard sees it, "men are only capable of reconciling their differences at the expense of a third party" (259). And judging by the scene in which (having just succeeded in stealing the ammunition from the troop train) the bunch relax by passing around a bottle of liquor, ensuring that it is all drunk by the time it gets to Lyle, I would say that this is Peckinpah's view, too. Group solidarity is always based on various kinds of exclusion or opposition, sometimes comic, as when the would-be excluder Lyle gets some of his own medicine, and sometimes deadly serious, as when the bunch go up against Mapache and his men at the end.

This latter is of course the one scene the western can't do without: the shoot-out. But what makes this particular shoot-out so distinctive is the difficulty we have separating the protagonists in terms of right and wrong. It isn't that there is *no* difference. When Dutch says that the Bunch are nothing like Mapache because they don't hang anybody he has a point. Unlike Mapache and his cohorts, the Bunch do not take pleasure in inflicting pain: their killings may be cruel but they are not sadistic. Still, Dutch exaggerates: it's simply not true to say that the Bunch are "*nothing* like Mapache." After all, if the Mapachistas are certainly represented as being the enemies of their fellow countrymen and women (whose true interests are defended by the Villistas), for their part, Pike and his men show no hesitation when asked to steal from their own government and to act as traitors to their own country. And while Mapache's behaviour towards Angel—first dragging him behind his car through the dirt and then cutting his throat—is contemptible (and no less horrific than the spectacle it obviously resembles, that of Hector being tortured in *The Iliad*), Angel himself is not quite as angelic as he sometimes appears. As we see, for example, when he shoots his former lover Teresa. It may be his pure-mindedness that prompts him to do this but if so then it has to be said that being pure-minded is not necessarily the same as being angelic.

Here, however, what seems to me to need stressing is Peckinpah's "imaginative impartiality," the kind of even-handed treatment that, as Seydor nicely puts it, "cannot help granting even the vilest characters a full measure of the rich, pulsating vitality that animates every frame of the film" (178). He makes sure, for example, that, on the one hand, we see how fearless Mapache can be—as when, in the midst of gunfire, he behaves towards an admiring youngster who hands him a cablegram as if he has all the time in the world; while, on the other, he takes care "to ironize Thornton's description of Pike as 'the best' " (Seydor 162), especially in those flashbacks that show his mistakes, miscalculations or equivocations.

As Seydor rightly insists, however, Peckinpah's ironies are not intended to debunk the Western, nor even to call into question "the idea of regeneration through violence." On the contrary, in fact, they are meant "to tighten the screws of the struggle, to make our assent more difficult, indeed, almost impossible, so that when the release comes and the heroic ideal is reclaimed in all its savage beauty and terror, it really is more miraculous than we had ever dreamed or imagined" (210).

But this only partially explains why we feel such release. "Let's go," says Pike and that's *all* he says. For that matter, it's just about all Wyatt Earp says as he and his brothers (and Doc Halliday) set out to meet the Clantons at the end of *My Darling Clementine*. So why do we find the spectacle of Pike, Lyle, Tector and Dutch setting off at the end of *The Wild Bunch* so much more moving and exhilarating than the earlier scene from Ford's film?[3] Partly, no doubt, we are stirred by the martial music that accompanies them; there is no music on the soundtrack as the Earp brothers walk to meet the Clantons. But over and above this is the fact that, while the Earps and Clantons are fairly even matched, the Bunch face such overwhelming odds—very much, I would say, like Coriolanus, when he leaves his army to follow his enemies inside the gates of Corioles, which then close behind him—that it makes sense to speak, as Seydor does, of their exhibiting "a suicidal passion for glory" (188). Suicidal or, at least, self-sacrificing. Small wonder, then, if we hear in Pike's utterance (but not, even though the words are the same, in Wyatt's) more or less what D. H. Lawrence once detected in what he referred to as the "[s]plendid word"—" 'Andiamo!'—let us go" (202)—*he* heard uttered during a marionette show in Palermo:

> Is there not the massive, brilliant, outflinging recklessness in the male soul, summed up in the sudden word: *Andiamo!* Andiamo! Let us go on. Andiamo!—let us go hell knows where, but let us go on. The splendid recklessness and passion that knows no precept and no school-teacher, whose very molten spontaneity is its own guide. (203)

After all, even if Pike and his men clearly do recognize *one* moral precept (loyalty, the obligation to stick together, to go back for Angel), what moves us so deeply is their lack of any kind of calculation as to what their action might reasonably accomplish; it is precisely, in other words, the splendid *recklessness* of their passionate and spontaneous commitment to a path of action almost certain to result in their own deaths.

In effect, if we recall the movie's opening scene, it is as if the Bunch voluntarily place themselves in the end in the position of "the scorpions on the anthill of *federale* soldiers" (Seydor 196), knowing full well—on some level, at least—that both the scorpions and the ants were consumed by flames, burnt alive. And for what? Other, that is to say, than glory, the point about which is that, as Falstaff famously pointed out, strictly speaking, it is useless. As useless, say, as beauty, the "terrible beauty" that is engendered just as surely by the final act of the Bunch as it is by the act of "MacDonagh and MacBride/And Connolly and Pearse" in Yeats's "Easter 1916." What, we can therefore say, the Bunch commit themselves to is the kind of "expenditure" Georges Bataille claimed humanity (recognizing only "the right to acquire, to conserve, and to consume rationally") tends to exclude in principle: the useless, nonproductive or unconditional kind of expenditure that involves great losses or spectacular destruction or sacrifices and that tends toward the "generous, orgiastic, and excessive" ("The Notion" 117, 118, 119, 124).

It seems appropriate to turn to Bataille at this point because, like Yeats (however reluctantly) and Peckinpah, he too *celebrates* this form of "expenditure," celebrates it, it's worth noting, as the kind of sacrificial consumption we associate with death by burning. In this Bataille differs from Girard, who encourages us to reject the phenomenon Yeats is referring to when he speaks of the birth of a "terrible beauty." Both Bataille and Girard agree, however, that what is at stake is the sacred, which they both understand as a contradictory, double-sided phenomenon, on the one side blessed, beautiful, pure and peaceful, on the other accursed, terrible, impure and violent. Hence, for example (with laughter, according to Bataille, being the key to "the enigma" of sacrifice, "the shared joy of laughter" representing "sacred communication" ["Sacrifice" 68]), our uneasy sense that the laughter we hear echoing throughout *The Wild Bunch* can turn at any moment from the one side of the sacred to the other. Right up to the ending, at any rate, when the successful resolution of the sacrificial crisis engenders the nucleus of a new community and a process of purification takes place as the sacred shows—for a while at least—only the more positive side of its face.

First Sykes invites Thornton to join him and the Villistas and as Thornton agrees to do so the two break out into laughter, which then gets amplified by the laughter of Pike, Dutch, Lyle, and Tector, and Angel who we now see resurrected at their best as they emerged days earlier from Angel's village. Positioned in a green and festive world, the Bunch are caught in a light—the kind we sometimes catch glimpses of in other westerns (as, for example, at the beginning and end of *The Outlaw Josey Wales*)—that unmistakeably cleanses and purifies them. As a result of which their villainy is sloughed off and they are effectively reborn.

Those who assume that nationalism is always reactionary will have an especially hard time with the ending of *The Wild Bunch* and also, if they open themselves to its challenge, with the western in general. If the western is a genre that engenders the nation it does so in a variety of forms, as in their different ways the meeting between Josey and the Comanche leader Ten Bears (in *The Outlaw Josey Wales*), the laughter of Mary's mother at the end of *The Ballad of Little Jo* and (in *The Wild Bunch*) the final identification of the Bunch with Angel's people—both the villagers and the revolutionary Villistas—all make clear.

Works Cited

Bataille, Georges. "Sacrifice" (1939–40), *October* 36 (Spring 1986): 61–74.

———. "The Notion of Expenditure" (1933), in *Visions of Excess: Selected Writings, 1927–1939,* ed. Allan Stoekle, trans. Allan Stoekle (Minneapolis: U of Minnesota P, 1985): 116–29.

Cawelti, John G. *The Six-Gun Mystique* (Bowling Green, Ohio; Bowling Green U Popular P, 1971).

Girard, René. *Things Hidden Since the Foundation of the World* (1978), trans. Stephen Bann and Michael Metteer (Stanford, Cal.: Stanford UP, 1987).

———. *Violence and the Sacred* (1972), trans. Patrick Gregory (Baltimore and London: Johns Hopkins UP, 1977).

Lawrence, D. H. *Sea and Sardinia* (1921), in *D. H. Lawrence in Italy,* intro. Anthony Burgess (Harmondsworth: Penguin, 1985): 1–205.

Seydor, Paul. "Men without Women: *The Wild Bunch as Epic,*" chapter five of *Peckinpah: The Western Films—A Reconsideration,* revised edition (Chicago: U of Illinois P, 1997): 137–212.

Notes

1. In his later work, from *Things Hidden Since the Foundation of the World* onwards, Girard argues that it is much more difficult for this to occur today than it used to be. How so? Mainly because of the long-term effects of the Christian revelation which, precisely to the degree that it exposes their workings to the light of day, makes all violent solutions unworkable. Our only remaining option is the *non*-violent and also—since "violence and the sacred are one and the same thing" (262)—non-*sacred* solution he associates with Christ. My own view is that we can and should disentangle the concept of the sacrificial crisis from the pro-Christian argument Girard wants it to serve. When I quote from Girard in this essay it is always from his *Violence and the Sacred.*
2. Of course in *High Noon* it is the sheriff's badge that gets contemptuously tossed into the dusty street, just as, in *High Noon,* the civics lesson ends with the US flag being taken down by the run-away judge. It has to be said, therefore, that unless we take it to be represented by the departing sheriff and his wife (and the youngster who brings them their wagon), in *High Noon* the community is *not* reborn. Hence, in part, no doubt, the need Hawks felt to remind us of the job the western is *supposed* to be performing in his inspired and still inspiring *Rio Bravo.*
3. As Seydor says, "[w]hen the Bunch strap on their guns and begin their march through the crowded streets of Agua Verde, they are reenacting a Western convention that is so generic it seems to dissolve into ritual before our very eyes" (208). In *The Wild Bunch: An Album in Montage* (1997), the movie Seydor put together from footage shot on the set of *The Wild Bunch,* we see how the idea for this magnificent scene occurred to Peckinpah at the last moment, in front of the cameras.

Sherman Alexie

Sherman Alexie, born in 1966, grew up on the Spokane Indian reservation about 50 miles from Spokane, Washington, and is a member of the Spokane and Coeur D'Alene tribes. Since 1992, Alexie has published several novels, as well as collections of poetry and short stories, and is considered to be one of the most important young writers in the twentieth century. Alexie has recently become involved in filmmaking. Smoke Signals *(Chris Eyre, 1998), the first feature film to be written, produced, and directed entirely by Native Americans, was based on Alexie's book of short stories* The Lone Ranger and Tonto Fistfight in Heaven *(New York: Atlantic Monthly Press, 1994). A short story from this book, "Because My Father Always Said He Was the Only Indian Who Saw Jimi Hendrix Play 'The Star-Spangled Banner' at Woodstock," appears in Chapter Eight, "Writing as Social Witness." Alexie made his directorial debut in 2001 at the Sundance Film Festival with the film* The Business of Fancydancing. *You can find out more about Sherman Alexie at his website, www.fallsapart.com. An accomplished basketball player and stand-up comic, Alexie currently lives and writes in Seattle. In this article, originally published in the* Los Angeles Times, *Alexie reflects on his own changing responses to the Western genre's representations of Native Americans.*

I Hated Tonto (Still Do)

I was a little Spokane Indian boy who read every book and saw every movie about Indians, no matter how terrible. I'd read those historical romance novels about the stereotypical Indian warrior ravaging the virginal white schoolteacher.

I can still see the cover art.

The handsome, blue-eyed warrior (the Indians in romance novels are always blue-eyed because half-breeds are somehow sexier than full-blooded Indians) would be nuzzling (the Indians in romance novels are always performing acts that are described in animalistic terms) the impossibly pale neck of a white woman as she reared her head back in primitive ecstasy (the Indians in romance novels always inspire white women to commit acts of primitive ecstasy).

Of course, after reading such novels, I imagined myself to be a blue-eyed warrior nuzzling the necks of various random, primitive, and ecstatic white women.

Reprinted from the *Los Angeles Times*, June 28, 1998, by permission of the author.

And I just as often imagined myself to be a cinematic Indian, splattered with Day-Glo Hollywood war paint as I rode off into yet another battle against the latest actor to portray Gen. George Armstrong Custer.

But I never, not once, imagined myself to be Tonto.

I hated Tonto then and I hate him now.

However, despite my hatred of Tonto, I loved movies about Indians, loved them beyond all reasoning and saw no fault with any of them.

I loved John Ford's "The Searchers."

I rooted for John Wayne as he searched for his niece for years and years. I rooted for John Wayne even though I knew he was going to kill his niece because she had been "soiled" by the Indians.

Hell, I rooted for John Wayne because I understood why he wanted to kill his niece.

I hated those savage Indians just as much as John Wayne did.

I mean, jeez, they had kidnapped Natalie Wood, transcendent white beauty who certainly didn't deserve to be nuzzled, nibbled, or nipped by some Indian warrior, especially an Indian warrior who only spoke in monosyllables and whose every movement was accompanied by ominous music.

In the movies, Indians are always accompanied by ominous music. And I've seen so many Indian movies that I feel like I'm constantly accompanied by ominous music. I always feel that something bad is about to happen.

I am always aware of how my whole life is shaped by my hatred of Tonto. Whenever I think of Tonto, I hear ominous music.

I walk into shopping malls or family restaurants, as the ominous music drops a few octaves, and imagine that I am Billy Jack, the half-breed Indian and Vietnam vet turned flower-power pacifist (now there's a combination) who loses his temper now and again, takes off his shoes (while his opponents patiently wait for him to do so), and then kicks the red out of the necks of a few dozen racist white extras.

You have to remember Billy Jack, right?

Every Indian remembers Billy Jack. I mean, back in the day, Indians worshipped Billy Jack.

Whenever a new Billy Jack movie opened in Spokane, my entire tribe would climb into two or three vans like so many circus clowns and drive to the East Trent Drive-In for a long evening of greasy popcorn, flat soda pop, fossilized licorice rope and interracial violence.

We Indians cheered as Billy Jack fought for us, for every single Indian.

Of course, we conveniently ignored the fact that Tom Laughlin, the actor who played Billy Jack, was definitely not Indian.

After all, such luminary white actors as Charles Bronson, Chuck Connors, Burt Reynolds, Burt Lancaster, Sal Mineo, Anthony Quinn and Charlton Heston had already portrayed Indians, so who were we to argue?

I mean, Tom Laughlin did have a nice tan and he spoke in monosyllables and wore cowboy boots and a jean jacket just like Indians. And he did have a Cherokee grandmother or grandfather or butcher, so he was Indian by proximity, and that was good enough in 1972, when disco music was about to rear its ugly head and bell-bottom pants were just beginning to change the shape of our legs.

When it came to the movies, Indians had learned to be happy with less.

We didn't mind that cinematic Indians never had jobs.

We didn't mind that cinematic Indians were deadly serious.

We didn't mind that cinematic Indians were rarely played by Indian actors.

We made up excuses.

"Well, that Tom Laughlin may not be Indian, but he sure should be."

"Well, that movie wasn't so good, but Sal Mineo looked sort of like Uncle Stubby when he was still living out on the reservation."

"Well, I hear Burt Reynolds is a little bit Cherokee. Look at his cheekbones. He's got them Indian cheekbones."

"Well, it's better than nothing."

Yes, that became our battle cry.

"Sometimes, it's a good day to die. Sometimes, it's better than nothing."

We Indians became so numb to the possibility of dissent, so accepting of our own lowered expectations, that we canonized a film like "Powwow Highway."

When it was first released, I loved "Powwow Highway." I cried when I first saw it in the theater, then cried again when I stayed and watched it again a second time.

I mean, I loved that movie. I memorized whole passages of dialogue. But recently, I watched the film for the first time in many years and cringed in shame and embarrassment with every stereotypical scene.

I cringed when Philbert Bono climbed to the top of a sacred mountain and left a Hershey chocolate bar as an offering.

I cringed when Philbert and Buddy Red Bow waded into a stream and sang Indian songs to the moon.

I cringed when Buddy had a vision of himself as an Indian warrior throwing a tomahawk through the window of a police cruiser.

I mean, I don't know a single Indian who would leave a chocolate bar as an offering. I don't know any Indians who have ever climbed to the top of any mountain. I don't know any Indians who wade into streams and sing to the moon. I don't know of any Indians who imagine themselves to be Indian warriors.

Wait—

I was wrong. I know of at least one Indian boy who always imagined himself to be a cinematic Indian warrior.

Me.

I watched the movies and saw the kind of Indian I was supposed to be.

A cinematic Indian is supposed to climb mountains.

I am afraid of heights.

A cinematic Indian is supposed to wade into streams and sing songs.

I don't know how to swim.

A cinematic Indian is supposed to be a warrior.

I haven't been in a fistfight since sixth grade and she beat the crap out of me.

I mean, I knew I could never be as brave, as strong, as wise as visionary, as white as the Indians in the movies.

I was just one little Indian boy who hated Tonto because Tonto was the only cinematic Indian who looked like me.

Gary Edgerton and Kathy Merlock Jackson

Gary Edgerton is professor and chair of the Communication and Theatre Arts Department at Old Dominion University in Norfolk, Virginia. He writes about film genres, Hollywood film and documentary film and television, and frequently publishes work in the Journal of American Culture *and the* Journal of Popular Film and Television. *His most recent book is* Ken Burns's America *(New York: St Martin's Palgrave, 2001), which traces the rise of the popular PBS documentary filmmaker Ken Burns.*

Kathy Merlock Jackson is professor and coordinator of communications at Virginia Wesleyan College. She frequently writes on topics in children's media and culture, particularly on Disney animation. This article, which focuses on Disney's re-telling of the story of Pocahontas, was first published in the Journal of Popular Film and Television. *Contributors to this journal tend to be scholars or graduate students who examine films and genres from a socio-cultural perspective. The journal concentrates on commercial film and television and appeals to both academics and a more general readership.*

Redesigning Pocahontas

> It is a story that is fundamentally about racism and intolerance and we hope that people will gain a greater understanding of themselves and of the world around them. It's also about having respect for each other's cultures.
>
> —Thomas Schumacher, senior vice president of Disney Feature Animation (*Pocahontas* 35)

> The challenge was how to do a movie with such themes and make it interesting, romantic, fun.
>
> —Peter Schneider, president of Disney Feature Animation (*Pocahontas* 37)

Thomas Schumacher and Peter Schneider are two of the key executives who have re-established the Walt Disney Company as the premier animation studio in Hollywood. Schneider, in particular, became president of Disney Feature Animation in 1985, and since that time has assembled a coterie of first-rate talent and guided

---

Reprinted from *Journal of Popular Film and Television*, (1996), pp. 90–98, by permission of The Helen Dwight Reid Educational Foundation. Published by Heldref Publications.

the division to a level of unprecedented success, boasting a lineup of recent productions that now includes *The Little Mermaid* (1989), *Beauty and the Beast* (1991), *Aladdin* (1992), *The Lion King* (1994), and *Pocahontas* (1995). Disney is the film industry's exemplar for creating blockbuster motion pictures, fueling the releases with highly sophisticated advertising and marketing campaigns, and then maximizing profit by licensing literally hundreds of ancillary products. For example, the film *The Lion King* and its merchandise have already grossed an estimated $2 billion worldwide (Biskind 81). With each subsequent feature, Disney executives try to equal or top their last success. Disney executives and animators had a related, though secondary, goal with *Pocahontas,* however. They wanted to address the rise in public criticism from various ethnic groups over racial stereotyping in their most recent productions. Arab American groups, for instance, protested against certain imagery and lyrics in *Aladdin* (Kim 24; Sharkey 22). African American critics similarly pointed out that the three hooligan hyenas in *The Lion King* were thinly disguised black and Hispanic characters who seemed to be living in a jungle equivalent of an inner-city ghetto (Sharkey 22). Disney executives understood from the outset that *Pocahontas* could be similarly problematic for the studio and planned to be more careful and sensitive in designing the film's portrayal of Native Americans.

The genesis of *Pocahontas* actually came from the eventual co-director, Mike Gabriel, who was trying to initiate a new project after finishing *The Rescuers Down Under* in 1990. He wanted to do a western, "a big scale epic that would lend itself to the kind of Broadway-oriented animated musicals that Disney had recently reinvigorated" (*Pocahontas* 36). Peter Schneider, for his part, had been considering an animated version of *Romeo and Juliet* for several years. The two seemingly disparate ideas merged for Gabriel when "somehow the name Pocahontas came into my mind . . . everyone knew the tale about her saving John Smith's life and it seemed like a natural for telling a story about two separate clashing worlds trying to understand each other" (*Pocahontas* 36). The Pocahontas narrative also furnished source material that could easily conform to the coming-of-age and romantic dictates of the Disney formula, as well as provide a spunky heroine as protagonist in the mold of Ariel in *The Little Mermaid,* Belle in *Beauty and the Beast,* and Jasmine in *Aladdin.*

Within this conventional framework, then, the talent at Disney Feature Animation began shaping its portrayals. Writers Carl Binder, Susannah Grant, and Philip LaZebnik drafted a script, while 12 interrelated teams of animators started experimental sketches of the characters and setting. Supervising animator Glen Keane journeyed to Tidewater, Virginia, hiring a number of local Native American consultants to advise his production team. Native American performers, moreover, were cast to provide the voices and characterizations for the main American Indian roles, including former American Indian Movement activist-turned-actor Russell Means, who would play Chief Powhatan, Pocahontas's father. The Walt Disney Company was apparently making all the appropriate and necessary preparations for an elaborate update of the Native American on film.

The "Hollywood Indian"

The "Hollywood Indian" is a well-established image that has appeared on movie screens around the world for nearly a century. The parameters of the stereotype are already outlined in a handful of useful studies (Bataille and Silet; Friar and Friar; Marsden and Nachbar; O'Connor). These analyses focus on representative types and traits, furnishing us with a composite that is deeply conflicted and contradictory, as is in the case of most racial, ethnic, and gender stereotypes. In the essay "The Indians in the Movies" in *Handbook of North American Indians,* Michael T. Marsden and Jack Nachbar described the cultural context of captivity narratives, dime novels, stage melodramas, and Wild West shows, all of which contributed to the film industry's rendition of the Native American. They also offer a three-part model of American Indian characterizations on film, in which men compose the first two stereotypes, as either "noble anachronisms" or "savage reactionaries," and women are presented as "Indian princesses" in the third, if they are presented on-screen at all.[1]

In this respect, Disney's *Pocahontas* (dir. Mike Gabriel and Eric Goldberg) promised to be an intriguing departure from the usual, male-centered storyline, as well as the general portrayal of American Indians. As the epigraphs suggest, the company's executives stressed a seriousness of purpose not usually connected with one of their animated pictures. For Roy Disney, Walt Disney's nephew and the board member who supervises the Feature Animation Division, "*Pocahontas* is a story that appeared to us because it was basically a story about people getting along together . . . which is particularly applicable to lots of places in the world today" (*Pocahontas* 33). Schneider confirmed, "It is an important message to a generation to stop fighting, stop killing each other because of the color of your skin" (*Pocahontas* 37).

Disney publicists asserted that "in every aspect of the storytelling, the filmmakers tried to treat Pocahontas with the respect she deserved and present a balanced and informed view of the Native American culture" (*Pocahontas* 34). Producer James Pentecost added, "We also tried to tap into [Pocahontas's] spirituality and the spirituality of the Native Americans, especially in the way they relate to nature" (*Pocahontas* 33). Finally, Russell Means conferred a much-welcomed imprimatur:

> When I first read the script, I was impressed with the beginning of the film. In fact, I was overwhelmed by it. It tells the truth about the motives for Europeans initially coming to the so-called New World. I find it astounding that Americans and the Disney Studios are willing to tell the truth. (*Pocahontas* 34).

Given the intentions voiced by the makers of *Pocahontas,* we intend in this article to examine the representation of Native Americans in the film, analyzing selected images, words, and sounds for their ideological content, particularly as they reflect points of view on race, gender, and social position. We assume that this newest version of the Pocahontas story resides in the fusion of movie and merchandise, generating a kind of cultural supertext that clearly has been a huge financial success for the Walt Disney Company on a global scale. We will next survey critical and corporate responses to the film, reflecting on those reactions as telling indicators of mainstream and alternative viewpoints toward Native Americans today, and we will conclude with suggestions on how to use *Pocahontas* as a teaching tool in our homes and classrooms.

The Disney Version

> You have to approach it carefully. The Disney version becomes the definitive version.
>
> —Glen Keane (qtd. in Gleiberman 42)

> Three things are inevitable in 1995: death, taxes, and Disney's *Pocahontas*.
>
> —Pat H. Broeske (8)

When Disney began marketing *Pocahontas* nearly five months before the film's eventual release, conventional wisdom in Hollywood alleged that the film could never approach the money-making performance of *The Lion King*. Insiders carped about the historical nature of the subject matter, and, more disturbingly, the so-called "girl factor." "Boys won't want to go to a girl picture" (Shapiro and Chang 57). What the rumor mill in the film industry underscored, of course, is how out-of-proportion Hollywood expectations are in the 1990s. To date, *Pocahontas*'s box-office and merchandising proceeds are still described as modest when compared to those of *The Lion King,* which with *E.T.* (1982) and *Jurassic Park* (1993) is one of the three most-profitable films of all time. On the other hand, *Pocahontas* has already generated over $1 billion in revenues on an $80 million investment (a $55 million production budget and $25 million for advertising and marketing), and its total earnings just keep on mounting (Walt Disney Company Annual Report, 1995: 13, 31, 50).

Disney's campaign to sell *Pocahontas* began on 3 February 1995 with a 24-city mall display, complete with an animation kiosk where shoppers could electronically paint a cel from the film and view a 26-foot model of John Smith's ship. The promotional juggernaut continued that spring with dozens of tie-ins; for example, Burger King distributed 55 million toy replicas of the film's characters with kids' meals, Payless Shoes featured a line of moccasins, and Mattel peddled a Barbie-like Pocahontas doll (Broeske 8). No doubt the most effective technique was attaching a *Pocahontas* trailer to the March release of *The Lion King* on home video, one which retailed 20 million units in just six days and ended by shattering all existing records, with more than 50 million tapes sold by year's end (Walt Disney Company Annual Report, 1995: 19).

Disney's marketing of *Pocahontas* peaked with a highly publicized 10 June premiere in New York's Central Park on four, eight-story-high screens, before 110,000 spectators. This extravaganza was not only covered amply by the print and electronic news media, but it was also telecast live as programming on the newly launched United Paramount Network. *Pocahontas* eventually earned $91 million in its first four weeks of domestic release and became a certifiable blockbuster by reaping more than $300 million at film theaters worldwide during the remainder of 1995 (Kilday and Thompson 28–29).

All told, *Pocahontas* entered the American mainstream during the spring and summer of 1995 to share space with O. J. Simpson, *Batman Forever,* Hootie and the Blowfish, and a handful of other high-profile popular cultural phenomena. Fashioned within the no-holds-barred commercial milieu of the Walt Disney Company, this animated feature erupted into the public sphere as the focal point of a massively successful advertising and marketing offensive. The film's storyline and characters were soon adapted into other media and provided the basis for an assortment of other widely retailed products, generating additional sales and promotions. Pocahontas, the 400-year-old legend, was expertly redesigned to Disney's usual specifications—meaning a full-length animated feature with a host of commodity tie-ins—thus becoming the version of the Pocahontas story that most people recognize today.

Don't Know Much About History

> Moviemakers shouldn't be handcuffed when using real stories as jumping-off places for works of entertainment.
>
> —James Pentecost (Kim 24)

> We never wanted to do a docu-drama, but something that was inspired by legend.
>
> —Peter Schneider (*Pocahontas* 37)

Representatives of the Walt Disney Company inadvertently alienated their chief Native American consultant, Shirley "Little Dove" Custalow McGowan, by sending her mixed signals about the kind of guidance they were seeking from her. Co-director Eric Goldberg, for example, remembers how "we met with surviving members of the Algonquin nation in Virginia and realized that it would be fascinating to show their culture in our film. We wanted to be as faithful as possible" (*Pocahontas* 34). In response, Custalow McGowan recalls

> I was honored to be asked by them . . . but I wasn't at the studio two hours before I began to make clear my objections to what they were doing . . . they had said that the film would be historically accurate. I soon found that it wasn't to be. . . . I wish my name wasn't on it. I wish Pocahontas' name wasn't on it. (Vincent, Disney E5)

The filmmakers at Disney never really intended *Pocahontas* to be historically accurate, despite all the sentimental rhetoric; they were producing yet another animated feature after all. Native American advisors were hired to secure a more positive, even hagiographic, portrayal of Native American characters within an earnestly sympathetic narrative. Studio executives were, therefore, banking on the likelihood that a postmodern restyling of Pocahontas and her legend would also be an immensely popular and profitable version for audiences in the mid-1990s. They were, moreover, attempting to favorably affect public opinion regarding "Disney's America," a historical theme park planned for Northern Virginia, which was subsequently abandoned.

Artists and authors have actually been reshaping Pocahontas and her history for nearly four centuries. In *Pocahontas: Her Life and Legend,* William M. S. Rasmussen and Robert S. Tilton surveyed literally dozens of depictions, beginning during Pocahontas's lifetime, when she was "living proof that American natives could be Christianized and civilized" (7). Fact and fiction were blended at the outset into this legendary personality who symbolized friendly and advantageous relations between American Indians and English settlers from a distinctly Anglo-American point of view. Disney's animators are merely part of that longer tradition, the latest in a series of storytellers, painters, poets, sculptors, and commercial artists who have taken liberties with Pocahontas's historical record for their own purposes (Rasmussen and Tilton).

Disney's *Pocahontas* is, once again, a parable of assimilation, although this time the filmmakers hinted at a change in outlook. Producer James Pentecost for instance reported that

> "Colors of the Wind" perhaps best sums up the entire spirit and essence of the film . . . this song was written before anything else. It set the tone of the movie and defined the character of Pocahontas. Once Alan [Menken] and Stephen [Schwartz] wrote that song, we knew what the film was about. (*Pocahontas* 51–52)

Schwartz agreed with Pentecost, adding that his lyrics were inspired by Chief Seattle's famous speech to the United States Congress that challenged white ascendancy in America and the appropriation of American Indian lands (*Pocahontas* 52).

"Colors of the Wind" functions as a rousing anthem for *Pocahontas,* extolling the virtues of tolerance, cross-cultural sensitivity, and respect for others and the natural environment:

> You think you own whatever land you land on
> The earth is just a dead thing you can claim
> But I know ev'ry rock and tree and creature
> Has a life, has a spirit, has a name
> You think the only people who are people
> Are the people who think and look like you
> But if you walk the footsteps of a stranger
> You'll learn things you never knew
> You never knew.

These lofty sentiments, however, are down-played by the film's overriding commitment to romantic fantasy. Pocahontas, for example, sings "Colors of the Wind" in response to John Smith's remark that her people are "savages," but the rest of the technically stirring sequence plays more like an adolescent seduction than a lesson teaching Smith those "things [he] never knew [he] never knew."

Pocahontas's search for her "dream," a classic Disney plot device, is a case in point. A great deal of dramatic energy is spent on Pocahontas's finding her "true path." She is sprightly, though troubled, in her conversations with Grandmother Willow. She is struggling with her own youthful uncertainties as well as her father's very definite plans for her:

> Should I choose the smoothest course
> Steady as a beating drum
> Should I marry Kocoum
> Is all my dreaming at an end?
> Or do you still wait for me, dreamgiver
> Just around the river bend?

Unsure of Kocoum, but regarding love and marriage as her only options, Pocahontas finally finds her answer in John Smith.

What this development discloses, of course, is the conventional viewpoint of the filmmakers: Pocahontas essentially falls in love with the first white man she sees. The film's scriptwriters chose certain episodes from her life, invented others, and in the process shaped a narrative that highlights some events, ideas, and values, while suppressing others. The historical Pocahontas and John Smith were never lovers; she was 12 and he was 27 when they met in 1607. In relying so completely on their romantic coupling, however, Disney's animators minimize the many challenging issues that they raise—racism, colonialism, environmentalism, and spiritual alienation.

The entire plot structure is similarly calculated to support the Disney game plan. The film begins in London in 1607 with John Smith and the Virginia Company crew setting out for the New World, and it concludes with Smith's return trip to England in 1609, although the duration of the movie seems to span weeks rather than years. The scriptwriters, nevertheless, terminate the narrative at the most expedient juncture, avoiding the more tragic business of Pocahontas's kidnapping by the English; her isolation from her people for a year; her ensuing conversion to Christianity; her marriage, and name change to Lady Rebecca Rolfe; and her untimely death from tuberculosis at age 21 in England (Barbour; Fritz; Mossiker; Woodward). Disney's filmmakers did, in fact, research those details of Pocahontas's life before starting production, but obviously their aim was to keep audiences as comfortable as possible by providing a predictable product.

Co-director Eric Goldberg later claimed that "it's important for us as filmmakers to be able to say not everything was entirely hunky-dory by the end . . . which it usually is in a traditionally Disneyesque movie" (Mallory 24). Given the eventual fate of Pocahontas and the Algonquins, though, Disney's animators could hardly have opted for the usual "happily ever after" finale. The filmmakers, after all, were genuinely trying to offend no one, including the Native American community and their consultants.

Pocahontas's climactic sequence further establishes the film's dominant, love-story narrative, albeit with some variations of the classic Disney formula. After

English settler Thomas shoots and kills Kocoum, tensions between the American Indians and the British mount. John Smith is captured by Kocoum's companions, blamed for his death, and immediately slated for execution. In a replay of the legendary rescue scene, Pocahontas risks her life to save John Smith, catalyzing peace between the English and the American Indians. In the process, the film's animators and scriptwriters complete their upgrade of the Indian princess characterization by making Pocahontas more assertive, determined to realize her "dream," and according to her father, "wis[e] beyond her years."

The film, moreover, concludes with Pocahontas standing alone on a rocky summit, watching the ship carrying a wounded John Smith sail for England. She has presumably resolved to stay behind in Virginia and take her rightful place alongside her father as a peacemaker, even though her actions in the previous 80 minutes of the film suggest that her "path" lies elsewhere. *Pocahontas* thus reinforces another resilient stereotype that the main purpose of a Disney heroine is to further the interests of love, notwithstanding the bittersweet coda. Pocahontas's newfound ambition to become a mediator, then, is a workable if somewhat disingenuous solution, especially considering the latent historical realities percolating beneath this romantic plotline.

The questions then arise: Can a Disney animated feature be substantive as well as entertaining? Can race, gender, and the rest of *Pocahontas*'s postmodernist agenda be presented in a thought-provoking way that still works for the animation audience, especially children? We believe the answer is yes, but we also believe the studio has an obligation to create a more forward-looking alternative to existing stereotypes and to deal more fully and maturely with the serious issues and charged imagery that it addresses.

Consider the redesigning of the character of Pocahontas. Supervising animator Glen Keane remembered how former studio chairman Jeffrey Katzenberg charged him with reshaping Pocahontas as "the finest creature the human race has to offer" (Kim 24). He also admitted, "I don't want to say a rut, but we've been doing mainly Caucasian faces" (Cochran 24). Keane, in turn, drew on four successive women for inspiration, beginning with paintings of Pocahontas herself; then Native American consultant Shirley "Little Dove" Custalow McGowan; then 21-year-old Filipino model Dyna Taylor; and finally white supermodel Christy Turlington (Cochran 24). After studio animators spent months sketching her, their Pocahontas emerged as a multicultural pastiche. They started with Native American faces but eventually gravitated to the more familiar and Anglicized looks of the statuesque Turlington. Not surprisingly, all the key decision makers and supervising artists on *Pocahontas* were white males. Disney and Keane's "finest creature" clearly is the result of a very conventional viewpoint.

Accordingly, what of avoiding old stereotypes? Native American actors were cast in all the native roles in the film; still, Pocahontas's screen image is less American Indian than fashionably exotic. Many critics, for example *Newsweek*'s Laura Shapiro, refer to the makeover as "Native American Barbie" (Shapiro and Chang 77)—in other words, Indian features, such as Pocahontas's eyes, skin color, and wardrobe, only provide a kind of Native American styling to an old stereotype.

The British colonists also replace the Indians as stock villains in *Pocahontas,* with Governor Ratcliffe, in particular, singing about gold, riches, and power in the appropriately titled song "Mine, Mine, Mine." The film's final impression, therefore, is that, with Ratcliffe bound, gagged, and headed back to England, American Indians and Europeans are now free to coexist peacefully. Race is a dramatic or stylistic device, but the more profound consequences of institutional racism are never allowed even momentarily to invade the audience's comfort zone.

Perhaps the Disney studio should trust its patrons more. Fairy tales and fantasies have traditionally challenged children (and adults) with the unpleasant realities lurking just beneath their placid exteriors. Audiences are likely to enjoy added depth and suggestiveness enough to buy plenty of tickets and merchandise. Disney's *Pocahontas* raises important issues but does not fully address them; it succeeds as a king-sized commercial vehicle, but fails as a half-hearted revision.

Contested Meanings

> The meaning of a text is always the site of a struggle.
> —Lawrence Grossberg (86)

> History is always interpreted. I'm not saying this film is accurate, but it is a start. I grew up being called Pocahontas as a derogatory term. They hissed that name at me, as if it was something dirty. Now, with this film, Pocahontas can reach a larger culture as a heroine. No, it doesn't make up for 500 years of genocide, but it is a reminder that we will have to start telling our own stories.
> —Irene Bedard (qtd. in Vincent E5)

The comments of Irene Bedard, the Native American actress who plays the voice of Pocahontas, augment many of the critical responses that surfaced after the release of *Pocahontas* in the summer of 1995. She offers audiences some valuable insights into the Native American perspective, especially with her painful recollection of being ridiculed with the surprising taunt, "Pocahontas." As she says, this film signals a welcomed counterbalance to such insults; most significantly, she calls for the emergence and development of a truly American Indian cinema that is the next needed step for fundamentally improving depictions of Native Americans on film.

Until that time, however, we can extend our understanding of *Pocahontas,* in particular, and established and alternative views toward Indian people in general, by examining the spectrum of critical reactions that the animated film engendered. The most striking aspect of *Pocahontas*'s critical reception is the contradictory nature of the responses: the film is alternately described as progressive or escapist, enlightened or racist, feminist or retrograde—depending on the critic. Inherently fraught with contradictions, Disney's *Pocahontas* sends an abundance of mixed messages, which probably underscores the limits of reconstructing the Native American image at Disney or, perhaps, any other major Hollywood studio that operates first and foremost as a marketer of conventional dreams and a seller of related consumer products.

As teachers, critics, parents, or students of popular culture, we can usefully extend the scope of our examinations of *Pocahontas* by studying the various critical communities that have engaged the Disney version with their own unique perspectives. These additional points of view help to illuminate not only what *Pocahontas* presented directly—such as mainstream representations of race and gender—but also what it underplayed or ignored—such as peripheral outlooks on those issues or the historical reality underlying the legend.

The Native Americans who worked on the film—such as Russell Means, the voice of Powhatan, and Irene Bedard—generally commended it. Means specifically called it "the single finest work ever done on American Indians by Hollywood" (*Pocahontas* 34). His comments especially drew fire from the Native American press, where a number of both columnists and readers who sent letters to the editor wondered if the former head of the American Indian Movement had "sold out to the white man and his money" (Rattler D1). Means's pronouncements evidently became a source of controversy in a debate that highlights the competing conceptions of American "Indian-ness" that co-exist in contemporary America.

A valuable place to start the discussion on *Pocahontas* is Robert Berkhofer Jr.'s seminal work *The White Man's Indian: Images of the American Indian from Columbus to the Present.* This insightful analysis underscores that the dominant view of Native Americans has always originated with Euro-American culture, reflecting Anglicized attitudes and preferences and ultimately pushing native perspectives to the margins of society, if not entirely out of view. Disney's *Pocahontas* is thus another example of the "white man's Indian," mostly because the studio was only willing to partially incorporate its consultants' advice. Berkhofer's book can also be supplemented with Daniel Francis's *The Imaginary Indian: The Image of the Indian in Canadian Culture,* which again emphasizes how most popular representations of Native Americans are the products of white needs, intentions, and purposes.

Pocahontas is, moreover, a text in which the issues of race and gender intersect. Bedard found herself at odds with several Native American women writers when she remarked, "When I was growing up, I wanted so much to be Barbie. Now, some little girl might want to be Pocahontas. That's a step in the right direction" (Vincent E5). Martina Whelshula and Faith Spotted Eagle countered Bedard's sentiment in their review of the film in the Spokane *Review-Perspective,* reprinted in *Indian Country Today*. They stated that Disney's *Pocahontas* is "part of Barbie culture. A culture that relies on sexism, capitalism, and lookism . . . where a woman is elevated only on her appearance . . . where a heroine lives only for approval from men" (D1).

This flashpoint again supplies a productive basis on which to encourage discussion on the social construction of beauty standards and race. From it can be gained a sense of the profound distress that is still elicited in the native community by the longstanding traditions of the "Hollywood Indian." Even Disney's relatively benign portrayal prompted consultant Shirley "Little Dove" Custalow

McGowan to say her "heart sorrowed" upon first seeing the film (Silver 61). Two letters to the editor of *Indian Country Today* likewise expressed dismay and anger, especially about Disney's use of the song "Savages," which the authors found highly offensive (Letters D2). University of Texas anthropologist Pauline Turner Strong aptly explains the reasons behind such a reaction when she writes that

> for many Native Americans "savage" is the "S" word, as potent and degrading as the word "nigger." I cannot imagine the latter epithet repeated so often, and set to music in a G-rated film and its soundtrack. it is even more shocking to write it in a review. Is "savage" more acceptable because it is used reciprocally? But then does this not downplay the role the colonial ideology of savagism played in the extermination and dispossession of indigenous people? (Strong, H-Net)

The portrayal of the English in *Pocahontas* similarly triggered outrage in the British press. The 30 July 1995 Times, for instance, referred to Pocahontas as

> history's most famous squaw. . . . The English are thugs, all greed, gold, and guns, and they treat natives like savages. The Indians, by contrast, are civilized, peace-loving, and eco-conscious. The animators have significantly made the Redskins look pretty much like modern paleface Americans, and speak like them, too. . . . Disney's fable of an arcadian American history wrecked by incursions from the Old World is obviously a means of allaying a bad conscience, while voicing xenophobic resentments about corrupt Europeans. (Adair 9)

Evidently the shoe is now on the other foot, and this symbolic inversion can lead to a fruitful exchange about multiculturalism and the function of stock villainy in popular film. As Betsy Sharkey writes in the *New York Times,* "British males seem to be one of the few safe villains in these politically correct times" (22). Paying attention to such cues can produce striking illustrations of intercultural differences in perspective, allowing us all to "learn [some] things [we] never knew [we] never knew."

The majority of America's mainstream press coverage also concentrated on *Pocahontas*'s racial and gender depictions, along with instances in which the film differed from the historical record. On one hand, Caryn James of the *New York Times* called *Pocahontas* "a sharp revision of the classic Disney fairy tale formula . . . [and] a model of how smartly those elements can be reinvigorated." She, moreover, viewed Pocahontas as "the most subversive heroine in the Disney canon" (F1). In contrast, Owen Gleiberman of *Entertainment Weekly* provided a more scathing, albeit glib, description:

> Pocahontas herself has been conceived as a strapping, high-cheekboned update of the usual Disney Princess—she's an aerobicized

> Native American superbabe, with long, muscular brown legs, regal shoulder blades, and silky black hair flowing down to her waist. With her vacuous Asian doll eyes, she looks ready to host *Pocahontas' House of Style*. (42)

Mal Vincent of the *Virginian-Pilot* and *Ledger-Star* (of Norfolk) concurred with James that "'Pocahontas' is a signal that Disney animators are willing to take new, and daring, risks" (Vincent, Pocahontas E2). David Sterritt of the *Christian Science Monitor* disagreed, saying that Disney is

> clinging to formulas that refuse to grow in any but superficial ways. True enough, "Pocahontas" tips its hat to such trendy (and worthy) causes as conservation and environmentalism, and even delivers a hearty endorsement of interracial dating. Yet the studio can hardly be congratulated for "taking a stand" on socially relevant issues, since it's careful to wrap its ideas in an aura of nostalgic fantasy that neutralizes their ability to challenge or stimulate us. (13)

Whether "subversive" or sexist, "daring" or reactionary, *Pocahontas* is a deeply conflicted text.

Finally, *Pocahontas*'s widespread popularity has produced a corresponding upsurge in interest in the historical Pocahontas and in Native Americans. After the release of *Pocahontas* in June 1995, admissions to the Jamestown Settlement rose 60 percent over those of July 1994 (Holland), eventually reaching 38 percent more than the average for the previous five summers (Renewed 3). Although other factors contributed to Jamestown's increased tourism, such as various marketing strategies and the 400th anniversary celebration of the birth of Pocahontas, the Disney film contributed greatly to the upturn.

In the words of one Jamestown historical interpreter, tourists are "coming here to learn. I've been pleasantly surprised at how much parental concern there is for children getting more than was shown in the movie" (Renewed 3). *Pocahontas* can be used as a springboard to encourage our students and children to look beyond the movie and the merchandise. Jean Fritz's young adult history, *The Double Life of Pocahontas,* is a wonderful place to start for adolescents. The informative books Philip Barbour's *Pocahontas and Her World,* William Rasmussen and Robert Tilton's *Pocahontas: Her Life and Legend,* and Robert Tilton's *Pocahontas: The Evolution of an American Narrative* and the 1995 half-hour documentary *Pocahontas: Ambassador of the New World* (A Perpetual Motions Production for the A&E Television Network) are other rewarding alternatives to the ubiquitous Disney version.

Works Cited

Adair, Gilbert. "Animating History." (London) *Sunday Times* 30 July 1995: 10.

Barbour, Philip L. *Pocahontas and Her World.* Boston: Houghton Mifflin, 1970.

Bataille, G., and C. Silet, eds. *The Pretend Indians: Images of Native Americans in the Movies.* Ames: Iowa State UP, 1980.

Berkhofer, Robert, Jr. *The White Man's Indian: Images of the American Indian from Columbus to the Present.* New York: Vintage, 1979.

Biskind, Peter. "Win, Lose—But Draw." *Premiere* July 1995: 81+.

Broeske, Pat H. "The Pocamotion: Promotion of Walt Disney's 'Pocahontas.'" *Entertainment Weekly* 5 Feb. 1995: 8.

Cochran, Jason. "What Becomes a Legend Most?" *Entertainment Weekly* 16 June 1995: 42.

Francis, Daniel. *The Imaginary Indian: The Image of the Indian in Canadian Culture.* Vancouver: Arsenal Pulp, 1992.

Friar, R., and N. Friar. *The Only Good Indian . . . The Hollywood Gospel.* New York: Drama Book Specialists, 1972.

Fritz, Jean. *The Double Life of Pocahontas.* New York: Puffin, 1983.

Gleiberman, Owen. "Disney's Indian Corn." *Entertainment Weekly* 16 June 1995: 42.

Grossberg, Lawrence. "Reply to the Critics." *Critical Studies in Mass Communication* 3 (1983): 86–95.

Holland, Erik. Telephone interview. Jamestown Settlement Interpreter Program Manager and Supervisor, Powhatan Village. 2 Oct. 1995.

James, Caryn. "Belle and Ariel Never Chose Duty Over Love." *New York Times* 18 June 1995: F1.

Kilday, Gregg, and Anne Thompson. "To Infinity and Beyond." *Entertainment Weekly* 2 Feb. 1996: 27–32.

Kim, Albert. "Whole New World?" *Entertainment Weekly* 23 June 1995: 22–25.

"Letters to the Entertainment Editor." *Indian Country Today* 6 July 1995: D2.

Mallory, Michael. "American History Makes Animation History." *The Disney Magazine* Spring 1995: 22–24.

Marsden, Michael T., and Jack Nachbar. "The Indians in the Movies." *Handbook of North American Indians.* Washington, D.C.: Smithsonian Institution, 1988.

Mossiker, Frances. *Pocahontas.* New York: Knopf, 1976.

O'Connor, J. *The Hollywood Indian: Stereotypes of Native Americans in Films.* Trenton: New Jersey State Museum, 1980.

"*Pocahontas:* Press Kit." Burbank: Walt Disney Pictures, 1995.

Rasmussen, William M. S., and Robert S. Tilton. *Pocahontas: Her Life and Legend.* Richmond: Virginia Historical Society, 1994.

Rattler, Terri. "Letters to the Entertainment Editor: Do We Teach History or Fiction to our Children?" *Indian Country Today* 6 July 1995: D1.

"Renewed National Interest in Pocahontas Has Impact at Jamestown Settlement." *Jamestown-Yorktown Foundation Dispatch* Fall 1995: 3.

Shapiro, Laura, and Yahlin Chang. "The Girls of Summer." *Newsweek* 22 May 1995: 56–57.

Sharkey, Betsy. "Beyond Teepees and Totem Poles." *New York Times* 11 June 1995: 2:1, 22.

Silver, Marc. "*Pocahontas* for Real." *U.S. News & World Report* 19 June 1995: 61.

Sterritt, David. "'Pocahontas' Doesn't Stray Far From Disney Game Plan." *The Christian Science Monitor* 23 June 1995: 13.

Strong, Pauline Turner. Rev. of *Pocahontas*. Online posting. Popular Culture and American Culture Associations/H-Net Discussion List. 30 June 1995. Availability: [H-PCAACA@msu.edu.]

Tilton, Robert S. *Pocahontas: The Evolution of an American Narrative*. Cambridge: Cambridge UP, 1994.

Vincent, Mal. "Disney vs. History . . . Again." *Virginian-Pilot* and *Ledger-Star* 20 June 1995: E1, E5.

———. "'Pocahontas': Discarding the History, It's still a Terrific Show." *Virginian-Pilot* and *Ledger-Star* 24 June 1995: E1–E2.

Whelshula, Martina, and Faith Spotted Eagle. "Pocahontas Rates an 'F' in Indian Country." *Indian Country Today* 6 July 1995: D1–2.

Woodward, Grace Steele. *Pocahontas*. Norman: U of Oklahoma P, 1969.

Notes

1. In the first category, a "noble anachronism" embodies Rousseau's notion of "natural man and his inherent goodness," who is ultimately doomed by the onslaught of Euro-American culture. Second, a "savage reactionary" confronts white manifest destiny with violent defiance but is also annihilated for the overall good of advancing civilization. Lastly, an "Indian princess" is rooted in the legend of Pocahontas. She is typically maidenly, demure, and deeply committed to some white man—for example, John Smith in the case of *Pocahontas*.
2. Keane was the animation supervisor for *Pocahontas*.

Rolando Romero

Rolando Romero is Associate Professor of Latina/Latino Studies in the Spanish, Italian, and Portuguese Department at the University of Illinois, Urbana-Champaign. He earned his Ph.D. at the University of California at Santa Barbara in Hispanic Languages and Literatures. Professor Romero's work has received many prestigious awards, including a Fulbright Fellowship, a Rockefeller Foundation grant, and a Ford Foundation Fellowship. You may visit his home page at: http://www.sip.uiuc.edu/rromero/index.htm. He has lectured and written widely about issues relating to border migration, Latinos in twentieth century literature and film, and Chicano art and culture. In this article, Romero questions why the popular science fiction film Blade Runner *(Ridley Scott, 1982) imagines 2019 Los Angeles as a postmodern urban environment devoid of Chicano/as, who currently represent a great majority of the city's population.*

The Postmodern Hybrid: Do Aliens Dream of Alien Sheep?

Critics have labeled Ridley Scott's *Blade Runner* (1982) the quintessential postmodern film. The film—which takes place in 2019 Los Angeles—centers around an enslaved group of replicants/humanoids who have escaped from an Off-World colony. Laws declare illegal their presence on earth and thus police hire blade runner/bounty hunter Rick Deckard (Harrison Ford) to destroy (or in the parlance of the film, retire) the replicants. The studio changed Scott's version of the film when test markets showed that the public did not appreciate the gloomy possibility that Deckard himself might be a humanoid (Kerman 141). Attempting to provide a happy ending, the studio released the film with a voice-over narration by the main character. This version did not include a sequence in which Deckard dreams of a unicorn in a forest. The last scene shows Deckard and Rachel (Sean Young) flying into the sunset, though in another version, the film concludes with Deckard taking Rachel out of the city and then, revealing the misogynist strand of film making, killing her, purportedly so she won't be killed by the police. The distributor pulled out the film from general release when, even with the addition of the happy ending, it still did not fare well commercially. Placed by the studio directly on the secondary markets the film acquired cult standing. In 1991 the studio released *Blade Runner: The Director's Cut,* Ridley Scott's version of the film.[1]

Reprinted from *Post Script: Essays in Film and the Humanities* 16.1, Fall 1996, pp. 41–52, by permission of the publisher.

The studio's cutting of the unicorn sequence in the first release, however, effectively eliminated the structural role Gaff (Edward James Olmos) plays in the film. Repeatedly, Gaff visually hints at the moral significance of the scenes by building origami figures. Gaff builds the figure of a chicken when Deckard hesitates to accept the Blade Runner assignment. Later when Deckard searches in Leon's hotel room, Gaff constructs the figure of a man with an erection, foreshadowing Deckard's and Rachel's physical relationship.

Gaff builds a third figure of a unicorn—the innocent beast lured into a trap by the "purity" of a virgin helping the captors. The unicorn sequence charges Gaff with the structural role of indicating to the audiences the possibility that the naive Deckard might himself be a replicant:

> The motivation of this unicorn sequence became clear in the final scenes. Gaff leaves behind an origami unicorn, indicating that he knows Deckard's private memories, and the only way this could possibly happen would be if Deckard was a replicant with all his memories nothing more than artificial transplants. (Instrell 164).

The director's cut clarifies the meaning of the unicorn by leading the audience to believe that Gaff's memories have been implanted on Deckard. The characters' sharing of memories would not only explain Gaff's sympathy towards the couple's relationship, it would also explain why Gaff decides not to hunt Rachel and Deckard.

What were the structural consequences of erasing the unicorn sequence from the final cut? Audiences perceive Olmos as the archetype of the Chicano character due to his roles in such noted Chicano canonical films as *Zoot Suit* (1982), *The Ballad of Gregorio Cortez* (1983), and *Stand and Deliver*. Thus the studio effectively erased the Chicano/a presence by erasing Gaff's structural role in the first release where Olmos's character functioned as a synechdoque for the Chicano/a population. Though Gaff does not exist in Philip K. Dick's original *Do Androids Dream of Electric Sheep?*, Hampton Fancher, the original script writer, introduced the character since, as he states, "I made him part-Mexican because I'm partly Chicano myself" (Sammon 113). It is also probable that initially the director did not deem the Chicano presence important because the movie had originally been scheduled for filming in England. When initially filmed "the street scenes were created on the New York Street set at the Burbank Studios" (Kerman 186). To add to the location confusion, the *Blade Runner* term is credited to William Burroughs, who secured the rights to a story by Alan Nourse with the same title. In Burroughs's ultimate welfare state, the blade runners were smugglers and runners who would take ". . . the actual drugs, instruments, and equipment from the suppliers to the clients and doctors and underground clinics" (Burroughs np). Burroughs's dystopia associates the "minorities" with decay from the very first sentence:

> Now B.J. you are asking me to tell you in one sentence what this film is about? . . . For starters it's about plain middle-class middle-income bracket Joe, the $15,000-a-year boy, sweating out two jobs, I.R.S. wringing the moon-light dollars out of him to

> keep the niggers and the spics on welfare and medicare so they can keep up their strength to mug his grandmother, rape his sister, and bugger his ten-year-old son. (Burroughs, n.p.)

Burroughs sets his *Blade Runner, A Movie* in a Manhattan of the future where mainland Puerto Ricans and African-Americans serve the author as props to characterize his American dystopia.

Though it could be argued that the *Blade Runner* script does not include more Chicano/as merely because the story takes place in the Los Angeles Chinatown, the representation of a future Los Angeles that obliterates a great majority of the population is inconceivable. Clearly, the ambivalence shown by the studio in releasing the two versions of the film in fact also reflects the ambivalence towards the Los Angeles Latino/a population which the dominant text would want to render invisible and non-existent, or at least, as alien.

My argument as to the causes of the ambivalence go far beyond material explanations of why the studio or the director opted for different versions. The ambivalence of the ending and of the structural role of Latino/as in the film reflects postmodernism's ambivalence towards hybridity itself. It is not coincidental that *Blade Runner,* as the "quintessential postmodern film" would also show indeterminacy towards the representation of the most visible population in the California landscape.

I should also note that the film acquired its critical resonance in postmodern circles no doubt thanks to the director's dystopian vision of the Los Angeles in the year 2019—"a city in the not-very-distant future of Western capitalism" (Kerman 16). *Blade Runner* turns the earth into a planetary run down inner city, with "demonic scene[s] of flaming towers, acid rain [suggesting atmospheric changes], and streets jammed with characters in a contemporary *Inferno*" (Kerman 42). David Desser compares the Los Angeles of *Blade Runner* to Milton's hell in *Paradise Lost:*

> A Dungeon horrible, on all sides round
> As one great Furnace flam'd, yet from those flames
> No light, but rather darkness visible
> Serve'd only to discover sight of woe,
> Regions of sorrow, doleful shades, where peace
> And rest can never dwell, hope never comes
> That comes to all; but torture without end
> Still urges, and a fiery Deluge, fed
> With ever-burning Sulphur unconsumed. (I: 61–9)

Another critic refers to the city as a Hades (Kerman 171). The people able to afford it "emigrated to the Off-World Colonies, and yet the streets swarm with Orientals, Hispanics, and punks" (Kerman 17). Society has completely fragmented, and to wit by the emphasis on the eyes (the green eye of the opening sequence, the owl, the Voight-Kampff test, the photographs, Deckard's Esper machine, Chow's laboratory, Tyrell's own death), only the ever present state control (represented by police vehicles and computers) can re-establish a social order. The film also borrows heavily from the tradition of the Private Eye film noir, and at least according to one critic, from Roman Polanski's *Chinatown*. As Kerman has noted, Deckard's and Tyrell's privileged panoramic position establish the relationship between control and the ability to see. Kerman goes as far as to establish that "Tyrell even looks a bit like the Nazi Angel of Death, Dr. Joseph Mengele" (Kerman 23). The Esper machine that Deckard uses also allows for the ultimate analysis of any picture taken in by the eye. It is clear from the commentaries that the film uses the mix of ethnicities to suggest the decrepitude of the future Los Angeles:

> In *Blade Runner,* race is structured into the film in both the traditional and the science fictional aspects of the issue. This futuristic Los Angeles is densely populated by a swarming mass of humanity, with a noticeable majority of Orientals, Latinos (the neon lights of a downtown Spanish-language movie theater flash prominently near J. F. Sebastian's apartment), and a smattering of Mediterranean types. The streets are also filled with a variety of midgets, punks, and decadent revelers (the latter among the few Caucasians). In fact, the sight of a white person is rare enough . . . for the replicant, Pris, to ask Sebastian why he hasn't emigrated off-world. (Kerman 111)

The film portrays visions of the possibilities of cultural contact with the Other. The subliminal need for "space" is another coded message to the dominant culture that sees itself pushed out by the "over breeding" of the migrant. This fear explains the usage of the replicants as metaphors for oppressed groups who historically have been subjected to exploitation, enslavement and extermination, and who have been deprived of such human rights as life, liberty, and the pursuit of happiness (Kerman 9). Since Ridley Scott came to direct the film after the success of the 1980 top grossing *Alien,* it is also hard not to view the replicants as subliminal metaphors for the California undocumented workers. In fact one of the characters in Dick's original novel on which the film was based calls the replicants "illegal aliens" (Dick 119). When Leon and Roy enter the eye shop, Chew tells them: "You not come here! Illegal!"[2] Clearly the film racializes the replicants as minorities: the viewer is told that the term "skin job" replaces the word "nigger" (Kerman 27). In the final scene in which Batty and Deckard square off, Batty ". . . strips down like a Comanche warrior in a kind of tribal ritual" (Kerman 168). "The replicants' association with people of color, with the masses at street level, and with frightful sexuality,[3] implicate the dehumanization process necessary at the political level to call forth the possibility of genocide" (Kerman 115). In the final scenes of the film, as Deckard hangs from the rooftop, Batty tells him: "Quite an experience to live in fear. That's what it is to be a slave." Batty's remarks subtly refer to the illegal immigrant constantly besieged by the threat of being turned in to the Immigration and Naturalization Service. The film depicts the replicants as indistinguishable from their human counterparts, except for their physical perfection and their limited four year life-span. The four-year life span might also be the ultimate dream for a society that uses and abuses the illegal alien with minimum wages, and would want to discard them before the abuse leads to the use of social services. And yet the hybrids remain: the androids, the minorities, the outcast. It is this vision of despair that is intermingled in the plot. The hybrid cop will let the protagonist escape with his humanoid lover because he understands hybridity.

The film also unmistakably speaks to the American dream. One of the scenes has Batty quote William Blake's poem "America: A Prophecy" which uses the American Revolution as an allegory for personal freedom and independence, according to Kolb (Kerman 160):

> Fiery the angels rose, and as they rose deep thunder rolled
> Around their shores: indignant burning with the fires of Orc. (Blake)

But Batty changes the poem to read "fiery the angels fell." Instrell believes that "the single alteration from 'rose' to 'fell' completely inverts Blake's original references to the rise of the American democratic Revolution and suggests instead its ultimate demise" (167). The allusion to the demise of the American dream is also allegorized by the month in which the story takes place: November, the Thanksgiving month. There is no mistaking the fact that the film attempts to portray the American dream gone awry, especially taking into account the genre of private eye films:

> Most of the characters in L.A. private eye fiction have come to California from somewhere else, often from sleepily innocent Midwestern towns, searching for the new Eden which Los Angeles advertised itself as being. California allowed the immigrants to cast aside their perceived failures and dare to hope for a new beginning, "the myth of a future." (Kerman 189)

The film puts to rest the myth of the East-West expansion with the ultimate story of doom. The west lies in outer space, now that the minorities have taken over California. Instrell writes:

> Similarly, racism seems to underlie the ethnic composition of the figures in the picture, with its 'normal' white hero, and white power figures, contrasted with the large number of exotic, mainly Asian, proletarians of the underclass inhabiting the city. This can all too easily be read as reflecting a white Anglo-Saxon fear of the Western cities of the future being overrun by foreigners of a different skin color. (169)

The visions of the postmodern dystopia are no doubt helped by the director's previous work directing television commercials for Hovis, Levi Jeans and Strongbow Cider. These visions are also present in *Blade Runner* with the ever present Coke Billboard over the city of Los Angeles.

Hybridity in *Blade Runner* is represented also by Olmos's persona and previous "ethnic" recognition. The script quite obviously characterizes the traits of the replicants by their names. Rachel, the replicant with whom Deckard will eventually fall in love, reincarnates the biblical wife of Israel in the Old Testament;

the mother of a culture that will rule the Earth: thus Deckard escapes "into a new Eden with a new Eve, hoping to regain at least a personal paradise" (Kerman 51). Leon Kowalski, by profession a nuclear waste engineer, is the instinctual beast that readily kills in self-defense. Not coincidentally his degree of intelligence and his profession fit the viewers' prejudices about ethnic stereotypes. Pris, the "pleasure model" clearly brings to the surface the ideas that the original French word connotes: "capture, prize, taken." Roy Batty, the bright bad boy and Aryan Superman, represents the original fallen angel.

Thus the viewer can also assume that the word "Gaff" highlights the character's traits. The British define "gaff" as "a public place of entertainment, especially a cheap or disreputable music hall or theater." Additionally, the dictionary defines gaff as "a clumsy social error; a faux pas; a blatant mistake or misjudgment." The word, originally derived from the French, translates into Spanish as "metida de pata." The production notes describe Gaff as "a man of the future, a multilingual bureaucrat with oriental skin, Japanese eyes, and blue irises. He is an intellectual and a sartorial dandy" (Kerman 156). Clearly, the audience will perceive Olmos as the director intended. The filmmakers obviously used Olmos's screen persona to convey the intentions on the script through Gaff, the quintessential figure of the hybrid character.[4]

The filmmakers also obliterated Spanish, the language of the hybrid, from the film. Though other languages are used in *Blade Runner* (German, for example, spoken by a street gang in the scene in which Deckard is about to enter Sebastian's apartment; Chinese, in the scene at the noodle bar; Mandarin in Chew's shop; Urdu in Ben-Hassan's shop), Spanish is conspicuously absent from the film (except in the Marquee of the Million Dollar Movie Theater that shows films in Spanish). Though Gaff uses "cityspeak"—a sort of future caló composed by combining the languages spoken in California: Spanish, English, Chinese—the Spanish is nowhere to be heard. In fact the script at one point called for the usage of Chicano caló in the film, but the sequence was also cut from the final versions. In the film, even the elevators speak with forked tongues—the elevator in Tyrell's building counts in six different languages; the elevator in Deckard's apartment thanks him in two languages. And yet, whether covertly or subliminally, the film suggests the Chicano/a presence, by the architecture of the retrofitted buildings that resemble Mayan pyramids, or the Mayan motifs of Deckard's apartment.

The erasure of hybridity is also textualized in the film. The director visually keeps the audiences off-balance by framing the characters, not centered, but screen left or screen right. The cutting of the unicorn segment that effectively erased the Chicano/Latino population is clearly apparent in the killing of Zhora and Leon in the public square and which is visibly the space that accommodates most of the minorities represented in the film. Scott described the scene thus:

> The hundreds of extras reflect the wide variety of people found in this future Times Square—soldiers from many countries, Asian peasants, hard-core punks and slumming society folks. (Kerman 163)

One of the critics believes that "the thronging population of the streets and the commercial signs suggest a tidal wave of immigration from the Third World" (Kerman 202). In a scene of total chaos, Zhora runs out of the club trying to escape her pursuer. The Blade Runner will eventually shoot her in the shoulder, and the audience will be exposed to the scene in slow motion from different angles as Zhora crumbles breaking the panes of glass in the display windows, ultimately resembling one of the store mannequins. Symptomatically, the scene takes place at the sight of everyone, while no one really pays attention to the fact that Deckard pursues Zhora with a gun. People seem to be unconcerned for their own safety, since no one gets out of the way. Nor is Deckard concerned about the other people, since he does not hesitate to fire the weapon risking the possibility of injuring innocent bystanders. The shooting is obviously intended as a spectacle of justice, like public hangings or tortures. It is intended to arrest the possibility of dissent. And there is no doubt as to who will be the recipient of that message; the minorities who dare to cross the line, who dare to question the status quo.

Notes

1. Paul Sammon has determined that the studios released as many as six different versions of the film: (1) The Workprint; (2) the San Diego Sneak Preview; (3) the Domestic Cut; (4) The International Cut; (5) the Director's Cut; (6) the TV Broadcast Version. His "Appendix B: Different Faces of *Blade Runner*—How Many Versions?" details the differences among them (394–408). The Workprint was used to test the market; the San Diego Sneak Preview incorporated the changes made to the Workprint. Changes to the San Diego Sneak Preview, the Domestic Cut, the International Cut, and the TV Broadcast Version—all similar among themselves—were made to accommodate the different markets without necessarily changing the film's structure (studios deem international audiences less prudish to violence, sex, and language than American audiences). The Director's Cut (1992), structurally closer to the Workprint, approximates Ridley Scott's original intentions.
2. In one of the *faux* newsstands in the set, "The cover of another magazine sported an in joke; a blurb for an article entitled 'Illegal Aliens,' bylined by one 'Ridley Scott'" (Sammon 104). Paul Sammon's subsection for "The T-Shirt War" details the ultimate irony, if not explanation for Scott's sympathy towards the replicants. According to Sammon, Scott had mentioned to a British newspaper that he found it frustrating to work in the U.S. since the crew often second-guessed his decisions. British crews, on the other hand, would perform as instructed with the words "Yes, Guv'nor." When members of the U.S. crew read the article, they had T-shirts made with the words "Yes, Guv'nor My Ass" to wear on the set. Scott and a couple of the producers responded by also having T-shirts made with the words "Xenophobia sucks." (Sammon 218)
3. The sexualization of the alien is quite apparent in *Blade Runner* suggesting, if not the close connection between self/another, at least the attraction of self to other. The equation between Zhora and the mannequins leaves no doubt: just

like the mannequins she is there to be looked at. But Zhora also represents temptation. She is the woman associated with the serpent. The serpent's scale allows Deckard to find her. While Deckard drinks at the bar, symptomatically swallowing worms with his drink, the announcer introduces Zhora with the following words: "Taffey Lewis presents Miss Salome and the snake. Watch her take the pleasure from the serpent that once corrupted man."

4. The script characterizes Gaff as part Chicano and part Japanese. Olmos made Gaff "more Asian." His skin was made-up in yellowish tones, according to the actor (Sammon 114). Linking Asian-American culture to Chicano culture simply reflects a California reality. Richard Rodríguez's *Days of Obligation* also ties Chicano/a culture to Asian-American concerns.

Peter Parshall

Peter Parshall, a professor of comparative literature and film, teaches at the Rose-Hulman Institute of Technology in Indiana. His writings have appeared in Literature/Film Quarterly, Film Criticism, *and* Perspectives on Contemporary Literature. *This essay on the film* Die Hard *was published in the* Journal of Popular Film and Television. *Contributors to this journal tend to be scholars or graduate students who examine films and genres from a socio-cultural perspective. The journal concentrates on commercial film and television and appeals to both academics and a general readership. In his case study of* Die Hard *(John McTiernan, 1988) Parshall demonstrates how some "outlaw hero" films provide simplistic solutions for today's social conflicts and complexities. Parshall's analysis, which compares contemporary films with classical mythology, draws on Joseph Campbell's and Claude Levi-Strauss's theories of mythology and the hero, and on Laura Mulvey's theory of the spectator and visual pleasure.*

Die Hard: *The American Mythos*

"Ah, take one consideration with another, / A policeman's lot is not a happy one." Such was the opinion of the Sergeant of Police in Gilbert and Sullivan's *The Pirates of Penzance*. His unhappiness stemmed from the fact that he and his timorous band of officers were ordered to apprehend a blood-thirsty gang of pirates. True to his misdoubts, the pirates quickly captured *them*. In contemporary times, the policeman's lot has become considerably unhappier, an unequal contest with the well-financed armies of the drug lords. As the law officer himself certainly recognizes, the problems he faces are symptoms of a sickness in the heart of society, which he can at best contain and cannot remedy. And yet, simply because he is in the front lines of the struggle, he is often cast in the role of the doctor who must find society's cure.

The most popular version of the policeman as hero is the rogue cop in the Dirty Harry mold, who takes over where the Western hero left off and inherits many traits from him. Robert B. Ray in *A Certain Tendency of the Hollywood Cinema* has argued for the centrality of the "outlaw hero" role in American film, typified in the cowboy loner, such as Shane, who rides into town and is persuaded to side temporarily with law and order before riding off again.[1] Variations of the role are found in other films from *Casablanca* to *Star Wars*. Ray suggests that

---

Reprinted from *Journal of Popular Film and Television*, Summer 1990, pp. 14–17, by permission of The Helen Dwight Reid Educational Foundation. Published by Heldref Publications.

such films show a struggle between the desire for law and order and profound mistrust of a legal establishment felt to be corrupt or impotent. In general, these films support the idea that the individual knows better than the group, that one's gut instincts about right and wrong are truer than society's laws, and that violence is often the best way to solve a problem. As Ray argues, these values typify American heroes back to Huckleberry Finn. The wave of popular support for Ollie North demonstrates that these values still enjoy widespread currency in America.

We may mourn the shallowness of the rogue cop and his ilk whose solution to the presence of human evil is to find the villain and gun him down. The higher the caliber of weapons used, the better. However, this very simplicity suggests an archetype at work, relating him to the epic hero, whose major task was "combat with an uncivilized monster (like the Cyclops or Grendel or Satan), an outsider who embodies the forces of anarchy."[2] While the epic simplified the problem by drawing a neat contrast between the hero and the chaos-monster from outside the society, the Greeks quickly discovered that those forces existed within the civilized citizenry as well. As Joseph Campbell suggests in *The Hero With a Thousand Faces,* the mythic hero's journey into the underworld to battle with dark forces represents an interior voyage to struggle with his own nature. King Minos of Crete kept for himself the bull sent by Poseidon for sacrifice, thus putting personal gain above public good. That bull engenders the Minotaur, but Minos is its symbolic father (as its name indicates), for it is the visible symbol of his corrupt rule. Theseus undertakes the task of defeating it to prove himself worthy to run Athens. The labyrinth he enters is a figuration of his own soul; the Minotaur he defeats is his own selfishness, for he risks his life to save others.[3] Heroes such as Theseus show the human spirit winning through to higher possibilities and returning to the ordinary world to manifest this potential to others.

Our current cultural heroes, typified more by macho toughness than depth of character, may seem to lack the inner struggle. However, we must remember that epics from the *Iliad* on were designed first and foremost to entertain, and their heroes have generally been known more for action than introspection. The hero's conflict may indeed be against inner forces, but these are typically personified as external monsters to which he must take sword or Uzi. Further, the hero is not without human failings: "He has a human heart and therefore a dimension of vulnerability and the possibility of failing."[4] Thus, Achilles and Roland were flawed by pride, and Lancelot betrayed his king. These flaws link us to the hero, suggesting that we may share his shortcomings and, like him, can overcome them.

One contemporary hero who battles both external and internal monsters and thus fits the archetypal mode is John McClane, the New York policeman in John McTiernan's 1988 film *Die Hard*. The success of the film—it tied for seventh in 1988 with a gross of $35 million[5] and spawned a big budget sequel—suggests that McClane personifies some of the heroic traits our culture finds most appealing. He arrives in Los Angeles to meet his wife Holly at the Nakatomi Corporation's Christmas party, taking place on the thirtieth floor of the Nakatomi Tower. John no sooner joins her and begins to argue about her putting her career before their marriage when the tower is invaded by a group of quasi-terrorists who take the partygoers hostage and set to work to crack the Nakatomi vault. The terrorists kill the Nakatomi security officers in cold blood, then the Los Angeles director,

Mr. Takagi, and finally Harry Ellis, Holly's co-worker, who tries to bargain with them. John escapes to wage guerilla warfare against the terrorists from the upper floors of the unfinished building, receiving little help from the regulation-bound police and even less from the FBI. His major ally is a sympathetic patrolman, Sgt. Al Powell, to whom he talks via a captured walkie-talkie. One by one, John dispatches the villains. Their leader, Hans Gruber, tries to escape using Holly as a shield, but John finally outwits him and sends him falling to his death from a building window. Holly and John are then driven away in the Nakatomi limo by Argyle, the chauffeur who brought John from the airport in the beginning.

In many regards, *Die Hard*'s story is an age-old one: A hero conquers the villains. Typical of Ray's "outlaw hero," John brings about justice single-handedly, trusting his own instincts rather than following official procedures. Indeed, the film makes a running joke of John as cowboy hero, culminating in the final shootout where John neatly plugs Hans and his remaining accomplice with his last two bullets and then, blowing imaginary smoke from his gun barrel, says, "Happy trails, Hans." Beyond its stereotypic dispatching of the villains, however, *Die Hard* functions on two additional levels. First, its hero attacks villains who personify major cultural problems and, second, he confronts problems in his own nature. As Campbell states, "The first work of the hero is to retreat from the world of secondary effects to those causal zones of the psyche where the difficulties really reside . . . [and] eradicate them." By wrestling with these problems, the hero presents a vision of how they may be dealt with by the larger society.

Christmas and the Family

According to Campbell, the hero's story begins with the "call to adventure"[7] that pulls him from his accustomed life. "The familiar life horizon has been outgrown; the old concepts, ideals, and emotional patterns no longer fit; the time for the passing of a threshold is at hand."[8] The film does not show the call that sets John McClane on his journey, but he has left the familiar territory of New York to come to Los Angeles. The hero must remedy society's blight, and California does appear blighted, for the action occurs on Christmas Eve and the holiday seems all wrong in this climate; there is no snow and the limousine radio is playing Christmas rap tunes instead of "Jingle Bells." Christmas is used as a benchmark throughout the film, with the good guys shown to be pro-Christmas and pro-family and the bad guys anti-Christmas and hence anti-family. John McClane is first seen dragging around a giant teddy bear he is bringing to his children as a Christmas present. He also declines Argyle's invitation to meet some "mama bears" because he's married. Al Powell, the black policeman, is first seen buying snacks for his pregnant wife and singing "Let It Snow" along with the store's Muzak. Al also has a Christmas ornament hanging from the mirror of his squad car. Obviously, he too is pro-family and pro-Christmas. Holly Gennero McClane (whose very name—Holly—links her to Christmas) is first seen fending off the advances of her fellow worker Ellis. She reminds him, "Harry, it's Christmas Eve. Family. Stockings. Chestnuts. Rudolf and Frosty. Any of these things ring a bell?"

He responds: "Actually, I was thinking more of a mulled wine, a nice aged Brie, a roaring fireplace. You know what I'm saying?" She thinks of Christmas as a time for family; he thinks of it as a time for sex.

If Ellis flunks the Christmas test, so does the Nakatomi Corporation, whose values he represents. It is Christmas Eve, but instead of being home with their children, the employees are at the office Christmas party. They are isolated on the thirtieth floor, the only people left in the building. Holly has to phone her children since she can't be there with them. John wanted to hear Christmas music and instead, when he walks into the party, the orchestra is playing Bach's Sixth Brandenburg Concerto. He is kissed by a man who may just be friendly but who may be homosexual—another suggestion that the corporate life is anti-family. This is suggested again by the couple found making out in an empty office. Further, the spirit of Christmas at Nakatomi is corrupted by the continual intrusion of business elements. Mr. Takagi, the head of the Los Angeles branch, thanks his employees "for making this one of the greatest years in the history of Nakatomi Corporation" and then wishes them a Merry Christmas. John is surprised that the Japanese celebrate Christmas and Takagi responds, "We're flexible. Pearl Harbor didn't work out, so we got you with tape decks." It's a joke, but one that subtly suggests the party is part of the Japanese business invasion. Ellis chimes in that the party is also a celebration of a successful business deal. Hollywood films like to set things right, and this film announces from the start that Christmas in the corporate world is all wrong. As Holly suggests to her co-worker Ginny, she feels like Ebeneezer Scrooge.

The terrorists also show themselves to be anti-Christmas and hence anti-family by their constant cynical remarks. Hans, the leader, promises Theo, the black computer wizard, that he will open the safe: "It's Christmas, Theo, the time of miracles. So be of good cheer." And when the safe finally does open, Theo says, "Merry Christmas." Also, when Theo is using the building security system to monitor the attacking police forces, he alerts his fellow conspirators by saying "T'was the night before Christmas and all through the house, not a creature was stirring . . . except the four assholes coming in the rear in standard two by two cover formation." The point is that John McClane is defending more than the Nakatomi employees: He is defending Christmas and, hence, traditional societal values.

The Role of Women

When the hero sets out to remedy society's problems, he often discovers that the illness that plagues society is also found within him. For example, when King Oedipus hears the chorus tell of a blight that has struck the city, he is unaware that he himself caused and contains the blight. In John McClane's case, he is forced to confess to Argyle, the limousine driver, that he has come to Los Angeles to win back his estranged wife. Thus, the loss of traditional values in the external world parallels his personal situation. On the social level, the film wrestles with a continuing problem in modern society—the changing structure of the family. American films have dealt with this problem from their inception, since the Industrial Revolution caused dramatic changes in the family, with fathers working in factories rather than on farms, and families moving from small towns to the city. By setting its action on Christmas Eve, possibly the most important time of the year for families to be together, *Die Hard* emphasizes that John and Holly McClane are *not* together. The major thrust of the film becomes to remove the barriers that keep this couple apart—a fairly typical Hollywood structure.

The film's concern with the changing nature of the family leads directly to a related issue, the changing role of women, which is a major dissonance in American culture at present. Women in the film are generally portrayed as empty-headed—the broadcaster Gail Wallens and the female police dispatcher—or as stereotypic sex objects, including the blonde girl whom the terrorists drag out of an office with her blouse off, the pin-up posters that John pats as he runs through the construction area, and Holly herself at the end as Hans's prisoner, with several buttons of her blouse undone. More specifically, the film criticizes the corporate woman as a poor mother. When Holly's pregnant co-worker Ginny heads to the party and asks if the baby can "handle a little sip," Holly replies, "That baby is ready to tend bar." Behind the joke, the implication is clear that corporate mothers are better at downing cocktails than in caring for their unborn offspring. Holly herself, the film suggests, has been "corrupted" by corporate thinking. Although she is portrayed positively in the film's opening, fending off Ellis' advances and showing concern for her children, she has put her career ahead of her family and her husband and she denies her married status. (She has retained her maiden name—Gennero—so as not to impede her career.) She says to her maid Pauline on the phone, "What would I do without you?"—suggesting that she cannot raise the children without help. The film's major project, second only to dispatching the terrorists, is thus to re-educate Holly.

It does so, first of all, by reducing this busy executive, first seen briskly walking the corporate corridors, to a passive victim, waiting to be rescued. It is true that she confronts Hans bravely and asks for a couch for the pregnant Ginny and trips to the bathroom for other employees. But that is female work: taking care of others. The important job of rescuing everyone is left to John. And when Hans asks, "What idiot put you in charge?" she replies, "You did. When you murdered my boss." It's a nice joke on Hans but also a reminder that women only receive authority when men choose to delegate it to them. The contrasting male/female roles are echoed in the methods of filming that follow Mulvey's well-known formulation that men do the looking and women are the object of the gaze.[9] When the terrorists first invade the thirtieth floor and begin rounding up employees, Holly is seen in one brief medium-closeup shot, looking around for John. The closeup shot traps her in the frame, giving her no space to move. Further, she is looking for John to help her, rather than running for an exit on her own. John is portrayed just the opposite. Hearing the commotion, he jumps to the door to peer out, and the camera does a 180° dolly around him, emphasizing the space he has and also adopting his point of view. With gun in hand, he sizes up the situation and spots the exit he will run to. Throughout the film, similarly, John is the active one: The camera has to pan and track frantically to keep up with him as he runs, shoots, dodges, dives for cover, leaps over parapets, swings from hoses, and smashes through windows. By contrast, Holly is filmed passively. There are eighteen closeup reaction shots of her, since the female's role is to express emotion and not to take action. Especially at the end, when Hans tries to use her as a shield, the film is filled with closeups of her face with his pistol jammed against her head.

The film implies that Holly reaccepts the "standard" feminine role because, surrounded by terrorists, she comes to appreciate John's courage and initiative. She also reevaluates her own role, shown in her reaction to her daughter, Lucy, talking on television. Prodded by the newscaster Thornburg to say something to her parents, Lucy looks into the camera and says, "Come home." That is followed immediately with two reaction shots of Holly watching wide-eyed. Clearly, the message "come home" is addressed to her. Lucy spoke those same words when she talked to her mother on the telephone at the very beginning of the film: "When are you coming home?" The film thus emphasizes that Holly has abandoned her family, as she has abandoned her married name. This may also explain the film's brutal and early murder of her boss, Takagi. He serves as Holly's alternative "husband," standing behind her as John first embraces her at the party saying, "She was made for the business. Tough as nails." The film seeks to break down the image of her toughness, to derail her career as an independent woman, and to return her to the accepted female role: weak and dependent. Takagi must be blown away so that John can step back into the picture and reestablish the traditional male/female roles. This is made very clear at the end when Hans nearly pulls Holly out the window with him. John saves her by unfastening the Rolex watch, symbol of her corporate success, allowing Hans to fall to his death.

Thus, on the social level, *Die Hard* seems to fall away from the true mythic journey. As Campbell suggests, "schism in the soul, schism in the body social, will not be resolved by any scheme to return to the good old days." Rather, the hero must be "reborn."[10] *Die Hard* dodges such a revolutionary step and reaffirms the traditional nuclear family and "standard" male/female roles. This is nicely encapsulated in the closing scene when John and Holly emerge slowly from the wreckage of the building. The black leather policeman's jacket she is wearing covers her suit and signals that her major role is now policeman's wife rather than corporate executive. She is no longer above John, sealed off on the thirtieth floor by security guards but has come down to his level. The woman Takagi described as "tough as nails" now leans on her husband and stares at him adoringly as he leads her to safety. When he introduces her to Al Powell as "Holly Gennero," she corrects it to "Holly McClane." At the end, she and John are driven away together, satisfying the film's drive to restore the family and to reestablish the male as its head.

The Terrorists and the Corporation

In *Die Hard*'s attack on forces separating John and Holly, one obvious obstacle to their reunion is the corporate world; a second is the terrorists, and it takes only a moment's thought to realize that the two overlap to a considerable degree. The fact that Hans clings so tightly to Holly's Rolex watch suggests a connection between him and the corporate world it represents. Most obviously, the terrorists are not terrorists at all—they are businessmen, seeking a profit, and using the latest technology to carry out their plan. Ellis, flashing the same insincere smile at

Hans, treats him as a compatriot, saying, "Business is business. You use a gun, I use a fountain pen. What's the difference?" Other references tie the terrorists even more specifically to the Nakatomi Corporation. When Hans confronts the Nakatomi employees, herded together into the main room, his first words are, "Ladies and Gentlemen," exactly the words Joe Takagi first used when he appeared on the balcony to wish the employees a Merry Christmas. The links between Hans and Takagi continue: As they ride up in the elevator together, the camera cuts between closeups of the two, portraying them as equals. Hans compliments Takagi on his London-tailored suit and says, "I have two myself." Hans also hums the "Ode to Joy" theme, which the party orchestra had been playing a few moments earlier when the terrorists first emerged from the elevator. That theme is associated with the terrorists throughout the film—first played when they enter the basement of the Nakatomi Tower, notably evident at the moment the safe finally opens, and occurring in the final credits. The fact that the theme is also played by the Nakatomi orchestra serves to emphasize the overlap in the two groups. The point is that, exactly as Ellis suggests, this is a "hostile takeover," with one organization co-opting another. The terrorists are a magnified, darker version of the corporate world.

One of the major traits of the terrorists is their robot-like mechanicality, which mirrors the conformity of the corporate world. When the truck first enters the garage and backs up to the loading dock, its ramp extends like a robot arm and its metal door flies up, both emphasized by the mechanical noise on the sound track. There are more mechanical sounds as Tony cuts open the telephone boxes in the basement and as his brother, Karl, flipping down his plastic visor, cuts through all the phone trunks with a chainsaw. Later on, there are shots of Theo with goggles on, drilling through the safe locks, the mechanical noises as the terrorists assemble the anti-tank gun, and the steam and noise of the roof compressors where the terrorists plant their explosives. This mechanicality is reflected even in the way they move in trained commando fashion. Particularly noteworthy is the teamwork of the three terrorists who attack John on the roof as he is broadcasting his appeal for help. Two of them chase him backward while, up above, Karl advances smoothly and stealthily to ambush him, his weapon ready, a deadly killing machine. Karl's machine-like qualities are emphasized also by the contrast with John's fighting style when the two battle near the end. John throws himself passionately into the fight, whereas Karl circles and kicks, a precise, detached, efficient karate robot.

These same traits—coldness, mechanicality, rigidity—are characteristic of the corporate world as symbolized by the Nakatomi Tower itself: its echoing marble lobby, its computers, its security guards and surveillance cameras, its automatic grills that clang down, its glaring stainless steel elevators, and all its glass. The geometric Nakatomi logo, found throughout the building, is a nice reminder of how the corporation invades every aspect of life. The terrorists are perfectly at home here and set up operations at desks in the corporate offices. John, who opposes this rigidity, operates in the upper floors still under construction where he has room to run and duck and improvise.

Terrence Rafferty in *The New Yorker* commented: "The most entertaining thing about this movie is the sheer joy it takes in destruction."[11] True. The film takes as much delight in John's demolishing the building as in his polishing off the terrorists. Scene after scene shows shot-up computers, overturned desks, smashed windows, and machine-gun fire sprayed in all directions. Particularly spectacular are the explosions when John blows out the entire third floor and when Hans detonates the roof. By the final scenes, the building has been reduced to shambles, suggesting considerable antagonism to the corporate values it represents. The building is a gigantic concrete and steel trap that tries to imprison John. It symbolizes the corporate life that captures people and squeezes them into its mold. The film is determined to break out of this cage, just as Argyle does at the end, crashing his limo through the grate that trapped him in the garage to take John and Holly home.

What the film is dealing with, then, is another major conflict in American culture: the individual versus corporate life. John represents the individual who chafes under bureaucracy and the need to work as a team member. He is at the other end of the spectrum from the corporate person. The film's first shot of him shows his hand clenched on the armrest of the plane seat. He is not a frequent flyer. He carries a duffel bag rather than a briefcase. He is more comfortable riding in the front seat of the limo with Argyle rather than in the back. In contrast to the yuppies who want to get as high up in the building as possible, he hates heights. Where the corporate workers wear suit and tie, he wears an open-collared sport shirt. In fairly short order, he is wearing even less, waging his guerrilla war barefoot and eventually barechested. In the final shootout, Hans still has on his suit and tie, whereas John, grimy and bloody, looks like some kind of primitive beast. That shootout is the showdown between the modern corporate leader and the ordinary individual. Hans has had "the benefit of a classical education"; he speaks several languages and talks polished English; he has an organization of a dozen professionals at his command. John is ordinary American, working class by speech and dress, uncomfortable in the cosmopolitan world, his only assets guts and determination and a quick mind. Where Hans uses anti-tank guns and computers, John uses a screwdriver, a cigarette lighter, and a roll of package tape. And he wins.

Evaluating the Values

Die Hard resolves the cultural problems portrayed by a return to traditional values, exalting the nuclear family and attacking the corporate world. Its portrayal of the terrorists as brutal thieves is especially disturbing, ruling out more complex cross-cultural values and implying that all terrorist actions may have similar venal motivation. It further simplifies the problem by suggesting that violence is the only way to deal with such people. Ellis' fate gives the film's judgment of those who try negotiation. The emphasis on violence and vigilante justice is reaffirmed in the conclusion when the terrorist Karl bursts from the building, threatening to kill John and Holly, and is shot by Al Powell. The film emphasizes the significance of this moment—arguably the most important outside of the killing of Hans—by three closeups of Al's gun firing and then a fourth slow rack focus from the gun to his face. There is also a shot of John looking at Al, giving his official hero's approval to his act, and the soundtrack swells with triumphant music. By this action, the film, after exalting the renegade cop throughout, cleverly turns law enforcement back over to the legitimate cop. Al is a goodhearted person who would prefer not to shoot because of his accidental killing of a thirteen-year-old boy. However, now he must do so to protect others. Besides exalting violence, this moment also suggests that we should trust immediate instinct rather than thought. The film reinforces this message a second later by having Holly punch out Thornburg, which the audience heartily applauds. He has been shown as sleazy throughout, invading the McClane home and endangering both John and Holly, so violence against him is perfectly acceptable. Besides, any man who can be punched out by a woman deserves to be laughed at. In sum, the film's value system is a distressingly common portrayal of vigilante justice.

Despite this superficial exploration of social problems, the fact that they are present at all may explain in part why *Die Hard* is more successful than the average rogue cop film. That is, Grendel gains resonance as the villain in *Beowolf* because he exemplifies the outer chaos that threatens to take over civilized society. The villains in *Die Hard,* likewise, personify the invasion of foreign concerns as well as American corporate life and are "stealing" Christmas as well as bearer bonds. Hence, they are all the more threatening. Most important, the social conflicts embodied in the film affect all of us. How does one resolve the conflicting demands of career and family? With both parents expending the majority of their effort at making a living, how do they remain caring, communicating human beings? The tensions caused by exactly such daily problems are conveniently personified in the film and then blown away—a satisfying fantasy that temporarily reduces the pressure and gives us the hope that the problems can indeed be overcome.

John McClane as Cultural Hero

On the personal level, the film's hero shares in these societal problems and his victory is over inner limitations as much as outer ones. Although not transfigured like a Buddha or a Christ, not able to discuss the inner truths he has discovered, John McClane's battles have important symbolic dimensions. In the first place, the person he kills at the end, Hans Gruber, is partly his own evil double. They both "crash" the Nakatomi party, they talk to one another at several points, and they even speak the same lines: John says "Trust me" to his seat mate on the plane who spots his Beretta pistol, and Hans says the same thing to Theo, promising to open the safe. Hans tries to trick John by pretending to be a frightened corporate executive when found near the roof compressors. John does the same thing more skillfully at the end as he also plays helpless, throwing his machine gun away and surrendering himself to Hans.

Hans represents the dark side of John, in particular, because he is a loner. Although part of a gang, he works only for himself, as when he blows up the roof at the end even though his own men are on it. Hans stands for isolation: The first act of the terrorists when they invade Nakatomi is to lock the doors, bring down the gates, and cut all the phone lines. Hans does not communicate with his underlings: He does not explain his plan for opening the final lock on the safe until the

FBI has cut the power that will do it. John, too, is isolated and uncommunicative. He has absented himself from his family for six months and plays the loner's game throughout the film. In the opening scenes, we note his reluctance to speak of his fear of flying to his seat mate on the plane and a similar reluctance to discuss his family situation with Argyle. He is a stranger at the Nakatomi party, observing the festivities without really participating. Most important, he and Holly no longer communicate well. He did not call before he took the flight and he blunders his attempt to talk with her in the executive washroom.

Somehow this loner learns communication. The first positive sign is that he leaves his world, New York, and journeys to Los Angeles to meet Holly on her territory. After allowing Holly to separate herself for six months, he now bends every effort to defeat the forces keeping them apart. He tells his alter ego Al Powell that he should have supported her and, in contrast to his joking with Argyle about the relationship, shows real feeling. (Typical of male adventure films, John discusses his marital relations more successfully with other men than with Holly herself. He does at least make his confession in a washroom, reminiscent of the executive washroom where he bungled his first conversation with Holly.) John has come to recognize her importance in his life, just as she comes to realize the importance of his police career. By the end of the film, John is reduced to some primitive, bloody creature, but still he mutters "Hang in here, honey" as he prepares his final assault on Hans, and calls out to her, "Hi, honey," as he limps forward out of the shambles of the building to the showdown. After operating as a loner throughout the film, he kills Hans—symbol of isolation—and emerges from the jungle of the Nakatomi Tower to rejoin Holly, his family, and civilization.

Linked to his closer connection with Holly is a key confrontation with himself: his fear of heights. The first shot of the film shows a plane landing, and the second shot shows John's hand clutching the armrest of his seat. John's fear of high places and his inability to accept Holly's career are related; he cannot accept the fact that she is above him. This is symbolized by the imposing height of the Nakatomi Tower, which he keeps glancing at as he rides with Argyle. This fear of heights becomes a major motif in the film, and John must confront it again and again. He hangs from a gun strap (in a shot that pays homage to *Vertigo*) and nearly falls to his death when the strap comes loose. The four times he goes to the roof all put him in danger: He is chased by three terrorists the first time, encounters Hans and three more terrorists the second time, and must fight to the death with Karl the third time. The fourth time—trying to herd the hostages out of danger—he is fired at by the FBI helicopter and must leap over the edge of the building, using a fire hose as a rappelling line. He breaks in through a window, but then the empty reel falls past and nearly pulls him to his death. The climax comes when he must leap to a window to keep Holly from being pulled out by Hans and let Hans take the death that had been stalking him all along. The terror of this fate is emphasized by the long tilting shot that follows Hans as he falls thirty stories to land with a crunch that makes the policemen below wince. Because John can confront his fear of high places he can accept his wife's position and introduce her as Holly Gennero to Al Powell at the end. Hence, John's actions suggest that a cultural solution to the new feminine roles requires men to overcome their fears of inadequacy and to ascend new heights themselves.

Sequel and Conclusion

Die Hard 2: Die Harder has even more action than its predecessor and yet is not as satisfying because it has lost the mythic resonance of the first film. The script is clever, but the jokes do not contain subtext messages as consistently as *Die Hard*. The film is set at Christmas again, but there is less sense of the villains being opposed to it and John a defender of it. There is little treatment of John and Holly's relationship and hence of male/female role conflicts. Her role becomes even more passive than in the first film as she sits on an airplane circling the airport, unable to do anything except beat on Thornburg the reporter one more time. John is fighting bureaucracy again, as one would expect of the rogue cop, but the airport hierarchy is a far less satisfying surrogate for corporate values. In particular, there is no sense of John fighting any internal battles—he never hesitates in his pursuit of the villains or doubts his abilities. The film's one interesting dimension is that John's two major opponents, Colonel Stuart and Captain Grant, are traitorous operatives, hinting at the dangers of the renegade cop's role if he adopts purely selfish ends.

Both films are simplistic in many ways. The complex global problems facing us cannot really be gunned down like villains in the Old West. Trusting gut instinct doesn't always work. The nuclear family will inevitably change. The earlier film, however, is able to make simplicity a virtue, transforming its story into something near myth. Myths reassure us that the culture will survive the changes it is undergoing (cf. Levi-Strauss[12]) because the mythic hero shows that the monsters within us can be defeated and a way out of the labyrinth can be found. Society may survive if we set personal concerns aside and throw Hans, symbol of selfishness, out the window. The family may endure if we have the confidence to assail the heights that daunt us and the sensitivity to communicate to those who love us. Perhaps most important, myth brings us a message of hope. We should all continue to be of good cheer, to expect miracles, and to believe in heroes. We should believe in Santa Claus, personified in John McClane, who whistles "Here Comes Santa Claus" when first entering the Nakatomi Tower and whose final words in the film are "Merry Christmas." Hans, the Scrooge figure, the man who would kill to amass wealth, has been dispatched. Hans, the killjoy, the man who smiles with mirth at Takagi before shooting him in cold blood, has been replaced by John, who can joke with Hans and Al Powell, talking about Twinkies and flat feet and cowboys. This joking Santa not only gets Mommy and Daddy together again, he actually brings Christmas to Nakatomi Land with bearer bonds drifting down through the sky as Vaughn Monroe sings "Let It Snow." Greed has been replaced by the spirit of giving; love and laughter have overcome violence; and we can have a white Christmas, even in L.A.

Acknowledgments

I would like to express my appreciation to the Lilly Endowment for granting me an Open Faculty Fellowship for sabbatical study at the University of Wisconsin 1988–1989. This paper was originally prepared as part of a sabbatical report for that year.

Notes

1. Robert B. Ray, *A Certain Tendency of the Hollywood Cinema, 1930–1980* (Princeton: Princeton University Press, 1985).
2. Beverle Houston and Marsha Kinder, *Self and Cinema* (Pleasantville, NY: Redgrave, 1980), p. 152.
3. Joseph Campbell, *The Hero With a Thousand Faces* (Cleveland: World Publishing, 1956), p. 15.
4. P. L. Travers, "The World of the Hero." *Parabola,* No. 1 (Winter 1976), pp. 46–47.
5. "Big Rental Films of '88 in U.S.-Canada," *Variety,* 11–17 January 1989, p. 16.
6. Campbell, p. 17.
7. Campbell, p. 51.
8. Campbell, p. 51.
9. Laura Mulvey, "Visual Pleasure and Narrative Cinema." *Screen* 16, No. 3 (Autumn 1975), pp. 6–19.
10. Campbell, pp. 16–17.
11. Terrence Rafferty "Current Cinema." *The New Yorker,* 8 August 1988, p. 79.
12. Claude Levi-Strauss, "The Structural Study of Myth." In Clair Jacobson and Brooke G. Schoepf, trans., *Structural Anthropology* (New York: Basic Books, 1963).

bell hooks

bell hooks is an internationally known cultural critic and scholar. In addition to her many books, hooks frequently contributes essays to various popular magazines. Her writings, which examine issues of race and gender, include Black Looks: Race and Representation *and* Teaching to Transgress: Education as the Practice of Freedom. *This essay, "Seduction and Betrayal," which originally appeared in* Visions Magazine *in the fall of 1993, compares the representations of African American female protagonists in films of two different genres.*

Seduction and Betrayal

Two recent films—Hollywood's *The Bodyguard* and the independent *The Crying Game*—highlight relationships that cross boundaries. *The Crying Game* explores the boundaries of race, gender, and nationality; *The Bodyguard,* boundaries of race and class. Within their particular genres, both films have been major box office successes. Yet critics acclaimed *The Crying Game* and overwhelmingly trashed *The Bodyguard.* Though *The Crying Game* was certainly a better film by artistic standards (superior acting, more complex plot, good screenwriting), it is more similar to *The Bodyguard* in the elements that make it work for audiences than it is different: both are romances that look at "desire" deemed taboo and exploit the theme of love on the edge.

At a time when critical theory and cultural criticism call us to interrogate the politics of race, nationality, and gender, these films locate reconciliation and redemption in the realm of desire, not politics. And while both exploit race as subject matter, both directors deny the significance of race in these films. Until *The Bodyguard,* American audiences had never seen a Hollywood film in which a major white star chooses a black female lover, yet the publicity for the film insisted that race was not important. In an interview in the black magazine *Ebony,* Kevin Costner insisted: "I don't think race is an issue here. The film is about a relationship between two people, and it would have been a failure if it became a film about interracial relationships." Similarly, in interviews about *The Crying Game,* director Neil Jordan identifies the female character only as "the woman," never as black. In his interview with Lawrence Chua in *Bomb* magazine, for example, Jordan says, "Fergus thinks the woman is one thing and he finds out she is something different." Their assertions expose the extent to which neither white male has interrogated his position. As progressive feminist thinkers and cultural

---

Reprinted from *Visions Magazine*, Fall 1993, by permission of the publisher.

critics have long noted, white supremacy allows those who exercise white privilege to behave as though race does not matter even as they help establish and maintain fixed and absolute racial hierarchies.

Both *The Crying Game* and *The Bodyguard* get their edge from the racial identity of the heroine. Long before the viewers of *The Crying Game* know that Dil is a transvestite, they are intrigued by her exoticism—marked by her race. Not just any ol' black woman, she/he embodies the "tragic mulatto" persona that has always characterized sexually desirable mixed-black female characters in Hollywood films. Kevin Costner's insistence that *The Bodyguard* is not about interracial relationships seems ludicrously arrogant when masses of viewers—including black women—flocked to see this film because it depicted a relationship between a black woman and a white man, portrayed by "big stars" Whitney Houston and Costner. Previously, the politics of racism and white supremacy in Hollywood had blocked the portrayal of such a relationship. And since the female lead is so often romantically linked with the male lead, this meant that black women were rarely given the female lead in movies.

The characters of Dil (Jaye Davidson) in *The Crying Game* and Rachel Marron (Whitney Houston) in *The Bodyguard* were portrayed unconventionally only in that they were the love objects of white men. Otherwise, they were stereotypically oversexed, aggressive, sexually experienced women—'ho's. Though Dil works as a hair stylist and Marron makes her money as an entertainer, their lure is in the realm of the sexual. As white racist and sexist stereotypes in mass media teach audiences, if you scratch the surface of any black woman's sexuality, you'll find a 'ho—someone sexually available, apparently indiscriminate, incapable of commitment, and likely to seduce and betray. Neither Dil nor Marron bothers to get to know the individual white male she falls in love with. In both cases, it is love—or should I say, lust—at first sight. Both films suggest that actual knowledge of the "other" would destroy the sexual mystery, the pleasure and danger caused by unknowing. Though Fergus (Stephen Rea) has sought Dil, she quickly becomes the sexual initiator, servicing him. Similarly, Marron seduces the bodyguard she has hired, Frank Farmer (Kevin Costner). Both films suggest that the sexual allure of these black females is so intense that the vulnerable white males lose all will to resist (even when Fergus must face the fact that Dil is not biologically female).

Before slavery was abolished in the United States, white government officials who supported sending black folks back to Africa warned of the danger of sexual relations between decent white men and licentious black females, asking specifically that the government "remove this temptation from us." They wanted the state to check their lust lest it get out of hand. Uncontrollable lust between white men and black women is not taboo. It becomes taboo only to the extent that such lust leads to the development of a committed relationship.

The Bodyguard assures its audience that no matter how magical, sexy, and thrilling the love between Rachel Marron and Frank Farmer is, it will not work. And should we dare to imagine otherwise, the powerful theme song sets us straight. Though the refrain declares, "I will always love you," other lyrics suggest that this relationship has been doomed from the start. "Bittersweet memories [are] all I am taking with me," the parting lover declares, since "We both know I am not what you need." Audiences can only presume that the unspoken, denied subject of interracial romance makes this love impossible. Conventionally, then, *The Bodyguard* promises a fulfilling romance between a white male and a black female only to declare that relationship doomed. Xenophobic and racist moviegoers who want to be titillated by taboo are thus comforted by having the status quo restored in the end.

In keeping with a colonizing mind set, the bodies of black men and women in these films are the playing field where white men work out their longing for transcendence. In Fergus's eyes, the black male prisoner Jody (Forest Whitaker) embodies the humanity his white comrades have lost. Though a grown man, Jody is childlike, innocent, a neo-primitive who, like Dil (another primitive), is not cut off from feeling or sensuality, and Fergus relates to him, according to Jordan, "like a mother." Jody alters the power relationship between himself and Fergus by emotionally seducing Fergus. Though, at the film's end, Jordan attempts to reverse his depiction of blacks as childlike and in need of white parents /protectors by turning Dil into Fergus's caretaker, he instead reinscribes racial stereotypes.

Fergus "eats the other" when he consumes Jody's life story, then usurps his place in Dil's affections. As the film ends, Fergus has not only cannibalized Jody but appropriated Jody's narrative to claim possession of Dil. As Jordan asserts, "his obsession with the man leads him to reshape her in the image of the guy he's lost." Black bodies, then, are like clay, to be shaped into anything the white man wants them to be. This paradigm romanticizes again the white colonizer's occupying of black territory, possessing it in a way that affirms his identity. Fergus never fully acknowledges Dil's race or sex. Like the real-life Costner and Jordan, he can make black bodies the site of his political and cultural "radicalism" without having to respect those bodies.

Few critical reviews of *The Crying Game* discussed race; indeed, most suggested that the film's power lies in its insistence that race and gender finally do not matter; what counts is what's inside. Yet, this message is undermined by the fact that all the people subordinated to white power are black. Even though the film (like *The Bodyguard*) seduces by suggesting that crossing boundaries, accepting difference, can be pleasurable, it does not disrupt conventional representations of subordination and domination. Black people allow white men to remake them in the film. And Dil's transvestism becomes less radical when she gives up her "womanly identity" to satisfy Fergus—whose actions are clearly paternalistic and patriarchal—without asking for an explanation. With her Billie Holiday "hush, now; don't explain" kind of love, Dil acts in complicity with Fergus's appropriation of Jody.

The Crying Game disrupts many of our conventional notions about identity. The British soldier is black. His girlfriend turns out to be a transvestite. Fergus readily abandons his role as an IRA freedom fighter (a group simplistically portrayed as only terrorists) to become an average working man. Much of this film invites us to interrogate the limits of identity politics by showing us how desire and feelings can disrupt fixed notions of who we are and what we stand for. Yet in the final scenes of the film, Fergus and Dil seem primarily concerned with fulfilling racist and sexist gender roles. He reverts to the passive, silent, unemotional, "rational" white man, an identity he earlier sought to escape. And Dil, no longer bold or defiant, becomes the "black woman" taking care of her white man; the "little woman" waiting for her man. Suddenly, heterosexism is evoked as the ideal relationship—so much for difference and ambiguity. Complex readings of identity are abandoned and everything is back in its place. No wonder mainstream viewers find this film so acceptable.

In a culture that systematically devalues black womanhood, that sees our presence as meaningful only to the extent that we serve others, it is not surprising that audiences would love a film that symbolically reinscribes us in this role. I say symbolically because the fact that Dil is really a black man suggests that in an ideal white supremacist, capitalist, patriarchal, imperialist world, females are not needed, women can be erased (no need for a real black woman) or annihilated (let the black man murder the white woman, not because she is a fascist terrorist but because she is biologically female). Ultimately, despite some magical transgressive moments, much of this film is conservative-reactionary. Crudely put, it suggests that transvestites hate and want to destroy "real" women; that straight white men want black mammies so badly that they will invent them, willingly vomiting up their own homophobia and entering a relationship with a black man to get that down-home service only a "black female" can give; that real homosexual men batter; and ultimately that the world would be a better place if we would forget about articulating race, gender, and sexual issues and become conventional white heterosexual couples. These reactionary messages echo *The Bodyguard's* conservative messages regarding difference.

Critics' rejection of *The Bodyguard* seems somehow fitting in a white supremacist, capitalist patriarchy. For despite its conventional plot, its representation of blackness in general and black femaleness in particular are far more radical than any image in *The Crying Game*. It disrupts, for example, Hollywood's conventional casting of black females in the role of servant. In fact, Rachel Marron is wealthy, and Frank Farmer is hired to serve her. However utopian this inversion is, it does challenge stereotypical assumptions about race, class, and gender hierarchies. When Frank Farmer acts to protect the life of Marron (how many films do we see in the United States in which black female life is deemed valuable, worth protecting or saving?), he takes her "home" to his white patriarchal father, who embraces her. Again, this representation breaks radically with racist stereotypes. It cannot be dismissed as mere coincidence that critics should trash a film that breaks significantly with racist and sexist norms in its representation of black womanhood even as they extol as more meaningful another film that reinscribes racist and sexist representations. Even though *The Bodyguard* conservatively suggests that interracial relationships are doomed, it still offers meaningful disruptions in the representation of race.

Despite flaws, both *The Crying Game* and *The Bodyguard* are daring works that evoke much beyond the screen dialogue about issues of race and gender, about difference and identity. Unfortunately, both films resolve the tensions of difference, of shifting roles and identity, by affirming the status quo. Both suggest that "otherness" can be the place where white folks—in both cases, white men—work through their troubled identity, their longing for transcendence. In this way they perpetuate white cultural imperialism and colonialism. Though compelling in those moments when they celebrate the possibility of accepting difference, of growing by shifting one's location, ultimately they seduce and betray.

Casey McKittrick

Casey McKittrick is a Ph.D. candidate in the Department of English at the University of Texas at Austin. He is finishing his dissertation on children in contemporary film and literature. His article examines comments made about the films American Beauty *(Sam Mendes, 1999) and* Happiness *(Todd Solondz, 1998) by everyday users of the Internet Movie Database (IMDb). The IMDb, which can be found on the internet at http://www.imdb.com, allows users to look up films, directors, actors—and even genres—and contribute their own thoughts and perspectives about the films. McKittrick uses these responses to explore the complex problem of pedophilia as it is presented in* American Beauty *and* Happiness.

"I Laughed and Cringed at the Same Time": Shaping Pedophilic Discourse around American Beauty *and* Happiness

The interrogation of suburbia's facades is hardly new fodder for Hollywood or independent filmmakers. The Academy Award-winning *Ordinary People* of 1981 was hailed as an incisive foray into middle-class malaise; it garnered praise as a subtly artful critique of family values and the importance of appearances and surfaces to the sustenance of bourgeois culture. Prior even to *Ordinary People,* movies such as *The Stepford Wives* (1975), *Bob and Carol and Ted and Alice* (1969), *The Graduate* (1967), and the melodramas of Douglas Sirk pushed the envelope by subjecting suburban life to intense scrutiny, raising issues of conformity, gender parity, the naturalness of monogamy, and the decay of the nuclear family.

The mid- to late nineties witnessed a number of films with similar aims of laying bare the pitfalls and contentions of suburban life. These films, however, have for the most part surpassed their predecessors in terms of their ambitions to expose or redefine subject matter heretofore regarded as taboo in mainstream cinema. Ang Lee's *The Ice Storm* (1997) explores preadolescent sexuality against the backdrop of the baby boomers' disenchantment with the enterprise of free love. Todd Solondz's *Welcome to the Dollhouse* (1995) dramatizes the collusive powers of home, school, and media to degrade or destroy the body image and self-esteem

Reprinted from *The Velvet Light Trap*, Spring 2001, pp. 3–14, University of Texas Press.

of adolescent girls. Greg Motolla's *Daytrippers* (1996) chronicles a family outing that facilitates another sort of "outing"—the husband's closeted homosexuality.

This essay focuses on two recent critically successful films of suburban life, Sam Mendes's *American Beauty* (1999) and Todd Solondz's *Happiness* (1998), as two events that have facilitated public discourse about social taboos and the moral and aesthetic implications of their representation in mainstream film. I examine the public reception of these two films vis-à-vis a popular online forum, the Internet Movie Database (IMDb). In recognizing this forum as a new audience formation, I attempt to delineate the cultural meanings ascribed to these film events by online citizen-critics.[1] In particular, I will address how the taboo of pedophilia, to some degree dramatized in both films, gets spoken through this online medium. I do not intend to affix any static or discrete meaning to the practices, situations, and effects that pedophilia as a category may come to signify. In fact, part of this project entails an examination of what people choose to identify or disavow as pedophilia and how gender, sexual object choice, and narrative strategies inform these choices. Additionally, I will explore the category of homosexuality as a "structuring absence" in the film events' public discourse.[2] Starting from the assumption that any critical map of public reception requires an examination of the silences and fissures contained within the event's emergent discourse, I contend that homosexuality's virtual absence in the body of popular critical discussion is worth exploring further. This absence, I suggest, is symptomatic of the cultural tendency to supplant rather than complicate categories of difference in the construction of textual meanings.

Before I attempt an analysis of the online discourse, I will give a brief history of the IMDb in order to give a sense of its institutional status as a significant and productive space for online public exchange. Next, I will situate these two films vis-à-vis their prominent popular critical reception in the "user comments" feature of the database. I then offer a reading of general trends in online public responses to each of the films with an eye toward issues of pedophilia, taboo, and aesthetic valuation. Finally, I will draw some conclusions about the general shape of the body of criticism found on the IMDb and discuss the cultural implications of locating homosexuality as a "structuring absence" in this discursive field.

The Internet Movie Database

The IMDb has existed in various forms and under various names for almost ten years. It began in 1990 as a Usenet bulletin/discussion board called rec.arts.movies. Access to the board required a Unix shell account, which could be provided predominantly by universities and corporations. Thus, the forum predated the point-and-click capabilities of the "Web browser," which would not surface until 1994. At its inception, the board provided a space for film buffs who had the technological resources to discuss current releases and collectively construct a knowledge base that would encompass most mainstream films, who acted in them, and who directed them. The board also solicited actor biographies and compiled a "Dead List" as an up-to-the-minute reference for its users.

By October 1990, the database included information for over 10,000 movies and television series. Over the next five years, the forum converted from a bulletin board to a more widely accessible and user-friendly Website, made possible through the institution of the World Wide Web. Character names were included in the films' cast sections, and the site incorporated trivia, extended actor biographies, box office numbers, plot summaries, and a voting system whereby films were ranked by the users from one to ten.

The IMDb in its current manifestation is a commercialized, incorporated entity that still offers free browsing services but also relies on advertisement and licensing via Amazon.com for its financial sustenance. Currently, the IMDb serves an average of 65 million accesses from over 3.5 million visitors every month. It is one of the three most widely used entertainment databases on the Web and has garnered several awards in the past two years for its popularity, comprehensiveness, and user-friendliness. Today, it catalogs over 200,000 films, 400,000 actors and actresses, and around 40,000 directors.

While the overwhelming popularity of the IMDb no doubt is due mostly to its free and unlimited usage, part of its appeal seems to be attributable to the ethos of its mission statement: "to provide useful and up to date movie information freely available online across as many platforms as possible." The database's appeal to the "film buff" is twofold. Not only does it provide easy access to knowledge about films and their stars, but it fosters an environment of recognizing online users as potential citizen-critics by providing a "platform" for them to speak to other users.

As the IMDb has developed, it has enhanced the possibilities for user feedback by adding to the simple one-to-ten voting system and including a function in which users can (again at no cost) post their own critiques of any film cataloged in the system. It is important to understand that this posting forum is not a message board, where threads of conversations emerge among users. Rather, it is a register of discretely posted critical pieces that are almost never in acknowledged dialogue with the other postings.[3] The tone of these responses predictably varies. Some users submit their critiques to convey their emotional responses to a film—to "vent" or applaud—or to relate a personal anecdote connected to their viewing experience. Others adopt a more distanced tone and rely on conventional popular critical models for their valuations. Often they programmatically discuss acting, plot, cinematography, genre conformity, and other familiar critical categories. Many users even employ a rating system of their own, offering "three out of four stars" or a "six out of ten" to sum up their appraisal. Still other citizen-critics use the posting forum as an opportunity to discuss broader social issues that emanate from a viewing experience or to discuss the current state of film and other media in terms of the moral climate they reflect, prescribe, or attempt to challenge.

American Beauty *and* Happiness *as IMDb Documents*

Both *American Beauty* and *Happiness* have received a phenomenal amount of attention on the IMDb. According to the one-to-ten ranking feature, *Beauty* is listed as the number two ranking movie of all time on the site, just below *The*

Godfather and above *Schindler's List, The Shawshank Redemption,* and *Casablanca.*[4] Over 6,970 votes have been cast for *Beauty*. Between its release in September 1999 and 25 November 1999, *Beauty* received 492 postings. The online users' attention to *American Beauty* is impressive, considering the other nine movies in the top ten of all time average only 140 comments per film.[5]

Happiness experienced a much more modest release in the fall of 1998 and had but a fraction of *Beauty*'s promotional costs. Yet it ranks an impressive number 177 of all time, with 1,944 votes cast. In fact, it has accrued 140 user comments, which is the average number of comments generated by the top ten films on the IMDb. Given the fact that the average film on the database has about five or six comments attached to it, the public response to these two films is indeed noteworthy. Even two months after *Beauty*'s release, four to five new comments appeared daily, probably due to its extended release. *Happiness* saw a resurgence in public comments after *American Beauty*'s release; in fact, over a third of the comments appeared for *Happiness* after *Beauty*'s release, possibly suggesting the public's conception of them as companion pieces.

American Beauty: *The Story of Lolita or Lazarus?*

> I loved the idea behind this movie, an average middle aged man has his rebirth and regains his youth.[6]
>
> A tired male fantasy [where] Spacey falls in sexual lust with a gorgeous high school blonde. Sooooo subversive!

American Beauty experienced enormous critical and box office success upon its release in September 1999. With a budget of only $15 million, it had earned $65.6 million in the United States by mid-November 1999. DreamWorks SKG marketed the film both to adults and teenagers, and two different trailers aired on television, one focusing on teens Thora Birch, Mena Suvari, and Wes Bentley, the other capitalizing on Academy Award nominees Kevin Spacey and Annette Bening.[7] The film depicts the midlife crisis of patriarch Lester Burnham (played by Spacey) and its manifestations in his professional and personal life. Most strikingly, Lester's "crisis" entails an obsessive fascination with his daughter's high school friend Angela (played by Mena Suvari) and a subsequent attempt to recapture his youth, his freedom from authority, and his sexual attractiveness. The film also focuses on Carolyn Burnham's (played by Annette Bening) professional travails and her extramarital affair with a rival real estate agent.[8] Added to this mélange is the budding relationship between daughter Jane (played by Thora Birch) and next-door neighbor Ricky Fitts (played by Wes Bentley), whose peculiar aesthetic vision has burgeoned despite or because of the repressive familial atmosphere generated by his homophobic military father (played by Chris Cooper), himself a repressed homosexual, and his catatonic mother (played by Allison Janney).

Although a sexual relationship between Lester and Angela is never fully realized in the film, much of the film's mise-en-scène is devoted to his fantasy of "getting," the adolescent girl. The scene in which Lester first glimpses teen-dream Angela segues into a dream sequence in which he and she alone are in the school gymnasium. The fantasy culminates in Angela's disrobing, whereupon rose petals emanate fantastically from her cheerleading uniform. While we are first introduced to the rose trope through Lester's watching the rigid Carolyn menacingly clip and trim her roses in the front yard, the petals emanating from Angela represent a pleasurable fragmentation. Other fantasy sequences include Angela in the Burnhams' bath, again adorned with rose petals, coyly beckoning Lester to join her, and Angela in the kitchen, kissing Lester passionately, at which point he pulls a rose petal from his mouth.[9] Lester's seduction of the girl at the film's end, thwarted by the realization that she is a virgin, gives way to a more paternal posturing, where he feeds and covers her and uses the opportunity to inquire about the well-being of his daughter.

While this unconventional relationship between Lester and Angela, so thematically resonant of Vladimir Nabokov's *Lolita,* arguably constitutes the crux of the film's attraction, it has rarely been characterized in online public discourse as a pedophilic one. In the broadest sense, pedophilia is defined simply as an adult's love for a child. Yet the term as it circulates in American culture connotes a moral evil; in the public imaginary, it evokes the sense of a lack of children's agency, the power imbalance of intergenerational relationships, and the inherent sexual and moral corruption involved in its realization.

Several factors may account for the virtual omission of pedophilia as a central trope in public discussion surrounding *American Beauty*. First, despite the final realization of Angela's sexual inexperience, she consciously presents herself as a sexual object and, to some degree, a sexual predator throughout the film. Thus, issues of sexual agency and consent can be more easily negotiated in the construction of Angela as an appropriate object choice for Lester or the viewer. Second, Angela is (obviously) female. Discourses of pedophilia often revolve around homosexuality, despite much social scientific evidence to the contrary.[10] Often, pedophilia and pederasty are conflated as concepts, and therefore pedophilia as a heterosexual activity is often illegible.[11] Third, the character of Angela is in her late high school years and is, therefore, close to or of the legal age of consent. Moreover, her bodily maturity may be a source of justification for a desiring male viewer. The specularization of her body, combined with her adultlike knowingness, may tip the scales from perceiving her as a "woman-child" to identifying her as a woman. Finally, the sexual relationship never comes to fruition; Angela's "deflowering" never takes place. Thus she remains an object of erotic fantasy, but her (filmic) body remains untouched or, at least, unpenetrated. These explanations, taken together, seem to point to a general need for the viewer to see his/her object choice as acceptable, natural, free of pathological meaning.[12] These facets of Angela's characterization perhaps mitigate the chances for reading her as an inappropriate object choice.

The IMDb discourse surrounding the dynamics between Lester and Angela elicits several ways of working through their potentially problematic relationship. One of the most prominent ways of dealing with the relationship was to foreground its importance as a catalyst in transforming Lester from a complacent potential cuckold to an exuberant aficionado of living for the moment. Over a third of the commentators framed Lester's affection for Angela as one that enables his transformation:

> *American Beauty* is the story of Lester's reincarnation. Once he lays eyes on the love of his dreams, . . . he instantly wakes up to the world around him.

> Lester's obsession becomes the catalyst for a life-wide make-over.

> The film's narrative offshoots revolve around Kevin Spacey's transitional quest to wrest joy and meaning from the vacancy of his life through an obsessive preoccupation with his daughter's alluring cheerleader friend, Angela. . . . One quickly recognizes the misplaced dreams and ideals in Lester Burnham's sleepwalk through a manicured life alongside his controlling and abusively compulsive wife.

> Spacey's character falls head over heels for a beautiful Barbie doll on his daughter's cheerleading squad. . . . It's terribly uplifting and somehow freeing to watch him liberate himself from a job he hates, a life he's bored with, and a middle-aged body he's neglected.

These respondents deal with the relationship by incorporating it into a more overarching narrative of Lester's self-development. In this vein, the desire for a teenager is not an end in itself but a means to masculine self-actualization and attaining (with the help of Ricky) a more highly cultivated aesthetic relationship to reality.

Other commentators made implicit and even occasional explicitly intertextual references to the *Lolita* story, using it as a touchstone to explicate the relationship between Lester and Angela. These respondents (about forty of them) generally adopted a tone of unapologetic investment in the progression of the relationship between the two:

> Fans of *Lolita* will immediately recognize the tortured agony of Kevin Spacey's character, drawn like a moth to a love that can never be. . . . Kevin is inextricably drawn to Mena, yet no attempt is made to challenge the tired Western stereotype that adult men cannot love teenage girls. And the ending of the film suggests a punishment that does not fit in with the overall message of the movie.

> [Lester Burnham] is tired of life until he meets his daughter's pretty Lolita-like girlfriend.

> Kevin Spacey's character [is] a kind of tragic figure who breaks his bonds, then dies for his trouble. . . . *American Beauty* adds humor, charm, sexy 18 year olds, and an intergenerational mind-meld that sucks you into the action.[13]

The commentators rely on a time-honored literary text to validate their readings of intergenerational desire. The first respondent above goes so far as to critique the film for not taking a stronger and more positive stand on intergenerational erotic love. In fact, the respondent reads Lester's death not as the result of homophobia and situational misunderstanding but as a punitive act for his desires, which are inappropriate within the film's parameters. Interestingly, this reading suggests the possibility that it is pedophilia, not homosexual desire or homophobic rage, as the sin that the film must exorcise to attain closure.

Only 2 of the 492 critics used the word "pedophilia" in their assessments of *American Beauty*. Aside from another mention of Lester's object choice as "jailbait," no other account gives a name to the relationship that bespeaks outright legal or moral illicitness. Interestingly, the two explicit references to pedophilia are used to widely different ends in their respective contexts:

> Was it just me that was disturbed by the Spacey love-a-child angle? Hmmm. . . . I'm not normally a prude, but this was maybe just a little too much for me. But then perhaps that was the point. I have no desire to see young girls/women getting deflowered/fantasized over. Smacks to me of a little pedophilia that is definitely *not* necessary. But then, films that don't provoke and push buttons are just fluff.[14]

> And what's the deal with the shock and outrage that I've seen expressed over [Lester's] fantasies about his daughter's friend, the blonde cheerleader, Hey, that's the way men are wired up. A drop-dead gorgeous young girl summons up all sorts of emotions in an older man. Pedophilic emotions? (There, I said it.) Yes and no. On the one hand he'd love to be able to have sex with her. ("Making love" is not the sort of experience that she represents to him.) But on the other hand, and waaay more importantly, that kind of girl represents "lost youth" more dramatically than any number of theatrical metaphors could. And that's exactly what a mid-life crisis is all about, isn't it? Failing powers: physical, sexual, and for Spacey and many of the men he represents—the loss of joy in life. She's just the trigger, the splash of cold water that wakes him from his coma.

The first respondent clearly reads the film's presentation of the relationship as complicitous with the eroticization of social and sexual imbalance. Her formulation, "X is disturbing, because X is pedophilia," reveals a reliance on the naming of social taboo as a self-evident indictment. Yet she tempers her accusation with a strange qualifier—"a little," indicating the presence of degrees to which acts or representations can fall into the realm of the taboo. Another interesting feature of her critique is her juxtaposition of "young girls" and "women"—a coupling that seems to indicate her uncertainty as to whether she should read Angela as woman or child. This hesitation is perhaps a logical corollary to her qualification of "how much" pedophilia the film is enacting or representing.

The second commentator echoes the earlier commentators' tendency to read Angela as instrumental to Lester's awakening, but he directly addresses the relationship as a social taboo. His self-congratulatory "There, I said it" foregrounds his willingness to face a social taboo head on and acknowledge it as a common experience among older men. He furthers his yes-and-no argument by suggesting that, just as Angela functions textually as a symbol for rejuvenation and youthful desire, young girls' bodies function similarly in our culture as emblems—even totems—of youth and desire.

The most prominent feature of the user responses to the film was the dismissal or incorporation of the film's controversial social issues, such as intergenerational sex and crises of masculinity, into a larger discussion of the film's aesthetic vision. For many of the online users, the interpersonal relationships of the film take a backseat to its more totalizing sense of life's profound beauty. This shift from the social realm to the aesthetic appears in a majority of the reviews:

> [Lester] is a corporate nobody who fantasizes about his daughter's best friend. . . . What seems to be a horrible ending is transformed into something wonderful and truly beautiful . . . American Beauty.

> I went to see this never thinking that a man's mid-life crisis and sexual fixation on his daughter's friend would make for a particularly fulfilling experience. . . . It was actually much more profound than that.

> There are those who would portray Lester's transformation as depraved (After all, its primary genesis is his lust for a teen cheerleader, and is fueled by marijuana use), but they would forget the final moments of the film, wherein he discovers peace by becoming so free with himself and others that he finally sees the family he had come to hate was the truly beautiful thing in his life.

> Beauty can also be found in the recognition that there are some things that can't change, and must be let go. These concepts and more are conveyed through humor and serious drama. . . . [T]he film does it superbly. It is truly a great American film.

In most of the critics' responses, this shift serves to hierarchize the film's formal and thematic elements. The problem of reading pedophilia into or against the film gets subsumed by pronouncements of the film's ability to enact a transcendence, whereby an often unspeakable social reality takes a backseat to the literally unspeakable omnipresence of "beauty."

Considering the amount of online criticism devoted to the social dimensions of the film's plot, it is perhaps surprising that very little mention is made of the subplot concerning the Fitts family—a plot that has an enormous bearing on the film's outcome. The manifestation of homosexual desire and homophobic violence that finally shapes the film's climax is all but completely effaced in the IMDb body of comments.[15] Ten of the 492 submissions refer to the strict colonel as homophobic, but none of these addresses the desires that his homophobia cloaks, despite the many clues in the film that point toward his repressed homosexuality.[16] Time and again throughout the film, we witness the colonel's lingering gazes at his son of what may be construed as longing. He watches Ricky primp before the mirror with a sense of awe. His violent attacks on his son come across as barely veiled expressions of desire. When Fitts brutally beats his son, his scolding words all but transparently decry the pain of his own repressive regime: "You can't just go around doing whatever you feel like. You can't! There are rules in life. You need structure; you need discipline." None of the unspoken but eroticized father/son dynamics is addressed in any of the postings.

Only one posting makes explicit mention of Colonel Fitts as a homosexual character. The comment reads, "Let's take Colonel Fitts's repressed homosexuality. His earlier comments about homosexuals, if taken at face value, totally belie his later actions. That is what makes his kiss with Kevin Spacey totally shocking." The comment's emphasis on the "shocking" nature of the kiss reveals the reviewer's unwillingness to make any hard-and-fast connections between homophobic behavior and repressed homosexual desire. Only two other postings mention Fitts's homosexuality, and they do so very obliquely. One commentator writes, "I was bothered by an extra twist that's thrown in near the end. It was unnecessary and made one character a little too implausible." The other adds, "The last switcheroo seemed tacked on and had no impact on the true themes of the movie." Most likely, these vague descriptions refer to Fitts's eleventh-hour attempt at seducing Lester, the failure of which leads to murder. Even though the suggestion of Fitts's sexual desires has evolved throughout the film, both commentators find the climactic moment out of place. For both respondents, the colonel's sexuality becomes "implausible" through its articulation; the revelation of it deviates from the "true themes" at stake in the film. I would suggest overall that homosexuality takes the form of a "structuring absence" in the body of *American Beauty* criticism on the IMDb. As indicated by the discursive choices made by the online respondents, the erasure of homosexuality as a critical framework is important for the sustenance of the film's aesthetic vision, which relies in part on a nostalgic encapsulation of the "beauty" of the heterosexual nuclear family.

Happiness: *The Transparent Pedophile and the Invisible Homosexual*

Todd Solondz's *Happiness* accrued much critical praise upon its release despite a disappointing showing at the box office. With a budget of $3 million, it earned only $2.76 million in theaters. Part of its disappointing performance stemmed from the lack of an NCAA rating. Solondz wanted to keep certain facets of his film intact that would have warranted only an NC-17 rating. He also went through several distributors before settling on Good Machine Releases and Killer Films, which finally agreed to release his version without editing.

Unlike *American Beauty* and its interpretive complexities, which make the assignation pedophilia quite a vexed issue, Solondz's film deals unabashedly with adult-child eroticism and even goes so far as to incorporate it into its black comedy. The film follows the lives of three sisters from suburban New Jersey and the relationships they try to establish and maintain to ward off loneliness and despair. Ironically, the most "successful" of the sisters—the one with a plush suburban home and three healthy children—is married to a therapist and serial pedophile, Bill Maplewood (played by Dylan Baker), who seduces his son's friends by drugging them (and his whole family) when they sleep over. The comedy emanates from the interspersed *Father Knows Best*–inspired father-son chats that Bill has with his son. The eleven-year-old boy's angst over not yet being able to orgasm and the length of his penis becomes the focal point of their interactions.

While the user comments on *American Beauty* used the word "pedophilia" only twice in 492 reviews, more than 35 of the 140 reviews of *Happiness* mention pedophilia explicitly; an additional 50 mention perversion or molestation. The adult-child eroticism differs from *American Beauty* in several important ways. First, the (multiple) victims are boys. Second, the boys are prepubescent or on the cusp of pubescence. The actors portraying them had not undergone a voice change, and they did not display any other visible secondary sex characteristics. Third, the relationships are consummated (off-screen) in the diegesis, with articulated physical consequences to the victims. Fourth, the sex is not consensual, and the victims are not conscious of the acts until a later date. Finally, the perpetrator views his sexual compulsions as pathological and verbally laments his inability to control them.

The ways in which IMDb commentators chose to deal with the overtly and often comically presented adult-child relationships in the film are quite disparate and revelatory of the ways that moral panic often gets translated into aesthetic judgments. Although the film ranks very highly in the IMDb's voting system, many of the comments posted about the film are staunchly condemning in tone. The following reviews are indicative of the content of roughly a quarter of the comments submitted:

> This 'movie' has left a greasy spot on my brain where it had lain; I now have hellish images of depravity stuck in my mind.[17]

> I'm sorry but a grown man talking to his kid about having sex with a little boy is just not funny.

> This movie is absolutely wrong. I could forgive the movie entirely, if it were to omit the pedofile [*sic*] section. . . . I think I am now worse off after seeing this movie.

> I don't see what is funny about pedophilic rape. Thankfully, we are spared the actual viewing of the act.

> I would compare this film to *Natural Born Killers,* except instead of promoting "violence," it promotes child rape!

> The characters lacked any conscience and morals, which overshadowed the whole movie and left you with a feeling of numbness.

> Solondz offers no solution. . . . While the types of problems he shows are becoming more common, they are individual and not universal. . . . *American Beauty* comes much closer to an accurate portrait of suburban life and does finally offer a solution to the unhappy. That movie was, at least, an attempt to create a work of art. *Happiness,* if it is remembered at all, will be remembered as the work of an unhappy craftsman, not an artist.

The commentators' disgust with the overtly sexual nature of the adult-child relationship gets translated as moral outrage, visceral damage, genre criticism, and a crisis in aesthetic representation. Many reviewers are quick to point out that pedophilia is a violence that the comedic form cannot acceptably encompass. Others portray the film as inflicting psychic damage, suggesting that the mere representation of certain taboos is traumatizing by nature. Still others equate representation of subject matter with promoting it. The last commentator mentioned above attempts to discredit *Happiness* as a piece of art on several levels. First, he defines art as that which provides a "solution to the unhappy." He cites *American Beauty* as a positive example of solution providing, whatever that may be. Second, he tries to establish true art as having "universal" qualities as opposed to merely "individual" ones. In doing so, he seems to locate adult-child eroticism as an "individual" issue—one that does not and cannot speak to the human condition as a whole. All of these interpretive frameworks ultimately appear as strategies of distanciation from and disavowal of the social taboo of pedophilia.

While many outspoken opponents of the film registered their complaints on the IMDb forum, many others praised the film both for its comedic success and its bravery in confronting the taboo of pedophilia and even creating a somewhat sympathetic character in the perpetrator:

> I loved the pedophile. I don't know why, but he really rang true for me.

> There are several difficult and conflicting situations [in the movie], like pedophilia and other sexual deviations. . . . One could ask if society provides channels to individuals to properly develop their sexuality?

> Dylan Baker's portrayal of the pederast . . . makes us understand how he's losing control of his attraction to little boys in a miraculous way.

> His treatment of pedophilia is sad, sensitive, and frightening, yet he even manages to draw some comedy from it.

> Solondz's scalpel is sharp, and he never flinches in depicting the unseemly (and generally taboo) subjects of child rape and pedophilia, which feature significantly in the narrative.
>
> My favorite characters were probably the pedophile and his eleven-year-old son. No transference there, but their problems weren't represented in a way that gave the audience any quick connections to their emotions. . . . I laughed and cringed at the same time, and then, afterwards, I just thought the whole thing was horrifically sad.

Those reviewing the film positively tended to focus on Solondz's success in accommodating such dark material in the genre of comedy. Further, they expressed admiration for putting a "human" face on a rarely represented perversion. Finally, they suggested the film's capacity for allowing the audience to empathize with the plight of a pedophile, though one respondent's qualifier, "No transference there," bespeaks a fear of being identified with him. Two atypical responses went so far as to admit a certain narrative identification with Dylan Baker's character.

> It was almost touching watching him trying to get the innocent victim to eat/drink the sleeping-potion-laced food.
>
> It's hard to admit but I was hoping the child molester, Bill Maplewood, wouldn't get caught. Just stop doing what he was doing. I sympathize with him rather than the "normal" people around him. Perhaps it is because Maplewood was able to find happiness when everyone else was beating up on each other.

In light of the many discussions of pedophilia that have surfaced in the IMDb forum around *Happiness,* it is again puzzling that any discussion of homosexuality is virtually nonexistent. Dr. Maplewood's predilection for young boys does not in and of itself require that his character be read as homosexual. In fact, many same-sex pedophiles do not identify as homosexual and view pedophilia and heterosexuality as two different, but not contradictory, facets of their identity. Yet I want to remark on a scene in *Happiness* that warrants attention in its suggestion of Bill Maplewood's orientation. Near the beginning of the film, Bill recounts a recurring dream to his own therapist in voice-over, while the dreamscape is represented visually. He dreams of taking an M-16 to a peaceful park, populated by happy couples and joggers, and opening fire. In the course of the dream, he manages to slay one half of a gay couple as they are walking along. At the dream's end, the surviving man sits weeping over his dead lover. An aerial view of the massacre reveals that the surviving gay man and Bill are wearing identical plaid shirts. This detail seems to convey an intentional sense of doubleness. While the dream may represent unfounded anxieties that his fondness for boys makes him "queer," the suggestion of his need to construct and punish a homosexual double, coupled with his often-noted resistance to sex with his wife, seems at least to warrant an inquiry into how the film constructs Bill's sexuality.

The virtual absence of discussion of sexual orientation in the *Happiness* forum may be indicative of several things. First, the online critics perhaps understand Bill to be a pedophile, assume that all pedophiles are homosexual, and therefore feel that any mention of his homosexuality would be tautological. On the other hand, the online critics may assume that his pedophilia indicates a sort of arrested development, making any discussion of his orientation toward "adult" sexual objects irrelevant. In a similar vein, the online critics may consider categories of social deviance such as "homosexual," "pedophile," or "pervert" interchangeable rather than overlapping, mutually determining, or complementary. That is to say, homosexuality becomes an irrelevant category when a "newer" or more threatening category of (dis)identification gets introduced into public discourse. Finally, homosexuality's eloquent silence here may suggest another facet of audience reception. I suggest that audiences need either to conflate categories of (specifically sexual) difference into one definable and visible Other or to see the categories as isolatable qualities that have no meaningful connections to other deviant categories in individual and social formations.

Conclusions

In this study, I have chosen to look at a broadly based, amateur-driven medium in order to perform a certain version of a cultural reception study. I chose the Internet Movie Database and its emergent audience formation as a means of gauging public discourse surrounding the taboo subject of pedophilia. I have avoided basing my analysis on the pronouncements of professional film critics, yet I do not pretend that my sampling possesses any sort of "innocence" from the taints of more institutionally grounded assessments of the subject. Certainly, many "citizen-critics" as I have at times called them had already internalized formally published reviews and simply replicated "Ebertian" responses. Also, while the comments I examined are not explicitly dialogic, I concede that many of the commentators probably read several, if not hundreds, of the preceding reviews before composing their own. What is more, I cannot account for the specificities of the vast majority of the citizen-critics that constitute the IMDb's critical mass. Their anonymity (or pseudonymity) precludes any kind of comprehensive understanding of their background regarding race, class, (often) gender, nationality, sexual orientation, and other life experiences and identifications.

As I have mentioned previously, other structuring absences have cropped up in the formation of pedophilic discourse around these two films, absences like voyeurism and incest that powerfully complicate the connections among discourse, taboo, and sexual identity that I have sought to develop in the course of this study. I have attempted to deal with the meaningfulness of homosexuality's silence in this discourse and to use pedophilia as a grounds for looking at how different taboos "compete" for space in public reception. I acknowledge that it is only one of many possible entry points into understanding these films' cultural reception.

Having conceded these limitations, I have cultivated some convictions over the course of the project concerning how this online audience formation negotiates social taboo in its readings and appraisals of films. In looking at this form of public reception of *American Beauty* and *Happiness,* I am convinced, first, that these audience members develop their own aesthetic criteria often as strategies for shoring up their own political identities and exorcising others. That is to say, these audience-critics deploy tropes like universality, verisimilitude, and moral uplift as aesthetic criteria in order to establish a fictive objectivity or distance from certain filmic situations—situations that perhaps threaten to challenge or dismantle their sexual or social identities. Second, while the labels of culturally ensconced taboos like "pedophilia" can be used as descriptive terms and to some degree can be challenged, justified, or redefined through their usage, it is difficult to strip them of their cultural connotations; often, the audience-critics circumvent the use of these labels in order to maintain the authority of their viewing positions.[18] In refusing to name certain desires or identifications, they avoid reifying their own (potentially stigmatized) identity. Third, the respondents are frequently at a loss when it comes to making sense of the various intersections of social and sexual differences; often they choose to recognize or interpret one category to the exclusion of others. Whether or not this one-category system of analysis entails the conflation of differences, the discursive isolation of differences, or both has yet to be determined. Finally, citizen-critics, whether they acknowledge it or not, thrive on the industry's breaking of taboo; as cultural events, films that represent what has heretofore been deemed unrepresentable elicit a multitude of responses. Indeed, it is not surprising that *American Beauty* and *Happiness* have been the object of such immediate, ardent, rich, and provocative examination. Both films provide a moment for audiences to "broaden their horizons," to act as judge and jury, to find new and different ways of self-identifying, or simply to pick a good fight.

Works Cited

American Beauty. Dir. Sam Mendes. DreamWorks SKG, 1999.

Eberly, Rosa. *Citizen-Critics: Literary Public Spheres.* Urbana: U of Illinois P, 2000.

Groth, A. N., and H. J. Birnbaum. "Adult Sexual Orientation and Attraction to Underage Persons." *Archives of Sexual Behavior* 7 (1978): 175–81.

Happiness. Dir. Todd Solondz. Good Machine Releases/Killer Films, 1998.

Jenny, C., T. A. Roesler, and K. L. Poyer. "Are Children at Risk for Sexual Abuse by Homosexuals?" *Pediatrics* 1 (1994): 41–44.

Staiger, Janet. "Taboos and Totems: Cultural Meanings of *The Silence of the Lambs.*" *Film Theory Goes to the Movies.* Ed. Jim Collins, Hilary Radner, and Ava Preacher Collins. New York: Routledge, 1993, 142–54.

Notes

My thanks go out to Jonathan Ayres, whose interest in and insights into *American Beauty* got me started on this project. Thanks also to Kelly Kessler, Jane Park, and Janet Staiger for their extremely helpful readings of the essay.

1. I wish to thank Rosa Eberly for an introduction to the idea of a "citizen-critic." She uses this concept to address the role of democratic participants and their actions in the public sphere. I find it useful as a descriptive category for these online users who take part in and construct the public discourse around these films. I borrow from her discussion in *Citizen-Critics*.
2. I am indebted to Janet Staiger and her suggestion of looking for structuring absences as part of the case study process in historical reception studies.
3. Occasionally, reviewers will speak to general trends that they have noticed in previous reviews, but most tend to take an insular tone and reject the forum as potentially dialogic.
4. The IMDb also has a feature that breaks down the rankings according to gender. For both male and female voters, *American Beauty* ranked number 2. Because the "gender" feature only lists the rankings for the top fifty films of all time, there is no way to access the reception of *Happiness* along gender lines, apart from looking at some of the comments on the film that I will later examine.
5. Certainly, part of the explanation for *Beauty*'s unparalleled attention in the voting and comments sections of the IMDb is due to its relatively recent release. Because more online users are discovering IMDb daily, it makes sense that current releases are more often the focus of evaluation than earlier movies. Still, the statistical significance of *Beauty*'s success on the Website is remarkable apart from this consideration.
6. This user comment on *American Beauty* is the first of many I will be examining in the course of the essay. I have chosen not to attribute the comments to the particular names given by the users because, in most cases, they are obvious pseudonyms. The body of comments on *American Beauty* can be found at the URL http://us.imdb.com/CommentsShow?0169547.
7. Tellingly, both trailers used the body (double) of teen Mena Suvari, clutching a rose across her navel, as the final image of the trailer.
8. I do not take up a discussion here of the mothers of both films because structurally, they fall outside of the triadic structures of pedophilic (and incestuous) desire in both films: Lester-Angela-Jane; Colonel Fitts-Lester-Ricky; in *Happiness,* Bill-Johnny/Ronald-Billy. Motherhood as a "structuring absence" in pedophilic discourse would be a provocative area of exploration as well, particularly as mothers are rarely mentioned in the descriptions of the pedophilic dynamics of the film, except as figures that are punished by the relationships, Carolyn in *American Beauty* for her frigidity, and Trish in *Happiness* for her delusions of "having it all." Resonant as this subject is, it is not in the province of this essay to develop the implications of this vein of reception.
9. I don't find it necessary to explore the "red rose" imagery at length other than to suggest its obvious connotations of beauty, ripeness, courtship, and pas-

sion. More interestingly, Lester's daughter Jane wears a sweater embroidered with red roses at some point in the film, which casts an incestuous light on his potentially deflected desires for her best friend. This suggestion gains force with Ricky's query into Jane's possibly jealous anger about her father's attraction to Angela: "You'd rather he had the crush on you?" This implication of incest is never raised in the online forum.

10. For example, see the findings of Jenny, Roesler, and Poyer; Groth and Birnbaum.
11. One reviewer mistakenly used the term *pederasty* for pedophilia in her discussion of *Happiness*.
12. This generalization may seem crude in light of so many emerging theories of spectatorship along the lines of gender; I am referring here both to the viewer who may be aligned with Lester in his specular desire for Angela and also to the viewer who is resistant to pedophilic taboo as an impediment to the narrative's progression.
13. It is noteworthy that the respondent refers to the characters of Jane and Angela as "sexy 18 year olds," even though their ages are never made explicit in the film. Lester, upon learning that Ricky is a classmate of Jane, assumes that he is sixteen. Thus, it seems unlikely that Jane and Angela would in fact be eighteen. This error seems strangely symptomatic of viewers' reluctance to identify the sexual object as an adolescent.
14. The commentator in another passage straightforwardly condemns the film's use of teenage nudity. This seems to be less of a gray area for her; while the pedophilia is a matter of "reading," the nudity is a "fact."
15. A few posters make mention of the neighboring gay couple as a presence in the movie, but they are explicitly identified as such in the film and are left at the margins—something a few posters noticed.
16. Issues of voyeurism and exhibitionism are also notably absent from discussion around the film. Perhaps this is attributable to the possibility that addressing voyeurism as a thematic concern would somehow implicate the viewer's own voyeuristic pleasures that the film generates. The lack of discussion surrounding the gaze, then, would constitute another sort of structuring absence, suggesting that voyeurism is central to textual pleasure but potentially traumatic if expressed in public discourse.
17. This user comment on *Happiness* is the first of many I will discuss in the essay. Like those of *American Beauty,* the comments are signed pseudonymously, and therefore the names are absent from the text. The body of user comments on *Happiness* can be found at the URL http://us.inidb.com/CommentsShow?0147612.
18. By "authority" here I mean to suggest a collectively imagined moral authority of sorts, one that is maintained through the understanding that social boundaries will be upheld, rather than challenged, and that taboos should not be articulated lest they be given some kind of public existence.

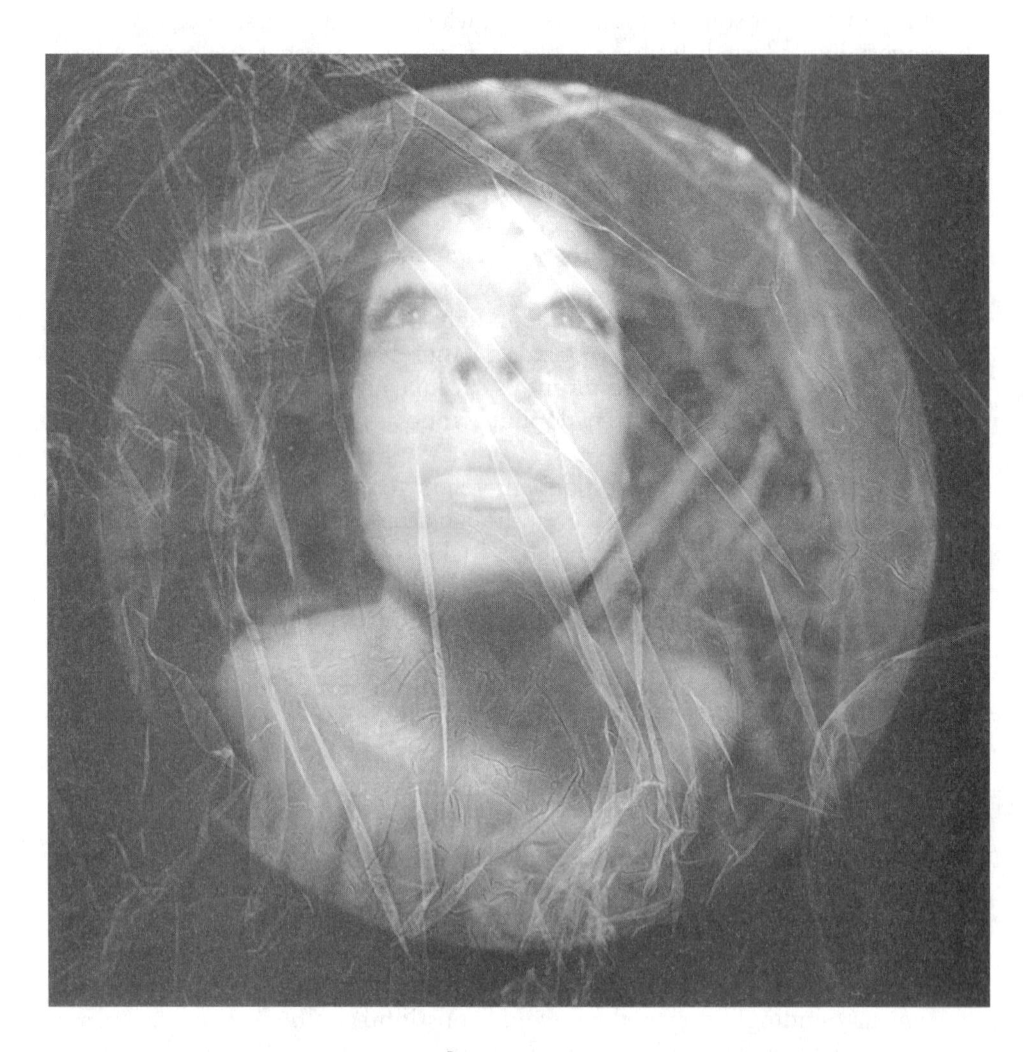

Limbo

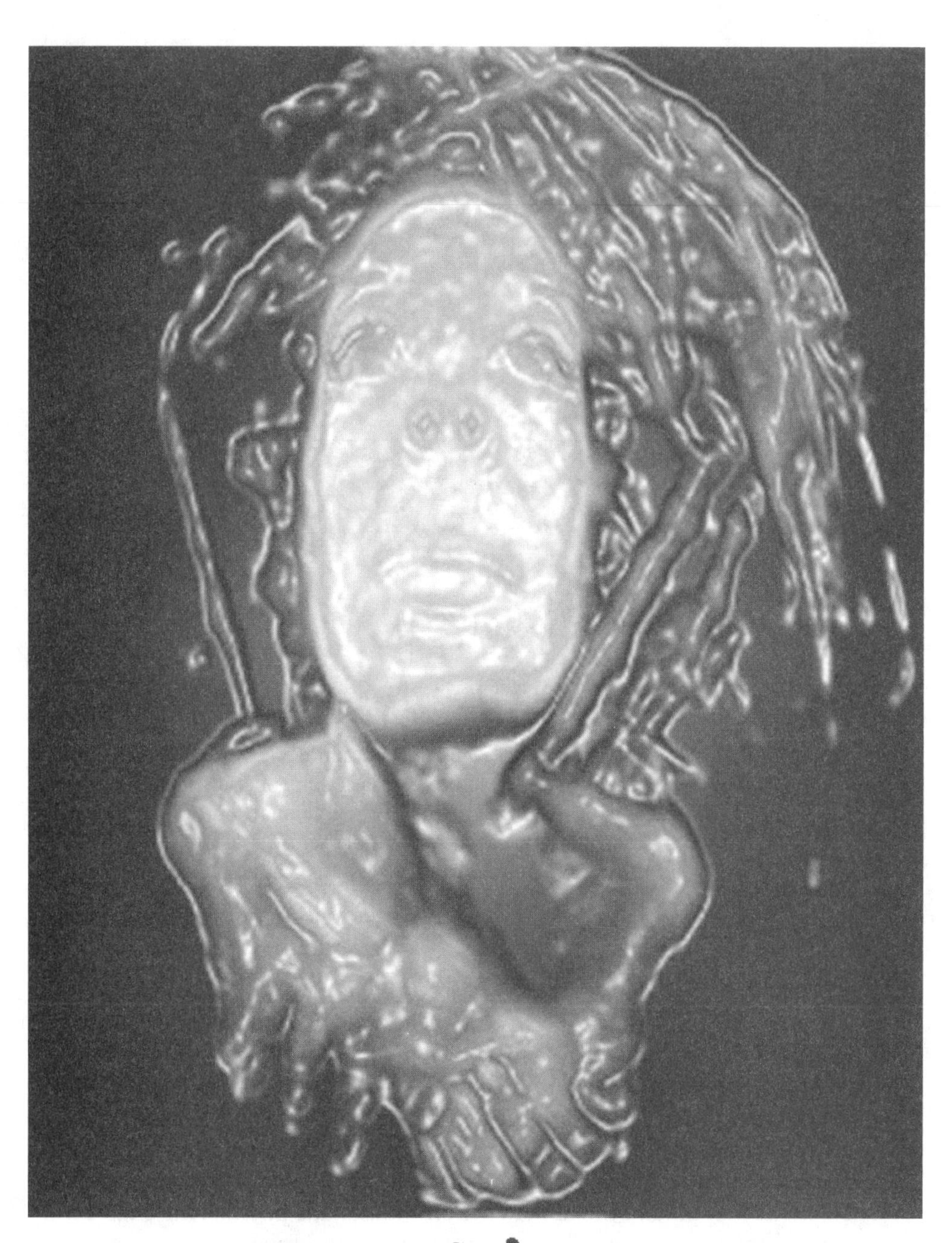

Digital Limbo

3

Rereading Science

Jocelyn D. White

> Electron waves, curved four-dimensional space-time, invisible black holes, concealed quarks, remote quasars, probabilistic atoms . . . are these elements of reality, figments of the imagination, or creations of an artist? Indeed, modern-day physics looks more and more like art, illusion, and show biz. It's hard to know what's real anymore.
>
> —Roger Jones, *Physics for the Rest of Us*

We live in an increasingly scientific world. Technology has made our world faster. Zipping a card through the automatic teller machine produces money in a few seconds. A click of a mouse delivers electronic mail instantly to someone halfway across the globe. Scientific advancements have made our lives longer and our world more intelligible. Illnesses that crippled thousands in previous decades are prevented with vaccines we receive within weeks of our birth. The late 20th century yielded the mapping of the human genome and made possible the engineering of our own genetic sequence. Because technology and scientific knowledge are such large parts of our lives, we may not always stop to critically examine the way that these advancements have shaped our lives and our views of the world. The readings in this chapter expose you to poetry and prose that deals with scientific issues or imagines new worlds with technology different from our own. As you read through these pieces, consider how science has shaped the world of the story, and how our attitudes toward science have shaped the stories that we tell.

We tend to think of science in terms of objective, verifiable facts, however, science is far from being a stable and remote body of knowledge. In fact, scientific beliefs function socially to shape how we envision the universe and what we see as our position within it. It's hard to believe that changes in a scientific field such as astronomy could affect a person individually. Even so, a shift in astronomical thought can have a profound impact on society. The medieval view of the cosmos, for example, relied on harmony and wholeness, where all is "a unified whole, in which the universe, the earth, society, and man were all images of one another" (Olson 9). The social stability and balance allowed by this worldview was challenged by the "new astronomy" of the 17th century, by theories of a sun-centered cosmos (rather than an earth-centered one) advanced by Copernicus, Kepler, and Galileo (Olson 10). This not only changed scientific thought, but had a profound effect on the people living at the time. The change literally forced people to reconsider their own place and value in a universe where they could no longer claim to be the center. "[T]o most seventeenth century thinkers," university professor Richard Olson explains, "the vastness and uncertainty of the new universe was terrifying" (10). More recently, in the 19th century, Charles Darwin's theories of evolution were adapted politically. Darwin's idea of the "survival of the fittest" was translated into a "philosophy of force" which was seen to justify colonization and make appropriate the cruelty that often accompanied it. Even sexuality has been shaped by technology. Radiologist Brian Lentle writes that "x-rays may have been the first intimation of what we now consider the sexual revolution of the 20th century" as the conservative Victorian society feared the x-ray's ability to see through their copious amounts of clothing (512).

Science shapes our views of the world, and as our scientific knowledge changes, so do our perceptions of reality. This phenomenon must be what inspired philosopher Friedrich Nietzsche to call Truth a "mobile army of metaphors" (359). Literature that deals with science frequently acknowledges this concept of our world as fluid and changing. In each story, readers find themselves confronted with a new set of scientific and technological "truths" and watch the effect that these truths have on the world of the story. As you read the selections in this chapter, consider how views of science and technology have shaped the social and personal realms of the text.

Science not only shapes how we see the world, but it is also shaped by us. Rather than existing independently from the political and social issues of our time, our cultural values and beliefs prefigure the knowledge that we gain. Scientist and writer Evelyn Fox Keller writes that "Careful attention to what questions get asked, of how research programs come to be legitimated and supported, of how theoretical disputes are resolved, of 'how experiments end' reveals the working of cultural and social norms at every stage" (45). The issue of funding became particularly pertinent in the light of debates over the scientific research on stem cells that considered arguments regarding ethics, morality, and human rights. Physicist Roger Jones concurs with Keller's beliefs. Jones writes: "Physics simply is not an objective body of facts and established theories. It incorporates its own system of beliefs, conventions, tacit knowledge, biases, assumptions, misconceptions, lore, and myth. It cannot stand above aesthetic judgement and psychological analysis" (316). Rereading science opens us to this dialogue between science and society. Represented in the stories we tell about science are our own views of the world, shaped by our technological and scientific knowledge, and our views of science which are coded with our cultural, religious, and social viewpoints. Our own anxieties are represented in the stories we tell, as is our need to work out our relationship to each other, to the planet, and to the universe.

As you read the selections in this chapter, look for current conflicts and social issues played out on unfamiliar landscapes. Even the frequency of machinery such as computers, spaceships, or cyborgs, which we may initially dismiss as a simple accessory of science fiction, may embody a current social or cultural issue. Adam Roberts, a critic of science fiction, points out that the technology plentiful in these texts "focuses our attitudes to difference" (147). Whether it is the difference of machines or the difference of the creature in Mary Shelley's *Frankenstein,* considered by many to be the first science fiction novel, difference is frequently a theme in science fiction writing. In considering what is different from us, we must also consider our own identity and what makes us who we are. In this way, writing involving science can probe questions that extend beyond the technical: How do we define humanity? What separates artificial intelligence from humans? How do we, as people, define ourselves in a time when machines are taking on more of the qualities we once deemed solely human?

Just as science provides a way to make the world understandable to us, it also gestures toward the areas that surpass our understanding and remain outside of our control. Some texts are hopeful, expressing the exciting possibility of the future. Some are more pessimistic, carrying trends like pollution, cloning, or our increasing reliance on computers to a terrifying extreme. Where science leaves off, the writer picks up, playing out imaginative, and sometimes horrifying, results of our scientific inquiry. The familiar plot of Mary Shelley's *Frankenstein* is an example of both hope and fear, as Victor Frankenstein's creature of beauty becomes a demon, the hideous, violent, and unexpected results of his experiments which will torment him. For Victor, "the cup of life is poisoned forever" as a result of his thirst for knowledge, and he is plagued by the "glimmer of [the] two eyes" of his creation (157). Shelley's theme resonated with the readers of her time, and this excitement and anxiety towards science resonates still. In our pursuit of the possibilities that science may provide, we harbor haunting fears of things that lie outside of our control. Texts about science may delve into questions of ethics: Should scientists perform experiments simply because they have the technology to carry them out? Are there areas that should be off limits to scientists? Is there a realm of faith or of the supernatural where humans should not tread? If this sacred realm exists, what would be the price for intrusion? As you read the texts in this chapter, consider the writer's attitude toward science, and the fears, doubts, confidence, or hopes embodied in the text. How do these attitudes play out? Are there any of your own attitudes that you recognize in the text?

If you are asked to do a close reading or textual analysis of one of the pieces in this chapter, there are several questions that you can explore. As you read, consider how the piece is written, the language that the writer uses, and how the writer has adapted the elements of the story or poem to include the subject of science. You may want to trace a specific theme in the story. How does character, or the sequence of the story for instance, contribute to a meaning or theme that you see? What is the connection between the form of the piece and its content? Are there ways in which the scientific content and the imaginative use of language collide?

If you're writing a text-in-context essay on one of the pieces in the chapter, you can begin by researching the specific scientific issues or concerns that the writer addresses in the piece you've chosen. You may want to research the context of the writer—what was the writer's own relationship to science? Is the writer a scientist, someone interested in science, or someone on the fringes, writing about science as an outsider? You may consider some of the various attitudes toward science exhibited by the authors. What is the writer's scientific context? What is his or her attitude toward the scientific notion that he or she discusses? You may also want to research the time in which the piece was written. What events surrounding this writer might have influenced him or her to write about this subject? How might those events have shaped the writer's attitudes toward the subject he or she has chosen?

If you are examining the piece in its cultural context, you may want to begin with an examination of your own attitudes. What are your attitudes toward the scientific issues of the story or poem? Are there themes that cause an extreme reaction as you read? What about your own beliefs and values might be challenged as you read? Compare your own context as a reader to the context of the writer of the piece. How might your context affect your understanding of and attitude toward the issues articulated in the story?

Whatever your approach to the selections in this chapter, try to view the texts critically. Consider what science contributes to the meaning of the story, what ideas the author is conveying in choosing science as a literary subject, and how your own ideas about science influence your perspective and beliefs.

Works Cited

Keller, Evelyn Fox. "Gender and Science: An Update." *Science and Technology Today*. Ed. Nancy MacKenzie. New York: St. Martin's P, 1995. 38–47.

Jones, Roger. *Physics for the Rest of Us*. Chicago: Contemporary Books, 1992.

Lentle, Brian. "X-rays and technology as metaphor." *Canadian Medical Association Journal* 162 :4, 2/22/2000, 512. Available from Academic Search Elite [database on-line]. Accessed 23 March 2002. <http://search.epnet.com>.

Nietzsche, Friedrich. "On Truth and Lying in an Extra-Moral Sense." *Literary Theory: An Anthology*. Ed. Julie Rivkin and Michael Ryan. Malden: Blackwell Publishers, 1998.

Olson, Richard. *Science as Metaphor*. Belmont: Wadsworth, 1971.

Roberts, Adam. *Science Fiction*. New York: Routledge, 2000.

Shelley, Mary. *Frankenstein*. 2nd ed. Ed. Johanna Smith. New York: Bedford/St. Martin's P, 2000.

Mark Akenside

Mark Akenside (1721–1770) was born and raised in Newcastle upon Tyne. He was sent to school in Edinburgh to become a dissenting minister (disagreeing with the doctrines of the Anglican church, the state church of England). However, Akenside was drawn to the study of medicine, which he went to study in Leyden (Netherlands) in 1741. Three years later he became a "doctor of physic," having published a thesis on "The Origin and Growth of the Human Foetus," which was apparently groundbreaking for its time. When he returned to London, he published his first collection of poetry (Odes). This collection helped him acquire a name as a poet while at the same time he was struggling to establish himself as a doctor. It seems that he never developed a very large practice as a physician, but he became a Fellow of the Royal Society and physician to the queen, obtained a degree from Cambridge, and was admitted to the college of physicians. Samuel Johnson, an important figure in the history of literary criticism, once commented of Akenside's poetry, "To examine such compositions singly cannot be required; they have doubtless brighter and darker parts: but, when they are once found to be generally dull, all further labour may be spared, for to what use can the work be criticised that will not be read?" While Akenside's poetry may not be considered skillful, it is his attitude toward science at an important time in history that makes his work worthy of our study here.

Hymn to Science

Science! thou fair effusive ray
From the great source of mental day,
Free, generous, and refin'd!
Descend with all thy treasures fraught,
Illumine each bewilder'd thought,
And bless my lab'ring mind.

But first with thy resistless light,
Disperse those phantoms from my sight,
Those mimic shades of thee;
The scholiast's learning, sophist's cant,
The visionary bigot's rant,
The monk's philosophy.

O! let thy powerful charms impart
The patient head, the candid heart,
Devoted to thy sway;
Which no weak passions e'er mislead,
Which still with dauntless steps proceed
Where Reason points the way.

Give me to learn each secret cause;
Let number's, figure's, motion's laws
Reveal'd before me stand;
These to great Nature's scenes apply,
And round the globe, and thro' the sky,
Disclose her working hand.

Next, to thy nobler search resign'd,
The busy, restless, human mind
Thro' ev'ry maze pursue;
Detect Perception where it lies,
Catch the ideas as they rise,
And all their changes view.

Say from what simple springs began
The vast, ambitious thoughts of man,
Which range beyond control;
Which seek Eternity to trace,
Dive thro' th' infinity of space,
And strain to grasp the whole.

Her secret stores let Memory tell,
Bid Fancy quit her fairy cell,
In all her colours drest;
While prompt her sallies to control,
Reason, the judge, recalls the soul
To Truth's severest test.

Let the fair scale, with just ascent,
And cautious steps, be trod;
And from the dead, corporeal mass,
Thro' each progressive order pass
To Instinct, Reason, God.

Nor dive too deep, nor soar too high,
In that divine abyss;
To Faith content thy beams to lend,
Her hopes t' assure, her steps befriend,
And light her way to bliss.

Then downwards take thy flight agen;
Mix with the policies of men,
And social nature's ties:

The plan, the genius of each state,
Its interest and its pow'rs relate,
Its fortunes and its rise.

Thro' private life pursue thy course,
Trace every action to its source,
And means and motives weigh:
Put tempers, passions in the scale,
Mark what degrees in each prevail,
And fix the doubtful sway.

That last, best effort of thy skill,
To form the life, and rule the will,
Propitious pow'r! impart:
Teach me to cool my passion's fires,
Make me the judge of my desires,
The master of my heart.

Raise me above the vulgar's breath,
Pursuit of fortune, fear of death,
And all in life that's mean.
Still true to reason be my plan,
Still let my action speak the man,
Thro' every various scene.

Hail! queen of manners, light of truth;
Hail! charm of age, and guide of youth;
Sweet refuge of distress:
In business, thou! exact, polite;
Thou giv'st Retirement its delight,
Prosperity its grace.

Of wealth, pow'r, freedom, thou! the cause;
Foundress of order, cities, laws,
Of arts inventress, thou!
Without thee what were human kind?
How vast their wants, their thoughts how blind!
Their joys how mean! how few!

Sun of the soul! thy beams unveil!
Let others spread the daring sail,
On Fortune's faithless sea;
While undeluded, happier I
From the vain tumult timely fly,
And sit in peace with thee.

Isaac Asimov

Isaac Asimov (1920–1992) was born in Petrovichi, Russia. As a teenager he was inspired by science fiction. While he was making progress through college and graduate school, Asimov wrote and published a number of important works in the genre, primarily concerning robots. When he graduated from Columbia with a Ph.D. in biochemistry, he managed to get a tenured teaching position at Boston University. Because he believed strongly in science as an important way of coming to understand the world, in the late fifties Asimov began writing popular science essays and books, which are considered to be the best of their time. Asimov's fictional work is considered to be a vital part of the body of "hard science fiction." During his lifetime, Asimov published more than 400 books, mostly nonfiction. As in other areas of his writing, "The Life and Times of Multivac," (written in 1973 at the request of New York Times Magazine*) reveals Asimov's belief that the application of knowledge gained through the study of science and mathematics can help human beings solve even the most complicated problems, although it may open up new ones.*

The Life and Times of Multivac

The whole world was interested. The whole world could watch. If anyone wanted to know how many did watch, Multivac could have told them. The great computer Multivac kept track—as it did of everything.

Multivac was the judge in this particular case, so coldly objective and purely upright that there was no need of prosecution or defense. There was only the accused, Simon Hines, and the evidence, which consisted, in part, of Ronald Bakst.

Bakst watched, of course. In his case, it was compulsory. He would rather it were not. In his tenth decade, he was showing signs of age and his rumpled hair was distinctly gray.

Noreen was not watching. She had said at the door, "If we had a friend left—" She paused, then added, "which I doubt!" and left.

Bakst wondered if she would come back at all, but at the moment, it didn't matter.

Hines had been an incredible idiot to attempt actual action, as though one could think of walking up to a Multivac outlet and smashing it—as though he

Reprinted from *The Ascent of Wonder: The Evolution of Hard SF*, (1994), edited by David G. Hartwell and Kathryn Cramer, TOR Books, a division of St. Martin's Press.

didn't know a world-girdling computer, *the* world-girdling Computer (capital letter, please) with millions of robots at its command, couldn't protect itself. And even if the outlet had been smashed, what would that have accomplished?

And Hines did it in Bakst's physical presence, too!

He was called, precisely on schedule—"Ronald Bakst will give evidence now."

Multivac's voice was beautiful, with a beauty that never quite vanished no matter how often it was heard. Its timbre was neither quite male nor, for that matter, female, and it spoke in whatever language its hearer understood best.

"I am ready to give evidence," Bakst said.

There was no way to say anything but what he had to say. Hines could not avoid conviction. In the days when Hines would have had to face his fellow human beings, he would have been convicted more quickly and less fairly—and would have been punished more crudely.

Fifteen days passed, days during which Bakst was quite alone. Physical aloneness was not a difficult thing to envisage in the world of Multivac. Hordes had died in the days of the great catastrophes and it had been the computers that had saved what was left and directed the recovery—and improved their own designs till all were merged into Multivac—and the five million human beings were left on Earth to live in perfect comfort.

But those five million were scattered and the chances of one seeing another outside the immediate circle, except by design, was not great. No one was designing to see Bakst, not even by television.

For the time, Bakst could endure the isolation. He buried himself in his chosen way—which happened to be, these last twenty-three years, the designing of mathematical games. Every man and woman on Earth could develop a way of life to self-suit, provided always that Multivac, weighing all of human affairs with perfect skill, did not judge the chosen way to be subtractive to human happiness.

But what could be subtractive in mathematical games? It was purely abstract—pleased Bakst—harmed no one else.

He did not expect the isolation to continue. The Congress would not isolate him permanently without a trial—a different kind of trial from that which Hines had experienced, of course, one without Multivac's tyranny of absolute justice.

Still, he was relieved when it ended, and pleased that it was Noreen coming back that ended it. She came trudging over the hill toward him and he started toward her, smiling. It had been a successful five-year period during which they had been together. Even the occasional meetings with her two children and two grandchildren had been pleasant.

He said, "Thank you for being back."

She said, "I'm not back." She looked tired. Her brown hair was windblown, her prominent cheeks a trifle rough and sunburned.

Bakst pressed the combination for a light lunch and coffee. He knew what she liked. She didn't stop him, and though she hesitated for a moment, she ate.

She said, "I've come to talk to you. The Congress sent me."

"The Congress!" he said. "Fifteen men and women—counting me. Self-appointed and helpless."

"You didn't think so when you were a member."

"I've grown older. I've learned."

"At least you've learned to betray your friends."

"There was no betrayal. Hines tried to damage Multivac; a foolish, impossible thing for him to try."

"You accused him."

"I had to. Multivac knew the facts without my accusation, and without my accusation, I would have been an accessory. Hines would not have gained, but I would have lost."

"Without a human witness, Multivac would have suspended sentence."

"Not in the case of an anti-Multivac act. This wasn't a case of illegal parenthood or life-work without permission. I couldn't take the chance."

"So you let Simon be deprived of all work permits for two years."

"He deserved it."

"A consoling thought. You may have lost the confidence of the Congress, but you have gained the confidence of Multivac."

"The confidence of Multivac is important in the world as it is," said Bakst seriously. He was suddenly conscious of not being as tall as Noreen.

She looked angry enough to strike him; her lips pressed whitely together. But then she had passed her eightieth birthday—no longer young—the habit of nonviolence was too ingrained. . . . Except for fools like Hines.

"Is that all you have to say, then?" she said.

"There could be a great deal to say. Have you forgotten? Have you all forgotten? Do you remember how it once was? Do you remember the Twentieth Century? We live long now; we live securely now; we live happily now."

"We live worthlessly now."

"Do you want to go back to what the world was like once?"

Noreen shook her head violently. "Demon tales to frighten us. We have learned our lesson. With the help of Multivac we have come through—but we don't need that help any longer. Further help will soften us to death. Without Multivac, *we* will run the robots, *we* will direct the farms and mines and factories."

"How well?"

"Well enough. Better, with practice. We need the stimulation of it in any case or we will all die."

Bakst said, "We have our work, Noreen; whatever work we choose."

"Whatever we choose, as long as it's unimportant, and even that can be taken away at will—as with Hines. And what's your work, Ron? Mathematical games? Drawing lines on paper? Choosing number combinations?"

Bakst's hand reached out to her, almost pleadingly. "That can be important. It is not nonsense. Don't underestimate—" He paused, yearning to explain but not quite knowing how he could, safely. He said, "I'm working on some deep problems in combinatorial analysis based on gene patterns that can be used to—"

"To amuse you and a few others. Yes, I've heard you talk about your games. You will decide how to move from A to B in a minimum number of steps and that will teach you how to go from womb to grave in a minimum number of risks and we will all thank Multivac as we do so."

She stood up. "Ron, you will be tried. I'm sure of it. *Our* trial. And you will be dropped. Multivac will protect you against physical harm, but you know it will not force us to see you, speak to you, or have anything to do with you. You will find that without the stimulation of human interaction, you will not be able to think—or to play your games. Goodbye."

"Noreen! Wait!"

She turned at the door. "Of course, you will have Multivac. You can talk to Multivac, Ron."

He watched her dwindle as she walked down the road through the parklands kept green, and ecologically healthy, by the unobtrusive labors of quiet, single-minded robots one scarcely ever saw.

He thought: Yes, I will have to talk to Multivac.

Multivac had no particular home any longer. It was a global presence knit together by wire, optical fiber, and microwave. It had a brain divided into a hundred subsidiaries but acting as one. It had its outlets everywhere and no human being of the five million was far from one.

There was time for all of them, since Multivac could speak to all individually at the same time and not lift its mind from the greater problems that concerned it.

Bakst had no illusions as to its strength. What was its incredible intricacy but a mathematical game that Bakst had come to understand over a decade ago? He knew the manner in which the connecting links ran from continent to continent in a huge network whose analysis could form the basis of a fascinating game. How do you arrange the network so that the flow of information never jams? How do you arrange the switching points? Prove that no matter what the arrangement, there is always at least one point which, on disconnection—

Once Bakst had learned the game, he had dropped out of the Congress. What could they do but talk and of what use was that? Multivac indifferently permitted talk of any kind and in any depth precisely because it was unimportant. It was only acts that Multivac prevented, diverted, or punished.

And it was Hines's act that was bringing on the crisis; and before Bakst was ready for it, too.

Bakst had to hasten now, and he applied for an interview with Multivac without any degree of confidence in the outcome.

Questions could be asked of Multivac at any time. There were nearly a million outlets of the type that had withstood Hines's sudden attack into which, or near which, one could speak. Multivac would answer.

An *interview* was another matter. It required time; it required privacy; most of all it required Multivac's judgment that it was necessary. Although Multivac had capacities that not all the world's problems consumed, it had grown chary, somehow, of its time. Perhaps that was the result of its ever-continuing self-improvement. It was becoming constantly more aware of its own worth and less likely to bear trivialities with patience.

Bakst had to depend on Multivac's good will. His leaving of the Congress, all his actions since, even the bearing of evidence against Hines, had been to gain that good will. Surely it was the key to success in this world.

He would have to assume the good will. Having made the application, he at once traveled to the nearest substation by air. Nor did he merely send his image.

He wanted to be there in person; somehow he felt his contact with Multivac would be closer in that way.

The room was almost as it might be if there were to be a human conference planned over closed multivision. For one flash-by moment, Bakst thought Multivac might assume an imaged human form and join him—the brain made flesh.

It did not, of course. There was the soft, whispering chuckle of Multivac's unceasing operations; something always and forever present in Multivac's presence; and over it, now, Multivac's voice.

It was not the usual voice of Multivac. It was a still, small voice, beautiful and insinuating, almost in his ear.

"Good day, Bakst. You are welcome. Your fellow human beings disapprove of you."

Multivac always comes to the point, thought Bakst. He said, "It does not matter, Multivac. What counts is that I accept your decisions as for the good of the human species. You were designed to do so in the primitive versions of yourself and—"

"And my self-designs have continued this basic approach. If *you* understand this, why do so many human beings fail to understand it? I have not yet completed the analysis of that phenomenon."

"I have come to you with a problem," said Bakst.

Multivac said, "What is it?"

Bakst said, "I have spent a great deal of time on mathematical problems inspired by the study of genes and their combinations. I cannot find the necessary answers and home-computerization is of no help."

There was an odd clicking and Bakst could not repress a slight shiver at the sudden thought that Multivac might be avoiding a laugh. It was a touch of the human beyond what even he was ready to accept. The voice was in his other ear and Multivac said:

"There are thousands of different genes in the human cell. Each gene has an average of perhaps fifty variations in existence and uncounted numbers that have never been in existence. If we were to attempt to calculate all possible combinations, the mere listing of them at my fastest speed, if steadily continued, would, in the longest possible lifetime of the Universe, achieve but an infinitesimal fraction of the total."

Bakst said, "A complete listing is not needed. That is the point of my game. Some combinations are more probable than others and by building probability upon probability, we can cut the task enormously. It is the manner of achieving this building of probability upon probability that I ask you to help me with."

"It would still take a great deal of my time. How could I justify this to myself?"

Bakst hesitated. No use in trying a complicated selling job. With Multivac, a straight line was the shortest distance between two points.

He said, "An appropriate gene combination might produce a human being more content to leave decisions to you, more willing to believe in your resolve to make men happy, more anxious to *be* happy. I cannot find the proper combination, but you might, and with guided genetic engineering—"

"I see what you mean. It is—good. I will devote some time to it."

Bakst found it difficult to hitch into Noreen's private wavelength. Three times the connection broke away. He was not surprised. In the last two months, there had been an increasing tendency for technology to slip in minor ways—never for long, never seriously—and he greeted each occasion with a somber pleasure.

This time it held. Noreen's face showed, holographically three-dimensional. It flickered a moment, but it held.

"I'm returning your call," said Bakst, dully impersonal.

"For a while it seemed impossible to get you," said Noreen. "Where have you been?"

"Not hiding. I'm here, in Denver."

"Why in Denver?"

"The world is my oyster, Noreen. I may go where I please."

Her face twitched a little. "And perhaps find it empty everywhere. We are going to try you, Ron."

"Now?"

"Now!"

"And here?"

"And here!"

Volumes of space flickered into different glitters on either side of Noreen, and further away, and behind. Bakst looked from side to side, counting. There were fourteen, six men, eight women. He knew every one of them. They had been good friends once, not so long ago.

To either side and beyond the simulacra was the wild background of Colorado on a pleasant summer day that was heading toward its end. There had been a city here once named Denver. The site still bore the name though it had been cleared, as most of the city sites had been. . . . He could count ten robots in sight, doing whatever it was robots did.

They were maintaining the ecology, he supposed. He knew no details, but Multivac did, and it kept fifty million robots all over the Earth in efficient order.

Behind Bakst was one of the converging grids of Multivac, almost like a small fortress of self-defense.

"Why now?" he asked. "And why here?"

Automatically he turned to Eldred. She was the oldest of them and the one with authority—if a human being could be said to have authority.

Eldred's dark-brown face looked a little weary. The years showed, all sixscore of them, but her voice was firm and incisive. "Because we have the final fact now. Let Noreen tell you. She knows best."

Bakst's eyes shifted to Noreen. "Of what crime am I accused?"

"Let us play no games, Ron. There are no crimes under Multivac except to strike for freedom and it is your human crime that you have committed no crime under Multivac. For that we will judge whether any human being alive wants your company any longer, wants to hear your voice, be aware of your presence, or respond to you in any way."

"Why am I threatened with isolation then?"

"You have betrayed all human beings."

"How?"

"Do you deny that you seek to breed mankind into subservience to Multivac?"

"Ah!" Bakst folded his arms across his chest. "You found out quickly, but then you had only to ask Multivac."

Noreen said, "Do you deny that you asked for help in the genetic engineering of a strain of humanity designed to accept slavery under Multivac without question?"

"I suggested the breeding of a more contented humanity. Is this a betrayal?"

Eldred intervened. She said, "We don't want your sophistry, Ron. We know it by heart. Don't tell us once again that Multivac cannot be withstood, that there is no use in struggling, that we have gained security. What you call security, the rest of us call slavery."

Bakst said, "Do you proceed now to judgment, or am I allowed a defense?"

"You heard Eldred," said Noreen. "We know your defense."

"We all heard Eldred," said Bakst, "but no one has heard me. What she says is my defense is not my defense."

There was a silence as the images glanced right and left at each other. Eldred said, "Speak!"

Bakst said, "I asked Multivac to help me solve a problem in the field of mathematical games. To gain his interest, I pointed out that it was modeled on gene combinations and that a solution might help in designing a gene combination that would leave man no worse off than he is now in any respect and yet breed into him a cheerful acceptance of Multivac's direction, and acquiescence in his decisions."

"So we have said," said Eldred.

"It was only on those terms that Multivac would have accepted the task. Such a new breed is clearly desirable for mankind by Multivac's standards, and by Multivac's standards he must labor toward it. And the desirability of the end will lure him on to examine greater and greater complications of a problem whose endlessness is beyond what even he can handle. You all witness that."

Noreen said, "Witness what?"

"Haven't you had trouble reaching me? In the last two months, hasn't each of you noticed small troubles in what has always gone smoothly? . . . You are silent. May I accept that as an affirmative?"

"If so, what then?"

Bakst said, "Multivac has been placing all his spare circuits on the problem. He has been slowly pushing the running of the world toward rather a skimpy minimum of his efforts, since nothing by his own sense of ethics, must stand in the way of human happiness and there can be no greater increase in that happiness than to accept Multivac."

Noreen said, "What does all this mean? There is still enough in Multivac to run the world—and us—and if this is done at less than full efficiency, that would only add temporary discomfort to our slavery. Only temporary, because it won't last long. Sooner or later, Multivac will decide the problem is insoluble, or will solve it, and in either case, his distraction will end. In the latter case, slavery will become permanent and irrevocable."

"But for now he is distracted," said Bakst, "and we can even talk like this—most dangerously—without his noticing. Yet I dare not risk doing so for long, so please understand me quickly.

"I have another mathematical game—the setting up of networks on the model of Multivac. I have been able to demonstrate that no matter how complicated and redundant the network is, there must be at least one place into which all the currents can funnel under particular circumstances. There will always be the fatal apopletic stroke if that one place is interfered with, since it will induce overloading elsewhere which will break down and induce overloading elsewhere—and so on indefinitely till all breaks down."

"Well?"

"And this is the point. Why else have I come to Denver? And Multivac knows it, too, and this point is guarded electronically and robotically to the extent that it cannot be penetrated."

"Well?"

"But Multivac is distracted, and Multivac trusts me. I have labored hard to gain that trust, at the cost of losing all of you, since only with trust is there the possibility of betrayal. If any of you tried to approach this point, Multivac might rouse himself even out of his present distraction. If Multivac were not distracted, he would not allow even me to approach. But he *is* distracted, and it *is* I!"

Bakst was moving toward the converging grid in a calm manner, and the fourteen images, keyed to him, moved along as well. The soft susurrations of a busy Multivac center were all about them.

Bakst said, "Why attack an invulnerable opponent? Make him vulnerable first, and then—"

Bakst fought to stay calm, but it all depended on this now. Everything! With a sharp yank, he uncoupled a joint. (If he had only had still more time to make more certain.)

He was not stopped—and as he held his breath, he became aware of the ceasing of noise, the ending of whisper, the closing down of Multivac. If, in a moment, that soft noise did not return, then he had had the right key point, and no recovery would be possible. If he were not quickly the focus of approaching robots—

He turned in the continuing silence. The robots in the distance were working still. None were approaching.

Before him, the images of the fourteen men and women of the Congress were still there and each seemed to be stupefied at the sudden enormous thing that had happened.

Bakst said, "Multivac is shut down, burnt out. It can't be rebuilt." He felt almost drunk at the sound of what he was saying. "I have worked toward this since I left you. When Hines attacked, I feared there might be other such efforts, that Multivac would double his guard, that even I—I had to work quickly—I wasn't sure." He was gasping, but forced himself steady, and said solemnly, "I have given us our freedom."

And he paused, aware at last of the gathering weight of the silence. Fourteen images stared at him, without any of them offering a word in response.

Bakst said sharply, "You have talked of freedom. You *have* it!"

Then, uncertainly, he said, "Isn't that what you want?"

Margaret Atwood

Canadian writer Margaret Atwood (b. 1939) is a leading literary artist of the twentieth century. Her work is highly regarded by both the general reader and the critics alike; she is the recipient of numerous literary and humanitarian awards, and, in 1986, was named Woman of the Year by Ms. Magazine. *Atwood was also honored with the Booker Prize in 2000 for her most recent novel* The Blind Assassin. *She has taught English literature at several colleges and universities. As a young author, Atwood was encouraged to pursue a career in writing as Canadians of her generation felt a need to develop a national literature. Among her many novels are the bestsellers* Surfacing *(1972),* The Handmaid's Tale *(1986),* Cat's Eye *(1989), and* The Robber Bride *(1993). She has also published three collections of short stories and several books of poetry. In an interview with Lindsy Van Gelder, Atwood says, "I began as a profoundly apolitical writer, but then . . . I began to describe the world around me." Her short story, "Happy Endings," appears in Chapter 5. "Speeches for Dr Frankenstein," from her collection entitled* Poems, 1965–1975, *takes the reader into the mind of Frankenstein as he attempts to mold his creature in the shape of his own desires, but ultimately fails.*

Speeches for Dr Frankenstein

I

I, the performer
in the tense arena, glittered
under the fluorescent moon. Was bent
masked by the table. Saw what focused
my intent: the emptiness

The air filled with an ether of cheers.

My wrist extended a scalpel.

II

The table is a flat void,
barren as total freedom. Though behold

A sharp twist
like taking a jar top off

Reprinted from *Selected Poems, 1965–1975*, (1976), by permission of Houghton Mifflin Company.

and it is a living
skeleton, mine, round,
that lies on the plate before me

red as a pomegranate,
every cell a hot light.

III

I circle, confront
my opponent. The thing

refuses to be shaped, it moves
like yeast. I thrust,

the thing fights back.
It dissolves, growls, grows crude claws;

The air is dusty with blood.

It springs. I cut
with delicate precision.

The specimens
ranged on the shelves, applaud.

The thing falls Thud. A cat
anatomized.

O secret
form of the heart, now I have you.

IV

Now I shall ornament you.
What would you like?

Baroque scrolls on your ankles?
A silver navel?

I am the universal weaver;
I have eight fingers.

I complicate you;
I surround you with intricate ropes.

What web shall I wrap you in?
Gradually I pin you down.

What equation shall
I carve and seal in your skull?

What size will I make you?
Where should I put your eyes?

V

I was insane with skill:
I made you perfect.

I should have chosen instead
to curl you small as a seed,

trusted beginnings. Now I wince
before this plateful of results:

core and rind, the flesh between
already turning rotten.

I stand in the presence
of the destroyed god:

a rubble of tendons,
knuckles and raw sinews.

Knowing that the work is mine
how can I love you?

These archives of potential
time exude fear like a smell.

VI

You arise, larval
and shrouded in the flesh I gave you;

I, who have no covering
left but a white cloth skin

escape from you. You are red,
you are human and distorted.

You have been starved,
you are hungry. I have nothing to feed you.

I pull around me, running,
a cape of rain.

What was my ravenous motive?
Why did I make you?

VII

Reflection, you have stolen
everything you needed:

my joy, my ability
to suffer.

You have transmuted
yourself to me: I am
a vestige, I am numb.

Now you accuse me of murder.

Can't you see
I am incapable?

Blood of my brain,
it is you who have killed these people.

VIII

Since I dared
to attempt impious wonders

I must pursue
that animal I once denied
was mine.

Over this vacant winter
plain, the sky is a black shell;
I move within it, a cold
kernel of pain.

I scratch huge rescue messages
on the solid
snow; in vain. My heart's
husk is a stomach. I am its food.

IX

The sparkling monster
gambols there ahead,
his mane electric:
This is his true place.

He dances in spirals on the ice,
his clawed feet
kindling shaggy fires.

His happiness
is now the chase itself:
he traces it in light,
his paths contain it.

I am the gaunt hunter
necessary for his patterns,
lurking, gnawing leather.

X

The creature, his arctic hackles
bristling, spreads
over the dark ceiling,
his paws on the horizons,
rolling the world like a snowball.

He glows and says:

Doctor, my shadow
shivering on the table,
you dangle on the leash
of your own longing;
your need grows teeth.

You sliced me loose

and said it was
Creation. I could feel the knife.
Now you would like to heal
that chasm in your side,
but I recede. I prowl.

I will not come when you call.

Roland Barthes

Roland Barthes (1915–1980) was a French social and literary critic whose work has had a great impact on how scholars in the humanities and social sciences approach their subjects. For example, Barthes's claimed that the starting point for literary analysis should not be value judgments and examinations of the author's intentions, the time-honored approach to texts, but rather should be an investigation of the system of signs of which the text is constructed. This underlying structure, then, forms the 'meaning of the work as a whole'. In "The Brain of Einstein," from a collection of short essays called Mythologies, *Barthes plays with traditional hierarchies in examining popular culture using the tools of literary criticism. After a lifetime full of such challenges to traditional thinking, Barthes died unexpectedly in 1980 in a street accident in Paris.*

The Brain of Einstein

Einstein's brain is a mythical object: paradoxically, the greatest intelligence of all provides an image of the most up-to-date machine, the man who is too powerful is removed from psychology, and introduced into a world of robots; as is well known, the supermen of science-fiction always have something reified about them. So has Einstein: he is commonly signified by his brain, which is like an object for anthologies, a true museum exhibit. Perhaps because of his mathematical specialization, superman is here divested of every magical character; no diffuse power in him, no mystery other than mechanical: he is a superior, a prodigious organ, but a real, even a physiological one. Mythologically, Einstein is matter, his power does not spontaneously draw one towards the spiritual, it needs the help of an independent morality, a reminder about the scientist's 'conscience' (*Science without conscience,* they said . . .).

Einstein himself has to some extent been a party to the legend by bequeathing his brain, for the possession of which two hospitals are still fighting as if it were an unusual piece of machinery which it will at last be possible to dismantle. A photograph shows him lying down, his head bristling with electric wires: the waves of his brain are being recorded, while he is requested to 'think of relativity'. (But for that matter, what does 'to think of' mean, exactly?) What this is meant to convey is probably that the seismograms will be all the more violent since 'relativity' is an arduous subject. Thought itself is thus represented as an energetic material, the

Reprinted from *Mythologies*, translated by Annette Lavers, (1972), Doubleday, a division of Random House.

measurable product of a complex (quasi-electrical) apparatus which transforms cerebral substance into power. The mythology of Einstein shows him as a genius so lacking in magic that one speaks about his thought as of a functional labour analogous to the mechanical making of sausages, the grinding of corn or the crushing of ore: he used to produce thought, continuously, as a mill makes flour, and death was above all, for him, the cessation of a localized function: *'the most powerful brain of all has stopped thinking'*.

What this machine of genius was supposed to produce was equations. Through the mythology of Einstein, the world blissfully regained the image of knowledge reduced to a formula. Paradoxically, the more the genius of the man was materialized under the guise of his brain, the more the product of his inventiveness came to acquire a magical dimension, and gave a new incarnation to the old esoteric image of a science entirely contained in a few letters. There is a single secret to the world, and this secret is held in one word; the universe is a safe of which humanity seeks the combination: Einstein almost found it, this is the myth of Einstein. In it, we find all the Gnostic themes: the unity of nature, the ideal possibility of a fundamental reduction of the world, the unfastening power of the word, the age-old struggle between a secret and an utterance, the idea that total knowledge can only be discovered all at once, like a lock which suddenly opens after a thousand unsuccessful attempts. The historic equation $E = mc^2$, by its unexpected simplicity, almost embodies the pure idea of the key, bare, linear, made of one metal, opening with a wholly magical ease a door which had resisted the desperate efforts of centuries. Popular imagery faithfully expresses this: *photographs* of Einstein show him standing next to a blackboard covered with mathematical signs of obvious complexity; but *cartoons* of Einstein (the sign that he has become a legend) show him chalk still in hand, and having just written on an empty blackboard, as if without preparation, the magic formula of the world. In this way mythology shows an awareness of the nature of the various tasks: research proper brings into play clockwork-like mechanisms and has its seat in a wholly material organ which is monstrous only by its cybernetic complication; discovery, on the contrary, has a magical essence, it is simple like a basic element, a principial substance, like the philosophers' stone of hermetists, tar-water for Berkeley, or oxygen for Schelling.

But since the world is still going on, since research is proliferating, and on the other hand since God's share must be preserved, some failure on the part of Einstein is necessary: Einstein died, it is said, without having been able to verify *'the equation in which the secret of the world was enclosed'*. So in the end the world resisted; hardly opened, the secret closed again, the code was incomplete. In this way Einstein fulfills all the conditions of myth, which could not care less about contradictions so long as it establishes a euphoric security: at once magician and machine, eternal researcher and unfulfilled discoverer, unleashing the best and the worst, brain and conscience. Einstein embodies the most contradictory dreams, and mythically reconciles the infinite power of man over nature with the 'fatality' of the sacrosanct, which man cannot yet do without.

Rick DeMarinis

At the age of 30 Rick DeMarinis (b. 1937) began to devote his time to writing, but was not published until the age of 40. A well-known poet Richard Hugo, who had been a technical writer at Boeing, taught him writing. From this teacher DeMarinis learned to "look at the fundamental atoms and molecules of writing." DeMarinis has himself taught English at the University of El Paso and at the University of Montana. The numerous prizes DeMarinis has won for his novels and short story collections evince his deep understanding of the craft of writing. The following story, "Weeds," is from an award winning (Drue Heinz Literature Prize) collection of short stories Under the Wheat *(1986). Dark humor is a notable characteristic of DeMarinis's fiction, which is evident in his critically acclaimed novel* The Burning Women of the Far Cry *(1986). While "Weeds" exhibits the darkly comic aspect of DeMarinis' fiction, it is also a fable about the triumph of the environment over humans and the chemicals they use to make the environment docile.*

Weeds

A black helicopter flapped out of the morning sun and dumped its sweet orange mist on our land instead of the Parley farm where it was intended. It was weed-killer, something strong enough to wipe out leafy spurge, knapweed and Canadian thistle, but it made us sick.

My father had a fatal stroke a week after that first spraying. I couldn't hold down solid food for nearly a month and went from 200 pounds to 170 in that time. Mama went to bed and slept for two days, and when she woke up she was not the same. She'd lost something of herself in that long sleep, and something that wasn't herself had replaced it.

Then it hit the animals. We didn't have much in the way of animals, but one by one they dropped. The chickens, the geese, the two old mules—Doc and Rex—and last of all, our only cow, Miss Milky, who was more or less the family pet.

Miss Milky was the only animal that didn't outright up and die. She just got sick. There was blood in her milk and her milk was thin. Her teats got so tender and brittle that she would try to mash me against the milk stall wall when I pulled at them. The white part of her eyes looked like fresh red meat. Her piss was so strong that the green grass whenever she stood died off. She got so bound up that

---

Reprinted from *Under the Wheat*, (1986), by permission of University of Pittsburgh.

when she'd lift her tail and bend with strain, only one black apple would drop. Her breath took on a burning sulphurous stink that would make you step back.

She also went crazy. She'd stare at me like she all at once had a desperate human mind and had never seen me before. Then she'd act as if she wanted to slip a horn under my ribs and peg me to the barn. She would drop her head and charge, blowing like a randy bull, and I would have to scramble out of the way. Several times I saw her gnaw on her hooves or stand stock-still in water up to her blistered teats. Or she would walk backward all day long, mewling like a lost cat that had been dropped off in a strange place. That mewling was enough to make you want to clap a set of noise dampers on your ears. The awful sound led Mama to say this: "It's the death song of the land, mark my words."

Mama never talked like that before in her life. She'd always been a cheerful woman who could never see the bad part of anything that was at least fifty percent good. But now she was dark and strange as a gypsy, and she would have spells of sheer derangement during which she'd make noises like a wild animal, or she'd play the part of another person—the sort of person she'd normally have nothing to do with at all. At Daddy's funeral, she got dressed up in an old and tattered evening gown the color of beet juice, her face painted and powdered like that of a barfly. And while the preacher told the onlookers what a fine man Daddy had been, Mama cupped her hands under her breasts and lifted them high, as if offering to appease a dangerous stranger. Then, ducking her head, she chortled, "Loo, loo, loo," her scared eyes scanning the trees for owls.

I was twenty-eight years old and my life had come to nothing. I'd had a girl but I'd lost her through neglect and a careless attitude that had spilled over into my personal life, souring it. I had no ambition to make something worthwhile of myself, and it nettled her. Toward the end, she began to parrot her mother: "You need to get yourself *established,* Jack," she would say. But I didn't want to get myself established. I was getting poorer and more aimless day by day, and I supposed she believed that "getting established" would put a stop to the downhill slide, but I had no desire to do whatever it took to accomplish that.

Shortly after Daddy died, the tax man came to our door with a paper in his hand. "Inheritance tax," he said, handing me the paper.

"What do you mean?" I asked.

"It's the law," he said. "Your father died, you see. And that's going to cost you some. You should have made better plans." He tapped his forehead with his finger and winked. He had a way of expressing himself that made me think he was country born and raised but wanted to seem citified. Or maybe it was the other way around.

"I don't understand this," I mumbled. I felt the weight of a world I'd so far been able to avoid. It was out there, tight-assed and squinty-eyed, and it knew to the dollar and dime what it needed to keep itself in business.

"Simple," he said. "Pay or move off. The government is the government, and it can't bend a rule to accommodate the confused. It's your decision. Pay or the next step is litigation."

He smiled when he said good-bye. I closed the door against the weight of his smile, which was the weight of the world. I went to a window and watched him head back to his green government car. The window was open and I could hear him. He was singing loudly in a fine tenor voice. He raised his right hand to hush an invisible audience that had broken into uncontrolled applause. I could still hear him singing as he slipped the car into gear and idled away. He was singing "Red River Valley."

Even though the farm was all ours, paid up in full, we had to give the government $7,000 for the right to stay on it. The singing tax man said we had inherited the land from my father, and the law was sharp on the subject.

I didn't know where the money was going to come from. I didn't talk it over with Mama because even in her better moments she would talk in riddles. To a simple question such as, "Should I paint the barns this year, Mama?" she might answer, "I've no eyes for glitter, nor ears for their ridicule."

One day I decided to load Miss Milky into the stock trailer and haul her into Saddle Butte where the vet, Doc Nevers, had his office. Normally, Doc Nevers would come out to your place, but he'd heard about the spraying that was going on and said he wouldn't come within three miles of our property until they were done.

The Parley farm was being sprayed regularly, for they grew an awful lot of wheat and almost as much corn, and they had the biggest haying operation in the county. Often, the helicopters they used were upwind from us and we were sprayed too. ("Don't complain," said Big Pete Parley when I called him up about it. "Think of it this way—you're getting your place weeded for *free*!" When I said I might have to dynamite some stumps on the property line and that he might get a barn or two blown away for free, he just laughed like hell, as if I had told one of the funniest jokes he'd ever heard.)

There was a good windbreak between our places, a thick grove of lombardy poplars, but the orange mist, sweet as a flower garden in full bloom, sifted through the trees and settled on our fields. Soon the poplars were mottled and dying. Some branches curled in an upward twist, as if flexed in pain, and others became soft and fibrous as if the wood were trying to turn itself into sponge.

With Miss Milky in the trailer, I sat in the truck sipping on a pint of Lewis and Clark bourbon and looking out across our unplanted fields. It was late—almost too late—to plant anything. Mama, in the state she was in, hadn't even noticed.

In the low hills on the north side of the property, some ugly looking things were growing. From the truck, they looked like white pimples on the smooth brown hill. Up close, they were big as melons. They were some kind of fungus, and they pushed up through the ground like the bald heads of fat babies. They gave off a rotten meat stink. I would get chillbumps just looking at them, and if I touched one, my stomach would rise. The bulbous heads had purple streaks on them that looked like blood vessels. I half expected to one day see human eyes clear the dirt and open. Big pale eyes that would see me and carry my image down to their deepest root. I was glad they seemed to prefer the hillside and bench and not the bottom land.

Justified or not, I blamed the growth of this fungus on the poison spray, just as I blamed it for the death of my father, the loss of our animals, and the strangeness of my mother. Now the land itself was becoming strange. And I thought, what about me? How am I being rearranged by that weedkiller?

I guess I should have gotten mad, but I didn't. Maybe I *had* been changed by the spray. Where once I had been a quick-to-take-offense hothead, I was now docile and thoughtful. I could sit on a stump and think for hours, enjoying the slow and complicated intertwinings of my own thoughts. Even though I felt sure the cause of all our troubles had fallen out of the sky, I would hold arguments with myself, as if there were always two sides to every question. If I said to myself, "Big Pete Parley has poisoned my family and farm and my father is dead because of it," I would follow it up with, "But Daddy was old anyway, past seventy-five, and he always had high blood pressure. Anything could have set off his stroke, from a wasp bite to a sonic boom."

"And what about Mama?" I would ask. "Senile with grief," came the quick answer, "Furthermore, Daddy himself used poison in his time. Cyanide traps for coyotes, DDT for mosquito larvae, arsenic for rats."

My mind was always doubling back on itself in this way, and it would often leave me standing motionless in a field for hours, paralyzed with indecision, sighing like a moonstruck girl of twelve. I imagined myself mistaken by passersby for a scarecrow.

Sometimes I saw myself as a human weed, useless to other people in general and maybe harmful in some weedy way. The notion wasn't entirely unpleasant. Jack Hucklebone: a weed among the well-established money crops of life.

On my way to town with Miss Milky, I crossed over the irrigation ditch my father had fallen into with the stroke that killed him. I pulled over onto the shoulder and switched off the engine. It was a warm, insect-loud day in early June. A spray of grasshoppers clattered over the hood of the truck. June bugs ticked past the windows like little flying clocks. The thirteen-year locusts were back and raising a whining hell. I was fifteen the last time they came, but I didn't remember them arriving in such numbers. I expected more helicopters to come flapping over with special sprays meant just for them, even though they would be around for only a few weeks and the damage they would do is not much more than measurable. But anything that looks like it might have an appetite for a money crop brings down the spraying choppers. I climbed out of the truck and looked up into the bright air. A lone jet, eastbound, too high to see or hear, left its neat chalk line across the top of the sky. The sky itself was like hot blue wax, north to south. A giant hammerhead sat on the west horizon as if it were a creamy oblong planet gone dangerously off-course.

There's where Daddy died. Up the ditch about fifty yards from here. I found him, buckled, white as paper, half under water. His one good eye, his right (he'd lost the left one thirty years ago when a tractor tire blew up in his face as he was filling it), was above water and wide open, staring at his hand as if it could focus on the thing it gripped. He was holding on to a root. He had big hands, strong, with fingers like thick hardwood dowels, but now they were soft and puffy, like the hands of a giant baby. Water bugs raced against the current toward him. His body blocked the ditch and little eddies swirled around it. The water bugs skated into the eddies and, fighting to hold themselves still in the roiling current, touched his face. They held still long enough to satisfy their curiosity, then slid back into the circular flow as if bemused by the strangeness of dead human flesh.

I started to cry, remembering it, thinking about him in the water, he had been so sure and strong, but then—true to my changed nature—I began to laugh at the memory, for his wide blue eye had had a puzzled cast to it, as if it had never before seen such a crazy thing as the ordinary root in his forceless hand. It was an expression he never wore in life.

"It was only a weed, Daddy," I said, wiping the tears from my face.

The amazed puzzlement stayed in his eye until I brushed down the lid.

Of course he had been dead beyond all talk and puzzlement. Dead when I found him, dead for hours, bloated dead. And this is how *I've* come to be—blame the spray or don't: the chores don't get done on time, the unplanted fields wait, Mama wanders in her mind, and yet I'll sit in the shade of my truck sipping on Lewis and Clark bourbon, inventing the thoughts of a stone-dead man.

Time bent away from me like a tail-dancing rainbow. It was about to slip the hook. I wasn't trying to hold it. Try to hold it and it gets all the more slippery. Try to let it go and it sticks like a cocklebur to cotton. I was drifting somewhere between the two kinds of not trying: not trying to hold anything, not trying to let anything go.

Then he sat down next to me. The old man.

"You got something for me?" he said.

He was easily the homeliest man I had ever seen. His bald head was bullet-shaped and his lumpy nose was warty as a crookneck squash. His little, close-set eyes sat on either side of that nose like hard black beans. He had shaggy eyebrows that climbed upward in a white and wiry tangle. There was a blue lump in the middle of his forehead the size of a pullet's egg, and his hairy ear lobes touched his grimy collar. He was mumbling something, but it could have been the noise of the ditch water as it sluiced through the culvert under the road.

He stank of whiskey and dung, and looked like he'd been sleeping behind barns for weeks. His clothes were rags, and he was caked with dirt from fingernail to jaw. His shoes were held together with strips of burlap. He untied some of these strips and took off the shoes, Then he slid his gnarled, dirt-crusted feet into the water. His eyes fluttered shut and he let out a hissing moan of pleasure. His toes were long and twisted, the arthritic knuckles painfully bright. They reminded me of the surface roots of a stunted oak that had been trying to grow in hardpan. Though he was only about five feet tall, his feet were huge. Easy size twelves, wide as paddles.

He quit mumbling, cleared his throat, spit. "You got something for me?" he said.

I handed him my pint. He took it, then held it up to the sunlight and looked through the rusty booze as if testing for its quality.

"If it won't do," I said, "I could run into town to get something a little smoother for you. Maybe you'd like some Canadian Club or some twelve-year-old Scotch. I could run into town and be back in less than an hour. Maybe you'd like me to bring back a couple of fried chickens and a sack of buttered rolls." This was my old self talking, the hothead. But I didn't feel mad at him, and was just being mouthy out of habit.

"No need to do that," he said, as if my offer had been made in seriousness. He took a long pull off my pint. "This snake piss is just fine by me, son." He raised the bottle to the sunlight again, squinted through it.

I wandered down the ditch again to the place where Daddy died. There was nothing there to suggest a recent dead man had blocked the current. Everything was as it always was. The water surged, the quick water bugs skated up and down, inspecting brown dumps of algae along the banks; underwater weeds waved like slim snakes whose tails had been staked to the mud. I looked for the thistle he'd grabbed on to. I guess he thought that he was going to save himself from drowning by hanging on to its root, not realizing that the killing flood was *inside* his head. But there were many roots along the bank and none of them seemed more special than any other.

Something silver glinted at me. It was a coin. I picked it out of the slime and polished it against my pants. It was a silver dollar, a real one. It could have been his. He carried a few of the old cartwheels around with him for luck. The heft and gleam of the old solid silver coin choked me up.

I walked back to the old man. He had stuffed his bindle under his head for a pillow and had dozed off. I uncapped the pint and finished it, then flipped it into the weeds. It hit a rock and popped. The old man grunted and his eyes snapped open. He let out a barking snort, and his black eyes darted around him fiercely, like the eyes of a burrow animal caught in a daylight trap. Then, remembering where he was, he calmed down.

"You got something for me?" he asked. He pushed himself up to a sitting position. It was a struggle for him.

"Not any more," I said. I sat down next to him. Then, from behind us, a deep groan cut loose. It sounded like siding being pried off an old barn with a crowbar. We both turned to look at whatever had complained so mightily.

It was Miss Milky, up in the trailer, venting her misery. I'd forgotten about her. Horseflies were biting her. Her red eyes peered sadly out at us through the bars. The corners of her eyes were swollen, giving her a Chinese look.

With no warning at all, a snapping hail fell on us. Only it wasn't hail. It was a moving cloud of thirteen-year locusts. They darkened the air and they covered us. The noise was like static on the radio, miles of static across the bug-peppered sky, static that could drown out all important talk and idle music, no matter how powerful the station.

The old man's face was covered with the bugs and he was saying something to me, but I couldn't make out what it was. His mouth opened and closed, opened and closed. When it opened, he'd have to brush away the locusts from his lips. They were like ordinary grasshoppers, only smaller, and they had big red eyes that seemed to glow with their own hellish light. Then, as fast as they had come, they were gone, scattered back into the fields. A few hopped here and there, but the main cloud had broken up.

I just sat there, brushing at the fingering feel of them on my skin and trying to readjust myself to uncluttered air, but my ears were still crackling with their racket.

The old man pulled at my sleeve, breaking me out of my daydream or trance. "You got something for me?" he asked.

I felt blue. Worse than blue. Sick. I felt incurable—ridden with the pointlessness of just about everything you could name. The farm struck me as a pointless wonder, and I found the idea depressing and fearsome. Pointless bugs lay waiting in the fields for the pointless crops as the pointless days and seasons ran on and on into the pointless forever.

"Shit," I said.

"I'll take that worthless cow off your hands, then," said the old man. "She's done for. All you have to do is look at her."

"No shit," I said.

He didn't seem so old or so wrecked to me now. He was younger and bigger, somehow, as if all his clocks had started spinning backwards, triggered by the locust cloud. He stood up. He looked thick across the shoulders like he'd done hard work all his life and could still do it. He showed me his right hand and it was yellow with hard calluses. His beady black eyes were quick and lively in their shallow sockets. The blue lump on his forehead glinted in the sun. It seemed deliberately polished, as if it were an ornament. He took a little silver bell out of his pocket and rang it for no reason at all.

"Let me have her," he said.

"You want Miss Milky?" I asked. I felt weak and childish. Maybe I was drunk. My scalp itched and I scratched it hard. He rang his little silver bell again. I wanted to have it, but he put it back into his pocket. Then he knelt down and opened his bindle. He took out a paper sack.

I looked inside. It was packed with seeds of some kind. I ran my fingers through them and did not feel foolish. I heard a helicopter putt-putting in the distance. In defense of what I did, let me say this much: I knew Miss Milky was done for. Doc Nevers would have told me to kill her. I don't think she was even good for hamburger. Old cow meat can sometimes make good hamburger, but Miss Milky looked wormy and lean. And I wouldn't have trusted her bones for soup. The poison that had wasted her flesh and ruined her udder had probably settled in her marrow.

And so I unloaded my dying cow. He took out his silver bell again and tied it to a piece of string. He tied the string around Miss Milky's neck. Then he led her away. She was docile and easy, as though this was exactly the way things were supposed to turn out.

My throat was dry. I felt too tired to move. I watched their slow progress down the path that ran along the ditch. They got smaller and smaller in the field until, against a dark hedge of box elders, they disappeared. I strained to see after them, but it was as if the earth had given them refuge, swallowing them into its deep, loamy, composting interior. The only sign that they still existed in the world was the tinkling of the silver bell he had tied around Miss Milky's neck. It was a pure sound, naked on the air.

Then a breeze opened a gap in the box elders and a long blade of sunlight pierced through them, illuminating and magnifying the old man and his cow, as if the air between us had formed itself into a giant lens, The breeze let up and the box elders shut off the sun again, and I couldn't see anything but a dense quiltwork of black and green shadows out of which a raven big as an eagle flapped. It cawed in raucous good humor as it veered over my head.

I went on into town anyway, cow or no cow, and hit some bars. I met a girl from the East in the Hobble who thought I was a cowboy and I didn't try to correct her mistaken impression, for it proved to be a free pass to good times.

When I got home, Mama had company. She was dressed up in her beet juice gown, and her face was powdered white. Her dark lips looked like a wine stain in snow. But her clear blue eyes were direct and calm. There was no distraction in them.

"Hi boy," said the visitor. It was Big Pete Parley. He was wearing a blue suit, new boots, a gray felt Stetson. He had a toothy grin on his fat red face.

I looked at Mama. "What's *he* want?" I asked.

"Mr. Parley is going to help us, Jackie," she said.

"What's going on, Mama?" I asked. Something was wrong. I could feel it but I couldn't see it. It was Mama, the way she was carrying herself maybe, or the look in her eyes and her whitened skin. Maybe she had gone all the way insane. She went over to Parley and sat next to him on the davenport. She had slit her gown and it fell away from her thigh, revealing the veiny flesh.

"We're going to be married," she said. "Pete's tired of being a widower. He wants a warm bed."

As if to confirm it was no fantasy dreamed up by her senile mind, Big Pete slipped his meaty hand into the slit dress and squeezed her thigh. He clicked his teeth and winked at me.

"Pete knows how to operate a farm," said Mama. "And you do not, Jackie." She didn't intend for it to sound mean or critical. It was just a statement of the way things were. I couldn't argue with her.

I went into the kitchen. Mama followed me in. I opened a beer. "I don't mean to hurt your feelings, Jackie," she said.

"He's scheming to get our land," I said. "He owns half the county, but it isn't enough."

"No," she said. "I'm the one who's scheming. I'm scheming for my boy who does not grasp the rudiments of the world."

I had the sack of seed with me. I realized that I'd been rattling them nervously.

"What do you have there?" she asked, narrowing her eyes.

"Seeds," I said.

"Seeds? What seeds? Who gave you seeds? Where'd you get them?"

I thought it best not to mention where I'd gotten them. "Big Pete Parley doesn't want to marry *you,*" I said. It was a mean thing to say, and I wanted to say it.

Mama sighed. "It doesn't matter what he wants, Jack. I'm dead anyway." She took the bag of seeds from me, picked some up, squinted at them.

"What is that supposed to mean?" I said, sarcastically.

She went to the window above the sink and stared out into the dark. Under the folds of her evening gown, I could see the ruined shape of her old body. "Dead, Jack," she said. "I've been dead for a while now. Maybe you didn't notice."

"No," I said. "I didn't."

"Well, you should have. I went to sleep shortly after your Daddy died and I had a dream. The dream got stronger and stronger as it went on until it was as vivid as real life itself. More vivid. When I woke up I knew that I had died. I also knew that nothing in the world would ever be as real to me as that dream."

I almost asked her what the dream was about, but I didn't, out of meanness. In the living room Big Pete Parley was whistling impatiently. The davenport was squeaking under his nervous weight.

"So, you see, Jackie," said Mama. "It doesn't matter if I marry Pete Parley or what his motives are in this matter. You are all that counts now. He will ensure your success in the world."

"I don't want to be a success, Mama," I said.

"Well, you have no choice. You cannot gainsay the dead."

She opened the window and dumped out the sack of seeds. Then Big Pete Parley came into the kitchen. "Let's go for a walk," he said. "It's too blame hot in this house."

They left by the kitchen door. I watched them walk across the yard and into the dark, unplanted field. Big Pete had his arm around Mama's shoulder. I wondered if he knew, or cared, that he was marrying a dead woman. Light from the half-moon painted their silhouettes for a while. Then the dark field absorbed them.

I went to bed and slept for what might have been days. In my long sleep I had a dream. I was canoeing down a whitewater river that ran sharply uphill. The farther up I got, the rougher the water became. Finally, I had to beach the canoe. I proceeded on foot until I came to a large gray house that had been built in a wilderness forest. The house was empty and quiet. I went in. It was clean and beautifully furnished. Nobody was home. I called out a few times before I understood that silence was a rule. I went from room to room, going deeper and deeper toward some dark interior place. I understood that I was involved in a search. The longer I searched, the more vivid the dream became.

When I woke up I was stiff and weak. Mama wasn't in the house. I made a pot of coffee and took a cup outside. Under the kitchen window there was a patch of green shoots that had not been there before. "You got something for me?" I said.

A week later that patch of green shoots had grown and spread. They were weeds. The worst kind of weeds I had ever seen. Thick, spiny weeds, with broad green leaves tough as leather. They rolled away from the house, out across the fields, in a viny carpet. Mean, deep-rooted weeds, too mean to uproot by hand. When I tried, I came away with a palm full of cuts.

In another week they were tall as corn. They were fast growers and I could not see where they ended. They covered everything in sight. A smothering blanket of deep green sucked the life out of every other growing thing. They crossed fences, irrigation ditches, and when they reached the trees of a windbreak, they became ropy crawlers that wrapped themselves around trunks and limbs.

When they reached the Parley farm, over which my dead mother now presided, they were attacked by squadrons of helicopters which drenched them in poisons, the best poisons chemical science knew how to brew. But the poisons only seemed to make the weeds grow faster, and after a spraying the new growths were tougher, thornier, and more determined than ever to dominate the land.

Some of the weeds sent up long woody stalks. On top of these stalks were heavy seedpods, fat as melons. The strong stalks pushed the pods high into the air.

The day the pods cracked, a heavy wind came up. The wind raised black clouds of seed in grainy spirals that reached the top of the sky, then scattered them, far and wide, across the entire nation.

Alison Hawthorne Deming

Connecticut born and raised, Alison Hawthorne Deming (b.1946) now makes her home in Tucson, Arizona. Currently she is an Associate Professor in Creative Writing at the University of Arizona. Deming attended Vermont College, where she received her MFA in 1983. She was awarded the Wallace Stegner Fellowship at Stanford University from 1987 to 1988. In Provincetown, she was a poetry Fellow from 1984–1985 at the Fine Arts Work Center. Among the multitude of awards Deming has received for her work is the prestigious Walt Whitman Award of the Academy of American Poets for her 1994 collection Science and Other Poems, *from which the following poem comes. She has earned two fellowships from the National Endowment for the Arts (1990 and 1995) for her writing. Deming has also won the Bayer Award in science writing for a creative nonfiction essay "Poetry and Science: A View from the Divide," which is reproduced in* The University Book: An Anthology of Writings From the University of Arizona. *Like Pattiann Rogers, whose poem appears later in this chapter, Deming (a direct descendant of Nathaniel Hawthorne) emphasizes the importance of making connections to the natural world in order to foster spiritual well-being. "Science" explores the childhood optimism reflected in entries for a science fair.*

Science

Then it was the future, though what's arrived
isn't what we had in mind, all chrome and
cybernetics, when we set up exhibits
in the cafeteria for the judges
to review what we'd made of our hypotheses.

The class skeptic (he later refused to sign
anyone's yearbook, calling it a sentimental
degradation of language) chloroformed mice,
weighing the bodies before and after
to catch the weight of the soul,

wanting to prove the invisible
real as a bagful of nails. A girl
who knew it all made cookies from euglena,

Reprinted from *Science and Other Poems*, (1994), Louisiana State University Press.

a one-celled compromise between animal and plant,
she had cultured in a flask.

We're smart enough, she concluded,
to survive our mistakes, showing photos of farmland,
poisoned, gouged, eroded. No one believed
he really had built it when a kid no one knew
showed up with an atom smasher, confirming that

the tiniest particles could be changed
into something even harder to break.
And one whose mother had cancer (hard to admit now,
it was me) distilled the tar of cigarettes
to paint it on the backs of shaven mice.

She wanted to know what it took,
a little vial of sure malignancy,
to prove a daily intake smaller
than a single aspirin could finish
something as large as a life. I thought of this

because, today, the dusky seaside sparrow
became extinct. It may never be as famous
as the pterodactyl or the dodo,
but the last one died today, a resident
of Walt Disney World where now its tissue samples

lie frozen, in case someday we learn to clone
one from a few cells. Like those instant dinosaurs
that come in a gelatin capsule—just add water
and they inflate. One other thing this
brings to mind. The euglena girl won first prize

both for science and, I think, in retrospect, for hope.

Nathaniel Hawthorne

With ancestral roots firmly planted in New England, Nathaniel Hawthorne's 1804 birth in Salem, Massachusetts marks a significant event in the creation of the American canon of literature. Almost two centuries after his first ancestors appeared in New England, Hawthorne was to write stories that were inspired by the subject matter of their lives, including a magistrate who presided over the witch trials of 1692 and a grandfather who was a heroic privateer during the Revolution. Although Hawthorne had a difficult beginning as an author (he attempted to destroy as many copies of his first published novel Fanshawe *as possible), eventually he was to be honored by his contemporaries. In a review of his earlier tales, Melville praises Hawthorne's American originality and freedom from European models, saying, "And now, my countrymen, as an excellent author of your own flesh and blood—. . . whom better can I commend to you, in the first place, than Nathaniel Hawthorne." In a number of his works, Hawthorne was preoccupied with the moral implications of science, portraying scientists as men who are driven to benefit humanity, but ultimately doomed because of an obsession with perfection. One of these works is "The Birthmark," originally published in the* Pioneer *in 1843. Hawthorne's attitude toward science was colored by the rapid rise of new experimental and empirical methods in the nineteenth century, which seemed to challenge conventional ways of understanding the physical world.*

The Birthmark

In the latter part of the last century, there lived a man of science—an eminent proficient in every branch of natural philosophy—who, not long before our story opens, had made experience of a spiritual affinity, more attractive than any chemical one. He had left his laboratory to the care of an assistant, cleared his fine countenance from the furnace-smoke, washed the stain of acids from his fingers, and persuaded a beautiful woman to become his wife. In those days, when the comparatively recent discovery of electricity, and other kindred mysteries of nature, seemed to open paths into the region of miracle, it was not unusual for the love of science to rival the love of woman, in its depth and absorbing energy. The higher intellect, the imagination, the spirit, and even the heart, might all find their congenial aliment in pursuits which, as some of their ardent votaries believed, would ascend from one step of powerful intelligence to another, until the philosopher should lay his hand on the secret of creative force, and perhaps make new worlds for himself. We know not whether Aylmer possessed this degree of faith in man's ultimate control over nature. He had devoted himself, however, too unreservedly to scientific studies, ever to be weaned from them by any second passion. His love for his young wife might prove the stronger of the two; but it could only be by intertwining itself with his love of science, and uniting the strength of the latter to his own.

Such a union accordingly took place, and was attended with truly remarkable consequences, and a deeply impressive moral. One day, very soon after their marriage, Aylmer sat gazing at his wife, with a trouble in his countenance that grew stronger, until he spoke.

"Georgiana," said he, "has it never occurred to you that the mark upon your cheek might be removed?"

"No, indeed," said she, smiling; but perceiving the seriousness of his manner, she blushed deeply. "To tell you the truth, it has been so often called a charm, that I was simple enough to imagine it might be so."

"Ah, upon another face, perhaps it might," replied her husband. "But never on yours! No, dearest Georgiana, you came so nearly perfect from the hand of Nature, that this slightest possible defect—which we hesitate whether to term a defect or a beauty—shocks me, as being the visible mark of earthly imperfection."

"Shocks you, my husband!" cried Georgiana, deeply hurt; at first reddening with momentary anger, but then bursting into tears. "Then why did you take me from my mother's side? You cannot love what shocks you!"

To explain this conversation, it must be mentioned, that, in the centre of Georgiana's left cheek, there was a singular mark, deeply interwoven, as it were, with the texture and substance of her face. In the usual state of her complexion,—a healthy though delicate bloom,—the mark wore a tint of deeper crimson, which imperfectly defined its shape amid the surrounding rosiness. When she blushed, it gradually became more indistinct, and finally vanished amid the triumphant rush of blood, that bathed the whole cheek with its brilliant glow. But, if any shifting motion caused her to turn pale, there was the mark again, a crimson stain upon the snow, in what Aylmer sometimes deemed an almost fearful distinctness. Its shape bore not a little similarity to the human hand, though of the smallest pygmy size. Georgiana's lovers were wont to say, that some fairy, at her birth-hour, had laid her tiny hand upon the infant's cheek, and left this impress there, in token of the magic endowments that were to give her such sway over all hearts. Many a desperate swain would have risked life for the privilege of pressing his lips to the mysterious hand. It must not be concealed, however, that the impression wrought by this fairy sign-manual varied exceedingly, according to the difference of temperament in the beholders. Some fastidious persons—but they were exclusively of her own sex—affirmed that the Bloody Hand, as they chose to call it, quite destroyed the effect of Georgiana's beauty, and rendered her countenance even hideous. But it would be as reasonable to say, that one of those small blue stains, which sometimes occur in the purest statuary marble, would convert the Eve of Powers to a monster. Masculine observers, if the birth-mark did not heighten their admiration, contented themselves with wishing it away, that the world might possess one living specimen of ideal loveliness, without the semblance of a flaw. After his marriage—for he thought little or nothing of the matter before—Aylmer discovered that this was the case with himself.

Had she been less beautiful—if Envy's self could have found aught else to sneer at—he might have felt his affection heightened by the prettiness of this mimic hand, now vaguely portrayed, now lost, now stealing forth again, and glimmering to-and-fro with every pulse of emotion that throbbed within her heart. But, seeing her otherwise so perfect, he found this one defect grow more and more intolerable, with every moment of their united lives. It was the fatal flaw of humanity, which Nature, in one shape or another, stamps ineffaceably on all her productions, either to imply that they are temporary and finite, or that their perfection must be wrought by toil and pain. The Crimson Hand expressed the ineludible gripe, in which mortality clutches the highest and purest of earthly mould, degrading them into kindred with the lowest, and even with the very brutes, like whom their visible frames return to dust. In this manner, selecting it as the symbol of his wife's liability to sin, sorrow, decay, and death, Aylmer's somber imagination was not long in rendering the birth-mark a frightful object, causing him more trouble and horror than ever Georgiana's beauty, whether of soul or sense, had given him delight.

At all the seasons which should have been their happiest, he invariably and without intending it—nay, in spite of a purpose to the contrary—reverted to this one disastrous topic. Trifling as it at first appeared, it so connected itself with innumerable trains of thought, and modes of feeling, that it became the central point of all. With the morning twilight, Aylmer opened his eyes upon his wife's face, and recognized the symbol of imperfection; and when they sat together at the evening hearth, his eyes wandered stealthily to her cheek, and beheld, flickering with the blaze of the wood fire, the spectral Hand that wrote mortality, where he would fain have worshiped. Georgiana soon learned to shudder at his gaze. It needed but a glance, with the peculiar expression that his face often wore, to change the roses of her cheek into a deathlike paleness, amid which the Crimson Hand was brought strongly out, like a bas-relief of ruby on the whitest marble.

Late, one night, when the lights were growing dim, so as hardly to betray the stain on the poor wife's cheek, she herself, for the first time, voluntarily took up the subject.

"Do you remember, my dear Aylmer," said she, with a feeble attempt at a smile—"have you any recollection of a dream, last night, about this odious Hand?"

"None!—none whatever!" replied Aylmer, starting; but then he added in a dry, cold tone, affected for the sake of concealing the real depth of his emotion:—"I might well dream of it; for before I fell asleep, it had taken a pretty firm hold of my fancy."

"And you did dream of it," continued Georgiana, hastily; for she dreaded lest a gush of tears should interrupt what she had to say—"A terrible dream! I wonder that you can forget it. Is it possible to forget this one expression?—Reflect, my husband; for by all means I would have you recall that dream."

The mind is in a sad note, when Sleep, the all-involving, cannot confine her specters within the dim region of her sway, but suffers them to break forth, affrighting this actual life with secrets that perchance belong to a deeper one. Aylmer now remembered his dream. He had fancied himself, with his servant Amindab, attempting an operation for the removal of the birth-mark. But the deeper went the knife, the deeper sank the Hand, until at length its tiny grasp appeared to have caught hold of Georgiana's heart; whence, however, her husband was inexorably resolved to cut or wrench it away.

When the dream had shaped itself perfectly in his memory, Aylmer sat in his wife's presence with a guilty feeling. Truth often finds its way to the mind close-muffled in robes of sleep, and then speaks with uncompromising directness of matters in regard to which we practice an unconscious self-deception, during our waking moments. Until now, he had not been aware of the tyrannizing influence acquired by one idea over his mind, and of the lengths which he might find in his heart to go, for the sake of giving himself peace.

"Aylmer," resumed Georgiana, solemnly, "I know not what may be the cost to both of us, to rid me of this fatal birth-mark. Perhaps its removal may cause cureless deformity. Or, it may be, the stain goes as deep as life itself. Again, do we know that there is a possibility, on any terms, of unclasping the firm grip of this little Hand, which was laid upon me before I came into the world?"

"Dearest Georgiana, I have spent much thought upon the subject," hastily interrupted Aylmer—"I am convinced of the perfect practicability of its removal."

"If there be the remotest possibility of it," continued Georgiana, "let the attempt be made, at whatever risk. Danger is nothing to me; for life—while this hateful mark makes me the object of your horror and disgust—life is a burthen which I would fling down with joy. Either remove this dreadful Hand, or take my wretched life! You have deep science! All the world bears witness of it. You have achieved great wonders! Cannot you remove this little, little mark, which I cover with the tips of two small fingers? Is this beyond your power, for the sake of your own peace, and to save your poor wife from madness?"

"Noblest—dearest—tenderest wife!" cried Aylmer, rapturously. "Doubt not my power. I have already given this matter the deepest thought—thought which might almost have enlightened me to create a being less perfect than yourself. Georgiana, you have led me deeper than ever into the heart of science. I feel myself fully competent to render this dear cheek as faultless as its fellow; and then, most beloved, what will be my triumph, when I shall have corrected what Nature left imperfect, in her fairest work! Even Pygmalion, when his sculptured woman assumed life, felt not greater ecstasy than mine will be."

"It is resolved, then," said Georgiana, faintly smiling,—"And, Aylmer, spare me not, though you should find the birth-mark take refuge in my heart at last."

Her husband tenderly kissed her cheek—her right cheek—not that which bore the impress of the Crimson Hand.

The next day, Aylmer apprised his wife of a plan that he had formed, whereby he might have opportunity for the intense thought and constant watchfulness, which the proposed operation would require; while Georgiana, likewise, would enjoy the perfect repose essential to its success. They were to seclude themselves in the extensive apartments occupied by Aylmer as a laboratory, and where, during his toil-some youth, he had made discoveries in the elemental powers of nature, that had roused the admiration of all the learned societies in Europe. Seated calmly in this laboratory, the pale philosopher had investigated the secrets of the highest cloud-region, and of the profoundest mines; he had satisfied himself of the causes that kindled and kept alive the fires of the volcano; and had explained the mystery of fountains, and how it is that they gush forth, some so bright and pure, and others with such rich medicinal virtues, from the dark bosom of the earth. Here, too, at an earlier period, he had studied the wonders of the human frame, and attempted to fathom the very process by which Nature assimilates all her precious influences from earth and air, and from the spiritual world, to create and foster Man, her masterpiece. The latter pursuit, however, Aylmer had long laid aside, in unwilling recognition of the truth, against which all seekers sooner or later stumble, that our great creative Mother, while she amuses us with apparently working in the broadest sunshine, is yet severely careful to keep her own secrets, and, in spite of her pretended openness, shows us nothing but results. She permits us indeed, to mar, but seldom to mend, and, like a jealous patentee, on no account to make. Now, however, Aylmer resumed these half-forgotten investigations; not, of course, with such hopes or wishes as first suggested them; but because they involved such physiological truth, and lay in the path of his proposed scheme for the treatment of Georgiana.

As he led her over the threshold of the laboratory, Georgiana was cold and tremulous. Aylmer looked cheerfully into her face, with intent to reassure her, but was so startled with the intense glow of the birth-mark upon the whiteness of her cheek, that he could not restrain a strong convulsive shudder. His wife fainted.

"Aminadab! Aminadab!" shouted Aylmer, stamping violently on the floor.

Forthwith, there issued from an inner apartment a man of low stature, but bulky frame, with shaggy hair hanging about his visage, which was grimed with the vapors of the furnace. This personage had been Aylmer's under-worker during his whole scientific career, and was admirably fitted for that office by his great mechanical readiness, and the skill with which, while incapable of comprehending a single principle, he executed all the details of his master's experiments. With his vast strength, his shaggy hair, his smoky aspect, and the indescribable earthiness that encrusted him, he seemed to represent man's physical nature; while Aylmer's slender figure, and pale, intellectual face, were no less apt a type of the spiritual element.

"Throw open the door of the boudoir, Aminadab," said Aylmer, "and burn a pastille."

"Yes, master," answered Aminadab, looking intently at the lifeless form of Georgiana; and then he muttered to himself:—"If she were my wife, I'd never part with that birth-mark."

When Georgiana recovered consciousness, she found herself breathing an atmosphere of penetrating fragrance, the gentle potency of which had recalled her from her deathlike faintness. The scene around her looked like enchantment. Aylmer had converted those smoky, dingy, sombre rooms, where he had spent his brightest years in recondite pursuits, into a series of beautiful apartments, not unfit to be the secluded abode of a lovely woman. The walls were hung with gorgeous curtains, which imparted the combination of grandeur and grace, that no other species of adornment can achieve; and as they fell from the ceiling to the floor, their rich and ponderous folds, concealing all angles and straight lines, appeared to shut in the scene from infinite space. For aught Georgiana knew, it might be a pavilion among the clouds. And Aylmer, excluding the sunshine, which would have interfered with his chemical processes, had supplied its place with perfumed lamps, emitting flames of various hue, but all uniting in a soft, empurpled radiance. He now knelt by his wife's side, watching her earnestly, but without alarm; for he was confident in his science, and felt that he could draw a magic circle round her, within which no evil might intrude.

"Where am I?—Ah, I remember!" said Georgiana, faintly; and she placed her hand over her cheek, to hide the terrible mark from her husband's eyes.

"Fear not, dearest!" exclaimed he. "Do not shrink from me! Believe me, Georgiana, I even rejoice in this single imperfection, since it will be such rapture to remove it."

"Oh, spare me!" sadly replied his wife—"Pray do not look at it again. I never can forget that convulsive shudder."

In order to soothe Georgiana, and, as it were, to release her mind from the burden of actual things, Aylmer now put in practice some of the light and playful secrets, which science had taught him among its profounder lore. Airy figures, absolutely bodiless ideas, and forms of unsubstantial beauty, came and danced before her, imprinting their momentary footsteps on beams of light. Though she had some indistinct idea of the method of these optical phenomena, still the illusion was almost perfect enough to warrant the belief, that her husband possessed sway over the spiritual world. Then again, when she felt a wish to look forth from her seclusion, immediately, as if her thoughts were answered, the procession of external existence flitted across a screen. The scenery and the figures of actual life were perfectly represented, but with that bewitching, yet indescribable difference, which always makes a picture, an image, or a shadow, so much more attractive than the original. When wearied of this, Aylmer bade her cast her eyes upon a vessel, containing a quantity of earth. She did so, with little interest at first, but was soon startled, to perceive the germ of a plant, shooting upward from the soil. Then came the slender stalk—the leaves gradually unfolded themselves—and amid them was a perfect and lovely flower.

"It is magical!" cried Georgiana. "I dare not touch it."

"Nay, pluck it," answered Aylmer, "pluck it, and inhale its brief perfume while you may. The flower will wither in a few moments, and leave nothing save its brown seed-vessels—but thence may be perpetuated a race as ephemeral as itself."

But Georgiana had no sooner touched the flower than the whole plant suffered a blight, its leaves turning coal-black, as if by the agency of fire.

"There was too powerful a stimulus," said Aylmer thoughtfully.

To make up for this abortive experiment, he proposed to take her portrait by a scientific process of his own invention. It was to be effected by rays of light striking upon a polished plate of metal. Georgiana assented—but, on looking at the result, was affrighted to find the features of the portrait blurred and indefinable; while the minute figure of a hand appeared where the cheek should have been. Aylmer snatched the metallic plate, and threw it into a jar of corrosive acid.

Soon, however, he forgot these mortifying failures. In the intervals of study and chemical experiment, he came to her, flushed and exhausted, but seemed invigorated by her presence, and spoke in glowing language of the resources of his art. He gave a history of the long dynasty of the Alchemists, who spent so many ages in quest of the universal solvent, by which the Golden Principle might be elicited from all things vile and base. Aylmer appeared to believe, that, by the plainest scientific logic, it was altogether within the limits of possibility to discover this long-sought medium; but, he added, a philosopher who should go deep enough to acquire the power, would attain too lofty a wisdom to stoop to the exercise of it. Not less singular were his opinions in regard to the Elixir Vitæ. He more than intimated, that it was at his option to concoct a liquid that should prolong life for years—perhaps interminably—but that it would produce a discord in nature, which all the world, and chiefly the quaffer of the immortal nostrum, would find cause to curse.

"Aylmer, are you in earnest?" asked Georgiana, looking at him with amazement and fear; "it is terrible to possess such power, or even to dream of possessing it!"

"Oh, do not tremble, my love!" said her husband, "I would not wrong either you or myself by working such inharmonious effects upon our lives. But I would have you consider how trifling, in comparison, is the skill requisite to remove this little Hand."

At the mention of the birth-mark, Georgiana, as usual, shrank, as if a red-hot iron had touched her cheek.

Again Aylmer applied himself to his labors. She could hear his voice in the distant furnace-room, giving directions to Aminadab, whose harsh, uncouth, misshapen tones were audible in response, more like the grunt or growl of a brute than human speech. After hours of absence, Aylmer reappeared, and proposed that she should now examine his cabinet of chemical products, and natural treasures of the earth. Among the former he showed her a small vial, in which, he remarked, was contained a gentle yet most powerful fragrance, capable of impregnating all the breezes that blow across a kingdom. They were of inestimable value, the contents of that little vial; and, as he said so, he threw some of the perfume into the air, and filled the room with piercing and invigorating delight.

"And what is this?" asked Georgiana, pointing to a small crystal globe, containing a gold-colored liquid. "It is so beautiful to the eye, that I could imagine it the Elixir of Life."

"In one sense it is," replied Aylmer, "or rather, the Elixir of Immortality. It is the most precious poison that ever was concocted in this world. By its aid, I could apportion the lifetime of any mortal at whom you might point your finger. The strength of the dose would determine whether he were to linger out years, or drop dead in the midst of a breath. No king, on his guarded throne, could keep his life, if I, in my private station, should deem that the welfare of millions justified me in depriving him of it."

"Why do you keep such a terrific drug?" inquired Georgiana in horror.

"Do not mistrust me, dearest," said her husband, smiling; "its virtuous potency is yet greater than its harmful one. But, see! here is a powerful cosmetic. With a few drops of this, in a vase of water, freckles may be washed away as easily as the hands are cleansed. A stronger infusion would take the blood out of the cheek, and leave the rosiest beauty a pale ghost."

"Is it with this lotion that you intend to bathe my cheek?" asked Georgiana, anxiously.

"Oh, no!" hastily replied her husband—"this is merely superficial. Your case demands a remedy that shall go deeper."

In his interviews with Georgiana, Aylmer generally made minute inquiries as to her sensations, and whether the confinement of the rooms, and the temperature of the atmosphere, agreed with her. These questions had such a particular drift, that Georgiana began to conjecture that she was already subjected to certain physical influences, either breathed in with the fragrant air, or taken with her food. She fancied, likewise—but it might be altogether fancy—that there was a stirring up of her system,—a strange indefinite sensation creeping through her veins, and tingling, half painfully, half pleasurably, at her heart. Still, whenever she dared to look into the mirror, there she beheld herself, pale as a white rose, and with the crimson birth-mark stamped upon her cheek. Not even Aylmer now hated it so much as she.

To dispel the tedium of the hours which her husband found it necessary to devote to the processes of combination and analysis, Georgiana turned over the volumes of his scientific library. In many dark old tomes, she met with chapters full of romance and poetry. They were the works of the philosophers of the middle ages, such as Albertus Magnus, Cornelius Agrippa, Paracelsus, and the famous friar who created the prophetic Brazen Head. All these antique naturalists stood in advance of their centuries, yet were imbued with some of their credulity, and therefore were believed, and perhaps imagined themselves, to have acquired from the investigation of nature a power above nature, and from physics a sway over the spiritual world. Hardly less curious and imaginative were the early volumes of the Transactions of the Royal Society, in which the members, knowing little of the limits of natural possibility, were continually recording wonders, or proposing methods whereby wonders might be wrought.

But, to Georgiana, the most engrossing volume was a large folio from her husband's own hand, in which he had recorded every experiment of his scientific career, its original aim, the methods adopted for its development, and its final success or failure, with the circumstances to which either event was attributable. The book, in truth, was both the history and emblem of his ardent, ambitious, imaginative, yet practical and laborious, life. He handled physical details, as if there were nothing beyond them; yet spiritualized them all, and redeemed himself from materialism, by his strong and eager aspiration towards the infinite. In his grasp, the veriest clod of earth assumed a soul. Georgiana, as she read, reverenced Aylmer, and loved him more profoundly than ever, but with a less entire dependence on his judgment than heretofore. Much as he had accomplished, she could not but observe that his most splendid successes were almost invariably failures, if compared with the ideal at which he aimed. His brightest diamonds were the merest pebbles, and felt to be so by himself, in comparison with the inestimable gems which lay hidden beyond his reach. The volume, rich with achievements that had won renown for its author, was yet as melancholy a record as ever mortal hand had penned. It was the sad confession, and continual exemplification, of the short-comings of the composite man—the spirit burdened with clay and working in matter—and of the despair that assails the higher nature, at finding itself so miserably thwarted by the earthly part. Perhaps every man of genius, in whatever sphere, might recognize the image of his own experience in Aylmer's journal.

So deeply did these reflections affect Georgiana, that she laid her face upon the open volume, and burst into tears. In this situation she was found by her husband.

"It is dangerous to read in a sorcerer's books," said he, with a smile, though his countenance was uneasy and displeased. "Georgiana, there are pages in that volume, which I can scarcely glance over and keep my senses. Take heed lest it prove as detrimental to you!"

"It has made me worship you more than ever," said she.

"Ah! wait for this one success," rejoined he, "then worship me if you will. I shall deem myself hardly unworthy of it. But, come! I have sought you for the luxury of your voice. Sing to me, dearest!"

So she poured out the liquid music of her voice to quench the thirst of his spirit. He then took his leave, with a boyish exuberance of gaiety, assuring her that her seclusion would endure but a little longer, and that the result was already certain. Scarcely had he departed, when Georgiana felt irresistibly impelled to follow him. She had forgotten to inform Aylmer of a symptom, which, for two or three hours past, had begun to excite her attention. It was a sensation in the fatal birth-mark, not painful, but which induced a restlessness throughout her system. Hastening after her husband, she intruded, for the first time, into the laboratory.

The first thing that struck her eye was the furnace, that hot and feverish worker, with the intense glow of its fire, which by the quantities of soot clustered above it, seemed to have been burning for ages. There was a distilling apparatus in full operation. Around the room were retorts, tubes, cylinders, crucibles, and other apparatus of chemical research. An electrical machine stood ready for immediate use. The atmosphere felt oppressively close, and was tainted with gaseous odors, which had been tormented forth by the processes of science. The severe and homely simplicity of the apartment, with its naked walls and brick pavement, looked strange, accustomed as Georgiana had become to the fantastic elegance of her boudoir. But what chiefly, indeed almost solely, drew her attention, was the aspect of Aylmer himself.

He was pale as death, anxious and absorbed, and hung over the furnace as if it depended upon his utmost watchfulness whether the liquid, which it was distilling, should be the draught of immortal happiness or misery. How different from the sanguine and joyous mien that he had assumed for Georgiana's encouragement!

"Carefully now, Aminadab! Carefully, thou human machine! Carefully, thou man of clay!" muttered Aylmer, more to himself than his assistant. "Now, if there be a thought too much or too little, it is all over!"

"Hoh! hoh!" mumbled Aminadab— "look, master, look!"

Aylmer raised his eyes hastily, and at first reddened, then grew paler than ever, on beholding Georgiana. He rushed towards her, and seized her arm with a grip that left the print of his fingers upon it.

"Why do you come hither? Have you no trust in your husband?" cried he impetuously. "Would you throw the blight of that fatal birth-mark over my labors? It is not well done. Go, prying woman, go!"

"Nay, Aylmer," said Georgiana, with the firmness of which she possessed no stinted endowment, "it is not you that have a right to complain. You mistrust your wife! You have concealed the anxiety with which you watch the development of this experiment. Think not so unworthily of me, my husband! Tell me all the risk we run; and fear not that I shall shrink, for my share in it is far less than your own!"

"No, no, Georgiana!" said Aylmer impatiently, "it must not be."

"I submit," replied she calmly. "And, Aylmer, I shall quaff whatever draught you bring me; but it will be on the same principle that would induce me to take a dose of poison, if offered by your hand."

"My noble wife," said Aylmer, deeply moved, "I knew not the height and depth of your nature, until now. Nothing shall be concealed. Know, then, that this Crimson Hand, superficial as it seems, has clutched its grasp into your being, with a strength of which I had no previous conception. I have already administered agents powerful enough to do aught except to change your entire physical system. Only one thing remains to be tried. If that fails us, we are ruined!"

"Why did you hesitate to tell me this?" asked she.

"Because, Georgiana," said Aylmer in a low voice, "there is danger!"

"Danger? There is but one danger—that this horrible stigma shall be left upon my cheek!" cried Georgiana. "Remove it! remove it!—whatever be the cost—or we shall both go mad!"

"Heaven knows, your words are too true," said Aylmer, sadly. "And now, dearest, return to your boudoir. In a little while, all will be tested."

He conducted her back, and took leave of her with a solemn tenderness, which spoke far more than his words how much was now at stake. After his departure, Georgiana became rapt in musings. She considered the character of Aylmer, and did it completer justice than at any previous moment. Her heart exulted, while it trembled, at his honorable love, so pure and lofty that it would accept nothing less than perfection, nor miserably make itself contented with an earthlier nature than he had dreamed of. She felt how much more precious was such a sentiment, than that meaner kind which would have borne with the imperfection for her sake, and have been guilty of treason to holy love, by degrading its perfect idea to the level of the actual. And, with her whole spirit, she prayed, that, for a single moment, she might satisfy his highest and deepest conception. Longer than one moment, she well knew, it could not be; for his spirit was ever on the march—ever ascending—and each instant required something that was beyond the scope of the instant before.

The sound of her husband's footsteps aroused her. He bore a crystal goblet, containing a liquor colorless as water, but bright enough to be the draught of immortality. Aylmer was pale; but it seemed rather the consequence of a highly wrought state of mind, and tension of spirit, than of fear or doubt.

"The concoction of the draught has been perfect," said he, in answer to Georgiana's look. "Unless all my science have deceived me, it cannot fail."

"Save on your account, my dearest Aylmer," observed his wife, "I might wish to put off this birth-mark of mortality by relinquishing mortality itself, in preference to any other mode. Life is but a sad possession to those who have attained precisely the degree of moral advancement at which I stand. Were I weaker and blinder, it might be happiness. Were I stronger, it might be endured hopefully. But, being what I find myself, methinks I am of all mortals the most fit to die."

"You are fit for heaven without tasting death!" replied her husband. "But why do we speak of dying? The draught cannot fail. Behold its effect upon this plant!"

On the window-seat there stood a geranium, diseased with yellow blotches, which had overspread all its leaves. Aylmer poured a small quantity of the liquid upon the soil in which it grew. In a little time, when the roots of the plant had taken up the moisture, the unsightly blotches began to be extinguished in a living verdure.

"There needed no proof," said Georgiana quietly. "Give me the goblet. I joyfully stake all upon your word."

"Drink then, thou lofty creature!" exclaimed Aylmer, with fervid admiration. "There is no taint of imperfection on thy spirit. Thy sensible frame, too, shall soon be all perfect!"

She quaffed the liquid, and returned the goblet to his hand.

"It is grateful," said she, with a placid smile. "Methinks it is like water from a heavenly fountain; for it contains I know not what of unobtrusive fragrance and deliciousness. It allays a feverish thirst, that had parched me for many days. Now, dearest, let me sleep. My earthly senses are closing over my spirit, like the leaves around the heart of a rose, at sunset."

She spoke the last words with a gentle reluctance, as if it required almost more energy than she could command to pronounce the faint and lingering syllables. Scarcely had they loitered through her lips, ere she was lost in slumber. Aylmer sat by her side, watching her aspect with the emotions proper to a man, the whole value of whose existence was involved in the process now to be tested. Mingled with this mood, however, was the philosophic investigation, characteristic of the man of science. Not the minutest symptom escaped him. A heightened flush of the cheek—a slight irregularity of breath—a quiver of the eyelid—a hardly perceptible tremor through the frame—such were the details which, as the moments passed, he wrote down in his folio volume. Intense thought had set its stamp upon every previous page of that volume; but the thoughts of years were all concentrated upon the last.

While thus employed, he failed not to gaze often at the fatal Hand, and not without a shudder. Yet once, by a strange and unaccountable impulse, he pressed it with his lips. His spirit recoiled, however, in the very act, and Georgiana, out of the midst of her deep sleep, moved uneasily and murmured as if in remonstrance. Again, Aylmer resumed his watch. Nor was it without avail. The Crimson Hand, which at first had been strongly visible upon the marble paleness of Georgiana's cheek now grew more faintly outlined. She remained not less pale than ever; but the birth-mark, with every breath that came and went, lost somewhat of its former distinctness. Its presence had been awful; its departure was more awful still. Watch the stain of the rainbow fading out of the sky; and you will know how that mysterious symbol passed away.

"By Heaven, it is well-nigh gone!" said Aylmer to himself, in almost irrepressible ecstasy. "I can scarcely trace it now. Success! Success! And now it is like the faintest rose-color. The lightest flush of blood across her cheek would overcome it. But she is so pale!"

He drew aside the window-curtain, and suffered the light of natural day to fall into the room, and rest upon her cheek. At the same time, he heard a gross, hoarse chuckle, which he had long known as his servant Aminadab's expression of delight.

"Ah clod! Ah, earthly mass!" cried Aylmer, laughing in a sort of frenzy. "You have served me well! Matter and Spirit—Earth and Heaven—have both done their part in this! Laugh, thing of senses! You have earned the right to laugh."

These exclamations broke Georgiana's sleep. She slowly unclosed her eyes, and gazed into the mirror, which her husband had arranged for that purpose. A faint smile flitted over her lips, when she recognized how barely perceptible was now that Crimson Hand, which had once blazed forth with such disastrous brilliancy as to scare away all their happiness. But then her eyes sought Aylmer's face, with a trouble and anxiety that he could by no means account for.

"My poor Aylmer!" murmured she.

"Poor? Nay, richest! Happiest! Most favored!" exclaimed he. "My peerless bride, it is successful! You are perfect!"

"My poor Aylmer!" she repeated, with a more than human tenderness. "You have aimed loftily!—you have done nobly! Do not repent, that, with so high and pure a feeling, you have rejected the best the earth could offer. Aylmer—dearest Aylmer—I am dying!"

Alas, it was too true! The fatal Hand had grappled with the mystery of life, and was the bond by which an angelic spirit kept itself in union with a mortal frame. As the last crimson tint of the birth-mark—that sole token of human imperfection—faded from her cheek, the parting breath of the now perfect woman passed into the atmosphere, and her soul, lingering a moment near her husband, took its heavenward flight. Then a hoarse, chuckling laugh was heard again! Thus ever does the gross Fatality of Earth exult in its invariable triumph over the immortal essence, which, in this dim sphere of half-development, demands the completeness of a higher state. Yet, had Aylmer reached a profounder wisdom, he need not thus have flung away the happiness, which would have woven his mortal life of the self-same texture with the celestial. The momentary circumstance was too strong for him; he failed to look beyond the shadowy scope of Time, and, living once for all in Eternity, to find the perfect Future in the present.

Richard Kadrey

Richard Kadrey is the multi-talented San Francisco–based author of such cyberpunk novels as Metrophage *and* Kamikaizi L'Amour. *He has also written the comic book* Accelerate, *the non-fiction catalog* Covert Culture Sourcebook, *and the illustrated erotic novel* Angel Scene. *In the past, Kadrey was senior editor at* Future Sex *magazine, which contributed to his involvement as a performer in HBO's* Real Sex 9, *and as an advisor in the CBC's* Wired for Sex. *He has also been a featured speaker on sex technology and the future on a number of television programs in Europe. Kadrey has published numerous articles and short fiction in magazines such as* Wired, Omni, Mondo 2000, Pulse!, Artforum, World Art, Reflex, Whole Earth Review, San Francisco Chronicle, *(and more), and his work has appeared in a number of anthologies. His story, "The First Man Not to Walk on the Moon," was nominated for Best Short Story of 1997 by the British Science Fiction Association. In addition to his writing, Kadrey has also published illustrations in magazines and anthologies all over the world. "Carbon Copy: Meet the First Human Clone," was first published in* Wired, *March 1998. Like most science fiction stories, this one poses a "what if" scenario, playing on contemporary fears about cloning in an eerily realistic journalistic style.*

Carbon Copy

She knew she'd have to explain it, probably even apologize for it, sooner or later, but Dr. Amanda Koteas didn't think she'd be doing it now. Nevertheless, after weeks of rumors and stolen memos and lab reports turning up in the tabloid press and on TV, Koteas, head of the University of Pennsylvania's Department of Molecular and Cellular Engineering and the school's Institute for Human Gene Therapy, decided to tell the full story. At a hastily pulled-together press conference last Friday, she announced to the world that not only is human cloning possible, but that she and her team had already done it—two years earlier, using an updated version of the techniques scientists at the Roslin Institute used to create the sheep Dolly, the first mammal cloned from an adult cell, in 1997.

The result of Koteas and company's bold experiment was a healthy 8-pound girl named Katy, born in secret to Virginia and Christopher Hytner at the institute on December 5, 1999.

Reprinted from *Wired*, March 1998, pp. 146–150, 180 & 182.

Why did Koteas wait so long to go public with the story? During our interview, it is clear that she remains moved by the child's birth, but ambivalent about discussing the cloning. "This was a medical procedure with a name and a child's face," she says. "We were hoping to keep the circumstances of Katy's birth out of the public eye for a few more years at least. She's a normal kid and deserves a normal childhood."

It's unlikely anything about Katy Hytner's life is going to be normal for years to come. Not only has the press descended on Pacifica, a coastal community 20 minutes south of San Francisco, but so have religious groups, film and book agents, and conspiracy buffs. While Pacifica is used to tourists, the current mix of curiosity-seekers is not sitting well with local residents. Says Thomas Winkler, owner of the Good Morning America coffee shop, "It's like there was an explosion at the idiot factory and all the debris landed here." Punching receipts into his cash register, Winkler reflects for a moment before adding, "They should all just leave that little girl alone."

The Hytners are not the only ones overwhelmed by the publicity surrounding this story. Koteas and her team are still trying to absorb the enormity of public reaction. "It's much more surreal than we ever imagined," she says. "Frightening, too."

Koteas and her colleagues have reason to be frightened. Several members of the cloning team have received death threats, while others, such as Adam Walken, whose studies into the genetics of aging encouraged the team that human cloning was possible, have been inundated with offers for movies and talk show appearances. In the corridors of the University of Pennsylvania, the words "Nobel Prize" and "jail time" are mentioned with equal frequency. School president James Osterberg has issued a terse press statement: "The university in no way condones the secret and unauthorized experiments conducted by doctors Amanda Koteas, Adam Walken, Eric Mortensen, Moriah Stoltz, and Albert Gomez. A full internal investigation is under way to determine whether any laws have been violated."

"We did the work using university facilities, so yes, technically, university funds were used for the work," admits Koteas. "And some of those funds were tied to government grants." The use of such funding, she acknowledges, defied the moratorium on human-cloning research encouraged by then-President Clinton in 1997. At her home in suburban Philadelphia, Koteas looks out the window. "We weren't conducting research for the sake of research. We were applying established scientific knowledge to a specific problem. I stand by that." She laughs anxiously. "If we win the Nobel Prize, I wonder if they'll let me keep mine in my cell?"

All this week, while the members of the Pennsylvania cloning team pondered their collective futures, Katy Hytner, an outwardly ordinary 2-year-old who had only last week been playing with Legos and Sesame Street dolls at the Oceanview Children's Center in Pacifica, was not yet aware of the controversy surrounding her birth.

Her "conception" began more than two years ago in the Prenatal Diagnosis Unit at the Institute for Human Gene Therapy. The university's cutting-edge combination of advanced computer analysis, genetic screening, and gene therapy had caused a stir in 1998, both as a scientific breakthrough and as a controversial moneymaking enterprise for the university (see "Buying the Future: Perfect Kids for Cold Cash" *Wired* 6.06, page 450).

Combining proprietary chemical and genetic tests for diseases and congenital abnormalities, all collated by the new "expert system" software developed at Carnegie Mellon University, the institute had developed a system that, according to its own publicity materials, "virtually guarantees not only a successful labor and delivery, but the healthy child every family dreams about."

Virginia and Christopher Hytner had talked about having children for years. "But we wanted to wait until the time was right," says Virginia, a part-time real estate agent. Her husband, a design engineer at Silicon Graphics in Mountain View, California, adds, "With our careers on track and our lives stable, the only things holding us back were health questions."

The Hytners, like a lot of the boomer generation, had waited until their late 30s to have children. While both were outwardly healthy, Virginia Hytner had some concerns about the health of any child she might bear. "Even though I don't have diabetes, my mother and an aunt do," she explains via phone. "I wanted to know about the possibility of passing that to my child. I also know that there are other problems that a child can have when coming from a diabetic background." Hearing of the University of Pennsylvania's successful screening program, the Hytners took their 1998 vacation in Philadelphia.

While much of the couple's concern centered on Virginia's genetic background, both prospective parents went through the screening process at the Prenatal Diagnosis Unit. This procedure is fairly simple for a man; only blood tests and sperm samples are required. Potential mothers, however, are injected with the hormone-based drug Metrodin to induce "superovulation." This bumper crop of eggs lets doctors collect samples for screening. Metrodin and related pharmaceuticals frequently bring on PMS-type cramps and other hormone-related discomforts.

Using the mother's eggs and the father's sperm, doctors fertilize several of the eggs in vitro. They then allow the fertilized eggs to grow until the eight-cell stage. Once the eggs have reached this phase, the doctors remove a cell from the egg and examine it using the university's proprietary tests, as well as a standard genetic-screening procedure known as nested PCR, a polymerase chain reaction that tags and amplifies DNA sequences so that doctors—or, in this case, a computer—can look for abnormalities.

For the Hytners, the tests indicated that the cell was clear of disease and congenital defects, and the couple chose to have the already-fertilized egg implanted in Virginia's uterus that day. Koteas, a native of San Francisco, performed that implantation herself, after meeting the Hytners during routine rounds at the Prenatal Diagnosis Unit. After an overnight stay and an exam the next morning, Virginia Hytner was released to rejoin her husband and plan the arrival of their first child.

But something went wrong.

It's not hard to believe the doctors and technicians at the Prenatal Diagnosis Unit when they say they still aren't sure what happened. Modern jet aircraft, handled by expert pilots and aided by the most advanced computers, still crash. In most of those cases, human error is the culprit. Was human error responsible for implanting a defective embryo in Virginia Hytner? We will probably never know. "There are nights I still lie awake wondering what went wrong," says Koteas.

"Did a tech mislabel a cell culture? Or enter data into the new computer incorrectly? Did someone read a chart wrong? Was there something *I* did wrong?"

Virginia gave birth to a daughter on January 3, 1999. The child, which had seemed sluggish in the womb, was pronounced dead two weeks later of multi-organ failure.

The cause of death was a subtle one: neonatal lactic acidosis, a problem brought about by a defect in the mitochondria—microscopic organelles that control the metabolism of individual cells—in her mother's egg. A woman can be unaffected by the defective mitochondria in her cells, only to have them wreak havoc in her developing offspring.

The death of the Hytners' daughter devastated the couple. Even now, two years later and after the birth of a healthy child, Virginia can't completely describe how she felt: "Numb. I felt dead. After all the assurances of the doctors, I felt alone and betrayed." Koteas, who years before had lost a child to a rare chromosomal disease, trisomy 13, was also shattered by the baby's death. "We had done so well at the screening clinic, we started to believe the university's hype about us," she says. "We were perfect, and then we weren't, and a child was dead. It was awful."

Enter Adam Walken, Koteas's friend and colleague at the Institute for Human Gene Therapy. Walken was studying how cells change and break down as they age and was interested in finding a way to arrest or reverse this process. He had been studying in particular tiny sections of chromosomes known as telomeres—chemical buffers at each end of a chromosome that act like the bumpers on a car. They protect the genes inside from damage, but each time a cell divides, the telomere buffer often decreases in length, Eventually, the telomeres become so short that they can't protect the chromosomes, and the cell stops dividing and dies.

The question Walken—and other researchers—wanted to answer was, if you could restore or stop the erosion of a cell's telomeres, could you stop or reverse the aging process? One way to find out was through studying primate cloning. Could the older, telomere-eroded cells of an adult primate be restored to their pristine condition in an embryo during the cloning process? When the Oregon Regional Primate Research Center in Beaverton cloned a rhesus monkey, Walken received a National Science Foundation grant to work and study there.

While the results of his studies on aging are still inconclusive (researchers don't yet understand all the proteins that produce telomeres, nor the mechanisms that erode the buffers), Walken did learn about the basic science of primate cloning and was a member of the team that in late 1998 first cloned a chimpanzee (an animal so similar to humans that it shares 98 percent of its DNA with us) using the technique employed by the Roslin Institute. Walken has admitted that while he was working at the primate center, he was convinced that human cloning was possible but didn't think he would ever really know in his lifetime. "The climate was all wrong. Even to say the words was a heresy," he says. "When the Hytners' daughter died, something clicked in my brain. It wasn't something planned, but the logic was inescapable."

It was during a discussion over dinner that the subject of human cloning became serious for Koteas and Walken. Both had been experiencing crises of faith in their areas of expertise and were questioning the possibilities of technical fixes to problems such as aging and childbirth. "I told Amanda about depressions we experienced at the primate center during some of the cloning trials, but said that with concentrated effort, we were confident we had worked out a straightforward and reliable process to produce identical primates for study. She told me about her despair over the Hytners. Then, all of a sudden, we just sort of looked at each other." Depending on your point of view, either a conspiracy or a bold scientific experiment was conceived that night.

Despite the almost mystical power of the word *cloning,* the process happens constantly in nature and has become routine in labs around the world. Identical twins—normal children born every day—are clones. Amoebae clone themselves when they divide. For several years cancer and retrovirus researchers have been using groups of cloned mice to test drug treatments. Plants clone themselves when they send off shoots and buds. Many common fruits and vegetables such as apples, bananas, grapes, garlic, and potatoes have become grocery-store staples because of plant breeding and cloning. Cloning large animals in a lab, however—especially mammals—is more complex.

When the Roslin Institute conceived the clone Dolly in July 1996, seven months before the sheep was presented to the world, the big question researchers had to answer was whether an adult cell that had become specialized for one part of the body (in the case of Dolly's "mother," an udder cell) could be made to "forget" that it was specialized and return to a nonspecialized, embryonic state. Dr. Ian Wilmut and his associates at Roslin made a breakthrough using a process called demethylation. Simply, they kept normal nutrients from the cell and starved it in a salt solution until it became dormant and stopped dividing. This intervention allowed the Roslin team to fuse the sleeping cell's genetic material with another sheep egg from which the DNA had already been removed—a process known as nuclear transfer.

It took the Roslin Institute 277 tries to bring a single pregnancy to term. Still, it worked. After experimenting with rhesus monkeys for a year, the Oregon Regional Primate Research Center could achieve pregnancy every 50 attempts. When researchers there developed the chemical procedures to demethylate chimpanzee cells, they hit every 20 tries.

Once scientists have cracked the method of returning cells to their embryonic state, the rest of the cloning procedure is a relatively simple, mechanical process. After the DNA is inserted into an egg, the team gives it a microshock of electricity to fuse them together, and then another minuscule jolt—a sort of jump-start—to begin cell division. When the cells begin dividing, they are transferred to the mother's womb, just as in any ordinary fertility treatment.

In February 1999 Koteas and Walken determined that they had intact cell samples from the Hytners' dead child, and the two scientists approached the couple with the idea of, in Koteas's words, "giving them back their child—this time, the way she should have been when she was born." The Hytners were resistant at first, still in pain from their daughter's death. But when Walken explained his cloning experience at the primate center, and added the idea of implanting the baby's DNA in a donated egg from another woman—one who had borne healthy children—the couple started to come around. By the next afternoon, they had decided to try it. "They explained the procedure to us and said that they needed to start work as soon as possible to make sure our daughter's DNA was fresh and undamaged—that she was still, in a sense, 'alive' in her genes, but lost without a body," says Virginia Hytner. "Amanda and Adam made me and my husband believe that they could give our daughter back her body." At that point, the Hytners were sworn to secrecy.

The team of five doctors—Koteas, Walken, Mortensen, Stoltz, and Gomez—plus a handful of trusted graduate student assistants, set to work culturing the child's cells, chemically returning them to their embryonic state using samples of the advanced demethylating drugs Walken had procured from the primate center. According to Koteas, they also "obtained" frozen human eggs from the gene clinic, checking them again and again for the donor's history and any possible disease traits.

After fusing a dormant cell nucleus with a donor egg, the doctors jolted the egg with electricity to see whether it would divide. After only 10 tries, an egg started dividing normally, and Koteas implanted it in Virginia Hytner.

Over the next nine months occurred one of the most closely watched pregnancies on record. All five doctors on the cloning team made trips from Pennsylvania to California to monitor Virginia Hytner's progress. By then the Hytners were already calling the growing fetus Katy, a name they'd selected for their first child, who they later started to think of as Katy's lost twin. In fact, the university team had already coined the term *serial twins* to refer among themselves to the products of the cloning process.

In late November 1999 Virginia and Christopher Hytner took leaves of absence from work and, accompanied by Walken, flew to Philadelphia one more time. At 1 A.M. on December 5, Katy Hytner was delivered by Dr. Albert Gomez via cesarean section. The team was elated, and the Hytners were speechless. "Our daughter was returned to us," says Christopher Hytner, "It was the miracle we'd prayed for."

Since their work had not been approved by the university, the cloning team kept all their records confidential, hidden in a filing cabinet in Koteas's office. Still sworn to secrecy, the team went back to its work at the university and the Hytners returned to California with Katy. Team members still made regular monthly visits to Pacifica to check on mother and child, who both appeared healthy and safe. The reality of the unprecedented experiment remained protected from public scrutiny for almost two years.

Then, last November, a chain of events began that revealed the Hytners' secret. Alice DeWitt, a graduate student who had worked on the cloning team screening donor eggs, filed for divorce from her husband. During the stormy divorce proceedings, Matthew DeWitt found a set of notes—copies of papers Alice had given to Koteas—while he was removing his wife's belongings from their apartment. Matthew, himself a pediatrician, recognized the implications of the notes and offered them through his lawyer for sale to the highest bidder.

When news crews from the Hard Copy cable network began scouring preschools in Pacifica for Katy Hytner, the members of the University of Pennsylvania cloning team knew they had to make a public announcement. "We could see how things were going," says Koteas. "HCTV was turning Katy's birth into a

Frankenstein story, portraying her as some frightening freak of science. As bad as things are now, we knew that if we didn't get hold of the story, the Hytners' lives would be ruined forever."

Koteas's press conference was beamed live around the world on CNN, MSNBC, HCTV, C-Span, and all 10 major broadcast networks. By then, the Hytner family had left Pacifica, and if anyone on the cloning team knows the family's whereabouts, they aren't saying.

Aside from the media, a number of other interested parties would like to find the Hytner family—among them Baby Gap, Pepsi, Benetton, and the Xerox Corporation, all waving lucrative endorsement contracts.

Now that human cloning has moved from science fiction films and research labs to the real world, what are we to make of it? No one seems to know yet. Dr. G. Richard Seed's operation, which moved from Chicago to San José, Costa Rica, in mid-1999 in response to pressure from the US government, has generated some interesting new approaches to large-scale cell culturing and fine DNA manipulation, but the facility has yet to bring any of its attempted pregnancies to term. Most of the European Union's member nations have passed strict laws preventing human-cloning work, though England and Germany remain holdouts. But it's generally known that Russia, Japan, and South Korea are setting up their own experimental cloning centers, perhaps in cooperation with Seed's lab.

One of the few unambiguous responses so far to Katy Hytner's birth has come from the Vatican, which released a statement urging people to recognize that clones have individual souls, even if they occupy identical bodies. Little else about what some are calling the Philadelphia Project is certain, even whether Katy is, in fact, a legitimate clone of her dead sibling.

Since she was produced in an egg that carried another woman's mitochondria, some scientists, including geneticists at MIT and Oxford University, question whether Katy can be truly considered a clone of the Hytners' first child. Perhaps the term *serial twin* is about to become common currency as Koteas and her colleagues try to calm a nervous public that, while admiring the motivations and technical skill of the cloning team, isn't sanguine about letting this genie out of the bottle.

"No one's about to start mass-producing copies of Adolf Hitler or rich people," assures Koteas. "This is one little girl—deeply loved by her ordinary mother and father. Trust me. There's nothing to worry about."

Alan Lightman

Born in Memphis, Tennessee (1948) to a father who owned a movie theatre and a mother who taught dance, Alan Lightman grew up trying to reconcile his love of art and science. He says of his early years, "Far back as I can remember, I built rockets and wrote poetry. . . . I always felt torn between two worlds." In 1970, Lightman received an AB degree in physics from Princeton University and moved on to a Ph.D. in theoretical physics from the California Institute of Technology, which he attained in 1974. As a postdoctoral fellow in astrophysics at Cornell (1974 to 1976), Lightman began publishing poetry in small literary magazines. Once an assistant professor at Harvard, Lightman now teaches at MIT, where he is able to combine his passion for teaching physics with his love of writing as the director of the Program in Writing and Humanistic studies. Like Isaac Asimov, Lightman began writing books and articles, such as Great Ideas in Physics *(1992 & 2000), which strive to make science understandable for the layman. Written in 1991,* Einstein's Dreams *was Lightman's first attempt at writing fiction. It has garnered praise from renowned authors, like Salman Rushdie, who compares his work to Italo Calvino. Lightman credits both of these authors with influence on his work. In combining his love of physics with art, the following chapters from his first novel lead us into the world of Albert Einstein's dreams about the multiple possibilities of time just before he publishes his theory of relativity. Lightman has been the recipient of a number of honors for both his artistic and scientific work. Most recently, his novel* The Diagnosis *was a finalist for the 2000 National Book Award in fiction.*

---

14 April 1905, 16 April 1905, & 14 May 1905

14 April 1905

Suppose time is a circle, bending back on itself. The world repeats itself, precisely, endlessly.

For the most part, people do not know they will live their lives over. Traders do not know that they will make the same bargain again and again. Politicians do not

Reprinted from *Einstein's Dreams*, (1993), Warner Books, Inc.

know that they will shout from the same lectern an infinite number of times in the cycles of time. Parents treasure the first laugh from their child as if they will not hear it again. Lovers making love the first time undress shyly, show surprise at the supple thigh, the fragile nipple. How would they know that each secret glimpse, each touch, will be repeated again and again and again, exactly as before?

On Marktgasse, it is the same. How could the shopkeepers know that each handmade sweater, each embroidered handkerchief, each chocolate candy, each intricate compass and watch will return to their stalls? At dusk, the shopkeepers go home to their families or drink beer in the taverns, calling happily to friends down the vaulted alleys, caressing each moment as an emerald on temporary consignment. How could they know that nothing is temporary, that all will happen again? No more than an ant crawling round the rim of a crystal chandelier knows that it will return to where it began.

In the hospital on Gerberngasse, a woman says goodbye to her husband. He lies in bed and stares at her emptily. In the last two months, his cancer has spread from his throat to his liver, his pancreas, his brain. His two young children sit on one chair in the corner of the room, frightened to look at their father, his sunken cheeks, the withered skin of an old man. The wife comes to the bed and kisses her husband softly on the forehead, whispers goodbye, and quickly leaves with the children. She is certain that this was the last kiss. How could she know that time will begin again, that she will be born again, will study at the gymnasium again, will show her paintings at the gallery in Zürich, will again meet her husband in the small library in Fribourg, will again go sailing with him in Thun Lake on a warm day in July, will give birth again, that her husband will again work for eight years at the pharmaceutical and come home one evening with a lump in his throat, will again throw up and get weak and end up in this hospital, this room, this bed, this moment. How could she know?

In the world in which time is a circle, every handshake, every kiss, every birth, every word, will be repeated precisely. So too every moment that two friends stop becoming friends, every time that a family is broken because of money, every vicious remark in an argument between spouses, every opportunity denied because of a superior's jealousy, every promise not kept.

And just as all things will be repeated in the future, all things now happening happened a million times before. Some few people in every town, in their dreams, are vaguely aware that all has occurred in the past. These are the people with unhappy lives, and they sense that their misjudgments and wrong deeds and bad luck have all taken place in the previous loop of time.

In the dead of night these cursed citizens wrestle with their bedsheets, unable to rest, stricken with the knowledge that they cannot change a single action, a single gesture. Their mistakes will be repeated precisely in this life as in the life before. And it is these double unfortunates who give the only sign that time is a circle. For in each town, late at night, the vacant streets and balconies fill up with their moans.

16 April 1905

In this world, time is like a flow of water, occasionally displaced by a bit of debris, a passing breeze. Now and then, some cosmic disturbance will cause a rivulet of time to turn away from the mainstream, to make connection backstream. When this happens, birds, soil, people caught in the branching tributary find themselves suddenly carried to the past.

Persons who have been transported back in time are easy to identify. They wear dark, indistinct clothing and walk on their toes, trying not to make a single sound, trying not to bend a single blade of grass. For they fear that any change they make in the past could have drastic consequences for the future.

Just now, for example, such a person is crouching in the shadows of the arcade, at no. 19 Kramgasse. An odd place for a traveler from the future, but there she is. Pedestrians pass, stare, and walk on. She huddles in a corner, then quickly creeps across the street and cowers in another darkened spot, at no. 22. She is terrified that she will kick up dust, just as a Peter Klausen is making his way to the apothecary on Spitalgasse this afternoon of 16 April 1905. Klausen is something of a dandy and hates to have his clothes sullied. If dust messes his clothes, he will stop and painstakingly brush them off, regardless of waiting appointments. If Klausen is sufficiently delayed, he may not buy the ointment for his wife, who has been complaining of leg aches for weeks. In that case, Klausen's wife, in a bad humor, may decide not to make the trip to Lake Geneva. And if she does not go to Lake Geneva on 23 June 1905, she will not meet a Catherine d'Épinay walking on the jetty of the east shore and will not introduce Mlle. d'Épinay to her son Richard. In turn, Richard and Catherine will not marry on 17 December 1908, will not give birth to Friedrich on 8 July 1912. Friedrich Klausen will not be father to Hans Klausen on 22 August 1938, and without Hans Klausen the European Union of 1979 will never occur.

The woman from the future, thrust without warning into this time and this place and now attempting to be invisible in her darkened spot at no. 22 Kramgasse, knows the Klausen story and a thousand other stories waiting to unfold, dependent on the births of children, the movement of people in the streets, the songs of birds at certain moments, the precise position of chairs, the wind. She crouches in the shadows and does not return the stares of people. She crouches and waits for the stream of time to carry her back to her own time.

When a traveler from the future must talk, he does not talk but whimpers. He whispers tortured sounds. He is agonized. For if he makes the slightest alteration in anything, he may destroy the future. At the same time, he is forced to witness events without being part of them, without changing them. He envies the people who live in their own time, who can act at will, oblivious of the future, ignorant of the effects of their actions. But he cannot act. He is an inert gas, a ghost, a sheet without soul. He has lost his personhood. He is an exile of time.

Such wretched people from the future can be found in every village and every town, hiding under the eaves of buildings, in basements, under bridges, in deserted fields. They are not questioned about coming events, about future marriages, births, finances, inventions, profits to be made. Instead, they are left alone and pitied.

14 May 1905

There is a place where time stands still. Raindrops hang motionless in air. Pendulums of clocks float mid-swing. Dogs raise their muzzles in silent howls.

Pedestrians are frozen on the dusty streets, their legs cocked as if held by strings. The aromas of dates, mangoes, coriander, cumin are suspended in space.

As a traveler approaches this place from any direction, he moves more and more slowly. His heartbeats grow farther apart, his breathing slackens, his temperature drops, his thoughts diminish, until he reaches dead center and stops. For this is the center of time. From this place, time travels outward in concentric circles—at rest at the center, slowly picking up speed at greater diameters.

Who would make pilgrimage to the center of time? Parents with children, and lovers.

And so, at the place where time stands still, one sees parents clutching their children, in a frozen embrace that will never let go. The beautiful young daughter with blue eyes and blond hair will never stop smiling the smile she smiles now, will never lose this soft pink glow on her cheeks, will never grow wrinkled or tired, will never get injured, will never unlearn what her parents have taught her, will never think thoughts that her parents don't know, will never know evil, will never tell her parents that she does not love them, will never leave her room with the view of the ocean, will never stop touching her parents as she does now.

And at the place where time stands still, one sees lovers kissing in the shadows of buildings, in a frozen embrace that will never let go. The loved one will never take his arms from where they are now, will never give back the bracelet of memories, will never journey far from his lover, will never place himself in danger in self-sacrifice, will never fail to show his love, will never become jealous, will never fall in love with someone else, will never lose the passion of this instant in time.

One must consider that these statues are illuminated by only the most feeble red light, for light is diminished almost to nothing at the center of time, its vibrations slowed to echoes in vast canyons, its intensity reduced to the faint glow of fireflies.

Those not quite at dead center do indeed move, but at the pace of glaciers. A brush of the hair might take a year, a kiss might take a thousand. While a smile is returned, seasons pass in the outer world. While a child is hugged, bridges rise. While a goodbye is said, cities crumble and are forgotten.

And those who return to the outer world . . . Children grow rapidly, forget the centuries-long embrace from their parents, which to them lasted but seconds. Children become adults, live far from their parents, live in their own houses, learn ways of their own, suffer pain, grow old. Children curse their parents for trying to hold them forever, curse time for their own wrinkled skin and hoarse voices. These now old children also want to stop time, but at another time. They want to freeze their own children at the center of time.

Lovers who return find their friends are long gone. After all, lifetimes have passed. They move in a world they do not recognize. Lovers who return still embrace in the shadows of buildings, but now their embraces seem empty and alone. Soon they forget the centuries-long promises, which to them lasted only seconds. They become jealous even among strangers, say hateful things to each other, lose passion, drift apart, grow old and alone in a world they do not know.

Some say it is best not to go near the center of time. Life is a vessel of sadness, but it is noble to live life, and without time there is no life. Others disagree. They would rather have an eternity of contentment, even if that eternity were fixed and frozen, like a butterfly mounted in a case.

Arthur Quinn

Arthur Quinn (1943–1997) was a third-generation Californian whose captivation with the state is reflected in the three books he wrote on California history: "The Broken Shore" (1981), "The Rivals" (1994), and "Hell With the Fire Out" (1997). As an undergraduate Quinn studied and played baseball at the University of San Francisco. He moved on to Princeton, where he attained a Ph.D. in the history and philosophy of science in 1970. Quinn began his teaching career at the University of Oregon in 1968 and moved to UC Berkeley two years later, where he remained until his death. During his tenure as chair of the department and director of the college of writing, Quinn reorganized the undergraduate major in rhetoric. His passion for teaching good writing is reflected in such texts as Figures of Speech *(1993), which provides colorful definitions of rhetorical terminology. Some of the honors Quinn received in his lifetime are the Woodrow Wilson, National Science Foundation, and Danforth fellowships; the Award of Merit of the California Historical Society; a UC Berkeley Distinguished Teaching Award; and a fellowship of Clare Hall, Cambridge, England. The following essay, "Science, Literature, and Rhetoric," is from an anthology he co-edited called* Audiences and Intentions: A Book of Arguments *(1997), which focuses on helping students master a sense of audience and purpose in their writing.*

Science, Literature, and Rhetoric

Rhetoric's most important contribution to the study of science and literature is a method to determine common ground between scientific discourse and literary, a method that does not prejudge in favor of either side. First I have to define what I mean by rhetoric and to distinguish its approach to discourse from those commonly employed in the evaluation of scientific and literary discourse, respectively, The most convenient way to do this is through the scheme that M. H. Abrams uses at the beginning of *The Mirror and the Lamp* (1953) to distinguish the four chief ways in which human discourse has been analyzed and evaluated within the Western tradition.

We can, like the scientist, attend to the relationship between the discourse and the world at large. Is the discourse true? Does it accurately represent or mirror the

Reprinted from *Audiences and Intentions: A Book of Arguments*, Second Edition, edited by Nancy Mason Bradbury, (1994), Prentice-Hall, Inc.

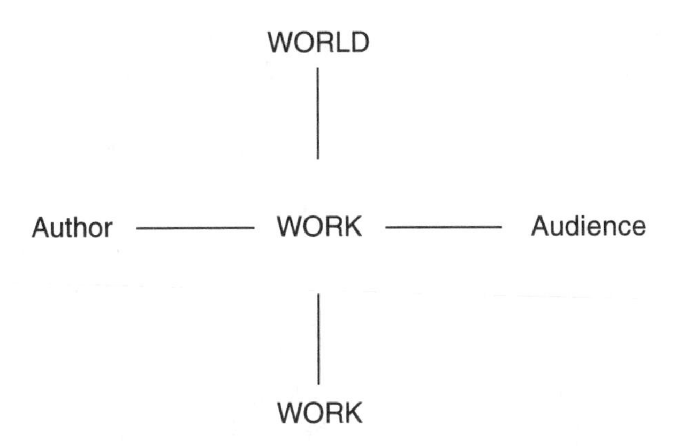

world? Second, we can attend to the relationship between the discourse and its author. Is it an adequate expression of the author's personality or feelings? Is it authentic, spontaneous, sincere? Third, we can evaluate the discourse in relation to itself. Then we are seeking the beauty of the discourse, intrinsically if possible, separate from the author or the world. We are treating it as an aesthetic object. Fourth, we can take a pragmatic, or rhetorical, approach to discourse.

Rhetoric focuses upon the relationship between the discourse and its audience. This relationship gives rise to characteristic questions: Who is the intended audience? What response from that audience does the author hope to get? How does the author's presentation of himself, his *ethos,* assist him in this task? How does the arrangement of the piece, as well as its style, shape the audience's response? The list of questions is hardly exhaustive. While the mimetic approach has dominated our understanding of scientific discourse, and the expressive and aesthetic approaches have, at least since the Romantics, dominated our understanding of literature, rhetoric, with its emphasis on audience, has been traditionally associated with oratory in general, and with political and legal discourse in particular. In oratory both the author and audience are physically present to one another, and their interaction is palpable. In politics and law the primary aim is power and influence—not beauty, or self-expression, or even truth.

The exemplary work of literary critics such as Wayne Booth in *The Rhetoric of Fiction* (1961), to give just one example, has demonstrated just how fruitful the application of rhetorical analysis to literary texts can be. Historians and philosophers of science have been moving in exactly the same direction, although less self-consciously, and with less recognition of the fact. Historians took the lead by showing that science is not as isomorphic, as methodologically homogeneous, as once was thought. Thomas Kuhn, in *The Structure of Scientific Revolutions* (2nd ed., 1970), calls the plurality of scientific methods "paradigms." Paul Feyerabend, in his *Against Method* (1975), argues simply that we should no longer seek *The* Scientific Method, but rather be satisfied with distinct rhetorics of science. Thus, following Feyerabend's line, when we deal with a great scientific work such as Darwin's *Origin of Species,* we should not try to reduce it to some method that philosophers of science in our own time happen to prefer. We should rather treat it as a great piece of deliberative rhetoric that did in fact convince many of the best young biologists of Darwin's time to use his theory as the basis for their own future research—this despite the many and fundamental objections to his theory that he himself could not answer. Let us look at his skill in a little more detail.

Darwin consistently seeks to soften his readers' opposition to his theory by showing that he sympathizes with their difficulties. A master of tactical concession, Darwin time and again places himself with his objecting readers, sympathizing with them, showing them he understands, and thereby mollifying them. Some of the difficulties facing his theory are, he says, "so grave that to this day I can never reflect on them without being staggered." Any attempt to explain the eye by natural selection seems, "I freely confess, absurd in the highest possible degree." And when Darwin must admonish his readers, he is careful always to do it at least partly at his own expense. The truth of the continual struggle for existence is difficult to bear constantly in mind—"at least I have found it so." The natural grouping of organisms into groups subordinate to groups is a fact "the wonder of which we are apt to overlook."

Darwin also seems to have been sensitive to the irrational resistance that his theory would provoke, particularly in its destruction of much of his readers' comforting sense of nature's harmony and beauty. Most of his figurative language is clustered in passages where he tries to retain the appearance of this beauty and harmony for his readers, partly at least by showing them that he still sees it. Adaptations are not just adaptations for Darwin—they are "beautiful adaptations." Nature at times becomes a personified "she" mothering over her children. The whole organic world becomes a lovely Tree of Life which "fills with its dead and broken branches the crust of the earth and covers the surface with its ever branching and beautiful ramifications." Darwin can even occasionally try to reassure his readers directly. "When we reflect on this struggle, we may console ourselves with the full belief that the war of nature is not incessant, that no fear is felt, that death is generally prompt, and that the vigorous, the healthy, and the happy survive and multiply." His readers may never again be able to believe rationally that this is the best of all possible worlds; Darwin will, nonetheless, for the time being, permit them to feel it may be so. Literary critics such as Stanley Edgar Hyman, writing in *The Tangled Bank* (1962), have understood the aesthetics of Darwin's style, but it has remained for rhetoric to make the connection between aesthetic effect and overall plausibility and persuasiveness.

What the Darwin example shows is that in the study of scientific discourse, as much as in the study of literature, rhetorical analysis is proving fruitful. The question remains one of how rhetorical analysis can help bring science and literature together. Rather than speaking in abstractions, I want, once again, to show how in one instance, the author-audience relationship in a great work of literature bears remarkable resemblance to the author-audience relationship implicit in a roughly contemporaneous great work of science. I want to point to a rhetorical similarity between Milton's *Paradise Lost* and Newton's *Principia*. (Newton is supposed to have "discovered" gravity in 1665–6; Milton published the first edition of his epic poem in 1667.)

One of the classic interpretive questions about *Paradise Lost* is, why does the snake have all the good lines? Or, to put it somewhat more elegantly, why are the virtuous characters so dull and the evil ones so interesting? Of course, there have been any number of attempted answers, Blake for one thinking that Milton was of the Devil's party whether he knew it or not. Stanley Fish, himself a prominent participant in the revival of rhetoric within literary studies, has suggested a rhetorical answer. In *Surprised by Sin* (1967), Fish argues that—*mirabile dictu*—Milton knew what he was doing, that he intended these effects.

Why would Milton have done such a thing? Fish believes the answer is clear once we consider Milton's view of his audience. Milton believed his audience to be composed of fallen men—men, indeed, who because of their fallen nature were not inclined to admit their own fundamental depravity, unless of course they were illuminated by grace. In *Paradise Lost* Milton was recounting for this audience the epic of how they became depraved. An important part of this recounting was for Milton's audience to realize, to realize fully, that they were indeed the sons and daughters of Adam and Eve, that they were fallen creatures, weak to the temptations of the Arch-Tempter. So Milton gave his Lucifer the tools of his trade, fully expecting his audience to fall again and again to Lucifer's charms, to fall only to be reminded again and again that they have listened in admiration to the embodiment of all evil. The saved in Milton's audience would be chastened by these reminders, the damned only perplexed.

No one might seem farther from this religious exchange between Milton and his audience than Isaac Newton, who was virtually deified by his eighteenth-century readers for his cold rationalism and objectivity. However, much of the most important work on Newton over the past twenty-five years has shown this Newton to be a figment of eighteenth-century scientific ideology. The real Newton was much closer to Milton than Voltaire would have liked to admit. But first let us look at Newton's idiosyncrasies as a writer.

Newton was extremely reluctant to make public his natural philosophy. As published, some of the most important parts of the *Principia* (1687) are tucked away in structurally unimportant sections. The discussion of absolute space and time, for instance, is included in a scholium. For a time he considered suppressing the whole third book of the *Principia,* the very book in which his mathematics is finally applied to the physical world. In short, his attitude to his own writing at times seems so secretive as to be almost pathological, leading at least one historian—Frank Manuel—to seek a psychoanalytic explanation. A different explanation is suggested by Newton's efforts at biblical exegesis.

Newton believed that he was living in the last days, the time prophesied in Daniel and the Apocalypse. The forces of the anti-Christ were on the march, and the people of God were being sorely tested. It was also a time when the people of God were recovering the revelation of God in its pristine form. No longer would this revelation be obscured in myth and allegory; now it could be rationally demonstrated, at least to those who were not wicked at heart.

The rhetorical implications of Newton's view of his own situation are striking. Newton faced a particularly acute form of the standard problem of the author forced to address a composite audience containing diverse and even opposed elements. It is the same audience problem that Milton had, but in a more extreme form.

In such a rhetorical context, Newton's reluctance to publish is understandable. His writing, once published, would be not just for Cambridge, but for the entire learned (Latin-literate) world. It was work that was going to be read by the wicked as well as the wise. With his work, the wise might be purified; but with it the wicked might just as easily try to do wickedly. Newton might decide to speak to this mixed audience, but he need not decide to speak to it candidly. He would write so that the good would understand, and the rest would be vexed. This decision is reflected, as I have tried to show in detail in my *Confidence of British Philosophers* (1977)—not just in Newton's general attitude toward his writing, but in the details of his presentation, or rather half-presentation, of his theories.

I think the kind of rhetorical affinity which I have sketched here between Milton and Newton should be found between other poets and scientists of other times and places—between, say, Victorian poets (and novelists) and Darwin. Noting these is one important way to create a bridge between the sciences and the humanities.

What I have been trying to suggest through my examples (at once so fragmentary and superficial in themselves) is that the rhetorical perspective on discourse, with its emphasis on audience, has a decisive contribution to make to our understanding of the relation between science and literature. The traditional philosophies of science have emphasized the difference between science and nonscience, emphasized what sets science apart, even above, other disciplines. So, too, traditional literary theory has emphasized the peculiarly aesthetic use of language, what sets literature apart, even above. Rhetoric simply offers a complementary perspective, one that emphasizes the common ground of all discourse by which one person endeavors to influence others. The great scientist and the great literary artist may be something more than skillful rhetors, but they are at least that—and this may be exactly what they share.

Patiann Rogers

Currently residing in Colorado with her retired geophysicist husband, Patiann Rogers (b. 1940) is considered to be a premier American poet. During her career as a writer, Rogers has created works that encourage readers to re-envision their relationship to the world, particularly the natural world. Her poetry frequently blends the spiritual and scientific, revealing, without sentimentalizing, the ways in which issues concerning love and sexuality are bound up with science. For her seven books of poetry Rogers has received numerous prizes: the Hokin Prize, the Tietjens Prize, and the Bock Prize from Poetry; *three awards from the Texas Institute of Letters; two Strousse Awards from the* Prairie Schooner; *the Theodore Roethke Prize from* Poetry Northwest; *and five Pushcart prizes. She has also been the beneficiary of two NEA grants: a Guggenheim fellowship and a Lannan Poetry fellowship. From 1993 to 1997 Rogers was an associate professor at the University of Arkansas, and she has been a visiting writer at many universities and colleges. The "Study of the Splinter Expert" was originally published in* Legendary Performance *(1987).*

The Study of the Splinter Expert

An expert on splinters was the guest lecturer
Featured at the academy last week. His career began
As a youthful hobby—a curiosity concerning
The minute lines in slivers of oak and ash, an expanding
Collection of glass splinters, purple, scarlet;
Metal shavings.

Spending two years as a student sorting
Through the refuse left from the explosion
Of a single pine, deciphering patterns in that tangled
Fall of feathered wood, he discovered and classified
Fifty varieties of splinters broken from splinters.

His meticulous investigation of the calls
Of the meadowlark splintering the spring afternoon
Led to his first book, *The Splinters of Time*.
Since then he has completed research on the splinters

Of moonlight made by the needles of icy firs, wind
Splintering the silver surface of the lake, the splintering
Of the wind by the blades of the bur reed.

In any entity he can only see the underlying
Truth of its splintered reality—the red
And yellow splinters composing rattle box
And hibiscus blooms, splinters forming
In the fertile egg of the swamp snake, the potential
Splinters of chill in future snow. He predicts
The eventual development of an instrument able to locate
And describe each splinter of space.

Concerned with the splintering action of analysis itself,
He has carefully studied photographs of himself
Taken as he scrutinized shavings from the femurs
Of unborn calves, shatters of hickory found
Before the rising of the sap. He has attempted
To locate in his own eye that splinter of light
Creating the original concept of "splinter."

Thursday evening he lectured on his recent
Proposal that the sharpest, most painful
Splinter experienced is not of micromagnesium
Or glass silk but the splinter of pure hypothesis.

A well-known seer has predicted that the death
Of this expert will come by steel splinter piercing
His eye and brain, whereby he will enter that coveted state—
The perfect union of object and idea.

Felicia, infatuated with the erudite demeanor
Of the splinter expert, hasn't left her bed during the five days
Since his departure. She is using a calculator to count
The splinters of loss filling the distance multiplying
Between them, and she's afraid that, should she rise,
The splinters of her despair, blending like moonlight
On the floor, would scatter like dust and be lost forever.

Richard Selzer

The son of a family doctor, Richard Selzer (b. 1928) was born in Troy, New York. He attended Union College in Schenectady, New York, and earned an M.D. at Albany Medical College in 1953. A former teacher of both surgery and writing at Yale, Selzer has devoted himself to his writing since 1984, when he quit his private practice in medicine. Selzer has commented on the fact that the impulse to write struck him unexpectedly, "Writing came to me late, like a wisdom tooth. I was 40 years old before the energy to write appeared. I had been a surgeon for a long time before that." His first published work was a collection of short horror stories (which he took to writing in the middle of the night) entitled Rituals of Surgery *(1974). He subsequently published numerous essays and stories in such magazines as* Redbook, Esquire, *and* Harper's, *which were then collected in two volumes of essays,* Mortal Lessons *(1977), in which "The Exact Location of the Soul" first appeared, and* Confessions of a Knife *(1979). Other important works include two essay collections,* Letters to a Young Doctor *(1982) and* Taking the World in for Repairs *(1986); and two books of memoirs,* Down from Troy: A Doctor Comes of Age *(1992) and* Raising the Dead *(1994). He has received many awards for his writing, including a National Magazine Award (1975), an American Medical Writer's Award (1984), a Pushcart Prize, and a Guggenheim fellowship (1985). In his writing, Selzer frequently brings together his experiences as a surgeon with his sense of humanity and morality, expressing these in tactile, evocative language.*

The Exact Location of the Soul

Someone asked me why a surgeon would write. Why, when the shelves are already too full? They sag under the deadweight of books. To add a single adverb is to risk exceeding the strength of the boards. A surgeon should abstain. A surgeon, whose fingers are more at home in the steamy gullies of the body than they are tapping the dry keys of a typewriter. A surgeon, who feels the slow slide of intestines against the back of his hand and is no more alarmed than were a family of snakes taking their comfort from such an indolent rubbing. A surgeon, who palms the human heart as though it were some captured bird.

Reprinted from *Mortal Lessons: Notes on the Art of Surgery*, (1976), Simon & Schuster

Why should he write? Is it vanity that urges him? There is glory enough in the knife. Is it for money? One can make too much money. No. It is to search for some meaning in the ritual of surgery, which is at once murderous, painful, healing, and full of love. It is a devilish hard thing to transmit—to find, even. Perhaps if one were to cut out a heart, a lobe of the liver, a single convolution of the brain, and paste it to a page, it would speak with more eloquence than all the words of Balzac. Such a piece would need no literary style, no mass of erudition or history, but in its very shape and feel would tell all the frailty and strength, the despair and nobility of man. What? Publish a heart? A little piece of bone? Preposterous. Still I fear that is what it may require to reveal the truth that lies hidden in the body. Not all the undressings of Rabelais, Chekhov, or even William Carlos Williams have wrested it free, although God knows each one of those doctors made a heroic assault upon it.

I have come to believe that it is the flesh alone that counts. The rest is that with which we distract ourselves when we are not hungry or cold, in pain or ecstasy. In the recesses of the body I search for the philosophers' stone. I know it is there, hidden in the deepest, dampest cul-de-sac. It awaits discovery. To find it would be like the harnessing of fire. It would illuminate the world. Such a quest is not without pain. Who can gaze on so much misery and feel no hurt? Emerson has written that the poet is the only true doctor. I believe him, for the poet, lacking the impediment of speech with which the rest of us are afflicted, gazes, records, diagnoses, and prophesies.

I invited a young diabetic woman to the operating room to amputate her leg. She could not see the great shaggy black ulcer upon her foot and ankle that threatened to encroach upon the rest of her body, for she was blind as well. There upon her foot was a Mississippi Delta brimming with corruption, sending its raw tributaries down between her toes. Gone were all the little web spaces that when fresh and whole are such a delight to loving men. She could not see her wound, but she could feel it. There is no pain like that of the bloodless limb turned rotten and festering. There is neither unguent nor anodyne to kill such a pain yet leave intact the body.

For over a year I trimmed away the putrid flesh, cleansed, anointed, and dressed the foot, staving off, delaying. Three times each week, in her darkness, she sat upon my table, rocking back and forth, holding her extended leg by the thigh, gripping it as though it were a rocket that must be steadied lest it explode and scatter her toes about the room. And I would cut away a bit here, a bit there, of the swollen blue leather that was her tissue.

At last we gave up, she and I. We could no longer run ahead of the gangrene. We had not the legs for it. There must be an amputation in order that she might live—and I as well. It was to heal us both that I must take up knife and saw, and cut the leg off. And when I could feel it drop from her body to the table, see the blessed *space* appear between her and that leg, I too would be well.

Now it is the day of the operation. I stand by while the anesthetist administers the drugs, watch as the tense familiar body relaxes into narcosis. I turn then to uncover the leg. There, upon her kneecap, she has drawn, blindly, upside down for me to see, a face; just a circle with two ears, two eyes, a nose, and a smiling upturned mouth. Under it she has printed SMILE, DOCTOR. Minutes later I listen to the sound of the saw, until a little crack at the end tells me it is done.

So, I have learned that man is not ugly, but that he is Beauty itself. There is no other his equal. Are we not all dying, none faster or more slowly than any other? I have become receptive to the possibilities of love (for it is love, this thing that happens in the operating room), and each day I wait, trembling in the busy air. Perhaps today it will come. Perhaps today I will find it, take part in it, this love that blooms in the stoniest desert.

All through literature the doctor is portrayed as a figure of fun. Shaw was splenetic about him; Molière delighted in pricking his pompous medicine men, and well they deserved it. The doctor is ripe for caricature. But I believe that the truly great writing about doctors has not yet been done. I think it must be done *by* a doctor, one who is through with the love affair with his technique, who recognizes that he has played Narcissus, raining kisses on a mirror, and who now, out of the impacted masses of his guilt, has expanded into self-doubt, and finally into the high state of wonderment. Perhaps he will be a nonbeliever who, after a lifetime of grand gestures and mighty deeds, comes upon the knowledge that he has done no more than meddle in the lives of his fellows, and that he has done at least as much harm as good. Yet he may continue to pretend, at least, that there is nothing to fear, that death will not come, so long as people depend on his authority. Later, after his patients have left, he may closet himself in his darkened office, sweating and afraid.

There is a story by Unamuno, in which a priest, living in a small Spanish village, is adored by all the people for his piety, kindness, and the majesty with which he celebrates the mass each Sunday. To them he is already a saint. It is a foregone conclusion, and they speak of him as Saint Immanuel. He helps them with their plowing and planting, tends them when they are sick, confesses them, comforts them in death, and every Sunday, in his rich, thrilling voice, transports them to paradise with his chanting. The fact is that Don Immanuel is not so much a saint as a martyr. Long ago his own faith left him. He is an atheist, a good man doomed to suffer the life of a hypocrite, pretending to a faith he does not have. As he raises the chalice of wine, his hands tremble, and a cold sweat pours from him. He cannot stop for he knows that the people need this of him, that their need is greater than his sacrifice. Still . . . still . . . could it be that Don Immanuel's whole life is a kind of prayer, a paean to God?

A writing doctor would treat men and women with equal reverence, for what is the "liberation" of either sex to him who knows the diagrams, the inner geographies of each? I love the solid heft of men as much as I adore the heated capaciousness of women—women in whose penetralia is found the repository of existence. I would have them glory in that. Women are physics and chemistry. They are matter. It is their bodies that tell of the frailty of men. Men have not their cellular, enzymatic wisdom. Man is albuminoid, proteinaceous, laked pearl; woman is yolky, ovoid, rich. Both are exuberant bloody growths. I would use the defects and deformities of each for my sacred purpose of writing, for I know that it is the marred and scarred and faulty that are subject to grace. I would seek the soul in the facts of animal economy and profligacy. Yes, it is the exact location of the soul that I am after. The smell of it is in my nostrils. I have caught glimpses of it in the body diseased. If only I could tell it. Is there no mathematical equation that can guide me? So much pain and pus equals so much truth? It is elusive as the whippoorwill that one hears calling incessantly from out the night window, but which, nesting as it does low in the brush, no one sees. No one but the poet, for he sees what no one else can. He was born with the eye for it.

Once I thought I had it: Ten o'clock one night, the end room off a long corridor in a college infirmary, my last patient of the day, degree of exhaustion suitable for the appearance of a vision, some manifestation. The patient is a young man recently returned from Guatemala, from the excavation of Mayan ruins. His left upper arm wears a gauze dressing which, when removed, reveals a clean punched-out hole the size of a dime. The tissues about the opening are swollen and tense. A thin brownish fluid lips the edge, and now and then a lazy drop of the overflow spills down the arm. An abscess, inadequately drained. I will enlarge the opening to allow better egress of the pus. Nurse, will you get me a scalpel and some . . . ?

What happens next is enough to lay Francis Drake avomit in his cabin. No explorer ever stared in wilder surmise than I into that crater from which there now emerges a narrow gray head whose sole distinguishing feature is a pair of black pincers. The head sits atop a longish flexible neck arching now this way, now that, testing the air. Alternately it folds back upon itself, then advances in new boldness. And all the while, with dreadful rhythmicity, the unspeakable pincers open and close. Abscess? Pus? Never. Here is the lair of a beast at whose malignant purpose I could but guess. A Mayan devil, I think, that would soon burst free to fly about the room, with horrid blanket-wings and iridescent scales, raking, pinching, injecting God knows what acid juice. And even now the irony does not escape me, the irony of my patient as excavator excavated.

With all the ritual deliberation of a high priest I advance a surgical clamp toward the hole. The surgeon's heart is become a bat hanging upside down from his rib cage. The rim achieved—now thrust—and the ratchets of the clamp close upon the empty air. The devil has retracted. Evil mocking laughter bangs back and forth in the brain. More stealth. Lying in wait. One must skulk. Minutes pass, perhaps an hour. . . . A faint disturbance in the lake, and once again the thing upraises, farther and farther, hovering. Acrouch, strung, the surgeon is one with his instrument; there is no longer any boundary between its metal and his flesh. They are joined in a single perfect tool of extirpation. It is just for this that he was born. Now—thrust—and clamp—and *yes*. Got him!

Transmitted to the fingers comes the wild thrashing of the creature. Pinned and wriggling, he is mine. I hear the dry brittle scream of the dragon, and a hatred seizes me, but such a detestation as would make of Iago a drooling sucktit. It is the demented hatred of the victor for the vanquished, the warden for his prisoner. It is the hatred of fear. Within the jaws of my hemostat is the whole of the evil of the world, the dark concentrate itself, and I shall kill it. For mankind. And, in so doing, will open the way into a thousand years of perfect peace. Here is Surgeon as Savior indeed.

Tight grip now . . . steady, relentless pull. How it scrabbles to keep its tentacle-hold. With an abrupt moist plop the extraction is complete. There, writhing in the teeth of the clamp, is a dirty gray body, the size and shape of an English walnut. He is hung everywhere with tiny black hooklets. Quickly . . . into the specimen jar of saline . . . the lid screwed tight. Crazily he swims round and round, wiping his slimy head against the glass, then slowly sinks to the bottom, the mass of hooks in frantic agonal wave.

"You are going to be all right," I say to my patient. "We are *all* going to be all right from now on."

The next day I take the jar to the medical school. "That's the larva of the botfly," says a pathologist. "The fly usually bites a cow and deposits its eggs beneath the skin. There, the egg develops into the larval form which, when ready, burrows its way to the outside through the hide and falls to the ground. In time it matures into a full-grown botfly. This one happened to bite a man. It was about to come out on its own, and, of course, it would have died."

The words *imposter, sorehead, servant of Satan* spring to my lips. But now he has been joined by other scientists. They nod in agreement. I gaze from one gray eminence to another, and know the mallet-blow of glory pulverized. I tried to save the world, but it didn't work out.

No, it is not the surgeon who is God's darling. He is the victim of vanity. It is the poet who heals with his words, stanches the flow of blood, stills the rattling breath, applies poultice to the scalded flesh.

Did you ask me why a surgeon writes? I think it is because I wish to be a doctor.

Mary Shelley

Born in 1797 to the radical thinkers Mary Wollstonecraft and William Godwin, Mary Shelley sometimes felt overshadowed by her famous parents. Her lack of confidence in her writing was not helped by her marriage to one of the most important poets of the Romantic period, Percy Bysshe Shelley. The most famous men in English Literature of the period, particularly Lord Byron, surrounded Mary Shelley. When she first dreamt up her most famous story Frankenstein *in 1815, the result of a contest with Lord Byron to create the best ghost story, Mary was only eighteen years old (and the runaway mistress of Percy Shelley). Mary married Shelley in 1816 after his first wife committed suicide, but he drowned in 1822 and she never remarried. Three of Mary's children, all under the age of four, died in those eight years she spent with Percy. Although Shelley was proud of her mother's independent mind and read her book,* A Vindication of the Rights of Woman, *numerous times, Wollstonecraft's death ten days after Mary's birth made it impossible for her to influence her daughter's upbringing. As a result, her stepmother, who did not share her mother's revolutionary ideas concerning education for women, educated Mary. Optimism concerning human perfectibility features in much Romantic literature, but Shelley's works often temper the desire for social change with skepticism. It is likely that Shelley's views were colored by the fact that both her parents were early supporters of the French Revolution, but they both withdrew this support when the excess of violence became impossible to ignore. Traces of these influences on her life can be found in the story reproduced here, "The Mortal Immortal," which was first published in 1833.*

The Mortal Immortal

July 16, 1833.—This is a memorable anniversary for me; on it I complete my three hundred and twenty-third year!

The Wandering Jew?—certainly not. More than eighteen centuries have passed over his head. In comparison with him, I am a very young Immortal.

Am I, then, immortal? This is a question which I have asked myself, by day and night, for now three hundred and three years, and yet cannot answer it. I detected a grey hair amidst my brown locks this very day—that surely signifies decay. Yet it may have remained concealed there for three hundred years—for some persons have become entirely white-headed before twenty years of age.

I will tell my story, and my reader shall judge for me. I will tell my story, and so contrive to pass some few hours of a long eternity, become so wearisome to me. For ever! Can it be? to live for ever! I have heard of enchantments, in which the victims were plunged into a deep sleep, to wake, after a hundred years, as fresh as ever: I have heard of the Seven Sleepers—thus to be immortal would not be so burthensome: but, oh! the weight of never-ending time—the tedious passage of the still-succeeding hours! How happy was the fabled Nourjahad!—But to my task.

All the world has heard of Cornelius Agrippa. His memory is as immortal as his arts have made me. All the world has also heard of his scholar, who, unawares, raised the foul fiend during his master's absence, and was destroyed by him. The report, true or false, of this accident, was attended with many inconveniences to the renowned philosopher. All his scholars at once deserted him—his servants disappeared. He had no one near him to put coals on his ever-burning fires while he slept, or to attend to the changeful colours of his medicines while he studied. Experiment after experiment failed, because one pair of hands was insufficient to complete them: the dark spirits laughed at him for not being able to retain a single mortal in his service.

I was then very young—very poor—and very much in love. I had been for about a year the pupil of Cornelius, though I was absent when this accident took place. On my return, my friends implored me not to return to the alchymist's abode. I trembled as I listened to the dire tale they told; I required no second warning; and when Cornelius came and offered me a purse of gold if I would remain under his roof, I felt as if Satan himself tempted me. My teeth chattered—my hair stood on end;—I ran off as fast as my trembling knees would permit.

My failing steps were directed whither for two years they had every evening been attracted,—a gently bubbling spring of pure living water, beside which lingered a dark-haired girl, whose beaming eyes were fixed on the path I was accustomed each night to tread. I cannot remember the hour when I did not love Bertha; we had been neighbours and playmates from infancy,—her parents, like mine were of humble life, yet respectable,—our attachment had been a source of pleasure to them. In an evil hour, a malignant fever carried off both her father and mother, and Bertha became an orphan. She would have found a home beneath my paternal roof, but, unfortunately, the old lady of the near castle, rich, childless, and solitary, declared her intention to adopt her. Henceforth Bertha was clad in silk—inhabited a marble palace—and was looked on as being highly favoured by fortune. But in her new situation among her new associates, Bertha remained true to the friend of her humbler days; she often visited the cottage of my father, and when forbidden to go thither, she would stray towards the neighbouring wood, and meet me beside its shady fountain.

She often declared that she owed no duty to her new protectress equal in sanctity to that which bound us. Yet still I was too poor to marry, and she grew weary of being tormented on my account. She had a haughty but an impatient spirit, and grew angry at the obstacle that prevented our union. We met now after an absence, and she had been sorely beset while I was away; she complained bitterly, and almost reproached me for being poor. I replied hastily,—

"I am honest, if I am poor!—were I not, I might soon become rich!"

This exclamation produced a thousand questions. I feared to shock her by owning the truth, but she drew it from me; and then, casting a look of disdain on me, she said,—

"You pretend to love, and you fear to face the Devil for my sake!"

I protested that I had only dreaded to offend her;—while she dwelt on the magnitude of the reward that I should receive. Thus encouraged—shamed by her—led on by love and hope, laughing at my later fears, with quick steps and a light heart, I returned to accept the offers of the alchymist, and was instantly installed in my office.

A year passed away. I became possessed of no insignificant sum of money. Custom had banished my fears. In spite of the most painful vigilance, I had never detected the trace of a cloven foot; nor was the studious silence of our abode ever disturbed by demoniac howls. I still continued my stolen interviews with Bertha, and Hope dawned on me—Hope—but not perfect joy: for Bertha fancied that love and security were enemies, and her pleasure was to divide them in my bosom. Though true of heart, she was something of a coquette in manner; I was jealous as a Turk. She slighted me in a thousand ways, yet would never acknowledge herself to be in the wrong. She would drive me mad with anger, and then force me to beg her pardon. Sometimes she fancied that I was not sufficiently submissive, and then she had some story of a rival, favoured by her protectress. She was surrounded by silk-clad youths—the rich and gay. What chance had the sad-robed scholar of Cornelius compared with these?

On one occasion, the philosopher made such large demands upon my time, that I was unable to meet her as I was wont. He was engaged in some mighty work, and I was forced to remain, day and night, feeding his furnaces and watching his chemical preparations. Bertha waited for me in vain at the fountain. Her haughty spirit fired at this neglect; and when at last I stole out during a few short minutes allotted to me for slumber, and hoped to be consoled by her, she received me with disdain, dismissed me in scorn, and vowed that any man should possess her hand rather than he who could not be in two places at once for her sake. She would be revenged! And truly she was. In my dingy retreat I heard that she had been hunting, attended by Albert Hoffer. Albert Hoffer was favoured by her protectress, and the three passed in cavalcade before my smoky window. Methought that they mentioned my name; it was followed by a laugh of derision, as her dark eyes glanced contemptuously towards my abode.

Jealousy, with all its venom and all its misery, entered my breast. Now I shed a torrent of tears, to think that I should never call her mine; and, anon, I imprecated a thousand curses on her inconstancy. Yet, still I must stir the fires of the alchymist, still attend on the changes of his unintelligible medicines.

Cornelius had watched for three days and nights, nor closed his eyes. The progress of his alembics was slower than he expected: in spite of his anxiety, sleep weighted upon his eyelids. Again and again he threw off drowsiness with more than human energy; again and again it stole away his senses. He eyed his crucibles wistfully. "Not ready yet," he murmured; "will another night pass before the work is accomplished? Winzy, you are vigilant—you are faithful—you have slept, my boy—you slept last night. Look at that glass vessel. The liquid it contains is of a soft rose-colour: the moment it begins to change hue, awaken me—till then I may close my eyes. First, it will turn white, and then emit golden flashes; but wait not till then; when the rose-colour fades, rouse me." I scarcely heard the last words, muttered, as they were, in sleep. Even then he did not quite yield to nature. "Winzy, my boy," he again said, "do not touch the vessel—do not put it to your lips; it is a philtre—a philtre to cure love; you would not cease to love your Bertha—beware to drink!"

And he slept. His venerable head sunk on his breast, and I scarce heard his regular breathing. For a few minutes I watched the vessel—the rosy hue of the liquid remained unchanged. Then my thoughts wandered—they visited the fountain, and dwelt on a thousand charming scenes never to be renewed—never! Serpents and adders were in my heart as the word "Never!" half formed itself on my lips. False girl!—false and cruel! Never more would she smile on me as that evening she smiled on Albert. Worthless, detested woman! I would not remain unrevenged—she should see Albert expire at her feet—she should die beneath my vengeance. She had smiled in disdain and triumph—she knew my wretchedness and her power. Yet what power had she?—the power of exciting my hate—my utter scorn—my—oh, all but indifference! Could I attain that—could I regard her with careless eyes, transferring my rejected love to one fairer and more true, that were indeed a victory!

A bright flash darted before my eyes. I had forgotten the medicine of the adept; I gazed on it with wonder: flashes of admirable beauty, more bright than those which the diamond emits when the sun's rays are on it, glanced from the surface of the liquid; an odour the most fragrant and grateful stole over my sense; the vessel seemed one globe of living radiance, lovely to the eye, and most inviting to the taste. The first thought, instinctively inspired by the grosser sense, was, I will—I must drink. I raised the vessel to my lips. "It will cure me of love—of torture!" Already I had quaffed half of the most delicious liquor ever tasted by the palate of man, when the philosopher stirred. I started—I dropped the glass—the fluid flamed and glanced along the floor, while I felt Cornelius's gripe at my throat, as he shrieked aloud, "Wretch! you have destroyed the labour of my life!"

The philosopher was totally unaware that I had drunk any portion of his drug. His idea was, and I gave a tacit assent to it, that I had raised the vessel from curiosity, and that, frightened at its brightness, and the flashes of intense light it gave forth, I had let it fall. I never undeceived him. The fire of the medicine was quenched—the fragrance died away—he grew calm, as a philosopher should under the heaviest trials, and dismissed me to rest.

I will not attempt to describe the sleep of glory and bliss which bathed my soul in paradise during the remaining hours of that memorable night. Words would be faint and shallow types of my enjoyment, or of the gladness that possessed my bosom when I woke. I trod air—my thoughts were in heaven. Earth appeared heaven, and my inheritance upon it was to be one trance of delight. "This it is to be cured of love," I thought; "I will see Bertha this day, and she will find her lover cold and regardless; too happy to be disdainful, yet how utterly indifferent to her!"

The hours danced away. The philosopher, secure that he had once succeeded, and believing that he might again, began to concoct the same medicine once more. He was shut up with his books and drugs, and I had a holiday. I dressed myself with care; I looked in an old but polished shield which served me for a mirror; methoughts my good looks had wonderfully improved. I hurried beyond the precincts of the town, joy in my soul, the beauty of heaven and earth around me. I turned my steps toward the castle—I could look on its lofty turrets with lightness of heart, for I was cured of love. My Bertha saw me afar off, as I came up the avenue. I know not what sudden impulse animated her bosom, but at the sight, she sprung with a light fawn-like bound down the marble steps, and was hastening towards me. But I had been perceived by another person. The old high-born hag, who called herself her protectress, and was her tyrant, had seen me also; she hobbled, panting, up the terrace; a page, as ugly as herself, held up her train, and fanned her as she hurried along, and stopped my fair girl with a "How, now, my bold mistress? whither so fast? Back to your cage—hawks are abroad!"

Bertha clasped her hands—her eyes were still bent on my approaching figure. I saw the contest. How I abhorred the old crone who checked the kind impulses of my Bertha's softening heart. Hitherto, respect for her rank had caused me to avoid the lady of the castle; now I disdained such trivial considerations. I was cured of love, and lifted above all human fears; I hastened forwards, and soon reached the terrace. How lovely Bertha looked! her eyes flashing fire, her cheeks glowing with impatience and anger, she was a thousand times more graceful and charming than ever. I no longer loved—oh no! I adored—worshipped—idolized her!

She had that morning been persecuted, with more than usual vehemence, to consent to an immediate marriage with my rival. She was reproached with the encouragement that she had shown him—she was threatened with being turned out of doors with disgrace and shame. Her proud spirit rose in arms at the threat; but when she remembered the scorn that she had heaped upon me, and how, perhaps, she had thus lost one whom she now regarded as her only friend, she wept with remorse and rage. At that moment I appeared. "Oh, Winzy!" she exclaimed, "take me to your mother's cot; swiftly let me leave the detested luxuries and wretchedness of this noble dwelling—take me to poverty and happiness."

I clasped her in my arms with transport. The old dame was speechless with fury, and broke forth into invective only when we were far on the road to my natal cottage. My mother received the fair fugitive, escaped from a gilt cage to nature and liberty, with tenderness and joy; my father, who loved her, welcomed her heartily; it was a day of rejoicing, which did not need the addition of the celestial potion of the alchymist to steep me in delight.

Soon after this eventful day, I became the husband of Bertha. I ceased to be the scholar of Cornelius, but I continued his friend. I always felt grateful to him for having, unaware, procured me that delicious draught of a divine elixir, which, instead of curing me of love (sad cure! solitary and joyless remedy for evils which seem blessings to the memory), had inspired me with courage and resolution, thus winning for me an inestimable treasure in my Bertha.

I often called to mind that period of trance-like inebriation with wonder. The drink of Cornelius had not fulfilled the task for which he affirmed that it had been prepared, but its effects were more potent and blissful than words can express.

They had faded by degrees, yet they lingered long—and painted life in hues of splendour. Bertha often wondered at my lightness of heart and unaccustomed gaiety; for, before, I had been rather serious, or even sad, in my disposition. She loved me the better for my cheerful temper, and our days were winged by joy.

Five years afterwards I was suddenly summoned to the bedside of the dying Cornelius. He had sent for me in haste, conjuring my instant presence. I found him stretched on his pallet, enfeebled even to death; all of life that yet remained animated his piercing eyes, and they were fixed on a glass vessel, full of roseate liquid.

"Behold," he said, in a broken and inward voice, "the vanity of human wishes! a second time my hopes are about to be crowned, a second time they are destroyed. Look at that liquor—you may remember five years ago I had prepared the same, with the same success;—then, as now, my thirsting lips expected to taste the immortal elixir—you dashed it from me! and at present it is too late."

He spoke with difficulty, and fell back on his pillow. I could not help saying,—

"How, revered master, can a cure for love restore you to life?"

A faint smile gleamed across his face as I listened earnestly to his scarcely intelligible answer.

"A cure for love and for all things—the Elixir of Immortality. Ah! if now I might drink, I should live for ever!"

As he spoke, a golden flash gleamed from the fluid; a well-remembered fragrance stole over the air; he raised himself, all weak as he was—strength seemed miraculously to re-enter his frame—he stretched forth his hand—a loud explosion startled me—a ray of fire shot up from the elixir, and the glass vessel which contained it was shivered to atoms! I turned my eyes towards the philosopher; he had fallen back—his eyes were glassy—his features rigid—he was dead!

But I lived, and was to live for ever! So said the unfortunate alchymist, and for a few days I believed his words. I remembered the glorious intoxication that had followed my stolen draught. I reflected on the change I had felt in my frame—in my soul. The bounding elasticity of the one—the buoyant lightness of the other. I surveyed myself in a mirror, and could perceive no change in my features during the space of the five years which had elapsed. I remembered the radiant hues and grateful scent of that delicious beverage—worthy the gift it was capable of bestowing—I was, then, **IMMORTAL**!

A few days after I laughed at my credulity. The old proverb, that "a prophet is least regarded in his own country," was true with respect to me and my defunct master. I loved him as a man—I respected him as a sage—but I derided the notion that he could command the powers of darkness, and laughed at the superstitious fears with which he was regarded by the vulgar. He was a wise philosopher, but had no acquaintance with any spirits but those clad in flesh and blood. His science was simply human; and human science, I soon persuaded myself, could never conquer nature's laws so far as to imprison the soul for ever within its carnal habitation. Cornelius had brewed a soul-refreshing drink—more inebriating than wine—sweeter and more fragrant than any fruit: it possessed probably strong medicinal powers, imparting gladness to the heart and vigour to the limbs; but its effects would wear out; already they were diminished in my frame. I was a lucky fellow to have quaffed health and joyous spirits, and perhaps a long life, at my master's hands; but my good fortune ended there: longevity was far different from immortality.

I continued to entertain this belief for many years. Sometimes a thought stole across me—Was the alchymist indeed deceived? But my habitual credence was, that I should meet the fate of all the children of Adam at my appointed time—a little late, but still at a natural age. Yet it was certain that I retained a wonderfully youthful look. I was laughed at for my vanity in consulting the mirror so often, but I consulted it in vain—my brow was untrenched—my cheeks—my eyes—my whole person continued as untarnished as in my twentieth year.

I was troubled. I looked at the faded beauty of Bertha—I seemed more like her son. By degrees our neighbors began to make similar observations, and I found at last that I went by the name of the Scholar bewitched. Bertha herself grew uneasy. She became jealous and peevish, and at length she began to question me. We had no children; we were all in all to each other; and though, as she grew older, her vivacious spirit became a little allied to ill-temper, and her beauty sadly diminished, I cherished her in my heart as the mistress I idolized, the wife I had sought and won with such perfect love.

At last our situation became intolerable: Bertha was fifty—I twenty years of age. I had, in very shame, in some measure adopted the habits of advanced age; I no longer mingled in the dance among the young and gay, but my heart bounded along with them while I restrained my feet; and a sorry figure I cut among the Nestors of our village. But before the time I mention, things were altered—we were universally shunned; we were—at least, I was—reported to have kept up an iniquitous acquaintance with some of my former master's supposed friends. Poor Bertha was pitied, but deserted. I was regarded with horror and detestation.

What was to be done? we sat by our winter fire—poverty had made itself felt, for none would buy the produce of my farm; and often I had been forced to journey twenty miles to some place where I was not known, to dispose of our property. It is true, we had saved something for an evil day—that day was come.

We sat by our lone fireside—the old-hearted youth and his antiquated wife. Again Bertha insisted on knowing the truth; she recapitulated all she had ever heard said about me, and added her own observations. She conjured me to cast off the spell; she described how much more comely grey hairs were than my chestnut locks; she descanted on the reverence and respect due to age—how preferable to the slight regard paid to mere children: could I imagine that the despicable gifts of youth and good looks outweighed disgrace, hatred and scorn? Nay, in the end I should be burnt as a dealer in the black art, while she, to whom I had not deigned to communicate any portion of my good fortune, might be stoned as my accomplice. At length she insinuated that I must share my secret with her, and bestow on her like benefits to those I myself enjoyed, or she would denounce me—and then she burst into tears.

Thus beset, methought it was the best way to tell the truth. I revealed it as tenderly as I could, and spoke only of a *very long life*, not of immortality—which representation, indeed, coincided best with my own ideas. When I ended I rose and said,—

"And now, my Bertha, will you denounce the lover of your youth?—You will not, I know. But it is too hard, my poor wife, that you should suffer for my ill-luck and the accursed arts of Cornelius. I will leave you—you have wealth enough, and friends will return in my absence. I will go; young as I seem and strong as I am, I can work and gain my bread among strangers, unsuspected and unknown. I loved you in youth; God is my witness that I would not desert you in age, but that your safety and happiness require it."

I took my cap and moved toward the door; in a moment Bertha's arms were round my neck, and her lips were pressed to mine. "No, my husband, my Winzy," she said, "you shall not go alone—take me with you; we will remove from this place, and, as you say, among strangers we shall be unsuspected and safe. I am not so old as quite to shame you, my Winzy; and I daresay the charm will soon wear off, and, with the blessing of God, you will become more elderly-looking, as is fitting; you shall not leave me."

I returned the good soul's embrace heartily. "I will not, my Bertha; but for your sake I had not thought of such a thing. I will be your true, faithful husband while you are spared to me, and do my duty by you to the last."

The next day we prepared secretly for our emigration. We were obliged to make great pecuniary sacrifices—it could not be helped. We realized a sum sufficient, at least, to maintain us while Bertha lived; and, without saying adieu to any one, quitted our native country to take refuge in a remote part of western France.

It was a cruel thing to transport poor Bertha from her native village, and the friends of her youth, to a new country, new language, new customs. The strange secret of my destiny rendered this removal immaterial to me; but I compassionated her deeply, and was glad to perceive that she found compensation for her misfortunes in a variety of little ridiculous circumstances. Away from all tell-tale chroniclers, she sought to decrease the apparent disparity of our ages by a thousand feminine arts—rouge, youthful dress, and assumed juvenility of manner. I could not be angry. Did I not myself wear a mask? Why quarrel with hers, because it was less successful? I grieved deeply when I remembered that this was my Bertha, whom I had loved so fondly and won with such transport—the dark-eyed, dark-haired girl, with smiles of enchanting archness and a step like a fawn—this mincing, simpering, jealous old woman. I should have revered her grey locks and withered cheeks; but thus!—It was my work, I knew; but I did not the less deplore this type of human weakness.

Her jealousy never slept. Her chief occupation was to discover that, in spite of outward appearances, I was myself growing old. I verily believe that the poor soul loved me truly in her heart, but never had woman so tormenting a mode of displaying fondness. She would discern wrinkles in my face and decrepitude in my walk, while I bounded along in youthful vigour, the youngest looking of twenty youths. I never dared address another woman. On one occasion, fancying that the belle of the village regarded me with favouring eyes, she brought me a grey wig. Her constant discourse among her acquaintances was, that though I looked so young, there was ruin at work within my frame; and she affirmed that the worst symptom about me was my apparent health. My youth was a disease, she said, and I ought at all times to prepare, if not for a sudden and awful death, at least to awake some morning white-headed and bowed down with all the marks of advanced years. I let her talk—I often joined in her conjectures. Her warnings chimed in with my never-ceasing speculations concerning my state, and I took an earnest, though painful, interest in listening to all that her quick wit and excited imagination could say on the subject.

Why dwell on these minute circumstances? We lived on for many long years. Bertha became bedrid and paralytic; I nursed her as a mother might a child. She grew peevish, and still harped upon one string—of how long I should survive her. It has ever been a source of consolation to me, that I performed my duty scrupulously towards her. She had been mine in youth, she was mine in age; and at last, when I heaped the sod over her corpse, I wept to feel that I had lost all that really bound me to humanity.

Since then how many have been my cares and woes, how few and empty my enjoyments! I pause here in my history—I will pursue it no further. A sailor without rudder or compass, tossed on a stormy sea—a traveller lost on a widespread heath, without landmark or stone to guide him—such I have been: more lost, more hopeless than either. A nearing ship, a gleam from some far cot, may save them; but I have no beacon except the hope of death.

Death! mysterious, ill-visaged friend of weak humanity! Why alone of all mortals have you cast me from your sheltering fold? Oh, for the peace of the grave! the deep silence of the iron-bound tomb! that thought would cease to work in my brain, and my heart beat no more with emotions varied only by new forms of sadness!

Am I immortal? I return to my first question. In the first place, is it not more probably that the beverage of the alchymist was fraught rather with longevity than eternal life? Such is my hope. And then be it remembered, that I only drank *half* of the potion prepared by him. Was not the whole necessary to complete the charm? To have drained half the Elixir of Immortality is but to be half-immortal—my For-ever is thus truncated and null.

But again, who shall number the years of the half of eternity? I often try to imagine by what rule the infinite may be divided. Sometimes I fancy age advancing upon me. One grey hair I have found. Fool! do I lament? Yes, the fear of age and death often creeps coldly into my heart; and the more I live, the more I dread death, even while I abhor life. Such an enigma is man—born to perish—when he wars, as I do, against the established laws of his nature.

But for this anomaly of feeling surely I might die: the medicine of the alchymist would not be proof against fire—sword—and the strangling waters. I have gazed upon the blue depths of many a placid lake, and the tumultuous rushing of many a mighty river, and have said, peace inhabits those waters; yet I have turned my steps away, to live yet another day. I have asked myself, whether suicide would be a crime in one to whom thus only the portals of the other world could be opened. I have done all, except presenting myself as a soldier or duelist, an objection of destruction to my—no, *not* my fellow mortals, and therefore I have shrunk away. They are not my fellows. The inextinguishable power of life in my frame, and their ephemeral existence, places us wide as the poles asunder. I could not raise a hand against the meanest or the most powerful among them.

Thus have I lived on for many a year—alone, and weary of myself—desirous of death, yet never dying—a mortal immortal. Neither ambition nor avarice can enter my mind, and the ardent love that gnaws at my heart, never to be returned—never to find an equal on which to expend itself—lives there only to torment me.

This very day I conceived a design by which I may end all—without self-slaughter, without making another man a Cain—an expedition, which mortal frame can never survive, even endued with the youth and strength that inhabits mine. Thus I shall put my immortality to the test, and rest for ever—or return, the wonder and benefactor of the human species.

Before I go, a miserable vanity has caused me to pen these pages. I would not die, and leave no name behind. Three centuries have passed since I quaffed the fatal beverage; another year shall not elapse before, encountering gigantic dangers—warring with the powers of frost in their home—beset by famine, toil, and tempest—I yield this body, too tenacious a cage for a soul which thirsts for freedom, to the destructive elements of air and water; or, if I survive, my name shall be recorded as one of the most famous among the sons of men; and, my task achieved, I shall adopt more resolute means, and, by scattering and annihilating the atoms that compose my frame, set at liberty the life imprisoned within, and so cruelly prevented from soaring from this dim earth to a sphere more congenial to its immortal essence.

4

Reconsidering Gender and Space

Wendy Weise-Smith and Damla Isik

A man perfects himself by working. Foul jungles are cleared away, fair seed-fields rise instead, and stately cities; and withal the man himself first ceases to be a jungle, and foul unwholesome desert thereby [. . .] The man is now a man.

—Thomas Carlyle, Scottish essayist, historian.
Past and Present, 1843.

The woman is the home. That's where she used to be, and that's where she still is. You might ask me, What if a man tries to be part of the home—will the woman let him? I answer yes. Because then he becomes one of the children.

—Marguerite Duras, French author, filmmaker.
"House and Home," *Practicalities,* 1987.

Nothing puzzles me more than time and space; and yet nothing troubles me less, as I never think about them.

—Charles Lamb, English poet, playwright, children's author, literary critic. Letter 9 Aug 1815 to Robert Southey, English poet laureate, historian, literary critic.

As the camera zooms out from the refrigerator, we see a well-groomed woman sitting at the kitchen table. A voice tells her that there is a better, faster way of preparing breakfast. All she has to do is microwave some frozen sausages and breakfast will be ready in a flash. The woman obeys, as her kids and husband rush into the kitchen. Smiling, the woman places the microwaved sausages on the table. The man takes a sausage, looks up at her and grins. Both are content. The scene changes and we are suddenly transported to a discount store where we watch a woman shop with her teenage son. As they walk down the aisles of the electronics section, another male teenager appears to highlight the various advantages of a new computer. The woman watches as her son excitedly talks and nods in agreement with the male representative. In the end we assume that the computer is bought for the son.

How many commercials can we recall in which the man makes and serves breakfast while the woman gets ready for work? How many commercials do we see in which a tech-savvy woman shops for a computer for herself? We do not tend to ask why the mother is always in the kitchen while the father is always preparing to leave or why technology departments are represented as a masculine domain in popular commercials. Because such spaces and the people we perceive within them are naturalized in our minds, we rarely think about them. This chapter invites you to question the spaces we inhabit and to consider how these spaces articulate gender roles. Why are there more stay-at-home moms than stay-at-home dads? Why do we expect a woman to sit behind the secretary's desk and not a man? Why do men dominate physics or chemistry departments, while women occupy most of the seats in humanities departments? Why are spaces gendered?

First, what do we mean by "gender"? There are various and sometimes contradictory definitions. According to the World Health Organization,

> The term "gender" is used to describe those characteristics of women and men that are socially constructed, in contrast to those that are biologically determined. People are born female or male, but learn to be girls and boys who grow into women and men. They are taught what the appropriate behaviour and attitudes, roles and activities are for them, and how they should relate to other people. These learned attributes are what make up gender identity and determine gender roles.

UNIFEM, a Gender-AIDS (HIV) Network, explains gender as

> the widely shared ideas and expectations (norms) about women and men: ideas about "typically" feminine and masculine characteristics and abilities and expectations about how women and men should behave in various situations. These ideas and expectations are learned from families, friends, opinion leaders, religious and cultural institutions, schools, the workplace and the media. They reflect and influence the different roles, social status, and the economic and political power of women and men in society.

Both definitions highlight the powerful cultural forces that help us see ourselves and other human beings as men and women. (You might think of the President's relationship with his wife, the way media figures such as Howard Stern, Rush Limbaugh, or Dr. Laura talk about men and women, your church's or synagogue's doctrines on marriage, images of men and women in popular books, magazines, and even video games). In today's world, where many people cross over and between these boundaries, perceiving of themselves as not entirely feminine nor masculine but sometimes femininely-masculine, masculinely-feminine, or even gender neutral (the "New [sensitive] Man," tomboys, or unisex clothing—*The Gap*), such definitions may be problematic and need modification. Nevertheless, as the commercials mentioned above reveal, society retains and the media perpetuates conservative stereotypes of gender. In this chapter, we ask you to think critically about gender roles, in the hope that we can de-naturalize these categories.

This chapter also asks you to reconsider conceptions of space. When we think about space, most of us think of astronauts or NASA, and at the University of Arizona in particular, we also think of the equipment produced in our Lunar and Planetary Lab that assists in space exploration. But how about the space that surrounds you on a daily basis? Perhaps because it seems so invisible and therefore, benign, as Charles Lamb confesses, most of us never give it a thought.

Consider how your living arrangements at the University impact your behavior or the choices you can make. As a first-year student, you're likely living in a dorm. How has the spatial arrangement of this new environment caused you to change your routine or modify the way you used to live at home? Your personal space—a room perhaps shared with one or more people—has become much smaller; your working space limited to a tiny desk, positioned in the same room in which you and your roommates all sleep; your closet holds *at most* a week's worth of clean laundry; and the kitchen and bathrooms are located down a hall rather than adjoined conveniently to your bedroom. These spatial and architectural arrangements impact everything from your decisions about whether you can take a nap or simply think uninterrupted to when you'll study or do laundry, and whether or not you can prepare a hot meal for yourself or walk in your underwear to the bathroom. This last observation leads us to the question of gender and the realization that these spaces are not gender-neutral. You might consider what additional accommodations to your lifestyle living on a co-ed versus same-sex floor would require. Perhaps you'd be more conscious of your appearance or of the articles you leave lying around your room, more aware of when your door is open or closed. Think about what's behind those doors as well. Can you tell when walking into another person's room what the gender of the inhabitant is? How does the inhabitant convey his or her gender and what sort of mental check list do you form to come to your conclusion?

It is not simply big spaces or architectural structures that influence us; the areas of smaller material objects affect us as well. Literary critics who study journals and diaries note how the size of a page and whether the pages are pre-dated and pre-lined, controls how much a diarist will write. They also consider the aesthetics of handwriting. Does it look feminine or masculine? Is it comparable to other female diarists, if studying a woman's text, or male diarists, if studying a man's text? If a woman's script looks masculine and a man's script looks feminine, what do these traits suggest? All of these factors, then, shape scholars' interpretations of the diary and the person—the story and sense of self this person crafts. Similarly, whether our notebooks are college- or wide-ruled (whether we have too much or too little space) determines the neatness of our writing and the number of notes we can and will take in our classes. If an archaeologist found your notebook for this course several hundred years from now, what would the way you take notes, whether you take notes, the decorations on your notebook, its color and size, your ink choice and handwriting style say about you? About your gender? In the essays that follow, you'll have the opportunity to do such investigative work, as you consider how everyday spaces influence, contradict, or function as a metaphor for another person's life.

Whether it is a woman hanging from the thirteenth-story window of a building—as in Joy Harjo's poem in this chapter—boys playing on a rugby field, or a woman alone in her bedroom, spaces and places shape and define our identities. In recent years, anthropologists, geologists, and architects have examined the different spaces men and women are allotted culturally and the specific role space plays in symbolizing, constructing, and enforcing gender roles. For example, the development of the suburban tract home in the 1950s and '60s changed American life as we knew it. No longer was the town center the center of a person's life. Rather, living in the suburbs required that one drive to the city, as opposed to having immediate access, to enjoy the theatre, cinema, or restaurants and to meet the necessities of life. This meant that those who worked were separated not only physically, but also geographically from the home, and since it was typically men who worked, the modernization of suburban life functioned to reinforce the patriarchal divide that associates woman with private or domestic space and man with public or worldly space. As Thomas Carlyle's and Marguerite Duras's quotes above observe: man needs to know how to survive in and organize public spaces in order to become a man, whereas a "woman is the home."

Because theories of gender are culturally constructed and people, to a certain extent, are products of their cultures, writers (sometimes purposely, sometimes unconsciously) incorporate social codes into their work, which can reflect or subvert cultural norms—or both. A critical understanding of these issues is central to deciphering the codes and multi-layered meanings within different kinds of texts. What we come to realize is that constructions of gender are political, and such stereotypes work to justify both the distribution and deployment of power. This paradigm, Doreen Massey argues in this chapter, is reinforced in modern times through architecture: some city spaces seem to be designed specifically to appeal to men but, as a result, deny women's contribution to and participation in men's lives and urban culture. In other words, we have found that spaces perpetuate gender ideologies. When we think of little girls' rooms, we imagine them as pink, decorated with frilly lace and dolls, and little boys' rooms as blue, studded with trucks, firemen and G.I. Joes. Similarly, we describe buildings or rooms with soft, round corners as feminine, but equate tall, erect, phallic structures with masculinity. In the selections in this chapter, then, you'll have an opportunity to watch these forces at play and re-consider how genders, spaces, and places are shaped. We hope you'll never look at architecture, geography, or the people who populate and construct these areas in quite the same way again.

As for the editors of this chapter, the politics of gender and space have influenced our lives in significant ways and changed our perspectives as well. Damla comes from a country that clearly distinguishes public space from private:

> Despite the fact that women in cities work side by side with men to provide for their families, women in rural places still prepare and wait for marriage. In villages, it is usually men who have the opportunity to go to school and learn how to read and write, while women, as the workers in the field and the workers in the home, do not have the same opportunity. Even in urban environments, which are considered enlightened and modern, this gendering of space still perpetuates. I can still picture my brother, who is 25 years old, entering the kitchen and not knowing where the pots and pans are. The kitchen is not his space; so, he simply never learns to operate within it. Just as spaces affect my brother's life, they affect mine as well. I experienced a distinct change of space three years ago when I came to the United States from Turkey. Izmir, the port city where I was born and where I grew up, lies sandwiched between mountains and the Aegean Sea. Here, the city of Tucson has a much wider space to grow. I remember seeing Tucson for the first time as my plane approached the city. It looked so massive and so flat. In many ways, I am still trying to get used to that flatness. In Izmir, Turkey, I was used to high apartment buildings; here everything is too close to the ground.

Wendy recalls the first time she realized the powerful connection between gender and space:

> The first academic conference I attended was held in New Haven, Connecticut. I was excited to visit Yale and see another part of the country. It was also the first time I stayed in a hotel alone. When I arrived the hotel turned out to be more of a motor inn, made up of separate buildings and rooms with doors facing the outside. At check-in, the room I had been assigned was located in the very last building on the bottom floor, adjacent to a defunct parking lot. The clerk chuckled as he mentioned that one of these rooms had been vandalized the night before. It took some convincing, but finally one of the managers agreed that it would be better for a single woman to have a room on the upper floor, closer to the lighted area of the front desk. Hungry, I asked if there was a place close-by to get some dinner and followed their advice on an Italian restaurant. I rarely eat out alone, but had brought some work with me, ordered my dinner, and tried to feel comfortable. Before my meal arrived, a man approached me. He and his friends had just ordered some more wine and wouldn't I like to join them? I looked over at their table, thanked him, but said I had quite a bit of work to do (a group of thirteen Italian men, alcohol, and one

> female in an area she didn't know didn't sound like a good mix to me). He walked back said something to the others and immediately returned. Pulling up a chair startlingly close and peering across my table in the dimly lit restaurant, he asked, "well, what are you working on . . . what are you doing *here*?" Eventually, he returned to his table, but as he did, the Don of the group hollered, 'So what's the situation?' The man who had approached me answered, 'She says she's a scholar.' 'A scholar?' the Don shouted. 'After all that?!? I knew a scholar once, she . . . She's a scholar? She comes in here, tall, thin, blonde, and all this, by herself. Who does she think she is? A scholar? No, she's got an air about her . . .' I was floored. Here I was, attending a conference on feminism and women in literature (an event dedicated to analyzing and deconstructing gender biases) and from the minute I'd arrived in New Haven, the spaces I occupy, my gender, and my sexuality had all been highlighted repeatedly. Later that night, I recorded the scene from the restaurant in my notebook and wondered, Why is it a woman can't go out alone at night? Why do we have to be constantly mindful of our safety—simply because we are women? Why does looking feminine somehow contradict what it means to be a serious scholar? These questions gave me much to think about during the critical, theoretical discussions of the conference, which somehow seemed so far removed from the previous night's events.

As you make your way through the readings in this chapter, you will find that they come together to illuminate the social ramifications of gendered spaces. Some more quietly and others more urgently draw our attention to the confinement or freedom women and men find in particular places, the ways in which they make sense of their identities, and the spaces they try to leave behind, destroy, or embrace in the process. What happens when spaces and genders meet? Let's find out together in this chapter.

Doreen Massey

Doreen Massey is Professor of Geography at The Open University in Milton Keynes, England. As just a few of her titles reveal— Cities for the Many Not the Few *(2000), "Imaging Globalization: Power-Geometries of Time-Space," "Spaces of Politics," and* High-Tech Fantasies: Science Parks in Society, Science, and Space *(1992), edited with Paul Quintas and David Wield—Massey studies the social and cultural politics of spaces and places. Her work ranges from the local to the global, from critiques of existing spaces to philosophically, conceptually, and/or politically re-theorizing future places.*

One of the forerunners in gender and special studies, Massey's 1994 text, Space, Place and Gender, *from which the following article is excerpted, was one of the first of its kind to call attention to the complex ways in which landscape, architecture, gender, and politics intersect. For this reason, her essay functions as a lens piece for the readings included in this chapter. Through three quite different examples—bodies on a football field, the decentralization of jobs in a coal mining town, and the geographic and architectural orientation of a high-tech town—Massey lays out clearly several of the critical elements involved in analyzing the relationships between space and gender and the gendering of spaces. She demonstrates why gender is political, how it can be reflected in local economics and politics, and how it is reinscribed in modern landscapes. Moreover, she extols the need for studying constructions of masculinity and femininity simultaneously, argues against essentialized or over-generalized analyses, and demonstrates how these goals shape her research and work.*

'Space, Place and Gender' from Space, Place and Gender *(1994)*

I can remember very clearly a sight which often used to strike me when I was nine or ten years old. I lived then on the outskirts of Manchester, and 'Going into Town' was a relatively big occasion; it took over half an hour and we went on the top deck of a bus. On the way into town we would cross the wide, shallow valley of the River Mersey, and my memory is of dank, muddy fields spreading away into a cold, misty distance. And all of it—all of these acres of Manchester—was

Reprinted from *LSE Magazine*, Spring 1992, London School of Economics Gender Institute.

divided up into football pitches and rugby pitches. And on Saturdays, which was when we went into Town, the whole vast area would be covered with hundreds of little people, all running around after balls, as far as the eye could see. (It seemed from the top of the bus like a vast, animated Lowry painting, with all the little people in rather brighter colours than Lowry used to paint them, and with cold red legs.)

I remember all this very sharply. And I remember, too, it striking me very clearly—even then as a puzzled, slightly thoughtful little girl—that all this huge stretch of the Mersey flood plain had been entirely given over to boys.

I did not go to those playing fields—they seemed barred, another world (though today, with more nerve and some consciousness of being a space-invader, I do stand on football terraces—and love it). But there were other places to which I did go, and yet where I still felt that they were not mine, or at least that they were designed to, or had the effect of, firmly letting me know my conventional subordination. I remember, for instance, in my late teens being in an Art Gallery (capital A capital G) in some town across the Channel. I was with two young men, and we were hitching around 'the Continent'. And this Temple of High Culture, which was one of The Places To Be Visited, was full of paintings, a high proportion of which were of naked women. They were pictures of naked women painted by men, and thus of women seen through the eyes of men. So I stood there with these two young friends, and they looked at these pictures which were of women seen through the eyes of men, and I looked at them, my two young friends, looking at pictures of naked women as seen through the eyes of men. And I felt objectified. This was a 'space' that clearly let me know something, and something ignominious, about what High Culture thought was my place in Society. The effect on me of being in that space/place was quite different from the effect it had on my male friends. (I remember that we went off to a café afterwards and had an argument about it. And I lost that argument, largely on the grounds that I was 'being silly'. I had not then had the benefit of reading Griselda Pollock, or Janet Wolff, or Whitney Chadwick . . . maybe I really *was* the only person who felt like that . . .)

I could multiply such examples, and so I am sure could anyone here today, whether woman or man. The only point I want to make is that space and place, spaces and places, and our senses of them (and such related things as our degrees of mobility) are gendered through and through. Moreover they are gendered in a myriad different ways, which vary between cultures and over time. And this gendering of space and place both reflects *and has effects back on* the ways in which gender is constructed and understood in the societies in which we live.

When I first started 'doing geography' these things were just not talked about. What I want to do here is simply to give one example of how issues of gender began to creep into our subject matter. The example is perhaps quite mundane; it concerns empirical issues of regional development which are now well established in debate; but in spite of that some interesting lessons can be drawn.

The example, then, is from studies of regional employment in the United Kingdom. It concerns the story of the regional decentralization of jobs which took place in this country between the mid-1960s and the early 1970s. There are some facts which ought to be known before the story begins. This was a period largely of Labour government, with Harold Wilson as Prime Minister. There were major losses of jobs in coal mining, in the north-east of England, in south Wales and in central Scotland. It was the great era of regional policy, when there were numerous incentives and inducements to firms to invest in the regions where job loss was taking place. And it was also an era of the decentralization of jobs from the high employment areas of the south-east and the west midlands to these 'northern' regions of high *un*employment. And the question which preoccupied many of us at that time was: how were we to put these facts together? Or, specifically, how were we to explain the decentralization of jobs to the regions of the north and the west?

The argument went through a series of stages. Or, at least, I shall present it as a series of stages—there are many occupants in what I label as the early stages who will doubtless disagree with what I say. Intellectual change is just not as linear as that.

The analysis, then, in 'stage one' was led primarily by people with computers and statistical packages, who correlated the timing and size of the decentralization of employment with the timing and distribution of regional policy. They found a high correlation between the two, and deduced that they were causally related: namely (although this was of course not directly shown by the statistics themselves) that regional policy was the cause of the decentralization of jobs. Thus regional policy, on this reading, was seen as having been quite successful.

But then came stage two. It was provoked by political rumblings of discontent, from male-dominated trade unions and local councils, and from evidence given to a parliamentary sub-committee. For jobs were not just jobs, it seemed: they were gendered. While the jobs which had been lost had been men's, the new jobs, arriving on the wave of decentralization, were largely being taken by women. And within academe, a whole new line of inquiry started as to *why* these jobs were for women. The answers which were found are now well known. Women workers were cheap; they were prepared to accept low wages, the result of years of negotiating in terms of 'the family wage'. Women were also more available than men for part-time work, an effect of the long-established domestic division of labour within the household. Both of these reasons were characteristic of male/female relations, within the home and within the employment market, across the country. But some reasons were more specific, or at least more important, to these particular regions to which the jobs had been decentralized. Thus, the women in these regions had very low rates of organization into trade unions, a result of the very low levels of their previous incorporation into paid employment. The female economic activity rates there were indeed amongst the lowest in the country. These women, in other words, were classic 'green labour'.

With this development of the argument a slightly more complex story evolved which recognized some differences within the labour market, which recognized certain constraints and specificities of women as potential employees, which, in brief, recognized that women and women's jobs were different. Such a revised understanding led also to a revised evaluation of the effectivity of regional policy. It was now clearly necessary to be more muted in any claims for its success. There were two versions of this re-evaluation. One, clearly sexist, persisted in its claim that the new jobs being made available in the regions should be criticized for being 'not real jobs', or for being 'only for women'. There was, however, also another form of re-evaluation, more academically respectable although still worrying in its implications: that the fact that the new jobs were for women was unfortunate in the sense that, because women's jobs were less well paid than were men's, aggregate regional income was still lower.

And yet there was a further stage in the development of this argument: stage three. For the more that one thought about it, the more the story seemed more complicated than that. Why, for example, had the economic activity rate for women in these regions been historically so low? This raised the whole question of local gender cultures. Many people, writing in both geography and sociology, commented upon the domestic labour burden of being a wife or mother to miners. They commented also on how the length and irregularity of shift-work made it problematical for the other partner in a couple also to seek paid employment outside the home. There was much detailed investigation of the construction of particular forms of masculinity around jobs such as mining. And all these investigations, and others besides, pointed to a deeper explanation of why, more than in most other regions of the country, there was in these areas a culture of the man being the breadwinner and of the woman being the homemaker.

We had, in other words, moved through a series of approaches; from not taking gender into account at all, we had moved first to looking at women, and from there to looking at gender roles, men, and locally constructed gender relations. Moreover this gave us, once again, both a different story of what had happened and a different evaluation of regional policy. The new story was again more complicated and more nuanced. Harold Wilson had come to power in 1964 on a programme of modernizing social democracy, part of which centred on the rationalization of old industries such as coal mining. Contradictorily for him, however, the loss of jobs which would be consequent upon that rationalization would occur precisely in the regions which were his main geographical power base—regions such as the north-east of England, south Wales, and the central area of Scotland. In order, therefore to proceed with this reconstruction of the old basic sectors of these regions, it was necessary to have as the other side of the deal a strong regional policy. Given this, acquiescence might be won from the trade unions and their members. However, it was the very fact that the men in the region were being made redundant which was important in creating the availability of female labour. For women were now for the first time in decades 'freed' on to the labour market. They needed paid employment, most particularly now in the absence of work for men, and there was less of a domestic labour burden upon them restraining them from taking it. Moreover these women had been constructed over the years, precisely by the specificity of the local gender culture, into just the kind of workforce the decentralizing industries were looking for.

Moreover, there was yet again a different evaluation of regional policy. For regional policy could no longer be accepted as the single dominant factor in the explanation of decentralization of employment because the labour-force which had been part of the attraction to the incoming industries had been created not by regional policy but by the simultaneous decline of men's jobs and as a result of the previous gender culture. It certainly remained true that regional policy had brought with it only low-paid jobs, but on the other hand there were some positive aspects to the jobs it did bring, which previously had been unrecognized. Most importantly, it did bring some independent income for women, and for the first time in decades. Moreover, as the very fact of the initial complaints indicated, precisely by bringing in those jobs it began to disrupt some of the old gender relations. In other words, on this score (though not on many others) regional policy can be seen to have had some quite positive effects—though in a wholly different way from that initially claimed in stage one of the development of the argument.

There are a number of reflections which can be drawn from this story of a developing analysis. First, and most obviously, taking gender seriously produced a more nuanced evaluation of regional policy, a far better understanding of the organization and reorganization of our national economic space, and indeed—since these decentralizing industries were moving north to cut costs in the face of increasing international competition—it has shown us how British industry was actively *using* regional differences in systems of gender relations in an early attempt to get out of what has become the crisis of the British economy. Second, this understanding was arrived at not just by looking at women—although that was a start—but by investigating geographical variations in the construction of masculinity and femininity and the relations between the two. Feminist geography is (or should be) as much about men as it is about women. Third, moreover, the very focus on geographical variation means that we are not here dealing with some essentialism of men and women, but with how they are constructed as such.

The fourth reflection is a rather different one. It is easy now to look back and criticize this old-time patriarchy in the coalfields. Indeed it has become a stick with which to beat 'the old labour movement'. But that should not let us slide into an assumption that because the old was bad the new is somehow unproblematical. So, partly in response to the last three reflections (the need to look at men and masculinity, the importance of recognizing geographical variations and of constructing a non-essentialist analysis, and the feeling that it is important to look at new jobs as well as at old) I am now involved in research on a 'new' region of economic growth—Cambridge. Cambridge: the very name of the place gives rise to thoughts of 'the Cambridge phenomenon' of high-technology growth, of science and innovation, and of white-collar work. It is all a million miles from coal mines, geographically, technologically, and—you would think—socially. In fact the picture is not as clear as that.

It is the highly qualified workers in high-technology sectors on which this new research is concentrating. Well over 90 per cent of these scientists and technologists are men. They frequently love their work. This is no bad thing, until one comes across statements like 'the boundary between work and play disappears', which immediately gives pause for thought. Is the only thing outside paid employment 'play'? Who does the domestic labour? These employees work long hours on knotty problems, and construct their image of themselves as people around the paid work that they do. But those long hours, and the flexibility of their organization, is someone else's constraint. Who goes to the launderette? Who picks up the children from school? In a previous project, from which this one derived, and from which we have some initial information, only one of these employees, and that one of the few women whom we found, mentioned using the flexibility of work hours in any relation to domestic labour—in this case she said that on occasions she left work at six o'clock to nip home to feed the cat![1] The point is that the whole design of these jobs requires that such employees do not do the work of reproduction and of caring for other people; indeed it implies that, best of all, they have someone to look after *them*. It is not therefore just the old labour movement, it is also the regions of the 'new man' which have their problems in terms of the construction of gender relations. What is being constructed in this region of new economic growth is a new version of masculinity, and a new—and still highly problematical—set of gender roles and gender relations.[2]

Notes

1. See Doreen Massey, Paul Quintas, and David Wield, *High-Tech Fantasies. Science Parks in Society, Science and Space,* London: Routledge, 1992.
2. This research is being undertaken with Nick Henry at the Open University and with funding from the Economic and Social Research Council (Grant no. R000233004, High-status growth? Aspects of home and work around high technology sectors).

Charlotte Perkins Gilman

Charlotte Perkins Gilman (1860–1935) was born in Hartford, Connecticut. Shortly after she was born, her father deserted the family and provided her mother with little financial support. She was raised by her mother and studied art at the Rhode Island School of Design. From the very beginning of her marriage to Charles Walter Stetson in 1884, she suffered from depression, which became serious after the birth of her daughter. A famous neurologist prescribed complete bed rest, which made matters worse for her. Eventually, Gilman left her husband and moved to California where she supported her mother and daughter by running a boarding house. During this time, she started publishing her writings. She became a very important figure as a prominent lecturer and a writer on feminism and the labor movement. Finally, in 1900, she found happiness in her marriage to George Houghton Gilman, her first cousin; however her happiness did not last. Weakened by cancer in her last years, Gilman decided to end her life. "The Yellow Wallpaper," which was first published in 1892, was followed by various publications including books on social and economic problems of women, utopian novels, and a posthumously published autobiography.

"The Yellow Wallpaper" is an excellent example of how gender and space function to shape identity. The story of the nameless narrator is the story of rebellion—a rebellion that tries to defy gendered conceptualizations of womanhood and raises important questions about social conventions that associate specific spaces with specific genders. What are the symbolic dimensions of the spaces in this story—the house, the nursery, etc.—and how are those spaces related to both the narrator and her husband? What happens to women who rebel against confinement and gender roles? How are they conceptualized? These are some important questions to bear in mind when reading this complicated, but fascinating story. "The Story of an Hour," which results in a different sort of rebellion, within similarly gendered spaces, also appears in this chapter and was written during the same period of history.

The Yellow Wallpaper

It is very seldom that mere ordinary people like John and myself secure ancestral halls for the summer.

A colonial mansion, a hereditary estate, I would say a haunted house and reach the height of romantic felicity—but that would be asking too much of fate!

Still I will proudly declare that there is something queer about it.

Else, why should it be let so cheaply? And why have stood so long untenanted?

John laughs at me, of course, but one expects that.

John is practical in the extreme. He has no patience with faith, an intense horror of superstition, and he scoffs openly at any talk of things not to be felt and seen and put down in figures.

John is a physician, and *perhaps*—(I would not say it to a living soul, of course, but this is dead paper and a great relief to my mind)—*perhaps* that is one reason I do not get well faster.

You see, he does not believe I am sick! And what can one do?

If a physician of high standing, and one's own husband, assures friends and relatives that there is really nothing the matter with one but temporary nervous depression—a slight hysterical tendency—what is one to do?

My brother is also a physician, and also of high standing, and he says the same thing.

So I take phosphates or phosphites—whichever it is—and tonics, and air and exercise, and journeys, and am absolutely forbidden to "work" until I am well again.

Personally, I disagree with their ideas.

Personally, I believe that congenial work, with excitement and change, would do me good.

But what is one to do?

I did write for a while in spite of them; but it *does* exhaust me a good deal—having to be so sly about it, or else meet with heavy opposition.

I sometimes fancy that in my condition, if I had less opposition and more society and stimulus—but John says the very worst thing I can do is to think about my condition, and I confess it always makes me feel bad.

So I will let it alone and talk about the house.

The most beautiful place! It is quite alone, standing well back from the road, quite three miles from the village. It makes me think of English places that you read about, for there are hedges and walls and gates that lock, and lots of separate little houses for the gardeners and people.

There is a *delicious* garden! I never saw such a garden—large and shady, full of box-bordered paths, and lined with long grape-covered arbors with seats under them.

There were greenhouses, but they are all broken now.

There was some legal trouble, I believe, something about the heirs and coheirs; anyhow, the place has been empty for years.

That spoils my ghostliness, I am afraid, but I don't care—there is something strange about the house—I can feel it.

I even said so to John one moonlight evening, but he said what I felt was a draught, and shut the window.

I get unreasonably angry with John sometimes. I'm sure I never used to be so sensitive. I think it is due to this nervous condition.

But John says if I feel so I shall neglect proper self-control; so I take pains to control myself—before him, at least, and that makes me very tired.

I don't like our room a bit. I wanted one downstairs that opened onto the piazza and had roses all over the window, and such pretty old-fashioned chintz hangings! But John would not hear of it.

He said there was only one window and not room for two beds, and no near room for him if he took another.

He is very careful and loving, and hardly lets me stir without special direction.

I have a schedule prescription for each hour in the day; he takes all care from me, and so I feel basely ungrateful not to value it more.

He said he came here solely on my account, that I was to have perfect rest and all the air I could get. "Your exercise depends on your strength, my dear," said he, "and your food somewhat on your appetite; but air you can absorb all the time." So we took the nursery at the top of the house.

It is a big, airy room, the whole floor nearly, with windows that look all ways, and air and sunshine galore. It was nursery first, and then playroom and gymnasium, I should judge, for the windows are barred for little children, and there are rings and things in the walls.

The paint and paper look as if a boys' school had used it. It is stripped off—the paper—in great patches all around the head of my bed, about as far as I can reach, and in a great place on the other side of the room low down. I never saw a worse paper in my life. One of those sprawling, flamboyant patterns committing every artistic sin.

It is dull enough to confuse the eye in following, pronounced enough constantly to irritate and provoke study, and when you follow the lame uncertain curves for a little distance they suddenly commit suicide—plunge off at outrageous angles, destroy themselves in unheard-of contradictions.

The color is repellent, almost revolting: a smouldering unclean yellow, strangely faded by the slow-turning sunlight. It is a dull yet lurid orange in some places, a sickly sulphur tint in others.

No wonder the children hated it! I should hate it myself if I had to live in this room long.

There comes John, and I must put this away—he hates to have me write a word.

We have been here two weeks, and I haven't felt like writing before, since that first day.

I am sitting by the window now, up in this atrocious nursery, and there is nothing to hinder my writing as much as I please, save lack of strength.

John is away all day, and even some nights when his cases are serious.

I am glad my case is not serious!

But these nervous troubles are dreadfully depressing.

John does not know how much I really suffer. He knows there is no reason to suffer, and that satisfies him.

Of course it is only nervousness. It does weigh on me so not to do my duty in any way!

I meant to be such a help to John, such a real rest and comfort, and here I am a comparative burden already!

Nobody would believe what an effort it is to do what little I am able—to dress and entertain, and order things.

It is fortunate Mary is so good with the baby. Such a dear baby!

And yet I *cannot* be with him, it makes me so nervous.

I suppose John never was nervous in his life. He laughs at me so about this wallpaper!

At first he meant to repaper the room, but afterward he said that I was letting it get the better of me, and that nothing was worse for a nervous patient than to give way to such fancies.

He said that after the wallpaper was changed it would be the heavy bedstead, and then the barred windows, and then that gate at the head of the stairs, and so on.

"You know the place is doing you good," he said, "and really, dear, I don't care to renovate the house just for a three months' rental."

"Then do let us go downstairs," I said. "There are such pretty rooms there."

Then he took me in his arms and called me a blessed little goose, and said he would go down cellar, if I wished, and have it whitewashed into the bargain.

But he is right enough about the beds and windows and things.

It is as airy and comfortable a room as anyone need wish, and, of course, I would not be so silly as to make him uncomfortable just for a whim.

I'm really getting quite fond of the big room, all but that horrid paper.

Out of one window I can see the garden—those mysterious deep-shaded arbors, the riotous old-fashioned flowers, and bushes and gnarly trees.

Out of another I get a lovely view of the bay and a little private wharf belonging to the estate. There is a beautiful shaded lane that runs down there from the house. I always fancy I see people walking in these numerous paths and arbors, but John has cautioned me not to give way to fancy in the least. He says that with my imaginative power and habit of story-making, a nervous weakness like mine is sure to lead to all manner of excited fancies, and that I ought to use my will and good sense to check the tendency. So I try.

I think sometimes that if I were only well enough to write a little it would relieve the press of ideas and rest me.

But I find I get pretty tired when I try.

It is so discouraging not to have any advice and companionship about my work. When I get really well, John says we will ask Cousin Henry and Julia down for a long visit; but he says he would as soon put fireworks in my pillow-case as to let me have those stimulating people about now.

I wish I could get well faster.

But I must not think about that. This paper looks to me as if it *knew* what a vicious influence it had!

There is a recurrent spot where the pattern lolls like a broken neck and two bulbous eyes stare at you upside down.

I get positively angry with the impertinence of it and the everlastingness. Up and down and sideways they crawl, and those absurd unblinking eyes are everywhere. There is one place where two breadths didn't match, and the eyes go all up and down the line, one a little higher than the other.

I never saw so much expression in an inanimate thing before, and we all know how much expression they have! I used to lie awake as a child and get more entertainment and terror out of blank walls and plain furniture than most children could find in a toy-store.

I remember what a kindly wink the knobs of our big old bureau used to have, and there was one chair that always seemed like a strong friend.

I used to feel that if any of the other things looked too fierce I could always hop into that chair and be safe.

The furniture in this room is no worse than inharmonious, however, for we had to bring it all from downstairs. I suppose when this was used as a playroom they had to take the nursery things out, and no wonder! I never saw such ravages as the children have made here.

The wallpaper, as I said before, is torn off in spots, and it sticketh closer than a brother—they must have had perseverance as well as hatred.

Then the floor is scratched and gouged and splintered, the plaster itself is dug out here and there, and this great heavy bed, which is all we found in the room, looks as if it had been through the wars.

But I don't mind it a bit—only the paper.

There comes John's sister. Such a dear girl as she is, and so careful of me! I must not let her find me writing.

She is a perfect and enthusiastic housekeeper, and hopes for no better profession. I verily believe she thinks it is the writing which made me sick!

But I can write when she is out, and see her a long way off from these windows.

There is one that commands the road, a lovely shaded winding road, and one that just looks off over the country. A lovely country, too, full of great elms and velvet meadows.

This wallpaper has a kind of sub-pattern in a different shade, a particularly irritating one, for you can only see it in certain lights, and not clearly then.

But in the places where it isn't faded and where the sun is just so—I can see a strange, provoking, formless sort of figure that seems to skulk about behind that silly and conspicuous front design.

There's sister on the stairs!

Well, the Fourth of July is over! The people are all gone, and I am tired out. John thought it might do me good to see a little company, so we just had Mother and Nellie and the children down for a week.

Of course I didn't do a thing. Jennie sees to everything now.

But it tired me all the same.

John says if I don't pick up faster he shall send me to Weir Mitchell[1] in the fall.

But I don't want to go there at all. I had a friend who was in his hands once, and she says he is just like John and my brother, only more so!

Besides, it is such an undertaking to go so far.

I don't feel as if it was worthwhile to turn my hand over for anything, and I'm getting dreadfully fretful and querulous.

I cry at nothing, and cry most of the time.

Of course I don't when John is here, or anybody else, but when I am alone.

And I am alone a good deal just now. John is kept in town very often by serious cases, and Jennie is good and lets me alone when I want her to.

So I walk a little in the garden or down that lovely lane, sit on the porch under the roses, and lie down up here a good deal.

I'm getting really fond of the room in spite of the wallpaper. Perhaps *because* of the wallpaper.

It dwells in my mind so!

I lie here on this great immovable bed—it is nailed down, I believe—and follow that pattern about by the hour. It is as good as gymnastics, I assure you. I start, we'll say, at the bottom, down in the corner over there where it has not been touched, and I determine for the thousandth time that I *will* follow that pointless pattern to some sort of a conclusion.

I know a little of the principle of design, and I know this thing was not arranged on any laws of radiation, or alternation, or repetition, or symmetry, or anything else that I ever heard of.

It is repeated, of course, by the breadths, but not otherwise.

Looked at in one way, each breadth stands alone; the bloated curves and flourishes—a kind of "debased Romanesque" with delirium tremens go waddling up and down in isolated columns of fatuity.

But, on the other hand, they connect diagonally, and the sprawling outlines run off in great slanting waves of optic horror, like a lot of wallowing sea-weeds in full chase.

The whole thing goes horizontally, too, at least it seems so, and I exhaust myself trying to distinguish the order of its going in that direction.

They have used a horizontal breadth for a frieze, and that adds wonderfully to the confusion.

There is one end of the room where it is almost intact, and there, when the crosslights fade and the low sun shines directly upon it, I can almost fancy radiation after all—the interminable grotesque seems to form around a common center and rush off in headlong plunges of equal distraction.

It makes me tired to follow it. I will take a nap, I guess.

I don't know why I should write this.

I don't want to.

I don't feel able.

And I know John would think it absurd. But I *must* say what I feel and think in some way—it is such a relief!

But the effort is getting to be greater than the relief.

Half the time now I am awfully lazy, and lie down ever so much. John says I mustn't lose my strength, and has me take cod liver oil and lots of tonics and things, to say nothing of ale and wines and rare meat.

Dear John! He loves me very dearly, and hates to have me sick. I tried to have a real earnest reasonable talk with him the other day, and tell him how I wish he would let me go and make a visit to Cousin Henry and Julia.

But he said I wasn't able to go, nor able to stand it after I got there; and I did not make out a very good case for myself, for I was crying before I had finished.

It is getting to be a great effort for me to think straight. Just this nervous weakness, I suppose.

And dear John gathered me up in his arms, and just carried me upstairs and laid me on the bed, and sat by me and read to me till it tired my head.

He said I was his darling and his comfort and all he had, and that I must take care of myself for his sake, and keep well.

He says no one but myself can help me out of it, that I must use my will and self-control and not let any silly fancies run away with me.

There's one comfort—the baby is well and happy, and does not have to occupy this nursery with the horrid wallpaper.

If we had not used it, that blessed child would have! What a fortunate escape! Why, I wouldn't have a child of mine, an impressionable little thing, live in such a room for worlds.

I never thought of it before, but it is lucky that John kept me here after all; I can stand it so much easier than a baby, you see.

Of course I never mention it to them any more—I am too wise—but I keep watch for it all the same.

There are things in the wallpaper that nobody knows about but me, or ever will.

Behind that outside pattern the dim shapes get clearer every day.

It is always the same shape, only very numerous.

And it is like a woman stooping down and creeping about behind that pattern. I don't like it a bit. I wonder—I begin to think—I wish John would take me away from here!

It is so hard to talk with John about my case, because he is so wise, and because he loves me so.

But I tried it last night.

It was moonlight. The moon shines in all around just as the sun does.

I hate to see it sometimes, it creeps so slowly, and always comes in by one window or another.

John was asleep and I hated to waken him, so I kept still and watched the moonlight on that undulating wallpaper till I felt creepy.

The faint figure behind seemed to shake the pattern, just as if she wanted to get out.

I got up softly and went to feel and see if the paper *did* move, and when I came back John was awake.

"What is it, little girl?" he said. "Don't go walking about like that—you'll get cold."

I thought it was a good time to talk, so I told him that I really was not gaining here, and that I wished he would take me away.

"Why, darling!" said he. "Our lease will be up in three weeks, and I can't see how to leave before.

"The repairs are not done at home, and I cannot possibly leave town just now. Of course, if you were in any danger, I could and would, but you really are better, dear, whether you can see it or not. I am a doctor, dear, and I know. You are gaining flesh and color, your appetite is better, I feel really much easier about you."

"I don't weigh a bit more," said I, "nor as much; and my appetite may be better in the evening when you are here but it is worse in the morning when you are away!"

"Bless her little heart!" said he with a big hug. "She shall be as sick as she pleases! But now let's improve the shining hours by going to sleep, and talk about it in the morning!"

"And you won't go away?" I asked gloomily.

"Why, how can I, dear? It is only three weeks more and then we will take a nice little trip for a few days while Jennie is getting the house ready. Really, dear, you are better!"

"Better in body perhaps—" I began, and stopped short, for he sat up straight and looked at me with such a stern, reproachful look that I could not say another word.

"My darling," said he, "I beg you, for my sake and for our child's sake, as well as for your own, that you will never for one instant let that idea enter your mind! There is nothing so dangerous, so fascinating, to a temperament like yours. It is a false and foolish fancy. Can you trust me as a physician when I tell you so?"

So of course I said no more on that score, and we went to sleep before long. He thought I was asleep first, but I wasn't, and lay there for hours trying to decide whether that front pattern and the back pattern really did move together or separately.

On a pattern like this, by daylight, there is a lack of sequence, a defiance of law, that is a constant irritant to a normal mind.

The color is hideous enough, and unreliable enough, and infuriating enough, but the pattern is torturing.

You think you have mastered it, but just as you get well under way in following, it turns a back-somersault and there you are. It slaps you in the face, knocks you down, and tramples upon you. It is like a bad dream.

The outside pattern is a florid arabesque, reminding one of a fungus. If you can imagine a toadstool in joints, an interminable string of toadstools, budding and sprouting in endless convolutions—why, that is something like it.

That is, sometimes!

There is one marked peculiarity about this paper, a thing nobody seems to notice but myself, and that is that it changes as the light changes.

When the sun shoots in through the east window—I always watch for that first long, straight ray—it changes so quickly that I never can quite believe it.

That is why I watch it always.

By moonlight—the moon shines in all night when there is a moon—I wouldn't know it was the same paper.

At night in any kind of light, in twilight, candlelight, lamplight, and worst of all by moonlight, it becomes bars! The outside pattern, I mean, and the woman behind it is as plain as can be.

I didn't realize for a long time what the thing was that showed behind, that dim sub-pattern, but now I am quite sure it is a woman.

By daylight she is subdued, quiet. I fancy it is the pattern that keeps her so still. It is so puzzling. It keeps me quiet by the hour.

I lie down ever so much now. John says it is good for me, and to sleep all I can.

Indeed he started the habit by making me lie down for an hour after each meal.

It is a very bad habit, I am convinced, for you see, I don't sleep.

And that cultivates deceit, for I don't tell them I'm awake—oh, no!

The fact is I am getting a little afraid of John.

He seems very queer sometimes, and even Jennie has an inexplicable look.

It strikes me occasionally, just as a scientific hypothesis, that perhaps it is the paper!

I have watched John when he did not know I was looking, and come into the room suddenly on the most innocent excuses, and I've caught him several times *looking at the paper!* And Jennie too. I caught Jennie with her hand on it once.

She didn't know I was in the room, and when I asked her in a quiet, a very quiet voice, with the most restrained manner possible, what she was doing with the paper, she turned around as if she had been caught stealing, and looked quite angry—asked me why I should frighten her so!

Then she said that the paper stained everything it touched, that she had found yellow smooches on all my clothes and John's and she wished we would be more careful!

Did not that sound innocent? But I know she was studying that pattern, and I am determined that nobody shall find it out but myself!

Life is very much more exciting now than it used to be. You see, I have something more to expect, to look forward to, to watch. I really do eat better, and am more quiet than I was.

John is so pleased to see me improve! He laughed a little the other day, and said I seemed to be flourishing in spite of my wallpaper.

I turned it off with a laugh. I had no intention of telling him it was *because* of the wallpaper—he would make fun of me. He might even want to take me away.

I don't want to leave now until I have found it out. There is a week more, and I think that will be enough.

I'm feeling so much better!

I don't sleep much at night, for it is so interesting to watch developments; but I sleep a good deal during the daytime.

In the daytime it is tiresome and perplexing.

There are always new shoots on the fungus, and new shades of yellow all over it. I cannot keep count of them, though I have tried conscientiously.

It is the strangest yellow, that wallpaper! It makes me think of all the yellow things I ever saw—not beautiful ones like buttercups, but old, foul, bad yellow things.

But there is something else about that paper—the smell! I noticed it the moment we came into the room, but with so much air and sun it was not bad. Now we have had a week of fog and rain, and whether the windows are open or not, the smell is here.

It creeps all over the house.

I find it hovering in the dining-room, skulking in the parlor, hiding in the hall, lying in wait for me on the stairs.

It gets into my hair.

Even when I go to ride, if I turn my head suddenly and surprise it—there is that smell!

Such a peculiar odor, too! I have spent hours in trying to analyze it, to find what it smelled like.

It is not bad—at first—and very gentle, but quite the subtlest, most enduring odor I ever met.

In this damp weather it is awful. I wake up in the night and find it hanging over me.

It used to disturb me at first. I thought seriously of burning the house—to reach the smell.

But now I am used to it. The only thing I can think of that it is like is the *color* of the paper! A yellow smell.

There is a very funny mark on this wall, low down, near the mopboard. A streak that runs round the room. It goes behind every piece of furniture, except the bed, a long, straight, even *smooch,* as if it had been rubbed over and over.

I wonder how it was done and who did it, and what they did it for. Round and round and round—round and round and round—it makes me dizzy!

I really have discovered something at last.

Through watching so much at night, when it changes so, I have finally found out.

The front pattern *does* move—and no wonder! The woman behind shakes it!

Sometimes I think there are a great many women behind, and sometimes only one, and she crawls around fast, and her crawling shakes it all over.

Then in the very bright spots she keeps still, and in the very shady spots she just takes hold of the bars and shakes them hard.

And she is all the time trying to climb through. But nobody could climb through that pattern—it strangles so; I think that is why it has so many heads.

They get through and then the pattern strangles them off and turns them upside down, and makes their eyes white!

If those heads were covered or taken off it would not be half so bad.

I think that woman gets out in the daytime!

And I'll tell you why—privately—I've seen her!

I can see her out of every one of my windows!

It is the same woman, I know, for she is always creeping, and most women do not creep by daylight.

I see her in that long shaded lane, creeping up and down. I see her in those dark grape arbors, creeping all around the garden.

I see her on that long road under the trees, creeping along, and when a carriage comes she hides under the blackberry vines.

I don't blame her a bit. It must be very humiliating to be caught creeping by daylight!

I always lock the door when I creep by daylight. I can't do it at night, for I know John would suspect something at once.

And John is so queer now that I don't want to irritate him. I wish he would take another room! Besides, I don't want anybody to get that woman out at night but myself.

I often wonder if I could see her out of all the windows at once.

But, turn as fast as I can, I can only see out of one at one time.

And though I always see her, she *may* be able to creep faster than I can turn! I have watched her sometimes away off in the open country, creeping as fast as a cloud shadow in a wind.

If only that top pattern could be gotten off from the under one! I mean to try it, little by little.

I have found out another funny thing, but I shan't tell it this time! It does not do to trust people too much.

There are only two more days to get this paper off, and I believe John is beginning to notice. I don't like the look in his eyes.

And I heard him ask Jennie a lot of professional questions about me. She had a very good report to give.

She said I slept a good deal in the daytime.

John knows I don't sleep very well at night, for all I'm so quiet!

He asked me all sorts of questions too, and pretended to be very loving and kind.

As if I couldn't see through him!

Still, I don't wonder he acts so, sleeping under this paper for three months.

It only interests me, but I feel sure John and Jennie are affected by it. Hurrah! This is the last day, but it is enough. John is to stay in town over night, and won't be out until this evening.

Jennie wanted to sleep with me—the sly thing; but I told her I should undoubtedly rest better for a night all alone.

That was clever, for really I wasn't alone a bit! As soon as it was moonlight and that poor thing began to crawl and shake the pattern, I got up and ran to help her.

I pulled and she shook. I shook and she pulled, and before morning we had peeled off yards of that paper.

A strip about as high as my head and half around the room.

And then when the sun came and that awful pattern began to laugh at me, I declared I would finish it today!

We go away tomorrow, and they are moving all my furniture down again to leave things as they were before.

Jennie looked at the wall in amazement, but I told her merrily that I did it out of pure spite at the vicious thing.

She laughed and said she wouldn't mind doing it herself, but I must not get tired.

How she betrayed herself that time!

But I am here, and no person touches this paper but Me—not *alive!*

She tried to get me out of the room—it was too patent! But I said it was so quiet and empty and clean now that I believed I would lie down again and sleep all I could, and not to wake me even for dinner—I would call when I woke.

So now she is gone, and the servants are gone, and the things are gone, and there is nothing left but that great bedstead nailed down, with the canvas mattress we found on it.

We shall sleep downstairs tonight, and take the boat home tomorrow.

I quite enjoy the room, now it is bare again.

How those children did tear about here!

This bedstead is fairly gnawed!

But I must get to work.

I have locked the door and thrown the key down into the front path.

I don't want to go out, and I don't want to have anybody come in, till John comes.

I want to astonish him.

I've got a rope up here that even Jennie did not find. If that woman does get out, and tries to get away, I can tie her!

But I forgot I could not reach far without anything to stand on!

This bed will *not* move!

I tried to lift and push it until I was lame, and then I got so angry I bit off a little piece at one corner—but it hurt my teeth.

Then I peeled off all the paper I could reach standing on the floor. It sticks horribly and the pattern just enjoys it! All those strangled heads and bulbous eyes and waddling fungus growths just shriek with derision!

I am getting angry enough to do something desperate. To jump out of the window would be admirable exercise, but the bars are too strong even to try.

Besides I wouldn't do it. Of course not. I know well enough that a step like that is improper and might be misconstrued.

I don't like to *look* out of the windows even—there are so many of those creeping women, and they creep so fast.

I wonder if they all come out of that wallpaper as I did?

But I am securely fastened now by my well-hidden rope—you don't get *me* out in the road there!

I suppose I shall have to get back behind the pattern when it comes night, and that is hard!

It is so pleasant to be out in this great room and creep around as I please!

I don't want to go outside. I won't, even if Jennie asks me to.

For outside you have to creep on the ground, and everything is green instead of yellow.

But here I can creep smoothly on the floor, and my shoulder just fits in that long smooch around the wall, so I cannot lose my way.

Why, there's John at the door!

It is no use, young man, you can't open it!

How he does call and pound!

Now he's crying to Jennie for an axe.

It would be a shame to break down that beautiful door!

"John, dear!" said I in the gentlest voice. "The key is down by the front steps, under a plantain leaf!"

That silenced him for a few moments.

Then he said, very quietly indeed, "Open the door, my darling!"

"I can't," said I. "The key is down by the front door under a plantain leaf!" And then I said it again, several times, very gently and slowly, and said it so often that he had to go and see, and he got it of course, and came in. He stopped short by the door.

"What is the matter?" he cried. "For God's sake, what are you doing!"

I kept on creeping just the same, but I looked at him over my shoulder.

"I've got out at last," said I, "in spite of you and Jane. And I've pulled off most of the paper, so you can't put me back!"

Now why should that man have fainted? But he did, and right across my path by the wall, so that I had to creep over him every time!

Note

1. American neurologist who treated Gilman.

Kate Chopin

Katherine O'Flaherty Chopin (1851–1904) was born and raised in St. Louis, Missouri. In 1870 she married a Louisiana Creole and it was only after her husband's death that she started to write about her experiences. She was almost forty when she published her first novel, At Fault *(1890). Her novel did not receive that much praise or recognition; however, her short stories (she wrote more than 100) brought her fame and acclaim. In 1899, Chopin published her most famous piece,* The Awakening, *which was highly condemned in her time because of its sexual frankness. The novel was taken out of the libraries and was out of print for some fifty years only to be rediscovered in the 1950's. Her famous short story "The Story of an Hour," (1894) also went against the conventional social behavior that was considered suitable for a woman and she felt like an outcast in the literary scene, which was very much against her liberal conceptualizations. It took more than half a century after her death for feminist critics to champion "The Story of an Hour" as a story about woman's condition in a patriarchal society that makes her dependent on the men.*

Like "The Yellow Wallpaper"—which also appears in this chapter and was written during the same time period—Kate Chopin's "The Story of an Hour" reveals how space can articulate gender roles by interrogating the gendered boundaries/spaces within a traditional marriage. As you read, consider, is there a tension that exists between what Mrs. Mallard sees from her window and what she encounters within her house? What does marriage symbolize for Mrs. Mallard and how does that affect her identity? What is her ultimate rebellion in the end and how does that define her future?

The Story of an Hour

Knowing that Mrs. Mallard was afflicted with a heart trouble, great care was taken to break to her as gently as possible the news of her husband's death.

It was her sister Josephine who told her, in broken sentences; veiled hints that revealed in half concealing. Her husband's friend Richards was there, too, near her. It was he who had been in the newspaper office when intelligence of the railroad disaster was received, with Brently Mallard's name leading the list of "killed." He had only taken the time to assure himself of its truth by a second telegram, and had hastened to forestall any less careful, less tender friend in bearing the sad message.

She did not hear the story as many women have heard the same, with a paralyzed inability to accept its significance. She wept at once, with sudden, wild abandonment, in her sister's arms. When the storm of grief had spent itself she went away to her room alone. She would have no one follow her.

There stood, facing the open window, a comfortable, roomy armchair. Into this she sank, pressed down by a physical exhaustion that haunted her body and seemed to reach into her soul.

She could see in the open square before her house the tops of trees that were all aquiver with the new spring life. The delicious breath of rain was in the air. In the street below a peddler was crying his wares. The notes of a distant song which someone was singing reached her faintly, and countless sparrows were twittering in the eaves.

There were patches of blue sky showing here and there through the clouds that had met and piled one above the other in the west facing her window.

She sat with her head thrown back upon the cushion of the chair, quite motionless, except when a sob came up into her throat and shook her, as a child who had cried itself to sleep continues to sob in its dreams.

She was young, with a fair, calm face, whose lines bespoke repression and even a certain strength. But now there was a dull stare in her eyes, whose gaze was fixed away off yonder on one of those patches of blue sky. It was not a glance of reflection, but rather indicated a suspension of intelligent thought.

There was something coming to her and she was waiting for it, fearfully. What was it? She did not know; it was too subtle and elusive to name. But she felt it, creeping out of the sky, reaching toward her through the sounds, the scents, the color that filled the air.

Now her bosom rose and fell tumultuously. She was beginning to recognize this thing that was approaching to possess her, and she was striving to beat it back with her will—as powerless as her two white slender hands would have been.

When she abandoned herself a little whispered word escaped her slightly parted lips. She said it over and over under her breath: "free, free, free!" The vacant stare and the look of terror that had followed it went from her eyes. They stayed keen and bright. Her pulses beat fast, and the coursing blood warmed and relaxed every inch of her body.

She did not stop to ask if it were or were not a monstrous joy that held her. A clear and exalted perception enabled her to dismiss the suggestion as trivial.

She knew that she would weep again when she saw the kind, tender hands folded in death; the face that had never looked save with love upon her, fixed and gray and dead. But she saw beyond that bitter moment a long procession of years to come that would belong to her absolutely. And she opened and spread her arms out to them in welcome.

There would be no one to live for her during those coming years: she would live for herself. There would be no powerful will bending hers in that blind persistence with which men and women believe they have a right to impose a private will upon a fellow-creature. A kind intention or a cruel intention made the act seem no less a crime as she looked upon it in that brief moment of illumination.

And yet she had loved him—sometimes. Often she had not. What did it matter! What could love, the unsolved mystery, count for in face of this possession of self-assertion which she suddenly recognized as the strongest impulse of her being!

"Free! Body and soul free!" she kept whispering.

Josephine was kneeling before the closed door with her lips to the keyhole, imploring for admission. "Louise, open the door! I beg; open the door—you will make yourself ill. What are you doing, Louise? For heaven's sake open the door."

"Go away. I am not making myself ill." No; she was drinking in a very elixir of life through that open window.

Her fancy was running riot along those days ahead of her. Spring days, and summer days, and all sorts of days that would be her own. She breathed a quick prayer that life might be long. It was only yesterday she had thought with a shudder that life might be long.

She arose at length and opened the door to her sister's importunities. There was a feverish triumph in her eyes, and she carried herself unwittingly like a goddess of Victory. She clasped her sister's waist, and together they descended the stairs. Richards stood waiting for them at the bottom.

Some one was opening the front door with a latchkey. It was Brently Mallard who entered, a little travel-stained, composedly carrying his gripsack and umbrella. He had been far from the scene of accident, and did not even know there had been one. He stood amazed at Josephine's piercing cry; at Richards' quick motion to screen him from the view of his wife.

But Richards was too late.

When the doctors came they said she had died of heart disease—of joy that kills.

Ernest Hemingway

Ernest Hemingway (1899–1961) was born in Oak Park, Illinois and began writing in high school. An active and outstanding student, he boxed and played football and, after graduating high school, worked as a reporter for the Kansas City Star. *In World War I, Hemingway joined the ambulance corps, since an eye problem disqualified him from serving in the army. He was wounded in Italy in 1918, hospitalized and fell in love with an American Red Cross nurse who declined to marry him, and later, returned home a decorated hero for rescuing one of his comrades. During the Spanish Civil War, Hemingway acted as a war correspondent and was an enthusiastic supporter of the Republican cause. Hemingway's fascination with war was evident throughout his writing career. In* A Farewell to Arms *(1929), he underlined war's pointlessness; in* For Whom the Bell Tolls *(1940), he celebrated comradeship. War was a potent symbol for Hemingway, whose writings about it not only centered on honor, courage, and dignity, but also on hardship, toil, pain, and destruction. "The Hemingway Code" was to behave honorably and courageously under pressure to overcome hardship. He received the Nobel Prize for Literature in 1954 and was famous for the forceful masculinity of his prose and for his public persona.*

In Hemingway's short story, "A Clean Well-Lighted Place," from The Short Stories of Ernest Hemingway, *an old man finds solace and comfort not at home but in a public place. To a certain extent space in this story functions similarly as it does in "The Yellow Wallpaper" and "The Story of an Hour": setting symbolizes the emotional state of the protagonist. Hemingway once claimed that he tries "to write on the principle of the iceberg. There is seven-eighths of it under water for every part that shows." With this in mind, how might the limited structure and action of the story provide us with further insights about the old man, about the culture in which he lives, about the other characters in the story? How might the old man's preference for one place over another defy social convention and why might his preference surprise us as readers?*

A Clean, Well-Lighted Place

It was late and every one had left the café except an old man who sat in the shadow the leaves of the tree made against the electric light. In the day time the street was dusty, but at night the dew settled the dust and the old man liked to sit late because he was deaf and now at night it was quiet and he felt the difference. The two waiters inside the café knew that the old man was a little drunk, and while he was a good client they knew that if he became too drunk he would leave without paying, so they kept watch on him.

"Last week he tried to commit suicide," one waiter said.

"Why?"

"He was in despair."

"What about?"

"Nothing."

"How do you know it was nothing?"

"He has plenty of money."

They sat together at a table that was close against the wall near the door of the café and looked at the terrace where the tables were all empty except where the old man sat in the shadow of the leaves of the tree that moved slightly in the wind. A girl and a soldier went by in the street. The street light shone on the brass number on his collar. The girl wore no head covering and hurried beside him.

"The guard will pick him up," one waiter said.

"What does it matter if he gets what he's after?"

"He had better get off the street now. The guard will get him. They went by five minutes ago."

The old man sitting in the shadow rapped on his saucer with his glass. The younger waiter went over to him.

"What do you want?"

The old man looked at him. "Another brandy," he said.

"You'll be drunk," the waiter said. The old man looked at him. The waiter went away.

"He'll stay all night," he said to his colleague. "I'm sleepy now. I never get into bed before three o'clock. He should have killed himself last week."

The waiter took the brandy bottle and another saucer from the counter inside the café and marched out to the old man's table. He put down the saucer and poured the glass full of brandy.

"You should have killed yourself last week," he said to the deaf man. The old man motioned with his finger. "A little more," he said. The waiter poured on into the glass so that the brandy slopped over and ran down the stem into the top saucer of the pile. "Thank you," the old man said. The waiter took the bottle back inside the café. He sat down at the table with his colleague again.

°*"He's drunk now," he said. "He's drunk every night":* The younger waiter says both these lines. A device of Hemingway's style is sometimes to have a character pause, then speak again—as often happens in actual speech.

"He's drunk now," he said.
"He's drunk every night."°
"What did he want to kill himself for?"
"How should I know."
"How did he do it?"
"He hung himself with a rope."
"Who cut him down?"
"His niece."
"Why did they do it?"
"Fear for his soul."
"How much money has he got?"
"He's got plenty."
"He must be eighty years old."
"Anyway I should say he was eighty."°
"I wish he would go home. I never get to bed before three o'clock. What kind of hour is that to go to bed?"
"He stays up because he likes it."
"He's lonely. I'm not lonely. I have a wife waiting in bed for me."
"He had a wife once too."
"A wife would be no good to him now."
"You can't tell. He might be better with a wife."
"His niece looks after him."
"I know. You said she cut him down."
"I wouldn't want to be that old. An old man is a nasty thing."
"Not always. This old man is clean. He drinks without spilling. Even now, drunk. Look at him."
"I don't want to look at him. I wish he would go home. He has no regard for those who must work."

The old man looked from his glass across the square, then over at the waiters.

"Another brandy," he said, pointing to his glass. The waiter who was in a hurry came over.

"Finished," he said, speaking with that omission of syntax stupid people employ when talking to drunken people or foreigners. "No more tonight. Close now."

"Another," said the old man.

"No. Finished." The waiter wiped the edge of the table with a towel and shook his head.

The old man stood up, slowly counted the saucers, took a leather coin purse from his pocket and paid for the drinks, leaving half a peseta tip.

The waiter watched him go down the street, a very old man walking unsteadily but with dignity.

"Why didn't you let him stay and drink?" the unhurried waiter asked. They were putting up the shutters. "It is not half-past two."

°*"He must be eighty years old." "Anyway I should say he was eighty"*: Is this another instance of the same character's speaking twice? Clearly, it is the younger waiter who says the next line, "I wish he would go home."

"I want to go home to bed."

"What is an hour?"

"More to me than to him."

"An hour is the same."

"You talk like an old man yourself. He can buy a bottle and drink at home."

"It's not the same."

"No, it is not," agreed the waiter with a wife. He did not wish to be unjust. He was only in a hurry.

"And you? You have no fear of going home before your usual hour?"

"Are you trying to insult me?"

"No, hombre, only to make a joke."

"No," the waiter who was in a hurry said, rising from pulling down the metal shutters. "I have confidence. I am all confidence."

"You have youth, confidence, and a job," the older waiter said. "You have everything."

"And what do you lack?"

"Everything but work."

"You have everything I have."

"No. I have never had confidence and I am not young."

"Come on. Stop talking nonsense and lock up."

"I am of those who like to stay late at the café," the older waiter said. "With all those who do not want to go to bed. With all those who need a light for the night."

"I want to go home and into bed."

"We are of two different kinds," the older waiter said. He was now dressed to go home. "It is not only a question of youth and confidence although those things are very beautiful. Each night I am reluctant to close up because there may be some one who needs the café."

"Hombre, there are bodegas° open all night long."

"You do not understand. This is a clean and pleasant café. It is well-lighted. The light is very good and also, now, there are shadows of the leaves."

"Good night," said the younger waiter.

"Good night," the other said. Turning off the electric light he continued the conversation with himself. It is the light of course but it is necessary that the place be clean and pleasant. You do not want music. Certainly you do not want music. Nor can you stand before a bar with dignity although that is all that is provided for these hours. What did he fear? It was not fear or dread. It was a nothing that he knew too well. It was all a nothing and a man was nothing too. It was only that and light was all it needed and a certain cleanness and order. Some lived in it and never felt it but he knew it all was nada y pues nada y nada y pues nada.° Our nada who art in nada, nada be thy name thy kingdom nada thy will be nada in nada as it is in nada. Give us this nada our daily nada and nada us our nada as we nada our nadas and nada us not into nada but deliver us from nada; pues nada.

°*bodegas:* wineshops.

°*nada y pues . . . nada:* nothing and then nothing and nothing and then nothing.

°*Otro loco más:* another lunatic.

Hail nothing full of nothing, nothing is with thee. He smiled and stood before a bar with a shining steam pressure coffee machine.

"What's yours?" asked the barman.

"Nada."

"Otro loco más,"° said the barman and turned away.

"A little cup," said the waiter.

The barman poured it for him.

"The light is very bright and pleasant but the bar is unpolished," the waiter said.

The barman looked at him but did not answer. It was too late at night for conversation.

"You want another copita?"° the barman asked.

"No, thank you," said the waiter and went out. He disliked bars and bodegas. A clean, well-lighted café was a very different thing. Now, without thinking further, he would go home to his room. He would lie in the bed and finally, with daylight, he would go to sleep. After all, he said to himself, it is probably only insomnia. Many must have it.

°*copita:* little cup.

Jonathan Swift

Jonathan Swift's "The Lady's Dressing Room" and Lady Mary Wortley Montagu's "The Reasons that Induced Dr. S. to write a Poem called The Lady's Dressing Room" are selected for this chapter as companion pieces, since Montagu was motivated to write "The Reasons" in response to Swift's poem. Both texts belong to the genre of satire, which means that at some level the poems are a form of attack. As readers, we must interpret what exactly they attack. But they also make clear the role that ocularity—the role that seeing*—plays in the gendering of space. It is significant that Swift's narrator is male and erects what he imagines as a female space, but one in which only man does the* looking *and woman is an object of visual consumption; likewise, it is particularly important that Montagu's narrator, who* sees *the "same event" in an entirely different way and turns these conventions on their heads, is female. As you read, consider how the power of the-one-who-does-the-looking influences constructions of gender and space.*

Jonathan Swift (1667–1745) was born in Dublin as part of the class of English who were sent to colonize Ireland, and though he would have preferred to live and rise to political prominence in England and though he did have an important role in Queen Anne's government for a spell in the early 1710s, he lived most of his life in Ireland, disappointed and disaffected. In 1682 Swift attended Trinity College, Dublin, just barely graduating with his B.A. "by special grace" in 1686. He worked for some time in England as Sir William Temple's secretary and earned an M.A from Hart Hall, Oxford in 1692. In 1694 Swift was ordained a deacon and in 1695 a priest in the Church of England. In 1700 he was named vicar of Laracor and awarded a prebend of St. Patrick's Cathedral, Dublin. In 1702, Swift earned a Doctor of Divinity degree from Trinity College, Dublin. Regardless of his education and advancement within his profession, however, a life in the church offered Swift little monetary, social, or political reward. It was the "Drapier Letters," which he began in 1720, that changed his career. Although Swift was not fond of his homeland, in the "Letters" he critiqued England's exploitation of Ireland and achieved literary acclaim. Students today are perhaps most familiar with Swift as author of Gulliver's Travels (1726), A Tale of A Tub *(1704), or* A Modest Proposal *(1729), but in addition to these satirical prose works, Swift was also an avid pamphleteer, which means he wrote political critiques from a quite partisan position, and a writer of miscellaneous verse, of which "The Lady's Dressing Room" is a fine example. Swift's brief description of Celia in the poem and incorporation of the term "Lady" in his title suggest that he is critiquing an aristocratic woman, which likely served as the impetus for Montagu's response.*

The Lady's Dressing Room

Five hours (and who can do it less in?)
By haughty Celia spent in dressing;
The goddess from her chamber issues,
Arrayed in lace, brocade, and tissues:
Strephon,[1] who found the room was void,
And Betty[2] otherwise employed,
Stole in, and took a strict survey,
Of all the litter as it lay:
Whereof, to make the matter clear,
An *inventory* follows here.

And first, a dirty smock appeared,
Beneath the arm-pits well besmeared;
Strephon, the rogue, displayed it wide,
And turned it round on every side.
In such a case few words are best,
And Strephon bids us guess the rest;
But swears how damnably the men lie,
In calling Celia sweet and cleanly.

Now listen while he next produces
The various combs for various uses,
Filled up with dirt so closely fixed,
No brush could force a way betwixt;
A paste of composition rare,
Sweat, dandruff, powder, lead,[3] and hair,
A forehead cloth with oil upon't
To smooth the wrinkles on her front;
Here alum flour[4] to stop the steams,
There night-gloves made of Tripsy's[5] hide,
Bequeathed by Tripsy when she died;
With puppy water,[6] beauty's help,
Distilled from Tripsy's darling whelp.
Here gallipots° and vials placed, — °ointment jars
Some filled with washes, some with paste;
Some with pomatum,° paints, and slops, — °hair ointment
And ointments good for scabby chops.° — °lips or cheeks

Hard° by a filthy basin stands, °close
Fouled with the scouring of her hands;
The basin takes whatever comes,
The scrapings of her teeth and gums,
A nasty compound of all hues,
For here she spits, and here she spews.

But oh! it turned poor Strephon's bowels,
When he beheld and smelt the towels;
Begummed, bemattered, and beslimed;
With dirt, and sweat, and ear-wax grimed.
No object Strephon's eye escapes,
Here, petticoats in frowzy° heaps; °unkempt
Nor be the handkerchiefs forgot,
All varnished o'er with snuff[7] and snot.
The stockings why should I expose,
Stained with the moisture of her toes;
Or greasy coifs and pinners° reeking, °night caps
Which Celia slept at least a week in?
A pair of tweezers next he found
To pluck her brows in arches round,
Or hairs that sink the forehead low,
Or on her chin like bristles grow.

The virtues we must not let pass
Of Celia's magnifying glass;
When frightened Strephon cast his eye on't,
It showed the visage of a giant:[8]
A glass that can to sight disclose
The smallest worm in Celia's nose,
And faithfully direct her nail
To squeeze it out from head to tail;
For catch it nicely by the head,
It must come out alive or dead.

Why, Strephon, will you tell the rest?
And must you needs describe the chest?
That careless wench! no creature warn her
To move it out from yonder corner,
But leave it standing full in sight,
For you to exercise your spite!
In vain the workman showed his wit
With rings and hinges counterfeit
To make it seem in this disguise
A cabinet to vulgar eyes;
Which Strephon ventured to look in,
Resolved to go through *thick and thin;*

He lifts the lid; there need no more,
He smelt it all the time before.

As, from within Pandora's box,
When Epimethus oped the locks,
A sudden universal crew
Of human evils upward flew;[9]
He still was comforted to find
That hope at last remained behind.

So, Strephon, lifting up the lid
To view what in the chest was hid,
The vapors flew from out the vent,
But Strephon cautious never meant
The bottom of the pan to grope,
And foul his hands in search of hope.

O! ne'er may such a vile machine° °construction
Be once in Celia's chamber seen!
O! may she better learn to keep
"Those secrets of the hoary deep."[10]

As mutton cutlets, prime of meat,
Which though with art you salt and beat
As laws of cookery require,
And roast them at the clearest fire;
If from adown the hopeful chops
The fat upon a cinder drops,
To stinking smoke it turns the flame
Poisoning the flesh from whence it came;
And up exhales a greasy stench
For which you curse the careless wench:
So things which must not be expressed,
When *plumped*° into the reeking chest, °dropped
Send up an excremental smell
To taint the parts from which they fell:
The petticoats and gown perfume,
And waft a stink round every room.

Thus finishing his grand survey,
The swain disgusted slunk away,
Repeating in his amorous fits,
"Oh! Celia, Celia, Celia shits!"

But Vengeance, goddess never sleeping,
Soon punished Strephon for his peeping.
His foul imagination links
Each dame he sees with all her stinks:
And if unsavory odors fly,

Conceives a lady standing by:
All women his description fits,
And both ideas jump° like wits
By vicious fancy coupled fast,
And still appearing in contrast.

°join together

I pity wretched Strephon, blind
To all the charms of womankind;
Should I the queen of love refuse,
Because she rose from stinking ooze?[11]
To him that looks behind the scene,
Statira's but some pocky quean.[12]

When Celia in her glory shows,
If Strephon would but stop his nose,
Who now so impiously blasphemes
Her ointments, daubs, and paints and creams;
Her washes, slops, and every clout,[13]
With which she makes so foul a rout;[14]
He soon would learn to think like me,
And bless his ravished eyes to see
Such order from confusion sprung,
Such gaudy *tulips* raised from *dung*.

c. 1730 1732

Notes

1. Strephon and Celia are names usually associated with pastoral poetry, and are therefore used mockingly here.
2. A typical maidservant's name.
3. White lead face paint, used to whiten the skin.
4. Powdered alum used like modern antiperspirant.
5. Celia's lapdog; no fashionable lady was without such a pet.
6. A recipe for this cosmetic, made from the innards of a pig or a fat puppy, was given in the "Fop's Dictionary" in *Mundus Muliebris* [Womanly Make-up]; *Or, the Ladies' Dressing Room Unlocked* (1690), which Swift also used for other terms.
7. Powdered tobacco, sniffed by fashionable men and women alike.
8. Cf. *Gulliver's Travels,* Part 2, "A Voyage to Brobdingnag," ch. 1: "This made me reflect upon the fair skins of our *English* ladies, who appear so beautiful to us, only because they are of our own size, and their defects not to be seen but through magnifying glass, where we find by experiment that the smoothest and whitest skins look tough and coarse, and ill colored."
9. In Greek mythology, Epimethus, acting against advice, opened the box Jove had given his wife Pandora, and all the evils and vices of the world flew out, leaving only hope in the box.

10. Quoting Milton's *Paradise Lost* 2.891, in which Sin is unleashing the chaotic forces of her infernal realm.
11. Venus, Roman goddess of sexual love and physical beauty, rose from the sea.
12. One of the heroines of Nathaniel Lee's highly popular tragedy *The Rival Queens* (1677); Swift's common slattern (quean) has had either smallpox or veneral disease.
13. Washes were either treated water used for the complexion or stale urine used as a detergent; clouts were rags.
14. Both of her skin and, presumably, of the men.

Lady Mary Wortley Montagu

Lady Mary Wortley Montagu (1689–1762) was extraordinary in a number of ways. In 1712, just as her father was to offer her in marriage to another man, Lady Mary eloped with Edward Wortley Montagu, who was appointed ambassador to Turkey in 1716. Breaking with tradition once again, Lady Mary accompanied her husband to Turkey, where she issued a number of letters detailing the Muslim country and celebrating the sexual freedom of Turkish women. The Turkish Embassy Letters first established Montagu's literary reputation in her lifetime, and because of critical interest in post-colonial theory, these letters continue to interest literary scholars today. Not unlike many aristocratic women, Montagu was self-educated. She taught herself Latin, French, Italian, and Persian, was an avid reader, and had a critical eye for social ironies—an intellectual proclivity that facilitated her witty and often satirical debates with fellow literary friends and foes. In addition to her letters, she wrote essays, fictional prose, poetry, and a play entitled Simplicity. *She also had a humanitarian nature: while in Turkey she fought to introduce inoculation against smallpox. In 1739, she grew bored with married life and ran away to France with the Italian Count Francesco Algarotti—a man half her age. In 1762, after the death of her husband and at her daughter's request, Lady Mary returned to England where she died a few months later.*

It is important to note in reading "The Reasons that Induced Dr. S to write a Poem call'd the Lady's Dressing room" that it is largely a matter of Montagu's social class that enables her to use the type of language she employs and it is likely a matter of class that prompted her response to Swift. She had a longtime dislike for Swift and his politics and often critiqued his social climbing, as his ambitions surpassed his rank. "The Reasons" was written sometime between June 1732, when Swift published "The Lady's Dressing Room" and February 1734, when Montagu's poem (significantly, one of the few she allowed to appear in print) was published. In it, she adopts Swift's poetic style and terminology as a means to mock him.

The Reasons that Induced Dr. S. to write a Poem called The Lady's Dressing Room[1]

The Doctor in a clean starched band,
His golden snuff box in his hand,
With care his diamond ring displays
And artful shows its various rays,
While grave he stalks down —— street
His dearest Betty —— to meet.[2]
Long had he waited for this hour,
Nor gained admittance to the bower,
Had joked and punned, and swore and writ,
Tried all his gallantry and wit,[3]
Had told her oft what part he bore
In Oxford's schemes in days of yore,[4]
But bawdy,° politics, nor satire °obscenity
Could move this dull hard hearted creature.
Jenny her maid could taste° a rhyme °enjoy
And, grieved to see him lose his time,
Had kindly whispered in his ear,
"For twice two pound you enter here;
My lady vows without that sum
It is in vain you write or come."
The destined offering now he brought,
And in a paradise of thought,
With a low bow approached the dame,
Who smiling heard him preach his flame.
His gold she takes (such proofs as these
Convince most unbelieving shes)
And in her trunk rose up to lock it
(Too wise to trust it in her pocket)
And then, returned with blushing grace,
Expects the doctor's warm embrace.
But now this is the proper place
Where morals stare me in the face,
And for the sake of fine expression
I'm forced to make a small digression.
Alas for wretched humankind,
With learning mad, with wisdom blind!
The ox thinks he's for saddle fit
(As long ago friend Horace writ[5])
And men their talents still mistaking,
The stutterer fancies his is speaking.

With admiration oft we see
Hard features heightened by toupée,
The beau affects° the politician, °pretends to be
Wit is the citizen's ambition,
Poor Pope philosophy displays on
With so much rhyme and little reason
And though he argues ne'er so long
That all is right, his head is wrong.[6]
None strive to know their proper merit
But strain for wisdom, beauty, spirit,
And lose the praise that is their due
While they've th' impossible in view.
So have I seen the injudicious heir
To add one window the whole house impair.
Instinct the hound does better teach,
Who never undertook to preach;
The frighted hare from dogs does run
But not attempts to bear a gun.
Here many noble thoughts occur
But I prolixity abhor,
And will pursue th' instructive tale
To show the wise in some things fail.
The reverend lover with surprise
Peeps in her bubbies, and her eyes,
And kisses both, and tries—and tries.
The evening in this hellish play,
Besides his guineas thrown away,
Provoked the priest to that degree
He swore, "The fault is not in me.
Your damned close stool° so near my nose, °chamber pot
Your dirty smock, and stinking toes
Would make a Hercules as tame
As any beau that you can name."
The nymph grown furious roared, "By God
The blame lies all in sixty odd,"[7]
And scornful pointing to the door
Cried, "Fumbler, see my face no more."
"With all my heart I'll go away,
But nothing done, I'll nothing pay.
Give back the money." "How," cried she,
"Would you palm such a cheat on me!
For poor four pound to roar and bellow—
Why sure you want some new Prunella?"[8]
"I'll be revenged, you saucy quean"° °whore
(Replies the disappointed Dean)
"I'll so describe your dressing room
The very Irish shall not come."

She answered short, "I'm glad you'll write.
You'll furnish paper when I shite."[9]

1734

Notes

1. In her riposte, Montagu mimics Swift's iambic tetrameter and other mannerisms.
2. In Swift's poem, Betty is the maid's name, Celia, the mistress's.
3. Montagu echoes Swift's poem *Cadenus and Vanessa,* where the clumsy lover "Had sighed and languished, vowed, and writ, / For pastime, or to show his wit" (542–543).
4. Swift had collaborated closely in the political schemes of Robert Harley, first Earl of Oxford (1661–1724).
5. "The ox desires the saddle" (Horace, *Epistles* 1.14.43).
6. Montagu ridicules Pope's conclusion to *An Essay on Man:* "Whatever IS, is RIGHT."
7. I.e., Swift's impotence derives not from her odors but from his age—65—at the time the poem was written).
8. "Prunella" is both a fabric used in clergy vestments (Swift was a clergyman), and the name of the promiscuous, low-born heroine in Richard Estcourt's comic interlude *Prunella* (1708).
9. Compare line 118 of Swift's poem.

Karen Brennan

Karen Brennan, who received her Ph.D. from the University of Arizona, is Associate Professor at the University of Utah, where she teaches creative writing and critical and feminist theories. Having published in a variety of genres, her work includes Here on Earth, a book of poems; Wild Desire, *a collection of short stories and winner of the prestigious Associated Writers Program Award for Fiction; and* Being with Rachel, *a memoir detailing the steps she took to facilitate her daughter's recovery from a serious motorcycle accident. She has also published several articles, poems, and essays in literary and scholarly journals.*

As you read "Floating," from Wild Desire, *reconsider your perceptions of traditional gender roles and gender hierarchies: Are such roles and hierarchies maintained in this story? How or how not? Then, reflect on how the types of spaces this woman and man occupy and how their physical positions within the home influence their relationship. The gap between the wife's lived experience and the husband's understanding of that experience makes "The Yellow Wallpaper" an especially powerful companion piece. In another of Brennan's stories, "Runaways"—reprinted in Chapter Eight, "Writing as Social Witness"—a mother and her four children take flight from her abusive husband out into the world.*

Floating

In the morning I levitated for the first time. I woke up and heard a tiny sound coming from the back of the house. It was a baby. She was wrapped in a white windbreaker and her face was raw from the cold. But she was ok. I unwrapped her and though she was wet, she was fine. I changed her diaper and even her little undershirt. She had all the plumpness of a baby; dimpled knees and folds around the wrists; pale baby skin. She had been crying for two days straight and had survived.

In my own room I realized I could float, simply by willing it. I ascended from the ground and spread my arms like an archangel's. Then I turned on my back and deadman's-floated parallel to the ceiling. My toes touched the plaster, I was wearing my new black boots that look like nun's bowling shoes according to my husband.

My husband was in the living room. I said, Look what I can do! and I floated up, I clasped my knees in my arms and floated across as if I was sitting on a rug. My

---

husband shook his head. He wasn't shocked, but annoyed. He took off his glasses and rubbed the bridge of his nose. I said, Isn't it amazing? But it didn't amaze him.

In the supermarket there are intriguing headlines: *Woman Meets Satan Face-to-Face*. Underneath is a picture of a monster done in fanciful swirls, reminiscent of an eighteenth-century tapestry. The woman said she had been out mowing the lawn. She had spread out a green plastic tarp and as she was heaving the first forkful (interesting that she used a pitchfork, I thought), Satan appeared on a cloud. Terrified, she ran inside to phone the police. Satan followed, opened her refrigerator, took out some of that Boursin cheese and fixed himself a snack. Then she snapped his picture with her Canon-Sure-Shot.

I wish I could float in the supermarket or even outside beneath the stars, over the treetops which would be so attractive from this angle. But I can only float through the rooms of my own house. I float like Chagall's bridal couple, slantwise, past the huge oak mirror my grandmother bequeathed me where I catch a glimpse of myself floating, hair swept back on one side as if there were a breeze. I smile to see myself this way, so uncharacteristically glamorous in this position.

Thinking back on my life as I float through these rooms, I try to remember what it was like before I could do this: How it was walking through rooms the regular way, picking up objects from the coffee table, dusting them, replacing them. A shell. A blue bowl made by my friend Eileen. An octagonal map of the world. I used to value these objects, their arrangement on my coffee table graceful but unpretentious, I thought, giving just the right sort of clue to my personality. A stone found in a Vermont creek; a number two pencil called Thor; a picture of my mother in a cloche hat smoking a cigarette.

My husband says: Come down now. It's six o'clock. This is no longer amusing. But it's a miracle! I say. I wonder if he knows about the baby, the other miracle. I wonder if she is sleeping or shivering. The back room where we store old photographs and old notebooks from law school and old clothes that are out of fashion, the back room is so cold. There is one cracked window where someone shot a beebee. I tacked a sheet over it and now, in addition to being cold, there is only the frailest light seeping through; no view of the mountain or even of the peach tree outside, or the apricot tree which is in bloom now, tiny white blossoms with pink centers and black needles like a bee's antennae. I put the baby in a drawer lined with dark blue velvet. I had imagined satin thick as cream but I could only find this dark blue velvet which belonged to my mother. The baby smiles at me as I float past; she lifts her hand as if to say *take it easy, have a great time*. She is very beautiful and around her chin which had been raw from the cold, little yellow flowers have sprung up. This is a secret baby: the baby of my after hours.

No one, especially my husband, would understand this. In the kitchen he is boiling water for the pasta, *spaghetti verdi*. My job is the sauce but from such a height he won't trust me with the garlic; I wish I had the nerve to go outside, I tell him. He grunts as if nothing was out of the ordinary. He peels an onion by himself, then puts a can of tomatoes in the Cuisinart. If I went outside I might go up and up, there might be no stopping me, I say.

How do we get this way? I was a perfectly ordinary girl. I went to sixteen years of Catholic school. I read three volumes of Thomas Aquinas's *Summa Theologica*. I made my debut on the St. Regis Roof in New York City. I imitated Ella Fitzgerald in a Boston nightclub called The Alibi. I married a nice responsible man who loved me. He gave me my first umbrella.

But now, what does it mean to be able to float through all these rooms? To roll over and over in sheer invisible air? I yell down to my husband, Watch this, it's a miracle! It's better than The Loaves and Fishes and The Marriage Feast at Cana. I love you, I yell down. He is straining the pasta in the colander. I could use some help, he says.

It took Satan hours to leave the woman's house. He ate cheese and crackers, bit the top off a bottle of Chablis and forced the woman to recite her life's story. So I had to, she told reporters. I began with my birth and worked my way up to this very minute. I never felt so embarrassed. Satan sat on the sofa and drank wine out of the broken Chablis bottle without cutting his mouth. He wore green cowboy boots and a turquoise ring. The woman remembers an eerie feeling whenever Satan would address her, as if his voice were resounding in an echo chamber. It gave me the creeps, said the woman, I will never forget that voice.

In the bedroom, the baby breathes in and out so softly I have to swoop down and touch her forehead to make sure she's alive. Her eyelids are like beautiful stones, but she is surviving. Nestled in dark blue velvet like a string of pearls or a magic good-luck stone, she is still breathing, and in each breath or rather between breaths, riding on that infinitesimal gap, I hear her thoughts. She is thinking about me. I let myself slowly down beside her, hold her in my arms, sing to her in almost a whisper. Then my husband opens the door. Dinner's served, he says sarcastically. I am kneeling over the baby in the drawer, but luckily he doesn't see. He turns on the light and kicks a pile of magazines across the room. What a mess, he says. Dust flies up and softly wafts to the ground and this reminds me of myself and my newfound power.

I float through the room, I float to the door on my stomach and push it open. My husband is angry but from this height his anger is so small; his footsteps which shake the floor and rattle the bric-a-brac on the shelves are so far away now. I feel sorry for him walking to the dining room, ladling our food into bowls, sitting down. So pathetic. I am way up here and will he be amazed? Will he believe in this extraordinary power? No. Nothing can impress him.

The woman confessed to reporters that at the end she had developed a kind of feeling for Satan. That he had been charming. He had listened to her stories about herself, even encouraged her to speak more openly. She confessed she found him attractive, sexually attractive.

No one knows about this baby and I'm not sure how long I can keep her. Sooner or later she'll want to fly off, just like me, only outside, over the trees, higher than the world. I hear her thinking to herself, making plans. . . . I wish her well, a good, intelligent baby with no crimp in her vision—for her the way is as clear as water, right through the clouds, like rain or tears. But no one owns anyone or owes anyone anything, I tell my husband as I float upside down over the dinner table, a long piece of spaghetti dangling from my mouth to tantalize him. Spaghetti kiss? I say. Because I want us to be friends, to be affectionate with one another. But he just looks down.

Raymond Carver

Raymond Carver was born in 1938 in a logging town in Oregon; his father was a laborer and his mother a housewife. After graduating from high school, Carver worked as a gas station attendant, a janitor, and a manual laborer in order to support his wife and children. In 1958 he enrolled in a creative writing course where he gained direction as a writer. In 1963 he received his A.B. from California State University Humboldt and in 1966 earned an MFA from the Iowa Writer's Workshop. Carver divorced his first wife in 1983. In 1988 shortly before he died of lung cancer, he married poet Tess Gallagher, his companion for almost a decade and who, like Carver, grew up poor in the Pacific Northwest.

Carver's first collection of short stories, Will You Please Be Quiet, Please?, *was nominated for a National Book Award in 1976. Later collections,* Cathedral *(1984) and* Where I'm Calling From *(1988) were both nominated for the Pulitzer Prize for Fiction in 1985 and 1989, respectively. Carver's frank depiction of the working class comes from his own experiences and critics' response to this depiction initially surprised Carver: In an interview with Bruce Weber of the* New York Times, *Carver discloses, "Until I started reading these reviews of my work, praising me, I never felt the people I was writing about were so bad. . . . The waitress, the bus driver, the mechanic, the hotel keeper. God, the country is filled with these people. They're good people. People doing the best they could." Carver's subject subsequently caught the eye of film director, Robert Altman, who adapted several of his short stories, including "So Much Water So Close to Home," for the film* Short Cuts. *Another of Carver's short stories, "What We Talk About When We Talk About Love," appears in Chapter Five, "Rereading Romance." In "So Much Water So Close to Home," from* Furious Seasons *(1977), space seems to be divided according to gender—woman is associated with the domestic and man with the "wilderness." But Carver also suggests how fragile these socially constructed boundaries are. How can what occurs in one space infect another?*

So Much Water So Close to Home

My husband eats with good appetite but he seems tired, edgy. He chews slowly, arms on the table, and stares at something across the room. He looks at me

---

Reprinted from *Furious Seasons*, (1976).

and looks away again. He wipes his mouth on the napkin. He shrugs and goes on eating. Something has come between us though he would like me to believe otherwise.

"What are you staring at me for?" he asks. "What is it?" he says and puts his fork down.

"Was I staring?" I say and shake my head stupidly, stupidly.

The telephone rings. "Don't answer it," he says.

"It might be your mother," I say. "Dean—it might be something about Dean."

"Watch and see," he says.

I pick up the receiver and listen for a minute. He stops eating. I bite my lip and hang up.

"What did I tell you?" he says. He starts to eat again, then throws the napkin onto his plate. "Goddamn it, why can't people mind their own business? Tell me what I did wrong and I'll listen! It's not fair. She was dead, wasn't she? There were other men there besides me. We talked it over and we all decided. We'd only just got there. We'd walked for hours. We couldn't just turn around, we were five miles from the car. It was opening day. What the hell, I don't see anything wrong. No, I don't. And don't look at me that way, do you hear? I won't have you passing judgment on me. Not you."

"You know," I say and shake my head.

"What do I know, Claire? Tell me. Tell me what I know. I don't know anything except one thing: you hadn't better get worked up over this." He gives me what he thinks is a *meaningful* look. "She was dead, dead, dead, do you hear?" he says after a minute. "It's a damn shame, I agree. She was a young girl and it's a shame, and I'm sorry, as sorry as anyone else, but she was dead, Claire, dead. Now let's leave it alone. Please, Claire. Let's leave it alone now."

"That's the point," I say. "She was dead. But don't you see? She needed help."

"I give up," he says and raises his hands. He pushes his chair away from the table, takes his cigarettes and goes out to the patio with a can of beer. He walks back and forth for a minute and then sits in a lawn chair and picks up the paper once more. His name is there on the first page along with the names of his friends, the other men who made the "grisly find."

I close my eyes for a minute and hold onto the drainboard. I must not dwell on this any longer. I must get over it, put it out of sight, out of mind, etc., and "go on." I open my eyes. Despite everything, knowing all that may be in store, I rake my arm across the drainboard and send the dishes and glasses smashing and scattering across the floor.

He doesn't move. I know he has heard, he raises his head as if listening, but he doesn't move otherwise, doesn't turn around to look. I hate him for that, for not moving. He waits a minute, then draws on his cigarette and leans back in the chair. I pity him for listening, detached, and then settling back and drawing on his cigarette. The wind takes the smoke out of his mouth in a thin stream. Why do I notice that? He can never know how much I pity him for that, for sitting still and listening, and letting the smoke stream out of his mouth. . . .

He planned his fishing trip into the mountains last Sunday, a week before the Memorial Day weekend. He and Gordon Johnson, Mel Dorn, Vern Williams. They play poker, bowl, and fish together. They fish together every spring and early summer, the first two or three months of the season, before family vacations, little league baseball, and visiting relatives can intrude. They are decent men, family men, responsible at their jobs. They have sons and daughters who go to school with our son, Dean. On Friday afternoon these four men left for a three-day fishing trip to the Naches River. They parked the car in the mountains and hiked several miles to where they wanted to fish. They carried their bedrolls, food and cooking utensils, their playing cards, their whiskey. The first evening at the river, even before they could set up camp, Mel Dorn found the girl floating face down in the river, nude, lodged near the shore in some branches. He called the other men and they all came to look at her. They talked about what to do. One of the men—Stuart didn't say which—perhaps it was Vern Williams, he is a heavy-set, easy man who laughs often—one of them thought they should start back to the car at once. The others stirred the sand with their shoes and said they felt inclined to stay. They pleaded fatigue, the late hour, the fact that the girl "wasn't going anywhere." In the end they all decided to stay. They went ahead and set up the camp and built a fire and drank their whiskey. They drank a lot of whiskey and when the moon came up they talked about the girl. Someone thought they should do something to prevent the body from floating away. Somehow they thought that this might create a problem for them if it floated away during the night. They took flashlights and stumbled down to the river. The wind was up, a cold wind, and waves from the river lapped the sandy bank. One of the men, I don't know who, it might have been Stuart, he could have done it, waded into the water and took the girl by the fingers and pulled her, still face down, closer to shore, into shallow water, and then took a piece of nylon cord and tied it around her wrist and then secured the cord to tree roots, all the while the flashlights of the other men played over the girl's body. Afterward, they went back to camp and drank more whiskey. Then they went to sleep. The next morning, Saturday, they cooked breakfast, drank lots of coffee, more whiskey, and then split up to fish, two men upriver, two men down.

That night, after they had cooked their fish and potatoes and had more coffee and whiskey, they took their dishes down to the river and rinsed them off a few yards from where the body lay in the water. They drank again and then they took out their cards and played and drank until they couldn't see the cards any longer. Vern Williams went to sleep, but the others told coarse stories and spoke of vulgar or dishonest escapades out of their past, and no one mentioned the girl until Gordon Johnson, who'd forgotten for a minute, commented on the firmness of the trout they'd caught, and the terrible coldness of the river water. They stopped talking then but continued to drink until one of them tripped and fell cursing against the lantern, and then they climbed into their sleeping bags.

The next morning they got up late, drank more whiskey, fished a little as they kept drinking whiskey. Then, at one o'clock in the afternoon, Sunday, a day earlier than they'd planned, they decided to leave. They took down their tents, rolled their sleeping bags, gathered their pans, pots, fish, and fishing gear, and hiked out. They didn't look at the girl again before they left. When they reached the car they drove the highway in silence until they came to a telephone. Stuart made the call to the sheriff's office while the others stood around in the hot sun and listened. He gave the man on the other end of the line all of their names—they had nothing to hide, they weren't ashamed of anything—and agreed to wait at the service station until someone could come for more detailed directions and individual statements.

He came home at eleven o'clock that night. I was asleep but woke when I heard him in the kitchen. I found him leaning against the refrigerator drinking a can of beer. He put his heavy arms around me and rubbed his hands up and down my back, the same hands he'd left with two days before, I thought.

In bed he put his hands on me again and then waited, as if thinking of something else. I turned slightly and then moved my legs. Afterward, I know he stayed awake for a long time, for he was awake when I fell asleep; and later, when I stirred for a minute, opening my eyes at a slight noise, a rustle of sheets, it was almost daylight outside, birds were singing, and he was on his back smoking and looking at the curtained window. Half-asleep I said his name, but he didn't answer. I fell asleep again.

He was up this morning before I could get out of bed to see if there was anything about it in the paper, I suppose. The telephone began to ring shortly after eight o'clock.

"Go to hell," I heard him shout into the receiver. The telephone rang again a minute later, and I hurried into the kitchen. "I have nothing else to add to what I've already said to the sheriff. That's right!" He slammed down the receiver.

"What is going on?" I said, alarmed.

"Sit down," he said slowly. His fingers scraped, scraped against his stubble of whiskers. "I have to tell you something. Something happened while we were fishing." We sat across from each other at the table, and then he told me.

I drank coffee and stared at him as he spoke. Then I read the account in the newspaper that he shoved across the table:

". . . unidentified girl eighteen to twenty-four years of age . . . body three to five days in the water . . . rape a possible motive . . . preliminary results show death by strangulation . . . cuts and bruises on her breasts and pelvic area . . . autopsy . . . rape, pending further investigation."

"You've got to understand," he said. "Don't look at me like that. Be careful now, I mean it. Take it easy, Claire."

"Why didn't you tell me last night?" I asked.

"I just . . . didn't. What do you mean?" he said.

"You know what I mean," I said. I looked at his hands, the broad fingers, knuckles covered with hair, moving, lighting a cigarette now, fingers that had moved over me, into me last night.

He shrugged. "What difference does it make, last night, this morning? It was late. You were sleepy, I thought I'd wait until this morning to tell you." He looked out to the patio: a robin flew from the lawn to the picnic table and preened its feathers.

"It isn't true," I said. "You didn't leave her there like that?"

He turned quickly and said, "What'd I do? Listen to me carefully now, once and for all. Nothing happened. I have nothing to be sorry for or feel guilty about. Do you hear me?"

I got up from the table and went to Dean's room. He was awake and in his pajamas, putting together a puzzle. I helped him find his clothes and then went back to the kitchen and put his breakfast on the table. The telephone rang two or three more times and each time Stuart was abrupt while he talked and angry when he hung up. He called Mel Dorn and Gordon Johnson and spoke with them, slowly, seriously, and then he opened a beer and smoked a cigarette while Dean ate, asked him about school, his friends, etc., exactly as if nothing had happened.

Dean wanted to know what he'd done while he was gone, and Stuart took some fish out of the freezer to show him.

"I'm taking him to your mother's for the day," I said.

"Sure," Stuart said and looked at Dean who was holding one of the frozen trout. "If you want to and he wants to, that is. You don't have to, you know. There's nothing wrong."

"I'd like to anyway," I said.

"Can I go swimming there?" Dean asked and wiped his fingers on his pants.

"I believe so," I said. "It's a warm day so take your suit, and I'm sure your grandmother will say it's okay."

Stuart lighted a cigarette and looked at us.

Dean and I drove across town to Stuart's mother's. She lives in an apartment building with a pool and a sauna bath. Her name is Catherine Kane. Her name, Kane, is the same as mine, which seems impossible. Years ago, Stuart has told me, she used to be called Candy by her friends. She is a tall, cold woman with white-blonde hair. She gives me the feeling that she is always judging, judging. I explain briefly in a low voice what has happened (she hasn't yet read the newspaper) and promise to pick Dean up that evening. "He brought his swimming suit," I say. "Stuart and I have to talk about some things," I add vaguely. She looks at me steadily from over her glasses. Then she nods and turns to Dean, saying "How are you, my little man?" She stoops and puts her arms around him. She looks at me again as I open the door to leave. She has a way of looking at me without saying anything.

When I return home Stuart is eating something at the table and drinking beer. . . .

After a time I sweep up the broken dishes and glassware and go outside. Stuart is lying on his back on the grass now, the newspaper and can of beer within reach, staring at the sky. It's breezy but warm out and birds call.

"Stuart, could we go for a drive?" I say. "Anywhere."

He rolls over and looks at me and nods. "We'll pick up some beer," he says. "I hope you're feeling better about this. Try to understand, that's all I ask." He gets to his feet and touches me on the hip as he goes past. "Give me a minute and I'll be ready."

We drive through town without speaking. Before we reach the country he stops at a roadside market for beer. I notice a great stack of papers just inside the door. On the top step a fat woman in a print dress holds out a licorice stick to a little girl. In a few minutes we cross Everson Creek and turn into a picnic area a few feet from the water. The creek flows under the bridge and into a large pond a few hundred yards away. There are a dozen or so men and boys scattered around the banks of the pond under the willows, fishing.

So much water so close to home, why did he have to go miles away to fish?

"Why did you have to go there of all places?" I say.

"The Naches? We always go there. Every year, at least once." We sit on a bench in the sun and he opens two cans of beer and gives one to me. "How the hell was I to know anything like that would happen?" He shakes his head and shrugs, as if it had all happened years ago, or to someone else. "Enjoy the afternoon, Claire. Look at this weather."

"They said they were innocent."

"Who? What are you talking about?"

"The Maddox brothers. They killed a girl named Arlene Hubly near the town where I grew up, and then cut off her head and threw her into the Cle Elum River. She and I went to the same high school. It happened when I was a girl."

"What a hell of a thing to be thinking about," he says. "Come on, get off it. You're going to get me riled in a minute. How about it now? Claire?"

I look at the creek. I float toward the pond, eyes open, face down, staring at the rocks and moss on the creek bottom until I am carried into the lake where I am pushed by the breeze. Nothing will be any different. We will go on and on and on and on. We will go on even now, as if nothing had happened. I look at him across the picnic table with such intensity that his face drains.

"I don't know what's wrong with you," he says. "I don't—"

I slap him before I realize. I raise my hand, wait a fraction of a second, and then slap his cheek hard. This is crazy, I think as I slap him. We need to lock our fingers together. We need to help one another. This is crazy.

He catches my wrist before I can strike again and raises his own hand. I crouch, waiting, and see something come into his eyes and then dart away. He drops his hand. I drift even faster around and around in the pond.

"Come on, get in the car," he says. "I'm taking you home."

"No, no," I say, pulling back from him.

"Come on," he says. "Goddamn it."

"You're not being fair to me," he says later in the car. Fields and trees and farmhouses fly by outside the window. "You're not being fair. To either one of us. Or to Dean, I might add. Think about Dean for a minute. Think about me. Think about someone else besides your goddamn self for a change."

There is nothing I can say to him now. He tries to concentrate on the road, but he keeps looking into the rearview mirror. Out of the corner of his eye, he looks across the seat to where I sit with my knees drawn up under my chin. The sun blazes against my arm and the side of my face. He opens another beer while he drives, drinks from it, then shoves the can between his legs and lets out breath. He knows. I could laugh in his face. I could weep.

Stuart believes he is letting me sleep this morning. But I was awake long before the alarm sounded, thinking, lying on the far side of the bed, away from his hairy legs and his thick, sleeping fingers. He gets Dean off for school, and then he shaves, dresses, and leaves for work. Twice he looks into the bedroom and clears his throat, but I keep my eyes closed.

In the kitchen I find a note from him signed "Love." I sit in the breakfast nook in the sunlight and drink coffee and make a coffee ring on the note. The telephone has stopped ringing, that's something. No more calls since last night. I look at the paper and turn it this way and that on the table. Then I pull it close and read what it says. The body is still unidentified, unclaimed, apparently unmissed. But for the last twenty-four hours men have been examining it, putting things into it, cutting, weighing, measuring, putting back again, sewing up, looking for the exact cause and moment of death. Looking for evidence of rape. I'm sure they hope for rape. Rape would make it easier to understand. The paper says the body will be taken to Keith & Keith Funeral Home pending arrangements. People are asked to come forward with information, etc.

Two things are certain: 1) people no longer care what happens to other people; and 2) nothing makes any real difference any longer. Look at what has happened. Yet nothing will change for Stuart and me. Really change, I mean. We will grow older, both of us, you can see it in our faces already, in the bathroom mirror, for instance, mornings when we use the bathroom at the same time. And certain things around us will change, become easier or harder, one thing or the other, but nothing will ever really be any different. I believe that. We have made our decisions, our lives have been set in motion, and they will go on and on until they stop. But if that is true, then what? I mean, what if you believe that, but you keep it covered up, until one day something happens that should change something, but then you see nothing is going to change after all. What then? Meanwhile, the people around you continue to talk and act as if you were the same person as yesterday, or last night, or five minutes before, but you are really undergoing a crisis, your heart feels damaged. . . .

The past is unclear. It's as if there is a film over those early years. I can't even be sure that the things I remember happening really happened to me. There was a girl who had a mother and father—the father ran a small cafe where the mother acted as waitress and cashier—who moved as if in a dream through grade school and high school and then, in a year or two, into secretarial school. Later, much later—what happened to the time in between?—she is in another town working as a receptionist for an electronics parts firm and becomes acquainted with one of the engineers who asks her for a date. Eventually, seeing that's his aim, she lets him seduce her. She had an intuition at the time, an insight about the seduction that later, try as she might, she couldn't recall. After a short while they decide to get married, but already the past, her past, is slipping away. The future is something she can't imagine. She smiles, as if she has a secret, when she thinks about the future. Once, during a particularly bad argument, over what she can't now remember, five years or so after they were married, he tells her that someday this affair (his words: "this affair") will end in violence. She remembers this. She files this away somewhere and begins repeating it aloud from time to time. Sometimes she spends the whole morning on her knees in the sandbox behind the garage playing with Dean and one or two of his friends. But every afternoon at four o'clock her head begins to hurt. She holds her forehead and feels dizzy with the pain. Stuart asks her to see a doctor and she does, secretly pleased at the doctor's solicitous attention. She goes away for a while to a place the doctor recommends. Stuart's mother comes out from Ohio in a hurry to care for the child. But she,

Claire, spoils everything and returns home in a few weeks. His mother moves out of the house and takes an apartment across town and perches there, as if waiting. One night in bed when they are both near sleep, Claire tells him that she heard some women patients at the clinic discussing fellatio. She thinks this is something he might like to hear. Stuart is pleased at hearing this. He strokes her arm. Things are going to be okay, he says. From now on everything is going to be different and better for them. He has received a promotion and a substantial raise. They've even bought another car, a station wagon, her car. They're going to live in the here and now. He says he feels able to relax for the first time in years. In the dark, he goes on stroking her arm. . . . He continues to bowl and play cards regularly. He goes fishing with three friends of his.

That evening three things happen: Dean says that the children at school told him that his father found a dead body in the river. He wants to know about it.

Stuart explains quickly, leaving out most of the story, saying only that, yes, he and three other men did find a body while they were fishing.

"What kind of body?" Dean asks. "Was it a girl?"

"Yes, it was a girl. A woman. Then we called the sheriff." Stuart looks at me.

"What'd he say?" Dean asks.

"He said he'd take care of it."

"What did it look like? Was it scary?"

"That's enough talk," I say. "Rinse your plate, Dean, and then you're excused."

"But what'd it look like?" he persists. "I want to know."

"You heard me," I say. "Did you hear me, Dean? Dean!" I want to shake him. I want to shake him until he cries.

"Do what your mother says," Stuart tells him quietly. "It was just a body, and that's all there is to it."

I am clearing the table when Stuart comes up behind and touches my arm. His fingers burn. I start, almost losing a plate.

"What's the matter with you?" he says, dropping his hand. "Claire, what is it?"

"You scared me," I say.

"That's what I mean. I should be able to touch you without you jumping out of your skin." He stands in front of me with a little grin, trying to catch my eyes, and then he puts his arm around my waist. With his other hand he takes my free hand and puts it on the front of his pants.

"Please, Stuart." I pull away and he steps back and snaps his fingers.

"Hell with it then," he says. "Be that way if you want. But just remember."

"Remember what?" I say quickly. I look at him and hold my breath.

He shrugs. "Nothing, nothing," he says.

The second thing that happens is that while we are watching television that evening, he in his leather recliner chair, I on the sofa with a blanket and magazine, the house quiet except for the television, a voice cuts into the program to say that the murdered girl has been identified. Full details will follow on the eleven o'clock news.

We look at each other. In a few minutes he gets up and says he is going to fix a nightcap. Do I want one?

"No," I say.

"I don't mind drinking alone," he says. "I thought I'd ask."

I can see he is obscurely hurt, and I look away, ashamed and yet angry at the same time.

He stays in the kitchen a long while, but comes back with his drink just when the news begins.

First the announcer repeats the story of the four local fishermen finding the body. Then the station shows a high school graduation photograph of the girl, a dark-haired girl with a round face and full, smiling lips. There's a film of the girl's parents entering the funeral home to make the identification. Bewildered, sad, they shuffle slowly up the sidewalk to the front steps to where a man in a dark suit stands waiting, holding the door. Then, it seems as if only seconds have passed, as if they have merely gone inside the door and turned around and come out again, the same couple is shown leaving the building, the woman in tears, covering her face with a handkerchief, the man stopping long enough to say to a reporter, "It's her, it's Susan. I can't say anything right now. I hope they get the person or persons who did it before it happens again. This violence. . . ." He motions feebly at the television camera. Then the man and woman get into an old car and drive away into the late afternoon traffic.

The announcer goes on to say that the girl, Susan Miller, had gotten off work as a cashier in a movie theater in Summit, a town 120 miles north of our town. A green, late-model car pulled up in front of the theater and the girl, who according to witnesses looked as if she'd been waiting, went over to the car and got in, leading the authorities to suspect that the driver of the car was a friend, or at least an acquaintance. The authorities would like to talk to the driver of the green car.

Stuart clears his throat, then leans back in the chair and sips his drink.

The third thing that happens is that after the news Stuart stretches, yawns, and looks at me. I get up and begin making a bed for myself on the sofa.

"What are you doing?" he says, puzzled.

"I'm not sleepy," I say, avoiding his eyes. "I think I'll stay up a while longer and then read something until I fall asleep."

He stares as I spread a sheet over the sofa. When I start to go for a pillow, he stands at the bedroom door, blocking the way.

"I'm going to ask you once more," he says. "What the hell do you think you're going to accomplish by this?"

"I need to be by myself tonight," I say. "I need to have time to think."

He lets out breath. "I'm thinking you're making a big mistake by doing this. I'm thinking you'd better think again about what you're doing. Claire?"

I can't answer. I don't know what I want to say. I turn and begin to tuck in the edges of the blanket. He stares at me a minute longer and then I see him raise his shoulders. "Suit yourself then. I could give a fuck less what you do," he says. He turns and walks down the hall scratching his neck.

This morning I read in the paper that services for Susan Miller are to be held in Chapel of the Pines, Summit, at two o'clock the next afternoon. Also, that police have taken statements from three people who saw her get into the green Chevrolet. But they still have no license number for the car. They are getting warmer, though, and the investigation is continuing. I sit for a long while holding the paper, thinking, then I call to make an appointment at the hairdresser's.

I sit under the dryer with a magazine on my lap and let Millie do my nails.

"I'm going to a funeral tomorrow," I say after we have talked a bit about a girl who no longer works there.

Millie looks up at me and then back at my fingers. "I'm sorry to hear that, Mrs. Kane. I'm real sorry."

"It's a young girl's funeral," I say.

"That's the worst kind. My sister died when I was a girl, and I'm still not over it to this day. Who died?" she says after a minute.

"A girl. We weren't all that close, you know, but still."

"Too bad. I'm real sorry. But we'll get you fixed up for it, don't worry. How's that look?"

"That looks . . . fine, Millie, did you ever wish you were somebody else, or else just nobody, nothing, nothing at all?"

She looks at me. "I can't say I ever felt that, no. No, if I was somebody else I'd be afraid I might not like who I was." She holds my fingers and seems to think about something for a minute. "I don't know, I just don't know. . . . Let me have your other hand now, Mrs. Kane."

At eleven o'clock that night I make another bed on the sofa and this time Stuart only looks at me, rolls his tongue behind his lips, and goes down the hall to the bedroom. In the night I wake and listen to the wind slamming the gate against the fence. I don't want to be awake, and I lie for a long while with my eyes closed. Finally I get up and go down the hall with my pillow. The light is burning in our bedroom and Stuart is on his back with his mouth open, breathing heavily. I go into Dean's room and get into bed with him. In his sleep he moves over to give me space. I lie there for a minute and then hold him, my face against his hair.

"What is it, Mama?" he says.

"Nothing, honey. Go back to sleep. It's nothing, it's all right."

I get up when I hear Stuart's alarm, put on coffee and prepare breakfast while he shaves.

He appears in the kitchen doorway, towel over his bare shoulder, appraising.

"Here's coffee," I say. "Eggs will be ready in a minute."

He nods.

I wake Dean and the three of us have breakfast. Once or twice Stuart looks at me as if he wants to say something, but each time I ask Dean if he wants more milk, more toast, etc.

"I'll call you today," Stuart says as he opens the door.

"I don't think I'll be home today," I say quickly. "I have a lot of things to do today. In fact, I may be late for dinner."

"All right. Sure." He moves his briefcase from one hand to the other. "Maybe we'll go out for dinner tonight? How would you like that?" He keeps looking at me. He's forgotten about the girl already. "Are you all right?"

I move to straighten his tie, then drop my hand. He wants to kiss me goodbye. I move back a step. "Have a nice day then," he says finally. He turns and goes down the walk to his car.

I dress carefully. I try on a hat that I haven't worn in several years and look at myself in the mirror. Then I remove the hat, apply a light makeup, and write a note for Dean.

> *Honey, Mommy has things to do this afternoon, but will be home later. You are to stay in the house or in the back/yard until one of us comes home.*
>
> *Love*

I look at the word "Love" and then I underline it. As I am writing the note I realize I don't know whether *back yard* is one word or two. I have never considered it before. I think about it and then I draw a line and make two words of it.

I stop for gas and ask directions to Summit. Barry, a forty-year-old mechanic with a mustache, comes out from the restroom and leans against the front fender while the other man, Lewis, puts the hose into the tank and begins to slowly wash the windshield.

"Summit," Barry says, looking at me and smoothing a finger down each side of his mustache. "There's no best way to get to Summit, Mrs. Kane. It's about a two-, two-and-a-half-hour drive each way. Across the mountains. It's quite a drive for a woman. Summit? What's in Summit, Mrs. Kane?"

"I have business," I say, vaguely uneasy. Lewis has gone to wait on another customer.

"Ah. Well, if I wasn't tied up there—" he gestures with his thumb toward the bay—"I'd offer to drive you to Summit and back again. Road's not all that good. I mean it's good enough, there's just a lot of curves and so on."

"I'll be all right. But thank you." He leans against the fender. I can feel his eyes as I open my purse.

Barry takes the credit card. "Don't drive it at night," he says. "It's not all that good a road, like I said. And while I'd be willing to bet you wouldn't have car trouble with this, I know this car, you can never be sure about blowouts and things like that. Just to be on the safe side I'd better check these tires." He taps one of the front tires with his shoe. "We'll run it onto the hoist. Won't take long."

"No, no, it's all right. Really, I can't take any more time. The tires look fine to me."

"Only takes a minute," he says. "Be on the safe side."

"I said no. No! They look fine to me. I have to go now. Barry. . . ."

"Mrs. Kane?"

"I have to go now."

I sign something. He gives me the receipt, the card, some stamps. I put everything into my purse. "You take it easy," he says. "Be seeing you."

As I wait to pull into the traffic, I look back and see him watching. I close my eyes, then open them. He waves.

I turn at the first light, then turn again and drive until I come to the highway and read the sign: SUMMIT 117 MILES. It is ten-thirty and warm.

The highway skirts the edge of town, then passes through farm country, through fields of oats and sugar beets and apple orchards, with here and there a small herd of cattle grazing in open pastures. Then everything changes, the farms become fewer and fewer, more like shacks now than houses, and stands of timber replace the orchards. All at once I'm in the mountains and on the right, far below, I catch glimpses of the Naches River.

In a little while I see a green pickup truck behind me, and it stays behind me for miles. I keep slowing at the wrong times, hoping it will pass, and then increasing my speed, again at the wrong times. I grip the wheel until my fingers hurt. Then on a clear stretch he does pass, but he drives along beside for a minute, a crew-cut man in a blue workshirt in his early thirties, and we look at each other. Then he waves, toots the horn twice, and pulls ahead of me.

I slow down and find a place, a dirt road off of the shoulder. I pull over and turn off the ignition. I can hear the river somewhere down below the trees. Ahead of me the dirt road goes into the trees. Then I hear the pickup returning.

I start the engine just as the truck pulls up behind me. I lock the doors and roll up the windows. Perspiration breaks on my face and arms as I put the car in gear, but there is no place to drive.

"You all right?" the man says as he comes up to the car. "Hello. Hello in there." He raps the glass. "You okay?" He leans his arms on the door and brings his face close to the window.

I stare at him and can't find any words.

"After I passed I slowed up some," he says. "But when I didn't see you in the mirror I pulled off and waited a couple of minutes. When you still didn't show I thought I'd better drive back and check. Is everything all right? How come you're locked up in there?"

I shake my head.

"Come on, roll down your window. Hey, are you sure you're okay? You know it's not good for a woman to be batting around the country by herself." He shakes his head and looks at the highway, then back at me. "Now come on, roll down the window, how about it? We can't talk this way."

"Please, I have to go."

"Open the door, all right?" he says, as if he isn't listening. "At least roll the window down. You're going to smother in there." He looks at my breasts and legs. The skirt has pulled up over my knees. His eyes linger on my legs, but I sit still, afraid to move.

"I want to smother," I say. "I am smothering, can't you see?"

"What in the hell?" he says and moves back from the door. He turns and walks back to his truck. Then, in the side mirror, I watch him returning, and I close my eyes.

"You don't want me to follow you toward Summit or anything? I don't mind. I got some extra time this morning," he says.

I shake my head.

He hesitates and then shrugs. "Okay, lady, have it your way then," he says. "Okay."

I wait until he has reached the highway, and then I back out. He shifts gears and pulls away slowly, looking back at me in his rearview mirror. I stop the car on the shoulder and put my head on the wheel.

The casket is closed and covered with floral sprays. The organ begins soon after I take a seat near the back of the chapel. People begin to file in and find chairs, some middle-aged and older people, but most of them in their early twenties or even younger. They are people who look uncomfortable in their suits and ties, sport coats and slacks, their dark dresses and leather gloves. One boy in flared pants and a yellow short-sleeved shirt takes the chair next to mine and begins to bite his lips. A door opens at one side of the chapel and I look up and for a minute the parking lot reminds me of a meadow. But then the sun flashes on car windows. The family enters in a group and moves into a curtained area off to the side. Chairs creak as they settle themselves. In a few minutes a slim, blond man in a dark suit stands and asks us to bow our heads. He speaks a brief prayer for us, the living, and when he finishes he asks us to pray in silence for the soul of Susan Miller, departed. I close my eyes and remember her picture in the newspaper and on television. I see her leaving the theater and getting into the green Chevrolet. Then I imagine her journey down the river, the nude body hitting rocks, caught at by branches, the body floating and turning, her hair streaming in the water. Then the hands and hair catching in the overhanging branches, holding, until four men come along to stare at her. I can see a man who is drunk (Stuart?) take her by the wrist. Does anyone here know about that? What if these people knew that? I look around at the other faces. There is a connection to be made of these things, these events, these faces, if I can find it. My head aches with the effort to find it.

He talks about Susan Miller's gifts: cheerfulness and beauty, grace and enthusiasm. From behind the closed curtain someone clears his throat, someone else sobs. The organ music begins. The service is over.

Along with the others I file slowly past the casket. Then I move out onto the front steps and into the bright, hot afternoon light. A middle-aged woman who limps as she goes down the stairs ahead of me reaches the sidewalk and looks around, her eyes falling on me. "Well, they got him," she says. "If that's any consolation. They arrested him this morning. I heard it on the radio before I came. A guy right here in town. A longhair, you might have guessed." We move a few steps down the hot sidewalk. People are starting cars. I put out my hand and hold on to a parking meter. Sunlight glances off polished hoods and fenders. My head swims. "He's admitted having relations with her that night, but he says he didn't kill her." She snorts. "They'll put him on probation and then turn him loose."

"He might not have acted alone," I say. "They'll have to be sure. He might be covering up for someone, a brother, or some friends."

"I have known that child since she was a little girl," the woman goes on, and her lips tremble. "She used to come over and I'd bake cookies for her and let her eat them in front of the TV." She looks off and begins shaking her head as the tears roll down her cheeks.

Stuart sits at the table with a drink in front of him. His eyes are red and for a minute I think he has been crying. He looks at me and doesn't say anything. For a wild instant I feel something has happened to Dean, and my heart turns.

"Where is he?" I say. "Where is Dean?"

"Outside," he says.

"Stuart, I'm so afraid, so afraid," I say, leaning against the door.

"What are you afraid of, Claire? Tell me, honey, and maybe I can help. I'd like to help, just try me. That's what husbands are for."

"I can't explain," I say. "I'm just afraid. I feel like, I feel like, I feel like. . . ."

He drains his glass and stands up, not taking his eyes from me. "I think I know what you need, honey. Let me play doctor, okay? Just take it easy now." He reaches an arm around my waist and with his other hand begins to unbutton my jacket, then my blouse. "First things first," he says, trying to joke.

"Not now, please," I say.

"Not now, please," he says, teasing. "Please nothing." Then he steps behind me and locks an arm around my waist. One of his hands slips under my brassiere.

"Stop, stop, stop," I say. I stamp on his toes.

And then I am lifted up and then falling. I sit on the floor looking up at him and my neck hurts and my skirt is over my knees. He leans down and says, "You go to hell then, do you hear, bitch? I hope your cunt drops off before I touch it again." He sobs once and I realize he can't help it, he can't help himself either. I feel a rush of pity for him as he heads for the living room.

He didn't sleep at home last night.

This morning, flowers, red and yellow chrysanthemums. I am drinking coffee when the doorbell rings.

"Mrs. Kane?" the young man says, holding his box of flowers.

I nod and pull the robe tighter at my throat.

"The man who called, he said you'd know." The boy looks at my robe, open at the throat, and touches his cap.

He stands with his legs apart, feet firmly planted on the top step. "Have a nice day," he says.

A little later the telephone rings and Stuart says, "Honey, how are you? I'll be home early, I love you. Did you hear me? I love you, I'm sorry, I'll make it up to you. Goodbye, I have to run now."

I put the flowers into a vase in the center of the dining room table and then I move my things into the extra bedroom.

Last night, around midnight, Stuart breaks the lock on my door. He does it just to show me that he can, I suppose, for he doesn't do anything when the door springs open except stand there in his underwear looking surprised and foolish while the anger slips from his face. He shuts the door slowly, and a few minutes later I hear him in the kitchen prying open a tray of ice cubes.

I'm in bed when he calls today to tell me that he's asked his mother to come stay with us for a few days. I wait a minute, thinking about this, and then hang up while he is still talking. But in a little while I dial his number at work. When he finally comes on the line I say, "It doesn't matter, Stuart. Really, I tell you it doesn't matter one way or the other."

"I love you," he says.

He says something else and I listen and nod slowly. I feel sleepy. Then I wake up and say, "For God's sake, Stuart, she was only a child."

Angela Carter

Angela Carter was a British novelist and short story writer whose work characteristically blends fantasy, fairy tales, and sexuality. Among her novels are The Magic Toy Shop, Several Perceptions, *and* Wise Children. *Critics have sometimes described her writing as an example of "magic realism," a term which has been used to describe the work of such Latin American authors as Jorge Luis Borges and Gabriel Garcia Marquez, but which has also been adopted to characterize the work of several younger fiction writers in Britain. Magic realist fiction typically mixes the realistic or the everyday with fantastic elements normally associated with dreams, fairy-tales, or mythological narratives. In her collection of short stories,* Saints and Strangers, *for example, Carter tells her version of "Peter and the Wolf." Carter was born in 1940 in Eastborne, England. She began her writing career as a journalist for a weekly London newspaper and later went on to study English Literature at the University of Bristol. She taught creative writing at Sheffield University in England between 1976 and 78. Of her death in 1992, the novelist Salman Rushdie wrote in* The New York Times: *"With Angela Carter's death English Literature has lost its high sorceress, its benevolent witch queen, a burlesque artist of genius and antic grace."*

Angela Carter's "The Fall River Axe Murders" brings a different and fantastical perspective to thinking about spaces and what they mean. Like "The Yellow Wallpaper," "The Fall River Axe Murders" borrows elements from the Gothic romance genre to comment on and infuse spaces with a variety of meanings that are both created and historical at the same time. When reading this story, it is important to pay attention to how Carter creates a certain atmosphere and how that affects the people who occupy it. How does Carter use imagery to give a specific character to the Borden residence? How are the descriptive details of the house used to comment on the murder that Lizzie Borden commits? Does the atmosphere Carter creates work to justify or further problematize Lizzie Borden's act?

The Fall River Axe Murders

Lizzie Borden with an axe
Gave her father forty whacks
When she saw what she had done
She gave her mother forty one.
Children's rhyme

Reprinted from *Saints and Strangers*, (1985), Penguin Books.

Early in the morning of the fourth of August, 1892, in the city of Fall River, Massachusetts.

Hot, hot, hot. Even though it is early in the morning, well before the factory whistle issues its peremptory summons from the dark, satanic mills to which the city owes its present pre-eminence in the cotton trade, the white, furious sun already shimmers and quivers high in the still air.

Nobody could call the New England summer a lovable thing; the inhabitants of New England have never made friends with it. More than the heat, it is the humidity that makes it scarcely tolerable. The weather clings, like a low fever you cannot shake off. The Indians who first lived here had the sense to take off their buckskins as soon as things hotted up and sit, thereafter, up to their necks in ponds. This behaviour is no longer permissible in the "City of Spindles."

However, as in most latitudes with similar summers, everything slows down in these dog days. The blinds are drawn, the shutters closed; all indoors becomes drowsy penumbra in which to nap away the worst heat of the day, and when they venture out again in the refreshed evening, they put on thin clothes loose enough to let cool air circulate refreshingly between the muslin and the skin, so that the warm weather, as nature intended, is a sweet, sensual, horizontal thing.

But the descendants of the industrious, self-mortifying saints who imported the Protestant ethic wholesale into a land intended for the siesta are proud of flying in the face of nature. The moment the factory whistle blares—bustle! bustle! bustle! And the stern fathers of Fall River will step briskly forth into the furnace, well wrapped up in flannel underclothes, linen shirts, vests and coats and trousers of good, thick wool, and—final touch—a strangulatory neck tie, as if discomfort were next to godliness.

On this burning morning when, after breakfast and the performance of a few household duties, Lizzie Borden will murder her parents, she will, on rising, don a simple cotton frock that, if worn by itself, might be right for the weather. But, underneath, has gone a long, starched cotton petticoat; another starched cotton petticoat, a short one; long drawers; woolen stockings; a chemise; and a whalebone corset that takes her viscera in an unkind hand and squeezes them very tightly.

There is also a heavy linen napkin strapped between her legs because she is menstruating.

In all these clothes, out of sorts and nauseous as she is, in this dementing heat, her belly in a vice, she will heat up a flatiron on a stove and press handkerchiefs with the heated iron until it is time for her to go down to the cellar wood-pile to collect the hatchet with which our imagination—"Lizzie Borden with an axe"—always equips her, just as we always visualize Saint Catherine rolling along her wheel, the emblem of her passion.

Soon, in just as many clothes as Miss Lizzie wears, if less fine, Bridget, the servant girl, will slop kerosene on a sheet of last night's newspaper, rumpled around a stick or two of kindling. When the fire settles down, she will cook breakfast. The fire will keep her company as she washes up afterward, when the mercury pauses briefly at eighty-five before recommencing its giddy ascent upwards.

In a blue serge suit one look at which would be enough to bring you out in prickly heat, old Andrew Borden will perambulate the perspiring town truffling for money like a pig until he will return home mid-morning when he will find his death, unannounced, waiting for him.

In a mean house on Second Street in the smoky city of Fall River, five living creatures are sleeping in the still, warm early morning. They comprise two old men and three women. The first old man owns all the women by either marriage, birth, or contract. His house is narrow as a coffin and that was how he made his fortune—he used to be an undertaker but he has recently branched out in several directions and all his branches bear fruit of the most fiscally gratifying kind.

But you would never think, to look at his house, that he is a successful and prosperous man. His house is cramped, comfortless—"unpretentious," you might say, if you were sycophantic, while Second Street itself saw better days some time ago. The Borden house—see "Andrew J. Borden" in flowing script on the brass plate next to the door—stands by itself with a few scant feet of yard on either side. On the left is a stable, out of use since he sold the horse. In the back lot grow a few pear trees, laden at this season.

On this particular morning, as luck would have it, only one of the two Borden girls sleep in their father's house. Emma Lenora, his oldest daughter, has taken herself off to nearby New Bedford for a few days, to catch the ocean breeze.

Few of their social class stay in sweltering Fall River in the sweating months of June, July, and August. But then, few of their social class live on Second Street, in the low part of town where heat gathers like fog. Lizzie was invited away, too, to a summer house by the sea to join a merry band of girls but, as if on purpose to mortify her flesh, as if important business kept her in the exhausted town, as if a wicked fairy spelled her on Second Street, she did not go.

The other old man is some kind of kin of Borden's. He doesn't belong here; he is a chance bystander, he is irrelevant.

Write him out of the script.

Even though his presence in the doomed house is historically unimpeachable, the colouring of this domestic apocalypse must be crude and the design profoundly simplified for the maximum emblematic effect.

Write John Vinnicum Morse out of the script.

One old man and three of his women sleep in the house on Second Street. These women comprise his second wife, his youngest daughter and his servant girl.

The City Hall clock whirs and sputters the prolegomena to the first stroke of six and Bridget's alarm clock gives a sympathetic skip and click as the minute hand stutters on the hour; back the little hammer jerks, about to hit the bell on top of her clock, but Bridget's damp eyelids do not shudder with premonition as she lies in her sticking flannel nightgown under one thin sheet on an iron bedstead, lies on her back, as the good nuns taught her in her Irish girlhood, in case she dies during the night, to make less trouble for the one who lays her out.

She is a good girl, on the whole, although her temper is sometimes uncertain and then she will talk back to the missus, sometimes, and will be forced to confess the sin of impatience to the priest. Overcome by heat and nausea—everyone in the house is going to wake up sick today—she will return to this little bed later on in the morning to snatch a few moments' rest. Fateful forty winks! While she indulges in them, the massacre takes place.

A rosary of brown glass beads, a cardboard-backed colour print of the Virgin bought from a Portuguese shop, a flyblown photograph of her solemn mother in Donegal—these lie or are propped on the mantelpiece that, however sharp the Massachusetts winter, has never seen a lit stick. A banged tin trunk at the foot of the bed holds all Bridget's worldly goods.

There is a stiff chair beside the bed with, upon it, a candlestick, matches, the alarm clock that resounds the room with a dyadic, metallic clang for it is a joke between Bridget and her mistress that the girl could sleep through anything, *anything,* and so she needs the alarm clock as well as all the factory whistles that are just about to blast off, just this very second about to blast off. . . .

A splintered pine washstand holds the jug and bowl she never uses; she isn't going to lug water all the way up to the third floor just to wipe herself down, is she? Not when there's water enough in the kitchen, where, in the sink, all will clean their teeth this morning.

Old Borden sees no necessity for baths. He does not believe in total immersion. To lose his natural oils would be to rob his body. Since he does not approve of baths, it goes without saying they do not maintain a bathroom.

A frameless square of mirror reflects in corrugated waves a cracked, dusty soap dish containing a quantity of black metal hair pins.

On bright rectangles of paper blinds move the beautiful shadows of the pear trees.

Although Bridget left the door open a crack in forlorn hopes of coaxing a draught into the room, all the spent heat of the previous day has packed itself tightly into her attic. A dandruff of spent whitewash flakes from the ceiling where a fly drearily whines.

Bridget's lopsided shoes stand together on a hand-braided rug of aged rags. The dress she wears for Mass on Sundays hangs from the hook on the back of the door. The calico dress she will wear for the morning's chores is folded up on the trunk where she left it last night, along with soiled underthings that will do another day.

The house is thickly redolent of sleep, that sweetish smell. Still, all still; in all the house nothing moves except the droning fly and the stillness on the staircase crushes him, he falls still. Stillness pressing against the blinds, stillness, mortal stillness in the room below, where Master and Mistress share the matrimonial bed.

Were the drapes open or the lamp lit, one could better observe the differences between this room and the austerity of the maid's room. Here is a carpet splashed with vigorous flowers even if the carpet is of the cheap and cheerful variety; there are mauve, ochre, and cerise flowers on the wallpaper, even though the wallpaper was old when the Bordens arrived in the house. A dresser with another distorting mirror; no mirror in this house does not take your face and twist it out of shape for you. On the dresser, a runner embroidered with forget-me-nots; on the runner, a bone comb missing three teeth and lightly threaded with grey hairs, a hairbrush backed with ebonized wood, and a number of lace mats underneath small china boxes holding safety pins, hairnets, et cetera. The little hairpiece that Mrs. Borden attaches to her balding scalp for daytime wear is curled up like a dead squirrel.

But of Borden's male occupation of this room there is no trace because he has a dressing-room of his own, through *that* door, on the left. . . .

What about the other door, the one next to it?

It leads to the back stairs.

And that yet other door, partially concealed behind the head of the heavy mahogany bed?

If it were not kept securely locked, it would take you into Miss Lizzie's room.

It is a peculiarity of the house, that the rooms are full of doors and—a further peculiarity—all these doors are always kept locked. A house full of locked doors that open only into other rooms with other locked doors. Upstairs and downstairs, all the rooms lead in and out of one another like a maze in a bad dream. It is a house without passages. There is no part of the house that has not been marked out as some inmate's personal territory; it is a house with no shared, no common spaces between one room and the next. It is a house of privacies sealed as close as if they had been sealed with wax on a legal document.

The only way to Emma's room is through Lizzie's. There is no way out of Emma's room. It is a dead end.

The Bordens' custom of locking all the doors, inside and outside, dates from a time, a few years ago, shortly before Bridget came to work for them, when the house was burgled. A person unknown came in through the side door while Borden and his wife had taken one of their rare trips out together. He had loaded her into a trap and set out for a farm they owned outside town, a surprise visit to ensure his tenant, a dour Swede, was not bilking him. The girls stayed at home in their rooms, napping on their beds or repairing ripped hems, or sewing loose buttons more securely, or writing letters, or contemplating acts of charity among the deserving poor, or staring vacantly into space.

I can't imagine what else they might do.

What the girls do when they are on their own is unimaginable to me.

Emma is even more of a mystery than Lizzie because we know less about her. She is a blank space. She has no life. The door from her room leads only into the room of her younger sister.

"Girls" is, of course, a courtesy term. Emma is well into her forties, Lizzie, her thirties, but they did not marry and so live on in their father's house, where they remain in a fictive, protracted childhood, "girls" for good.

In this city of working women, the most visible sign of the status of the Borden girls is that they toil not. "Clickety clack, clickety clack, You're got to work till it breaks your back!" the looms sing to the girls they lured here, the girls fresh from Lancashire, the dark-browed Portuguese, the French Canadian farmers' daughters, the up-country girls, the song whose rhythms now govern the movements of their dexterous fingers. But the Borden girls are deaf to it.

Strange, that endless confinement of these perpetual "girls" who do not labour in the mean house of the rich man. Strange, marginal life that those who lived it believed to be the very printing on the page, to be just exactly why the book was printed in the first place, to be the way all decent folks lived.

While the master and mistress were away and the girls asleep or otherwise occupied, some person or persons unknown tiptoed up the back stairs to the matrimonial bedroom and pocketed Mrs. Borden's gold watch and chain, the collar necklace and silver bangle of her remote childhood, and a roll of dollar bills old Borden kept under his clean union suits in the third drawer of the bureau on the left. The intruder attempted to force the lock of the safe, that featureless block of black iron like a slaughtering block or an altar sitting squarely next to the bed on Old Borden's side, but it would have taken a crowbar to adequately penetrate the safe and the intruder tackled it with a pair of nail scissors that were lying handy on the dresser, so *that* didn't come off.

Then the intruder pissed and shitted on the cover of the Bordens' bed, knocked the clutter of this and that on the dresser to the floor, smashing a brace of green and violet porcelain parakeets into a thousand fragments in the process, swept into Old Borden's dressing room, there to maliciously assault his funeral coat as it hung in the moth-balled dark of his closet with the selfsame nail scissors that had been used on the safe, which now split in two and were abandoned on the closet floor, retired to the kitchen, smashed the flour crock and the treacle crock, and then scrawled an obscenity or two on the parlour window with the cake of soap that lived beside the scullery sink.

What a mess! Lizzie stared with vague surprise at the parlor window; she heard the soft bang of the open screen door, swinging idly, although there was no breeze. What was she doing, standing clad only in her corset in the middle of the sitting room? How had she got there? Had she crept down when she heard the screen door rattle? She did not know. She could not remember.

It was well known in polite circles in Fall River that Lizzie suffered from occasional "peculiar spells," as the idiom of the place and time called odd lapses of behaviour, unexpected, involuntary trances, moments of disconnection—those times when the mind misses a beat.

The Indians cursed the land with madness and death.

Even on the sunniest days, you could not say the landscape smiled; the ragged woodland, the ocean beaten out of steel. Not much, here, to cheer the heart, and all beneath the avenging light. The Indians stuck a few flints of their hard-cornered language onto the map, those names like meals of stone—Massachusetts, Pawtuxet, Woonsocket. And there are certain fruits of the region, such as the corn, especially those strange ears of crimson corn—some of the kernels are black, they dry out and rattle, you cannot eat them but people, nowadays, like to hang them on their doors for decoration in the fall—that strange, archaic-looking corn; and various squashes, the long-necked, pale yellow butternut, and the squat, whorled acorn squash, pine-green with a splatter of orange on one flank—squash and pumpkin that look and feel like votive objects carved from wood; you must boil them for hours to make them soft and then they taste flat, insipid, alien. These fruits have the ineradicable somberness of the aborigines.

From puberty, she had been troubled by these curious lapses of consciousness that often, though not always, came at the time of her menses; at these times, everyday things appeared to her with a piercing, appalling clarity that rendered them mysterious beyond words, so that the harsh, serrated leaves knocking against the window were those of a tree whose name she did not know in which sat birds whose names were not yet invented, whirring, clicking, and chucking like no birds known before, while a sputtering radiance emanated from everything. All the familiar things, at those times, seemed to her not only unknown but also unknowable, always unknowable.

So the strangers must have felt after they watched the boat that brought them slide away from them over the horizon and, abandoned, turned their faces inland towards the wilderness with the anguish of the newborn confronted with infinite space.

Time opened in two; suddenly she was not continuous any more.

Dull headaches announced the approaches of these trances, from which she returned as from an electric elsewhere. She would quiver with exhaustion; her sister would bathe her temples with a handkerchief moistened with eau de cologne, she lying on her bedroom sofa.

She had no words with which to describe the over-clarity with which she had seen the everyday things around her, even had she wished to do so, She kept the knowledge she was discontinuous to herself—or, rather, she steadfastly ignored the knowledge that she was discrete because the notion had no meaning to her, or, perhaps, too much meaning for her to assimilate since she believed that either a person was, or else was not. But don't think because she believed this that she believed it *in so many words* . . . she believed it in the same way that she believed she lived in Fall River, Massachusetts, and in the same way that she believed the second Mrs. Borden had married her father for his money. She did not believe she believed in these things; she thought she *knew* them for a fact, just as she knew the Portuguese were pigs and God was the Father Almighty.

Therefore these intermittent lapses in day-to-day consciousness, in which she was and was not at the same time, were unaccountable in every way and she did not dare to think of them once she came back to herself. So she remained a stranger to herself.

A trap rattled by in the street outside. A child burst out crying in a house across the way. Lizzie experienced the departure of vision as though it were the clearing of a haze.

"Help! We have been burgled! Help!"

I cannot tell you what effect the burglary had on Borden. It utterly disconcerted him; he was a man stunned. It violated him, even. He was a man raped. It took away his hitherto unshakeable confidence in the integrity inherent in things.

The family broke its habitual silence with one another in order to discuss the burglary, it moved them so. They blamed it on the Portuguese, mostly, but sometimes on the Canucks. If their outrage remained constant and did not diminish with time, the focus of it varied according to their moods, although they always pointed the finger of suspicion at the strangers who lived in the dark ramparts of the company housing a few stinking blocks away. They did not always suspect the dark strangers exclusively; sometimes they thought the culprit might very well have been one of the mill hands fresh from saucy Lancashire across the ocean who did the deed, for a slum landlord has few friends among the criminal classes. Sometimes Lizzie voiced the notion that the lugubrious and monosyllabic Swede out on Old Borden's bit of property at Swansea might have been harbouring a grudge against her father for some reason and, when the old man gruffly reminded her the Swede had the unshakeable alibi of Borden's own presence at the time of the offence, she would fall silent and fix upon the middle distance the large, accusing, blue stare of her pale eyes.

The possibility of a poltergeist occurred to Mrs. Borden, although she does not know the word; she knows, however, that her younger step-daughter could make the plates jump out of sheer spite, if she wanted to. But the old man adores his daughter. Perhaps it is then, after the shock of the burglary, that he decided she needed a change of scene, a dose of sea air, a long voyage.

The only defence against further depredation was to lock everything and then lock it again, to lock and relock everything and then lock it up once more for luck.

After the burglary, the front door and the side door were always locked three times if one of the inhabitants of the house left it for just so long as to go into the yard and pick up a basket of fallen pears when pears were in season, or if the maid went out to hang a bit of washing or Old Borden, after supper, took a piss under a tree.

From this time dated the custom of locking all the bedroom doors on the inside when one was on the inside oneself or on the outside when one was on the outside. Old Borden locked his bedroom door in the morning, when he left it, and put the key in sight of all on the kitchen shelf.

The burglary awakened Old Borden to the evanescent nature of private property. He thereafter undertook an orgy of investment. He would forthwith invest his surplus in good brick and mortar for who can make away with an office block?

A number of leases fell in simultaneously at just this time on a certain street in the downtown area of the city and Borden snapped them up. When he owned the block, he pulled it down. He planned the Borden building, an edifice of shops and offices, dark red brick, deep tan stone, with cast iron detail, from whence, in perpetuity, he might reap a fine harvest of unsaleable rents, and this monument, like that of Ozymandias, would long survive him—indeed, still stands, foursquare and handsome, the Andrew Borden Building on South Main Street.

Not bad for a fish peddler's son, eh? To turn yourself into a solid piece of real estate?

For, although "Borden" is an ancient name in New England and the Borden clan between them owned the better part of Fall River, our Borden, Old Borden, these Bordens, did not spring from a wealthy branch of the family. There were Bordens and Bordens and he was the son of a man who sold fresh fish in a wicker basket from house to house. Old Borden's parsimony was bred of poverty but learned to thrive best on prosperity for thrift has a different meaning for the poor; they get no joy of it, it is stark necessity to them. But a penniless miser is a contradiction in terms.

Morose and gaunt, this self-made man is one of few pleasures. His vocation is capital accumulation.

What is his hobby?

Why, grinding the faces of the poor.

First, Andrew Borden was an undertaker and death, recognizing an accomplice, did well by him. In the city of spindles, few made old bones; the little children who laboured in the mills died with especial frequency. When he was an undertaker, no!—it was not true he cut the feet of corpses to fit into a job lot of coffins bought cheap as Civil War surplus! That was a rumour put about by his enemies!

With the profits from his coffins, he bought up a tenement or two and made fresh profit from the living. He bought shares in the mills. Then he invested in a brace of banks, so that now he makes a profit on money itself, which is the purest form of profit of all.

Foreclosures and evictions are meat and drink to him. He loves nothing better than a little usury. He is halfway on the road to his first million.

At night, to save the kerosene, he sits in lampless dark. He waters the pear trees with his own urine; waste not, want not. As soon as the daily newspapers are done with, he rips them into squares and stores them in the cellar privy so that they can wipe their arses with them. He mourns the loss of the good organic waste that goes down the privy. He would like to charge the very cockroaches in the kitchen rent. And yet he has not grown fat on all this; the pure flame of his passion has melted off his flesh, his skin sticks to his bones out of sheer parsimony. Perhaps it is from his first profession that he has acquired his bearing, for he walks with the stately dignity of a hearse.

To watch Old Borden bearing down the street toward you was to be filled with an instinctual respect for mortality, whose gaunt ambassador he seemed to be. And it made you think, too, what a triumph over nature it was when we rose up to walk on two legs instead of four, in the first place! For he held himself upright with such ponderous assertion it was a perpetual reminder to all who witnessed his progress how it is not *natural* to be upright, it is a triumph of the will over gravity, in itself a transcendence of the spirit over matter.

His spine is like an iron rod, forged, not born, impossible to imagine that spine of Old Borden's curled up in the womb in the big C-shape of the fetus; he walks as if his legs had joints at neither knee or ankle so that his feet strike at the trembling earth like a bailiff pounding a door with an iron bar.

He has a white, chin-strap beard, old-fashioned already in those days. His lips are so thin it looks as if he'd gnawed them off. He is at peace with his god for he has used his talents as the Good Book says he should.

Yet do not think he has no soft spot. Like Old Lear, like Old Goriot, his heart—and, more than that, his cheque-book—is putty in his youngest daughter's hands. On his pinky—you, cannot see it, it lies under the covers—he wears a gold ring, not a wedding ring but a high school ring, a singular trinket for a fabulously misanthropic miser. His youngest daughter gave it to him when she left school and asked him to wear it, always, and so he always does, and will wear it to the grave.

He sleeps fully dressed in a flannel nightshirt over his long-sleeved underwear, and a flannel nightcap, and his back is turned toward his wife of thirty years, as is hers to his.

They are Mr. and Mrs. Jack Spratt in person, he, tall and gaunt as a hanging judge and she, such a spreading, round little doughball. He is a miser, while she—

she is a glutton, a solitary eater, most innocent of vices and yet the shadow or parodic vice of his, for he would like to eat up all the world, or, failing that, since fate has not spread him a sufficiently large table for his ambitions—he is a mute, inglorious Napoleon, he does not know what he might have done because he never had the opportunity—since he has not access to the entire world, he would like to gobble up the city of Fall River. But she, well, she just gently, continuously stuffs herself, doesn't she, she's always nibbling away at something, at the cud, perhaps.

Not that she gets much pleasure from it, either; no gourmet, she, forever meditating the exquisite difference between a mayonnaise sharpened with a few drops of Orleans vinegar or one pointed up with a squeeze of fresh lemon juice. No. Abby never aspired so high, nor would she ever think to do so even if she had the option; she is satisfied to stick to simple gluttony and she eschews all overtones of the sensuality of consumption. Since she relishes not one single mouthful of the food she eats, she knows her ceaseless gluttony is no transgression.

Here they lie in bed together, living embodiments of two of the Seven Deadly Sins, but he knows his avarice is no offence because he never spends any money and she knows she is not greedy because the grub she shovels down gives her dyspepsia. Gives her dyspepsia and worse; in those days, great-grandmother's days, summer and salmonella came in together.

Refrigeration is, perhaps, the only unmitigated blessing that the Age of Technology has brought us, a blessing that has brought no bane in tow, a wholly positive good that can be welcomed without reluctance or qualification. The white-enamelled refrigerator is the genius of every home, the friendly chill of whose breath has banished summer sickness and the runs for good! How often, nowadays, in summer does your milk turn into a sour jelly, or your butter separate itself out into the liquid fat and the corrupt-smelling whey? When did you last see the waxy clusters of the seed-pearl eggs of the blowfly materialise disgustingly on the left-over joint? Perhaps, perfect child of the Frigidaire, you've known none of all this! In those days, however, you took your life in your hands each time you picked up your knife and fork.

On the Saturday preceding the murders, for dinner, at twelve, the Bordens had a big joint of roast mutton, hot. Bridget cooked it. They must have had potatoes with it. Mashed, probably. With flour gravy. I don't know if they had greens or not. The documents don't say. But we know the main items of the Bordens' diet during their last week living because the police thoroughly investigated the rumour that the parents had been poisoned before they had been butchered and so the week's dolorous bill of fair was recorded in full.

On Saturday, they had more mutton, cold, for supper. They ate their roast on Saturdays because they were Sabbatarians and did not believe work should be done on Sundays, so Bridget had Sunday off, to go to church.

Because Bridget had Sundays off, they ate more cold mutton for Sunday dinner, with bread and butter, I dare say, and pickles, perhaps.

On Monday, they had mutton for midday dinner. I don't know how Bridget fixed the mutton; perhaps she warmed it up in left-over gravy, to make a change from having it cold. They had mutton for breakfast on Tuesday, too. It must have been a veritably gargantuan joint of mutton—or did the fault lie with Old Borden; did he carve thin as paper money and lay the slice on the plate with as much disinclination as if he'd been paying back a loan, so the eaters felt he grudged each bite?

There was an ice-box of the old-fashioned, wooden kind, the doors of which must be kept tightly shut at all times or else the ice melts and everything inside goes rotten. Every morning, Bridget put out the pan for the ice-man and filled up the dripping ice-compartment.

In this ice-box, she lodged the remains of the mutton.

In and out of the ice-box went the joint of mutton.

On Tuesday, it was time for a change. They had sword-fish for midday dinner. Bridget bought the thick steaks of sword-fish in a fish-market that smelled like a brothel after a busy night. She put the sword-fish in the ice-box until it was time to grill it. Then the left-over sword-fish went back into the ice-box until supper time, when she warmed it up again. That was the night they vomited again and again.

Bridget kept back the knuckle from the leg of mutton in order to make broth; perhaps the broth was comforting to an upset stomach and perhaps not. They had the broth for Wednesday dinner, followed by mutton, again. Was that warmed over, too? On Wednesday, they had cold mutton for supper, again.

There is nothing quite like cold mutton. The sinewy, grey, lean meat amidst the veined lumps of congealed fat, varicosed with clotted blood; it must be the sheep's Pyrrhic vengeance on the carnivore! Considering that which lay upon her plate, Mrs. Borden's habitual gluttony takes on almost an heroic quality. Undeterred by the vileness of the table, still she pigs valiantly away while the girls look on, push their own plates away, wince to see the grease on her chin.

Oh, how she loves to eat! She is Mrs. Jack Spratt in person, round as a ball, fat as butter . . . the heavy fare of New England, the chowders, the cornmeal puddings, the boiled dinners, have shaped her, and continue to shape her.

See her rub her bread round her plate. "Is there a little more gravy, Bridget, just to finish up my bread?" She pours cold gravy, lumpy with flour, onto her plate, so much gravy she's forced, in the end, to cut herself just another little corner of bread with which to finish up the gravy.

The sisters think, she eats and eats and eats; she eats everything, she will eat up every single thing, crunch up the plate from which she eats when no more gravy is forthcoming, munch through the greenbacks in father's safe for a salad, for dessert she will polish off the gingerbread house in which they live.

If the old woman thought to deceive them as to her true nature by affecting to confine her voracity only to comestibles, Lizzie knew better; her guzzling stepmother's appetite terrified and appalled her, for it was the only thing within the straight and narrow Borden home that was not kept within confinement.

There had never been any conversation at table; that was not their style. Their stiff lips would part to request the salt, the bread, the butter, yes; but, apart from that, only the raucous squawk of knife on plate and private sounds of chewing and swallowing amplified and publicised and rendered over-intimate, obscene, by the unutterable silence of the narrow dining room. A strip of flypaper hung from a nail over the table, bearing upon it a mourning band of dead flies. A stopped clock of black marble, shaped like a Greek mausoleum, stood on the sideboard, becalmed. Father sat at the head of the table and shaved the meat. Mrs. Borden sat at the foot and ate it.

"I won't eat with her; I won't," said Lizzie. "I refuse to sit at the trough with that sow."

After this little explosion of ill temper, Bridget served the meal twice, once for Mr. and Mrs. Borden, then kept all warm and brought it out again for Lizzie and Emma, since Emma knew it was her duty to take the part of her little sister, her little dearest, the tender and difficult one. After this interruption, calm returned to the household; calm continued to dominate the household.

Saturday, Sunday, Monday, Tuesday, Wednesday. In and out of the ice-box went the slowly dwindling leg of mutton until Thursday dinner was cancelled because corpses and not places were laid out on the table as if the eaters had become the meal.

Back to back they lie. You could rest a sword in the space between the old man and his wife, between the old man's backbone, the old rigid thing he ever offered her, and her soft, warm, enormous bum. Her flannel nightdress is cut on the same lines as his nightshirt except for the limp flannel frill around the neck. She weighs two hundred pounds. She is five feet nothing tall. The bed sags on her side. It is the bed in which his first wife died.

Last night, they dosed themselves with castor oil, due to the indisposition that kept them both awake and vomiting the whole night before that; the copious results of their purges brim the chamberpots beneath the bed.

Their purges flailed them. Their faces show up decomposing green in the dim, curtained room, in which the air is too thick for flies to move.

The youngest daughter dreams behind the locked door.

She threw back the top sheet and her window is wide open but there is no breeze outside this morning to deliciously shiver the screen. Bright sun floods the blinds so that the linen-coloured light shows us how Lizzie has gone to bed as for a levée in a pretty, ruffled nightdress of starched white muslin with ribbons of pastel pink satin threaded through the eyelets of the lace, for is it not the "naughty nineties" everywhere but dour Fall River? Don't the gilded steamships of the Fall River Line signify all the squandered luxury of the Gilded Age within their mahogany and chandeliered interiors? Elsewhere, it is the Belle Epoque. In New York, Paris, London, champagne corks pop and women fall backwards in a crisp meringue of petticoats for fun and profit but not in Fall River. Oh, no. So, in the immutable privacy of her bedroom, for her own delight, Lizzie puts on a rich girl's pretty nightdress, although she lives in a mean house, because she is a rich girl, too.

But she is plain.

The hem of her nightdress is rucked up above her knees because she is a restless sleeper. Her light, dry, reddish hair, crackling with static, slipping loose from the nighttime plait, crisps and stutters over the square pillow at which she clutches as she sprawls on her stomach, having rested her cheek on the starched pillowcase for coolness's sake at some earlier hour.

Lizzie was not an affectionate diminutive but the name with which she had been christened. Since she would always be known as "Lizzie," so her father reasoned, why burden her with the effete and fancy prolongation of "Elizabeth"? A miser in everything, he even cropped off half her name before he gave it to her. So "Lizzie" it was, stark and unadorned, and she is a motherless child, orphaned at two years old, poor thing.

Now she is two-and-thirty and yet the memory of that mother whom she cannot remember remains an abiding source of grief: "If mother had lived, everything would have been different."

How? Why? Different in what way? She wouldn't have been able to answer that, lost in a nostalgia for lost affection. Yet how could she have been loved better than by her sister, Emma, who lavished the pent-up treasures of a New England spinster's heart upon the little thing? Different, perhaps, because her natural mother, the first Mrs. Borden, subject as she was to fits of sudden, wild, inexplicable rage, might have taken the hatchet to Old Borden on her own account? But Lizzie *loves* her father. All are agreed on that. Lizzie adores the adoring father who, after her mother died, took to himself another wife.

Her bare feet twitch a little, like those of a dog dreaming of rabbits. Her sleep is thin and unsatisfying, full of vague terrors and indeterminate menaces to which she cannot put a name or form once she is awake. Sleep opens within her a disorderly house. But all she knows is, she sleeps badly, and this last, stifling night has been troubled, too, by vague nausea and the gripes of her female pain; her room is harsh with the metallic smell of menstrual blood.

Yesterday evening she slipped out of the house to visit a woman friend. Lizzie was agitated; she kept picking nervously at the shirring on the front of her dress.

"I am afraid . . . that somebody . . . will *do* something," said Lizzie.

"Mrs. Borden . . ." and here Lizzie lowered her voice and her eyes looked everywhere in the room except at Miss Russell . . . "Mrs. Borden—oh! will you ever believe? Mrs. Borden thinks somebody is trying to *poison* us!"

She used to call her stepmother "mother," as duty bade, but after a quarrel about money after her father deeded half a slum property to her stepmother five years before, Lizzie always, with cool scrupulosity, spoke of "Mrs. Borden" when she was forced to speak of her and called her "Mrs. Borden" to her face, too.

"Last night, Mrs. Borden and poor father were so sick! I hear them, through the wall. And, as for me, I haven't felt myself all day, I have felt so strange. So very . . . strange."

Miss Russell hastened to discover an explanation within reason; she was embarrassed to mention the "peculiar spells." Everyone knew there was nothing odd about the Borden girls. It was Lizzie's difficult time of the month, too; her friend could tell by a certain haggard, glazed look on Lizzie's face when it was happening. Yet her gentility forbade her to mention that.

"Something you ate? It must have been something you have eaten. What was yesterday's supper?" solicitously enquired Miss Russell.

"Warmed-over swordfish. We had it hot for dinner though I could not take much. Then Bridget heated up the left-overs for supper but, again, for myself, I could only get down a forkful. Mrs. Borden ate up the remains and scoured her plate with her bread. She smacked her lips but then was sick all night." (Note of smugness, here.)

"Oh, Lizzie! In all this heat, this dreadful heat! Twice-cooked fish! You know how quickly fish goes off in this heat! Bridget should have known better than to give you twice-cooked fish!"

"There have been threats," Lizzie pursued remorselessly, keeping her eyes on her nervous fingertips. "So many people, you understand, dislike father."

This cannot be denied. Miss Russell politely remained mute.

"Mrs. Borden was so very sick she called the doctor in and Father was abusive toward the doctor and shouted at him and told him he would not pay a doctor's bills whilst we had our own good castor oil in the house. He shouted at the doctor and all the neighbours heard and I was so ashamed. There is a man, you see . . ." and here she ducked her head, while her short, pale eyelashes beat on her cheekbones . . . "such a man, a *dark* man, Portuguese, Italian, I've seen him outside the house at odd, at unexpected hours, early in the morning, late at night, whenever I cannot sleep in this dreadful heat if I raise the blind and peep out, there I see him in the shadows of the pear trees, in the yard . . . perhaps he puts poison in the milk, in the mornings, after the milk-man fills his can.

"Perhaps he poisons the ice, when the ice-man comes."

"How long has he been haunting you?" asked Miss Russell, properly dismayed.

"Since . . . the burglary," said Lizzie and suddenly looked Miss Russell full in the face with a kind of triumph. How large her eyes were, prominent, yet veiled. And her well-manicured fingers went on pecking away at the front of her dress as if she were trying to unpick the shirring.

Miss Russell knew, she just *knew,* this dark man was a figment of Lizzie's imagination. All in a rush, she lost patience with the girl; dark men standing outside her bedroom window, indeed! Yet she was kind and cast about for ways to reassure her.

"But Bridget is up and about when the milk-man and the ice-man call and the whole street is busy and bustling, too; who would dare to put poison in either milk or ice-bucket while half of Second Street looks on? Oh, Lizzie, it is the dreadful summer, the heat, the intolerable heat that's put us all out of sorts, makes us fractious and nervous, makes us sick. So easy to imagine things in this terrible weather, that taints the food and sows worms in the mind. . . . I thought you'd planned to go away, Lizzie, to the ocean. Didn't you plan to take a little holiday, by the sea? Oh, do go! Sea air would blow away all these silly fancies!"

Lizzie neither nods nor shakes her head but continues to worry at her shirring. For does she not have important business in Fall River? Only that morning, had she not been down to the drug-store to try to buy some prussic acid? But how can she tell kind Miss Russell she is gripped by an imperious need to stay in Fall River and murder her parents?

Had all that talk of poison in the vomiting house put her in mind of poison? She went to the drug-store on the corner of Main Street in order to buy prussic acid but nobody would sell it to her so she came home empty-handed. When she asked the corner pharmacist only that morning for a little prussic acid to kill the moth in her seal-skin cape, the man looked at her oddly. "Moths don't breed in seal-skin," he opined. The autopsy will reveal no trace of poison in the stomachs of either parent. She did not try to poison them; she only had it in mind to poison them.

"And this dark man," she pursued to the unwilling Miss Russell, "oh! I have seen the moon glint upon his knife!"

When she wakes up, she can never remember her dreams; she only remembers she slept badly.

Hers is a pleasant room of not ungenerous dimensions, seeing the house is so very small. Besides the bed and the dresser, there is a sofa and a desk; it is her bedroom and also her sitting room and her office, too, for the desk is stacked with account books of various charitable organizations with which she occupies her ample spare time. The Fruit and Flower Mission, under whose auspices she visits the indigent old in the hospital with gifts; the Women's Christian Temperance Union, for whom she extracts signatures for petitions against the Demon Drink; Christian Endeavour, whatever that is—this is the golden age of good works and she flings herself into committees with a vengeance. What would the daughters of the rich do with themselves if the poor ceased to exist?

Then there is the Newsboys Thanksgiving Dinner Fund; and the Horsetrough Association; and the Chinese Conversion Association—no class nor kind is safe from her merciless charity.

She used to teach a Sunday school class of little Chinese children but they did not like her; they teased her, they played an unpleasant trick on her, one Sunday afternoon they put a dead dog inside her desk, a trick of which one would have thought the Chinese were incapable because they are so impassive and did not even giggle when she shrieked.

First, she shrieked, then she caught hold of the shoulder of the little Chinese boy sitting at the end of the front row—the nearest child she could get at—and started in on hitting him but then the class instantly abandoned its impassivity and let out such a racket the superintendent came before much damage was done. The children were severely punished. They were forbidden to come to Sunday school again.

Bureau; dressing-table; closet; bed; sofa. She spends her days in this room, moving between each of these dull items of furniture in a circumscribed, undeviating, planetary round. She loves her privacy, she loves her room, she locks herself up in it all day. A shelf contains a book or two: *Heros of the Mission Field, The Romance of Trade*. On the walls, framed photographs of high school friends, sentimentally inscribed, with, tucked inside one frame, a picture postcard showing a black kitten peeking through a horseshoe. A watercolour of a Cape Cod seascape executed with poignant amateur incompetence. A monochrome photograph of two works of art, a Delia Robbia madonna and the Mona Lisa; these she bought in the Uffizi and the Louvre, respectively, when she went to Europe.

Europe!

For don't you remember What Katy Did Next? The storybook heroine took the steamship to smoky old London, to elegant, fascinating Paris, to sunny, antique Rome and Florence; the storybook heroine sees Europe reveal itself before her like an interesting series of magic lantern slides on a gigantic screen. All is present and all unreal. The Tower of London; click. Notre Dame; click. The Sistine Chapel; click. Then the lights go out and she is in the dark again.

Of this journey she retained only the most circumspect of souvenirs, that madonna, that Mona Lisa, reproductions of objects of art consecrated by a universal approval of taste. If she came back with a bag full of memories stamped "Never to be Forgotten," she put the bag away under the bed on which she had dreamed of the world before she set out to see it and on which, at home again, she continued to dream, the dream having been transformed not into lived experience but into memory, which is only another kind of dreaming.

Wistfully: "When I was in Florence . . ."

But then, with pleasure, she corrects herself. "When *we* were in Florence . . ."

Because a good deal, in fact, most of the gratification the trip gave her came from having set out from Fall River with a select group of the daughters of respectable and affluent mill owners. Once away from Second Street, she was able to move comfortably in the segment of Fall River society to which she belonged by right of old name and new money but from which, when she was at home, her father's plentiful personal eccentricities excluded her. Sharing bedrooms, sharing staterooms, sharing berths, the girls travelled together in a genteel gaggle that bore its doom already upon it for they were girls who would not marry, now, and any pleasure they might have obtained from the variety and excitement of the trip was spoiled in advance by the knowledge they were eating up what might have been their own wedding-cake, using up what should have been, if they'd had any luck, their marriage settlements.

All girls pushing thirty, privileged to go out and look at the world before they resigned themselves to the thin condition of New England spinsterhood; but it was a case of look, don't touch. They knew they must not get their hands dirtied or their dresses crushed by the world, while their affectionate companionship en route had a certain steadfast, determined quality about it as they bravely made the best of the second-best.

It was a sour tour, in some ways, and it was a round trip; it ended at the sour place from which it had set out. Home, again, the narrow house, the rooms all locked like those in Bluebeard's Castle, and the fat, white stepmother whom nobody loves sitting in the middle of the spider web; she has not budged a single inch while Lizzie was away but she has grown fatter.

This stepmother oppressed her like a spell. Lizzie will immediately correct the judge at her trial: "She is not my mother, sir; she is my stepmother: my mother died when I was a child." But Old Borden brought his new bride home when his younger girl was five!

Another mystery—how the Bordens contrived to live together for twenty, nearly thirty years without generating amongst themselves a single scrap of the grumbling, irritable, everyday affection without which proximity becomes intolerable; yet their life cannot have been truly intolerable, because they lived it for so long. They bore it. They did not rub along together, somehow; they rubbed each other up the wrong way all the time, and yet they lived in each others' pockets.

Correction: they lived in Old Borden's pocket and all they had in common was the contents of that pocket.

The days open their cramped spaces into other cramped spaces and old furniture and never anything to look forward to, nothing. Empty days. Oppressive afternoons. Nights stalled in calm. Empty days.

When Old Borden dug in his pocket to shell out for Lizzie's trip to Europe, the eye of God on the pyramid blinked to see daylight but no extravagance is too excessive for the miser's younger daughter who is the wild card in this house and, it seems, can have anything she wants, play ducks and drakes with her father's silver dollars if it so pleases her. He pays all her dressmakers' bills on the dot and how she loves to dress up fine! In her unacknowledged, atrocious solitude, she has become addicted to dandyism. He gives her each week in pin money the same as the cook gets for wages and Lizzie gives that which she does not spend on personal adornment to the deserving poor.

He would give his Lizzie anything, anything in the world that lives under the green sign of the dollar.

She would like a pet, a kitten or a puppy; she loves small animals and birds, too, poor, helpless things. She piles high the bird-table all winter. She used to keep some white pouter pigeons in the disused stable, the kind that look like shuttlecocks and go "vroo croo" soft as a cloud.

Surviving photographs of Lizzie Borden show a face it is difficult to look at as if you knew nothing about her; coming events cast their shadow across her face, or else you see the shadows these events have cast—something terrible, something ominous in this face with its jutting, rectangular jaw and those mad eyes of the New England saints, eyes that belong to a person who does not listen . . . fanatic's eyes, you might say, if you knew nothing about her. If you were sorting through a box of old photographs in a junk shop and came across this particular sepia, faded face above the choker collars of the eighteen-nineties, you might murmur when you saw her: "Oh, what big eyes you have!" as Red Riding Hood said to the wolf, but then you might not even pause to pick her out and look at her more closely, for hers is not, in itself, a striking face.

But as soon as the face has a name, once you recognise her, when you know who she is and what it was she did, the face becomes as if of one possessed, and now it haunts you, you look at it again and again, it secretes mystery.

This woman, with her jaw of a concentration camp attendant; and such eyes . . .

In her old age, she wore pince-nez and truly with the years the mad light has departed from those eyes or else is deflected by her glasses—if, indeed, it *was* a mad light, in the first place, for don't we all conceal somewhere photographs of ourselves that make us look like crazed assassins? And, in those early photographs of her young womanhood, she herself does not look so much like a crazed assassin as somebody in extreme solitude, oblivious of that camera in whose direction she obscurely smiles, so that it would not surprise you to learn that she is blind.

There is a mirror on the dresser in which she sometimes looks at those times when time snaps in two and then she sees herself with clairvoyant eyes, as though she were another person.

"Lizzie is not herself, today."

At those times, those irremediable times, she could have raised her muzzle to an aching moon, and howled.

At other times, she watches herself doing her hair and trying her clothes on. The distorting mirror reflects her with the queasy fidelity of water. She puts on dresses and then she takes them off. She looks at herself in her corset. She measures herself with the tape measure. She pulls the measure tight. She pats her hair. She tries on a hat, a little hat, a chic little straw toque. She punctures it with a hatpin. She pulls the veil down. She pulls it up. She takes the hat off. She drives the hatpin into it with a vivacious strength she did not know she possessed.

Time goes by and nothing happens.

She traces the outlines of her face with an uncertain hand as if she were thinking of unfastening the bandages on her soul but it isn't time to do that, yet; her new face isn't ready to be seen, yet.

She is a girl of Sargasso calm.

She used to keep her pigeons in the loft above the disused stable and feed them grain out of the palms of her cupped hands. She liked to feel the soft scratch of their little beaks. They murmured "vroo croo" with infinite tenderness. She changed their water every day and cleaned up their leprous messes but Old Borden took a dislike to their cooing, it got on his nerves—who'd have thought he *had* any nerves? But he invented some, they got on them, and one afternoon he took out the hatchet from the wood-pile in the cellar and chopped the pigeons' heads off.

Abby fancied the slaughtered pigeons for a pie but Bridget the servant girl put her foot down, at that; What?!? Make a pie out of Miss Lizzie's beloved turtle-doves? JesusMaryandJoseph!!! she exclaimed with characteristic impetuousness; what can they be thinking of! Miss Lizzie so nervy with her funny turns and all! (The maid is the only one in the house with any sense and that's the truth of it.) Lizzie came home from the Fruit and Flowers Mission where she had been reading a tract to an old woman in a poorhouse: "God bless you, Miss Lizzie." At home all was blood and feathers.

She doesn't weep, this one, it isn't her nature, she is still waters, but, when moved, she changes colour, her face flushes, it goes dark, angry, mottled red, marbling up like the marbling on the inner covers of the family Bible. The old man loves his daughter this side of idolatry and pays for everything she wants but all the same he killed her pigeons when his wife wanted to gobble them up.

That is how she sees it. That is how she understands it. Now she cannot bear to watch her stepmother eat. Each bite the woman takes seems to go "vroo croo."

Old Borden cleaned off the hatchet and put it back in the cellar, next to the wood-pile. The red receding from her face, Lizzie went down to inspect the instrument of destruction. She picked it up and weighed it in her hand.

That was a few weeks before, at the beginning of the spring.

Her hands and feet twitch in her sleep; the nerves and muscles of this complicated mechanism won't relax, just won't relax; she is all twang, all tension; she is as taut as the strings of a wind-harp from which random currents of air pluck out tunes that are not our tunes.

At the first stroke of the City Hall clock, the first factory hooter blares, and then, on another note, another, and another, the Metacomet Mill, the American

Mill, the Mechanics Mill . . . until every mill in the entire town sings out aloud in a common anthem of summoning and the hot alleys where the factory folk live blacken with the hurrying throng, hurry! scurry! to loom, to bobbin, to spindle, to dye-shop as to places of worship, men, and women, too, and children, the street blackens, the sky darkens as the chimneys now belch forth, the clang, bang, and clatter of the mills commences.

Bridget's clock leaps and shudders on its chair, about to sound its own alarm. Their day, the Bordens' fatal day, trembles on the brink of beginning.

Outside, above, in the already burning air, see! the angel of death roosts on the roof-tree.

Joy Harjo

Poet and saxophonist, Joy Harjo, the daughter of a Cherokee-French mother and a Creek father, was born in 1951 in Tulsa, Oklahoma. She was educated at University of New Mexico (B.A. 1976) and University of Iowa (MFA 1978). She has published three books of poetry: What Moon Drove Me to This? *(1980),* She Had Some Horses *(1983), and* In Mad Love and War *(1990). She also published, with photographer Steven Strom, a prose piece entitled* Secrets from the Center of the World *(1989). She is currently a professor at the University of New Mexico in Albuquerque. Harjo uses Native American symbolism, imagery, and history in her poetry. Her poetry also deals with social and personal issues, especially feminism. She also performs her poetry and plays saxophone with her band called "Poetic Justice." Harjo has written, "Each time I write I am in a different and wild place, and travel toward something I do not know the name of. Each poem is a jumping-off edge and I am not safe, but I take more risks and understand better now how to take them." In her poem, "The Woman Hanging from the Thirteenth Floor Window," the nature imagery, the city-scape, the building the speaker lives in, the thirteenth floor, and the window ledge may all symbolize different aspects of the woman's life. It might be interesting to consider how these spaces are related to her roles, her identity, and the conflicts that have driven her to the edge.*

The Woman Hanging from the Thirteenth Floor Window

She is the woman hanging from the 13th floor
window. Her hands are pressed white against the
concrete moulding of the tenement building. She
hangs from the 13th floor window in east Chicago,
with a swirl of birds over her head. They could
be a halo, or a storm of glass waiting to crush her.

She thinks she will be set free.

The woman hanging from the 13th floor window
on the east side of Chicago is not alone.

She is a woman of children, of the baby, Carlos,
and of Margaret, and of Jimmy who is the oldest.
She is her mother's daughter and her father's son.
She is several pieces between the two husbands
she has had. She is all the women of the apartment
building who stand watching her, watching themselves.

When she was young she ate wild rice on scraped down
plates in warm wood rooms. It was in the farther
north and she was the baby then. They rocked her.

She sees Lake Michigan lapping at the shores of
herself. It is a dizzy hole of water and the rich
live in tall glass houses at the edge of it. In some
places Lake Michigan speaks softly, here, it just sputters
and butts itself against the asphalt. She sees
other buildings just like hers. She sees other
women hanging from many-floored windows
counting their lives in the palms of their hands
and in the palms of their children's hands.

She is the woman hanging from the 13th floor window
on the Indian side of town. Her belly is soft from
her children's births, her worn levis swing down below
her waist, and then her feet, and then her heart.
She is dangling.

The woman hanging from the 13th floor hears voices.
They come to her in the night when the lights have gone
dim. Sometimes they are little cats mewing and scratching
at the door, sometimes they are her grandmother's voice,
and sometimes they are gigantic men of light whispering
to her to get up, to get up, to get up. That's when she wants
to have another child to hold onto in the night, to be able
to fall back into dreams.

And the woman hanging from the 13th floor window
hears other voices. Some of them scream out from below
for her to jump, they would push her over. Others cry softly
from the sidewalks, pull their children up like flowers and gather
them into their arms. They would help her, like themselves.

But she is the woman hanging from the 13th floor window,
and she knows she is hanging by her own fingers, her
own skin, her own thread of indecision.

She thinks of Carlos, of Margaret, of Jimmy.
She thinks of her father, and of her mother.
She thinks of all the women she has been, of all
the men. She thinks of the color of her skin, and

of Chicago streets, and of waterfalls and pines.
She thinks of moonlight nights, and of cool spring storms.
Her mind chatters like neon and northside bars.
She thinks of the 4 a.m. lonelinesses that have folded
her up like death, discordant, without logical and
beautiful conclusion. Her teeth break off at the edges.
She would speak.

The woman hangs from the 13th floor window crying for
the lost beauty of her own life. She sees the
sun falling west over the grey plane of Chicago.
She thinks she remembers listening to her own life
break loose, as she falls from the 13th floor
window on the east side of Chicago, or as she
climbs back up to claim herself again.

Jamaica Kincaid

Jamaica Kincaid, whose original name was Elaine Potter Richardson, (b. 1949) was born in St. John's, Antigua, in the West Indies, and educated there in government schools. She left Antigua at the age of 16 and worked as an au pair in Manhattan. In 1973, she took the name Jamaica Kincaid, and began submitting articles to The New Yorker *magazine, where she became a staff member in 1976. Her essays and stories were published in other magazines as well. In 1983, Kincaid published her first book,* At the Bottom of the River, *which was a collection of short stories and reflections. Her work was often concerned with Caribbean culture and emphasized mother-daughter relationships in an effort to criticize the consequences of colonialism. "Girl" (1978) is a good example of the mother-daughter theme and her rhythmic style of writing about intense emotional experiences. As the critic Susan Freeman states, "What Kincaid has to tell me, she tells, with her singsong style, in a series of images that are as sweet and mysterious as the secrets that children whisper in your ear." In "Girl" Jamaica Kincaid relies on the mother-daughter "dialog" to comment on women's roles and how those specific roles inevitably cause women to be located in specific places.*

Girl

Wash the white clothes on Monday and put them on the stone heap; wash the color clothes on Tuesday and put them on the clothesline to dry; don't walk barehead in the hot sun; cook pumpkin fritters in very hot sweet oil; soak your little cloths right after you take them off; when buying cotton to make yourself a nice blouse, be sure that it doesn't have gum on it, because that way it won't hold up well after a wash; soak salt fish overnight before you cook it; is it true that you sing benna in Sunday school?; always eat your food in such a way that it won't turn someone else's stomach; on Sundays try to walk like a lady and not like the slut you are so bent on becoming; don't sing benna in Sunday school; you mustn't speak to wharf-rat boys, not even to give directions; don't eat fruits on the street—flies will follow you; *but I don't sing benna on Sundays at all and never in Sunday school;* this is how to sew on a button; this is how to make a buttonhole for the button you have just sewed on; this is how to hem a dress when you see the hem coming down and so to prevent yourself from looking like the slut I know

---

Reprinted from *At the Bottom of the River*, (1983), by permission of Farrar, Straus & Giroux.

you are so bent on becoming; this is how you iron your father's khaki shirt so that it doesn't have a crease; this is how you iron your father's khaki pants so that they don't have a crease; this is how you grow okra—far from the house, because okra tree harbors red ants; when you are growing dasheen, make sure it gets plenty of water or else it makes your throat itch when you are eating it; this is how you sweep a corner; this is how you sweep a whole house; this is how you sweep a yard; this is how you smile to someone you don't like too much; this is how you smile to someone you don't like at all; this is how you smile to someone you like completely; this is how you set a table for tea; this is how you set a table for dinner; this is how you set a table for dinner with an important guest; this is how you set a table for lunch; this is how you set a table for breakfast; this is how to behave in the presence of men who don't know you very well, and this way they won't recognize immediately the slut I have warned you against becoming; be sure to wash every day, even if it is with your own spit; don't squat down to play marbles—you are not a boy, you know; don't pick people's flowers—you might catch something; don't throw stones at blackbirds, because it might not be a blackbird at all; this is how to make a bread pudding; this is how to make doukona; this is how to make pepper pot; this is how to make a good medicine for a cold; this is how to make a good medicine to throw away a child before it even becomes a child; this is how to catch a fish; this is how to throw back a fish you don't like, and that way something bad won't fall on you; this is how to bully a man; this is how a man bullies you; this is how to love a man, and if this doesn't work there are other ways, and if they don't work don't feel too bad about giving up; this is how to spit up in the air if you feel like it and this is how to move quick so that it doesn't fall on you; this is how to make ends meet; always squeeze bread to make sure it's fresh; *but what if the baker won't let me feel the bread?;* you mean to say that after all you are really going to be the kind of woman who the baker won't let near the bread?

Boyer Rickel

Boyer Rickel, a recent National Endowment for the Arts fellow, is the author of a collection of poetry, arreboles *(Wesleyan University Press, 1991) and a collection of autobiographical essays,* Taboo *(The University of Wisconsin Press, 1999). His work has appeared in* Poetry, Ploughshares, Iowa Review, Puerto del Sol, *and many other literary magazines. He is Assistant Director of the Creative Writing Program at the University of Arizona in Tucson.*

Pass

Born in 1951, I was reared in Tempe, Arizona, fifty years ago a mix of family farms, small businesses on a short, hooked main drag, Mill Avenue, and a state college where my father taught on the piano faculty. Tempe then was of a knowable dimension, one bank, one drugstore, one haberdashery. And even more important for my early boyhood formation, one place for the flat-top haircut I preferred, Ray's Barbershop. A low, narrow structure, Ray's was just down from the newspaper office on Mill, and marked by a revolving barber pole, the red stripe spinning forever down or up, I couldn't decide. At age five and six, propped on a smooth board laid across the arms of the barber chair, a white smock fanning out from my neck, I'd fuss—I hated the buzzing clippers, and being confined—till some treat, usually a piece of Dentyne gum, could be found to pacify me.

Entering Ray's, to the right one saw three black leather swivel chairs that rose and turned on pedestals like carnival rides; to the left, against the wall, a line of five or six green naugahyde-covered chairs with chrome tube arm-rests. These waiting chairs I loved because their surfaces stung with coolness the skin on my arms and bare legs in the many hot months of the year. Having used up the cool of one spot, I'd lift my legs and shift my arms to a new position—enjoying even the unsticking sound—and use up the cool in the new location.

Despite the chairs, each time we neared Ray's those first few years, my fingers wrapped in my father's hand, I felt an odd sense of dread. Ray's was a world of men, men without women. If a mother had the job of seeing to her son's haircut, she'd usher him through the door, ask Ray to keep an eye out till she got some other errand done, and be on her way. This charged the atmosphere in some way that made me uncomfortable. Though the talk was generally good-natured, it took on the quality of a public competition, voices chiming in from all parts of the room, the volume rising and falling and rising again quickly.

And the talk seemed to follow a pattern. Whether a man agreed or disagreed with what had just been said—"What a lousy baseball team the college has this

---

Reprinted from *Taboo*, (1999), University of Wisconsin Press, by permission of the author.

year," or "We need to pass those road bonds"—he'd have to up the ante, speaking more loudly, making a point, or countering a point, with greater intensity. A break in the build-up and he was out.

What made me most uneasy, though, was how my father, stepping through Ray's door, became someone else; how he suddenly treated me as an other, to be discussed as if not present, located in the third-person: "I hope he's not too much trouble today, Ray." My father's voice would dip to a lower register, sounding flat and less gentle.

"A bad time to be in the stock market, Ray?" he'd ask, chin raised. I could see his shoulders, even beneath the smock, flatten against the chair back—my father, who was otherwise noticeably round-shouldered. I could see that rather than take part in the actual contest, my father asked questions, deferring somewhat to the others. I was puzzled by the changes that took place in him; I was embarrassed by his awkwardness.

Some years later, as a member of the high school tennis team, I'd stand with about a dozen naked boys every day after practice in the open showers, the air thick with steam and the stink of gym clothes.

—"What a fuck-up Jimmy was in his match Thursday."

—"It'd serve that asshole right if Sally didn't let him touch her for a month."

—"Hey, Jimmy, she let you do stuff to her with that little wang of yours?"

Though we made our points with quick insults and sarcasm, the pattern was the same as in Ray's, each comment an attempt to top the one before.

Without calling too much attention to myself, I discovered how to add in a sentence here and there, not unlike my father's practice of posing questions. I'd snort at the appropriate moments, and find safe places (the splintered foot of an old wooden bench, a pile of discarded towels) to direct my gaze—away, always, from what interested and confused me most: the other boys' bodies.

By age twelve I visited Ray's alone, riding my bike downtown after school or on Saturday. Not only had I begun to figure out what made me uncomfortable there, I was becoming a student of character, intrigued by the manners of speech and dress and movement that gave adults their distinctive places in my small universe. Ray's was no good for this, the cast changing too quickly for long observation. But just a few blocks up and across the street, I found in another men's place, The Q, a pool hall, a cast of characters who daily arrived to take up their roles. Allowed, perhaps encouraged, to watch—these men knew how to play to an audience—I'd rent a table for half an hour, then sit with a cherry coke at a distance to observe the drama.

The Q was cavernous, a huge open rectangle with lights like giant plungers hanging down over the green felt-covered tables. Entering through the heavy glass door at one end of the storefront, you were met by a squinty little man with stringy dark hair and a stringy body, a body dried and smoked like beef jerky, and a few fading tattoos on his forearms. He sat at the register at the near-end of a long snack counter. From any of the high stools along this counter one could turn and watch the nearby tables. The real action, though, was usually at a back corner snooker table, where the older characters—the Mex, Doc, Walter—would mix it up with the younger hustlers like Smitty and the Rail—and my brother, Richard.

Richard, four years my senior and in high school already, was friends with Smitty and the others; he could hold his own at this table. Always voluble, and tall, with a broad smile and crisp flat-top haircut like mine, he could smoke and curse and talk about sex in conspiratorial ways with the other guys, hinting at conquests, winking, cigarette jittering between his lips, breaking into a growling laugh. All this carried off as he sighted along his cue to make a shot. Between turns he sat with three or four others in high plastic scooped chairs along the wall. They'd slouch in their seats, sticks standing straight up and held with both hands between their legs, comments floating side to side, heads rolling back and forth along the cool painted cinder-block.

I was his kid brother, OK as long as he said so; he said so as long as I never made a point of being his brother. For hours I'd lurk outside the circle, witness to the give and take of men—from late adolescents like my brother, through the older unemployed or retired ones, some of them drunks, noses red and porous from years on the bottle.

Walter and the Mex were the lords of this latter group. Though Walter was light and the Mex dark, their bodies matched in almost every other way, paunches overlapping their belts, skin puffy and creased, brown eyes bloodshot as if they never slept. And their voices were ragged. Walter barked out phrases in hoarse bursts, tugging at his pants from the belt-loops to emphasize a point. The Mex, quieter, was more inclined to ribbing Walter and the others than telling whole stories. "Better pull hard, my friend," he'd wheeze, "you got no ass to hold those pants up." They always looked and acted so settled, small grins and chuckles punctuating their remarks, I figured they had some secret to life.

The younger men handled themselves differently. If the rumpled Walter approached the snooker table like a respectful lover, deliberately considering each shot, gently placing the bridge-hand on the felt, his elbow coming to rest in one slow graceful motion, the young ones said with their bodies they would dominate. Volatile, loud, with quick eyes that knifed in anger or pleasure, Smitty charged the table, swiftly finding the desired angle, pulling the cue back in precise but sudden preliminary jerks. Missing an important shot, Rail, nicknamed both for his skill with bank shots and his skinny frame, would slam the butt of his cue against a wall, spitting a curse. And there were actual fights—over debts (these games were played for money), over occasional insults (about little peckers and never getting laid, or somebody's dumpy girlfriend). Sometimes I couldn't see the explosion coming. There'd be the thud of bodies against a table, arms and grunts and teeth in a blur, and then five or six men rushing in to pull the bodies apart. Those of us just watching would scatter to the walls like so many water droplets shaken from a rag.

I was scared almost to trembling each time I walked into The Q—and excited by my fear. But it wasn't because of the fights. It had to do with my role as a watcher. I felt no kinship with either group, the fiery young hustlers or their blowsy elders, though both I found fascinating. I knew I was a spy, an imposter. I was terrified some comment or some stupid stumbling gesture would show them who and what I was. And though I didn't know what that would be, I felt certain something fundamental in my nature would be different, and to these men, to my brother, even, unacceptable. And so I held myself in absolute, nearly frozen, reserve. If I was blank, I thought, if I didn't try to show I was anybody, if I simply watched, smiled, smirked, laughed at the right moments, slouched down in my chair, I'd pass.

Erec Toso

Erec Toso, a Tucson writer, is a Senior Lecturer and Teaching Advisor at the University of Arizona. He has published essays in The Sun—A Magazine of Ideas, Northern Lights, The Arizona Literary Magazine, The Arizona Daily Star, *and other local publications. This essay first appeared in the November 1993 issue of* The Sun, *a magazine devoted to publishing creative writing and black and white photographs. Toso also has two other pieces in "Chapter Six: Writing the Environment." In this essay, Toso explores his relationship to his young son and his son's eagerness to explore the world.*

Setting the Borders on Desire

He looked odd, hardly lovable. His head was elongated from the pounding it had taken against a cervix that did not fully dilate. He was covered with blood and amniotic fluid. When he took his first breath, he closed his eyes and screamed. The sound, the sight of him, and the profound terror of being a parent took my breath away.

It has been a year and a half since Kyle was born, and I can only now admit how little I understand about being a parent. I still don't really know him. I am daily surprised by him. I feel awkward, and marvel, watching him change.

Today I walked him home from the babysitter. I am in a hurry; he wants to stop and dig in the dirt. He knows there is soft potting soil in a barrel planter along our path. I am tired. I want to drop off the bag of diapers he has used today, and I want to sit down. He picks up a spade near the barrel and plunges it into the dry mixture of dirt and manure.

At first I feel annoyed. "House," I say, hoping to encourage him to follow me home so that I can cook dinner, catch the news, and unwind after a day of graduate school.

He is deliberate. "Nuh no." He roots in the loose, brown humus with the spade and dumps some soil onto his sleeve. He turns the soil, examining its texture, then plunges in with the spade again.

I hang there between diapers and book bag, a harried cargo carrier, suddenly aware that I am witnessing worship. I want to drop the bags and join him. But I only watch and wait for him to finish. It takes more than this simple testimony to mindfulness for me to undo years of impatience.

Reprinted from *The Sun*, November 1993, pp. 30–32.

I set down my heavy book bag. He notices but goes back to his digging. Then he walks across the paving stones with a load of earth, intending to dump it on my bag. Part of me thinks that burying my books would not be a bad idea, but I counter, "No no," and lead him back to his work.

Watching him, sometimes, I feel time jump its track. I don't know who he is, yet he seems so much like me.

I know he has a fear of mine. When he was about three months old, he had a walker that played "It's a Small World After All" when you wound a flower-shaped crank on the side. I felt relieved that he could move now under his own power; he looked less like a baby, more like a boy. Sometimes on his trips around the house, he would stop in the kitchen and look up at me with a piercing expression, appealing, desperate. *Dad,* his look said, *please love me.* I'd scoop him up and hold him close, smelling his hair, his fragility. I'd try to tell him, chasing away his baby fear with the sum of my conviction and sincerity, that of course I loved him. How could I not love him?

There have been other times when I've been sound asleep and his voice rose from a chant to a plaintive wail. The noise got behind my eyes and burned there. I remember the peculiar pounding, unlike any I had felt before. Often I was angry. On those nights, Megan would tell me not to get up, not until I wanted to comfort him. Then she would go to him. On those nights I wasn't able to be a parent. I was still a child myself.

Sometimes, lately, my reluctance falls away, and he and I speak the same language. He lies on the table as I change him, and he begins, "Haab daab daab yow," gesturing exaggeratedly with his arms. I forget who I am and join him, chattering, "Yaab bo daab haand oh." Passionate assertion, legal argument, the big questions fill the weight of our debate. Sometimes I broadly assent with giant nods and swinging arms, Desitin in one hand, in the other a pair of plastic pants. Sometimes I disagree but keep the tone conversational. His eyes show that he understands. He giggles, and I speak from deep within myself, saying truths I dare not utter to any other. He senses the communion, contributing secrets of his own. He laughs, showing two perfect but lonely lower teeth.

In the morning, he is very small. He cries before beginning to name his world. "Kitty . . . milk . . . on (turn on the light) . . . Papa . . . Mama . . . truck." When the world is named, he strides into it, confident, unbroken. I feel the impossible desire to protect him, keep him from ever breaking. But the thought burns off as we both move into the day. Again, I hurry. I want him to eat his bananas so I can get out the door to make my eight o'clock class. "Ah pea," he asks, *open.* He wants me to help him with his curriculum: opening and closing juice bottles, milk bottles, toothpaste tubes. This morning, "ah pea" is for his green, plastic turtle that houses different shapes—stars, triangles, hexagons—in its shell. He is holding it up to me. "Ah pea." I sit down, open the turtle, take the cylindrical piece, put it in my mouth, lie back, and shoot it skyward. He takes the oval piece, lies back, and blows until it puffs above his head. I guess I will be late.

Sometimes I think he holds me back. I don't have all the time I once did. I don't know when I last went to an art exhibit or talked over a beer. I feel that I will never have the energy necessary to excel at anything. But, perhaps by way of detour, I feel pushed ahead, too. He shows me things. I have had a cordless phone for more than a year, but there are buttons on it I've never understood. Within a week of picking it up, he had found the intercom, page, and finder buttons. He made the answering machine respond to commands I didn't know existed. He speaks into the phone, and the answering machine amplifies his voice; he pushes "page" and gets great, shrill beeps from the distant machine. He sees a world I barely notice.

Once in a while we go into the back yard after dinner, when it's almost dark. A light illuminates only a small part of the yard, and I like to stay under it, rolling the ball back and forth, but he charges ahead and flings the ball into the darkest corners of the yard. I walk back there to get it through dust that fills my sandals, through the shit of neighborhood cats. I don't like it, wouldn't walk there if I didn't have to retrieve the ball. He stands on the edge of shadow, a silhouette, swinging his hands, walking in circles, half dancing, half waiting for me to bring back the ball. I don't know who he is, really, this person in my care, but he seems very close to knowing himself.

When he sees me coming back out of the dark, he runs. His feet do not touch the dirt as they disappear, too short for his body, in a galloping blur. He is pleased that I have come back. I toss the ball toward the light, hoping to move us in that direction. He retrieves it and flings it back into the darkness, then swings his arms, or touches his fingertips to fingertips, or walks in circles, waiting.

He stays with a neighbor couple while I am at school. To them, he is part of the family. He goes walking with the retired husband. They go where Kyle wants to go. Sometimes they walk over to the bus stop. He knows the buses. They sit and watch them squeak to a stop. They breathe in the released air of the brakes and feet the air-conditioned whooshes of hydraulic doors opening and closing. They are in no hurry. They stay until they get tired of the view, then move on to another. Kyle knows the park and can speak a few words of Spanish with some of the homeless regulars who stay there. He knows the library. He knows the fountains in the mall. The two of them move slowly, deliberately. About a week ago, I came home early and found them watering trees in the back yard. "*Hola, este . . .* Erec," the husband said to me, as if he couldn't quite remember my name. That is his way. "*Buenos dias,*" I answered. I followed up the salutation with a broad-armed stoop that I thought would elicit a hug and called out, "Kylito!" Kyle turned to look at me. He seemed a little surprised or annoyed. He turned back to the neighbor, grabbed his hand, looked back at me, and said, "Buh bye." They turned off the water, and the two of them walked away together, the one old and a little bent, the other brand-new, trying out his body.

He changes between the time I drop him off in the morning and when I return for him in the afternoon. His new words, gestures, surprise me. I try to find a continuity. He offers to reacquaint us. "Bao?" he says, pointing up at an orange tree we pass on our walk home. Tight, green oranges hang from the branches. They look like the ball we toss around the yard. I jump to grab one for him. When I give it to him, he is pleased and holds it with both hands before tossing it down the driveway. I race him to pick it up.

The oranges in my reach have now been all but exhausted, so I sometimes plant an orange in the crotch of a branch. On our walks home, I harvest oranges that are reruns.

Kyle has gotten used to being outside, to walking. One day, I closed the gate when he wanted to go out. He stood next to it and demanded that I open it. "Ah pea."

"No no. It's time to stay in the yard."

He crossed his hands, wrung them, and said again, a little more desperately, "Ahhhh pea."

"No no."

It became clear to him that he couldn't leave. The pleas gave way to whimpers, then a pout, then a full scream. It was difficult to walk away, quietly asserting "no no." I sat at the other end of the yard while he stood facing me with his back against the gate, berating me in every way he knew. We stood off for almost an hour. Only when I went into the house for some fruit did he relent and come join me on the porch.

It's just me and him for now. In the future, he will have teachers, peers, schedules, but those years still seem distant. I watch him wield a long piece of plastic pipe. It is twice as long as he is tall. With it, he is a warrior of the yard and trots around reciting victory incantations. He holds his arms up in triumphant glory when he doesn't know I'm watching. He sometimes chases the cats with his lance. They elude him, jumping onto high adobe walls, warily unwinding and flicking their tails. They are adversaries, dragons, full of animal cunning. He pursues them fearlessly.

I admire him. His movements betray his unbroken desires, his trust, his confidence of place. Someday, I know he will doubt, will see me pull the orange from behind the branch, will sense my discomfort when playing his games. Without another player, enthusiasm—*en theo,* in God—will eventually wither. He will forget his wonder. I am reluctant to play my inevitable role, the instructor of limitation, yet the dance my son and I do is fated, I believe, inexorable as the tides. He will forget how to walk slowly, as I have forgotten. But I want him to know how for as long as he can so that maybe, someday, he will begin to remember.

Robert Frost

Robert Frost (1874–1963) was an American poet famous for his depictions of the rural life in New England and his realistic verse that dealt with ordinary people and everyday life. He was born in San Francisco and lived there until his father's death. After his father's death, his mother moved to Lawrence, Massachusetts, where Frost attended high school. He married three years later and constantly struggled to support his family with various poorly paid jobs. His grandfather provided support during these impoverished years; however, Frost came close to emotional collapse due to his failure to become an established writer. He took his family to England and his constant conversations with British poets helped him in developing his poetic skills. After getting published in England, he was able to return to America and work as a teacher at various schools among them Harvard University and Dartmouth College. What makes Frost's poetic style famous is its readability. He avoids obscure language and avoids political, economic references and prefers to use traditional poetic forms that rely on coherence instead of the fragmentary style of his contemporaries. For Frost, poetry "begins in delight and ends in wisdom. The figure is the same as for love. No one can really hold that the ecstasy should be static and stand still in one place. It begins in delight, it inclines to the impulse, it assumes direction with the first line laid down, it runs a course of lucky events, and ends in clarification of life."

"Home Burial" offers a glimpse into the life of a married couple who have lost their first-born child, and the disruption that results from the husband's having carved out a geographical space in which to bury the child. In the aftermath of this emotional and spatial change, the wife and husband confront each other. This poem raises questions that are also important in Carver's story "So Much Water So Close to Home" such as how do we create boundaries between "inside" and "outside"? Are these boundaries definitive and always stable, or can they shift, melt into each other and alter each other's meanings? How do we face such disruptions and how can those disruptions change who we are and how we communicate with one another?

Home Burial

He saw her from the bottom of the stairs
Before she saw him. She was starting down,
Looking back over her shoulder at some fear.
She took a doubtful step and then undid it
To raise herself and look again. He spoke
Advancing toward her: "What is it you see
From up there always—for I want to know."
She turned and sank upon her skirts at that,
And her face changed from terrified to dull.
He said to gain time: "What is it you see,"
Mounting until she cowered under him.
"I will find out now—you must tell me, dear."
She, in her place, refused him any help
With the least stiffening of her neck and silence.
She let him look, sure that he wouldn't see,
Blind creature; and awhile he didn't see.
But at last he murmured, "Oh," and again, "Oh."

"What is it—what?" she said.

"Just that I see."

"You don't," she challenged. "Tell me what it is."

"The wonder is I didn't see at once.
I never noticed it from here before.
I must be wonted to it—that's the reason.
The little graveyard where my people are!
So small the window frames the whole of it.
Not so much larger than a bedroom, is it?
There are three stones of slate and one of marble,
Broad-shouldered little slabs there in the sunlight
On the sidehill. We haven't to mind *those*.
But I understand: it is not the stones,
But the child's mound—"

"Don't, don't, don't, don't," she cried.

She withdrew, shrinking from beneath his arm
That rested on the banister, and slid downstairs;
And turned on him with such a daunting look,
He said twice over before he knew himself:
"Can't a man speak of his own child he's lost?"

"Not you!—Oh, where's my hat? Oh, I don't need it!
I must get out of here. I must get air.
I don't know rightly whether any man can."

"Amy! Don't go to someone else this time.
Listen to me. I won't come down the stairs."
He sat and fixed his chin between his fists.
"There's something I should like to ask you, dear."

"You don't know how to ask it."
"Help me, then."

Her fingers moved the latch for all reply.

"My words are nearly always an offense.
I don't know how to speak of anything
So as to please you. But I might be taught,
I should suppose. I can't say I see how.
A man must partly give up being a man
With women-folk. We could have some arrangement
By which I'd bind myself to keep hands off
Anything special you're a-mind to name.
Though I don't like such things 'twixt those that love.
Two that don't love can't live together without them.
But two that do can't live together with them."
She moved the latch a little. "Don't—don't go.
Don't carry it to someone else this time.
Tell me about it if it's something human.
Let me into your grief. I'm not so much
Unlike other folks as your standing there
Apart would make me out. Give me my chance.
I do think, though, you overdo it a little.
What was it brought you up to think it the thing
To take your mother-loss of a first child
So inconsolably—in the face of love.
You'd think his memory might be satisfied—"

"There you go sneering now!"

"I'm not, I'm not!
You make me angry. I'll come down to you.
God, what a woman! And it's come to this,
A man can't speak of his own child that's dead."

"You can't because you don't know how to speak.
If you had any feelings, you that dug
With your own hand—how could you?—his little grave;
I saw you from that very window there,
Making the gravel leap and leap in air,
Leap up, like that, like that, and land so lightly
And roll back down the mound beside the hole.
I thought, Who is that man? I didn't know you.
And I crept down the stairs and up the stairs
To look again, and still your spade kept lifting.

Then you came in. I heard your rumbling voice
Out in the kitchen, and I don't know why,
But I went near to see with my own eyes.
You could sit there with the stains on your shoes
Of the fresh earth from your own baby's grave
And talk about your everyday concerns.
You had stood the spade up against the wall
Outside there in the entry, for I saw it."

"I shall laugh the worst laugh I ever laughed.
I'm cursed. God, if I don't believe I'm cursed."

"I can repeat the very words you were saying.
'Three foggy mornings and one rainy day
Will rot the best birch fence a man can build.'
Think of it, talk like that at such a time!
What had how long it takes a birch to rot
To do with what was in the darkened parlor.
You *couldn't* care! The nearest friends can go
With anyone to death, comes so far short
They might as well not try to go at all.
No, from the time when one is sick to death,
One is alone, and he dies more alone.
Friends make pretense of following to the grave.
But before one is in it, their minds are turned
And making the best of their way back to life
And living people, and things they understand.
But the world's evil. I won't have grief so
If I can change it. Oh, I won't, I won't!"

"There, you have said it all and you feel better.
You won't go now. You're crying. Close the door.
The heart's gone out of it: why keep it up.
Amy! There's someone coming down the road!"

"*You*—oh, you think the talk is all. I must go—
Somewhere out of this house. How can I make you—"

"If—you—do!" She was opening the door wider.
"Where do you mean to go? First tell me that.
I'll follow and bring you back by force. I *will!*—"

1912–13 1914

5

Rereading Romance

Jillian Cantor and Leta McGaffey Sharp

Attraction, seduction, lust, and true love. These powerful elements compose what we call "romance." Rarely does a novel or movie of any genre seem complete without romance. In our North American culture, we begin to think about love, romance, sexuality, and beauty at a very young age. Most of us have been bombarded with the fairy tale version of romance since we were children, taken to an extreme by Disney: a desolate, beautiful young woman is swept off her feet by a handsome young prince searching for meaning in his life. We see the same essential story in *Cinderella, Snow White, Rapunzel, Mulan, The Little Mermaid,* and *Beauty and the Beast.* Hollywood has provided us with more similar versions: the "chick flick" romance where the man and woman realize they are made for each other, or the macho hero riding off into the sunset with the beautiful maiden tucked under his arm. Indeed, the definition of romance as a "love affair" implies a certain fanciful, exciting, and ideal air to it. But these notions of romance reveal a cultural bias—depicting one version of romance: it is heterosexual, it is for "the beautiful people," almost always of the same race, women are won by sensitive men with chocolates and flowers, men are dazzled with beauty and wit, and life is not complete without a happy marriage and children. This single, narrowly defined perspective leaves many people in the dust with, so it seems, little chance for romance and love. If you don't fit into this story line, you seem to be destined to die alone—and miserable about it. This chapter invites you to look at the way you think about romance. How do we define romance today? How does our culture/gender/age/sexuality change the way we define romance?

As you have encountered romance in your own lives, you may have also encountered a set of "implied rules" or norms. Hundreds of books about dating and relationships line bookstore shelves. The recent bestseller *A Man's Field Guide to Dating* by Robert A. Wray guides men through "the dating game," attempting to solve the eternal mystery of what women want. Wray focuses on men's fear of rejection from attractive women and becoming able to commit to a relationship. In another example, *The Rules,* a self-help guide to romance for women, authors Ellen Fein and Sherrie Schneider give women 35 rules they must follow to "catch" the perfect man. They write, "Follow *The Rules,* and he will not just marry you, but feel crazy about you, forever! What we are promising you is 'happily ever after.' A marriage truly made in heaven" (6). But to get this "happily ever after" women must "Let Him Take the Lead" (Rule #17), "Don't Tell Him What to Do" (Rule 16), and "Stop Dating Him if He Doesn't Buy You a Romantic Gift for Your Birthday or Valentine's Day" (Rule 12). Can happily ever after really only exist if women follow behind men, don't speak their mind, and focus on gifts? And why does society still believe in this traditional notion of romance where men are expected to take the lead and face the risk of rejection and where women are expected to be coy and deferential? Should we consider this idea of "happily ever after" flawed, considering we live in a society where one out of every two marriages ends in divorce? (2002 Census). Perhaps our notions about exciting romance and easy, ever-lasting love are even part of the reason for our high divorce rates.

We invite you to critique this narrow vision of romantic love as you read the stories, essays, and poems in this chapter. "Reread" your own definition of romance by thinking about different cultural values, sexual orientations, gender roles, generational differences, and situations that may be vastly different from your own. Think about what "true love" and "romance" mean to you. Think about your parents, your schools, and your groups of friends over time. Think about the romantic relationships you have been exposed to throughout your life. How have others influenced your definition of romance and love? What are you "supposed to feel" when you are in love? Do you believe in the Hollywood/Disney version? Do you fight that version? Do you think romance itself is a silly notion? Does it have anything to do with love? How is romance defined differently in other cultures, including the thousands of subcultures, within America?

We chose the selections in this chapter to help you explore the multiple perspectives that do exist surrounding romance and romantic love. The first two stories, "Happy Endings" by Margaret Atwood and "What We Talk About When We Talk About Love" by Raymond Carver help us examine our definitions of romance, love, and "happily ever after," exploring what men and women want from romantic relationships.

Because cultural values influence the way individuals think and feel about romance, we have included stories that present views from various cultures in time and place. Romance is not always the main driving force behind choosing a partner. Money, social class, and the desire/need for progeny have often been much more important than romance and love when making partnerships. In "The Tenant," for instance, Bharati Mukherjee explores how an East Indian woman feels conflicted about dating, sex, and marriage while living in the very different culture of America. And Thomas Raddall tells an interesting tale from the nineteenth century in "The Wedding Gift" about a young woman's choices during a time of arranged marriages.

You can also explore how age affects your view of romance and love in the stories by Boswell and Oates. Robert Boswell's story, "Dancing in the Movies" provides a divergent version of the traditional hero rescuing the damsel in distress romance where a college age student tries to "save" his junkie girlfriend. Joyce Carol Oates also dramatically reveals the excitement and danger of temptation and obsessions of a teenage girl.

Another important question concerns whether romance is viewed differently within same-sex romantic relationships. Is it basically the same as heterosexual attraction, dating, and romance? Terry Castle's essay, "First Ed," examines those first awakening moments of sexual attraction from the viewpoint of a young girl who has a crush on an older woman. It explores the questions: How do we define romance as children? How do we define romance from a lesbian perspective? Mark Doty's poem "Days of 1981" depicts a young man's first desire to be swept away into a wild romance by another man. It explores his feelings of humiliation at his own naiveté. The poem also explores the way we look back at early romance, tainted by life's hard lessons, remembering with idealization.

Bodies also play a major role in relationships. Ideas of what is beautiful, sexy, and attractive obviously influence romantic relationships. Attraction is in turn influenced by age, gender, sexual orientation, religion, and culture. Body self-image plays a major role as well. People who don't feel attractive tend to be insecure about their chances for finding a partner. But how important are bodies in life-long relationships? How important are other material influences like money? The poems by Charles Simic and Marge Piercy both delve into sexual attraction and body image and how they change over time.

We see each of these stories and poems as helpful in examining romance in a rich and more encompassing way than is traditionally presented. Rewrite your own fairy tales. It may be interesting and fun to get into same-gender groups, coming up with a list of what women want, and then what men want. Have fun while re-envisioning "traditional" American notions of romance, challenging stereotypes and opening possibilities for everyone—no matter what they look like, who they find attractive, what their life goals are, or what they find romantic or rewarding.

Works Cited

Wray, Robert A. *A Man's Field Guide to Dating*. NetImage, 1999.

Fein, Ellen and Sherrie Schneider. *The Rules: Time-tested Secrets for Capturing the Heart of Mr. Right*. New York: Warner Books, 1996.

Margaret Atwood

Canadian writer, Margaret Atwood (b.1939), is a leading literary artist of the twentieth century. Her work is highly regarded by both critics and readers. She is the recipient of numerous literary and humanitarian awards and, in 1986, was named Woman of the Year by Ms. *magazine. She has taught English literature at several colleges and universities. As a young author, Atwood was encouraged to pursue a career in writing as Canadians of her generation felt a need to develop a national literature. Among her many novels are the bestsellers,* Surfacing *(1972),* The Handmaid's Tale *(1986),* Cat's Eye *(1989) and* The Robber Bride *(1993). She has also published three collections of short stories and several books of poetry. In an interview with Lindsy van Gelder, Atwood says, "I began as a profoundly apolitical writer, but then . . . I began to describe the world around me." "Happy Endings," published in* Murder in the Dark (Good Bones and Simple Murders) *in the US in 1983, plays with the notion of the typical fairytale ending.*

Happy Endings

John and Mary meet.
What happens next?
If you want a happy ending, try A.

A

John and Mary fall in love and get married. They both have worthwhile and remunerative jobs which they find stimulating and challenging. They buy a charming house. Real estate values go up. Eventually, when they can afford live-in help, they have two children, to whom they are devoted. The children turn out well. John and Mary have a stimulating and challenging sex life and worthwhile friends. They go on fun vacations together. They retire. They both have hobbies which they find stimulating and challenging. Eventually they die. This is the end of the story.

Reprinted from *Good Bones and Simple Murders*, (1983), Doubleday.

B

Mary falls in love with John but John doesn't fall in love with Mary. He merely uses her body for selfish pleasure and ego gratification of a tepid kind. He comes to her apartment twice a week and she cooks him dinner, you'll notice that he doesn't even consider her worth the price of a dinner out, and after he's eaten the dinner he fucks her and after that he falls asleep, while she does the dishes so he won't think she's untidy, having all those dirty dishes lying around, and puts on fresh lipstick so she'll look good when he wakes up, but when he wakes up he doesn't even notice, he puts on his socks and his shorts and his pants and his shirt and his tie and his shoes, the reverse order from the one in which he took them off. He doesn't take off Mary's clothes, she takes them off herself, she acts as if she's dying for it every time, not because she likes sex exactly, she doesn't, but she wants John to think she does because if they do it often enough surely he'll get used to her, he'll come to depend on her and they will get married, but John goes out the door with hardly so much as a good-night and three days later he turns up at six o'clock and they do the whole thing over again.

Mary gets run-down. Crying is bad for your face, everyone knows that and so does Mary but she can't stop. People at work notice. Her friends tell her John is a rat, a pig, a dog, he isn't good enough for her, but she can't believe it. Inside John, she thinks, is another John, who is much nicer. This other John will emerge like a butterfly from a cocoon, a Jack from a box, a pit from a prune, if the first John is only squeezed enough.

One evening John complains about the food. He has never complained about the food before. Mary is hurt.

Her friends tell her they've seen him in a restaurant with another woman, whose name is Madge. It's not even Madge that finally gets to Mary: it's the restaurant. John has never taken Mary to a restaurant. Mary collects all the sleeping pills and aspirins she can find, and takes them and a half a bottle of sherry. You can see what kind of a woman she is by the fact that it's not even whiskey. She leaves a note for John. She hopes he'll discover her and get her to the hospital in time and repent and then they can get married, but this fails to happen and she dies.

John marries Madge and everything continues as in A.

C

John, who is an older man, falls in love with Mary, and Mary, who is only twenty-two, feels sorry for him because he's worried about his hair falling out. She sleeps with him even though she's not in love with him. She met him at work. She's in love with someone called James, who is twenty-two also and not yet ready to settle down.

John on the contrary settled down long ago: this is what is bothering him. John has a steady, respectable job and is getting ahead in his field, but Mary isn't impressed by him, she's impressed by James, who has a motorcycle and a fabulous record collection. But James is often away on his motorcycle, being free. Freedom isn't the same for girls, so in the meantime Mary spends Thursday evenings with John. Thursdays are the only days John can get away.

John is married to a woman called Madge and they have two children, a charming house which they bought just before the real estate values went up, and hobbies which they find stimulating and challenging, when they have the time. John tells Mary how important she is to him, but of course he can't leave his wife because a commitment is a commitment. He goes on about this more than is necessary and Mary finds it boring, but older men can keep it up longer so on the whole she has a fairly good time.

One day James breezes in on his motorcycle with some top-grade California hybrid and James and Mary get higher than you'd believe possible and they climb into bed. Everything becomes very underwater, but along comes John, who has a key to Mary's apartment. He finds them stoned and entwined. He's hardly in any position to be jealous, considering Madge, but nevertheless he's overcome with despair. Finally he's middle-aged, in two years he'll be bald as an egg and he can't stand it. He purchases a handgun, saying he needs it for target practice—this is the thin part of the plot, but it can be dealt with later—and shoots the two of them and himself.

Madge, after a suitable period of mourning, marries an understanding man called Fred and everything continues as in A, but under different names.

D

Fred and Madge have no problems. They get along exceptionally well and are good at working out any little difficulties that may arise. But their charming house is by the seashore and one day a giant tidal wave approaches. Real estate values go down. The rest of the story is about what caused the tidal wave and how they escape from it. They do, though thousands drown, but Fred and Madge are virtuous and lucky. Finally on high ground they clasp each other, wet and dripping and grateful, and continue as in A.

E

Yes, but Fred has a bad heart. The rest of the story is about how kind and understanding they both are until Fred dies. Then Madge devotes herself to charity work until the end of A. If you like, it can be "Madge," "cancer," "guilty and confused," and "bird watching."

F

If you think this is all too bourgeois, make John a revolutionary and Mary a counterespionage agent and see how far that gets you. Remember, this is Canada. You'll still end up with A, though in between you may get a lustful brawling saga of passionate involvement, a chronicle of our times, sort of.

You'll have to face it, the endings are the same however you slice it. Don't be deluded by any other endings, they're all fake, either deliberately fake, with malicious intent to deceive, or just motivated by excessive optimism if not by downright sentimentality.

The only authentic ending is the one provided here:

John and Mary die. John and Mary die. John and Mary die.

So much for endings. Beginnings are always more fun. True connoisseurs, however, are known to favor the stretch in between, since it's the hardest to do anything with.

That's about all that can be said for plots, which anyway are just one thing after another, a what and a what and a what.

Now try How and Why.

[1983]

Raymond Carver

Raymond Carver (1938–1988) is an acclaimed short story writer whose stories often reflect the difficulties people have communicating with one another. His candid depiction of the working class is based upon his own experiences and history, which he discusses in his book, Fires, *a collection of essays about his life and his influences as a writer. "What We Talk About When We Talk About Love" discusses both the meaning of love itself and the difficulty couples have in communicating its meaning. It was published in a collection of stories of the same name in 1981. His story "So Much Water So Close to Home" appears in Chapter Four.*

What We Talk About When We Talk About Love

My friend Mel McGinnis was talking. Mel McGinnis is a cardiologist, and sometimes that gives him the right.

The four of us were sitting around his kitchen table drinking gin. Sunlight filled the kitchen from the big window behind the sink. There were Mel and me and his second wife, Teresa—Terri, we called her—and my wife, Laura. We lived in Albuquerque then. But we were all from somewhere else.

There was an ice bucket on the table. The gin and the tonic water kept going around, and we somehow got on the subject of love. Mel thought real love was nothing less than spiritual love. He said he'd spent five years in a seminary before quitting to go to medical school. He said he still looked back on those years in the seminary as the most important years in his life.

Terri said the man she lived with before she lived with Mel loved her so much he tried to kill her. Then Terri said, "He beat me up one night. He dragged me around the living room by my ankles. He kept saying, 'I love you, I love you, you bitch.' He went on dragging me around the living room. My head kept knocking on things." Terri looked around the table. "What do you do with love like that?"

She was a bone-thin woman with a pretty face, dark eyes, and brown hair that hung down her back. She liked necklaces made of turquoise, and long pendant earrings.

"My God, don't be silly. That's not love, and you know it," Mel said. "I don't know what you'd call it, but I sure know you wouldn't call it love."

"Say what you want to, but I know it was," Terri said. "It may sound crazy to you, but it's true just the same. People are different, Mel. Sure, sometimes he may have acted crazy. Okay. But he loved me. In his own way maybe, but he loved me. There was love there, Mel. Don't say there wasn't."

Mel let out his breath. He held his glass and turned to Laura and me. "The man threatened to kill me," Mel said. He finished his drink and reached for the gin bottle. "Terri's a romantic. Terri's of the kick-me-so-I'll-know-you-love-me school. Terri, hon, don't look that way." Mel reached across the table and touched Terri's cheek with his fingers. He grinned at her.

"Now he wants to make up," Terri said.

"Make up what?" Mel said. "What is there to make up? I know what I know. That's all."

"How'd we get started on this subject, anyway?" Terri said. She raised her glass and drank from it. "Mel always has love on his mind," she said. "Don't you, honey?" She smiled, and I thought that was the last of it.

"I just wouldn't call Ed's behavior love. That's all I'm saying, honey," Mel said. "What about you guys?" Mel said to Laura and me. "Does that sound like love to you?"

"I'm the wrong person to ask," I said. "I didn't even know the man. I've only heard his name mentioned in passing. I wouldn't know. You'd have to know the particulars. But I think what you're saying is that love is an absolute."

Mel said, "The kind of love I'm talking about is. The kind of love I'm talking about, you don't try to kill people."

Laura said, "I don't know anything about Ed, or anything about the situation. But who can judge anyone else's situation?"

I touched the back of Laura's hand. She gave me a quick smile. I picked up Laura's hand. It was warm, the nails polished, perfectly manicured. I encircled the broad wrist with my fingers, and I held her.

"When I left, he drank rat poison," Terri said. She clasped her arms with her hands. "They took him to the hospital in Sante Fe. That's where we lived then, about ten miles out. They saved his life. But his gums went crazy from it. I mean they pulled away from his teeth. After that, his teeth stood out like fangs. My God," Terri said. She waited a minute, then let go of her arms and picked up her glass.

"What people won't do!" Laura said.

"He's out of the action now," Mel said. "He's dead."

Mel handed me the saucer of limes. I took a section, squeezed it over my drink, and stirred the ice cubes with my finger.

"It gets worse," Terri said. "He shot himself in the mouth. But he bungled that too. Poor Ed," she said. Terri shook her head.

"Poor Ed nothing," Mel said. "He was dangerous."

Mel was forty-five years old. He was tall and rangy with curly soft hair. His face and arms were brown from the tennis he played. When he was sober, his gestures, all his movements, were precise, very careful.

"He did love me though, Mel. Grant me that," Terri said. "That's all I'm asking. He didn't love me the way you love me. I'm not saying that. But he loved me. You can grant me that, can't you?"

"What do you mean, he bungled it?" I said.

Laura leaned forward with her glass. She put her elbows on the table and held her glass in both hands. She glanced from Mel to Terri and waited with a look of bewilderment on her open face, as if amazed that such things happened to people you were friendly with.

"How'd he bungle it when he killed himself?" I said.

"I'll tell you what happened," Mel said. "He took this twenty-two pistol he'd bought to threaten Terri and me with. Oh, I'm serious, the man was always threatening. You should have seen the way we lived in those days. Like fugitives. I even bought a gun myself. Can you believe it? A guy like me? But I did. I bought one for self-defense and carried it in the glove compartment. Sometimes I'd have to leave the apartment in the middle of the night. To go to the hospital, you know? Terri and I weren't married then, and my first wife had the house and kids, the dog, everything, and Terri and I were living in this apartment here. Sometimes, as I say, I'd get a call in the middle of the night and have to go in to the hospital at two or three in the morning. It'd be dark out there in the parking lot, and I'd break into a sweat before I could even get to my car. I never knew if he was going to come up out of the shrubbery or from behind a car and start shooting. I mean, the man was crazy. He was capable of wiring a bomb, anything. He used to call my service at all hours and say he needed to talk to the doctor, and when I'd return the call, he'd say, 'Son of a bitch, your days are numbered.' Little things like that. It was scary, I'm telling you."

"I still feel sorry for him," Terri said.

"It sounds like a nightmare," Laura said. "But what exactly happened after he shot himself?"

Laura is a legal secretary. We'd met in a professional capacity. Before we knew it, it was a courtship. She's thirty-five, three years younger than I am. In addition to being in love, we like each other and enjoy one another's company. She's easy to be with.

"What happened?" Laura said.

Mel said, "He shot himself in the mouth in his room. Someone heard the shot and told the manager. They came in with a passkey, saw what had happened, and called an ambulance. I happened to be there when they brought him in, alive but past recall. The man lived for three days. His head swelled up to twice the size of a normal head. I'd never seen anything like it, and I hope I never do again. Terri wanted to go in and sit with him when she found out about it. We had a fight over it. I didn't think she should see him like that. I didn't think she should see him, and I still don't."

"Who won the fight?" Laura said.

"I was in the room with him when he died," Terri said. "He never came up out of it. But I sat with him. He didn't have anyone else."

"He was dangerous," Mel said. "If you call that love, you can have it."

"It was love," Terri said. "Sure, it's abnormal in most people's eyes. But he was willing to die for it. He did die for it."

"I sure as hell wouldn't call it love," Mel said. "I mean, no one knows what he did it for. I've seen a lot of suicides, and I couldn't say anyone ever knew what they did it for."

Mel put his hands behind his neck and tilted his chair back. "I'm not interested in that kind of love," he said. "If that's love, you can have it."

Terri said, "We were afraid. Mel even made a will out and wrote to his brother in California who used to be a Green Beret. Mel told him who to look for if something happened to him."

Terri drank from her glass. She said, "But Mel's right—we lived like fugitives. We were afraid. Mel was, weren't you, honey? I even called the police at one point, but they were no help. They said they couldn't do anything until Ed actually did something. Isn't that a laugh?" Terry said.

She poured the last of the gin into her glass and waggled the bottle. Mel got up from the table and went to the cupboard. He took down another bottle.

"Well, Nick and I know what love is," Laura said. "For us, I mean," Laura said. She bumped my knee with her knee. "You're supposed to say something now," Laura said, and turned her smile on me.

For an answer, I took Laura's hand and raised it to my lips. I made a big production out of kissing her hand. Everyone was amused.

"We're lucky," I said.

"You guys," Terri said. "Stop that now. You're making me sick. You're still on the honeymoon, for God's sake. You're still gaga, for crying out loud. Just wait. How long have you been together now? How long has it been? A year? Longer than a year?"

"Going on a year and a half," Laura said, flushed and smiling.

"Oh, now," Terri said. "Wait awhile."

She held her drink and gazed at Laura.

"I'm only kidding," Terri said.

Mel opened the gin and went around the table with the bottle.

"Here, you guys," he said. "Let's have a toast. I want to propose a toast. A toast to love. To true love," Mel said.

We touched glasses.

"To love," we said.

Outside in the backyard, one of the dogs began to bark. The leaves of the aspen that leaned past the window ticked against the glass. The afternoon sun was like a presence in this room, the spacious light of ease and generosity. We could have been anywhere, somewhere enchanted. We raised our glasses again and grinned at each other like children who had agreed on something forbidden.

"I'll tell you what real love is," Mel said. "I mean, I'll give you a good example. And then you can draw your own conclusions." He poured more gin into his glass. He added an ice cube and a sliver of lime. We waited and sipped our drinks. Laura and I touched knees again. I put a hand on her warm thigh and left it there.

"What do any of us really know about love?" Mel said. "It seems to me we're just beginners at love. We say we love each other and we do, I don't doubt it. I love Terri and Terri loves me, and you guys love each other too. You know the kind of love I'm talking about now. Physical love, that impulse that drives you to someone special, as well as love of the other person's being, his or her essence, as it were. Carnal love and, well, call it sentimental love, the day-to-day caring about the other person. But sometimes I have a hard time accounting for the fact that I must have loved my first wife too. But I did, I know I did. So I suppose I am like Terri in that regard. Terri and Ed." He thought about it and then he went on. "There was a time when I thought I loved my first wife more than life itself. But now I hate her guts. I do. How do you explain that? What happened to that love? What happened to it, is what I'd like to know. I wish someone could tell me. Then there's Ed. Okay, we're back to Ed. He loves Terri so much he tries to kill her and he winds up killing himself." Mel stopped talking and swallowed from his glass. "You guys have been together eighteen months and you love each other. It shows all over you. You glow with it. But you both loved other people before you met each other. You've both been married before, just like us. And you probably loved other people before that too, even. Terri and I have been together five years, been married for four. And the terrible thing, the terrible thing is, but the good thing too, the saving grace, you might say, is that if something happened to one of us—excuse me for saying this—but if something happened to one of us tomorrow I think the other one, the other person, would grieve for a while, you know, but then the surviving party would go out and love again, have someone else soon enough. All this, all of this love we're talking about, it would just be a memory. Maybe not even a memory. Am I wrong? Am I way off base? Because I want you to set me straight if you think I'm wrong. I want to know. I mean, I don't know anything, and I'm the first one to admit it."

"Mel, for God's sake," Terri said. She reached out and took hold of his wrist. "Are you getting drunk? Honey? Are you drunk?"

"Honey, I'm just talking," Mel said. "All right? I don't have to be drunk to say what I think. I mean, we're all just talking, right?" Mel said. He fixed his eyes on her.

"Sweetie, I'm not criticizing," Terri said.

She picked up her glass.

"I'm not on call today," Mel said. "Let me remind you of that. I am not on call," he said.

"Mel, we love you," Laura said.

Mel looked at Laura. He looked at her as if he could not place her, as if she was not the woman she was.

"Love you too, Laura," Mel said. "And you, Nick, love you too. You know something?" Mel said. "You guys are our pals," Mel said.

He picked up his glass.

Mel said, "I was going to tell you about something. I mean, I was going to prove a point. You see, this happened a few months ago, but it's still going on right now, and it ought to make us feel ashamed when we talk like we know what we're talking about when we talk above love."

"Come on now," Terri said. "Don't talk like you're drunk if you're not drunk."

"Just shut up for once in your life," Mel said very quietly. "Will you do me a favor and do that for a minute? So as I was saying, there's this old couple who had this car wreck out on the interstate. A kid hit them and they were all torn to shit and nobody was giving them much chance to pull through."

Terri looked at us and then back at Mel. She seemed anxious, or maybe that's too strong a word.

Mel was handing the bottle around the table.

"I was on call that night," Mel said. "It was May or maybe it was June. Terri and I had just sat down to dinner when the hospital called. There'd been this thing out on the interstate. Drunk kid, teenager, plowed his dad's pickup into this camper with this old couple in it. They were up in their mid-seventies, that couple. The kid—eighteen, nineteen, something—he was DOA. Taken the steering wheel through his sternum. The old couple, they were alive, you understand. I mean, just barely. But they had everything. Multiple fractures, internal injuries, hemorrhaging, contusions, lacerations, the works, and they each of them had themselves concussions. They were in a bad way, believe me. And, of course, their age was two strikes against them. I'd say she was worse off than he was. Ruptured spleen along with everything else. Both kneecaps broken. But they'd been wearing their seatbelts and, God knows, that's what saved them for the time being."

"Folks, this is an advertisement for the National Safety Council," Terri said. "This is your spokesman, Dr. Melvin R. McGinnis, talking." Terri laughed. "Mel," she said, "sometimes you're just too much. But I love you, hon," she said.

"Honey, I love you," Mel said.

He leaned across the table. Terri met him halfway. They kissed.

"Terri's right," Mel said as he settled himself again. "Get those seatbelts on. But seriously, they were in some shape, those oldsters. By the time I got down there, the kid was dead, as I said. He was off in a corner, laid out on a gurney. I took one look at the old couple and told the ER nurse to get me a neurologist and an orthopedic man and a couple of surgeons down there right away."

He drank from his glass. "I'll try to keep this short," he said. "So we took the two of them up to the OR and worked like fuck on them most of the night. They had these incredible reserves, those two. You see that once in a while. So we did everything that could be done, and toward morning we're giving them a fifty-fifty chance, maybe less than that for her. So here they are, still alive the next morning. So, okay, we move them into the ICU, which is where they both kept plugging away at it for two weeks, hitting it better and better on all the scopes. So we transfer them out to their own room."

Mel stopped talking. "Here," he said, "let's drink this cheapo gin the hell up. Then we're going to dinner, right? Terri and I know a new place. That's where we'll go, to this new place we know about. But we're not going until we finish up this cut-rate, lousy gin."

Terri said, "We haven't actually eaten there yet. But it looks good. From the outside, you know."

"I like food," Mel said. "If I had it to do all over again, I'd be a chef, you know? Right, Terri?" Mel said.

He laughed. He fingered the ice in his glass.

"Terri knows," he said. "Terri can tell you. But let me say this. If I could come back again in a different life, a different time and all, you know what? I'd like to come back as a knight. You were pretty safe wearing all that armor. It was all right being a knight until gunpowder and muskets and pistols came along."

"Mel would like to ride a horse and carry a lance," Terri said.

"Carry a woman's scarf with you everywhere," Laura said.

"Or just a woman," Mel said.

"Shame on you," Laura said.

Terri said, "Suppose you came back as a serf. The serfs didn't have it so good in those days," Terri said.

"The serfs never had it good," Mel said. "But I guess even the knights were vessels to someone. Isn't that the way it worked? But then everyone is always a vessel to someone. Isn't that right? Terri? But what I liked about knights, besides their ladies, was that they had that suit of armor, you know, and they couldn't get hurt very easy. No cars in those days, you know? No drunk teenagers to tear into your ass."

"Vassals," Terri said.

"What?" Mel said.

"Vassals," Terri said. "They were called vassals, not vessels."

"Vassals, vessels," Mel said, "what the fuck's the difference? You knew what I meant anyway. All right," Mel said. "So I'm not educated. I learned my stuff. I'm a heart surgeon, sure, but I'm just a mechanic. I go in and I fuck around and I fix things. Shit," Mel said.

"Modesty doesn't become you," Terri said.

"He's just a humble sawbones," I said. "But sometimes they suffocated in all that armor, Mel. They'd even have heart attacks if it got too hot and they were too tired and worn out. I read somewhere that they'd fall off their horses and not be able to get up because they were too tired to stand with all that armor on them. They got trampled by their own horses sometimes."

"That's terrible," Mel said. "That's a terrible thing, Nicky. I guess they'd just lay there and wait until somebody came along and made a shish kebab out of them."

"Some other vessel," Terri said.

"That's right," Mel said. "Some vassal would come along and spear the bastard in the name of love. Or whatever the fuck it was they fought over in those days."

"Same things we fight over these days," Terri said.

Laura said, "Nothing's changed."

The color was still high in Laura's cheeks. Her eyes were bright. She brought her glass to her lips.

Mel poured himself another drink. He looked at the label closely as if studying a long row of numbers. Then he slowly put the bottle down on the table and slowly reached for the tonic water.

"What about the old couple?" Laura said. "You didn't finish that story you started."

Laura was having a hard time lighting her cigarette. Her matches kept going out.

The sunshine inside the room was different now, changing, getting thinner. But the leaves outside the window were still shimmering, and I stared at the pattern they made on the panes and on the Formica counter. They weren't the same patterns, of course.

"What about the old couple?" I said.

"Older but wiser," Terri said.

Mel stared at her.

Terri said, "Go on with your story, hon. I was only kidding. Then what happened?"

"Terri, sometimes," Mel said.

"Please, Mel," Terri said. "Don't always be so serious, sweetie. Can't you take a joke?"

"Where's the joke?" Mel said.

He held his glass and gazed steadily at his wife.

"What happened?" Laura said.

Mel fastened his eyes on Laura. He said, "Laura, if I didn't have Terri and if I didn't love her so much, and if Nick wasn't my best friend, I'd fall in love with you, I'd carry you off, honey," he said.

"Tell your story," Terri said. "Then we'll go to that new place, okay?"

"Okay," Mel said. "Where was I?" he said. He stared at the table and then he began again.

"I dropped in to see each of them every day, sometimes twice a day if I was up doing other calls anyway. Casts and bandages, head to foot, the both of them. You know, you've seen it in the movies. That's just the way they looked, just like in the movies. Little eye-holes and nose-holes and mouth-holes. And she had to have her legs slung up on top of it. Well, the husband was very depressed for the longest while. Even after he found out that his wife was going to pull through, he was still very depressed. Not about the accident, though. I mean, the accident was one thing, but it wasn't everything. I'd get up to his mouth-hole, you know, and he'd say no, it wasn't the accident exactly but it was because he couldn't see her through his eye-holes. He said that was what was making him feel so bad. Can you imagine? I'm telling you, the man's heart was breaking because he couldn't turn his goddamn head and *see* his goddamn wife."

Mel looked around the table and shook his head at what he was going to say.

"I mean, it was killing the old fart just because he couldn't *look* at the fucking woman."

We all looked at Mel.

"Do you see what I'm saying?" he said.

Maybe we were a little drunk by then. I know it was hard keeping things in focus. The light was draining out of the room, going back through the window where it had come from. Yet nobody made a move to get up from the table to turn on the overhead light.

"Listen," Mel said. "Let's finish this fucking gin. There's about enough left here for one shooter all around. Then let's go eat. Let's go to the new place."

"He's depressed," Terri said. "Mel, why don't you take a pill?"

Mel shook his head. "I've taken everything there is."

"We all need a pill now and then," I said.

"Some people are born needing them," Terri said.

She was using her finger to rub at something on the table. Then she stopped rubbing.

"I think I want to call my kids," Mel said. "Is that all right with everybody? I'll call my kids," he said.

Terri said, "What if Marjorie answers the phone? You guys, you've heard us on the subject of Marjorie? Honey, you know you don't want to talk to Marjorie. It'll make you feel even worse."

"I don't want to talk to Marjorie," Mel said. "But I want to talk to my kids."

"There isn't a day goes by that Mel doesn't say he wishes she'd get married again. Or else die," Terri said. "For one thing," Terri said, "she's bankrupting us. Mel says it's just to spite him that she won't get married again. She has a boyfriend who lives with her and the kids, so Mel is supporting the boyfriend too."

"She's allergic to bees," Mel said. "If I'm not praying she'll get married again, I'm praying she'll get herself stung to death by a swarm of fucking bees."

"Shame on you," Laura said.

"Bzzzzzzz," Mel said, turning his fingers into bees and buzzing them at Terri's throat. Then he let his hands drop all the way to his sides.

"She's vicious," Mel said. "Sometimes I think I'll go up there dressed like a beekeeper. You know, that hat that's like a helmet with the plate that comes down over your face, the big gloves, and the padded coat? I'll knock on the door and let loose a hive of bees in the house. But first I'd make sure the kids were out, of course."

He crossed one leg over the other. It seemed to take him a lot of time to do it. Then he put both feet on the floor and leaned forward, elbows on the table, his chin cupped in his hands.

"Maybe I won't call the kids, after all. Maybe it isn't such a hot idea. Maybe we'll just go eat. How does that sound?"

"Sounds fine to me," I said. "Eat or not eat. Or keep drinking. I could head right on out into the sunset."

"What does that mean, honey?" Laura said.

"It just means what I said," I said. "It means I could just keep going. That's all it means."

"I could eat something myself," Laura said. "I don't think I've ever been so hungry in my life. Is there something to nibble on?"

"I'll put out some cheese and crackers," Terri said.

But Terri just sat there. She did not get up to get anything.

Mel turned his glass over. He spilled it out on the table.

"Gin's gone," Mel said.

Terri said, "Now what?"

I could hear my heart beating. I could hear everyone's heart. I could hear the human noise we sat there making, not one of us moving, not even when the room went dark.

[1981]

Terry Castle

Terry Castle (b. 1953) is a prize-winning essayist and a professor of English at Stanford University. She won the William Riley Parker Prize of the Modern Language Association in 1985 and the Crompton-Noll Prize of the Lesbian and Gay Caucus of the Modern Language Association in 1993. She has also been nominated for the PEN Spielvogel-Diamondstein Award for the Art of the Essay. She has written five books including Clarissa's Ciphers: Meaning and Disruption in Richardson's 'Clarissa' *(1982)* Masquerade and Civilization: The Carnivalesque in Eighteenth-Century English Culture and Fiction *(1986), and* The Female Thermometer: Eighteenth-Century Culture and the Invention of the Uncanny *(1995). Castle calls lesbianism the "ghost" of sexual love between women; yet, she also views lesbianism as a central theme in the imagination of the Western world. "First Ed," a personal essay, was published in* The Apparitional Lesbian: Female Homosexuality and Modern Culture *(1993), a collection of essays that explores lesbianism and its role in Western literature and life.*

First Ed

First, Ed—who, for all the sense of drama her memory evokes, is surrounded with a certain haze, a nimbus of uncertainty. Did our encounter, the one I remember, take place in 1963 or 1964? It must, I think, have been 1964, if only because the Dixie Cups' "Chapel of Love" (a crucial clue) was on the radio that summer, lilting out of dashboards all over San Diego, along with "Don't Worry Baby," "Pretty Woman," and "I Want to Hold Your Hand." It was the summer that my father's large brown and white Oldsmobile got a cracked block from the heat, and his hair, which had gone gray after my mother divorced him, went completely white, like Marie Antoinette's. A few months later the Dodgers, resplendent with Koufax, won the Series, and I and my fellow sixth-graders, transistors in hand, celebrated with loud huzzahs on the rough gravel playgrounds of Whittier Elementary School.

All during the long hot months of vacation, I went once a week for a swimming lesson at the old YWCA downtown at 10th and C Street. We had recently returned (my mother, my younger sister, and I) from two years on the English coast, where we had lived in a gloomy village near Dover. My British-born mother had taken us there—in a flurry of misguided nostalgia and emotional confusion—

Reprinted from *The Apparitional Lesbian: Female Homosexuality and Modern Culture*, (1995), Columbia University Press.

immediately after her divorce in 1961, and we had stayed on, in a strange state of immobility and shared melancholia, until mid-1963. In the summer of 1964, however, things seemed better. While my sister and I reaccustomed ourselves to the unfamiliar sunshine, my mother exulted in being back in California, in living as a "bachelorette" (with two children) in the pink Buena Vista apartments, and in the hope—not yet dashed by various Jamesian revelations—of her imminent marriage to the handsome Chuck, the mustachioed ensign in the Navy with whom she had committed the sweetest of adulteries before her divorce.

My mother had been a swimming instructor for the Y during the ten years she had been married to my father, and the organization kept her loyalty, being associated with water, freedom, light, pools, and "living in San Diego"—with everything, indeed, that she had dreamed of as a teenager working for the gasworks in St. Albans. She herself had taken a number of classes at the downtown Y: the intermediate and advanced swim course, synchronized swimming, and beginning and advanced lifeguard training, during which she learned to divest herself of numerous layers of clothing, including laced snow boots, while submerged in eight feet of water. Despite my mother's demonstrated aquatic skills, however, I adamantly refused to let her teach me any of them, and remained, at the relatively advanced age of ten, a coy nonswimmer. After several abortive sessions at the bathroom sink, during which she tried to make me open my eyes under water, it became clear that I was not going to learn anything under her tutelage, but would require instruction from some more neutral party. Hence my introduction to the Y, the children's evening swim program, and the delicious orchestrated flutterings of breast, elbow, and ankle.

The YWCA was an antiquated building by southern California standards—Julia Morganish, from the teens or twenties, though not a work of her hand. It preserved the dowdy grandeur of turn-of-the-century California women's buildings, manifest in its square white facade, Mission-style touches, and cool, cavernous interior. Of the actual decor of the building, I remember little: only, vaguely, some seedy fifties leatherette furniture parked at odd angles in the reception area, peeling bulletin boards, the ancient candy machine expelling Paydays and Snickers with a frightful death rattle, and the small front office staffed—inevitably—by a middle aged, short-haired woman in slacks. The place had an interesting air of desolation: various lost or ill-fitting souls lingered in the front area especially—off-duty sailors, people speaking Spanish, Negroes and Filipinas, mysterious solitary women. I never saw any of the guest rooms, and did not know that they existed: it would not have occurred to me that anyone might actually live there.

The indoor pool was deep in the netherworld of the building, seemingly underground—a greenish, Bayreuthian extravagance, reeking of chlorine and steam. Entering from the women's locker room, one found oneself immediately at one of the pool's deep-end corners. A wobbly diving board jutted out here in dangerous invitation, while at the opposite end a set of pale scalloped steps beckoned to the less adventurous. Running around the pool on all sides was an ornate white tile gutter, cheerfully decorated—by the same wayward deco hand, presumably, that had done the steps—with tiny mosaic flowers and swastikas. The water itself was cloudy, awash with dead moths and floating Band-Aids, but nonetheless, in its foggy Byzantine way, also warm-seeming and attractive. A slippery tiled walkway, inset with more flowers and swastikas and the imprinted words DO NOT RUN, completed the scene. Along this elevated platform our blond-haired teacher, an athletic woman named Pam, would slap up and down in bathing suit and bare feet, calling out instructions in a plaintive Midwestern tongue.

We were five or six in all, a sprinkling of little girls in cotton suits with elastic waists, and one or two even smaller boys in minuscule trunks. Under Pam's guidance we soon mastered the basics: the dog paddle, a variety of elementary crawls and backstrokes, flapping sidestrokes, "sculling" and "treading water"—all with much gasping and excitement. It was on one of these occasions, while struggling to float on my back without inhaling water, that I must first have seen Ed. The ceiling over the pool was high up, some thirty or forty feet, with tall windows of opaque glass near the roof line, through which a few dim green rays of evening sunlight would sometimes penetrate to the fluorescent fog below. A dusty balcony overhung the pool at this level, stacked with seldom-used folding chairs for the spectators who came to observe the water ballet displays put on by the synchronized swimming class. Ed stood up there aloft, along with a few seamen in whites, waiting for the adult free swim hour that immediately followed our class.

Even from my unusual angle I could see that Ed was spectacularly good-looking—in a hoodish fifties way that had not yet, by mid-1964, been utterly superseded by the incoming styles of the era. I might grace my bedroom bulletin board with the toothy images of John, Paul, George, and Ringo, but Ed's "look" (as I knew even then) was far more compelling. Indeed I felt oddly giddy those times when she met my gaze—as though our positions had reversed, water and air had changed places, and I was the one looking down from above. She wore men's clothes of a decade earlier, Sears and Roebuck style, the tightest of black pants (with a discreet fly), a dark leather belt and white shirt, a thin striped tie, and, as I saw later, the same pointy-toed black dress shoes worn by the Mexican "bad boys" at Clairemont High School, down the street from the Buena Vista apartments. Her hair was excessively, almost frighteningly groomed into a narrow scandalous pompadour, and had been oiled with brilliantine to a rich black-brown, against which her face stood out with stark and ravishing paleness. She appeared to be in her late twenties or early thirties—definitely "old" to me—though something about the drastic formality of her costume also gave her the look of a teenage boy, one dressed up, perhaps, for a senior prom. She spoke to no one, smoked a cigarette, and seemed, despite her great beauty, consumed by sadness. She had a thin face of the sort I would later find irresistible in women.

One evening, more sultry than usual, my mother, who normally dropped me off and picked me up after class in the front foyer, was unable to collect me, owing to some sudden disorder in the radiator of our bulbous green Studebaker. My teacher, Pam, and her mother, the gamy old Peg, a short tanned woman who wore pants and also taught swimming classes at the Y, agreed to drive me home to Clairemont in their car. As soon as they had closed up the office we were to leave.

I had already finished changing and sat by myself in the locker room, waiting for my ride, when Ed came in. The other little girls were long gone. The floor was still wet with the footprints of the departed; the thick damp air hung about like a dream. At the same time everything seemed to open up, as if I—or she and I together—had suddenly entered a clearing in a forest. Ed said nothing, yet seemed, in some distant way, to recognize me. I sat still, not knowing where to go. She scrutinized me ambiguously for a few moments. Then, as if some complex agreement had been reached between us, she began to strip away, vertiginously, the emblems of her manhood.

Ed, Ed, my first, my only undressing. She moved gracefully, like a Pierrot, her pallid face a mask in the dim light. She removed her jacket and unbuckled her belt first, laying them carefully on the bench next to me. Then she slipped off her shoes and socks. I gazed down at her bare feet. Her eyes met mine and looked away. Then she loosened her tie with one hand, and pulled it off, followed by her heavy cuff links. Glancing again in my direction, she began to unbutton her shirt, twisting her torso in an uneasy fashion as she did so. She wore, heart-stoppingly, a woman's white brassiere. This she unhooked slowly from behind, and watching me intently now, let her breasts fall forward. Her breasts were full and had dark nipples. She stopped to flick back some wet-looking strands of hair that had come down, Dion-like, over her brow. Then rather more quickly, with a practiced masculine gesture, she began to undo her fly. She removed her trousers, revealing a pair of loose Jockey shorts. She hesitated a moment before uncovering the soft hairiness beneath—that mystery against which I would thrust my head, blindly, in years to come. I stared childishly at the curly black V between her legs. She took off her watch, a man's gold Timex, last of all.

Her transfiguration was not complete, of course: now she took out a rusty-looking woman's swimsuit from a metal locker and began, uncannily, stepping into it. She became a woman. Then she folded up her clothes neatly and put them away. Still she did not speak—nor, it seemed, did she ever remove her eyes from mine.

I am aware, too late, how almost painfully sexy Ed was—and perhaps, at the level of hallucination, intended to be. Even now I seem to see the disquieting movement of her chest and shoulders as she leaned over the bench between us, the damp pressed-in look of her thighs when she began to pull the resistant nylon swimsuit up her body, her breasts poignantly hanging, then confined, with the aid of diffident fingers, in the suits's stiff built-in cups. Indeed, I seem to be assisting her, leaning into her, even (slyly) inhaling her. She bends slightly at the knees, balances herself with one hand against the locker, begins to hold me around the neck—but this is a fantasy of the present. In that moment my feelings were of a far more polite, delicate, even sentimental nature. Astonishment gave way to, resolved into, embarrassment. When at last Ed drew on, over the dark crown of her head, a flowered Esther Williams-style bathing cap—the final clownish touch of femininity—I felt, obscurely, the pathos of her transformation: she had become somehow less than herself. But her eyes, with their mute, impassive challenge, never faltered. They seemed to say, I own you now. And I realized too, though I had no words for it at the time, how much I adored her, and what tumult lay ahead.

The other women came and got me soon enough—Ed must have gone—for the next thing I remember is sitting deep in the well of the backseat of my teacher's Plymouth, the warm night breeze blowing in my face, and the lights of downtown glinting in the background as we drove away. Pam and her mother talked in a desultory, friendly way in the front seat. They used slang with each other and swore softly—almost as if I weren't there, or were much older, which I enjoyed. I looked at the back of their heads, at Pam's blond nape and her mother's cropped gray thatch, while the sounds of the radio—KCBQ—wafted sweetly through the summer air:

> We're going to the chapel
> And we're
> Gonna get ma-a-a-rried
>
> Going to the Chapel of Love

Then, as we wound our way down 101 through Balboa Park, under the tall bridge by the zoo, the two of them began—as if to the music—to talk about Ed. They seemed to know her; they spoke almost tenderly, referring to her by name. Ed looked more like a guy than ever, my teacher remarked. The words hung about softly in the air. I began listening hard, as I did at school. Her mother, Peg, reflected for a moment, then glanced back and smiled at me in the dark, enigmatically, before murmuring in reply, "Yeah, but she don't have the superior plumbing system." And into the night we sped away.

Many years later, when I had just turned twenty-two, and lay in bed with a much older woman with whom I was greatly in love, I told the story of Ed, this story, for the first time. I was already getting on Helen's nerves by that point; she tried to find the fastest way through my postcoital maunderings. Ed was, she concluded, "just an externalization." As she often reminded me, Helen had spent fifty thousand dollars a year for eight years of psychoanalysis in Chicago. She wore her hair in a long braid down her back to represent, she told me, her "missing part." She was thin and dark, and, when she wasn't teaching, wore a man's watch and lumberman's jacket. My mother, she said, "sounded like a hysteric." A lot of things happened later, and I finally got to resenting Helen back, but that's a winter, not a summer story.

Joyce Carol Oates

Joyce Carol Oates (b. 1938) is a writer, critic, and professor at Princeton University. She majored in English at Syracuse University and received an MA from the University of Wisconsin in 1961. After she discovered by chance that a story she'd written had been noted in the honor roll of The Best American Short Stories, *she put together her first book of stories,* By the North Gate, *in 1963. Today, she has published nearly 70 books, including* Heat and Other Stories *(1991),* Haunted: Tales of the Grotesque *(1994), and* Will You Always Love Me? *(1996). First published in* Epoch *in 1966, "Where Are You Going, Where Have You Been?" also appeared in the* Best American Short Stories *of 1967 and* Prize Stories: The O'Henry Awards 1968. *Additionally, it was made into the film* Smooth Talk. *Oates based this story on an article in* Life *magazine about a serial murderer in Tucson, Arizona, known as "The Pied Piper of Tucson." In* The Story and Its Writer *Ann Charters quotes Oates as saying that this story has been "constantly misunderstood by one generation, and intuitively understood by another," and the story deals with a human being "struggling heroically to define personal identity in the face of incredible opposition, even in the face of death itself" (Charters 591).*

Where Are You Going, Where Have You Been?

For Bob Dylan

Her name was Connie. She was fifteen and she had a quick nervous giggling habit of craning her neck to glance into mirrors, or checking other people's faces to make sure her own was all right. Her mother, who noticed everything and knew everything and who hadn't much reason any longer to look at her own face, always scolded Connie about it. "Stop gawking at yourself, who are you? You think you're so pretty?" she would say. Connie would raise her eyebrows at these familiar complaints and look right through her mother, into a shadowy vision of herself as she was right at that moment: she knew she was pretty and that was everything. Her mother had been pretty once too, if you could believe those old snapshots in the album, but now her looks were gone and that was why she was always after Connie.

Reprinted from *The Wheel of Love*, (1970), John Hawkins & Associates, Inc..

"Why don't you keep your room clean like your sister? How've you got your hair fixed—what the hell stinks? Hair spray? You don't see your sister using that junk."

Her sister June was twenty-four and still lived at home. She was a secretary in the high school Connie attended, and if that wasn't bad enough—with her in the same building—she was so plain and chunky and steady that Connie had to hear her praised all the time by her mother and her mother's sisters. June did this, June did that, she saved money and helped clean the house and cooked and Connie couldn't do a thing, her mind was all filled with trashy daydreams. Their father was away at work most of the time and when he came home he wanted supper and he read the newspaper at supper and after supper he went to bed. He didn't bother talking much to them, but around his bent head Connie's mother kept picking at her until Connie wished her mother was dead and she herself was dead and it was all over. "She makes me want to throw up sometimes," she complained to her friends. She had a high, breathless, amused voice which made everything she said a little forced, whether it was sincere or not.

There was one good thing: June went places with girl friends of hers, girls who were just as plain and steady as she, and so when Connie wanted to do that her mother had no objections. The father of Connie's best girl friend drove the girls the three miles to town and left them off at a shopping plaza, so that they could walk through the stores or go to a movie, and when he came to pick them up again at eleven he never bothered to ask what they had done.

They must have been familiar sights, walking around that shopping plaza in their shorts and flat ballerina slippers that always scuffed the sidewalk, with charm bracelets jingling on their thin wrists; they would lean together to whisper and laugh secretly if someone passed by who amused or interested them. Connie had long dark blond hair that drew anyone's eye to it, and she wore part of it pulled up on her head and puffed out and the rest of it she let fall down her back. She wore a pullover jersey blouse that looked one way when she was at home and another way when she was away from home. Everything about her had two sides to it, one for home and one for anywhere that was not home: her walk that could be childlike and bobbing, or languid enough to make anyone think she was hearing music in her head, her mouth which was pale and smirking most of the time, but bright and pink on these evenings out, her laugh which was cynical and drawling at home—"Ha, ha, very funny"—but high-pitched and nervous anywhere else, like the jingling of the charms on her bracelet.

Sometimes they did go shopping or to a movie, but sometimes they went across the highway, ducking fast across the busy road, to a drive-in restaurant where older kids hung out. The restaurant was shaped like a big bottle, though squatter than a real bottle, and on its cap was a revolving figure of a grinning boy who held a hamburger aloft. One night in midsummer they ran across, breathless with daring, and right away someone leaned out a car window and invited them over, but it was just a boy from high school they didn't like. It made them feel good to be able to ignore him. They went up through the maze of parked and cruising cars to the bright-lit, fly-infested restaurant, their faces pleased and expectant as if they were entering a sacred building that loomed out of the night to give them what haven and what blessing they yearned for. They sat at the counter and crossed their legs at the ankles, their thin shoulders rigid with excitement and listened to the music that made everything so good: the music was always in the background like music at a church service, it was something to depend upon.

A boy named Eddie came in to talk with them. He sat backwards on his stool, turning himself jerkily around in semi-circles and then stopping and turning again, and after a while he asked Connie if she would like something to eat. She said she did and so she tapped her friend's arm on her way out—her friend pulled her face up into a brave droll look—and Connie said she would meet her at eleven, across the way. "I just hate to leave her like that," Connie said earnestly, but the boy said that she wouldn't be alone for long. So they went out to his car and on the way Connie couldn't help but let her eyes wander over the windshields and faces all around her, her face gleaming with the joy that had nothing to do with Eddie or even this place; it might have been the music. She drew her shoulders up and sucked in her breath with the pure pleasure of being alive, and just at that moment she happened to glance at a face just a few feet from hers. It was a boy with shaggy black hair, in a convertible jalopy painted gold. He stared at her and then his lips widened into a grin. Connie slit her eyes at him and turned away, but she couldn't help glancing back and there he was still watching her. He wagged a finger and laughed and said, "Gonna get you, baby," and Connie turned away again without Eddie noticing anything.

She spent three hours with him, at the restaurant where they ate hamburgers and drank Cokes in wax cups that were always sweating, and then down an alley a mile or so away, and when he left her off at five to eleven only the movie house was still open at the plaza. Her girl friend was there, talking with a boy. When Connie came up the two girls smiled at each other and Connie said, "How was the movie?" and the girl said, "*You* should know." They rode off with the girl's father, sleepy and pleased, and Connie couldn't help but look at the darkened shopping plaza with its big empty parking lot and its signs that were faded and ghostly now, and over at the drive-in restaurant where cars were still circling tirelessly. She couldn't hear the music at this distance.

Next morning June asked her how the movie was and Connie said, "So-so."

She and that girl and occasionally another girl went out several times a week that way, and the rest of the time Connie spent around the house—it was summer vacation—getting in her mother's way and thinking, dreaming, about the boys she met. But all the boys fell back and dissolved into a single face that was not even a face, but an idea, a feeling, mixed up with the urgent insistent pounding of the music and the humid night air of July. Connie's mother kept dragging her back to the daylight by finding things for her to do or saying suddenly, "What's this about the Pettinger girl?"

And Connie would say nervously, "Oh, her. That dope." She always drew thick clear lines between herself and such girls, and her mother was simple and kindly enough to believe her. Her mother was so simple, Connie thought, that it was maybe cruel to fool her so much. Her mother went scuffling around the house in old bedroom slippers and complained over the telephone to one sister about the other, then the other called up and the two of them complained about the third one. If June's name was mentioned her mother's tone was approving, and if Connie's name was mentioned it was disapproving. This did not really mean she disliked Connie and actually Connie thought that her mother preferred her to June because she was prettier, but the two of them kept up a pretense of exasperation, a sense that they were tugging and struggling over something of little value to either of them. Sometimes, over coffee, they were almost friends, but something would come up—some vexation that was like a fly buzzing suddenly around their heads—and their faces went hard with contempt.

One Sunday Connie got up at eleven—none of them bothered with church—and washed her hair so that it could dry all day long, in the sun. Her parents and sister were going to a barbecue at an aunt's house and Connie said no, she wasn't interested, rolling her eyes, to let mother know just what she thought of it. "Stay home alone then," her mother said sharply. Connie sat out back in a lawn chair and watched them drive away, her father quiet and bald, hunched around so that he could back the car out, her mother with a look that was still angry and not at all softened through the windshield, and in the back seat poor old June all dressed up as if she didn't know what a barbecue was, with all the running yelling kids and the flies. Connie sat with her eyes closed in the sun, dreaming and dazed with the warmth about her as if this were a kind of love, the caresses of love, and her mind slipped over onto thoughts of the boy she had been with the night before and how nice he had been, how sweet it always was, not the way someone like June would suppose but sweet, gentle, the way it was in movies and promised in songs; and when she opened her eyes she hardly knew where she was, the back yard ran off into weeds and a fenceline of trees and behind it the sky was perfectly blue and still. The asbestos "ranch house" that was now three years old startled her—it looked small. She shook her head as if to get awake.

It was too hot. She went inside the house and turned on the radio to drown out the quiet. She sat on the edge of her bed, barefoot, and listened for an hour and a half to a program called XYZ Sunday Jamboree, record after record of hard, fast, shrieking songs she sang along with, interspersed by exclamations from "Bobby King": "An' look here you girls at Napoleon's—Son and Charley want you to pay real close attention to this song coming up!"

And Connie paid close attention herself, bathed in a glow of slow-pulsed joy that seemed to rise mysteriously out of the music itself and lay languidly about the airless little room, breathed in and breathed out with each gentle rise and fall of her chest.

After a while she heard a car coming up the drive. She sat up at once, startled, because it couldn't be her father so soon. The gravel kept crunching all the way in from the road—the driveway was long—and Connie ran to the window. It was a car she didn't know. It was an open jalopy, painted a bright gold that caught the sun opaquely. Her heart began to pound and her fingers snatched at her hair, checking it, and she whispered "Christ. Christ," wondering how bad she looked. The car came to a stop at the side door and the horn sounded four short taps as if this were a signal Connie knew.

She went into the kitchen and approached the door slowly, then hung out the screen door, her bare toes curling down off the step. There were two boys in the car and now she recognized the driver: he had shaggy, shabby black hair that looked crazy as a wig and he was grinning at her.

"I ain't late, am I?" he said.

"Who the hell do you think you are?" Connie said.

"Toldja I'd be out, didn't I?"

"I don't even know who you are."

She spoke sullenly, careful to show no interest or pleasure, and he spoke in a fast bright monotone. Connie looked past him to the other boy, taking her time. He had fair brown hair, with a lock that fell onto his forehead. His sideburns gave him a fierce, embarrassed look, but so far he hadn't even bothered to glance at her. Both boys wore sunglasses. The driver's glasses were metallic and mirrored everything in miniature.

"You wanta come for a ride?" he said.

Connie smirked and let her hair fall loose over one shoulder.

"Don'tcha like my car? New paint job," he said. "Hey."

"What?"

"You're cute."

She pretended to fidget, chasing flies away from the door.

"Don'tcha believe me, or what?" he said.

"Look, I don't even know who you are," Connie said in disgust.

"Hey, Ellie's got a radio, see. Mine's broke down." He lifted his friend's arm and showed her the little transistor the boy was holding, and now Connie began to hear the music. It was the same program that was playing inside the house.

"Bobby King?" she said.

"I listen to him all the time. I think he's great."

"He's kind of great," Connie said reluctantly.

"Listen, that guy's *great*. He knows where the action is."

Connie blushed a little, because the glasses made it impossible for her to see just what this boy was looking at. She couldn't decide if she liked him or if he was just a jerk, and so she dawdled in the doorway and wouldn't come down or go back inside. She said, "What's all that stuff painted on your car?"

"Can'tcha read it?" He opened the door very carefully, as if he was afraid it might fall off. He slid out just as carefully, planting his feet firmly on the ground, the tiny metallic world in his glasses slowing down like gelatine hardening and in the midst of it Connie's bright green blouse. "This here is my name, to begin with," he said. ARNOLD FRIEND was written in tar-like black letters on the side, with a drawing of a round grinning face that reminded Connie of a pumpkin, except it wore sunglasses. "I wanta introduce myself, I'm Arnold Friend and that's my real name and I'm gonna be your friend, honey, and inside the car's Ellie Oscar, he's kinda shy." Ellie brought his transistor up to his shoulder and balanced it there. "Now these numbers are a secret code, honey," Arnold Friend explained. He read off the numbers 33, 19, 17 and raised his eyebrows at her to see what she thought of that, but she didn't think much of it. The left rear fender had been smashed and around it was written, on the gleaming gold background: DONE BY CRAZY WOMAN DRIVER. Connie had to laugh at that. Arnold Friend was pleased at her laughter and looked up at her. "Around the other side's a lot more—you wanta come and see them?"

"No."
"Why not?"
"Why should I?"
"Don'tcha wanta see what's on the car? Don'tcha wanta go for a ride?"
"I don't know."
"Why not?"
"I got things to do."
"Like what?"
"Things."

He laughed as if she had said something funny. He slapped his thighs. He was standing in a strange way, leaning back against the car as if he were balancing himself. He wasn't tall, only an inch or so taller than she would be if she came down to him. Connie liked the way he was dressed, which was the way all of them dressed: tight faded jeans stuffed into black, scuffed boots, a belt that pulled his waist in and showed how lean he was, and a white pull-over shirt that was a little soiled and showed the hard small muscles of his arms and shoulders. He looked as if he probably did hard work, lifting and carrying things. Even his neck looked muscular. And his face was a familiar face, somehow: the jaw and chin and cheeks slightly darkened, because he hadn't shaved for a day or two, and the nose long and hawk-like, sniffing as if she were a treat he was going to gobble up and it was all a joke.

"Connie, you ain't telling the truth. This is your day set aside for a ride with me and you know it," he said, still laughing. The way he straightened and recovered from his fit of laughing showed that it had been all fake.

"How do you know what my name is?" she said suspiciously.

"It's Connie."

"Maybe and maybe not."

"I know my Connie," he said, wagging his finger. Now she remembered him even better, back at the restaurant, and her cheeks warmed at the thought of how she sucked in her breath just at the moment she passed him—how she must have looked to him. And he had remembered her. "Ellie and I come out here especially for you," he said. "Ellie can sit in back. How about it?"

"Where?"

"Where what?"

"Where're we going?"

He looked at her. He took off the sunglasses and she saw how pale the skin around his eyes was, like holes that were not in shadow but instead in light. His eyes were like chips of broken glass that catch the light in an amiable way. He smiled. It was as if the idea of going for a ride somewhere, to some place, was a new idea to him.

"Just for a ride, Connie sweetheart."

"I never said my name was Connie," she said.

"But I know what it is. I know your name and all about you, lots of things," Arnold Friend said. He had not moved yet but stood still leaning back against the side of his jalopy. "I took a special interest in you, such a pretty girl, and found out all about you like I know your parents and sister are gone somewheres and I know where and how long they're going to be gone, and I know who you were with last night, and your best friend's name is Betty. Right?"

He spoke in a simple lilting voice, exactly as if he were reciting the words to a song. His smile assured her that everything was fine. In the car Ellie turned up the volume on his radio and did not bother to look around at them.

"Ellie can sit in the back seat," Arnold Friend said. He indicated his friend with a casual jerk of his chin, as if Ellie did not count and she could not bother with him.

"How'd you find out all that stuff?" Connie said.

"Listen: Betty Schultz and Tony Fitch and Jimmy Pettinger and Nancy Pettinger," he said, in a chant. "Raymond Stanley and Bob Hutter—"

"Do you know all those kids?"

"I know everybody."

"Look, you're kidding. You're not from around here."

"Sure."

"But—how come we never saw you before?"

"Sure you saw me before," he said. He looked down at his boots, as if he were a little offended. "You just don't remember."

"I guess I'd remember you," Connie said.

"Yeah?" He looked up at this, beaming. He was pleased. He began to mark time with the music from Ellie's radio, tapping his fists lightly together. Connie looked away from his smile to the car, which was painted so bright it almost hurt her eyes to look at it. She looked at that name, ARNOLD FRIEND. And up at the front fender was an expression that was familiar—MAN THE FLYING SAUCERS. It was an expression kids had used the year before, but didn't use this year. She looked at it for a while as if the words meant something to her that she did not yet know.

"What're you thinking about? Huh?" Arnold Friend demanded. "Not worried about your hair blowing around in the car, are you?"

"No."

"Think I maybe can't drive good?"

"How do I know?"

"You're a hard girl to handle. How come?" he said. "Don't you know I'm your friend? Didn't you see me put my sign in the air when you walked by?"

"What sign?"

"My sign." And he drew an X in the air, leaning out toward her. They were maybe ten feet apart. After his hand fell back to his side the X was still in the air, almost visible. Connie let the screen door close and stood perfectly still inside it, listening to the music from her radio and the boy's blend together. She stared at Arnold Friend. He stood there so stiffly relaxed, pretending to be relaxed, with one hand idly on the door handle as if he were keeping himself up that way and had no intention of ever moving again. She recognized most things about him, the tight jeans that showed his thighs and buttocks and the greasy leather boots and the tight shirt, and even that slippery friendly smile of his, that sleepy dreamy smile that all the boys used to get across ideas they didn't want to put into words. She recognized all this and also the singsong way he talked, slightly mocking, kidding, but serious and a little melancholy, and she recognized the way he tapped one fist against the other in homage to the perpetual music behind him. But all these things did not come together.

She said suddenly, "Hey, how old are you?"

His smile faded. She could see then that he wasn't a kid, he was much older—thirty, maybe more. At this knowledge her heart began to pound faster.

"That's a crazy thing to ask. Can'tcha see I'm your own age?"

"Like hell you are."

"Or maybe a coupla years older, I'm eighteen."

"Eighteen?" she said doubtfully.

He grinned to reassure her and lines appeared at the corners of his mouth. His teeth were big and white. He grinned so broadly his eyes became slits and she saw how thick the lashes were, thick and black as if painted with a black tar-like material. Then he seemed to become embarrassed, abruptly, and looked over his shoulder at Ellie. "*Him,* he's crazy," he said. "Ain't he a riot, he's a nut, a real character." Ellie was still listening to the music. His sunglasses told nothing about what he was thinking. He wore a bright orange shirt unbuttoned halfway to show his chest, which was a pale, bluish chest and not muscular like Arnold Friend's. His shirt collar was turned up all around and the very tips of the collar pointed out past his chin as if they were protecting him. He was pressing the transistor radio up against his ear and sat there in a kind of daze, right in the sun.

"He's kinda strange," Connie said.

"Hey, she says you're kinda strange! Kinda strange!" Arnold Friend cried. He pounded on the car to get Ellie's attention. Ellie turned for the first time and Connie saw with shock that he wasn't a kid either—he had a fair, hairless face, cheeks reddened slightly as if the veins grew too close to the surface of his skin, the face of a forty-year-old baby. Connie felt a wave of dizziness rise in her at this sight and she stared at him as if waiting for something to change the shock of the moment, make it all right again. Ellie's lips kept shaping words, mumbling along with the words blasting his ear.

"Maybe you two better go away," Connie said faintly.

"What? How come?" Arnold Friend cried. "We come out here to take you for a ride. It's Sunday." He had the voice of the man on the radio now. It was the same voice, Connie thought. "Don'tcha know it's Sunday all day and honey, no matter who you were with last night today you're with Arnold Friend and don't you forget it!—Maybe you better step out here," he said, and this last was in a different voice. It was a little flatter, as if the heat was finally getting to him.

"No. I got things to do."

"Hey."

"You two better leave."

"We ain't leaving until you come with us."

"Like hell I am—"

"Connie, don't fool around with me. I mean—I mean, don't fool *around,*" he said, shaking his head. He laughed incredulously. He placed his sunglasses on top of his head, carefully, as if he were indeed wearing a wig, and brought the stems down behind his ears. Connie stared at him, another wave of dizziness and fear rising in her so that for a moment he wasn't even in focus but was just a blur, standing there against his gold car, and she had the idea that he had driven up the driveway all right but had come from nowhere before that and belonged nowhere and that everything about him and even the music that was so familiar to her was only half real.

"If my father comes and sees you—"

"He ain't coming. He's at a barbecue."

"How do you know that?"

"Aunt Tillie's. Right now they're—uh—they're drinking. Sitting around," he said vaguely, squinting as if he were staring all the way to town and over to Aunt Tillie's back yard. Then the vision seemed to clear and he nodded energetically. "Yeah. Sitting around. There's your sister in a blue dress, huh? And high heels, the poor sad bitch—nothing like you, sweetheart! And your mother's helping some fat woman with the corn, they're cleaning the corn—husking the corn—"

"What fat woman?" Connie cried.

"How do I know what fat woman. I don't know every goddamn fat woman in the world!" Arnold Friend laughed.

"Oh, that's Mrs. Hornby. . . . Who invited her?" Connie said. She felt a little light-headed. Her breath was coming quickly.

"She's too fat. I don't like them fat. I like them the way you are, honey," he said, smiling sleepily at her. They stared at each other for a while, through the screen door. He said softly, "Now what you're going to do is this: you're going to come out that door. You're going to sit up front with me and Ellie's going to sit in the back, the hell with Ellie, right? This isn't Ellie's date. You're my date. I'm your lover, honey."

"What? You're crazy—"

"Yes, I'm your lover. You don't know what that is but you will," he said. "I know that too. I know all about you. But look: it's real nice and you couldn't ask for nobody better than me, or more polite. I always keep my word. I'll tell you how it is, I'm always nice at first, the first time. I'll hold you so tight you won't think you have to try to get away or pretend anything because you'll know you can't. And I'll come inside you where it's all secret and you'll give in to me and you'll love me—"

"Shut up! You're crazy!" Connie said. She backed away from the door. She put her hands against her ears as if she'd heard something terrible, something not meant for her. "People don't talk like that, you're crazy," she muttered. Her heart was almost too big now for her chest and its pumping made sweat break out all over her. She looked out to see Arnold Friend pause and then take a step toward the porch lurching. He almost fell. But, like a clever drunken man, he managed to catch his balance. He wobbled in his high boots and grabbed hold of one of the porch posts.

"Honey?" he said. "You still listening?"

"Get the hell out of here!"

"Be nice, honey. Listen."

"I'm going to call the police—"

He wobbled again and out of the side of his mouth came a fast spat curse, an aside not meant for her to hear. But even this "Christ!" sounded forced. Then he began to smile again. She watched this smile come, awkward as if he were smiling from inside a mask. His whole face was a mask, she thought wildly, tanned down onto his throat but then running out as if he had plastered make-up on his face but had forgotten about his throat.

"Honey—? Listen, here's how it is. I always tell the truth and I promise you this: I ain't coming in that house after you."

"You better not! I'm going to call the police if you—if you don't—"

"Honey," he said, talking right through her voice, "honey, I'm not coming in there but you are coming out here. You know why?"

She was panting. The kitchen looked like a place she had never seen before, some room she had run inside but which wasn't good enough, wasn't going to help her. The kitchen window had never had a curtain, after three years, and there were dishes in the sink for her to do—probably—and if you ran your hand across the table you'd probably feel something sticky there.

"You listening, honey? Hey?"

"—going to call the police—"

"Soon as you touch the phone I don't need to keep my promise and can come inside. You won't want that."

She rushed forward and tried to lock the door. Her fingers were shaking. "But why lock it," Arnold Friend said gently, talking right into her face. "It's just a screen door. It's just nothing." One of his boots was at a strange angle, as if his foot wasn't in it. It pointed out to the left, bent at the ankle. "I mean, anybody can break through a screen door and glass and wood and iron or anything else if he needs to, anybody at all and specially Arnold Friend. If the place got lit up with a fire, honey, you'd come running out into my arms, right into my arms an' safe at home—like you knew I was your lover and'd stopped fooling around, I don't mind a nice shy girl but I don't like no fooling around." Part of those words were spoken with a slight rhythmic lilt, and Connie somehow recognized them—the echo of a song from last year, about a girl rushing into her boy friend's arms and coming home again—

Connie stood barefoot on the linoleum floor, staring at him. "What do you want?" she whispered.

"I want you," he said.

"What?"

"Seen you that night and thought, that's the one, yes sir. I never needed to look any more."

"But my father's coming back. He's coming to get me. I had to wash my hair first—" She spoke in a dry, rapid voice, hardly raising it for him to hear.

"No, your daddy is not coming and yes, you had to wash your hair and you washed it for me. It's nice and shining and all for me. I thank you, sweetheart," he said, with a mock bow, but again he almost lost his balance. He had to bend and adjust his boots. Evidently his feet did not go all the way down; the boots must have been stuffed with something so that he would seem taller. Connie stared out at him and behind him at Ellie in the car, who seemed to be looking off toward Connie's right, into nothing. This Ellie said, pulling the words out of the air one after another as if he were just discovering them, "You want me to pull out the phone?"

"Shut your mouth and keep it shut," Arnold Friend said, his face red from bending over or maybe from embarrassment because Connie had seen his boots. "This ain't none of your business."

"What—what are you doing? What do you want?" Connie said. "If I call the police they'll get you, they'll arrest you—"

"Promise was not to come in unless you touch that phone, and I'll keep that promise," he said. He resumed his erect position and tried to force his shoulders back. He sounded like a hero in a movie, declaring something important. He spoke too loudly and it was as if he were speaking to someone behind Connie. "I ain't made plans for coming in that house where I don't belong but just for you to come out to me, the way you should. Don't you know who I am?"

"You're crazy," she whispered. She backed away from the door but did not want to go into another part of the house, as if this would give him permission to come through the door. "What do you. . . . You're crazy, you. . . ."

"Huh? What're you saying, honey?"

Her eyes darted everywhere in the kitchen. She could not remember what it was, this room.

"This is how it is, honey: you come out and we'll drive away, have a nice ride. But if you don't come out we're gonna wait till your people come home and then they're all going to get it."

"You want that telephone pulled out?" Ellie said. He held the radio away from his ear and grimaced, as if without the radio the air was too much for him.

"I toldja shut up, Ellie," Arnold Friend said, "You're deaf, get a hearing aid, right? Fix yourself up. This little girl's no trouble and's gonna be nice to me, so Ellie keep to yourself, this ain't your date—right? Don't hem in on me, don't hog, don't crush, don't bird dog, don't trail me," he said in a rapid, meaningless voice, as if he were running through all the expressions he'd learned but was no longer sure which one of them was in style, then rushing on to new ones, making them up with his eyes closed. "Don't crawl under my fence, don't squeeze in my chipmunk hole, don't sniff my glue, suck my popsicle, keep your own greasy fingers on yourself!" He shaded his eyes and peered in at Connie, who was backed against the kitchen table. "Don't mind him, honey, he's just a creep. He's a dope. Right? I'm the boy for you and like I said, you come out here nice like a lady and give me your hand, and nobody else gets hurt, I mean, your nice old bald-headed daddy and your mummy and your sister in her high heels. Because listen: why bring them in this?"

"Leave me alone," Connie whispered.

"Hey, you know that old woman down the road, the one with the chickens and stuff—you know her?"

"She's dead!"

"Dead? What? You know her?" Arnold Friend said.

"She's dead—"

"Don't you like her?"

"She's dead—she's—she isn't here any more—"

"But don't you like her, I mean, you got something against her? Some grudge or something?" Then his voice dipped as if he were conscious of rudeness. He touched the sunglasses on top of his head as if to make sure they were still there. "Now you be a good girl."

"What are you going to do?"

"Just two things, or maybe three," Arnold Friend said. "But I promise it won't last long and you'll like me that way you get to like people you're close to. You will. It's all over for you here, so come on out. You don't want your people in any trouble, do you?"

She turned and bumped against a chair or something, hurting her leg, but she ran into the back room and picked up the telephone. Something roared in her ear, a tiny roaring, and she was so sick with fear that she could do nothing but listen to it—the telephone was clammy and very heavy and her fingers groped down to the dial but were too weak to touch it. She began to scream into the phone, into the roaring. She cried out, she cried for her mother, she felt her breath start jerking back and forth in her lungs as if it were something Arnold Friend was stabbing her with again and again with no tenderness. A noisy sorrowful wailing rose all about her and she was locked inside it the way she was locked inside this house.

After a while she could hear again. She was sitting on the floor, with her wet back against the wall.

Arnold Friend was saying from the door, "That's a good girl. Put the phone back."

She kicked the phone away from her.

"No, honey. Pick it up. Put it back right."

She picked it up and put it back. The dial tone stopped.

"That's a good girl. Now you come outside."

She was hollow with what had been fear but what was now just an emptiness. All that screaming had blasted it out of her. She sat, one leg cramped under her, and deep inside her brain was something like a pinpoint of light that kept going and would not let her relax. She thought, I'm not going to see my mother again. She thought, I'm not going to sleep in my bed again. Her bright green blouse was all wet.

Arnold Friend said, in a gentle-loud voice that was like a stage voice, "The place where you came from ain't there any more, and where you had in mind to go is cancelled out. This place you are now—inside your daddy's house—is nothing but a cardboard box I can knock down any time. You know that and always did know it. You hear me?"

She thought, I have got to think. I have got to know what to do.

"We'll go out to a nice field, out in the country here where it smells so nice and it's sunny," Arnold Friend said. "I'll have my arms tight around you so you won't need to try to get away and I'll show you what love is like, what it does. The hell with this house! It looks solid all right," he said. He ran a fingernail down the screen and the noise did not make Connie shiver, as it would have the day before. "Now put your hand on your heart, honey. Feel that? That feels solid too but we know better. Be nice to me, be sweet like you can because what else is there for a girl like you but to be sweet and pretty and give in?—and get away before her people come back?"

She felt her pounding heart. Her hands seemed to enclose it. She thought for the first time in her life that it was nothing that was hers, that belonged to her, but just a pounding, living thing inside this body that wasn't hers either.

"You don't want them to get hurt," Arnold Friend went on. "Now get up, honey. Get up all by yourself."

She stood.

"Now turn this way. That's right. Come over to me—Ellie, put that away, didn't I tell you? You dope. You miserable creepy dope," Arnold Friend said. His words were not angry but only part of an incantation. The incantation was kindly. "Now come out through the kitchen to me honey and let's see a smile, try it, you're a brave sweet little girl and now they're eating corn and hotdogs cooked to bursting over an outdoor fire, and they don't know one thing about you and never did and honey you're better than them because not one of them would have done this for you."

Connie felt the linoleum under her feet; it was cool. She brushed her hair back out of her eyes. Arnold Friend let go of the post tentatively and opened his arms for her, his elbows pointing up toward each other and his wrist limp, to show that this was an embarrassed embrace and a little mocking, he didn't want to make her self-conscious.

She put out her hand against the screen. She watched herself push the door slowly open as if she were safe back somewhere in the other doorway, watching this body and this head of long hair moving out into the sunlight where Arnold Friend waited.

"My sweet little blue-eyed girl," he said in a half-sung sigh that had nothing to do with her brown eyes but was taken up just the same by the vast sunlit reaches of the land behind him and on all sides of him, so much land that Connie had never seen before and did not recognize except to know that she was going to it.

[1966]

Robert Boswell

Robert Boswell (b. 1953) is an award-winning fiction writer and playwright. He was born in Missouri, spent his early childhood in Kentucky, and moved to Yuma, Arizona when he was in sixth grade. Boswell completed both his undergraduate and graduate studies at The University of Arizona. Among his honors are the prestigious Guggenheim Fellowship, two National Endowment for the Arts Fellowships, the Iowa School of Letters Award for Fiction, and the 1995 PEN West Award for Fiction. He teaches at New Mexico State University and in the Warren Wilson MFA Program for Writers. He has written seven books including Crooked Hearts *(1987),* The Geography of Desire *(1989), and* American Owned Love *(1997). "Dancing in the Movies" examines what people are willing to give up for love, exploring the idea that love can be both dangerous and selfish. It was published in* Dancing in the Movies *in 1986.*

Dancing in the Movies

"Bob Marley dead," Eugene said, hand at his dick as he walked in the door, brown face yellowed from heroin, eyes puffy like a boxer's. He stared hard at me, leaned against a barstool. His shoulders made a big spread, but he was junk skinny, that all-sucked-out look. "Bob Marley *dead,*" he said again, like I couldn't hear.

I wanted to call him a lemon-faced nigger, but I didn't like that ugly side and kept it quiet, even with Eugene. I got straight to the point. "You seen Dee?"

"Didn't you hear me?" He gripped at the air, making two large fists, his voice full of anger and familiarity, as if I hadn't been gone for months.

"I already heard," I said. My best friend, Lonnie, had picked me up at the bus station and given me the news. "It's all over the radio," he said. "The industrialists killed him." I felt weak, twenty hours on a Greyhound, then I hear Marley is gone. I asked Lonnie how they killed him. "Cancer," he said, "white man's disease." It had sounded like an accusation.

"Shit," Eugene said, bending close to study my face for signs of anguish. He crossed his arms to make himself bigger. "Go listen at your fucking Elton John."

I felt accused again, as if my white skin had contributed to Marley's death. I would not apologize for being white, especially not to a bone-hollow junkie like Eugene. I stood and threw what was left of my beer in his face. "Where's Dee?"

Reprinted from *Dancing in the Movies*, (1986), by permission of University of Iowa Press.

For a moment his eyes sparked, but they clouded quickly. He seemed to shrink. "Shit, Freddie, why you always got a hard-on?" He wiped at his face, eyebrows. Beer ran down his fingers and dripped onto the concrete floor. "I don't know where she is. We ain't in no club."

"I need to find her." I sat again on the wood ladder-back chair, already regretting throwing the beer. "I need to find her, Eugene."

He turned away from me, wiping the last of the beer on his jeans, and walked to the jukebox. "Ask Wilson," he said.

Wilson was Lonnie's little brother. "Wilson's clean," I said. With Lonnie's help, Wilson had put down heroin and begun avoiding junkies, which meant he would have nothing to do with Dee. "Wilson is clean," I said again, louder.

Eugene paid no attention, slipping coins into the machine. As kids, Eugene and I had been friends, part of the neighborhood crowd that centered around Lonnie. Dee had been the only girl in the group and my girlfriend, off and on, since fourth grade. It was hard for me to remember a time I didn't love Dee. We cheated together on spelling, stole cigarettes from Quick Mart, made a wreath from oleander leaves for her mother's grave.

I knew where to find Wilson, although I didn't think he'd know where to find Dee. From noon to five Wilson sat in front of the Unemployment office, hoping to find *his* girlfriend. She left him because he couldn't quit heroin. Now he was clean, but she was gone.

Eugene bent over the jukebox, ran his index finger down the song list. He looked like a Norman Rockwell parody, big and childish, black and gaunt. He reminded me of a letter from Lonnie. *I used to think junkies were like little kids,* he wrote. *They're more like dead people playing human.* I decided to look for Wilson. He, at least, would be sympathetic—we were both looking for girlfriends.

I walked out of the Bree Lounge. The rain had stopped but the sky was still hooded with clouds. Music started up inside the bar, too muffled to be recognizable. I thought it must be Bob Marley. Dee and I had seen Bob Marley once in LA, so stoned we had to dance in our chairs. Lonnie had been with us, doing spins and dancing funk to reggae. Some song made us cry, just the sound of it, the way it moved inside. Lonnie enjoyed crying, but Dee and I weren't criers. It was Marley himself, singing with his whole body, moving like a marionette, then a dancer, that made the music into something liquid. I pictured Marley, bare to his waist, the blue light shining off his sweaty back, his dark hands on the silver microphone stand, but all I could hear was the muffled music from the Bree. I headed for the Unemployment building.

Downtown was noisy as a bad movie. Vested men carrying briefcases hurried past. They looked straight ahead, their thin, high-polish shoes finding the dry spots of the sidewalks. I almost fit in, wearing my best blue slacks and olive shirt, wanting to look good when I found Dee. In her last letter, she had written, *All the streets in Langston run the wrong way—that's why we grew up lost.* In response, I sent her a bus ticket. I didn't hear from her after that. My letters were returned.

Wilson sat in Lonnie's cream Coupe de Ville, drinking Burgie from the can. He rolled down the window on the passenger side and yelled. "Get in before it rains some more." He put a cold Burgie in my hand. "I love the rain," he said, "but from the inside."

I nodded, drank a swallow of beer. Flower vendors were back on the corners. The thin green paper tore when they tried to pull it off the stems of the rain-flattened flowers. The women with the flowers reminded me of Dee. Why? Because they smiled and waved the bouquets like Dee finding the phone book under a pile of magazines? Because I bought her flowers once? Lonnie told me I have a blindness for Dee; whatever I did, I was thinking how she could fit in, even if I was with my parents, who hated her, or in a class hundreds of miles from her. Then I remembered the cemetery. We had bought flowers for the graves last December, the day before I left Langston. Dee took me to where her mother, grandmother, and aunt were buried. She started crying, not because those dead women were dead, but because they didn't have any better imagination than to keep planting themselves one next to another. She had told me she wanted to be buried where everyone was a stranger. It was then she promised to come to Oregon in the summer.

Wilson was wearing a long-sleeved T-shirt and jeans speckled with white paint. He worked from six to noon, then watched the Unemployment building. The flecks of paint in his hair made him look like an old man. "Any sign of Angela?" I asked.

"It's tough," Wilson said. "Paper says unemployment is up though. I'm optimistic."

I could tell from his eyes he was still clean, although I didn't know him as a first-rate friend but through his brother Lonnie. I knew heroin enough to know clean, even though Dee told me that was bullshit. She said I didn't know heroin because I was straight, that I didn't know women because I was male, that I didn't know black because I was white. I just threw it back at her upside down to make her hush.

Wilson was two years younger than Lonnie and me, a junkie since he was thirteen. He used to stumble through our parties, giggling and scratching at himself. Lonnie had tried to get him to put down junk, but nothing had worked. When Wilson moved in with Angela, who was also a junkie, Lonnie bore down on her until she quit. But she couldn't endure Wilson's trying, especially when he'd get sick from shooting up again. It was her leaving that finally got him to quit. I had never felt close to Wilson before then, sharing the front seat of Lonnie's car, each of us looking for a woman who probably didn't want to be found. And something more—Wilson had been a junkie for years and quit. It gave me hope for Dee.

A Mexican woman with a sour-looking kid walked out of the Unemployment building. "You think of Welfare?" I asked. The first drop of rain hit center like a huge bug splat just below the rearview mirror.

"Starting again," Wilson said. He leaned forward, looked up to the dark sky. "Welfare's a waste of time. She's too proud. Too crazy. Too stupid."

I looked at the way his long neck curved as he stared at the sky. I pictured Angela walking by, seeing Wilson craning his head up and knowing instantly that he was clean. Thinking about it reminded me of my own problems. "You know where Dee is?"

Wilson gave a short laugh. "I can't find my own woman."

"Eugene said you might know."

"Fuck Eugene." Another drop hit right above his face. "They look like stars exploding," he said, then straightened. "Why don't you just get another woman?"

I shook my head, thinking that was what Eugene wanted to say in the bar, only he would have come out and said, "Why don't you get a *white* woman?" I didn't get angry with Wilson. We both had our ugly sides. "I love Dee," I said.

"Yeah," he said, looking at the Unemployment door as a man in a tie walked out. "They closing up. You need a ride somewhere?"

Wilson dropped me off at Lonnie's apartment, saying only that Dee got junk from Eugene. If I stayed close to Eugene, she would show.

Lonnie was smoking a joint. I didn't want any, even though he acted hurt and told me how wonderful it was with that effeminate twist in his voice. Everyone thought he was queer, but Lonnie was always after women and women were always after him.

"Maybe you should forget about Dee," Lonnie said, sitting with his legs crossed under him at one end of his record collection, flipping through the albums. He wore a smoke-colored shirt with a short collar and pleated beige pants, though he wasn't going anywhere and expecting no one but me.

"I love Dee." I squatted at the other end of the records. We looked for Bob Marley, moving crablike across the floor, checking each of the albums that lined the wall. Lonnie decided he must have lent the albums out. We settled for Peter Tosh, *Equal Rights*.

The five months I had been at college, Lonnie and Dee were the only ones who had written. Lonnie's letters covered everything—from how well he was doing at work to how hard it was for his brother to quit junk. He had his own stationery—heavy blue paper with thick and thin black lines bordering it and a big *L.W.* at the top. Dee's letters came on whatever was handy while she was high and missing me. Once she had mailed a napkin from the Bree, scribbled up and blurred from wet-glass circles. Her letters were short, choppy, full of things that only half made sense. *I can't talk on telephones,* she wrote, *my throat swells up the size of testicles you seen in pictures—you love me or you just love niggers?* Her last letter said, *The birds are loose in Langston and all the streets run the wrong way, I eat drugs, Freddie.* When I had left, she'd just been fooling with heroin. With each letter she seemed more and more a junkie, until she started calling herself one. *Which your parents going to hate worser? Dee the nigger or Dee the junkie?*

"It's such a tacky love," Lonnie said. He sat, recrossed his legs, twisting his top foot behind a knee, like pretzels. "You need a cleaner love."

"I'm taking her back. I've got school housing and work study. I can afford it."

"Oh, Freddie, why on earth do you want to love Dee?" He leaned against the long fingers of his left hand, pushing his mouth into a half smile.

"Didn't say I want to. I just do."

"Huck Finn and Nigger Jim," Lonnie said.

"What's that supposed to mean?"

"It's a complex boys get where they feel they have to love what they hate." His head gave a little waggle as he said it.

"That'd explain why *you* chase after women," I said, happy for the chance to turn it upside down on him.

"You're such a clever boy," he said, flipping both hands open and spreading his fingers, then letting them fall limp at the wrists—his best fake fag gesture. "I suppose it would also explain why you hang out with me." He laughed, a giggle, and not fake. "Really, Dee and I are perfect for you: multiple outcasts."

He wanted me to laugh, forget about Dee for now, but I wouldn't buy it. "I've known you and Dee all my life."

"She smokes constantly. It's such a dirty habit." Suddenly he stood, twisting as he came out of the pretzel. "Wait here. Bob Marley may be in my closet."

"It's time someone came out of your closet," I said.

Lonnie couldn't find the album he wanted but returned with some old Temptations. "You remember?" he asked, flashing the album cover and doing a crossover step.

When we were kids we sang backup together on Temptations and Four Tops albums, complete with steps and hand moves. Lonnie had been the best in the neighborhood and he still loved to do it. I jumped up beside him. We rocked together to get in time. "Just My Imagination" was the song and it called for finger snapping at the hips, lots of hand movements to show nothing was real. The steps were just a little box with plenty of sway. We worked well together. All that was missing was Dee to sing the Eddie Kendricks high notes. Once I thought about that, I knew I would only dance through one song. Wherever I was, Dee was what was missing.

The Bree was quiet—a couple of the regular drunks at the bar, a heavy-thighed black woman we used to call Sisters because she was so fat, a dog-faced junkie who knew me and had breath like turpentine, a few others sipping beer or sleeping head down on the cheap tables. In the corner, an ugly red dog with a pointed nose chewed his leg. Nobody was saying where Eugene might be.

I was ready to leave when Dee walked in, hair knotted back on her head and body too thin, but still beautiful in jeans and a purple blouse, baggy so her ribs didn't show. She smiled when she saw me and came straight over. Dee carried heroin in her eyes. They became milky and thick, moved too slow.

Her arms went right around me, elbows at my ribs, hands pressed against my shoulder blades. The kissing took me back to December, before I left, as if time were something people carried with them, the way some carried pictures.

"I've been looking for you," I said.

"Wilson told me." She ran her hands down then up my sides. "You look good," she said. "You got your Lonnie clothes on."

I laughed. I hadn't realized it, but everything I had on had been given to me at Christmases or birthdays by Lonnie.

"How's your college?" she said.

"I've got a place now. I want you to come back with me."

She smiled and sat at the table. "Get me a Coke."

I came back with a Coke and a beer. Dee sat, legs crossed, arms folded, leaning back and smiling, lipstick too red and smeared under her nose where she'd missed her lip.

"I mean it, Dee. This is a way out."

"Can't be." She took a big swallow of Coke.

"Why not?"

"If it was, we wouldn't know about it." Her upper lip glistened with Coke. She took another big drink, wiped her mouth with her hand. "Anyway, I don't like mixed marriages."

"Fuck that."

"They don't work, junkies and straights." She reached over and twisted one of my shirt buttons. "You'd have to take to junk."

I leaned back. The chair squeaked. Her milky eyes caught up with me. "I was thinking you could quit," I said.

Her hand moved up and down the glass. "You want to consume me." She wiped the cold sweat from the glass onto her forehead, the bridge of her nose, her eyelids.

"Wilson quit."

Her hand dropped to her lap. "That's what got you all excited, ain't it?"

"Lonnie got him through it."

She glared at me, only it was a fake look, like Lonnie's fake fag moves, meaning just the opposite. I tilted my head to show her I knew what she was doing. It must have reminded her of how long I had loved her because she went soft, showed her tongue as she smiled. Then she moved in another direction. Something came to her and her eyes flitted down to the table. "I'm one up on you," she said. "You go to college to figure out what it is *worth* getting up for." She looked up at me, thick eyes set hard against mine. "I got my reason to live."

She made me feel small, like junkies were the only full-grown people. "I tried the shit," I said, feeling stupid as soon as I said it because she knew I only snorted it. It was the needles I couldn't stand. I couldn't even look at them. But it was more than that. Junkies made me angry, especially gone junkies like Eugene, but even the clever ones, the pretty ones, the ones who could be anybody.

Dee's laugh was like a gurgle, but low enough to be a moan. "Snorting junk is like jacking off, a waste of good stuff."

I couldn't get mad at Dee. Every expression on her face was one I'd seen before, like old songs I never got tired of. "I love you, Dee."

"Love is the spike." Someone said this to her or she read it, because she just spat it out the way some people say "dig it," as if rehearsed. She couldn't even look at me, but I didn't know what to say or how to explain. I said what she already knew.

"I'm scared of needles."

"I'm scared of white college boys in short sleeves." She looked at me, started to look away, but I took her chin and turned her toward me.

"I want you to come with me."

"I want a Marlboro, all I've got are Kents." She lifted her purse from her lap. "Eugene smokes Kents."

"I got Luckies."

"Lucky Strikes are for lunatics."

"Then don't smoke." I leaned back. The chair squeaked again.

"I always smoke with heroin. It's what I do best. Or go with Eugene and get our shoes shined at Kresge's." She leaned way over the table, cupped *my* chin in her palm. "It's just like making love. That brush move through you like words move through your throat." She laughed, pulled me close, whispered as if it were a secret. "It's like dancing in the movies, when the music starts up and everyone knows their steps even though they're all strangers," She let go of my chin. "You try it. You *really* love me, then try it."

We sat without talking. I needed to convince her to leave goons like Eugene and the dog-faced black bastard at the next table, but I couldn't come up with the words. I knew what I didn't want to talk about—she was always wanting me to try the needle just once. Before she had become a junkie, when she was just using it now and then, she thought it would prove something. "You want to love me, you got to get a little dirty," she had said. I couldn't. I tried to change the subject. "Bob Marley died. Cancer."

She rocked her head without showing any emotion at all.

I needed the words to say how I had missed her, how other girls seemed plain and empty, how we could beat it if she'd just come with me. All that came in my head were the old clichés—*You have to believe in our love—we could make it if we believed in each other.* Dee hated those kinds of things, called them blind talking. I knew she wouldn't like it but said, "You have to have some faith."

Saying this, I reminded her of something, maybe something she'd heard, maybe just the way I could be, my limitations. Some little recognition flashed in and she came up with one of her Dee-isms. "Faith is the wooden pistol that gets you killed."

"What's that mean?"

She bit her lower lip, looked to the right, the left. "You try it once and I'll go with you."

My throat knotted. It came down to a trade. She'd try my way if I'd try hers. She smiled at me, knowing I was too scared to do it. I decided to throw her fear back at her. "Clean?"

"Jesus, Freddie."

"You've got to quit. We can talk to Lonnie and Wilson."

"I know this shit inside out," she said, her voice flat with real anger. "Heard it in the churchhouse, heard it in the schoolhouse, heard it in the flapbox in my own house, heard it up to here." She sliced her hand across her throat. "And you telling me again? What the fuck for?" She slid her chair back and stood. "Tell me I got hands. Tell me I got feet."

"Clean," I said.

"Fuck you, Freddie. Your world's got no place to shit. You fuck it up by being there." She walked to the door, opened it, leaned on it. "This much is mine," she said.

I looked around at the wooden chairs and card tables, the strung-out clowns propping up their faces with their bony fists. "You can have it," I said and looked back at Dee, but she was gone.

I caught up with her fifty yards down the street. She was crying. "Tonight," she said, arms around me again, elbows at my ribs, hands on my shoulder blades, breasts pressed tight against my chest. "We do it tonight, together, and I'll go with you."

"I can't. The whole idea . . ."

"Clean," she said. "You do it once with me, and I'll quit."

"Why?"

"No questions." She thudded my chest with the heel of her hand.

"Okay," I said. Even as I said it, I knew I wouldn't.

Lonnie didn't answer the door, but I could hear Steel Pulse on the stereo. I tried the knob. The door was unlocked. Lonnie sat on the floor across the room, arms around his long legs, back against the off-white wall. He was wearing white pants with perfect creases and a soft gray V-neck sweater that gathered at the waist. His eyes focused on the carpet, a blank stare that made him look older than he was and tired, really tired. Even after I closed the door, he didn't look up.

"I found Dee," I said. My stomach jerked just saying it, thinking of the needle. She needed something, like an act of faith, before she could come with me, but I had to think of an alternative, like cutting off an arm or walking barefoot through fire. I wanted to tell Lonnie all this, but he'd say Huck Finn and Nigger Jim, the more I hated her the more I'd love her. "Junkies are dead people," he told me once, while his brother lay in bed in the next room, groaning and sweating through withdrawals. "You can't invest in the dead," he'd said. "You get them back or give them up." Lonnie would want to know why I loved Dee. That was like wanting to know the why of my thoughts, the why of my walk. If my reasons for loving her were bad, I didn't care. I couldn't. Lonnie still just sat, so I said again, "I found Dee."

He nodded, staring at the carpet. His right hand went to his mouth.

I stared at the carpet where he was looking. Nothing was there. "She's going to leave with me."

He moved his head up slowly. "Angela was just here."

"Wilson's Angela?"

"She wanted to borrow money." He lowered his eyes again.

"What's the story, Lonnie?" I squatted to look at him eye to eye. He wouldn't look up. "She with Wilson now?"

His head shook slowly from side to side, eyes still down. "I didn't tell him." His long brown hands covered his eyes, then he raised his head level with mine. "I just gave her the money." He didn't move, hands over his eyes like when we were kids playing hide-and-seek. For a moment, he became a kid, nine years old. I must have become one too, because I looked around the room for a couch to crawl under, a door to squeeze behind.

Just when I expected Lonnie to say "ready or not," he said, "You *know* what she wanted that money for," and dropped his hands. For an instant he must have seen me still as a little boy, because the corners of his mouth pulled back into a surprised smile before falling back into line.

"I thought she was clean. I thought that was the whole point."

"*Was.* She said she kept getting sad." His head started shaking again, back and forth, slowly.

I thought of Wilson in the Coupe de Ville, his long neck curved up, watching the rain explode on the windshield and the people coming and going from the Unemployment building. "You've got to tell your brother," I said.

Lonnie's head stopped moving. He looked me straight on. "No, I don't." His stare was so solid I could feel it on my face, like an open hand, one of Lonnie's big hands across my face. He stood. The hand lifted. "I made her promise to leave town. I wouldn't give her the money until she promised."

I stood next to him. "You trust her?"

"No, I don't *trust* her." He brushed his hand across the rear of his immaculate pants. "You want to come with me?"

"Where?"

"I'm going to get my brother and we're going to eat out, some place expensive, then maybe we'll see a movie, or come here and watch television and smoke, or anything."

"Dee and I . . ."

"Dee can't come."

I nodded. "We've got plans."

Lonnie put his arms around me, pulled me close. "You should come with us, Freddie. I'll buy you a steak."

"I can't," I said.

He leaned back, smiled. "A lobster, then, and I'll introduce you to a woman. Black, if you want black. I even know a very lovely paraplegic who's half Puerto Rican."

Then I surprised myself by putting my arms around Lonnie. "I love Dee," I whispered, right in his ear.

I spent the afternoon with my parents. We couldn't find much to talk about and sat in the TV room watching "Star Trek"—the crew had beamed down to a planet where everyone's dreams came true and all it did was cause them trouble. My parents had moved from the old neighborhood to a trailer park called Happy Trails Trailer Lots. All the mailbox poles looked like hitching posts. My mother said it was very quiet.

Dee had grown up less than a block from where we used to live, but she had never seen the inside of our house until we were in high school. She was quiet around my parents in a way she was with no one else. "They praying I'm a phase," she'd say, once we were out of the house. It became a routine. "Your number 1 phase wants to go dancing," she'd say. "This phase is getting fat and fat phases never last." One night my parents were having a party. I was in the shower when my father barged into the bathroom, drunk. He pulled the curtain aside, saying we needed to talk. I tried to pull the curtain shut again, but he put his arms around me and pressed his face against my chest, even though the water was spraying all over. "Honey," he said, a name he used when he got drunk and sentimental. "She's not just black, she's a nigger. There's a difference." I clubbed him with the soap and he left.

He apologized the next day, the same day Dee made her biggest effort to get next to them. She told a joke about a dog that loses his tail so he has to wag his tongue. Halfway through it, my father said excuse me and left the room. Mother was ironing and never laughed, but went right into a story about a dog we used to have that died under the house and made a stink. Dee quit trying after that.

"Police Woman" was on after "Star Trek." No one liked it, but the TV made it easier for us all to be in the same room. My father got out his needlepoint, which he had taken up after I left. He never wrote letters, but sent ugly needlepoint flowers or doodads and notes mentioning that Rosie Grier did needlepoint.

He included the note so I wouldn't think he'd gone queer. Mother drank her beer and said an actress got her start on "The Edge of Night."

On TV, a sniper wearing a red ski mask aimed his rifle at a woman carrying a shopping bag. Right then it hit me that I was going to have to shoot heroin or lose Dee. I couldn't do either one. The show became a marker. By the time it was over, I would have to go to Dee's and do *something*. I could see the needle pressing against my skin. A little cup in the flesh formed around the point as the needle pressed in more. The skin broke, needle sank in, flesh rose around it.

I had to get Dee out of Langston without doing junk. Angie Dickinson, tied with a yellow extension cord to a chair, waggled her butt to scoot the chair across the floor, closer to the window. She was being held hostage by the man in the red ski mask. The show was almost over. I left, trusting my parents to see how Angie escaped.

Dee named the biggest vein in my arm Mississippi and pinched it out with her fingers. She sucked the last of her Pepsi out of the paper cup and set it behind her on the floor. It caught the edge of a magazine and tipped over, spilling beads of ice across the faded yellow tile. Her apartment was one little room in the back of a grocery store. Magazines littered the floor. A thin striped mattress lay flat in one corner, partially covered by a dirty pink sheet. A TV rattled on in another corner, but I didn't look. I didn't want to see the needle. Instead, I looked at a poster, curling at the edges, hanging crooked on the wall, a picture of the earth taken from space. The world was blue, streaked with white. It looked like a great place. Paper-clipped to the poster was a photo of Dee, Lonnie, and me from our trip to LA to see Bob Marley and the Wailers. I had my arm around Dee and Lonnie had his arm around me.

I had delayed as much as I could, talking about my classes, where we would live, my parents, "Star Trek," how I threw beer at Eugene, Angela borrowing money from Lonnie. I tried to distract myself from the needle, couldn't, tried to think of it as walking barefoot through fire.

I pumped up my arm when Dee told me to. The photograph was dark. We were all smiling. She tied my arm off with a vinyl belt. I tried to remember the Wailers live. She pinched out the vein again. "Put some Bob Marley on," I said, head still turned.

"Traded all I had to Eugene."

"For what?" I asked. Instead of answering, she stuck the needle in my arm.

My arm tensed hard as wood, but the needle was already out, the belt off. Something like sleep turned in my chest, came up my throat on a wave of static, then flooded out all over. Even my fingers filled with light. "Jesus," I said.

"Our savior," Dee laughed.

I started to turn to her but began yawning. In the TV in the blue corner: Chef Boyardee, Tony the Tiger, the Shell Answer Man, the flat yellow hat the laughing blonde presses against her breasts. Beside the set: a sour gray apple whose skin curls around a missing piece like lips protecting teeth. A gurgle from Dee I had to laugh with. Dolphins standing straight up in the television like children choosing sides for baseball. It was like a movie, this life. The crushed cup, drained of Pepsi, had bunches of ice that looked like caviar. I said "caviar" and slipped a piece into Dee's mouth.

"When *you* ever seen caviar?" She was laughing.

I decided we should make love. Little legs began crawling across my cheek, but I scratched them off. Dee lay back on the pink sheet, kissing me once, her lips fibrous as peaches. I couldn't get it up, even though my currents sizzled like rain on asphalt, like a scaled fish in salt water.

"You don't need to fuck on junk," Dee said. "You don't need to do anything."

"I want to," I said. "It's Christmas," meaning we hadn't made love since I left in December. A fly landed on my face, but it was not a fly. "Is there something on my face?"

She smiled, lit a Kent 100. The smoke came inside my lungs liquid. If you listened to a smoking cigarette, it sounded like TV static, like locusts, like heroin humming through the veins inside your skull.

Dee laughed and that started me laughing. She walked from the mattress to the TV, stepping only on magazines. "Piranhas," she said and pointed to the yellow tile.

I joined her. We stepped from magazine to magazine, as if from stone to stone, above the man-eaters. At the TV, she turned off the sound, abandoned the game, and walked to the stereo. She put on an album of saxophones I didn't recognize, then locked her arms around me. "You do love me," she said.

"I must," I said. My stomach started twisting. Dee led me to the bathroom. I knelt in front of the toilet but didn't vomit. We began dancing to the saxophones, slow at first, then faster, pushing off the walls to send us across the floor faster. We slid on the magazines, and that became part of the step.

I began throwing up and that became part of the dance too. We were both laughing. She kissed me hard. Our tongues became part of the dance. Vomit trailed across her mouth and down her cheek. We danced back to the mattress and pulled at each other's clothes. The music was over, maybe for a long time.

I kissed her breasts, bit her ribs. My fingers sank into the soft of her butt. "Freddie," she said, and I raised my head. "We can really get out?" I kissed her again, wiped the vomit from her face. "Freddie," she said again.

"We can get out," I said. "Eight hundred miles." I entered her. We made love for what may have been a long while. And all the time, inside the frenzy was the calm. Memory hovered about my head, becoming visible at intervals, like particles of dust in twilight—the alley behind the Bree where we bought pot, beneath the slide in the Woodard schoolyard where Dee and I first made love, the corner of 5th and Main where the knobby prostitutes hawked, the vacant lot behind the Mesa Drive-In where we made up dialogue for the huge silent screen, all the places we grew up lost—the men in suits and vests with high-polish shoes, the bearded transvestite who collected bottles in the basket of his bicycle, the black butcher with red slabs of meat, the abandoned Sinclair station covered with names, my name, Dee's, Lonnie's, Wilson's, Eugene's—the curtains of my parents' house drawn closed, the liquor store on 49th with the neon dinosaur, the all-night diner on 4th Avenue, Lonnie's Coupe de Ville, the asphalt bedrooms, the Unemployment building, my mother, who told me the last people who lived here didn't know how to behave.

"It's like dancing in the movies," Dee said, her hand on my chest. She laughed, looked confused. "Did I already say that?" She pulled gently at my dick. "I love you, Freddie. A lot. A very lot."

We slept.

"She just wasn't there," I said to Lonnie. The windows were starting to go dark and no sign of Dee all day. My head was clear, arm a little sore, and that grown-up feeling, age that just fell into me like a brick into a pond. Not that I liked needles or wanted junk, but I knew I couldn't tell Lonnie about heroin ever, and knowing that put a distance between us, made me feel older. "I slept late and she was just gone."

"You know where she is." He was on the floor, propping himself up with his elbows. Lonnie always sat on the floor if he had a choice.

"I know what she's doing. I don't know where she is."

Lonnie let his head drop back. He had the same long neck as his brother. He and Wilson had eaten last night across town, then drank beer at the Mesa Drive-In, laughing and watching James Bond. All the tension Lonnie had the night before was gone. His brother was at a local concert in memory of Bob Marley. Lonnie believed he was safe, at least for the night. He lifted his head, smiled at me, straightened his black pinstripe shirt. "We'll look for her," he said. "Then we'll put you both on a bus."

We drove the old streets, checked the regular spots—like the old times, me and Lonnie cruising, looking for familiar cars, waiting for something to happen. There was no sign of Dee. We decided to try the reggae concert, although neither of us thought she would have the money for it. On our way, Lonnie spotted Eugene's old Chrysler parked on a dark stretch of 32nd Street. We cut around and pulled up to the car.

A Mexican with long frizzy hair lay on the hood of the Chrysler. Eugene sat behind the wheel, hand tapping the dash. Beside him, the dog-faced junkie from the Bree. "Don't stop," Eugene said as we pulled up next to the car. "We waiting here. You can't stop."

"You seen Dee?" I leaned over next to Lonnie, tried to see in the car.

"No, no, fuck." Eugene looked in his rearview mirror. Headlights appeared from around the corner, then stopped a hundred yards before reaching the cars. "She ain't here, come on." His hand hammered the dash faster.

I started to ask again, but Lonnie pulled out, U-turned so we didn't go by the other car. "Let them be," he said. "Let them rest in peace."

The headlights neared Eugene's car. A head rose from the backseat of the Chrysler. "There's somebody in the backseat," I said.

Lonnie shrugged. "Doesn't mean it's Dee. Besides, we can't stop what's going on there."

The reggae concert was in an old warehouse and was sold out. From the outside, all we could hear was the bass. I tried to imagine it as part of a song, but it distorted everything. We drove again. Lonnie produced a joint. I only smoked a little. The night was dark, sky empty. I remembered something from the night before. "Let's go to the old Sinclair station," I said.

"They tore it down," Lonnie said.

We drove out on the loop we always used to take. I caught Lonnie staring at his reflection in the dark window and we laughed. The neon sign for the Oasis Motel read *as s Mot l,* gas gauge read under a quarter of a tank. Lonnie's car had only AM radio. All we could find was cowboy music and people talking on telephones.

Lonnie turned the radio off. He looked straight ahead, one hand pinching the crease in his pants. "I love you, Freddie," he said, "but you're not strong enough. She'll drag you down. It's dirty, Freddie. It's ugly."

I turned to him, opened my mouth to speak, and suddenly I realized why Dee had wanted me to shoot heroin. She had to see if I could be strong, if I could do the thing I hated most *for her*. It hit me so hard I almost told Lonnie, so I would never hear about Huck Finn and Nigger Jim again. Instead, I said, "I can be stronger than you think."

We turned back.

Lonnie took 5th. It was mainly residential, good at night because there was never any traffic and no cops. He wanted to smoke another joint. I fumbled through the glove box to find one. The yards were green all year round, trimmed straight to give them edges. I lit the joint just before we reached 5th Street Park, a big grassy area with trees and swings. A car pulled out of the park and approached with its lights off. As it passed, I recognized Eugene and his beat-up Chrysler. I tried to see who else was in the car but couldn't make out anyone. Lonnie just shrugged.

As we drew nearer to the park, I saw a dark mound in the grass twenty yards from the street. I pointed. Lonnie stopped the car. We looked at it through the windshield. It didn't move. I couldn't tell whether the mound was a man or a woman. Lonnie cut the engine. The night was perfectly quiet. Fear entered me like heroin had, turning in my chest, filling me. I hoped it was that dog-faced junkie from the Bree or the Mexican who had lain on the hood of Eugene's Chrysler or someone I had never seen or heard of. I felt like we should run to it, but we walked close to one another, very slowly.

"No," Lonnie said. "No, no."

Wilson's head twisted to the side, vomit was spattered across his chin, shoulder.

We squatted beside the body. Lonnie began crying. Neither of us wanted to touch the body, but one of his arms was wrenched behind his back. I couldn't leave him that way. I pulled on the arm at the elbow.

The arm jerked, eyelids rose. "Hey, brother," Wilson said. He smiled a goofy smile and lifted himself up on his elbows.

"Jesus," I said. "We thought you were dead."

"I puked all over Eugene's car," he said, still smiling.

Lonnie raised his hand and slapped Wilson hard. He was still crying, trembling.

Wilson just fell back. "I'm sorry," he said.

Lonnie stood, one hand over his eyes. He brought up the other to cover his mouth.

I kissed Lonnie on the cheek, a love kiss, but not a lover's kiss.

"She promised she'd leave," Lonnie said.

"You can't blame Angela for this," Wilson said, up again on one elbow. "Angela?" he called out. He turned to the dark and vacant park. "Angela?"

The bus out of Langston moved like a sick dog. Dee, in the window seat, looked at the same streets she'd seen all her life. The early morning light made everything look fake, like movie scenery. We went by the liquor store on 49th, the neon dinosaur flickering blue, past the grocery store Dee lived behind, still lit by its nighttime lights. Eugene squatted next to the grocery door. His back partially covered the diagonal yellow band advertising bread. WONDER, the sign read. Dee put her head on my shoulder. "I guess this street don't owe me nothing I ain't already took."

I put my hand on her cheek. She had been sleeping on the porch of Lonnie's apartment when we pulled in. We had taken Wilson inside, then I woke her. "Eight hundred miles," she had said, high on junk but ready to go. And we were going. I tilted our seats back and closed my eyes.

"Your place have carpet?" Dee asked. "I hate carpet."

"We can pull it out," I said.

"It's a few things I can't tolerate and carpet's one."

"You don't have to talk," I said. "I'm too tired to laugh."

She kissed my cheek and we rode on, but I couldn't sleep. I didn't want to think about Lonnie and Wilson starting over again and again or about Eugene sitting in the Chrysler beating the dash, waiting for headlights. I didn't even want to think about me and Dee—it made me tired. And scared.

I tried again to hear Bob Marley, but his music just wouldn't come. I pictured him on stage in the blue light with the silver mike. Instead, I saw him skinny in some hospital bed, shitting in his sleep, his breath already the color of death, thinking, *It all comes down to this moment,* trying to say what was left inside, what hadn't been strangled by the white hands of cancer. I tried to hear Marley's words and wondered if the vision grew soft before the mind or the mind before the vision.

Then I heard Bob Marley.

His voice was nothing like the living Marley's voice. It was flat, even, without any Jamaican accent. "Bury the swollen tongues of the dead," he said, and I understood that the faith of the living was with the dead and the faith of the dead with the living.

The bus rattled across a hole in the road, then lugged as it entered the freeway. Dee slept. The driver downshifted. We picked up speed. The sky grew light but without color, like concrete. I looked at Dee and she opened her eyes.

"Shh," she said, then fell back to sleep.

Bharati Mukherjee

Bharati Mukherjee was born a Bengali Brahmin in Calcutta, India in 1940. In her adult life she has lived in Canada and the United States. She received her MFA in Creative Writing in 1963 and her Ph.D. in English and Comparative Literature in 1969, both from the University of Iowa. Today she teaches at the Univeristy of California, Berkeley. In her work she frequently explores Indian women and their struggles, in addition to the themes of immigration and the alienation of expatriates. Her novels include the following: The Tiger's Daughter *(1971),* Wife *(1975), and* Jasmine *(1989). She has also published several short story collections, and she co-authored two books with her husband, Clark Blaise. Focusing on an Indian woman's struggles with love in the United States, "The Tenant" explores the relationship between culture and romance. It was published in* The Middleman and Other Stories *in 1988.*

The Tenant

Maya Sanyal has been in Cedar Falls, Iowa, less than two weeks. She's come, books and clothes and one armchair rattling in the smallest truck that U-Haul would rent her, from New Jersey. Before that she was in North Carolina. Before that, Calcutta, India. Every place has something to give. She is sitting at the kitchen table with Fran drinking bourbon for the first time in her life. Fran Johnson found her the furnished apartment and helped her settle in. Now she's brought a bottle of bourbon which gives her the right to stay and talk for a bit. She's breaking up with someone named Vern, a pharmacist. Vern's father is also a pharmacist and owns a drugstore. Maya has seen Vern's father on TV twice already. The first time was on the local news when he spoke out against the selling of painkillers like Advil and Nuprin in supermarkets and gas stations. In the matter of painkillers, Maya is a universalist. The other time he was in a barbershop quartet. Vern gets along all right with his father. He likes the pharmacy business, as business goes, but he wants to go back to graduate school and learn to make films. Maya is drinking her first bourbon tonight because Vern left today for San Francisco State.

"I understand totally," Fran says. She teaches Utopian Fiction and a course in Women's Studies and worked hard to get Maya hired. Maya has a Ph.D. in Comparative Literature and will introduce writers like R. K. Narayan and Chinua

---

Achebe to three sections of sophomores at the University of Northern Iowa. "A person has to leave home. Try out his wings."

Fran has to use the bathroom. "I don't feel abandoned." She pushes her chair away from the table. "Anyway, it was a sex thing totally. We were good together. It'd be different if I'd loved him."

Maya tries to remember what's in the refrigerator. They need food. She hasn't been to the supermarket in over a week. She doesn't have a car yet and so she relies on a corner store—a longish walk—for milk, cereal, and frozen dinners. Someday these exigencies will show up as bad skin and collapsed muscle tone. No folly is ever lost. Maya pictures history as a net, the kind of safety net travelling trapeze artists of her childhood fell into when they were inattentive, or clumsy. Going to circuses in Calcutta with her father is what she remembers vividly. It is a banal memory, for her father, the owner of a steel company, is a complicated man.

Fran is out in the kitchen long enough for Maya to worry. They need food. Her mother believed in food. What is love, anger, inner peace, etc., her mother used to say, but the brain's biochemistry. Maya doesn't want to get into that, but she is glad she has enough stuff in the refrigerator to make an omelette. She realizes Indian women are supposed to be inventive with food, whip up exotic delights to tickle an American's palate, and she knows she should be meeting Fran's generosity and candor with some sort of bizarre and effortless countermove. If there's an exotic spice store in Cedar Falls or in neighboring Waterloo, she hasn't found it. She's looked in the phone book for common Indian names, especially Bengali, but hasn't yet struck up culinary intimacies. That will come—it always does. There's a six-pack in the fridge that her landlord, Ted Suminski, had put in because she'd be thirsty after unpacking. She was thirsty, but she doesn't drink beer. She probably should have asked him to come up and drink the beer. Except for Fran she hasn't had anyone over. Fran is more friendly and helpful than anyone Maya has known in the States since she came to North Carolina ten years ago, at nineteen. Fran is a Swede, and she is tall, with blue eyes. Her hair, however, is a dull, darkish brown.

"I don't think I can handle anything that heavy-duty," Fran says when she comes back to the room. She means the omelette. "I have to go home in any case." She lives with her mother and her aunt, two women in their mid-seventies, in a drafty farmhouse. The farmhouse now has a computer store catty-corner from it. Maya's been to the farm. She's been shown photographs of the way the corner used to be. If land values ever rebound, Fran will be worth millions.

Before Fran leaves she says, "Has Rab Chatterji called you yet?"

"No." She remembers the name, a good, reliable Bengali name, from the first night's study of the phone book. Dr. Rabindra Chatterji teaches Physics.

"He called the English office just before I left." She takes car keys out of her pocketbook. She reknots her scarf. "I bet Indian men are more sensitive than Americans. Rab's a Brahmin, that's what people say."

A Chatterji has to be a Bengali Brahmin—last names give ancestral secrets away—but Brahminness seems to mean more to Fran than it does to Maya. She was born in 1954, six full years after India became independent. Her India was Nehru's India: a charged, progressive place.

"All Indian men are wife beaters," Maya says. She means it and doesn't mean it. "That's why I married an American." Fran knows about the divorce, but nothing else. Fran is on the Hiring, Tenure, and Reappointment Committee.

Maya sees Fran down the stairs and to the car which is parked in the back in the spot reserved for Maya's car, if she had owned one. It will take her several months to save enough to buy one. She always pays cash, never borrows. She tells herself she's still recovering from the U-Haul drive halfway across the country. Ted Suminski is in his kitchen watching the women. Maya waves to him because waving to him, acknowledging him in that way, makes him seem less creepy. He seems to live alone though a sign, THE SUMINSKIS, hangs from a metal horse's head in the front yard. Maya hasn't seen Mrs. Suminski. She hasn't seen any children either. Ted always looks lonely. When she comes back from campus, he's nearly always in the back, throwing darts or shooting baskets.

"What's he like?" Fran gestures with her head as she starts up her car. "You hear these stories."

Maya doesn't want to know the stories. She has signed a year's lease. She doesn't want complications. "He's all right. I keep out of his way."

"You know what I'm thinking? Of all the people in Cedar Falls, you're the one who could understand Vern best. His wanting to try out his wings, run away, stuff like that."

"Not really." Maya is not being modest. Fran is being impulsively democratic, lumping her wayward lover and Indian friend together as headstrong adventurers. For Fran, a utopian and feminist, borders don't count. Maya's taken some big risks, made a break with her parents' ways. She's done things a woman from Ballygunge Park Road doesn't do, even in fantasies. She's not yet shared stories with Fran, apart from the divorce. She's told her nothing of men she picks up, the reputation she'd gained, before Cedar Falls, for "indiscretions." She has a job, equity, three friends she can count on for emergencies. She is an American citizen. But.

Fran's Brahmin calls her two nights later. On the phone he presents himself as Dr. Chatterji, not Rabindra or Rab. An old-fashioned Indian, she assumes. Her father still calls his closest friend, "Colonel." Dr. Chatterji asks her to tea on Sunday. She means to say no but hears herself say, "Sunday? Fiveish? I'm not doing anything special this Sunday."

Outside, Ted Suminski is throwing darts into his garage door. The door has painted-on rings: orange, purple, pink. The bull's-eye is gray. He has to be fifty at least. He is a big, thick, lonely man about whom people tell stories. Maya pulls the phone cord as far as it'll go so she can look down more directly on her landlord's large, bald head. He has his back to her as he lines up a dart. He's in black running shoes, red shorts, he's naked to the waist. He hunches his right shoulder, he pulls the arm back; a big, lonely man shouldn't have so much grace. The dart is ready to cut through the September evening. But Ted Suminski doesn't let go. He swings on worn rubber soles, catches her eye in the window (she has to have imagined this), takes aim at her shadow. Could she have imagined the noise of the dart's metal tip on her windowpane?

Dr. Chatterji is still on the phone. "You are not having any mode of transportation, is that right?"

Ted Suminski has lost interest in her. Perhaps it isn't interest, at all; perhaps it's aggression. "I don't drive," she lies, knowing it sounds less shameful than not owning a car. She has said this so often she can get in the right degree of apology and Asian upper-class helplessness. "It's an awful nuisance."

"Not to worry, please." Then, "It is a great honor to be meeting Dr. Sanyal's daughter. In Calcutta business circles he is a legend."

On Sunday she is ready by four-thirty. She doesn't know what the afternoon holds; there are surely no places for "high tea"—a colonial tradition—in Cedar Falls, Iowa. If he takes her back to his place, it will mean he has invited other guests. From his voice she can tell Dr. Chatterji likes to do things correctly. She has dressed herself in a peach-colored nylon georgette sari, jade drop-earrings and a necklace. The color is good on dark skin. She is not pretty, but she does her best. Working at it is a part of self-respect. In the mid-seventies, when American women felt rather strongly about such things, Maya had been in trouble with her women's group at Duke. She was too feminine. She had tried to explain the world she came out of. Her grandmother had been married off at the age of five in a village now in Bangladesh. Her great-aunt had been burned to death over a dowry problem. She herself had been trained to speak softly, arrange flowers, sing, be pliant. If she were to seduce Ted Suminski, she thinks as she waits in the front yard for Dr. Chatterji, it would be minor heroism. She has broken with the past. But.

Dr. Chatterji drives up for her at about five ten. He is a hesitant driver. The car stalls, jumps ahead, finally slams to a stop. Maya has to tell him to back off a foot or so; it's hard to leap over two sacks of pruned branches in a sari. Ted Suminski is an obsessive pruner and gardener.

"My sincerest apologies, Mrs. Sanyal," Dr. Chatterji says. He leans across the wide front seat of his noisy, very old, very used car and unlocks the door for her. "I am late. But then, I am sure you're remembering that Indian Standard Time is not at all the same as time in the States." He laughs. He could be nervous—she often had that effect on Indian men. Or he could just be chatty. "These Americans are all the time rushing and rushing but where it gets them?" He moves his head laterally once, twice. It's the gesture made famous by Peter Sellers. When Peter Sellers did it, it had seemed hilarious. Now it suggests that Maya and Dr. Chatterji have three thousand years plus civilization, sophistication, moral virtue, over people born on this continent. Like her, Dr. Chatterji is a naturalized American.

"Call me Maya," she says. She fusses with the seat belt. She does it because she needs time to look him over. He seems quite harmless. She takes in the prominent teeth, the eyebrows that run together. He's in a blue shirt and a beige cardigan with the K-Mart logo that buttons tightly over the waist. It's hard to guess his age because he has dyed his hair and his moustache. Late thirties, early forties. Older than she had expected. "Not Mrs. Sanyal."

This isn't the time to tell about ex-husbands. She doesn't know where John is these days. He should have kept up at least. John had come into her life as a graduate student at Duke, and she, mistaking the brief breathlessness of sex for love, had married him. They had stayed together two years, maybe a little less. The pain that John had inflicted all those years ago by leaving her had subsided into a cozy feeling of loss. This isn't the time, but then she doesn't want to be a legend's daughter all evening. She's not necessarily on Dr. Chatterji's side is what she wants to get across early; she's not against America and Americans. She makes the story—of marriage outside the Brahminic pale, the divorce—quick, dull. Her unsentimentality seems to shock him. His stomach sags inside the cardigan.

"We've each had our several griefs," the physicist says. "We're each required to pay our karmic debts."

"Where are we headed?"

"Mrs. Chatterji has made some Indian snacks. She is waiting to meet you because she is knowing your cousin-sister who studied in Scottish Church College. My home is okay, no?"

Fran would get a kick out of this. Maya has slept with married men, with nameless men, with men little more than boys, but never with an Indian man. Never.

The Chatterjis live in a small blue house on a gravelly street. There are at least five or six other houses on the street; the same size but in different colors and with different front yard treatments. More houses are going up. This is the cutting edge of suburbia.

Mrs. Chatterji stands in the driveway. She is throwing a large plastic ball to a child. The child looks about four, and is Korean or Cambodian. The child is not hers because she tells it, "Chung-Hee, ta-ta, bye-bye. Now I play with guest," as Maya gets out of the car.

Maya hasn't seen this part of town. The early September light softens the construction pits. In that light the houses too close together, the stout woman in a striped cotton sari, the child hugging a pink ball, the two plastic lawn chairs by a tender young tree, the sheets and saris on the clothesline in the back, all seem miraculously incandescent.

"Go home now, Chung-Hee. I am busy." Mrs. Chatterji points the child homeward, then turns to Maya, who has folded her hands in traditional Bengali greeting. "It is an honor. We feel very privileged." She leads Maya indoors to a front room that smells of moisture and paint.

In her new, deliquescent mood, Maya allows herself to be backed into the best armchair—a low-backed, boxy Goodwill item draped over with a Rajasthani bedspread—and asks after the cousin Mrs. Chatterji knows. She doesn't want to let go of Mrs. Chatterji. She doesn't want husband and wife to get into whispered conferences about their guest's misadventures in America, as they make tea in the kitchen.

The coffee table is already laid with platters of mutton croquettes, fish chops, onion pakoras, ghugni with puris, samosas, chutneys. Mrs. Chatterji has gone to too much trouble. Maya counts four kinds of sweetmeats in Corning casseroles on an end table. She looks into a see-through lid; spongy, white dumplings float in rosewater syrup. Planets contained, mysteries made visible.

"What are you waiting for, Santana?" Dr. Chatterji becomes imperious, though not unaffectionate. He pulls a dining chair up close to the coffee table. "Make some tea." He speaks in Bengali to his wife, in English to Maya. To Maya he says, grandly, "We are having real Indian Green Label Lipton. A nephew is bringing it just one month back."

His wife ignores him. "The kettle's already on," she says. She wants to know about the Sanyal family. Is it true her great-grandfather was a member of the Star Chamber in England?

Nothing in Calcutta is ever lost. Just as her story is known to Bengalis all over America, so are the scandals of her family, the grandfather hauled up for tax evasion, the aunt who left her husband to act in films. This woman brings up the Star Chamber, the glories of the Sanyal family, her father's philanthropies, but it's a way of saying, *I know the dirt.*

The bedrooms are upstairs. In one of those bedrooms an unseen, tormented presence—Maya pictures it as a clumsy ghost that strains to shake off the body's shell—drops things on the floor. The things are heavy and they make the front room's chandelier shake. Light bulbs, shaped like tiny candle flames, flicker. The Chatterjis have said nothing about children. There are no tricycles in the hallway, no small sandals behind the doors. Maya is too polite to ask about the noise, and the Chatterjis don't explain. They talk just a little louder. They flip the embroidered cover off the stereo. What would Maya like to hear? Hemanta Kumar? Manna Dey? Oh, that young chap, Manna Dey? What sincerity, what tenderness he can convey!

Upstairs the ghost doesn't hear the music of nostalgia. The ghost throws and thumps. The ghost makes its own vehement music. Maya hears in its voice madness, self-hate.

Finally the water in the kettle comes to a boil. The whistle cuts through all fantasy and pretense. Dr. Chatterji says, "I'll see to it," and rushes out of the room. But he doesn't go to the kitchen. He shouts up the stairwell. "Poltoo, kindly stop this nonsense straightaway! We're having a brilliant and cultured lady-guest and you're creating earthquakes?" The kettle is hysterical.

Mrs. Chatterji wipes her face. The face that had seemed plump and cheery at the start of the evening is now flabby. "My sister's boy," the woman says.

So this is the nephew who has brought with him the cartons of Green Label tea, one of which will be given to Maya.

Mrs. Chatterji speaks to Maya in English as though only the alien language can keep emotions in check. "Such an intelligent boy! His father is government servant. Very highly placed."

Maya is meant to visualize a smart, clean-cut young man from south Calcutta, but all she can see is a crazy, thwarted, lost graduate student. Intelligence, proper family guarantee nothing. Even Brahmins can do self-destructive things, feel unsavory urges. Maya herself had been an excellent student.

"He was First Class First in B. Sc. from Presidency College," the woman says. "Now he's getting Master's in Ag. Science at Iowa State."

The kitchen is silent. Dr. Chatterji comes back into the room with a tray. The teapot is under a tea cozy, a Kashmiri one embroidered with the usual chinar leaves, loops, and chains. "*Her* nephew," he says. The dyed hair and dyed moustache are no longer signs of a man wishing to fight the odds. He is a vain man, anxious to cut losses. "Very unfortunate business."

The nephew's story comes out slowly, over fish chops and mutton croquettes. He is in love with a student from Ghana.

"Everything was A-Okay until the Christmas break. Grades, assistantship for next semester, everything."

"I blame the college. The office for foreign students arranged a Christmas party. And now, *baapre baap!* Our poor Poltoo wants to marry a Negro Muslim."

Maya is known for her nasty, ironic one-liners. It has taken her friends weeks to overlook her malicious, un-American pleasure in others' misfortunes. Maya would like to finish Dr. Chatterji off quickly. He is pompous; he is reactionary; he wants to live and work in America but give back nothing except taxes. The confused world of the immigrant—and lostness that Maya and Poltoo feel—that's what Dr. Chatterji wants to avoid. She hates him. But.

Dr. Chatterji's horror is real. A good Brahmin boy in Iowa is in love with an African Muslim. It shouldn't be a big deal. But the more she watches the physicist, the more she realizes that "Brahmin" isn't a caste; it's a metaphor. You break one small rule, and the constellation collapses. She thinks suddenly that John Cheever—she is teaching him as a "world writer" in her classes, cheek-by-jowl with Africans and West Indians—would have understood Dr. Chatterji's dread. Cheever had been on her mind, ever since the late afternoon light slanted over Mrs. Chatterji's drying saris. She remembers now how full of a soft, Cheeverian light Durham had been the summer she had slept with John Hadwen; and how after that, her tidy graduate-student world became monstrous, lawless. All men became John Hadwen; John became all men. Outwardly, she retained her poise, her Brahminical breeding. She treated her crisis as a literary event; she lost her moral sense, her judgment, her power to distinguish. Her parents had behaved magnanimously. They had cabled from Calcutta: WHAT'S DONE IS DONE WE ARE CONFIDENT YOU WILL HANDLE NEW SITUATIONS WELL, ALL LOVE. But she knows more than do her parents. Love is anarchy.

Poltoo is Mrs. Chatterji's favorite nephew. She looks as though it is her fault that the Sunday has turned unpleasant. She stacks the empty platters methodically. To Maya she says, "It is the goddess who pulls the strings. We are puppets. I know the goddess will fix it. Poltoo will not marry that African woman." Then she goes to the coat closet in the hall and staggers back with a harmonium, the kind sold in music stores in Calcutta, and sets it down on the carpeted floor. "We're nothing but puppets," she says again. She sits at Maya's feet, her pudgy hands on the harmonium's shiny, black bellows. She sings, beautifully, in a virgin's high voice, "Come, goddess, come, muse, come to us hapless peoples' rescue."

Maya is astonished. She has taken singing lessons at Dakshini Academy in Calcutta. She plays the sitar and the tanpur, well enough to please Bengalis, to astonish Americans. But stout Mrs. Chatterji is a devotee, talking to God.

A little after eight, Dr. Chatterji drops her off. It's been an odd evening and they are both subdued.

"I want to say one thing," he says. He stops her from undoing her seat belt. The plastic sacks of pruned branches are still at the corner.

"You don't have to get out," she says.

"Please. Give me one more minute of your time."

"Sure."

"Maya is my favorite name."

She says nothing. She turns away from him without making her embarrassment obvious.

"Truly speaking, it is my favorite. You are sometimes lonely, no? But you are lucky. Divorced women can date, they can go to bars and discos. They can see mens, many mens. But inside marriage there is so much loneliness." A groan, low, horrible, comes out of him.

She turns back toward him, to unlatch the seat belt and run out of the car. She sees that Dr. Chatterji's pants are unzipped. One hand works hard under his Jockey shorts; the other rests, limp, penitential, on the steering wheel.

"Dr. Chatterji—*really!*" she cries.

The next day, Monday, instead of getting a ride home with Fran—Fran says she *likes* to give rides, she needs the chance to talk, and she won't share gas expenses, absolutely not—Maya goes to the periodicals room of the library. There are newspapers from everywhere, even from Madagascar and New Caledonia. She thinks of the periodicals room as an asylum for homesick aliens. There are two aliens already in the room, both Orientals, both absorbed in the politics and gossip of their far off homes.

She goes straight to the newspapers from India. She bunches her raincoat like a bolster to make herself more comfortable. There's so much to catch up on. A village headman, a known Congress-Indira party worker, has been shot by scooter-riding snipers. An Indian pugilist has won an international medal—in Nepal. A child drawing well water—the reporter calls the child "a neo-Buddhist, a convert from the now-outlawed untouchable caste"—has been stoned. An editorial explains that the story about stoning is not a story about caste but about failed idealism; a story about promises of green fields and clean, potable water broken, a story about bribes paid and wells not dug. But no, thinks Maya, it's about caste.

Out here, in the heartland of the new world, the India of serious newspapers unsettles. Maya longs again to feel what she had felt in the Chatterjis' living room: virtues made physical. It is a familiar feeling, a longing. Had a suitable man presented himself in the reading room at that instant, she would have seduced him. She goes on to the stack of *India Abroads,* reads through matrimonial columns, and steals an issue to take home.

Indian men want Indian brides. Married Indian men want Indian mistresses. All over America, "handsome, tall, fair" engineers, doctors, data processors—the new pioneers—cry their eerie love calls.

Maya runs a finger down the first column; her fingertip, dark with newsprint, stops at random.

> Hello! Hi! Yes you *are* the one I'm looking for. You are the new emancipated Indo-American woman. You have a zest for life. You are at ease in USA and yet your ethics are rooted in Indian tradition. The man of your dreams has come. Yours truly is handsome, ear-nose-throat specialist, well-settled in Connecticut. Age is 41 but never married, physically fit, sportsmanly, and strong. I adore

> idealism, poetry, beauty. I abhor smugness, passivity, caste system. Write with recent photo. Better still, call!!!.

Maya calls. Hullo, hullo, hullo! She hears immigrant lovers cry in crowded shopping malls. Yes, you who are at ease in both worlds, you are the one. She feels she has a fair chance.

A man answers. "Ashoke Mehta speaking."

She speaks quickly into the bright-red mouthpiece of her telephone. He will be in Chicago, in transit, passing through O'Hare. United counter, Saturday, two P.M. As easy as that.

"Good," Ashoke Mehta says. "For these encounters, I, too, prefer a neutral zone."

On Saturday at exactly two o'clock the man of Maya's dreams floats toward her as lovers used to in shampoo commercials. The United counter is a loud, harrassed place but passengers and piled-up luggage fall away from him. Full-cheeked and fleshy-lipped, he is handsome. He hasn't lied. He is serene, assured, a Hindu god touching down in Illinois.

She can't move. She feels ugly and unworthy. Her adult life no longer seems miraculously rebellious; it is grim, it is perverse. She has accomplished nothing. She has changed her citizenship but she hasn't broken through into the light, the vigor, the *bustle* of the New World. She is stuck in dead space.

"Hullo, hullo!" Their fingers touch.

Oh, the excitement! Ashoke Mehta's palm feels so right in the small of her back. Hullo, hullo, hullo. He pushes her out of the reach of anti-Khomeini Iranians, Hare Krishnas, American Fascists, men with fierce wants, and guides her to an empty gate. They have less than an hour.

"What would you like, Maya?"

She knows he can read her mind, she knows her thoughts are open to him. *You,* she's almost giddy with the thought, with simple desire. "From the snack bar," he says, as though to clarify. "I'm afraid I'm starved."

Below them, where the light is strong and hurtful, a Boeing is being serviced. "Nothing," she says.

He leans forward. She can feel the nap of his scarf—she recognizes the Cambridge colors—she can smell the wool of his Icelandic sweater. She runs her hand along the scarf, then against the flesh of his neck. "Only the impulsive ones call," he says.

The immigrant courtship proceeds. It's easy, he's good with facts. He knows how to come across to a stranger who may end up a lover, a spouse. He makes over a hundred thousand. He owns a house in Hartford, and two income properties in Newark. He plays the market but he's cautious. He's good at badminton but plays handball to keep in shape. He watches all the sports on television. Last August he visited Copenhagen, Helsinki, and Leningrad. Once upon a time he collected stamps but now he doesn't have hobbies, except for reading. He counts himself an intellectual, he spends too much on books. Ludlum, Forsyth, MacInnes; other names she doesn't catch. She suppresses a smile, she's told him only she's a graduate student. He's not without his vices. He's a spender, not a saver. He's a sensualist: good food—all foods, but easy on the Indian—good wine. Some temptations he doesn't try to resist.

And I, she wants to ask, do I tempt?

"Now tell me about yourself, Maya." He makes it easy for her. "Have you ever been in love?"

"No."

"But many have loved you, I can see that." He says it not unkindly. It is the fate of women like her, and men like him. Their karmic duty, to be loved. It is expected, not judged. She feels he can see them all, the sad parade of need and demand. This isn't the time to reveal all.

And so the courtship enters a second phase.

When she gets back to Cedar Falls, Ted Suminski is standing on the front porch. It's late at night, chilly. He is wearing a down vest. She's never seen him on the porch. In fact there's no chair to sit on. He looks chilled through. He's waited around a while.

"Hi." She has her keys ready. This isn't the night to offer the six-pack in the fridge. He looks expectant, ready to pounce.

"Hi." He looks like a man who might have aimed the dart at her. What has he done to his wife, his kids? Why isn't there at least a dog? "Say, I left a note upstairs."

The note is written in Magic Marker and thumb-tacked to her apartment door. DUE TO PERSONAL REASONS, NAMELY REMARRIAGE, I REQUEST THAT YOU VACATE MY PLACE AT THE END OF THE SEMESTER.

Maya takes the note down and retacks it to the kitchen wall. The whole wall is like a bulletin board, made of some new, crumbly building-material. Her kitchen, Ted Suminski had told her, was once a child's bedroom. Suminski in love: the idea stuns her. She has misread her landlord. The dart at her window speaks of no twisted fantasy. The landlord wants the tenant out.

She gets a glass out of the kitchen cabinet, gets out a tray of ice, pours herself a shot of Fran's bourbon. She is happy for Ted Suminski. She is. She wants to tell someone how moved she'd been by Mrs. Chatterji's singing. How she'd felt in O'Hare, even about Dr. Rab Chatterji in the car. But Fran is not the person. No one she's ever met is the person. She can't talk about the dead space she lives in. She wishes Ashoke Mehta would call. Right now.

Weeks pass. Then two months. She finds a new room, signs another lease. Her new landlord calls himself Fred. He has no arms, but he helps her move her things. He drives between Ted Suminski's place and his twice in his station wagon. He uses his toes the way Maya uses her fingers. He likes to do things. He pushes garbage sacks full of Maya's clothes up the stairs.

"It's all right to stare," Fred says. "Hell, I would."

That first afternoon in Fred's rooming house, they share a Chianti. Fred wants to cook her pork chops but he's a little shy about Indians and meat. Is it beef, or pork? Or any meat? She says it's okay, any meat, but not tonight. He has an ex-wife in Des Moines, two kids in Portland, Oregon. The kids are both normal; he's the only freak in the family. But he's self-reliant. He shops in the supermarket like anyone else, he carries out the garbage, shovels the snow off the sidewalk. He needs Maya's help with one thing. Just one thing. The box of Tide is a bit too heavy to manage. Could she get him the giant size every so often and leave it in the basement?

The dead space need not suffocate. Over the months, Fred and she will settle into companionship. She has never slept with a man without arms. Two wounded people, he will joke during their nightly contortions. It will shock her, this assumed equivalence with a man so strikingly deficient. She knows she is strange, and lonely, but being Indian is not the same, she would have thought, as being a freak.

One night in spring, Fred's phone rings. "Ashoke Mehta speaking." None of this "do you remember me?" nonsense. The god has tracked her down. He hasn't forgotten. "Hullo," he says, in their special way. And because she doesn't answer back, "Hullo, hullo, hullo." She is aware of Fred in the back of the room. He is lighting a cigarette with his toes.

"Yes," she says, "I remember."

"I had to take care of a problem," Ashoke Mehta says. "You know that I have my vices. That time at O'Hare I was honest with you."

She is breathless.

"Who is it, May?" asks Fred.

"You also have a problem," says the voice. His laugh echoes. "You will come to Hartford, I know."

When she moves out, she tells herself, it will not be the end of Fred's world.

[1988]

Thomas H. Raddall

Thomas Head Raddall (1903–1994) was born in Kent, England and moved with his family to Canada when he was ten years old. Before becoming a full time writer in 1934, Raddall was an accountant for wood pulp and paper firms in Nova Scotia. He was a multifaceted prolific author writing novels, short stories, history, children's literature, journalism, memoirs, radio plays, and travel literature. His many awards include the Canadian Governor General's Award for best Canadian book of the year in fiction for The Pied Piper of Dipper Creek and Other Tales *in 1944, and in nonfiction for* Halifax, Warden of the North *in 1948, and* The Path of Destiny: Canada from the British Conquest to Home Rule, 1763–1850 *in 1957. Many of his books recreate life in Nova Scotia from the founding of Halifax in 1749 to the twentieth century. His characters are frequently swept up against their will in the tide of events as we see in Kezia and Mr. Mears in "The Wedding Gift," which was first published in* The Wedding Gift and Other Stories *in 1947. This story is an excellent example of Raddall's treatment of historical material in the short-story form.*

The Wedding Gift

Nova Scotia, in 1794. Winter. Snow on the ground. Two feet of it in the woods, less by the shore, except in drifts against Port Marriott's barns and fences; but enough to set sleigh bells ringing through the town, enough to require a multitude of paths and burrows from doors to streets, to carpet the wharves and the decks of the shipping, and to trim the ships' yards with tippets of ermine. Enough to require fires roaring in the town's chimneys, and blue wood smoke hanging low over the roof tops in the still December air. Enough to squeal under foot in the trodden places and to muffle the step everywhere else. Enough for the hunters, whose snowshoes now could overtake the floundering moose and caribou. Even enough for the always-complaining loggers, whose ox sleds now could haul their cut from every part of the woods. But not enough, not nearly enough snow for Miss Kezia Barnes, who was going to Bristol Creek to marry Mr Hathaway.

Kezia did not want to marry Mr Hathaway. Indeed she had told Mr and Mrs Barclay in a tearful voice that she didn't want to marry anybody. But Mr Barclay had taken snuff and said 'Ha! Humph!' in the severe tone he used when he was

---

Reprinted from *The New Oxford Book of Canadian Short Stories in English*, edited by Margaret Atwood and Robert Weaver, (1997), by permission of Dalhousie University.

displeased; and Mrs Barclay had sniffed and said it was a very good match for her, and revolved the cold blue eyes in her fat moon face, and said Kezia must not be a little fool.

There were two ways of going to Bristol Creek. One was by sea, in one of the fishing sloops. But the preacher objected to that. He was a pallid young man lately sent out from England by Lady Huntingdon's Connexion, and seasick five weeks on the way. He held Mr Barclay in some awe, for Mr Barclay had the best pew in the meetinghouse and was the chief pillar of godliness in Port Marriott. But young Mr Mears was firm on this point. He would go by road, he said, or not at all. Mr Barclay had retorted 'Ha! Humph!' The road was twenty miles of horse path through the woods, now deep in snow. Also the path began at Harper's Farm on the far side of the harbour, and Harper had but one horse.

'I shall walk,' declared the preacher calmly, 'and the young woman can ride.'

Kezia had prayed for snow, storms of snow, to bury the trail and keep anyone from crossing the cape to Bristol Creek. But now they were setting out from Harper's Farm, with Harper's big brown horse, and all Kezia's prayers had gone for naught. Like any anxious lover, busy Mr Hathaway had sent Black Sam overland on foot to find out what delayed his wedding, and now Sam's day-old tracks marked for Kezia the road to marriage.

She was a meek little thing, as became an orphan brought up as househelp in the Barclay home; but now she looked at the preacher and saw how young and helpless he looked so far from his native Yorkshire, and how ill-clad for this bitter trans-Atlantic weather, and she spoke up.

'You'd better take my shawl, sir. I don't need it. I've got Miss Julia's old riding cloak. And we'll go ride-and-tie.'

'Ride and what?' murmured Mr Mears.

'I'll ride a mile or so, then I'll get down and tie the horse to a tree and walk on. When you come up to the horse, you mount and ride a mile or so, passing me on the way, and you tie him and walk on. Like that. Ride-and-tie, ride-and-tie. The horse gets a rest between.'

Young Mr Mears nodded and took the proffered shawl absently. It was a black thing that matched his sober broadcloth coat and smallclothes, his black woollen stockings and his round black hat. At Mr Barclay's suggestion he had borrowed a pair of moose-hide moccasins for the journey. As he walked a prayer-book in his coat-skirts bumped the back of his legs.

At the top of the ridge above Harper's pasture, where the narrow path led off through gloomy hemlock woods, Kezia paused for a last look back across the harbour. In the morning sunlight the white roofs of the little lonely town resembled a tidal wave flung up by the sea and frozen as it broke against the dark pine forest to the west. Kezia sighed, and young Mr Mears was surprised to see tears in her eyes.

She rode off ahead. The saddle was a man's, of course, awkward to ride modestly, woman-fashion. As soon as she was out of the preacher's sight she rucked her skirts and slid a leg over to the other stirrup. That was better. There was a pleasant sensation of freedom about it, too. For a moment she forgot that she was going to Bristol Creek, in finery second-hand from the Barclay girls, in a new linen shift and drawers that she had sewn herself in the light of the kitchen candles, in white cotton stockings and a bonnet and shoes from Mr Barclay's store, to marry Mr Hathaway.

The Barclays had done well for her from the time when, a skinny weeping creature of fourteen, she was taken into the Barclay household and, as Mrs Barclay so often said, 'treated more like one of my own than a bond-girl from the poorhouse'. She had first choice of the clothing cast off by Miss Julia and Miss Clara. She was permitted to sit in the same room, and learn what she could, when the schoolmaster came to give private lessons to the Barclay girls. She waited on table, of course, and helped in the kitchen, and made beds, and dusted and scrubbed. But then she had been taught to spin and to sew and to knit. And she was permitted, indeed encouraged, to sit with the Barclays in the meetinghouse, at the convenient end of the pew, where she could worship the Barclays' God and assist with the Barclay wraps at the beginning and end of the service. And now, to complete her rewards, she had been granted the hand of a rejected Barclay suitor.

Mr Hathaway was Barclay's agent at Bristol Creek, where he sold rum and gunpowder and corn meal and such things to the fishermen and hunters, and bought split cod—fresh, pickled or dry—and ran a small sawmill, and cut and shipped firewood by schooner to Port Marriott, and managed a farm, all for a salary of fifty pounds, Halifax currency, per year. Hathaway was a most capable fellow, Mr Barclay often acknowledged. But when after fifteen capable years he came seeking a wife, and cast a sheep's eye first at Miss Julia, and then at Miss Clara, Mrs Barclay observed with a sniff that Hathaway was looking a bit high.

So he was. The older daughter of Port Marriott's most prosperous merchant was even then receiving polite attentions from Mr Gamage, the new collector of customs, and a connection of the Halifax Gamages, as Mrs Barclay was fond of pointing out. And Miss Clara was going to Halifax in the spring to learn the gentle art of playing the pianoforte, and incidentally to display her charms to the naval and military young gentlemen who thronged the Halifax drawingrooms. The dear girls laughed behind their hands whenever long solemn Mr Hathaway came to town aboard one of the Barclay vessels and called at the big house under the elms. Mrs Barclay bridled at Hathaway's presumption, but shrewd Mr Barclay narrowed his little black eyes and took snuff and said 'Ha! Humph!'

It was plain to Mr Barclay that an emergency had arisen. Hathaway was a good man—in his place; and Hathaway must be kept content there, to go on making profit for Mr Barclay at a cost of only £50 a year. 'Twas a pity Hathaway couldn't satisfy himself with one of the fishermen's girls at the Creek, but there 'twas. If Hathaway had set his mind on a town miss, then a town miss he must have; but she must be the right kind, the sort who would content herself and Hathaway at Bristol Creek and not go nagging the man to remove and try his capabilities elsewhere. At once Mr Barclay thought of Kezia—dear little Kezzie. A colourless little creature but quiet and well-mannered and pious, and only twenty-two.

Mr Hathaway was nearly forty and far from handsome, and he had a rather cold, seeking way about him—useful in business of course—that rubbed women the wrong way. Privately Mr Barclay thought Hathaway lucky to get Kezia. But it was a nice match for the girl, better than anything she could have expected.

He impressed that upon her and introduced the suitor from Bristol Creek. Mr Hathaway spent two or three evenings courting Kezia in the kitchen—Kezia in a quite good gown of Miss Clara's, gazing out at the November moon on the snow, murmuring now and again in the tones of someone in a rather dismal trance, while the kitchen help listened behind one door and the Barclay girls giggled behind another.

The decision, reached mainly by the Barclays, was that Mr Hathaway should come to Port Marriott aboard the packet schooner on December twenty-third, to be married in the Barclay parlour and then take his bride home for Christmas. But an unforeseen circumstance had changed all this. The circumstance was a ship, 'from Mogador in Barbary' as Mr Barclay wrote afterwards in the salvage claim, driven off her course by gales and wrecked at the very entrance to Bristol Creek. She was a valuable wreck, laden with such queer things as goatskins in pickle, almonds, wormseed, pomegranate skins and gum arabic, and capable Mr Hathaway had lost no time in salvage for the benefit of his employer.

As a result he could not come to Port Marriott for a wedding or anything else. A storm might blow up at any time and demolish this fat prize. He dispatched a note by Black Sam, urging Mr Barclay to send Kezia and the preacher by return. It was not the Orthodox note of an impatient sweetheart, but it said that he had moved into his new house by the Creek and found it 'extream empty lacking a woman', and it suggested delicately that while his days were full, the nights were dull.

Kezia was no judge of distance. She rode for what she considered a reasonable time and then slid off and tied the brown horse to a maple tree beside the path. She had brought a couple of lamp wicks to tie about her shoes, to keep them from coming off in the snow, and she set out afoot in the big splayed tracks of Black Sam. The soft snow came almost to her knees in places and she lifted her skirts high. The path was no wider than the span of a man's arms, cut out with axes years before. She stumbled over a concealed stump from time to time, and the huckleberry bushes dragged at her cloak, but the effort warmed her. It had been cold, sitting on the horse with the wind blowing up her legs.

After a time the preacher overtook her, riding awkwardly and holding the reins in a nervous grip. The stirrups were too short for his long black stockinged legs. He called out cheerfully as he passed, 'Are you all right, Miss?' She nodded, standing aside with her back to a tree. When he disappeared ahead, with a last flutter of black shawl tassels in the wind, she picked up her skirts and went on. The path climbed and dropped monotonously over a succession of wooded ridges. Here and there in a hollow she heard water running, and the creak of frosty poles underfoot, and knew she was crossing a small stream, and once the trail ran across a wide swamp on half-rotten corduroy, wind-swept and bare of snow.

She found the horse tethered clumsily not far ahead, and the tracks of the preacher going on. She had to lead the horse to a stump so she could mount, and when she passed Mr Mears again she called out, 'Please, sir, next time leave the horse by a stump or a rock so I can get on.' In his quaint old-country accent he murmured, 'I'm very sorry,' and gazed down at the snow. She forgot she was riding astride until she had passed him, and then she flushed, and gave the indignant horse a cut of the switch. Next time she remembered and swung her right leg back where it should be, and tucked the skirts modestly about her ankles; but young Mr Mears looked down at the snow anyway, and after that she did not trouble to shift when she overtook him.

The ridges became steeper, and the streams roared under the ice and snow in the swales. They emerged upon the high tableland between Port Marriott and Bristol Creek, a gusty wilderness of young hardwood scrub struggling up amongst the gray snags of an old forest fire, and now that they were out of the gloomy softwoods they could see a stretch of sky. It was blue-grey and forbidding, and the wind whistling up from the invisible sea felt raw on the cheek. At their next meeting Kezia said, 'It's going to snow.'

She had no knowledge of the trail but she guessed that they were not much more than half way across the cape. On this high barren the track was no longer straight and clear, it meandered amongst the meagre hardwood clumps where the path-makers had not bothered to cut, and only Black Sam's footprints really marked it for her unaccustomed eyes. The preacher nodded vaguely at her remark. The woods, like everything else about his chosen mission field, were new and very interesting, and he could not understand the alarm in her voice. He looked confidently at Black Sam's tracks.

Kezia tied the horse farther on and began her spell of walking. Her shoes were solid things, the kind of shoes Mr Barclay invoiced as 'a Common Strong sort, for women, Five Shillings'; but the snow worked into them and melted and saturated the leather. Her feet were numb every time she slid down from the horse and it took several minutes of stumbling through the snow to bring back an aching warmth. Beneath her arm she clutched the small bundle which contained all she had in the world—two flannel nightgowns, a shift of linen, three pairs of stout wool stockings—and of course Mr Barclay's wedding gift for Mr Hathaway.

Now as she plunged along she felt the first sting of snow on her face and, looking up, saw the stuff borne on the wind in small hard pellets that fell amongst the bare hardwoods and set up a whisper everywhere. When Mr. Mears rode up to her the snow was thick in their faces, like flung salt.

'It's a nor-easter!' she cried up to him. She knew the meaning of snow from the sea. She had been born in a fishing village down the coast.

'Yes,' mumbled the preacher, and drew a fold of the shawl about his face. He disappeared. She struggled on, gasping, and after what seemed a tremendous journey came upon him standing alone and bewildered, looking off somewhere to the right.

'The horse!' he shouted. 'I got off him, and before I could fasten the reins some snow fell off a branch—startled him, you know—and he ran off, over that way.' He gestured with a mittened hand. 'I must fetch him back,' he added confusedly.

'No!' Kezia cried. 'Don't you try. You'd only get lost. So would I. Oh, dear! This is awful. We'll have to go on, the best we can.'

He was doubtful. The horse tracks looked very plain. But Kezia was looking at Black Sam's tracks, and tugging his arm. He gave in, and they struggled along for half an hour or so. Then the last trace of the old footprints vanished.

'What shall we do now?' the preacher asked, astonished.

'I don't know,' whispered Kezia, and leaned against a dead pine stub in an attitude of weariness and indifference that dismayed him.

'We must keep moving, my dear, mustn't we? I mean, we can't stay here.'

'Can't stay here,' she echoed.

'Down there—a hollow, I think. I see some hemlock trees, or are they pines?—I'm never quite sure. Shelter, anyway.'

'Shelter,' muttered Kezia.

He took her by the hand and like a pair of lost children they dragged their steps into the deep snow of the hollow. The trees were tall spruces, a thick bunch in a ravine, where they had escaped an old fire. A stream thundered amongst them somewhere. There was no wind in this place, only the fine snow whirling thickly down between the trees like a sediment from the storm overhead.

'Look!' cried Mr Mears. A hut loomed out of the whiteness before them, a small structure of moss-chinked logs with a roof of poles and birch-bark. It had an abandoned look. Long streamers of moss hung out between the logs. On the roof shreds of birch-bark wavered gently in the drifting snow. The door stood half open and a thin drift of snow lay along the split-pole floor. Instinctively Kezia went to the stone hearth. There were old ashes sodden with rain down the chimney and now frozen to a cake.

'Have you got flint and steel?' she asked. She saw in his eyes something dazed and forlorn. He shook his head, and she was filled with a sudden anger, not so much at him as at Mr Barclay and that—that Hathaway, and all the rest of mankind. They ruled the world and made such a sorry mess of it. In a small fury she began to rummage about the hut.

There was it crude bed of poles and brushwood by the fireplace—brushwood so old that only a few brown needles clung to the twigs. A rough bench whittled from a pine log, with round birch sticks for legs. A broken earthenware pot in a corner. In another some ash-wood frames such as trappers used for stretching skins. Nothing else. The single window was covered with a stretched moose-bladder, cracked and dry-rotten, but it still let in some daylight while keeping out the snow.

She scooped up the snow from the floor with her mittened hands, throwing it outside, and closed the door carefully, dropping the bar into place, as if she could shut out and bar the cold in such a fashion. The air inside was frigid. Their breath hung visible in the dim light from the window. Young Mr Mears dropped on his wet knees and began to pray in a loud voice. His face was pinched with cold and his teeth rattled as he prayed. He was a pitiable object.

'Prayers won't keep you warm,' said Kezia crossly.

He looked up, amazed at the change in her. She had seemed such a meek little thing. Kezia was surprised at herself, and surprisingly she went on, 'You'd far better take off those wet moccasins and stockings and shake out the snow of your clothes.' She set the example, vigorously shaking out her skirts and Miss Julia's cloak, and she turned her small back on him and took off her own shoes and stockings, and pulled on dry stockings from her bundle. She threw him a pair.

'Put those on.'

He looked at them and at his large feet, hopelessly.

'I'm afraid they wouldn't go on.'

She tossed him one of her flannel nightgowns. 'Then take off your stockings and wrap your feet and legs in that.'

He obeyed, in an embarrassed silence. She rolled her eyes upward, for his modesty's sake, and saw a bundle on one of the low rafters—the late owner's bedding, stowed away from mice. She stood on the bench and pulled down three bearskins, marred with bullet holes. A rank and musty smell arose in the cold. She considered the find gravely.

'You take them,' Mr Mears said gallantly. 'I shall be quite all right.'

'You'll be dead by morning, and so shall I,' she answered vigorously, 'if you don't do what I say. We've got to roll up in these.'

'Together?' he cried in horror.

'Of course! To keep each other warm. It's the only way.'

She spread the skins on the floor, hair uppermost, one overlapping another, and dragged the flustered young man down beside her, clutched him in her arms, and rolled with him, over, and over again, so that they became a single shapeless heap in the corner farthest from the draft between door and chimney.

'Put your arms around me,' commanded the new Kezia, and he obeyed.

'Now,' she said, 'you can pray. God helps those that help themselves.'

He prayed aloud for a long time, and privately called upon heaven to witness the purity of his thoughts in this strange and shocking situation. He said 'Amen' at last; and 'Amen', echoed Kezia, piously.

They lay silent a long time, breathing on each other's necks and hearing their own hearts—poor Mr Mears' fluttering in an agitated way, Kezia's steady as a clock. A delicious warmth crept over them. They relaxed in each other's arms. Outside, the storm hissed in the spruce tops and set up an occasional cold moan in the cracked clay chimney. The down-swirling snow brushed softly against the bladder pane.

'I'm warm now,' murmured Kezia. 'Are you?'

'Yes. How long must we stay here like this?'

'Till the storm's over, of course. Tomorrow, probably. Nor'easters usually blow themselves out in a day and a night, 'specially when they come up sharp, like this one. Are you hungry?'

'No.'

'Abigail—that's the black cook at Barclay's—gave me bread and cheese in a handkerchief. I've got it in my bundle. Mr Barclay thought we ought to reach Bristol Creek by supper time, but Nabby said I must have a bite to eat on the road. She's a good kind thing, old Nabby. Sure you're not hungry?'

'Quite. I feel somewhat fatigued but not hungry.'

'Then we'll eat the bread and cheese for breakfast. Have you got a watch?'

'No, I'm sorry. They cost such a lot of money. In Lady Huntingdon's Connexion we—'

'Oh well, it doesn't matter. It must be about four o'clock—the light's getting dim. Of course, the dark comes very quick in a snowstorm.'

'Dark,' echoed young Mr Mears drowsily. Kezia's hair, washed last night for the wedding journey, smelled pleasant so close to his face. It reminded him of something. He went to sleep dreaming of his mother, with his face snug in the curve of Kezia's neck and shoulder, and smiling, and muttering words that Kezia could not catch. After a time she kissed his check. It seemed a very natural thing to do.

Soon she was dozing herself, and dreaming, too; but her dreams were full of forbidding faces—Mr Barclay's, Mrs Barclay's, Mr Hathaway's; especially Mr Hathaway's. Out of a confused darkness Mr Hathaway's hard acquisitive gaze searched her shrinking flesh like a cold wind. Then she was shuddering by the kitchen fire at Barclay's, accepting Mr Hathaway's courtship and wishing she was dead. In the midst of that sickening wooing she wakened sharply.

It was quite dark in the hut. Mr Mears was breathing quietly against her throat. But there was a sound of heavy steps outside, muffled in the snow and somehow felt rather than heard. She shook the young man and he wakened with a start, clutching her convulsively.

'Sh-h-h!' she warned. 'Something's moving outside.' She felt him stiffen.

'Bears?' he whispered.

Silly! thought Kezia. People from the old country could think of nothing but bears in the woods. Besides, bears holed up in winter. A caribou, perhaps. More likely a moose. Caribou moved inland before this, to the wide mossy bogs up the river, away from the coastal storms. Again the sound.

'There!' hissed the preacher. Their hearts beat rapidly together.

'The door—you fastened it, didn't you?'

'Yes,' she said. Suddenly she knew.

'Unroll, quick!' she cried. . . . 'No, not this way—your way.'

They unrolled, ludicrously, and the girl scrambled up and ran across the floor in her stockinged feet, and fumbled with the rotten door-bar. Mr Mears attempted to follow but he tripped over the nightgown still wound about his feet, and fell with a crash. He was up again in a moment, catching up the clumsy wooden bench for a weapon, his bare feet slapping on the icy floor. He tried to shoulder her aside, crying 'Stand back! Leave it to me!' and waving the bench uncertainly in the darkness.

She laughed excitedly. 'Silly!' she said. 'It's the horse.' She flung the door open. In the queer ghostly murk of a night filled with snow they beheld a large dark shape. The shape whinnied softly and thrust a long face into the doorway. Mr Mears dropped the bench, astonished.

'He got over his fright and followed us here somehow,' Kezia said, and laughed again. She put her arms about the snowy head and laid her face against it.

'Good horse! Oh, good, good horse!'

'What are you going to do?' the preacher murmured over her shoulder. After the warmth of their nest in the furs they were shivering in this icy atmosphere.

'Bring him in, of course. We can't leave him out in the storm.' She caught the bridle and urged the horse inside with expert clucking sounds. The animal hesitated, but fear of the storm and a desire for shelter and company decided him. In he came, tramping ponderously on the split-pole floor. The preacher closed and barred the door.

'And now?' he asked.

'Back to the furs. Quick! It's awful cold.'

Rolled in the furs once more, their arms went about each other instinctively, and the young man's face found the comfortable nook against Kezia's soft throat. But sleep was difficult after that. The horse whinnied gently from time to time, and stamped about the floor. The decayed poles crackled dangerously under his hoofs whenever he moved, and Kezia trembled, thinking he might break through and frighten himself, and flounder about till he tumbled the crazy hut about their heads. She called out to him 'Steady, boy! Steady!'

It was a long night. The pole floor made its irregularities felt through the thickness of fur; and because there seemed nowhere to put their arms but about each other the flesh became cramped, and spread its protest along the bones. They were stiff and sore when the first light of morning stained the window. They unrolled and stood up thankfully, and tramped up and down the floor, threshing their arms in an effort to fight off the gripping cold. Kezia undid her bundle in a corner and brought forth Nabby's bread and cheese, and they ate it sitting together on the edge of the brushwood bed with the skins about their shoulders. Outside the snow had ceased.

'We must set off at once,' the preacher said. 'Mr Hathaway will be anxious."

Kezia was silent. She did not move, and he looked it her curiously. She appeared very fresh, considering the hardships of the previous day and the night. He passed a hand over his cheeks and thought how unclean he must appear in her eyes, with this stubble on his pale face.

'Mr Hathaway—' he began again.

'I'm not going to Mr Hathaway,' Kezia said quietly.

'But—the wedding!'

'There'll be no wedding. I don't want to marry Mr Hathaway. 'Twas Mr Hathaway's idea, and Mr and Mrs Barclay's. They wanted me to marry him.'

'What will the Barclays say, my dear?'

She shrugged. 'I've been their bond-girl ever since I was fourteen, but I'm not a slave like poor black Nabby, to be handed over, body and soul, whenever it suits.'

'Your soul belongs to God,' said Mr Mears devoutly.

'And my body belongs to me.'

He was a little shocked at this outspokenness but he said gently, 'Of course. To give oneself in marriage without true affection would be an offense in the sight of heaven. But what will Mr Hathaway say?'

'Well, to begin with, he'll ask where I spent the night, and I'll have to tell the truth. I'll have to say I bundled with you in a hut in the woods.'

'Bundled?'

'A custom the people brought with them from Connecticut when they came to settle in Nova Scotia. Poor folk still do it. Sweethearts, I mean. It saves fire and candles when you're courting on a winter evening. It's harmless—they keep their clothes on, you see, like you and me—but Mr Barclay and the other Methody people are terrible set against it. Mr Barclay got old Mr Mings—he's the Methody preacher that died last year—to make a sermon against it. Mr Mings said bundling was an invention of the devil.'

'Then if you go back to Mr Barclay—'

'He'll ask me the same question and I'll have to give him the same answer. I couldn't tell a lie, could I?' She turned a pair of round blue eyes and met his embarrassed gaze.

'No! No, you mustn't lie. Whatever shall we do?' he murmured in a dazed voice. Again she was silent, looking modestly down her small nose.

'It's so very strange,' he floundered. 'This country—there are so many things I don't know, so many things to learn. You—I—we shall have to tell the truth, of course. Doubtless I can find a place in the Lord's service somewhere else, but what about you, poor girl?'

'I heard say the people at Scrod Harbour want a preacher.'

'But—the tale would follow me, wouldn't it, my dear? This—er—bundling with a young woman?'

'Twouldn't matter if the young woman was your wife.'

'Eh?' His mouth fell open. He was like an astonished child, for all his preacher's clothes and the new beard on his jaws.

'I'm a good girl,' Kezia said, inspecting her foot. 'I can read and write and know all the tunes in the psalter. And—and you need someone to look after you.'

He considered the truth of that. Then he murmured uncertainly, 'We'd be very poor, my dear. The Connexion gives some support, but of course—'

'I've always been poor,' Kezia said. She sat very still but her cold fingers writhed in her lap.

He did something then that made her want to cry. He took hold of her hands and bowed his head and kissed them.

'It's strange—I don't even know your name, my dear.'

'It's Kezia—Kezia Barnes.'

He said quietly 'You're a brave girl, Kezia Barnes, and I shall try to be a good husband to you. Shall we go?'

'Hadn't you better kiss me, first?' Kezia said faintly.

He put his lips awkwardly to hers; and then, as if the taste of her clean mouth itself provided strength and purpose, he kissed her again, and firmly. She threw her arms about his neck.

'Oh, Mr Mears!'

How little he knew about everything! He hadn't even known enough to wear two or three pairs of stockings inside those roomy moccasins, nor to carry a pair of dry ones. Yesterday's wet stockings were lying like sticks on the frosty floor. She showed him how to knead the hard-frozen moccasins into softness, and while he worked at the stiff leather she tore up one of her wedding bed-shirts and wound the flannel strips about his legs and feet. It looked very queer when she had finished, and they both laughed.

They were chilled to the bone when they set off, Kezia on the horse and the preacher walking ahead, holding the reins. When they regained the slope where they had lost the path, Kezia said, 'The sun rises somewhere between east and southeast, at this time of year. Keep it on your left shoulder a while. That will take us back towards Port Marriott.'

When they came to the green timber she told him to shift the sun to his left eye.

'Have you changed your mind?' he asked cheerfully. The exercise had warmed him.

'No, but the sun moves across the sky.'

'Ah! What a wise little head it is!'

They came over a ridge of mixed hemlock and hardwood and looked upon a long swale full of bare hackmatacks.

'Look!' the girl cried. The white slot of the axe path showed clearly in the trees at the foot of the swale, and again where it entered the dark mass of the pines beyond.

'Praise the Lord!' said Mr Mears.

When at last they stood in the trail, Kezia slid down from the horse.

'No!' Mr Mears protested.

'Ride-and-tie,' she said firmly. 'That's the way we came, and that's the way we'll go. Besides, I want to get warm.'

He climbed up clumsily and smiled down at her.

'What shall we do when we get to Port Marriott, my dear?'

'Get the New Light preacher to marry us, and catch the packet for Scrod Harbour.'

He nodded and gave a pull at his broad hat brim. She thought of everything, A splendid helpmeet for the world's wilderness. He saw it all very humbly now as a dispensation of Providence.

Kezia watched him out of sight. Then, swiftly, she undid her bundle and took out the thing that had lain there (and on her conscience) through the night—the tinderbox—Mr Barclay's wedding gift to Mr Hathaway. She flung it into the woods and walked on, skirts lifted, in the track of the horse, humming a psalm tune to the silent trees and the snow.

Mark Doty

Mark A. Doty (b.1953) is the son of an army engineer and grew up in a succession of suburbs in Tennessee, Florida, southern California, and Arizona. Since the publication of his first volume of verse, Turtle, Swan, *in 1987, Mark Doty has become recognized as one of the most accomplished poets in America. Doty's utterings transcend the category of "gay poetry" to appeal to a diverse cross-section of readers. Fittingly, Doty has won a number of prestigious literary awards for his poetry and his two memoirs, including the Whiting Writer's Award, the T. S. Eliot Prize, the National Poetry Series, and the* Los Angeles Times *Book Award. Doty described himself, in* Publishers Weekly, *as having been "a sissy" in childhood. Frightened by his emerging sexual identity, he married hastily at age eighteen. After completing his undergraduate studies at Drake University in Iowa, he got a divorce and moved to Manhattan, where he paid his dues as a temporary office worker. He earned a master's degree in creative writing from Goddard College. During the same period, he met his lasting love, Wally Roberts. Wally's illness and death from AIDS, with which he was diagnosed in 1989 and to which he finally succumbed in January, 1994, was to be the central event of Doty's maturation as person and poet. Doty's poem, "Days of 1981," was published in* My Alexandria *in 1993, which won the National Poetry Series contest. Here Doty explores the exhilaration and confusion of discovering a new kind of romance and sexual identity as a gay man.*

Days of 1981

Cambridge Street, summer,
and a boy in a blue bandanna brought the bartender
flowers: delphiniums, splendid, blackened

in the dim room, though it was still afternoon, "tea
dance," in the heat of early July. Men in too-tight jeans
—none of them dancing—watched

the black women singing. Secret advocates of our hearts,
they urged us on as they broke apart
in painterly chaos on the video screen,

gowns and wigs, perfectly timed gestures
becoming bits of iridescent weather

Reprinted from *My Alexandria*, (1993), University of Illinois Press.

in the club's smoked atmosphere. The Supremes

—by then historical, lushly ascetic—then the endless
stream of women we loved, emblematic, reckless
in their attachments, or so the songs would have us think.

The man I met, slight and dark as Proust, a sultry flirt,
introduced himself because he liked my yellow shirt.
I don't remember who bought who drinks,

or why I liked him; I think it was simply
that I *could*. The heady rush of quickly
leaving together, late sun glaring over the Charles,

those last white sails blinding: it was so easy,
and strangely exhilarating, and free
as the women singing: a tidal, glimmering whirl

into which you could ease down, without thinking,
and simply be swept away. I was ready and waiting
to be swept. After the subway ride,

he knelt in front of me on the bleachers
in an empty suburban park, and I reached
for anything to hold onto, my head thrown back

to blueblack sky rinsed at the rim
with blazing city lights, then down to him:
relentless, dazzling, anyone. The smokestacks

and office towers loomed, a half-lit backdrop
beyond the baseball diamond. I didn't want him to ever stop,
and he left me breathless and unsatisfied.

He was a sculptor, and for weeks afterward I told myself
I loved him, because I'd met a man and wasn't sure
I could meet another—I'd never tried—

and because the next morning, starting
off to work, the last I saw of him, he gave me a heart,
ceramic, the marvel of a museum school show

his class had mounted. No one could guess
how he'd fired hollow clay entirely seamless
and kept it from exploding. I thought it beautiful, though

I was wrong about so much: him,
my prospects, the charm of the gift.
Out of context, it was a cool,

lumpish thing, earth-toned, lop-sided,
incapable of standing on its own. I propped
it up with books, then left it somewhere, eventually,

though I don't mind thinking of it now,
when I don't have the first idea where it's gone.
I called him more than twice.

If I knew where he was, even his last name,
(something French?) I might call again
to apologize for my naive

persistence, my lack of etiquette,
my ignorance of the austere code of tricks.
I didn't know then how to make love like that.

I thought of course we'd go on learning
the fit of chest to chest, curve to curve.
I didn't understand the ethos, the drama

of the search,
the studied approach to touch
as brief and recklessly enjambed

as the magic songs: *Give me just a little more time,*
I'm so excited, I will survive.
Nothing was promised, nothing sustained

or lethal offered. I wish I'd kept the heart.
Even the emblems of our own embarrassment
become acceptable to us, after a while,

evidence of someone we'd once have wished to erase:
a pottery heart,
an unrecaptured thing that might represent

the chancy exhilaration of a day, years ago
—*1981*—bleached sails on the Charles blowing,
the blueblack women in their rapture on the screen,

their perfected longing and release.
The astonishing flowers, seething
a blue I could barely see.

Charles Simic

Charles Simic was born in 1938 in Belgrade, Yugoslavia where his childhood coincided with World War II. Several times his family evacuated their home to escape indiscriminate bombing—or as he put it in an online interview for Cortland Review, *"My travel agents were Hitler and Stalin." The atmosphere of violence and desperation continued after the war. When he and his family finally managed to leave Eastern Europe in 1954 and move to Chicago, he became interested in literature, particularly poetry. Although he admits that one reason he began exploring the art form was to meet girls. Since 1973 Simic has taught English, creative writing, and criticism at the University of New Hampshire. In addition to poetry and prose poems, Simic has also written several works of prose nonfiction. Although he writes in English, Simic draws upon his experiences of growing up in war-torn Belgrade to compose poems about the physical and spiritual poverty of modern life. He has been hailed as one of his adopted homeland's finest poets. Simic's work, which includes* Unending Blues, Walking the Black Cat, *and* Hotel Insomnia, *has won numerous awards, among them the 1990 Pulitzer Prize for* The World Doesn't End *and the coveted MacArthur Foundation "genius grant." Some of Simic's best-known works challenge the dividing line between the ordinary and extraordinary. He gives substance and even life to inanimate objects, discerning the strangeness in household items as ordinary as a knife or a spoon. We see such themes in "Crazy about her Shrimp" which was originally published in* A Wedding in Hell *in 1994. Simic commented to* Artful Dodge: *"When you start putting words on the page, an associative process takes over. And, all of a sudden, there are surprises. All of a sudden you say to yourself, 'My God, how did this come into your head? Why is this on the page?' I just simply go where it takes me."*

Crazy about Her Shrimp

We don't even take time
To come up for air.
We keep our mouths full and busy
Eating bread and cheese.
And smooching in between.

No sooner have we made love
Than we are back in the kitchen.
While I chop the hot peppers,
She wiggles her ass
And stirs the shrimp on the stone.

How good the wine tastes
That has run red
Out of a laughing mouth!
Down her chin
And onto her naked tits.

"I'm getting fat," she says,
Turning this way and that way
Before the mirror.
"I'm crazy about her shrimp!"
I shout to the gods above.

Marge Piercy

Marge Piercy (b.1936) is a prominent and sometimes controversial writer of poetry and fiction. She grew up poor and white in a predominantly black section of Detroit. Her mother was a housewife with a tenth-grade education and her father a millwright who repaired and installed machinery. From her surroundings, Piercy learned about the inequities of the capitalist system. By winning a scholarship to the University of Michigan, Piercy became the first person in her family to attend college. She was an enthusiastic student and encouraged in her writing by winning several Hopwood awards. But professional success did not come easily. Ten years elapsed before Piercy was able to give up a series of odd jobs and support herself by writing. Piercy first became politically active in the 1960s, when she joined the Civil Rights movement and became an organizer for Students for a Democratic Society (SDS). Piercy writes about the oppression of individuals she sees in our society, infusing her works with political statements, autobiographical elements, and realist and utopian perspectives. Piercy openly acknowledges that she wants her writing—particularly some of her poems—to be "useful." "What I mean by useful," she explains in the introduction to Circles on the Water, *"is simply that readers will find poems that speak to and for them, will take those poems into their lives." Piercy's poetry recounts not only the injustices of sexism, but also such pleasures of daily life as making love or gardening. She also writes of sensuality, humor, playfulness, and the strength that lies buried in all women and the ways it can be tapped. "Cats like Angels" was originally published in* The Moon Is Always Female *in 1984 and reprinted in* Circles on the Water.

Cats like Angels

Cats like angels are supposed to be thin;
pigs like cherubs are supposed to be fat.
People are mostly in between, a knob
of bone sticking out in the knee you might
like to pad, a dollop of blab hanging
over the belt. You punish yourself,
one of those rubber balls kids have

that come bouncing back off their own
paddles, rebounding on the same slab.
you want to be slender and seamless
as a bolt.
When I was a girl
I loved spiny men with ascetic grimaces
all elbows and words and cartilage
ribbed like cast up fog-grey hulls,
faces to cut the eyes blink
on the glittering blade, chins
of Aegean prows bent on piracy.

Now I look for men whose easy bellies
show a love for the flesh and the table,
men who will come in the kitchen
and sit, who don't think peeling potatoes
makes their penis shrink, men with broad
fingers and purple figgy balls,
men with rumpled furrows and the slightly
messed look at ease of beds recently
we used.
We are not all supposed
to look like undernourished fourteen year
old boys, no matter what the fashions
ordain. You are built to pull a cart,
to lift a heavy load and bear it,
to haul up the long slope, and so
am I, peasant bodies, earthy, solid
shapely dark glazed clay pots that can
stand on the fire. When we put our
bellies together we do not clatter
but bounce on the good upholstery.

Pablo Neruda

Pablo Neruda (1904–1973) was a Chilean poet who became known as the greatest poet writing in the Spanish language during his lifetime, although many readers in the United States find it difficult to disassociate his poetry from his fervent commitment to communism. He won the highly prestigious Nobel Prize in literature in 1971 and the International Peace Prize in 1950. Born Ricardo Eliezer Neftali Reyes y Basoalto, Neruda adopted the pseudonym under which he would become famous in his early teens. He was a rather indifferent student, however, and other than writing love poetry, he spent most of his time engrossed in love affairs, books, daydreams, and long hours looking at the sunset from his window. By the time he finished high school, he had published in local papers and in Santiago, Chile's magazines, and had won several literary competitions. Neruda is widely known internationally for his vivid love poetry as well as his political poetry and prose. In his later life, his work advocated an active role in social change rather than simply describing his feelings. This poem describing the world of two lovers is labeled simply "XLVIII" from his collection "Cien Sonetos de Amour" or "100 Love Sonnets."

XLVIII

Two happy lovers make one bread,
a single moon drop in the grass.
Walking, they cast two shadows that flow together;
waking, they leave one sun empty in their bed.

Of all the possible truths, they chose the day;
they held it, not with ropes but with an aroma.
They did not shred the peace; they did not shatter words;
their happiness is a transparent tower.

The air and wine accompany the lovers.
The night delights them with its joyous petals.
They have a right to all the carnations.

Two happy lovers, without an ending, with no death,
they are born, they die, many times while they live:
they have the eternal life of the Natural.

Reprinted from *Cien Sonetos de Amor*, (1960), Fundacion Pablo Neruda.

Boyer Rickel

Boyer Rickel, a recent National Endowment for the Arts fellow, is the author of a collection of poetry, arreboles *(Wesleyan University Press, 1991) and a collection of autobiographical essays,* Taboo *(The University of Wisconsin Press, 1999). His work has appeared in* Poetry, Ploughshares, Iowa Review, Puerto del Sol, *and many other literary magazines. He is Assistant Director of the Creative Writing Program at the University of Arizona in Tucson.*

Beach Reading

The morning is warm and hazy, mysterious,
as if translated from Spanish. Just seeing
that from the country of Lorca a poem has been brought
into English, one is warmed as one is warmed by the sight
of boys who lie on a beach. A boys-only section. Though
a mild chill breeze crosses the sand
and their isolation—islands unto themselves and their personal rituals—
and nobody talks. By the look of them,
there are many languages represented.
This is a beach known internationally for the beauty of its boys.

Reading further, the second stanza disappoints.
There could never be another Lorca. But there's the action
of the waves, the caustic talking of gulls and the cliffs back of the beach
that crumble in cascades like brown dry waterfalls.
Everything disappoints, even Lorca, abandoning
lovers on train station platforms and in the smoke of bars.

The boom box reports: a soldier's body
has been found in the undergrowth at a public park. It's made to sound
like a scandal. A secret life is supposed. Documents were faxed to explain
the circumstances, to paper over the incident, the unanswered questions.

A boy carves initials in the sand with a stick.
His initials? Those of a new lover?
What about your new love? Just hoped-for. A love
you would surely have
if you could speak in the language of anemones.
The boy erases the initials with a sweep of his foot.

It's all in your mind. Nothing disappoints or happens
in isolation. A fighter jet streaks low over the coast
where the boys lie on pastel towels at careful intervals,
pale rosettes on a sepia wedding cake.

The poem translated from Spanish preens on its own intelligence, that's
   the problem.
Had it oiled and combed its hair with a part
down the middle like a Spanish sailor just off a freighter
so that a thing of beauty lay before the reader, a thing
in isolation but not in isolation, as if among others on a famous beach,
one might have thought of the perfume Lorca favored
or the tanned foot of a stranger kicking at surf, testing it—*Too cold
   for me?*—
not looking at those arrayed on the sand like unwrapped sweets.

Intelligence, surely, is not the enemy.
Distance, coldness, a regard
only for one's own island—

which is fear.
So that's the secret.
OK, then. I'll remove my shirt so that you might have a clear target.

Double Entendre

There was every reason for us to call it quits,
though careful management of our facial expressions helped us cope
with the daily subterfuges—vague, upbeat accounts to family and
   friends.
Not that we didn't slam doors or curse.

Careful management of our facial expressions helped us cope
with how we felt about each other, even in desire.
Not that we didn't slam doors or curse
within minutes of our usual tender fucking.

Given how we felt about each other, given our desire,
the contour of our emotional lives was complex, as you might expect.
One Sunday A.M., within minutes of our usual tender fucking,
news broke that the national leader had been caught in lies like ours.

This complicated the contour of our emotional lives, as you might
   expect.
The morning headlines provided unintended personal ironies

as more news of the leader, caught in lies like ours, unfolded.
Stand-up comics on late night shows cracked jokes

derived from the morning headlines—with unintended personal ironies.
All over the globe people could talk of nothing else.
As night after night the comics cracked jokes,
the leader's troubles, so over-exposed, grew to seem trivial.

Still, people all over the globe talked of nothing else—
as though one's private life were fit matter for public discussion—
until our troubles, as if they'd been widely exposed, seemed trivial.
We were lucky, I suppose, to be led by such a fool,

whose private life became a matter of public discussion
revealing subterfuges—vague, upbeat accounts to family and friends;
lucky, beyond reckoning, to be led by such a fool,
who could help us see we had no good reason to call it quits.

Wislawa Szymborska

Wislawa Szymborska (b.1923) was thrust into the international spotlight in 1996 after receiving the Nobel Prize for Literature for her direct, distinctive poetry. The Polish poet had been famous in her homeland for many years before she received critical acclaim for the first translation of her poetry into English: Sounds, Feelings, Thoughts: Seventy Poems. *Szymborska is praised for her seductively simple verse that captures the wit and wisdom of everyday life. She is considered rather reclusive, a gentle subversive, stubbornly refusing to see anything in the world as ordinary. The poem "True Love" is from her 1995 collection,* View with a Grain of Sand: Selected Poems *that was highly praised by many critics who extol Szymborska's directness, distinctive voice, and fierce humor.*

True Love

True love. Is it normal,
is it serious, is it practical?
What does the world get from two people
who exist in a world of their own?

Placed on the same pedestal for no good reason,
drawn randomly from millions, but convinced
it had to happen this way—in reward for what?
   For nothing.
The light descends from nowhere.
Why on these two and not on others?
Doesn't this outrage justice? Yes it does.
Doesn't it disrupt our painstakingly erected principles,
and cast the moral from the peak? Yes on both accounts.

Look at the happy couple.
Couldn't they at least try to hide it,
fake a little depression for their friends' sake!
Listen to them laughing—it's an insult.
The language they use—deceptively clear.
And their little celebrations, rituals,
the elaborate mutual routines—
it's obviously a plot behind the human race's back!

It's hard even to guess how far things might go
if people start to follow their example.
What could religion and poetry count on?
What would be remembered? What renounced?
Who'd want to stay within bounds?

True love. Is it really necessary?
Tact and common sense tell us to pass over it in silence,
like a scandal in Life's highest circles.
Perfectly good children are born without its help.
It couldn't populate the planet in a million years,
it comes along so rarely.

Let the people who never find true love
keep saying that there's no such thing.

Their faith will make it easier for them to live and die.

6

Writing the Environment

Ute Haker and Sharon Wright-Harris

To see a world in a grain of sand,
And a heaven in a wild flower,
Hold infinity in the palm of your hand,
And eternity in an hour.

—William Blake (1757–1827)

Each morning in the backcountry is exhilarating and full of promise. The sun bursts over the ridge, moves up the west wall of the valley, and brushes the camp as I (Ute) finish breakfast. My friends and I take down the tents, someone does the dishes, someone else packs the pots and pans. The rest straighten the camp to make it look like no one has been here at all. By the time we hit the trail, the sun has gained strength. By noon, heaving from the morning climb, I drink from a river born of glaciers and snow packs. Next to my foot I notice a counterpoint to the mountain grandeur, a tiny blue flower no more than a fraction of an inch above the ground.

Being out and about, to me, means noticing details and attempting to understand relationships. North America is home to some 290 species of land mammals and 40 of marine mammals. Beach walking, tide-pooling, snorkeling, and scuba diving show me a wealth of ocean life. Land mammals are active mostly at dawn, dusk, and night. During the day, I watch for tracks and scat. Bare patches on tree trunks may have been caused by deer or elk cleaning velvet off new antler growth. Claw marks might be a sign of a mountain lion or bear.

Visiting different parts of the U.S. at different seasons allows me to see many of North America's 850 species of birds. I watch for land birds in the morning and late afternoon, ducks and geese all day, shorebirds at ebb tide, and nightjars and owls at night. A bird's size and shape, particularly the shape of the bill, help me identify its family. Additional details—color patterns, behavior, song, habitat, and range—point me to the species.

A drama is always unfolding, if I look and listen carefully. If I see a salamander, I lie on my belly and watch it climb over rocks and dive into a stream. Close to 300 species of reptiles (turtles, lizards, snakes, and crocodiles) and almost 200 species of amphibians (frogs, toads, salamanders) live in North America, but insects are by far the world's most numerous animals: over 100,000 species live on the North American continent alone. Fortunately, the number of pesky insects is relatively small. I can see insects that live in social groups—ants and bees, for instance—and creatures that undergo amazing metamorphoses—butterflies, moths, and beetles. Open-air, wire-encased bug jars allow me to catch insects, observe them for a while, then set them free unharmed.

Writing and roaming in nature go hand in hand for me because both use all that I am. When I'm in the backcountry, I use my senses more intensely than at other times and I intimately belong to everything around me. I melt into the land and am just another form of life who depends on the soil, water, and air for survival and for inspiration.

When I write, I go deep inside myself and remember the things that I've seen, heard, smelled, tasted, and felt. I mix these flashbacks with my city life and take stock of the totality of my experience. I become more than a busy graduate student sitting in front of the computer, typing these lines. I connect with the rest of the world and all the places I've been. I re-vise who I am.

But who I am, who any of us are, and how we see the world cannot be separated from our ideological positions within our culture and time. Much of our thinking still adheres to a mechanistic worldview, which reduces the complexities of the world to isolated parts, organisms, and mechanisms, rather than to an ecological one, which considers organisms in relation to each other and their surroundings and which focuses on the interdependence of all living and nonliving systems of the universe. Although the German biologist Ernst Haeckel coined the term *ecology* in 1866, it took another hundred years to infiltrate the vernacular, and even today we generally regard the universe, and everything in it, as made up of distinct parts.

Under the ecological model, the parts, organisms, and mechanisms of the universe are part of complex webs of relationships and interdependencies that in turn belong to ever larger webs. Every organism, for example—from the smallest bacterium to human beings—is a living system. Cells are living systems, and so are the tissues and organs formed by the cells. Social systems, such as beehives, anthills, and human families, exhibit the same aspects of wholeness as individual organisms, and so do the ecosystems in which the individual organisms and their social systems interact with the wider world. All of these systems are integrated wholes whose forms are not rigid structures but dynamic yet stable manifestations of underlying processes; in other words, their forms are defined by the interactions and interdependencies of their parts. When a system is dissected into isolated ingredients—either physically or theoretically—its systemic properties are lost. Although we can recognize the individual parts of the system, the nature of the whole is different from the sum of its parts.

A paradigm shift toward an ecological worldview is well underway in many disciplines, especially physics and the life sciences. Writing, too—whether environmental writing or writing about other topics—benefits from our awareness of the essential interrelatedness and interdependence of all aspects of the world, whether inorganic, biological, or social. Because writing depends on—and in turn shapes—how people think and communicate, writing is central to the conception and exchange of human knowledge and ideas. Language, textual format, and style are part of how we create meaning, and they reflect our concepts of what exists, what is possible, and what is good.

Writers and readers benefit by understanding themselves in relation to texts' social, economic, political, and ecological implications. We can do this by constantly asking questions such as "Who benefits from a given version of truth? How are the material benefits of society distributed? What is the relation of this distribution to social relations? Do these relations encourage conflict? To whom does our knowledge designate power? Who is privileged at the expense of others? And how we can accomplish the greatest good for all?"

So what about you, the reader of this "Writing the Environment" section? How do you define your environment? Do you think of it as nature? The local landscape? The campus community? The global community? Your own modes of life? Do you think of the environment as an ecological unit? This chapter will encourage you to think in terms of relationships, and where we as humans fit within these various definitions of natural and human-made environments.

When you think of the natural environment, you probably immediately think "environmental problems," and this may seem like a depressing subject. And, yes, environmental problems continue to mount in this country and worldwide. According to a recent U.N.-sponsored report, during the past 100 years half of the world's wetlands have disappeared. Fishing fleets are taking in far greater amounts of fish than the oceans can replenish: seventy percent of the sea fish stocks are overfished worldwide. Twenty percent of the world's freshwater fish have vanished or are close to extinction. Dams and other diversions have fragmented 60 percent of the planet's largest rivers. Half of all forests are gone.

Perhaps hearing these statistics is depressing because you feel powerless and don't know what to do. One thing you can do is read how other people think about the environment and about how they view humanity's responsibilities. Then, you can do some thinking and researching of your own and respond through your own writing. And while you are writing and thinking, you'll probably want to spend a bit of quality time out in the backcountry among the cacti or high up in the mountains, beyond where roads go, and see for yourself what it's like.

Each writer in this chapter, like each of you, writes about the environment in her or his own way. What the writers share is a respect for looking close and noticing things—a respect for opening their eyes and seeing details and relationships. What they also share is an ability to translate the details of their experience into words, to create images on the page that draw readers into the scene and make them feel like they are there, too.

When you study such craft and practice it yourself, all of a sudden you aren't so powerless anymore. You can communicate your experiences to your class and the wider community. You are able to make us see how you think about your immediate environment and the relationships rippling out from there.

Barry Lopez

Barry Lopez once said in an interview that he doesn't believe that it is necessary for a reader to know much about him in order to understand his work, that the writer of the text should not intrude upon the voice of the text. In the essay printed here, Lopez discusses the nature of the relationship between the external and internal worlds of the writer and the manifestations of that relationship on the written page. A nature writer, Lopez is well-known for such nonfiction collections as Desert Notes, Giving Birth to Thunder, *and* River Notes. *His most notable work is perhaps* Arctic Dreams, *for which he received a National Book Award. The essay "Landscape and Narrative" comes from his nonfiction collection* Crossing Open Ground.

Landscape and Narrative

One summer evening in a remote village in the Brooks Range of Alaska, I sat among a group of men listening to hunting stories about the trapping and pursuit of animals. I was particularly interested in several incidents involving wolverine, in part because a friend of mine was studying wolverine in Canada, among the Cree, but, too, because I find this animal such an intense creature. To hear about its life is to learn more about fierceness.

Wolverines are not intentionally secretive, hiding their lives from view, but they are seldom observed. The range of their known behavior is less than that of, say, bears or wolves. Still, that evening no gratuitous details were set out. This was somewhat odd, for wolverine easily excite the imagination; they can loom suddenly in the landscape with authority, with an aura larger than their compact physical dimensions, drawing one's immediate and complete attention. Wolverine also have a deserved reputation for resoluteness in the worst winters, for ferocious strength. But neither did these attributes induce the men to embellish.

I listened carefully to these stories, taking pleasure in the sharply observed detail surrounding the dramatic thread of events. The story I remember most vividly was about a man hunting a wolverine from a snow machine in the spring. He followed the animal's tracks for several miles over rolling tundra in a certain valley. Soon he caught sight ahead of a dark spot on the crest of a hill—the wolverine pausing to look back. The hunter was catching up, but each time he came over a rise the wolverine was looking back from the next rise, just out of range. The hunter topped one more rise and met the wolverine bounding toward him. Before he could pull his rifle from its scabbard the wolverine flew across the engine cowl and the windshield,

Reprinted from *Crossing Open Ground*, (1998), Macmillan Publishing Company.

hitting him square in the chest. The hunter scrambled his arms wildly, trying to get the wolverine out of his lap, and fell over as he did so. The wolverine jumped clear as the snow machine rolled over, and fixed the man with a stare. He had not bitten, not even scratched the man. Then the wolverine walked away. The man thought of reaching for the gun, but no, he did not.

The other stories were like this, not so much making a point as evoking something about contact with wild animals that would never be completely understood.

When the stories were over, four or five of us walked out of the home of our host. The surrounding land, in the persistent light of a far northern summer, was still visible for miles—the striated, pitched massifs of the Brooks Range; the shy, willow-lined banks of the John River flowing south from Anaktuvuk Pass; and the flat tundra plain, opening with great affirmation to the north. The landscape seemed alive because of the stories. It was precisely these ocherous tones, this kind of willow, exactly this austerity that had informed the wolverine narratives. I felt exhilaration, and a deeper confirmation of the stories. The mundane tasks which awaited me I anticipated now with pleasure. The stories had renewed in me a sense of the purpose of my life.

This feeling, an inexplicable renewal of enthusiasm after storytelling, is familiar to many people. It does not seem to matter greatly what the subject is, as long as the context is intimate and the story is told for its own sake, not forced to serve merely as the vehicle for an idea. The tone of the story need not be solemn. The darker aspects of life need not be ignored. But I think intimacy is indispensable—a feeling that derives from the listener's trust and a storyteller's certain knowledge of his subject and regard for his audience. This intimacy deepens if the storyteller tempers his authority with humility, or when terms of idiomatic expression, or at least the physical setting for the story, are shared.

I think of two landscapes—one outside the self, the other within. The external landscape is the one we see—not only the line and color of the land and its shading at different times of the day, but also its plants and animals in season, its weather, its geology, the record of its climate and evolution. If you walk up, say, a dry arroyo in the Sonoran Desert you will feel a mounding and rolling of sand and silt beneath your foot that is distinctive. You will anticipate the crumbling of the sedimentary earth in the arroyo bank as your hand reaches out, and in that tangible evidence you will sense a history of water in the region. Perhaps a black-throated sparrow lands in a paloverde bush—the resiliency of the twig under the bird, that precise shade of yellowish-green against the milk-blue sky, the fluttering whir of the arriving sparrow, are what I mean by "the landscape." Draw on the smell of creosote bush, or clack stones together in the dry air. Feel how light is the desiccated dropping of the kangaroo rat. Study an animal track obscured by the wind. These are all elements of the land, and what makes the landscape comprehensible are the relationships between them. One learns a landscape finally not by knowing the name or identity of everything in it, but by perceiving the relationships in it—like that between the sparrow and the twig. The difference between the relationships and the elements is the same as that between written history and a catalog of events.

The second landscape I think of is an interior one, a kind of projection within a person of a part of the exterior landscape. Relationships in the exterior landscape include those that are named and discernible, such as the nitrogen cycle, or a vertical sequence of Ordovician limestone, and others that are uncodified or ineffable, such as winter light falling on a particular kind of granite, or the effect of humidity on the frequency of a blackpoll warbler's burst of song. That these relationships have purpose and order, however inscrutable they may seem to us, is a tenet of evolution. Similarly, the speculations, intuitions, and formal ideas we refer to as "mind" are a set of relationships in the interior landscape with purpose and order; some of these are obvious, many impenetrably subtle. The shape and character of these relationships in a person's thinking, I believe, are deeply influenced by where on this earth one goes, what one touches, the patterns one observes in nature—the intricate history of one's life in the land, even a life in the city, where wind, the chirp of birds, the line of a falling leaf, are known. These thoughts are arranged, further, according to the thread of one's moral, intellectual, and spiritual development. The interior landscape responds to the character and subtlety of an exterior landscape; the shape of the individual mind is affected by land as it is by genes.

In stories like those I heard at Anaktuvuk Pass about wolverine, the relationship between separate elements in the land is set forth clearly. It is put in a simple framework of sequential incidents and apposite detail. If the exterior landscape is limned well, the listener often feels that he has heard something pleasing and authentic—trustworthy. We derive this sense of confidence I think not so much from verifiable truth as from an understanding that lying has played no role in the narrative. The storyteller is obligated to engage the reader with a precise vocabulary, to set forth a coherent and dramatic rendering of incidents—and to be ingenuous.

When one hears a story one takes pleasure in it for different reasons—for the euphony of its phrases, an aspect of the plot, or because one identifies with one of the characters. With certain stories certain individuals may experience a deeper, more profound sense of well-being. This latter phenomenon, in my understanding, rests at the heart of storytelling as an elevated experience among aboriginal peoples. It results from bringing two landscapes together. The exterior landscape is organized according to principles or laws or tendencies beyond human control. It is understood to contain an integrity that is beyond human analysis and unimpeachable. Insofar as the storyteller depicts various subtle and obvious relationships in the exterior landscape accurately in his story, and insofar as he orders them along traditional lines of meaning to create the narrative, the narrative will "ring true." The listener who "takes the story to heart" will feel a pervasive sense of congruence within himself and also with the world.

Among the Navajo and, as far as I know, many other native peoples, the land is thought to exhibit a sacred order. That order is the basis of ritual. The rituals themselves reveal the power in that order. Art, architecture, vocabulary, and costume, as well as ritual, are derived from the perceived natural order of the universe—from observations and meditations on the exterior landscape. An indigenous philosophy—metaphysics, ethics, epistemology, aesthetics, and logic—

may also be derived from a people's continuous attentiveness to both the obvious (scientific) and ineffable (artistic) orders of the local landscape. Each individual, further, undertakes to order his interior landscape according to the exterior landscape. To succeed in this means to achieve a balanced state of mental health.

I think of the Navajo for a specific reason. Among the various sung ceremonies of this people—Enemyway, Coyoteway, Red Antway, Uglyway—is one called Beautyway. In the Navajo view, the elements of one's interior life—one's psychological makeup and moral bearing—are subject to a persistent principle of disarray. Beautyway is, in part, a spiritual invocation of the order of the exterior universe, that irreducible, holy complexity that manifests itself as all things changing through time (a Navajo definition of beauty, hózhṕó). The purpose of this invocation is to recreate in the individual who is the subject of the Beautyway ceremony that same order, to make the individual again a reflection of the myriad enduring relationships of the landscape.

I believe story functions in a similar way. A story draws on relationships in the exterior landscape and projects them onto the interior landscape. The purpose of storytelling is to achieve harmony between the two landscapes, to use all the elements of story—syntax, mood, figures of speech—in a harmonious way to reproduce the harmony of the land in the individual's interior. Inherent in story is the power to reorder a state of psychological confusion through contact with the pervasive truth of those relationships we call "the land."

These thoughts, of course, are susceptible to interpretation. I am convinced, however, that these observations can be applied to the kind of prose we call nonfiction as well as to traditional narrative forms such as the novel and the short story, and to some poems. Distinctions between fiction and nonfiction are sometimes obscured by arguments over what constitutes "the truth." In the aboriginal literature I am familiar with, the first distinction made among narratives is to separate the authentic from the inauthentic. Myth, which we tend to regard as fictitious or "merely metaphorical," is as authentic, as real, as the story of a wolverine in a man's lap. (A distinction is made, of course, about the elevated nature of myth—and frequently the circumstances of myth-telling are more rigorously prescribed than those for the telling of legends or vernacular stories—but all of these narratives are rooted in the local landscape. To violate *that* connection is to call the narrative itself into question.)

The power of narrative to nurture and heal, to repair a spirit in disarray, rests on two things: the skillful invocation of unimpeachable sources and a listener's knowledge that no hypocrisy or subterfuge is involved. This last simple fact is to me one of the most imposing aspects of the Holocene history of man.

We are more accustomed now to thinking of "the truth" as something that can be explicitly stated, rather than as something that can be evoked in a metaphorical way outside science and Occidental culture. Neither can truth be reduced to aphorism or formulas. It is something alive and unpronounceable. Story creates an atmosphere in which it becomes discernible as a pattern. For a storyteller to insist on relationships that do not exist is to lie. Lying is the opposite of story. (I do not mean to confuse ignorance with deception, or to imply that a storyteller can perceive all that is inherent in the land. Every storyteller falls short of a perfect limning of the landscape—perception and language both fail. But to make up something that is not there, something which can never be corroborated in the land, to knowingly set forth a false relationship, is to be lying, no longer telling a story.)

Because of the intricate, complex nature of the land, it is not always possible for a storyteller to grasp what is contained in a story. The intent of the storyteller, then, must be to evoke, honestly, some single aspect of all that the land contains. The storyteller knows that because different individuals grasp the story at different levels, the focus of his regard for truth must be at the primary one—with who was there, what happened, when, where, and why things occurred. The story will then possess similar truth at other levels—the integrity inherent at the primary level of meaning will be conveyed everywhere else. As long as the storyteller carefully describes the order before him, and uses his storytelling skill to heighten and emphasize certain relationships, it is even possible for the story to be more successful than the storyteller himself is able to imagine.

I would like to make a final point about the wolverine stories I heard at Anaktuvuk Pass. I wrote down the details afterward, concentrating especially on aspects of the biology and ecology of the animals. I sent the information on to my friend living with the Cree. When, many months later, I saw him, I asked whether the Cree had enjoyed these insights of the Nunamiut into the nature of the wolverine. What had they said?

"You know," he told me, "how they are. They said, 'That could happen.' "

In these uncomplicated words the Cree declared their own knowledge of the wolverine. They acknowledged that although they themselves had never seen the things the Nunamiut spoke of, they accepted them as accurate observations, because they did not consider story a context for misrepresentation. They also preserved their own dignity by not overstating their confidence in the Nunamiut, a distant and unknown people.

Whenever I think of this courtesy on the part of the Cree I think of the dignity that is ours when we cease to demand the truth and realize that the best we can have of those substantial truths that guide our lives is metaphorical—a story. And the most of it we are likely to discern comes only when we accord one another the respect the Cree showed the Nunamiut. Beyond this—that the interior landscape is a metaphorical representation of the exterior landscape, that the truth reveals itself most fully not in dogma but in the paradox, irony, and contradictions that distinguish compelling narratives—beyond this there are only failures of imagination: reductionism in science; fundamentalism in religion; fascism in politics.

Our national literatures should be important to us insofar as they sustain us with illumination and heal us. They can always do that so long as they are written with respect for both the source and the reader, and with an understanding of why the human heart and the land have been brought together so regularly in human history.

John Steinbeck

Born and raised in the Salinas Valley region of California, John Steinbeck draws his stories from his native land and experiences. Although he began as a journalist, Steinbeck's turn to fiction produced success with works such as Tortilla Flat, Of Mice and Men, *and the Pulitzer Prize-winning novel* The Grapes of Wrath. *Steinbeck also received the Nobel Prize for Literature in 1962. The chapter excerpted from Steinbeck's novel,* The Grapes of Wrath, *explores personal and fiscal relationships to the land.*

Chapter Five

The owners of the land came onto the land, or more often a spokesman for the owners came. They came in closed cars, and they felt the dry earth with their fingers, and sometimes they drove big earth augers into the ground for soil tests. The tenants, from their sun-beaten dooryards, watched uneasily when the closed cars drove along the fields. And at last the owner men drove into the dooryards and sat in their cars to talk out of the windows. The tenant men stood beside the cars for a while, and then squatted on their hams and found sticks with which to mark the dust.

In the open doors the women stood looking out, and behind them the children—corn-headed children, with wide eyes, one bare foot on top of the other bare foot, and the toes working. The women and the children watched their men talking to the owner men. They were silent.

Some of the owner men were kind because they hated what they had to do, and some of them were angry because they hated to be cruel, and some of them were cold because they had long ago found that one could not be an owner unless one were cold. And all of them were caught in something larger than themselves. Some of them hated the mathematics that drove them, and some were afraid, and some worshiped the mathematics because it provided a refuge from thought and from feeling. If a bank or a finance company owned the land, the owner man said, The Bank—or the Company—needs—wants—insists—must have—as though the Bank or the Company were a monster, with thought and feeling, which had ensnared them. These last would take no responsibility for the banks or the companies because they were men and slaves, while the banks were machines and masters all at the same time. Some of the owner men were a little proud to be slaves to such cold and powerful masters. The owner men sat in the cars and explained. You know the land is poor. You've scrabbled at it long enough, God knows.

Reprinted from *The Grapes of Wrath*, (1976), Penguin Books.

The squatting tenant men nodded and wondered and drew figures in the dust, and yes, they knew, God knows. If the dust only wouldn't fly. If the top would only stay on the soil, it might not be so bad.

The owner men went on leading to their point: You know the land's getting poorer. You know what cotton does to the land; robs it, sucks all the blood out of it.

The squatters nodded—they knew, God knew. If they could only rotate the crops they might pump blood back into the land.

Well, it's too late. And the owner men explained the workings and the thinkings of the monster that was stronger than they were. A man can hold land if he can just eat and pay taxes; he can do that.

Yes, he can do that until his crops fail one day and he has to borrow money from the bank.

But—you see, a bank or a company can't do that, because those creatures don't breathe air, don't eat side-meat. They breathe profits; they eat the interest on money. If they don't get it, they die the way you die without air, without side-meat. It is a sad thing, but it is so. It is just so.

The squatting men raised their eyes to understand. Can't we just hang on? Maybe the next year will be a good year. God knows how much cotton next year. And with all the wars—God knows what price cotton will bring. Don't they make explosives out of cotton? And uniforms? Get enough wars and cotton'll hit the ceiling. Next year, maybe. They looked up questioningly.

We can't depend on it. The bank—the monster has to have profits all the time. It can't wait. It'll die. No, taxes go on. When the monster stops growing, it dies. It can't stay one size.

Soft fingers began to tap the sill of the car window, and hard fingers tightened on the restless drawing sticks. In the doorways of the sun-beaten tenant houses, women sighed and then shifted feet so that the one that had been down was now on top, and the toes working. Dogs came sniffing near the owner cars and wetted on all four tires one after another. And chickens lay in the sunny dust and fluffed their feathers to get the cleansing dust down to the skin. In the little sties the pigs grunted inquiringly over the muddy remnants of the slops.

The squatting men looked down again. What do you want us to do? We can't take less share of the crop—we're half starved now. The kids are hungry all the time. We got no clothes, torn an' ragged. If all the neighbors weren't the same, we'd be ashamed to go to meeting.

And at last the owner men came to the point. The tenant system won't work any more. One man on a tractor can take the place of twelve or fourteen families. Pay him a wage and take all the crop. We have to do it. We don't like to do it. But the monster's sick. Something's happened to the monster.

But you'll kill the land with cotton.

We know. We've got to take cotton quick before the land dies. Then we'll sell the land. Lots of families in the East would like to own a piece of land.

The tenant men looked up alarmed. But what'll happen to us? How'll we eat?

You'll have to get off the land. The plows'll go through the dooryard.

And now the squatting men stood up angrily. Grampa took up the land, and he had to kill the Indians and drive them away. And Pa was born here, and he killed weeds and snakes. Then a bad year came and he had to borrow a little money. An' we was born here. There in the door—our children born here. And Pa had to borrow money. The bank owned the land then, but we stayed and we got a little bit of what we raised.

We know that—all that. It's not us, it's the bank. A bank isn't like a man. Or an owner with fifty thousand acres, he isn't like a man either. That's the monster.

Sure, cried the tenant men, but it's our land. We measured it and broke it up. We were born on it, and we got killed on it, died on it. Even if it's no good, it's still ours. That's what makes it ours—being born on it, working it, dying on it. That makes ownership, not a paper with numbers on it.

We're sorry. It's not us. It's the monster. The bank isn't like a man.

Yes, but the bank is only made of men.

No, you're wrong there—quite wrong there. The bank is something else than men. It happens that every man in a bank hates what the bank does, and yet the bank does it. The bank is something more than men, I tell you. It's the monster. Men made it, but they can't control it.

The tenants cried, Grampa killed Indians, Pa killed snakes for the land. Maybe we can kill banks—they're worse than Indians and snakes. Maybe we got to fight to keep our land, like Pa and Grampa did.

And now the owner men grew angry. You'll have to go.

But it's ours, the tenant men cried. We—

No. The bank, the monster owns it. You'll have to go.

We'll get our guns, like Grampa when the Indians came. What then?

Well—first the sheriff, and then the troops. You'll be stealing if you try to stay, you'll be murderers if you kill to stay. The monster isn't men, but it can make men do what it wants.

But if we go, where'll we go? How'll we go? We got no money.

We're sorry, said the owner men. The bank, the fifty-thousand-acre owner can't be responsible. You're on land that isn't yours. Once over the line maybe you can pick cotton in the fall. Maybe you can go on relief. Why don't you go on west to California? There's work there, and it never gets cold. Why, you can reach out anywhere and pick an orange. Why, there's always some kind of crop to work in. Why don't you go there? And the owner men started their cars and rolled away.

The tenant men squatted down on their hams again to mark the dust with a stick, to figure, to wonder. Their sunburned faces were dark, and their sun-whipped eyes were light. The women moved cautiously out of the doorways toward their men, and the children crept behind the women, cautiously, ready to run. The bigger boys squatted beside their fathers, because that made them men. After a time the women asked, What did he want?

And the men looked up for a second, and the smolder of pain was in their eyes. We got to get off. A tractor and a superintendent. Like factories.

Where'll we go? the women asked.

We don't know. We don't know.

And the women went quickly, quietly back into the houses and herded the children ahead of them. They knew that a man so hurt and so perplexed may turn in anger, even on people he loves. They left the men alone to figure and to wonder in the dust.

After a time perhaps the tenant man looked about—at the pump put in ten years ago, with a goose-neck handle and iron flowers on the spout, at the chopping block where a thousand chickens had been killed, at the hand plow lying in the shed, and the patent crib hanging in the rafters over it.

The children crowded about the women in the houses. What we going to do, Ma? Where we going to go?

The women said, We don't know, yet. Go out and play. But don't go near your father. He might whale you if you go near him. And the women went on with the work, but all the time they watched the men squatting in the dust—perplexed and figuring.

The tractors came over the roads and into the fields, great crawlers moving like insects, having the incredible strength of insects. They crawled over the ground, laying the track and rolling on it and picking it up. Diesel tractors, puttering while they stood idle; they thundered when they moved, and then settled down to a droning roar. Snub-nosed monsters, raising the dust and sticking their snouts into it, straight down the country, across the country, through fences, through dooryards, in and out of gullies in straight lines. They did not run on the ground, but on their own roadbeds. They ignored hills and gulches, water courses, fences, houses.

The man sitting in the iron seat did not look like a man; gloved, goggled, rubber dust mask over nose and mouth, he was a part of the monster, a robot in the seat. The thunder of the cylinders sounded through the country, became one with the air and the earth, so that earth and air muttered in sympathetic vibration. The driver could not control it—straight across country it went, cutting through a dozen farms and straight back. A twitch at the controls could swerve the cat', but the driver's hands could not twitch because the monster that built the tractor, the monster that sent the tractor out, had somehow got into the driver's hands, into his brain and muscle, had goggled him and muzzled him—goggled his mind, muzzled his speech, goggled his perception, muzzled his protest. He could not see the land as it was, he could not smell the land as it smelled; his feet did not stamp the clods or feel the warmth and power of the earth. He sat in an iron seat and stepped on iron pedals. He could not cheer or beat or curse or encourage the extension of his power, and because of this he could not cheer or whip or curse or encourage himself. He did not know or own or trust or beseech the land. If a seed dropped did not germinate, it was nothing. If the young thrusting plant withered in drought or drowned in a flood of rain, it was no more to the driver than to the tractor.

He loved the land no more than the bank loved the land. He could admire the tractor—its machined surfaces, its surge of power, the roar of its detonating cylinders; but it was not his tractor. Behind the tractor rolled the shining disks, cutting the earth with blades—not plowing but surgery, pushing the cut earth to the right where the second row of disks cut it and pushed it to the left; slicing blades shining, polished by the cut earth. And pulled behind the disks, the harrows combing with iron teeth so that the little clods broke up and the earth lay smooth. Behind the harrows, the long seeders—twelve curved iron penes erected in the foundry, orgasms set by gears, raping methodically, raping without passion. The driver sat in his iron seat and he was proud of the straight lines he did not will, proud of the tractor he did not own or love, proud of the power he could not control. And when that crop grew, and was harvested, no man had crumbled a hot clod in his fingers and let the earth sift past his fingertips. No man had touched the seed, or lusted for the growth. Men ate what they had not raised, had no connection with the bread. The land bore under iron, and under iron gradually died; for it was not loved or hated, it had no prayers or curses.

At noon the tractor driver stopped sometimes near a tenant house and opened his lunch: sandwiches wrapped in waxed paper, white bread, pickle, cheese, Spam, a piece of pie branded like an engine part. He ate without relish. And tenants not yet moved away came out to see him, looked curiously while the goggles were taken off, and the rubber dust mask, leaving white circles around the eyes and a large white circle around nose and mouth. The exhaust of the tractor puttered on, for fuel is so cheap it is more efficient to leave the engine running than to heat the Diesel nose for a new start. Curious children crowded close, ragged children who ate their fried dough as they watched. They watched hungrily the unwrapping of the sandwiches, and their hunger-sharpened noses smelled the pickle, cheese, and Spam. They didn't speak to the driver. They watched his hand as it carried food to his mouth. They did not watch him chewing; their eyes followed the hand that held the sandwich. After a while the tenant who could not leave the place came out and squatted in the shade beside the tractor.

"Why, you're Joe Davis's boy!"

"Sure," the driver said.

"Well, what you doing this kind of work for—against your own people?"

"Three dollars a day. I got damn sick of creeping for my dinner—and not getting it. I got a wife and kids. We got to eat. Three dollars a day, and it comes every day."

"That's right," the tenant said. "But for your three dollars a day fifteen or twenty families can't eat at all. Nearly a hundred people have to go out and wander on the roads for your three dollars a day. Is that right?"

And the driver said, "Can't think of that. Got to think of my own kids. Three dollars a day, and it comes every day. Times are changing, mister, don't you know? Can't make a living on the land unless you've got two, five, ten thousand acres and a tractor. Crop land isn't for little guys like us any more. You don't kick up a howl because you can't make Fords, or because you're not the telephone company. Well, crops are like that now. Nothing to do about it. You try to get three dollars a day someplace. That's the only way."

The tenant pondered. "Funny thing how it is. If a man owns a little property, that property is him, it's part of him, and it's like him. If he owns property only so he can walk on it and handle it and be sad when it isn't doing well, and feel fine when the rain falls on it, that property is him, and some way he's bigger because he owns it. Even if he isn't successful he's big with his property. That is so."

And the tenant pondered more. "But let a man get property he doesn't see, or can't take time to get his fingers in, or can't be there to walk on it—why, then the property is the man. He can't do what he wants, he can't think what he wants. The property is the man, stronger than he is. And he is small, not big. Only his possessions are big—and he's the servant of his property. That is so, too."

The driver munched the branded pie and threw the crust away. "Times are changed, don't you know? Thinking about stuff like that don't feed the kids. Get your three dollars a day, feed your kids. You got no call to worry about anybody's kids but your own. You get a reputation for talking like that, and you'll never get three dollars a day. Big shots won't give you three dollars a day if you worry about anything but your three dollars a day."

"Nearly a hundred people on the road for your three dollars. Where will we go?"

"And that reminds me," the driver said, "you better get out soon. I'm going through the dooryard after dinner."

"You filled in the well this morning."

"I know. Had to keep the line straight. But I'm going through the dooryard after dinner. Got to keep the lines straight. And—well, you know Joe Davis, my old man, so I'll tell you this. I got orders wherever there's a family not moved out—if I have an accident—you know, get too close and cave the house in a little—well, I might get a couple of dollars. And my youngest kid never had no shoes yet."

"I built it with my hands. Straightened old nails to put the sheathing on. Rafters are wired to the stringers with baling wire. It's mine. I built it. You bump it down—I'll be in the window with a rifle. You even come too close and I'll pot you like a rabbit."

"It's not me. There's nothing I can do. I'll lose my job if I don't do it. And look—suppose you kill me? They'll just hang you, but long before you're hung there'll be another guy on the tractor, and he'll bump the house down. You're not killing the right guy."

"That's so," the tenant said. "Who gave you orders? I'll go after him. He's the one to kill."

"You're wrong. He got his orders from the bank. The bank told him, 'Clear those people out or it's your job.' "

"Well, there's a president of the bank. There's a board of directors. I'll fill up the magazine of the rifle and go into the bank."

The driver said, "Fellow was telling me the bank gets orders from the East. The orders were, 'Make the land show profit or we'll close you up.' "

"But where does it stop? Who can we shoot? I don't aim to starve to death before I kill the man that's starving me."

"I don't know. Maybe there's nobody to shoot. Maybe the thing isn't men at all. Maybe, like you said, the property's doing it. Anyway I told you my orders."

"I got to figure," the tenant said. "We all got to figure. There's some way to stop this. It's not like lightning or earthquakes. We've got a bad thing made by men, and by God that's something we can change." The tenant sat in his doorway, and the driver thundered his engine and started off, tracks falling and curving, harrows combing, and the phalli of the seeder slipping into the ground. Across the dooryard the tractor cut, and the hard, foot-beaten ground was seeded field, and the tractor cut through again; the uncut space was ten feet wide. And back he came. The iron guard bit into the house-corner, crumbled the wall, and wrenched the little house from its foundation so that it fell sideways, crushed like a bug. And the driver was goggled and a rubber mask covered his nose and mouth. The tractor cut a straight line on, and the air and the ground vibrated with its thunder. The tenant man stared after it, his rifle in his hand. His wife was beside him, and the quiet children behind. And all of them stared after the tractor.

Richard Shelton

Richard Shelton, a professor in the University of Arizona English Department's Creative Writing Program, is the author of nine books of poetry. His poems and prose pieces have appeared in more than 200 magazines and journals, including The New Yorker, The Atlantic, The Paris Review, *and* The Antioch Review. *He won the International Poetry Forum's U.S. Award for his first major collection of poems,* The Tattooed Desert, *and has been honored with many subsequent awards, including nominations for the Pulitzer Prize and the National Book Award.* Going Back to Bisbee, *Shelton's first book of nonfiction, won the 1992 Western States Book Award for Creative Nonfiction. He also teaches writing in Arizona prisons. The poem "Sonora for Sale," from his* Selected Poems: 1969–1981, *addresses the human threat to the spiritual paradise of the desert.*

Sonora for Sale

this is the land of gods in exile
they are fragile and without pride
they require no worshipers

we come down a white road in the moonlight
dragging our feet like innocents
to find the guilty already arrived
and in possession of everything

we see the stars as they were years ago
but for us it is the future
they warn us too late

we are here we cannot turn back
soon we hold out our hands
full of money
this is the desert
it is all we have left to destroy

Reprinted from *Selected Poems: 1969–1981*, (1982), by permission of University of Pittsburgh Press.

Lucille Clifton

Lucille Clifton has published numerous volumes of poetry, including Good Times, Good News about the Earth, *and* An Ordinary Woman. *Although she is most widely known as an award-winning poet, Clifton has also written a number of children's books. Named Poet Laureate of Maryland in 1979, Clifton is currently a Distinguished Professor of Humanities at St. Mary's College of Maryland. "sonora desert poem", from the collection* Two-Headed Woman, *reflects on what we can learn when we open our senses to the details of the desert landscape.*

---

sonora desert poem

for lois and richard shelton

1.

the ones who live in the desert,
if you knew them
you would understand everything.
they see it all and
never judge any
just drink the water when
they get the chance.
if i could grow arms on my scars
like them,
if i could learn
the patience they know
i wouldn't apologize for my thorns either
just stand in the desert
and witness.

2.

directions for watching the sun set in the desert

come to the landscape that was hidden under the sea.
look in the opposite direction.
reach for the mountain.
the mountain will ignore your hand.
the sun will fall on your back.

Reprinted from *Two-Headed Woman*, (1980), Curtis Brown, Ltd.

the landscape will fade away.
you will think you're alone until a flash
of green incredible light.

3.
directions for leaving the desert

push the bones back
under your skin.
finish the water.
they will notice your thorns and
ask you to testify.
turn toward the shade.
smile.
say nothing at all.

1980

Erec Toso

Erec Toso has published essays in The Sun—A Magazine of Ideas, Northern Lights, The Arizona Literary Magazine, *the* Arizona Daily Star, *and other local publications. He is a Senior Lecturer and Teaching Advisor at the University of Arizona.*

His short prose pieces probe the tension between the desert as a place and metaphor for spiritual searching and the current role of the desert as playground and object to be packaged, sold, and consumed. His work shows how we may be loving the desert to death, missing what we came to the desert to find. The heat, sparse resources, and emptiness, which permit no excess, he says, have become home to superfluity and material indulgence. His work asks that we re-examine our wants and let the desert help replace a hunger for things with a desire for rich experience of living.

When the Waters Recede in Tucson

It is Sunday night in our little mesquite bosque. I grab a key lime soda from the fridge and find a chair on the porch next to my wife. We can hear the highway up the hill behind the house but the light of the setting sun and the breeze off the mountains—a breeze still carrying the chill of last night's snow—quiets the drone of traffic.

No gauzy film, billboard, corporate-sponsored dreamscape, or media hype could capture this subtle shift of the season, this last, cool, goodbye kiss of spring-time that spills over and through us as we sip drinks and make small talk.

Snowbirds, busy packing, worry what summer will do to the garden, hastily apply lip-gloss, and stow golf carts. More of the desert will be given to them next year, more water too. The lock snaps shut on the hasp. Doors close. Engines whine, then fade into the distance.

The last of the snow runoff is withdrawing back to the high country. Clear water still runs over the sand at the foot of the mountains, but has disappeared just today here in the valley. I followed it upstream as the mouth of our winter creek retreated, growing silent, its piece said, overtaken by the thirsty sand.

Shadows lengthen. Trees have gone opaque with blossom and leaf in this last week. I watch my wife read, study her crossed legs, and wonder how many times I will see her again in a light like this, a breeze like this, my shoes wet with the last drops of a vanishing desert river. Once more? Twice? Not more than a few, if any.

The shadows overtake the light, and the sounds of the highway come down to us, no longer held at bay by the breeze. She gets up. It is too dark to read, and friends are coming over. I sit and listen for the sounds of coyotes, somewhere. How dear this moment, how elusive, exquisite, and unbearable its taste.

April 22, 2001, Erec Toso, Tucson, AZ

Hungry Soul

The table feels empty
Despite heaps of food.
I am hungry for the wrong things.

A cereus bloomed last night
But I did not see it.
One night of the year
Luminous velvet edges
Spring from a neck
Of spines and gnarled
Armor.

I walked past it
Breathing hard
Lungs straining against
A straitjacket
Woven from the hunger
For more than I could ever use.

Lightning struck the roof
Frying our habits.
Phones died.
Tools are silent, inert.

I am angry at being set free.
I am sure I need them
To slake my appetite
For something to fill
Empty places.

In the silence sprouts a question:
For what are you hungry?

Fog clears
And I see with right eyes
Roots of thick appetite
Rising to
Stems, fruit
A ripening
Seed,
Liquid, timeless
Desire.

I want to witness
The night bloom of the cereus
And sit with it as the night gives way to day
As the sun exposes the blossom,

Piercing its defiant glory.
I want to attend to the bloom as it
  wilts, kneels, fades, drains,
And prays to the ground.

I want to abide with the cereus
To call it by its sacred name,
  wonder.
I long to gaze directly at this
  reminder
Of the brevity and passing
  impermanence
Of me,
And all things,
To turn away from neither
The beauty and miracle of the bloom nor
The certainty of its demise.

I hear the spines of the cacti
Whispering in my dreams.
Withered and thirsty in this
Place bathed in light
They remember.

Rachel Carson

A marine biologist and writer, Rachel Carson's works include The Sea Around Us *and* The Edge of the Sea. *Her most prominent and influential work,* Silent Spring, *publicized the dangers of pesticide use to environmental health. The excerpt printed here focuses on "The Human Price" of using toxic pesticides.*

The Human Price

As the tide of chemicals born of the Industrial Age has arisen to engulf our environment, a drastic change has come about in the nature of the most serious public health problems. Only yesterday mankind lived in fear of the scourges of smallpox, cholera, and plague that once swept nations before them. Now our major concern is no longer with the disease organisms that once were omnipresent; sanitation, better living conditions, and new drugs have given us a high degree of control over infectious disease. Today we are concerned with a different kind of hazard that lurks in our environment—a hazard we ourselves have introduced into our world as our modern way of life has evolved.

The new environmental health problems are multiple—created by radiation in all its forms, born of the never-ending stream of chemicals of which pesticides are a part, chemicals now pervading the world in which we live, acting upon us directly and indirectly, separately and collectively. Their presence casts a shadow that is no less ominous because it is formless and obscure, no less frightening because it is simply impossible to predict the effects of lifetime exposure to chemical and physical agents that are not part of the biological experience of man.

"We all live under the haunting fear that something may corrupt the environment to the point where man joins the dinosaurs as an obsolete form of life," says Dr. David Price of the United States Public Health Service. "And what makes these thoughts all the more disturbing is the knowledge that our fate could perhaps be sealed twenty or more years before the development of symptoms."

Where do pesticides fit into the picture of environmental disease? We have seen that they now contaminate soil, water, and food, that they have the power to make our streams fishless and our gardens and woodlands silent and birdless. Man, however much he may like to pretend the contrary, is part of nature. Can he escape a pollution that is now so thoroughly distributed throughout our world?

We know that even single exposures to these chemicals, if the amount is large enough, can precipitate acute poisoning. But this is not the major problem. The sudden illness or death of farmers, spraymen, pilots, and others exposed to appre-

---

ciable quantities of pesticides are tragic and should not occur. For the population as a whole, we must be more concerned with the delayed effects of absorbing small amounts of the pesticides that invisibly contaminate our world.

Responsible public health officials have pointed out that the biological effects of chemicals are cumulative over long periods of time, and that the hazard to the individual may depend on the sum of the exposures received throughout his lifetime. For these very reasons the danger is easily ignored. It is human nature to shrug off what may seem to us a vague threat of future disaster. "Men are naturally most impressed by diseases which have obvious manifestations," says a wise physician, Dr. René Dubos, "Yet some of their worst enemies creep on them unobtrusively."

For each of us, as for the robin in Michigan or the salmon in the Miramichi, this is a problem of ecology, of interrelationships, of interdependence. We poison the caddis flies in a stream and the salmon runs dwindle and die. We poison the gnats in a lake and the poison travels from link to link of the food chain and soon the birds of the lake margins become its victims. We spray our elms and the following springs are silent of robin song, not because we sprayed the robins directly but because the poison traveled, step by step, through the now familiar elm leaf-earthworm-robin cycle. These are matters of record, observable, part of the visible world around us. They reflect the web of life—or death—that scientists know as ecology.

But there is also an ecology of the world within our bodies. In this unseen world minute causes produce mighty effects; the effect, moreover, is often seemingly unrelated to the cause, appearing in a part of the body remote from the area where the original injury was sustained. "A change at one point, in one molecule even, may reverberate throughout the entire system to initiate changes in seemingly unrelated organs and tissues," says a recent summary of the present status of medical research. When one is concerned with the mysterious and wonderful functioning of the human body, cause and effect are seldom simple and easily demonstrated relationships. They may be widely separated both in space and time. To discover the agent of disease and death depends on a patient piecing together of many seemingly distinct and unrelated facts developed through a vast amount of research in widely separated fields.

We are accustomed to look for the gross and immediate effect and to ignore all else. Unless this appears promptly and in such obvious form that it cannot be ignored, we deny the existence of hazard. Even research men suffer from the handicap of inadequate methods of detecting the beginnings of injury. The lack of sufficiently delicate methods to detect injury before symptoms appear is one of the great unsolved problems in medicine.

"But," someone will object, "I have used dieldrin sprays on the lawn many times but I have never had convulsions like the World Health Organization spraymen—so it hasn't harmed me." It is not that simple. Despite the absence of sudden and dramatic symptoms, one who handles such materials is unquestionably storing up toxic materials in his body. Storage of the chlorinated hydrocarbons, as we have seen, is cumulative, beginning with the smallest intake. The toxic materials become lodged in all the fatty tissues of the body. When these reserves of fat are drawn upon the poison may then strike quickly. A New Zealand medical journal recently provided an example. A man under treatment for obesity suddenly developed symptoms of poisoning. On examination his fat was found to contain stored dieldrin, which had been metabolized as he lost weight. The same thing could happen with loss of weight in illness.

The results of storage, on the other hand, could be even less obvious. Several years ago the *Journal* of the American Medical Association warned strongly of the hazards of insecticide storage in adipose tissue, pointing out that drugs or chemicals that are cumulative require greater caution than those having no tendency to be stored in the tissues. The adipose tissue, we are warned, is not merely a place for the deposition of fat (which makes up about 18 per cent of the body weight), but has many important functions with which the stored poisons may interfere. Furthermore, fats are very widely distributed in the organs and tissues of the whole body, even being constituents of cell membranes. It is important to remember, therefore, that the fat-soluble insecticides become stored in individual cells, where they are in position to interfere with the most vital and necessary functions of oxidation and energy production. This important aspect of the problem will be taken up in the next chapter.

One of the most significant facts about the chlorinated hydrocarbon insecticides is their effect on the liver. Of all organs in the body the liver is most extraordinary. In its versatility and in the indispensable nature of its functions it has no equal. It presides over so many vital activities that even the slightest damage to it is fraught with serious consequences. Not only does it provide bile for the digestion of fats, but because of its location and the special circulatory pathways that converge upon it the liver receives blood directly from the digestive tract and is deeply involved in the metabolism of all the principal foodstuffs. It stores sugar in the form of glycogen and releases it as glucose in carefully measured quantities to keep the blood sugar at a normal level. It builds body proteins, including some essential elements of blood plasma concerned with blood-clotting. It maintains cholesterol at its proper level in the blood plasma, and inactivates the male and female hormones when they reach excessive levels. It is a storehouse of many vitamins, some of which in turn contribute to its own proper functioning.

Without a normally functioning liver the body would be disarmed—defenseless against the great variety of poisons that continually invade it. Some of these are normal by-products of metabolism, which the liver swiftly and efficiently makes harmless by withdrawing their nitrogen. But poisons that have no normal place in the body may also be detoxified. The "harmless" insecticides malathion and methoxychlor are less poisonous than their relatives only because a liver enzyme deals with them, altering their molecules in such a way that their capacity for harm is lessened. In similar ways the liver deals with the majority of the toxic materials to which we are exposed.

Our line of defense against invading poisons or poisons from within is now weakened and crumbling. A liver damaged by pesticides is not only incapable of protecting us from poisons, the whole wide range of its activities may be interfered with. Not only are the consequences far-reaching, but because of their variety and the fact that they may not immediately appear they may not be attributed to their true cause.

In connection with the nearly universal use of insecticides that are liver poisons, it is interesting to note the sharp rise in hepatitis that began during the 1950s and is continuing a fluctuating climb. Cirrhosis also is said to be increasing. While it is admittedly difficult, in dealing with human beings rather than laboratory animals, to "prove" that cause A produces effect B, plain common sense suggests that the relation between a soaring rate of liver disease and the prevalence of liver poisons in the environment is no coincidence. Whether or not the chlorinated hydrocarbons are the primary cause, it seems hardly sensible under the circumstances to expose ourselves to poisons that have a proven ability to damage the liver and so presumably to make it less resistant to disease.

Both major types of insecticides, the chlorinated hydrocarbons and the organic phosphates, directly affect the nervous system, although in somewhat different ways. This has been made clear by an infinite number of experiments on animals and by observations on human subjects as well. As for DDT, the first of the new organic insecticides to be widely used, its action is primarily on the central nervous system of man; the cerebellum and the higher motor cortex are thought to be the areas chiefly affected. Abnormal sensations as of prickling, burning, or itching, as well as tremors or even convulsions may follow exposure to appreciable amounts, according to a standard textbook of toxicology.

Our first knowledge of the symptoms of acute poisoning by DDT was furnished by several British investigators, who deliberately exposed themselves in order to learn the consequences. Two scientists at the British Royal Navy Physiological Laboratory invited absorption of DDT through the skin by direct contact with walls covered with a water-soluble paint containing 2 per cent DDT, overlaid with a thin film of oil. The direct effect on the nervous system is apparent in their eloquent description of their symptoms: "The tiredness, heaviness, and aching of limbs were very real things, and the mental state was also most distressing . . . [there was] extreme irritability . . . great distaste for work of any sort . . . a feeling of mental incompetence in tackling the simplest mental task. The joint pains were quite violent at times."

Another British experimenter who applied DDT in acetone solution to his skin reported heaviness and aching of limbs, muscular weakness, and "spasms of extreme nervous tension." He took a holiday and improved, but on return to work his condition deteriorated. He then spent three weeks in bed, made miserable by constant aching in limbs, insomnia, nervous tension, and feelings of acute anxiety. On occasion tremors shook his whole body—tremors of the sort now made all too familiar by the sight of birds poisoned by DDT. The experimenter lost 10 weeks from his work, and at the end of a year, when his case was reported in a British medical journal, recovery was not complete.

(Despite this evidence, several American investigators conducting an experiment with DDT on volunteer subjects dismissed the complaint of headache and "pain in every bone" as "obviously of psychoneurotic origin.")

There are now many cases on record in which both the symptoms and the whole course of the illness point to insecticides as the cause. Typically, such a victim has had a known exposure to one of the insecticides, his symptoms have subsided under treatment which included the exclusion of all insecticides from his environment, and most significantly *have returned with each renewed contact* with the offending chemicals. This sort of evidence—and no more—forms the basis of a vast amount of medical therapy in many other disorders. There is no reason why it should not serve as a warning that it is no longer sensible to take the "calculated risk" of saturating our environment with pesticides.

Why does not everyone handling and using insecticides develop the same symptoms? Here the matter of individual sensitivity enters in. There is some evidence that women are more susceptible than men, the very young more than adults, those who lead sedentary, indoor lives more than those leading a rugged life of work or exercise in the open. Beyond these differences are others that are no less real because they are intangible. What makes one person allergic to dust or pollen, sensitive to a poison, or susceptible to an infection whereas another is not is a medical mystery for which there is at present no explanation. The problem nevertheless exists and it affects significant numbers of the population. Some physicians estimate that a third or more of their patients show signs of some form of sensitivity, and that the number is growing. And unfortunately, sensitivity may suddenly develop in a person previously insensitive. In fact, some medical men believe that intermittent exposures to chemicals may produce just such sensitivity. If this is true, it may explain why some studies on men subjected to continuous occupational exposure find little evidence of toxic effects. By their constant contact with the chemicals these men keep themselves desensitized—as an allergist keeps his patients desensitized by repeated small injections of the allergen.

The whole problem of pesticide poisoning is enormously complicated by the fact that a human being, unlike a laboratory animal living under rigidly controlled conditions, is never exposed to one chemical alone. Between the major groups of insecticides, and between them and other chemicals, there are interactions that have serious potentials. Whether released into soil or water or a man's blood, these unrelated chemicals do not remain segregated; there are mysterious and unseen changes by which one alters the power of another for harm.

There is interaction even between the two major groups of insecticides usually thought to be completely distinct in their action. The power of the organic phosphates, those poisoners of the nerve-protective enzyme cholinesterase, may become greater if the body has first been exposed to a chlorinated hydrocarbon which injures the liver. This is because, when liver function is disturbed, the cholinesterase level drops below normal. The added depressive effect of the organic phosphate may then be enough to precipitate acute symptoms. And as we have seen, pairs of the organic phosphates themselves may interact in such a way as to increase their toxicity a hundredfold. Or the organic phosphates may interact with various drugs, or with synthetic materials, food additives—who can say what else of the infinite number of man-made substances that now pervade our world?

The effect of a chemical of supposedly innocuous nature can be drastically changed by the action of another; one of the best examples is a close relative of DDT called methoxychlor. (Actually, methoxychlor may not be as free from dangerous qualities as it is generally said to be, for recent work on experimental animals shows a direct action on the uterus and a blocking effect on some of the powerful pituitary hormones—reminding us again that these are chemicals with enormous biologic effect. Other work shows that methoxychlor has a potential ability to damage the kidneys.) Because it is not stored to any great extent when given alone, we are told that methoxychlor is a safe chemical. But this is not necessarily true. If the liver has been damaged by another agent, methoxychlor is stored in the body at *100 times* its normal rate, and will then imitate the effects of DDT with long-lasting effects on the nervous system. Yet the liver damage that brings this about might be so slight as to pass unnoticed. It might have been the result of any of a number of commonplace situations—using another insecticide, using a cleaning fluid containing carbon tetrachloride, or taking one of the so-called tranquilizing drugs, a number (but not all) of which are chlorinated hydrocarbons and possess power to damage the liver.

Damage to the nervous system is not confined to acute poisoning; there may also be delayed effects from exposure. Long-lasting damage to brain or nerves has been reported for methoxychlor and others. Dieldrin, besides its immediate consequences, can have long delayed effects ranging from "loss of memory, insomnia, and nightmares to mania." Lindane, according to medical findings, is stored in significant amounts in the brain and functioning liver tissue and may induce "profound and long lasting effects on the central nervous system." Yet this chemical, a form of benzene hexachloride, is much used in vaporizers, devices that pour a stream of volatilized insecticide vapor into homes, offices, restaurants.

The organic phosphates, usually considered only in relation to their more violent manifestations in acute poisoning, also have the power to produce lasting physical damage to nerve tissues and, according to recent findings, to induce mental disorders. Various cases of delayed paralysis have followed use of one or another of these insecticides. A bizarre happening in the United States during the prohibition era about 1930 was an omen of things to come. It was caused not by an insecticide but by a substance belonging chemically to the same group as the organic phosphate insecticides. During that period some medicinal substances were being pressed into service as substitutes for liquor, being exempt from the prohibition law. One of these was Jamaica ginger. But the *United States Pharmacopeia* product was expensive, and bootleggers conceived the idea of making a substitute Jamaica ginger. They succeeded so well that their spurious product responded to the appropriate chemical tests and deceived the government chemists. To give their false ginger the necessary tang they had introduced a chemical known as triorthocresyl phosphate. This chemical, like parathion and its relatives, destroys the protective enzyme cholinesterase. As a consequence of drinking the bootleggers' product some 15,000 people developed a permanently crippling type of paralysis of the leg muscles, a condition now called "ginger paralysis." The paralysis was accompanied by destruction of the nerve sheaths and by degeneration of the cells of the anterior horns of the spinal cord.

About two decades later various other organic phosphates came into use as insecticides, as we have seen, and soon cases reminiscent of the ginger paralysis episode began to occur. One was a greenhouse worker in Germany who became paralyzed several months after experiencing mild symptoms of poisoning on a few occasions after using parathion. Then a group of three chemical plant workers developed acute poisoning from exposure to other insecticides of this group. They recovered under treatment, but ten days later two of them developed muscular weakness in the legs. This persisted for 10 months in one; the other, a young woman chemist, was more severely affected, with paralysis in both legs and some involvement of the hands and arms. Two years later when her case was reported in a medical journal she was still unable to walk.

The insecticide responsible for these cases has been withdrawn from the market, but some of those now in use may be capable of like harm. Malathion (beloved of gardeners) has induced severe muscular weakness in experiments on chickens. This was attended (as in ginger paralysis) by destruction of the sheaths of the sciatic and spinal nerves.

All these consequences of organic phosphate poisoning, if survived, may be a prelude to worse. In view of the severe damage they inflict upon the nervous system, it was perhaps inevitable that these insecticides would eventually be linked with mental disease. That link has recently been supplied by investigators at the University of Melbourne and Prince Henry's Hospital in Melbourne, who reported on 16 cases of mental disease. All had a history of prolonged exposure to organic phosphorus insecticides. Three were scientists checking the efficacy of sprays; 8 worked in greenhouses; 5 were farm workers. Their symptoms ranged from impairment of memory to schizophrenic and depressive reactions. All had normal medical histories before the chemicals they were using boomeranged and struck them down.

Echoes of this sort of thing are to be found, as we have seen, widely scattered throughout medical literature, sometimes involving the chlorinated hydrocarbons, sometimes the organic phosphates. Confusion, delusions, loss of memory, mania—a heavy price to pay for the temporary destruction of a few insects, but a price that will continue to be exacted as long as we insist upon using chemicals that strike directly at the nervous system.

Terry Tempest Williams

In the spring of 1983, Terry Tempest Williams (born 1955) learned that her mother was dying of breast cancer. That same spring, Great Salt Lake started to rise to record heights, threatening the Bear River Migratory Bird Refuge that Williams frequently visited. Williams combined these two events into Refuge: An Unnatural History of Family and Place, *a collection of essays published in 1991, from which "The Clan of One-Breasted Women" is taken. In "The Clan of One-Breasted Women," Williams connects the breast cancers of nine women in her Utah family (mother, both grandmothers, six aunts) to nuclear testing, especially at the Nevada Test Site. Although the essay is focused on the testing, it also speaks of the love of landscape.*

Williams is Naturalist-in-Residence at the Utah Museum of Natural History in Salt Lake City and sometimes teaches at the University of Utah. Her first book, Pieces of White Shell: A Journey to Navajoland *(1984), received the 1984 Southwest Book Award. She also is the author of* Coyote's Canyon *and of two children's books.*

The Clan of One-Breasted Women

I belong to a Clan of One-Breasted Women. My mother, my grandmothers, and six aunts have all had mastectomies. Seven are dead. The two who survive have just completed rounds of chemotherapy and radiation.

I've had my own problems: two biopsies for breast cancer and a small tumor between my ribs diagnosed as a "borderline malignancy."

This is my family history.

Most statistics tell us that breast cancer is genetic, hereditary, with rising percentages attached to fatty diets, childlessness, or becoming pregnant after thirty. What they don't say is that living in Utah may be the greatest hazard of all.

We are a Mormon family with roots in Utah since 1847. The "word of wisdom" in my family aligned us with good foods—no coffee, no tea, tobacco, or alcohol. For the most part, our women were finished having their babies by the time they were thirty. And only one faced breast cancer prior to 1960. Traditionally, as a group of people, Mormons have a low rate of cancer.

Is our family a cultural anomaly? The truth is, we didn't think about it. Those who did, usually the men, simply said, "bad genes." The women's attitude was

---

stoic. Cancer was part of life. On February 16, 1971, the eve of my mother's surgery, I accidentally picked up the telephone and overheard her ask my grandmother what she could expect.

"Diane, it is one of the most spiritual experiences you will ever encounter."

I quietly put down the receiver.

Two days later, my father took my brothers and me to the hospital to visit her. She met us in the lobby in a wheelchair. No bandages were visible. I'll never forget her radiance, the way she held herself in a purple velvet robe, and how she gathered us around her.

"Children, I am fine. I want you to know I felt the arms of God around me."

We believed her. My father cried. Our mother, his wife, was thirty-eight years old.

A little over a year after Mother's death, Dad and I were having dinner together. He had just returned from St. George, where the Tempest Company was completing the gas lines that would service southern Utah. He spoke of his love for the country, the sandstoned landscape, bare-boned and beautiful. He had just finished hiking the Kolob trail in Zion National Park. We got caught up in reminiscing, recalling with fondness our walk up Angel's Landing on his fiftieth birthday and the years our family had vacationed there.

Over dessert, I shared a recurring dream of mine. I told my father that for years, as long as I could remember, I saw this flash of light in the night in the desert—that this image had so permeated my being that I could not venture south without seeing it again, on the horizon, illuminating buttes and mesas.

"You did see it," he said.

"Saw what?"

"The bomb. The cloud. We were driving home from Riverside, California. You were sitting on Diane's lap. She was pregnant. In fact, I remember the day, September 7, 1957. We had just gotten out of the Service. We were driving north, past Las Vegas. It was an hour or so before dawn, when this explosion went off. We not only heard it, but felt it. I thought the oil tanker in front of us had blown up. We pulled over and suddenly, rising from the desert floor, we saw it, clearly, this golden-stemmed cloud, the mushroom. The sky seemed to vibrate with an eerie pink glow. Within a few minutes, a light ash was raining on the car."

I stared at my father.

"I thought you knew that," he said. "It was a common occurrence in the fifties."

It was at this moment that I realized the deceit I had been living under. Children growing up in the American Southwest, drinking contaminated milk from contaminated cows, even from the contaminated breasts of their mothers, my mother—members, years later, of the Clan of One-Breasted Women.

It is a well-known story in the Desert West, "The Day We Bombed Utah," or more accurately, the years we bombed Utah: above ground atomic testing in Nevada took place from January 27, 1951 through July 11, 1962. Not only were the winds blowing north covering "low-use segments of the population" with fallout and leaving sheep dead in their tracks, but the climate was right. The United States of the 1950s was red, white, and blue. The Korean War was raging.

McCarthyism was rampant. Ike was it, and the cold war was hot. If you were against nuclear testing, you were for a communist regime.

Much has been written about this "American nuclear tragedy." Public health was secondary to national security. The Atomic Energy Commissioner, Thomas Murray, said, "Gentlemen, we must not let anything interfere with this series of tests, nothing."

Again and again, the American public was told by its government, in spite of burns, blisters, and nausea, "It has been found that the tests may be conducted with adequate assurance of safety under conditions prevailing at the bombing reservations." Assuaging public fears was simply a matter of public relations. "Your best action," an Atomic Energy Commission booklet read, "is not to be worried about fallout." A news release typical of the times stated, "We find no basis for concluding that harm to any individual has resulted from radioactive fallout."

On August 30, 1979, during Jimmy Carter's presidency, a suit was filed, *Irene Allen v. The United States of America.* Mrs. Allen's case was the first on an alphabetical list of twenty-four test cases, representative of nearly twelve hundred plaintiffs seeking compensation from the United States government for cancers caused by nuclear testing in Nevada.

Irene Allen lived in Hurricane, Utah. She was the mother of five children and had been widowed twice. Her first husband, with their two oldest boys, had watched the tests from the roof of the local high school. He died of leukemia in 1956. Her second husband died of pancreatic cancer in 1978.

In a town meeting conducted by Utah Senator Orrin Hatch, shortly before the suit was filed, Mrs. Allen said, "I am not blaming the government, I want you to know that, Senator Hatch. But I thought if my testimony could help in any way so this wouldn't happen again to any of the generations coming up after us. . . I am happy to be here this day to bear testimony of this."

God-fearing people. This is just one story in an anthology of thousands.

On May 10, 1984, Judge Bruce S. Jenkins handed down his opinion. Ten of the plaintiffs were awarded damages. It was the first time a federal court had determined that nuclear tests had been the cause of cancers. For the remaining fourteen test cases, the proof of causation was not sufficient. In spite of the split decision, it was considered a landmark ruling. It was not to remain so for long.

In April 1987, the Tenth Circuit Court of Appeals overturned Judge Jenkins's ruling on the ground that the United States was protected from suit by the legal doctrine of sovereign immunity, a centuries-old idea from England in the days of absolute monarchs.

In January 1988, the Supreme Court refused to review the Appeals Court decision. To our court system it does not matter whether the United States government was irresponsible, whether it lied to its citizens, or even that citizens died from the fallout of nuclear testing. What matters is that our government is immune: "The King can do no wrong."

In Mormon culture, authority is respected, obedience is revered, and independent thinking is not. I was taught as a young girl not to "make waves" or "rock the boat."

"Just let it go," Mother would say. "You know how you feel, that's what counts."

For many years, I have done just that—listened, observed, and quietly formed my own opinions, in a culture that rarely asks questions because it has all the answers. But one by one, I have watched the women in my family die common, heroic deaths. We sat in waiting rooms hoping for good news, but always receiving the bad. I cared for them, bathed their scarred bodies, and kept their secrets. I watched beautiful women become bald as Cytoxan, cisplatin, and Adriamycin were injected into their veins. I held their foreheads as they vomited green-black bile, and I shot them with morphine when the pain became inhuman. In the end, I witnessed their last peaceful breaths, becoming a midwife to the rebirth of their souls.

The price of obedience has become too high.

The fear and inability to question authority that ultimately killed rural communities in Utah during atmospheric testing of atomic weapons is the same fear I saw in my mother's body. Sheep. Dead sheep. The evidence is buried.

I cannot prove that my mother, Diane Dixon Tempest, or my grandmothers, Lettie Romney Dixon and Kathryn Blackett Tempest, along with my aunts developed cancer from nuclear fallout in Utah. But I can't prove they didn't.

My father's memory was correct. The September blast we drove through in 1957 was part of Operation Plumbbob, one of the most intensive series of bomb tests to be initiated. The flash of light in the night in the desert, which I had always thought was a dream, developed into a family nightmare. It took fourteen years, from 1957 to 1971, for cancer to manifest in my mother—the same time, Howard L. Andrews, an authority in radioactive fallout at the National Institutes of Health, says radiation cancer requires to become evident. The more I learn about what it means to be a "downwinder," the more questions I drown in.

What I do know, however, is that as a Mormon woman of the fifth generation of Latter-day Saints, I must question everything, even if it means losing my faith, even if it means becoming a member of a border tribe among my own people. Tolerating blind obedience in the name of patriotism or religion ultimately takes our lives.

When the Atomic Energy Commission described the country north of the Nevada Test Site as "virtually uninhabited desert terrain," my family and the birds at Great Salt Lake were some of the "virtual uninhabitants."

One night, I dreamed women from all over the world circled a blazing fire in the desert. They spoke of change, how they hold the moon in their bellies and wax and wane with its phases. They mocked the presumption of even-tempered beings and made promises that they would never fear the witch inside themselves. The women danced wildly as sparks broke away from the flames and entered the night sky as stars.

And they sang a song given to them by Shoshone grandmothers:

Ah ne nah, nah	Consider the rabbits
nin nah nah—	How gently they walk on the earth—
ah ne nah, nah	Consider the rabbits

nin nah nah—	How gently they walk on the earth—
Nyaga mutzi	We remember them
oh ne nay—	We can walk gently also—
Nyaga mutzi	We remember them
oh ne nay—	We can walk gently also—

The women danced and drummed and sang for weeks, preparing themselves for what was to come. They would reclaim the desert for the sake of their children, for the sake of the land.

A few miles downwind from the fire circle, bombs were being tested. Rabbits felt the tremors. Their soft leather pads on paws and feet recognized the shaking sands, while the roots of mesquite and sage were smoldering. Rocks were hot from the inside out and dust devils hummed unnaturally. And each time there was another nuclear test, ravens watched the desert heave. Stretch marks appeared. The land was losing its muscle.

The women couldn't bear it any longer. They were mothers. They had suffered labor pains but always under the promise of birth. The red hot pains beneath the desert promised death only, as each bomb became a stillborn. A contract had been made and broken between human beings and the land. A new contract was being drawn by the women, who understood the fate of the earth as their own.

Under the cover of darkness, ten women slipped under a barbed-wire fence and entered the contaminated country. They were trespassing. They walked toward the town of Mercury, in moonlight, taking their cues from coyote, kit fox, antelope squirrel, and quail. They moved quietly and deliberately through the maze of Joshua trees. When a hint of daylight appeared they rested, drinking tea and sharing their rations of food. The women closed their eyes. The time had come to protest with the heart, that to deny one's genealogy with the earth was to commit treason against one's soul.

At dawn, the women draped themselves in mylar, wrapping long streamers of silver plastic around their arms to blow in the breeze. They wore clear masks, that became the faces of humanity. And when they arrived at the edge of Mercury, they carried all the butterflies of a summer day in their wombs. They paused to allow their courage to settle.

The town that forbids pregnant women and children to enter because of radiation risks was asleep. The women moved through the streets as winged messengers, twirling around each other in slow motion, peeking inside homes and watching the easy sleep of men and women. They were astonished by such stillness and periodically would utter a shrill note or low cry just to verify life.

The residents finally awoke to these strange apparitions. Some simply stared. Others called authorities, and in time, the women were apprehended by wary soldiers dressed in desert fatigues. They were taken to a white, square building on the other edge of Mercury. When asked who they were and why they were there, the women replied, "We are mothers and we have come to reclaim the desert for our children."

The soldiers arrested them. As the ten women were blindfolded and handcuffed, they began singing:

You can't forbid us everything
You can't forbid us to think—
You can't forbid our tears to flow
And you can't stop the songs that we sing.

The women continued to sing louder and louder, until they heard the voices of their sisters moving across the mesa:

Ah ne nah, nah
nin nah nah—
Ah ne nah, nah
nin nah nah—
Nyaga mutzi
oh ne nay—
Nyaga mutzi
oh ne nay—

"Call for reinforcements," one soldier said.

"We have," interrupted one woman, "we have—and you have no idea of our numbers."

I crossed the line at the Nevada Test Site and was arrested with nine other Utahns for trespassing on military lands. They are still conducting nuclear tests in the desert. Ours was an act of civil disobedience. But as I walked toward the town of Mercury, it was more than a gesture of peace. It was a gesture on behalf of the Clan of One-Breasted Women.

As one officer cinched the handcuffs around my wrists, another frisked my body. She found a pen and a pad of paper tucked inside my left boot.

"And these?" she asked sternly.

"Weapons," I replied.

Our eyes met. I smiled. She pulled the leg of my trousers back over my boot.

"Step forward, please," she said as she took my arm.

We were booked under an afternoon sun and bused to Tonopah, Nevada. It was a two-hour ride. This was familiar country. The Joshua trees standing their ground had been named by my ancestors, who believed they looked like prophets pointing west to the Promised Land. These were the same trees that bloomed each spring, flowers appearing like white flames in the Mojave. And I recalled a full moon in May, when Mother and I had walked among them, flushing out mourning doves and owls.

The bus stopped short of town. We were released.

The officials thought it was a cruel joke to leave us stranded in the desert with no way to get home. What they didn't realize was that we were home, soul-centered and strong, women who recognized the sweet smell of sage as fuel for our spirits.

Edward Abbey

One of the most vocal advocates for wilderness protection, particularly in the Southwest, Edward Abbey (1927–1989) believed that responsible individuals must defend natural areas by whatever means, except violence against life. Born in Pennsylvania, Abbey hitchhiked west as a young man and made the arid landscapes of New Mexico, Arizona, and Utah his permanent home. In between treks deep into the desert, he lived in Albuquerque, where he studied philosophy and literature at the University of New Mexico and earned a master's degree. For many years, he worked as a fire lookout and seasonal park ranger for the National Park Service, especially at today's Arches National Park in Utah.

After becoming a respected writer of both fiction and nonfiction, Abbey taught part-time at the University of Arizona in Tucson. He is best known for Desert Solitaire *(1968), a collection of essays describing his life as a park ranger at Arches back in the late 1950s, and for* The Monkey Wrench Gang *(1976), a novel about four saboteurs who undermine the construction of dams. Abbey's love for natural landscapes was fierce and this fierceness is reflected in his usually funny-cranky writing style. "Abbey is not for everybody" reviewer Kerry Luft once wrote. "He's about as subtle as a wrecking ball." In "Even the Bad Guys Wear White Hats," Edward Abbey takes us back to his twenty-year-old self. He's just arrived in the West and wants to be a cowboy.*

Even the Bad Guys Wear White Hats

When I first came West in 1948, a student at the University of New Mexico, I was only twenty years old and just out of the Army. I thought, like most simple-minded Easterners, that a cowboy was a kind of mythic hero. I idolized those scrawny little red-nosed hired hands in their tight jeans, funny boots, and comical hats.

Like other new arrivals in the West, I could imagine nothing more romantic than becoming a cowboy. Nothing more glorious than owning my own little genuine working cattle outfit. About the only thing better, I thought, was to be a big league baseball player. I never dreamed that I'd eventually sink to writing books for a living. Unluckily for me—coming from an Appalachian hillbilly background and with a poor choice of parents—I didn't have much money. My father was a small-time logger. He ran a one-man sawmill and a submarginal side-hill farm.

Reprinted from *Writing Nature: An Ecological Reader for Writers*, edited by Carolyn Ross, (1995), Don Congdon Associates.

There wasn't any money in our family, no inheritance you could run 10,000 cattle on. I had no trust fund to back me up. No Hollywood movie deals to finance a land acquisition program. I lived on what in those days was called the G.I. Bill, which paid about $150 a month while I went to school. I made that last as long as I could—five or six years. I couldn't afford a horse. The best I could do in 1947 and '48 was buy a thirdhand Chevy sedan and roam the West, mostly the Southwest, on holidays and weekends.

I had a roommate at the University of New Mexico. I'll just call him Mac. I don't want him to come looking for me. Mac came from a little town in southwest New Mexico where his father ran a feed store. Mackie was a fair bronc rider, eager to get into the cattle-growing business. And he had some money, enough to buy a little cinder-block house and about forty acres in the Sandia Mountains east of Albuquerque, near a town we called Landfill. Mackie fenced those forty acres, built a corral, and kept a few horses there, including an occasional genuine bronco for fun and practice.

I don't remember exactly how Mackie and I became friends in the first place. I was majoring in classical philosophy. He was majoring in screwworm management. But we got to know each other through the mutual pursuit of a pair of nearly inseparable Kappa Kappa Gamma girls. I lived with him in his little cinder-block house. Helped him meet the mortgage payments. Helped him meet the girls. We were both crude, shy, ugly, obnoxious—like most college boys.

My friend Mac also owned a 1947 black Lincoln convertible, the kind with the big grille in front, like a cowcatcher on a locomotive, chrome plated. We used to race to classes in the morning, driving the twenty miles from his house to the campus in never more than fifteen minutes. Usually Mac was too hung over to drive, so I'd operate the car, clutching the wheel while Mac sat beside me waving his big .44, taking potshots at jackrabbits and road signs and billboards and beer bottles. Trying to wake up in time for his ten o'clock class in brand inspection.

I'm sorry to say that my friend Mac was a little bit gun-happy. Most of his forty acres was in tumbleweed. He fenced in about half an acre with chicken wire and stocked that little pasture with white rabbits. He used it as a target range. Not what you'd call sporting, I suppose, but we did eat the rabbits. Sometimes we even went deer hunting with handguns. Mackie with his revolver, and me with a chrome-plated Colt .45 automatic I had liberated from the U.S. Army over in Italy. Surplus government property.

On one of our deer hunting expeditions, I was sitting on a log in a big clearing in the woods, thinking about Plato and Aristotle and the Kappa Kappa Gamma girls. I didn't really care whether we got a deer that day or not. It was a couple of days before opening, anyway. The whole procedure was probably illegal as hell. Mac was out in the woods somewhere looking for deer around the clearing. I was sitting on the log, thinking, when I saw a chip of bark fly away from the log all by itself, about a foot from my left hand. Then I heard the blast of Mac's revolver—that big old .44 he'd probably liberated from his father. Then I heard him laugh.

"That's not very funny, Mackie," I said.

"Now, don't whine and complain, Ed," he said. "You want to be a real hunter like me, you gotta learn to stay awake."

We never did get a deer with handguns. But that's when I had my first little doubts about Mackie, and about the cowboy type in general. But I still loved him. Worshiped him, in fact. I was caught in the grip of the Western myth. Anybody said a word to me against cowboys, I'd jump down his throat with my spurs on. Especially if Mac was standing nearby.

Sometimes I'd try to ride those broncs that he brought in, trying to prove that I could be a cowboy too. Trying to prove it more to myself than to him. I'd be on this crazy, crackpot horse, going up, down, left, right, and inside out. Hanging on to the saddle horn with both hands. And Mac would sit on the corral fence, throwing beer bottles at us and laughing. Every time I got thrown off, Mac would say, "Now get right back on there, Ed. Quick, quick. Don't spoil 'im."

It took me a long time to realize I didn't have to do that kind of work. And it took me another thirty years to realize that there's something wrong at the heart of our most popular American myth—the cowboy and his cow.

You may have guessed by now that I'm thinking of criticizing the livestock industry. And you are correct. I've been thinking about cows and sheep for many years. Getting more and more disgusted with the whole business. There are some Western cattlemen who are nothing more than welfare parasites. They've been getting a free ride on the public lands for over a century, and I think it's time we phased it out. I'm in favor of putting the public lands livestock grazers out of business.

First of all, we don't need the public lands beef industry. Even beef lovers don't need it. According to most government reports (Bureau of Land Management, Forest Service), only about 2 percent of our beef, our red meat, comes from the eleven Western states. By those eleven I mean Montana, Nevada, Utah, Colorado, New Mexico, Arizona, Idaho, Wyoming, Oregon, Washington, and California. Most of our beef, aside from imports, comes from the Midwest and the East, especially the Southeast—Georgia, Alabama, Florida—and from other private lands across the nation. More than twice as many beef cattle are raised in the state of Georgia than in the sagebrush empire of Nevada. And for a very good reason: back East, you can support a cow on maybe half an acre. Out here, it takes anywhere from twenty-five to fifty acres. In the red rock country of Utah, the rule of thumb is one section—a square mile—per cow.

Since such a small percentage of the cows are produced on public lands in the West, eliminating that industry should not raise supermarket beef prices very much. Furthermore, we'd save money in the taxes we now pay for various subsidies to these public lands cattlemen. Subsidies for things like "range improvement"—tree chaining, sagebrush clearing, mesquite poisoning, disease control, predator trapping, fencing, wells, stock ponds, roads. Then there are the salaries of those who work for government agencies like the BLM and the Forest Service. You could probably also count in a big part of the salaries of the overpaid professors engaged in range-management research at the Western land-grant colleges.

Moreover, the cattle have done, and are doing, intolerable damage to our public lands—our national forests, state lands, BLM-administered lands, wildlife preserves, even some of our national parks and monuments. In Utah's Capital Reef National Park, for example, grazing is still allowed. In fact, it's recently been extended for another ten years, and Utah politicians are trying to make the arrangement permanent. They probably won't get away with it. But there we have at least one case where cattle are still tramping about in a national park, transforming soil and grass into dust and weeds.

Overgrazing is much too weak a term. Most of the public lands in the West, and especially in the Southwest, are what you might call "cowburnt." Almost anywhere and everywhere you go in the American West you find hordes of these ugly, clumsy, stupid, bawling, stinking, fly-covered, disease-spreading brutes. They are a pest and a plague. They pollute our springs and streams and rivers. They infest our canyons, valleys, meadows, and forests. They graze off the native bluestem and grama and bunch grasses, leaving behind jungles of prickly pear. They trample down the native forbs and shrubs and cactus. They spread the exotic cheat grass, the Russian thistle, and the crested wheat grass. *Weeds.*

Even when the cattle are not physically present, you'll see the dung and the flies and the mud and the dust and the general destruction. If you don't see it, you'll smell it. The whole American West stinks of cattle. Along every flowing stream, around every seep and spring and water hole and well, you'll find acres and acres of what range-management specialists call "sacrifice areas"—another understatement. These are places denuded of forage, except for some cactus or a little tumbleweed or maybe a few mutilated trees like mesquite, juniper, or hackberry.

I'm not going to bombard you with graphs and statistics, which don't make much of an impression on intelligent people anyway. Anyone who goes beyond the city limits of almost any Western town can see for himself that the land is overgrazed. There are too many cows and horses and sheep out there. Of course, cattlemen would never publicly confess to overgrazing, any more than Dracula would publicly confess to a fondness for blood. Cattlemen are interested parties. Many of them will not give reliable testimony. Some have too much at stake: their Cadillacs and their airplanes, their ranch resale profits and their capital gains. (I'm talking about the corporation ranchers, the land-and-cattle companies, the investment syndicates.) Others, those ranchers who have only a small base property, flood the public lands with their cows. About 8 percent of the federal land permittees have cattle that consume approximately 45 percent of the forage on the government rangelands.

Beef ranchers like to claim that their cows do not compete with deer. Deer are browsers, cows are grazers. That's true. But when a range is overgrazed, when the grass is gone (as it often is for seasons at a time), then cattle become browsers too, out of necessity. In the Southwest, cattle commonly feed on mesquite, cliff rose, cactus, acacia, or any other shrub or tree they find biodegradable. To that extent, they compete with deer. And they tend to drive out other and better wildlife. Like elk, or bighorn sheep, or pronghorn antelope.

How much damage have cattle done to the Western rangelands? Large-scale beef ranching has been going on since the 1870s. There's plenty of documentation of the effects of this massive cattle grazing on the erosion of the land, the character of the land, the character of the vegetation. Streams and rivers that used to flow on the surface all year round are now intermittent, or underground, because of overgrazing and rapid runoff.

Our public lands have been overgrazed for a century. The BLM knows it; the Forest Service knows it. The Government Accounting Office knows it. And overgrazing means eventual ruin, just like strip mining or clear-cutting or the damming of rivers. Much of the Southwest already looks like Mexico or Southern Italy or North Africa: a cow-burnt wasteland. As we destroy our land, we destroy our agricultural economy and the basis of modern society. If we keep it up, we'll gradually degrade American life to the status of life in places like Mexico or southern Italy or Libya or Egypt.

In 1984 the Bureau of Land Management, which was required by Congress to report on its stewardship of our rangelands—the property of all Americans, remember—confessed that 31 percent of the land it administered was in "good condition," 42 percent in "fair condition," and 18 percent in "poor condition." And it reported that only 18 percent of the rangelands were improving, while 68 percent were "stable" and 14 percent were getting worse. If the BLM said that, we can safely assume that range conditions are actually much worse.

What can we do about this situation? This is the fun part—this is the part I like. It's not too easy to argue that we should do away with cattle ranching. The cowboy myth gets in the way. But I do have some solutions to overgrazing.

I'd begin by reducing the number of cattle on public lands. Not that range managers would go along with it, of course. In their eyes, and in the eyes of the livestock associations they work for, cutting down on the number of cattle is the worst possible solution—an impossible solution. So they propose all kinds of gimmicks. More cross-fencing. More wells and ponds so that more land can be exploited. These proposals are basically a maneuver by the Forest Service and the BLM to appease their critics without offending their real bosses in the beef industry.

I also suggest that we open a hunting season on range cattle. I realize that beef cattle will not make very sporting prey at first. Like all domesticated animals (including most humans), beef cattle are slow, stupid, and awkward. But the breed will improve if hunted regularly. And as the number of cattle is reduced, other and far more useful, beautiful, and interesting animals will return to the rangelands and will increase.

Suppose, by some miracle of Hollywood or inheritance or good luck, I should acquire a respectable-sized working cattle outfit. What would I do with it? First, I'd get rid of the stinking, filthy cattle. Every single animal. Shoot them all, and stock the place with real animals, real game, real protein: elk, buffalo, pronghorn antelope, bighorn sheep, moose. And some purely decorative animals, like eagles. We need more eagles. And wolves. We need more wolves. Mountain lions and bears. Especially, of course, grizzly bears. Down in the desert, I would stock every water tank, every water hole, every stock pond, with alligators.

You may note that I have said little about coyotes or deer. Coyotes seem to be doing all right on their own. They're smarter than their enemies. I've never heard of a coyote as dumb as a sheepman. As for deer, especially mule deer, they, too, are surviving—maybe even thriving, as some game and fish departments claim, though nobody claims there are as many deer now as there were before the cattle industry was introduced in the West. In any case, compared to elk the deer is a second-rate game animal, nothing but a giant rodent—a rat with antlers.

I've suggested that the beef industry's abuse of our Western lands is based on the old mythology of the cowboy as natural nobleman. I'd like to conclude this diatribe with a few remarks about this most cherished and fanciful of American fairy tales. In truth, the cowboy is only a hired hand. A farm boy in leather britches and a comical hat. A herdsman who gets on a horse to do part of his work. Some ranchers are also cowboys, but many are not. There is a difference. There are many ranchers out there who are bigtime farmers of the public lands—our property. As such, they do not merit any special consideration or special privileges. There are only about 31,000 ranchers in the whole American West who use the public lands. That's less than the population of Missoula, Montana.

The rancher (with a few honorable exceptions) is a man who strings barbed wire all over the range; drills wells and bulldozes stock ponds; drives off elk and antelope and bighorn sheep; poisons coyotes and prairie dogs; shoots eagles, bears, and cougars on sight; supplants the native grasses with tumbleweed, snakeweed, povertyweed, anthills, mud, dust, and flies. And then leans back and grins at the TV cameras and talks about how much he loves the American West. Cowboys are also greatly overrated. Consider the nature of their work. Suppose you had to spend most of your working hours sitting on a horse, contemplating the hind end of a cow. How would that affect your imagination? . . .

Do cowboys work hard? Sometimes. But most ranchers don't work very hard. They have a lot of leisure time for politics and belly-aching. Anytime you go into a small Western town you'll find them at the nearest drugstore, sitting around all morning drinking coffee, talking about their tax breaks.

Is a cowboy's work socially useful? No. As I've already pointed out, subsidized Western range beef is a trivial item in the national beef economy. If all of our 31,000 Western public land ranchers quit tomorrow, we'd never miss them. Any public school teacher does harder work, more difficult work, more dangerous work, and far more valuable work than any cowboy or rancher. The same thing applies to registered nurses and nurses' aides, garbage collectors, and traffic cops. Harder work, tougher work, more necessary work. We need those people in our complicated society. We do not need cowboys or ranchers. We've carried them on our backs long enough.

"This Abbey," the cowboys and their lovers will say, "this Abbey is a wimp. A chicken-hearted sentimentalist with no feel for the hard realities of practical life." Especially critical of my attitude will be the Easterners and Midwesterners newly arrived here from their Upper West Side apartments, their rustic lodges in upper Michigan. Our nouveau Westerners with their toy ranches, their pickup trucks with the gun racks, their pointy-toed boots with the undershot heels, the gigantic hats. And, of course, their pet horses. The *instant rednecks*.

To those who might accuse me of wimpery and sentimentality, I'd like to say this in reply. I respect real men. I admire true manliness. But I despise arrogance and brutality and bullies. So let me close with some nice remarks about cowboys and cattle ranchers. They are a mixed lot, like the rest of us. As individuals, they range from the bad to the ordinary to the good. A rancher, after all, is only a farmer, cropping the public rangelands with his four-legged lawnmowers, stashing our grass into his bank account. A cowboy is a hired hand trying to make an honest living. Nothing special.

I have no quarrel with these people as fellow humans. All I want to do is get their cows off our property. Let those cowboys and ranchers find some harder way to make a living, like the rest of us have to do. There's no good reason why we should subsidize them forever. They've had their free ride. It's time they learned to support themselves.

In the meantime, I'm going to say goodbye to all you cowboys and cowgirls. I love the legend, too—but keep your sacred cows and your dead horses off of my elk pastures.

David Quammen

Essayist and fiction writer David Quammen (born 1948) earned his B.A. from Yale University, where he was a Rhodes Scholar, and his B.Litt. from Oxford University in England. Although he was not trained as a scientist, much of Quammen's writing is on natural history and other scientific topics and has been praised for its accuracy and intelligence. He also is noted for his "funky New Journalistic" writing style, as reviewer James Kaufmann has pointed out, which makes complex subjects accessible and appealing to a wide readership. Quammen's early works include two well-received novels, To Walk a Line, *published in 1970 when he was only 22, and the political thriller* The Zolta Configuration, *published in 1983. Currently, he is the author of a popular monthly column, "Natural Acts," in* Outside *magazine. He lives and writes in Montana.*

In "Animal Rights and Beyond: The Search for a New Moral Framework and a Righteous Gumbo"—borrowed from his collection Natural Acts: A Sidelong View of Science and Nature *(1985)—Quammen responds to the arguments of two key animal rights advocates: Peter Singer and Tom Regan. He questions the line they draw between species and wonders how humans should behave toward animals "other than"* homo sapiens.

Animal Rights and Beyond: The Search for a New Moral Framework and a Righteous Gumbo

Do non-human animals have rights? Should we humans feel morally bound to exercise consideration for the lives and well-being of individual members of other animal species? If so, how much consideration, and by what logic? Is it permissible to torture and kill? Is it permissible to kill cleanly, without prolonged pain? To abuse or exploit without killing? For a moment, don't think about whales or wolves or the California condor; don't think about the cat or the golden retriever with whom you share your house. Think about chickens. Think about laboratory monkeys and then think about lab rats and then also think about lab frogs. Think about scallops. Think about mosquitoes.

Reprinted from *Natural Acts*, (1985), Lyons & Burford Publishers.

It's a Gordian question, by my lights, but one not very well suited to Alexandrian answers. Some people would disagree, judging the matter simply enough settled, one way or the other. *Of course they have rights. Of course they don't.* I say beware any such snappy, steel-trap thinking. Some folk would even—this late in the evolution of human sensibility—call it a frivolous question, a time-filling diversion for emotional hemophiliacs and cranks. *Women's rights, gay rights, now for Christ sake they want ANIMAL rights.* Notwithstanding the ridicule, the strong biases toward each side, it is certainly a serious philosophical issue, important and tricky, with almost endless implications for the way we humans live and should live on this planet.

Philosophers of earlier ages, if they touched the subject at all, were likely to be dismissive. Thomas Aquinas announced emphatically that animals "are intended for man's use in the natural order. Hence it is no wrong for man to make use of them, either by killing or in any other way whatever." Descartes held that animals are merely machines. As late as 1901, a moral logician named Joseph Rickaby (who happened to be a Jesuit, but don't necessarily hold that against him) declared: "Brute beasts, not having understanding and therefore not being persons, cannot have any rights. The conclusion is clear." Maybe not quite so clear. Recently, just during the past decade, professional academic philosophers have at last begun to address the matter more open-mindedly.

Two thinkers in particular have been influential: an Australian named Peter Singer, an American named Tom Regan. In 1975 Singer published a book titled *Animal Liberation,* which stirred up the debate among his colleagues and is still treated as a landmark. Eight years later Tom Regan published *The Case for Animal Rights,* a more thorough and ponderous opus that stands now as a sort of companion piece to the Singer book. In between there came a number of other discussions of animal rights—including a collection of essays edited jointly by Singer and Regan. Despite the one-time collaboration, Peter Singer and Tom Regan represent two distinct schools of thought: They reach similar conclusions about the obligations of humans to other animals, but the moral logic is very different, and possibly also the implications. Both men have produced some formidable work and both, to my simple mind, show some shocking limitations of vision.

I've spent the past week amid these books, Singer's and Regan's and the rest. It has been an edifying experience, and now I'm more puzzled than ever. I keep thinking about monkeys and frogs and mosquitoes and—sorry, but I'm quite serious—carrots.

Peter Singer's view is grounded upon the work of Jeremy Bentham, that eighteenth-century British philosopher generally known as the founder of utilitarianism. "The greatest good for the greatest number" is a familiar cartoon version of what, according to Bentham, should be achieved by the ethical ordering of society and behavior. A more precise summary is offered by Singer: "In other words, the interests of every being affected by an action are to be taken into account and given the same weight as the like interests of any other being." If this much is granted, the crucial next point is deciding what things constitute *interests* and who or what qualifies as a *being*. Evidently Bentham did not have just humans in mind. Back in 1789, optimistically and perhaps presciently, he wrote: "The day *may* come when the rest of the animal creation may acquire those rights which never could have been withholden from them but by the hand of tyranny." Most philosophers of his day were inclined (as most in our day are still inclined) to extend moral coverage only to humans, because only humans (supposedly) are rational and communicative. Jeremy Bentham took exception: "The question is not, Can they *reason*? nor, Can they *talk*? but, Can they *suffer*?" On this crucial point, Peter Singer follows Bentham.

The capacity to suffer, says Singer, is what separates a being with legitimate interests from an entity without interests. A stone has no interests that must be respected, because it cannot suffer. A mouse can suffer; therefore it has interests and those interests must be weighed in the moral balance. Fine, that much seems simple enough. Certain people of sophistic or Skinnerian bent would argue that there is no proof a mouse can in fact suffer, that it's merely an anthropomorphic assumption; but since each of us has no proof that *anyone* else actually suffers besides ourselves, we are willing, most of us, to grant the assumption. More problematic is that very large gray area between stones and mice.

Peter Singer declares: "If a being suffers, there can be no moral justification for disregarding that suffering, or for refusing to count it equally with the like suffering of any other being. But the converse of this is also true. If a being is not capable of suffering, or of enjoyment, there is nothing to take into account." Where is the boundary? Where falls the line between creatures who suffer and those that are incapable? Singer's cold philosophic eye travels across the pageant of living species—chickens suffer, mice suffer, fish suffer, um, lobsters most likely suffer, *look alive, you other creatures!*—and his damning stare lands on the oyster.

No I'm not making this up. The oyster, by Singer's best guess, doesn't suffer. Its nervous system lacks the requisite complexity. Therefore, while lobsters and crawfish and shrimp possess inviolable moral status, the oyster has none. It is a difficult judgment, Singer admits, by no means an infallible one but "somewhere between a shrimp and an oyster seems as good a place to draw the line as any, and better than most."

Moral philosophy, no one denies, is an imperfect science.

Tom Regan takes exception with Singer on two important points. First, he disavows the utilitarian framework, with its logic that abuse or killing of animals by humans is wrong because it yields a net *overall* decrease in welfare, among all beings who qualify for moral status. No, argues Regan, that logic is false and pernicious. The abuse or killing is wrong in its *essence*—however the balance comes out on overall welfare—because it violates the rights of those individual animals. Individual rights, in other words, take precedence over the maximizing of the common good. Second, in Regan's opinion the capacity to suffer is not what marks the elect. Mere suffering is not sufficient. Instead he posits the concept of *inherent value,* a complex and magical quality possessed by some living creatures but not others.

A large portion of Regan's book is devoted to arguing toward this concept. He is more uncompromisingly protective of certain creatures—those with rights—than Singer, but he is also more selective; the hull of his ark is sturdier, but the gangplank is narrower. According to Regan, individual beings possess inherent value (and therefore inviolable rights) if they "are able to perceive and remember; if they have beliefs, desires, and preferences; if they are able to act intentionally in pursuit of their desires or goals; if they are sentient and have an emotional life; if they have a sense of the future, including a sense of their own future; if they have a psychophysical identity over time; and if they have an individual experiential welfare that is logically independent of their utility for, and the interests of, others." So Tom Regan is not handing rights around profligately, to every cute little beast that crawls over his foot. In fact we all probably know a few humans who, at least on a bad night, might have trouble meeting those standards. But how would Regan himself apply them? Where does he see the line falling? Who qualifies for inherent value, and what doesn't?

Like Singer, Regan has thought this point through. Based on his grasp of biology and ethology, he is willing to grant rights to "mentally normal mammals of a year or more."

Also like Singer, he admits that the judgment is not infallible: "Because we are uncertain where the boundaries of consciousness lie, it is not unreasonable to advocate a policy that bespeaks moral caution." So chickens and frogs should be given the benefit of the doubt, as should all other animals that bear a certain degree of anatomical and physiological resemblance to us mentally normal mammals.

But Regan does not specify just what degree.

The books by Singer and Regan leave me with two very separate reactions. The first combines admiration and gratitude. These men are applying the methods of systematic philosophy to an important and much-neglected question. Furthermore, they don't content themselves with just understanding and describing a pattern of gross injustice; they also emphatically say *Let's stop it!* They are fighting a good fight. Peter Singer's book in particular has focused attention on the outrageous practices that are routine in American factory farms, in "psychological" experimentation, in research on the toxicity of cosmetics. Do you know how chickens are dealt with on the large poultry operations? How veal is produced? How the udders of dairy cows are kept flowing? Do you know the sorts of ingenious but pointless torment that thousands of monkeys and millions of rats endure, each year, to fill the time and the dissertations of uninspired graduate students? If you don't, by all means read Singer's *Animal Liberation.*

The second reaction is negative. Peter Singer and Tom Regan, it seems to me, share a breathtaking smugness and myopia not too dissimilar to the brand they so forcefully condemn. Theirs is a righteous and vigorous smugness, not a passive and unreflective one. But still.

Singer inveighs against a sin he labels *speciesism*—discrimination against certain creatures based solely upon the species to which they belong. Regan uses a slightly less confused and less clumsy phrase, *human chauvinism,* to indicate roughly the same thing. Both of them arrive (supposedly by sheer logic) at the position that vegetarianism is morally obligatory: To kill and eat a "higher" animal represents absolute violation of one being's rights; to kill and eat a plant evidently violates nothing at all. Both Singer and Regan claim to disparage the notion—pervasive in Western philosophy since Protagoras—that "Man is the measure of all things." Both argue elaborately against anthropocentrism, while creating new moral frameworks that are also decidedly anthropocentric. Make no mistake: Man is still the measure for Singer and Regan. The test for inherent value has changed only slightly. Instead of asking *Is the creature a human?*, they simply ask *How similar to human is similar enough?*

Peter Singer explains that shrimp deserve brotherly treatment but oysters, so different from us, are fair game for the gumbo. In Tom Regan's vocabulary, the redwood tree is an "inanimate natural object," sharing that category with clouds and rocks. But some simple minds would say: Life is life.

Aldo Leopold

Aldo Leopold (1887–1948) held a master's degree from Yale's School of Forestry, the United States' first graduate program of its kind. In 1909, he joined the U.S. Forestry Service, which had been established only three years before, and went to the Southwest as a forest ranger. When he first arrived, his approach to wildlife management was traditional and focused on killing large predators like wolves and grizzly bears who seemed to pose a threat to livestock. Gradually, however, he came to believe that wildlife and land management could not be looked at separately, and that understanding larger ecological systems was essential to maintaining healthy lands.

By 1919 Leopold began advocating the preservation of wilderness for recreational and aesthetic values. His ideas bore fruit in 1924 with the establishment of New Mexico's Gila Wilderness as the world's first designated wilderness area. But as the Gila gained public attention, Leopold saw that people appreciated wilderness areas for more than just recreational use. He came to see wilderness as society's capacity for self-restraint in growth and development. "An action is right," Leopold said, "when it tends to preserve the integrity, stability, and beauty of the biotic community."

In 1933, Leopold was appointed professor of wildlife management at the University of Wisconsin, the first such position in the country, created especially for him. He wrote a major textbook on wildlife management and many professional papers, but is best known for the essays he wrote with the general public in mind. A Sand County Almanac, *his classic collection of essays that includes "Escudilla," was published the year after Leopold died of a heart attack while helping to fight a forest fire on a Wisconsin neighbor's land.*

"Escudilla" stems from Aldo Leopold's days as a forester in New Mexico and Arizona and describes the Arizonan mountain "Escudilla" before and after the killing of its last grizzly. Although chronologically "Escudilla" should be at the front of this "Writing the Environment" chapter because it was published in 1949, it makes an excellent end piece if we understand the chapter's other authors as Aldo Leopold's literary descendants.

Escudilla

Life in Arizona was bounded under foot by grama grass, overhead by sky, and on the horizon by Escudilla.

To the north of the mountain you rode on honey-colored plains. Look up anywhere, any time, and you saw Escudilla.

To the east you rode over a confusion of wooded mesas. Each hollow seemed its own small world, soaked in sun, fragrant with juniper, and cozy with the chatter of piñon jays. But top out on a ridge and you at once became a speck in an immensity. On its edge hung Escudilla.

To the south lay the tangled canyons of Blue River, full of whitetails, wild turkeys, and wilder cattle. When you missed a saucy buck waving his goodbye over the skyline, and looked down your sights to wonder why, you looked at a far blue mountain: Escudilla.

To the west billowed the outliers of the Apache National Forest. We cruised timber there, converting the tall pines, forty by forty, into notebook figures representing hypothetical lumber piles. Panting up a canyon, the cruiser felt a curious incongruity between the remoteness of his notebook symbols and the immediacy of sweaty fingers, locust thorns, deer-fly bites, and scolding squirrels. But on the next ridge a cold wind, roaring across a green sea of pines, blew his doubts away. On the far shore hung Escudilla.

The mountain bounded not only our work and our play, but even our attempts to get a good dinner. On winter evenings we often tried to ambush a mallard on the river flats. The wary flocks circled the rosy west, the steel-blue north, and then disappeared into the inky black of Escudilla. If they reappeared on set wings, we had a fat drake for the Dutch oven. If they failed to reappear, it was bacon and beans again.

There was, in fact, only one place from which you did not see Escudilla on the skyline: that was the top of Escudilla itself. Up there you could not see the mountain, but you could feel it. The reason was the big bear.

Old Bigfoot was a robber-baron, and Escudilla was his castle. Each spring, when the warm winds had softened the shadows on the snow, the old grizzly crawled out of his hibernation den in the rock slides and, descending the mountain, bashed in the head of a cow. Eating his fill, he climbed back to his crags, and there summered peaceably on marmots, conies, berries, and roots.

I once saw one of his kills. The cow's skull and neck were pulp, as if she had collided head-on with a fast freight.

No one ever saw the old bear, but in the muddy springs about the base of the cliffs you saw his incredible tracks. Seeing them made the most hard-bitten cowboys aware of bear. Wherever they rode they saw the mountain, and when they saw the mountain they thought of bear. Campfire conversation ran to beef, *bailes,* and bear. Bigfoot claimed for his own only a cow a year, and a few square miles of useless rocks, but his personality pervaded the county.

Those were the days when progress first came to the cow country. Progress had various emissaries.

One was the first transcontinental automobilist. The cowboys understood this breaker of roads; he talked the same breezy bravado as any breaker of bronchos.

They did not understand, but they listened to and looked at, the pretty lady in black velvet who came to enlighten them, in a Boston accent, about woman suffrage.

They marveled, too, at the telephone engineer who strung wires on the junipers and brought instantaneous messages from town. An old man asked whether the wire could bring him a side of bacon.

One spring, progress sent still another emissary, a government trapper, a sort of St. George in overalls, seeking dragons to slay at government expense. Were there, he asked, any destructive animals in need of slaying? Yes, there was the big bear.

The trapper packed his mule and headed for Escudilla.

In a month he was back, his mule staggering under a heavy hide. There was only one barn in town big enough to dry it on. He had tried traps, poison, and all his usual wiles to no avail. Then he had erected a set-gun in a defile through which only the bear could pass, and waited. The last grizzly walked into the string and shot himself.

It was June. The pelt was foul, patchy, and worthless. It seemed to us rather an insult to deny the last grizzly the chance to leave a good pelt as a memorial to his race. All he left was a skull in the National Museum, and a quarrel among scientists over the Latin name of the skull.

It was only after we pondered on these things that we began to wonder who wrote the rules for progress.

Since the beginning, time had gnawed at the basaltic hulk of Escudilla, wasting, waiting, and building. Time built three things on the old mountain, a venerable aspect, a community of minor animals and plants, and a grizzly.

The government trapper who took the grizzly knew he had made Escudilla safe for cows. He did not know he had toppled the spire off an edifice a-building since the morning stars sang together.

The bureau chief who sent the trapper was a biologist versed in the architecture of evolution, but he did not know that spires might be as important as cows. He did not foresee that within two decades the cow country would become tourist country, and as such have greater need of bears than of beefsteaks.

The Congressmen who voted money to clear the ranges of bears were the sons of pioneers. They acclaimed the superior virtues of the frontiersman, but they strove with might and main to make an end of the frontier.

We forest officers, who acquiesced in the extinguishment of the bear, knew a local rancher who had plowed up a dagger engraved with the name of one of Coronado's captains. We spoke harshly of the Spaniards who, in their zeal for gold and converts, had needlessly extinguished the native Indians. It did not occur to us that we, too, were the captains of an invasion too sure of its own righteousness.

Escudilla still hangs on the horizon, but when you see it you no longer think of bear. It's only a mountain now.

7

Writing from the Borderlands

Beth Alvarado

> There is a rock tower in northwestern New Mexico that bears the mark of many travelers. For thousands of years, people who have journeyed through this region have carved names, images, and symbols into the rock's surface, preserving their memory on the landscape. The rock tower is known as Inscription Rock, or *El Morro*. . . . The writing on Inscription Rock reminds us that many people—from the Ancient Anasazi to Spanish Conquistadores to White American settlers—have lived and moved here and have tried to make sense of what they have experienced here in various written forms. And in spite of the fences that today protect *El Morro* from further 'graffiti,' this rock still stands as a figurative as well as literal crossroads, as a cross-cultural marker, as an indicator of the rich history and heritage of the landscape that we now journey into—the American Southwest.
>
> —Alesia Garcia and Maureen Salzer

The first time I encountered the landscape of the Sonoran desert, it seemed surreal, a vision from some science fiction movie: the saguaros were tall and forbidding, the spiny fingers of the ocotillo scratched at the sky, and the flat disks of the prickly pear were studded with spikes. The heat. As a native of Colorado, what can I say about the heat? I've seen rain turn to steam as soon as it hits the asphalt.

Summer air scorches the tissues in my lungs. My skin can tell the minute the thermometer climbs over one hundred. It seems unnatural. Of course, if you are from here, or once you have spent time here, the desert can seem lush. Nothing is the velvet green of the mesquite in early spring; by April, the palo verde are golden. You begin to believe what the natives tell you: there *are* seasons. You can feel the subtle shift in the morning air as we enter autumn. In summer, you feel rain long before you see clouds or smell the moisture.

My husband, who was born here and who works outside in the sun, no matter how hot it gets, tells me there is a zen to surviving summer. I would like to believe him. Instead, even after having lived here for three decades, I still move from air conditioned house to air conditioned car to air conditioned building. Every summer, as I stand at the window and gaze at mountains flattened by the glare of a relentless sun, I realize how dependent on technology we are. Electric pumps deliver water from the rapidly shrinking aquifers that lie deep beneath the surface of the earth. How long could we survive without that water? After all, every summer people die trying to cross the desert. There are portions of it where there is no water, where daytime temperatures can reach 125 degrees in the shade, but even here, in Tucson, we live in a place where we could not survive out of our own resources, where the forces of nature—the heat and lack of water—could kill us.

The border is another reality of this part of the country and, again, it might be good to begin with our own experiences. When we imagine a border, we may visualize any number of things. We may see ourselves sitting aboard a stopped train or bus, armed policemen walking down the aisles, scrutinizing passengers' passports, speaking a language we don't understand. Their gestures or facial expressions may make us feel nervous—no matter that we've done nothing wrong. Or we may remember sitting in a long line of cars while children try to sell us *chicle* or while they ask to wash the windshield, hoping we'll give them loose change. The border itself might be clearly marked with a wall and armed men in trucks patrolling the tops of nearby hills or it might be marked by a small station house on a lonely highway, or there may be nothing at all, not even a road sign, not even a piece of rusted barbed wire or a line on the ground.

For instance, just last autumn, my brother-in-law Alfonso had been hunting with his sons in the desert south of Arivaca. He asked a rancher how far it was to the border and the rancher told him six miles. Alfonso told me, "I remember, when we stepped across this old fence, Gabriel asked me if it was the border and I said, 'Nah.' " They continued on until they came to a canyon. At the bottom of it, where the canyon widened, there were trees and a pond, the surface covered with ducks. It was beautiful. They were going to start climbing down when Alfonso noticed a tall tower that said, "Mexico." They had crossed the border without knowing it. There they were, illegally in Mexico, with rifles. Had they been spotted by the authorities, they could have been thrown in jail. How long would they have been there before the family was notified? Would they have been able to convince either the *Federales* or the U. S. Border Patrol that it was an innocent mistake? They quickly traveled north, back across the border and, of course, as soon as they crossed to this side, they saw a deer. A buck. At least three points on his antlers. But because he was on the other side, safe in Mexico, they couldn't shoot him.

When it is that easy to forget about the line between "here" and "there," the border may seem completely arbitrary. In her essay in this chapter, "The Homeland, *Aztlán/El Otro Mexico,*" Gloria Anzaldúa acknowledges that "Borders are set up to define the places that are safe and unsafe, to distinguish us from them. A border is a dividing line, a narrow strip along a steep edge." However, from her point of view, the border divides a people, a culture, a *pueblo*—tribes and families. She thinks of the border as being an "unnatural boundary," calling it an open wound, "*una herida abierta* where the Third World grates against the first and bleeds." Many of us would never think of the border in this way although, when the Iron Curtain divided West Germany from East, Americans often lamented the fact that families had been divided. Further, when East Germans risked their lives to cross into the West, whether to reunite with family members or simply to find better opportunities, we found them heroic and supported their efforts to cross over to freedom. Many authors from the southwest, including Leslie Marmon Silko and Luis Alberto Urrea, compare the U.S./Mexican border to the Iron Curtain and the Gaza Strip, hoping, perhaps, that such analogies will provoke readers to re-see the border and re-think their assumptions about it.

While the border seems, at least geographically, fairly easy to define, "borderlands" is much more difficult. How far do the borderlands extend? Past Colorado? Is Los Angeles a part of them? Do we think of the area south of the border as being a part of our borderlands? In Spanish, the word for the border is *la frontera*. Annette Kolodny, a professor of American literature at the University of Arizona, builds on the work of two historians when she says that a frontier is not a "boundary or line, but . . . a territory or zone of interpenetration between . . . previously distinct societies" (Lamar and Thompson as cited in Kolodny 313). Because of the way we've been taught American history, we tend to think of the frontier in terms of expansion westward, of the white settlers displacing the Indians, but Kolodny notes that indigenous cultures and languages were coming together in both conflict and trade—and therefore were exchanging stories and knowledge—long before the Spanish Conquistadors and European-American settlers ever showed up. In fact, while there are 21 Native American tribes in Arizona today, Kolodny tells us that in precolonial North America there were 550 different languages in use north of the Rio Grande (314).

Because of this history, Kolodny argues that we need to think of *la frontera* as a "liminal landscape of changing meanings," and she and other literary scholars use the image of a "continuously unfolding palimpsest" in order to illustrate this view of the history of the region (315). As Garcia and Salzer explain it, a "palimpsest is a document that has been constructed in layers. . . . The early writing [on the wall or on the stone, like El Morro] may be completely or imperfectly covered up. It may, at times, begin to bleed through and color later inscriptions" (307). We've probably all heard the old saying that the conqueror gets to write history, but the image of history as a palimpsest complicates that idea. Even though we can't deny that conquest and colonialism took place here and that we continue to be defined by that legacy, the palimpsest encourages us to look for the various stories and histories of this region and asks us to resist privileging one over the other. Further, it suggests that because older stories will "bleed through" the new layers, history cannot be completely erased. Here, though, it seems important to note that in cultures that rely on oral storytelling, where there is no written record, the stories are always only one generation away from being lost.

While Kolodny describes what happened in history, Mary Louise Pratt, a professor of Spanish and Comparative Literature at Stanford, uses the term "Contact Zone" to describe "social places where cultures meet, clash, and grapple with each other, often in contexts of highly asymmetrical relations of power, such as colonialism, slavery, or their aftermaths as they are lived out in many parts of the world today" (34). In other words, the term "Contact Zone" acknowledges that this contact between cultures, this hybridizing process, is mutual and is still going on. For instance, we often hear Spanglish words and, if you go to the *Yaqui* deer dances here in Tucson, you can see that some dancers have integrated contemporary items like Burger King Crowns into their traditional costumes. San Xavier Mission, on the *Tohono O'Odahm* reservation south of Tucson, is another visual representation of the fusion of cultures: the architecture is obviously Spanish but, inside, the geometric designs reveal Native American influences.

Pratt also notes that, in texts created in the Contact Zones, we will often find stories that use more than one language, old stories retold in ways that question or critique the dominant culture, stories told in ways that appropriate or critique representations from both cultures, and stories that parody or redefine representations (37). In these narratives, people are redefining themselves as they clash or mingle with people from other cultures. Because texts from the Contact Zone call cultural assumptions into question, Pratt notes that they are often met with miscomprehension or incomprehension.

The texts in this chapter contain many of the characteristics Pratt describes. As you read them, you will see that *la frontera* is a place not only where cultures and languages come together, but also where the past and present meet, where the surreal emerges from the real, and where the mythical world coexists with the physical. *La frontera* is a place where surprising things can happen. For instance, when my mother-in-law was a child, she heard stories about how Geronimo used to sneak into Tucson and play pool in the bars on Cushing Street. Meanwhile, the troops stationed at Fort Lowell were out scouring the desert for him. "*Se dice que los Apaches podrian correr todo el día en el sol, sin agua, y podrian desaparecer en el desierto, como fantasmos.*" (They say that the Apaches could run all day in the sun, without water, and that they could disappear into the desert, like ghosts.) Likewise, many old Tucson families tell stories about Pancho Villa crossing the border at will, showing up at their great-grandmother's door for a midnight snack. In Kimi Eisele's essay, Mexican children and their parents tell stories of La Llorona and ask Eisele if it's true that there are vampires on this side of the line. In "Yellow Woman" by Leslie Silko, the character Silva may be a man or a spirit. And what about the state trooper in Silko's "Tony's Story"—is he from this world or another? Can anyone know for sure?

As you read the selections in this chapter, consider yourself in a frontier, where reading is a way to encounter other cultures as well as other perspectives and realities. Even if you are from Tucson or from this region, you might think of yourself as a traveler, someone who is taking note of the place and the people who inhabit it and of the stories they tell. Because we often come away from our travels feeling as if *we* have been changed, you'll also want to take careful note of your interior landscape. You might write about passages where you connect with the authors and understand their points of view, but also note points where you feel tension or have strong reactions. What details stand out for you and why? How might someone else interpret them? In other words, you'll want to use your Writer's Journal to record your journey through this territory and to create a dialogue with the writers and characters you encounter.

Works Cited

Garcia, Alesia and Maureen Salzer. "Introduction to 'Writing Southwestern Journeys'." *Writing as Revision,* 1st Edition. Eds. Beth Alvarado and Barbara Cully. Needham Heights, MA: Simon and Schuster Education Group, 1996. 305–309.

Kolodny, Annette. "Letting Go Our Grand Obsessions: Notes Toward a New Literary History of the American Frontiers." *Writing as Revision,* 1st Edition. 310–319.

Pratt, Mary Louise. "Arts of the Contact Zone." *Profession 91,* 33–40.

Gloria Anzaldúa

Gloria Anzaldúa self-identifies as a Tejana, Chicana, feminist, lesbian, poet. She is widely known through her contributions to the anthologies of writing by radical women of color This Bridge Called My Back *and* Haciendo Caras/Making Face, Making Soul. *Her own collection,* Borderlands/La Frontera: The New Mestiza, *is a groundbreaking collection of essays and poetry because it represents one of the first books of feminist writing that discusses feminism from a Chicana point of view.*

In the preface to that book, Anzaldúa states, "The psychological borderlands, the sexual borderlands and the spiritual borderlands are not particular to the Southwest. In fact the Borderlands are physically present wherever two or more cultures edge each other, where people of different races occupy the same territory, where under, lower, middle and upper classes touch, where the space between two individuals shrinks with intimacy." In the piece below, the first chapter of Borderlands/La Frontera, *Anzaldúa uses the concept of Aztlán, what is known as the mythical Chicano homeland that is traditionally situated in the Southwest, to describe her understanding of borders from the literal United States/Mexico border to ethnic and racial borders to intellectual borders.*

The Homeland, Aztlán/El Otro Mexico

El otro México que acá hemos construido
el espacio es lo que ha sido
territorio nacional.
Es del esfuerzo de todos nuestros hermanos
y latinoamericanos que han sabido
progresar.

—Los Tigres del Norte[1]

"The *Aztecas del norte* . . . compose the largest single tribe or nation of Anishinabeg (Indians) found in the United States today. . . . Some call themselves Chicanos and see themselves as people whose true homeland is Aztlán [the U.S. Southwest]."[2]

Wind tugging at my sleeve
feet sinking into the sand
I stand at the edge where earth touches ocean
where the two overlap
a gentle coming together
at other times and places a violent clash.

Across the border in Mexico
 stark silhouette of houses gutted by waves,
  cliffs crumbling into the sea,
   silver waves marbled with spume
    gashing a hole under the border fence.
     Miro el mar atacar
    la cerca en Border Field Park
   con sus buchones de agua,
an Easter Sunday resurrection
of the brown blood in my veins.

Oigo el llorido del mar, el respiro del aire,
 my heart surges to the beat of the sea.
  In the gray haze of the sun
   the gulls' shrill cry of hunger,
    the tangy smell of the sea seeping into me.

     I walk through the hole in the fence
      to the other side.
  Under my fingers I feel the gritty wire
    rusted by 139 years
     of the salty breath of the sea.

Beneath the iron sky
Mexican children kick their soccer ball across,
run after it, entering the U.S.

  I press my hand to the steel curtain—
 chainlink fence crowned with rolled barbed wire—
rippling from the sea where Tijuana touches San Diego
 unrolling over mountains
    and plains
     and deserts,
this "Tortilla Curtain" turning into *el Río Grande*
  flowing down to the flatlands
    of the Magic Valley of South Texas
 its mouth emptying into the Gulf.

1,950 mile-long open wound
     dividing a *pueblo,* a culture,
     running down the length of my body,
      staking fence rods in my flesh,

splits me splits me
me raja me raja

This is my home
this thin edge of
barbwire.

But the skin of the earth is seamless.
The sea cannot be fenced,
el mar does not stop at borders
To show the white man what she thought of his
arrogance,
Yemaya blew that wire fence down.

This land was Mexican once,
was Indian always
and is.
And will be again.

Yo soy un puente tendido
del mundo gabacho al del mojado.
lo pasado me estirá pa' 'trás
y lo presente pa' 'delante.
Que la Virgen de Guadalupe me cuide
Ay ay ay, soy mexicana de este lado.

The U.S.-Mexican border es una herida abierta where the Third World grates against the first and bleeds. And before a scab forms it hemorrhages again, the lifeblood of two worlds merging to form a third country—a border culture. Borders are set up to define the places that are safe and unsafe, to distinguish us from them. A border is a dividing line, a narrow strip along a steep edge. A borderland is a vague and undetermined place created by the emotional residue of an unnatural boundary. It is in a constant state of transition. The prohibited and forbidden are its inhabitants. Los atravesados live here: the squint-eyed, the perverse, the queer, the troublesome, the mongrel, the mulato, the half-breed, the half dead; in short, those who cross over, pass over, or go through the confines of the "normal." Gringos in the U.S. Southwest consider the inhabitants of the borderlands transgressors, aliens—whether they possess documents or not, whether they're Chicanos, Indians or Blacks. Do not enter, trespassers will be raped, maimed, strangled, gassed, shot. The only "legitimate" inhabitants are those in power, the whites and those who align themselves with whites. Tension grips the inhabitants of the borderlands like a virus. Ambivalance and unrest reside there and death is no stranger.

> In the fields, *la migra.* My aunt saying, "*No corran,* don't run. They'll think you're *del otro lado.*" In the confusion, Pedro ran, terrified of being caught. He couldn't speak English, couldn't tell them he was fifth generation American. *Sin papeles*—he did not

> carry his birth certificate to work in the fields. *La migra* took him away while we watched. *Se lo llevaron.* He tried to smile when he looked back at us, to raise his fist. But I saw the shame pushing his head down, I saw the terrible weight of shame hunch his shoulders. They deported him to Guadalajara by plane. The furthest he'd ever been to Mexico was Reynosa, a small border town opposite Hidalgo, Texas, not far from McAllen. Pedro walked all the way to the Valley. *Se lo llevaron sin un centavo al pobre. Se vino andando desde Guadalajara.*

During the original peopling of the Americas, the first inhabitants migrated across the Bering Straits and walked south across the continent. The oldest evidence of humankind in the U.S.—the Chicanos' ancient Indian ancestry—was found in Texas and has been dated to 35,000 B.C.[3] In the Southwest United States archeologists have found 20,000-year-old campsites of the Indians who migrated through, or permanently occupied, the Southwest, Aztlán—land of the herons, land of whiteness, the Edenic place of origin of the Azteca.

In 1000 B.C., descendants of the original Cochise people migrated into what is now Mexico and Central America and became the direct ancestors of many of the Mexican people. (The Cochise culture of the Southwest is the parent culture of the Aztecs. The Uto-Aztecan languages stemmed from the language of the Cochise people.)[4] The Aztecs (the Nahuatl word for people of Aztlán) left the Southwest in 1168 A.D.

> Now let us go,
> *Tihueque, tihueque,*
> Vámonos, vámonos.
> *Un pájaro cantó.*
> *Con sus ocho tribus salieron*
> *de la "cueva del origen."*
> *Los aztecas siguieron al dios*
> *Huitzilopochtli.*

Huitzilopochtli, the God of War, guided them to the place (that later became Mexico City) where an eagle with a writhing serpent in its beak perched on a cactus. The eagle symbolizes the spirit (as the sun, the father); the serpent symbolizes the soul (as the earth, the mother). Together, they symbolize the struggle between the spiritual/celestial/male and the underworld/earth/feminine. The symbolic sacrifice of the serpent to the "higher" masculine powers indicates that the patriarchal order had already vanquished the feminine and matriarchal order in pre-Columbian America.

At the beginning of the 16th century, the Spaniards and Hernán Cortéz invaded Mexico and, with the help of tribes that the Aztecs had subjugated, conquered it. Before the Conquest, there were twenty-five million Indian people in Mexico and the Yucatán. Immediately after the Conquest, the Indian population had been reduced to under seven million. By 1650, only one-and-a-half-million pure-blooded Indians remained. The *mestizos* who were genetically equipped to survive small pox, measles, and typhus (Old World diseases to which the natives had no immunity), founded a new hybrid race and inherited Central and South America.[5] *En 1521 nació una nueva raza, el mestizo, el mexicano* (people of mixed Indian and Spanish blood), a race that had never existed before. Chicanos, Mexican-Americans, are the offspring of those first matings.

Our Spanish, Indian, and *mestizo* ancestors explored and settled parts of the U.S. Southwest as early as the sixteenth century. For every gold-hungry *conquistador* and soul-hungry missionary who came north from Mexico, ten to twenty Indians and *mestizos* went along as porters or in other capacities.[6] For the Indians, this constituted a return to the place of origin, Aztlán, thus making Chicanos originally and secondarily indigenous to the Southwest. Indians and *mestizos* from central Mexico intermarried with North American Indians. The continual intermarriage between Mexican and American Indians and Spaniards formed an even greater *mestizaje*.

EL DESTIERRO/THE LOST LAND

Entonces corre la sangre
no sabe el indio que hacer,
le van a quitar su tierra,
la tiene que defender,
el indio se cae muerto,
y el afuerino de pie.
Levántate, Manquilef.

Arauco tiene una pena
más negra que su chamal,
ya no son los españoles
los que les hacen llorar,
hoy son los propios chilenos
los que les quitan su pan.
Levántate, Pailahuan.

—Violeta Parra,
"*Arauco tiene una pena*"[7]

In the 1800s, Anglos migrated illegally into Texas, which was then part of Mexico, in greater and greater numbers and gradually drove the *tejanos* (native Texans of Mexican descent) from their lands, committing all manner of atrocities against them. Their illegal invasion forced Mexico to fight a war to keep its Texas territory. The Battle of the Alamo, in which the Mexican forces vanquished the whites, became, for the whites, the symbol for the cowardly and villainous character of the Mexicans. It became (and still is) a symbol that legitimized the white imperialist takeover. With the capture of Santa Anna later in 1836, Texas became a republic. *Tejanos* lost their land and, overnight, became the foreigners.

Y la mitad del terreno
les vendió el traidor Santa Anna,
con lo que se ha hecho muy rica
la nación americana.

¿Qué acaso no se conforman
con el oro de las minas?
Ustedes muy elegantes
y aquí nosotros en ruinas.
—*from the Mexican corrido,*
"Del peligro de la Intervención"[8]

In 1846, the U.S. incited Mexico to war. U.S. troops invaded and occupied Mexico, forcing her to give up almost half of her nation, what is now Texas, New Mexico, Arizona, Colorado and California.

With the victory of the U.S. forces over the Mexican in the U.S.-Mexican War, *los norteamericanos* pushed the Texas border down 100 miles from *el Río Nueces* to *el Río Grande*. South Texas ceased to be part of the Mexican state of Tamaulipas. Separated from Mexico, the Native Mexican-Texan no longer looked toward Mexico as home; the Southwest became our homeland once more. The border fence that divides the Mexican people was born on February 2, 1848 with the signing of the Treaty of Guadalupe Hidalgo. It left 100,000 Mexican citizens on this side, annexed by conquest along with the land. The land established by the treaty as belonging to Mexicans was soon swindled away from its owners. The treaty was never honored and restitution, to this day, has never been made.

The justice and benevolence of God
will forbid that . . . Texas should again
become a howling wilderness
trod only by savages, or . . . benighted
by the ignorance and superstition,
the anarchy and rapine of Mexican misrule
The Anglo-American race are destined
to be forever the proprietors of
this land of promise and fulfillment.
Their laws will govern it,
their learning will enlighten it,
their enterprise will improve it.
Their flocks range its boundless pastures,
for them its fertile lands will yield . . .
luxuriant harvests. . . .
The wilderness of Texas has been redeemed
by Anglo-American blood & enterprise.
—William H. Wharton[9]

The Gringo, locked into the fiction of white superiority, seized complete political power, stripping Indians and Mexicans of their land while their feet were still rooted in it. *Con el destierro y el exilo fuimos desuñados, destroncados, destripados*—we were jerked out by the roots, truncated, disemboweled, dispossessed, and separated from our identity and our history. Many, under the threat of Anglo terrorism, abandoned homes and ranches and went to Mexico. Some stayed and protested. But as the courts, law enforcement officials, and government officials not only ignored their pleas but penalized them for their efforts, *tejanos* had no other resource but armed retaliation.

After Mexican-American resisters robbed a train in Brownsville, Texas on October 18, 1915, Anglo vigilante groups began lynching Chicanos. Texas Rangers would take them into the brush and shoot them. One hundred Chicanos were killed in a matter of months, whole families lynched. Seven thousand fled to Mexico, leaving their small ranches and farms. The Anglos, afraid that the *mexicanos*[10] would seek independence from the U.S., brought in 20,000 army troops to put an end to the social protest movement in South Texas. Race hatred had finally fomented into an all out war.[11]

> My grandmother lost all her cattle,
> they stole her land.

"Drought hit South Texas," my mother tells me. "*La tierra se puso bien seca y los animales comenzaron a morirse de se'. Mí papá se murió de un* heart attack *dejando a mamá* pregnant *y con ocho huercos,* with eight kids and one on the way. *Yo fui la mayor, tenía diez años*. The next year the drought continued *y el ganado* got hoof and mouth. *Se cayeron* in droves *en las pastas y el* brushland, *panzas blancas* ballooning to the skies. *El siguiente año* still no rain. *Mi pobre madre viuda perdió* two-thirds of her *ganado*. A smart *gabacho* lawyer took the land away *mamá* hadn't paid taxes. *No hablaba inglés,* she didn't know how to ask for time to raise the money." My father's mother, Mama Locha, also lost her *terreno*. For a while we got $12.50 a year for the "mineral rights" of six acres of cemetery, all that was left of the ancestral lands. Mama Locha had asked that we bury her there beside her husband. *El cementerio estaba cercado*. But there was a fence around the cemetery, chained and padlocked by the ranch owners of the surrounding land. We couldn't even get in to visit the graves, much less bury her there. Today, it is still padlocked. The sign reads: "Keep out. Trespassers will be shot."

In the 1930s, after Anglo agribusiness corporations cheated the small Chicano landowners of their land, the corporations hired gangs of *mexicanos* to pull out the brush, chaparral and cactus and to irrigate the desert. The land they toiled over had once belonged to many of them, or had been used communally by them. Later the Anglos brought in huge machines and root plows and had the Mexicans scrape the land clean of natural vegetation. In my childhood I saw the end of dryland farming. I witnessed the land cleared; saw the huge pipes connected to underwater sources sticking up in the air.

As children, we'd go fishing in some of those canals when they were full and hunt for snakes in them when they were dry. In the 1950s I saw the land, cut up into thousands of neat rectangles and squares, constantly being irrigated. In the 340-day growth season, the seeds of any kind of fruit or vegetable had only to be stuck in the ground in order to grow. More big land corporations came in and bought up the remaining land.

To make a living my father became a sharecropper. Rio Farms Incorporated loaned him seed money and living expenses. At harvest time, my father repaid the loan and forked over 40% of the earnings. Sometimes we earned less than we owed, but always the corporations fared well. Some had major holdings in vegetable trucking, livestock auctions and cotton gins. Altogether we lived on three successive Rio farms; the second was adjacent to the King Ranch and included a dairy farm; the third was a chicken farm. I remember the white feathers of three thousand Leghorn chickens blanketing the land for acres around. My sister, mother and I cleaned, weighed and packaged eggs. (For years afterwards I couldn't stomach the sight of an egg.) I remember my mother attending some of the meetings sponsored by well-meaning whites from Rio Farms. They talked about good nutrition, health, and held huge barbeques. The only thing salvaged for my family from those years are modern techniques of food canning and a food-stained book they printed made up of recipes from Rio Farms' Mexican women. How proud my mother was to have her recipe for *enchiladas coloradas* in a book.

EL CRUZAR DEL MOJADO/ILLEGAL CROSSING

> *"Ahora sí ya tengo una tumba para llorar,"*
> *dice Conchita,* upon being reunited with
> her unknown mother just before the mother dies
> —from Ismael Rodríguez' film,
> *Nosotros los pobres*[12]

La crisis. Los gringos had not stopped at the border. By the end of the nineteenth century, powerful landowners in Mexico, in partnership with U.S. colonizing companies, had dispossessed millions of Indians of their lands. Currently, Mexico and her eighty million citizens are almost completely dependent on the U.S. market. The Mexican government and wealthy growers are in partnership with such American conglomerates as American Motors, IT&T and Du Pont which own factories called *maquiladoras*. One-fourth of all Mexicans work at *maquiladoras:* most are young women. Next to oil, *maquiladoras* are Mexico's second greatest source of U.S. dollars. Working eight to twelve hours a day to wire in backup lights of U.S. autos or solder miniscule wires in TV sets is not the Mexican way. While the women are in the *maquiladoras,* the children are left on their own. Many roam the street, become part of *cholo* gangs. The infusion of the values of the white culture, coupled with the exploitation by that culture, is changing the Mexican way of life.

The devaluation of the *peso* and Mexico's dependency on the U.S. have brought on what the Mexicans call *la crisis. No hay trabajo.* Half of the Mexican people are unemployed. In the U.S. a man or woman can make eight times what they can in Mexico. By March, 1987, 1,088 pesos were worth one U.S. dollar. I remember when I was growing up in Texas how we'd cross the border at Reynosa or Progreso to buy sugar or medicines when the dollar was worth eight *pesos* and fifty *centavos.*

La travesía. For many *mexicanos del otro lado,* the choice to stay in Mexico and starve or move north and live. *Dicen que cada mexicano siempre sueña de la conquista en los brazos de cuatro gringas rubias, la conquista del país poderoso del norte, los Estados Unidos. En cada Chicano y mexicano vive el mito del tesoro territorial perdido.* North Americans call this return to the homeland the silent invasion.

> *"A la cueva volverán"*
> —El Puma *en la canción "Amalia"*

South of the border, called North America's rubbish dump by Chicanos, *mexicanos* congregate in the plazas to talk about the best way to cross. Smugglers, *coyotes, pasadores, enganchadores* approach these people or are sought out by them. *"¿Qué dicen muchachos a echársela de mojado?"*

> "Now among the alien gods with
> weapons of magic am I."
> —Navajo protection song,
> sung when going into battle.[13]

We have a tradition of migration, a tradition of long walks. Today we are witnessing *la migración de los pueblos mexicanos,* the return odyssey to the historical/mythological Aztlán. This time, the traffic is from south to north.

El retorno to the promised land first began with the Indians from the interior of Mexico and the *mestizos* that came with the *conquistadores* in the 1500s. Immigration continued in the next three centuries, and, in this century, it continued with the *braceros* who helped to build our railroads and who picked our fruit. Today thousands of Mexicans are crossing the border legally and illegally; ten million people without documents have returned to the Southwest.

Faceless, nameless, invisible, taunted with "Hey cucaracho" (cockroach). Trembling with fear, yet filled with courage, a courage born of desperation. Barefoot and uneducated, Mexicans with hands like boot soles gather at night by the river where two worlds merge creating what Reagan calls a frontline, a war zone. The convergence has created a shock culture, a border culture, a third country, a closed country.

Without benefit of bridges, the *"mojados"* (wetbacks) float on inflatable rafts across *el Río Grande,* or wade or swim across naked, clutching their clothes over their heads. Holding onto the grass, they pull themselves along the banks with a prayer to *Virgen de Guadalupe* on their lips: *Ay virgencita morena, mi madrecita, dame tu bendición.*

The Border Patrol hides behind the local McDonalds on the outskirts of Brownsville, Texas or some other border town. They set traps around the river beds beneath the bridge.[14] Hunters in army-green uniforms stalk and track these economic refugees by the powerful nightvision of electronic sensing devices planted in the ground or mounted on Border Patrol vans. Cornered by flashlights, frisked while their arms stretch over their heads, *los mojados* are handcuffed, locked in jeeps, and then kicked back across the border.

One out of every three is caught. Some return to enact their rite of passage as many as three times a day. Some of those who make it across undetected fall prey to Mexican robbers such as those in Smugglers' Canyon on the American side of the border near Tijuana. As refugees in a homeland that does not want them, many find a welcome hand holding out only suffering, pain, and ignoble death.

Those who make it past the checking points of the Border Patrol find themselves in the midst of 150 years of racism in Chicano *barrios* in the Southwest and in big northern cities. Living in a no-man's-borderland, caught between being treated as criminals and being able to eat, between resistance and deportation, the illegal refugees are some of the poorest and the most exploited of any people in the U.S. It is illegal for Mexicans to work without green cards. But big farming combines, farm bosses and smugglers who bring them in make money off the "wetbacks"' labor—they don't have to pay federal minimum wages, or ensure adequate housing or sanitary conditions.

The Mexican woman is especially at risk. Often the *coyote* (smuggler) doesn't feed her for days or let her go to the bathroom. Often he rapes her or sells her into prostitution. She cannot call on county or state health or economic resources because she doesn't know English and she fears deportation. American employers are quick to take advantage of her helplessness. She can't go home. She's sold her house, her furniture, borrowed from friends in order to pay the *coyote* who charges her four or five thousand dollars to smuggle her to Chicago. She may work as a live-in maid for white, Chicano or Latino households for as little as $15 a week. Or work in the garment industry, do hotel work. Isolated and worried about her family back home, afraid of getting caught and deported, living with as many as fifteen people in one room, the *mexicana* suffers serious health problems. *Se enferma de los nervios, de alta presión.*[15]

La mojada, la mujer indocumentada, is doubly threatened in this country. Not only does she have to contend with sexual violence, but like all women, she is prey to a sense of physical helplessness. As a refugee, she leaves the familiar and safe homeground to venture into unknown and possibly dangerous terrain.

This is her home
this thin edge of
barbwire.

Notes

1. Los Tigres del Norte is a *conjunto* band.
2. Jack D. Forbes, *Aztecas del Norte: The Chicanos of Aztlán.* (Greenwich, CT: Fawcett Publications, Premier Books, 1973), 13, 183; Eric R. Wolf, *Sons of Shaking Earth* (Chicago, IL: University of Chicago Press, Phoenix books, 1959), 32.
3. John R. Chávez, *The Lost Land: The Chicano Images of the Southwest* (Albuquerque, NM: University of New Mexico Press, 1984), 9.
4. Chávez, 9. Besides the Aztecs, the Ute, Gabrillino of California, Pima of Arizona, some Pueblo of New Mexico, Comanche of Texas, Opata of Sonora, Tarahumara of Sinaloa and Durango, and the Huichol of Jalisco speak Uto-Aztecan languages and are descended from the Cochise people.

5. Reay Tannahill, *Sex In History* (Briarcliff Manor, NY: Stein and Day/Publishers/Scarborough House, 1980), 308.
6. Chávez, 21.
7. Isabel Parra, *El Libro Mayor de Violeta Parra* (Madrid, España: Ediciones Michay, S.A., 1985), 156–7.
8. From the Mexican *corrido, "Del peligro de la intervención,"* Vicente T. Mendoza, *El Corrido Mexicano* (México. D.F.: Fondo De Cultura Económica, 1954), 42.
9. Arnoldo De León, *They Called Them Greasers: Anglo Attitudes Toward Mexicans in Texas, 1821–1900* (Austin, TX: University of Texas Press, 1983), 2–3.
10. The Plan of San Diego, Texas, drawn up on January 6, 1915, called for the independence and segregation of the states bordering Mexico: Texas, New Mexico, Arizona, Colorado, and California. Indians would get their land back, Blacks would get six states from the south and form their own independent republic. Chávez, 79.
11. Jesús Mena, "Violence in the Rio Grande Valley," *Nuestro* (Jan./Feb. 1983), 41–42.
12. *Nosotros los pobres* was the first Mexican film that was truly Mexican and not an imitation European film. It stressed the devotion and love that children should have for their mother and how its lack would lead to the dissipation of their character. This film spawned a generation of mother-devotion/ungrateful-sons films.
13. From the Navajo "Protection Song" (to be sung upon going into battle). George W. Gronyn, ed., *American Indian Poetry: The Standard Anthology of Songs and Chants* (New York, NY: Liveright, 1934), 97.
14. Grace Halsell, *Los ilegales,* trans. Mayo Antonio Sánchez (Editorial Diana Mexica, 1979).
15. Margarita B. Melville, "Mexican Women Adapt to Migration," *International Migration Review,* 1978.

Kimi Eisele

Kimi Eisele is a Tucson resident who received her Master of Arts in Geography at the University of Arizona where she also founded You Are Here: The Journal of Creative Geography. *She is currently the managing editor and mentor for* 110 Degrees, *a magazine about Tucson produced by teenagers and published by Voices, Inc. This essay, "The Space in Between" is based on her master's degree project in which she held geography and art workshops with children in Nogales, Sonora in order to understand how they viewed their place in the world. Over a period of a year, she worked most extensively with about fifteen children, ages 8–12, from nine families. The Arizona-Sonora Desert Museum's "Sense of Place Project" funded her work. Eisele has written several essays on her experiences with the children in Nogales, Sonora and on the environmental issues their community faces. One of them, "The Other Side of the Wires," documents the health problems that can result from contaminated water. It was published in* Orion *magazine in Spring 2000; this essay is forthcoming in* Fourth Genre.

The Space in Between

Always it began with the drive down Highway 19, not a particularly exciting stretch of highway, but an access road of sorts, a gateway. I'd pass the Duvall copper mine to the west, blue and glowing; the spiky Santa Rita Mountains to the east; the senior citizen sprawl of Green Valley on both sides. The speeding and swerving shuttle vans from Phoenix would invariably pass me in my clunky truck.

The only peculiar thing about this highway was where it ended—at the southern edge of the United States. It steered me into Nogales, Arizona, pushed me under an overpass, and spilled me into Mexico. There, I'd feel either pleasantly received or violently accosted. This, I suppose, is the mercurial nature of borders.

If it was still early in the morning, the city cool and just waking up, I felt at ease. The foreignness was a rush. Suddenly I was in another language, and it changed everything. The movement was what I liked—a man towed a burro across the street, hunched *doñas* carried baskets of tortillas, old men stood eating stew on the corner. This was a part of the West that had not been paved over by wide slabs of asphalt. In some places, it wasn't paved at all. People did not hide inside homes. On the street, I could hear the tapping of women's feet on the

---

pavement, the shouts of boys on their way to school, the trilling exchanges between mothers and babes.

But if it was hot, late, and I was in a hurry, the motion was what I most disliked. Buses pulled out in front of me. Potholes in the road compressed my spine. I swerved to miss mangy dogs. Everyone honked. Too often I smelled the sour stench of rotting fruit and sewage. I felt like a warrior on a mission to get through town. I could not fully enter the language, and my tongue stumbled.

Then there was the space in between. A friend in Tucson finally installed a new horn in the truck in an ingeniously Mexican style—I had to keep my eyes on the road and reach for a large white plastic button under the dash. Still, I was deeply satisfied with making my own noise and used little discretion. With the radio tuned to loud, bouncy *Norteño* music, I stared back at people. I gained full control of Spanish, and in it, I cursed eloquently. I relished the chaos.

I drove this stretch of highway into the city of Nogales, Sonora, mostly because I had to cross a line to get there. With this, there was an instinctual and endless fascination. And also, of course, a certain sort of privilege.

The trips I made were regular visits to a community called Colonia Solidaridad on the outskirts of the burgeoning Mexican border city of Nogales. There, I gathered together a group of children to find out what it meant to grow up right next to the world's most powerful country, my own. Over the course of several months, I asked children to describe to me, in words, drawings, and photographs, where they lived.

I picked the place because it was close and because it seemed an appropriate vantage point from which to understand something about the impacts of global economic change on Mexico in general and on its young people in particular. Since 1964, when the Mexican government lured foreign-owned assembly plants known as *maquiladoras* to its northern border through tax-incentives, people had left an ailing countryside and flocked to the border in search of more permanent work. And not just in the factories, but also as hot dog salesmen, chauffeurs, homebuilders, waiters, seamstresses, hairstylists, photographers, or merchants in the tourist district. Decades later the city still struggled to keep up. In Nogales, as in other border cities, houses of cardboard, shipping pallets, and aluminum are tacked together almost overnight. Solidaridad represents a fairly typical self-help neighborhood on the border. Today, over half of the houses there still do not have running water or plumbing. Water is delivered by a truck and poured into metal drums supplied by the factories. Garbage collection is sporadic at best, and when it rains, the refuse flows in rivers down gravel streets. Walls made of stacked tires hold up the hillsides.

Before I began to cross the border regularly, I heard stories about it. Some I read in the newspapers, some I watched on the local nightly news, some I heard on the streets. Most of these stories were about desperate souls who'd do anything to get north. There were the eight migrants who drowned in a drainage ditch, the seventeen who suffocated in an airless van en route to Phoenix, and the countless dry and desiccated bodies that end up in the deserts of the American Southwest.

I traveled to Solidaridad because I wanted to understand the other side of things in as many ways as possible. I wanted to revision the border, to understand what the line really separated. How does it define difference? What limits does it place on those who cannot cross it easily? On those who can? What would the present life of children reveal about the future of the border? How far north would children's imaginations wander? How far would my own imagination wander? These were the nagging questions. To answer them, I crossed again and again. Eventually, in the crossing, I learned to invert the world, to rearrange north and south.

Late one morning, after a walk through the neighborhood, twelve children didn't want to go home yet. We sat in the fifth-grade classroom, the one room I had been given the key to, a dim concrete room that often smelled of petrol, and told stories.

Suzi, at twelve, was the oldest of the group. She was tall with dark round eyes and a leftover scar from a cleft palate. Her hair, long and shiny and black, stood straight up in the front. I had seen her shower her entire head with hair spray. She wore mini-skirts and thick-soled shoes and liked to paint her nails sky blue.

"I know a story but I don't know where it's from," she said. "There once was a little girl whose mother told her to pay attention when she was speaking to her. The mother said, 'I don't know what's wrong with you. If you don't pay attention to me, the devil will get you and turn you to stone.' And the bad little girl didn't pay attention, so the devil grabbed her, and they say that he turned her to stone and that now every night, she opens one eye and lets out la Llorona."

"La Llorona!" Maria Fernanda said. "I know that story."

"So do I!" said Grillo, Suzi's eight-year-old brother.

I knew the story too. La Llorona—the woman who weeps. It's like a Grimm's fairy tale, a bit twisted, and everyone knows it. The versions of La Llorona are all slightly different, but at base, it's the story of a woman who long ago drowned her own children in a river. Now the woman wanders the banks of rivers everywhere, looking for her children, wailing.

"Any stories about the *border*?" I asked again.

Yesenia chimed in with a story about a man named Nahuatl. "He was a drunk and a wanderer and his mother said, 'You will travel the world for all your life.' They say that the devil told him if he didn't change when he was little, he would be cursed for his whole life. And I've seen him. My mother said he's not bad, he takes care of children, he's just cursed."

The children told tale after tale like these, never really answering my question. None mentioned anything about an uncle who headed for *"el Norte"* in the dead of night with only the clothes on his back. None spoke of treacherous river crossings. Of falsified passports, crooked *coyotes,* or flashflood drownings in storm drains—the kind of border stories I'd heard before, the kind I expected them to have heard too.

The tales they told were all of mother's curses and devils. Didactic stories, they scared children into paying attention and following orders. They modeled correct behavior, the way to find your right position in relation to others. They reminded me of fables and ghost stories. They were not about the border at all. It might as well not have existed.

One day Yesenia looked at me and said, "I thought Americans were bad until I met you." Then she cited the battle of Santa Anna, the Treaty of Guadalupe

Hidalgo, and La Mesilla (the Gadsden Purchase), three events that in the 19th century significantly shrunk the territory of Mexico.

The teaching of history engenders nationalism, and the children in Solidaridad seemed full of it. On the fifth of May, the day that commemorates the 1862 Battle of Puebla when Mexico thwarted France's attempt to install a monarch, several children marched in the city parade. Both Yesenia and Blanca walked down the main street through town in their school uniforms. Amidst the crowd of people watching that day were many who visited parents, aunts and uncles, children, siblings, and spouses in the United States. Some of those watching could slip effortlessly between Spanish and English with perfectly trilled r's and hardened d's. Many bought sneakers, chicken, plastic dishes, and underwear regularly in Nogales, Arizona. Even more knew how to say "Hello" and "How much?" and sing the lyrics to "Hotel California."

The director of Solidaridad's school, Antonio Arán, told me that children are not taught much about the international border in the classroom. "The line marks the line of our work," he said. "We focus mostly on our own history. They don't know much about the United States, and there, you don't know much about us. That seems obvious because that line divides us for so many kilometers."

Almost 2,000 miles long, the border between Mexico and the United States stretches from the Gulf of Mexico to the Pacific, from eastern Texas and Tamaulipas to western California and Baja. Nogales, Sonora and its twin city, Nogales, Arizona, were officially founded in 1882 when the railroad from Guaymas met the line from Kansas City. Since then, goods and people have moved with varying degrees of ease across the border. In the 1920s, Prohibition and antigambling laws in the United States sent Americans on brief visits to the Mexican side where they could get their fill of alcohol, games, and women. Since then, tourism has been one of the economic mainstays of Mexico's northern frontier.

Despite a few setbacks brought about by economic hardships and recessions over the years, the Nogales tourist strip today still thrives. When I walked through it vendors persistently tried to sell me gold chains, cigars, ceramic suns, rugs, leather bags, baskets, tequila, fertility pills, and Viagra. Amidst the chaos, I spotted Nikes and Arizona license plates. I heard words in English.

In the 1980s, several journalists popularized the notion of the U.S.-Mexico border region as a "third country" between the two nations, a country with its own distinct culture. Perhaps, perhaps not—it depends on where you stand.

From the highest hill behind Solidaridad, I could look north to an American landscape. It was only American because I knew so. The mountains ahead were remarkably similar to those behind. If I descended the hill and wandered the streets of Solidaridad—where ramshackle houses were built and rebuilt daily, where tinny *Ranchera* music squeezed out of pocket radios, where on good days the smell of fresh tortillas swirled in the air—I was most certainly and fully in Mexico.

Figuring out what children in Solidaridad knew about the other side of the line, for me, bordered on an obsession. I finally got through, via television, to Lupita, a sharp 11-year-old girl with a propensity for asking questions repeatedly. "On TV, they say people in the United States are getting richer," she said.

"How do you imagine it there?" I asked.

"I imagine that it's a city with many buildings, that there's almost no garbage. And I imagine that there are only blondes. Well, some kids are the same as me."

Lupita told me she wanted to cross the border because of what they sell on the other side. "When I was very little we went, and there was a bicycle, very cheap, and my Papí said that someday he's going to buy it for me."

Nine-year-old Lucero also said she had seen the United States on television. "On TV, I have seen that they rob a lot, that there are a lot of *cholos*." Lucero had watched the home movies her aunt had brought from the U.S. side. "She videotapes when there is a party." Though it looks fun sometimes, Lucero said she would rather live in Nogales, Mexico. "There," she said, "there are no houses, only trailers."

The first time I asked Lucero's older sister Blanca what she imagined the other side is like, she gave me a blank stare. A moment later she looked up and said, "There's a pool."

Carmen, a mother of two, said, "[The other side] doesn't affect me at all. We don't go there."

"You've never wanted to go across to the other side""

"What you don't know, you don't want," Carmen said. Then she leaned over in her chair. "Is it true?" she whispered. "Is it true there are vampires there? On the other side?"

Sometimes on my way through town, I'd stop just south of the port of entry, in one of the tourist strip locales, a corner stall in an open-air market. There, the father of Josué, one of the kids I worked with, ran a small photography stand he inherited from his father. On Saturdays Josué and his three younger sisters sometimes assisted him.

On good days, Ricardo took as many as 40 photos a day of retirees, families, and fraternity boys who crossed the border for a day long "Mexican experience." In front of the camera, they'd don a sombrero and a colored shawl, some would mount María the burro and pose in front of a sanguine painting of the Mexican countryside titled with "Mexico 1999" or "2000" or "2001."

Josué had learned to say things in English like "Cahmon, meester," "Betty cheep" and "Tayka peecher!" Sometimes he got tips from the posers. He told me that someday he too wanted to be a photographer. With the camera I gave him, he took pictures of María the burro, the green hills outside of the neighborhood, and the inside of his house.

Josué's house was bigger and sturdier than other houses in Solidaridad. Built on two lots, it had cement walls, a full roof, glass windows, and steel doors. Inside were a cement floor, a living room, a kitchen, and a fully furnished separate bedroom, where the whole family slept. Sometimes, because of the extra space, I spent the night there on a spare sofa, which sagged, but gave me enough of a good night's sleep.

Josué's father told me his job was lucrative enough to earn him three times what he'd make in the factories. During the months I spent with the family, he finished the roof, purchased a new double bed, and gave new bicycles to Josué and his two sisters for Christmas.

In the evenings I helped Ricardo's wife, Rosario, with dinner. In the dark kitchen, I learned to flatten balls of flour, water, and lard into tortillas. Habitually, I steered the conversation toward the other side. "There, people live better for the comforts they have," Rosario said. "I've never tried to explain [the differences] to [my children]. It all really depends on each person. If God wanted me to be Mexican, then that's why I am Mexican and my children are Mexican. Maybe if he didn't plan that, we wouldn't live so humbly. We're Mexicans whether the country is strong or failing, but we have to look for the way to move forward here."

Ricardo told me he had no intention of ever moving his family north across the border. "I wouldn't leave here to go struggle in the United States," he said. "I realize that most leave behind their own property, their own house; they go, supposedly to work, to progress, but I don't call that progress to go to the United States and begin to pay rent. For me, it would be like starting over. Because here in Mexico, thanks to God, there's a little hill and you climb it and make your house of wood, but it's your own—the land and the house. We struggle with little problems, but it's our own."

One morning I asked the children to draw maps of their world. Met with confused stares, I explained it over and over. "Here. The place where you live. Your neighborhood." Slowly, they caught on. I held up a variety of different maps and applauded each effort.

Eventually Josué made two maps. The first showed a bird's-eye view of the school grounds and the route to his house. With a pencil he drew a roller-coaster-like line then colored in brown the space below it—the steep, dusty hills he walks over to get home. In the second map, drawn more hastily, Josué recorded both his house and the school, along with the hills, María the burro's house, and this time the border itself—a thick pencil line at the top of the page.

Blanca drew an irregular triangle shape. She colored in a one-inch brown stripe at the top and filled the rest in with orange. In the center of the line dividing the two colors, she drew a small gray square. Above Mexico she wrote "Los Estados Unidos." Inside the gray square she wrote "Sonora," and placed a small dot, which she labeled "Nogales."

I was still marveling at Blanca's sense of space and scale two weeks later when she drew another map, almost identical. When I suggested adding more details, she drew in two squares, one on each side of the country. In each she wrote "La Ley," the name of a local super-store with two Nogales locations.

Yesenia made a detailed map of her street. Meticulously, she drew a row of houses and behind several of them included the walls of tires built to hold up the eroding hillsides. She colored the hills beyond the neighborhood green and decorated them with tiny flower stickers. Lucero rendered two houses, labeled them "My house" and "My Nana's house," and connected them with a thick road. Other children drew floor plans of the interior of their houses, mostly one-room sketches crammed with beds, chairs, a refrigerator, and always, a television. My favorite included a single light bulb dangling by a wire from the ceiling.

Of all the information these maps revealed, the border was conspicuously absent from all but two. Only Blanca and Josué drew lines to signify it, though neither rendered anything on the other side.

When I asked the children to draw their visions of utopia, the perfect place, they drew pictures of large sturdy houses, green fields, castles, sports complexes, and pools—landscapes of wealth they had seen on TV, perhaps, or right in Nogales, where on the west side of town a neighborhood of large bright houses along paved streets looms over the self-help colonias that circle the city. From what I could see, there was nothing unequivocally American in their pictures. But I knew that as always, our world is as big or as small as our experience. The children's lack of curiosity and conceptual understanding of the border was likely the result of their youth and limited knowledge. Few had traveled to the states and towns their parents left years ago. Few had traveled across the border north.

The repeated blank stares, the simple drawings, and the silent answers to my diligent questions, revealed that for now at least the border was less of a boundary in the children's geography as it was in my own.

In April, a department at the University of Arizona in Tucson organized a meeting on border health and environmental issues. Representatives from organizations on both sides of the border, all the way across it, would meet for a long weekend in Tijuana, Baja California, Mexico. I rallied funds together to take three girls with me to present the project. We would drive on the Mexican side, a ten-hour journey, because none had a passport.

Two months ahead of time I talked to their parents, explained the trip, hoped that they'd trust me. The morning of our departure, I arrived in a large, white university van. Yesenia told me right away that Blanca wasn't allowed to go. When I walked up the hill, Blanca stepped out of the house. She told me it was because she couldn't miss her catechism class. She kicked the ground and never looked me in the eye. Her parents didn't come out of the house.

While we waited for Karla, the immediate substitute, Lupita's mother told me that she trusted me fully, but that Blanca's parents feared I might steal the girls and take them across the border to sell. I had heard this before. For a time, a popular rumor in the borderlands and throughout Latin America told that Americans, women especially, kidnapped children, carried them north, and sold off their organs to keep white babies alive.

The words crawled into my gut and lodged themselves there. Was this for real? After months of activities with these children, lunches in their house, long conversations with their parents, had I not won any trust? Was I still the same light-haired, blue-eyed foreigner to them that I had been when I first arrived? I went outside to wait. Though I fought hard against them, the tears came in torrents.

In her book *Translated Woman,* American anthropologist Ruth Behar documents the life history of a sixty-year-old Mexican woman from a small village and reflects on her own position as the collector and translator of a story told by a woman of a different race, class, and social position as her own. Lamenting the fact that many people in Mexico assumed things about her that were not true, that she was there to exploit them for instance, Behar gets the "gringa blues."

Though she knew it was impossible, she wanted to be disconnected from associations that invariably linked her to the *other* side of the border.

That morning, the gringa blues overwhelmed me. Feeling foolish and fragile, I fought the urge to get back in the van, drive home, and stay there forever. In the moment, I arrived at the horrible realization that no matter what I did, no matter how much I gave, no matter how patient I was, no matter how close I became to the children and their families, I would always be someone else from somewhere else. South of the border, this simple fact would forever slant both the way I saw and the way I was seen.

Despite its beginnings, the trip was a stunning success. In Tijuana, the girls presented their photographs and stories confidently. The accolades poured in. Although they attended some of the other sessions, the girls spent most of the time riding the elevators, watching *telenovelas,* and taking baths. Every time I entered their room, one of them was in the bathtub. It was a new and wonderful phenomenon—to turn a knob and have water pour endlessly out of the faucet.

For a time, I worried that the luxury of that hotel room would raise their expectations about material comforts and set them up for disappointment. But after four long days the girls were more than ready to go home. To that, I could relate.

For many weeks, I made a habit out of buying *bolillos,* knobs of fresh bread, before I crossed back into Arizona. From time to time, I thought to buy watermelon and mangos, too, but then I remembered I couldn't carry produce into the United States. This law, like many of them, was so bizarre I often forgot it was one.

Depending on the hour I left Sonora, I either had little time to think or I was forced to meditate for thirty minutes or more. More often it was the latter, as the queue was usually long. If I was lucky, women sold fresh green corn tamales there and I could buy a dozen for half of what I paid for them in Tucson. Otherwise, I cursed the length of the wait and how arbitrary this boundary could seem. A cruel trick of politics, it was both convenient and inconvenient. It was, as one writer put it, "a word game." I tried continuously to crack it.

Often a man wearing alligator-skin boots and an oversized cowboy hat wound his way in and out of the traffic twirling a lasso. There was something patient and talented about him, and I gave him coins off my dashboard. Women with Mayan faces paced back and forth, their arms struggling to not to drop their wares—large plastic Tweety Birds and oversized crucifixes. On these crosses, Jesus was hard and lean and muscular; squiggles of dark red paint trailed down his arms.

I said the same thing every time: children, colonia, research project. Sometimes the customs agents or immigration officers pretended to be interested. But I was just one of thousands. Sometimes they smacked my tires, sometimes the dog came, panting, to smell circles around the truck.

I crossed the line easily. Still, there was another kind of toll. On either side, I stumbled into a confusing blend of relief and anxiety. I expected this in crossing from the United States to Mexico, where I could feel nervous, uncomfortable, foreign. I was not supposed to feel this upon returning.

In 1939 Graham Greene wrote, "The border means more than a customs house, a passport officer, a man with a gun. Over there everything is going to be different; life is never going to be quite the same again. . . . The atmosphere of the border—it is like starting over again, there is something about it like a good confession: poised for a few happy moments between sin and sin."

Leaving Mexico, I carried with me drawings, tape recordings, and undeveloped film. These items filled the room in my house I use as an office. Suddenly the whole house felt too big, too empty, too clean. I tried to compensate. I taped drawings of flowers and houses to the wall. When I sat at my desk I could read the sweet words written on them in Spanish with crayon, "I'll never forget you." Looking at these drawings, these words, gave me an uncomfortable comfort.

I sorted through the children's photographs and assembled them in a large three-ring binder. There was a stunning image of a girl looking out of a shop window, a contemplative boy sitting on boards in the schoolyard, a young boy's self-portrait with the Virgin and a lollipop. I showed these pictures to others and tried to deliver impressive statements about the children—how talented they were, how young, how challenged. I told the stories. Inevitably, things got lost in translation.

I eased back into my American life. I swam in a pool, made long-distance phone calls, read books, watched the news. The border got thicker. It became a broad barrier separating two worlds, indeed different from each other. I could still cross it whenever I want, but the consequences of doing so were greater than the ease in which I made the action. There grew in me a desire to remain poised on the line, in the space between.

Perhaps I could have done better to ignore the border, to disregard what lies beyond it. After all, to do that would be to do what the families of the children I know did. But to deny the border would be to ignore what I now know—that not all of the stories about what's on the other side are true. That not everyone is yearning to jump the fence, give up their identity in exchange for dollar bills. That the shiny country I call my own is not everyone's dream destination.

Though perhaps unpatriotic of me, I found it refreshing that the children in Solidaridad were not overflowing with knowledge nor longing to know more about the place where I come from. Despite what the media, the economists, and a century of cartographic projections would have me believe, my country is not the center of the world. Ultimately, the stories that children told and didn't tell shifted my view of the world.

Now, if someone were to ask me to draw a map of my own world, I would expand my range. I would still draw the adobe house I rent, the garden and mesquite trees, the train tracks, and the interstate highway. But on the lower half of the page, I would add an hour's worth of line, Highway 19, and I'd scribble in a few red-tailed hawks alongside it. I would intersect the page with a solid line, but I would leave a space for easy crossing. On the other side of that line, I would drag a road through traffic, across a set of train tracks, and through a series of neighborhoods. In one of them, I would draw a handful of pink cement buildings and a basketball court in a big lot. Around it, I'd put houses, and draw X's in ten of them. Then I would park a yellow truck next to the basketball court, get out, and greet a gathering of children who I hope would be there, waiting.

Richard Shelton

Richard Shelton was born in 1933 in Boise, Idaho, though he has lived in Southern Arizona since 1956. Much of his writing reflects his impressions of the Sonoran Desert. Shelton has written several books of poetry and his work has been translated into Spanish, French, Swedish, Polish and Japanese. Going Back to Bisbee, *published in 1992, won the Western States Book Award for creative non-fiction. Shelton is a Regent Professor at the University of Arizona. Since 1974 he has been the director of a creative writing workshop at Arizona State Prison in Florence, Arizona; in the twenty-one years he has been working at the prison eight books of poetry, written by inmates, have been published.*

The Bus to Veracruz

The mail is slow here. If I died, I wouldn't find out about it for a long time. Perhaps I am dead already. At any rate, I am living in the wrong tense of a foreign language and have almost no verbs and only a few nouns to prove I exist. When I need a word, I fumble among the nouns and find one, but so many are similar in size and color. I am apt to come up with *caballo* instead of *caballero,* or *carne* instead of *casa*. When that happens, I become confused and drop the words. They roll across the tile floor in all directions. Then I get down on my hands and knees and crawl through a forest of legs, reaching under tables and chairs to retrieve them. But I am no longer embarrassed about crawling around on the floor in public places. I have come to realize that I am invisible most of the time and have been since I crossed the border.

All the floors are tile. All the tiles are mottled with the same disquieting pattern in one of three muddy colors—shades of yellow, purple, or green. They make me think of dried vomit, desiccated liver, and scum on a pond. The floor of my room is dried vomit with a border of scum on a pond, and like most of the floors it has several tiles missing, which is a great blessing to me. These lacunae are oases in the desert where I can rest my eyes. The nausea from which I suffer so much of the time is not caused by food or water, but by the floors. I know this because when I sit in the town square, which is covered with concrete of no particular color, the nausea subsides.

The town is small, although larger than it would seem to a visitor—if there are any visitors—and remote. It has no landing field for even small planes, and the nearest railroad is almost one hundred kilometers to the east. The only bus goes to Veracruz. Often I stop at the bus terminal to ask about the bus to Veracruz. The

---

Reprinted from *The Other Side of the Story*, (1987), by permission of the author.

floor of the bus terminal is scum on a pond with a border of desiccated liver, but there are many tiles missing. The terminal is always deserted except for Rafael and Esteban, sometimes sitting on the bench inside, sometimes lounging just outside the door. They are young, barefoot, and incredibly handsome. I buy them Cocas from the machine, and we have learned to communicate in our fashion. When I am with them, I am glad to be invisible, glad that they never look directly at me. I could not bear the soft vulnerability of those magnificent eyes.

"When does the bus leave for Veracruz?" I ask them. I have practiced this many times and am sure I have the right tense. But the words rise to the ceiling, burst, and fall as confetti around us. A few pieces catch in their dark hair and reflect the light like jewels. Rafael rubs his foot on the floor. Esteban stares out the filthy window. Are they sad, I wonder, because they believe there is no bus to Veracruz or because they don't know when it leaves.

"Is there a bus to Veracruz?" Suddenly they are happy again. Their hands fly like vivacious birds. *"¡Sí, hay! ¡Por supuesto, Señor! ¡Es verdad!"* They believe, truly, in the bus to Veracruz. Again I ask them when it leaves. Silence and sadness. Rafael studies on the tiles on the floor if it contains the answer. Esteban turns back to the window, I buy them *Cocas* from the machine and go away.

Once a week I stop at the post office to get my mail from the ancient woman in the metal cage, and each week I receive one letter. Actually, the letters are not mine, and the ancient woman has probably known this for a long time, but we never speak of it and she continues to hand me the letters, smiling and nodding in her coquettish way, eager to please me. Her hair is braided with colored ribbons, and her large silver earrings jingle when she bobs her head, which she does with great enthusiasm when I appear. I could not estimate how old she is. Perhaps even she has forgotten. But she must have been a great beauty at one time. Now she sits all day in the metal cage in the post office, a friendly apparition whose bright red lipstick is all the more startling because she has no teeth.

The first time I entered the post office, it was merely on an impulse to please her. I was expecting no mail, since no one knew where I was. But each time I passed, I had seen her through the window, seated in her metal cage with no customers to break the monotony. She always smiled and nodded at me through the window, eager for any diversion. Finally one day I went in on the pretext of calling for my mail, although I knew there would be none. To avoid the confusion which my accent always causes, I wrote my name on a slip of paper and presented it to her. Her tiny hands darted among the pigeonholes, and to my astonishment she presented me with a letter which was addressed to me in care of general delivery. She was so delighted with her success that I simply took the letter and went away, unwilling to disillusion her.

As soon as I opened the letter, the mystery was solved. My name is fairly common. The letter was intended for someone else with the same name. It was written on blue paper, in flawless Palmer Method script, and signed by a woman. It was undated and there was no return address. But it was in English, and I read it shamelessly, savoring each phrase. I rationalized by convincing myself that the mail was so slow the man to whom the letter had been written was probably already dead and could not object to my reading his mail. But I knew before I finished the letter that I would return to the post office later on the chance there might be others. She loved him. She thought he was still alive.

Since then I have received one letter each week, to the enormous delight of my ancient friend in the post office. I take the letters home and steam them open, careful to leave no marks on the delicate paper. They are always from the same woman, and I feel by now that I know her. Sometimes I dream about her, as if she were someone I knew in the past. She is blond and slender, no longer young but far from old. I can see her long, graceful fingers holding the pen as she writes, and sometimes she reaches up to brush a strand of hair away from her face. Even that slight gesture has the eloquence of a blessing.

When I have read each letter until I can remember it word for word, I reseal it, Then, after dark, I take it back to the post office by a circuitous route, avoiding anyone who might be on the street at that hour. The post office is always open, but the metal cage is closed and the ancient one is gone for the night. I drop the letter into the dead letter box and hurry away.

At first I had no curiosity about what happened to the letters after they left my hands. Then I began to wonder if they were destroyed or sent to some central office where, in an attempt to locate the sender and return them, someone might discover that they had been opened. Still later, the idea that some nameless official in a distant city might be reading them became almost unbearable to me. It was more and more difficult to remember that they were not my letters. I could not bear to think of anyone else reading her words, sensing her hesitations and tenderness. At last I decided to find out.

It took months of work, but with practice I became clever at concealing myself in shadowy doorways and watching. I have learned that once each week a nondescript man carrying a canvas bag enters the post office through the back door, just as the ancient woman is closing her metal cage for the night. She empties the contents of the dead letter box into his canvas bag, and he leaves by the door he came in. The man then begins a devious journey which continues long into the night. Many nights I have lost him and have had to begin again the following week. He doubles back through alleys and down obscure streets. Several times he enters deserted buildings by one door and emerges from another. He crosses the cemetery and goes through the Cathedral.

But finally he arrives at his destination—the bus terminal. And there, concealed behind huge doors which can be raised to the ceiling, is the bus to Veracruz. The man places his canvas bag in the luggage compartment, slams the metal cover with a great echoing clang, and goes away.

And later, at some unspecified hour, the bus to Veracruz rolls silently out of the terminal, a luxury liner leaving port with all its windows blazing. It has three yellow lights above the windshield and three gold stars along each side. The seats are red velvet and there are gold tassels between the windows. The dashboard is draped with brocade in the richest shades of yellow, purple, and green; and on this altar is a statue of the Virgin, blond and shimmering. Her slender fingers are extended to bless all those who ride the bus to Veracruz, but the only passenger is an ancient woman with silver earrings who sits by the window, nodding and smiling to the empty seats around her. There are two drivers who take turns during the long journey. They are young and incredibly handsome, with eyes as soft as the wings of certain luminous brown moths.

The bus moves through sleeping streets without making a sound. When it gets to the highway, it turns toward Veracruz and gathers speed. Then nothing can stop it: not the rain, nor the washed-out bridges, nor the sharp mountain curves, nor the people who stand by the road to flag it down.

I believe in the bus to Veracruz. And someday, when I am too tired to struggle any longer with the verbs and nouns, when the ugliness and tedium of this place overcome me, I will be on it. I will board the bus with my ticket in my hand. The doors of the terminal will rise to the ceiling, and we will move out through the darkness, gathering speed, like a great island of light.

Leslie Marmon Silko

Leslie Marmon Silko, a Laguna Pueblo (New Mexico) woman whose heritage includes White and Mexican forebears, is best known for her novels Ceremony *and* Almanac of the Dead. *Her work stems from the Pueblo world of her childhood and is grounded in the oral tradition in which culture and values are maintained through story. Silko's political concerns range from local water rights issues to global concerns regarding the rights of indigenous peoples.*

In the essay below, Silko recounts an experience she and a companion had while driving home one evening from a poetry reading. As they drove south down a New Mexico state road, they were stopped by United States Border Patrol agents and questioned. Silko's experience inspired her to write about the meaning of borders, particularly the meaning of official borders as defined by the United States government and law enforcement in the Southwest. The piece was originally published in The Nation.

The Border Patrol State

I used to travel the highways of New Mexico and Arizona with a wonderful sensation of absolute freedom as I cruised down the open road and across the vast desert plateaus. On the Laguna Pueblo reservation, where I was raised, the people were patriotic despite the way the U.S. government had treated Native Americans. As proud citizens, we grew up believing the freedom to travel was our inalienable right, a right that some Native Americans had been denied in the early twentieth century. Our cousin, old Bill Pratt, used to ride his horse 300 miles overland from Laguna, New Mexico, to Prescott, Arizona, every summer to work as a fire lookout.

In school in the 1950s, we were taught that our right to travel from state to state without special papers or threat of detainment was a right that citizens under communist and totalitarian governments did not possess. That wide open highway told us we were U.S. citizens: we were free. . . .

Not so long ago, my companion Gus and I were driving south from Albuquerque, returning to Tucson after a book promotion for the paperback edition of my novel *Almanac of the Dead*. I had settled back and gone to sleep while Gus drove, but I was awakened when I felt the car slowing to a stop. It was nearly midnight on New Mexico State Road 26, a dark, lonely stretch of two-lane highway between Hatch and Deming. When I sat up, I saw the headlights and emergency flashers of six vehicles—Border Patrol cars and a van were blocking both lanes of

Reprinted from the *Nation*, October 1994, pp. 412–416.

the highway. Gus stopped the car and rolled down the window to ask what was wrong. But the closest Border Patrolman and his companion did not reply; instead, the first agent ordered us to "step out of the car." Gus asked why, but his question seemed to set them off. Two more Border Patrol agents immediately approached our car, and one of them snapped, "Are you looking for trouble?" as if he would relish it.

I will never forget that night beside the highway. There was an awful feeling of menace and violence straining to break loose. It was clear that the uniformed men would be only too happy to drag us out of the car if we did not speedily comply with their request (asking a question is tantamount to resistance, it seems). So we stepped out of the car and they motioned for us to stand on the shoulder of the road. The night was very dark, and no other traffic had come down the road since we had been stopped. All I could think about was a book I had read—*Nunca Más*—the official report of a human rights commission that investigated and certified more than 12,000 "disappearances" during Argentina's "dirty war" in the late 1970s.

The weird anger of these Border Patrolmen made me think about descriptions in the report of Argentine police and military officers who became addicted to interrogations, torture and the murder that followed. When the military and police ran out of political suspects to torture and kill, they resorted to the random abduction of citizens off the streets. I thought how easy it would be for the Border Patrol to shoot us and leave our bodies and car beside the highway, like so many bodies found in these parts and ascribed to "drug runners."

Two other Border Patrolmen stood by the white van. The one who had asked if we were looking for trouble ordered his partner to "get the dog," and from the back of the van another patrolman brought a small female German shepherd on a leash. The dog apparently did not heel well enough to suit him, and the handler jerked the leash. They opened the doors of our car and pulled the dog's head into it, but I saw immediately from the expression in her eyes that the dog hated them, and that she would not serve them. When she showed no interest in the inside of our car, they brought her around back to the trunk, near where we were standing. They half-dragged her up into the trunk, but still she did not indicate any stowed-away human beings or illegal drugs.

Their mood got uglier; the officers seemed outraged that the dog could not find any contraband, and they dragged her over to us and commanded her to sniff our legs and feet. To my relief, the strange violence the Border Patrol agents had focused on us now seemed shifted to the dog. I no longer felt so strongly that we would be murdered. We exchanged looks—the dog and I. She was afraid of what they might do, just as I was. The dog's handler jerked the leash sharply as she sniffed us, as if to make her perform better, but the dog refused to accuse us: She had an innate dignity that did not permit her to serve the murderous impulses of those men. I can't forget the expression in the dog's eyes; it was as if she were embarrassed to be associated with them. I had a small amount of medicinal marijuana in my purse that night, but she refused to expose me. I am not partial to dogs, but I will always remember the small German shepherd that night.

Unfortunately, what happened to me is an everyday occurrence here now. Since the 1980s, on top of greatly expanding border checkpoints, the Immigration and Naturalization Service and the Border Patrol have implemented policies that interfere with the rights of U.S. citizens to travel freely within our borders. I.N.S. agents now patrol all interstate highways and roads that lead to or from the U.S.-Mexico border in Texas, New Mexico, Arizona and California. Now, when you drive east from Tucson on Interstate 10 toward El Paso, you encounter an I.N.S. check station outside Las Cruces, New Mexico. When you drive north from Las Cruces up Interstate 25, two miles north of the town of Truth or Consequences, the highway is blocked with orange emergency barriers, and all traffic is diverted into a two-lane Border Patrol checkpoint—ninety-five miles north of the U.S.-Mexico border.

I was detained once at Truth or Consequences, despite my and my companion's Arizona driver's licenses. Two men, both Chicanos, were detained at the same time, despite the fact that they too presented ID and spoke English without the thick Texas accents of the Border Patrol agents. While we were stopped, we watched as other vehicles—whose occupants were white—were waved through the checkpoint. White people traveling with brown people, however, can expect to be stopped on suspicion they work with the sanctuary movement, which shelters refugees. White people who appear to be clergy, those who wear ethnic clothing or jewelry and women with very long hair or very short hair (they could be nuns) are also frequently detained; white men with beards or men with long hair are likely to be detained, too, because Border Patrol agents have "profiles" of "those sorts" of white people who may help political refugees. (Most of the political refugees from Guatemala and El Salvador are Native American or mestizo because the indigenous people of the Americas have continued to resist efforts by invaders to displace them from their ancestral lands.) Alleged increases in illegal immigration by people of Asian ancestry means that the Border Patrol now routinely detains anyone who appears to be Asian or part Asian, as well.

Once your car is diverted from the Interstate Highway into the checkpoint area, you are under the control of the Border Patrol, which in practical terms exercises a power that no highway patrol or city patrolman possesses: They are willing to detain anyone, for no apparent reason. Other law-enforcement officers need a shred of probable cause in order to detain someone. On the books, so does the Border Patrol; but on the road, it's another matter. They'll order you to stop your car and step out; then they'll ask you to open the trunk. If you ask why or request a search warrant, you'll be told that they'll have to have a dog sniff the car before they can request a search warrant, and the dog might not get there for two or three hours. The search warrant might require an hour or two past that. They make it clear that if you force them to obtain a search warrant for the car, they will make you submit to a strip search as well.

Traveling in the open, though, the sense of violation can be even worse. Never mind high-profile cases like that of former Border Patrol agent Michael Elmer, acquitted of murder by claiming self-defense, despite admitting that as an officer he shot an "illegal" immigrant in the back and then hid the body, which remained undiscovered until another Border Patrolman reported the event. (Last month, Elmer was convicted of reckless endangerment in a separate incident, for shooting at least ten rounds from his M-16 too close to a group of immigrants as they were crossing illegally into Nogales in March 1992). Or that in El Paso, a high school football coach driving a vanload of his players in full uniform was pulled over on the freeway and a Border Patrol agent put a cocked revolver to his head. (The football coach was Mexican-American, as were most of the players in his van; the incident eventually caused a federal judge to issue a restraining order against the Border Patrol.) We've a mountain of personal experiences like that which never make the newspapers. A history professor at U.C.L.A. told me she had been traveling by train from Los Angeles to Albuquerque twice a month doing research. On each of her trips, she had noticed that the Border Patrol agents were at the station in Albuquerque scrutinizing the passengers. Since she is six feet tall and of Irish and German ancestry, she was not particularly concerned. Then one day when she stepped off the train in Albuquerque, two Border Patrolmen accosted her, wanting to know what she was doing, and why she was traveling between Los Angeles and Albuquerque twice a month. She presented identification and an explanation deemed "suitable" by the agents, and was allowed to go about her business.

Just the other day, I mentioned to a friend that I was writing this article and he told me about his 73-year-old father, who is half Chinese and had set out alone by car from Tucson to Albuquerque the week before. His father had become confused by road construction and missed a turnoff from Interstate 10 to Interstate 25; when he turned around and circled back, he missed the turnoff a second time. But when he looped back for yet another try, Border Patrol agents stopped him and forced him to open his trunk. After they satisfied themselves that he was not smuggling Chinese immigrants, they sent him on his way. He was so rattled by the event that he had to be driven home by his daughter.

This is the police state that has developed in the southwestern United States since the 1980s. No person, no citizen, is free to travel without the scrutiny of the Border Patrol. In the city of South Tucson, where 80 percent of the respondents were Chicano or Mexicano, a joint research project by the University of Wisconsin and the University of Arizona recently concluded that one out of every five people there had been detained, mistreated verbally or nonverbally, or questioned by I.N.S. agents in the past two years.

Manifest Destiny may lack its old grandeur of theft and blood—"lock the door" is what it means now, with racism a trump card to be played again and again, shamelessly, by both major political parties. "Immigration," like "street crime" and "welfare fraud," is a political euphemism that refers to people of color. Politicians and media people talk about "illegal aliens" to dehumanize and demonize undocumented immigrants, who are for the most part people of color. Even in the days of Spanish and Mexican rule, no attempts were made to interfere with the flow of people and goods from south to north and north to south. It is the U.S. government that has continually attempted to sever contact between the tribal people north of the border and those to the south.[1]

Now that the "Iron Curtain" is gone, it is ironic that the U.S. government and its Border Patrol are constructing a steel wall ten feet high to span sections of the border with Mexico. While politicians and multinational corporations extol the virtues of NAFTA and "free trade" (in goods, not flesh), the ominous curtain is already up in a six-mile section at the border crossing at Mexicali; two miles are being erected but are not yet finished at Naco; and at Nogales, sixty miles south of Tucson, the steel wall has been all rubber-stamped and awaits construction likely to begin in March. Like the pathetic multimillion-dollar "antidrug" border surveillance balloons that were continually deflated by high winds and made only a couple of meager interceptions before they blew away, the fence along the border is a theatrical prop, a bit of pork for contractors. Border entrepreneurs have already used blowtorches to cut passageways through the fence to collect "tolls," and are doing a brisk business. Back in Washington, the I.N.S. announces a $300 million computer contract to modernize its record-keeping and Congress passes a crime bill that shunts $255 million to the I.N.S. for 1995, $181 million earmarked for border control, which is to include 700 new partners for the men who stopped Gus and me in our travels, and the history professor, and my friend's father, and as many as they could from South Tucson.

It is no use; borders haven't worked, and they won't work, not now, as the indigenous people of the Americas reassert their kinship and solidarity with one another. A mass migration is already under way; its roots are not simply economic. The Uto-Aztecan languages are spoken as far north as Taos Pueblo near the Colorado border, all the way south to Mexico City. Before the arrival of the Europeans, the indigenous communities throughout this region not only conducted commerce, the people shared cosmologies, and oral narratives about the Maize Mother, the Twin Brothers and their Grandmother, Spider Woman, as well as Quetzalcoatl the benevolent snake. The great human migration within the Americas cannot be stopped; human beings are natural forces of the Earth, just as rivers and winds are natural forces.

Deep down the issue is simple: The so-called "Indian Wars" from the days of Sitting Bull and Red Cloud have never really ended in the Americas. The Indian people of southern Mexico, of Guatemala and those left in El Salvador, too, are still fighting for their lives and for their land against the "cavalry" patrols sent out by the governments of those lands. The Americas are Indian country, and the "Indian problem" is not about to go away.

One evening at sundown, we were stopped in traffic at a railroad crossing in downtown Tucson while a freight train passed us, slowly gaining speed as it headed north to Phoenix. In the twilight I saw the most amazing sight: Dozens of human beings, mostly young men, were riding the train; everywhere, on flat cars, inside open boxcars, perched on top of boxcars, hanging off ladders on tank cars and between boxcars. I couldn't count fast enough, but I saw fifty or sixty people headed north. They were dark young men, Indian and mestizo; they were smiling and a few of them waved at us in our cars. I was reminded of the ancient story of Aztlán, told by the Aztecs but known in other Uto-Aztecan communities as well. Aztlán is the beautiful land to the north, the origin place of the Aztec people. I don't remember how or why the people left Aztlán to journey farther south, but the old story says that one day, they will return.

Note

1. The Treaty of Guadalupe Hidalgo, signed in 1848, recognizes the right of the Tohano O'Odom (Papago) people to move freely across the U.S.-Mexico border without documents. A treaty with Canada guarantees similar rights to those of the Iroquois nation in traversing the U.S.-Canada border.

Leslie Marmon Silko

Leslie Silko's story "Yellow Woman" is based on a female character from ancient Laguna stories. In the traditional stories, Yellow Woman has many, and sometimes contradictory, characteristics, from being loyal to being selfish to being a witch. The particular version that Silko re-tells here is based on the abduction stories; in those, a powerful, mythical male figure takes Yellow Woman away from her husband and children. The setting of Silko's version, though, is contemporary, and because it follows the woman's journey into adultery and myth and back again, the story focuses on her identity, her sexuality, and her relationships to family, community and tradition. In order to research stories about Yellow Woman, both traditional and contemporary, you might see Spider Woman's Granddaughters *by Paula Gunn Allen, which has a chapter on Yellow Woman stories.* Yellow Woman *by Leslie Silko, a book edited by Melody Graulich, is part of a series called* Women Writers: Text and Context; *it contains articles about the story as well as other sources, such as interviews with Silko.*

Yellow Woman

One

My thigh clung to his with dampness, and I watched the sun rising up through the tamaracks and willows. The small brown water birds came to the river and hopped across the mud, leaving brown scratches in the alkali-white crust. They bathed in the river silently. I could hear the water, almost at our feet where the narrow fast channel bubbled and washed green ragged moss and fern leaves. I looked at him beside me, rolled in the red blanket on the white river sand. I cleaned the sand out of the cracks between my toes, squinting because the sun was above the willow trees. I looked at him for the last time, sleeping on the white river sand.

I felt hungry and followed the river south the way we had come the afternoon before, following our footprints that were already blurred by the lizard tracks and bug trails. The horses were still lying down, and the black one whinnied when he saw me but he did not get up—maybe it was because the corral was made out of thick cedar branches and the horses had not yet felt the sun like I had. I tried to

---

Reprinted from *Storyteller*, (1981), by permission of Seaver Books.

look beyond the pale red mesas to the pueblo. I knew it was there, even if I could not see it, on the sand rock hill above the river, the same river that moved past me now and had reflected the moon last night.

The horse felt warm underneath me. He shook his head and pawed the sand. The bay whinnied and leaned against the gate trying to follow, and I remembered him asleep in the red blanket beside the river. I slid off the horse and tied him close to the other horse. I walked north with the river again, and the white sand broke loose in footprints over footprints.

"Wake up."

He moved in the blanket and turned his face to me with his eyes still closed. I knelt down to touch him.

"I'm leaving."

He smiled now, eyes still closed. "You are coming with me, remember?" He sat up now with his bare dark chest and belly in the sun.

"Where?"

"To my place."

"And will I come back?"

He pulled his pants on. I walked away from him, feeling him behind me and smelling the willows.

"Yellow Woman," he said.

I turned to face him. "Who are you?" I asked.

He laughed and knelt on the low, sandy bank, washing his face in the river. "Last night you guessed my name, and you knew why I had come."

I stared past him at the shallow moving water and tried to remember the night, but I could only see the moon in the water and remember his warmth around me.

"But I only said that you were him and that I was Yellow Woman—I'm not really her—I have my own name and I come from the pueblo on the other side of the mesa. Your name is Silva and you are a stranger I met by the river yesterday afternoon."

He laughed softly. "What happened yesterday has nothing to do with what you will do today, Yellow Woman."

"I know—that's what I'm saying—the old stories about the ka'tsina spirit and Yellow Woman can't mean us."

My old grandpa liked to tell those stories best. There is one about Badger and Coyote who went hunting and were gone all day, and when the sun was going down they found a house. There was a girl living there alone, and she had light hair and eyes and she told them that they could sleep with her. Coyote wanted to be with her all night so he sent Badger into a prairie-dog hole, telling him he thought he saw something in it. As soon as Badger crawled in, Coyote blocked up the entrance with rocks and hurried back to Yellow Woman.

"Come here," he said gently.

He touched my neck and I moved close to him to feel his breathing and to hear his heart. I was wondering if Yellow Woman had known who she was—if she knew that she would become part of the stories. Maybe she'd had another name that her husband and relatives called her so that only the ka'tsina from the north and the storytellers would know her as Yellow Woman. But I didn't go on; I felt him all around me, pushing me down into the white river sand.

Yellow Woman went away with the spirit from the north and lived with him and his relatives. She was gone for a long time, but then one day she came back and she brought twin boys.

"Do you know the story?"

"What story?" He smiled and pulled me close to him as he said this. I was afraid lying there on the red blanket. All I could know was the way he felt, warm, damp, his body beside me. This is the way it happens in the stories, I was thinking, with no thought beyond the moment she meets the ka'tsina spirit and they go.

"I don't have to go. What they tell in stories was real only then, back in time immemorial, like they say."

He stood up and pointed at my clothes tangled in the blanket. "Let's go," he said.

I walked beside him, breathing hard because he walked fast, his hand around my wrist. I had stopped trying to pull away from him, because his hand felt cool and the sun was high, drying the river bed into alkali. I will see someone, eventually I will see someone, and then I will be certain that he is only a man—some man from nearby—and I will be sure that I am not Yellow Woman. Because she is from out of time past and I live now and I've been to school and there are highways and pickup trucks that Yellow Woman never saw.

It was an easy ride north on horseback. I watched the change from the cottonwood trees along the river to the junipers that brushed past us in the foothills, and finally there were only piñons, and when I looked up at the rim of the mountain plateau I could see pine trees growing on the edge. Once I stopped to look down, but the pale sandstone had disappeared and the river was gone and the dark lava hills were all around. He touched my hand, not speaking, but always singing softly a mountain song and looking into my eyes.

I felt hungry and wondered what they were doing at home now—my mother, my grandmother, my husband, and the baby. Cooking breakfast, saying, "Where did she go?—maybe kidnapped," and Al going to the tribal police with the details: "She went walking along the river."

The house was made with black lava rock and red mud. It was high above the spreading miles of arroyos and long mesas. I smelled a mountain smell of pitch and buck brush. I stood there beside the black horse, looking down on the small, dim country we had passed, and I shivered.

"Yellow Woman, come inside where's it's warm."

Two

He lit a fire in the stove. It was an old stove with a round belly and an enamel coffeepot on top. There was only the stove, some faded Navajo blankets, and a bedroll and cardboard box. The floor was made of smooth adobe plaster, and there was one small window facing east. He pointed at the box.

"There's some potatoes and the frying pan." He sat on the floor with his arms around his knees pulling them close to his chest and he watched me fry the potatoes. I didn't mind him watching me because he was always watching me—he had been watching me since I came upon him sitting on the river bank trimming leaves from a willow twig with his knife. We ate from the pan and he wiped the grease from his fingers on his Levis.

"Have you brought women here before?" He smiled and kept chewing, so I said, "Do you always use the same tricks?"

"What tricks?" He looked at me like he didn't understand.

"The story about being a ka'tsina from the mountains. The story about Yellow Woman."

Silva was silent; his face was calm.

"I don't believe it. Those stories couldn't happen now," I said.

He shook his head and said softly, "But someday they will talk about us, and they will say, 'Those two lived long ago when things like that happened.'"

He stood up and went out. I ate the rest of the potatoes and thought about things—about the noise the stove was making and the sound of the mountain wind outside. I remembered yesterday and the day before, and then I went outside.

I walked past the corral to the edge where the narrow trail cut through the black rim rock. I was standing in the sky with nothing around me but the wind that came down from the blue mountain peak behind me. I could see faint mountain images in the distance miles across the vast spread of mesas and valleys and plains. I wondered who was over there to feel the mountain wind on those sheer blue edges—who walks on the pine needles in those blue mountains.

"Can you see the pueblo?" Silva was standing behind me.

I shook my head. "We're too far away."

"From here I can see the world." He stepped out on the edge. "The Navajo reservation begins over there." He pointed to the east. "The Pueblo boundaries are over here." He looked below us to the south, where the narrow trail seemed to come from. "The Texans have their ranches over there, starting with that valley, the Concho Valley. The Mexicans run some cattle over there too."

"Do you ever work for them?"

"I steal from them," Silva answered. The sun was dropping behind us and shadows were filling the land below. I turned away from the edge that dropped forever into the valleys below.

"I'm cold," I said; "I'm going inside," I started wondering about this man who could speak the Pueblo language so well but who lived on a mountain and rustled cattle. I decided that this man Silva must be Navajo, because Pueblo men didn't do things like that.

"You must be a Navajo."

Silva shook his head gently. "Little Yellow Woman," he said, "you never give up, do you? I have told you who I am. The Navajo people know me, too." He knelt down and unrolled the bedroll and spread the extra blankets out on a piece of canvas. The sun was down, and the only light in the house came from outside—the dim orange light from sundown.

I stood there and waited for him to crawl under the blankets.

"What are you waiting for?" he said, and I lay down beside him. He undressed me slowly like the night before beside the river—kissing my face gently and running his hands up and down my belly and legs. He took off my pants and then he laughed.

"Why are you laughing?"

"You are breathing so hard."

I pulled away from him and turned my back to him.

He pulled me around and pinned me down with his arms and chest. "You don't understand, do you, little Yellow Woman? You will do what I want."

And again he was all around me with his skin slippery against mine, and I was afraid because I understood that his strength could hurt me. I lay underneath him and I knew that he could destroy me. But later, while he slept beside me, I touched his face and I had a feeling—the kind of feeling for him that overcame me that morning along the river. I kissed him on the forehead and he reached out for me.

When I woke up in the morning he was gone. It gave me a strange feeling because for a long time I sat there on the blankets and looked around the little house for some object of his—some proof that he had been there or maybe that he was coming back. Only the blankets and the cardboard box remained. The .30–.30 that had been leaning in the corner was gone, and so was the knife I had used the night before. He was gone, and I had my chance to go now. But first I had to eat, because I knew it would be a long walk home.

I found some dried apricots in the cardboard box, and I sat down on a rock at the edge of the plateau rim. There was no wind and the sun warmed me. I was surrounded by silence. I drowsed with apricots in my mouth, and I didn't believe that there were highways or railroads or cattle to steal.

When I woke up, I stared down at my feet in the black mountain dirt. Little black ants were swarming over the pine needles around my foot. They must have smelled the apricots. I thought about my family far below me. They would be wondering about me, because this had never happened to me before. The tribal police would file a report. But if old Grandpa weren't dead he would tell them what happened—he would laugh and say, "Stolen by a ka'tsina, a mountain spirit. She'll come home—they usually do." There are enough of them to handle things. My mother and grandmother will raise the baby like they raised me. Al will find someone else, and they will go on like before, except that there will be a story about the day I disappeared while I was walking along the river. Silva had come for me; he said he had. I did not decide to go. I just went. Moonflowers blossom in the sand hills before dawn, just as I followed him. That's what I was thinking as I wandered along the trail through the pine trees.

It was noon when I got back. When I saw the stone house I remembered that I had meant to go home. But that didn't seem important any more, maybe because there were little blue flowers growing in the meadow behind the stone house and the gray squirrels were playing in the pines next to the house. The horses were standing in the corral, and there was a beef carcass hanging on the shady side of a big pine in front of the house. Flies buzzed around the clotted blood that hung from the carcass. Silva was washing his hands in a bucket full of water. He must have heard me coming because he spoke to me without turning to face me.

"I've been waiting for you."

"I went walking in the big pine trees."

I looked into the bucket full of bloody water with brown-and-white animal hairs floating in it. Silva stood there letting his hand drip, examining me intently.

"Are you coming with me?"

"Where?" I asked him.

"To sell the meat in Marquez."

"If you're sure it's O.K."

"I wouldn't ask you if it wasn't," he answered.

He sloshed the water around in the bucket before he dumped it out and set the bucket upside down near the door. I followed him to the corral and watched him saddle the horses. Even beside the horses he looked tall, and I asked him again if he wasn't Navajo. He didn't say anything; he just shook his head and kept cinching up the saddle.

"But Navajos are tall."

"Get on the horse," he said, "and let's go."

The last thing he did before we started down the steep trail was to grab the .30–30 from the corner. He slid the rifle into the scabbard that hung from his saddle.

"Do they ever try to catch you?" I asked.

"They don't know who I am."

"Then why did you bring the rifle?"

"Because we are going to Marquez where the Mexicans live."

Three

The trail leveled out on a narrow ridge that was steep on both sides like an animal spine. On one side I could see where the trail went around the rocky gray hills and disappeared into the southeast where the pale sandrock mesas stood in the distance near my home. On the other side was a trail that went west, and as I looked far into the distance I thought I saw the little town. But Silva said no, that I was looking in the wrong place, that I just thought I saw houses. After that I quit looking off into the distance; it was hot and the wildflowers were closing up their deep-yellow petals. Only the waxy cactus flowers bloomed in the bright sun, and I saw every color that a cactus blossom can be; the white ones and the red ones were still buds, but the purple and the yellow were blossoms, open full and the most beautiful of all.

Silva saw him before I did. The white man was riding a big gray horse, coming up the trail toward us. He was traveling fast and the gray horse's feet sent rocks rolling off the trail into the dry tumbleweeds. Silva motioned for me to stop and we watched the white man. He didn't see us right away, but finally his horse whinnied at our horses and he stopped. He looked at us briefly before he loped the gray horse across the three hundred yards that separated us. He stopped his horse in front of Silva, and his young fat face was shadowed by the brim of his hat. He didn't look mad, but his small, pale eyes moved from the blood-soaked gunny sacks hanging from my saddle to Silva's face and then back to my face.

"Where did you get the fresh meat?" the white man asked.

"I've been hunting," Silva said, and when he shifted his weight in the saddle the leather creaked.

"The hell you have, Indian. You've been rustling cattle. We've been looking for the thief for a long time."

The rancher was fat, and sweat began to soak through his white cowboy shirt and the wet cloth stuck to the thick rolls of belly fat. He almost seemed to be panting from the exertion of talking, and he smelled rancid, maybe because Silva scared him.

Silva turned to me and smiled. "Go back up the mountain, Yellow Woman."

The white man got angry when he heard Silva speak in a language he couldn't understand. "Don't try anything, Indian. Just keep riding to Marquez. We'll call the state police from there."

The rancher must have been unarmed because he was very frightened and if he had a gun he would have pulled it out then. I turned my horse around and the rancher yelled, "Stop!" I looked at Silva for an instant and there was something ancient and dark—something I could feel in my stomach—in his eyes, and when I glanced at his hand I saw his finger on the trigger of the .30–30 that was still in the saddle scabbard. I slapped my horse across the flank and the sacks of raw meat swung against my knees as the horse leaped up the trail. It was hard to keep my balance, and once I thought I felt the saddle slipping backward; it was because of this that I could not look back.

I didn't stop until I reached the ridge where the trail forked. The horse was breathing deep gasps and there was a dark film of sweat on its neck. I looked down in the direction I had come from, but I couldn't see the place. I waited. The wind came up and pushed warm air past me. I looked up at the sky, pale blue and full of thin clouds and fading vapor trails left by jets.

I think four shots were fired—I remember hearing four hollow explosions that reminded me of deer hunting. There could have been more shots after that, but I couldn't have heard them because my horse was running again and the loose rocks were making too much noise as they scattered around his feet.

Horses have a hard time running downhill, but I went that way instead of uphill to the mountain because I thought it was safer. I felt better with the horse running southeast past the round gray hills that were covered with cedar trees and black lava rock. When I got to the plain in the distance I could see the dark green patches of tamaracks that grew along the river; and beyond the river I could see the beginning of the pale sandrock mesas. I stopped the horse and looked back to see if anyone was coming; then I got off the horse and turned the horse around, wondering if it would go back to its corral under the pines on the mountain. It looked back at me for a moment and then plucked a mouthful of green tumbleweeds before it trotted back up the trail with its ears pointed forward, carrying its head daintily to one side to avoid stepping on the dragging reins. When the horse disappeared over the last hill, the gunny sacks full of meat were still swinging and bouncing.

Four

I walked toward the river on a wood-hauler's road that I knew would eventually lead to the paved road. I was thinking about waiting beside the road for someone to drive by, but by the time I got to the pavement I had decided it wasn't very far to walk if I followed the river back the way Silva and I had come.

The river water tasted good, and I sat in the shade under a cluster of silvery willows. I thought about Silva, and I felt sad at leaving him; still, there was something strange about him, and I tried to figure it out all the way back home.

I came back to the place on the river bank where he had been sitting the first time I saw him. The green willow leaves that he had trimmed from the branch were still lying there, wilted in the sand. I saw the leaves and I wanted to go back to him—to kiss him and to touch him—but the mountains were too far away now. And I told myself, because I believe it, he will come back sometime and be waiting again by the river.

I followed the path up from the river into the village. The sun was getting low, and I could smell supper cooking when I got to the screen door of my house. I could hear their voices inside—my mother was telling my grandmother how to fix the Jell-O and my husband, Al, was playing with the baby. I decided to tell them that some Navajo had kidnapped me, but I was sorry that old Grandpa wasn't alive to hear my story because it was the Yellow Woman stories he liked to tell best.

Leslie Marmon Silko

The misuse of power is a common theme in Leslie Silko's work and she often uses the figure of the witch to represent someone who both misunderstands and abuses power. In Native American tradition, witchery can throw things out of balance; it can cause drought, destruction, and death. In "Tony's Story," Silko tells her fictional version of a true story about a deadly conflict between a traditional Indian and a white state trooper. Since the story is told from Tony's perspective, readers are taken into a borderland between cultures and between different realities. We are left, at the end of the story, pondering the significance of all of the characters' actions.

Tony's Story

It happened one summer when the sky was wide and hot and the summer rains did not come; the sheep were thin, and the tumbleweeds turned brown and died. Leon came back from the army. I saw him standing by the Ferris wheel across from the people who came to sell melons and chili on San Lorenzo's Day. He yelled at me, "Hey Tony—over here!" I was embarrassed to hear him yell so loud, but then I saw the wine bottle with the brown-paper sack crushed around it.

"How's it going, buddy?"

He grabbed my hand and held it tight like a white man. He was smiling. "It's good to be home again. They asked me to dance tomorrow—it's only the Corn Dance, but I hope I haven't forgotten what to do."

"You'll remember—it will all come back to you when you hear the drum." I was happy, because I knew that Leon was once more a part of the pueblo. The sun was dusty and low in the west, and the procession passed by us, carrying San Lorenzo back to his niche in the church.

"Do you want to get something to eat?" I asked.

Leon laughed and patted the bottle. "No, you're the only one who needs to eat. Take this dollar—they're selling hamburgers over there." He pointed past the merry-go-round to a stand with cotton candy and a snow-cone machine.

It was then that I saw the cop pushing his way through the crowds of people gathered around the hamburger stand and bingo tent; he came steadily toward us. I remembered Leon's wine and looked to see if the cop was watching us; but he was wearing dark glasses and I couldn't see his eyes.

He never said anything before he hit Leon in the face with his fist. Leon collapsed into the dust, and the paper sack floated in the wine and pieces of glasses.

Reprinted from *Storyteller*, (1981), by permission of Seaver Books.

He didn't move and blood kept bubbling out of his mouth and nose. I could hear a siren. People crowded around Leon and kept pushing me away. The tribal policemen knelt over Leon, and one of them looked up at the state cop and asked what was going on. The big cop didn't answer. He was staring at the little patterns of blood in the dust near Leon's mouth. The dust soaked up the blood almost before it dripped to the ground—it had been a very dry summer. The cop didn't leave until they laid Leon in the back of the paddy wagon.

The moon was already high when we got to the hospital in Albuquerque. We waited a long time outside the emergency room with Leon propped between us. Siow and Gaisthea kept asking me, "What happened, what did Leon say to the cop?" and I told them how we were just standing there, ready to buy hamburgers—we'd never even seen him before.

They put stitches around Leon's mouth and gave him a shot; he was lucky, they said—it could've been a broken jaw instead of broken teeth.

They dropped me off near my house. The moon had moved lower into the west and left the close rows of houses in long shadows. Stillness breathed around me, and I wanted to run from the feeling behind me in the dark; and the stories about witches ran with me. That night I had a dream—the big cop was pointing a long bone at me—they always use human bones, and the whiteness flashed silver in the moonlight where he stood. He didn't have a human face—only little, round, white-rimmed eyes on a black ceremonial mask.

Leon was better in a few days. But he was bitter, and all he could talk about was the cop. "I'll kill the big bastard if he comes around here again," Leon kept saying.

With something like the cop it is better to forget, and I tried to make Leon understand. "It's over now. There's nothing you can do."

I wondered why men who came back from the army were troublemakers on the reservation. Leon even took it before the pueblo meeting. They discussed it, and the old men decided that Leon shouldn't have been drinking. The interpreter read a passage out of the revised pueblo law-and-order code about possessing intoxicants on the reservation, so we got up and left.

Then Leon asked me to go with him to Grants to buy a roll of barbed wire for his uncle. On the way we stopped at Cerritos for gas, and I went into the store for some pop. He was inside. I stopped in the doorway and turned around before he saw me, but if he really was what I feared, then he would not need to see me—he already knew we were there. Leon was waiting with the truck engine running almost like he knew what I would say.

"Let's go—the big cop's inside."

Leon gunned it and the pickup skidded back on the highway. He glanced back in the rearview mirror. "I didn't see his car."

"Hidden," I said.

Leon shook his head. "He can't do it again. We are just as good as them."

The guys who came back always talked like that.

The sky was hot and empty. The half-grown tumbleweeds were dried up flat and brown beside the highway, and across the valley, heat shimmered above wilted fields of corn. Even the mountains high beyond the pale sandrock mesas were dusty blue. I was afraid to fall asleep so I kept my eyes on the blue mountains—not letting them close—soaking in the heat; and then I knew why the drought had come that summer.

Leon shook me. "He's behind us—the cop's following us!"

I looked back and saw the red light on top of the car whirling around, and I could make out the dark image of a man, but where the face should have been there were only the silvery lenses of the dark glasses he wore.

"Stop, Leon! He wants us to stop!"

Leon pulled over and stopped on the narrow gravel shoulder.

"What in the hell does he want?" Leon's hands were shaking.

Suddenly the cop was standing beside the truck, gesturing for Leon to roll down his window. He pushed his head inside, grinding the gum in his mouth; the smell of Doublemint was all around us.

"Get out. Both of you."

I stood beside Leon in the dry weeds and tall yellow grass that broke through the asphalt and rattled in the wind. The cop studied Leon's driver's license. I avoided his face—I knew that I couldn't look at his eyes, so I stared at his black half-Wellingtons, with the black uniform cuffs pulled over them; but my eyes kept moving, upward past the black gun belt. My legs were quivering, and I tried to keep my eyes away from his. But it was like the time when I was very little and my parents warned me not to look into the masked dancers' eyes because they would grab me, and my eyes would not stop.

"What's your name?" His voice was high-pitched and it distracted me from the meaning of the words.

I remember Leon said, "He doesn't understand English so good," and finally I said that I was Antonio Sousea, while my eyes strained to look beyond the silver frosted glasses that he wore; but only my distorted face and squinting eyes reflected back.

And then the cop stared at us for a while, silent; finally he laughed and chewed his gum some more slowly. "Where were you going?"

"To Grants." Leon spoke English very clearly. "Can we go now?"

Leon was twisting the key chain around his fingers, and I felt the sun everywhere. Heat swelled up from the asphalt and when cars went by, hot air and the motor smell rushed past us.

"I don't like smart guys, Indian. It's because of you bastards that I'm here. They transferred me here because of Indians. They thought there wouldn't be as many for me here. But I find them." He spit his gum into the weeds near my foot and walked back to the patrol car. It kicked up gravel and dust when he left.

We got back in the pickup, and I could taste sweat in my mouth, so I told Leon that we might as well go home since he would be waiting for us up ahead.

"He can't do this," Leon said. "We've got a right to be on this highway."

I couldn't understand why Leon kept talking about "rights," because it wasn't "rights" that he was after, but Leon didn't seem to understand; he couldn't remember the stories that old Teofilo told.

I didn't feel safe until we turned off the highway and I could see the pueblo and my own house. It was noon, and everybody was eating—the village seemed empty—even the dogs had crawled away from the heat. The door was open, but there was only silence, and I was afraid that something had happened to all of them. Then as soon as I opened the screen door the little kids started crying for more Kool-Aid, and my mother said "no," and it was noisy again like always. Grandfather commented that it had been a fast trip to Grants, and I said "yeah" and didn't explain because it would've only worried them.

"Leon goes looking for trouble—I wish you wouldn't hang around with him." My father didn't like trouble. But I knew that the cop was something terrible, and even to speak about it risked bringing it close to all of us; so I didn't say anything.

That afternoon Leon spoke with the Governor, and he promised to send letters to the Bureau of Indian Affairs and to the State Police Chief. Leon seemed satisfied with that. I reached into my pocket for the arrowhead on the piece of string.

"What's that for?"

I held it out to him. "Here, wear it around your neck—like mine. See? Just in case," I said, "for protection."

"You don't believe in *that,* do you?" He pointed to a .30–30 leaning against the wall. "I'll take this with me whenever I'm in the pickup."

"But you can't be sure that it will kill one of them."

Leon looked at me and laughed. "What's the matter," he said, "have they brainwashed you into believing that a .30–30 won't kill a white man?" He handed back the arrowhead. "Here, you wear two of them."

Leon's uncle asked me if I wanted to stay at the sheep camp for a while. The lambs were big, and there wouldn't be much for me to do, so I told him I would. We left early, while the sun was still low and red in the sky. The highway was empty, and I sat there beside Leon imagining what it had been like before there were highways or even horses. Leon turned off the highway onto the sheep-camp road that climbs around the sandstone mesas until suddenly all the trees are piñons.

Leon glanced in the rearview mirror. "He's following us!"

My body began to shake and I wasn't sure if I would be able to speak. "There's no place left to hide. It follows us everywhere."

Leon looked at me like he didn't understand what I'd said. Then I looked past Leon and saw that the patrol car had pulled up beside us; the piñon branches were whipping and scraping the side of the truck as it tried to force us off the road. Leon kept driving with the two right wheels in the rut—bumping and scraping the trees. Leon never looked over at it so he couldn't have known how the reflections kept moving across the mirror lenses of the dark glasses. We were in the narrow canyon with pale sandstone close on either side—the canyon that ended with a spring where willows and grass and tiny blue flowers grow.

"We've got to kill it, Leon. We must burn the body to be sure."

Leon didn't seem to be listening. I kept wishing that old Teofilo could have been there to chant the proper words while we did it. Leon stopped the truck and got out—he still didn't understand what it was. I sat in the pickup with the .30–30 across my lap, and my hands were slippery.

The big cop was standing in front of the pickup, facing Leon. "You made your mistake, Indian. I'm going to beat the shit out of you." He raised the billy club slowly. "I like to beat Indians with this."

He moved toward Leon with the stick raised high, and it was like the long bone in my dream when he pointed it at me—a human bone painted brown to look like wood, to hide what it really was; they'll do that, you know—carve the bone into a spoon and use it around the house until the victim comes within range.

The shot sounded far away and I couldn't remember aiming. But he was motionless on the ground and the bone wand lay near his feet. The tumbleweeds and tall yellow grass were sprayed with glossy, bright blood. He was on his back, and the sand between his legs and along his left side was soaking up the dark, heavy blood—it had not rained for a long time, and even the tumbleweeds were dying.

"Tony! You killed him—you killed the cop!"

"Help me! We'll set the car on fire."

Leon acted strange, and he kept looking at me like he wanted to run. The head wobbled and swung back and forth, and the left hand and the legs left individual trails in the sand. The face was the same. The dark glasses hadn't fallen off and they blinded me with their hot-sun reflections until I pushed the body into the front seat.

The gas tank exploded and the flames spread along the underbelly of the car. The tires filled the wide sky with spirals of thick black smoke.

"My God, Tony. What's wrong with you? That's a state cop you killed." Leon was pale and shaking.

I wiped my hands on my Levi's. "Don't worry, everything is O.K. now, Leon. It's killed. They sometimes take on strange forms."

The tumbleweeds around the car caught fire, and little heat waves shimmered up toward the sky; in the west, rain clouds were gathering.

Luci Tapahonso

Luci Tapahonso grew up in Shiprock, New Mexico, in the Navajo Nation. She has published five books of poetry: One More Shiprock Night, Seasonal Woman, A Breeze Swept Through, The Women Are Singing, *and* Blue Horses Rush In. *Tapahonso currently teaches here at the University of Arizona. Her work is anchored in the land she shares with her people and in Navajo traditions.*

In her short essay, "A Sense of Myself," Tapahonso explores her relationship to both the Navajo and English languages. Her poetry also reflects her awareness of the interfaces always present between Indian and non-Indian worlds. In her short story, "What I Am," she explores her connection to her mother, grandmother, and her great-grandmother, whom she knew only through stories. In the narrative poem, "In 1864," she tells of the notorious Long Walk that the Navajo people endured and survived at the hands of the United States troops. The many storytellers within the poem create a sense of the continual presence of the past—of history—in individual memory and therefore in culture. In the lyrical poems "This is How They Were Placed for Us" and "Blue Horses Rush In," she weaves together images of nature and family so that readers can witness her culture's spiritual connection to the land and the journey of a cherished child's birth.

A Sense of Myself

Earlier this year, as I was driving to a poetry reading in southern Colorado, I was trying to remember a certain part of a song that I wanted to sing that evening.

In the last part of the song, there were a few notes that seemed to dip and lower, then the song repeated itself again. I felt I had to get that tiny part accurate before it was sung in public. I asked my father if he remembered it and he did. He was sitting in the back seat and looking out at the mountains, then leaning forward towards me to listen as I sang. He sang it over and over again. After a half-hour or so, I finally learned it right and we sang it all the way into Durango where I was to read.

Before the reading, I asked my father if he thought I should sing that particular song as it was attached to the poem. He said, "If you know the song and like it when you sing, then sing it. It's your song. The English in the poems, though, is not yours. You are only borrowing that. Once you read it to others, it becomes theirs also. You are responsible for what that may create. You should be careful with that particular use of English."

Reprinted from *Dine Be'iina: A Journal of Navajo Life* 1, no. 1, pp. 372–373, (1987).

He is right in that the language I have chosen to write in and express myself with is not truly mine. I have adopted it and learned to use it for myself. Because I was born into and come out of an oral culture, I learned early that the use of words involves responsibility and respect for oneself. A person is known primarily by his use of language and song. One's family and upbringing are reflected in the way he or she talks among others. So one does not act alone in the use of words or songs; it always involves his parents, his family and distant relatives. In telling me this again, in English no less, my father was essentially saying, "Remember you are talking for us all, the things you write will come back to us, because you are part of us. We are together whole."

And so it is in this way of learning and being spoken to, that I have come to see my work as not even really being mine but as an outlet for those whom I belong to. So that I do not write alone and I am responsible and held accountable for what I write in terms of my history, my family and myself.

It is this sense of having "borrowed" that increases the value of the language for me. In Navajo, there is a song or oration that goes with every activity in daily life. To use these out of context, whether carelessly or in jest, is frowned upon greatly. As I write in English, I am aware of how this particular line or feeling would be in Navajo first so that I am translating roughly into English the song or the prayer, the story that accompanies whatever I happen to be writing about. Thus it becomes important for my work to carry the "rhythm" or the "feeling" of the story or event as it would if I were sitting at my mother's kitchen table telling about the event.

After the reading that night, it was snowing as we drove home. As we neared Shiprock, the snow started to thin out, becoming lighter and clearer. "It was like this the night your sister was born," my mother said and she went on to tell about that night and why this sister possessed this or that characteristic because of her birth-night long ago. In my mother's telling of that event, the weather that night became synonymous with my sister's birth in my mind and the songs she sang immediately after will remember that.

It has been that way my whole life, and my sense of language, my awareness of words becomes entangled with songs, memories, history and the land. It is not separate—the borrowing of English—from the way I would use it in Navajo. My sense of poetics, in this case, becomes a sense of myself.

What I Am

Nineteen hundred thirty-five. KinLichíi'nii Bitsí waited, looking across the snow-covered desert stretching out before her. Snow was falling lightly and the desert

---

Reprinted from *Saani Dahataal: The Women Are Singing*, (1993), by permission of University of Arizona Press.

was flat and white. From where she stood at the foothills of the Carriso Mountains, she could see for miles.

She would see him when he approached—a small, dark speck on the vast whiteness, moving slowly, but closer. Her son, Prettyboy, tall and lanky on the sure-footed horse. She would see him.

All evening, she kept watch, stepping out every once in a while. He had gone to visit some relatives at Little Shiprock and should have returned by now. It had begun snowing early and continued into the evening. She knew Prettyboy had started home before the storm and would be arriving soon. She kept watch, looking out on the horizon.

In those days, hogans had no windows so she stood at the front door, a shawl around her shoulders. Only her eyes were uncovered as she squinted, looking out into the desert night. "Nihimá, deesk'aaz. Our mother, it's cold," her children called her inside. She would come in for a while, then go back out to watch for him again. All evening she waited, and her children urged her not to worry. He would be home soon they said. She continued watching for him, insisting that she wasn't cold.

Finally, she saw him, a dark speck on the horizon. She rushed in and stirred up the fire, heated up the stew, and put on a fresh pot of coffee. She heated up the grease for frybread. He came in, damp and cold with snow. They laughed because his eyebrows were frozen white. "Tell us everything about your trip," they said to him. "Tell us about your trip." While he ate, he talked about the relatives he visited and the news that he had heard. He said the horse seemed to know the way by itself through the snow and wind. He kept his head down most of the way, he said. The snow was blowing and it was hard to see. The family finally went to bed, relieved that Prettyboy was safely home. Outside the wind blew and the snow formed drifts around the hogan.

In the morning, KinŁichíi'nii Bitsí was sick—feverish and dizzy. She didn't get up and they fed her blue corn mush and weak Navajo tea to drink. She slept most of the day and felt very warm. Her family began to worry. The nearest medical doctor was in Shiprock, fifty miles to the east. On horseback, it was a full day's journey. Even then, the doctor was at the agency only two days a week, and they couldn't remember which days he was there. A medicineman lived nearby on the mountainside, and they decided to wait until morning to go over there and alert him, if they had to. She would get better, they said, and they prayed and sang songs for strength and for the children. Very late that night, she became very ill and talked incessantly about her children and grandchildren.

She died before morning, and Prettyboy went out into the snow and blowing wind to tell other relatives who lived at distances from the hogan of KinŁichíi'nii Bitsí. People gathered quickly despite the snow; they came from all around to help out with the next four days.

Nineteen hundred sixty-eight. The granddaughter of KinŁichíi'nii Bitsí said:

My Uncle Prettyboy died today, and we went over to his house. His aunt, my grandma, was sweeping out her hogan next door and scolding the young people for not helping out. They were listening to the radios in their pickups and holding hands. You know, they are teenagers. My grandma is 104 years old. My real grandma, Kinlichíi'nii Bitsí, would have been 106 if she hadn't died in the 1930s. I know a lot about her through stories they told me. I know how she was. I think I'm like her in some ways.

At Prettyboy's house, his wife and children were sitting in the front room, and people came in and spoke to them quietly. They were crying and crying; sometimes loudly, sometimes sobbing. In the kitchen, and outside over open fires, we were cooking and preparing food for everyone who had come following his death.

Prettyboy was a tall man and he died of cancer. It was awful because he didn't even smoke. But he had worked in the uranium mines near Red Valley, like many other Navajo men, and was exposed to radioactive materials.

Last week when we were hoeing in the field, my mother told me, "Having a mother is everything. Your mother is your home. When children come home, the mother is always ready with food, stories, and songs for the little ones. She's always happy to see her children and grandchildren."

She had always told me this as I was growing up. That day when we were hoeing corn, I asked her, "Tell me about my grandmother and how you knew something was wrong that time. Tell me the story, shima."

She told me, saying:

That night Prettyboy was coming home, I knew something was wrong. The wind blew hard and roared through the tall pine trees. We lived in the mountains at Oak Springs, ten miles above where my mother lived. We were just married then. Our first baby, your oldest sister, was a month old.

That night the dogs started barking wildly and loudly; they were afraid of something. Then they stopped suddenly. Your father and I looked at each other across the room. Then we heard the coyotes barking and yelping outside. He opened the door and they were circling the hogan, running around and around, yelping the whole time. Your father grabbed the rifle and shot at the coyotes, but he missed each time. He missed. He had been a sharpshooter in the army, and he couldn't shoot them. Finally, they ran off, and we were both afraid. We talked and prayed into the night. We couldn't go anywhere. The snow was deep, and even the horses would have a hard time.

In the morning, I went out to pray and I saw my brother, Prettyboy, riding up to our hogan. He was still far away, but even then, I knew something had happened. I tried not to cry, but I knew in my bones something had happened. My brother would not ride out in that weather just to visit. Even though the sun was out, the snow was frozen, and the wind blew steadily. I held the baby and prayed, hoping I was wrong.

Finally, as he came up to our hogan, I went out and I could see that he was crying. He wasn't watching where he was going. The horse led my brother who was crying. I watched him, and then he saw me. I called out, "Shínaaí, my older brother!" He got off the horse and ran to me, crying out, "Shideezhí, nihimá adin. My younger sister, our mother's gone!" My heart fell. We cried. The wind stopped blowing and we went inside.

I held my baby girl and told her she would not see her grandmother. Neither would our other children. My mother died, and I realized that she was my home.

She had always welcomed us, and since I was the youngest, she called me "baby." "Even if you are a grandmother, you will be my baby always," she often said to me.

When my mother told this story, we always cried. Even if I had known KinLichíi'nii Bitsî, I couldn't love her more than I do now—knowing her only through stories and my mother's memory.

My grandmother had talked to my father about a week before she died. She told him, "Take care of her. She is my youngest, my baby. I trust you, and I have faith that you will care for her as I have all these years. She is my baby, but she knows what to do. Listen to her and remember that a woman's wisdom is not foolish. She knows a lot, because I have raised her to be a good and kind person."

My father listened, and he treats my mother well. He listens to her and abides by her wishes.

Nineteen hundred eighty-seven. The great-granddaughter of KinLichíi'nii Bitsí said:

Early in the morning, we went out to pray. The corn pollen drifted into the swimming pool, becoming little specks of yellow on the blue water. The water lapped quietly against the edges. We prayed and asked the holy ones and my ancestors who died before to watch over me.

I was going so far away to Europe. What a trip it would be. My grandma called the evening before I left and said, "Remember who you are. You're from Oak Springs, and all your relatives are thinking about you and praying that you will come back safely. Do well on your trip, my little one." I was nervous and couldn't sleep. I felt like changing my mind, but my mother had already spent all that money. She promised she wouldn't cry at the airport, then she did. I know that my little sister teased her about it.

I put the bag of pollen in my purse. At La Guardia Airport, I went to the bathroom and tasted some. My mother, I thought, my grandmother, help me. Everything was confusing and loud, so many people smoking and talking loudly. I wanted my mother's soft, slow voice more than anything. I was the only Indian in the group, and no one knew how I felt. The other girls were looking at boys and giggling.

At least I had the corn pollen. I was afraid they would arrest me at customs for carrying an unknown substance, but they didn't. I knew I was meant to go to Paris.

I prayed on top of the Eiffel Tower, and the pollen floated down to the brick plaza below. I was so far away from home, so far above everything. The tower swayed a bit in the wind. I never missed Indians until I went abroad. I was lonely to see an Indian the whole time. People thought I was "neat"—being a "real" Indian. They asked all kinds of questions and wanted to learn Navajo. It was weird to be a "real" Indian. All along, I was just regular, one of the bunch, laughing with relatives and friends, mixing Navajo and English. We were always telling jokes about cowboys, computer warriors, and stuff.

It was while I stood on top of the Eiffel Tower that I understood that who I am is my mother, her mother, and my great-grandmother, KinLichíi'nii Bitsí. It was she who made sure I got through customs and wasn't mugged in Paris. When I returned, my grandmother was at the airport. She hugged me tightly. My mother stood back, then came forward and held me. I was home.

In 1864

In 1864, 8,354 Navajos were forced to walk from Dinetah to Basque Redondo in southern New Mexico, a distance of three hundred miles. They were held for four years until the U.S. government declared the assimilation attempt a failure. More than 2,500 died of smallpox and other illnesses, depression, severe weather conditions, and starvation. The survivors returned to Dinetah* in June of 1868.

While the younger daughter slept, she dreamt of mountains,
the wide blue sky above, and friends laughing.

We talked as the day wore on. The stories and highway beneath
became a steady hum. The center lines were a blurred guide.
As we neared the turn to Fort Sumner,† I remembered this story:

A few winters ago, he worked as an electrician on a crew
installing power lines on the western plains of New Mexico.
He stayed in his pickup camper, which was connected to a generator.
The crew parked their trucks together and built a fire in the center.
The nights were cold and there weren't any trees to break the wind.
It snowed off and on, a quiet, still blanket. The land was like
he had imagined from the old stories—flat and dotted with shrubs.
The arroyos and washes cut through the soft dirt.
They were unsuspectingly deep.
During the day, the work was hard and the men were exhausted.
In the evenings, some went into the nearby town to eat and drink
a few beers. He fixed a small meal for himself and tried to relax.
Then at night, he heard cries and moans carried by the wind
and blowing snow. He heard the voices wavering and rising
in the darkness. He would turn over and pray, humming songs
he remembered from his childhood. The songs returned to him
as easily as if he had heard them that very afternoon.
He sang for himself, his family, and the people whose spirits
lingered on the plains, in the arroyos, and in the old windswept plants.
No one else heard the thin wailing.
After the third night, he unhooked his camper, signed his time card,
and started the drive north to home. He told the guys,
"Sure, the money's good. But I miss my kids and it sure gets lonely
out here for a family man." He couldn't stay there any longer.
The place contained the pain and cries of his relatives,
the confused and battered spirits of his own existence.

* "Dinetah" means "Navajo country" or "homeland of The People."
†Fort Sumner was also called "Bosque Redondo" owing to its location.

After we stopped for a Coke and chips, the storytelling resumed:

My aunt always started the story saying, "You are here
because of what happened to your great-grandmother long ago."

They began rounding up the people in the fall.
Some were lured into surrendering by offers of food, clothes,
and livestock. So many of us were starving and suffering
that year because the bilagáana* kept attacking us.
Kit Carson and his army had burned all the fields,
and they killed our sheep right in front of us.
We couldn't believe it. I covered my face and cried.
All my life, we had sheep. They were like our family.
It was then I knew our lives were in great danger.
We were all so afraid of that man, Redshirt,* and his army.
Some people hid in the foothills of the Chuska Mountains
and in Canyon de Chelly. Our family talked it over,
and we decided to go to this place. What would our lives
be like without sheep, crops, and land? At least, we thought
we would be safe from gunfire and our family would not starve.

The journey began, and the soldiers were all around us.
All of us walked, some carried babies. Little children and the elderly
stayed in the middle of the group. We walked steadily each day,
stopping only when the soldiers wanted to eat or rest.
We talked among ourselves and cried quietly.
We didn't know how far it was or even where we were going.
All that was certain was that we were leaving Dinetah, our home.
As the days went by, we grew more tired, and soon,
the journey was difficult for all of us, even the military.
And it was they who thought all this up.

We had such a long distance to cover.
Some old people fell behind, and they wouldn't let us go back to help them.
It was the saddest thing to see—my heart hurts so to remember that.
Two women were near the time of the births of their babies,
and they had a hard time keeping up with the rest.
Some army men pulled them behind a huge rock, and we screamed out
loud
when we heard the gunshots. The women didn't make a sound,
but we cried out loud for them and their babies.
I felt then that I would not live through everything.
When we crossed the Rio Grande, many people drowned.
We didn't know how to swim—there was hardly any water deep enough
to swim in at home. Some babies, children, and some of the older men
and women were swept away by the river current.

*"Bilagáana" is the Navajo word for Anglos.
*Kit Carson's name was "Redshirt" in Navajo.

We must not ever forget their screams and the last we saw of them—
hands, a leg, or strands of hair floating.

There were many who died on the way to Hwééldi.* All the way
we told each other, "We will be strong as long as we are together."
I think that was what kept us alive. We believed in ourselves
and the old stories that the holy people had given us.
"This is why," she would say to us. "This is why we are here.
Because our grandparents prayed and grieved for us."

The car hums steadily, and my daughter is crying softly.
Tears stream down her face. She cannot speak. Then I tell her that
it was at Bosque Redondo the people learned to use flour and now
fry bread is considered to be the "traditional" Navajo bread.
It was there that we acquired a deep appreciation for strong coffee.
The women began to make long, tiered calico skirts
and fine velvet shirts for the men. They decorated their dark velvet
blouses with silver dimes, nickels, and quarters.
They had no use for money then.
It is always something to see—silver flashing in the sun
against dark velvet and black, black hair.

This Is How They Were Placed for Us

I

HayooLkáaLgo Sisnaajiní nihi neL'iih Leh.
Blanca Peak is adorned with white shell.
Blanca Peak is adorned with morning light.
She watches us rise at dawn.
Nidoohjeeh shá'áLchíní, nii leh.
Get up, my children, she says.

She is the brightness of spring.
She is Changing Woman returned.
By Sisnaajiní, we set our standards for living.
Bik'ehgo da'iiná.

Because of her, we think and create.
Because of her, we make songs.
Because of her, the designs appear as we weave.

*Hwééldi is the Navajo name for Fort Sumner.

Reprinted from *Blue Horses Rush In*, (1997), by permission of University of Arizona.

Because of her, we tell stories and laugh.
We believe in old values and new ideas.
HayooLkáaLgo Sisnaajiní bik'ehgo hózhónígo naashá.

II

This is how they were placed for us.
ALní' ní' áago Tsoo dziL ánii Leh, "Da'oosá, shá'áLchíní."
In the midday sunlight, Mount Taylor tells us,
"It's time to eat, my little ones."
She is adorned with turquoise.
She is adorned with lakes that sparkle in the sunlight.
Jó 'éí biniinaa nihitah yá'áhoot'ééh.
Tsoo dziL represents our adolescence.
Mount Taylor gave us turquoise to honor all men,
thus we wear turquoise to honor our brothers,
we wear turquoise to honor our sons,
we wear turquoise to honor our fathers.
Because of Tsoo dziL, we do this.

We envision our goals as we gaze southward.
Each summer, we are reminded of our own strength.
T'áá hó' ájít' iigo t'éiya dajinii Leh.
Tsoo dziL teaches us to believe in all ways of learning
ALní' ní' áago TsoodziL bik'ehgo hózhónígo naashá.

III

This is how they were placed for us.
E'e'aahjigo, Dook'o'oosLiíd sida.
To the west, the San Francisco Peaks are adorned with abalone.
Each evening she is majestic.
She is adorned with snow.
She is adorned with the white light of the moon.

The San Francisco Peaks represent the autumn of our lives.
Asdzání dahiniLníí doo.
Dinééh dahiniLníí doo.
In the autumn of our lives,
they will call us woman.
In the autumn of our lives,
they will call us man.

The San Francisco Peaks taught us to believe in strong families.
Dook'o'oosLiíd binahji' danihidziiL.
The San Francisco Peaks taught us to value our many relatives.
E'e'aahjígo Dook'o'oosLiíd bik'ehgo hózhónígo naashá.

IV

This is how they were placed for us.
ChahaLheeLgo Dibé Nitsaa, "Da'oLwosh, shá'áLchíní," níi Leh.
From the north, darkness arrives—Hesperus Peak—
urges us to rest. "Go to sleep, my children," she says.
She is adorned with jet.
She is our renewal, our rejuvenation.
Dibé Nitsaa binahji' laanaa daniidzin Leh.
Hesperus Peak taught us to have hope for good things.

Haigo sáanii, dahiniLníí doo.
Haigo hastóíí, dahiniLíí doo.
In the winter of our life, they will call us elderly woman.
In the winter of our life, they will call us elderly man.
In the winter of our life, we will be appreciated.
In the winter of our life, we will rest.
ChahaLheeLgo Dibé Nitsaa bik'ehgo hózhónígo naashá.
This is how the world was placed for us.
In the midst of this land, Huerfano Mountain
is draped in precious fabrics.
Her clothes glitter and sway in the bright sunlight.
Gobernador Knob is clothed in sacred jewels.
She wears mornings of white shell.
She wears the midday light of turquoise.
She wears evenings of abalone, the light of the moon.
She wears nights of black jet.

This is how they were placed for us.
We dress as they have taught us,
adorned with precious jewels
and draped in soft fabrics.

All these were given to us to live by.
These mountains and the land keep us strong.
From them, and because of them, we prosper.

With this we speak,
with this we think,
with this we sing,
with this we pray.

This is where our prayers began.

Blue Horses Rush In

For Chamisa Bah Edmo,
who was born March 6, 1991

Before the birth, she moved and pushed inside her mother.
Her heart pounded quickly and we recognized the sound of horses running:

the thundering of hooves on the desert floor.

Her mother clenched her fists and gasped.
She moans ageless pain and pushes: This is it!

Chamisa slips out, glistening wet and takes her first breath.
The wind outside swirls small leaves
and branches in the dark.
Her father's eyes are wet with gratitude.
He prays and watches both mother and baby—stunned.

This baby arrived amid a herd of horses,
horses of different colors.

White horses ride in on the breath of the wind.
White horses from the west
where plants of golden chamisa shimmer in the moonlight.
She arrived amid a herd of horses.
Yellow horses enter from the east
bringing the scent of prairie grasses from the small hills outside.
She arrived amid a herd of horses.

Blue horses rush in, snorting from the desert in the south.
It is possible to see across the entire valley to Niist'áá from Tó.
Bah, from here your grandmothers went to war long ago.

She arrived amid a herd of horses.

Black horses came from the north.
They are the lush summers of Montana and still white winters of Idaho.

Chamisa, Chamisa Bah. It is all this that you are.
You will grow: laughing, crying,
and we will celebrate each change you live.

You will grow strong like the horses of your past.
You will grow strong like the horses of your birth.

Luis Alberto Urrea

Although Luis Alberto Urrea was born in Tijuana, Mexico, he was raised from the age of three in San Diego, California. Because his father was from Mexico and his mother from the United States, he grew up fluent in both languages and cultures. For about ten years, he did relief work on the Mexican Border with San Diego's Spectrum Ministries, a Protestant Organization. He began writing about this work for the San Diego Reader *and later further documented it in his critically acclaimed book* Across the Wire: Life and Hard Times on the Mexican Border. *This book, which combines investigative reporting with vivid and powerful storytelling, is the first of his border trilogy.* By the Lake of Sleeping Children: The Secret Life of the Mexican Border, *the second book of the trilogy, published in 1996, is a passionate argument in response to NAFTA and California's Proposition 187. The third book of the trilogy,* Nobody's Son: Notes from an American Life, *is a memoir that was published by University of Arizona Press in 1998. In all of his work, Urrea gives us the opportunity to see border issues from unfamiliar angles. In his introduction to* By the Lake of Sleeping Children, *he says, "If, as some have suggested lately, I am some sort of 'voice of the border,' it is because the border runs down the middle of me. I have a barbed-wire fence neatly bisecting my heart." In this excerpt of* Nobody's Son, *he recounts stories from his childhood.*

Nobody's Son

III

How is this for a name: Aethelberht Urias of the Visigoths.

It doesn't sound too Mexican, whatever *Mexican* is.

Aethelberht Urias begat Hlutwig Aethelberht Urias of the Visigoths. From Old German, Hlutwig means "famous warrior." Note to the Nazis: mine is a truly Aryan name. Hlutwig—Ludwig—Louis—Luis. Me.

If you trace the Urrea bloodline back far enough, you find that our Aryan looks are attributed to the Visigoths, when they entered Spain and generously dispersed gallons of genetic material in every burning village. And one of the Visigoth warriors who blitzed our part of Spain, siring many blond ancestors of mine, was Urias. Urias—Uria—Urria—Urrea.

It confuses me too, Homes. Here I am, a Luis Alberto, a *greaser,* and I still could have been enrolled in the SS. Did I tell you about the border patrol truck idling between my ribs?

My cousin is Apache. My other cousin is Mayo. My second cousin is black. My niece is German. One branch of the Urreas is Chinese. Other Urreas claim to be Basques. One great-grandmother was Tarascan. As I mentioned above, my paternal grandmother was a Murray—Irish. My cousins are Hubbards. Somebody tell me, please, what a Mexican is.

Mexico—the true melting pot.

We called Dad "Papa." All of us—his kids from his first marriage, my cousins, my mother, and me.

He came out of a small yet famous mining town in the south of Sinaloa. It was called Rosario, and it slumbered on the banks of the Baluarte River, beneath the strange profile of a mountain called El Yauco. My uncle always swore there was a town nearby called Palo Cagado, which means, I'm afraid, "shit on a stick."

Students of magic realism in graduate school today need only to live in a small Mexican town for a few weeks. They will soon see that this mad literary genre is based on truth. My father's memories were full of ghosts, natural catastrophes, demons, miracles, weird sex, weirder pranks, floods, appalling deaths, flying saucers, Indian spirits, and tall tales. Rosario had, for example, a self-proclaimed Practical Joke King of All Mexico. This man—Pancho Mena—terrorized the town for decades with ever more elaborate stunts. His masterpiece was a hog's head barrel suspended over the town square on a web work of ropes. In the barrel, several hundred pounds of feces collected from his outhouse. Inside the feces, a charge of dynamite with a time fuse.

My father was present when the bomb exploded. It had been timed to blow right at 7:00 A.M., when everyone who was on the way to market would have been in the square and stopped to gawk at the levitating barrel. My father was behind an adult when the barrel blew, but he remembers peeking around the man's side and being hit in the face, as if by a noxious cream pie.

Mena never saw this *tour de force,* since he had wisely boarded the dawn train for the north, never to return.

One summer, when I was living in Rosario, spending many idle boyhood hours hunting iguanas and snapping turtles, eating mangos fresh off the tree, I spent some time with my father's first girlfriend. She was famous in family lore as his lost love. She didn't call him "Papa"; she called him "Beto."

One day, she showed me a mountain with a cleft in it. She—like many Sinaloans, not at all afraid of crude speech—informed me it was known as "La Pucha," The Pussy. I stared at it, thinking, *So that's what they look like!* Inside La Pucha's caves, supposedly there was a rope that dangled out of a sheer rock wall. This was because the Spanish monks from Rosario had hidden their vast treasure of gold bars in the cave, then either died of mysterious afflictions, committed suicide, or were murdered. Their ghastly spirits still wandered the cave, often leading explorers to the gold—*but the explorers never found the gold again when they went back to collect it.* One expedition reasoned that a rope, played out behind them, would give them an easy egress from the treasure chamber. When they didn't return, rescuers followed them *and found the rope sticking out of a blank rock wall!* The other side of La Pucha was round—it featured two wooded hills meeting in a deep vertical crack. "Guess what we call this side," she said.

My father, fully steeped in Rosario's occult atmosphere, swore that the angry spirit of an Indian warrior pursued him through time. He had stolen several Aztec figurines when he was working for the president. (I have one of them still—it's a thick bead covered in small designs.) And the warrior wanted them back.

My father dreaded this spirit. It rapped on his bedroom furniture and woke him several times a night. It appeared to him in dreams. It shook him awake.

One night, he came for me well after midnight. He whispered, "Come in my room." I followed him down the hall and into his bedroom. "Touch the bed," he said. I put my hand on it. The bed was vibrating, jumping up and down as if alive. "I told you," Papa said, "that he was after me."

He was my hero and my greatest source of terror.

He was brilliant and kindhearted, and at times painfully funny. His wit was such that you couldn't tell if he was putting you on or not. When I was little, for example, he would insist that cows were horses, and horses, cows. With a perfectly straight face, he would argue the point with me until I was exasperated. He never relented. On another occasion, he brought home Mexican translations of *The Iliad* and *The Odyssey.* He claimed it was time for me to study them "in their original Spanish."

He was always a great storyteller.

On car trips, he delighted in constructing a Paul Bunyanesque alternate history of my grandfather's exploits. The Painted Desert was painted by my grandfather, for example. The bubbling "paint pots" of Yellowstone were heated by my grandfather. The Grand Canyon was excavated by my grandfather sometime around 1936—he carried the dirt and rocks out in buckets, and he used the mounds to build the Sierras.

He delighted in the foolishness of others. One of his favorite jokes (he was a walking library of off-color jokes) was about a Mexican sleeping in the shade behind a donkey. An American came by and asked him, "What time is it?" The Mexican reached up and lifted the donkey's testicles, looking under them. "It's noon," he said. Astounded, the American said, "Could you check again?" The Mexican reached up, took the donkey's testicles in hand, lifted, and peeked again. "Twelve-oh-one," he said. The American thought this was sheer magic, an ancient Mexican ritual. He rushed to get his wife. When they got back to the Mexican, the man said, "Excuse me, but could you tell my wife what time it is?" The Mexican repeated the lifting ritual and said, "Five minutes after twelve." Overcome with awe, the American fell to his knees and said, "Please, you must teach me this occult mystery! How do you do it?" The Mexican looked up at him, then gestured for the American to join him on the ground. "You see," he said, "I reach up here and lift the donkey's balls. Then I can look under his belly at the clock tower across the street. It's twelve-ten."

Americans often got the worst of my father's jokes.

* * *

"Oh Papa!" Mom would say when he told one of his stories. They slept apart, in separate bedrooms. They sat sometimes in the living room, chatting, smoking. And sometimes they towered far above me, laughing, their heads lost in blue-white clouds of smoke. Sometimes, they'd even start to reach for each other, almost embrace. But they'd stop. Look away. Leave the room. Mom would go to the kitchen. Papa would go bowling, or put on a record album with the turntable set at 45 rpms. The squeaky, sped-up voices of Vaughn Monroe or Pedro Infante would knock me to the floor, laughing.

These were the best moments.

But Papa was also consumed by rage. A burning, purple rage. Nobody knew what caused it, and nobody could predict what would set it off. Sometimes he would just explode—seem to open his chest and let a roar escape that shook the windows. At other times, he would turn cold, harsh, mechanical in his anger. This was more frightening than his eruptions.

And always, the stories. He never stopped telling stories. When the rage was upon him, he would betray my mother by telling his first wife that she staggered around the house swilling whiskey from a bottle of Jack Daniels, so drunk she couldn't make the beds. In our home, however, he would betray his first wife by telling my mother that she picked lice out of her hair, cracking them on her dirty thumbnails, or flicking them away into a corner, there to join the other vermin.

He had a favorite dog, Palito. Palito lived at my grandmother's house in Tijuana. My father adored this old dog—saved Fritos for him, loved for him to sit on his feet as he watched television. Still, one day, for no apparent reason, he drop-kicked Palito down a flight of stairs and walked away, unflustered. Later, in San Diego, neighbors were appalled to see him kicking our new dog down the street, kicking him as they ran, until they were out of sight. The dog screaming all the way.

The Machine appeared when I was to learn anything that a macho man should know how to do. Riding a bike, for example. He said to me one day when I was in first grade, "Do you want to learn to ride a bike like a real man? Get rid of these." He gestured at the training wheels, which he hated. He had called me "Pussy" once, when I'd rattled past.

Of course I wanted to please him. He was Papa! So I said yes, and he immediately broke out a tool and undid the training wheels. Balancing me on the bike seat, in the middle of the street, with cars rushing by beside us, he said, "Ready?"

"Yeah!" I cried.

And we started to run. I felt like I was flying, with Papa's strong hands holding me upright. Until he let go.

I flew down the street. Not very far. It couldn't have been far at all. And I tumbled, sliding on the blacktop, crashing into the curb. Cars honked. I started to cry, but I realized it was a mistake. "Get up," he said. I stopped crying right away. We did it again. I was a little bloodied after the second crackup. "Again," he said. And, "Otra vez."

It may not have been tender, but I learned to ride the bike. It only took about five crashes to get it. I suddenly knew that either I'd learn to ride it, or he'd keep at it until I was knocked out or the bike broken. It didn't matter which—a lesson, some sort of lesson, would have been learned. I am still guessing about his lessons.

I suspect they had something to do with that peculiar and sometimes lamentable state called "manhood." Whatever that is.

He was ashamed that I was afraid of the waves at the beach. He enlisted the aid of another man, and they took me to the ocean and carried me into the water. I begged them not to do it. They laughed. The harder I fought, the more they laughed. They had me by the hands and feet, and they swung me back and forth, counting, "One! Two! Three!" and throwing me into the oncoming waves. The water drove me under, sand up my nose.

When I crawled out on the beach, they'd be there, waiting. Laughing. I would begin to beg again, crying; I even ran, but I couldn't outrun them. And he'd always tell me I should learn to stop crying. Maybe if I had refused to beg for mercy, they would have let me go.

Because I cried easily, he always volunteered to take me to the dentist. It would be better with Papa there was the line my mother bought. And Tijuana would be a better place for dental work because it was cheaper. We were poor. It made sense to Phyl.

The dentist was a man from Sinaloa, and he apparently had the same ethic of masculinity as my father. They agreed to work on my teeth without an anesthetic, with my father in the room. The drill wailed in my mouth, the pain forever equated in my mind with the smell of my smoking teeth. The dentist's breath. And my father staring over his shoulder. "Be a *man,* God damn it," my father said.

When I cried, they both yelled at me, using the word that, in their language, translated as "asshole."

"He wasn't always bitter," Papa's first wife told me. "He was sweet. He was sweet and innocent. He never cursed, never misbehaved. Something happened to him."

He was tight-lipped about what happened. I caught glimpses of his story, but often from others, witnesses or those who heard from a friend of a friend. My father was the superstar of his own life. They talk about "Beto" still—about his jokes, his music (he played piano and organ), his adventures, his bowling, his women. If you had a wife, and my father entered your house, chances were he'd have made some sort of significant contact with her that would leave her touched and intrigued. Often, women fell in love with him at their first meeting. And my father would find a way to come back to see them. He could wait ten years to collect on their infatuations.

I never knew the legendary dapper Mexican officer. The Papa I knew best worked all night in bowling alleys. My hero, dusting bowling shoes with Quinsana foot powder and renting them to winos. Or waxing the lanes with a long-handled dust mop. Or sitting in the deafening roar of the walkways behind the big Brunswick pin-tending machines. I can see him there now, under the sole lightbulb, bent over a *Playboy,* smoking his Pall Malls. He also hid nudist magazines back there. I was enthralled by the absurd photographs of middle-aged volleyball players, caught in midair, breasts and privates flapping. He liked this stuff. He wanted me to know all about it.

I still remember a book he gave me. It was called *Diary of a Dirty Old Man.* It was about masturbating in every imaginable situation. Perhaps one reason he was so interested in printed, two-dimensional sex was because Mom would have none of it. Sex seemed to scare her almost as much as her worst terror, snakes. I could make her shudder just by saying "rattlesnake." If I said "python," she would actually cry out and leave the room.

"Sex" wasn't as bad as snakes. She delighted in James Bond's exploits with the "Bond girls." She just didn't want me to ever come near the evil deed. And the idea of sex with Papa . . . well.

One day, I got home from school to find her in a fury. She had a way of going wild—her hair would be in disarray and she would have a crazy gleam in her eye. She'd purse her lips, as though she were about to whistle. There was no reasoning with her in those moments.

She dragged me into his room and tore the mattress off the bed. *Oh-oh,* I thought. I couldn't believe she'd found his stash of "naughty" magazines. What was she doing lifting his mattress? He made his own bed—we were not often welcome in his room.

My mother ranted and raved, waving the magazines in front of my face. They were all low-rent nudie rags, third raters like *Pix* and *Adam* and *Knight.* All I remember her saying is the phrase, "I can understand *Playboy,* but not this FILTH!" I kept hearing that word: filth. She dragged me into the back yard, where she had a bonfire going. She tore the books and magazines apart—including the *Diary*—and threw them into the fire. She seemed insane with rage. Yelling in my face, as if I had written the things, as if the pictures were all my idea. She emptied his room of any trace of nude women, but when he came home, he didn't mention a thing. Neither did she. We all kept quiet, and there was never any mention of it again.

What happened to him? There were rumors that he suffered a serious head injury while deep in the silver mines of Rosario; others tell me this didn't happen at all. Once, he told me he'd seen a terrible accident in the mines. "I had to hold a man down when I was fourteen," he told me. "They sawed his leg off."

Rumors that his first lost love enraged him at a party by dancing with another, and my father, drunk and insane with jealousy, stole his first wife and rode away with her on a horse. Or not. Whatever happened, they were married. They had six children—one died at birth. Then he fell in love with his cousin, and the marriage ended.

He told me that the president of Mexico kept a black DC-3 airplane in a secret hangar in Mexico City. When political enemies of the PRI party were caught, the plane flew them out to the Pacific. It returned empty. He said he sometimes flew DC-3s. Was he on these flights? He never said.

Finally, what brought him to the border? Survivors say he came north to try to reconnect with that cousin. She is portrayed as a dragon lady who used my father and then cast him off. When he realized that he had been played for a fool, he married my mother on the rebound. That's their story.

His story was considerably different. He told me that after years of service to the president, he had accrued a great deal of trust and influence in the Mexican government. One day, the president of Mexico called him in to a private meeting. Papa would never tell me what was said. It still upset him. The only things he ever told me, and he said them many times over the years, were that they asked him to do something he could not do, and that they had paid him $2,000 in American money. This was quite a lot of money in Mexico City in 1951.

Relatives who heard this tale didn't believe me. Then, when he died, I was put in charge of sifting through his things. In a shoebox, mixed in with his papers and old government documents, was an uncashed check. It was made out to Alberto Urrea Murray. It was for $2,000. It was signed by the president of Mexico.

Nothing broke my father. Except for the U.S. He couldn't find his footing here. He couldn't rise again, and he knew it. He tried many jobs—busboy, cannery worker, bakery truck driver. I often think he settled on bowling alleys because he was the most erudite man there, even if he was a greaser. Al was the smart one. Al was the one who read. Al was the lover who swept Norma and all the other burgerbar waitresses off their feet with sweet Spanish, love songs, and his looks.

Whenever I think of the bowling alley, I hear Patsy Cline echoing over the lanes. "Crazy" and "I Fall to Pieces" and "Walkin' after Midnight" were the big hits in the Rip Van Winkle Lounge. The old drunks slumped in there among red vinyl booths and blue lights, smoking and staring out of the darkened windows at Papa, manning the main desk like a captain again. And Norma tipping up on her toes to steal a quick kiss, her peach waitress uniform skirt hiking up to reveal the tops of her white stockings, her tender thighs, her petticoat's hem. Maybe it wasn't the drunks. Maybe it was me, sipping a chocolate malt.

What happened? I don't think even he knew. I can tell you what happened to them, what caused the wrong turn. It was Tijuana. It was San Diego. My mother went from aristocratic surroundings to a dirt street in Tijuana, where the Mexicans didn't want her and subjected her to mental cruelties like taking a hammer to her jewelry and cutting her clothes up with shears. And my father went from being a superstar to just another beaner, doing it all legally—green-carded and registered—but still unable to touch the American Dream. Scrubbing the urinals used by white men who were far below him in every way.

Betrayed by life, by the border, by each other, my parents clung to lives they hated. It seems heroic now, looking back.

They managed to carry on when every dream they'd ever had was dashed and scattered.

They even tried to be a family when every possible definition of that word was lost to them.

They tried to be parents when they'd never even had the chance to be children.

He often told people, "Luis is not my son! He is my best friend!"

Whenever he did something, he'd touch me on the head first, for good luck.

He bought me every book and every record I wanted, even sitting through Jimi Hendrix's "Star-Spangled Banner" and saying, "Those are rockets!" as the guitar screamed.

When he met my first steady girlfriend, and I kissed her in front of him, he said, "Don't count your money in front of a pauper."

When he made chili, he went for the world record heartstopping atomic recipe: four pork chops, two large cans of Dennison's chili, refried beans, red onions, chiles, a pound of monterey jack cheese, and a pan of Spanish rice.

He thought pancakes were exotic, and buttermilk or blueberry pancakes drove him mad with lust.

Before he left us, he would sit for hours playing his organ. Clad in blue pajamas, chain smoking, drinking cup after cup of black coffee, he'd play. Over and over, he'd play one song, trying to get it perfect. He'd go into a kind of trance, staring at the wall, or sitting with his head thrown back, eyes closed, smiling vaguely, and oom-pa-pa-ing through "Red Roses for a Blue Lady." He was dreaming, he said, of being the lounge organist in the Rip Van Winkle Room, a glass snifter full of dollar bills, and blonde American women leaning toward him as he played.

At night, he ground his teeth. He ground them so hard that they broke in his mouth. Sometimes he swallowed the pieces. Sometimes he spit them out in the morning. By the time I was in my early teens, every tooth in his mouth was shattered. All that was left was a row of small stumps.

I learned insomnia in our house, between Al and Phyl. She was whimpering and crying out all night. He was snoring and grinding his teeth with a loud cheeping sound. All night, cries and grinding. Not even pillows over my head could keep the noise of their horrible nights out of my ears.

IV

Here's a story about a family that comes from Tijuana and settles into the 'hood, hoping for the American Dream. It's a small picture of a few moves in the chess game of disaster. The family game starting to fall apart from the buried rage and broken souls. I'm not saying it's our story. I'm not saying it isn't. It might be yours.

They lived at 3935 National Avenue.

When she was feeling well, Mother fed the birds on their narrow strip of lawn. She tore chunks from three or four slices of bread, and she and the boy tossed them out in the middle of the grass. Then they watched through the living room window, hiding behind the edge of the venetian blinds, as sparrows, pigeons, and the occasional mockingbird descended to squabble over the food. The boy thought the blinds came from Venus.

Their apartment was in the last building of the development, and the pavement of National Avenue didn't extend to the alley that ran behind their kitchen door. They lived in the lower back corner, in a two-bedroom apartment with a small kitchen/dining alcove and a living room. The boy shared one bedroom with his mother. His father slept in the other room, alone. Outside, there were the kinds of bushes that passed for greenery in Southern California. A dark-leaved hibiscus covered the opening beneath the concrete stairs to the second-story apartments. The boy had his cave there behind the bush. Sometimes, after he'd watched a Hercules movie with his father, he'd climb the outside of the stairway and leap onto the lawn, swinging a plastic sword.

Drunken men sometimes slept on the lawn, dark-skinned skinny men, lying comatose in the creeping sun after some ghetto dance party. On those days, the birds did not come. And the boy watched the men from his window, watched their bony chests rise and fall, watched the stain of urine spread sometimes, watched their fingers curl and their feet twitch as they dreamed. The soles of their feet were yellow, cracked. His mother called them terrible names, and they thought worse things about her but dared not say them.

On the Fourth of July, Dad was usually out with friends, and Mom was too afraid of the neighborhood to walk the mile and a half to the public park for the fireworks. So she'd make popcorn, and she and the boy would climb to the landing halfway up. From there, they could see the colored flashes lighting the sky behind a stand of trees. It looked like lightning inside a cloud, only it was red, violet, yellow, blue. Sometimes, slim puffs of smoke angled out from the tree crowns, and they turned dark before the reflected glow of the explosions. Every once in a while, a bit of the actual fireworks would rise high enough to clear the treetops. It was shocking—like a chunk of the sky catching fire and throwing an ember. Years later, those balmy nights remained precious to him. His mother in her dresses, her dark hair pulled back by a pale headband, flickering in silhouette against the colored sky. She sat primly, knees together, hands in lap, looking over her shoulder. As he stared up at her so lost in the spectacle, she sometimes seemed one hundred feet tall, a sorrowful monument thrown up against the dark.

Burr clover grew all over the lawn. It had tiny yellow flowers, and its tightly rolled burrs could be peeled open if you were patient and careful. You could unroll them, and minuscule yellow-green seeds revealed themselves. The boy often harvested the seeds and put them in his plastic army helmet. Then he'd go to other parts of the lawn and scatter them, trying to make something grow.

There was sourweed in the shade around the base of the biggest bushes. Pill bugs and snails could always be found there, and sometimes beetles. The occasional earwig frightened him—he thought the pincers on their tails meant they were baby scorpions. The pill bugs looked like Volkswagens. He suspected they might be baby armadillos. He picked sourweed stalks and chewed them, his lips puckering at the bitter taste. The black kids said the taste was from dog pee, but he didn't believe them. He was in third grade.

Across the lawn, Their apartments began. *They.*

They had some fuchsias and poinsettias left over from the days of white families, but the lawn was already going yellow between the buildings. The landlords sold out to welfare leases, then promptly stopped attending to their buildings. The boy didn't venture into the further reaches of the complex, but he knew there was a mattress moldering on the lawn at 3930, a broken television set on the walkway at 3929, and a wall coming down at 3925. His father offered reports of each new development when he got home from work.

"There's a God-damned television out there," he'd say. "The first thing they buy is a television."

"Or a Cadillac," Mom said.

"Then they don't know how to take care of them," Dad said.

Mom had decided to block off the stairs. She used potted geraniums—three pots per step, nine in all, because "those people will just walk up to your door and stare in at you. Looking for something to steal."

One day, while they were out, one of Their fathers came up on the porch and broke every pot. The boy's family came home to dirt and fragments of brightly painted clay scattered all over the steps. The little geranium twigs lay murdered in the dirt. They reminded him of broken umbrellas. He stood and watched Mom and Dad clean the mess, afraid less of the violence than of his parents' response to it.

The boy didn't know what Mom did in there when she sent him out to play. The apartment was usually dark—they didn't like the blinds open to let in too much sun. His father was off driving a bread truck.

He'd started out as a waiter. Then he'd worked at Chicken of the Sea canning tuna. He was restless. Nothing suited him. He was small, compact. Supercharged. The boy thought his father's hands had the thickest, strongest fingers in the world.

Now, he was driving a 1961 Chevy panel truck, leased out from Helm's Bakery. It was two-tone—pale yellow with black fenders—and in back there were large wooden drawers full of doughnuts, cookies, pies, cakes. The area directly behind the driver's seat had racks of bread and bins of rolls. On the roof of the cab was a little train whistle, and the driver could pull a chain and the truck would go *woo-woo.*

In spite of his nasty racial views, he couldn't bear to see the poor mothers on his route. Black mothers. He extended so much credit to them that he was going out of business. He drove longer hours, longer miles, and earned less by a dollar or two a day. He was driving himself to bankruptcy. In the afternoons when Mom came home from work, she'd send the boy outdoors. Then she'd go inside and shut the door and stay shut in until six o'clock, when Dad came home.

And the boy would pull himself slowly out of the dusk, into the painful light of the kitchen.

He liked the back of the apartment more than the front. In the front, there was the cave under the stairs. But the back offered poisonous plants. When he was sure Mom wasn't looking, he broke open poinsettia stalks and watched the milk seep out. Everyone said it would kill you. It fascinated him. It smelled bland, like the smell in all the other plants when you crumpled their leaves. It also smelled a little like the black soil beneath the rocks at the edge of the alley. He'd almost let the milk touch his fingers before he pulled them away. Death, right in his hand. He thought it might be like falling asleep.

Then, of course, there was the alley. He delighted in the alley—its wide dirt and rock surface was a wilderness to him, a desert in the middle of the neighborhood. When it rained, he saw swamps, dark King Kong rivers teeming with monsters: he sank his plastic dinosaurs in up to their haunches.

The alley sloped downhill and turned left, behind the row of detached garages. At the far end of the garages was a small washroom with two washing machines and two dryers. Dad had the first garage. When he came home from work, the boy raced to the door and pulled it open. Dad drove in and set the hand brake. He and the boy checked the daddy longlegs that hung upside down beneath the dashboard in its paltry web.

"He's my buddy," Dad said. "My pet."

The boy always liked it when Dad was in his gooder mood. Sometimes Dad had his cranky mood, and the whole house turned dark gray inside and nobody spoke too loud. The gooder mood was full of jokes and Bert Kaempfert records. When Mom was in her cranky mood, they would crash together and everything would be broken, lights out, Dad gone, Mom in bed howling boo-hoos, just like in fairy tales. Boo-hoo!

They walked to the rear of the truck.

"Let's check the inventory," Dad said.

Yep, definitely feeling gooder today.

He opened the big door at the back and pulled open the top drawer. The indelible odor of bakeries escaped: chocolate, cinnamon, dough. In their wax-paper-lined compartments, doughnuts stood on end, tightly packed.

"I don't know . . ." Dad said. "It seems to me the best doughnut ever made is the glazed."

"No, Dad," the boy said. "It's a chocolate-coated."

"What!"

"Really." He pointed at the row of chocolate-coated cake doughnuts, pushed together like the coils of some delicious snake. "The best."

Dad reached in and plucked a huge glazed one out with a square of wax paper.

"But look at this," he said. He turned it like some fine piece of jewelry.

"Chocolate," the boy said.

Dad took out a chocolate doughnut with the other hand.

"No comparison," he said.

"Cho-co-late, Dad," the boy said.

Dad shook his head sadly.

"Well," he sighed. "I suppose we're going to have to taste them." He took a bite of the glazed. "Mf," he said.

The boy grabbed his doughnut from his father and took a bite. The hard chocolate cracked, and the golden fried cake dough broke all over his tongue.

They sat on the back bumper eating their doughnuts, the boy's legs swinging.

"Mine's better," he said.

They got done, slammed the truck door shut, pulled down the garage door, and headed up the alley. It was turning dark. His father smelled of sweat and cigarette smoke. He poked the boy in the gut with one finger and said, "Butterball."

He did not smile.

The boy laughed really loud.

"Wipe your mouth," Dad said. "And don't tell your mother I gave you a doughnut."

The boy's lips, in the gloom, looked like they were covered in blood.

She was in the kitchen heating TV dinners. Dad always ate turkey with gravy. Mom and the boy ate "fried" chicken, with apple cobbler in one triangular compartment. She was cutting lettuce in small pieces for a salad.

Dad put his lunch bucket on the aluminum table and said, "Hi." She kept her back to him. The boy shook a little turtle food into the turtle tank. The yellow-eyed turtle inside was stretched out on the plastic ramp beneath the palm tree. "Don't feed him too much," Dad said. "You'll make him fat."

He rummaged in the fridge.

"Would you like some sherry?" he said, taking a bottle out.

"Oh, a little Thunderbird might be nice," she said.

He put one bottle back, took out another. He filled two small glasses.

"Can I have a sip?" the boy said.

"No," Mom said.

Dad said, "Just a little sip." He winked.

"You want it here or out there?" he said to Mom.

"I'll join you," she said.

"Fine," he said.

She glanced at him.

"Hm," she said.

Dad took a small soup bowl and emptied a bag of Fritos into it. Then he shook a bunch of cashews into the bowl on top of the Fritos.

"I'll carry it," the boy said.

They went into the other room, Dad carrying the glasses, the boy carrying the bowl. They set it all down on a small TV tray table beside Dad's favorite white chair. He sat and said, "Ah."

He shook the last Pall Mall out of the pack on the tray.

"Turn on the TV," he said. "Channel eight. Cronkite."

The boy switched on the television.

Dad lit his cigarette.

There was a small crash in the kitchen.

"Shit," Mom muttered.

"That's nice," said Dad. "Isn't that nice, Son, to talk like that?"

Thinking he was in on a joke, the boy said, "Yeah, Mom. Real nice!"

He and Dad giggled.

Dad gave him a small sip of Thunderbird.

Mom came in and sat in her chair, placed exactly three feet from Dad's. Its feet had made four precise little holes in the carpet. She picked up one Frito with her nails and bit it. Then she sipped her drink. She lit a cigarette.

"Aren't we hilarious?" she said.

Cronkite's brow was furrowed as he reported on Negro unrest and strange developments in Cuba. "President Kennedy," he was saying.

"Rub my feet," Dad said.

The boy sat between his feet and began to unlace Dad's work shoes. They had thick, rippled rubber soles.

"Must you do that before supper?" said Mom.

"He can wash his hands," said Dad.

He worked the shoes off. Dad always wore black socks. He had about twelve pairs of identical black socks. He was never without a match in his sock drawer. Still, he carefully rolled each pair together and kept them neat. When he ended up with an extra sock, he threw it away. The boy rolled his socks down, over Dad's high arches, and off. Dad's feet were white as grubs. His toes were square and stubby. The boy put the socks inside the shoes.

"Get between my toes," Dad said.

The boy massaged Dad's feet, starting on the ball and moving up to the toes then back to the heel. He reached between Dad's toes and peeled out the tattered little flags of skin blistered up by athlete's foot. First the right foot, then the left, pushing in between Dad's toes with his fingertips.

He could tell it felt good.

When things felt good to Dad, he made a little sucking gasp: *Sst-unh. Sst-unh.*

Dad waited till the boy was absorbed by his work, then he snapped his ear. He liked to flick it with one nail when he wasn't expecting it, make the kid jump. Old Jug Ear.

"Ow!" the boy said.

Dad laughed, prodded the boy away with his foot.

"Don't talk back to me," he said.

"Wash your hands," Mom said.

As he ran the water over his hands, he could hear them in there sniping at each other. When he turned the water off, it ended. Like magic.

Dinner was served when he came out. Mom and Dad had their small trays of food set on their TV tables, with saucers of salad. Their glasses full of amber liquid jittered as they cut their food.

His supper was set out on the kitchen table. His napkin was folded in a neat triangle. He ate alone.

Whenever he complained, he was told, "You will learn to eat like a decent human being, at a fully set table."

Mom with her weird little rules.

He stared at the turtle. It stared at him. The batter on the chicken was soggy. It stuck to his mouth. He avoided the compartment with the gray peas and perfectly cubed cooked carrots.

"Drink your milk," Mom said.

"I will."

"Want some bread?" said Dad.

"Would you *like* some bread?" Mom corrected.

"Jesus Christ," muttered Dad.

He could hear him gobbling his food. Dad breathed through his nose as he ate. He sounded like an engine. He ate like a starving dog. Sometimes the way Dad ate scared him.

"Yeah."

"Manners," Mom said. "We won't have our boy speaking like white trash."

"Yes," the boy said. "Please."

Mom came into the kitchen and buttered two slices of bread. She cut the bread diagonally and set it on a saucer, then placed the saucer on the table. She ruffled his hair.

"How's supper, Honey?"

"Fine."

She patted his head.

"That's good." Then, suddenly overcome with emotion, she grabbed him in a desperate hug. Her forearm dug into his throat and choked him.

"My eensie-teensie-weensie baby boy," she said.

She kissed him. He ducked his head away from her. The turtle slid off its ramp and plopped into the water.

"A little more Thunderbird?" Mom called out.

"Don't you think you've had enough?" Dad said.

"Let's not be ridiculous," Mom said. "I've only had one glass. The way you carry on, a person would think you're an old woman!"

The boy turned in his chair and looked at Dad.

Dad was staring at the television, his face red. His jaw muscle worked furiously in his cheek. He took a drag on his cigarette and glanced at his son. He let smoke leak out of his mouth.

"*Eensie-teensie,*" Dad said.

Back to supper. The cobbler was gooey and sweet. He chewed it carefully, in little tiny bites to make it last. The baked cinnamon apple chunks burst between his molars.

Mom poured herself another little glass.

"Papa's going *bowling* tonight," she said brightly. "Doesn't that sound like fun?" She walked out of the kitchen. "I can't imagine a more fascinating evening! So athletic!"

"Have another drink," Dad said. "Show us how sophisticated you are."

"Oh, *Papa!* You have put me in my place."

"Bitch, bitch, bitch," Dad muttered.

On TV the mystery guest was signing his name on a card. The audience applauded wildly.

"Can I come out?" the boy said.

Dad stubbed out his cigarette butt.

"Bring me a new pack when you come," he said.

The boy rummaged under the sink, broke open a red carton, and peeled the cellophane off the new pack. He came out and sat between Dad's legs again. Dad tapped the pack against his knuckle, shaking one cigarette loose.

Dad must have gotten the idea right then—he got those ideas all the time. Real good ones. Creative. He liked to play little pranks, scare his *hijo* a little, toughen him up. Like, when they were up high, on a cliff above the ocean or on a high bridge, Dad liked to grab him and start to throw him off, yanking him back at the last second. The boy fell for it every time. Dad would go "Whoo!" when he did it. The boy would scream.

Pendejo.

Dad was about to strike the match to light his fresh cigarette. He was looking at the back of the boy's head, the flatness of it and the cowlick. The boy's ears drove Dad nuts. Dad put the match on the sandpaper strip, ready to strike it; it had to be perfect for the gag.

"Hey," he said.

"Hub?" said the boy, still staring at the TV.

"Hey. Look."

The boy turned around.

Dad struck the match and thrust it at his face. Mom shouted. Dad said: "Whoo!" The boy, startled, opened his mouth in a gasp. Dad had already started to laugh. The match went between the boy's lips as the sulfur ignited. The match head burst into flame, searing the corner of his mouth. His lips sealed around the flame and stuck together. Dad's eyes widened. The boy clawed at his face, screamed, ran out of the room. Mom knocked over her chair as she ran after him.

"What'd I do?" Dad was shouting.

He sat there in his white chair, waving his cigarette.

"It was a joke, God damn it! What do you think, I did it on purpose?"

He could hear them in the bathroom, making a fuss.

"Stop crying, you baby!"

He ate some Fritos.

"It was a God-damned joke!"

V

"Joke" is a Latin word. "God" is Old English. "Damn" is Latin. "Mother" is Old English, as is "Father," as is "Son."

"Family" is Latin.

"Forgive" is English.

William Carlos Williams, that most American of poets, was half Puerto Rican. "Carlos" wasn't just a New England WASP affectation. He was a Latino, just like me. He was a half-breed, just like me. He was an American. And he said: "Of mixed ancestry, I felt from earliest childhood that America was the only home I could ever possibly call my own. I felt that it was expressedly founded for me, personally, and that it must be my first business in life to possess it."

America is home. It's the only home I have. Both Americas. All three Americas, from the Arctic circle to Tierra del Fuego.

I'm not old enough to write my memoir. Yet I'd feel as if I'd cheated if I didn't try to share some observations. So many of us live in a nightmare of silence. We are sons and daughters of a middle region, nobody's children, marching under a starless flag. Some of us wave a black flag of anarchy, and others a red flag of revolution. But most of us are waving a white flag of surrender.

My life isn't so different from yours. My life is utterly alien compared to yours. You and I have nothing to say to each other. You and I share the same story. I am Other. I am you.

So, I've offered here a few words about my part of the journey. We're all heading the same way, after all. Whether we choose to walk together or separately, we're going toward night. I am lucky. I have the angels of words beside me. So many of us are silent.

Words are the only bread we can really share.

When I say "we," I mean every one of us, everybody, all of you reading this. Each border patrol agent and every trembling Mexican peering through a fence. Every Klansman and each NAACP office worker. Each confused mother and every disappointed dad.

For I am nobody's son.

But I am everyone's brother.

So come here to me.

Walk me home.

Helena María Viramontes

Helena María Viramontes is a professor of creative writing at Cornell University. Her first collection of short stories received wide acclaim for its representations of the lives of Mexican-American women in nontraditional roles.

The Moths, *Viramontes's most widely anthologized short story, is an excellent example of how she pushes the boundaries of Chicana identity and challenges popular stereotypes about Mexican-American women.*

The Moths

I was fourteen years old when Abuelita requested my help. And it seemed only fair. Abuelita had pulled me through the rages of scarlet fever by placing, removing and replacing potato slices on the temples of my forehead; she had seen me through several whippings, an arm broken by a dare jump off Tío Enrique's toolshed, puberty, and my first lie. Really, I told Amá, it was only fair.

Not that I was her favorite granddaughter or anything special. I wasn't even pretty or nice like my older sisters and I just couldn't do the girl things they could do. My hands were too big to handle the fineries of crocheting or embroidery and I always pricked my fingers or knotted my colored threads time and time again while my sisters laughed and called me bull hands with their cute waterlike voices. So I began keeping a piece of jagged brick in my sock to bash my sisters or anyone who called me bull hands. Once, while we all sat in the bedroom, I hit Teresa on the forehead, right above her eyebrow and she ran to Amá with her mouth open, her hand over her eye while blood seeped between her fingers. I was used to the whippings by then.

I wasn't respectful either. I even went so far as to doubt the power of Abuelita's slices, the slices she said absorbed my fever. "You're still alive, aren't you?" Abuelita snapped back, her pasty gray eye beaming at me and burning holes in my suspicions. Regretful that I had let secret questions drop out of my mouth, I couldn't look into her eyes. My hands began to fan out, grow like a liar's nose until they hung by my side like low weights. Abuelita made a balm out of dried moth wings and Vicks and rubbed my hands, shaped them back to size and it was the strangest feeling. Like bones melting. Like sun shining through the darkness of your eyelids. I didn't mind helping Abuelita after that, so Amá would always send me over to her.

Reprinted from *The Moths and Other Stories*, (1995), by permission of Arte Publico Press.

In the early afternoon Amá would push her hair back, hand me my sweater and shoes, and tell me to go to Mama Luna's. This was to avoid another fight and another whipping, I knew. I would deliver one last direct shot on Marisela's arm and jump out of our house, the slam of the screen door burying her cries of anger, and I'd gladly go help Abuelita plant her wild lilies or jasmine or heliotrope or cilantro or hierbabuena in red Hills Brothers coffee cans. Abuelita would wait for me at the top step of her porch holding a hammer and nail and empty coffee cans. And although we hardly spoke, hardly looked at each other as we worked over root transplants, I always felt her gray eye on me. It made me feel, in a strange sort of way, safe and guarded and not alone. Like God was supposed to make you feel.

On Abuelita's porch, I would puncture holes in the bottom of the coffee cans with a nail and a precise hit of a hammer. This completed, my job was to fill them with red clay mud from beneath her rose bushes, packing it softly, then making a perfect hole, four fingers round, to nest a sprouting avocado pit, or the spidery sweet potatoes that Abuelita rooted in mayonnaise jars with toothpicks and daily water, or prickly chayotes that produced vines that twisted and wound all over her porch pillars, crawling to the roof, up and over the roof, and down the other side, making her small brick house look like it was cradled within the vines that grew pear-shaped squashes ready for the pick, ready to be steamed with onions and cheese and butter. The roots would burst out of the rusted coffee cans and search for a place to connect. I would then feed the seedlings with water.

But this was a different kind of help, Amá said, because Abuelita was dying. Looking into her gray eye, then into her brown one, the doctor said it was just a matter of days. And so it seemed only fair that these hands she had melted and formed found use in rubbing her caving body with alcohol and marihuana, rubbing her arms and legs, turning her face to the window so that she could watch the Bird of Paradise blooming or smell the scent of clove in the air. I toweled her face frequently and held her hand for hours. Her gray wiry hair hung over the mattress. Since I could remember, she'd kept her long hair in braids. Her mouth was vacant and when she slept, her eyelids never closed all the way. Up close, you could see her gray eye beaming out the window, staring hard as if to remember everything. I never kissed her. I left the window open when I went to the market.

Across the street from Jay's Market there was a chapel. I never knew its denomination, but I went in just the same to search for candles. I sat down on one of the pews because there were none. After I cleaned my fingernails, I looked up at the high ceiling. I had forgotten the vastness of these places, the coolness of the marble pillars and the frozen statues with blank eyes. I was alone. I knew why I had never returned.

That was one of Apá's biggest complaints. He would pound his hands on the table, rocking the sugar dish or spilling a cup of coffee and scream that if I didn't go to mass every Sunday to save my goddamn sinning soul, then I had no reason to go out of the house, period. Punto final. He would grab my arm and dig his nails into me to make sure I understood the importance of catechism. Did he make himself clear? Then he strategically directed his anger at Amá for her lousy ways of bringing up daughters, being disrespectful and unbelieving, and my older sisters would pull me aside and tell me if I didn't get to mass right this minute, they were all going to kick the holy shit out of me. Why am I so selfish? Can't you see what it's doing to Amá, you idiot? So I should wash my feet and stuff them in my black Easter shoes that shone with Vaseline, grab a missal and veil, and wave good-bye to Amá.

I would walk slowly down Lorena to First to Evergreen, counting the cracks on the cement. On Evergreen I would turn left and walk to Abuelita's. I liked her porch because it was shielded by the vines of the chayotes and I could get a good look at the people and car traffic on Evergreen without them knowing. I would jump up the porch steps, knock on the screen door as I wiped my feet and call Abuelita? mi Abuelita? As I opened the door and stuck my head in, I would catch the gagging scent of toasting chile on the placa. When I entered the sala, she would greet me from the kitchen, wringing her hands in her apron. I'd sit at the corner of the table to keep from being in her way. The chiles made my eyes water. Am I crying? No, Mama Luna, I'm sure not crying. I don't like going to mass, but my eyes watered anyway, the tears dropping on the tablecloth like candle wax. Abuelita lifted the burnt chiles from the fire and sprinkled water on them until the skins began to separate. Placing them in front of me, she turned to check the menudo. I peeled the skins off and put the flimsy, limp looking green and yellow chiles in the molcajete and began to crush and crush and twist and crush the heart out of the tomato, the clove of garlic, the stupid chiles that made me cry, crushed them until they turned into liquid under my bull hand. With a wooden spoon, I scraped hard to destroy the guilt, and my tears were gone. I put the bowl of chile next to a vase filled with freshly cut roses. Abuelita touched my hand and pointed to the bowl of menudo that steamed in front of me. I spooned some chile into the menudo and rolled a corn tortilla thin with the palms of my hands. As I ate, a fine Sunday breeze entered the kitchen and a rose petal calmly feathered down to the table.

I left the chapel without blessing myself and walked to Jay's. Most of the time Jay didn't have much of anything. The tomatoes were always soft and the cans of Campbell soups had rusted spots on them. There was dust on the tops of cereal boxes. I picked up what I needed: rubbing alcohol, five cans of chicken broth, a big bottle of Pine Sol. At first Jay got mad because I thought I had forgotten the money. But it was there all the time, in my back pocket.

When I returned from the market, I heard Amá crying in Abuelita's kitchen. She looked up at me with puffy eyes. I placed the bags of groceries on the table and began putting the cans of soup away. Amá sobbed quietly. I never kissed her. After a while, I patted her on the back for comfort. Finally: "¿Y mi Amá?" she asked in a whisper, then choked again and cried into her apron.

Abuelita fell off the bed twice yesterday, I said, knowing that I shouldn't have said it and wondering why I wanted to say it because it only made Amá cry harder. I guess I became angry and just so tired of the quarrels and beatings and unanswered prayers and my hands just there hanging helplessly by my side. Amá looked at me again, confused, angry, and her eyes were filled with sorrow. I went outside and sat on the porch swing and watched the people pass. I sat there until she left. I dozed off repeating the words to myself like rosary prayers: when do you stop giving when do you start giving when do you . . . and when my hands fell from my lap, I awoke to catch them. The sun was setting, an orange glow, and I knew Abuelita was hungry.

There comes a time when the sun is defiant. Just about the time when moods change, inevitable seasons of a day, transitions from one color to another, that hour or minute or second when the sun is finally defeated, finally sinks into the realization that it cannot with all its power to heal or burn, exist forever, there comes an illumination where the sun and earth meet, a final burst of burning red orange fury reminding us that although endings are inevitable, they are necessary for rebirths, and when that time came, just when I switched on the light in the kitchen to open Abuelita's can of soup, it was probably then that she died.

The room smelled of Pine Sol and vomit and Abuelita had defecated the remains of her cancerous stomach. She had turned to the window and tried to speak, but her mouth remained open and speechless. I heard you, Abuelita, I said, stroking her cheek, I heard you. I opened the windows of the house and let the soup simmer and overboil on the stove. I turned the stove off and poured the soup down the sink. From the cabinet I got a tin basin, filled it with lukewarm water and carried it carefully to the room. I went to the linen closet and took out some modest bleached white towels. With the sacredness of a priest preparing his vestments, I unfolded the towels one by one on my shoulders. I removed the sheets and blankets from her bed and peeled off her thick flannel nightgown. I toweled her puzzled face, stretching out the wrinkles, removing the coils of her neck, toweled her shoulders and breasts. Then I changed the water. I returned to towel the creases of her stretch-marked stomach, her sporadic vaginal hairs, and her sagging thighs. I removed the lint from between her toes and noticed a mapped birthmark on the fold of her buttock. The scars on her back which were as thin as the life lines on the palms of her hands made me realize how little I really knew of Abuelita. I covered her with a thin blanket and went into the bathroom. I washed my hands, and turned on the tub faucets and watched the water pour into the tub with vitality and steam. When it was full, I turned off the water and undressed. Then, I went to get Abuelita.

She was not as heavy as I thought and when I carried her in my arms, her body fell into a V, and yet my legs were tired, shaky, and I felt as if the distance between the bedroom and bathroom was miles and years away. Amá, where are you?

I stepped into the bathtub one leg first, then the other. I bent my knees slowly to descend into the water slowly so I wouldn't scald her skin. There, there, Abuelita, I said, cradling her, smoothing her as we descended, I heard you. Her hair fell back and spread across the water like eagle's wings. The water in the tub overflowed and poured onto the tile of the floor. Then the moths came. Small, gray ones that came from her soul and out through her mouth fluttering to light, circling the single dull light bulb of the bathroom. Dying is lonely and I wanted to go to where the moths were, stay with her and plant chayotes whose vines would crawl up her fingers and into the clouds; I wanted to rest my head on her chest with her stroking my hair, telling me about the moths that lay within the soul and slowly eat the spirit up; I wanted to return to the waters of the womb with her so that we would never be alone again. I wanted. I wanted my Amá. I removed a few strands of hair from Abuelita's face and held her small light head within the hollow of my neck. The bathroom was filled with moths, and for the first time in a long time I cried, rocking us, crying for her, for me, for Amá, the sobs emerging from the depths of anguish, the misery of feeling half born, sobbing until finally the sobs rippled into circles and circles of sadness and relief. There, there, I said to Abuelita, rocking us gently, there, there.

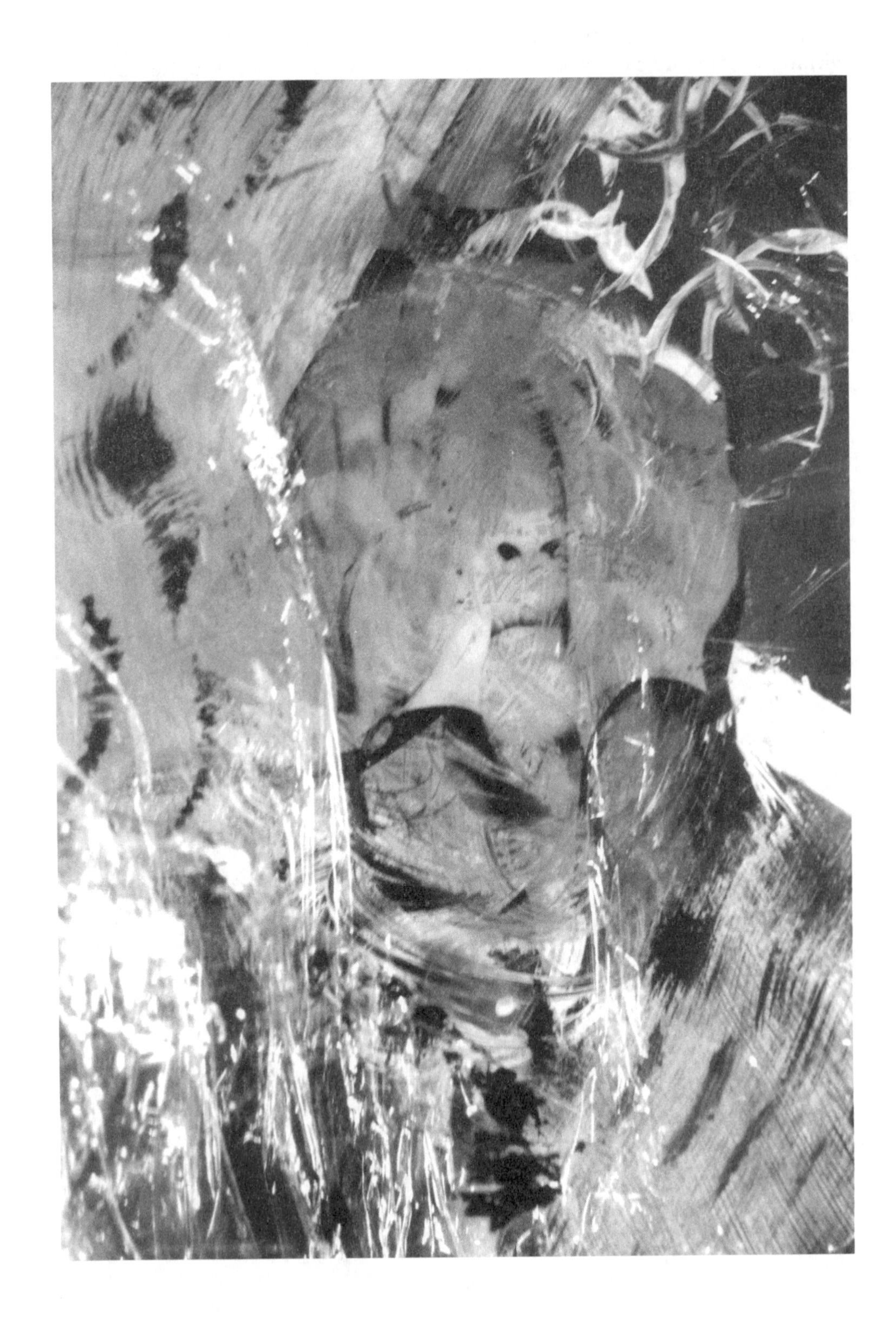

8

Writing as Social Witness

Patty Malesh and Deborah Margolis

My silences had not protected me.
Your silence will not protect you.

—Audre Lorde

I was a witness, not a victim. I was a witness for those who for one reason or another would never have a place of their own, would never have the opportunity to make their lives stable enough because resources weren't available or because they just could not get it together. My job was to witness and record the "it" of their lives, to celebrate those who don't have a place in this world to stand and call home. For those people, my journals, poems, and writing are home. My pen and heart chronicle their hopes, doubts, regrets, loves, despairs, and dreams. I do this partly out of selfishness, because it helps to heal my own impermanence, my own despair. My role as witness is to give voice to the voiceless and hope to the hopeless, of which I am one.

—Jimmy Santiago Baca

'Witnessing' can take many forms. It can be an eyewitness account of a historical event, like the Vietnam War or the tragedies of September 11, 2001. It can be testimony in a courtroom about a crime, a poem about a family secret, or a story that reveals the horrors of everyday life. But to be a witness means more than being an observer, a passive recipient of an experience. To bear witness is to take action—to tell a story, to recreate an event, to reflect on an experience, to alert outsiders to the struggles of particular individuals and communities. It can expose secrets, redefine experience, and change understanding for both speaker and listener. Through witnessing, we learn and develop. When we share a story, especially in writing, it can take on a life of its own. It can influence and be remembered by an audience that transcends the time and place of its author. That story can speak to people across boundaries of time, generation, nationality, class, education, sexuality, and gender.

In "The Necessity to Speak," Sam Hamill explores the importance of bearing witness not only to our private lives, but also to our shared social lives. This is what is meant by "social witness." We cannot separate the public and political world from the private sphere. This kind of writing reaches beyond a mere reiteration of experience and dispels the myth of neutrality. Whether we are participants or witnesses, we are never neutral. Our own perspectives, opinions, biases, values, and culture always inform our actions—even if it is through *inaction* that we take our stand. Ignorance is not an excuse for complacency. As Cassie Premo Steele, in her book *We Heal from Memory,* writes, "We are neither only victims nor only oppressors, but . . . all of us inherit the legacies of a history of violence" (12). Those who bear witness and those who refuse to bear witness are similarly obligated to consider and reconsider their morality and their social responsibility. Because of this, those who bear witness become involved in the processes of meaning making and transforming experience.

What does "bearing witness" mean for us as readers? One way to think about it is that "to witness" means "to participate—not only with the head but with the heart—in the experience of another, an experience so painful that it must be shared in order to be confronted" (Steele 2). Writing as social witness asks you to engage with your heart, soul, and imagination—to allow the unknown, the "other," into yourself (Steele 4-5). The poetry, short stories, and essays in this chapter have the power to transform individual horror and trauma into a common narrative. The words these individuals share with us can show us our connections to each other—our guilt, complicity, wounds, healing potential, common bonds, and saving grace.

As Hamill points out, this knowledge often involves "the loss of innocence" as we struggle to accept our histories, good and bad. This struggle is important, even though storytelling can be risky. As Audre Lorde explains, "the transformation of silence into language and action is an act of self-revelation, and that always seems fraught with danger" (43). By speaking out about even our most painful, personal, and shameful experiences, we expose ourselves to the criticism or, even worse, the apathy of others. Silence, however, is more dangerous. Lorde, a self-proclaimed black woman warrior poet, speaks to the danger of silence:

> We can learn to work and speak when we are afraid in the same way we have learned to work and speak when we are tired. For we have been socialized to respect fear more than our own needs for language and definition, and while we wait in silence for that

> final luxury of fearlessness, the weight of that silence will choke us. (44)

If silence keeps our wounds hidden until they fester and ooze, giving a voice to our pain begins the process of healing. When we share our pain with others, we often discover that we are not alone in our suffering. Identifying our common struggles can comfort us, and it can also allow us to explore those experiences—to make meaning. For Lorde, this means that she has "come to believe over and over again that what is most important to me must be spoken, made verbal and shared, even at the risk of having it bruised or misunderstood" (40). We take risks when we share our experiences with others because we never know if we will be understood or accepted.

By bearing witness, the silent and oppressed are transformed into public figures with agency and voice. In this speaking out, healing is possible. As Steele tells us, witnessing both makes the promise of healing and acknowledges "the breaking of the promise, the hope, that things can return to the way they were before the trauma" (9). She continues:

> Successful witnessing, then, leads to an acknowledgement of many losses: the loss of the experience, the loss of others through death, the loss of a life untouched by trauma, and the loss of the memories and histories of civilizations. (Steele 9-10)

Through literature of witness, we find both a recognition of difference and the possibility of reconciliation and change. Steele concludes with these significant words about witnessing through writing and the healing potential of recognizing the connections between the present and past:

> History may be a solution if we remember, witness, and mourn our traumatic past. The recognition of the problem of memory—that our seemingly most personal, individual memories are not only connected to the collective past but are also shaped by it—is the necessary first step toward our being able to say that, indeed, we heal from memory. The tremendous hope of these writers' visions, then, comes from their courage in remembering the enormous horror of their pasts. To create from horror, to regain the power of hope: these are the promises that arise when we heal from memory. (12)

Borrowing Steele's phrase, the "legacies of different kinds of historical violence" presented in this chapter's selections can show us how we are different from and similar to each other. As we read these texts, we can think about how violence (physical and psychological) arises, who is targeted, and how the manifestations of violence grow out of different histories (Steele 5).

These writings offer us insights about circumstances outside our own, and, more importantly, they complicate experience and demand reflection. These writers have been defined by social circumstance and standards; their writing is an attempt to re-define themselves and their experiences on their own terms. Similarly, these texts help us to realize that how we define ourselves and how others define us is often determined by social circumstance and standards. Language and writing are key in our struggle to survive, heal, and change; we need, as Audre Lorde suggests, a shared "commitment to language and to the power of language" in an attempt to reclaim "that language that has been made to work against us" (43). As the outcasts and the reflective participants move out of the silent shadows and bring their experiences to light, they are empowered because "writing is a form of human communication expressing ideas regarding the human condition" (Hamill). In other words, the writings in this chapter recognize and validate experience. In breaking the silence, they pave the way for others to speak, and their experience is no longer a solitary or shameful one.

This chapter attempts to capture the essence of witnessing across differences in genre and form. Nonfiction often allows us to speak candidly about our experiences; fiction allows us to illustrate our experiences and encourages the readers to come to their own conclusions; and poetry captures the detail of experience. As readers, we need to explore a variety of literature, that which sustains as well as that which challenges our values and beliefs. These readings illustrate how experience shapes identity and how speaking out helps us to heal and others to grow. They expose the consequences of social values and explore gendered identity, racial identity, and class values so that we can create positive change. By exposing us to experiences outside our own, these stories challenge us to reach for new understandings. We must acknowledge the reality of trauma and oppression, even if these are horrors that do not touch each of us equally. We must negotiate between complicity in oppression and facing marginalization ourselves. We must define our own identity in relation to our experience in the world and our understanding of the way the world works.

As you read the selections in this chapter, think about all the different kinds of "witnessing" being suggested. We are encouraged to try to understand experiences that may be quite foreign to us, and to re-examine more familiar experiences through unfamiliar voices. We are challenged to take action, yet we must also struggle with the consequences of inaction. In Harriet Levin's poem "The Christmas Show" and Mark Doty's poem "Charlie Howard's Descent" especially, inaction and inattentiveness become what Hamill describes as "silence [that] grants violence permission." Sometimes witnessing is more subtle, asking us to question our experiences and explore how our situated understanding shapes our perception, like in Bob Dylan's "Last Thoughts on Woody Guthrie" and Jimmy Santiago Baca's "Coming into Language." Social witness can be about giving a voice to those who have fallen victim to social expectation, like in Alice Walker's "Everyday Use" and James Baldwin's "Sonny's Blues." Witnessing can initialize a broader audience to the experiences of the few, like in Carolyn Forché's "The Colonel" and Sherman Alexie's "Because My Father Always Said He Was the Only Indian Who Saw Jimi Hendrix Play 'The Star Spangled Banner' at Woodstock." Witnessing involves exposing us, as readers, to worlds outside our own in order to help us understand identity as the complex relationship between social influence and resistant individual responses to it.

Finally, in order to truly understand the concept of "bearing witness," we must acknowledge that who we are and how we understand the world is shaped by the histories that we learn, the stories we tell, the literature we read, and the traditions we carry. Although these cultural narratives often endorse the experiences of the many and silence the voices of the few, they can also be powerful tools in awakening us to the realities of injustice. Voices that have been drowned out by the tide of tradition can be resurrected by the power of the written word. Through writing, victims find the strength and freedom to rob silence of its power. Because writing is reflective and redemptive, it can give strength and freedom to both readers and writers. What we choose to read can lead us to challenge our understanding of the world, and make us question our values, prejudices, and morals. Witnessing, then, is two-fold. As writers bear witness, they redefine their experience. However, as readers, we are not simply passive recipients; rather, we also gain understanding and reshape our worldviews. Because writing encourages us to question our place in the world and how the world works, it can inspire both personal and social transformation. Through language, we can reinvent ourselves.

Works Cited

Baca, Jimmy Santiago. *A Place to Stand: The Making of a Poet*. New York: Grove Press, 2001. 244.

Lorde, Audre. "The Transformation of Silence into Language and Action." *Sister Outsider*. Freedom, CA: The Crossing Press, 1984. 40–44.

Steele, Cassie Premo. *We Heal From Memory: Sexton, Lorde, Anzaldúa, and the Poetry of Witness*. New York: Palgrave, 2000.

Sam Hamill

Sam Hamill was born in 1942, perhaps in Northern California. He was abandoned in Northern Utah and spent the years during World War II in an orphanage before being adopted by a Utah farm family. His adolescent years are marked by time spent in and out of jails and on the streets until his late teens, when he joined the United States Marine Corps in order to eradicate his juvenile record and visit Japan. While in the Marine Corps, serving in Okinawa, Hamill began to study Zen Buddhist literature. He became a social activist and campaigned against the Vietnam War in the 1960s. Hamill is a poet and translator of extraordinary range who has taught in prisons, public schools and universities. He is the recipient of many prestigious awards, a longtime editor of Copper Canyon Press and author of A Poet's Work: The Other Side of Poetry *(1990), the collection from which the following essay is taken.*

The Necessity to Speak

> One must understand what fear means: what it implies and what it rejects. It implies and rejects the same fact: a world where murder is legitimate, and where human life is considered trifling. . . . All I ask is that, in the midst of a murderous world, we agree to reflect on murder and to make a choice. After that, we can distinguish those who accept the consequences of being murderers themselves or the accomplices of murderers, and those who refuse to do so with all their force and being. Since this terrible dividing line does actually exist, it will be a gain if it be clearly marked.
>
> —Albert Camus, *Neither Victims Nor Executioners*

And yet we go on living closed lives, pretending we are not each personally responsible for the deaths we buy and sell. We go on living our sheltered lives among the potted plants and automobiles and advertising slogans. We don't want to know what the world is like, we can't bear very much reality.

The man in prison remembers. The man who's been in prison remembers. Cesare Pavese brings the message home most forcefully: "The lonely man, who's been in prison, goes back to prison every time he eats a piece of bread." The woman who was battered remembers. The woman who was raped will never forget. The convict and the ex-con, the rape victim, the battered child—each, reading these words, will remember.

I teach creative writing in the prisons because I have been in prison. Writing is a form of human communication expressing ideas regarding the human condition. Because writing creates emotion in the audience, the writer's responsibility is enormous. Arousing passion, exploring the grief of loss, making another laugh, showing someone how to care—these are the concerns of the writer, and they do not come free of responsibility. But the creative writing itself is only a by-product. What I teach cannot be simply stated.

The women I have escorted to shelters where they can be protected from the rage of sick men have also been my friends and my students and my teachers. Three of every four of these victims, men and women, will return—the men will go back to prison, and the women will return to battering relationships. The battered child will grow into the child batterer.

There are presently fifteen hundred men on Death Row in the United States. There are over two hundred in Florida alone, and they are let out of their cells twice per week for a quick shower, and once per week for one hour of exercise. Ninety-two percent of these men were battered children. They have had a lengthy schooling. But they are beginning to understand how we as a society establish acceptable levels of violence. We pay the bill for murder in Nicaragua. We say the $27 million we send there this year, like the $40 million we sent last year, is for "humanitarian purposes," and we tell ourselves the money is not for murder. We weep for the battered woman, but we are stingy when it comes time to pay for groceries and bandages at the shelter. The victim of rape earns our sympathy. But we discipline our children with a belt or a stick or a fist. The battered woman learns that violence is one of the forms love takes. The battered child learns that there are two possibilities in human life: one can remain the victim, or one can seize power and become the executioner. The mother who was battered typically understands that the only condition worse than being a victim is to become an executioner.

The convict writes himself out of prison, he writes his brothers out of prison. The battered woman makes peace in the world with tender words chosen with deep care.

A true poet, someone once said, is often faced with the difficult task of telling people what they already know and do not want to hear. Sharon Olds, in *The Dead and the Living* (Alfred A. Knopf, 1983), writes of being a victim of domestic violence herself, and her poems are painful to read, very painful, but beautiful because they are true.

> When Mother divorced you, we were glad. She took it and
> took it, in silence, all those years and then
> kicked you out, suddenly, and her
> kids loved it.

We can't bear very much reality. When the rape victim cries out for help, we are frozen. Our emotions are mute. We are seized as though we are catatonic. We have not been taught how to properly express our feelings. We find poetry embarrassing.

A critic writing of Kenneth Rexroth's love poems in the *New York Times* declares, "Rexroth has issued a volume of breasts-and-thighs poems. What would I say, should I chance to meet his wife in public?" The poet Deena Metzger makes a beautiful, joyous poster of herself, naked, arms outstretched, following a radical mastectomy of her left breast. We are embarrassed by her naked body and by her joy, but mostly we are embarrassed because we do not know how or what to think confronted by that long ragged scar. Our vocabulary of the emotions has become critically impoverished.

Veterans returning from Viet Nam often found it impossible to discuss what transpired there. Delayed Stress Syndrome has probably taken as many American lives as Agent Orange. And yet, in high schools today, no one has heard of My Lai. Unless we learn to articulate our own emotions, we cannot prevent other My Lais and other Viet Nams from recurring, nor will we ever properly address the domestic violence so common in the American home.

"All wisdom," Kung-fu Tze says, "is rooted in learning to call things by the right name."

I became a conscientious objector while serving in the U.S. Marine Corps. I am proud of my decision to practice non-cooperation, and I am shamed by my complicity. In the vocabulary of human emotions, the terms "guilt" and "innocence" are insufficient. Like "right" and "wrong," they reject compassionate wisdom.

Once each month the recruiters for the business of death are permitted into our high schools to recruit more cannon fodder. There is no voice for non-violence inside those same institutions; the children who listen and enlist are being trained to become both victims and executioners. And we are all co-conspirators. Our silence grants permission to the military to establish all critical vocabulary pertaining to the armed forces. The *armed forces* are precisely what that name implies: a resort to armed force, a complete collapse of compassionate communication.

The battering of women and children is the most common felony committed in the United States. No one knows how often it happens because it is so rarely reported. But every cop on a beat will tell you that the most feared call of all is the domestic dispute. One never knows what to expect. It kills more cops than dope-dealers and bank robbers combined.

When James Cagney shoves half a grapefruit in a woman's face, we all laugh and applaud. Nobody likes an uppity woman. And a man who is a man, when all else fails, asserts his "masculinity." It is easy to learn to be a man. I learned to be a batterer without ever thinking about it. That's the way we learn. When I was an adolescent, it was taken for granted that real men sometimes had to slap their women around. Just like John Wayne did to Maureen O'Hara in the movies. How very often in our movies and popular fiction the assaulted woman falls in love with the assaulting "hero."

The man who slips off his belt to spank his naughty child is about to commit felony assault. If he behaves like this toward any other human being but those of his immediate family, he is locked up for the protection of society. The child is about to get a practical lesson in adult behavior when reason breaks down. This incident, repeated over the years, will help to form the growing child's sense of justice, it will inform the definition of compassion. The father will say, "I'm sorry I have to do this. It will hurt me more than it hurts you." Because this father believes himself a good man, a kind and compassionate father. But the child won't believe a word of it. The child fears the wound. The child has learned that might makes right, that parents sometimes lie, and that there are acceptable limits of violence.

If a belt is acceptable, why not a stick? If a stick is acceptable, why not a baseball bat? If broken bones are unacceptable, what about cuts or welts or bruises?

The first duty of the writer is the rectification of names—to name things properly, for, as Kung-fu Tze said, "All wisdom is rooted in learning to call things by the right name."

"The names of things bring them closer," Robert Sund wrote. This applies to the terrible as well as to the sublime. The writer learns from the act of writing. "I write to find out what's on my mind," Gary Snyder once said. What the writer invents is its own reality.

The writer is aware that verbs show action and that precision in the use of nouns and verbs frees one from the muddiness of most modifiers. The writer accepts responsibility for every implication derived from what is stated. The writer is also eternally vulnerable.

The writer *is* the battered woman in her blossoming pain; the writer *is* the lonely face behind the steel door; the writer *is* the good man with the belt wrapped around his fist. Before the first word is written, the writer is a witness who struggles not to flinch, not to look away.

We hear all around us our language being de-valued. Our president tells us that a missile with one thousand times the power of the bomb we dropped on Hiroshima is a "peacekeeper." We remember the bitter irony with which Colt named its pistol the Peacemaker. Our president tells us that $27 million is being sent to aid one side of a civil war in Nicaragua, but that the money won't be used for military purposes. The writer is in the service of the language. The writer is accountable.

We live in a culture in which "real men" don't often touch and often don't even like to be touched. Touch is a primary language in the discourse of emotions. There is eighteen square feet of skin on the average human being, and that skin holds about five million sensory perceptors. A University of Wisconsin study determined that denial of touch in young monkeys resulted in deformation in the cerebellum. D. H. Lawrence, in a story called "You Touched Me!," describes how simple human physical contact can restore the health of a life. Our president is a tough guy. He shakes hands, presumably with a firm grip, but he doesn't hug the foreign dignitaries. John Wayne didn't hug. Sylvester Stallone, Hollywood's male role model for our children, doesn't touch much.

We are embarrassed when the poet weeps publicly during the recitation of a poem. The physical expression of emotion makes many people uncomfortable. I was taught as a child—like most of my contemporaries—that men should not express emotion.

Men envy women their friendships with other women. Men secretly wish they, too, could have friends like that. Men have learned that ours is a lonely and insular country. We think poetry is about emotions. We are dead wrong. Poetry is not *about*. Take the rhyme out of poetry, and there is still poetry; take the rhythm out of it, and there is still poetry; take even the words themselves away, and poetry remains, as Yang Wan-li said a thousand years ago. The poet identifies a circumstance in which the poetry reveals itself. The poet is the vehicle used by poetry so that *it* can touch us. From the inside out. The words are only the frame which focuses the epiphany we name poetry. We say the poem touches us, sometimes even deeply. We often say the poet is a bit touched. Adrienne Rich dreams of a common language.

In the language of violence all argument is solipsistic. Those who pay tithing at the altar of violence are afraid: they fear the here-and-now and they fear the hereafter, but most of all, they fear the truth of knowledge. Knowledge is the loss of innocence. How desperately we want our innocence. How desperately we protect the innocence of our children! Our children don't know what has happened. They have never heard of Auschwitz or Treblinka, they have never heard of Canyon de Chelly. They do not know that it was their European-immigrant great-great-grandfathers who invented scalp-taking, they have never dreamed of the tortured flesh that has subtly informed our attitudes since those long-ago trials in Salem. They do not know that German death camps were modeled on U.S. camps, our own nineteenth-century Final Solution to "the Indian problem."

The past we name History. Out of it, today. Every day there are people who die to know. Every day, people die because they know. In El Salvador, in Chile, in the Philippines, in Korea, Nicaragua, and Lebanon. In the U.S.S.R. and in the U.S. of A.

And the murderers, the dirty little dictators who order the heads brought in upon a platter? Our money sustains their power. Just as our indifference permits gangs to run our prisons where men also die for knowing and for speaking up. Just as we continue to permit the deaths of 2500 women per year at the hands of their "lovers," one every three-and-a-half hours, and just as we permit a woman to be battered senseless every eighteen seconds of every day in this country.

And our money brings us television to distract us from what we know we are responsible for but do not want to know. It is difficult to explain things to our children. It is convenient to declare international conflict too large, too ugly, or too confusing to explain. And we likewise declare the personal too embarrassing. How else do we account for the fact that ten percent of all teenage girls get pregnant? We perform forty-five abortions per every thousand teenage girls every year, or about one out of every twenty-five girls. One in three sixteen-year-old girls is sexually active and knows almost nothing about birth control. Her seventeen-year-old lover knows nothing, typically, or doesn't care. Our silence contributes to the shame and misery of these girls and to the deaths of millions of unborn children.

We warn our daughters lest they become "loose" with their affections. We don't want them to care for the wrong people. We don't want to wound them with the knowledge that womankind has been singled out for special suffering throughout history, so we protect them from *her-story*. We persuade ourselves that perhaps, if we don't talk about sex, sexual involvement won't happen too soon. And perhaps, if we don't think about our daughters loving a batterer, that won't happen either. Our silence grants violence permission. We sacrifice our daughters to protect our own beloved innocence. In the language of violence, every speech is a solipsism and silence a conspirator.

* * *

The true poet gives up the self. The *I* of my poem is not *me*. It is the first person impersonal, it is permission for you to enter the experience which we name Poem.

Although the poem itself is often a "given" thing, in the justice of poetry we often earn the gift in some way. The disciplining of the self helps the poet clarify the experience so that the experience itself may be yours with as little superficial clutter as possible. The true poet asks for nothing "in return" because the poem itself is given to the poet who, in turn, gives it away and gives it away again. The poet is grateful for the opportunity to serve.

The poet wants neither fame nor money, but simply to be of use.

I am not the *I* of my poem. But I am responsible for the poem and, therefore, for that *I*. The poet invents a being, and that being, man or woman, stands before the world, naked and feeling. Thus, the poet who invents the persona of the poem is reflected similarly "undressed," and we say, "This poet takes risks," because there is neither false modesty nor the arrogance of exhibitionism, but the truth of human experience as it is, all somehow beyond the mere words of the poem.

The poet may speak for the speechless, for the suffering and the wounded. The poet may be a conscience, walking. The poet honors the humble most of all because poetry is gift-giving. The poet adores the erotic because in a world of pain there is charity and hope and because the poet aspires to a condition of perpetual vulnerability.

But there are poets who murder and poets who lie. Dante placed the corrupters of language in the seventh circle of Hell, and there are poets among them. Christopher Marlowe was an assassin.

I was strapped belly-down with webbing ripped from beds in a prison for the young, my face in a pillow to muffle my screams, my mouth gagged with my own socks—I was gang-raped by I-don't-know-how-many boys, ice-picked in the face, and left, presumably to die, alone all night before the guards discovered me, bloody and crazed. Fourteen years old and in the custody of the State. It has been thirty years, and I remember it like yesterday at noon. Out of my own guilt and shame over having been raped, out of my own guilt and shame over having been a batterer, out of my own silence over these terrible events, I began to articulate needs; out of defining my own needs, I discovered a necessity for believing that justice is possible; out of a commitment to a sense of justice, I found it necessary, essential, to bear witness.

Some of my students are women who begin writing because a writing class is permission to speak, which they do not have at home. Some of these women are battered because they have taken my class. Some have been battered when their "lovers" discovered that I talk about violence and responsibility in class. One of the kindest women I have ever known was murdered by her husband because he feared she would tell the truth. Our last conversation took place over a leisurely brunch; we discussed the origins and history of Kuan Yin, bodhisattva of compassion.

We are all impoverished by our silence.

There are more men in prison in the United States than there are people in South Dakota. Many of these men are eager to work, eager to learn, and dream of learning another way of life. They exist in a moment-to-moment despair that is utterly beyond the comprehension of anyone who has not been there.

The history of our prisons is a study of cruelty and stupidity so savage and so constant that almost no one wants to know a thing about it. Poor men go to prison. Men from minority races go to prison. But batterers come from every station, even from Reagan's Administration. The rich are as likely to commit sexual violence as are the poor. The batterer cannot name his fear, the thing inside that makes him strike out blindly at the very things he loves. It is his own inability to articulate his needs, his own speechlessness, that makes him crazy. Because he has been denied his language, he cannot name things clearly; because he cannot name, he cannot see what frightens him so terribly; therefore, the fear is invisible and is everywhere and consumes him.

Only when those of us who have overcome the terrible cycle of violence bear witness can we demonstrate another possibility. Because I have been both victim and executioner, I am able to speak from the bleak interior, and, perhaps, bring a little light into a vast darkness. An apology from a reformed batterer means nothing. The only conceivable good that can come from my confession is that of example for other sick men, a little hope for change amidst the agony of despair.

She took a class in creative writing. There was much talk of naming things correctly: objects, feelings, acts, deeds. And each time there was talk, there was also responsibility. "You will be held accountable," she was told, "just as you will be expected to hold others accountable."

And then one night it happened. She got home a little late from class. He was drunk. She tried to be especially nice, she tried to calm and soothe him. But his voice got louder and louder. He screamed. He grabbed her by the throat and shook her like a rag. And then he hit her. He hit her hard.

And then he apologized. He begged her not to leave. She was crumpled in a corner, her lip bleeding, her whole body trembling out of control. He got her a wet towel and tried to touch her face. She turned her face away and held up her hands for protection. Tears streamed down his face. He begged her not to go, he swore he'd never do that again, he swore he'd gone crazy. She knew it would happen again. It had *already* happened again.

She went that night to the shelter. She spent weeks talking to a counselor every day. She was lucky. She didn't have children. He didn't find her. She was lucky to be alive. For a while, she hated men. She hated being a victim. But she made friends in the shelter. Later, she made more friends outside. And through friendship, learned to love. True love is not without its own accountability.

The violence we learn at home we take with us everywhere we go. It shapes the way we look at a man or a woman, it colors our foreign policy and our tax structure. It is outright theft to pay a woman fifty-eight cents on the dollar we pay a man for doing the same job; it is economic violence.

In Viet Nam, the soldiers, those young men conscripted or enlisted from our high schools and colleges to do our killing for us, called the enemy "Gook," an epithet first used in Nicaragua in the 1920s, China in the 1930s, Japan in the

1940s, and in the Philippines since the 1940s, because that removed an element of the enemy's humanity, making it more like killing a thing than murdering a man, a woman, or a child.

I see them every day, the wounded women in the supermarket or in the bookstore, the children beaten to a whimper until all life has grayed in them. I've learned to recognize Fear's signature scrawled across their faces. The way one learns to recognize a man who walks with a "prison shuffle."

It is essential to make it clear that these things are personal. Our nuclear arms have 180,000 times the blast of the charge that leveled Hiroshima forty years ago. Our ability to deliver death is so unspeakably potent that it is far beyond the range of all human imagination. And we add to that arsenal every day. Nothing will change until we demolish the "we-and-they" mentality. We are human, and therefore all human concerns are ours. And those concerns are personal. "Everywhere we go," George Seferis said, "we walk on the faces of the dead."

Children in our public schools are paddled, whipped, slapped, locked in closets, lockers, and bathrooms—all quite legally. Every fourth homosexual male in a U.S. high school is the victim of a major assault during his tenure. Virtually all of them are victims of harassment. Homophobia is so rampant in our culture that it is common to see people fly into a rage over the mere sight of a gay couple holding hands in public. We excuse racism, sexism, homophobia—all the mindless violence of others—by refusing to make a *personal* issue of the problem.

We lend a helping hand to the mugger when we don't educate our children (of both sexes) about self- defense; we lend a hand to the rapist when we don't readily discuss rape. Our silence grants permission to the child molester. Because we have not learned how to name things properly, the batterer beats his child or lover in public, and we stand to one side, crippled inside, fearful and guilty.

If we really do believe that felony assault has no place in the home, we must encourage all victims to name names, to come forward and bear witness. We must find a way to save the victims. And we must find a way to save the executioners, as well.

There is a way. I know. Poetry has been a means for me, a way to find my way out of Hell. But it takes an iron will or a deeply spiritual conviction not unlike that of many poets toward poetry, the way James Wright spoke with compassion for drunkards and murderers, the way Richard Hugo testified on behalf of the dying farm towns and lonely saloons of the Northwest, or the way we might learn from Denise Levertov how to accept the loss of our mothers or to accept responsibility for our own violent realpolitik or for a marriage that was "good in its time" after that time has passed.

There *is* a third way. It begins with the end of lies and silence about violence. It begins with accepting responsibility for our own words and deeds. It begins with searching one's own heart for the compassionate justice which is located *only* there. It begins with the articulation of one's truest and deepest response to a world where, as Camus said, murder is legitimate and human life is considered trifling. Only from such a profoundly articulated *No!* can we hope to achieve a final, irrefutable affirmation of the human soul.

Jane Miller

Jane Miller's newest collection of poetry is Wherever You Lay Your Head *(Copper Canyon Press, 1999). Among earlier collections are* Memory at These Speeds: New and Selected Poems; The Greater Leisures, *a National Poetry Series Selection; and* August Zero, *winner of the Western States Book Award. She has also written* Working Time: Essays on Poetry, Culture, and Travel, *in the University of Michigan's Poets on Poetry Series. She is a recipient of a Lila Wallace-Reader's Digest Award for Poetry, as well as a Guggenheim Fellowship and two National Endowment for the Arts Fellowships. She lives in Tucson and is Director of the Creative Writing Program at The University of Arizona. Currently, she is writing a novel,* Seven Mediterraneans.

The poems of Wherever You Lay Your Head *are modeled after the 19th century woodcut artist Hiroshige's "Pictures of the Floating World," intimate prints of ordinary folks' hardships and pleasures. His scenes recall, in spirit, early American life on the open road. Following the thread up to the present, the poems depict images of the trauma of war and its aftermath on both sides of the Pacific. They highlight the development of the bomb in laboratories in the Southwest, where Miller lives, and the dropping of the bomb on Nagasaki. The closer the poet gets to the mass deaths caused by the bomb, the shorter the poems become, and the smaller the details, as the poet gets overwhelmed by grief, fear, and compassion.*

The Grand Waterfall Plunges Unbending into the Pool Below

with only a tiny wreath of waves.
It is 1942 and Edward Teller pushes back from his station,
uncomfortable since his lamb lunch
in the cafeteria, and unbuckles a notch.
His stomach gases are on fire.
What fat he hasn't wiped from his hands
has greased and blurred his slide rule.
He hasn't stopped into the washroom

because he is preoccupied calculating
that a nitrogen reaction
could kindle an explosion beyond
the team's control.
For this bomb
Oppenheimer and Compton
stake the odds at three times
in a million. Here are men who feel
they distinguish among sleep,
delusion, and reality,
tiny flashes of mica
on a bare-branched green pine.
Foxes leap under the branches
spitting flames,
and from their height and merriment
farmers foretell harvest.
Countdown begins in darkness.
Dawn quiet over the Oscura hills to the east.
General Farrell prays the test
is a boy—a winner—rather than a girl.
A small sun slowly rises
surrounded by blue light
fixed to earth by a charcoal stem.
Silence. Then the blast. In God's eyes,
tiny flashes of mica leap spitting flames.
"First of all,"
Teller, the heavy, confides, "I have no hope
of clearing my conscience." The fungal blue glow
sits and thinks of Winston Churchill
in an unzipped siren suit, hearing the success
of the experiment, sucking a cigar and smiling
through a facsimile of atomic smoke.
People march from twin cities in a dream
we are at once forbidden to see
and at the same time required.
A charred common skin
at least someone and probably many
could have saved,
figures climbing through a craggy garden
toward a bright pavilion,
small factories, and shops.
Two men indulge in a comic dance with fans.
Ladies chat, drawing in their parasols
to absorb the warm summer sun.

In Such a Way That Nothing Could Go Wrong

A low stratum of mushroom cloud
begins shortly to move over the park
in a north-northwesterly direction
& twenty or thirty minutes later
to rain radioactive
building block & human remains
onto still living stick figures
& thus with a fireball to evaporate
a paradise of hackberry trees

Two waitresses pedaling to a noodle shop downtown
see the last of the freshness of dawn
fume into the regular traffic & trade of oblivion
a hundred thousand fall in the city like blossoms
 along a riverbank
some crawl burned
& faceless into the rising river
poor memory
too tired to rest
especially in summer or in the sun

Reprinted from *Wherever You Lay Your Head*, (1999), by permission of Copper Canyon Press.

School

A Hispanic gentleman familiar
with piñon in the adobe fireplace
shovels on soft coal
which pours acrid smoke
through the ventilators in the mirror-image
apartments of the evacuated
Los Alamos, New Mexico, Ranch School,
straightening slowly. *Bueno.*
Kitty Oppenheimer's name is on a list
of wives waiting for her maid to arrive
by bus from the valley this weekday morning,
and is awake enough in her log and stone house

Reprinted from *Wherever You Lay Your Head*, (1999), by permission of Copper Canyon Press.

on a quiet road partly shielded
by shrubs and a small garden
to smell the regular disturbance again.

She and her husband haven't the time
to advise the janitor of his error,
or to enjoy the pine-covered promontory,
or the Rio Grande Valley, or hike the old trails
of the Valle Grande,
or even to gaze out beyond the fence and the military patrol
toward the Pajarito Plateau,
because they live in a magic place which vanishes
in the blowing dust of construction this summer,
and they can only retrieve it
by getting beyond the sun behind the Jemez skyline
along bad roads ten miles back
by hairpin turns and precipitous drops,
and that is impossible now. It is dawn
and a long day ahead, the nearest railroad
sixty miles away, and the many secluded
canyons and mesas host experiments
beyond the broad two-mile-long mesa
which spits up the bus this morning.
Buenos días.

Here is pregnant Anna,
firm and big as a gourd.
Anna is using the money
for her family, who cannot believe
the price gringos will pay
so she can ride the bus into the country
a few hours a day to polish the laboratories,
resident quarters, and dining hall.
Anna has heard that Kitty's husband is lost
in a mountain snowdrift or in the desert.
She knows because everyone knows
he is searching for a secret
site three hundred miles south
in the desolate Jornada del Muerto, near Alamogordo,
where anyone goes who wants to
die for a day. *Dios mío.*

Anna loves Kitty because she is fair
and Kitty loves Anna because she is dear.
They come from far away and meet
between the familiar and the unknown,
to which Kitty's husband gives the name
Trinity, from "Batter my heart, three-person'd God,"
a line little understood

and which might otherwise do some good,
muchas gracias.
We fly straight in at medium height
at rather low speed over the city
and drop one bomb with the energy
of fifteen thousand tons of TNT,
killing more than a hundred thousand people
and wounding at least a hundred thousand people.
We destroy the medium-sized city.
It is not a question of one bomb.
It is a question of ten, and then
one hundred, and then a thousand,
and then, maybe, one hundred thousand.
We know or, rather, do not know,
but think that it is not a question
of ten thousand tons
but of one hundred thousand
and then a million tons, or ten million,
and then, perhaps, of one hundred million.
When Grant, at Appomattox, looked beyond
the slaughter to nature and to time
he could tell Lee to let his troops keep
their horses because they would need them
for plowing in the early spring.
Oppenheimer himself drops by briefly

during the celebration at the school
on August 15, 1945, after hostilities cease
of a sudden, as planned, after we drop
a plutonium bomb on Nagasaki
and a uranium bomb on Hiroshima,
only to find a level-headed young scientist
vomiting in the shrubs,
to whom he says, and who can in no way
emerge to consciousness to hear him
nor be able to entertain the instant of brilliance
required to recommend him to us
and to this place, much like the future,
in which the poor body is defeated
and the spirit transformed,
where all has been reclassified
and all are being
informed of our acts,
"The reaction has begun."
Jesus Cristo.

Carolyn Forché

Carolyn Forché's first poetry collection, Gathering The Tribes *(Yale University Press, 1976), won the Yale Series of Younger Poets Award.*

In 1977, she traveled to Spain to translate the work of Salvadoran-exiled poet Claribel Alegría, and upon her return, received a John Simon Guggenheim Foundation Fellowship, which enabled her to live in El Salvador for two years, where she worked as a human rights activist. Her experiences there informed her second book, The Country Between Us *(Harper and Row, 1982), which received the Poetry Society of America's Alice Fay di Castagnola Award, and was chosen as the Lamont Selection of the Academy of American Poets. "The Colonel," and "As Children Together," which appear here, are from this collection.*

Forché has held three fellowships from The National Endowment for the Arts, and her work has been translated into Swedish, German, Czech, Slovak, French, Spanish, Russian, Bulgarian, Romanian, Thai, Vietnamese, Greek, Hebrew and Arabic. She teaches in the Master of Fine Arts Program in Poetry at George Mason University in Virginia. In 1992 she received a Lannan Foundation Literary Fellowship. Her anthology, Against Forgetting: Twentieth Century Poetry of Witness, *a collection of poetry in English and in translation by poets who endured conditions of social, historical and political extremity during the 20th century, was published by W.W. Norton & Co. in 1993.*

In 1994, her third book of poetry, The Angel of History *(HarperCollins, Publishers), received* The Los Angeles Times Book Award. *An excerpt of this work, about a woman named Ellie, appears here. Her new collection of poetry,* Blue Hour, *is forthcoming in 2003 from HarperCollins Publishers.*

The Colonel

What you have heard is true. I was in his house. His wife carried a tray of coffee and sugar. His daughter filed her nails, his son went out for the night. There were daily papers, pet dogs, a pistol on the cushion beside him. The moon swung bare on its black cord over the house. On the television was a cop show. It was in English. Broken bottles were embedded in the walls around the house to scoop the kneecaps from a man's legs or cut his hands to lace. On the windows there were

Reprinted from *The Country Between Us*, (1980), HarperCollins.

gratings like those in liquor stores. We had dinner, rack of lamb, good wine, a gold bell was on the table for calling the maid. The maid brought green mangoes, salt, a type of bread. I was asked how I enjoyed the country. There was a brief commercial in Spanish. His wife took everything away. There was some talk then of how difficult it had become to govern. The parrot said hello on the terrace. The colonel told it to shut up, and pushed himself from the table. My friend said to me with his eyes: say nothing. The colonel returned with a sack used to bring groceries home. He spilled many human ears on the table. They were like dried peach halves. There is no other way to say this. He took one of them in his hands, shook it in our faces, dropped it into a water glass. It came alive there. I am tired of fooling around he said. As for the rights of anyone, tell your people they can go fuck themselves. He swept the ears to the floor with his arm and held the last of his wine in the air. Something for your poetry, no? he said. Some of the ears on the floor caught this scrap of his voice. Some of the ears on the floor were pressed to the ground.

May 1978

As Children Together

Under the sloped snow
pinned all winter with Christmas
lights, we waited for your father
to whittle his soap cakes
away, finish the whisky,
your mother to carry her coffee
from room to room closing lights
cubed in the snow at our feet.
Holding each other's
coat sleeves we slid down
the roads in our tight
black dresses, past
crystal swamps and the death
face of each dark house,
over the golden ice
of tobacco spit, the blue
quiet of ponds, with town
glowing behind the blind
white hills and a scant
snow ticking in the stars.
You hummed *blanche comme*
la neige and spoke of Montreal

Reprinted from *The Country Between Us*, (1980), HarperCollins.

where a *quebeçoise* could sing,
take any man's face
to her unfastened blouse
and wake to wine
on the bedside table.
I always believed this,
Victoria, that there might
be a way to get out.

You were ashamed of that house,
its round tins of surplus flour,
chipped beef and white beans,
relief checks and winter trips
that always ended in deer
tied stiff to the car rack,
the accordion breath of your uncles
down from the north, and what
you called the stupidity
of the Michigan French.

Your mirror grew ringed
with photos of servicemen
who had taken your breasts
in their hands, the buttons
of your blouses in their teeth,
who had given you the silk
tassles of their graduation,
jackets embroidered with dragons
from the Far East. You kept
the corks that had fired
from bottles over their beds,
their letters with each city
blackened, envelopes of hair
from their shaved heads.

I am going to have it, you said.
Flowers wrapped in paper from carts
in Montreal, a plane lifting out
of Detroit, a satin bed, a table
cluttered with bottles of scent.
So standing in a platter of ice
outside a Catholic dance hall
you took their collars
in your fine chilled hands
and lied your age to adulthood.

I did not then have breasts of my own,
nor any letters from bootcamp,
and when one of the men who had

gathered around you took my mouth
to his own there was nothing
other than the dance hall music
rising to the arms of iced trees.

I don't know where you are now, Victoria.
They say you have children, a trailer
in the snow near our town,
and the husband you found as a girl
returned from the Far East broken
cursing holy blood at the table
where nightly a pile of white shavings
is paid from the edge of his knife.

If you read this poem, write to me.
I have been to Paris since we parted.

From *The Angel of History*

We lived in Ste. Monique ward over the main corridor, Ellie and myself,
in the Hôtel-Dieu on the Place du Parvis Notre Dame.
Below us jonquils opened.
Ellie was afflicted with scales again, tiny Ellie, at the edge of her bed,
peeling her skin from her arm as if it were an opera glove,
and weeping *cachée, cachée, cachée* all during the war.

Barn to barn in the haylight, field to cellar. Winter took one of her sons,
and her own attempt to silence him, the other.

Le Dieu? Le Dieu est un feu. A psychopath. Le Dieu est feu.

It isn't normal for a mother to outlive her children.
It isn't normal that my sons should be dead.

Paris! Oh, how I loathe this city because of its past.

Then you wish to leave Paris?

Mais oui. I wish to leave life, *my dear.*
My parents? Deported. My aunts and uncles? Deported. My friends? All of them deportees.
I don't know what became of a single one. How they came to the end.
My papers said I was Polish. When the money ran out, we ran. When the Nazis came, we ran. Cachée, cachée, cachée!

Reprinted from *The Angel of History*, (1994), HarperCollins.

The tubercular man offers his cigarette and the snow falls, patiently, across the spring flowers.

My life, triste. Do you understand? This place. No good! France. No good! Germany. No good! Ni l'Union soviétique. Fascists! It is no good.

Then why not leave Paris?

I am Jewish. Do you understand? Alone in a small room on the third floor, always alone.
To remain sane, I sing librettos to myself, and German lullabies, can you imagine?

Mein Flügel ist zum Schwung bereit
ich kehrte gern zurück,
denn bleib ich auch lebendige Zeit
ich hätte wenig Glück

My husband was a soldier against the Nazis. Résistance. Agir. He wasn't killed in the war.
He even returned to me. It was after the war he died. He died of cholera. And the world is worse now than it was then.

Worse?
Mais oui!

Sharon Olds

Sharon Olds (b. 1942) is a poet who holds degrees from Stanford University (BA) and Columbia (Ph.D.). She is currently an associate professor at New York University and acting director of the graduate program in Creative Writing. She has published numerous collections of poetry including Satan Says *(1980),* The Gold Cell *(1987), and* Blood, Tin, Straw *(1999). Her poetry often challenges conventions and asks the reader to do the same.*

On the Subway

The boy and I face each other.
His feet are huge, in black sneakers
laced with white in a complex pattern like a
set of intentional scars. We are stuck on
opposite sides of the car, a couple of
molecules stuck in a rod of light
rapidly moving through darkness. He has the
casual cold look of a mugger,
alert under hooded lids. He is wearing
red, like the inside of the body
exposed. I am wearing dark fur, the
whole skin of an animal taken and
used. I look at his raw face,
he looks at my fur coat, and I don't
know if I am in his power—
he could take my coat so easily, my
briefcase, my life—
or if he is in my power, the way I am
living off his life, eating the steak
he does not eat, as if I am taking
the food from his mouth. And he is black
and I am white, and without meaning or
trying to I must profit from his darkness,
the way he absorbs the murderous beams of the
nation's heart, as black cotton
absorbs the heat of the sun and holds it. There is
no way to know how easy this

---

white skin makes my life, this
life he could take so easily and
break across his knee like a stick the way his
own back is being broken, the
rod of his soul that at birth was dark and
fluid and rich as the heart of a seedling
ready to thrust up into any available light.

Michael Lassell

Michael Lassell (b. 1947) often writes about life as a gay man. He speaks bravely about sexuality and vulnerability. His work expresses his anger, his loss, and his hope in the face of hopelessness. In a review of his book The Hard Way *(1995), Philip Gambone praises Lassell's writing because it embodies "his humanity—his bruised and burning embrace of life." His other works include* Poems for Lost and Un-lost Boys *(1985),* Decade Dance *(1990), and* Eros in Boystown *(1996). He has been a recipient of a Lambda Literary Award and is currently the articles director for* Metropolitan Home.

In "How to Watch Your Brother Die," the speaker candidly shares his struggles as he attempts to come to terms with his brother as a gay man, an AIDS victim, and a loved one. In the poem, the speaker steps into his brother's world just as he is leaving it, which forces the speaker to recognize the humanity of those in the gay community and the inhumanity of those who fear it. It was first published in 1985 and serves as an early response to AIDS.

How to Watch Your Brother Die

When the call comes, be calm.
Say to your wife, "My brother is dying. I have to fly
to California."
Try not to be shocked that he already looks like
a cadaver.
Say to the young man sitting by your brother's side,
"I'm his brother."
Try not to be shocked when the young man says,
"I'm his lover. Thanks for coming."

Listen to the doctor with a steel face on.
Sign the necessary forms.
Tell the doctor you will take care of everything.
Wonder why doctors are so remote.

Watch the lover's eyes as they stare into
your brother's eyes as they stare into
space.
Wonder what they see there.

Reprinted from *Decade Dance*, (1990), by permission of the author.

Remember the time he was jealous and
opened your eyebrow with a sharp stick.
Forgive him out loud
even if he can't
understand you.
Realize the scar will be
all that's left of him.

Over coffee in the hospital cafeteria
say to the lover, "You're an extremely good-looking
young man."
Hear him say,
"I never thought I was good enough looking to
deserve your brother."

Watch the tears well up in his eyes. Say,
"I'm sorry. I don't know what it means to be
the lover of another man."
Hear him say,
"It's just like a wife, only the commitment is
deeper because the odds against you are so much
greater."
Say nothing, but
take his hand like a brother's.

Drive to Mexico for unproven drugs that might
help him live longer.
Explain what they are to the border guard.
Fill with rage when he informs you,
"You can't bring those across."
Begin to grow loud.
Feel the lover's hand on your arm
restraining you. See in the guard's eye
how much a man can hate another man.
Say to the lover. "How can you stand it?"
Hear him say, "You get used to it."
Think of one of your children getting used to
another man's hatred.

Call your wife on the telephone. Tell her,
"He hasn't much time.
I'll be home soon." Before you hang up say,
"How could anyone's commitment be deeper than
a husband and wife?" Hear her say,
"Please. I don't want to know all the details."

When he slips into an irrevocable coma,
hold his lover in your arms while he sobs,
no longer strong. Wonder how much longer

you will be able to be strong.
Feel how it feels to hold a man in your arms
whose arms are used to holding men.
Offer God anything to bring your brother back.
Know you have nothing God could possibly want.
Curse God, but do not
abandon Him.

Stare at the face of the funeral director
when he tells you he will not
embalm the body for fear of
contamination. Let him see in your eyes
how much a man can hate another man.

Stand beside a casket covered in flowers,
white flowers. Say,
"Thank you for coming," to each of several hundred men
who file past in tears, some of them
holding hands. Know that your brother's life
was not what you imagined. Overhear two
mourners say, "I wonder who'll be next?" and
"I don't care anymore,
as long as it isn't you."

Arrange to take an early flight home.
His lover will drive you to the airport.
When your flight is announced say,
awkwardly, "If I can do anything, please
let me know." Do not flinch when he says,
"Forgive yourself for not wanting to know him
after he told you. He did."
Stop and let it soak in. Say,
"He forgave me, or he knew himself?"
"Both," the lover will say, not knowing what else
to do. Hold him like a brother while he
kisses you on the cheek. Think that
you haven't been kissed by a man since
your father died. Think,
"This is no moment not to be strong."

Fly first class and drink Scotch. Stroke
your split eyebrow with a finger and
think of your brother alive. Smile
at the memory and think
how your children will feel in your arms,
warm and friendly and without challenge.

Mark Doty

Mark A. Doty (b. 1953) is the son of an army engineer and grew up in a succession of suburbs in Tennessee, Florida, southern California, and Arizona. Since the publication of his first volume of verse, Turtle, Swan, *in 1987, Mark Doty has become recognized as one of the most accomplished poets in America. Doty's work transcends the category of "gay poetry" to appeal to a diverse cross-section of readers. Fittingly, Doty has won a number of prestigious literary awards for his poetry and his two memoirs, including the Whiting Writer's Award, the T. S. Eliot Prize, the National Poetry Series, and the* Los Angeles Times *Book Award. Doty described himself, in* Publishers Weekly, *as having been "a sissy" in childhood. Frightened by his emerging sexual identity, he married hastily at age eighteen. After completing his undergraduate studies at Drake University in Iowa, he got a divorce and moved to Manhattan, where he paid his dues as a temporary office worker. He earned a master's degree in creative writing from Goddard College. During the same period, he met his lasting love, Wally Roberts. Wally's illness and death from AIDS, with which he was diagnosed in 1989 and to which he finally succumbed in January, 1994, was to be the central event of Doty's maturation as person and poet. Doty's poem, "Days of 1981," which is reprinted in Chapter Five, "Rereading Romance," was first published in* My Alexandria *in 1993, which won the National Poetry Series contest.*

Charlie Howard's Descent

Between the bridge and the river
he falls through
a huge portion of night;
it is not as if falling

is something new. Over and over
he slipped into the gulf
between what he knew and how
he was known. What others wanted

opened like an abyss: the laughing
stock-clerks at the grocery, women
at the luncheonette amused by his gestures.
What could he do, live

---

with one hand tied
behind his back? So he began to fall
into the star-faced section
of night between the trestle

and the water because he could not meet
a little town's demands,
and his earrings shone and his wrists
were as limp as they were.

I imagine he took the insults in
and made of them a place to live;
we learn to use the names
because they are there,

familiar furniture: *faggot*
was the bed he slept in, hard
and white, but simple somehow,
queer something sharp

but finally useful, a tool,
all the jokes a chair,
stiff-backed to keep the spine straight,
a table, a lamp. And because

he's fallen for twenty-three years,
despite whatever awkwardness
his flailing arms and legs assume
he is beautiful

and like any good diver
has only an edge of fear
he transforms into grace.
Or else he is not afraid,

and in this way climbs back
up the ladder of his fall,
out of the river into the arms
of the three teenage boys

who hurled him from the edge—
really boys now, afraid,
their fathers' cars shivering behind them,
headlights on—and tells them

it's all right, that he knows
they didn't believe him
when he said he couldn't swim,
and blesses his killers

in the way that only the dead
can afford to forgive.

Harriet Levin

Harriet Levin, whose poems have appeared in The Partisan Review, New Letters, The Iowa Review, Nimrod, *and elsewhere, is described by poet Eavan Boland as a compelling political poet, who tells "the story of [her] nation through the lens of [her] sexuality." Among her poetry prizes is the Alice Fay di Dastagnola Award from The Poetry Society of America. A graduate of the Iowa Writers' Workshop, she teaches at Drexel University. Of her collection of poetry,* The Christmas Show *(1997), the poet Andrew Hudgins writes: "Early in her powerful new book, Harriet Levin, with stunning tenderness, says. . . . 'But this / is how my life is different from my sister's, / I have not been forced to struggle for it.' But she is wrong. She has struggled honorably with her sister's pain and the pain of others, and out of her struggle she has brought this passionate and eloquent book." In the introduction to the book, Boland says of the poem that it "insists on a world where contraries exist: The young girl is violated in the very society which is trying out its legend of innocence in a festive show. In this way, the loneliness of sexual violence is allowed to comment on that other construct which all societies hide behind: the myth of inviolable childhood."*

The Christmas Show

While my youngest sister lies
on a cold cellar floor
in a house whose broken windows hold back nothing
and three boys pin down her shoulders
and force their way past her belt buckle, I am watching
The Christmas Show at Radio City Music Hall, seeing
a full moon accentuate the otherworldliness
of children dressed as elves, skating snowmen
and cardboard reindeer.
While my youngest sister lies on her back, stripped naked,
and three boys, one at a time, move over her, I am applauding
when an entire row of girls
wearing bright red bathing suits
fleeced with white fur
kick open their legs, the whole house applauds
at that moment. While my youngest sister looks into the dark

Reprinted from *The Christmas Show*, (1997), Beacon Press.

wide pupils she will look into
for the rest of her life, the boys
who prick her throat with a knife
feel only a momentary pleasure.
And just when I think The Christmas Show is over,
the curtain opens once more
with sheep, straw and stars
and the story of the nativity begins,
of a birth with no sex in it.
A real live camel is led across the stage
in a caravan with sheiks, children, and beggars
waiting to be touched and saved,
but at that moment
my mother is rushing to open the front door
my sister pounds
and pounds on, blood on her face, her lips
swollen, her cheek swollen, her
eyes swollen, having seen enough.

Jimmy Santiago Baca

Today, Jimmy Santiago Baca (b. 1952) is recognized as a le Chicano writer. He is a poet and essayist, and has written screenplays and a memoir, A Place to Stand: The Making of a Poet. *His list of awards is distinguished: Pushcart Prize, National Endowment of Poetry Award, Vogelstein Foundation Award, National Hispanic Heritage Award, Berkeley Regents Award, Southwest Book Award, and American Book Award. He has been a poet in residence at the University of California, Berkeley, and at Yale University.*

Yet, at the age of twenty-one Baca was illiterate and incarcerated. He had been sentenced to five years in a maximum-security prison for selling drugs. In prison, Baca became determined to change his life. He spent long hours studying grammar books and teaching himself to read and write. Soon he was writing letters and poems for other prisoners in exchange for cigarettes and coffee. Baca used poetry to work through the pain of his traumatic childhood in Santa Fe, New Mexico, his adolescence spent in orphanages and detention centers, and his experiments with crime and dealing drugs. His poetry is a product of his efforts to heal and make sense of a life filled with poverty, struggle, and betrayal. Baca's poems and prose are powerful testaments to the power of the written word to effect personal transformation and give voice to the marginalized. Further, his writing is important in exposing the harsh realities of poverty, discrimination, and prison life for those of us lucky enough to be unfamiliar with those kinds of hardships.

Coming into Language

On weekend graveyard shifts at St. Joseph's Hospital I worked the emergency room, mopping up pools of blood and carting plastic bags stuffed with arms, legs, and hands to the outdoor incinerator. I enjoyed the quiet, away from the screams of shotgunned, knifed, and mangled kids writhing on gurneys outside the operating rooms. Ambulance sirens shrieked and squad car lights reddened the cool nights, flashing against the hospital walls: gray—red, gray—red. On slow nights I would lock the door of the administration office, search the reference library for a book on female anatomy and, with my feet propped on the desk, leaf through the illustrations, smoking my cigarette. I was seventeen.

Reprinted from *Working in the Dark*, (1992), Red Crane Books.

One night my eye was caught by a familiar-looking word on the spine of a book. The title was *450 Years of Chicano History in Pictures*. On the cover were black-and-white photos: Padre Hidalgo exhorting Mexican peasants to revolt against the Spanish dictators; Anglo vigilantes hanging two Mexicans from a tree; a young Mexican woman with rifle and ammunition belts crisscrossing her breast; César Chávez and field workers marching for fair wages; Chicano railroad workers laying creosote ties; Chicanas laboring at machines in textile factories; Chicanas picketing and hoisting boycott signs.

From the time I was seven, teachers had been punishing me for not knowing my lessons by making me stick my nose in a circle chalked on the blackboard. Ashamed of not understanding and fearful of asking questions, I dropped out of school in the ninth grade. At seventeen I still didn't know how to read, but those pictures confirmed my identity. I stole the book that night, stashing it for safety under the slopsink until I got off work. Back at my boardinghouse, I showed the book to friends. All of us were amazed; this book told us we were alive. We, too, had defended ourselves with our fists against hostile Anglos, gasping for breath in fights with the policemen who outnumbered us. The book reflected back to us our struggle in a way that made us proud.

Most of my life I felt like a target in the cross hairs of a hunter's rifle. When strangers and outsiders questioned me I felt the hang-rope tighten around my neck and the trapdoor creak beneath my feet. There was nothing so humiliating as being unable to express myself, and my inarticulateness increased my sense of jeopardy, of being endangered. I felt intimidated and vulnerable, ridiculed and scorned. Behind a mask of humility, I seethed with mute rebellion.

Before I was eighteen, I was arrested on suspicion of murder after refusing to explain a deep cut on my forearm. With shocking speed I found myself handcuffed to a chain gang of inmates and bused to a holding facility to await trial. There I met men, prisoners, who read aloud to each other the works of Neruda, Paz, Sabines, Nemerov, and Hemingway. Never had I felt such freedom as in that dormitory. Listening to the words of these writers, I felt that invisible threat from without lessen—my sense of teetering on a rotting plank over swamp water where famished alligators clapped their horny snouts for my blood. While I listened to the words of the poets, the alligators slumbered powerless in their lairs. Their language was the magic that could liberate me from myself, transform me into another person, transport me to other places far away.

And when they closed the books, these Chicanos, and went into their own Chicano language, they made barrio life come alive for me in the fullness of its vitality. I began to learn my own language, the bilingual words and phrases explaining to me my place in the universe. Every day I felt like the paper boy taking delivery of the latest news of the day.

Months later I was released, as I had suspected I would be. I had been guilty of nothing but shattering the windshield of my girlfriend's car in a fit of rage.

Two years passed. I was twenty now, and behind bars again. The federal marshals had failed to provide convincing evidence to extradite me to Arizona on a drug charge, but still I was being held. They had ninety days to prove I was guilty. The only evidence against me was that my girlfriend had been at the scene of the crime with my driver's license in her purse. They had to come up with something else. But there was nothing else. Eventually they negotiated a deal with the actual drug dealer, who took the stand against me. When the judge hit me with a million-dollar bail, I emptied my pockets on his booking desk: twenty-six cents.

One night in my third month in the county jail, I was mopping the floor in front of the booking desk. Some detectives had kneed an old drunk and handcuffed him to the booking bars. His shrill screams raked my nerves like a hacksaw on bone, the desperate protest of his dignity against their inhumanity. But the detectives just laughed as he tried to rise and kicked him to his knees. When they went to the bathroom to pee and the desk attendant walked to the file cabinet to pull the arrest record, I shot my arm through the bars, grabbed one of the attendant's university textbooks, and tucked it in my overalls. It was the only way I had of protesting.

It was late when I returned to my cell. Under my blanket I switched on a pen flashlight and opened the thick book at random, scanning the pages. I could hear the jailer making his rounds on the other tiers. The jangle of his keys and the sharp click of his boot heels intensified my solitude. Slowly I enunciated the words . . . p-o-n-d, ri-pple. It scared me that I had been reduced to this to find comfort. I always had thought reading a waste of time, that nothing could be gained by it. Only by action, by moving out into the world and confronting and challenging the obstacles, could one learn anything worth knowing.

Even as I tried to convince myself that I was merely curious, I became so absorbed in how the sounds created music in me and happiness, I forgot where I was. Memories began to quiver in me, glowing with a strange but familiar intimacy in which I found refuge. For a while, a deep sadness overcame me, as if I had chanced on a long-lost friend and mourned the years of separation. But soon the heartache of having missed so much of life, that had numbed me since I was a child, gave way, as if a grave illness lifted itself from me and I was cured, innocently believing in the beauty of life again. I stumblingly repeated the author's name as I fell asleep, saying it over and over in the dark: Words–worth, Words–worth.

Before long my sister came to visit me, and I joked about taking her to a place called Kubla Khan and getting her a blind date with this *vato* named Coleridge who lived on the seacoast and was *malías* on morphine. When I asked her to make a trip into enemy territory to buy me a grammar book, she said she couldn't. Bookstores intimidated her, because she, too, could neither read nor write.

Days later, with a stub pencil I whittled sharp with my teeth, I propped a Red Chief notebook on my knees and wrote my first words. From that moment, a hunger for poetry possessed me.

Until then, I had felt as if I had been born into a raging ocean where I swam relentlessly, flailing my arms in hope of rescue, of reaching a shoreline I never sighted. Never solid ground beneath me, never a resting place. I had lived with only the desperate hope to stay afloat; that and nothing more.

But when at last I wrote my first words on the page, I felt an island rising beneath my feet like the back of a whale. As more and more words emerged, I could finally rest: I had a place to stand for the first time in my life. The island grew, with each page, into a continent inhabited by people I knew and mapped with the life I lived.

I wrote about it all—about people I had loved or hated, about the brutalities and ecstasies of my life. And, for the first time, the child in me who had witnessed and endured unspeakable terrors cried out not just in impotent despair, but with the power of language. Suddenly, through language, through writing, my grief and my joy could be shared with anyone who would listen. And I could do this all alone; I could do it anywhere. I was no longer a captive of demons eating away at me, no longer a victim of other people's mockery and loathing, that had made me clench my fist white with rage and grit my teeth to silence. Words now pleaded back with the bleak lucidity of hurt. They were wrong, those others, and now I could say it.

Through language I was free. I could respond, escape, indulge; embrace or reject earth or the cosmos. I was launched on an endless journey without boundaries or rules, in which I could salvage the floating fragments of my past, or be born anew in the spontaneous ignition of understanding some heretofore concealed aspect of myself. Each word steamed with the hot lava juices of my primordial making, and I crawled out of stanzas dripping with birth-blood, reborn and freed from the chaos of my life. The child in the dark room of my heart, that had never been able to find or reach the light switch, flicked it on now; and I found in the room a stranger, myself, who had waited so many years to speak again. My words struck in me lightning crackles of elation and thunderhead storms of grief.

When I had been in the county jail longer than anyone else, I was made a trustee. One morning, after a fist fight, I went to the unlocked and unoccupied office used for lawyer-client meetings, to think. The bare white room with its fluorescent tube lighting seemed to expose and illuminate my dark and worthless life. And yet, for the first time, I had something to lose—my chance to read, to write; a way to live with dignity and meaning, that had opened for me when I stole that scuffed, second-hand book about the Romantic poets. In prison, the abscess had been lanced.

"I will never do any work in this prison system as long as I am not allowed to get my G.E.D." That's what I told the reclassification panel. The captain flicked off the tape recorder. He looked at me hard and said, "You'll never walk outta here alive. Oh, you'll work, put a copper penny on that, you'll work."

After that interview I was confined to deadlock maximum security in a subterranean dungeon, with ground-level chickenwired windows painted gray. Twenty-three hours a day I was in that cell. I kept sane by borrowing books from the other cons on the tier. Then, just before Christmas, I received a letter from Harry, a charity house samaritan who doled out hot soup to the homeless in Phoenix. He had picked my name from a list of cons who had no one to write to them. I wrote back asking for a grammar book, and a week later received one of Mary Baker Eddy's treatises on salvation and redemption, with Spanish and English on opposing pages. Pacing my cell all day and most of each night, I grappled with grammar until I was able to write a long true-romance confession for a con to send to his pen pal. He paid me with a pack of smokes. Soon I had a thriving barter business, exchanging my poems and letters for novels, commissary pencils, and writing tablets.

One day I tore two flaps from the cardboard box that held all my belongings and punctured holes along the edge of each flap and along the border of a ream of state-issue paper. After I had aligned them to form a spine, I threaded the holes with a shoestring, and sketched on the cover a hummingbird fluttering above a rose. This was my first journal.

Whole afternoons I wrote, unconscious of passing time or whether it was day or night. Sunbursts exploded from the lead tip of my pencil, words that grafted me into awareness of who I was; peeled back to a burning core of bleak terror, an embryo floating in the image of water, I cracked out of the shell wide-eyed and insane. Trees grew out of the palms of my hands, the threatening otherness of life dissolved, and I became one with the air and sky, the dirt and the iron and concrete. There was no longer any distinction between the other and I. Language made bridges of fire between me and everything I saw. I entered into the blade of grass, the basketball, the con's eye and child's soul.

At night I flew. I conversed with floating heads in my cell, and visited strange houses where lonely women brewed tea and rocked in wicker rocking chairs listening to sad Joni Mitchell songs.

Before long I was frayed like a rope carrying too much weight, that suddenly snaps. I quit talking. Bars, walls, steel bunk and floor bristled with millions of poem-making sparks. My face was no longer familiar to me. The only reality was the swirling cornucopia of images in my mind, the voices in the air. Mid-air a cactus blossom would appear, a snakeflame in blinding dance around it, stunning me like a guard's fist striking my neck from behind.

The prison administrators tried several tactics to get me to work. For six months, after the next monthly prison board review, they sent cons to my cell to hassle me. When the guard would open my cell door to let one of them in, I'd leap out and fight him—and get sent to thirty-day isolation. I did a lot of isolation time. But I honed my image-making talents in that sensory-deprived solitude. Finally they moved me to death row, and after that to "nut-run," the tier that housed the mentally disturbed.

As the months passed, I became more and more sluggish. My eyelids were heavy, I could no longer write or read. I slept all the time.

One day a guard took me out to the exercise field. For the first time in years I felt grass and earth under my feet. It was spring. The sun warmed my face as I sat on the bleachers watching the cons box and run, hit the handball, lift weights. Some of them stopped to ask how I was, but I found it impossible to utter a syllable. My tongue would not move, saliva drooled from the corners of my mouth. I had been so heavily medicated I could not summon the slightest gesture. Yet inside me a small voice cried out, I am fine! I am hurt now but I will come back! I am fine!

Back in my cell, for weeks I refused to eat. Styrofoam cups of urine and hot water were hurled at me. Other things happened. There were beatings, shock therapy, intimidation.

Later, I regained some clarity of mind. But there was a place in my heart where I had died. My life had compressed itself into an unbearable dread of being. The strain had been too much. I had stepped over that line where a human being has lost more than he can bear, where the pain is too intense, and he knows he is changed forever. I was now capable of killing, coldly and without feeling. I was empty, as I have never, before or since, known emptiness. I had no connection to this life.

But then, the encroaching darkness that began to envelop me forced me to reform and give birth to myself again in the chaos. I withdrew even deeper into the world of language, cleaving the diamonds of verbs and nouns, plunging into the brilliant light of poetry's regenerative mystery. Words gave off rings of white energy, radar signals from powers beyond me that infused me with truth. I believed what I wrote, because I wrote what was true. My words did not come from books or textual formulas, but from a deep faith in the voice of my heart.

I had been steeped in self-loathing and rejected by everyone and everything—society, family, cons, God and demons. But now I had become as the burning ember floating in darkness that descends on a dry leaf and sets flame to forests. The word was the ember and the forest was my life.

I was born a poet one noon, gazing at weeds and creosoted grass at the base of a telephone pole outside my grilled cell window. The words I wrote then sailed me out of myself, and I was transported and metamorphosed into the images they made. From the dirty brown blades of grass came bolts of electrical light that jolted loose my old self; through the top of my head that self was released and reshaped in the clump of scrawny grass. Through language I became the grass, speaking its language and feeling its green feelings and black root sensations. Earth was my mother and I bathed in sunshine. Minuscule speckles of sunlight passed through my green skin and metabolized in my blood.

Writing bridged my divided life of prisoner and free man. I wrote of the emotional butchery of prisons, and of my acute gratitude for poetry. Where my blind doubt and spontaneous trust in life met, I discovered empathy and compassion. The power to express myself was a welcome storm rasping at tendril roots, flooding my soul's cracked dirt. Writing was water that cleansed the wound and fed the parched root of my heart.

I wrote to sublimate my rage, from a place where all hope is gone, from a madness of having been damaged too much, from a silence of killing rage. I wrote to avenge the betrayals of a lifetime, to purge the bitterness of injustice. I wrote with a deep groan of doom in my blood, bewildered and dumbstruck; from an indestructible love of life, to affirm breath and laughter and the abiding innocence of things. I wrote the way I wept, and danced, and made love.

Ancestor

It was a time when they were afraid of him.
My father, a bare man, a gypsy, a horse
with broken knees no one would shoot.
Then again, he was like the orange tree,
and young women plucked from him sweet fruit.
To meet him, you must be in the right place,

even his sons and daughter, we wondered
where was papa now and what was he doing.
He held the mystique of travelers
that pass your backyard and disappear into the trees.
Then, when you follow, you find nothing,
not a stir, not a twig displaced from its bough.
And then he would appear one night.
Half covered in shadows and half in light,
his voice quiet, absorbing our unspoken thoughts.
When his hands lay on the table at breakfast,
they were hands that had not fixed our crumbling home,
hands that had not taken us into them
and the fingers did not gently rub along our lips.
They were hands of a gypsy that filled our home
with love and safety, for a moment;
with all the shambles of boards and empty stomachs,
they filled us because of the love in them.
Beyond the ordinary love, beyond the coordinated life,
beyond the sponging of broken hearts,
came the untimely word, the fallen smile, the quiet tear,
that made us grow up quick and romantic.
Papa gave us something: when we paused from work,
my sister fourteen years old working the cotton fields,
my brother and I running like deer,
we would pause, because we had a papa no one could catch,
who spoke when he spoke and bragged and drank,
he bragged about us: he did not say we were smart,
nor did he say we were strong and were going to be rich someday.
He said we were good. He held us up to the world for it to see,
three children that were good, who understood love in a quiet way,
who owned nothing but calloused hands and true freedom,
and that is how he made us: he offered us to the wind,
to the mountains, to the skies of autumn and spring.
He said, "Here are my children! Care for them!"
And he left again, going somewhere like a child
with a warrior's heart, nothing could stop him.
My grandmother would look at him for a long time,
and then she would say nothing.
She chose to remain silent, praying each night,
guiding down like a root in the heart of earth,
clutching sunlight and rains to her ancient breast.
And I am the blossom of many nights.
A threefold blossom: my sister is as she is,
my brother is as he is, and I am as I am.
Through sacred ceremony of living, daily living,
arose three distinct hopes, three loves,
out of the long felt nights and days of yesterday.

Healing Earthquakes

Through little garden plots I was mesmerized by,
Through streets torn and twisted like gnawed bark,
Through all the writers and artists of Americas
Parading by my fathers, I with their quills and
brushes,
Through all the stately documents,
Those of the Bible and political bodies of the
world,
And quietly by itself is the Healing Earthquake,
From all sides it comes,
Through the black-knotted drunkenness of my
father,
Through the cold deep bowels of hope,
Through the trowels of sombrero'd brick-layers
And wall-builders spreading the moist mortar,
Through the blacks in the South in grimy torn
t-shirts,
To the snarling CIA that broke loose from their
chains,
To the crumbled houses of my people,
Through the scorpion-tailed magnums and
carbines
Held at their heads,
Healing Earthquake comes up from the debris
and rubble,
Splitting its own body and heart,
Mumbling below in its own discontented winds,
Threading slowly my torn soul in a grip of fury,
To the eye of its mark it leans undaunted,
I am Healing Earthquake,
Not in the commotion swirling upwards of the atom
bomb,
Nor the blast and heraldic upshoot of a rocket,
A lesser man by all the law books,
A man awaking to the day with ground to stand upon
and defend.

Karen Brennan

Karen Brennan, who received her Ph.D. from the University of Arizona, is Associate Professor at the University of Utah, where she teaches creative writing and critical and feminist theories. Having published in a variety of genres, her work includes Here on Earth, *a book of poems,* Wild Desire, *a collection of short stories and winner of the prestigious Associated Writers Program Award for Fiction, and* Being with Rachel, *a memoir detailing the steps she took to facilitate her daughter's recovery from a serious motorcycle accident. "Runaways" and "Floating," which is reprinted in Chapter Four, "Reconsidering Gender and Space," were both first published in* Wild Desire.

Runaways

The day I escaped from my husband was ninety degrees and humid. Nevertheless, my neighbor Mrs. Williams stuffed all our winter clothes in the back of the blue VW station wagon. I told her to run up to the closets and get our things and what she grabbed were ski sweaters, my long yellow wool coat, the kids' flannel-lined corduroys, and a green garbage bag full of Finnish socks. She smashed everything into a box. The kids in the back seat were howling, on account of the heat, and because the box was crowding them. When they weren't howling, they poked each other. The oldest sat in the front and sucked her thumb.

Good-bye, life. Already we could see Mrs. Williams's flowered blouse merging with the driveway shrubbery. I felt fine, though my heart raced.

First we drove a long way to the bank. It was four towns over, and we drove on country roads since I avoid highways when possible. At the bank parking lot, I left the kids in the car and opened the windows. Don't move, I told them. Don't fight.

I felt conspicuous in the bank because of my clothes. I felt people looking at my torn blue jeans and my plaid shirt and thinking that I was a runaway. I *was* a runaway. I was very thin. No one would believe I had four children waiting for me in the car. The teller asked me for three forms of identification which, luckily, I was able to produce. Then I took exactly half from our joint checking account: six hundred dollars.

From then, things took a happier turn. I never had much sense about money—I couldn't seem to see into the future with it and so I drove straight to a Holiday Inn and rented a large suite of rooms. The children were very excited. They felt good about me.

Reprinted from *Wild Desire*, (1991), by permission of University of Massachusetts Press.

In the rooms they found ballpoints and pads of paper in the night-table drawers and they all crammed on one king-sized bed. I lay back on the double and clicked on the TV news. Maybe they had something about us escaping. But there was only a clip about a fire. Two children burned to death in an apartment. Their mother had been smoking a cigarette. I hated this kind of story. I turned it off and nursed the baby. I noticed a little rash on her arm.

After a while the kids went swimming in their underwear and for dinner we all had steak.

We stayed at the Holiday Inn for three days. I tried to think, but there was a cloud in my head. I knew my husband would be searching for us and it scared me to think about it. I lay on the double bed and watched the kids tear apart the suite of rooms. They dragged a giant bedspread into the bathroom and made a tent over the dressing counter. They pushed the box of clothes into the tent. They took all the hangers out of the closet and made a path. This is our new house, they said. Why don't you come over?

They drew pictures on the pads and scotch-taped them to the bedspread tent. My oldest daughter drew a picture of a princess who was rescued by an old man who lived in the woods and gave her a many-tiered castle and lots of jewelry. My son drew a few dozen triceratops. The baby lay next to me on the bed and nursed. It always gave me a light-headed feeling.

What next? they asked me.

It was still very hot and the car was not running properly. It had a failing battery. I wasn't sure what to do. We went shopping at the Holiday Inn gift store and bought T-shirts that said Holiday Inn A Great Resort Hotel across the backs. In the lounge I ran into a former babysitter.

Oh, Mrs., how are you and how are the children? she asked me. I poured out my whole story to her, the way you do.

She seemed surprised, but interested. Her face became animated and she called me by my first name, Lou. Stay with me, Lou, she said.

She meant I could stay with her at her parents' house. It was a ridiculous idea, but there was a cloud in my head. I said OK.

Her parents were very hospitable. They lived in a small cozy house with green wall-to-wall carpeting and a TV in the living room. They had five kids themselves. They were Christians. You could see their love of mankind twirling around in their kind eyes. But it was impersonal. We could have been anyone. This way I didn't need to feel beholden.

They gave us a nice bedroom and made their sons sleep on the fold-out living-room couch. They fed us fat slabs of ham with pineapple rings and creamed corn, and scrambled eggs for breakfast. My son asked me if he could stay there for a while. No, I said, though I felt a certain regret because what did I have to offer?

A woman without a husband is like a ship without a sea, I said to myself. I said it again and again. Even though I was the one who left. Some different husband, I said to God. A regular one. I prayed just in case, out of habit. Also, these were hard times—anything was worth a try. I am fighting for my life, I told God, I'll do anything you suggest.

I only spent one night at the babysitter's parents. I told them I was planning to go to my sister's in Rhode Island. I didn't feel desperate. Rather I was escaping a desperate situation. My husband beat me. The night before I left, I lay on the living-room couch with the front door ajar in case he came down in the middle of the night in one of his furies. I was afraid to go to sleep. Then it came to me out of nowhere: *this is no life*. Exactly, I thought. That night I slept like a baby and so, thank god, did my husband.

In the morning I stood over our bed and watched him. I felt I owed him a last look. He hated sheets. He slept rolled into a sleeping bag even in the hottest weather. He pulled the sleeping bag over his ears and a tuft of his blond hair poked over the top. It made me feel tender toward him, so I left the room. I knew what I had to do, but I needed to steel myself. I woke the children and piled them into the car as if they were tires. It felt that way. Then I called Mrs. Williams from a phone booth.

My sister lived in Rhode Island with her wealthy husband. They had a beautiful home with white pillars and a garden. I thought I'd go there for a while, even though my sister and I were not on the best of terms. Before I knew it, I was driving on the New England throughway headed for her house. It was a long drive and very hot. The children complained in the back seat, but I never lost my temper.

I am not one of those mothers who turns around in the car and swats the kids on the legs and tells them to shut up. I never believed in that. When they whined, I told stories. I told them about a family who sailed away in an orange balloon and visited different planets and had adventures. My children loved these stories. They made me tell the same ones over and over. If I changed something, they'd correct me. I was trying to give them hope, but the stories made me tired. I would have rather not talked. I would have rather looked straight ahead at the cars and the bridges and the sky. But it was my job to cheer them up. I had robbed them of their father, after all. But we were safe.

My husband didn't always beat me. In the beginning he was just irresponsible. I could live with that. He drank too much and in the worst times he drove too fast with the babies in the car. I would beg him to slow down or to let me drive, but he was a maniac when he was drunk. Once he stopped the car in the middle of the George Washington Bridge and got out. It was during an ice storm and the bridge shook. He called me a fucking bitch. He yelled it at the top of his lungs. I drove alongside of him while he weaved through the traffic. I was sure he'd get killed, but finally he got into the car.

In those days, I hit him back. I punched his arm with all my strength, but he'd just laugh. It's unfair, the advantage that men have. But what can you do about it? In those days, I was a little plumper than when I left him. I had all the babies in a row and put on some weight. I wore the right kinds of clothes—little wool skirts and white blouses with a pin. I was appropriate, but unhappy. My husband was tall and blond and handsome. He liked taking risks, and coming home bored him. We had difficulty talking to each other. Many times I could feel his contempt for me, for this plumpish wife who screamed at him to slow down.

Around that time I remember dancing with him at an outdoor wedding. He held me at arm's length, but it didn't matter. I was wearing a gray silk dress which made my hair look black. I felt attractive. The band was playing a song I liked very much, "My Funny Valentine." It was the song they played at our wedding.

My husband looked at me and winked. He gave me a little squeeze. For a moment, I felt relaxed and happy. Then a man with prematurely silver hair leaned over and said something. That's not the way you were dancing with that girl the other night, said this man. He didn't even bother to lower his voice. I might have been invisible. I remember breaking away from my husband's arms and walking over to some bushes. I thought I would never stop crying. A woman loaned me her handkerchief.

Then a man fell in love with me. It was so unexpected. He was one of the men who played cards with my husband on Wednesdays. His name was Nardo. This one Wednesday I was in the upstairs bathroom, trimming my hair. Suddenly, Nardo appeared next to me in the medicine cabinet mirror.

Don't cut your hair, he was saying. It's pretty.

His face was muscular, stubbled, weathered in a way because he had seen hard times. The children were sleeping, I had had a struggle getting them to bed because of the card-playing men and the noise they made.

Keep your voice down, was all I could think to tell Nardo.

Our eyes met in the mirror—oh, there was a cool challenge in that look—and he put his arms around me. He lowered his face so that his tough dark beard was just grazing my cheek. We stayed like that for a minute, me with my wet half-clipped hair and the scissors and Nardo holding on. It was like a photograph, very odd and beautiful, and it made me shiver.

I was never good at duplicity and so it went downhill from there. Nardo and I met a few times at the bar where he worked and in these meetings Nardo tried to persuade me to have an affair with him.

What's wrong with you, he finally said in exasperation, your old man is plugging every twenty-year-old in town and you're so passive, for God's sake. Or maybe you're a lesbian.

I had to laugh, but inside it was like a sword ripping through me. On the way home that day, I felt unable to breathe. After that, I became thin and beautiful.

On the way to Rhode Island, we stopped at the usual rest stations for bags of Fritos and hot dogs. Each time, I had the service station personnel charge up my battery. Whenever I saw a cop car I made the children duck down. I was sure there was an all-points bulletin out for me. Even the people sitting at the counter ordering coffees and root beers looked like spies sent by my husband. I told the children not to talk or look around. It was crazy, but I was sure we'd be dragged back to that house, we'd be dragged back and we'd never get free.

I was so thin I looked like a fourteen-year-old. My hair was long and shiny, very dark. I had no lines in my face and my clothes were not suitable for a mother. People eyed me suspiciously at the counter, they watched as I fed the baby sips of Coke and let her suck the salt from a Frito. The baby had a bad rash on her arm. She didn't look well tended.

From one of the rest stops I called Nardo. I could have depended on him for my escape, but it didn't seem right. I felt I could not go from one dependency to another. Also, our relationship lately was limited to phone calls. Now I called him from Massachusetts and told him we had run away. He was very surprised, but he couldn't talk long. He was busy in the bar.

Come to my place, he said. We'll figure out what to do from there.

What with the cloud in my head, it sounded reasonable. I turned around and headed south again. I drove about twenty miles and pulled off on the shoulder.

Let's take a vote, I told the kids. All in favor of going to Rhode Island, say ay, all in favor of going to Nardo's, say ay. No one said anything.

Let's just go home, said my daughter after a minute. She was clutching her doll with no hair and spoke with her thumb in her mouth.

We can't go home yet, I said.

Then, right there on the shoulder of the throughway, I burst into tears. I sobbed in big noisy gulps and pounded the steering wheel with my head. The children looked frightened and serious. They sat as still as statues.

I cried for about ten minutes, then I felt immeasurably better. Let's go to Cape Cod, I said. The kids liked that idea. So I turned around and headed north again.

My relationship with Nardo was limited to phone calls, as I've said, because I could not bear to sleep with him. I could not bear infidelity, even though my marriage had disintegrated. Why was that?

On the Wednesday nights when Nardo came to play cards, we hardly talked to each other, but on the phone he called me hon. On the phone he'd say, you're looking good hon. He was obsessed with my new thin body. You ought to tone up the thighs just a tad, hon, he'd say. I'd try to look sexy on those Wednesday nights in short shorts because, oh, what else was there. But it was laughable really.

And here I was, driving to Cape Cod and it was so beautiful, the ocean and the little houses. We checked into a motel, which was really more of a house that the people had converted to a motel. We got there at night and a woman in a blue terrycloth robe wrote all of our names in the loose-leaf register. In the morning we awoke to the sound of the waves, but at first I thought it was traffic. It's funny how sounds imitate each other. My daughter looked contented, for once. My sons pulled me out of bed and begged me to go swimming. The baby's rash was clearing up.

While the children played on the beach, arranging rows of shells on the wet part of the sand and watching the waves rumble in and sweep them away, I talked to the woman in the blue terrycloth robe who had checked us in. Only now she was wearing a black skirted bathing suit and a wide brimmed straw hat. Her name was Rose. She was saying how unusual it was to see a woman as young as myself with four children.

I'm actually the right age, I told her, it's because I'm thin.

Too thin, said Rose. If you ask me.

Rose had been living at the Cape all her life. Her husband's name was Charley and her son's name was Flea. Flea was about nineteen with long dark hair and eyes and narrow but nicely modulated shoulders. He didn't look like either Rose or Charley. He looked more like me. He offered to watch the kids if I wanted to go shopping. I didn't want to go shopping, but I needed a nap. Flea said he didn't mind watching them while I slept.

I slept right on the beach towel Rose gave me. When I woke up, I had a sunburn. Flea said he'd put some lotion on my shoulders since they looked sore. He and the kids had built a huge fortress out of sand. We could live here, Mom, said my son. Flea winked at me. He was handsome in a quiet unmasculine way and I could tell he liked me.

So how long do you figure on staying? said Rose that night. We all ate supper together, it was part of the deal—supper and breakfast and the one big room with two beds. Flea sat next to my son and helped him cut his meat.

We're not sure, I said. I tried to sound lighthearted, but I could tell I didn't fool Rose. She knew I was escaping. Her eyes narrowed as they surveyed me sitting there in my Holiday Inn T-shirt and the same old torn jeans.

Where are your people from? asked Charley. He was a big man in a coverall. He worked for the sanitation department. I could tell he didn't approve of us.

The next day, I sat on the bed for a long time and looked at the ocean through the window. I invented a story which would please Rose: we were on a real vacation, me and the kids, and my husband, a prominent lawyer who had just had a tumor removed from his brain, would join us in a few days. He would drive up in the Porsche and then we'd go shopping for clothes. We'd probably check out of this place and move to one which suited my husband a bit more—the Sheraton or someplace. I could imagine Rose's stern New England face dissolving into soft folds of sympathy if I told her this story.

It made me quite peaceful, imagining Rose's sympathetic face. I stacked the kids' drawings in a pile and folded the clean clothes from the box. I gathered the little bit of laundry we'd accumulated and stuffed it all into a plastic shopping bag which I found in the closet. The kids were on the beach with Flea, running and jumping around. I saw them from the window looking so happy.

I decided to call Nardo. I woke him up. What the hell do you think you're doing? he said. I've been waiting for you. We're with relatives on the Cape, I told him. We're having fun.

Oh great, said Nardo sarcastically. Then he paused to riffle through some newspapers and gag and cough and spit. He was always doing that. Once I had a dream about him and in the dream he was wearing a white three-piece suit and a panama hat. He looked impossibly aged. We were standing in some kind of tropical city with white buildings and awnings jutting over the windows. Nardo, in his white suit, stood in an angular shadow. I got the feeling he was dying. Good-bye Nardo, I said in the dream.

Now I got the feeling again, only it was stronger. His voice sounded far away and ill.

You could make it by six if you leave in the next half hour, he was saying.

I think not, I said. My heart was racing because I am usually not so direct.

What the hell are you talking about? he said. Then he calmed down. OK hon, he said. Keep in touch.

When I hung up the phone my heart was still racing.

Leaving my husband was hard enough, but leaving Nardo was harder. I wondered why that was. Perhaps because he thought I was beautiful. Perhaps because he didn't beat me.

I sat on the bed cradling the phone on my lap and looking at the kids playing on the beach. My sons sped by with towels tied over their shoulders like Superman. My daughter was crouched in the sand, tying the baby's hat under her chin. Flea turned toward the window and shaded his eyes. He waved up at me.

That night I went to bed with Flea. It happened like this. After the kids fell asleep, we went to the beach with a bottle of wine. Flea opened the wine with a corkscrew and we passed the bottle back and forth.

At first we were shy, since we were used to being with the kids. Now that we were alone, we couldn't think of what to say. There was a round moon, almost but not quite full, and Flea pointed out that its blurriness meant rain for tomorrow. Then I tried to identify a few constellations, but I was always hopeless at that. I only got the Little Dipper and the Pleiades, my favorite.

When the wine hit us, we started to talk nonstop. Flea talked about his old girlfriend and how she got married at sixteen to this guy who had been in jail for car theft, and I talked all about my husband and even about Nardo.

You're young to have so many kids, said Flea.

I'm not as young as I look, I said, and Flea touched the part of my hair that was streaked with gray. Hmmm, he said.

In the moonlight, how can I explain it? Flea looked even more like me. His long dark hair, his thinness, even the way he stretched out on the sand and leaned on his elbows and crossed his feet at the ankles. There was something loose and unself-conscious about him, and it reminded me of myself in my best moments.

Now he was winging little pebbles toward the ocean and humming something. I blew on his neck. Hi, he said. He turned toward me and lowered his eyes. The moonlight flickered on his serious face.

After four days at Flea's parents' motel, I realized I was running out of money. I had about sixty-four dollars left. But we had had four days of paradise. The kids were tan and healthy, the baby's rash was almost completely gone, and I didn't feel so alone. As I gathered their clothes from where they lay scattered on the floor of our room and under the bed, I felt the tears pressing behind my eyes. I didn't want to leave, but what choice did I have?

Just then my son came into the room with a live mussel shell. We pried it open and peeked in at the slimy animal, pale yellow with pulpy blue veins around the edges. We thought we could see it breathing.

I wonder if it dreams, my son said.

Of course it dreams, I said. It dreams that someone comes, some giant god with a giant hand, a hand so big that the mussel can't tell it's a hand, and it picks up the mussel and his little shell and pries it open. And the mussel dreams that of all the mussels in the world for some reason, for some bad luck reason or other, he was chosen for this awful adventure.

That's a horrible dream, said my son. I agreed with him. It was a nightmare.

In the afternoon, the baby and I were lying on the bed, nursing, when Rose knocked on the door. When she came in she didn't sit down. I understand you'll be leaving us then, she said.

I didn't know how she knew, but I said yes, that was right, we had to be going to my sister's in Rhode Island, we were expected. Rose fingered the plastic lace on the bureau and breathed in sharply through her nose. I suppose she didn't believe me. Then she looked at me and the baby. The baby had fallen asleep at my breast and her head was lolling to one side. There was a chill in the room and my exposed nipple got small and hard.

Rose shook her head. I don't know what you could be thinking about, she said in a clear voice.

I took it she was referring to Flea and me, but I couldn't be sure. She closed the door carefully on her way out.

I have no choice, I told Flea. We were standing on the shore letting the little waves slip over our bare feet. The children were splashing nearby. I had checked out of our room and given Rose what I owed which, as I said, left me with about sixty-four dollars. The car was packed and Flea had given me a new battery he happened to have around. This was good-bye.

What if I come along? asked Flea. I shook my head. There was no room in the car. But my son heard and said he'd stay in the caboose part and that Flea could have his seat.

There you go, said Flea. He took the baby from my arms and whirled her around.

What do you think, Snookers, he said to the baby. The baby howled with laughter.

I wasn't sure though. What would my sister say when we got to Rhode Island? Also, I wasn't sure we were really going to Rhode Island. Everything was so vague and confusing. I looked at the ocean, way out there, nothing but a line, where the mystery stops. I was hoping an answer would spring up from somewhere. Dear god, I said under my breath. But god didn't answer.

Flea whirled the baby around some more and the baby started to cry. Give her to me, I said. Flea looked wounded, his long dark hair, his thinnish shoulders, like mine.

I wasn't always thin, but I became thin as a result of life's circumstances. My husband plugging twenty-year-old girls, I guess that was it. I was so devastated that I didn't eat for months. I sat in the backyard on a blanket with the baby, who was an infant at the time, and felt nothing for anyone. I felt that they could come with stones and throw them at me, they could come with rope and lash at me, and it wouldn't change anything. My husband stopped drinking and became mean. He may have even stopped with the twenty-year-old girls. I had no way of knowing. He stood by me as I sat on the blanket and he beat the ground with a long rusty shovel. Snap out of it, he'd say, then he'd slap me around. It was during this period of my life that I gave Nardo a call. It was Nardo who pointed out that my looks had improved. He'd been watching me those Wednesday card-playing nights and he said I was a knockout now. It's amazing what a few pounds will do to a woman, he said.

My new beauty did not go unnoticed by my husband. It made him angry. He beat the ground with the shovel and slapped me around. I sat there, on the blanket, and nothing he could do could make me cry. I smiled at him, meanly. I don't care what you do anymore, I told him.

I watched the children as if from the wrong end of a telescope. They played and ran and ate and watched TV, but they weren't my children. They were like little specks scattered across a landscape. They were not connected to me. This made me sad, but it was a sadness I could not feel in my body. My body may have been thin and beautiful, but my soul had floated away. Sometimes I caught a glimpse of it in the trees, stuck up there like a kite.

Now it was different. We had escaped and the children were mine again. There they were on the beach, stuffing their pockets with stones and shells. There they were shrieking and lumping, their faces inexpressibly happy. Only the baby seemed disconsolate. She looked at me with her round blue eyes and I thought I saw the faint ugly traces of the rash reappearing on her arm.

Flea touched my shoulder. Lou, he said.

In Rhode Island, my sister sat on the screened patio with her two impeccably dressed children. In comparison, my own kids seemed like wild animals.

Why are they wearing corduroys in this heat? asked my sister.

She didn't say anything about my outfit, the Holiday Inn shirt and torn jeans that I'd been wearing on and off for a week. You look like a skeleton, she said.

She was not exactly pleased to see me. Her husband was away on business. You're not the only one in the world with problems, she said. I knew that, I told her. Flea was outside with the kids walking around their big yard. Her well-behaved children sat on the patio chairs at the glass table and played cards. Daniel is dyslexic, she told me. She sighed deeply.

I had never been close to my sister. We had different imaginations. She always knew exactly what she wanted. This was it: two impeccably dressed, well-behaved children, a wealthy husband, a beautiful house. I never knew what to wish for. This was my problem. I never had a big picture of my life, though as time went on I believed I saw little slivers of things that would fall into place and satisfy me. Maybe Flea was one of these.

Who is he anyway? said my sister. Don't tell me he's your lover.

I shrugged, embarrassed. He's good with the kids, I said. But my voice lacked conviction. Why was that?

My sister tossed her head impatiently. She wasn't one for sitting and talking. She stood up and looked into the garden. Lilacs and zinnia beds. Grass so evenly cut and of such a uniform green color that it looked artificial. The garden is amazing, I said. She pretended not to hear me.

Later she offered me a sundress that was way too big. It's better than what you have, she said. She wasn't one for sitting and talking, she believed in action. Put it on anyway, she said. She handed me a comb. Do you need anything else?

No thanks, I said. I was feeling a little humiliated.

Then my daughter wandered in holding the baby who was holding a lilac bloom. She loves the smell, said my daughter.

We don't pick those, please, said my sister.

My sister was not a mean person, she was only a bit cold. Her life had been superficially easy what with her wealthy husband, her nice house, her quiet children. It was exactly this life which made her bitter, you felt. You could spot it in the set of her mouth and the way she always stood up so abruptly. Twice I caught her looking at me with a peculiar expression on her face—once, as I wiped the drool from the baby's chin and again, when Flea came and touched my hair.

I suppose you two can share a bed, she said.

In the morning I put on the sundress and tied my hair back in a ribbon. The dress was big, but my sister found a sash made of silk grosgrain and we tied it around my waist. That looks great, she said. She was calmer now. We sat at the kitchen table and ate cinnamon toast.

I'm not planning on staying long, I said. I'm just trying to figure out things.

She nodded. Robert called yesterday, she said. Robert was my husband.

What did you tell him? I shuddered involuntarily at the sound of Robert's name. I could imagine him calling my sister and giving her some line on the phone.

I felt sorry for him, my sister said. She picked up the salt shaker and turned it in her hands. He wanted to know where his children were.

I see, I said. I took a bite of the toast just to be doing something, but I had trouble swallowing.

She sprinkled a few grains of salt into her palm and clapped them off. I told him I didn't know where you were.

Thanks, I said. I wanted to hug her, but as I've said there's something formidable about my sister—she didn't take well to hugs. I appreciate it, I said in lieu of a hug.

Oh well, she shrugged. I have enough problems of my own.

What are they? I asked her. I mean besides Daniel's dyslexia. Is it Michael? Is that it?

Michael was my sister's husband. He was always away on business trips.

Never mind, she said. I'd rather not talk about it. She brushed a few cinnamon toast crumbs into a napkin. Don't start, she said.

Your sister is nothing like you, said Flea later. We were lying on the bed in our room. The children were making seashell necklaces on the rug beside us. The baby was nursing. Your sister is old and pinched and nervous. You are full of life, said Flea.

I hated to hear him talk about my sister this way. I closed my eyes, felt the baby's long pulls on my breast. When I opened my eyes, Flea was looking at my face, regarding it as you might an interesting stone.

I pretend better, I said. I chucked him under the chin with my free hand.

That's what counts, he said.

We are never going home, are we Mom, my son said. He had climbed up on the bed with us and was straddling Flea's knee.

We have to go home, said my daughter from her place on the rug. I left my sandals there. And my bed.

She held up the necklace she'd made from the shells. Then she knelt on a pillow in back of me and tied it around my neck. It's perfect with your new sundress, she said.

During dinner, my sister received a phone call from her husband. When she came back to the table she was visibly upset. Her mouth trembled as she talked. Continue without me, she said.

I followed her to her room, but she slipped into the adjoining bathroom and locked the door. Leave me alone, she said from inside the locked bathroom.

I sat on the small tufted chair by her dressing table and waited. The room was eerily peaceful. Soft recessed lights played over the lace pillows on the bed, on the little Limoges china boxes on the dressing table, on the embroidered cushions set carefully in each corner of the divan with the expensive English print, on the filmy white curtains swaying in the long windows. Everything lovely and intact: crystal perfume bottles, silver picture frames, a tall walnut armoir with burled wood inlay, its brass key dangling from the knob, like a jewel. My sister liked to keep things. No, she liked to preserve things.

Finally, she unlocked the door. Her eyes were red and puffed up.

What is it? I said. Is it Michael?

Do me one favor, she said, don't talk to me.

You could leave him, I said.

A harsh note crept into her voice. It's not so easy for some of us, she said.

My sister hated good-byes. She disappeared behind the white pillars of her big house as soon as I turned on the ignition. But I could see her shadow slanted on the porch, motionless. I had no idea where we were going.

What next? said my son. He taped a picture of a triceratops on the back vent window. Flea held the baby on his lap in the passenger seat.

My other son produced the mussel shell from Cape Cod. Look Mom, he said. The mussel is still dreaming.

This time things have gotten better in the mussel's dream, I said. He's going to Texas with his family. He's excited about the beaches around the Gulf of Mexico.

He'll meet new relatives, my son added.

Yes, I said, and maybe he'll crawl out of his shell in this dream. He'll pop his little suckers loose and he'll slither away and have adventures.

The only thing is, Lou, said my son, is that he's dead I think.

It was true. The mussel didn't smell right.

It's gross, said my daughter. I think you should make him throw it out the window, Lou.

I didn't say anything. I drove straight into the glorious sunset, thinking of the mussel dead in my son's pocket this whole time. Thinking that if God's very hand were reaching down and nudging us along this flat shiny road or the next, I'd have no way of knowing.

Sherman Alexie

Sherman Alexie (b. 1966), a Spokane/Coeur d'Alene Indian, is the author of several novels, collections of poetry, and a collection of short stories, The Lone Ranger and Tonto Fistfight in Heaven *(1993). He adapted some of the stories from that collection into a screenplay, and the result was the award-winning movie* Smoke Signals. *Alexie's stories are fun and easy to read, yet carry complex messages about the nature of reservation life and the grim reality of alcoholism, loss of tradition, and the history of oppression that Native Americans have faced. Although often set on the Spokane Indian Reservation, his work has implications for all of us, particularly in considering our place in American society, the distances that separate us from each other, and the ties that bind us together. Survival, forgiveness, resistance, community, humor, and mythmaking are important themes for Alexie, who writes, "Survival = Anger x Imagination. Imagination is the only weapon on the reservation."*

Because My Father Always Said He Was the Only Indian Who Saw Jimi Hendrix Play "The Star-Spangled Banner" at Woodstock

During the sixties, my father was the perfect hippie, since all the hippies were trying to be Indians. Because of that, how could anyone recognize that my father was trying to make a social statement?

But there is evidence, a photograph of my father demonstrating in Spokane, Washington, during the Vietnam war. The photograph made it onto the wire service and was reprinted in newspapers throughout the country. In fact, it was on the cover of *Time*.

In the photograph, my father is dressed in bell-bottoms and flowered shirt, his hair in braids, with red peace symbols splashed across his face like war paint. In his hands my father holds a rifle above his head, captured in that moment just before he proceeded to beat the shit out of the National Guard private lying prone on the ground. A fellow demonstrator holds a sign that is just barely visible over my father's left shoulder. It read MAKE LOVE NOT WAR.

Reprinted from *The Lone Ranger and Tonto Fistfight in Heaven*, (1994), by permission of Grove/Atlantic, Inc.

The photographer won a Pulitzer Prize, and editors across the country had a lot of fun creating captions and headlines. I've read many of them collected in my father's scrapbook, and my favorite was run in the *Seattle Times*. The caption under the photograph read DEMONSTRATOR GOES TO WAR FOR PEACE. The editors capitalized on my father's Native American identity with other headlines like ONE WARRIOR AGAINST WAR and PEACEFUL GATHERING TURNS INTO NATIVE UPRISING.

Anyway, my father was arrested, charged with attempted murder, which was reduced to assault with a deadly weapon. It was a high-profile case so my father was used as an example. Convicted and sentenced quickly, he spent two years in Walla Walla State Penitentiary. Although his prison sentence effectively kept him out of the war, my father went through a different kind of war behind bars.

"There was Indian gangs and white gangs and black gangs and Mexican gangs," he told me once. "And there was somebody new killed every day. We'd hear about somebody getting it in the shower or wherever and the word would go down the line. Just one word. Just the color of his skin. Red, white, black, or brown. Then we'd chalk it up on the mental scoreboard and wait for the next broadcast."

My father made it through all that, never got into any serious trouble, somehow avoided rape, and got out of prison just in time to hitchhike to Woodstock to watch Jimi Hendrix play "The Star-Spangled Banner."

"After all the shit I'd been through," my father said, "I figured Jimi must have known I was there in the crowd to play something like that. It was exactly how I felt."

Twenty years later, my father played his Jimi Hendrix tape until it wore down. Over and over, the house filled with the rockets' red glare and the bombs bursting in air. He'd sit by the stereo with a cooler of beer beside him and cry, laugh, call me over and hold me tight in his arms, his bad breath and body odor covering me like a blanket.

Jimi Hendrix and my father became drinking buddies. Jimi Hendrix waited for my father to come home after a long night of drinking. Here's how the ceremony worked:

1. I would lie awake all night and listen for the sounds of my father's pickup.
2. When I heard my father's pickup, I would run upstairs and throw Jimi's tape into the stereo.
3. Jimi would bend his guitar into the first note of "The Star-Spangled Banner" just as my father walked inside.
4. My father would weep, attempt to hum along with Jimi, and then pass out with his head on the kitchen table.
5. I would fall asleep under the table with my head near my father's feet.
6. We'd dream together until the sun came up.

The days after, my father would feel so guilty that he would tell me stories as a means of apology.

"I met your mother at a party in Spokane," my father told me once. "We were the only two Indians at the party. Maybe the only two Indians in the whole town. I thought she was so beautiful. I figured she was the kind of woman who could make buffalo walk on up to her and give up their lives. She wouldn't have needed to hunt. Every time we went walking, birds would follow us around. Hell, tumbleweeds would follow us around."

Somehow my father's memories of my mother grew more beautiful as their relationship became more hostile. By the time the divorce was final, my mother was quite possibly the most beautiful woman who ever lived.

"Your father was always half crazy," my mother told me more than once. "And the other half was on medication."

But she loved him, too, with a ferocity that eventually forced her to leave him. They fought each other with the kind of graceful anger that only love can create. Still, their love was passionate, unpredictable, and selfish. My mother and father would get drunk and leave parties abruptly to go home and make love.

"Don't tell your father I told you this," my mother said. "But there must have been a hundred times he passed out on top of me. We'd be right in the middle of it, he'd say *I love you,* his eyes would roll backwards, and then out went his lights. It sounds strange, I know, but those were good times."

I was conceived, during one of those drunken nights, half of me formed by my father's whiskey sperm, the other half formed by my mother's vodka egg. I was born a goofy reservation mixed drink, and my father needed me just as much as he needed every other kind of drink.

One night my father and I were driving home in a near blizzard after a basketball game, listening to the radio. We didn't talk much. One, because my father didn't talk much when he was sober, and two, because Indians don't need to talk to communicate.

"Hello out there, folks, this is Big Bill Baggins, with the late-night classics show on KROC, 97.2 on your FM dial. We have a request from Betty in Tekoa. She wants to hear Jimi Hendrix's version of 'The Star-Spangled Banner' recorded live at Woodstock."

My father smiled, turned the volume up, and we rode down the highway while Jimi led the way like a snowplow. Until that night, I'd always been neutral about Jimi Hendrix. But, in that near-blizzard with my father at the wheel, with the nervous silence caused by the dangerous roads and Jimi's guitar, there seemed to be more to all that music. The reverberation came to mean something, took form and function.

That song made me want to learn to play guitar, not because I wanted to be Jimi Hendrix and not because I thought I'd ever play for anyone. I just wanted to touch the strings, to hold the guitar tight against my body, invent a chord, and come closer to what Jimi knew, to what my father knew.

"You know," I said to my father after the song was over, "my generation of Indian boys ain't ever had no real war to fight. The first Indians had Custer to fight. My great-grandfather had World War I, my grandfather had World War II, you had Vietnam. All I have is video games."

My father laughed for a long time, nearly drove off the road into the snowy fields.

"Shit," he said. "I don't know why you're feeling sorry for yourself because you ain't had to fight a war. You're lucky. Shit, all you had was that damn Desert Storm. Should have called it Dessert Storm because it just made the fat cats get fatter. It was all sugar and whipped cream with a cherry on top. And besides that, you didn't even have to fight it. All you lost during that war was sleep because you stayed up all night watching CNN."

We kept driving through the snow, talked about war and peace.

"That's all there is," my father said. "War and peace with nothing in between. It's always one or the other."

"You sound like a book," I said.

"Yeah, well, that's how it is. Just because it's in a book doesn't make it not true. And besides, why the hell would you want to fight a war for this country? It's been trying to kill Indians since the very beginning. Indians are pretty much born soldiers anyway. Don't need a uniform to prove it."

Those were the kinds of conversations that Jimi Hendrix forced us to have. I guess every song has a special meaning for someone somewhere. Elvis Presley is still showing up in 7-11 stores across the country, even though he's been dead for years, so I figure music just might be the most important thing there is. Music turned my father into a reservation philosopher. Music had powerful medicine.

"I remember the first time your mother and I danced," my father told me once. "We were in this cowboy bar. We were the only real cowboys there despite the fact that we're Indians. We danced to a Hank Williams song. Danced to that real sad one, you know. 'I'm So Lonesome I Could Cry.' Except your mother and I weren't lonesome or crying. We just shuffled along and fell right goddamn down into love."

"Hank Williams and Jimi Hendrix don't have much in common," I said.

"Hell, yes, they do. They knew all about broken hearts," my father said.

"You sound like a bad movie."

"Yeah, well, that's how it is. You kids today don't know shit about romance. Don't know shit about music either. Especially you Indian kids. You all have been spoiled by those drums. Been hearing them beat so long, you think that's all you need. Hell, son, even an Indian needs a piano or guitar or saxophone now and again."

My father played in a band in high school. He was the drummer. I guess he'd burned out on those. Now, he was like the universal defender of the guitar.

"I remember when your father would haul that old guitar out and play me songs," my mother said. "He couldn't play all that well but he tried. You could see him thinking about what chord he was going to play next. His eyes got all squeezed up and his face turned all red. He kind of looked that way when he kissed me, too. But don't tell him I said that."

Some nights I lay awake and listened to my parents' lovemaking. I know white people keep it quiet, pretend they don't ever make love. My white friends tell me they can't even imagine their own parents getting it on. I know exactly what it sounds like when my parents are touching each other. It makes up for knowing exactly what they sound like when they're fighting. Plus and minus. Add and subtract. It comes out just about even.

Some nights I would fall asleep to the sounds of my parents' lovemaking. I would dream Jimi Hendrix. I could see my father standing in the front row in the dark at Woodstock as Jimi Hendrix played "The Star-Spangled Banner." My mother was at home with me, both of us waiting for my father to find his way back home to the reservation. It's amazing to realize I was alive, breathing and wetting my bed, when Jimi was alive and breaking guitars.

I dreamed my father dancing with all these skinny hippie women, smoking a few joints, dropping acid, laughing when the rain fell. And it did rain there. I've seen actual news footage. I've seen the documentaries. It rained. People had to share food. People got sick. People got married. People cried all kinds of tears.

But as much as I dream about it, I don't have any clue about what it meant for my father to be the only Indian who saw Jimi Hendrix play at Woodstock. And maybe he wasn't the only Indian there. Most likely there were hundreds but my father thought he was the only one. He told me that a million times when he was drunk and a couple hundred times when he was sober.

"I was there," he said. "You got to remember this was near the end and there weren't as many people as before. Not nearly as many. But I waited it out. I waited for Jimi."

A few years back, my father packed up the family and the three of us drove to Seattle to visit Jimi Hendrix's grave. We had our photograph taken lying down next to the grave. There isn't a gravestone there. Just one of those flat markers.

Jimi was twenty-eight when he died. That's younger than Jesus Christ when he died. Younger than my father as we stood over the grave.

"Only the good die young," my father said.

"No," my mother said. "Only the crazy people choke to death on their own vomit."

"Why you talking about my hero that way?" my father asked.

"Shit," my mother said. "Old Jesse WildShoe choked to death on his own vomit and he ain't anybody's hero."

I stood back and watched my parents argue. I was used to these battles. When an Indian marriage starts to fall apart, it's even more destructive and painful than usual. A hundred years ago, an Indian marriage was broken easily. The woman or man just packed up all their possessions and left the tipi. There were no arguments, no discussions. Now, Indians fight their way to the end, holding onto the last good thing, because our whole lives have to do with survival.

After a while, after too much fighting and too many angry words had been exchanged, my father went out and bought a motorcycle. A big bike. He left the house often to ride that thing for hours, sometimes for days. He even strapped an old cassette player to the gas tank so he could listen to music. With that bike, he learned something new about running away. He stopped talking as much, stopped drinking as much. He didn't do much of anything except ride that bike and listen to music.

Then one night my father wrecked his bike on Devil's Gap Road and ended up in the hospital for two months. He broke both his legs, cracked his ribs, and punctured a lung. He also lacerated his kidney. The doctors said he could have died easily. In fact, they were surprised he made it through surgery, let alone survived those first few hours when he lay on the road, bleeding. But I wasn't surprised. That's how my father was.

And even though my mother didn't want to be married to him anymore and his wreck didn't change her mind about that, she still came to see him every day. She sang Indian tunes under her breath, in time with the hum of the machines hooked into my father. Although my father could barely move, he tapped his finger in rhythm.

When he had the strength to finally sit up and talk, hold conversations, and tell stories, he called for me.

"Victor," he said. "Stick with four wheels."

After he began to recover, my mother stopped visiting as often. She helped him through the worst, though. When he didn't need her anymore, she went back to the life she had created. She traveled to powwows, started to dance again. She was a champion traditional dancer when she was younger.

"I remember your mother when she was the best traditional dancer in the world," my father said. "Everyone wanted to call her sweetheart. But she only danced for me. That's how it was. She told me that every other step was just for me."

"But that's only half of the dance," I said.

"Yeah," my father said. "She was keeping the rest for herself. Nobody can give everything away. It ain't healthy."

"You know," I said, "sometimes you sound like you ain't even real."

"What's real? I ain't interested in what's real. I'm interested in how things should be."

My father's mind always worked that way. If you don't like the things you remember, then all you have to do is change the memories. Instead of remembering the bad things, remember what happened immediately before. That's what I learned from my father. For me, I remember how good the first drink of that Diet Pepsi tasted instead of how my mouth felt when I swallowed a wasp with the second drink.

Because of all that, my father always remembered the second before my mother left him for good and took me with her. No. I remembered the second before my father left my mother and me. No. My mother remembered the second before my father left her to finish raising me all by herself.

But however memory actually worked, it was my father who climbed on his motorcycle, waved to me as I stood in the window, and rode away. He lived in Seattle, San Francisco, Los Angeles, before he finally ended up in Phoenix. For a while, I got postcards nearly every week. Then it was once a month. Then it was on Christmas and my birthday.

On a reservation, Indian men who abandon their children are treated worse than white fathers who do the same thing. It's because white men have been doing that forever and Indian men have just learned how. That's how assimilation can work.

My mother did her best to explain it all to me, although I understood most of what happened.

"Was it because of Jimi Hendrix?" I asked her.

"Part of it, yeah," she said. "This might be the only marriage broken up by a dead guitar player."

"There's a first time for everything, enit?"

"I guess. Your father just likes being alone more than he likes being with other people. Even me and you."

Sometimes I caught my mother digging through old photo albums or staring at the wall or out the window. She'd get that look on her face that I knew meant she missed my father. Not enough to want him back. She missed him just enough for it to hurt.

On those nights I missed him most I listened to music. Not always Jimi Hendrix. Usually I listened to the blues. Robert Johnson mostly. The first time I heard Robert Johnson sing I knew he understood what it meant to be Indian on the edge of the twenty-first century, even if he was black at the beginning of the twentieth. That must have been how my father felt when he heard Jimi Hendrix. When he stood there in the rain at Woodstock.

Then on the night I missed my father most, when I lay in bed and cried, with that photograph of him beating that National Guard private in my hands, I imagined his motorcycle pulling up outside. I knew I was dreaming it all but I let it be real for a moment.

"Victor," my father yelled. "Let's go for a ride."

"I'll be right down. I need to get my coat on."

I rushed around the house, pulled my shoes and socks on, struggled into my coat, and ran outside to find an empty driveway. It was so quiet, a reservation kind of quiet, where you can hear somebody drinking whiskey on the rocks three miles away. I stood on the porch and waited until my mother came outside.

"Come on back inside," she said. "It's cold."

"No," I said. "I know he's coming back tonight."

My mother didn't say anything. She just wrapped me in her favorite quilt and went back to sleep. I stood on the porch all night long and imagined I heard motorcycles and guitars, until the sun rose so bright that I knew it was time to go back inside to my mother. She made breakfast for both of us and we ate until we were full.

Bob Dylan

Bob Dylan (b. 1941 as Robert Zimmerman) is a prolific songwriter and folk singer who has won several Grammys and written over three hundred songs. He has been called the "poet of the people" for speaking out with his lyrics and his poetry. His major collection of poems and prose is entitled Tarantula *(1971), but he has published his poetry in several places including* Writings and Drawings *(1973) and* Lyrics 1962–1999 *(1999). "Last Thoughts on Woody Guthrie" is a tribute to one of his most profound early influences. Guthrie, perhaps America's most well known folk singer, transformed the folk ballad into a vehicle for social commentary and protest during the 1930's and 1940's. He died in 1967 after suffering with Huntington's Chorea, a degenerative disorder of the nervous system, for over fifteen years. In "Last Thoughts on Woody Guthrie," Dylan honors Guthrie by using the poem as a space for social commentary instead of creating a straight-forward tribute to Guthrie himself. As all witnessing strives to do, he blends private experience with cultural influence to better help us see our responses as social manifestations.*

Last Thoughts on Woody Guthrie

When yer head gets twisted and yer mind grows numb
When you think you're too old, too young, too smart or too dumb
When yer laggin' behind an' losin' yer pace
In a slow-motion crawl or life's busy race
No matter what yer doing if you start givin' up
If the wine don't come to the top of yer cup
If the wind's got you sideways with one hand holdin' on
And the other starts slipping and the feeling is gone
And yer train engine fire needs a new spark to catch it
And the wood's easy findin' but yer lazy to fetch it
And yer sidewalk starts curlin' and the street gets too long
And you start walkin' backwards though you know that it's wrong
And lonesome comes up as down goes the day
And tomorrow's mornin' seems so far away
And you feel the reins from yer pony are slippin'
And yer rope is a-slidin' 'cause yer hands are a-drippin'
And yer sun-decked desert and evergreen valleys
Turn to broken down slums and trash-can alleys

Reprinted from *Bob Dylan Lyrics, 1962–1985*, (1998).

And yer sky cries water and yer drain pipe's a-pourin'
And the lightnin's a-flashing and the thunder's a-crashin'
And the windows are rattlin' and breakin' and the roof tops a-shakin'
And yer whole world's a-slammin' and bangin'
And yer minutes of sun turn to hours of storm
And to yourself you sometimes say
"I never knew it was gonna be this way
Why didn't they tell me the day I was born"
And you start gettin' chills and yer jumping from sweat
And you're lookin' for somethin' you ain't quite found yet
And yer knee-deep in dark water with yer hands in the air
And the whole world's a-watchin' with a window-peek stare
And yer good gal leaves and she's long gone a-flying
And yer heart feels sick like fish when they're fryin'
And yer jackhammer falls from yer hands to yer feet
And you need it badly but it lays on the street
And yer bell's bangin' loudly but you can't hear its beat
And you think yer ears might a been hurt
Or yer eyes've turned filthy from the sight-blindin' dirt
And you figured you failed in yesterday's rush
When you were faked out an' fooled while facing a four flush
And all the time you were holdin' three queens
And it's makin' you mad, it's makin' you mean
Like in the middle of *Life* magazine
Bouncin' around a pinball machine
And there's something on yer mind that you wanna be saying
That somebody someplace oughta be hearin'
But it's trapped on yer tongue and sealed in yer head
And it bothers you badly when you're layin' in bed
And no matter how you try you just can't say it
And yer scared to yer soul you just might forget it
And yer eyes get swimmy from the tears in yer head
And yer pillows of feathers turn to blankets of lead
And the lion's mouth opens and yer staring at his teeth
And his jaws start closin' with you underneath
And yer flat on yer belly with yer hands tied behind
And you wish you'd never taken that last detour sign
And you say to yerself just what am I doin'
On this road I'm walkin', on this trail I'm turnin'
On this curve I'm hanging
On this pathway I'm strolling, in the space I'm taking
In this air I'm inhaling
Am I mixed up too much, am I mixed up too hard
Why am I walking, where am I running
What am I saying, what am I knowing
On this guitar I'm playing, on this banjo I'm frailin'
On this mandolin I'm strummin', in the song I'm singin'

In the tune I'm hummin', in the words that I'm writin'
In the words that I'm thinkin'
In this ocean of hours I'm all the time drinkin'
Who am I helping, what am I breaking
What am I giving, what am I taking
But you try with yer whole soul best
Never to think these thoughts and never to let
Them kind of thoughts gain ground
Or make yer heart pound
But then again you know why they're around
Just waiting for a chance to slip and drop down
'Cause sometime you hear 'em when the night time comes creeping
And you fear that they might catch you a-sleeping
And you jump from yer bed, from yer last chapter of dreamin'
And you can't remember for the best of yer thinking
If that was you in the dream that was screaming
And you know that it's somethin' special you're needin'
And you know that there's no drug that'll do for the healin'
And no liquor in the land to stop yer brain from bleeding
And you need something special
Yeah, you need something special all right
You need a fast flyin' train on a tornado track
To shoot you someplace and shoot you back
You need a cyclone wind on a steam engine howler
That's been banging and booming and blowing forever
That knows yer troubles a hundred times over
You need a Greyhound bus that don't bar no race
That won't laugh at yer looks
Your voice or your face
And by any number of bets in the book
Will be rollin' long after the bubblegum craze
You need something to open up a new door
To show you something you seen before
But overlooked a hundred times or more
You need something to open yer eyes
You need something to make it known
That it's you and no one else that owns
That spot that yer standing, that space that you're sitting
That the world ain't got you beat
That it ain't got you licked
It can't get you crazy no matter how many
Times you might get kicked
You need something special all right
You need something special to give you hope
But hope's just a word
That maybe you said or maybe you heard
On some windy corner 'round a wide-angled curve

But that's what you need man, and you need it bad
And yer trouble is you know it too good
'Cause you look an' you start getting the chills

'Cause you can't find it on a dollar bill
And it ain't on Macy's window sill
And it ain't on no rich kid's road map
And it ain't in no fat kid's fraternity house
And it ain't made in no Hollywood wheat germ
And it ain't on that dimlit stage
With that half-wit comedian on it
Ranting and raving and taking yer money
And you think it's funny
No you can't find it in no night club or no yacht club
And it ain't in the seats of a supper club
And sure as hell you're bound to tell
That no matter how hard you rub
you just ain't a-gonna find it on yer ticket stub
No, and it ain't in the rumors people're tellin' you
And it ain't in the pimple-lotion people are sellin' you
And it ain't in no cardboard-box house
Or down any movie star's blouse
And you can't find it on the golf course
And Uncle Remus can't tell you and neither can Santa Claus
And it ain't in the cream puff hair-do or cotton candy clothes
And it ain't in the dime store dummies or bubblegum goons
And it ain't in the marshmallow noises of the chocolate cake voices
That come knockin' and tappin' in Christmas wrappin'
Sayin' ain't I pretty and ain't I cute and look at my skin
Look at my skin shine, look at my skin glow
Look at my skin laugh, look at my skin cry
When you can't even sense if they got any insides
These people so pretty in their ribbons and bows
No you'll not now or no other day
Find it on the doorsteps made out-a paper maché
And inside it the people made of molasses
That every other day buy a new pair of sunglasses
And it ain't in the fifty-star generals and flipped-out phonies
Who'd turn yuh in for a tenth of a penny
Who breathe and burp and bend and crack
And before you can count from one to ten
Do it all over again but this time behind yer back
My friend
The ones that wheel and deal and whirl and twirl
And play games with each other in their sand-box world
And you can't find it either in the no-talent fools
That run around gallant

And make all rules for the ones that got talent
And it ain't in the ones that ain't got any talent but think they do
And think they're foolin' you
The ones who jump on the wagon
Just for a while 'cause they know it's in style
To get their kicks, get out of it quick
And make all kinds of money and chicks
And you yell to yourself and you throw down yer hat
Sayin', "Christ do I gotta be like that
Ain't there no one here that knows where I'm at
Ain't there no one here that knows how I feel
Good God Almighty
THAT STUFF AIN'T REAL"

No but that ain't yer game, it ain't even yer race
You can't hear yer name, you can't see yer face
You gotta look some other place
And where do you look for this hope that yer seekin'
Where do you look for this lamp that's a-burnin'
Where do you look for this oil well gushin'
Where do you look for this candle that's glowin'
Where do you look for this hope that you know is there
And out there somewhere
And your feet can only walk down two kinds of roads
Your eyes can only look through two kinds of windows
Your nose can only smell two kinds of hallways
You can touch and twist
And turn two kinds of doorknobs
You can either go to the church of your choice
Or you can go to Brooklyn State Hospital
You'll find God in the church of your choice
You'll find Woody Guthrie in Brooklyn State Hospital

And though it's only my opinion
I may be right or wrong
You'll find them both
In the Grand Canyon
At sundown

James Baldwin

James Baldwin (1924–1987) was born and raised in New York City. He graduated from De Witt Clinton High School in 1942. After high school, he was variously employed as a handyman, dishwasher, waiter and office boy. In 1948 Baldwin moved to France because he felt artistically inhibited as a gay, black man in the United States. In France, he was able to write critically about race, sexual identity and social injustice in America, producing his first two novels Go Tell It on the Mountain *(1953) and* Giovanni's Room *(1956), and a collection of essays,* Notes of a Native Son *(1955). Nearly a decade later, Baldwin returned to New York where he became a national figure in the civil rights movement. Later, he returned to St. Paul de Vence, France, where he continued to live and write until his death of cancer in 1987. The short story* Sonny's Blues *was written in 1955, and the essay "The Uses of the Blues" was first published in* Playboy *in 1964.*

Sonny's Blues

I read about it in the paper, in the subway, on my way to work. I read it, and I couldn't believe it, and I read it again. Then perhaps I just stared at it, at the newsprint spelling out his name, spelling out the story. I stared at it in the swinging lights of the subway car, and in the faces and bodies of the people, and in my own face, trapped in the darkness which roared outside.

It was not to be believed and I kept telling myself that, as I walked from the subway station to the high school. And at the same time I couldn't doubt it. I was scared, scared for Sonny. He became real to me again. A great block of ice got settled in my belly and kept melting there slowly all day long, while I taught my classes algebra. It was a special kind of ice. It kept melting, sending trickles of ice water all up and down my veins, but it never got less. Sometimes it hardened and seemed to expand until I felt my guts were going to come spilling out or that I was going to choke or scream. This would always be at a moment when I was remembering some specific thing Sonny had once said or done.

When he was about as old as the boys in my classes his face had been bright and open, there was a lot of copper in it; and he'd had wonderfully direct brown eyes, and great gentleness and privacy. I wondered what he looked like now. He had been picked up, the evening before, in a raid on an apartment downtown, for peddling and using heroin.

I couldn't believe it: but what I mean by that is that I couldn't find any room for it anywhere inside me. I had kept it outside me for a long time. I hadn't wanted to know. I had had suspicions, but I didn't name them, I kept putting them away. I told myself that Sonny was wild, but he wasn't crazy. And he'd always been a good boy, he hadn't ever turned hard or evil or disrespectful, the way kids can, so quick, so quick, especially in Harlem. I didn't want to believe that I'd ever see my brother going down, coming to nothing, all that light in his face gone out, in the condition I'd already seen so many others. Yet it had happened and here I was, talking about algebra to a lot of boys who might, every one of them for all I knew, be popping off needles every time they went to the head.[1] Maybe it did more for them than algebra could.

I was sure that the first time Sonny had ever had horse,[2] he couldn't have been much older than these boys were now. These boys, now, were living as we'd been living then, they were growing up with a rush and their heads bumped abruptly against the low ceiling of their actual possibilities. They were filled with rage. All they really knew were two darknesses, the darkness of their lives, which was now closing in on them, and the darkness of the movies, which had blinded them to that other darkness, and in which they now, vindictively, dreamed, at once more together than they were at any other time, and more alone.

When the last bell rang, the last class ended, I let out my breath. It seemed I'd been holding it for all that time. My clothes were wet—I may have looked as though I'd been sitting in a steam bath, all dressed up, all afternoon. I sat alone in the classroom a long time. I listened to the boys outside, downstairs, shouting and cursing and laughing. Their laughter struck me for perhaps the first time. It was not the joyous laughter which—God knows why—one associates with children. It was mocking and insular, its intent to denigrate. It was disenchanted, and in this, also, lay the authority of their curses. Perhaps I was listening to them because I was thinking about my brother and in them I heard my brother. And myself.

One boy was whistling a tune, at once very complicated and very simple, it seemed to be pouring out of him as though he were a bird, and it sounded very cool and moving through all that harsh, bright air, only just holding its own through all those other sounds.

I stood up and walked over to the window and looked down into the courtyard. It was the beginning of the spring and the sap was rising in the boys. A teacher passed through them every now and again, quickly, as though he or she couldn't wait to get out of that courtyard, to get those boys out of their sight and off their minds. I started collecting my stuff. I thought I'd better get home and talk to Isabel.

The courtyard was almost deserted by the time I got downstairs. I saw this boy standing in the shadow of a doorway, looking just like Sonny. I almost called his name. Then I saw that it wasn't Sonny, but somebody we used to know, a boy from around our block. He'd been Sonny's friend. He'd never been mine, having been too young for me, and, anyway, I'd never liked him. And now, even though he was a grown-up man, he still hung around that block, still spent hours on the street corners, was always high and raggy. I used to run into him from time to time and he'd often work around to asking me for a quarter or fifty cents. He always had some real good excuse, too, and I always gave it to him, I don't know why.

But now, abruptly, I hated him. I couldn't stand the way he looked at me, partly like a dog, partly like a cunning child. I wanted to ask him what the hell he was doing in the school courtyard.

He sort of shuffled over to me, and he said, "I see you got the papers. So you already know about it."

"You mean about Sonny? Yes, I already know about it. How come they didn't get you?"

He grinned. It made him repulsive and it also brought to mind what he'd looked like as a kid. "I wasn't there. I stay away from them people."

"Good for you." I offered him a cigarette and I watched him through the smoke. "You come all the way down here just to tell me about Sonny?"

"That's right." He was sort of shaking his head and his eyes looked strange, as though they were about to cross. The bright sun deadened his damp dark brown skin and it made his eyes look yellow and showed up the dirt in his kinked hair. He smelled funky. I moved a little away from him and I said, "Well, thanks. But I already know about it and I got to get home."

"I'll walk you a little ways," he said. We started walking. There were a couple of kids still loitering in the courtyard and one of them said goodnight to me and looked strangely at the boy beside me.

"What're you going to do?" he asked me. "I mean, about Sonny?"

"Look. I haven't seen Sonny for over a year. I'm not sure I'm going to do anything. Anyway, what the hell *can* I do?"

"That's right," he said quickly, "ain't nothing you can do. Can't much help old Sonny no more, I guess."

It was what I was thinking and so it seemed to me he had no right to say it.

"I'm surprised at Sonny, though," he went on—he had a funny way of talking, he looked straight ahead as though he were talking to himself—"I thought Sonny was a smart boy, I thought he was too smart to get hung."

"I guess he thought so too," I said sharply, "and that's how he got hung. And how about you? You're pretty goddamn smart, I bet."

Then he looked directly at me, just for a minute. "I ain't smart," he said. "If I was smart, I'd have reached for a pistol a long time ago."

"Look. Don't tell *me* your sad story, if it was up to me, I'd give you one." Then I felt guilty—guilty, probably, for never having supposed that the poor bastard *had* a story of his own, much less a sad one, and I asked, quickly, "What's going to happen to him now?"

He didn't answer this. He was off by himself some place.

"Funny thing," he said, and from his tone we might have been discussing the quickest way to get to Brooklyn, "when I saw the papers this morning, the first thing I asked myself was if I had anything to do with it. I felt sort of responsible."

I began to listen more carefully. The subway station was on the corner, just before us, and I stopped. He stopped, too. We were in front of a bar and he ducked slightly, peering in, but whoever he was looking for didn't seem to be there. The juke box was blasting away with something black and bouncy and I half watched the barmaid as she danced her way from the juke box to her place behind the bar. And I watched her face as she laughingly responded to something someone said to her, still keeping time to the music. When she smiled one saw the little girl, one sensed the doomed, still-struggling woman beneath the battered face of the semi-whore.

"I never *give* Sonny nothing," the boy said finally, "but a long time ago I come to school high and Sonny asked me how it felt." He paused, I couldn't bear to watch him, I watched the barmaid, and I listened to the music which seemed to be causing the pavement to shake. "I told him it felt great." The music stopped, the barmaid paused and watched the juke box until the music began again. "It did."

All this was carrying me some place I didn't want to go. I certainly didn't want to know how it felt. It filled everything, the people, the houses, the music, the dark, quicksilver barmaid, with menace; and this menace was their reality.

"What's going to happen to him now?" I asked again.

"They'll send him away some place and they'll try to cure him." He shook his head. "Maybe he'll even think he's kicked the habit. Then they'll let him loose"—he gestured, throwing his cigarette into the gutter. "That's all."

"What do you mean, that's *all*?"

But I knew what he meant.

"I *mean,* that's *all.*" He turned his head and looked at me, pulling down the corners of his mouth. "Don't you know what I mean?" he asked, softly.

"How the hell *would* I know what you mean?" I almost whispered it, I don't know why.

"That's right," he said to the air, "how would *he* know what I mean?" He turned toward me again, patient and calm, and yet I somehow felt him shaking, shaking as though he were going to fall apart. I felt that ice in my guts again, the dread I'd felt all afternoon; and again I watched the barmaid, moving about the bar, washing glasses, and singing. "Listen. They'll let him out and then it'll just start all over again. That's what I mean."

"You mean—they'll let him out. And then he'll just start working his way back in again. You mean he'll never kick the habit. Is that what you mean?"

"That's right," he said, cheerfully. "*You* see what I mean."

"Tell me," I said at last, "why does he want to die? He must want to die, he's killing himself, why does he want to die?"

He looked at me in surprise. He licked his lips. "He don't want to die. He wants to live. Don't nobody want to die, ever."

Then I wanted to ask him—too many things. He could not have answered, or if he had, I could not have borne the answers. I started walking. "Well, I guess it's none of my business."

"It's going to be rough on old Sonny," he said. We reached the subway station. "This is your station?" he asked. I nodded. I took one step down. "Damn!" he said, suddenly. I looked up at him. He grinned again. "Damn it if I didn't leave all my money home. You ain't got a dollar on you, have you? Just for a couple of days, is all."

All at once something inside gave and threatened to come pouring out of me. I didn't hate him any more. I felt that in another moment I'd start crying like a child.

"Sure," I said. "Don't sweat." I looked in my wallet and didn't have a dollar, I only had a five. "Here," I said. "That hold you?"

He didn't look at it—he didn't want to look at it. A terrible closed look came over his face, as though he were keeping the number on the bill a secret from him and me. "Thanks," he said, and now he was dying to see me go. "Don't worry about Sonny. Maybe I'll write him or something."

"Sure," I said. "You do that. So long."

"Be seeing you," he said. I went on down the steps.

And I didn't write Sonny or send him anything for a long time. When I finally did, it was just after my little girl died, he wrote me back a letter which made me feel like a bastard.

Here's what he said:

> Dear brother,
>
> You don't know how much I needed to hear from you. I wanted to write you many a time but I dug how much I must have hurt you and so I didn't write. But now I feel like a man who's been trying to climb up out of some deep, real deep and funky hole and just saw the sun up there, outside. I got to get outside.
>
> I can't tell you much about how I got here. I mean I don't know how to tell you. I guess I was afraid of something or I was trying to escape from something and you know I have never been very strong in the head (smile). I'm glad Mama and Daddy are dead and can't see what's happened to their son and I swear if I'd known what I was doing I would never have hurt you so, you and a lot of other fine people who were nice to me and who believed in me.
>
> I don't want you to think it had anything to do with me being a musician. It's more than that. Or maybe less than that. I can't get anything straight in my head down here and I try not to think about what's going to happen to me when I get outside again. Sometime I think I'm going to flip and *never* get outside and sometime I think I'll come straight back. I tell you one thing, though, I'd rather blow my brains out than go through this again. But that's what they all say, so they tell me. If I tell you when I'm coming to New York and if you could meet me, I sure would appreciate it. Give my love to Isabel and the kids and I was sure sorry to hear about little Gracie. I wish I could be like Mama and say the Lord's will be done, but I don't know it seems to me that trouble is the one thing that never does get stopped and I don't know what good it does to blame it on the Lord. But maybe it does some good if you believe it.
>
> Your brother,
> Sonny

Then I kept in constant touch with him and I sent him whatever I could and I went to meet him when he came back to New York. When I saw him many things I thought I had forgotten came flooding back to me. This was because I had begun, finally, to wonder about Sonny, about the life that Sonny lived inside. This life, whatever it was, had made him older and thinner and it had deepened the distant stillness in which he had always moved. He looked very unlike my baby brother. Yet, when he smiled, when we shook hands, the baby brother I'd never known looked out from the depths of his private life, like an animal waiting to be coaxed into the light.

"How you been keeping?" he asked me.

"All right. And you?"

"Just fine." He was smiling all over his face. "It's good to see you again."

"It's good to see you."

The seven years' difference in our ages lay between us like a chasm: I wondered if these years would ever operate between us as a bridge. I was remembering, and it made it hard to catch my breath, that I had been there when he was born; and I had heard the first words he had ever spoken. When he started to walk, he walked from our mother straight to me. I caught him just before he fell when he took the first steps he ever took in this world.

"How's Isabel?"

"Just fine. She's dying to see you."

"And the boys?"

"They're fine, too. They're anxious to see their uncle."

"Oh, come on. You know they don't remember me."

"Are you kidding? Of course they remember you."

He grinned again. We got into a taxi. We had a lot to say to each other, far too much to know how to begin.

As the taxi began to move, I asked, "You still want to go to India?"

He laughed. "You still remember that. Hell, no. This place is Indian enough for me."

"It used to belong to them," I said.

And he laughed again. "They damn sure knew what they were doing when they got rid of it."

Years ago, when he was around fourteen, he'd been all hipped on the idea of going to India. He read books about people sitting on rocks, naked, in all kinds of weather, but mostly bad, naturally, and walking barefoot through hot coals and arriving at wisdom. I used to say that it sounded to me as though they were getting away from wisdom as fast as they could. I think he sort of looked down on me for that.

"Do you mind," he asked, "if we have the driver drive alongside the park? On the west side—I haven't seen the city in so long."

"Of course not," I said. I was afraid that I might sound as though I were humoring him, but I hoped he wouldn't take it that way.

So we drove along, between the green of the park and the stony, lifeless elegance of hotels and apartment buildings, toward the vivid, killing streets of our childhood. These streets hadn't changed, though housing projects jutted up out of them now like rocks in the middle of a boiling sea. Most of the houses in which we had grown up had vanished, as had the stores from which we had stolen, the basements in which we had first tried sex, the rooftops from which we had hurled tin cans and bricks. But houses exactly like the houses of our past yet dominated the landscape, boys exactly like the boys we once had been found themselves smothering in these houses, came down into the streets for light and air and found themselves encircled by disaster. Some escaped the trap, most didn't. Those who got out always left something of themselves behind, as some animals amputate a leg and leave it in the trap. It might be said, perhaps, that I had escaped, after all, I was a school teacher; or that Sonny had, he hadn't lived in Harlem for years. Yet, as the cab moved uptown through streets which seemed, with a rush, to darken with dark people, and as I covertly studied Sonny's face, it came to me that what we both were seeking through our separate cab windows was that part of ourselves which had been left behind. It's always at the hour of trouble and confrontation that the missing member aches.

We hit 110th Street and started rolling up Lenox Avenue. And I'd known this avenue all my life, but it seemed to me again, as it had seemed on the day I'd first heard about Sonny's trouble, filled with a hidden menace which was its very breath of life.

"We almost there," said Sonny.

"Almost." We were both too nervous to say anything more.

We live in a housing project. It hasn't been up long. A few days after it was up it seemed uninhabitably new, now, of course, it's already rundown. It looks like a parody of the good, clean, faceless life—God knows the people who live in it do their best to make it a parody. The beat-looking grass lying around isn't enough to make their lives green, the hedges will never hold out the streets, and they know it. The big windows fool no one, they aren't big enough to make space out of no space. They don't bother with the windows, they watch the TV screen instead. The playground is most popular with the children who don't play at jacks, or skip rope, or roller skate, or swing, and they can be found in it after dark. We moved in partly because it's not too far from where I teach, and partly for the kids; but it's really just like the houses in which Sonny and I grew up. The same things happen, they'll have the same things to remember. The moment Sonny and I started into the house I had the feeling that I was simply bringing him back into the danger he had almost died trying to escape.

Sonny has never been talkative. So I don't know why I was sure he'd be dying to talk to me when supper was over the first night. Everything went fine, the oldest boy remembered him, and the youngest boy liked him, and Sonny had remembered to bring something for each of them; and Isabel, who is really much nicer than I am, more open and giving, had gone to a lot of trouble about dinner and was genuinely glad to see him. And she's always been able to tease Sonny in a way that I haven't. It was nice to see her face so vivid again and to hear her laugh and watch her make Sonny laugh. She wasn't, or, anyway, she didn't seem to be, at all uneasy or embarrassed. She chatted as though there were no subject which had to be avoided and she got Sonny past his first, faint stiffness. And thank God she was there, for I was filled with that icy dread again. Everything I did seemed awkward to me, and everything I said sounded freighted with hidden meaning. I was trying to remember everything I'd heard about dope addiction and I couldn't help watching Sonny for signs. I wasn't doing it out of malice. I was trying to find out something about my brother. I was dying to hear him tell me he was safe.

"Safe!" my father grunted, whenever Mama suggested trying to move to a neighborhood which might be safer for children. "Safe, hell! Ain't no place safe for kids, nor nobody."

He always went on like this, but he wasn't, ever, really as bad as he sounded, not even on weekends, when he got drunk. As a matter of fact, he was always on the lookout for "something a little better," but he died before he found it. He died suddenly, during a drunken weekend in the middle of the war, when Sonny was fifteen. He and Sonny hadn't ever got on too well. And this was partly because Sonny was the apple of his father's eye. It was because he loved Sonny so much and was frightened for him, that he was always fighting with him. It doesn't do any good to fight with Sonny. Sonny just moves back, inside himself, where he can't be reached. But the principal reason that they never hit it off is that they were so much alike. Daddy was big and rough and loud-talking, just the opposite of Sonny, but they both had—that same privacy.

Mama tried to tell me something about this, just after Daddy died. I was home on leave from the army.

This was the last time I ever saw my mother alive. Just the same, this picture gets all mixed up in my mind with pictures I had of her when she was younger. The way I always see her is the way she used to be on a Sunday afternoon, say, when the old folks were talking after the big Sunday dinner. I always see her wearing pale blue. She'd be sitting on the sofa. And my father would be sitting in the easy chair, not far from her. And the living room would be full of church folks and relatives. There they sit, in chairs all around the living room, and the night is creeping up outside, but nobody knows it yet. You can see the darkness growing against the windowpanes and you hear the street noises every now and again, or maybe the jangling beat of a tambourine from one of the churches close by, but it's real quiet in the room. For a moment nobody's talking, but every face looks darkening, like the sky outside. And my mother rocks a little from the waist, and my father's eyes are closed. Everyone is looking at something a child can't see. For a minute they've forgotten the children. Maybe a kid is lying on the rug, half asleep. Maybe somebody's got a kid in his lap and is absent-mindedly stroking the kid's head. Maybe there's a kid, quiet and big-eyed, curled up in a big chair in the corner. The silence, the darkness coming, and the darkness in the faces frightens the child obscurely. He hopes that the hand which strokes his forehead will never stop—will never die. He hopes that there will never come a time when the old folks won't be sitting around the living room, talking about where they've come from, and what they've seen, and what's happened to them and their kinfolk.

But something deep and watchful in the child knows that this is bound to end, is already ending. In a moment someone will get up and turn on the light. Then the old folks will remember the children and they won't talk any more that day. And when light fills the room, the child is filled with darkness. He knows that every time this happens he's moved just a little closer to that darkness outside. The darkness outside is what the old folks have been talking about. It's what they've come from. It's what they endure. The child knows that they won't talk any more because if he knows too much about what's happened to *them,* he'll know too much too soon, about what's going to happen to *him.*

The last time I talked to my mother, I remember I was restless. I wanted to get out and see Isabel. We weren't married then and we had a lot to straighten out between us.

There Mama sat, in black, by the window. She was humming an old church song, *Lord, you brought me from a long ways off.* Sonny was out somewhere. Mama kept watching the streets.

"I don't know," she said, "if I'll ever see you again, after you go off from here. But I hope you'll remember the things I tried to teach you."

"Don't talk like that," I said, and smiled. "You'll be here a long time yet."

She smiled, too, but she said nothing. She was quiet for a long time. And I said, "Mama, don't you worry about nothing. I'll be writing all the time, and you be getting the checks. . . ."

"I want to talk to you about your brother," she said, suddenly. "If anything happens to me he ain't going to have nobody to look out for him."

"Mama," I said, "ain't nothing going to happen to you *or* Sonny. Sonny's all right. He's a good boy and he's got good sense."

"It ain't a question of his being a good boy," Mama said, "nor of his having good sense. It ain't only the bad ones, nor yet the dumb ones that gets sucked under." She stopped, looking at me. "Your Daddy once had a brother," she said, and she smiled in a way that made me feel she was in pain. "You didn't never know that, did you?"

"No," I said, "I never knew that," and I watched her face.

"Oh, yes," she said, "your Daddy had a brother." She looked out of the window again. "I know you never saw your Daddy cry. But *I* did—many a time, through all these years."

I asked her, "What happened to his brother? How come nobody's ever talked about him?"

This was the first time I ever saw my mother look old.

"His brother got killed," she said, "when he was just a little younger than you are now. I knew him. He was a fine boy. He was maybe a little full of the devil, but he didn't mean nobody no harm."

Then she stopped and the room was silent, exactly as it had sometimes been on those Sunday afternoons. Mama kept looking out into the streets.

"He used to have a job in the mill," she said, "and, like all young folks, he just liked to perform on Saturday nights. Saturday nights, him and your father would drift around to different places, go to dances and things like that, or just sit around with people they knew, and your father's brother would sing, he had a fine voice, and play along with himself on his guitar. Well, this particular Saturday night, him and your father was coming home from some place, and they were both a little drunk and there was a moon that night, it was bright like day. Your father's brother was feeling kind of good, and he was whistling to himself, and he had his guitar slung over his shoulder. They was coming down a hill and beneath them was a road that turned off from the highway. Well, your father's brother, being always kind of frisky, decided to run down this hill, and he did, with that guitar banging and clanging behind him, and he ran across the road, and he was making water behind a tree. And your father was sort of amused at him and he was still coming down the hill, kind of slow. Then he heard a car motor and that same minute his brother stepped from behind the tree, into the road, in the moonlight. And he started to cross the road. And your father started to run down the hill, he says he don't know why. This car was full of white men. They was all drunk, and when they seen your father's brother they let out a great whoop and holler and they aimed the car straight at him. They was having fun, they just wanted to scare him, the way they do sometimes, you know. But they was drunk. And I guess the boy, being drunk, too, and scared, kind of lost his head. By the time he jumped it was too late. Your father says he heard his brother scream when the car rolled over him, and he heard the wood of that guitar when it give, and he heard them strings go flying, and he heard them white men shouting, and the car kept on a-going and it ain't stopped till this day. And, time your father got down the hill, his brother weren't nothing but blood and pulp."

Tears were gleaming on my mother's face. There wasn't anything I could say.

"He never mentioned it," she said, "because I never let him mention it before you children. Your Daddy was like a crazy man that night and for many a night thereafter. He says he never in his life seen anything as dark as that road after the lights of that car had gone away. Weren't nothing, weren't nobody on that road, just your Daddy and his brother and that busted guitar. Oh, yes. Your Daddy never did really get right again. Till the day he died he weren't sure but that every white man he saw was the man that killed his brother."

She stopped and took out her handkerchief and dried her eyes and looked at me.

"I ain't telling you all this," she said, "to make you scared or bitter or to make you hate nobody. I'm telling you this because you got a brother. And the world ain't changed."

I guess I didn't want to believe this. I guess she saw this in my face. She turned away from me, toward the window again, searching those streets.

"But I praise my Redeemer," she said at last, "that He called your Daddy home before me. I ain't saying it to throw no flowers at myself, but, I declare, it keeps me from feeling too cast down to know I helped your father get safely through this world. Your father always acted like he was the roughest, strongest man on earth. And everybody took him to be like that. But if he hadn't had me there—to see his tears!"

She was crying again. Still, I couldn't move. I said, "Lord, Lord, Mama, I didn't know it was like that."

"Oh, honey," she said, "there's a lot that you don't know. But you are going to find out." She stood up from the window and came over to me. "You got to hold on to your brother," she said, "and don't let him fall, no matter what it looks like is happening to him and no matter how evil you gets with him. You going to be evil with him many a time. But don't you forget what I told you, you hear?"

"I won't forget," I said. "Don't you worry, I won't forget. I won't let nothing happen to Sonny."

My mother smiled as though she were amused at something she saw in my face. Then, "You may not be able to stop nothing from happening. But you got to let him know you's *there.*"

Two days later I was married, and then I was gone. And I had a lot of things on my mind and I pretty well forgot my promise to Mama until I got shipped home on a special furlough for her funeral.

And, after the funeral, with just Sonny and me alone in the empty kitchen, I tried to find out something about him.

"What do you want to do?" I asked him.

"I'm going to be a musician," he said.

For he had graduated, in the time I had been away, from dancing to the juke box to finding out who was playing what, and what they were doing with it, and he had bought himself a set of drums.

"You mean, you want to be a drummer?" I somehow had the feeling that being a drummer might be all right for other people but not for my brother Sonny.

"I don't think," he said, looking at me very gravely, "that I'll ever be a good drummer. But I think I can play a piano."

I frowned. I'd never played the role of the older brother quite so seriously before, had scarcely ever, in fact, *asked* Sonny a damn thing. I sensed myself in the presence of something I didn't really know how to handle, didn't understand. So I made my frown a little deeper as I asked: "What kind of musician do you want to be?"

He grinned. "How many kinds do you think there are?"

"Be *serious,*" I said.

He laughed, throwing his head back, and then looked at me. "I *am* serious."

"Well, then, for Christ's sake, stop kidding around and answer a serious question. I mean, do you want to be a concert pianist, you want to play classical music and all that, or—or what?" Long before I finished he was laughing again. "For Christ's *sake,* Sonny!"

He sobered, but with difficulty. "I'm sorry. But you sound so—*scared!*" and he was off again.

"Well, you may think it's funny now, baby, but it's not going to be so funny when you have to make your living at it, let me tell you *that.*" I was furious because I knew he was laughing at me and I didn't know why.

"No," he said, very sober now, and afraid, perhaps, that he'd hurt me, "I don't want to be a classical pianist. That isn't what interests me. I mean"—he paused, looking hard at me, as though his eyes would help me to understand, and then gestured helplessly, as though perhaps his hand would help—"I mean, I'll have a lot of studying to do, and I'll have to study *everything,* but, I mean, I want to play *with*—jazz musicians." He stopped. "I want to play jazz," he said.

Well, the word had never before sounded as heavy, as real, as it sounded that afternoon in Sonny's mouth. I just looked at him and I was probably frowning a real frown by this time. I simply couldn't see why on earth he'd want to spend his time hanging around nightclubs, clowning around on bandstands, while people pushed each other around a dance floor. It seemed—beneath him, somehow. I had never thought about it before, had never been forced to, but I suppose I had always put jazz musicians in a class with what Daddy called "good-time people."

"Are you *serious?*"

"Hell, *yes,* I'm serious."

He looked more helpless than ever, and annoyed, and deeply hurt.

I suggested, helpfully: "You mean—like Louis Armstrong?"

His face closed as though I'd struck him. "No. I'm not talking about none of that old-time, down home crap."

"Well, look, Sonny, I'm sorry, don't get mad. I just don't altogether get it, that's all. Name somebody—you know, a jazz musician you admire."

"Bird."

"Who?"

"Bird! Charlie Parker![3] Don't they teach you nothing in the goddamn army?"

I lit a cigarette. I was surprised and then a little amused to discover that I was trembling. "I've been out of touch," I said. "You'll have to be patient with me. Now. Who's this Parker character?"

"He's just one of the greatest jazz musicians alive," said Sonny, sullenly, his hands in his pockets, his back to me. "Maybe *the* greatest," he added, bitterly, "that's probably why *you* never heard of him."

"All right," I said, "I'm ignorant. I'm sorry. I'll go out and buy all the cat's records right away, all right?"

"It don't," said Sonny, with dignity, "make any difference to me. I don't care what you listen to. Don't do me no favors."

I was beginning to realize that I'd never seen him so upset before. With another part of my mind I was thinking that this would probably turn out to be one of those things kids go through and that I shouldn't make it seem important by pushing it too hard. Still, I didn't think it would do any harm to ask: "Doesn't all this take a lot of time? Can you make a living at it?"

He turned back to me and half leaned, half sat, on the kitchen table. "Everything takes time," he said, "and—well, yes, sure, I can make a living at it. But what I don't seem to be able to make you understand is that it's the only thing I want to do."

"Well, Sonny," I said, gently, "you know people can't always do exactly what they *want* to do—"

"*No,* I don't know that," said Sonny, surprising me. "I think people *ought* to do what they want to do, what else are they alive for?"

"You getting to be a big boy," I said desperately, "it's time you started thinking about your future."

"I'm thinking about my future," said Sonny, grimly. "I think about it all the time."

I gave up. I decided, if he didn't change his mind, that we could always talk about it later. "In the meantime," I said, "you got to finish school." We had already decided that he'd have to move in with Isabel and her folks. I knew this wasn't the ideal arrangement because Isabel's folks are inclined to be dicty[4] and they hadn't especially wanted Isabel to marry me. But I didn't know what else to do. "And we have to get you fixed up at Isabel's."

There was a long silence. He moved from the kitchen table to the window. "That's a terrible idea. You know it yourself."

"Do you have a *better* idea?"

He just walked up and down the kitchen for a minute. He was as tall as I was. He had started to shave. I suddenly had the feeling that I didn't know him at all.

He stopped at the kitchen table and picked up my cigarettes. Looking at me with a kind of mocking, amused defiance, he put one between his lips. "You mind?"

"You smoking already?"

He lit the cigarette and nodded, watching me through the smoke. "I just wanted to see if I'd have the courage to smoke in front of you." He grinned and blew a great cloud of smoke to the ceiling. "It was easy." He looked at my face. "Come on, now. I bet you was smoking at my age, tell the truth."

I didn't say anything but the truth was on my face, and he laughed. But now there was something very strained in his laugh. "Sure. And I bet that ain't all you was doing."

He was frightening me a little. "Cut the crap," I said. "We already decided that you was going to go and live at Isabel's. Now what's got into you all of a sudden?"

"*You* decided it," he pointed out. "*I* didn't decide nothing." He stopped in front of me, leaning against the stove, arms loosely folded. "Look, brother. I don't want to stay in Harlem no more, I really don't." He was very earnest. He looked at me, then over toward the kitchen window. There was something in his eyes I'd never seen before, some thoughtfulness, some worry all his own. He rubbed the muscle of one arm. "It's time I was getting out of here."

"Where do you want to *go,* Sonny?"

"I want to join the army. Or the navy, I don't care. If I say I'm old enough, they'll believe me."

Then I got mad. It was because I was so scared. "You must be crazy. You goddamn fool, what the hell do you want to go and join the *army* for?"

"I just told you. To get out of Harlem."

"Sonny, you haven't even finished *school.* And if you really want to be a musician, how do you expect to study if you're in the *army*?"

He looked at me, trapped, and in anguish. "There's ways. I might be able to work out some kind of deal. Anyway, I'll have the G.I. Bill when I come out."

"*If* you come out." We stared at each other. "Sonny, please. Be reasonable. I know the setup is far from perfect. But we got to do the best we can."

"I ain't learning nothing in school," he said. "Even when I go." He turned away from me and opened the window and threw his cigarette out into the narrow alley. I watched his back. "At least, I ain't learning nothing you'd want me to learn." He slammed the window so hard I thought the glass would fly out, and turned back to me. "And I'm sick of the stink of these garbage cans!"

"Sonny," I said, "I know how you feel. But if you don't finish school now, you're going to be sorry later that you didn't." I grabbed him by the shoulders. "And you only got another year. It ain't so bad. And I'll come back and I swear I'll help you do *whatever* you want to do. Just try to put up with it till I come back. Will you please do that? For me?"

He didn't answer and he wouldn't look at me.

"Sonny. You hear me?"

He pulled away. "I hear you. But you never hear anything *I* say."

I didn't know what to say to that. He looked out of the window and then back at me. "OK," he said, and sighed. "I'll try."

Then I said, trying to cheer him up a little, "They got a piano at Isabel's. You can practice on it."

And as a matter of fact, it did cheer him up for a minute. "That's right," he said to himself. "I forgot that." His face relaxed a little. But the worry, the thoughtfulness, played on it still, the way shadows play on a face which is staring into the fire.

But I thought I'd never hear the end of that piano. At first, Isabel would write me, saying how nice it was that Sonny was so serious about his music and how, as soon as he came in from school, or wherever he had been when he was supposed to be at school, he went straight to that piano and stayed there until suppertime. And, after supper, he went back to that piano and stayed there until everybody went to bed. He was at the piano all day Saturday and all day Sunday. Then he bought a record player and started playing records. He'd play one record over and over again, all day long sometimes, and he'd improvise along with it on the piano. Or he'd play one section of the record, one chord, one change, one progression, then he'd do it on the piano. Then back to the record. Then back to the piano.

Well, I really don't know how they stood it. Isabel finally confessed that it wasn't like living with a person at all, it was like living with sound. And the sound didn't make any sense to her, didn't make any sense to any of them—naturally. They began, in a way, to be afflicted by this presence that was living in their home. It was as though Sonny were some sort of god, or monster. He moved in an atmosphere which wasn't like theirs at all. They fed him and he ate, he washed himself, he walked in and out of their door; he certainly wasn't nasty or unpleasant or rude, Sonny isn't any of those things; but it was as though he were all wrapped up in some cloud, some fire, some vision all his own; and there wasn't any way to reach him.

At the same time, he wasn't really a man yet, he was still a child, and they had to watch out for him in all kinds of ways. They certainly couldn't throw him out. Neither did they dare to make a great scene about that piano because even they dimly sensed, as I sensed, from so many thousands of miles away, that Sonny was at that piano playing for his life.

But he hadn't been going to school. One day a letter came from the school board and Isabel's mother got it—there had, apparently, been other letters but Sonny had torn them up. This day, when Sonny came in, Isabel's mother showed him the letter and asked where he'd been spending his time. And she finally got it out of him that he'd been down in Greenwich Village, with musicians and other characters, in a white girl's apartment. And this scared her and she started to scream at him and what came up, once she began—though she denies it to this day—was what sacrifices they were making to give Sonny a decent home and how little he appreciated it.

Sonny didn't play the piano that day. By evening, Isabel's mother had calmed down but then there was the old man to deal with, and Isabel herself. Isabel says she did her best to be calm but she broke down and started crying. She says she just watched Sonny's face. She could tell, by watching him, what was happening with him. And what was happening was that they penetrated his cloud, they had reached him. Even if their fingers had been a thousand times more gentle than human fingers ever are, he could hardly help feeling that they had stripped him naked and were spitting on that nakedness. For he also had to see that his presence, that music, which was life or death to him, had been torture for them and that they had endured it, not at all for his sake, but only for mine. And Sonny couldn't take that. He can take it a little better today than he could then but he's still not very good at it and, frankly, I don't know anybody who is.

The silence of the next few days must have been louder than the sound of all the music ever played since time began. One morning, before she went to work, Isabel was in his room for something and she suddenly realized that all of his records were gone. And she knew for certain that he was gone. And he was. He went as far as the navy would carry him. He finally sent me a postcard from some place in Greece and that was the first I knew that Sonny was still alive. I didn't see him any more until we were both back in New York and the war had long been over.

He was a man by then, of course, but I wasn't willing to see it. He came by the house from time to time, but we fought almost every time we met. I didn't like the way he carried himself, loose and dreamlike all the time, and I didn't like his friends, and his music seemed to be merely an excuse for the life he led. It sounded just that weird and disordered.

Then we had a fight, a pretty awful fight, and I didn't see him for months. By and by I looked him up, where he was living, in a furnished room in the Village, and I tried to make it up. But there were lots of other people in the room and Sonny just lay on his bed, and he wouldn't come downstairs with me, and he treated these other people as though they were his family and I weren't. So I got mad and then he got mad, and then I told him that he might just as well be dead as live the way he was living. Then he stood up and he told me not to worry about him any more in life, that he *was* dead as far as I was concerned. Then he pushed me to the door and the other people looked on as though nothing were happening, and he slammed the door behind me. I stood in the hallway, staring at the door. I heard somebody laugh in the room and then the tears came to my eyes. I started down the steps, whistling to keep from crying, I kept whistling to myself, *You going to need me, baby, one of these cold, rainy days.*

I read about Sonny's trouble in the spring. Little Grace died in the fall. She was a beautiful little girl. But she only lived a little over two years. She died of polio and she suffered. She had a slight fever for a couple of days, but it didn't seem like anything and we just kept her in bed. And we would certainly have called the doctor, but the fever dropped, she seemed to be all right. So we thought it had just been a cold. Then, one day, she was up, playing, Isabel was in the kitchen fixing lunch for the two boys when they'd come in from school, and she heard Grace fall down in the living room. When you have a lot of children you don't always start running when one of them falls, unless they start screaming or something. And, this time, Grace was quiet. Yet, Isabel says that when she heard that *thump* and then that silence, something happened in her to make her afraid. And she ran to the living room and there was little Grace on the floor, all twisted up, and the reason she hadn't screamed was that she couldn't get her breath. And when she did scream, it was the worst sound, Isabel says, that she'd ever heard in all her life, and she still hears it sometimes in her dreams. Isabel will sometimes wake me up with a low, moaning, strangling sound and I have to be quick to awaken her and hold her to me and where Isabel is weeping against me seems a mortal wound.

I think I may have written Sonny the very day that little Grace was buried. I was sitting in the living room in the dark, by myself, and I suddenly thought of Sonny. My trouble made his real.

One Saturday afternoon, when Sonny had been living with us, or, anyway, been in our house, for nearly two weeks, I found myself wandering aimlessly about the living room, drinking from a can of beer, and trying to work up the courage to search Sonny's room. He was out, he was usually out whenever I was home, and Isabel had taken the children to see their grandparents. Suddenly I was standing still in front of the living room window, watching Seventh Avenue. The idea of searching Sonny's room made me still. I scarcely dared to admit to myself what I'd be searching for. I didn't know what I'd do if I found it. Or if I didn't.

On the sidewalk across from me, near the entrance to a barbecue joint, some people were holding an old-fashioned revival meeting. The barbecue cook, wearing a dirty white apron, his conked[5] hair reddish and metallic in the pale sun, and a cigarette between his lips, stood in the doorway, watching them. Kids and older people paused in their errands and stood there, along with some older men and a couple of very tough-looking women who watched everything that happened on the avenue, as though they owned it, or were maybe owned by it. Well, they were watching this, too. The revival was being carried on by three sisters in black, and a brother. All they had were their voices and their Bibles and a tambourine. The brother was testifying[6] and while he testified two of the sisters stood together, seeming to say, amen, and the third sister walked around with the tambourine outstretched and a couple of people dropped coins into it. Then the brother's testimony ended and the sister who had been taking up the collection dumped the coins into her palm and transferred them to the pocket of her long black robe. Then she raised both hands, striking the tambourine against the air, and then against one hand, and she started to sing. And the two other sisters and the brother joined in.

It was strange, suddenly, to watch, though I had been seeing these meetings all my life. So, of course, had everybody else down there. Yet, they paused and watched and listened and I stood still at the window. "*Tis the old ship of Zion,*" they sang, and the sister with the tambourine kept a steady, jangling beat, "*it has rescued many a thousand!*" Not a soul under the sound of their voices was hearing this song for the first time, not one of them had been rescued. Nor had they seen much in the way of rescue work being done around them. Neither did they especially believe in the holiness of the three sisters and the brother, they knew too much about them, knew where they lived, and how. The woman with the tambourine, whose voice dominated the air, whose face was bright with joy, was divided by very little from the woman who stood watching her, a cigarette between her heavy, chapped lips, her hair a cuckoo's nest, her face scarred and swollen from many beatings, and her black eyes glittering like coal. Perhaps they both knew this, which was why, when, as rarely, they addressed each other, they addressed each other as Sister. As the singing filled the air the watching, listening faces underwent a change, the eyes focusing on something within; the music seemed to soothe a poison out of them; and time seemed, nearly, to fall away from the sullen, belligerent, battered faces, as though they were fleeing back to their first condition, while dreaming of their last. The barbecue cook half shook his head and smiled, and dropped his cigarette and disappeared into his joint. A man fumbled in his pockets for change and stood holding it in his hand impatiently, as though he had just remembered a pressing appointment further up the avenue. He looked furious. Then I saw Sonny, standing on the edge of the crowd. He was carrying a wide, flat notebook with a green cover, and it made him look, from where I was standing, almost like a schoolboy. The coppery sun brought out the copper in his skin, he was very faintly smiling, standing very still. Then the singing stopped, the tambourine turned into a collection plate again. The furious man dropped in his coins and vanished, so did a couple of the women, and Sonny dropped some change in the plate, looking directly at the woman with a little smile. He started across the avenue, toward the house. He has a slow, loping walk, something like the way Harlem hipsters walk, only he's imposed on this his own half-beat. I had never really noticed it before.

I stayed at the window, both relieved and apprehensive. As Sonny disappeared from my sight, they began singing again. And they were still singing when his key turned in the lock.

"Hey," he said.

"Hey, yourself. You want some beer?"

"No. Well, maybe." But he came up to the window and stood beside me, looking out. "What a warm voice," he said.

They were singing *If I could only hear my mother pray again!*

"Yes," I said, "and she can sure beat that tambourine."

"But what a terrible song," he said, and laughed. He dropped his notebook on the sofa and disappeared into the kitchen. "Where's Isabel and the kids?"

"I think they went to see their grandparents. You hungry?"

"No." He came back into the living room with his can of beer. "You want to come some place with me tonight?"

I sensed, I don't know how, that I couldn't possibly say no. "Sure. Where?"

He sat down on the sofa and picked up his notebook and started leafing through it. "I'm going to sit in with some fellows in a joint in the Village."

"You mean, you're going to play, tonight?"

"That's right." He took a swallow of his beer and moved back to the window. He gave me a sidelong look. "If you can stand it."

"I'll try," I said.

He smiled to himself and we both watched as the meeting across the way broke up. The three sisters and the brother, heads bowed, were singing *God be with you till we meet again.* The faces around them were very quiet. Then the song ended. The small crowd dispersed. We watched the three women and the lone man walk slowly up the avenue.

"When she was singing before," said Sonny, abruptly, "her voice reminded me for a minute of what heroin feels like sometimes—when it's in your veins. It makes you feel sort of warm and cool at the same time. And distant. And—and sure." He sipped his beer, very deliberately not looking at me. I watched his face. "It makes you feel—in control. Sometimes you've got to have that feeling."

"Do you?" I sat down slowly in the easy chair.

"Sometimes." He went to the sofa and picked up his notebook again. "Some people do."

"In order," I asked, "to play?" And my voice was very ugly, full of contempt and anger.

"Well"—he looked at me with great, troubled eyes, as though, in fact, he hoped his eyes would tell me things he could never otherwise say—"they *think* so. And *if* they think so—!"

"And what do *you* think?" I asked.

He sat on the sofa and put his can of beer on the floor. "I don't know," he said, and I couldn't be sure if he were answering my question or pursuing his thoughts. His face didn't tell me. "It's not so much to *play.* It's to *stand* it, to be able to make it at all. On any level." He frowned and smiled: "In order to keep from shaking to pieces."

"But these friends of yours," I said, "they seem to shake themselves to pieces pretty goddamn fast."

"Maybe." He played with the notebook. And something told me that I should curb my tongue, that Sonny was doing his best to talk, that I should listen. "But of course you only know the ones that've gone to pieces. Some don't—or at least they haven't *yet* and that's just about all *any* of us can say." He paused. "And then there are some who just live, really, in hell, and they know it and they see what's happening and they go right on. I don't know." He sighed, dropped the notebook, folded his arms. "Some guys, you can tell from the way they play, they on something *all* the time. And you can see that, well, it makes something real for them. But of course," he picked up his beer from the floor and sipped it and put the can down again, "they *want* to, too, you've got to see that. Even some of them that say they don't—*some,* not all."

"And what about you?" I asked—I couldn't help it. "What about you? Do *you* want to?"

He stood up and walked to the window and remained silent for a long time. Then he sighed. "Me," he said. Then: "While I was downstairs before, on my way here, listening to that woman sing, it struck me all of a sudden how much suffering she must have had to go through—to sing like that. It's *repulsive* to think you have to suffer that much."

I said: "But there's no way not to suffer—is there, Sonny?"

"I believe not," he said and smiled, "but that's never stopped anyone from trying." He looked at me. "Has it?" I realized, with this mocking look, that there stood between us, forever, beyond the power of time or forgiveness, the fact that I had held silence—so long!—when he had needed human speech to help him. He turned back to the window. "No, there's no way not to suffer. But you try all kinds of ways to keep from drowning in it, to keep on top of it, and to make it seem—well, like *you.* Like you did something, all right, and now you're suffering for it. You know?" I said nothing. "Well you know," he said, impatiently, "why *do* people suffer? Maybe it's better to do something to give it a reason, *any* reason."

"But we just agreed," I said, "that there's no way not to suffer. Isn't it better, then, just to—take it?"

"But nobody just takes it," Sonny cried, "that's what I'm telling you! *Everybody* tries not to. You're just hung up on the *way* some people try—it's not *your* way!"

The hair on my face began to itch, my face felt wet. "That's not true," I said, "that's not true. I don't give a damn what other people do, I don't even care how they suffer. I just care how *you* suffer." And he looked at me. "Please believe me," I said, "I don't want to see you—die—trying not to suffer."

"I won't," he said, flatly, "die trying not to suffer. At least, not any faster than anybody else."

"But there's no need," I said, trying to laugh, "is there? in killing yourself."

I wanted to say more, but I couldn't. I wanted to talk about will power and how life could be—well, beautiful. I wanted to say that it was all within; but was it? or, rather, wasn't that exactly the trouble? And I wanted to promise that I would never fail him again. But it would all have sounded—empty words and lies.

So I made the promise to myself and prayed that I would keep it.

"It's terrible sometimes, inside," he said, "that's what's the trouble. You walk these streets, black and funky and cold, and there's not really a living ass to talk to, and there's nothing shaking, and there's no way of getting it out—that storm inside. You can't talk it and you can't make love with it, and when you finally try to get with it and play it, you realize *nobody's* listening. So *you've* got to listen. You got to find a way to listen."

And then he walked away from the window and sat on the sofa again, as though all the wind had suddenly been knocked out of him. "Sometimes you'll do *anything* to play, even cut your mother's throat." He laughed and looked at me. "Or your brother's." Then he sobered. "Or your own." Then: "Don't worry. I'm all right now and I think I'll *be* all right. But I can't forget—where I've been. I don't mean just the physical place I've been, I mean where I've *been.* And *what* I've been."

"What have you been, Sonny?" I asked.

He smiled—but sat sideways on the sofa, his elbow resting on the back, his fingers playing with his mouth and chin, not looking at me. "I've been something I didn't recognize, didn't know I could be. Didn't know anybody could be." He stopped, looking inward, looking helplessly young, looking old. "I'm not talking about it now because I feel *guilty* or anything like that—maybe it would be better if I did, I don't know. Anyway, I can't really talk about it. Not to you, not to anybody," and now he turned and faced me. "Sometimes, you know, and it was actually when I was most *out* of the world, I felt that I was in it, that I was *with* it, really, and I could play or I didn't really have to *play,* it just came out of me, it was there. And I don't know how I played, thinking about it now, but I know I did awful things, those times, sometimes, to people. Or it wasn't that I *did* anything to them—it was that they weren't real." He picked up the beer can; it was empty; he rolled it between his palms: "And other times—well, I needed a fix, I needed to find a place to lean, I needed to clear a space to *listen*—and I couldn't find it, and I—went crazy, I did terrible things to *me,* I was terrible *for* me." He began pressing the beer can between his hands, I watched the metal begin to give. It glittered, as he played with it like a knife, and I was afraid he would cut himself, but I said nothing. "Oh well. I can never tell you. I was all by myself at the bottom of something, stinking and sweating and crying and shaking, and I smelled it, you know? *my* stink, and I thought I'd die if I couldn't get away from it and yet, all the same, I knew that everything I was doing was just locking me in with it. And I didn't know," he paused, still flattening the beer can, "I didn't know, I still *don't* know, something kept telling me that maybe it was good to smell your own stink, but I didn't think that *that* was what I'd been trying to do—and—who can stand it?" and he abruptly dropped the ruined beer can, looking at me with a small, still smile, and then rose, walking to the window as though it were the lodestone rock. I watched his face, he watched the avenue. "I couldn't tell you when Mama died—but the reason I wanted to leave Harlem so bad was to get away from drugs. And then, when I ran away, that's what I was running from—really. When I came back, nothing had changed, *I* hadn't changed, I was just—older." And he stopped, drumming with his fingers on the windowpane. The sun had vanished, soon darkness would fall. I watched his face. "It can come again," he said, almost as though speaking to himself. Then he turned to me. "It can come again," he repeated. "I just want you to know that."

"All right," I said, at last. "So it can come again, All right."

He smiled, but the smile was sorrowful. "I had to try to tell you," he said.

"Yes," I said. "I understand that."

"You're my brother," he said, looking straight at me, and not smiling at all.

"Yes," I repeated, "yes. I understand that."

He turned back to the window, looking out. "All that hatred down there," he said, "all that hatred and misery and love. It's a wonder it doesn't blow the avenue apart."

We went to the only nightclub on a short, dark street, downtown. We squeezed through the narrow, chattering, jam-packed bar to the entrance of the big room, where the bandstand was. And we stood there for a moment, for the lights were very dim in this room and we couldn't see. Then, "Hello, boy," said a voice and an enormous black man, much older than Sonny or myself, erupted out of all that atmospheric lighting and put an arm around Sonny's shoulder. "I been sitting right here," he said, "waiting for you."

He had a big voice, too, and heads in the darkness turned toward us.

Sonny grinned and pulled a little away, and said, "Creole, this is my brother. I told you about him."

Creole shook my hand. "I'm glad to meet you, son," he said, and it was clear that he was glad to meet me *there,* for Sonny's sake. And he smiled, "You got a real musician in *your* family," and he took his arm from Sonny's shoulder and slapped him, lightly, affectionately, with the back of his hand.

"Well. Now I've heard it all," said a voice behind us. This was another musician, and a friend of Sonny's, a coal-black, cheerful-looking man, built close to the ground. He immediately began confiding to me, at the top of his lungs, the most terrible things about Sonny, his teeth gleaming like a lighthouse and his laugh coming up out of him like the beginning of an earthquake. And it turned out that everyone at the bar knew Sonny, or almost everyone; some were musicians, working there, or nearby, or not working, some were simply hangers-on, and some were there to hear Sonny play. I was introduced to all of them and they were all very polite to me. Yet, it was clear that, for them, I was only Sonny's brother. Here, I was in Sonny's world. Or, rather: his kingdom. Here, it was not even a question that his veins bore royal blood.

They were going to play soon and Creole installed me, by myself, at a table in a dark corner. Then I watched them, Creole, and the little black man, and Sonny, and the others, while they horsed around, standing just below the bandstand. The light from the bandstand spilled just a little short of them and, watching them laughing and gesturing and moving about, I had the feeling that they, nevertheless, were being most careful not to step into that circle of light too suddenly; that if they moved into the light too suddenly, without thinking, they would perish in flame. Then, while I watched, one of them, the small black man, moved into the light and crossed the bandstand and started fooling around with his drums. Then—being funny and being, also, extremely ceremonious—Creole took Sonny by the arm and led him to the piano. A woman's voice called Sonny's name and a few hands started clapping. And Sonny, also being funny and being ceremonious, and so touched, I think, that he could have cried, but neither hiding it nor showing it, riding it like a man, grinned, and put both hands to his heart and bowed from the waist.

Creole then went to the bass fiddle and a lean, very bright-skinned brown man jumped up on the bandstand and picked up his horn. So there they were, and the atmosphere on the bandstand and in the room began to change and tighten. Someone stepped up to the microphone and announced them. Then there were all kinds of murmurs. Some people at the bar shushed others. The waitress ran around, frantically getting in the last orders, guys and chicks got closer to each other, and the lights on the bandstand, on the quartet, turned to a kind of indigo. Then they all looked different there. Creole looked about him for the last time, as though he were making certain that all his chickens were in the coop, and then he— jumped and struck the fiddle. And there they were.

All I know about music is that not many people ever really hear it. And even then, on the rare occasions when something opens within, and the music enters, what we mainly hear, or hear corroborated, are personal, private, vanishing evocations. But the man who creates the music is hearing something else, is dealing with the roar rising from the void and imposing order on it as it hits the air. What is evoked in him, then, is of another order, more terrible because it has no words, and triumphant, too, for that same reason. And his triumph, when he triumphs, is ours. I just watched Sonny's face. His face was troubled, he was working hard, but he wasn't with it. And I had the feeling that, in a way, everyone on the bandstand was waiting for him, both waiting for him and pushing him along. But as I began to watch Creole, I realized that it was Creole who held them all back. He had them on a short rein. Up there, keeping the beat with his whole body, wailing on the fiddle, with his eyes half closed, he was listening to everything, but he was listening to Sonny. He was having a dialogue with Sonny. He wanted Sonny to leave the shoreline and strike out for the deep water. He was Sonny's witness that deep water and drowning were not the same thing—he had been there, and he knew. And he wanted Sonny to know. He was waiting for Sonny to do the things on the keys which would let Creole know that Sonny was in the water.

And, while Creole listened, Sonny moved, deep within, exactly like someone in torment. I had never before thought of how awful the relationship must be between the musician and his instrument. He has to fill it, this instrument, with the breath of life, his own. He has to make it do what he wants it to do. And a piano is just a piano. It's made out of so much wood and wires and little hammers and big ones, and ivory. While there's only so much you can do with it, the only way to find this out is to try; to try and make it do everything.

And Sonny hadn't been near a piano for over a year. And he wasn't on much better terms with his life, not the life that stretched before him now. He and the piano stammered, started one way, got scared, stopped; started another way, panicked, marked time, started again; then seemed to have found a direction, panicked again, got stuck. And the face I saw on Sonny I'd never seen before. Everything had been burned out of it, and, at the same time, things usually hidden were being burned in, by the fire and fury of the battle which was occurring in him up there.

Yet, watching Creole's face as they neared the end of the first set, I had the feeling that something had happened, something I hadn't heard. Then they finished, there was scattered applause, and then, without an instant's warning, Creole started into something else, it was almost sardonic, it was *Am I Blue.*[7] And, as though he commanded, Sonny began to play. Something began to happen. And Creole let out the reins. The dry, low, black man said something awful on the drums, Creole answered, and the drums talked back. Then the horn insisted, sweet and high, slightly detached perhaps, and Creole listened, commenting now and then, dry, and driving, beautiful and calm and old. Then they all came together again, and Sonny was part of the family again. I could tell this from his face. He seemed to have found, right there beneath his fingers, a damn brand-new piano. It seemed that he couldn't get over it. Then, for awhile, just being happy with Sonny, they seemed to be agreeing with him that brand-new pianos certainly were a gas.

Then Creole stepped forward to remind them that what they were playing was the blues. He hit something in all of them, he hit something in me, myself, and the music tightened and deepened, apprehension began to beat the air. Creole began to tell us what the blues were all about. They were not about anything very new. He and his boys up there were keeping it new, at the risk of ruin, destruction, madness, and death, in order to find new ways to make us listen. For, while the tale of how we suffer, and how we are delighted, and how we may triumph is never new, it always must be heard. There isn't any other tale to tell, it's the only light we've got in all this darkness.

And this tale, according to that face, that body, those strong hands on those strings, has another aspect in every country, and a new depth in every generation. Listen, Creole seemed to be saying, listen. Now these are Sonny's blues. He made the little black man on the drums know it, and the bright, brown man on the horn. Creole wasn't trying any longer to get Sonny in the water. He was wishing him Godspeed. Then he stepped back, very slowly, filling the air with the immense suggestion that Sonny speak for himself.

Then they all gathered around Sonny and Sonny played. Every now and again one of them seemed to say, amen. Sonny's fingers filled the air with life, his life.

But that life contained so many others. And Sonny went all the way back, he really began with the spare, flat statement of the opening phrase of the song. Then he began to make it his. It was very beautiful because it wasn't hurried and it was no longer a lament. I seemed to hear with what burning he had made it his, with what burning we had yet to make it ours, how we could cease lamenting. Freedom lurked around us and I understood, at last, that he could help us to be free if we would listen, that he would never be free until we did. Yet, there was no battle in his face now. I heard what he had gone through, and would continue to go through until he came to rest in earth. He had made it his: that long line, of which we knew only Mama and Daddy. And he was giving it back, as everything must be given back, so that, passing through death, it can live forever. I saw my mother's face again, and felt, for the first time, how the stones of the road she had walked on must have bruised her feet. I saw the moonlit road where my father's brother died. And it brought something else back to me, and carried me past it. I saw my little girl again and felt Isabel's tears again, and I felt my own tears begin to rise. And I was yet aware that this was only a moment, that the world waited outside, as hungry as a tiger, and that trouble stretched above us, longer than the sky.

Then it was over. Creole and Sonny let out their breath, both soaking wet, and grinning. There was a lot of applause and some of it was real. In the dark, the girl came by and I asked her to take drinks to the bandstand. There was a long pause, while they talked up there in the indigo light and after awhile I saw the girl put a Scotch and milk on top of the piano for Sonny. He didn't seem to notice it, but just before they started playing again, he sipped from it and looked toward me, and nodded. Then he put it back on top of the piano. For me, then, as they began to play again, it glowed and shook above my brother's head like the very cup of trembling.[8]

1957

Notes

1. Lavatory.
2. Heroin.
3. Charlie ("Bird") Parker (1920–1955), brilliant saxophonist and innovator of jazz; working in New York in the mid-1940s, he developed, with Dizzy Gillespie and others, the style of jazz called "bebop." He was a narcotics addict.
4. Snobbish, bossy.
5. Processed: straightened and greased.
6. Publicly professing belief.
7. A favorite jazz standard, brilliantly recorded by Billie Holiday.
8. See Isaiah 51:17, 22–23: "Awake, awake, stand up, O Jerusalem, which hast drunk at the hand of the Lord the cup of his fury; thou hast drunken the dregs of the cup of trembling, and wrung them out. . . . Behold, I have taken out of thine hand the cup of trembling, even the dregs of the cup of my fury; thou shalt no more drink it again: But I will put it into the hand of them that afflict thee; . . ."

The Uses of the Blues

The title, *The Uses of the Blues,* does not refer to music; I don't know anything about music. It does refer to the experience of life, or the state of being, out of which the blues come. Now, I am claiming a great deal for the blues; I'm using them as a metaphor—I might have titled this, for example, *The Uses of Anguish* or *The Uses of Pain.* But I want to talk about the blues, not only because they speak of this particular experience of life and this state of being, but because they contain the toughness that manages to make this experience articulate. I am engaged, then, in a discussion of craft or, to use a very dangerous word, art. And I want to suggest that the acceptance of this anguish one finds in the blues, and the expression of it, creates also, however odd this may sound, a kind of joy. Now joy is a true state, it is a reality; it has nothing to do with what most people have in mind when they talk of happiness, which is not a real state and does not really exist.

Consider some of the things the blues are about. They're about work, love, death, floods, lynchings; in fact, a series of disasters which can be summed up under the arbitrary heading, "Facts of Life." Bessie Smith, who is dead now, came out of somewhere in the Deep South. I guess she was born around 1898, a great blues singer; died in Mississippi after a very long, hard—not *very* long, but very *hard*—life: pigs' feet and gin, many disastrous lovers, and a career that first went up, then went down; died on the road on the way from one hospital to another. She was in an automobile accident and one of her arms was wrenched out of its socket; and because the hospital attendants argued whether or not they could let her in because she was colored, she died. Not a story Horatio Alger would write. Well, Bessie saw a great many things, and among those things was a flood. And she talked about it and she said, "It rained five days and the skies turned dark as night" and she repeated it: "It rained five days and the skies turned dark as night." Then, "Trouble take place in the lowlands at night." And she went on: "Then it thundered and lightnin'd and the wind began to blow/Then it thundered and lightnin'd and the wind began to blow/There's thousands of people ain't got no place to go." As the song makes clear, she was one of those people. But she ended in a fantastic way: "Backwater blues done caused me to pack my things and go/Because my house fell down/And I can't live there no mo'."

Billie Holiday came along a little later and she had quite a story, too, a story which *Life* magazine would never print except as a tough, bittersweet sob-story obituary—in which, however helplessly, the dominant note would be relief. She was a little girl from the South, and she had quite a time with gin, whiskey and dope. She died in New York in a narcotics ward under the most terrifying and—in terms of crimes of the city and the country against her—disgraceful circumstances, and she had something she called *Billie's Blues:* "My man wouldn't give me no dinner/Wouldn't give me no supper/Squawked about my supper and turned me outdoors/And had the nerve to lay a padlock on my clothes/I didn't have so many, but I had a long, long way to go."

And one more, one more—Bessie Smith had a song called *Gin House Blues*. It's another kind of blues, and maybe I should explain this to you—a Negro has his difficult days, the days when everything has gone wrong and on top of it, he has a fight with the elevator man, or the taxi driver, or somebody he never saw before, who seems to decide to prove he's white and you're black. But this particular Tuesday it's more than you can take—sometimes, you know, you can take it. But Bessie didn't this time, and she sat down in the gin house and sang: "Don't try me, nobody/'Cause you will never win/I'll fight the Army and the Navy/Just me and my gin."

Well, you know, that is all very accurate, all very concrete. I know, I watched, I was there. You've seen these black men and women, these boys and girls; you've seen them on the streets. But I know what happened to them at the factory, at work, at home, on the subway, what they go through in a day, and the way they sort of ride with it. And it's very, very tricky. It's kind of a fantastic tightrope. They may be very self-controlled, very civilized; I like to think of myself as being very civilized and self-controlled, but I know I'm not. And I know that some improbable Wednesday, for no reason whatever, the elevator man or the doorman, the policeman or the landlord, or some little boy from the Bronx will say something, and it will be the wrong day to say it, the wrong moment to have it said to me; and God knows what will happen. I have seen it all, I have seen that much. What the blues are describing comes out of all this.

Gin House Blues is a real gin house. *Backwater Flood* is a real flood. When Billie says, "My man don't love me," she is not making a fantasy out of it. This is what happened, this is where it is. This is what it is. Now, I'm trying to suggest that the triumph here—which is a very un-American triumph—is that the person to whom these things happened watched with eyes wide open, saw it happen. So that when Billie or Bessie or Leadbelly stood up and sang about it, they were commenting on it, a little bit outside it: they were accepting it. And there's something funny—there's always something a little funny in all our disasters, if one can face the disaster. So that it's this passionate detachment, this inwardness coupled with outwardness, this ability to know that, All right it's a mess, and you can't do anything about it . . . so, well, you have to do something about it. You can't stay there, you can't drop dead, you can't give up, but all right, OK, as Bessie said: "Picked up my bag, baby, and I tried it again." This made life, however horrible that life was, bearable for her. It's what makes life bearable for any person, because every person, everybody born, from the time he's found out about people until the whole thing is over is certain of one thing: he is going to suffer. There is no way not to suffer.

Now, this brings us to two things. It brings us to the American Negro's experience of life, and it brings us to the American dream or sense of life. It would be hard to find any two things more absolutely opposed. I want to make it clear that when I talk about Negroes in this context I am not talking about race; I don't know what race means. I am talking about a social fact. When I say Negro, it is a digression; it is important to remember that I am not talking about a people, but a person. I am talking about a man who, let's say, was once 17 and who is now, let's say, 40, who has four children and can't feed them. I am talking about what happens to that man in this time and during this effort. I'm talking about what happens to you if, having barely escaped suicide, or death, or madness, or yourself, you watch your children growing up and no matter what you do, no matter *what* you do, you are powerless, you are really powerless, against the force of the world that is out to tell your child that he has no right to be alive. And no amount of liberal jargon, and no amount of talk about how well and how far we have progressed, does anything to soften or to point out any solution to this dilemma. In every generation, ever since Negroes have been here, every Negro mother and father has had to face that child and try to create in that child some way of surviving this particular world, some way to make the child who will be despised, not despise himself. I don't know what the Negro problem means to white people, but this is what it means to Negroes. Now, it would seem to me, since this is so, that one of the reasons we talk about the Negro problem in the way we do is in order precisely to avoid any knowledge of this fact. Imagine Doris Day trying to sing:

> *Papa may have, Mama may have*
> *But God bless the child that's got his own.*

People talk to me absolutely bathed in a bubble bath of self-congratulation. I mean, I walk into a room and everyone there is terribly proud of himself because I managed to get to the room. It proves to him that he is getting better. It's funny, but it's terribly sad. It's sad that one needs this kind of corroboration and it's terribly sad that one can be so self-deluded. The fact that Harry Belafonte makes as much money as, let's say, Frank Sinatra, doesn't really mean anything in this context. Frank can still get a house anywhere, and Harry can't. People go to see Harry and stand in long lines to watch him. They love him onstage, or at a cocktail party, but they don't want him to marry their daughters. This has nothing to do with Harry; this has everything to do with America. All right. Therefore, when we talk about what we call the Negro problem we are simply evolving means of avoiding the facts of this life. Because in order to face the facts of a life like Billie's or, for that matter, a life like mine, one has got to—the American white has got to—accept the fact that what he thinks he is, he is not. He has to give up, he has to surrender his image of himself and, apparently, this is the last thing white Americans are prepared to do.

But anyway, it is not a question now of accusing the white American of crimes against the Negro. It is too late for that. Besides, it is irrelevant. Injustice, murder, the shedding of blood, unhappily, are commonplace. These things happen all the time and everywhere. There is always a reason for it. People will always give themselves reasons for it. What I'm much more concerned about is what white Americans have done to themselves; what has been done to me is irrelevant simply because there is nothing more you can do to me. But, in doing it, you've done something to yourself. In evading my humanity, you have done something to your own humanity. We all do this all the time, of course. One labels people; one labels them Jew, one labels them Fascist, one labels them Communist, one labels them Negro, one labels them white man. But in the doing of this, you have not described anything—you have not described me when you call me a nigger or when you call me a Negro leader. You have only described yourself. What I think of you says more about me than it can possibly say about you. This is a very simple law and every Negro who intends to survive has to learn it very soon. Therefore, the Republic, among other things, has managed to create a body of people who have very little to lose, and there is nothing more dangerous in any republic, any state, any country, any time, than men who have nothing to lose.

Because you have thus given him his freedom, the American Negro can do whatever he wills; you can no longer do anything to him. He doesn't want anything you've got, he doesn't believe anything you say. I don't know why and I don't know how America arrived at this peculiar point of view. If one examines American history, there is no apparent reason for it. It's a bloody history, as bloody as everybody else's history, as deluded, as fanatical. One has only to look at it from the time we all got here. Look at the Pilgrims, the Puritans—the people who presumably fled oppression in Europe only to set up a more oppressed society here—people who wanted freedom, who killed off the Indians. Look at all the people moving into a new era, and enslaving all the blacks. These are the facts of American history as opposed to the legend. We came from Europe, we came from Africa, we came from all over the world. We brought whatever was in us from China or from France. We *all* brought it with us. We were not transformed when we crossed the ocean. Something else happened. Something much more serious. We no longer had any way of finding out, of knowing who we were.

Many people have said in various tones of voice, meaning various things that the most unlucky thing that happened in America was the presence of the Negro. Freud said, in a kind of rage that the black race was the folly of America and that it served America right. Well, of course, I don't quite know what Freud had in mind. But I can see that, in one way, it may have been the most unlucky thing that happened to America, since America, unlike any other Western power, had its slaves on the mainland. They were here. We had our slaves at a time, unluckily for us, when slavery was going out of fashion. And after the Bill of Rights. Therefore, it would seem to me that the presence of this black mass here as opposed to all the things we said we believed in and also at a time when the whole doctrine of white supremacy had never even been questioned is one of the most crucial facts of our history. It would be nightmarish now to read the handbooks of colonialists a hundred years ago: even ten years ago, for that matter. But in those days, it was not even a question of black people being inferior to white people. The American found himself in a very peculiar position because he knew that black people were people. Frenchmen could avoid knowing it—they never met a black man. Englishmen could avoid knowing it. But Americans could not avoid knowing it because, after all, here he was and he was, no matter how it was denied, a man, just like everybody else. And the attempt to avoid this, to avoid this fact, I consider one of the keys to what we can call loosely the American psychology. For one thing, it created in Americans a kind of perpetual, hidden, festering and entirely unadmitted guilt. Guilt is a very peculiar emotion. As long as you are guilty about something, no matter what it is, you are not compelled to change it. Guilt is like a warm bath or, to be rude, it is like masturbation—you can get used to it, you can prefer it, you may get to a place where you cannot live without it, because in order to live without it, in order to get past this guilt, you must act. And in order to act, you must be conscious and take great chances and be responsible for the consequences. Therefore, liberals, and people who are not even liberals, much prefer to discuss the Negro problem than to try to deal with what this figure of the Negro really means personally to them. They still prefer to read statistics, charts, Gallup polls, rather than deal with the reality. They still tell me, to console me, how many Negroes bought Cadillacs, Cutty Sark, Coca-Cola, Schweppes last year; how many more will buy Cadillacs, Cutty Sark, Coca-Cola and Schweppes next year. To prove to me that things are getting better. Now, of course, I think it is a very sad matter if you suppose that you or I have bled and suffered and died in this country in order to achieve Cadillacs, Cutty Sark, Schweppes and Coca-Cola. It seems to me if one accepts this speculation about the luxury of guilt that the second reason must be related to the first. That has to do with the ways in which we manage to project onto the Negro face, because it is so visible, all of our guilts and aggressions and desires. And if you doubt this, think of the legends that surround the Negro to this day. Think, when you think of these legends, that they were not invented by Negroes, but they were invented by the white republic. Ask yourself if Aunt Jemima or Uncle Tom ever existed anywhere and why it was necessary to invent them. Ask yourself why Negroes until today are, in the popular imagination, at once the most depraved people under heaven and the most saintly. Ask yourself what William Faulkner really was trying to say in *Requiem for a Nun,* which is about a nigger, whore, dope addict, saint. Faulkner wrote it. I never met Nancy, the nun he was writing about. He never met her either, but the question is, why was it necessary for him and for us to hold onto this image? We needn't go so far afield. Ask yourself why liberals are so delighted with the movie *The Defiant Ones.* It ends, if you remember, when Sidney Poitier, the black man, having been chained interminably to Tony Curtis, the white man, finally breaks the chain, is on the train, is getting away, but no, he doesn't go, doesn't leave poor Tony Curtis down there on the chain gang. Not at all. He jumps off the train and they go buddy-buddy back together to the same old Jim Crow chain gang. Now this is a fable. Why? Who is trying to prove what to whom? I'll tell you something. I saw that movie twice. I saw it downtown with all my liberal friends who were delighted when Sidney jumped off the train. I saw it uptown with my less liberal friends, who were furious. When Sidney jumped off that train they called him all kinds of unmentionable things. Well, their reaction was at least more honest and more direct. Why is it necessary at this late date, one screams at the world, to prove that the Negro doesn't really hate you, he's forgiven and forgotten all of it. Maybe he has. That's not the problem. *You* haven't. And that *is* the problem:

I love you, baby,
But can't stand your dirty ways.

There's one more thing I ought to add to this. The final turn of the screw that created this peculiar purgatory which we call America is that aspect of our history that is most triumphant. We really did conquer a continent, we have made a lot of money, we're better off materially than anybody else in the world. How easy it is as a person or as a nation to suppose that one's well-being is proof of one's virtue; in fact, a great many people are saying just that right now. You know, we're the best nation in the world because we're the richest nation in the world. The American way of life has proven itself, according to these curious people, and that's why we're so rich. This is called Yankee virtue and it comes from Calvin, but my point is that I think this has again something to do with the American failure to face reality. Since we have all these things, we can't be so bad and, since we have all these things, we are robbed, in a way, of the incentive to walk away from the TV set, the Cadillac, and go into the chaos out of which and only out of which we can create ourselves into human beings.

To talk about these things in this country today is extremely difficult. Even the words mean nothing anymore. I think, for example, what we call the religious revival in America means that more and more people periodically get more and more frightened and go to church in order to make sure they don't lose their investments. This is the only reason that I can find for the popularity of men who have nothing to do with religion at all, like Norman Vincent Peale, for example—only for example; there's lots of others just like him. I think this is very sad. I think it's very frightening. But Ray Charles, who is a great tragic artist, makes of a genuinely religious confession something triumphant and liberating. He tells us that he cried so loud he gave the blues to his neighbor next door.

How can I put it? Let us talk about a person who is no longer very young, who somehow managed to get to, let us say, the age of 40, and a great many of us do, without ever having been touched, broken, disturbed, frightened—40-year-old virgin, male or female. There is a sense of the grotesque about a person who has spent his or her life in a kind of cotton batting. There is something monstrous about never having been hurt, never having been made to bleed, never having lost anything, never having gained anything because life is beautiful, and in order to keep it beautiful you're going to stay just the way you are and you're not going to test your theory against all the possibilities outside. America is something like that. The failure on our part to accept the reality of pain, of anguish, of ambiguity, of death has turned us into a very peculiar and sometimes monstrous people. It means, for one thing, and it's very serious, that people who have had no experience have no compassion. People who have had no experience suppose that if a man is a thief, he is a thief; but, in fact, that isn't the most important thing about him. The most important thing about him is that he is a man and, furthermore, that if he's a thief or a murderer or whatever he is, *you* could also be and you would know this, anyone would know this who had really dared to live. Miles Davis once gave poor Billie Holiday $100 and somebody said, "Man, don't you know she's going to go out and spend it on dope?" and Miles said, "Baby, have you ever been sick?"

Now, you don't know that by reading, by looking. You don't know what the river is like or what the ocean is like by standing on the shore. You can't know anything about life and suppose you can get through it clean. The most monstrous people are those who think they are going to. I think this shows in everything we see and do, in everything we read about these peculiar private lives, so peculiar that it is almost impossible to write about them, because what a man *says* he's doing has nothing to do with what he's *really* doing. If you read such popular novelists as John O'Hara, you can't imagine what country he's talking about. If you read *Life* magazine, it's like reading about the moon. Nobody lives in that country. That country does not exist and, what is worse, everybody knows it. But everyone pretends that it does. Now this is panic. And this is terribly dangerous, because it means that when the trouble comes, and trouble always comes, you won't survive it. It means that if your son dies, you may go to pieces or find the nearest psychiatrist or the nearest church, but you won't survive it on your own. If you don't survive your trouble out of your own resources, you have not really survived it; you have merely closed yourself against it. The blues are rooted in the slave songs; the slaves discovered something genuinely terrible, terrible because it sums up the universal challenge, the universal hope, the universal fear:

The very time I thought I was lost
My dungeon shook and my chains
fell off.

Well, that is almost all I am trying to say. I say it out of great concern. And out of a certain kind of hope. If you can live in the full knowledge that you are going to die, that you are not going to live forever, that if you live with the reality of death, you can live. This is not mystical talk, it is a fact. It is a principal fact of life. If you can't do it, if you spend your entire life in flight from death, you are also in flight from life. For example, right now you find the most unexpected people building bomb shelters, which is very close to being a crime. It is a private panic which creates a public delusion that some of us will be saved by bomb shelters. If we had, as human beings, on a personal and private level, our personal authority, we would know better, but because we are so uncertain of all these things, some of us, apparently, are willing to spend the rest of our lives underground in concrete. Perhaps, if we had a more working relationship with ourselves and with one another, we might be able to turn the tide and eliminate the propaganda for building bomb shelters. People who in some sense know who they are can't change the world always, but they can do something to make it a little more, to make life a little more human. Human in the best sense. Human in terms of joy, freedom which is always private, respect, respect for one another, even such things as manners. All these things are very important, all these old-fashioned things. People who don't know who they are privately, accept as we have accepted for nearly 15 years, the fantastic disaster which we call American politics and which we call American foreign policy, and the incoherence of the one is an exact reflection of the incoherence of the other. Now, the only way to change all this is to begin to ask ourselves very difficult questions.

I will stop now. But I want to quote two things. A very great American writer, Henry James, writing to a friend of his who had just lost her husband, said, "Sorrow wears and uses us but we wear and use it too, and it is blind. Whereas we, after a manner, see." And Bessie said:

Good mornin' blues.
Blues, how do you do?
I'm doin' all right.
Good mornin'.
How are you?

Alice Walker

Alice Walker (b. 1944) is a celebrated author of short stories, essays, children's literature, and poetry, and novels, including The Temple of My Familiar, Possessing the Secret of Joy, *and the Pulitzer-Prize winning* The Color Purple. *Much of her early non-fiction is collected in the acclaimed* In Search of Our Mother's Gardens *(1983). Born in Georgia, Walker attended college in Atlanta and New York, and earned a B.A. in 1965. She became involved in the civil rights movement and worked as an editor for* Ms. *magazine. She published her first book of poetry,* Once, *in 1968. Her many awards include National Endowment for the Arts grant, Guggenheim grant, American Book award, as well as honorary doctorates from Russell-Sage College in Troy, New York and University of Massachusetts, Amherst. Her work is especially noted for its exploration of black American culture and the realities of women's lives. A political and social activist in her life and in her writing, Walker defines "what is real [as] what is happening. What is real is what did happen. What happened to me and happens to me is most real of all. I write then, out of that." (from "Duties of the Black Revolutionary Artist" in* In Search of Our Mother's Gardens*)*

In "Everyday Use," Walker complicates how we perceive tradition and heritage. She challenges us to look at our motives and she emphasizes our often silent susceptibility to the changing social climate that defines us. In "The Flowers," Walker contrasts innocence and peaceful beauty with racial violence and its repercussions in order to emphasize the importance of recognizing each.

Everyday Use

for your grandmama

I will wait for her in the yard that Maggie and I made so clean and wavy yesterday afternoon. A yard like this is more comfortable than most people know. It is not just a yard. It is like an extended living room. When the hard clay is swept clean as a floor and the fine sand around the edges lined with tiny, irregular grooves, anyone can come and sit and look up into the elm tree and wait for the breezes that never come inside the house.

Maggie will be nervous until after her sister goes: she will stand hopelessly in corners, homely and ashamed of the burn scars down her arms and legs, eyeing her sister with a mixture of envy and awe. She thinks her sister has held life always in the palm of one hand, that "no" is a word the world never learned to say to her.

You've no doubt seen those TV shows where the child who has "made it" is confronted, as a surprise, by her own mother and father, tottering in weakly from backstage. (A pleasant surprise, of course: What would they do if parent and child came on the show only to curse out and insult each other?) On TV mother and child embrace and smile into each other's faces. Sometimes the mother and father weep, the child wraps them in her arms and leans across the table to tell how she would not have made it without their help. I have seen these programs.

Sometimes I dream a dream in which Dee and I are suddenly brought together on a TV program of this sort. Out of a dark and soft-seated limousine I am ushered into a bright room filled with many people. There I meet a smiling, gray, sporty man like Johnny Carson who shakes my hand and tells me what a fine girl I have. Then we are on the stage and Dee is embracing me with tears in her eyes. She pins on my dress a large orchid, even though she has told me once that she thinks orchids are tacky flowers.

In real life I am large, big-boned woman with rough, man-working hands. In the winter I wear flannel nightgowns to bed and overalls during the day. I can kill and clean a hog as mercilessly as a man. My fat keeps me hot in zero weather. I can work outside all day, breaking ice to get water for washing. I can eat pork liver cooked over the open fire minutes after it comes steaming from the hog. One winter I knocked a bull calf straight in the brain between the eyes with a sledge hammer and had the meat hung up to chill before nightfall. But of course all this does not show on television. I am the way my daughter would want me to be: a hundred pounds lighter, my skin like an uncooked barley pancake. My hair glistens in the hot bright lights. Johnny Carson has much to do to keep up with my quick and witty tongue.

But that is a mistake. I know even before I wake up. Who ever knew a Johnson with a quick tongue? Who can even imagine me looking a strange white man in the eye? It seems to me I have talked to them always with one foot raised in flight, with my head turned in whichever way is farthest from them. Dee, though. She would always look anyone in the eye. Hesitation was not part of her nature.

"How do I look, Mama?" Maggie says, showing just enough of her thin body enveloped in pink skirt and red blouse for me to know she's there, almost hidden by the door.

"Come out into the yard," I say.

Have you ever seen a lame animal, perhaps a dog run over by some careless person rich enough to own a car, sidle up to someone who is ignorant enough to be kind to him? That is the way my Maggie walks. She has been like this, chin on chest, eyes on ground, feet in shuffle, ever since the fire that burned the other house to the ground.

Dee is lighter than Maggie, with nicer hair and a fuller figure. She's a woman now, though sometimes I forget. How long ago was it that the other house burned?

Ten, twelve years? Sometimes I can still hear the flames and feel Maggie's arms sticking to me, her hair smoking and her dress falling off her in little black papery flakes. Her eyes seemed stretched open, blazed open by the flames reflected in them. And Dee. I see her standing off under the sweet gum tree she used to dig gum out of; a look of concentration on her face as she watched the last dingy gray board of the house fall in toward the red-hot brick chimney. Why don't you do a dance around the ashes? I'd wanted to ask her. She had hated the house that much.

I used to think she hated Maggie, too. But that was before we raised the money, the church and me, to send her to Augusta to school. She used to read to us without pity; forcing words, lies, other folks' habits, whole lives upon us two, sitting trapped and ignorant underneath her voice. She washed us in a river of make-believe, burned us with a lot of knowledge we didn't necessarily need to know. Pressed us to her with the serious way she read, to shove us away at just the moment, like dimwits, we seemed about to understand.

Dee wanted nice things. A yellow organdy dress to wear to her graduation from high school; black pumps to match a green suit she'd made from an old suit somebody gave me. She was determined to stare down any disaster in her efforts. Her eyelids would not flicker for minutes at a time. Often I fought off the temptation to shake her. At sixteen she had a style of her own: and knew what style was.

I never had an education myself. After second grade the school was closed down. Don't ask me why: in 1927 colored asked fewer questions than they do now. Sometimes Maggie reads to me. She stumbles along good-naturedly but can't see well. She knows she is not bright. Like good looks and money, quickness passed her by. She will marry John Thomas (who has mossy teeth in an earnest face) and then I'll be free to sit here and I guess just sing church songs to myself. Although I never was a good singer. Never could carry a tune. I was always better at a man's job. I used to love to milk till I was hoofed in the side in '49. Cows are soothing and slow and don't bother you, unless you try to milk them the wrong way.

I have deliberately turned my back on the house. It is three rooms, just like the one that burned, except the roof is tin; they don't make shingle roofs any more. There are no real windows, just some holes cut in the sides, like the portholes in a ship, but not round and not square, with rawhide holding the shutters up on the outside. This house is in a pasture, too, like the other one. No doubt when Dee sees it she will want to tear it down. She wrote me once that no matter where we "choose" to live, she will manage to come see us. But she will never bring her friends. Maggie and I thought about this and Maggie asked me, "Mama, when did Dee ever *have* any friends?"

She had a few. Furtive boys in pink shirts hanging about on washday after school. Nervous girls who never laughed. Impressed with her they worshiped the well-turned phrase, the cute shape, the scalding humor that erupted like bubbles in lye. She read to them.

When she was courting Jimmy T she didn't have much time to pay to us, but turned all her faultfinding power on him. He *flew* to marry a cheap gal from a family of ignorant flashy people. She hardly had time to recompose herself.

When she comes I will meet—but there they are!

Maggie attempts to make a dash for the house, in her shuffling way, but I stay her with my hand. "Come back here," I say. And she stops and tries to dig a well in the sand with her toe.

It is hard to see them clearly through the strong sun. But even the first glimpse of leg out of the car tells me it is Dee. Her feet were always neat-looking, as if God himself had shaped them with a certain style. From the other side of the car comes a short, stocky man. Hair is all over his head a foot long and hanging from his chin like a kinky mule tail. I hear Maggie suck in her breath. "Uhnnnh," is what it sounds like. Like when you see the wriggling end of a snake just in front of your foot on the road. "Uhnnnh."

Dee next. A dress down to the ground, in this hot weather. A dress so loud it hurts my eyes. There are yellows and oranges enough to throw back the light of the sun. I feel my whole face warming from the heat waves it throws out. Earrings too, gold, and hanging down to her shoulders. Bracelets dangling and making noises when she moves her arm up to shake the folds of the dress out of her armpits. The dress is loose and flows, and as she walks closer, I like it. I hear Maggie go "Uhnnnh" again. It is her sister's hair. It stands straight up like the wool on a sheep. It is black as night and around the edges are two long pigtails that rope about like small lizards disappearing behind her ears.

"Wa-su-zo-Tean-o!" she says, coming on in that gliding way the dress makes her move. The short stocky fellow with the hair to his navel is all grinning and he follows up with "Asalamalakim, my mother and sister!" He moves to hug Maggie but she falls back, right up against the back of my chair. I feel her trembling there and when I look up I see the perspiration falling off her chin.

"Don't get up," says Dee. Since I am stout it takes something of a push. You can see me trying to move a second or two before I make it. She turns, showing white heels through her sandals, and goes back to the car. Out she peeks next with a Polaroid. She stoops down quickly and lines up picture after picture of me sitting there in front of the house with Maggie cowering behind me. She never takes a shot without making sure the house is included. When a cow comes nibbling around the edge of the yard she snaps it and me and Maggie *and* the house. Then she puts the Polaroid in the back seat of the car, and comes up and kisses me on the forehead.

Meanwhile Asalamalakim is going through motions with Maggie's hand. Maggie's hand is as limp as a fish, and probably as cold, despite the sweat, and she keeps trying to pull it back. It looks like Asalamalakim wants to shake hands but wants to do it fancy. Or maybe he don't know how people shake hands. Anyhow, he soon gives up on Maggie.

"Well," I say. "Dee."

"No, Mama," she says. "Not 'Dee,' Wangero Leewanika Kemanjo!"

"What happened to 'Dee'?" I wanted to know.

"She's dead," Wangero said. "I couldn't bear it any longer, being named after the people who oppress me."

"You know as well as me you was named after your aunt Dicie," I said. Dicie is my sister. She named Dee. We called her "Big Dee" after Dee was born.

"But who was *she* named after?" asked Wangero.

"I guess after Grandma Dee," I said.

"And who was she named after?" asked Wangero.

"Her mother," I said, and saw Wangero was getting tired. "That's about as far back as I can trace it," I said. Though, in fact, I probably could have carried it back beyond the Civil War through the branches.

"Well," said Asalamalakim, "there you are."

"Uhnnnh," I heard Maggie say.

"There I was not," I said, "before 'Dicie' cropped up in our family, so why should I try to trace it that far back?"

He just stood there grinning, looking down on me like somebody inspecting a Model A car. Every once in a while he and Wangero sent eye signals over my head.

"How do you pronounce this name?" I asked.

"You don't have to call me by it if you don't want to," said Wangero.

"Why shouldn't I?" I asked. "If that's what you want us to call you, we'll call you."

"I know it might sound awkward at first," said Wangero.

"I'll get used to it," I said. "Ream it out again."

Well, soon we got the name out of the way. Asalamalakim had a name twice as long and three times as hard. After I tripped over it two or three times he told me to just call him Hakim-a-barber. I wanted to ask him was he a barber, but I didn't really think he was, so I didn't ask.

"You must belong to those beef-cattle peoples down the road," I said. They said "Asalamalakim" when they met you, too, but they didn't shake hands. Always too busy: feeding the cattle, fixing the fences, putting up salt-lick shelters, throwing down hay. When the white folks poisoned some of the herd the men stayed up all night with rifles in their hands. I walked a mile and a half just to see the sight.

Hakim-a-barber said, "I accept some of their doctrines, but farming and raising cattle is not my style." (They didn't tell me, and I didn't ask, whether Wangero [Dee] had really gone and married him.)

We sat down to eat and right away he said he didn't eat collards and pork was unclean. Wangero, though, went on through the chitlins and corn bread, the greens and everything else. She talked a blue streak over the sweet potatoes. Everything delighted her. Even the fact that we still used the benches her daddy made for the table when we couldn't afford to buy chairs.

"Oh, Mama!" she cried. Then turned to Hakim-a-barber. "I never knew how lovely these benches are. You can feel the rump prints," she said, running her hands underneath her and along the bench. Then she gave a sigh and her hand closed over Grandma Dee's butter dish. "That's it!" she said. "I knew there was something I wanted to ask you if I could have." She jumped up from the table and went over in the corner where the churn stood, the milk in it clabber by now. She looked at the churn and looked at it.

"This churn top is what I need," she said. "Didn't Uncle Buddy whittle it out of a tree you all used to have?"

"Yes," I said.

"Uh huh," she said happily. "And I want the dasher, too."

"Uncle Buddy whittle that, too?" asked the barber.

Dee (Wangero) looked up at me.

"Aunt Dee's first husband whittled the dash," said Maggie so low you almost couldn't hear her. "His name was Henry, but they called him Stash."

"Maggie's brain is like an elephant's," Wangero said, laughing. "I can use the churn top as a centerpiece for the alcove table," she said, sliding a plate over the churn, "and I'll think of something artistic to do with the dasher."

When she finished wrapping the dasher the handle stuck out. I took it for a moment in my hands. You didn't even have to look close to see where hands pushing the dasher up and down to make butter had left a kind of sink in the wood. In fact, there were a lot of small sinks; you could see where thumbs and fingers had sunk into the wood. It was beautiful light yellow wood, from a tree that grew in the yard where Big Dee and Stash had lived.

After dinner Dee (Wangero) went to the trunk at the foot of my bed and started rifling through it. Maggie hung back in the kitchen over the dishpan. Out came Wangero with two quilts. They had been pieced by Grandma Dee and then Big Dee and me had hung them on the quilt frames on the front porch and quilted them. One was in the Lone Star pattern. The other was Walk Around the Mountain. In both of them were scraps of dresses Grandma Dee had worn fifty and more years ago. Bits and pieces of Grandpa Jarrell's Paisley shirts. And one teeny faded blue piece, about the size of a penny matchbox, that was from Great Grandpa Ezra's uniform that he wore in the Civil War.

"Mama," Wangero said sweet as a bird. "Can I have these old quilts?"

I heard something fall in the kitchen, and a minute later the kitchen door slammed.

"Why don't you take one or two of the others?" I asked. "These old things was just done by me and Big Dee from some tops your grandma pieced before she died."

"No," said Wangero. "I don't want those. They are stitched around the borders by machine."

"That'll make them last better," I said.

"That's not the point," said Wangero. "These are all pieces of dresses Grandma used to wear. She did all this stitching by hand. Imagine!" She held the quilts securely in her arms, stroking them.

"Some of the pieces, like those lavender ones, come from old clothes her mother handed down to her," I said, moving up to touch the quilts. Dee (Wangero) moved back just enough so that I couldn't reach the quilts. They already belonged to her.

"Imagine!" she breathed again, clutching them closely to her bosom.

"The truth is," I said, "I promised to give them quilts to Maggie, for when she marries John Thomas."

She gasped like a bee had stung her.

"Maggie can't appreciate these quilts!" she said. "She'd probably be backward enough to put them to everyday use."

"I reckon she would," I said. "God knows I been saving 'em for long enough with nobody using 'em. I hope she will!" I didn't want to bring up how I had offered Dee (Wangero) a quilt when she went away to college. Then she had told me they were old-fashioned, out of style.

"But they're *priceless!*" she was saying now, furiously; for she has a temper. "Maggie would put them on the bed and in five years they'd be in rags. Less than that!"

"She can always make some more," I said. "Maggie knows how to quilt."

Dee (Wangero) looked at me with hatred. "You just will not understand. The point is these quilts, *these* quilts!"

"Well," I said, stumped. "What would *you* do with them?"

"Hang them," she said. As if that was the only thing you *could* do with quilts.

Maggie by now was standing in the door. I could almost hear the sound her feet made as they scraped over each other.

"She can have them, Mama," she said, like somebody used to never winning anything, or having anything reserved for her. "I can 'member Grandma Dee without the quilts."

I looked at her hard. She had filled her bottom lip with checkerberry snuff and it gave her face a kind of dopey, hangdog look. It was Grandma Dee and Big Dee who taught her how to quilt herself. She stood there with her scarred hands hidden in the folds of her skirt. She looked at her sister with something like fear but she wasn't mad at her. This was Maggie's portion. This was the way she knew God to work.

When I looked at her like that something hit me in the top of my head and ran down to the soles of my feet. Just like when I'm in church and the spirit of God touches me and I get happy and shout. I did something I never had done before: hugged Maggie to me, then dragged her on into the room, snatched the quilts out of Miss Wangero's hands and dumped them into Maggie's lap. Maggie just sat there on my bed with her mouth open.

"Take one or two of the others," I said to Dee.

But she turned without a word and went out to Hakim-a-barber.

"You just don't understand," she said, as Maggie and I came out to the car.

"What don't I understand?" I wanted to know.

"Your heritage," she said. And then she turned to Maggie, kissed her, and said, "You ought to try to make something of yourself, too, Maggie. It's really a new day for us. But from the way you and Mama still live you'd never know it."

She put on some sunglasses that hid everything above the tip of her nose and her chin.

Maggie smiled; maybe at the sunglasses. But a real smile, not scared. After we watched the car dust settle I asked Maggie to bring me a dip of snuff. And then the two of us sat there just enjoying, until it was time to go in the house and go to bed.

[1973]

The Flowers

It seemed to Myop as she skipped lightly from hen house to pigpen to smokehouse that the days had never been as beautiful as these. The air held a keenness that made her nose twitch. The harvesting of the corn and cotton, peanuts and squash, made each day a golden surprise that caused excited little tremors to run up her jaws.

Myop carried a short, knobby stick. She struck out at random at chickens she liked, and worked out the beat of a song on the fence around the pigpen. She felt light and good in the warm sun. She was ten, and nothing existed for her but her song, the stick clutched in her dark brown hand, and the tat-de-ta-ta-ta of accompaniment.

Turning her back on the rusty boards of her family's sharecropper cabin, Myop walked along the fence till it ran into the stream made by the spring. Around the spring, where the family got drinking water, silver ferns and wildflowers grew. Along the shallow banks pigs rooted. Myop watched the tiny white bubbles disrupt the thin black scale of soil and the water that silently rose and slid away down the stream.

She had explored the woods behind the house many times. Often, in late autumn, her mother took her to gather nuts among the fallen leaves. Today she made her own path, bouncing this way and that way, vaguely keeping an eye out for snakes. She found, in addition to various common but pretty ferns and leaves, an armful of strange blue flowers with velvety ridges and a sweetsuds bush full of the brown, fragrant buds.

By twelve o'clock, her arms laden with sprigs of her findings, she was a mile or more from home. She had often been as far before, but the strangeness of the land made it not as pleasant as her usual haunts. It seemed gloomy in the little cove in which she found herself. The air was damp, the silence close and deep.

Myop began to circle back to the house, back to the peacefulness of the morning. It was then she stepped smack into his eyes. Her heel became lodged in the broken ridge between brow and nose, and she reached down quickly, unafraid, to free herself. It was only when she saw his naked grin that she gave a little yelp of surprise.

He had been a tall man. From feet to neck covered a long space. His head lay beside him. When she pushed back the leaves and layers of earth and debris Myop saw that he'd had large white teeth, all of them cracked or broken, long fingers, and very big bones. All his clothes had rotted away except some threads of blue denim from his overalls. The buckles of the overalls had turned green.

Myop gazed around the spot with interest. Very near where she'd stepped into the head was a wild pink rose. As she picked it to add to her bundle she noticed a raised mound, a ring, around the rose's root. It was the rotted remains of a noose, a bit of shredding plowline, now blending benignly into the soil. Around an overhanging limb of a great spreading oak clung another piece. Frayed, rotted, bleached, and frazzled—barely there—but spinning restlessly in the breeze. Myop laid down her flowers.

And the summer was over.

Audre Lorde

Audre Lorde (1934–1992) was born in New York City to parents who had immigrated from Grenada. Lorde earned a B.A. from Hunter College and a Masters of Library Science from Columbia University and later taught English at John Jay College of Justice in New York and Hunter College. Although as a young woman, Lorde married a man and had two children, she was an outspoken lesbian whose bravery and audacity both shocks and enthralls her readers. Lorde's work is often anthologized and widely celebrated for its honesty, directness, and strength. Although Lorde is best known for her poetry, she published in several genres. In 1980, Lorde published The Cancer Journals, *a blend of essays, journal entries, and memoir that offers a painful account of Lorde's battle with breast cancer. In it, she writes, "I have been wanting to write a piece of meaning words on cancer as it affects my life and my consciousness as a woman, a black lesbian feminist mother lover poet all I am." In 1984, she published* Sister Outsider: Essays and Speeches, *a collection of her nonpoetry that spans two decades and addresses a wide range of social issues. Her poetry and prose have earned her many honors, including two National Book Awards. She died of cancer on November 11, 1992.*

A Litany for Survival

For those of us who live at the shoreline
standing upon the constant edges of decision
crucial and alone
for those of us who cannot indulge
the passing dreams of choice
who love in doorways coming and going
in the hours between dawns
looking inward and outward
at once before and after
seeking a now that can breed
futures
like bread in our children's mouths
so their dreams will not reflect
the death of ours;

Reprinted from *The Black Unicorn*, (1978), W.W. Norton & Company.

For those of us
who were imprinted with fear
like a faint line in the center of our foreheads
learning to be afraid with our mother's milk
for by this weapon
this illusion of some safety to be found
the heavy-footed hoped to silence us
For all of us
this instant and this triumph
We were never meant to survive.

And when the sun rises we are afraid
it might not remain
when the sun sets we are afraid
it might not rise in the morning
when our stomachs are full we are afraid
of indigestion
when our stomachs are empty we are afraid
we may never eat again
when we are loved we are afraid
love will vanish
when we are alone we are afraid
love will never return
and when we speak we are afraid
our words will not be heard
nor welcomed
but when we are silent
we are still afraid.

So it is better to speak
remembering
we were never meant to survive.

Tomb of Tu Doc

Near Hue in Central Vietnam

9

Writing of Witness: Perspectives on the Vietnam War

Patty Malesh

I was born the same year the last American troops left Vietnam. I lost no one to the war. Bill Malesh, my father, joined Bill Clinton and many others as a National Guardsman. He did not go to Vietnam. My uncles were too old for the draft, my cousins too young. For me, Vietnam happened in the 1980s. It happened to Charlie Sheen in *Platoon* (1986) and Matthew Modine in *Full Metal Jacket* (1987). It happened a few years earlier to Martin Sheen in *Apocalypse Now* (1979) and to Christopher Walken and Robert DeNiro in the *Deer Hunter* (1978). It even happened to Tom Cruise in *Born on the Fourth of July* (1989). It happened on primetime in *China Beach* and *Tour of Duty*. For me, Vietnam wasn't a place; it was a form of entertainment.

When Americans hear the word Vietnam, we tend to respond to an event that shaped *our* history instead of a country with a history all its own. Vietnam is no stranger to occupation and resistance. The fight for a sovereign Vietnam began over a century ago. By 1883, Vietnam fell under French Colonial rule and Catholic missionaries began to gain influence in the historically Buddhist country. During World War II, French Vietnam suffered military occupation by Japan. While these French and Japanese forces battled for power in Vietnam from 1940 to the Japanese surrender in 1945, Ho Chi Minh, leader of the Indochinese Communist party, formed the Vietminh Front as a resistance movement against outside occupation. After the Japanese surrender, the Vietminh, or Vietnam Doc Lap Dong Minh (League for the Independence of Vietnam), declared an Independent Republic of Hanoi but French occupation continued, resulting in the outbreak of war in 1946. After eight years of fighting, Vietnam was divided into a communist North and an anti-communist South pending a national election that both governments agreed would take place two years later in 1956. But as tensions between the neighboring factions grew, the likelihood of a national election diminished. South-Vietnamese president Ngo Dinh Diem refused to hold elections. Instead, he began aggressive attempts to drive Vietnamese communists out of South Vietnam. As a result, the Vietcong emerged as a rebel faction and, in 1959, civil war erupted (www.viettouch.com).

United States involvement in these escalating conflicts began as early as 1950 when President Truman sent thirty-five noncombatant "advisors" to help the French maintain their colonial control (Fussell 651). In the early 1960s, President Kennedy's administration increased support to the South Vietnamese army (ARVN). The first American was killed in 1961. By 1965 Lyndon Johnson was sending significant numbers of U.S. troops to South Vietnam, ultimately reaching about half a million. In addition to supplying manpower, Johnson began intensive bombing in North Vietnam. Over the next eight years "the air force dropped on the Communists three times the bomb tonnage dropped in the whole of the Second World War" (654). As American casualties and North Vietnamese offensives grew, Lyndon Johnson, and later Richard Nixon, began withdrawing U.S. troops from Vietnam. By 1973, the last American troops returned to American soil. Even with U.S. involvement, the South Vietnamese army was weakening. Within two years after the U.S. pulled out of the conflict in Vietnam, the country was united under a communist government as the New Socialist Republic of Vietnam. By the end of the war, "2 million people were dead in Vietnam, 200,000 in Cambodia, 100,000 in Laos. Over 3 million were wounded in Southeast Asia, and 14 million became refugees. Of the American troops and marines, 58,135 were killed. Over 300,000 people were wounded, of whom 33,000 are permanently paralyzed" (653). Since its reunification, Vietnam has had conflicts with Cambodia and China, but it and much of Eastern Asia has vanished from American political interest and concern.

As the previous chapter on Social Witness exemplifies and Carolyn Forché recognizes in her essay "Introduction: *Against Forgetting*" in this chapter, witnessing takes many forms. "It will be impassioned or ironic. It will speak in the language of the common man or in an esoteric language of paradox or literary privilege. It will curse and it will bless; it will blaspheme against or ignore the holy." It may be the ravings of a political prisoner carved into a prison wall hours before his execution or the words of a child tucked into her doll's pocket as she leaves the Warsaw Ghetto for Auchschwitz. These accounts stand as the only record of their pain and their experience. As with other forms of witness, writing about Vietnam prevents forgetting by exorcising the demons of its authors and exposing its listeners to what they often try not to hear.

Not all accounts of witness, however, come from victims. Although many of the atrocities committed during the Vietnam conflict are captured by those who experienced them, some are recorded by those who committed them. Still other accounts leak out of those who suffer the consequences—the legacy of war. All of these stories evoke the intensity of personal struggle to speak to the political forces that often shape or are shaped by those struggles. In Forché's introduction to *Against Forgetting*, an anthology of poetry of witness, she argues that poetry of witness forces us to acknowledge the reality of brutal acts so unspeakable that "it becomes easier to forget than remember, and this forgetfulness becomes our defense against remembering." But as American soldiers returned home from Vietnam, charged political protests and media responses to acts of inhumanity made forgetting impossible. Unlike those who fought in WWII and the Korean War, returning soldiers were condemned for their participation in the violence of Vietnam instead of being hailed as heroes for democracy. Incidents like the massacre at My Lai and similar accounts served to reinforce these popular perceptions. In his essay in this chapter, "The Vietnam in Me," veteran Tim O'Brien discusses the lingering political and personal ramifications of this incident and, at the same time, makes distinctions between soldiers who did and those who did *not* commit such atrocities.

These accounts of our own inhumanity make it more difficult for us to stand in judgement of the inhumanity of others. In his essay "Vietnam," Paul Fussell faults the mental anguish of war as the force which drove American soldiers to acts of hatred that dehumanized the Viet Cong. He suggests that "the terrible things the troops had to do and see, and . . . their anger at the Vietnamese, both North and South, and their frustration and fear at the absence of a front line and a locatable enemy" all played their parts (655). Unlike the World Wars, the war in Vietnam did not abide by clear geographical boundaries. The enemy looked no different from the ally. Vietnam was a war "where anyone might be an enemy and where the enemy was unidentifiable and everywhere" causing American soldiers to "kill people, uniformed or not, old or young, male or female, proven Viet Cong or not" (654). In Vietnam, we were fighting an enemy that did not play by our rules, the same rules that we rejected in our fight to become Americans. In his novel, *In the Lake of the Woods,* O'Brien quotes a British soldier after the revolutionary war battles at Lexington and Concord. The soldier claims that the colonists "did not fight us like a regular army, only like savages behind trees and stone walls, and out of the woods and houses . . . [they were] as bad as the Indians for scalping and cutting the dead men's ears and noses off" (qtd. in O'Brien 259). Much like our frustrated response to the Viet Cong's unorthodox brand of warfare, British soldiers responded by their own acts of hatred. The British troops were "so enraged at suffering from an unseen enemy that they forced open many of the houses . . . and put to death all those found in them" (qtd. in O'Brien 259). For the British on American soil, the colonists seemed as barbaric and misguided as the Vietcong did to U.S. soldiers in Vietnam. These parallel accounts document the experiences of soldiers fighting for independence—American independence from British colonial rule and Vietnamese independence from what many Vietnamese believed was the remnant of French colonial rule. These accounts of witness capture the moment for those outside the experience and encourage insight into the experience for those who lived through it.

Because witnessing has a power that extends beyond the moment, it keeps us from forgetting. Distance can threaten witnessing and blur memories, but distance can also encourage and enable reflection. When we craft our experiences into language, we represent and recreate them. We do not merely reflect our experiences, we reflect on them. And when we do, "experience [becomes] historical and ongoing, constantly reconstituting itself" (Lu and Horner 261). For instance, O'Brien uses the quotations of the British soldier in his fiction as a way of showing that atrocities have been committed during wars throughout history; he is also recreating the psychology of the soldier, allowing us to reflect on the ways a soldier's morality can be affected by traumatic experiences. On first reading, we may think that O'Brien is explaining the causes of such behavior as a way of justifying it, especially since such atrocities were not peculiar to Vietnam. However, in his nonfiction essay, "The Vietnam in Me," O'Brien says very bluntly that, even in war, there is a difference between killing others in combat and committing murder:

> Justifications are empty and outrageous . . . . I know the boil that precedes butchery. At the same time, however, the men in [my] Company did not commit murder. We did not turn our machine guns on civilians; we did not cross that conspicuous line between rage and homicide. I know what occurred here, yes, but I also feel betrayed by a nation that so widely shrugs off barbarity, by a military judicial system that treats murderers and common soldiers as one and the same.

The ideas in his fiction may seem, on first reading, to contradict his ideas in his nonfiction, but as readers, we can more fully understand his intentions when we consider his work in context: perhaps in the fiction, he recreates the soldier's experiences so the reader can come to an understanding of them through the soldier's perspective; however, in his nonfiction, he steps back and reflects on his own experiences, drawing distinctions, making judgments, and trying to come to an understanding of the larger forces at work. Too, in his nonfiction, he more directly challenges his readers to consider for themselves their own complicity.

Only in retrospect, perhaps, can a writer explore these moral complexities. Through reflection, we ground personal experience in political and social situations. In doing so, "we can use experience not simply to affirm our state of being but to raise questions about that material being, to critique and bring about changes in the conditions of our existence and, in turn, to transform our experience" (Lu and Horner 261). The readings in this chapter bear witness in one way or another to the Vietnam War. Each selection was written post-war, allowing the writers to reflect on their experiences and offer witness. These writings stand in contrast to the selections in Chapter 10 which document the September 11th, 2001 attacks. While the Vietnam selections grow from reflection and distance, most of the September 11th accounts are initial reactions and responses. For us, the process of healing has just begun; for the writers in this chapter, the process of healing is still going on, some thirty years later.

Today, many people in Vietnam still follow the peaceful agrarian way of life they have for centuries. Despite this, reminders of the violence in its past shape the landscape and her people. In a letter to his family in February 2001, JD Roberto, enroute from Cambodia to Vietnam, writes:

> Every time a one-legged child or mother hops by on the street, I am sickened to think of the damages and horror. . . . It's a real, day to day danger for the people working the fields and uncharted back hills of the country. . . . The Khmer Rogue, the French, the U.S., the Viet Cong all laid mines here. . . . And it's inevitably children playing alone in a field that find them.

In Saigon the Cu Chi Tunnels designed by the Vietcong to move soldiers and weapons into the city have become a tourist attraction for American visitors. Tourists can move freely from a cybercafe in Hanoi to the Great Khmer Ruins at Angkor Wat near Siem Reap, Cambodia, from stunning beauty to abject poverty, from the present to the past. Even those of us who did not live through the Vietnam War can still be haunted by its effects. Vietnam holds a piece of our past just as we have become a piece of theirs and by holding a piece of our past, it shapes our present and our selves. Although many of us may not have lived through the conflict in Vietnam, it still impacts who we, as a nation and as a people, have become. In his correspondence from Vietnam to his family, JD's friend Michael writes:

> I can't help but think as I lie awake at night trying to fall asleep to "Who Let the Dogs Out?" that thirty years ago I would have been cramped up in a fox hole, without my wife, without my dearest friends, afraid to light a cigarette. . . . There is still that awkward moment before you say "I'm American," and every now and then a "checkpoint" reminds you where you are.

JD and Michael saw Vietnam through the lens of a war that took place before they were born: what they knew about our involvement there shaped how they experienced the country and how they expected the Vietnamese people to react to them.

Likewise, your reading of the selections in this chapter will be shaped by what you know of our history, by movies you've seen about the war, by stories you may have heard people in your family tell and, inevitably, by the current conflicts we're involved in in the Middle East. As you read, you'll want to note the connections you make. What do these writers tell us about the choices people make during war and about how extreme experiences shape or reshape the people who survive them? At the end of "How to Tell a True War Story," O'Brien's narrator says, "It *wasn't* a war story. It was a *love* story." In his essay, "The Vietnam in Me" he writes: "I'm on war time, which is the time we're all on at one point or another: when fathers die, when husbands ask for divorce, when women you love are fast asleep beside men you wish you were." In both texts, he is clearly making connections between war and our everyday lives, trying to say that the moral and emotional issues of war transcend war; they may be intensified by war but they are relevant to our everyday lives, to the conflicts we have and the choices we make as human beings.

Works Cited

Forché, Carolyn. "Introduction to *Against Forgetting.*" *Writing as Revision.*

Fussell, Paul. "Vietnam." *The Bloody Game: An Anthology of Modern War.* Ed. Paul Fussell. London: Scribners, 1991. 651–656.

Lu, Min-Zhan and Bruce Horner. "The Problematic of Experience: Redefining Critical Work in Ethnography and Pedagogy." *College English* 60.3 (1998).

O'Brien, Tim. "How to Tell a True War Story." *Writing as Revision.*

———. *In the Lake of the Woods.* Boston: Houghton Mifflin, 1994.

———. "The Vietnam in Me." *Writing as Revision.*

Roberto, JD and Michael Alvarado. E-mail correspondence. February 2001.

www.viettouch.com

Carolyn Forché

Carolyn Forché (b. 1950) is one of the most powerful and affecting poets of her generation. Her first collection of poetry, Gathering the Tribes *(1975), won the Yale Series of Younger Poets Award. Her second collection,* The Country Between Us *(1981), written after a period of time spent doing human rights work in El Salvador during the People's Revolution, is a best-selling book of poetry and was named the Lamont Selection of the Academy of American Poets. Forché's more recent books are* The Angel of History *and* Blue Hour, *which will be published in 2003. In Chapter Eight,* "Writing as Social Witness," *you will find three of her poems. Here, we excerpt the introductory essay she wrote for her anthology of poetry by survivors of extremity,* Against Forgetting: Twentieth Century Poetry of Witness.

Introduction: Against Forgetting

In 1944, the Hungarian poet Miklós Radnóti was sent to a forced-labor camp in what became Yugoslavia. While there, he was able to procure a small notebook, in which he wrote his last ten poems, along with the following message in Hungarian, Croatian, German, French, and English: ". . . [this] contains the poems of the Hungarian poet Miklós Radnóti . . . to Mr. Gyula Ortutay, Budapest University lecturer. . . . Thank you in advance."

When it was clear that they would be defeated, the Germans decided to evacuate the camp and return the workers to Hungary. Radnóti, assuming that the first column would be the safest, volunteered for the march and recorded it in his poetry. Once in Hungary, the soldiers in charge, unable to find hospital room for these prisoners, took Radnóti and twenty-one others to a mass grave and executed them. Had Radnóti not volunteered to return to Hungary, he might have been saved by Marshal Tito's partisans. However, the story does not end—as millions of such stories ended—with execution and the anonymity of a mass grave. After the war was over, Radnóti's wife was among those who found and exhumed the mass grave in the village of Abda. The coroner's report for corpse #12 read:

> A visiting card with the name Dr. Miklós Radnóti printed on it. An ID card stating the mother's name as Ilona Grosz. Father's name illegible. Born in Budapest, May 5, 1909. Cause of death: shot in the nape. In the back pocket of the trousers a small

---

Reprinted from *Against Forgetting: Twentieth-Century Poetry of Witness*, (1993), W.W. Norton & Company.

> notebook was found soaked in the fluids of the body and blackened by wet earth. This was cleaned and dried in the sun.

Radnóti's final poems [survived him] along with the poems of other significant poets who endured conditions of historical and social extremity during the twentieth century—through exile, state censorship, political persecution, house arrest, torture, imprisonment, military occupation, warfare, and assassination. Many poets did not survive, but their works remain with us as poetic witness to the dark times in which they lived.

This attempt to assemble such work in a single volume is the result of a thirteen-year effort to understand the impress of extremity upon the poetic imagination. My own journey began in 1980, upon my return from El Salvador—where I had worked as a human rights activist—and led me through the occupied West Bank, Lebanon, and South Africa. Something happened along the way to the introspective poet I had been. My new work seemed controversial to my American contemporaries, who argued against its "subject matter," or against the right of a North American to contemplate such issues in her work, or against any mixing of what they saw as the mutually exclusive realms of the personal and the political. Like many other poets, I felt that I had no real choice regarding the impulse of my poems, and had only to wait, in meditative expectancy. In attempting to come to terms with the question of poetry and politics, and seeking the solace of poetic camaraderie, I turned to the works of Anna Akhmatova, Yannis Ritsos, Paul Celan, Federico García Lorca, Nazim Hikmet, and others. I began collecting their work, and soon found myself a repository of what began to be called "the poetry of witness." In thinking about these poems, I realized that the arguments about poetry and politics had been too narrowly defined. Regardless of "subject matter," these poems bear the trace of extremity within them, and they are, as such, evidence of what occurred. They are also poems which are as much "about" language as are poems that have no subject other than language itself.

This anthological history of our century begins with the genocide of the Armenians and follows extremity in its various forms. The volume is arranged in sections according to regions and major events, with historical headnotes. Within each section, poets appear in chronological order by date of birth, with biographical notes to illuminate the experience of extremity for each poet, and a selection of poetry from available works in the English originals or in translation. The criteria for inclusion were these: poets must have personally endured such conditions; they must be considered important to their national literatures; and their work, if not in English, must be available in a quality translation. The necessarily brief biographies included here provide information relevant to the poets' experience of extremity. In instances where it was possible to place poets in more than one section, they appear according to their first significant experience of this kind, even though their poems might reflect later experiences as well. Finally, not all poems address extreme conditions, nor do all appear relevant in terms of their subject matter. I was interested in what these poets wrote, regardless of the explicit content.

This collection reflects the abundance of works in translation from European languages, but unfortunately underscores the scarcity of works translated from Asian and African literatures. In addition, fewer women poets seem to have survived the horrors of our century than their male counterparts, and many fewer have been translated. Despite these limitations, the present volume makes available only about one quarter of the material I was able to gather. It is, however, not my intention to propose a canon of such works; this is, rather, a poetic memorial to those who suffered and resisted through poetry itself.

Poetry of witness presents the reader with an interesting interpretive problem. We are accustomed to rather easy categories: we distinguish between "personal" and "political" poems—the former calling to mind lyrics of love and emotional loss, the latter indicating a public partisanship that is considered divisive, even when necessary. The distinction between the personal and the political gives the political realm too much and too little scope; at the same time, it renders the personal too important and not important enough. If we give up the dimension of the personal, we risk relinquishing one of the most powerful sites of resistance. The celebration of the personal, however, can indicate myopia, an inability to see how larger structures of the economy and the state circumscribe, if not determine, the fragile realm of individuality.

We need a third term, one that can describe the space between the state and the supposedly safe havens of the personal. Let us call this space "the social." As North Americans, we have been fortunate: wars for us (provided we are not combatants) are fought elsewhere, in other countries. The cities bombed are other people's cities. The houses destroyed are other people's houses. We are also fortunate in that we do not live under martial law; there are nominal restrictions on state censorship; our citizens are not sent into exile. We are legally and juridically free to choose our associates, and to determine our communal lives. But perhaps we should not consider our social lives as merely the products of our choice: the social is a place of resistance and struggle, where books are published, poems read, and protest disseminated. It is the sphere in which claims against the political order are made in the name of justice.

By situating poetry in this social space, we can avoid some of our residual prejudices. A poem that calls on us from the other side of a situation of extremity cannot be judged by simplistic notions of "accuracy" or "truth to life." It will have to be judged, as Ludwig Wittgenstein said of confessions, by its consequences, not by our ability to verify its truth. In fact, the poem might be our only evidence that an event has occurred: it exists for us as the sole trace of an occurrence. As such, there will be nothing for us to base the poem on, no independent account that will tell us whether or not we can see a given text as being "objectively" true. Poem as trace, poem as evidence. Radnóti's final notebook entry, dated October 31, 1944, read:

> I fell beside him; his body turned over,
> already taut as a string about to snap.
> Shot in the back of the neck. That's how you too will end,
> I whispered to myself; just lie quietly.
> Patience now flowers into death.
> *Der springt noch auf,* a voice said above me.
> On my ear, blood dried, mixed with filth.

This verse describes the death of his fellow prisoner Miklós Lorsi, a violinist, and remains the only trace of his dying.

Miklós Radnóti's poems evade easy categories. They are not merely personal, nor are they, strictly speaking, political. What is one to make of the first lines of "Forced March"?:

> The man who, having collapsed,   rises, takes steps, is insane;
> he'll move an ankle, a knee,   an errant mass of pain,
> and take to the road again . . .

The poem becomes an apostrophe to a fellow marcher, and so it is not only a record of experience but an exhortation and a plea against despair. It is not a cry for sympathy but a call for strength. The hope that the poem relies on, however, is not "political" as such: it is not a celebration of solidarity in the name of a class or common enemy. It is not partisan in any accepted sense. It opposes the dream of future satisfaction to the reality of current pain. One could argue that it uses the promise of personal happiness against a politically induced misery, but it does so in the name of the poet's fellows, in a spirit of communality.

We all know that atrocities have taken place on an unprecedented scale in the last one hundred years. Such monstrous acts have come to seem almost normal. It becomes easier to forget than to remember, and this forgetfulness becomes our defense against remembering—a rejection of unnecessary sentimentality, a hard-headed acceptance of "reality." Modernity, as twentieth-century German Jewish philosophers Walter Benjamin and Theodor Adorno argued, is marked by a superstitious worship of oppressive force and by a concomitant reliance on oblivion. Such forgetfulness, they argue, is willful and isolating: it drives wedges between the individual and the collective fate to which he or she is forced to submit. These poems will not permit us diseased complacency. They come to us with claims that have yet to be filled, as attempts to mark us as they have themselves been marked. . . .

The poetry of witness reclaims the social from the political and in so doing defends the individual against illegitimate forms of coercion. It often seeks to register through indirection and intervention the ways in which the linguistic and moral universes have been disrupted by events. When I began this project, I was hard pressed to find a significant poet who could not be included, who in some important way or another did *not* bear witness to the ravages of our time. But clearly it was impossible to contemplate a book of such length. I was therefore forced to develop criteria for inclusion that would do justice to the poets I would necessarily have to exclude, criteria that would begin to describe the trajectory of our modernity. I decided to limit the poets in the anthology to those for whom the social had been irrevocably invaded by the political in ways that were sanctioned neither by law nor by the fictions of the social contract. The writers I have chosen are those for whom the normative promises of the nation-state have failed. They have not been afforded the legal or the physical protections that the modern state is supposed to lend its citizens, nor have they been able to enjoy the solidarity that the concept of the nation is supposed to provide. If my selection seems to include an inordinate number of writers whose human rights have been abused, it is because those rights, in the tradition of political theory, were supposed to police the boundaries between the government and personal self-determination, between citizenship and autonomy.

For decades, American literary criticism has sought to oppose "man" and "society," the individual against the communal, alterity against universality. Perhaps we can learn from the practice of the poets in this anthology that these are not oppositions based on mutual exclusion but are rather dialectical complementaries that invoke and pass through each other. Extremity is born of the simplifying desire to split these dyads into separate parts. It is the product of the drive to expunge one category in the name of another, to sacrifice the individual on the altar of the communal or vice versa. The poetry of witness is itself born in dialectical opposition to the extremity that has made such witness necessary. In the process, it restores the dynamic structure of dialectics.

Because the poetry of witness marks a resistance to false attempts at unification, it will take many forms. It will be impassioned or ironic. It will speak in the language of the common man or in an esoteric language of paradox or literary privilege. It will curse and it will bless; it will blaspheme against or ignore the holy. Its protest might rest on an odd grammatical inversion, on a heady peroration to an audience, or on a bizarre flight of fancy. It can be partisan in a limited sense but is more often partisan in the best of senses, that is, it speaks for what might, with less than crippling irony be called "the party of humanity." I do not mean this in an unreflective way, as a celebration of some mythological "inherent" goodness in man's "innate" nature. Rather, I take the partisanship of humanity as a rejection of unwarranted pain inflicted on some humans by others, of illegitimate domination. I am guided in this by Hannah Arendt's meditation on the self-justifications of collaboration with oppression, on the claim that the resistance of the single individual does not count in the face of the annihilating superiority of totalitarian regimes which make all resistance disappear into "holes of oblivion":

> The holes of oblivion do not exist. Nothing human is that perfect and there are simply too many people in the world to make oblivion possible. One man will always be left alive to tell the story . . . the lesson of such stories is simple and within everybody's grasp. Politically speaking, it is that under conditions of terror, most people will comply but *some people will not*. . . . Humanly speaking, no more is required, and no more can reasonably be asked, for this planet to remain a place fit for human habitation.

The resistance to terror is what makes the world habitable: the protest against violence will not be forgotten and this insistent memory renders life possible in communal situations. As Desnos wrote in a poem called "Epitaph":

> You who are living, what have you done with these treasures?
> Do you regret the time of my struggle?
> Have you raised your crops for a common harvest?
> Have you made my town a richer place?

If we have not, if we do not, what, in the end, have we become? And if we do not, what, in the end, shall we be?

Le Ly Hayslip

Le Ly Hayslip (b. 1949) is originally from near Da Nang, Vietnam and lived through the war in Vietnam. She first came to the U.S. after she married an American civilian working in Vietnam. She has written two critically acclaimed books that reflect on her experiences. When Heaven and Earth Changed Places *(1989), her first book, was later made into the movie* Heaven and Earth *(1993) by Oliver Stone who is a Vietnam vet. Her second book,* Child of War, Woman and Peace, *was published in 1993. The following selection is the Prologue to* When Heaven and Earth Changed Places *that addresses the Vietnam war from a Vietnamese perspective.*

Prologue: Dedication to Peace

For my first twelve years of life, I was a peasant girl in Ky La, now called Xa Hoa Qui, a small village near Danang in Central Vietnam. My father taught me to love god, my family, our traditions, and the people we could not see: our ancestors. He taught me that to sacrifice one's self for freedom—like our ancient kings who fought bravely against invaders; or in the manner of our women warriors, including Miss Trung Nhi Trung Trac who drowned herself rather than give in to foreign conquerors—was a very high honor. From my love of my ancestors and my native soil, he said, I must never retreat.

From my mother I learned humility and the strength of virtue. I learned it was no disgrace to work like an animal on our farm, provided I did not complain. "Would you be less than our ox," she asked, "who works to feed us without grumbling?" She also taught me, when I began to notice village boys, that there is no love beyond faithful love, and that in my love for my future husband, my ancestors, and my native soil, I must always remain steadfast.

For my next three years of life, I loved, labored, and fought steadfastly for the Viet Cong against American and South Vietnamese soldiers.

Everything I knew about the war I learned as a teenaged girl from the North Vietnamese cadre leaders in the swamps outside Ky La. During these midnight meetings, we peasants assumed everything we heard was true because what the Viet Cong said matched, in one way or another, the beliefs we already had.

The first lesson we learned about the new "American" war was why the Viet Cong was formed and why we should support it. Because this lesson came on the

---

Reprinted from *When Heaven and Earth Changed Places: a Vietnamese Women's Journey from War to Peace*, (1990), Doubleday, a division of Random House.

heels of our war with the French (which began in 1946 and lasted, on and off, for eight years), what the cadre leaders told us seemed to be self-evident.

First, we were taught that Vietnam was *con rong chau tien*—a sovereign nation which had been held in thrall by Western imperialists for over a century. That all nations had a right to determine their own destiny also seemed beyond dispute, since we farmers subsisted by our own hands and felt we owed nothing to anyone but god and our ancestors for the right to live as we saw fit. Even the Chinese, who had made their own disastrous attempt to rule Vietnam in centuries past, had learned a painful lesson about our country's zeal for independence. "Vietnam," went the saying that summarized their experience, "is nobody's lapdog."

Second, the cadres told us that the division of Vietnam into North and South in 1954 was nothing more than a ploy by the defeated French and their Western allies, mainly the United States, to preserve what influence they could in our country.

"Chia doi dat nuoc?" the Viet Cong asked, "Why should outsiders divide the land and tell some people to go north and others south? If Vietnam were truly for the Vietnamese, wouldn't we choose for ourselves what kind of government our people wanted? A nation cannot have *two* governments," they said, "anymore than a family can have two fathers."

Because those who favored America quickly occupied the seats of power formerly held by the French, and because the North remained pretty much on its own, the choice of which side best represented independence was, for us, a foregone conclusion. In fact, the Viet Cong usually ended our indoctrination sessions with a song that played on our worst fears:

> Americans come to kill our people,
> Follow America, and kill your relatives!
> The smart bird flies before it's caught.
> The smart person comes home before Tet.
> Follow us, and you'll always have a family.
> Follow America, and you'll always be alone!

After these initial "lessons," the cadre leaders introduced us to the two Vietnamese leaders who personified each view—the opposite poles of our tiny world. On the South pole was President Ngo Dinh Diem, America's staunch ally, who was Catholic like the French. Although he was idolized by many who said he was a great humanitarian and patriot, his religion alone was enough to make him suspicious to Buddhists on the Central Coast. The loyalty we showed him, consequently, was more duty to a landlord than love for a founding father. Here is a song the Republican schoolteachers made us learn to praise the Southern president:

> In stormy seas, Vietnam's boat rolls and pitches.
> Still we must row; our President's hand upon the helm.
> The ship of state plows through heavy seas,
> Holding fast its course to democracy.
> Our President is celebrated from Europe to Asia,
> He is the image of philanthropy and love.

> He has sacrificed himself for our happiness.
> He fights for liberty in the land of the Viet.
> Everyone loves him earnestly, and behind him we will march
> Down the street of freedom, lined with fresh flowers,
> The flag of liberty crackling above our heads!

In the North, on the other pole, was Ho Chi Minh, whom we were encouraged to call *Bac Ho*—Uncle Ho—the way we would refer to a trusted family friend. We knew nothing of his past beyond stories of his compassion and his love for our troubled country—the independence of which, we were told, he had made the mission of his life.

Given the gulf between these leaders, the choice of whom we should support again seemed obvious. The cadre leaders encouraged our natural prejudices (fear of outsiders and love of our ancestors) with stirring songs and tender stories about Uncle Ho in which the Communist leader and our ancient heroes seemed to inhabit one congenial world. Like an unbroken thread, the path from our ancestors and legends seemed to lead inevitably to the Northern leader—then past him to a future of harmony and peace.

But to achieve that independence, Ho said, we must wage total war. His cadremen cried out "We must hold together and oppose the American empire. There is nothing better than freedom, independence, and happiness!"

To us, these ideas seemed as obvious as everything else we had heard. *Freedom* meant a Vietnam free of colonial domination. *Independence* meant one Vietnamese people—not two countries, North and South—determining its own destiny. *Happiness* meant plenty of food and an end to war—the ability, we assumed, to live our lives in accordance with our ancient ways. We wondered: how can the Southerners oppose these wonderful things? The answer the Viet Cong gave us was that the Republicans prized Yankee dollars more than the blood of their brothers and sisters. We did not think to question with our hearts what our minds told us must be true.

Although most of us thought we knew what the Viet Cong meant by freedom, independence, and happiness, a few of us dared to ask what life the Northerners promised when the war was over. The answer was always the same: "Uncle Ho promises that after our victory, the Communist state will look after your rights and interests. Your highest interest, of course, is the independence of our fatherland and the freedom of our people. Our greatest right is the right to determine our own future as a state." This always brought storms of applause from the villagers because most people remembered what life was like under the French.

Nonetheless, despite our vocal support, the Viet Cong never took our loyalty for granted. They rallied and rewarded and lectured us sternly, as the situation demanded, while the Republicans assumed we would be loyal because we lived south of a line some diplomats had drawn on a map. Even when things were at their worst—when the allied forces devastated the countryside and the Viet Cong themselves resorted to terror to make us act the way they wanted—the villagers clung to the vision the Communists had drummed into us. When the Republicans put us in jail, we had the image of "Communist freedom"—freedom from war—to see us through. When the Viet Cong executed a relative, we convinced ourselves that it was necessary to bring "Communist happiness"—peace in the village—a little closer. Because the Viet Cong encouraged us to voice our basic human feelings through patriotic songs, the tortured, self-imposed silence we endured around Republicans only made us hate the government more. Even on those occasions when the Republicans tried to help us, we saw their favors as a trick or sign of weakness. Thus, even as we accepted their kindness, we despised the Republicans for it.

As the war gathered steam in the 1960s, every villager found his or her little world expanded—usually for the worse. The steady parade of troops through Ky La meant new opportunities for us to fall victim to outsiders. Catholic Republicans spurned and mistreated Buddhists for worshiping their ancestors. City boys taunted and cheated the "country bumpkins" while Vietnamese servicemen from other provinces made fun of our funny accents and strange ways. When the tactics on both sides got so rough that people were in danger no matter which side they favored, our sisters fled to the cities where they learned about liquor, drugs, adultery, materialism, and disrespect for their ancestors. More than one village father died inside when a "stranger from Saigon" returned in place of the daughter he had raised.

In contrast to this, the Viet Cong were, for the most part, our neighbors. Even though our cadre leaders had been trained in Hanoi, they had all been born on the Central Coast. They did not insult us for our manners and speech because they had been raised exactly like us. Where the Republicans came into the village overburdened with American equipment designed for a different war, the Viet Cong made do with what they had and seldom wasted their best ammunition—the goodwill of the people. The cadremen pointed out to us that where the Republicans wore medals, the Viet Cong wore rags and never gave up the fight. "Where the Republicans pillage, rape, and plunder," they said, "we preserve your houses, crops, and family"; for they knew that it was only by these resources—our food for rations, our homes for hiding, our sons and brothers for recruits—that they were able to keep the field.

Of course, the Viet Cong cadremen, like the Republicans, had no desire (or ability, most of them) to paint a fairer picture. For them, there could be no larger reason for Americans fighting the war than imperialist aggression. Because we peasants knew nothing about the United States, we could not stop to think how absurd it would be for so large and wealthy a nation to covet our poor little country for its rice fields, swamps, and pagodas. Because our only exposure to politics had been through the French colonial government (and before that, the rule of Vietnamese kings), we had no concept of democracy. For us, "Western culture" meant bars, brothels, black markets, and *xa hoi van minh*—bewildering machines—most of them destructive. We couldn't imagine that life in the capitalist world was anything other than a frantic, alien terror. Because, as peasants, we defined "politics" as something other people did someplace else, it had no relevance to our daily lives—except as a source of endless trouble. As a consequence, we overlooked the power that lay in our hands: our power to achieve virtually anything we wanted if only we acted together. The Viet Cong and the North, on the other hand, always recognized and respected this strength.

We children also knew that our ancestral spirits demanded we resist the outsiders. Our parents told us of the misery they had suffered from the invading Japanese ("small death," our neighbors called them) in World War II, and from the French, who returned in 1946. These soldiers destroyed our crops, killed our livestock, burned our houses, raped our women, and tortured or put to death anyone who opposed them—as well as many who did not. Now, the souls of all those people who had been mercilessly killed had come back to haunt Ky La—demanding revenge against the invaders. This we children believed with all our hearts. After all, we had been taught from birth that ghosts were simply people we could not see.

There was only one way to remove this curse. Uncle Ho had urged the poor to take up arms so that everyone might be guaranteed a little land on which to cultivate some rice. Because nearly everyone in Central Vietnam was a farmer, and because farmers must have land, almost everyone went to war: with a rifle or a hoe; with vigilance to give the alarm; with food and shelter for our fighters; or, if one was too little for anything else, with flowers and songs to cheer them up. Everything we knew commanded us to fight. Our ancestors called us to war. Our myths and legends called us to war. Our parents' teachings called us to war. Uncle Ho's cadre called us to war. Even President Diem had called us to fight for the very thing we now believed he was betraying—an independent Vietnam. Should an obedient child be less than an ox and refuse to do her duty?

And so the war began and became an insatiable dragon that roared around Ky La. By the time I turned thirteen, that dragon had swallowed me up.

In 1986, after living for sixteen years in America and becoming a U.S. citizen, I went back to Vietnam—to find out what had happened to my family, my village, my people, and to the man I loved who had given me my first son. I went with many memories and many questions. This book is the story of what I remember and what I found.

It is dedicated to all those who fought for their country, wherever it may be. It is dedicated, too, to those who did not fight—but suffered, wept, raged, bled, and died just the same. We all did what we had to do. By mingling our blood and tears on the earth, god has made us brothers and sisters.

If you were an American GI, I ask you to read this book and look into the heart of one you once called enemy. I have witnessed, firsthand, all that you went through. I will try to tell you who your enemy was and why almost everyone in the country you tried to help resented, feared, and misunderstood you. It was not your fault. It could not have been otherwise. Long before you arrived, my country had yielded to the terrible logic of war. What for you was normal—a life of peace and plenty—was for us a hazy dream known only in our legends. Because we had to appease the allied forces by day and were terrorized by Viet Cong at night, we slept as little as you did. We obeyed both sides and wound up pleasing neither. We were people in the middle. We were what the war was all about.

Your story, however, was different. You came to Vietnam, willingly or not, because your country demanded it. Most of you did not know, or fully understand, the different wars my people were fighting when you got here. For you, it was a simple thing: democracy against communism. For us, that was not our fight at all. How could it be? We knew little of democracy and even less about communism. For most of us it was a fight for independence—like the American Revolution. Many of us also fought for religious ideals, the way the Buddhists fought the Catholics. Behind the religious war came the battle between city people and country people—the rich against the poor—a war fought by those who wanted to change Vietnam and those who wanted to leave it as it had been for a thousand years. Beneath all that, too, we had vendettas: between native Vietnamese and immigrants (mostly Chinese and Khmer) who had fought for centuries over the land. Many of these wars go on today. How could you hope to end them by fighting a battle so different from our own?

The least you did—the least any of us did—was our duty. For that we must be proud. The most that any of us did—or saw—was another face of destiny or luck or god. Children and soldiers have always known it to be terrible. If you have not yet found peace at the end of your war, I hope you will find it here. We have important new roles to play.

In the war many Americans—and many more Vietnamese—lost limbs, loved ones, and that little light we see in babies' eyes which is our own hope for the future. Do not despair. As long as you are alive, that light still burns within you. If you lost someone you love, his light burns on in you—so long as you remember. Be happy every day you are alive.

If you are a person who knows the Vietnam war, or any war, only by stories and pictures, this book is written for you too. For you see, the face of destiny or luck or god that gives us war also gives us other kinds of pain: the loss of health and youth; the loss of loved ones or of love; the fear that we will end our days alone. Some people suffer in peace the way others suffer in war. The special gift of that suffering, I have learned, is how to be strong while we are weak, how to be brave when we are afraid, how to be wise in the midst of confusion, and how to let go of that which we can no longer hold. In this way, anger can teach forgiveness, hate can teach us love, and war can teach us peace.

Phung Thi Le Ly Hayslip
San Diego, California
October 1988

Vu Bao

Vu Bao (b. 1931) is a decorated veteran of both the French and American wars in Vietnam. He has numerous collections of short stories including Your Father was a Woman, To Be God *and* The Eldest and the Youngest *as well as novels and film scripts. In 1988 and 1989 he was awarded best short story by the Army Literature and Arts magazine. In 1991 he received best novel from the Hanoi Writer's Association. In "The Man Who Stained His Soul," he juxtaposes the reality of war with the perceptions of war that are created as representations of that reality.*

The Man Who Stained His Soul

If everything had gone as we'd planned, I would have nothing now to write about the battle against Che post that year.

Painstakingly accurate plans had been drawn up under the close guidance of the Command Staff. New intelligence about shifts in the enemy's effective strength and weaponry was received every day. The diagram of Che post's defenses was drawn and redrawn so many times it reached a point of absolute perfection. Each enemy fire point was scouted over and over and marked by a different symbol on the diagram. Victory couldn't be more certain.

But war isn't a game in which only one side fires and the other eats bullets. The enemy major in charge of Che post was an experienced soldier. Ignoring the deliberate provocations of our recons-by-fire, he kept the two heavy machine guns he had concealed in the command bunker silent. It wasn't until our company burst through the barbed wire and advanced to the center of the compound in an arrow-shape formation that those guns opened up, catching us in a cross fire.

Our attack was stopped dead. The company was pinned down, with everyone's belly glued to the earth and no one daring to lift his head. It was a miracle we could keep our heads and limbs intact without breathing dirt.

This tactic hadn't been anticipated in the combat plan, and now the commanders couldn't react. Usually, once the company engaged, the Party cell would confer urgently, exchange ideas and make timely decisions. But this time, Luat, the company commander, was stuck with our front unit, the commissar was in the rear of the formation, and the deputy commissar was helping to get the wounded dragged out of the barbed wire and bandaged up. Pulling out his revolver, the commissar fired up into the air and sprang forward, yelling; "Comrades, advance . . ."

His order was cut short by a bullet.

Reprinted from *The Other Side of Heaven: Postwar Fiction by Vietnamese and American Writers*, edited by Wayne Karlin, Le Minh Khue, and Truong Vu, (1995), Curbstone Press.

Luat crawled down the column to me and jerked his chin at the fire point: "Take out the left side and leave the right to me."

We divided the front unit into two V-shaped lines. Half of the men crept after Luat, the other half after me. Only Vinh lay prostrate in his place.

I crawled back to him.

"What the hell are you doing?"

Vinh's voice was strained. "How can we advance—the bullets are pouring in like rain."

"Would you rather lie here waiting for death?"

"Death's waiting up there also."

With the bullets zeroing in on us, this wasn't the time or place to try to turn a coward into a brave soldier. "Give me your cartridge belt and grenades," I yelled at him.

"Then I'll be killed in the enemy's counterattack."

My blood was boiling. I yanked his submachine gun from his hands. "I have to advance. Hang onto the company flag."

I crawled low under the fire, keeping my eyes on the muzzle flashes. Suddenly the fire pecking at us from the bunker's loophole ceased. The enemy gunners must have been changing the belt. I sprang up and rushed the bunker. Someone threw a grenade at me. I snatched it up and tossed it back into the loophole. Then I thrust the barrel of my rifle through the opening and sprayed in a full magazine, sweeping the area inside.

Shouts of joy sounded from all around. Fourth Company had penetrated the base. But what followed was our hardest battle. We struggled to take one fortified position after another, and it was nearly morning before we managed to blow up their headquarters.

Afterwards, the battalion commander ran up to us. "Hurry and scrounge up whatever supplies and equipment you can," he said. "It's nearly dawn—you'll start shitting when the enemy's long range artillery begins firing."

I turned around to see Vinh standing nearby. His left trouser leg was sticking like glue to his thigh. I tore out the bandage I had tucked into my belt.

Luat seized my hand. "Don't bother. He just pissed himself," he said, nodding at Vinh's saturated trouser. "Pissed on his own soul."

We withdrew to Noi hamlet, four kilometers from Che post. Air raid shelters had been dug there by the local militia. Those units that had been held in reserve during the attack were now sent out to guard the perimeter of the hamlet, and huge sauce pans full of chicken gruel were prepared for us in each house. But after our night of shooting, crawling and rolling through the mud, we could only take a few perfunctory mouthfuls. It was better to sleep than to eat. As soon as we lay down on our straw mats, we didn't know if heaven was up or earth was down.

Suddenly I was awakened by someone pulling me to my feet. Still in a daze, my eyes half-sealed, I dimly heard Luat order me to get the unit dressed in full uniform and equipment. "Get everybody over to battalion headquarters—they have a new job for you."

"Yes, commander."

When we arrived at headquarters, the battalion commander told me that a foreign comrade had come to shoot a documentary film. Since the battle was over, it would be necessary to reconstruct the fighting for him. The first shot would be the raising of the company flag over the roof of Che post.

I stood dumbfounded for a moment. "Commander, after the fighting we policed up the battlefield and returned here at once. We didn't have time to raise a flag."

"Then you'll have to raise one now."

"Sir, we don't have a flag."

"What do you mean—what about the Victory flag the regimental commander handed to you before you left? Didn't he give it to you, unit commander, in front of all your men?"

"I passed it to Vinh when the C.O. ordered us to advance. After I took out the heavy machine gun, the rest of the company charged forward. Vinh came along with them, but he forgot to bring the flag."

"Why didn't you look for it?"

"I did, but I couldn't find it. When I went back to that place, all I saw were three mortar craters."

The battalion commander turned to the press liaison officer and told him to get Third Company's Victory flag instead.

The foreign comrade was waiting for us at regimental headquarters. Smiling, he shook our hands. "Glory to Vietnam; of thou I'm proud," he said.

We tightened our lips to keep from bursting into laughter.

The "reconstruction" of the flag-raising didn't go as easily as we thought it would. The machine gun company took positions along the outer perimeter. The heavy artillery company set up four observation posts to watch for air raids. An infantry company deployed inside Che post, ready to take on any enemy parachutists who might try to pounce upon us. And our unit, directed by the foreign comrade, had the task of reenacting the destruction of the command bunker. Unfortunately, when the explosive charges were blown, a piece of concrete from the bunker hurled itself at my knee, knocking me to the ground. I immediately tried to rise, but I couldn't stay on my feet. A medic helped me off the site and stopped my bleeding with a bandage. But I was unable to act in the next scene.

Luat asked the interpreter if the director would like to choose another soldier to raise the flag. The foreign comrade nodded and strolled along our ranks, gazing at us one by one. He turned and coming down the line once again, then stopped in front of Vinh and pointed at his chest.

"All right. This soldier will be the flag bearer."

Before we began the reenactment again, the battalion commander reiterated once again how important making the film was, how it would be seen all over the world. Any idea the director had was to be obeyed as strictly as an order on the battlefield.

Luat raised his hand, as if to object, but dropped it back down. After that, he didn't seem to act out his role with any enthusiasm.

The sappers exploded eight "square cakes" (satchel charges) around the post, allowing the cameraman to shoot the scene through a haze of smoke and fire.

Then came the raising-of-the-flag scene. Under the foreign comrade's direction, Luat waved his revolver and sprang forward, followed by Vinh, raising his flag pole high, and then the rest of the unit. Stop, the director called. Then—

action! Vinh scrambled up to the roof of the headquarters bunker and struck the enemy's flag pole with the sole of his foot, sending their flag to the ground. With his legs firmly spread, he stood and waved the Victory flag. The rest of the unit flanked him on both sides. They raised their submachine guns and shouted joyfully.

But the scene had to be reshot three times, as we seemed somewhat sluggish. Taking Che post had been a difficult task, the director explained through the interpreter. Could we please then try a little harder to demonstrate to the whole world how high the morale was in our army?

Finally the filming was over. Staggering with fatigue, we stumbled back to Noi hamlet. Before packing up his equipment, the foreign comrade shook our hands.

"Glory to Vietnam. Of thou I'm proud."

Soon after we were back in battle and had no time to think about that scene. We were happy enough after a fight to simply find that our friends had come through intact. Then the war ended and after a while we turned in our rifles and came home and each of us tried to find ways to make a living. We forgot all about the flag raising at Che post.

One day, not long after the war, I was getting my hair cut and reading a newspaper to pass the time. A large headline flashed up at me. The documentary film, *The Path of Blood and Fire* had just premiered. The words: "Of thou I'm proud" came unbidden into my mind. Under the headline was a photograph of Vinh, spreading his legs on the roof of the headquarters' bunker, waving the Victory flag. He was flanked on both sides by my friends, raising their submachine guns, shouting joyfully.

I knew it was merely a reenactment of the battle. But still my heart beat swiftly in my chest as I read the caption: "A still from *The Path of Blood and Fire:* 'Raising the flag at Che post.' "

I felt it wasn't worth talking about. Like most veterans, my life was taken up with a day by day struggle just to make ends meet. None of us displayed our citations on the wall or pinned our medals on our chests. It was better to spend our energy keeping our plates full. At any rate, the movies were always full of such tricks and gimmicks. When the pig shed in my village cooperative had been filmed, the crew had gathered the biggest pigs from each family and stuck them all together, rubbing crushed garlic on their mouths to keep them from biting each other. And when they'd wanted to shoot our model fish pond, they'd brought baskets full of huge fish and loaded them into the boats so it looked as if the fish had been drawn into the boats with nets.

The victory over Che post had not only been the proudest moment of our battalion, but of the entire division. The division commander had even had the photo of the flag raising enlarged to the size of a double bed sheet and displayed on the center wall of the division museum. The veterans of the engagement knew very well that it was only a reenacted scene. But raw recruits gazed admiringly at Vinh waving the Victory flag and thought the photo had been taken on the spot, under enemy fire.

That still from the film was, admittedly, very beautiful: a People's Army soldier standing dignified and undaunted on top of the enemy's headquarters. One artist used the photograph as a model for a drawing put on a stamp to be distributed on Army Day. It was also featured in calendars, though after the veterans saw that they began to mutter among themselves. Finally, on Division Day, they approached the commissar. He shrugged and said that it was up to the artists to decide what particular images and symbols should be used—it wasn't possible to capture the entire division in one photograph.

Twenty years passed.

One day a director named T. Stevenson came to Vietnam to shoot a film called *Blood and Flowers*. After visiting several studios to view films made during the war, he asked the Minister of Culture to arrange interviews with those people who were in the sequences he wished to buy.

The ministry telephoned the army's political department, which in turn rang up the division. By this time, the old commanders had retired and their replacements believed it had been Vinh who'd advanced through enemy fire to plant the flag on Che post. The division commander ordered his political officers to locate Vinh and bring him to headquarters in order to meet Stevenson.

The original *Blood and Fire* was screened again, all over the country.

And everything Vinh told Stevenson fit the reenactment filmed by the foreign comrade, as if it had all really occurred. He managed to forget that at the time he had been glued to the earth, so filled with fear that he'd pissed on his own soul.

Luat came to see me. "Vinh must have thought we'd all died," he said.

I tried to console him. "What earthly good can the truth of the matter do for us soldiers now?"

"If something that we saw with our own eyes can be distorted this way, then what can happen to other events that happened fifty or a hundred years ago. I've written a letter to the Central Committee confirming that there was no flag raising at Che post. Will you sign it?"

"All right—I'll sign."

"Good. Add your rank, please, and the code word for our unit."

I wrote it all down. Months later, I found out that Luat's wife had had to sell their only pig in order to finance Luat's trips to visit his former comrades-in-arms and get their signatures. He made scores of copies of his letter and sent them all to the appropriate agencies.

The whole division was thrown into an uproar. But no one dared take down the huge photograph hanging in the Division Museum. And no one dared throw away the millions of stamps and thousands of calendars that had been printed.

The division commander arranged a private meeting with us. He asked us not to put everyone into a quandary. The attack against Che post had been the largest battle in the history of the division; it was the pride of the entire unit. Although he couldn't take down the photograph right at the moment, he assured us he would eventually find a substitute.

But I was certain one would never be found, not in a hundred years.

One day, Luat's son rushed to my house.

"Uncle, there's something wrong with my father's stomach. He asked to see you before he went onto the operating table."

I cycled over to the hospital.

Luat signalled to me to approach his bed. He grasped my hand firmly.

"You're a writer. You should never write a half-truth or turn a lie into truth. You have to write what you saw: there was no flag raising at Che post. Write it immediately and read it to me."

"Don't speak so ominously. A lie can't be corrected in a day. But don't worry, of course I'll write about it."

The operation was successful. Luat survived. The photo of Vinh waving the flag still hangs in the Division Museum. And recently, Vinh was invited by Stevenson to visit the director's country and talk about the flag raising as a way of promoting *Blood and Flowers*. He was lucky, that guy. If he'd been so mortified and humiliated when I'd asked him to give me his cartridge belt and grenades that he'd gotten up and charged the loophole and blocked it with his body, he wouldn't have been alive now to brag to foreigners.

Abroad, how can people know that Vinh pissed on his own soul and his trousers were only a prop?

Translated by Ho Ahn Thai
Edited by Wayne Karlin

Phan Huy Duong

Phan Huy Duong (b. 1945) is from South Vietnam but left in 1955 and finally settled in France in 1965. He translates contemporary Vietnamese fiction and has published a collection of Short Stories in French called Metic Love. *"The Billion Dollar Skeleton" addresses the pain of those whose loved ones are still considered "missing in action" or whose bodies were never recovered.*

The Billion Dollar Skeleton

Richard Steel, the richest American—that is to say, the richest man in the world—the one they call simply "The Billionaire," leaps into his private jet. Destination: Saigon. His entourage is impressive. More than one hundred people. He isn't taking any chances. Everyone who can contribute to the success of his operation has been included. Mission impossible: To find his son, John, missing in action since 1972 during a bombing raid over the seventeenth parallel. John, his only son. He'll find him, he'll bring his remains back to the United States. The Billionaire promised his wife on her deathbed, one day their little boy would rest next to her in the family plot. The Steel Dynasty. When the Billionaire decides to do something, nothing stops him. In his whole life he's never known an obstacle he couldn't overcome. No one and nothing can stop him. He's a fighter. He *always* wins.

The Billionaire's staff is silent. They've all worked hard to prepare the mission. Everyone is fascinated by the Billionaire's insatiable drive. But no one believes he can succeed.

"Everything in order for tomorrow, Colonel Wood?" said the Billionaire, emptying his glass of whiskey in one swig.

Colonel Wood had been hired as Staff Commander. When he'd worked for the State Department, the MIA/POW problem was his issue. It was the Colonel who had negotiated with the Vietnamese government; he was the one who had personally sifted through the four thousand documents delivered by the Vietnamese before the embargo was lifted. But there had been no trace of John Steel.

"Everything is ready, sir," the Colonel said gruffly. "The warehouses, the buildings, the equipment, the telecommunications network. The entire area has been ready for a week now. You'll have direct satellite links to the rest of the world. You'll be able to follow the operations closely. The command post is located in a wing of your villa; Your wife's Bible is on the altar, in the little chapel next to your bedroom. I've checked everything."

"What about the publicity campaign?"

Reprinted from *The Other Side of Heaven: Postwar Fiction by Vietnamese and American Writers*, edited by Wayne Karlin, Le Minh Khue, and Truong Vu, (1995), Curbstone Press.

"Yes, sir. Radio stations, the television networks—the entire national and local press corps will be there for your conference tomorrow morning. Almost a thousand of them. We've bought the front page of every newspaper, a radio spot every hour, and the national television station every night for a hundred days. Prime time. We've got all the publicity spots in the country. There are billboards all over the place. No one will be able to miss the offer. We start tomorrow morning. You just need to choose your service woman."

The Colonel passed a photo album to the Billionaire: "We've already bought them all. There's no risk of AIDS or infection. Your doctor has examined them—they're virgins, healthy girls. Whoever you choose will be brought to your suite tonight. She won't be allowed out for any reason. The villa is well guarded."

The Billionaire flipped through the album. Indeed the girls were young and beautiful. But that didn't really interest him. He had never been particularly attracted to a pretty face. But doctor's orders were doctor's orders: he had been advised to make love once a day to maintain his physical and psychological equilibrium. The Billionaire quickly skimmed through the candidates' resumes, and stopped at the first girl who spoke English fluently.

Colonel Wood coughed. "There's still time to change your mind. The mission is impossible. I've managed this portfolio for more than twenty years. It's absolutely crazy . . . you've got one chance in a million.'

"Well, I'll buy that chance. I've got a budget of a billion dollars for it. The GNP of this country is $164 per head. We've got enough to *buy* that one chance in a million. I'm giving you one hundred days to find it. We're going to win, Colonel. You just leave your bureaucracy, your dossiers, your politics, your strategies, and all your stupid diplomatic tactics in the closet. I don't investigate, I don't negotiate, I act. I buy. I'm going to succeed where your Pentagon has failed."

The next morning, the entire national and local press swarmed into the Billionaire's vast conference room. The Billionaire wasn't a man to waste his time on a long speech. He got right to the point: "I've got a billion dollars to find my son, John Steel. U.S. Air Force. Disappeared in combat on the 24th of December 1972 over the seventeenth parallel. I'll make the person who helps me find him—dead or alive—a millionaire for the rest of his life. What's more, I pay cash: $164 for all unidentified skeletons. And I mean *all* of 'em—whether they're men, women, or children. Find 'em, bring 'em to me, I'll pay. No questions asked. Our offices are open twenty-four hours a day for exactly one hundred days. Everybody's welcome." And he left.

The news spread like wildfire. Every morning, on their front pages, every newspaper in Vietnam published a photo of John Steel, his measurements, his facial traits, the phone, address, and fax number of the Research Center, a map to get there, bus schedules from the surrounding cities, train timetables, planes . . . the $164 reward for each whole skeleton, and a range of fees for separate bones. The radio stations announced the offer every hour. National television repeated it each evening. In one night, Hanoi, Saigon, all the provincial towns, even the most remote villages, were covered with posters. *A skull . . . $164 per skeleton . . . public offer to purchase* . . . repeated millions and millions of times throughout the entire country. The Billionaire's operation was passionately debated, from the highest ranks of the Vietnamese Communist Party to the most squalid slums.

Some were for it, others were against it. No one thought of forbidding it. Such an indisputably humanitarian project. The Vietnamese worship their ancestors, the memory of the dead. They couldn't oppose this. And then, the Vietnamese economy had never had such a windfall. A billion dollars for a skeleton! And everyone had a chance—from the most powerful to the most humble. Never had they known such justice, such democracy.

On the first day, no one showed up at the Research Center.

The second day, as night fell, a suspicious-looking man with scruffy hair and a face half-masked by a bushy beard slipped into the reception room, a dirty sack slung over his shoulder. The man unpacked the contents of his sack—a large male skeleton—pocketed the $164 and disappeared.

The Billionaire immediately ordered forensic work on the skeleton. In a specially conceived laboratory, Professor Smith and his team had all the data, all the instruments needed to identify even the smallest bone that might belong to John. They had all the photos, all the X rays of John from the day of his birth to his disappearance. The shape and size of the bones—everything had been photographed, measured, calculated, and cataloged in a precise graphic and numerical data base. A camera scanned images of the skeleton and transmitted them to a neuronic computer, where artificial-intelligence software gave an exact reading on whether or not they belonged to John Steel.

The Professor: "It's not him. But the skeleton is unusual. From its configuration, it could be either Vietnamese or American. According to the computer, it's fifty-fifty. Probably a half-breed. What do we do with it?"

"Put it aside. It's the first. An authentic unknown soldier. When we find John, we're gonna give this boy a coffin cut to the measure of his tragedy."

By the third day, people in rags were swarming up to the counters. They were all well received and paid according to the set rates: $164 for a whole skeleton, $10 dollars for a skull, $5 for a tibia . . . and ten cents for bone fragments.

Colonel Wood's carefully conceived sorting warehouse bustled. Women's and children's bones were dumped into specially tagged bins. Men's bones were stocked in bins close to the command headquarters and directly linked to the laboratory by remote-control belts. Intelligent robots sorted the bones into their 214 known parts: the skull bone, the vertebrae, the clavicle. . . . They passed them one by one under the eyes of the cameras for the first sort. Vietnamese bones were put into the refuse bins. The American bones were given a final examination by neuronic computer.

In Vietnam, as in all poor countries of the world, the grapevine works wonders. Barely a week had passed, but everyone already knew that the Billionaire kept his word, that he paid cash, no questions asked, for any kind of bones brought to him. The Research Center was besieged. People came bearing skulls, tibiae, ribs, a phalanx, a femur. You just presented your bones at a counter, placed them on a conveyor belt to be scanned by the cameras, and pocketed the money. Only dog, cat, and monkey bones were refused.

Long lines of human beings converged from every province in the country to the Research Center. Never had the land, the rice fields, the forests been scoured so thoroughly. Sometimes men, women, and children stumbled onto long-buried mines, undetonated bombs. The Billionaire generously reimbursed the families of the deceased. He bought their skeletons at twice the normal rate.

Never in human memory had so many human bones been piled up by the square meter. Men women children old people Viets Laos Khmers Thais Koreans Australians New Zealanders French black white red yellow brown Australopithecus, and . . . even a few Americans. The Billionaire sent the Western bones to their respective national governments, and the prehistoric bones to the museums. He had the rest stacked in warehouses kept for this purpose. Men with men, women with women, children with children, old people with old people, babies with babies. Some of the bones were recent, barely clean, scraped down with knives. Sometimes, bits of nerves, shreds of flesh still stuck to the bones. But that didn't matter. The Billionaire didn't want to discourage anyone. He paid. No questions asked.

By the end of a month, the bins were overflowing.

"What do we do now? Do we put them in the bins with the Americans?" asked Colonel Wood.

"Absolutely not. Buy all the rice paddies in the area, and pile them up there. How are we doing?"

"More than 400,000 so far, sir."

"Terrific. We're ahead of schedule. You'll have more than one chance in a million. If it exists, we're going to find it."

The rice paddies were immediately transformed into stocking areas. Men to the north. Women to the south. Children to the east. Babies to the west. At the beginning, the piles formed tiny hills. But day by day, the bones scattered over the Vietnamese land slid toward the center. Soon the hills formed huge mountains visible from several miles away. A dense network of trains was rapidly extended. The four asphalt roads to the Research Center stretched toward the four horizons. Now, you drove to the Center through a mountain range, at the bottom of a gorge, between two steep walls of bones.

The New York Times published a huge aerial photo with the headline: FOR THE LOVE OF A SON: THE MOST EXTRAVAGANT ENTERPRISE IN HUMAN HISTORY. A few intellectuals from the Old World protested. They hadn't understood a thing about the market economy. A few brighter, hipper young philosophers rapped about the operation on CNN. A handful of Vietnamese artists cried scandal. A lone deputy dared suggest setting up an investigative committee. Alarmed, the Vietnamese government published a convoluted communiqué about human rights and the importance of humanitarian missions. It couldn't have done less. It couldn't have done much more. Thanks to the billion dollars, unemployment had vanished from the province. And, if you took the country as a whole, hunger had been reduced.

By the sixty-sixth day—two-thirds of the way into the Billionaire's schedule—land for stocking bones was scarce. On the last few available acres, he had crematoriums built. The Billionaire led all the operations, assisted with the sorting. He seldom ate, slept only about four hours a day, working nonstop from dawn to dusk. In the evenings, after ten o'clock, he would retire to his villa, shower, gulp down a sandwich, wash it down with a half-bottle of whiskey, make love with the service woman, and then retreat to the chapel to pray and commune with his wife. Every evening he would remember his son. Such a tall, handsome young man. So intelligent. Such blue eyes. A life full of such promise, such a future. That was yesterday, some twenty years ago. Every night, the Billionaire would place his hand on the Bible and renew the vow. And every morning, at four o'clock, he was back at the command post.

By the eightieth day, the tide of bones began to subside. Old bones became rarer and rarer. On the ninetieth day, the supply tapered off completely. The Billionaire stepped up his efforts, encouraging, motivating, tirelessly inspiring his men. "If there's one chance in a million to find him, it's now that it's going to happen."

The fateful day approached. Skeleton sellers were scarce now. At the most a dozen per day. Now they either brought new skeletons, or those over a hundred years old. The next to last day, only an old beggar walked up to one of the counters with a big toe bone. And that was the last ten cents of the billion dollars.

The one hundredth day. No one came. From his armchair, the Billionaire watched the hands of the clock on the wall inch along. The office was aglow in the sunset, the rosewood furniture aflame with its rays. The clock chimed, announcing the end of the day. The Billionaire sighed, pushed aside his glass of whiskey, and stood up to go.

Just then, three discrete knocks on the door. The interpreter slipped into the office, shuffling his way to the Billionaire's desk.

"There's an old man here who would like to speak to you, sir."

"Give him the dollars and throw the bones in the pile. The campaign's over."

"He doesn't have a skeleton to sell. He just wanted to give you this."

The interpreter opened his hand. In his palm lay a tiny black velvet satchel. Irritated, the Billionaire picked it up, and distractedly pulled it open. A tiny platinum cross with a ruby heart encrusted at the intersection of the two branches. The Billionaire shuddered. Now it was certain. John was dead. His son would never have parted with the cross. His mother had it made for him by the best jeweler in Paris. The Billionaire slumped back into his armchair.

"Show him in," he said, in a low voice.

A frail old man with white hair and eyebrows and a long white goatee entered. He seemed to float in his peasant pajamas, the earthy, ocher color of the High Plateaus. He advanced softly, leaning on a bamboo cane. He stopped at the desk. The Billionaire offered him a seat. The old man shook his head.

"Where did you find this cross?"

"It belongs to me."

"Do you know where my son is?"

"Yes."

"Show me the place. I'll cover you in gold to the third generation."

The old man shook his head.

"Tell me what you want then," said the Billionaire.

"You will burn the mountains of bones. You will sow the ashes on the Vietnamese land, from the Gate of Nam Quan to the tip of Ca Mau. When you have done it, come to my house, in the Village of Man, at the foot of the Mountain of Peace. I'll give you back your son's bones."

"I'll be there in seven days."

The old man didn't respond. He turned his head, left the office slowly. His cane resonated on the floor. Sharp, regular taps, as if to announce the beginning of a play.

The Billionaire summoned his staff. He ordered the cremation of the bones within six days. The Colonel paled. "But that's impossible! The furnaces are working at full tilt. The locals are already complaining about the smell and the smoke. We've got enough trouble calming the authorities."

"Shut up! What's impossible? God created the world in seven days. Why can't we burn this lousy pile of bones in less time? Quadruple the teams, double the salaries, but make sure that production continues. If there aren't enough furnaces, bring wood, coal, and gasoline. Light as many bonfires as it takes. In seven days, I want my jets to scatter those damn ashes from Nam Quan to Ca Mau. Execute!"

Never in human memory had so much fire and smoke filled one corner of the earth. A hellish furnace swarming with men, women, and children blackened with soot. Human chains crisscrossed and encircled the furnaces—burning embers in the chaotic links of an immense net. They passed the bones hand to hand down from the mountains to the gaping mouths of the furnaces. A thick, acrid smoke hung in the air. By the third day, you could no longer distinguish night from day. Shadows darted in and out of the murky twilight. For six days and six nights running, the smoke covered the province in a mantle of gloom, searing faces, blinding eyes, scratching throats. People burrowed into their homes, barricading doors and windows. They prayed. Babies stopped crying. The earth became as still as a prayer, a silence broken only by the crackling of the bonfires.

By the evening of the sixth day, the furnaces, the bonfires, the prayers, had all flickered out. A bloodied sun appeared and, for an instant, set the sky aflame, and then night engulfed the earth. A warm wind rose in the east, slowly dispersing the smoke. A few pale stars twinkled. And a chill moon lit the silence.

A cock crowed. In the distance, a dog barked. You could hear a baby cry. The sun emerged, shivering, from the fog. On the horizon, a dull rumbling as a squadron of planes took off, howling across the sky, scattering long gray streaks in their wake. Ashes rained to the earth. Not a single rice paddy was spared. Ash suffused the air, dusting the trees, the plants, the flowers, penetrating every human dwelling. It blinded the eyes, blocked the nose, stuck in the throat. All day, from north to south, a tornado of gray ash against the screeching of jet planes. That evening, the tempest subsided. The night returned the silence.

The next morning, the Billionaire went to the old man's house.

"Old man, I have fulfilled your wish. Now, give me my son's bones."

The old man looked at him with tenderness. "I thank you," he said in a soft, low voice. "Our dead have finally been returned to their ancestors. The dead belong there where men build civilizations. Go find your son. He is in my garden, under the altar."

The Billionaire rushed into the old man's garden. At the foot of an old banyan tree stood a brick altar, a few joss sticks smoldering there. The Billionaire ordered his men to unearth the coffin. The men advanced, shovels and pails in hand.

Nearby, crouched against the root of the banyan tree, a child watched in silence. The Billionaire approached him, and bent down to give him a dollar. The boy pushed his hand away, and as he ran to hide behind the old man, his bamboo-leaf hat fell into the open grave. The Billionaire picked it up, and walked toward the boy. He shuddered. The child's eyes, brimming with tears, were blue with hatred.

* * *

The Billionaire sipped his whiskey and gazed at the luxurious coffin where his son lay. He had won. He had fulfilled his duty as a father, his wife's last wish. The Billionaire's jet had been ready to return to the U.S. for over a week. But now he hesitated. He couldn't leave Vietnam without knowing how his son had died. He had the interpreter sent to the Village of Man, at the foot of the Mountain of Peace.

The interpreter slid into the office with a feline step. The Billionaire swiveled around in his armchair. "Well?"

"It worked. I spent a fortune. They finally talked."

"Well done. Go ahead."

"Do you really want to know everything?"

"Yes, everything."

"They killed him. John jumped from his plane before it exploded and broke his left leg. He must have crawled through the jungle for a long time. The old man found him lying unconscious next to a stream and carried him home. We don't know how long he lived with the old man. One night, he snuck out to the stream. A child saw him and alerted the village. They arrested him immediately. The village had been routinely bombed. A lot of people died, there was a lot of hatred. The villagers formed a kangaroo court and condemned your son and the old man's daughter to death. They shot your son on the spot. The girl was pregnant, so she got a reprieve. When the kid was born, they gave him to the old man."

"Thanks. You can go now. Not a word to anyone. That's an order. Understand?"

"Of course."

The Billionaire continued to sip his whiskey, staring at the coffin, overcome by a mixture of pain and tenderness. And he stayed there for hours, without moving. Suddenly, he shook his head, got up, and called the service woman.

"Please, help me."

He opened the coffin. Together they carried the bones to the furnace. While the skeleton burned, they laid the bones of the unknown soldier in the coffin.

The next morning, the Billionaire went to the old man's house. He clutched an urn of ashes to his chest. The old man was seated in the shade of the banyan tree. The boy stood behind him, his skinny arms enlaced the old man's neck. His eyes were intense, blue, full of hate. The Billionaire sighed.

"Old man, I've brought you your son's ashes. This is his final resting place. And now, I must say good-bye."

"Farewell. May peace be with you."

The Billionaire looked over at the boy with the blue eyes one last time. He walked away, his step calm, assured. His heart filled with a strange sense of relief.

He brought the unknown soldier's skeleton back to the United States. He buried it with great pomp and circumstance in the family plot next to his wife's grave. He married the service woman. They had many children. And they lived happily ever after. Among their vast progeny were many learned people, famous women and men of letters, beloved citizens. One of them became the first woman president of the United States.

—Translated by Nina McPherson and Phan Huy Duong

Tim O'Brien

Tim O'Brien (b. 1946) graduated summa cum laude *from Macalester College (B.A. 1968) and did graduate study at Harvard University. O'Brien was drafted into the United States Army to serve in the Vietnam War. In his two years of service he was promoted to sergeant and received a Purple Heart. In 1973 he published his first book,* If I Die in a Combat Zone, Box Me Up and Ship Me Home, *a synthesis of autobiography and fiction. His third novel* Going after Cacciato *(1978) won the National Book Award and is considered to be one of the best books by a U.S. veteran about the Vietnam War. In "How to Tell a True War Story," which is from his collection* The Things They Carried, *and in his recent novel* In The Lake of the Woods, *O'Brien continues to blur distinctions between autobiography, fiction and history. His article, "The Vietnam in Me," was published in the* New York Times Magazine *in 1994.*

How to Tell a True War Story

This is true.

I had a buddy in Vietnam. His name was Bob Kiley, but everybody called him Rat.

A friend of his gets killed, so about a week later Rat sits down and writes a letter to the guy's sister. Rat tells her what a great brother she had, how together the guy was, a number one pal and comrade. A real soldier's soldier, Rat says. Then he tells a few stories to make the point, how her brother would always volunteer for stuff nobody else would volunteer for in a million years, dangerous stuff, like doing recon or going out on these really badass night patrols. Stainless steel balls, Rat tells her. The guy was a little crazy, for sure, but crazy in a good way, a real daredevil, because he liked the challenge of it, he liked testing himself, just man against gook. A great, great guy, Rat says.

Anyway, it's a terrific letter, very personal and touching. Rat almost bawls writing it. He gets all teary telling about the good times they had together, how her brother made the war seem almost fun, always raising hell and lighting up villes and bringing smoke to bear every which way. A great sense of humor, too. Like the time at this river when he went fishing with a whole damn crate of hand grenades. Probably the funniest thing in world history, Rat says, all that gore, about twenty zillion dead gook fish. Her brother, he had the right attitude. He knew how to have a good time. On Halloween, this real hot spooky night, the

---

Reprinted from *The Things They Carried*, (1991), Houghton Mifflin Company.

dude paints up his body all different colors and puts on this weird mask and hikes over to a ville and goes trick-or-treating almost stark naked, just boots and balls and an M-16. A tremendous human being, Rat says. Pretty nutso sometimes, but you could trust him with your life.

And then the letter gets very sad and serious. Rat pours his heart out. He says he loved the guy. He says the guy was his best friend in the world. They were like soul mates, he says, like twins or something, they had a whole lot in common. He tells the guy's sister he'll look her up when the war's over.

So what happens?

Rat mails the letter. He waits two months. The dumb cooze never writes back.

A true war story is never moral. It does not instruct, nor encourage virtue, nor suggest models of proper human behavior, nor restrain men from doing the things they have always done. If a story seems moral, do not believe it. If at the end of a war story you feel uplifted, or if you feel that some small bit of rectitude has been salvaged from the larger waste, then you have been made the victim of a very old and terrible lie. There is no rectitude whatsoever. There is no virtue. As a first rule of thumb, therefore, you can tell a true war story by its absolute and uncompromising allegiance to obscenity and evil. Listen to Rat Kiley. Cooze, he says. He does not say bitch. He certainly does not say woman, or girl. He says cooze. Then he spits and stares. He's nineteen years old—it's too much for him—so he looks at you with those big sad gentle killer eyes and says *cooze,* because his friend is dead, and because it's so incredibly sad and true: she never wrote back.

You can tell a true war story if it embarrasses you. If you don't care for obscenity, you don't care for the truth; if you don't care for the truth, watch how you vote. Send guys to war, they come home talking dirty.

Listen to Rat: "Jesus Christ, man, I write this beautiful fuckin' letter, I slave over it, and what happens? The dumb cooze never writes back."

The dead guy's name was Curt Lemon. What happened was, we crossed a muddy river and marched west into the mountains, and on the third day we took a break along a trail junction in deep jungle. Right away, Lemon and Rat Kiley started goofing. They didn't understand about the spookiness. They were kids; they just didn't know. A nature hike, they thought, not even a war, so they went off into the shade of some giant trees—quadruple canopy, no sunlight at all—and they were giggling and calling each other yellow mother and playing a silly game they'd invented. The game involved smoke grenades, which were harmless unless you did stupid things, and what they did was pull out the pin and stand a few feet apart and play catch under the shade of those huge trees. Whoever chickened out was a yellow mother. And if nobody chickened out, the grenade would make a light popping sound and they'd be covered with smoke and they'd laugh and dance around and then do it again.

It's all exactly true.

It happened, to *me,* nearly twenty years ago, but I still remember that trail junction and the giant trees and a soft dripping sound somewhere beyond the trees. I remember the smell of moss. Up in the canopy there were tiny white blossoms, but no sunlight at all, and I remember the shadows spreading out under the trees where Curt Lemon and Rat Kiley were playing catch with smoke grenades. Mitchell Sanders sat flipping his yo-yo. Norman Bowker and Kiowa and Dave Jensen were dozing, or half-dozing, and all around us were those ragged green mountains.

Except for the laughter things were quiet.

At one point, I remember, Mitchell Sanders turned and looked at me, not quite nodding, as if to warn me about something, as if he already *knew,* then after a while he rolled up his yo-yo and moved away.

It's hard to tell you what happened next.

They were just goofing. There was a noise, I suppose, which must've been the detonator, so I glanced behind me and watched Lemon step from the shade into bright sunlight. His face was suddenly brown and shining. A handsome kid, really. Sharp gray eyes, lean and narrow-waisted, and when he died it was almost beautiful, the way the sunlight came around him and lifted him up and sucked him high into a tree full of moss and vines and white blossoms.

In any war story, but especially a true one, it's difficult to separate what happened from what seemed to happen. What seems to happen becomes its own happening and has to be told that way. The angles of vision are skewed. When a booby trap explodes, you close your eyes and duck and float outside yourself. When a guy dies, like Curt Lemon, you look away and then look back for a moment and then look away again. The pictures get jumbled; you tend to miss a lot. And then afterward, when you go to tell about it, there is always that surreal seemingness, which makes the story seem untrue, but which in fact represents the hard and exact truth as it *seemed.*

In many cases a true war story cannot be believed. If you believe it, be skeptical. It's a question of credibility. Often the crazy stuff is true and the normal stuff isn't, because the normal stuff is necessary to make you believe the truly incredible craziness.

In other cases you can't even tell a true war story. Sometimes it's just beyond telling.

I heard this one, for example, from Mitchell Sanders. It was near dusk and we were sitting at my foxhole along a wide muddy river north of Quang Ngai. I remember how peaceful the twilight was. A deep pinkish red spilled out on the river, which moved without sound, and in the morning we would cross the river and march west into the mountains. The occasion was right for a good story.

"God's truth," Mitchell Sanders said. "A six-man patrol goes up into the mountains on a basic listening-post operation. The idea's to spend a week up there, just lie low and listen for enemy movement. They've got a radio along, so if they hear anything suspicious—anything—they're supposed to call in artillery or gunships, whatever it takes. Otherwise they keep strict field discipline. Absolute silence. They just listen."

Sanders glanced at me to make sure I had the scenario. He was playing with his yo-yo, dancing it with short, tight little strokes of the wrist.

His face was blank in the dusk.

"We're talking regulation, by-the-book LP. These six guys, they don't say boo for a solid week. They don't got tongues. *All* ears."

"Right," I said.

"Understand me?"

"Invisible."

Sanders nodded.

"Affirm," he said. "Invisible. So what happens is, these guys get themselves deep in the bush, all camouflaged up, and they lie down and wait and that's all they do, nothing else, they lie there for seven straight days and just listen. And man, I'll tell you—it's spooky. This is mountains. You don't *know* spooky till you been there. Jungle, sort of, except it's way up in the clouds and there's always this fog—like rain, except it's not raining—everything's all wet and swirly and tangled up and you can't see jack, you can't find your own pecker to piss with. Like you don't even have a body. Serious spooky. You just go with the vapors—the fog sort of takes you in. . . . And the sounds, man. The sounds carry forever. You hear stuff nobody should *ever* hear."

Sanders was quiet for a second, just working the yo-yo, then he smiled at me.

"So, after a couple days the guys start hearing this real soft, kind of wacked-out music. Weird echoes and stuff. Like a radio or something, but it's not a radio, it's this strange gook music that comes right out of the rocks. Faraway, sort of, but right up close, too. They try to ignore it. But it's a listening post, right? So they listen. And every night they keep hearing this crazyass gook concert. All kinds of chimes and xylophones. I mean, this is wilderness—no way, it can't be real—but there it *is,* like the mountains are tuned in to Radio fucking Hanoi. Naturally they get nervous. One guy sticks Juicy Fruit in his ears. Another guy almost flips. Thing is, though, they can't report music. They can't get on the horn and call back to base and say, 'Hey, listen, we need some firepower, we got to blow away this weirdo gook rock band.' They can't do that. It wouldn't go down. So they lie there in the fog and keep their mouths shut. And what makes it extra bad, see, is the poor dudes can't horse around like normal. Can't joke it away. Can't even talk to each other except maybe in whispers, all hush-hush, and that just revs up the willies. All they do is listen."

Again there was some silence as Mitchell Sanders looked out on the river. The dark was coming on hard now, and off to the west I could see the mountains rising in silhouette, all the mysteries and unknowns.

"This next part," Sanders said quietly, "you won't believe."

"Probably not," I said.

"You won't. And you know why?" He gave me a tired smile. "Because it happened. Because every word is absolutely dead-on true."

Sanders made a little sound in his throat, like a sigh, as if to say he didn't care if I believed it or not. But he did care. He wanted me to feel the truth, to believe by the raw force of feeling. He seemed sad, in a way.

"These six guys," he said, "they're pretty fried out by now, and one night they start hearing voices. Like at a cocktail party. That's what it sounds like, this big swank gook cocktail party somewhere out there in the fog. Music and chitchat and stuff. It's crazy, I know, but they hear the champagne corks. They hear the actual martini glasses. Real hoity-toity, all very civilized, except this isn't civilization. This is Nam.

"Anyway, the guys try to be cool. They just lie there and groove, but after a while they start hearing—you won't believe this—they hear chamber music. They hear violins and cellos. They hear this terrific mama-san soprano. Then after a while they hear gook opera and a glee club and the Haiphong Boys Choir and a barbershop quartet and all kinds of weird chanting and Buddha-Buddha stuff. And the whole time, in the background, there's still that cocktail party going on. All these different voices. Not human voices, though. Because it's the mountains. Follow me? The rock—it's *talking*. And the fog, too, and the grass and the goddamn mongooses. Everything talks. The trees talk politics, the monkeys talk religion. The whole country. Vietnam. The place talks. It talks. Understand? Nam—it truly *talks*.

"The guys can't cope. They lose it. They get on the radio and report enemy movement—a whole army, they say—and they order up the firepower. They get arty and gunships. They call in air strikes. And I'll tell you, they fuckin' crash that cocktail party. All night long, they just smoke those mountains. They make jungle juice. They blow away trees and glee clubs and whatever else there is to blow away. Scorch time. They walk napalm up and down the ridges. They bring in the Cobras and F-4s, they use Willie Peter and HE and incendiaries. It's all fire. They make those mountains burn.

"Around dawn things finally get quiet. Like you never even *heard* quiet before. One of those real thick, real misty days—just clouds and fog, they're off in this special zone—and the mountains are absolutely dead-flat silent. Like Brigadoon—pure vapor, you know? Everything's all sucked up inside the fog. Not a single sound, except they still *hear* it.

"So they pack up and start humping. They head down the mountain, back to base camp, and when they get there they don't say diddly. They don't talk. Not a word, like they're deaf and dumb. Later on this fat bird colonel comes up and asks what the hell happened out there. What'd they hear? Why all the ordnance? The man's ragged out, he gets down tight on their case. I mean, they spent six trillion dollars on firepower, and this fatass colonel wants answers, he wants to know what the fuckin' story is.

"But the guys don't say zip. They just look at him for a while, sort of funny like, sort of amazed, and the whole war is right there in that stare. It says everything you can't ever say. It says, man, you got *wax* in your ears. It says, poor bastard, you'll never know—wrong frequency—you don't *even* want to hear this. Then they salute the fucker and walk away, because certain stories you don't ever tell."

You can tell a true war story by the way it never seems to end. Not then, not ever. Not when Mitchell Sanders stood up and moved off into the dark.

It all happened.

Even now, at this instant, I remember that yo-yo. In a way, I suppose, you had to be there, you had to hear it, but I could tell how desperately Sanders wanted me to believe him, his frustration at not quite getting the details right, not quite pinning down the final and definitive truth.

And I remember sitting at my foxhole that night, watching the shadows of Quang Ngai, thinking about the coming day and how we would cross the river and march west into the mountains, all the ways I might die, all the things I did not understand.

Late in the night Mitchell Sanders touched my shoulder.

"Just came to me," he whispered. "The moral, I mean. Nobody listens. Nobody hears nothin'. Like that fatass colonel. The politicians, all the civilian types. Your girlfriend. My girlfriend. Everybody's sweet little virgin girlfriend. What they need is to go out on LP. The vapors, man. Trees and rocks—you got to *listen* to your enemy."

And then again, in the morning, Sanders came up to me. The platoon was preparing to move out, checking weapons, going through all the little rituals that preceded a day's march. Already the lead squad had crossed the river and was filing off toward the west.

"I got a confession to make," Sanders said. "Last night, man, I had to make up a few things."

"I know that."

"The glee club. There wasn't any glee club."

"Right."

"No opera."

"Forget it, I understand."

"Yeah, but listen, it's still true. Those six guys, they heard wicked sound out there. They heard sound you just plain won't believe."

Sanders pulled on his rucksack, closed his eyes for a moment, then almost smiled at me.

I knew what was coming but I beat him to it.

"All right," I said, "what's the moral?"

"Forget it."

"No, go ahead."

For a long while he was quiet, looking away, and the silence kept stretching out until it was almost embarrassing. Then he shrugged and gave me a stare that lasted all day.

"Hear that quiet, man?" he said. "That quiet—just listen. There's your moral."

In a true war story, if there's a moral at all, it's like the thread that makes the cloth. You can't tease it out. You can't extract the meaning without unraveling the deeper meaning. And in the end, really, there's nothing much to say about a true war story, except maybe "Oh."

True war stories do not generalize. They do not indulge in abstraction or analysis.

For example: War is hell. As a moral declaration the old truism seems perfectly true, and yet because it abstracts, because it generalizes, I can't believe it with my stomach. Nothing turns inside.

It comes down to gut instinct. A true war story, if truly told, makes the stomach believe.

This one does it for me. I've told it before—many times, many versions—but here's what actually happened.

We crossed the river and marched west into the mountains. On the third day, Curt Lemon stepped on a booby-trapped 105 round. He was playing catch with

Rat Kiley, laughing, and then he was dead. The trees were thick; it took nearly an hour to cut an LZ for the dustoff.

Later, higher in the mountains, we came across a baby VC water buffalo. What it was doing there I don't know—no farms or paddies—but we chased it down and got a rope around it and led it along to a deserted village where we set for the night. After supper Rat Kiley went over and stroked its nose.

He opened up a can of C rations, pork and beans, but the baby buffalo wasn't interested.

Rat shrugged.

He stepped back and shot it through the right front knee. The animal did not make a sound. It went down hard, then got up again, and Rat took careful aim and shot off an ear. He shot it in the hindquarters and in the little hump at its back. He shot it twice in the flanks. It wasn't to kill; it was to hurt. He put the rifle muzzle up against the mouth and shot the mouth away. Nobody said much. The whole platoon stood there watching, feeling all kinds of things, but there wasn't a great deal of pity for the baby water buffalo. Curt Lemon was dead. Rat Kiley had lost his best friend in the world. Later in the week he would write a long personal letter to the guy's sister, who would not write back, but for now it was a question of pain. He shot off the tail. He shot away chunks of meat below the ribs. All around us there was the smell of smoke and filth and deep greenery, and the evening was humid and very hot. Rat went to automatic. He shot randomly, almost casually, quick little spurts in the belly and butt. Then he reloaded, squatted down, and shot it in the left front knee. Again the animal fell hard and tried to get up, but this time it couldn't quite make it. It wobbled and went down sideways. Rat shot it in the nose. He bent forward and whispered something, as if talking to a pet, then he shot it in the throat. All the while the baby buffalo was silent, or almost silent, just a light bubbling sound where the nose had been. It lay very still. Nothing moved except the eyes, which were enormous, the pupils shiny black and dumb.

Rat Kiley was crying. He tried to say something, but then cradled his rifle and went off by himself.

The rest of us stood in a ragged circle around the baby buffalo. For a time no one spoke. We had witnessed something essential, something brand-new and profound, a piece of the world so startling there was not yet a name for it.

Somebody kicked the baby buffalo.

It was still alive, though just barely, just in the eyes.

"Amazing," Dave Jensen said. "My whole life, I never seen anything like it."

"Never?"

"Not hardly. Not once."

Kiowa and Mitchell Sanders picked up the baby buffalo. They hauled it across the open square, hoisted it up, and dumped it in the village well.

Afterward, we sat waiting for Rat to get himself together.

"Amazing," Dave Jensen kept saying. "A new wrinkle. I never seen it before."

Mitchell Sanders took out his yo-yo. "Well, that's Nam," he said. "Garden of Evil. Over here, man, every sin's real fresh and original."

How do you generalize?

War is hell, but that's not the half of it, because war is also mystery and terror and adventure and courage and discovery and holiness and pity and despair and longing and love. War is nasty; war is fun. War is thrilling; war is drudgery. War makes you a man; war makes you dead.

The truths are contradictory. It can be argued, for instance, that war is grotesque. But in truth war is also beauty. For all its horror, you can't help but gape at the awful majesty of combat. You stare out at tracer rounds unwinding through the dark like brilliant red ribbons. You crouch in ambush as a cool, impassive moon rises over the nighttime paddies. You admire the fluid symmetries of troops on the move, the harmonies of sound and shape and proportion, the great sheets of metal-fire streaming down from a gunship, the illumination rounds, the white phosphorous, the purply orange glow of napalm, the rocket's red glare. It's not pretty, exactly. It's astonishing. It fills the eye. It commands you. You hate it, yes, but your eyes do not. Like a killer forest fire, like cancer under a microscope, any battle or bombing raid or artillery barrage has the aesthetic purity of absolute moral indifference—a powerful, implacable beauty—and a true war story will tell the truth about this, though the truth is ugly.

To generalize about war is like generalizing about peace. Almost everything is true. Almost nothing is true. At its core, perhaps, war is just another name for death, and yet any soldier will tell you, if he tells the truth, that proximity to death brings with it a corresponding proximity to life. After a firefight, there is always the immense pleasure of aliveness. The trees are alive. The grass, the soil—everything. All around you things are purely living, and you among them, and the aliveness makes you tremble. You feel an intense, out-of-the-skin awareness of your living self—your truest self, the human being you want to be and then become by the force of wanting it. In the midst of evil you want to be a good man. You want decency. You want justice and courtesy and human concord, things you never knew you wanted. There is a kind of largeness to it, a kind of godliness. Though it's odd, you're never more alive than when you're almost dead. You recognize what's valuable. Freshly, as if for the first time, you love what's best in yourself and in the world, all that might be lost. At the hour of dusk you sit at your foxhole and look out on a wide river turning pinkish red, and at the mountains beyond, and although in the morning you must cross the river and go into the mountains and do terrible things and maybe die, even so, you find yourself studying the fine colors on the river, you feel wonder and awe at the setting of the sun, and you are filled with a hard, aching love for how the world could be and always should be, but now is not.

Mitchell Sanders was right. For the common soldier, at least, war has the feel—the spiritual texture—of a great ghostly fog, thick and permanent. There is no clarity. Everything swirls. The old rules are no longer binding, the old truths no longer true. Right spills over into wrong. Order blends into chaos, love into hate, ugliness into beauty, law into anarchy, civility into savagery. The vapors suck you in. You can't tell where you are, or why you're there, and the only certainty is overwhelming ambiguity.

In war you lose your sense of the definite, hence your sense of truth itself, and therefore it's safe to say that in a true war story nothing is ever absolutely true.

Often in a true war story there is not even a point, or else the point doesn't hit you until twenty years later, in your sleep, and you wake up and shake your wife and start telling the story to her, except when you get to the end you've forgotten the point again. And then for a long time you lie there watching the story happen in your head. You listen to your wife's breathing. The war's over. You close your eyes. You smile and think, Christ, what's the point?

This one wakes me up.

In the mountains that day, I watched Lemon turn sideways. He laughed and said something to Rat Kiley. Then he took a peculiar half step, moving from shade into bright sunlight, and the booby-trapped 105 round blew him into a tree. The parts were just hanging there, so Dave Jensen and I were ordered to shinny up and peel him off. I remember the white bone of an arm. I remember pieces of skin and something wet and yellow that must've been the intestines. The gore was horrible, and stays with me, but what wakes me up twenty years later is Dave Jensen singing "Lemon Tree" as we threw down the parts.

You can tell a true war story by the questions you ask. Somebody tells a story, let's say, and afterward you ask, "Is it true?" and if the answer matters, you've got your answer.

For example, we've all heard this one. Four guys go down a trail. A grenade sails out. One guy jumps on it and takes the blast and saves his three buddies.

Is it true?

The answer matters.

You'd feel cheated if it never happened. Without the grounding reality, it's just a trite bit of puffery, pure Hollywood, untrue in the way all such stories are untrue. Yet even if it did happen—and maybe it did, anything's possible—even then you know it can't be true, because a true war story does not depend upon that kind of truth. Absolute occurrence is irrelevant. A thing may happen and be a total lie; another thing may not happen and be truer than the truth. For example: four guys go down a trail. A grenade sails out. One guy jumps on it and takes the blast, but it's a killer grenade and everybody dies anyway. Before they die, though, one of the dead guys says, "The fuck you do *that* for?" and the jumper says, "Story of my life, man," and the other guy starts to smile but he's dead.

That's a true story that never happened.

Twenty years later, I can still see the sunlight on Lemon's face. I can see him turning, looking back at Rat Kiley, then he laughed and took that curious half step from shade into sunlight, his face suddenly brown and shining, and when his foot touched down, in that instant, he must've thought it was the sunlight that was killing him. It was not the sunlight. It was a rigged 105 round. But if I could ever get the story right, how the sun seemed to gather around him and pick him up and lift him into a tree, if I could somehow recreate the fatal whiteness of that light, the quick glare, the obvious cause and effect, then you would believe the last thing Curt Lemon believed, which for him must've been the final truth.

Now and then, when I tell this story, someone will come up to me afterward and say she liked it. It's always a woman. Usually it's an older woman of kindly temperament and humane politics. She'll explain that as a rule she hates war stories; she can't understand why people want to wallow in blood and gore. But this one she liked. The poor baby buffalo, it made her sad. Sometimes, even, there are little tears. What I should do, she'll say, is put it all behind me. Find new stories to tell.

I won't say it but I'll think it.

I'll picture Rat Kiley's face, his grief, and I'll think, *You dumb cooze.*

Because she wasn't listening.

It *wasn't* a war story. It was a *love* story.

But you can't say that. All you can do is tell it one more time, patiently, adding and subtracting, making up a few things to get at the real truth. No Mitchell Sanders, you tell her. No Lemon, no Rat Kiley. No trail junction. No baby buffalo. No vines or moss or white blossoms. Beginning to end, you tell her, it's all made up. Every goddamn detail—the mountains and the river and especially that poor dumb baby buffalo. None of it happened. *None* of it. And even if it did happen, it didn't happen in the mountains, it happened in this little village on the Batangan Peninsula, and it was raining like crazy, and one night a guy named Stink Harris woke up screaming with a leech on his tongue. You can tell a true war story if you just keep on telling it.

And in the end, of course, a true war story is never about war. It's about sunlight. It's about the special way that dawn spreads out on a river when you know you must cross the river and march into the mountains and do things you are afraid to do. It's about love and memory. It's about sorrow. It's about sisters who never write back and people who never listen.

The Vietnam in Me

LZ Gator, Vietnam, February 1994

I'm home, but the house is gone. Not a sandbag, not a nail or a scrap of wire. On Gator, we used to say, the wind doesn't blow, it sucks. Maybe that's what happened—the wind sucked it all away. My life, my virtue.

In February 1969, 25 years ago, I arrived as a young, terrified pfc. on this lonely little hill in Quang Ngai Province. Back then, the place seemed huge and imposing and permanent. A forward firebase for the Fifth Battalion of the 46th infantry, 198th Infantry Brigade, LZ Gator was home to 700 or 800 American soldiers, mostly grunts. I remember a tar helipad, a mess hall, a medical station, mortar and artillery emplacements, two volleyball courts, numerous barracks and offices and supply depots and machine shops and entertainment clubs. Gator was our castle. Not safe, exactly, but far preferable to the bush. No land mines here. No paddies bubbling with machine-gun fire.

Maybe once a month, for three or four days at a time, Alpha Company would return to Gator for stand-down, where we took our comforts behind a perimeter of bunkers and concertina wire. There were hot showers and hot meals, ice chests packed with beer, glossy pinup girls, big, black Sony tape decks booming "We gotta get out of this place" at decibels for the deaf. Thirty or 40 acres of almost-America. With a little weed and a lot of beer, we would spend the days of stand-down in flat-out celebration, purely alive, taking pleasure in our own biology, kidneys and livers and lungs and legs, all in their proper alignments. We could

---

Reprinted from the *New York Times Magazine*, October 2, 1994, pp. 48–57, by permission of The New York Times Company.

breathe here. We could feel our fists uncurl, the pressures approaching normal. The real war, it seemed, was in another solar system. By day, we'd fill sandbags or pull bunker guard. In the evenings, there were outdoor movies and sometimes live floor shows—pretty Korean girls breaking our hearts in their spangled miniskirts and high leather boots—then afterward we'd troop back to the Alpha barracks for some letter writing or boozing or just a good night's sleep.

So much to remember. The time we filled a nasty lieutenant's canteen with mosquito repellent; the sounds of choppers and artillery fire; the slow dread that began building as word spread that in a day or two we'd be heading back to the bush. Pinkville, maybe. The Batangan Peninsula. Spooky, evil places where the land itself could kill you.

Now I stand in this patch of weeds, looking down on what used to be the old Alpha barracks. Amazing, really, what time can do. You'd think there would be *something* left, some faint imprint, but LZ (Landing Zone) Gator has been utterly and forever erased from the earth. Nothing here but ghosts and wind

At the foot of Gator, along Highway 1, the little hamlet of Nuoc Man is going bonkers over our arrival here. As we turn and walk down the hill, maybe 200 people trail along, gawking and chattering, the children reaching out to touch our skin. Through our interpreter, Mrs. Le Hoai Phuong, I'm told that I am the first American soldier to return to this place in the 24 years since Gator was evacuated in 1970. In a strange way, the occasion has the feel of a reunion—happy faces, much bowing. "Me Wendy," says a middle-aged woman. Another says, "Flower." Wendy and Flower: G.I. nicknames retrieved from a quarter-century ago.

An elderly woman, perhaps in her late 70's, tugs at my shirt and says, "My name Mama-san."

Dear God. We should've bombed these people with love.

Cambridge, Mass., June 1994

Last night suicide was on my mind. Not whether, but how. Tonight it will be on my mind again. Now it's 4 A. M., June the 5th. The sleeping pills have not worked. I sit in my underwear at this unblinking fool of a computer and try to wrap words around a few horrid truths.

I returned to Vietnam with a woman whose name is Kate, whom I adored and have since lost. She's with another man, seven blocks away. This I learned yesterday afternoon. My own fault, Kate would say, and she would be mostly right. Not entirely. In any case, these thoughts are probably too intimate, too awkward and embarrassing for public discussion. But who knows? Maybe a little blunt human truth will send you off to church, or to confession, or inside yourself.

Not that it matters. For me, with one eye on these smooth yellow pills, the world must be written about as it is or not written about at all.

LZ Gator, February 1994

By chance, Kate and I have arrived in Nuoc Man on a day of annual commemoration, a day when the graves of the local war dead are blessed and repaired and decorated and wept over.

The village elders invite us to a feast, a picnic of sorts, where we take seats before a low lacquered table at an outdoor shrine. Children press up close, all around. The elders shoo them away, but the shooing doesn't do much. I'm getting nervous. The food on display seems a bit exotic. Not to my taste. I look at Kate, Kate looks at me. "Number one chop-chop," an old woman says, a wrinkled, gorgeous, protective, scarred, welcoming old woman. "Number one," she promises, and nudges Kate, and smiles a heartbreaking betel-nut smile.

I choose something white. Fish, I'm guessing. I have eaten herring; I have enjoyed herring. This is not herring.

There are decisions to be made.

The elders bow and execute chewing motions. Do not forget: our hosts are among the maimed and widowed and orphaned, the bombed and rebombed, the recipients of white phosphorus, the tenders of graves. Chew, they say, and by God I chew.

Kate has the good fortune to find a Kleenex. She's a pro. She executes a polite wiping motion and it's over for her. Eddie Keating, the *Times* photographer whose pictures accompany this text, tucks his portion between cheek and gum, where it remains until the feast concludes. Me—I imagine herring. I remember Sunday afternoons as a boy, the Vikings on TV, my dad opening up the crackers and creamed herring, passing it out at half-time. Other flashes too. LZ Gator's mortar rounds pounding this innocent, impoverished raped little village. Eight or nine corpses piled not 50 yards from where we now sit in friendly union. I prepare myself. Foul, for sure, but things come around. Nuoc Man swallowed plenty.

The Song Tra Hotel, Quang Ngai City, February 1994

It's late in the evening. The air-conditioner is at full Cuban power. Kate's eyes sparkle, she's laughing. "Swallowed!" she keeps saying.

In 1969, when I went to war, Kate was 3 years old. Kennedy, Johnson, Nixon, McNamara, Bunker, Rogers, Bundy, Rusk, Abrams, Rostow—for her, these names are like the listings on a foreign menu. Some she recognizes not at all, some she recalls from books or old television clips. But she never tasted the dishes. She does not know ice cream from Brussels sprouts. Three years old—how could she? No more than I could know the Southern California of her own youth.

Still it was Kate who insisted we come here. I was more than reluctant—I was petrified. I looked for excuses. Bad dreams and so on. But Kate's enthusiasm won me over; she wanted to share in my past, the shapes of things, the smells and sunlight.

As it turns out, the sharing has gone both ways. In any other circumstances, I would have returned to this country almost purely as a veteran, caught up in memory, but Kate's presence has made me pay attention to the details of here and now, a Vietnam that exists outside the old perimeter of war. She takes delight in things alive: a chicken wired to someone's bicycle, an old woman's enormous fingernails, an infant slung casually on the hip of a tiny 7-year-old girl. Kate has the eyes and spirit of an adventurer, wide open to the variety of the world and these qualities have pushed me toward some modest adventurism of my own.

Now I watch her fiddle with the air-conditioner. "Swallowed!" she keeps saying.

Later in the night, as on many other nights, we talk about the war. I try to explain—ineptly, no doubt—that Vietnam was more than terror. For me, at least, Vietnam was partly love. With each step, each light-year of a second, a foot soldier is always almost dead, or so it feels, and in such circumstances you can't *help* but love. You love your mom and dad, the Vikings, hamburgers on the grill, your pulse, your future—everything that might be lost or never come to be. Intimacy with death carries with it a corresponding new intimacy with life. Jokes are funnier, green is greener. You love the musty morning air. You love the miracles of your own enduring capacity for love. You love your friends in Alpha Company—a kid named Chip, my buddy. He wrote letters to my sister, I wrote letters to his sister. In the rear, back at Gator, Chip and I would go our separate ways, by color, both of us ashamed but knowing it had to be that way. In the bush, though, nothing kept us apart. "Black and White" we were called. In May of 1969, Chip was blown high into a hedge of bamboo. Many pieces. I loved the guy, he loved me. I'm alive. He's dead. An old story, I guess.

Cambridge, June 1994

It's 5:25 in the morning, June 7. I have just taken my first drug of the day, a prescription drug, Oxazepam, which files the edge off anxiety. Thing is, I'm not anxious. I'm slop. This is despair. This is a valance of horror that Vietnam never approximated. If war is hell what do we call hopelessness?

I have not killed myself. That day, this day, maybe tomorrow. Like Nam, it goes.

For some time, years in fact, I have been treated for depression, $8,000 or $9,000 worth. Some of it has worked. Or was working. I had called back to memory—not to memory, exactly, but to significance—some pretty painful feelings of rejection as a child. Chubby and friendless and lonely. I had come to acknowledge, more or less, the dominant principle of love in my life, how far I would go to get it, how terrified I was of losing it. I have done bad things for love, bad things to stay loved. Kate is one case. Vietnam is another. More than anything, it was this desperate love craving that propelled me into a war I considered mistaken, probably evil. In college, I stood in peace vigils. I rang doorbells for Gene McCarthy, composed earnest editorials for the school newspaper. But when the draft notice arrived after graduation, the old demons went to work almost instantly. I thought about Canada. I thought about jail. But in the end I could not bear the prospect of rejection: by my family, my country, my friends, my hometown. I would risk conscience and rectitude before risking the loss of love.

I have written some of this before, but I must write it again. I was a coward. I went to Vietnam.

My Lai, Quang Ngai Province, February 1994

Weird, but I know this place. I've been here before. Literally, but also in my nightmares.

One year after the massacre, Alpha Company's area of operations included the village of My Lai 4, or so it was called on American military maps. The Vietnamese call it Thuan Yen, which belongs to a larger hamlet called Tu Cung, which in turn belongs to an even larger parent village called Son My. But names are finally irrelevant. I am just here.

Twenty-five years ago, knowing nothing of the homicides committed by American troops on the morning of March 16, 1968, Alpha Company walked through and around this hamlet on numerous occasions. Now, standing here with Kate, I can't recognize much. The place blends in with all the other poor, scary, beleaguered villes in this area we called Pinkville. Even so, the feel of the place is as familiar as the old stucco house of my childhood. The clay trails, the cow dung, the blank faces, the unknowns and unknowables. There is the smell of sin here. Smells of terror, too, and enduring sorrow.

What happened briefly, was this. At approximately 7:30 on the morning of March 16, 1968, a company of roughly 115 American solders were inserted by helicopter just outside the village of My Lai. They met no resistance. No enemy. No incoming fire. Still, for the next four hours, Charlie Company killed whatever could be killed. They killed chickens. They killed dogs and cattle. They killed people too. Lots of people. Women, infants, teen-agers, old men. The United States Army's Criminal Investigation Division compiled a list of 343 fatalities and an independent Army inquiry led by Lieut. Gen. William R. Peers estimated that the death count may have exceeded 400. At the Son My Memorial a large tablet lists 504 names. According to Col. William Wilson, one of the original Army investigators, "The crimes visited on the inhabitants of Son My Village included individual and group acts of murder, rape, sodomy, maiming, assault on noncombatants and the mistreatment and killing of detainees."

The testimony of one member of Charlie Company, Salvadore LaMartina, suggests the systematic, cold-blooded character of the slaughter.

Q: Did you obey your orders?
A: Yes, sir.
Q: What were your orders?
A: Kill anything that breathed.

Whether or not such instructions were ever directly issued is a matter of dispute. Either way, a good many participants would later offer the explanation that they were obeying orders, a defense explicitly prohibited by the Nuremberg Principles and the United States Army's own rules of war. Other participants would argue that the civilians at My Lai were themselves Vietcong. A young soldier named Paul Meadlo, who was responsible for numerous deaths on that bright March morning, offered this appalling testimony:

Q: What did you do?
A: I held my M-16 on them.
Q: Why?
A: Because they might attack.
Q: They were children and babies?
A: Yes.
Q: And they might attack? Children and babies?
A: They might've had a fully loaded grenade on them. The mothers might have throwed them at us.

Q: Babies?
A: Yes. . . .
Q: Were the babies in their mothers' arms?
A: I guess so.
Q: And the babies moved to attack?
A: I expected at any moment they were about to make a counterbalance.

Eventually, after a cover-up that lasted more than a year and after the massacre made nationwide headlines, the Army's Criminal Investigation Division produced sufficient evidence to charge 30 men with war crimes. Of these, only a single soldier, First Lieut. William Laws Calley Jr., was ever convicted or spent time in prison. Found guilty of the premeditated murder of "not less than" 22 civilians, Calley was sentenced to life at hard labor, but after legal appeals and sentence reductions, his ultimate jail time amounted to three days in a stockade and four and a half months in prison.

In some cases, judicial action was never initiated; in other cases, charges were quietly dropped. Calley aside, only a handful of men faced formal court-martial proceedings, either for war crimes or for subsequent cover-up activities, with the end result of five acquittals and four judicially ordered dismissals. Among those acquitted was Capt. Ernest Medina, who commanded Charlie Company on the morning of March 16, 1968.

All this is history. Dead as those dead women and kids. Even at the time, most Americans seemed to shrug it off as a cruel, nasty, inevitable consequence of war. There were numerous excuses, numerous rationalizations. Upright citizens decried even the small bit of justice secured by the conviction of Lieutenant Calley. Now, more than 25 years later, the villainy of that Saturday morning in 1968 has been pushed off to the margins of memory. In the colleges and high schools I sometimes visit, the mention of My Lai brings on null stares, a sort of puzzlement, disbelief mixed with utter ignorance.

Evil has no place, it seems, in our national mythology. We erase it. We use ellipses. We salute ourselves and take pride in America the White Knight, America the Lone Ranger, America's sleek laser-guided weaponry beating up on Saddam and his legion of devils.

It's beginning to rain when Kate and I sit down to talk with two survivors of the slaughter here. Mrs. Ha Thi Quy is a woman of 69 years. Her face is part stone, part anguish as she describes through an interpreter the events of that day. It's hard stuff to hear. "Americans came here twice before," Mrs. Quy says. "Nothing bad happened, they were friendly to us. But on that day the solders jumped out of their helicopters and immediately began to shoot. I prayed, I pleaded." As I take notes, I'm recalling other prayers, other pleadings. A woman saying "No VC, no VC," while a young lieutenant pistol-whipped her without the least expression on his face, without the least sign of distress or moral uncertainty. Mad Mark, we called him. But he wasn't mad. He was numb. He'd lost himself. His gyroscope was gone. He didn't know up from down, good from bad.

Mrs. Quy is crying now. I can feel Kate crying off to my side, though I don't dare look.

"The Americans took us to a ditch. I saw two soldiers with red faces—sunburned—and they pushed a lot of people into the ditch. I was in the ditch. I fell down and many fell on top of me. Soldiers were shooting. I was shot in the hip. The firing went on and on. It would stop and then start again and then stop." Now I hear Kate crying, not loud just a certain breathiness I've come to recognize. This will be with us forever. This we'd have.

My notes take a turn for the worse. "I lay under the dead in the ditch. Around noon, when I heard no more gunfire, I came out of the ditch and saw many more. Brains, pieces of body. My house was burned. Cattle were shot. I went back to the ditch. Three of my four children were killed."

I'm exhausted when Mrs. Quy finishes. Partly it's the sheer magnitude of horror, partly some hateful memories of my own.

I can barely wire myself together as Mrs. Truong Thi Le, another survivor, recounts those four hours of murder. Out of her family of 10, 9 died that day. "I fell down," Mrs. Le tells us. "But I was not shot. I lay with three other bodies on me, all blood. Did not move at all. Pretended dead. Saw newborn baby near a woman. Woman died. Infant still alive. Soldiers came up. Shot baby."

Outside, the rain has let up. Kate, Eddie and I take a walk through the hamlet. We stare at foundations where houses used to stand. We admire a harsh, angular, defiant, beautiful piece of sculpture, a monument to the murdered.

Mrs. Quy accompanies us for a while. She's smiling, accommodating. Impossible, but she seems to like us.

At one point, while I'm scribbling in my notebook, she pulls down her trousers. She shows Kate the scarred-over bullet hole in her hip.

Kate nods and makes sounds of sympathy. What does one say? Bad day. World of hurt.

Now the rain is back, much harder. I'm drenched, cold and something else. Eddie and I stand at the ditch where maybe 50, maybe 80, maybe 100 innocent human beings perished. I watch Eddie snap his pictures.

Here's the something else: I've got the guilt chills.

Years ago, ignorant of the massacre, I hated this place, and places much like it. Two miles away, in an almost identical hamlet, Chip was blown into his hedge of bamboo. A mile or so east, Roy Arnold was shot dead, I was slightly wounded. A little farther east, a kid named McElhaney died. Just north of here, on a rocky hillside, another kid, named Slocum, lost his foot to a land mine. It goes on.

I despised everything—the soil, the tunnels, the paddies, the poverty and myself. Each step was an act of the purest self-hatred and self-betrayal, yet, in truth, because truth matters, my sympathies were rarely with the Vietnamese. I was mostly terrified. I was lamenting in advance my own pitiful demise. After fire fights, after friends died there was also a great deal of anger—black, fierce, hurting anger—the kind you want to take out on whatever presents itself. This is not to justify what occurred here. Justifications are empty and outrageous. Rather, it's to say that I more or less understand what happened on that day in March 1968, how it happened, the wickedness that soaks into your blood and heats up and starts to sizzle. I know the boil that precedes butchery. At the same time, however, the men in Alpha Company did not commit murder. We did not turn our machine guns on civilians; we did not cross that conspicuous line between rage and homicide. I know what occurred here, yes, but I also feel betrayed by a nation that so widely shrugs off barbarity, by a military judicial system that treats murderers and common soldiers as one and the same.

Apparently we're all innocent—those who exercise moral restraint and those who do not, officers who control their troops and officers who do not. In a way, America has declared *itself* innocent.

I look away for a time, and then look back.

By most standards, this is not much of a ditch. A few feet deep, a few feet wide. The rain makes the greenish brown water bubble like a thousand tiny mouths.

The guilt has turned to a gray, heavy sadness. I have to take my leave but don't know how.

After a time, Kate walks up, hooks my arm, doesn't say anything, doesn't have to, leads me into a future that I know will hold misery for both of us. Different hemispheres, different scales of atrocity. I don't want it to happen. I want to tell her things and be understood and live happily ever after. I want a miracle. That's the final emotion. The terror at this ditch, the certain doom, the need for God's intervention.

Cambridge, June 1994

I've been trying to perform good deeds. I bought a Father's Day card three days early. I made appointments for a physical exam, dental work, a smoke-ender's program. I go for walks every day. I work out, draw up lists, call friends, visit lawyers, buy furniture, discharge promises, keep my eyes off the sleeping pills. The days are all right.

Now the clock shows 3:55 A.M. I call NERVOUS and listen to an automated female voice confirm it. The nights are not all right.

I write these few words, which seem useless, then get up and pull out an album of photographs from the Vietnam trip. The album was Kate's parting gift. On the cover she inserted a snapshot that's hard to look at but harder still to avoid. We stand on China Beach near Danang. Side by side, happy as happy will ever be, our fingers laced in a fitted, comfortable, half-conscious way that makes me feel a gust of hope. It's a gust though, here and gone.

Numerous times over the past several days, at least a dozen, this piece has come close to hyperspace. Twice it lay at the bottom of a wastebasket. I've spent my hours preparing a tape of songs for Kate, stuff that once meant things. Corny songs, some of them. Happy songs, love-me songs.

Today, scared stiff, I deposited the tape on her doorstep. Another gust of hope, then a whole lot of stillness.

The Song Tra Hotel, Quang Ngai City, February 1994

Kate's in the shower, I'm in history. I sit with a book propped up against the air-conditioner, underlining sentences, sweating out my own ignorance. Twenty-five years ago, like most other grunts in Alpha Company, I knew next to nothing about this place—Vietnam in general, Quang Ngai in particular. Now I'm learning. In the years preceding the murders at My Lai, more than 70 percent of the villages in this province had been destroyed by air strikes, artillery fire, Zippo lighters, napalm, white phosphorus, bulldozers, gunships and other such means.

Roughly 40 percent of the population had lived in refugee camps, while civilian casualties in the area were approaching 50,000 a year. These numbers, reported by the journalist Jonathan Schell in 1967, were later confirmed as substantially correct by Government investigators. Not that I need confirmation. Back in 1969 the wreckage was all around us, so common it seemed part of the geography, as natural as any mountain or river. Wreckage was the rule. Brutality was S.O.P. Scalded children, pistol-whipped women, burning hootches, free-fire zones, body counts, indiscriminate bombing and harassment fire, villages in ash, M-60 machine guns hosing down dark green tree lines and any human life behind them.

In a war without aim, you tend not to aim. You close your eyes, close your heart. The consequences become hit or miss in the most general sense.

With so few military targets, with an enemy that was both of and among the population, Alpha Company began to regard Quang Ngai itself as the true enemy—the physical place, the soil and paddies. What had started for us as a weird, vicious little war soon evolved into something far beyond vicious, a hopped-up killer strain of nihilism, waste without want, aimlessness of deed mixed with aimlessness of spirit. As Schell wrote after the events at My Lai, "There can be no doubt that such an atrocity was possible only because a number of other methods of killing civilians and destroying their villages had come to be the rule, and not the exception, in our conduct of the war."

I look up from my book briefly, listen to Kate singing in the shower. A doctoral candidate at Harvard University, smart and sophisticated, but she's also fluent in joy, attuned to the pleasures and beauty of the world. She knows the lyrics to "Hotel California," start to finish, while here at the air-conditioner I can barely pick out the simplest melodies of Vietnam, the most basic chords of history. It's as if I never heard the song, as if I'd gone to war in some mall or supermarket. I discover that Quang Ngai Province was home to one of Vietnam's fiercest, most recalcitrant, most zealous revolutionary movements. Independent by tradition, hardened by poverty and rural isolation, the people of Quang Ngai were openly resistant to French colonialism as far back as the 19th century and were among the first to rebel against France in the 1930's. The province remained wholly under Vietminh control throughout the war against France; it remained under Vietcong control, at least by night, throughout the years of war against America. Even now, in the urbane circles of Hanoi and Ho Chi Minh City, the people of Quang Ngai are regarded as a clan of stubborn country bumpkins, coarse and insular, willfully independent, sometimes defiant of the very Government they had struggled to install.

"Like a different country," our interpreter told us after a long, frustrating session with representatives of the Quang Ngai People's Committee. "These people I don't like much, very crude, very difficult. I think you had horrible bad luck to fight them."

At noon, by appointment, a Vietnamese journalist named Pham Van Duong knocks on our door. It's a secret meeting of sorts. Nothing illegal—a couple of writers, a couple of beers—but I've still got the buzz of some low-level paranoia. Earlier in the day, our joint request for this interview had been denied by a stern, rather enigmatic functionary of the People's Committee. Impossible, we were told. Not on the schedule. The official offered little sympathy for our interpreter's reminder that schedules are man-made, that blocks of time appeared wide open. Logic went nowhere. Bureaucratic scowls, stare-into-space silence. A few minutes later, just outside the provincial offices, we quietly huddled to make our own unsanctioned arrangements.

Now, as Mr. Duong sits down and accepts a beer, I'm feeling the vigilant, slightly illicit anxiety of a midday drug buy. Kate locks the door; I close the drapes. Ridiculous, or almost ridiculous but for the first 10 minutes I sit picturing prison food, listening for footsteps in the hallway. Our interpreter explains to Mr. Duong that I will happily guard his identity in any written account of this conversation.

Mr. Duong snorts at the suggestion. "Only a problem in Quang Ngai," he says. "Officials in Hanoi would be glad for our talking. They wish good relations with America—good new things to happen. Maybe I get a medal. Sell the medal, buy Marlboros."

We click beer bottles. For the next two hours we chat about books, careers, memories of war. I ask about My Lai. Mr. Duong looks at the wall. There is a short hesitation—the hesitation of tact, I suppose. He was 8 years old when news of the massacre reached his village nearby. He recalls great anger among his relatives and friends, disgust and sadness, but no feelings of shock or surprise. "This kind of news came often," he says. "We did not then know the scale of the massacre, just that Americans had been killing people. But killing was everywhere."

Two years later, Mr. Duong's brother joined the 48th Vietcong Battalion. He was killed in 1972.

"My mother fainted when she heard this. She was told that his body had been buried in a mass grave with seven comrades who died in the same attack. This made it much worse for my mother—no good burial. After liberation in 1975, she began to look for my brother's remains. She found the mass grave 20 kilometers south of Quang Ngai City. She wished to dig, to rebury my brother, but people told her no, don't dig and in the beginning she seemed to accept this. Then the Americans returned to search for their own missing, and my mother became very angry. *Why them? Not me?* So she insisted we dig. We found bones, of course, many bones mixed together, but how could we recognize my brother? How could anyone know? But we took away some bones in a box. Reburied them near our house. Every day now, my mother passes by this grave. She feels better, I think. Better at least to tell herself *maybe*."

Kate looks up at me. She's silent, but she knows what I'm thinking. At this instant, a few blocks away, an American M.I.A. search team is headquartered at the Quang Ngai Government guesthouse. With Vietnamese assistance, this team and others like it are engaged in precisely the work of Mr. Duong's mother, digging holes, picking through bones, seeking the couple thousand Americans still listed as missing.

Which is splendid.

And which is also utterly one-sided. A perverse and outrageous double standard.

What if things were reversed? What if the Vietnamese were to ask us, or to require us, to locate and identify each of their own M.I.A.'s? Numbers alone make it impossible: 100,000 is a conservative estimate. Maybe double that. Maybe triple. From my own sliver of experience—one year at war, one set of eyes—I can testify to the lasting anonymity of a great many Vietnamese dead. I watched napalm turn villages into ovens. I watched burials by bulldozer. I watched bodies being flung into trucks, dumped into wells, used for target practice, stacked up and burned like cordwood.

Even in the abstract, I get angry at the stunning, almost cartoonish narcissism of American policy on this issue. I get angrier yet at the narcissism of an American public that embraces and breathes life into the policy—so arrogant, so ignorant, so self-righteous, so wanting in the most fundamental qualities of sympathy and fairness and mutuality. Some of this I express aloud to Mr. Duong, who nods without comment. We finish off our beers. Neither of us can find much to say. Maybe we're both back in history, snagged in brothers and bones. I feel hollow. So little has changed it seems, and so much will always be missing.

Cambridge, June 1994

June 11, I think—I'm too tired to find a calendar. Almost 5 A.M. In another hour it'll be 5:01. I'm on war time, which is the time we're all on at one point or another: when fathers die, when husbands ask for divorce, when women you love are fast asleep beside men you wish were you.

The tape of songs did nothing. Everything will always do nothing.

Kate hurts, too, I'm sure, and did not want it this way. I didn't want it either. Even so, both of us have to live in these slow-motion droplets of now, doing what we do, choosing what we choose, and in different ways both of us are now responsible for the casualty rotting in the space between us.

If there's a lesson in this, which there is not, it's very simple. You don't have to be in Nam to be in Nam.

The Batangan Peninsula, Quang Ngai Province, February 1994

The Graveyard we called it. Littered with land mines, almost completely defoliated, this spit of land jutting eastward into the South China Sea was a place Alpha Company feared the way others might fear snakes, or the dark, or the bogyman. We lost at least three men here; I couldn't begin to count the arms and legs.

Today our little caravan is accompanied by Mr. Ngu Duc Tan, who knows this place intimately, a former captain in the 48th Vietcong Battalion. It was the 48th that Alpha Company chased from village to village, paddy to paddy, during my entire tour in Vietnam. Chased but never found. They found us: ambushes, sniper fire, nighttime mortar attacks. Through our interpreter, who passes along commodious paragraphs in crisp little packets, Mr. Tan speaks genially of military tactics while we make the bumpy ride out toward the Batangan. "U.S. troops not hard to see, not hard to fight," he says. "Much noise, much equipment. Big columns. Nice green uniforms." Sitting ducks, in other words, though Mr. Tan is too polite to express it this way. He explains that the United States Army was never a primary target. "We went after Saigon puppet troops, what you called ARVN. If we beat them, everything collapse, the U.S. would have nothing more to fight for. You brought many soldiers, helicopters, bombs, but we chose not to fight you, except sometimes. America was not the main objective."

God help us, I'm thinking, if we *had* been. All those casualties. All that blood and terror. Even at this moment, more than half a lifetime later, I remember the feel of a bull's-eye pinned to my shirt, a prickly when-will-it-happen sensation, as if I alone had been the main objective.

Meanwhile, Kate is taking her own notes, now and then asking questions through the interpreter. She's better than I am at human dynamics, more fluid and spontaneous, and after a time she gets Mr. Tan to display a few war scars—arms, legs, hands, cheek, chest, skull. Sixteen wounds altogether. The American war, he says, was just one phase in his career as a soldier which began in 1961 and encompassed combat against the South Vietnamese, Khmer Rouge and Chinese.

Talk about bad dreams. One year gave me more than enough to fill up the nights.

My goal on the Batangan peninsula was to show Kate one of the prettiest spots on earth. I'm looking for a lagoon, a little fishing village, an impossibly white beach along the South China Sea.

First, though, Mr. Tan attends to his own agenda. We park the van in one of the inland hamlets, walk without invitation into a small house, sit down for lunch with a man named Vo Van Ba. Instantly, I'm thinking herring. Kate and Eddie have the sense to decline, to tap their stomachs and say things like "Full, full, thanks, thanks." Cans are opened. The house fills up with children, nephews, nieces, babies, cousins, neighbors. There are flies, too. Many, many flies. Many thousand.

Mr. Tan and Mr. Ba eat lunch with their fingers, fast and hungry, chatting amiably while our interpreter does her best to put the gist of it into English. I'm listening hard, chewing hard. I gather that these two men had been comrades of a sort during the war. Mr. Ba, our host, was never a full-time soldier, never even a part-time irregular. As I understand it, he belonged to what we used to call the VC infrastructure, offering support and intelligence to Mr. Tan and his fighting troops.

I lean forward, nod my head. The focus, however, is on the substance I'm swallowing, its remarkable texture, the flies trying to get at it. For five years, Mr. Ba explains, he lived entirely underground with a family of eight. Five years, he repeats. Cooking, bathing, working, sleeping. He waits for the translation, waits a bit longer, then looks at me with a pair of silvery, burned-out, cauterized, half-blind, underground eyes. "You had the daylight, but I had the earth." Mr. Ba turns to Mr. Tan. After a second he chuckles. "Many times I might reach up and take this man's leg. Many times. Very easy. I might just pull him down to where the war was."

We're on foot now. Even at 59, Mr. Tan moves swiftly, with the grace and authority of a man who once led solders in combat. He does not say much. He leads us toward the ocean, toward the quaint fishing village I'm hoping to show Kate, but along the way there is one last item Mr. Tan wishes to show me. We move down a trail through two or three adjacent hamlets, seem to circle back for a time, end up in front of another tiny house.

Mr. Tan's voice goes into command tone—two or three sharp, snapping words. A pair of boys dart into the house. No wasted time, they come out fast, carrying what's left of a man named Nguyen Van Ngu. They balance this wreckage on a low chair. Both legs are gone at the upper-upper thigh. We shake hands. Neither of us knows what to say—there is nothing worth saying—so for a few minutes we exchange stupidities in our different languages, no translator available to wash away the helplessness. We pose for photographs. We try for smiles.

Mr. Tan does not smile. He nods to himself—maybe to me. But I get the point anyway. Here is your paradise. Here is your pretty little fishing village by the sea.

Two minutes later, we're on the beach. It *is* beautiful, even stunning. Kate wades out into the water. She's surrounded by kids. They giggle and splash her, she splashes back, and I stand there like an idiot, grinning, admiring the view, while Mr. Tan waits patiently in the shade.

Cambridge, July 1994

Outside, it's the Fourth of July. Lovely day, empty streets. Kate is where Kate is, which is elsewhere, and I am where I am, which is also elsewhere. Someday, no doubt, I'll wish happiness for myself, but for now it's still war time, minute to minute. Not quite 11 A.M. Already I've been out for two walks, done the laundry, written a few words, bought groceries, lifted weights, watched the Fourth of July sunlight slide across my street-side balcony.

And Kate?

The beach, maybe? A backyard cookout?

The hardest part, by far, is to make the bad pictures go away. On war time, the world is one long horror movie, image after image, and if it's anything like Vietnam, I'm in for a lifetime of wee-hour creeps.

Meanwhile, I try to plug up the leaks and carry through on some personal resolutions. For too many years I've lived in paralysis—guilt, depression, terror, shame—and now it's either move or die. Over the past weeks, at profound cost, I've taken actions with my life that are far too painful for any public record. But at least the limbo has ended. Starting can start.

There's a point here: Vietnam, Cambridge, Paris, Neptune—these are states of mind. Minds change.

My Khe, Quang Ngai Province, February 1994

There is one piece of ground I wish to revisit above all others in this country. I've come . . . prepared with a compass, a military map, grid coordinates, a stack of after-action reports recovered from a dusty box in the National Archives.

We're back near Pinkville, a mile or so east of My Lai. We are utterly lost, the interpreter, the van driver, the People's Committee representative, Eddie, Kate, me. I unfold the map and place a finger on the spot I'm hoping to find. A group of villagers puzzle over it. They chatter among themselves—arguing, it seems—then one of them points west, another north, most at the heavens.

Lost, that was the Vietnam of 25 years ago. The war came at us as a blur, raw confusion, and my fear now is that I would not recognize the right spot even while standing on it.

For well over an hour we drive from place to place. We end up precisely where we started. Once more, everyone spills out of the van. The thought occurs to me that this opportunity may never come again. I find my compass, place it on the map and look up for a geographical landmark. A low green hill rises to the west—not much, just a hump on the horizon.

I'm no trailblazer; but this works. One eye on the compass, one eye on some inner rosary, I lead our exhausted column 200 yards eastward, past a graveyard and out along a narrow paddy lake, where suddenly the world shapes itself exactly as it was shaped a quarter-century ago—the curvatures, the tree lines, the precise angles and proportions. I stop there and wait for Kate. *This* I dreamed of giving her. *This* I dreamed of sharing.

Our fingers lock, which happens without volition, and we stand looking out on a wide and very lovely field of rice. The sunlight gives it some gold and yellow. There is no wind at all. Before us is how peace would be defined in a dictionary for the speechless. I don't cry. I don't know what to do. At one point I hear myself talking about what happened here so long ago, motioning out at the rice, describing chaos and horror beyond anything I would experience until a few months later. I tell her how Paige lost his lower leg, how we had to probe for McElhaney in the flooded paddy, how the gunfire went on and on, how in the course of two hell-on-earth hours we took 13 casualties.

I doubt Kate remembers a word. Maybe she shouldn't. But I do hope she remembers the sunlight striking that field of rice. I hope she remembers the feel of our fingers. I hope she remembers how I fell silent after a time, just looking out at the golds and yellows, joining the peace, and how in those fine sunlit moments, which were ours, Vietnam took a little Vietnam out of me.

Ho Chi Minh City, February 1994

We hate this place.

Even the names—Saigon, Ho Chi Minh City. A massive identity crisis. Too loud, too quiet. Too alive, too dead.

For all the discomforts of Quang Ngai Province, which were considerable, Kate and I had taken pleasure in those qualities of beauty and equanimity that must have vanished from Saigon when the first oil barge steamed into port.

But we give it our best. An hour in the Chinese market district which is like an hour in combat. Two hours at the old presidential palace—as tawdry and corrupt as its former inhabitants. We risk periodic excursions into streets where the American dollar remains more valuable than oxygen, of which there is precious little. Maybe we've hit some interior wall. Maybe it's the diesel-heat. We visit a war-crimes museum, the old American Embassy and order lunch by way of room service. Western pop music blares at full volume from Government loudspeakers just outside our hotel. For hours, even with earplugs, we listen to "As Tears Go By" and "My Way." What happened to Ho Chi Minh? What happened to revolution? All we've heard comes from the Beatles.

In mid-afternoon, the music ceases. We go out for a short walk, do some shopping, then retreat to the rooftop swimming pool of the Rex Hotel. It could as well be Las Vegas. We don't say so, not directly, but both Kate and I are ready to evacuate, we're humming "We gotta get out of this place." Pretty soon we'll be singing it over loudspeakers.

For now, Kate lounges at the pool. She writes postcards. She catches me watching. She snaps pictures to show her children someday.

Bruce Weigl

American poet Bruce Weigl (b. 1949) served in the First Air Cavalry of the Vietnam War during 1967 and 1968. He has written many books of poetry and received several awards. Weigl has returned to Vietnam two times. On his second visit, in 1990, he went with fellow writers Larry Heineman and Tim O'Brien, whose work also appears in this chapter.

What Saves Us

We are wrapped around each other
in the back of my father's car parked
in the empty lot of the high school
of our failures, sweat on her neck
like oil. The next morning I would leave
for the war and I thought I had something
coming for that, I thought to myself
that I would not die never having
been inside her body. I lifted
her skirt above her waist like an umbrella
blown inside out by the storm. I pulled
her cotton panties up as high
as she could stand. I was on fire. Heaven
was in sight. We were drowning
on our tongues and I tried
to tear my pants off when she stopped
so suddenly we were surrounded
only by my shuddering
and by the school bells
grinding in the empty halls.
She reached to find something,
a silver crucifix on a silver chain,
the tiny savior's head
hanging, and stakes through his hands and his feet.
She put it around my neck and held me
so long my heart's black wings were calmed.
We are not always right
about what we think will save us.
I thought that dragging the angel down that night

Reprinted from *What Saves Us*, (1992), by permission of Northwestern University.

would save me, but I carried the crucifix in my pocket
and rubbed it on my face and lips
nights the rockets roared in.
People die sometimes so near you,
you feel them struggling to cross over,
the deep untangling, of one body from another.

The Way of Tet

Year of the monkey, year of the human wave,
the people smuggled weapons in caskets through the city
in long processions undisturbed
and buried them in Saigon graveyards.
At the feet of their small Buddhas
weary bar girls burned incense
before the boy soldiers arrived
to buy them tea and touch them
where they pleased. Twenty years
and the feel of a girl's body
so young there's no hair
is like a dream, but living is a darker thing,
the iron burning bee who drains the honey,
and he remembers her
twisting in what evening
light broke into the small room in the shack
in the labyrinth of shacks
in the alley where the lost and corrupted kept house.
He undressed her for the last time,
each piece of clothing
a sacrifice she surrendered to the war
the way the world had become.
Tomorrow blood would run in every province.
Tomorrow people would rise from tunnels everywhere
and resurrect something ancient from inside them,
and the boy who came ten thousand miles to touch her
small self lies beside the girl whose words he can't understand,
their song a veil between them.

She is a white bird in the bamboo, fluttering.
She is so small he imagines

---

he could hold all of her
in his hands and lift her to the black
sky beyond the illumination round's white light
where she would fly from her life
and the wounds from the lovers would heal,
the broken skin grow back.
But he need only touch her, only
lift the blanket from her shoulders
and the automatic shape of love unfolds,
the flare's light burning down on them,
lost in a wave that arrives
after a thousand years of grief
at their hearts.

Song of Napalm

for my wife

After the storm, after the rain stopped pounding,
we stood in the doorway watching horses
walk off lazily across the pasture's hill.
We stared through the black screen,
our vision altered by the distance
so I thought I saw a mist
kicked up around their hooves when they faded
like cut-out horses
away from us.
The grass was never more blue in that light, more
scarlet; beyond the pasture
trees scraped their voices into the wind, branches
crisscrossed the sky like barbed wire
but you said they were only branches.

Okay. The storm stopped pounding.
I am trying to say this straight: for once
I was sane enough to pause and breathe
outside my wild plans and after the hard rain
I turned my back on the old curses. I believed
they swung finally away from me . . .

But still the branches are wire
and thunder is the pounding mortar,
still I close my eyes and see the girl
running from her village, napalm
stuck to her dress like jelly,
her hands reaching for the no one
who waits in waves of heat before her.

So I can keep on living,
so I can stay here beside you,
I try to imagine she runs down the road and wings
beat inside her until she rises
above the stinking jungle and her pain
eases, and your pain, and mine.

But the lie swings back again.
The lie works only as long as it takes to speak
and the girl runs only as far
as the napalm allows
until her burning tendons and crackling
muscles draw her up
into that final position
burning bodies so perfectly assume. Nothing
can change that, she is burned behind my eyes
and not your good love and not the rain-swept air
and not the jungle-green
pasture unfolding before us can deny it.

Nguyen Duy

Nguyen Duy (b. 1948) was born Nguyen Duy Nhue. He holds degrees in linguistics and literature and currently lives in Ho Chi Minh City. During the Vietnam War, he served in the signal corps and also served as a militia squad leader. He has ten collections of poetry, three collections of memoirs, and a novel. His poetry has won awards in Vietnam and in the U. S. As Liz Rosenberg of The Boston Globe *writes, "Few poets have written as powerfully, consistently, and passionately against war . . . [his] poetry is inextricably woven with a larger sense of history." In "Stop" Duy exposes his readers to the thoughts of a Vietnamese soldier.*

Stop

Stop! . . .
He ran three steps ahead of me,
a ranger with the face of a child.
His shot just missed my temple.

My fingers tightened on the trigger,
the AK's clip pressed to my stomach.
Only half a second.
No! Only a tenth of a second.
If my finger moved half a millimeter
he'd be dead.

Stop!
He kept running.
I kept running after him, rifle ready.
Chasing him was much harder
than pulling the trigger. A tenth of a second
    was all it would take.

I knew that so well.
Just as I knew
if the situation had been reversed,
and I ran in front empty handed,
and he ran behind, M-16 in hand,
very likely I'd have been dead.
Life and death crossing in a tenth of a second.

Reprinted from *Mountain River: Vietnamese Poetry from the Wars, 1948—1993*, edited by Kevin Bowen, Nguyen Ba Chung, and Bruce Wiegl, (1998), by permission of University of Massachusetts Press.

The clip pressed hard to my stomach,
beating harder, a disquieting thought:
"It's easy to kill him,
to save him is harder . . ."
"It's easy to kill him,
save him, it's harder . . ."
The thought ran forward through me,
forward . . .
forward.
With all my strength,
I forced him
to stop!

Quang Tri Campaign, 1972
Translated by Nguyen Ba Chung

10

Writing of Witness: Perspectives on September 11, 2001

Josh Carney

On August 7th of 1998 I was in Malawi, Africa, nearing the end of a yearlong ethnobotanical research project. I recall that morning because a number of people stopped me on my walk to the University, where I was working at the time, and told me how sorry they were. "Sorry for what?" was my response, but I wasn't able to get the whole story. Something about bombs going off and killing Americans.

It was not until I reached the commons room—and the one TV with satellite news, since there are no TV stations in Malawi—that I learned about the embassy bombings in Dar-es-Salaam and Nairobi. As I sat there watching, the apologies kept coming, and I couldn't help but wonder why. I didn't know anyone killed in the bombings; besides, the news was telling me that more Kenyans and Tanzanians had died than Americans. Though I had been in Malawi for nine months, it wasn't until the bombings that I realized the significance of my citizenship—realized that I carried my national identity with me whether I wanted to or not.

I stayed in front of the TV in the commons room for much of the next few days and I began to notice something else: the coverage differed greatly between stations. We received the international versions of CNN and the BBC (British Broadcasting Corporation) and, especially after President Clinton ordered a retaliatory strike—with attacks in Sudan hitting a pharmaceutical plant mistaken for a chemical weapons facility, and a missile meant for Afghanistan straying into Pakistan—the stories were different. CNN was loath to cover what was being called "collateral damage." The BBC began asking hard questions about the strikes.

Shortly after the bombings, I made a friend—a Londoner of Pakistani heritage studying for his Ph.D. in law. He was also researching in Malawi; was also struck by the difference in coverage on the TV stations. What struck him even more, though, as we came to know each other, was my absolute ignorance about world events. I was in Malawi on a scholarship from the U.S. Government, supposedly one of the best and brightest picked to represent our country, and I didn't know the simplest facts about geography, politics, or recent world history. A typical conversation:

"Any idea what the conflict in Kosovo was about, mate?"

"Uh, something ethnic, right?"

"Capital of Djibouti?"

"Is that a country?"

"Do you know what your military did in Somalia?"

"Not really."

"At least tell me you know what a test match is in cricket."

"No, can you tell me who won the World Series last year?"

The questions always ended in cricket, and I was unashamed on only one count after conversations like this.

Weeks before September 11, 2001, this friend sent me a number of web links. "To educate you," he told me, "You need to get a bit of independent media in your life." I glanced at the pages, even browsed through a few articles, but I didn't spend much time there. I was in school, I was teaching, trying to get back in shape. Like most Americans, I had other things to do.

Then the planes hit.

That morning I was in conferences with students. I didn't hear anything until mid-morning; then the details were sketchy. A plane had hit a building—I thought maybe a Cessna or a commuter jet; couldn't imagine more than a few casualties. By noon, fewer and fewer students started showing up for conferences; another teacher came in and told me it was two planes, big ones. It was not until that evening that I made it to a TV and saw the images that many of us will remember for the rest of our lives: a plane running into a tower, disappearing in flame; bodies leaping from windows; two of the largest buildings on earth folding to dust, their deafening rumble drowning thousands of cries.

By the time I got to the TV, the calls for revenge had begun. We wanted to fight, but we didn't know whom, exactly, we should be after. One place I went to watch had over fifteen televisions, many turned to different channels. But though most of them carried news of the day's events, I noticed they were, for the most part, saying the same things. This continued the next day and the next and I began to wonder if maybe the media wasn't doing its job. Where was the BBC to question? What about a point of view that wasn't all about war? In '98, CNN had rallied around Clinton's bombing—avoided asking the tough questions—I wondered if something similar could be happening now.

So I turned to the independent media. I checked out the web pages my friend had sent, started listening to *Democracy Now* on the radio (91.3 FM), read the editorials in the *Tucson Weekly*. And I heard a lot of things that I wasn't hearing in the mainstream media of TV and newspaper. I learned about the U.S.'s long history of involvement in Afghanistan—how our CIA had funded and supplied much of the military force that had now become the Taliban. I read Arundhati Roy's piece and began to think there might be some alternative answers to President Bush's question, "Why do they hate us?" I read Edward Said, who linked the anger felt in the Arab world with U.S. policy in Israel, and made concrete suggestions about ways that relations might be improved. And my understanding of the term "terrorism" was complicated when I read Noam Chomsky's discussion of U.S. sponsored terror in Nicaragua, which had been condemned in a world court and virtually ignored in our country.

I also began to see different ways of looking at the events. Slavoj Zizek commented on the way that the terrorist attacks seemed almost unreal—like a movie—and went on to formulate a theory on American conceptions of reality mediated by Hollywood and television. This hit right home when I realized that I was one of the Americans who had not wanted to hear the news of the world that didn't affect me—that it only became real when it happened in America. Following this, Barbara Kingsolver's piece gave me a thoughtful way to look at one of our reactions—the nationwide raising of our Flag—which was a more complex symbol than many were giving it credit for.

As the events of 9.11 grew further away, voices of critical questioning began to emerge. Robert Jensen wondered whether the concept of patriotism might be doing more harm than good. Judith Butler evaluated the U.S. reaction, taking a critical look at both the "right" and the "left"; the mainstream and the alternative media reactions to the terror, and the way that the attacks were being used by all sides.

For me, it was important to hear the alternative voices in the discussion. I listened and read not necessarily to agree with them—for all acts of communication are loaded with their own agendas—but rather to have a framework within which to formulate my own account: my own witness and interpretation of the events. I felt that I needed to be exposed to as many points of view as possible when trying to understand what had happened and how our country was responding. This was especially true because alternative points of view were not being heard by much of our population—as a nation, our witness account of 9.11 was severely lopsided.

This chapter contains a number of the articles that I came across in my search and my teaching that fall. They represent views from the mainstream media as well as the alternative, though emphasis is put on the latter, as many students may not have been exposed to them. The pieces here were all published in 2001, after the 9.11 attacks. As such, they serve as a particular sort of witness to an event that will certainly undergo many interpretations in the course of history: they are snapshots of thought and feeling from within the experience of 9.11. Those written days after the events as accounts of personal witness are compiled in Section One. They include poetry, narratives, essays and letters, written amidst the immediacy of experience and attesting to the numbing shock felt by the authors and those who surrounded them. (Although Auden's poem in this section was written over half a century before the attacks, it was then a work of immediate witness, and appears highly prescient of the events of 9.11 in image, theme and concern.)

Section Two examines the rhetoric of Terror and Patriotism, looking at the way words and symbols took on a new meaning in the wake of the attacks—bearing witness to the power of rhetoric and the necessity of critical analysis. Here, the reader is invited to take part in the witness process on a level removed from the immediacy of the event: with rhetoric at the forefront, we can examine the terms that were redefined after 9.11, and the ideologies that may have lurked behind them. What are the implications, for instance, of Bush's claim that this is a war of good versus evil? How are these terms to be defined? Does everyone agree on what a terrorist is; what it means to be patriotic? As readers, we can witness the definition of these terms taking place, and from our distanced perspective one, three or ten years after the events, we can look back to these first pieces and see them as historical artifacts.

The articles in Section Three can also be interpreted as artifacts of a time period. The pieces are clearly dated in their concerns and knowledge. For instance, writers arguing for peace before the U.S. began bombing Afghanistan wrote from a perspective that had no idea where a war might lead. They bore the precedents of Vietnam and the Persian Gulf War foremost in their minds. What draws these pieces together is not only their historical significance as witness, however, but also that they begin to interpret witness. These authors have begun the task of making meaning out of the events and accounts of others; in doing so, they have turned witness into a tool. This tool can have clear political implications, as when Vijay Prashad and Arundhati Roy use past accounts of U.S. sponsored violence to argue for peace, or it can be more theoretical as when Slavoj Zizek interprets the hijackings as the dark fulfillment of an American fantasy born in Hollywood, or when Judith Butler critiques the rhetoric and assumptions of both the "left" and "right" in political and academic spheres.

While I believe it is worthwhile to examine the pieces in this chapter in light of these three functions of witness—the personal account, the rhetorical artifact, and the interpretive tool—I don't want to overstate the distinction. Pieces can overlap these somewhat arbitrary boundaries. Ansary's letter, for instance, clearly had intended political implications, as did Kingsolver's essay.

As you read these accounts, then, perhaps the most important thing to keep in mind is your own experience of witness—both to the texts before you and the events of 9.11. How does the information in the texts modify your preconceived notions about the U.S., the flag, the meaning of terror, the clear line between good and evil? Do the accounts in this chapter contradict what you learned while watching coverage of 9.11 on TV? At the most basic level, witness is an act of acquiring knowledge, but we can only witness that which is available to us. For the most part, the pieces in this chapter were far less readily available to the U.S. public than the nightly news. Reading and thinking about them, then, letting them wash through what you've come to know or believe about 9.11 may be the most important thing you can do in response.

As these accounts demonstrate a specific time and sense of being, you should pay attention to the date of publication as you read. Also note the author and original source of publication. Ask yourself, "Where is the author from? With whom is she aligned politically? What source published the work and why might it have done so?" These are all matters of the context surrounding a piece of writing, and they are especially relevant when looking at an event as politically charged as this one.

Additional Resources for Study

Videos (Available in the U of Arizona Library)

9.11

Edward Said On Orientalism

Manufacturing Consent: Noam Chomsky and the Media

Web Sites

Z Magazine Online: *www.zmag.org*

Independent Media Center: *www.indymedia.org*

The Progressive: *www.progressive.org*

Articles

Kingsolver, Barbara. "A Pure, High Note of Anguish." *L.A. Times*. 23 Sept. 2001.

Max, D.T. "The 2,988 Words That Changed A Presidency: An Etymology." *The New York Times Magazine*. 7 Oct. 2001.

Nagy, Thomas. "The Secret Behind the Sanctions." *The Progressive*. 65:9, Sept. 2001.

Said, Edward. "America's Last Taboo." *New Left Review*. 6. Nov–Dec 2000.

Section One

Personal Witness

W. H. Auden

W. H. Auden (1907–1973) was born in England but became a U.S. citizen in 1946. A modernist poet who was a major influence on poetry of the 20th century, he was concerned with moral, social and political issues. He once wrote that "All genuine poetry is in a sense the formation of private spheres out of public chaos." One of his collections of poems, Journey to War, *was concerned with the moral issues humankind was facing as they found themselves on the brink of World War II. In fact, this poem, "September 1, 1939," is one of his most famous. Written on the occasion of the German invasion of Poland, it both witnessed and reflected upon the outbreak of the war.*

September 1, 1939

I sit in one of the dives
On Fifty-second Street
Uncertain and afraid
As the clever hopes expire
Of a low dishonest decade:
Waves of anger and fear
Circulate over the bright

Reprinted from *Another Time*, by W.H. Auden, (1940), Curtis Brown, Ltd. (NY).

And darkened lands of the earth,
Obsessing our private lives;
The unmentionable odour of death
Offends the September night.

Accurate scholarship can
Unearth the whole offence
From Luther until now
That has driven a culture mad,
Find what occurred at Linz,
What huge imago made
A psychopathic god:
I and the public know
What all schoolchildren learn,
Those to whom evil is done
Do evil in return.

Exiled Thucydides knew
All that a speech can say
About Democracy,
And what dictators do,
The elderly rubbish they talk
To an apathetic grave;
Analysed all in his book,
The enlightenment driven away,
The habit-forming pain,
Mismanagement and grief:
We must suffer them all again.

Into this neutral air
Where blind skyscrapers use
Their full height to proclaim
The strength of Collective Man,
Each language pours its vain
Competitive excuse:
But who can live for long
In an euphoric dream;
Out of the mirror they stare,
Imperialism's face
And the international wrong.

Faces along the bar
Cling to their average day:
The lights must never go out,
The music must always play,
All the conventions conspire
To make this fort assume
The furniture of home;
Lest we should see where we are,
Lost in a haunted wood,

Children afraid of the night
Who have never been happy or good.

The windiest militant trash
Important Persons shout
Is not so crude as our wish:
What mad Nijinsky wrote
About Diaghilev
Is true of the normal heart;
For the error bred in the bone
Of each woman and each man
Craves what it cannot have,
Not universal love
But to be loved alone.

From the conservative dark
Into the ethical life
The dense commuters come,
Repeating their morning vow;
'I will be true to the wife,
I'll concentrate more on my work,'
And helpless governors wake
To resume their compulsory game:
Who can release them now,
Who can reach the dead,
Who can speak for the dumb?

All I have is a voice
To undo the folded lie,
The romantic lie in the brain
Of the sensual man-in-the-street
And the lie of Authority
Whose buildings grope the sky:
There is no such thing as the State
And no one exists alone;
Hunger allows no choice
To the citizen or the police;
We must love one another or die.

Defenseless under the night
Our world in stupor lies;
Yet, dotted everywhere,
Ironic points of light
Flash out wherever the Just
Exchange their messages:
May I, composed like them
Of Eros and of dust,
Beleaguered by the same
Negation and despair,
Show an affirming flame.

Talk of the Town

"Talk of the Town" is a regular column in the New Yorker. *While it is usually devoted to a fairly random collection of anecdotes and observations dealing with life in New York City, the 24 September 2001 edition was composed entirely of pieces about 9.11 and its aftermath. Four of the original ten pieces from the column have been included in this selection.*

Hendrik Hertzberg worked as a speechwriter for President Jimmy Carter and served on the White House Staff during the Carter administration. He has been a correspondent for Newsweek, *Editor of* New Republic *and is currently Editorial Director for the* New Yorker.

Aharon Appelfeld is an Israeli writer who escaped from Nazi concentration camps at the age of eight. Eleven of his novels, which tend to deal with the legacy of the holocaust, have been translated into English.

Susan Sontag is a novelist, essayist, and theorist who has written extensively on art and interpretation. Her work had a fundamental role in the activist movements of the 60's and 70's, and she is considered to be one of America's leading intellectuals.

Amitav Ghosh is an Indian novelist who writes regularly for the New Yorker. *He teaches at Queens College in the City University of New York.*

Comment
Tuesday, and After

The catastrophe that turned the foot of Manhattan into the mouth of Hell on the morning of September 11, 2001, unfolded in four paroxysms. At a little before nine, a smoldering scar on the face of the north tower of the World Trade Center (an awful accident, like the collision of a B-25 bomber with the Empire State Building on July 28, 1945?); eighteen minutes later, the orange and gray blossoming of the second explosion, in the south tower; finally, at a minute before ten and then at not quite ten-thirty, the sickening slide of the two towers, collapsing one after the other. For those in the immediate vicinity, the horror was of course immediate and unmistakable; it occurred in what we have learned to call real time, and in real space. For those farther away—whether a few dozen blocks or

Reprinted from the *New Yorker*, September 24, 2001, pp. 27–33, by permission of Conde Nast.

halfway around the world—who were made witnesses by the long lens of television, the events were seen as through a glass, brightly. Their reality was visible but not palpable. It took hours to begin to comprehend their magnitude; it is taking days for the defensive numbness they induced to wear off; it will take months—or years—to measure their impact and meaning.

New York is a city where, however much strangers meet and mix on the streets and in the subways, circles of friends are usually demarcated by work and family. The missing and presumed dead—their number is in the thousands—come primarily from the finance, international trade, and government service workers in the doomed buildings, and from the ranks of firefighters and police officers drawn there by duty and courage. The umbra of personal grief already encompasses scores or even hundreds of thousands of people; a week or two from now, when the word has spread from friend to colleague to relative to acquaintance, the penumbra will cover millions. The city has never suffered a more shocking calamity from any act of God or man.

The calamity, of course, goes well beyond the damage to our city and to its similarly bereaved rival and brother Washington. It is national; it is international; it is civilizational. In the decade since the end of the Cold War, the human race has become, with increasing rapidity, a single organism. Every kind of barrier to the free and rapid movement of goods, information, and people has been lowered. The organism relies increasingly on a kind of trust—the unsentimental expectation that people, individually and collectively, will behave more or less in their rational self-interest. (Even the anti-globalizers of the West mostly embrace the underlying premises of the new dispensation; their demand is for global democratic institutions to mitigate the cruelties of the global market.) The terrorists made use of that trust. They rode the flow of the world's aerial circulatory system like lethal viruses.

With growing ferocity, officials from the President on down have described the bloody deeds as acts of war. But, unless a foreign government turns out to have directed the operation (or, at least, to have known and approved its scope in detail and in advance), that is a category mistake. The metaphor of war—and it is more metaphor than description—ascribes to the perpetrators a dignity they do not merit, a status they cannot claim, and a strength they do not possess. Worse, it points toward a set of responses that could prove futile or counterproductive. Though the death and destruction these acts caused were on the scale of war, the acts themselves were acts of terrorism, albeit on a wholly unprecedented level. From 1983 until last week, according to the *Times,* ten outrages had each claimed the lives of more than a hundred people. The worst—the destruction of an Air-India 747 in 1985—killed three hundred and twenty-nine people; the Oklahoma City bombing, which killed a hundred and sixty-eight, was the seventh worst. Last week's carnage surpassed that of any of these by an order of magnitude. It was also the largest violent taking of life on American soil on any day since the Civil War, including December 7, 1941. And in New York and Washington, unlike at Pearl Harbor, the killed and maimed were overwhelmingly civilians.

The tactics of the terrorists were as brilliant as they were depraved. The nature of those tactics and their success—and there is no use denying that what they did was, on its own terms, successful—points up the weakness of the war metaphor. Authorities estimated last week that "as many as" fifty people may have been involved. The terrorists brought with them nothing but knives and the ability to fly a jumbo jet already in the air. How do you take "massive military action" against the infrastructure of a stateless, compartmentalized "army" of fifty, or ten times fifty, whose weapons are rental cars, credit cards, and airline tickets?

The scale of the damage notwithstanding, a more useful metaphor than war is crime. The terrorists of September 11th are outlaws within a global polity. They may enjoy the corrupt protection of a state (and corruption, like crime, can be ideological or spiritual as well as pecuniary in motive). But they do not constitute or control a state and do not even appear to aspire to control one. Their status and numbers are such that the task of dealing with them should be viewed as a police matter, of the most urgent kind. As with all criminal fugitives, the essential job is to find out who and where they are. The goal of foreign and military policy must be to induce recalcitrant governments to coöperate, a goal whose attainment may or may not entail the use of force but cannot usefully entail making general war on the peoples such governments rule and in some cases (that of Afghanistan, for example) oppress. Just four months ago, at a time when the whole world was aware both of the general intentions of the terrorist Osama bin Laden and of the fact that the Afghan government was harboring him, the United States gave the Taliban a forty-three-million-dollar grant for banning poppy cultivation. The United States understands that on September 11th the line between the permissible and the impermissible shifted. The Taliban must be made to understand that, too.

As for America's friends, they have rallied around us with alacrity. On Wednesday, the NATO allies, for the first time ever, invoked the mutual-defense clause of the alliance's founding treaty, formally declaring that "an armed attack" against one—and what happened on September 11th, whether you call it terrorism or war, was certainly an armed attack—constitutes an attack against all. This gesture of solidarity puts to shame the contempt the Bush Administration has consistently shown for international treaties and instruments, including those in areas relevant to the fight against terrorism, such as small-arms control, criminal justice, and nuclear proliferation. By now, it ought to be clear to even the most committed ideologues of the Bush Administration that the unilateralist approach it was pursuing as of last Tuesday is in urgent need of reëvaluation. The world will be policed collectively or it will not be policed at all.

—*Hendrik Hertzberg*

For almost a year now, Jerusalem has been under siege. Not a day goes by without something terrible happening: a man stabbed in a quiet street, a bomb exploding from a watermelon, a booby-trapped car. Just weeks ago, a suicide bomber blew himself up in the center of town, injuring dozens of innocent people. Shrewd enemies, hidden from sight, are fighting in this city of stone.

Every day, I go to Ticho, my coffee shop, which is in a garden in an old house in the heart of the city. Despite the threat of danger, everyone seems to go out. Often, it seems as if life is able to continue because of the shared illusion that "this won't happen to me." At Ticho, I read a newspaper or a book, or work on a manuscript. In the past, people who recognized me didn't interfere with my privacy. But recently they have stopped to inquire after my health and to ask my opinion of the stressful situation.

I am a writer, not a prophet or a political analyst. Like everyone else, I am groping in this darkness. From a writer, people expect a wise word or a joke. But what can one say when what is happening blunts the few thoughts that one has? I try to overcome the uncertainty by working every day. I am in the middle of a novel, progressing sluggishly, writing and erasing. It seems that the daily disturbances are stronger than internal motivation. It is hard to be with oneself when everything around is burning.

I used to feel that those of us who had suffered in the Holocaust were immune to fear. I was wrong. We are more sensitive to danger. We can smell it. A few days ago, a Holocaust survivor came over to my table and enumerated the dangers ahead of us. During the war, he had been in three death camps. He was a master of dangers. There wasn't a danger that he didn't know in the most minute detail.

The daily disasters evoke images of the Holocaust. Fifty-six years have passed, and the images don't go away. Last night, a man approached me and said that he reads all my books with great diligence. Like me, he was an orphaned child during the war, roaming the forests and taking refuge with farmers. He, too, arrived in Israel. He is an engineer, and he is worried about Jewish destiny. Why do the Jews arouse such hatred? he asked. We had naïvely thought that all the anger and hatred toward us would disappear once we had our own state. I didn't know what to say. I have never dealt in abstract questions—I try to see the world in pictures. And so I kept quiet while he, dismayed, also kept quiet.

After the attack on America, I stayed up all night watching television. It had been a long time since I'd felt such identification, with events that were happening so far away. The next day, when I arrived at Ticho, it occurred to me that all of us here were feeling this blow in our flesh. In modern Jewish mythology, America is the father figure who saved many Jews from the cruel Bolsheviks and Nazis by granting us a home. Now the loving father is united with his sons in a Jerusalem coffee shop, in grief over the evil that refuses to disappear from the world.

—*Aharon Appelfeld*

(Translated, from the Hebrew, by Dina Fein.)

The disconnect between last Tuesday's monstrous dose of reality and the self-righteous drivel and outright deceptions being peddled by public figures and TV commentators is startling, depressing. The voices licensed to follow the event seem to have joined together in a campaign to infantilize the public. Where is the acknowledgment that this was not a "cowardly" attack on "civilization" or "liberty" or "humanity" or "the free world" but an attack on the world's self-proclaimed superpower, undertaken as a consequence of specific American alliances and actions? How many citizens are aware of the ongoing American bombing of Iraq? And if the word "cowardly" is to be used, it might be more aptly applied to those who kill from beyond the range of retaliation, high in the sky, than to those willing to die themselves in order to kill others. In the matter of courage (a morally neutral virtue): whatever may be said of the perpetrators of Tuesday's slaughter, they were not cowards.

Our leaders are bent on convincing us that everything is O.K. America is not afraid. Our spirit is unbroken, although this was a day that will live in infamy and America is now at war. But everything is not O.K. And this was not Pearl Harbor. We have a robotic President who assures us that America still stands tall. A wide spectrum of public figures, in and out of office, who are strongly opposed to the policies being pursued abroad by this Administration apparently feel free to say nothing more than that they stand united behind President Bush. A lot of thinking needs to be done, and perhaps is being done in Washington and elsewhere, about the ineptitude of American intelligence and counter-intelligence, about options available to American foreign policy, particularly in the Middle East, and about what constitutes a smart program of military defense. But the public is not being asked to bear much of the burden of reality. The unanimously applauded, self-congratulatory bromides of a Soviet Party Congress seemed contemptible. The unanimity of the sanctimonious, reality-concealing rhetoric spouted by American officials and media commentators in recent days seems, well, unworthy of a mature democracy.

Those in public office have let us know that they consider their task to be a manipulative one: confidence-building and grief management. Politics, the politics of a democracy—which entails disagreement, which promotes candor—has been replaced by psychotherapy. Let's by all means grieve together. But let's not be stupid together. A few shreds of historical awareness might help us understand what has just happened, and what may continue to happen. "Our country is strong," we are told again and again. I for one don't find this entirely consoling. Who doubts that America is strong? But that's not all America has to be.

—*Susan Sontag*

In 1999, soon after moving to Fort Greene, in Brooklyn, my wife and I were befriended by Frank and Nicole De Martini, two architects. As construction manager of the World Trade Center, Frank worked in an office on the eighty-eighth floor of the north tower. Nicole is an employee of the engineering firm that built the World Trade Center, Leslie E. Robertson Associates. Hired as a "surveillance engineer," she was a member of a team that conducted year-round structural-integrity inspections of the Twin Towers. Her offices were on the thirty-fifth floor of the south tower.

Frank is forty-nine, sturdily built, with wavy salt-and-pepper hair and deeply etched laugh lines around his eyes. His manner is expansively avuncular. The Twin Towers were both a livelihood and a passion for him: he would speak of them with the absorbed fascination with which poets sometimes speak of Dante's canzones. Nicole is forty-two, blond and blue-eyed, with a gaze that is at once brisk and friendly. She was born in Basel, Switzerland, and met Frank while studying design in New York. They have two children—Sabrina, ten, and Dominic, eight. It was through our children that we first met.

Shortly after the basement bomb explosion of 1993, Frank was hired to do bomb-damage assessment at the World Trade Center. An assignment that he thought would last only a few months quickly turned into a consuming passion. "He fell in love with the buildings," Nicole told me. "For him, they represented an incredible human feat. He was awed by their scale and magnitude, by their design, and by the efficiency of the use of materials. One of his most repeated sayings about the towers is that they were built to take the impact of a light airplane."

On Tuesday morning, Frank and Nicole dropped their children off at school, in Brooklyn Heights, and then drove on to the World Trade Center. Traffic was light, and they arrived unexpectedly early, so Nicole decided to go up to Frank's office for a cup of coffee. It was about a quarter past eight when they got upstairs. A half hour later, she stood up to go. She was on her way out when the walls and the floor suddenly heaved under the shock of a massive impact. Through the window, she saw a wave of flame bursting out overhead, like a torrent spewing from the floodgates of a dam. The blast was clearly centered on the floor directly above; she assumed that it was a bomb. Neither she nor Frank was unduly alarmed: few people knew the building's strength and resilience better than they. They assumed that the worst was over and that the structure had absorbed the impact. Sure enough, within seconds of the initial tumult, a sense of calm descended on their floor. Frank herded Nicole and a group of some two dozen other people into a room that was relatively free of smoke. Then he went off to scout the escape routes and stairways. Minutes later, he returned to announce that he had found a stairway that was intact. They could reach it fairly easily, by climbing over a pile of rubble.

The bank of rubble that barred the entrance to the fire escape was almost knee-high. Just as Nicole was about to clamber over, she noticed that Frank was hanging back. She begged him to come with her. He shook his head and told her to go on without him. There were people on their floor who had been hurt by the blast, he said; he would follow her down as soon as he had helped the injured.

Frank must have gone back to his office shortly afterward, because he made a call from his desk at about nine o' clock. He called his sister Nina, on West Ninety-third Street in Manhattan, and said, "Nicole and I are fine. Don't worry."

Nicole remembers the descent as quiet and orderly. The evacuees went down in single file, leaving room for the firemen who were running in the opposite direction. On many floors, there were people to direct the evacuees, and in the lower reaches of the building there was even electricity. The descent took about half an hour, and, on reaching the plaza, Nicole began to walk in the direction of the Brooklyn Bridge. She was within a few hundred feet of the bridge when the first tower collapsed. "It was like the onset of a nuclear winter," she said. "Suddenly, everything went absolutely quiet and you were in the middle of a fog that was as blindingly bright as a snowstorm on a sunny day."

It was early evening by the time Nicole reached Fort Greene. She had received calls from several people who had seen Frank on their way down the fire escape, but he had not been heard from directly. Their children stayed with us that night while Nicole sat up with Frank's sister Nina, waiting by the telephone.

The next morning, Nicole decided that her children had to be told that there was no word of their father. Both she and Nina were calm when they arrived at our door, even though they had not slept all night. Nicole's voice was grave but unwavering as she spoke to her children about what had happened the day before.

The children listened with wide-eyed interest, but soon afterward they went back to their interrupted games. A little later, my son came to me and whispered, "Guess what Dominic's doing?"

"What?" I said, steeling myself.

"He's learning to wiggle his ears."

This was, I realized, how my children—or any children, for that matter—would have responded: turning their attention elsewhere before the news could begin to gain purchase in their minds.

At about noon, we took the children to the park. It was a bright, sunny day, and they were soon absorbed in riding their bicycles. My wife, Deborah, and I sat on a shaded bench and spoke with Nicole. "Frank could easily have got out in the time that passed between the blast and the fall of the building," Nicole said. "The only thing I can think of is that he stayed back to help with the evacuation. Nobody knew the building like he did, and he must have thought he had to."

Nicole paused. "I think it was only because Frank saw me leave that he decided he could stay," she said. "He knew that I would be safe and the kids would be looked after. That was why he felt he could go back to help the others. He loved the towers and had complete faith in them. Whatever happens, I know that what he did was his own choice."

—*Amitav Ghosh*

Sonia Shah

Sonia Shah was born in 1969. She received her B.A. in Philosophy from Oberlin college in 1990. She is an activist and writer whose work on feminism and Asian American issues has appeared in Z Magazine, The Progressive, Ms., In These Times, The Indian American, Nuclear Times, *and* Gay Community News. *She has worked as both editor and publisher at South End Press and has been anthologized in books such as* Listen Up! Voices from the Next Feminist Generation; The State of Asian America: Activism and Resistance in the 1990s; A Patchwork Shawl: Chronicles of South Asian Women in America. *She currently lives in Queensland, Australia. This article gives a witness account of the prejudices and difficulties faced by people of Asian and Arabic appearance in the days after the terrorist attacks, before moving on to critique the use of polls by corporate media. It originally appeared in on the* Z Magazine *web site www.zmag.org a week after the attacks.*

Revenge Comes Home

"What are you looking at, terrorist bitch?"

So said a surly gentleman on a Manhattan-bound subway to my sister, who violated the rules of overcrowded-island etiquette by stealing a glance at him as he discussed the pros and cons of prejudice.

Ordinarily, racist slurs would make her angry. As it was, having just watched stricken people jump from burning towers to their certain deaths, her eyes filled with tears and she hurried off the train.

A few days later, some thugs visited my cousin's convenience store/gas station, demanding "Where are you people from?" and "Why don't you have a flag up?" My cousin rushed out and bought two gigantic flags and installed them prominently on his house and the store.

At least five South Asian or Middle Eastern Americans have been slain so far and dozens of incidents of harassment, intimidation, and terror have been reported, against Arab-Americans, Muslims, Sikhs, Pakistanis, and other South and West Asians, according to the Asian Pacific American Legal Center. In Mesa, Arizona, a Sikh man was shot, the suspect shouting "I stand for America all the way" as he was handcuffed. In Los Angeles, an Egyptian American man was shot; a Persian woman was beaten; a gun was shoved into another woman's face; a Spanish-speaking woman was attacked after being told "you foreigners caused all

Reprinted from Z *Magazine*, ZNet Magazine.

this trouble!"; and another was attacked after being told "America is only for white people." In San Francisco, a bag of blood was thrown on the doorstep of an immigrant-services center. In Chicago, 300 people waving flags and shouting "USA! USA!" tried to march into a mosque; a firebomb was tossed into an Arab-American community center; and a Morrocan man was attacked with a machete. In New York, two Pakistanis were killed on Coney Island, a Sikh man was attacked with a baseball bat; two others attacked with a paint-ball gun; another was fired upon with rubber bullets; a taxi driver was pulled out of his cab and beaten; and a Pakistani woman was chased by a car, whose driver threatened to kill her for "destroying my country." In Cleveland, a Sikh temple was attacked with lit bottles of gasoline. In Tulsa, a Pakistani was beaten by three men. In Dallas, a Pakistani grocer was shot dead; elsewhere in the state shots and firebombs were lobbed at mosques, and a Molotov cocktail was thrown at the Islamic Society building.

There have been others. Most of those who suffer such attacks won't report them. They'll just hide, lay low, wear baseball caps or bindis, as the Indian consul-general advised, and pray they won't be targeted again. As word spreads, their friends and families will do the same. Even my liberal family says I shouldn't take my small boys to the anti-war rallies, because they have brown skin, hair and eyes, and even Muslim names. What if they are targeted? What if someone throws a rock?

Hate crimes hotlines have been set up, and I hope anyone who witnesses or suffers harassment or violence will use them, at least so this wave of violence can be accurately recorded for posterity. For anti-Asian violence organizations, calling these episodes of domestic terror "hate crimes" is tragically understated. For the news media and administration officials, however, it is offensively, dangerously hypocritical. These are not just isolated acts committed by crazed individuals, driven mad by fear and trauma. This wave of violence is a necessary extension of today's warmongering patriotism as defined by our political and media elites.

"There is only one way to begin to deal with people like this," said former Secretary of State Lawrence Eagleburger on CNN, "and that is you have to kill some of them even if they are not immediately directly involved in this thing." "People like this need to feel pain," said National Review editor Rich Lowry in the *Washington Post*. "This is no time to be precious about locating the exact individuals directly involved in this particular terrorist attack," wrote syndicated columnist Ann Coulter in the *New York Daily News*.

In other words, indiscriminate revenge, whether on millions of Afghans or against some random brown person on the subway, is what flag-waving patriots must do. "They" need to be punished, commentators say, whoever "they" may be. On a recent episode of PBS's *Newshour with Jim Lehrer*, even the learned commentators couldn't or wouldn't distinguish between Arabs, Muslims, Afghans (who are not Arabs), fundamentalists, and terrorists. All were just simply "they."

It must be clear to most now. "We" are white. "They" are brown. "They" celebrated—not only in Palestine, as the news media would have us believe, but also in Pakistan, in Nigeria, and elsewhere. This is taken as evidence of their inhumanity. But of course when the jocks in the sports bar in my old neighborhood cheered when Scud missiles hit Iraq years ago, that was good old red-blooded Americanism in action. "They" hate "us" not because of our government's violence and arrogance, but because . . . well, because "we" are so damn great. Because we are so modern, so advanced, so free, and so rich.

How sad to have to say that all of this is nothing compared to the carnage of the plane attacks, and will be entirely insignificant compared to the massive, sustained slaughter of innocent people that Bush is threatening.

Bush's tepid response to the wave of anti-Asian violence at home was to say that the perpetrators should be "ashamed" of themselves. Ashamed? Like how you feel when you steal a cookie from a baby? Like how you feel when you think you might be reproached? Will Bush be "ashamed" when his bombs kill, maim, and further impoverish desperate men, women and children in South and West Asia?

Polls Paint Public Opinion Red

And who is this "we" who hate some unspecified, brown "them" so much and are so willing to forego all the rules and procedures usually insisted upon (for even the most disgusting, murderous American thug) in order to hunt "them" down and kill them . . . whoever "they" are?

A spate of polls paid for and trumpeted by the warmongering news media in the two weeks following the September 11th attacks told us who. They are us.

But these polls asked loaded questions to handfuls of people who by any measure were still in shock. Their "findings" intensified in each re-telling, as reporters referred to them in their articles, columnists referred to the articles, and letter writers referred to the columnists. The sense of widespread blood-thirst calcified into a basic truism rationalizing the rush to war.

Although most news reports on public support for war simply cited "numerous polls" or some such, most referred to the two ongoing, nationally representative polling efforts on this topic—by CBS News/*New York Times* and by Gallup/ CNN/*USA Today*. Both circumscribed and contained people's potential responses to paint a portrait of a vengeful, angry America, one that will support Bush's war in South Asia and not coincidentally, sell a few newspapers too.

Questions aren't neutral. Their timing and wording reveal the questioners' expectations and assumptions. Gallup's and CBS News's crude questions seem designed to gauge the extent of U.S. rage and vengeance and couldn't have captured a complex, nuanced perspective even if they wanted to.

For instance, on the dark evening of the attacks themselves, CBS pollsters called 402 shell-shocked people and asked them the following incendiary questions. "Are these attacks another Pearl Harbor? they wanted to know. "Should the U.S. retaliate even if innocent people are killed?" About 6 in 10 said yes, 2 said no, and 2 said . . . well whatever they said went unrecorded. Then the interviewers went on to goad people into apportioning blame—at least toward the two immediate culprits they could think of. "Should U.S. intelligence have known about the attacks?" they asked. "Could the attacks have been prevented by tighter airport security?"

And then, click, interview over. The "findings"—two-thirds of Americans want retaliation even if innocents are killed, as they put it—were trumpeted eagerly. "America Wants Retaliation" their headline proclaimed.

The next day, our intrepid pollsters bothered another 638 people. Do you feel bad? Do you feel angry? Horrified? Or shocked? pollsters asked. Assuming each respondent picked just one answer (a big assumption, unilluminated by CBS's poll website), about 80 percent felt one of those ways.

So how did the other 20 percent feel? Nobody asked. (How about scared? How about sad? That's how I felt.)

About 25 percent said they were angry, and despite the fact that pollsters had no idea how many people would have said they were angry the previous day (it's within the realm of possibility that some portion of Americans are always angry)—CBS announced that "Americans are no longer shocked, they're angry." Seventy-one percent wanted retaliation, they found.

Over the next two days—Thursday September 13 and Friday September 14—our pollsters again took to the phones. They demanded answers from 959 people. They asked essentially the same questions, except this time they added a new one.

"Are Arab Americans more sympathetic to terrorists?" they wanted to know.

Twenty-seven percent said yes, CBS noted ominously.

(But this is a meaningless question, by itself. Which terrorists? Irish ones? Sympathetic how? Like they know how to pronounce their names? Like they know where they are coming from? Like they'd give them loads of cash and their passport? What?)

The Gallup Organization, "one of the world's leading management consulting firms" according to their website, in partnership with *USA Today* and CNN have also been conducting ongoing much-cited national polling. They asked much the same questions that CBS did, with much the same results, but they also wanted to know how many people attended memorial services, cried, displayed a flag, or prayed in response to the attacks.

How many wrote letters to their editors? How many gave flowers to their Muslim neighbors? How many attended peace rallies? Gallup won't say. The unasked goes unanswered.

Since my whole argument here is that these polls are worse than useless, it may not be fair to note one underreported finding. When asked whether the U.S. should act immediately against known terrorists or only against those responsible, over sixty percent said that only the proven perpetrators should be targeted.

Doesn't that just blow all the other findings about wanting war, indiscriminate revenge, and all the rest of it out of the water?

Gallup's and CBS News' numbers frighten me. But I'm going to try not to make much of them either way. As a statistician friend of mine who used to work at Harris Polls says, "polling companies burn through hundreds if not thousands of phone numbers to get the sample sizes they need. But there is probably good reason to think people who refuse to participate, who aren't home, who don't answer the phone, who don't have phones would respond quite differently from those people who do participate."

"In other words the samples are not truly representative of the American public," he says.

That's good to hear.

Tamim Ansary

Ansary, a writer who came to the United States from Afghanistan in 1966, wrote this letter to his friend Gary within days of the bombing of the World Trade Center and the Pentagon. His friend then forwarded it to his friends; soon the letter had been informally "published" through e-mail before it was picked up by Salon, *an on-line news magazine. In some ways this piece is both witness—informing Americans, who knew little about the Taliban at the time, about the oppressive conditions in Afghanistan—and an argument about how the U.S. should respond. As you read it, you might note features of the letter that made it so compelling that readers immediately forwarded it to one another.*

From an Afghani-American September 14, 2001

I've been hearing a lot of talk about "bombing Afghanistan back to the Stone Age." Ronn Owens, on KGO Talk Radio today, allowed that this would mean killing innocent people, people who had nothing to do with this atrocity, but "we're at war, we have to accept collateral damage. What else can we do?" Minutes later I heard some TV pundit discussing whether we "have the belly to do what must be done."

And I thought about the issues being raised especially hard because I am from Afghanistan, and even though I've lived here for 35 years I've never lost track of what's going on there. So I want to tell anyone who will listen how it all looks from where I'm standing.

I speak as one who hates the Taliban and Osama bin Laden. There is no doubt in my mind that these people were responsible for the atrocity in New York. I agree that something must be done about those monsters.

But the Taliban and bin Laden are not Afghanistan. They're not even the government of Afghanistan. The Taliban are a cult of ignorant psychotics who took over Afghanistan in 1997. Bin Laden is a political criminal with a plan. When you think Taliban, think Nazis. When you think bin Laden, think Hitler. And when you think "the people of Afghanistan" think "the Jews in the concentration camps." It's not only that the Afghan people had nothing to do with this atrocity. They were the first victims of the perpetrators. They would exult if someone would come in there, take out the Taliban and clear out the rats nest of international thugs holed up in their country.

Reprinted from *Salon.com*, September 14, 2001, by permission of the publisher.

Some say, why don't the Afghans rise up and overthrow the Taliban?

The answer is, they're starved, exhausted, hurt, incapacitated, suffering.

A few years ago, the United Nations estimated that there are 500,000 disabled orphans in Afghanistan—a country with no economy, no food. There are millions of widows. And the Taliban has been burying these widows alive in mass graves. The soil is littered with land mines, the farms were all destroyed by the Soviets. These are a few of the reasons why the Afghan people have not overthrown the Taliban.

We come now to the question of bombing Afghanistan back to the Stone Age. Trouble is, that's been done. The Soviets took care of it already. Make the Afghans suffer? They're already suffering. Level their houses? Done. Turn their schools into piles of rubble? Done. Eradicate their hospitals? Done. Destroy their infrastructure? Cut them off from medicine and health care? Too late. Someone already did all that.

New bombs would only stir the rubble of earlier bombs. Would they at least get the Taliban? Not likely. In today's Afghanistan, only the Taliban eat, only they have the means to move around. They'd slip away and hide. Maybe the bombs would get some of those disabled orphans, they don't move too fast, they don't even have wheelchairs. But flying over Kabul and dropping bombs wouldn't really be a strike against the criminals who did this horrific thing. Actually it would only be making common cause with the Taliban—by raping once again the people they've been raping all this time.

So what else is there? What can be done, then? Let me now speak with true fear and trembling. The only way to get bin Laden is to go in there with ground troops. When people speak of "having the belly to do what needs to be done" they're thinking in terms of having the belly to kill as many as needed. Having the belly to overcome any moral qualms about killing innocent people. Let's pull our heads out of the sand.

What's actually on the table is Americans dying. And not just because some Americans would die fighting their way through Afghanistan to bin Laden's hideout. It's much bigger than that folks. Because to get any troops to Afghanistan, we'd have to go through Pakistan. Would they let us? Not likely. The conquest of Pakistan would have to be first.

Will other Muslim nations just stand by? You see where I'm going. We're flirting with a world war between Islam and the West. And guess what: that's bin Laden's program. That's exactly what he wants. That's why he did this. Read his speeches and statements. It's all right there. He really believes Islam would beat the West. It might seem ridiculous, but he figures if he can polarize the world into Islam and the West, he's got a billion soldiers. If the West wreaks a holocaust in those lands, that's a billion people with nothing left to lose, that's even better from bin Laden's point of view. He's probably wrong, in the end the West would win, whatever that would mean, but the war would last for years and millions would die, not just theirs but ours. Who has the belly for that?

Bin Laden does. Anyone else?

Section Two

Rhetoric of Terror and Patriotism

George W. Bush

When George W. Bush delivered this "Address of the president to the joint Session of Congress" on September 20, 2001, he was interrupted for applause 31 times and, afterwards, the consensus in the media seemed to be that the speech had redefined his presidency. "Pundits wrote that the president had said just the right thing in a time of crisis" (Max 9). Ted Kennedy remarked that "The speech was exactly what the nation needed—a message of determination and hope, strength and compassion" (9). When you read it, you might annotate for phrases that would make the speech so successful with an American audience. For instance, some phrases, like the sound bite "freedom versus fear," were distributed to the press before he gave the speech because his communications team could anticipate that such a phrase would appeal to our values (9).

Like many presidents and politicians, however, Bush does not write his own speeches. For this speech, a team of six writers, led by Michael Gerson, consulted with Condoleeza Rice, the national security advisor, and President Bush as well as others, in order to write it. Rice pointed out that he had to speak to "multiple audiences. . . .the American people, foreign leaders, to the Congress, and to the Taliban" (2). Another challenge was writing a speech that fit Bush's persona. Earlier in the week, he had been quoted as saying things that seemed rash, calling the coming battle a "crusade" and calling for "revenge" by remarking that the U.S. wanted bin Laden "dead or alive" (1). On the other hand, at the National Cathedral, he had delivered a meditation, also written by Gerson, that began, "We are in the middle hour of our grief," which was a marked contrast from his extemporaneous remarks (1). As you read the speech, you might note the ways that the writers tried to keep the tone within a conversational range, neither too eloquent, nor too informal. What parts of the speech seem calculated to appeal to the various audiences that Rice listed? If you would like to do further research on the background of the speech, you might want to read the article cited in this head note, "The 2,988 Words that Changed a Presidency: An Etymology" by D.T. Max, which was published in the New York Times *on October 7, 2001.*

Address to a Joint Session of Congress and the American People

United States Capitol
Washington, D.C.
9:00 P.M. EDT

THE PRESIDENT:

Mr. Speaker, Mr. President Pro Tempore, members of Congress, and fellow Americans:

In the normal course of events, Presidents come to this chamber to report on the state of the Union. Tonight, no such report is needed. It has already been delivered by the American people.

We have seen it in the courage of passengers, who rushed terrorists to save others on the ground—passengers like an exceptional man named Todd Beamer. And would you please help me to welcome his wife, Lisa Beamer, here tonight. (Applause.)

We have seen the state of our Union in the endurance of rescuers, working past exhaustion. We have seen the unfurling of flags, the lighting of candles, the giving of blood, the saying of prayers—in English, Hebrew, and Arabic. We have seen the decency of a loving and giving people who have made the grief of strangers their own.

My fellow citizens, for the last nine days, the entire world has seen for itself the state of our Union—and it is strong. (Applause.)

Tonight we are a country awakened to danger and called to defend freedom. Our grief has turned to anger, and anger to resolution. Whether we bring our enemies to justice, or bring justice to our enemies, justice will be done. (Applause.)

I thank the Congress for its leadership at such an important time. All of America was touched on the evening of the tragedy to see Republicans and Democrats joined together on the steps of this Capitol, singing "God Bless America." And you did more than sing; you acted, by delivering $40 billion to rebuild our communities and meet the needs of our military.

Speaker Hastert, Minority Leader Gephardt, Majority Leader Daschle and Senator Lott, I thank you for your friendship, for your leadership and for your service to our country. (Applause.)

And on behalf of the American people, I thank the world for its outpouring of support. America will never forget the sounds of our National Anthem playing at Buckingham Palace, on the streets of Paris, and at Berlin's Brandenburg Gate.

We will not forget South Korean children gathering to pray outside our embassy in Seoul, or the prayers of sympathy offered at a mosque in Cairo. We will not forget moments of silence and days of mourning in Australia and Africa and Latin America.

Nor will we forget the citizens of 80 other nations who died with our own: dozens of Pakistanis; more than 130 Israelis; more than 250 citizens of India; men and women from El Salvador, Iran, Mexico and Japan; and hundreds of British citizens. America has no truer friend than Great Britain. (Applause.) Once again, we are joined together in a great cause—so honored the British Prime Minister has crossed an ocean to show his unity of purpose with America. Thank you for coming, friend. (Applause.)

On September the 11th, enemies of freedom committed an act of war against our country. Americans have known wars—but for the past 136 years, they have been wars on foreign soil, except for one Sunday in 1941. Americans have known the casualties of war—but not at the center of a great city on a peaceful morning. Americans have known surprise attacks—but never before on thousands of civilians. All of this was brought upon us in a single day—and night fell on a different world, a world where freedom itself is under attack.

Americans have many questions tonight. Americans are asking: Who attacked our country? The evidence we have gathered all points to a collection of loosely affiliated terrorist organizations known as al Qaeda. They are the same murderers indicted for bombing American embassies in Tanzania and Kenya, and responsible for bombing the USS Cole.

Al Qaeda is to terror what the mafia is to crime. But its goal is not making money; its goal is remaking the world—and imposing its radical beliefs on people everywhere.

The terrorists practice a fringe form of Islamic extremism that has been rejected by Muslim scholars and the vast majority of Muslim clerics—a fringe movement that perverts the peaceful teachings of Islam. The terrorists' directive commands them to kill Christians and Jews, to kill all Americans, and make no distinction among military and civilians, including women and children.

This group and its leader—a person named Osama bin Laden—are linked to many other organizations in different countries, including the Egyptian Islamic Jihad and the Islamic Movement of Uzbekistan. There are thousands of these terrorists in more than 60 countries. They are recruited from their own nations and neighborhoods and brought to camps in places like Afghanistan, where they are trained in the tactics of terror. They are sent back to their homes or sent to hide in countries around the world to plot evil and destruction.

The leadership of al Qaeda has great influence in Afghanistan and supports the Taliban regime in controlling most of that country. In Afghanistan, we see al Qaeda's vision for the world.

Afghanistan's people have been brutalized—many are starving and many have fled. Women are not allowed to attend school. You can be jailed for owning a television. Religion can be practiced only as their leaders dictate. A man can be jailed in Afghanistan if his beard is not long enough.

The United States respects the people of Afghanistan—after all, we are currently its largest source of humanitarian aid—but we condemn the Taliban regime. (Applause.) It is not only repressing its own people, it is threatening people everywhere by sponsoring and sheltering and supplying terrorists. By aiding and abetting murder, the Taliban regime is committing murder.

And tonight, the United States of America makes the following demands on the Taliban: Deliver to United States authorities all the leaders of al Qaeda who hide in your land. (Applause.) Release all foreign nationals, including American citizens, you have unjustly imprisoned. Protect foreign journalists, diplomats and aid workers in your country. Close immediately and permanently every terrorist training camp in Afghanistan, and hand over every terrorist, and every person in their support structure, to appropriate authorities. (Applause.) Give the United States full access to terrorist training camps, so we can make sure they are no longer operating.

These demands are not open to negotiation or discussion. (Applause.) The Taliban must act, and act immediately. They will hand over the terrorists, or they will share in their fate.

I also want to speak tonight directly to Muslims throughout the world. We respect your faith. It's practiced freely by many millions of Americans, and by millions more in countries that America counts as friends. Its teachings are good and peaceful, and those who commit evil in the name of Allah blaspheme the name of Allah. (Applause.) The terrorists are traitors to their own faith, trying, in effect, to hijack Islam itself. The enemy of America is not our many Muslim friends; it is not our many Arab friends. Our enemy is a radical network of terrorists, and every government that supports them. (Applause.)

Our war on terror begins with al Qaeda, but it does not end there. It will not end until every terrorist group of global reach has been found, stopped and defeated. (Applause.)

Americans are asking, why do they hate us? They hate what we see right here in this chamber—a democratically elected government. Their leaders are self-appointed. They hate our freedoms—our freedom of religion, our freedom of speech, our freedom to vote and assemble and disagree with each other.

They want to overthrow existing governments in many Muslim countries, such as Egypt, Saudi Arabia, and Jordan. They want to drive Israel out of the Middle East. They want to drive Christians and Jews out of vast regions of Asia and Africa.

These terrorists kill not merely to end lives, but to disrupt and end a way of life. With every atrocity, they hope that America grows fearful, retreating from the world and forsaking our friends. They stand against us, because we stand in their way.

We are not deceived by their pretenses to piety. We have seen their kind before. They are the heirs of all the murderous ideologies of the 20th century. By sacrificing human life to serve their radical visions—by abandoning every value except the will to power—they follow in the path of fascism, and Nazism, and totalitarianism. And they will follow that path all the way, to where it ends: in history's unmarked grave of discarded lies. (Applause.)

Americans are asking: How will we fight and win this war? We will direct every resource at our command—every means of diplomacy, every tool of intelligence, every instrument of law enforcement, every financial influence, and every necessary weapon of war—to the disruption and to the defeat of the global terror network.

This war will not be like the war against Iraq a decade ago, with a decisive liberation of territory and a swift conclusion. It will not look like the air war above Kosovo two years ago, where no ground troops were used and not a single American was lost in combat.

Our response involves far more than instant retaliation and isolated strikes. Americans should not expect one battle, but a lengthy campaign, unlike any other we have ever seen. It may include dramatic strikes, visible on TV, and covert operations, secret even in success. We will starve terrorists of funding, turn them one against another, drive them from place to place, until there is no refuge or no rest. And we will pursue nations that provide aid or safe haven to terrorism. Every nation, in every region, now has a decision to make. Either you are with us, or you are with the terrorists. (Applause.) From this day forward, any nation that continues to harbor or support terrorism will be regarded by the United States as a hostile regime.

Our nation has been put on notice: We are not immune from attack. We will take defensive measures against terrorism to protect Americans. Today, dozens of federal departments and agencies, as well as state and local governments, have responsibilities affecting homeland security. These efforts must be coordinated at the highest level. So tonight I announce the creation of a Cabinet-level position reporting directly to me—the Office of Homeland Security.

And tonight I also announce a distinguished American to lead this effort, to strengthen American security: a military veteran, an effective governor, a true patriot, a trusted friend—Pennsylvania's Tom Ridge. (Applause.) He will lead, oversee and coordinate a comprehensive national strategy to safeguard our country against terrorism, and respond to any attacks that may come.

These measures are essential. But the only way to defeat terrorism as a threat to our way of life is to stop it, eliminate it, and destroy it where it grows. (Applause.)

Many will be involved in this effort, from FBI agents to intelligence operatives to the reservists we have called to active duty. All deserve our thanks, and all have our prayers. And tonight, a few miles from the damaged Pentagon, I have a message for our military: Be ready. I've called the Armed Forces to alert, and there is a reason. The hour is coming when America will act, and you will make us proud. (Applause.)

This is not, however, just America's fight. And what is at stake is not just America's freedom. This is the world's fight. This is civilization's fight. This is the fight of all who believe in progress and pluralism, tolerance and freedom.

We ask every nation to join us. We will ask, and we will need, the help of police forces, intelligence services, and banking systems around the world. The United States is grateful that many nations and many international organizations have already responded—with sympathy and with support. Nations from Latin America, to Asia, to Africa, to Europe, to the Islamic world. Perhaps the NATO Charter reflects best the attitude of the world: An attack on one is an attack on all.

The civilized world is rallying to America's side. They understand that if this terror goes unpunished, their own cities, their own citizens may be next. Terror, unanswered, can not only bring down buildings, it can threaten the stability of legitimate governments. And you know what—we're not going to allow it. (Applause.)

Americans are asking: What is expected of us? I ask you to live your lives, and hug your children. I know many citizens have fears tonight, and I ask you to be calm and resolute, even in the face of a continuing threat.

I ask you to uphold the values of America, and remember why so many have come here. We are in a fight for our principles, and our first responsibility is to live by them. No one should be singled out for unfair treatment or unkind words because of their ethnic background or religious faith. (Applause.)

I ask you to continue to support the victims of this tragedy with your contributions. Those who want to give can go to a central source of information, libertyunites.org, to find the names of groups providing direct help in New York, Pennsylvania, and Virginia.

The thousands of FBI agents who are now at work in this investigation may need your cooperation, and I ask you to give it.

I ask for your patience, with the delays and inconveniences that may accompany tighter security; and for your patience in what will be a long struggle.

I ask your continued participation and confidence in the American economy. Terrorists attacked a symbol of American prosperity. They did not touch its source. America is successful because of the hard work, and creativity, and enterprise of our people. These were the true strengths of our economy before September 11th, and they are our strengths today. (Applause.)

And, finally, please continue praying for the victims of terror and their families, for those in uniform, and for our great country. Prayer has comforted us in sorrow, and will help strengthen us for the journey ahead.

Tonight I thank my fellow Americans for what you have already done and for what you will do. And ladies and gentlemen of the Congress, I thank you, their representatives, for what you have already done and for what we will do together.

Tonight, we face new and sudden national challenges. We will come together to improve air safety, to dramatically expand the number of air marshals on domestic flights, and take new measures to prevent hijacking. We will come together to promote stability and keep our airlines flying, with direct assistance during this emergency. (Applause.)

We will come together to give law enforcement the additional tools it needs to track down terror here at home. (Applause.) We will come together to strengthen our intelligence capabilities to know the plans of terrorists before they act, and find them before they strike. (Applause.)

We will come together to take active steps that strengthen America's economy, and put our people back to work.

Tonight we welcome two leaders who embody the extraordinary spirit of all New Yorkers: Governor George Pataki, and Mayor Rudolph Giuliani. (Applause.) As a symbol of America's resolve, my administration will work with Congress, and these two leaders, to show the world that we will rebuild New York City. (Applause.)

After all that has just passed—all the lives taken, and all the possibilities and hopes that died with them—it is natural to wonder if America's future is one of fear. Some speak of an age of terror. I know there are struggles ahead, and dangers to face. But this country will define our times, not be defined by them. As long as the United States of America is determined and strong, this will not be an age of terror; this will be an age of liberty, here and across the world. (Applause.)

Great harm has been done to us. We have suffered great loss. And in our grief and anger we have found our mission and our moment. Freedom and fear are at war. The advance of human freedom—the great achievement of our time, and the great hope of every time—now depends on us. Our nation—this generation—will lift a dark threat of violence from our people and our future. We will rally the world to this cause by our efforts, by our courage. We will not tire, we will not falter, and we will not fail. (Applause.)

It is my hope that in the months and years ahead, life will return almost to normal. We'll go back to our lives and routines, and that is good. Even grief recedes with time and grace. But our resolve must not pass. Each of us will remember what happened that day, and to whom it happened. We'll remember the moment the news came—where we were and what we were doing. Some will remember an image of a fire, or a story of rescue. Some will carry memories of a face and a voice gone forever.

And I will carry this: It is the police shield of a man named George Howard, who died at the World Trade Center trying to save others. It was given to me by his mom, Arlene, as a proud memorial to her son. This is my reminder of lives that ended, and a task that does not end. (Applause.)

I will not forget this wound to our country or those who inflicted it. I will not yield; I will not rest; I will not relent in waging this struggle for freedom and security for the American people.

The course of this conflict is not known, yet its outcome is certain. Freedom and fear, justice and cruelty, have always been at war, and we know that God is not neutral between them. (Applause.)

Fellow citizens, we'll meet violence with patient justice—assured of the rightness of our cause, and confident of the victories to come. In all that lies before us, may God grant us wisdom, and may He watch over the United States of America.

Thank you. (Applause.)

END 9:41 P.M. EDT

Noam Chomsky

Noam Chomsky was born in Philadelphia, Pennsylvania in 1928. His father, a Hebrew scholar, passed an interest in linguistics onto Noam, who received his Ph.D. in that field from the University of Pennsylvania in 1955. He is famous for his work on generative grammar as well as his political activism and leanings towards socialism and anarchism. He was an outspoken critic of U.S. involvement in Vietnam, and has continued to critique U.S. foreign and domestic policy on many levels. He is the author of numerous books including 9–11, Manufacturing Consent: The Political Economy of the Mass Media *(with Edward S. Herman),* Propaganda and the Public Mind *(with David Barsamian),* Generative Grammar: Its Basis, Development and Prospects, Knowledge of Language: Its Nature, Origin, and Use. *He currently teaches linguistics at MIT and lectures throughout the world. This excerpt from a composite interview of Chomsky's responses to questions after 9–11, originally appeared on the web site www.zmag.org. It examines the way terror is defined based on who is speaking.*

Chomsky Interview 5

1. Do you condemn terrorism? How can we decide which act is terrorism and which one is an act of resistance of a desperate nation against a tyrant or an occupying force? In which of the previous categories do you "classify" the recent strike against USA?

I understand the term "terrorism" exactly in the sense defined in official U.S. documents: "the calculated use of violence or threat of violence to attain goals that are political, religious, or ideological in nature. This is done through intimidation, coercion, or instilling fear."

In accord with this—entirely appropriate—definition, the recent attack on the U.S. is certainly an act of terrorism, in fact, a horrifying terrorist crime. There is scarcely any disagreement about this throughout the world, nor should there be.

But alongside the literal meaning of the term, as just quoted from U.S. official documents, there is also a propagandistic usage, which unfortunately is the standard one: the term "terrorism" is used to refer to terrorist acts committed by enemies against us or our allies. Political scientist Michael Stohl is quite correct when he writes that "we must recognize that by convention—and it must be emphasized

---

Reprinted from Z *Magazine*, ZNet Magazine.

only by convention—great power use and the threat of the use of force is normally described as coercive diplomacy and not as a form of terrorism," though it commonly involves "the threat and often the use of violence for what would be described as terroristic purposes were it not great powers who were pursuing the very same tactic."

This propagandistic use is virtually universal. Everyone "condemns terrorism," in this sense of the term. The Nazis harshly condemned terrorism, and carried out counter-terrorism against the terrorist partisans—in Greece, for example. The U.S. basically agreed. It organized and conducted similar "counter-terrorism" in Greece and elsewhere in the postwar years. Furthermore, U.S. counterinsurgency programs drew quite explicitly from the Nazi model, which was treated with respect: Wehrmacht officers were consulted and their manuals were used in designing postwar counterinsurgency programs worldwide, typically called "counter-terrorism."

Given these conventions, even the very same people and actions can quickly shift from "terrorists" to "freedom fighters" and back again. That's been happening right next door to Greece in recent years. The KLA-UCK were officially condemned by the U.S. as "terrorists" in 1998, because of their attacks on Serb police and civilians in an effort to elicit a disproportionate and brutal Serbian response, as they openly declared. As late as January 1999, the British—the most hawkish element in NATO on this matter—believed that the KLA-UCK was responsible for more deaths than Serbia, which is hard to believe, but at least tells us something about perceptions at high levels in NATO. If one can trust the voluminous documentation provided by the state department, NATO, the OSCE, and other western sources, nothing materially changed on the ground until the withdrawal of the K.V.M. monitors and the bombing in late March 1999. But policies did change: the U.S. and U.K. decided to launch an attack on Serbia, and the "terrorists" instantly became "freedom fighters." After the war, they became "terrorists," "thugs," and "murderers" as they carried out similar actions in Macedonia, a U.S. ally. Everyone condemns terrorism, but we have to ask what they mean. You can find the answer to your question about my views in many books and articles that I have written about terrorism in the past several decades, though I use the term in the literal sense, and hence condemn all terrorist actions, not only those that are called "terrorist" for propagandistic reasons.

It should be unnecessary to point out that massive terrorism is a standard device of powerful states, just as Stohl observes. Some cases are not even controversial. Take the U.S. war against Nicaragua, leaving tens of thousands dead and the country in ruins. Nicaragua appealed to the world court, which condemned the U.S. for international terrorism ("the unlawful use of force"), ordering it to desist and pay substantial reparations. The U.S. responded to the court ruling by sharply escalating the war, and vetoing a security council resolution calling on all states to observe international law. The escalation included official orders to attack "soft targets"—undefended civilian targets, like agricultural collectives and health clinics—and to avoid the Nicaraguan army. The terrorists were able to carry out these instructions, thanks to the complete control of Nicaraguan air space by the U.S. and the advanced communications equipment provided to them by their supervisors. It should also be recognized that these terrorist actions were widely approved. One prominent commentator, Michael Kinsley, at the liberal extreme of the mainstream, argued that we should not simply dismiss state department justifications for terrorist attacks on "soft targets": a "sensible policy" must "meet the test of cost-benefit analysis," an analysis of "the amount of blood and misery that will be poured in, and the likelihood that democracy will emerge at the other end"—"democracy" as the U.S. understands the term, an interpretation illustrated quite clearly in the region. It is taken for granted that U.S. elites have the right to conduct the analysis and pursue the project if it passes their tests. When the terrorist project succeeded, and Nicaragua succumbed, Americans were "united in joy," the *New York Times* proclaimed, knowing full well how the goal was achieved. As *Time* magazine put it joyfully, the methods were to "wreck the economy and prosecute a long and deadly proxy war until the exhausted natives overthrow the unwanted government themselves," with a cost to us that is "minimal," leaving the victim "with wrecked bridges, sabotaged power stations, and ruined farms," and thus providing the U.S. candidate with "a winning issue": ending the "impoverishment of the people of Nicaragua." Euphoria over the achievement was unconstrained among elites.

But the U.S. terrorist war was not "terrorism," it was "counter-terrorism" by doctrinal standards. And U.S. standards prevail in much of the world, as a result of U.S. power and the cost of defying it.

This is by no means the most extreme example; I mention it because it is uncontroversial, given the world court decision, and because the failed efforts of Nicaragua to pursue lawful means, instead of setting off bombs in Washington, provide a model for today, not the only one.

Barbara Kingsolver

Barbara Kingsolver, a Tucson writer who is best known for her novels such as Bean Trees *and* The Poisonwood Bible, *began her career by working as a technical writer for the office of Arid Land Studies at the University of Arizona and as a freelance journalist.*

She is also a political activist, interested in both environmental and human rights issues, and has established the Bellwether Prize for fiction that promotes awareness of social and political issues. Her editorial, "And Our Flag Was Still There" was written in response to the "human flag" that Tucsonans created to express their solidarity just after September 11. This article, which was first published in the San Francisco Chronicle *on September 25, 2001, generated a great deal of controversy across the nation. She responded to angry charges of anti-Americanism in a further article that appeared in the* Tucson Weekly *of January 10th, 2001.*

And Our Flag Was Still There

My daughter came home from kindergarten and announced, "Tomorrow we all have to wear red, white and blue."

"Why?" I asked, trying not to sound wary.

"For all the people that died when the airplanes hit the buildings."

I fear the sound of saber-rattling, dread that not just my taxes but even my children are being dragged to the cause of death in the wake of death. I asked quietly, "Why not wear black, then? Why the colors of the flag, what does that mean?"

"It means we're a country. Just all people together."

So we sent her to school in red, white and blue, because it felt to her like something she could do to help people who are hurting. And because my wise husband put a hand on my arm and said, "You can't let hateful people steal the flag from us."

He didn't mean terrorists, he meant Americans. Like the man in a city near us who went on a rampage crying "I'm an American" as he shot at foreign-born neighbors, killing a gentle Sikh man in a turban and terrifying every brown-skinned person I know. Or the talk-radio hosts, who are viciously bullying a handful of members of Congress for airing sensible skepticism at a time when the White House was announcing preposterous things in apparent self-interest, such as the "revelation" that terrorists had aimed to hunt down Air Force One with a hijacked commercial plane. Rep. Barbara Lee cast the House's only vote against

---

Reprinted from the *San Francisco Chronicle*, September 25, 2001, HarperCollins.

handing over virtually unlimited war powers to one man that a whole lot of us didn't vote for. As a consequence, so many red-blooded Americans have now threatened to kill her, she has to have additional bodyguards.

Patriotism seems to be falling to whoever claims it loudest, and we're left struggling to find a definition in a clamor of reaction. This is what I'm hearing: Patriotism opposes the lone representative of democracy who was brave enough to vote her conscience instead of following an angry mob. (Several others have confessed they wanted to vote the same way, but chickened out.) Patriotism threatens free speech with death. It is infuriated by thoughtful hesitation, constructive criticism of our leaders and pleas for peace. It despises people of foreign birth who've spent years learning our culture and contributing their talents to our economy. It has specifically blamed homosexuals, feminists and the American Civil Liberties Union. In other words, the American flag stands for intimidation, censorship, violence, bigotry, sexism, homophobia, and shoving the Constitution through a paper shredder? Who are we calling terrorists here? Outsiders can destroy airplanes and buildings, but it is only we, the people, who have the power to demolish our own ideals.

It's a fact of our culture that the loudest mouths get the most airplay, and the loudmouths are saying now that in times of crisis it is treasonous to question our leaders. Nonsense. That kind of thinking let fascism grow out of the international depression of the 1930s. In critical times, our leaders need most to be influenced by the moderating force of dissent. That is the basis of democracy, in sickness and in health, and especially when national choices are difficult, and bear grave consequences.

It occurs to me that my patriotic duty is to recapture my flag from the men now waving it in the name of jingoism and censorship. This isn't easy for me.

The last time I looked at a flag with unambiguous pride, I was 13. Right after that, Vietnam began teaching me lessons in ambiguity, and the lessons have kept coming. I've learned of things my government has done to the world that made me direly ashamed. I've been further alienated from my flag by people who waved it at me declaring I should love it or leave it. I search my soul and find I cannot love killing for any reason. When I look at the flag, I see it illuminated by the rocket's red glare.

This is why the warmongers so easily gain the upper hand in the patriot game: Our nation was established with a fight for independence, so our iconography grew out of war. Our national anthem celebrates it; our language of patriotism is inseparable from a battle cry. Our every military campaign is still launched with phrases about men dying for the freedoms we hold dear, even when this is impossible to square with reality. In the Persian Gulf War we rushed to the aid of Kuwait, a monarchy in which women enjoyed approximately the same rights as a 19th century American slave. The values we fought for and won there are best understood, I think, by oil companies. Meanwhile, a country of civilians was devastated, and remains destroyed.

Stating these realities does not violate the principles of liberty, equality, and freedom of speech; it exercises them, and by exercise we grow stronger. I would like to stand up for my flag and wave it over a few things I believe in, including but not limited to the protection of dissenting points of view. After 225 years, I vote to retire the rocket's red glare and the bullet wound as obsolete symbols of Old Glory. We desperately need a new iconography of patriotism. I propose we rip stripes of cloth from the uniforms of public servants who rescued the injured and panic-stricken, remaining at their post until it fell down on them. The red glare of candles held in vigils everywhere as peace-loving people pray for the bereaved, and plead for compassion and restraint. The blood donated to the Red Cross. The stars of film and theater and music who are using their influence to raise money for recovery. The small hands of schoolchildren collecting pennies, toothpaste, teddy bears, anything they think might help the kids who've lost their moms and dads.

My town, Tucson, Ariz., has become famous for a simple gesture in which some 8,000 people wearing red, white or blue T-shirts assembled themselves in the shape of a flag on a baseball field and had their photograph taken from above. That picture has begun to turn up everywhere, but we saw it first on our newspaper's front page. Our family stood in silence for a minute looking at that photo of a human flag, trying to know what to make of it. Then my teenage daughter, who has a quick mind for numbers and a sensitive heart, did an interesting thing. She laid her hand over a quarter of the picture, leaving visible more or less 6,000 people, and said, "That many are dead." We stared at what that looked like—all those innocent souls, multi-colored and packed into a conjoined destiny—and shuddered at the one simple truth behind all the noise, which is that so many beloved people have suddenly gone from us. That is my flag, and that's what it means: We're all just people together.

Robert Jensen

Robert Jensen was born in 1958 in Devil's Lake, North Dakota. He is Professor in the School of Journalism at the University of Texas at Austin. He holds a Ph.D. in media law and ethics from the University of Minnesota, and has worked as a freelance journalist for many years. Writing for both mainstream and alternative press, he has combined political activism with his career, and has written extensively on issues including race, white privilege, radical feminism, pornography, the UN embargo against Iraq and the events leading up to and following 9.11. In this piece, he questions the value of patriotism for an increasingly globalized world in the aftermath of the attacks.

Saying Goodbye to Patriotism A talk delivered to the Peace Action National Congress, November 10, 2001

This summer I wrote a book review for an academic journal—one of those terribly important pieces of writing that will be read by tens and tens of people, some of them actually people outside my own family. The book is about the history of governmental restrictions on U.S. news media during war, and it's a good book in many ways. But I faulted the author for accepting the American mythology about the nobility of our wars and their motivations. I challenged his uncritical use of the term patriotism, which I called "perhaps the single most morally and intellectually bankrupt concept in human history."

By coincidence, the galley proofs for the piece came back to me for review a few days after September 11. I paused as I reread my words, and I thought about the reaction those words might spark, given the reflexive outpouring of patriotism in the wake of the terrorist attacks. I thought about the controversy that some of my writing had already sparked on campus and, it turned out, beyond the campus. I thought about how easy it would be to take out that sentence.

I thought about all that for some time before deciding to let it stand. My reason was simple: I think that statement was true on September 10, and if anything, I'm more convinced it is true after September 11.

I also believe that nestled in the truth of that assertion is a crucial question for the U.S.-based peace movement, one that we cannot avoid after 9–11:

Are we truly internationalist? Can we get beyond patriotism? Or, in the end, are we just Americans?

Reprinted from Z *Magazine*, ZNet Magazine.

That is a way, I think, of asking whether we are truly for peace and justice.

I realize that framing of the question may seem harsh. It may rub the wrong way people who want to hold onto a positive notion of patriotism.

I mean the statement to be harsh because I believe the question is crucial. If in the end we are just Americans, if we cannot move beyond patriotism, then we cannot claim to be internationalists. And, if we are not truly internationalist in our outlook—all the way to the bone—then I do not think we truly call ourselves people committed to peace and justice.

Let me try to make the case for this by starting with definitions.

My dictionary defines patriotism as "love and loyal or zealous support of one's own country." We'll come back to that, but let's also look beyond the dictionary to how the word is being used at this moment in history, in this country. I would suggest there are two different, and competing, definitions of patriotism circulating these days.

Definition #1: Patriotism as loyalty to the war effort.

It's easy to get a handle on this use of the word. Just listen to the president of the United States speak. Or watch the TV anchors. Or, as I have done, be a guest on a lot of talk radio shows. This view of patriotism is pretty simple: We were attacked. We must defend ourselves. The only real way to defend ourselves is by military force. If you want to be patriotic, you should—you must—support the war.

I have been told often that it is fine for me to disagree with that policy, but now is not the time to disagree publicly. A patriotic person, I am told, should remain quiet and support the troops until the war is over, at which point we can all have a discussion about the finer points of policy. If I politely disagree with that, then the invective flows: Commie, terrorist-lover, disloyal, unpatriotic. Love it or leave it.

It is easy to take apart this kind of patriotism. It is a patriotism that is incompatible with democracy or basic human decency. To see just how intellectually and morally bankrupt a notion it is, just ask this question: What would we have said to Soviet citizens who might have made such an argument about patriotic duty as the tanks rolled into Prague in 1968? To draw that analogy is not to say the two cases are exactly alike. Rather, it is to point out that a decision to abandon our responsibility to evaluate government policy and surrender our power to think critically is a profound failure, intellectually and morally.

Definition #2: Patriotism as critique of the war effort.

Many in the peace-and-justice movement, myself included, have suggested that to be truly patriotic one cannot simply accept policies because they are handed down by leaders or endorsed by a majority of people, even if it is an overwhelming majority. Being a citizen in a real democracy, we have said over and over, means exercising our judgment, evaluating policies, engaging in discussion, and organizing to try to help see that the best policies are enacted. When the jingoists start throwing around terms like "anti-American" and "traitor," we point out that true patriotism means staying true to the core commitments of democracy and the obligations that democracy puts on people. There is nothing un-American, we contend, about arguing for peace.

That's all clear enough. As I have said, I have used that line of argument many times. It is the best way—maybe the only way—to respond in public at this moment if one wants to be effective in building an antiwar movement. We all remind ourselves, over and over, that we have to start the discussion where people are, not where we wish people were. If people feel "love and loyal or zealous support of one's own country," then we have to be aware of that and respond to it.

But increasingly, I feel uncomfortable arguing for patriotism, even with this second definition. And as I listen to friends and allies in the peace-and-justice movement, I have started to wonder whether that claim to patriotism-as-critical-engagement is indeed merely strategic. Or is it motivated by something else? Are we looking for a way to hold onto patriotism because we really believe in it?

I think it is valuable to ask the question: Is there any way to define the term that doesn't carry with it arrogant and self-indulgent assumptions? Is there any way to salvage patriotism?

I want to argue that invoking patriotism puts us on dangerous ground and that we must be careful about our strategic use of it.

At its ugliest, patriotism means a ranking of the value of the lives of people based on boundaries. To quote Emma Goldman: "Patriotism assumes that our globe is divided into little spots, each one surrounded by an iron gate. Those who had the fortune of being born on some particular spot, consider themselves better, nobler, grander, more intelligent than the living beings inhabiting any other spot. It is, therefore, the duty of everyone living on that chosen spot to fight, kill, and die in the attempt to impose his superiority upon all others."

People have said this directly to me: Yes, the lives of U.S. citizens are more important than the lives of Afghan citizens. If innocent Afghans have to die, have to starve—even in large numbers—so that we can achieve our goals, well, that's the way it is, and that's the way it should be. I assume no argument here is needed as to why this type of patriotism is unacceptable. We may understand why people feel it, but it is barbaric.

But what of the effort to hold onto a kinder and gentler style of patriotism by distinguishing it from this kind of crude nationalism? We must ask: What are the unstated assumptions of this other kind of patriotism we have been defending? If patriotism is about loyalty of some sort, to what are we declaring our loyalty?

If we are pledging loyalty to a nation-state, we have already touched on the obvious problems: What if that nation-state pursues an immoral objective? Should we remain loyal to it? The same question is obvious if our loyalty is to a specific government or set of government officials. If they pursue immoral objectives or pursue moral objectives in an immoral fashion, what would it mean to be loyal to them?

Some suggest we should be loyal to the ideals of America, a set of commitments and practices connected with the concepts of freedom and democracy. That's all well and good; freedom and democracy are good things, and I try to not only endorse those values but live them. I assume everyone in this room does as well.

But what makes those values uniquely American? Is there something about the United States or the people who live here that make us more committed to, or able to act out, the ideals of freedom and democracy—more so than, say, Canadians or Indians or Brazilians? Are not people all over the world—including those who live in countries that do not guarantee freedom to the degree the United States does—capable of understanding and acting on those ideals? Are not different systems possible for making real those ideals in a complex world?

If freedom and democracy are not unique to us, then they are simply human ideals, endorsed to varying degrees in different places and realized to different degrees by different people acting in different places? If that's true, then they are not distinctly American ideals. They were not invented here, and we do not have a monopoly on them. So, if one is trying to express a commitment to those ideals, why do it in the limiting fashion of talking of patriotism?

Let me attempt an analogy to gender. After 9–11, a number of commentators have argued that criticisms of masculinity should be rethought. Yes, masculinity is often connected to, and expressed through, competition, domination, and violence, they said. But as male firefighters raced into burning buildings and risked their lives to save others, cannot we also see that masculinity encompasses a kind of strength that is rooted in caring and sacrifice?

My response is, yes, of course men often exhibit such strength. But do not women have the capacity for that kind of strength rooted in caring and sacrifice? Do they not exhibit such strength on a regular basis? Why of course they do, most are quick to agree. Then the obvious question is, what makes these distinctly masculine characteristics? Are they not simply human characteristics?

We identify masculine tendencies toward competition, domination, and violence because we see patterns of different behavior; we see that men are more prone to such behavior in our culture. We can go on to observe and analyze the ways in which men are socialized to behave in those ways. We do all that work, I would hope, to change those behaviors.

But that is a very different exercise than saying that admirable human qualities present in both men and women are somehow primarily the domain of one of those genders. To assign them to a gender is misguided, and demeaning to the gender that is then assumed not to possess them to the same degree. Once you start saying "strength and courage are masculine traits," it leads to the conclusion that woman are not as strong or courageous. To say "strength and courage are masculine traits," then, is to be sexist.

The same holds true for patriotism. If we abandon the crude version of patriotism but try to hold onto an allegedly more sophisticated version, we bump up against this obvious question: Why are human characteristics being labeled as American if there is nothing distinctly American about them?

If people want to argue that such terminology is justified because those values are realized to their fullest degree in the United States, then there's some explaining to do. Some explaining to the people of Guatemala and Iran, Nicaragua and South Vietnam, East Timor and Laos, Iraq and Panama. We would have to explain to the victims of U.S. aggression—direct and indirect—how it is that our political culture, the highest expression of the ideals of freedom and democracy, has managed routinely to go around the world overthrowing democratically elected governments, supporting brutal dictators, funding and training proxy terrorist armies, and unleashing brutal attacks on civilians when we go to war. If we want to make the claim that we are the fulfillment of history and the ultimate expression of the principles of freedom and justice, our first stop might be Hiroshima. We might want to explain that claim there.

If we are serious about peace and justice in the world, we need to subject this notion of patriotism to scrutiny. If we do that, I would suggest, it is clear that any use of the concept of patriotism is bound to be chauvinistic at some level. At its worst, patriotism can lead easily to support for barbarism. At its best, it is self-indulgent and arrogant in its assumptions about the uniqueness of U.S. culture.

None of what I have said should be taken as a blanket denunciation of the United States, our political institutions, or our culture. People often tell me, "You start with the assumption that everything about the United States is bad." Of course I do not assume that. That would be as absurd a position as the assumption that everything about the United States is good. I can't imagine any reasonable person making either statement. That does raise the question, of course, of who is a reasonable person. We might ask that question about, for example, George Bush, the father. In 1988, after the U.S. Navy warship Vincennes shot down an Iranian commercial airliner in a commercial corridor, killing 290 civilians, Bush said, "I will never apologize for the United States of America. I don't care what the facts are."

I want to put forward the radical proposition that we should care what the facts are. We should start with the assumption that everything about the United States, like everything about any country, needs to be examined and assessed. That is what it means to be a moral person.

There is much about this country a citizen can be proud of, and I am in fact proud of those things. The personal freedoms guaranteed (to most people) in this culture, for example, are quite amazing. As someone who regularly tries to use those freedoms, I am as aware as anyone of how precious they are.

There also is much to be appalled by. The obscene gaps in wealth between rich and poor, for example, are quite amazing as well, especially in a wealthy society that claims to be committed to justice.

In that sense, we are like any other grouping of people. That doesn't mean one can't analyze various societies and judge some better than others by principles we can articulate and defend—so long as they are truly principles, applied honestly and uniformly. But one should maintain a bit of humility in the endeavor. Perhaps instead of saying "The United States is the greatest nation on earth"—a comment common among politicians, pundits, and the public—we would be better off saying, "I live in the United States and have deep emotional ties to the people, land, and ideals of this place. Because of these feelings, I want to highlight the positive while working to change what is wrong." That is not moral relativism—it is a call for all of us to articulate and defend our positions.

We can make that statement without having to argue that we are, in some essential way, better than everyone else. We can make that statement without arrogantly suggesting that other people are inherently less capable of articulating or enacting high ideals. We can make that statement and be ready and willing to engage in debate and discussion about the merits of different values and systems.

We can make that statement, in other words, and be true internationalists, people truly committed to peace and justice. If one wants to call that statement an expression of patriotism, I will not spend too much time arguing. But I will ask: If we make a statement like that, why do we need to call it an expression of patriotism? What can we learn by asking ourselves: What makes us, even people in the peace-and-justice community, want to hold onto the notion of patriotism with such tenacity?

When I write or talk with the general public and raise questions like these, people often respond, "If you hate America so much, why don't you leave?"

But what is this America that I allegedly hate? The land itself? The people who live here? The ideals in the country's founding documents? I do not hate any of those things.

When people say to me "love it or leave it," what is the "it" to which they refer?

No one can ever quite answer that. Still, I have an answer for them.

I will not leave "it" for a simple reason: I have nowhere else to go. I was born here. I was given enormous privileges here. My place in the world is here, where I feel an obligation to use that privilege to be part—a very small part of, as we all are only a small part—of a struggle to make real a better world. Whatever small part I can play in that struggle, whatever I can achieve, I will have to achieve here, in the heart of the beast.

I love it, which is to say that I love life—I love the world in which I live and the people who live in it with me. I will not leave that "it."

That "it" may not be specific enough for some, but it's the best I can do. Maybe it will help to answer in the negative, for I can say more clearly what the "it" is not. I can describe more clearly what is the America I do not love.

The America I love is not this administration, or any other collections of politicians, or the corporations they serve.

It is not the policies of this administration, or any other collection of politicians, or the corporations they serve.

The America I love is not wrapped up in a mythology about "how good we are" that ignores the brutal realities of our own history of conquest and barbarism.

Most of all, I want no part of the America that arrogantly claims that the lives and hopes and dreams of people who happen to live within the boundaries of the United States have more value than those in other places. Nor will I indulge America in the belief that our grief is different. Since September 11, the United States has demanded that the world take our grief more seriously. When some around the world have not done so, we express our outrage.

But we should ask: What makes the grief of a parent who lost a child in the World Trade Center any deeper than the grief of a parent who lost a child in Baghdad when U.S. warplanes rained death on the civilian areas of Iraq in the Gulf War? Or the parents of a child in Nicaragua when the U.S. terrorist proxy army ravaged that country? Soon after 9–11, I heard a television reporter describe lower Manhattan as "Beirut on the Hudson." We might ask, how did Beirut come to look like Beirut, and what is our responsibility in that? And what of the grief of those who saw their loved ones die during the shelling of that city?

We should ask: Where was the empathy of America for the grief of those people?

Certainly we grieve differently, more intensely, when people close to us die. We don't feel the loss of a family member the same way as a death of a casual friend. We feel something different over the death of someone we knew compared with the death of a stranger. But we must understand that the grief we feel when our friends and neighbors became victims of political violence is no different than what people around the world feel. We must understand that each of those lives lost abroad has exactly the same value as the life of any one of our family, friends and neighbors.

Goodbye to patriotism

September 11 was a dark day. I still remember what it felt like to watch those towers come down, the darkness that settled over me that day, the hopelessness, how tangible death felt—for me, not only the deaths of those in the towers but also the deaths of those who would face the bombs in the war that might follow, the war that did follow, the war that goes on.

But humans are resilient; in the darkness we tend to look for light, for a way out of the darkness.

I believe there is a light shining out of September 11, out of all that darkness. It is a light that I believe we Americans can follow to our own salvation. That light is contained in a simple truth that is obvious, but which Americans have never really taken to heart: We are part of the world. We cannot any longer hide from that world. We cannot allow our politicians, and generals, and corporate executives to do their dirty business around the world while we hide from the truths about just how dirty that business really is. We can no longer hide from the coups they plan, the wars they start, the sweatshops they run.

For me, all this means saying goodbye to patriotism.

That is the paradox: September 11 has sparked a wave of patriotism, a patriotism that has in many cases been overtly hateful, racist and xenophobic. A patriotism that can lead people to say, as one person wrote to me, "We should bomb [Afghanistan] until there's no more earth to bomb."

But the real lesson of September 11, which I believe we will eventually learn, is that if we are to survive as a free people, as decent people who want honestly to claim the ideals we say we live by, we must say goodbye to patriotism. That patriotism will not relieve our grief, but only deepen it. It will not solve our problems but only extend them. I believe there is no hope for ourselves or for the world if we continue to embrace patriotism, no matter what the definition.

We must give up our "love and loyal or zealous support of one's own country" and transfer that love, loyalty and zealousness to the world, and especially the people of the world who have suffered most so that we Americans can live in affluence.

We must be able to say, as the great labor leader of the early 20th century Eugene Debs said, "I have no country to fight for; my country is the earth, and I am a citizen of the world."

I am with Debs. I believe it is time to declare: I am not patriotic. I am through with trying to redefine the term patriotic to make sense. There is no sense to it.

That kind of statement will anger many, but at some point we must begin to take that risk, for this is not merely an academic argument over semantics.

This is both a struggle to save ourselves and a struggle to save the lives of vulnerable people around the world.

We must say goodbye to patriotism because the kind of America the peace-and-justice movement wants to build cannot be built on, or through, the patriotism of Americans.

We must say goodbye to patriotism because the world cannot survive indefinitely the patriotism of Americans.

Section Three

Witness Interpreted and Politicized

Arundhati Roy

Arundahti Roy was born circa 1960 in Kerala, India to Syrian Christian and Hindu parents. She has acted in films and has written for film and television. Her first novel, 1997's The God of Small Things, *which has been published in nineteen countries and sixteen languages, won the Booker Prize. This was the first time an Indian citizen had ever won Britain's most prestigious literary award. At the awards ceremony, Roy hinted that she might not write another novel. Instead, she focused her work on social issues by writing an essay called "The Greater Common Good"—later published in book form—which criticized a dam project in India. Even though proponents claimed that the dam would solve water and energy problems, Roy argued it would displace an estimated 40 million people and harm the environment. She also protested India's testing of nuclear weapons in her essay, "The End of Imagination." The essay we include here, "The Algebra of Infinite Justice," first published in the London newspaper,* The Guardian, *on September 29, 2001 advances a political critique of the rapid U.S. response to 9.11, attempting to contextualize this response with some historical background on prior U.S. foreign policy in the Middle East. This article caused quite a bit of controversy in London, while large U.S. newspapers refused to publish it.*

The Algebra of Infinite Justice

In the aftermath of the unconscionable September 11 suicide attacks on the Pentagon and the World Trade Centre, an American newscaster said: "Good and evil rarely manifest themselves as clearly as they did last Tuesday. People who we don't know massacred people who we do. And they did so with contemptuous glee." Then he broke down and wept.

Here's the rub: America is at war against people it doesn't know, because they don't appear much on TV. Before it has properly identified or even begun to comprehend the nature of its enemy, the U.S. government has, in a rush of publicity and embarrassing rhetoric, cobbled together an "international coalition against terror," mobilised its army, its air force, its navy and its media, and committed them to battle.

The trouble is that once America goes off to war, it can't very well return without having fought one. If it doesn't find its enemy, for the sake of the enraged folks back home, it will have to manufacture one. Once war begins, it will develop a momentum, a logic and a justification of its own, and we'll lose sight of why it's being fought in the first place.

What we're witnessing here is the spectacle of the world's most powerful country reaching reflexively, angrily, for an old instinct to fight a new kind of war. Suddenly, when it comes to defending itself, America's streamlined warships, cruise missiles and F-16 jets look like obsolete, lumbering things. As deterrence, its arsenal of nuclear bombs is no longer worth its weight in scrap. Box-cutters, penknives, and cold anger are the weapons with which the wars of the new century will be waged. Anger is the lock pick. It slips through customs unnoticed. Doesn't show up in baggage checks.

Who is America fighting? On September 20, the FBI said that it had doubts about the identities of some of the hijackers. On the same day President George Bush said, "We know exactly who these people are and which governments are supporting them." It sounds as though the president knows something that the FBI and the American public don't.

In his September 20 address to the U.S. Congress, President Bush called the enemies of America "enemies of freedom." "Americans are asking, 'Why do they hate us?'" he said. "They hate our freedoms—our freedom of religion, our freedom of speech, our freedom to vote and assemble and disagree with each other." People are being asked to make two leaps of faith here. First, to assume that The Enemy is who the U.S. government says it is, even though it has no substantial evidence to support that claim. And second, to assume that The Enemy's motives are what the U.S. government says they are, and there's nothing to support that either.

For strategic, military and economic reasons, it is vital for the U.S. government to persuade its public that their commitment to freedom and democracy and the American Way of Life is under attack. In the current atmosphere of grief, outrage and anger, it's an easy notion to peddle. However, if that were true, it's

---

Reprinted from the *Guardian* (London), September 29, 2001.

reasonable to wonder why the symbols of America's economic and military dominance—the World Trade Centre and the Pentagon—were chosen as the targets of the attacks. Why not the Statue of Liberty? Could it be that the stygian anger that led to the attacks has its taproot not in American freedom and democracy, but in the U.S. government's record of commitment and support to exactly the opposite things—to military and economic terrorism, insurgency, military dictatorship, religious bigotry and unimaginable genocide (outside America)? It must be hard for ordinary Americans, so recently bereaved, to look up at the world with their eyes full of tears and encounter what might appear to them to be indifference. It isn't indifference. It's just augury. An absence of surprise. The tired wisdom of knowing that what goes around eventually comes around. American people ought to know that it is not them but their government's policies that are so hated. They can't possibly doubt that they themselves, their extraordinary musicians, their writers, their actors, their spectacular sportsmen and their cinema, are universally welcomed. All of us have been moved by the courage and grace shown by firefighters, rescue workers and ordinary office staff in the days since the attacks.

America's grief at what happened has been immense and immensely public. It would be grotesque to expect it to calibrate or modulate its anguish. However, it will be a pity if, instead of using this as an opportunity to try to understand why September 11 happened, Americans use it as an opportunity to usurp the whole world's sorrow to mourn and avenge only their own. Because then it falls to the rest of us to ask the hard questions and say the harsh things. And for our pains, for our bad timing, we will be disliked, ignored and perhaps eventually silenced.

The world will probably never know what motivated those particular hijackers who flew planes into those particular American buildings. They were not glory boys. They left no suicide notes, no political messages; no organisation has claimed credit for the attacks. All we know is that their belief in what they were doing outstripped the natural human instinct for survival, or any desire to be remembered. It's almost as though they could not scale down the enormity of their rage to anything smaller than their deeds. And what they did has blown a hole in the world as we knew it. In the absence of information, politicians, political commentators and writers (like myself) will invest the act with their own politics, with their own interpretations. This speculation, this analysis of the political climate in which the attacks took place, can only be a good thing.

But war is looming large. Whatever remains to be said must be said quickly. Before America places itself at the helm of the "international coalition against terror," before it invites (and coerces) countries to actively participate in its almost godlike mission—called Operation Infinite Justice until it was pointed out that this could be seen as an insult to Muslims, who believe that only Allah can mete out infinite justice, and was renamed Operation Enduring Freedom—it would help if some small clarifications are made. For example, Infinite Justice/Enduring Freedom for whom? Is this America's war against terror in America or against terror in general? What exactly is being avenged here? Is it the tragic loss of almost 7,000 lives, the gutting of five million square feet of office space in Manhattan, the destruction of a section of the Pentagon, the loss of several hundreds of thousands of jobs, the bankruptcy of some airline companies and the dip in the New York Stock Exchange? Or is it more than that? In 1996, Madeleine Albright, then the

U.S. secretary of state, was asked on national television what she felt about the fact that 500,000 Iraqi children had died as a result of U.S. economic sanctions. She replied that it was "a very hard choice," but that, all things considered, "we think the price is worth it." Albright never lost her job for saying this. She continued to travel the world representing the views and aspirations of the U.S. government. More pertinently, the sanctions against Iraq remain in place. Children continue to die.

So here we have it. The equivocating distinction between civilisation and savagery, between the "massacre of innocent people" or, if you like, "a clash of civilisations" and "collateral damage." The sophistry and fastidious algebra of infinite justice. How many dead Iraqis will it take to make the world a better place? How many dead Afghans for every dead American? How many dead women and children for every dead man? How many dead mojahedin for each dead investment banker? As we watch mesmerised, Operation Enduring Freedom unfolds on TV monitors across the world. A coalition of the world's superpowers is closing in on Afghanistan, one of the poorest, most ravaged, war-torn countries in the world, whose ruling Taliban government is sheltering Osama bin Laden, the man being held responsible for the September 11 attacks.

The only thing in Afghanistan that could possibly count as collateral value is its citizenry. (Among them, half a million maimed orphans. There are accounts of hobbling stampedes that occur when artificial limbs are airdropped into remote, inaccessible villages.) Afghanistan's economy is in a shambles. In fact, the problem for an invading army is that Afghanistan has no conventional coordinates or signposts to plot on a military map—no big cities, no highways, no industrial complexes, no water treatment plants. Farms have been turned into mass graves. The countryside is littered with land mines—10 million is the most recent estimate. The American army would first have to clear the mines and build roads in order to take its soldiers in.

Fearing an attack from America, one million citizens have fled from their homes and arrived at the border between Pakistan and Afghanistan. The UN estimates that there are eight million Afghan citizens who need emergency aid. As supplies run out—food and aid agencies have been asked to leave—the BBC reports that one of the worst humanitarian disasters of recent times has begun to unfold. Witness the infinite justice of the new century. Civilians starving to death while they're waiting to be killed.

In America there has been rough talk of "bombing Afghanistan back to the stone age." Someone please break the news that Afghanistan is already there. And if it's any consolation, America played no small part in helping it on its way. The American people may be a little fuzzy about where exactly Afghanistan is (we hear reports that there's a run on maps of the country), but the U.S. government and Afghanistan are old friends.

In 1979, after the Soviet invasion of Afghanistan, the CIA and Pakistan's ISI (Inter Services Intelligence) launched the largest covert operation in the history of the CIA. Their purpose was to harness the energy of Afghan resistance to the Soviets and expand it into a holy war, an Islamic jihad, which would turn Muslim countries within the Soviet Union against the communist regime and eventually destabilise it. When it began, it was meant to be the Soviet Union's Vietnam. It turned out to be much more than that. Over the years, through the ISI, the CIA funded and recruited almost 100,000 radical mojahedin from 40 Islamic countries as soldiers for America's proxy war. The rank and file of the mojahedin were unaware that their jihad was actually being fought on behalf of Uncle Sam. (The irony is that America was equally unaware that it was financing a future war against itself.)

In 1989, after being bloodied by 10 years of relentless conflict, the Russians withdrew, leaving behind a civilisation reduced to rubble.

Civil war in Afghanistan raged on. The jihad spread to Chechnya, Kosovo and eventually to Kashmir. The CIA continued to pour in money and military equipment, but the overheads had become immense, and more money was needed. The mojahedin ordered farmers to plant opium as a "revolutionary tax." The ISI set up hundreds of heroin laboratories across Afghanistan. Within two years of the CIA's arrival, the Pakistan-Afghanistan borderland had become the biggest producer of heroin in the world, and the single biggest source of the heroin on American streets. The annual profits, said to be between $100bn and $200bn, were ploughed back into training and arming militants.

In 1995, the Taliban—then a marginal sect of dangerous, hardline fundamentalists—fought its way to power in Afghanistan. It was funded by the ISI, that old cohort of the CIA, and supported by many political parties in Pakistan. The Taliban unleashed a regime of terror. Its first victims were its own people, particularly women. It closed down girls' schools, dismissed women from government jobs, and enforced sharia laws under which women deemed to be "immoral" are stoned to death, and widows guilty of being adulterous are buried alive. Given the Taliban government's human rights track record, it seems unlikely that it will in any way be intimidated or swerved from its purpose by the prospect of war, or the threat to the lives of its civilians.

After all that has happened, can there be anything more ironic than Russia and America joining hands to re-destroy Afghanistan? The question is, can you destroy destruction? Dropping more bombs on Afghanistan will only shuffle the rubble, scramble some old graves and disturb the dead.

The desolate landscape of Afghanistan was the burial ground of Soviet communism and the springboard of a unipolar world dominated by America. It made the space for neocapitalism and corporate globalisation, again dominated by America. And now Afghanistan is poised to become the graveyard for the unlikely soldiers who fought and won this war for America.

And what of America's trusted ally? Pakistan too has suffered enormously. The U.S. government has not been shy of supporting military dictators who have blocked the idea of democracy from taking root in the country. Before the CIA arrived, there was a small rural market for opium in Pakistan. Between 1979 and 1985, the number of heroin addicts grew from zero to one-and-a-half million. Even before September 11, there were three million Afghan refugees living in tented camps along the border. Pakistan's economy is crumbling. Sectarian violence, globalisation's structural adjustment programmes and drug lords are tearing the country to pieces. Set up to fight the Soviets, the terrorist training centres and madrasahs, sown like dragon's teeth across the country, produced fundamentalists with tremendous popular appeal within Pakistan itself. The Taliban, which the Pakistan government has supported, funded and propped up for years, has material and strategic alliances with Pakistan's own political parties.

Now the U.S. government is asking (asking?) Pakistan to garotte the pet it has hand-reared in its backyard for so many years. President Musharraf, having pledged his support to the U.S., could well find he has something resembling civil war on his hands.

India, thanks in part to its geography, and in part to the vision of its former leaders, has so far been fortunate enough to be left out of this Great Game. Had it been drawn in, it's more than likely that our democracy, such as it is, would not have survived. Today, as some of us watch in horror, the Indian government is furiously gyrating its hips, begging the U.S. to set up its base in India rather than Pakistan. Having had this ringside view of Pakistan's sordid fate, it isn't just odd, it's unthinkable, that India should want to do this. Any third world country with a fragile economy and a complex social base should know by now that to invite a superpower such as America in (whether it says it's staying or just passing through) would be like inviting a brick to drop through your windscreen.

Operation Enduring Freedom is ostensibly being fought to uphold the American Way of Life. It'll probably end up undermining it completely. It will spawn more anger and more terror across the world. For ordinary people in America, it will mean lives lived in a climate of sickening uncertainty: will my child be safe in school? Will there be nerve gas in the subway? A bomb in the cinema hall? Will my love come home tonight? There have been warnings about the possibility of biological warfare—smallpox, bubonic plague, anthrax—the deadly payload of innocuous crop-duster aircraft. Being picked off a few at a time may end up being worse than being annihilated all at once by a nuclear bomb.

The U.S. government, and no doubt governments all over the world, will use the climate of war as an excuse to curtail civil liberties, deny free speech, lay off workers, harass ethnic and religious minorities, cut back on public spending and divert huge amounts of money to the defence industry. To what purpose? President Bush can no more "rid the world of evil-doers" than he can stock it with saints. It's absurd for the U.S. government to even toy with the notion that it can stamp out terrorism with more violence and oppression. Terrorism is the symptom, not the disease. Terrorism has no country. It's transnational, as global an enterprise as Coke or Pepsi or Nike. At the first sign of trouble, terrorists can pull up stakes and move their "factories" from country to country in search of a better deal. Just like the multi-nationals.

Terrorism as a phenomenon may never go away. But if it is to be contained, the first step is for America to at least acknowledge that it shares the planet with other nations, with other human beings who, even if they are not on TV, have loves and griefs and stories and songs and sorrows and, for heaven's sake, rights. Instead, when Donald Rumsfeld, the U.S. defence secretary, was asked what he would call a victory in America's new war, he said that if he could convince the world that Americans must be allowed to continue with their way of life, he would consider it a victory.

The September 11 attacks were a monstrous calling card from a world gone horribly wrong. The message may have been written by bin Laden (who knows?) and delivered by his couriers, but it could well have been signed by the ghosts of the victims of America's old wars. The millions killed in Korea, Vietnam and Cambodia, the 17,500 killed when Israel—backed by the U.S.—invaded Lebanon in 1982, the 200,000 Iraqis killed in Operation Desert Storm, the thousands of Palestinians who have died fighting Israel's occupation of the West Bank. And the millions who died, in Yugoslavia, Somalia, Haiti, Chile, Nicaragua, El Salvador, the Dominican Republic, Panama, at the hands of all the terrorists, dictators and genocidists whom the American government supported, trained, bankrolled and supplied with arms. And this is far from being a comprehensive list.

For a country involved in so much warfare and conflict, the American people have been extremely fortunate. The strikes on September 11 were only the second on American soil in over a century. The first was Pearl Harbour. The reprisal for this took a long route, but ended with Hiroshima and Nagasaki. This time the world waits with bated breath for the horrors to come.

Someone recently said that if Osama bin Laden didn't exist, America would have had to invent him. But, in a way, America did invent him. He was among the jihadis who moved to Afghanistan in 1979 when the CIA commenced its operations there. Bin Laden has the distinction of being created by the CIA and wanted by the FBI. In the course of a fortnight he has been promoted from suspect to prime suspect and then, despite the lack of any real evidence, straight up the charts to being "wanted dead or alive."

From all accounts, it will be impossible to produce evidence (of the sort that would stand scrutiny in a court of law) to link bin Laden to the September 11 attacks. So far, it appears that the most incriminating piece of evidence against him is the fact that he has not condemned them.

From what is known about the location of bin Laden and the living conditions in which he operates, it's entirely possible that he did not personally plan and carry out the attacks—that he is the inspirational figure, "the CEO of the holding company." The Taliban's response to U.S. demands for the extradition of bin Laden has been uncharacteristically reasonable: produce the evidence, then we'll hand him over. President Bush's response is that the demand is "nonnegotiable."

(While talks are on for the extradition of CEOs—can India put in a side request for the extradition of Warren Anderson of the U.S.? He was the chairman of Union Carbide, responsible for the Bhopal gas leak that killed 16,000 people in 1984. We have collated the necessary evidence. It's all in the files. Could we have him, please?)

But who is Osama bin Laden really? Let me rephrase that. What is Osama bin Laden? He's America's family secret. He is the American president's dark doppelgänger. The savage twin of all that purports to be beautiful and civilised. He has been sculpted from the spare rib of a world laid to waste by America's foreign policy: its gunboat diplomacy, its nuclear arsenal, its vulgarly stated policy of "full-spectrum dominance," its chilling disregard for non-American lives, its barbarous military interventions, its support for despotic and dictatorial regimes, its merciless economic agenda that has munched through the economies of poor countries like a cloud of locusts. Its marauding multinationals who are taking over the air we breathe, the ground we stand on, the water we drink, the thoughts we think. Now that the family secret has been spilled, the twins are blurring into one another and gradually becoming interchangeable. Their guns, bombs, money and drugs have been going around in the loop for a while. (The Stinger missiles that will greet U.S. helicopters were supplied by the CIA. The heroin used by America's drug addicts comes from Afghanistan. The Bush administration recently gave Afghanistan a $43m subsidy for a "war on drugs". . . .)

Now Bush and bin Laden have even begun to borrow each other's rhetoric. Each refers to the other as "the head of the snake." Both invoke God and use the loose millenarian currency of good and evil as their terms of reference. Both are engaged in unequivocal political crimes. Both are dangerously armed—one with the nuclear arsenal of the obscenely powerful, the other with the incandescent, destructive power of the utterly hopeless. The fireball and the ice pick. The bludgeon and the axe. The important thing to keep in mind is that neither is an acceptable alternative to the other.

President Bush's ultimatum to the people of the world—"If you're not with us, you're against us"—is a piece of presumptuous arrogance. It's not a choice that people want to, need to, or should have to make.

Vijay Prashad

Vijay Prashad is Associate Professor and Director of International Studies at Trinity College in Hartfort Connecticut. As a political columnist, he has written extensively for Z Magazine, Dollars and Sense, the Monthly Review, Political Affairs, Frontline, *and* People's Democracy. *He has authored five books including* Fat Cats and Running Dogs: The Enron Stage of Capitalism, *and* War Against the Planet: The Fifth Afghan War, U.S. Imperialism and Other Assorted Fundamentalisms. *In this piece, which came out on the web site www.zmag.org a week after 9.11, Prashad provides a historical context to for U.S. involvement in Afghanistan and the Middle East.*

War Against the Planet

President George W. Bush of the United States appeared on television sets across the world on the 11th of September and declared war against the planet. Not only will those who committed the dreadful crimes of the morning be brought to justice, he declared, but so too will those who once harbored and now continue to harbor them.

Supply ships have started their way to Diego Garcia in the Indian Ocean, and toward Spain. A large part of the $40 billion designated by the U.S. Congress will go toward the preparations that have already begun within the U.S. military establishment, in close contact with its allies.

The Taliban, in Afghanistan, quickly pleaded that the suffering of its poor should not be increased with the wrath of the cruise missiles. So did Libya's Gaddafi.

Others, such as Pakistan, hastily declared their fealty to the U.S. strike back, and pledged to allow planes to fly over its territory. India was not far behind, eager to allow its land for what may be the largest assault since the bombardment of Cambodia and Iraq.

One commentator on the U.S. television networks lamented that the U.S. lost its virginity at 8:45 A.M. on 9/11 when the first plane struck the World Trade Center.

But the war did not begin at that time. This was not Pearl Harbor. The war has been ongoing for quite some time now, at least for five decades.

Indeed, five decades ago the United States assumed charge of that band of nations that stretches from Libya to Afghanistan, most of whom are oil rich and

---

Reprinted from Z *Magazine*, ZNet Magazine.

therefore immensely important for global capitalism. The civilizational mandate held by France and Britain came to a close when World War II devastated Europe, and it fell to the U.S. to adopt the white man's burden. It did so with glee, indeed on behalf, for the most part, of the Seven Sisters, the largest oil conglomerates in the world (most of them U.S.-based transnational corporations).

Alliances forged with right-wing forces in these regions found fellowship from the U.S., just as the Left fashioned relations with the USSR. The United States participated in the decimation of the Left in north Africa and west Asia, from the destruction of the Egyptian Communist Party, the largest in the region, to the rise of people like Saddam Hussein to take out the vibrant Iraqi Communist Party, and of the Saudi financier Osama bin Laden to take down the Communist Afghan regime.

We hear that 9/11 was the "worst terrorist attack in history," but this ignores the vast history of bombardment, in general, tracked by Sven Lindquist in his new book (for the New Press), and it certainly ignores the many terrorist massacres conducted in the name of the United States, for instance, such as at Hallabja in Iraq or else in South America by Operation Condor. These are just a few examples. But what is that history before 8:45 A.M. on 9/11, and will it show us that "retaliation" misses out the fact that the U.S. has been at war for many decades already?

I. The Afghan Concession.

In 1930, a U.S. State Department "expert" on Afghanistan offered an assessment which forms the backbone of U.S. social attitudes and state policy towards the region: "Afghanistan is doubtless the most fanatic hostile country in the world today." Given this, the U.S. saw Afghanistan simply as a *tool* in foreign policy terms and as a *mine* in economic terms. When the Taliban (lit. "religious students") entered Kabul on 27 September 1996, the U.S. state welcomed the development with the hope that the new rulers might bring stability to the region despite the fact that they are notoriously illiberal in social terms. The U.S. media offered a muted and clichéd sense of horror at the social decay of the Taliban, but without any sense of the U.S. hand in the manufacture of such theocratic fascists for its own hegemonic ends. In thirty years, Afghanistan has been reduced to a "concession" in which corporations and states vie for control over commodities and markets without concern for the dignity and destiny of the people of the region. Oil, guns, landmines and heroin are the coordinates for policy-makers, not the shadowy bodies that hang from the scaffolds like paper-flags of a nation without sovereignty.

Shortly after the Taliban took power in Kabul, the U.S. State Department offered the following assessment: "Taliban leaders have announced that Afghans can return to Kabul without fear, and that Afghanistan is the common home of all Afghans," announced spokesperson Glyn Davies. The U.S. felt that the Taliban's assertion in Kabul would allow "an opportunity for a process of reconciliation to begin." Reconciliation was a distant dream as the troops led by the Tajik warlord, Ahmed Shah Masood and the troops led by General Abdul Rashid Dostum and the Hazara-dominated Hezb-e-Wahdat party disturbed the vales of Afghanistan with warfare. Citizens of the advanced industrial states mouthed clichés about "timeless ethnic warfare" and "tribal blood-feuds" without any appreciation of the history of Afghanistan that produced these political conflicts (in much the same way as the media speaks of the Tutsi-Hutu turmoil without a sense of colonial Belgium's role in the production of these politico-ethnic conflicts).

In 1964, King Zahir Shah responded to popular pressure from his subjects with a constitution and initiated a process known as "New Democracy." Three main forces grew after this phase: (1) the communists (who split into two factions in 1967, Khalq [the masses] and Parcham [the flag]); (2) the Islamic populists, among whom Burhanuddin Rabbani's Jamiat-i-Islami from 1973 was the main organization (whose youth leader was the engineering student, Gulbuddin Hikmatyar); (3) constitutional reformers (such as Muhammad Daoud, cousin of Zahir Shah, whose coup of July 1973 abolished the monarchy). Daoud's consequent repression against the theocratic elements pushed them into exile from where they began, along with the Pakistani Jamaat-I-Islami and the Saudi Rabitat al-Alam al-Islami, to plot against the secular regime in Afghanistan. In 1975, for instance, the theocratic elements, led by Hikmatyar in Paktia, attempted an uprising with Pakistani assistance, but the "Panjsher Valley incident" was promptly squashed. The first split amongst the theocratic elements occurred in the aftermath of this incident. Instability in Afghanistan led to the communist coup in 1978 and the eventual Soviet military presence in the region from 1979. The valiant attempts to create a democratic state failed as a result of the inability of hegemonic states to allow the nation to come into its own.

From 1979, Afghanistan became home to violence and heroin production. Money from the most unlikely sources poured into the band of mujahidin forces located in Pakistan: the U.S., the Saudis (notably their general intelligence service, al-Istakhbara al-'Ama), the Kuwaitis, the Iraqis, the Libyans and the Iranians paid the theocratic elements over $1 billion per year during the 1980s. The U.S.-Saudi dominance in funding enabled them to choose amongst the various exiled forces—they, along with the Pakistanis, chose seven parties in 1981 that leaned more towards theocratic fascism than toward secular nationalism. One of the main financiers was the Saudi businessman, Osama bin Laden. Five years later, these seven parties joined the Union of Mujahidin of Afghanistan. Its monopoly over access to the U.S.-Saudi link emboldened it to assassinate Professor Sayd Bahauddin Majrooh in Peshawar in 1988 when he reported that 70% of the Afghan refugees wanted a return to the monarchism of Zahir Shah (who waited in a Roman suburb playing chess). Further, the Interim Islamic Government of Afghanistan called a shura (council) in 1989; the seven parties nominated all the representatives to the body. All liberal and left wing elements came under systematic attack from the shura and its armed representatives. The U.S.-Saudi axis anointed the theocratic fascists as the heirs to Afghanistan.

With over $1 billion per year, the mujahidin and its Army of Sacrifice (Lashkar-i Isar) led by Hikmatyar (who was considered the main "factor of stability" until 1988) built up ferocious arsenals. In 1986, they received shoulder-fired Stinger missiles that they began to fire indiscriminately into civilian areas of Afghanistan. Asia Watch, in 1991, reported that Hikmatyar paid his commanders for each rocket fired into Kabul. Claymore mines and other U.S.-made antipersonnel directional fragmentation mines became a staple of the countryside. Today, about 10 million mines still litter the vales of Afghanistan (placed there by the Soviets and by the U.S.-Saudi backed mujahidin). In 1993, the U.S. State Department noted that landmines "may be the most toxic and widespread pollution facing mankind." Nevertheless, the U.S. continues to sell mines at $3/mine (mines cost about $300–$1000/mine to detect and dismantle). Motorola manufactures many of the plastic components inside the mines, which makes the device undetectable by metal-detectors.

The CIA learnt to extend its resources during the Southeast Asian campaigns in the 1970s by sale of heroin from the Golden Triangle. In Afghanistan, the Inter-Service Intelligence (ISI) [Pakistan's CIA], the Pakistani military and civilian authorities (notably Governor Fazle Huq) and the mujahidin became active cultivators, processors and sellers of heroin (a commodity which made its Southern Asian appearance in large numbers only after 1975, and whose devastation can be gleaned in Mohsin Hamid's wonderful novel, *Moth Smoke*). The opium harvest at the Pakistan-Afghan border doubled between 1982 and 1983 (575 tons), but by the end of the decade it would grow to 800 tons. On 18 June 1986, the *New York Times* reported that the mujahidin "have been involved in narcotics activities as a matter of policy to finance their operations." The opium warlords worked under cover of the U.S.-Saudi-Pakistani axis that funded their arms sales and aided the conveyance of the drugs into the European and North American markets where they account for 50% of heroin sales.

Heroin is not the only commodity flogged by the mujahidin. They are the front-line troops of an ensemble that wants "commercial freedom" in Afghanistan so that the Afghan people and land can be utilized for "peaceful" exploitation. The California-based oil company Unocal (76), then busy killing the Karens and other ethnic groups in alliance with the Burmese junta and with the French oil company Total, had its eyes on a pipeline from Central Asia to the Indian Ocean, through Afghanistan. Only with an end to hostilities, at any cost, will the international corporations be able to benefit from the minerals and cheap labor of the Afghans. So far, the corporations have reaped a profit from sales of arms to the Afghans; now they want to use the arms of the Afghans for sweatshops and mines.

For corporations and for corporatized states (such as the U.S.), an unprincipled peace allows them to extract their needs without the bother of political dissent. The Taliban briefly offered the possibility of such a peace. Formed in 1994 under the tutelage of the ISI and General Naseerullah Khan (Pakistan's Interior Minister), the Taliban comprises southern Pashtun tribes who are united by a vision of a society under Wahhabism which extols a form of Islam *(Tariqa Muhammadiya)* based on its interpretation of the Quran without the benefit of the centuries of elaboration of the complexities of the Islamic tradition. In late September 1996, Radio Kabul broadcast a statement from Mullah Agha Gulabi: "God says that those committing adultery should be stoned to death. Anybody who drinks and says that that is not against the Koran, you have to kill him and hang his body for three days until people say this is the body of the drinker who did not obey the Koran and Allah's order." The Taliban announced that women must be veiled and that education would cease to be available for women. Najmussahar Bangash, editor of *Tole Pashtun,* pointed out shortly thereafter that there are 40,000 war widows in Kabul alone and their children will have a hard time with their subsistence. Further, she wrote, "if girls are not allowed to study, this will affect a whole generation." For the U.S.-Saudi-Unocal-Pakistan axis, geopolitics and economics make the Taliban a worthy regime for Afghanistan. Drugs, weapons and social brutalities will continue, but Washington extended a warm hand towards Mullah Mohammed Omar and the Taliban. U.S. foreign policy is driven by the dual modalities of containment (of rebellion inspired by egalitarianism) and concession (of goods which will bring profit to corporate entities). Constrained by these parameters, the U.S. government was able to state, in 1996, "there's on the face of it nothing objectionable at this stage."

Certainly, on 10 October 1996, the State Department revised its analysis of the Taliban on the basis of sustained pressure from Human Rights and women's groups in the advanced industrial states as well as pressure from the conferences held by Iran (at which numerous regional nations, such as India participated). In conflict with its earlier statement, the U.S. declared "we do not see the Taliban as the savior of Afghanistan. We never really welcomed them." The main reason offered for this was the Taliban's "uniquely discriminatory manner" with women. The U.S. state department would have done well to mention the heroic attempt made by the communist regime to tackle the "woman question." In late 1978, the regime of Nur Mohammad Taraki, President of the Revolutionary Council of Afghanistan, promulgated Decree no. 7 which aimed at a transformation of the marriage institution by attacking its monetary basis and which promoted equality between men and women. Women took leadership positions in the regime and fought social conservatives and theological fascists on various issues. Anahita Ratebzad was a major Marxist leader who sat on the Revolutionary Council; other notable leaders included Sultana Umayd, Suraya, Ruhafza Kamyar, Firouza, Dilara Mark, Professor R. S. Siddiqui, Fawjiyah Shahsawari, Dr. Aziza, Shirin Afzal and Alamat Tolqun. Ratebzad wrote the famous *Kabul Times* editorial (28 May 1978) which declared that "Privileges which women, by right, must have are equal education, job security, health services, and free time to rear a healthy generation for building the future of the country. . . . Educating and enlightening women is now the subject of close government attention." The hope of 1978 is now lost and the pessimism must not be laid at the feet of the Taliban alone, but also of those who funded and supported the Taliban-like theocratic fascists, states such as the U.S., Saudi Arabia and Pakistan.

The real reason for the U.S. frustration with the Taliban was its recalcitrance toward global capitalism (as an example, the Unocal scheme fell apart). The Taliban, created by many social forces, but funded by the Saudis (such as bin Laden) and the CIA, was now in the saddle in the center of Asia, and it soon became a haven for disgruntled and alienated young men who wanted to take out their wrath on the U.S. rather than fight against the contradictions of global capital. Bin Laden, the CIA asset, became the fulcrum of many of their inchoate fears and angers.

II. Oil, Guns and Saddam.

During the Gulf War of 1991, a decade ago, the U.S.-Europe discovered the Kurds for a few years. The Kurds and the Kuwaitis provided the war aims for the Alliance, since we kept hearing how Saddam Hussein's armies had exploited both. Oil is not the reason, we were repeatedly told; we are only concerned for the ordinary people of the region oppressed by these madmen, such as Saddam Hussein, Hafez al-Assad and the Ayatollahs. We heard little about the recently closed Iran-Iraq war, about the various contradictions in the region, indeed about the role of the U.S.-Europe for several decades in the fabrication of the regimes that ruled here. As the cruise missiles fell on Iraq, we did not then hear that the first major aerial bombardment in modern times took place in December 1923 when the Royal Air Force pummeled the rebellious Kurds (they felt the wrath of the guns again in March 1924, not being disciplined firmly enough by Headmaster Britain).

In 1932 the British put in place the puppet royal dynasty, the al-Saud family to rule the Arabian Peninsula as Saudi Arabia. This regime was to protect the "interests" of global capitalism, particularly after oil was discovered there in the early 1930s. The British put King Faisal over the newly created Iraq, a Sunni leader over a predominantly Shi'ite land. Workers movements in the region came under attack from these regimes, many of which violently crushed democratic dissent in the name of the dollar. Henry Kissinger was later to create political theory of a policy that had been long in the works: that the U.S. should lock arms with any political leader who will resist the will of socialism, who will ensure that international capitalism's dictates be maintained and who can therefore be a "factor of stability." The rogue gallery of this policy includes a host of CIA assets, such as the Noreiga, Marcos, Pinochet, Suharto, the Shah of Iran, the various Gulf Sheikhs, and latterly such fundamentalist friends as the BJP in India. Even when some of these leaders flirted with the Soviets (Saddam and al-Assad), their usefulness to U.S. policy prevented a break in their links to the CIA, mainly to contain domestic left-wing dissent. The Ayatollah may have been a natural asset, but his regime was stamped by a radical and patriarchially egalitarian Shi'ism that terrified the Oil Kingdoms, whose tenuous rule was now bolstered even further by the armies of the imperial powers and their proxy state at this time, Iraq. When the Iran-Iraq war broke out, people spoke of it as a sectarian war between Shias and Sunnis, but few pointed out that Iraq has a large Shia population and that Iraq fought primarily with the backing of the U.S. and its alliance to "contain" the Iranian revolution and the rule of the Mullahs. Saddam, then, was friend not foe.

During these years, no one mentioned the Kurds. For decades the communist movement grew amongst the Kurds, both in Turkey and in northern Iraq. But by the early 1970s, the CIA entered the battlefield to cut down the left and bolster the right. Between 1972 and 1975 the CIA paid $16 million to the eccentric and untrustworthy Mullah Mustafa Barzani as a "moral guarantee" of U.S. support for this activities. In 1959, Barzani had expelled the communists from his mainly Iraqi party and he had sent Iranian Kurds to their death in the camps of the Shah. Barzani was an asset that the U.S. cultivated, and is now a close ally of Saddam Hussein, another U.S. asset. In 1975, Marxist-Leninists within the Kurdish resistance formed the Patriotic Union of Kurdistan (PUK), which pushed many Kurds to the Left, including those in the Iraqi Kurdish Front formed in 1988. Saddam Hussein was given the green light by Washington to take out the PUK, and he conducted chemical bombing on them in 1983 (at Arbil) and most spectacularly in 1988 (at Halabja, where five thousand died, and many thousand continue to suffer). The outrage of Halabja created a momentary stir in the Left media, but nothing was done then because Saddam was a U.S. ally and asset—it returned to do ideological work during the Gulf War. As many died at Halabja as on 9/11, but their death does not factor in when NPR announces that 9/11 was the "worst terrorist attack in history." When terror is conducted in our name, then it is not terror but "retaliation."

III. Revenge or Justice?

President Bush promises to get those who did the bombings in New York and Washington, but he also promises that those who harbor them will feel the wrath of the U.S.. This is the most dangerous statement so far. Not only does it violate all manner of international laws, it ignores the fact that the U.S. has harbored these criminals for years, mainly at the expense of the global Left. Saddam and bin Laden are products of the U.S., even as they, like Frankenstein's beast, turn against their master now. The lesson is not to continue the madness, to go after the symptom with $40 billion of firepower. The lesson, for all democratic minded people, is to undermine the basis of our global insecurity.

First those people who did the horrendous deed on 9/11 must be found, arrested and brought to trial. The path of justice should not be short-circuited by the emotions of the moment.

Second, our fight in the U.S. continues, as we continue to point out that U.S. foreign policy engenders these acts of barbarism by its own desire to set-up strong-arm "factors of stability" in those zones of raw materials and markets that must be subservient to U.S. corporate interests. Vast areas of anger, zones of resentment will continue to emerge—this is not the way forward. Another indiscriminate bombardment will bring forth more body bags for the innocent.

History shows us that the U.S. was not innocent on 9/11, even as thousands of innocent people died. We should not confuse these two things: the terrorists made no distinction between those who conduct political and economic terror over their lives, between a regime that they dislike, corporate interests that they revile and innocent people who live in the same spaces. The terror of the frustrated works alongside the terror of the behemoth to undermine the powerful and democratic urges of the people. Both of those terrors must be condemned.

Slavoj Zizek

Slavoj Zizek was born in Ljubljana, Slovenia in 1949. He approaches his work as a writer, political activist and educator from the theoretical background of psychologist Jacques Lacan. His political views have been strongly influenced by the works of Karl Marx, Georg W.F. Hegel, and Friedrich W.J. Schelling, and he integrates politics into both his academic work and his everyday life. (In 1990, he ran for president of Slovenia.) He has published over fifty books and his work has been translated into twelve languages. This piece was originally published on the web site www.lacan.com in the week after 9.11. It underwent three major revisions before appearing as a book early in 2002. With the exception of the final paragraphs—taken from the third version—the text printed here is Zizek's original.

Welcome to the Desert of the Real

The ultimate American paranoiac fantasy is that of an individual living in a small idyllic Californian city, a consumerist paradise, who suddenly starts to suspect that the world he lives in is a fake, a spectacle staged to convince him that he lives in a real world, while all people around him are effectively actors and extras in a gigantic show. The most recent example of this is Peter Weir's *The Truman Show* (1998), with Jim Carrey playing the small town clerk who gradually discovers the truth that he is the hero of a 24-hours permanent TV show: his hometown is constructed on a gigantic studio set, with cameras following him permanently. Among its predecessors, it is worth mentioning Philip Dick's *Time Out of Joint* (1959), in which a hero living a modest daily life in a small idyllic Californian city of the late 50s, gradually discovers that the whole town is a fake staged to keep him satisfied. . . . The underlying experience of *Time Out of Joint* and of *The Truman Show* is that the late capitalist consumerist Californian paradise is, in its very hyper-reality, in a way IRREAL, substanceless, deprived of the material inertia.

So it is not only that Hollywood stages a semblance of real life deprived of the weight and inertia of materiality—in the late capitalist consumerist society, "real social life" itself somehow acquires the features of a staged fake, with our neighbors behaving in "real" life as stage actors and extras. . . . / Again, the ultimate truth of the capitalist utilitarian de-spiritualized universe is the de-materialization of the "real life" itself, its reversal into a spectral show. Among them, Christopher Isherwood gave expression to this unreality of the American daily life, exemplified

---

Reprinted from *Lacanian Ink*, November 2001, by permission of the publisher.

in the motel room: "American motels are unreal!/ . . . they are deliberately designed to be unreal. / . . . / The Europeans hate us because we've retired to live inside our advertisements, like hermits going into caves to contemplate." Peter Sloterdijk's notion of the "sphere" is here literally realized, as the gigantic metal sphere that envelopes and isolates the entire city. Years ago, a series of science-fiction films like *Zardoz* or *Logan's Run* forecasted today's postmodern predicament by extending this fantasy to the community itself. The isolated group living an aseptic life in a secluded area longs for the experience of the real world of material decay.

The Wachowski brothers' hit *Matrix* (1999) brought this logic to its climax: the material reality we all experience and see around us is a virtual one, generated and coordinated by a gigantic mega-computer to which we are all attached; when the hero (played by Keanu Reeves) awakens into the "real reality," he sees a desolate landscape littered with burned ruins—what remained of Chicago after a global war. The resistance leader Morpheus utters the ironic greeting: "Welcome to the desert of the real." Was it not something of the similar order that took place in New York on September 11? Its citizens were introduced to the "desert of the real"—to us, corrupted by Hollywood, the landscape and the shots we saw of the collapsing towers could not but remind us of the most breathtaking scenes in the catastrophe big productions.

When we hear how the bombings were a totally unexpected shock, how the unimaginable Impossible happened, one should recall the other defining catastrophe from the beginning of the XXth century, that of Titanic: it was also a shock, but the space for it was already prepared in ideological fantasizing, since Titanic was the symbol of the might of the XIXth century industrial civilization. Does the same not hold also for these bombings? Not only were the media bombarding us all the time with the talk about the terrorist threat; this threat was also obviously libidinally invested—just recall the series of movies from *Escape From New York* to *Independence Day*. The unthinkable which happened was thus the object of fantasy: in a way, America got what it fantasized about, and this was the greatest surprise.

It is precisely now, when we are dealing with the raw Real of a catastrophe, that we should bear in mind the ideological and fantasmatic coordinates which determine its perception. If there is any symbolism in the collapse of the WTC towers, it is not so much the old-fashioned notion of the "center of financial capitalism," but, rather, the notion that the two WTC towers stood for the center of the VIRTUAL capitalism, of financial speculations disconnected from the sphere of material production. The shattering impact of the bombings can only be accounted for only against the background of the borderline which today separates the digitalized First World from the Third World "desert of the Real." It is the awareness that we live in an insulated artificial universe which generates the notion that some ominous agent is threatening us all the time with total destruction.

Is, consequently, Osama bin Laden, the suspected mastermind behind the bombings, not the real-life counterpart of Ernst Stavro Blofeld, the master-criminal in most of the James Bond films, involved in the acts of global destruction? What one should recall here is that the only place in Hollywood films where we see the production process in all its intensity is when James Bond penetrates the master-criminal's secret domain and locates there the site of intense labor (distilling and packaging the drugs, constructing a rocket that will destroy New York . . .). When the master-criminal, after capturing Bond, usually takes him on a tour of his illegal factory, is this not the closest Hollywood comes to the socialist-realist proud presentation of the production in a factory? And the function of Bond's intervention, of course, is to explode in fireworks this site of production, allowing us to return to the daily semblance of our existence in a world with the "disappearing working class." Is it not that, in the exploding WTC towers, this violence directed at the threatening Outside turned back at us? The safe Sphere in which Americans live is experienced as under threat from the Outside of terrorist attackers who are ruthlessly self-sacrificing AND cowards, cunningly intelligent AND primitive barbarians. Whenever we encounter such a purely evil Outside, we should gather the courage to endorse the Hegelian lesson: in this pure Outside, we should recognize the distilled version of our own essence. For the last five centuries, the (relative) prosperity and peace of the "civilized" West was bought by the export of ruthless violence and destruction into the "barbarian" Outside: the long story from the conquest of America to the slaughter in Congo. Cruel and indifferent as it may sound, we should also, now more than ever, bear in mind that the actual effect of these bombings is much more symbolic than real. The U.S. just got the taste of what goes on around the world on a daily basis, from Sarajevo to Grozny, from Rwanda and Congo to Sierra Leone. If one adds to the situation in New York snipers and gang rapes, one gets an idea about what Sarajevo was a decade ago.

It is when we watched on TV screen the two WTC towers collapsing, that it became possible to experience the falsity of the "reality TV shows": even if this shows are "for real," people still act in them—they simply play themselves. The standard disclaimer in a novel ("characters in this text are a fiction, every resemblance with the real life characters is purely contingent") holds also for the participants of the reality soaps: what we see there are fictional characters, even if they play themselves for the real. Of course, the "return to the Real" can be given different twists: Rightist commentators like George Will also immediately proclaimed the end of the American "holiday from history"—the impact of reality shattering the isolated tower of the liberal tolerant attitude and the Cultural Studies focus on textuality. Now, we are forced to strike back, to deal with real enemies in the real world. . . . However, WHOM to strike? Whatever the response, it will never hit the RIGHT target, bringing us full satisfaction. The ridicule of America attacking Afghanistan cannot but strike the eye: if the greatest power in the world will destroy one of the poorest countries in which peasants barely survive on barren hills, will this not be the ultimate case of the impotent acting out?

There is a partial truth in the notion of the "clash of civilizations" attested here—witness the surprise of the average American: "How is it possible that these people have such a disregard for their own lives?" Is not the obverse of this surprise the rather sad fact that we, in the First World countries, find it more and more difficult even to imagine a public or universal Cause for which one would be ready to sacrifice one's life? When, after the bombings, even the Taliban foreign minister said that he can "feel the pain" of the American children, did he not thereby confirm the hegemonic ideological role of this Bill Clinton's trademark phrase? Furthermore, the notion of America as a safehaven, of course, also is a fantasy: when a New Yorker commented on how, after the bombings, one can no longer walk safely on the city's streets, the irony of it was that, well before the bombings, the streets of New York were well-known for the dangers of being attacked or, at least, mugged—if anything, the bombings gave rise to a new sense of solidarity, with the scenes of young African-Americans helping an old Jewish gentlemen to cross the street, scenes unimaginable a couple of days ago.

Now, in the days immediately following the bombings, it is as if we dwell in the unique time between a traumatic event and its symbolic impact, like in those brief moments after we are deeply cut, and before the full extent of the pain strikes us—it is open how the events will be symbolized, what their symbolic efficiency will be, what acts they will be evoked to justify. Even here, in these moments of utmost tension, this link is not automatic but contingent. There are already the first bad omens; the day after the bombing, I got a message from a journal which was just about to publish a longer text of mine on Lenin, telling me that they decided to postpone its publication—they considered in opportune to publish a text on Lenin immediately after the bombing. Does this not point towards the ominous ideological rearticulations which will follow?

We don't yet know what consequences in economy, ideology, politics, war, this event will have, but one thing is sure: the U.S., which, till now, perceived itself as an island exempted from this kind of violence, witnessing this kind of things only from the safe distance of the TV screen, is now directly involved. So the alternative is: will Americans decide to fortify further their "sphere," or to risk stepping out of it? Either America will persist in, strengthen even, the deeply immoral attitude of "Why should this happen to us? Things like this don't happen HERE!," leading to more aggressivity towards the threatening Outside, in short: to a paranoiac acting out. Or America will finally risk stepping through the fantasmatic screen separating it from the Outside World, accepting its arrival into the Real world, making the long-overdue move from "A thing like this should not happen HERE!" to "A thing like this should not happen ANYWHERE!". Therein resides the true lesson of the bombings: the only way to ensure that it will not happen HERE again is to prevent it going on ANYWHERE ELSE. In short, America should learn to humbly accept its own vulnerability as part of this world, enacting the punishment of those responsible as a sad duty, not as an exhilarating retaliation.

The WTC bombings again confront us with the necessity to resist the temptation of a double blackmail. If one simply, only and unconditionally condemns it, one cannot but appear to endorse the blatantly ideological position of the American innocence under attack by the Third World Evil; if one draws attention to the deeper socio-political causes of the Arab extremism, one cannot but appear to blame the victim which ultimately got what it deserved. . . . The only consequent solution is here to reject this very opposition and to adopt both positions simultaneously, which can only be done if one resorts to the dialectical category of totality: there is no choice between these two positions, each one is one-sided and false. Far from offering a case apropos of which one can adopt a clear ethical stance, we encounter here the limit of moral reasoning: from the moral standpoint, the victims are innocent, the act was an abominable crime; however, this very innocence is not innocent—to adopt such an "innocent" position in today's global capitalist universe is in itself a false abstraction. The same goes for the more ideological clash of interpretations: one can claim that the attack on the WTC was an attack on what is worth fighting for in democratic freedoms—the decadent Western way of life condemned by Muslim and other fundamentalists is the universe of women's rights and multiculturalist tolerance; however, one can also claim that it was an attack on the very center and symbol of global financial capitalism. This, of course, in no way entails the compromise notion of shared guilt (terrorists are to blame, but, partially, also Americans are also to blame . . .)—the point is, rather, that the two sides are not really opposed, that they belong to the same field. The fact that global capitalism is a totality means that it is the dialectical unity of itself and of its other, of the forces which resist it on "fundamentalist" ideological grounds.

Consequently, of the two main stories which emerged after September 11, both are worse, as Stalin would have put it. The American patriotic narrative—the innocence under siege, the surge of patriotic pride—is, of course, vain; however, is the Leftist narrative (with its Schadenfreude: the U.S. got what they deserved, what they were for decades doing to others) really any better? The predominant reaction of European, but also American, Leftists was nothing less than scandalous: all imaginable stupidities were said and written, up to the "feminist" point that the WTC towers were two phallic symbols, waiting to be destroyed ("castrated"). Was there not something petty and miserable in the mathematics reminding one of the holocaust revisionism (what are the 6000 dead against millions in Ruanda, Kongo, etc.)? And what about the fact that CIA (co)created Taliban and bin Laden, financing and helping them to fight the Soviets in Afghanistan? Why was this fact quoted as an argument AGAINST attacking them? Would it not be much more logical to claim that it is precisely their duty to get us rid of the monster they created? The moment one thinks in the terms of "yes, the WTC collapse was a tragedy, but one should not fully solidarize with the victims, since this would mean supporting U.S. imperialism," the ethical catastrophe is already here: the only appropriate stance is the unconditional solidarity with ALL victims. The ethical stance proper is here replaced with the moralizing mathematics of guilt and horror which misses the key point: the terrifying death of each individual is absolute and incomparable. In short, let us make a simple mental experiment: if you detect in yourself any restraint to fully empathize with the victims of the WTC collapse, if you feel the urge to qualify your empathy with "yes, but what about the millions who suffer in Africa . . .", you are not demonstrating your Third World sympathies, but merely the mauvaise foi which bears witness to your implicit patronizing racist attitude towards the Third World victims. (More precisely, the problem with such comparative statements is that they are necessary and inadmissible: one HAS to make them, one HAS to make the point that much worse horrors are taken place around the world on a daily basis—but one has to do it without getting involved in the obscene mathematics of guilt.)

It must be said that, within the scope of these two extremes (the violent retaliatory act versus the new reflection about the global situation and America's role in it), the reaction of the Western powers till now was surprisingly considerate (no wonder it caused the violent anti-American outburst of Ariel Sharon!). Perhaps the greatest irony of the situation is that the main "collateral damage" of the Western reaction is the focus on the plight of the Afghani refugees, and, more generally, on the catastrophic food and health situation in Afghanistan, so that, sometimes, military action against Taliban is almost presented as a means to guarantee the safe delivery of the humanitarian aid—as Tony Blair said, perhaps, we will have to bomb Taliban in order to secure the food transportation and distribution. Although, of course, such large-scale publicized humanitarian actions are in themselves ideologically charged, involving the debilitating degradation of the Afghani people to helpless victims, and reducing the Taliban to a parasite terrorizing them, it is significant to acknowledge that the humanitarian crisis in Afghanistan presents a much larger catastrophe than the WTC bombings. [. . .]

Edward Said

Edward Said was born in 1935 in Jerusalem, Palestine. He left Palestine as a child when his family sought refuge in Egypt because of the turmoil that led to Israel's declaration of independence and the Israeli-Arab war of 1948. After the war, because Israel refused to allow the Palestinian refugees return, his family immigrated to the United States in 1950 and Said became a naturalized citizen in 1953. He was educated in Cairo and in the United States, earning a Ph.D. from Harvard in 1964. He has taught at several universities, including Harvard, Stanford, and Colombia, and has earned several awards for his writing, including the National Book Critics Circle Award for Orientalism *and the* New Yorker *Award for non-fiction for* Out of Place in 2000. *Said, a widely read and respected proponent of Palestinian national rights, is regarded as a moderate. This piece, originally published on the web site www.lacan.com a month after 9.11, questions the idea that the war in Afghanistan was to be a "clash of civilizations," suggesting that westerners should become more aware of the groups they are labeling and the implications of that labeling. Said attempts to contextualize the actions of many groups involved in the aftermath of 9.11, and it is this contextualization—learning more about the groups involved—that he believes could lead to a productive solution to the various instances of strife in the Middle East.*

Backlash and Backtrack

For the seven million Americans who are Muslims (only two million of them Arab) and have lived through the catastrophe and backlash of 11 September, it's been a harrowing, especially unpleasant time. In addition to the fact that there have been several Arab and Muslim innocent casualties of the atrocities, there is an almost palpable air of hatred directed at the group as a whole that has taken many forms. George W. Bush immediately seemed to align America and God with each other, declaring war on the "folks"—who are now, as he says, wanted dead or alive—who perpetrated the horrible deeds. And this means, as no one needs any further reminding, that Osama bin Laden, the elusive Muslim fanatic who represents Islam to the vast majority of Americans, has taken center stage. TV and radio have run file pictures and potted accounts of the shadowy (former playboy,

Reprinted *Lacan.com*, October 12, 2001, by permission of Lacanian Ink.

they say) extremist almost incessantly, as they have of the Palestinian women and children caught "celebrating" America's tragedy.

Pundits and hosts refer non-stop to "our" war with Islam, and words like "jihad" and "terror" have aggravated the understandable fear and anger that seem widespread all over the country. Two people (one a Sikh) have already been killed by enraged citizens who seem to have been encouraged by remarks like Defense Department official Paul Wolfowitz's to literally think in terms of "ending countries" and nuking our enemies. Hundreds of Muslim and Arab shopkeepers, students, hijab-ed women and ordinary citizens have had insults hurled at them, while posters and graffiti announcing their imminent death spring up all over the place. The director of the leading Arab-American organization told me this morning that he averages 10 messages an hour of insult, threat, bloodcurdling verbal attack. A Gallup poll released yesterday states that 49 per cent of the American people said yes (49 per cent no) to the idea that Arabs, including those who are American citizens, should carry special identification; 58 per cent demand (41 per cent don't) that Arabs, including those who are Americans, should undergo special, more intense security checks in general.

Then, the official bellicosity slowly diminishes as George W. discovers that his allies are not quite as unrestrained as he is, as (undoubtedly) some of his advisers, chief among them the altogether more sensible-seeming Colin Powell, suggest that invading Afghanistan is not quite as simple as sending in the Texas militias might have been, even as the enormously confused reality forced on him and his staff dissipates the simple Manichean imagery of good versus evil that he has been maintaining on behalf of his people. A noticeable de-escalation sets in, even though reports of police and FBI harassment of Arabs and Muslim continue to flood in. Bush visits a Washington mosque; he calls on community leaders and the Congress to damp down hate speech; he starts trying to make at least rhetorical distinctions between "our" Arab and Muslim friends (the usual ones—Jordan, Egypt, Saudi Arabia) and the still undisclosed terrorists. In his speech to the joint session of Congress, Bush did say that the U.S. is not at war with Islam, but said regrettably nothing about the rising wave of both incidents and rhetoric that has assailed Muslims, Arabs and people resembling Middle Easterners all across the country. Powell here and there expresses displeasure with Israel and Sharon for exploiting the crisis by oppressing Palestinians still more, but the general impression is that U.S. policy is still on the same course it has always been on—only now a huge war seems to be in the making.

But there is little positive knowledge of the Arabs and Islam in the public sphere to fall back on and balance the extremely negative images that float around: the stereotypes of lustful, vengeful, violent, irrational, fanatical people persist anyway. Palestine as a cause has not yet gripped the imagination here, especially not after the Durban conference. Even my own university, justly famous for its intellectual diversity and the heterogeneity of its students and staff, rarely offers a course on the Qur'an. Philip Hitti's *History of the Arabs*, by far the best modern, one-volume book in English on the subject, is out of print. Most of what is available is polemical and adversarial: the Arabs and Islam are occasions for controversy, not cultural and religious subjects like others. Film and TV are packed with horrendously unattractive, bloody-minded Arab terrorists; they were there, alas, before the terrorists of the World Trade Center and Pentagon hijacked the planes and turned them into instruments of a mass slaughter that reeks of criminal pathology much more than of any religion.

There seems to be a minor campaign in the print media to hammer home the thesis that "we are all Israelis now," and that what has occasionally occurred in the way of Palestinian suicide bombs is more or less exactly the same as the World Trade Center and Pentagon attacks. In the process, of course, Palestinian dispossession and oppression are simply erased from memory; also erased are the many Palestinian condemnations of suicide bombing, including my own. The overall result is that any attempt to place the horrors of what occurred on 11 September in a context that includes U.S. actions and rhetoric is either attacked or dismissed as somehow condoning the terrorist bombardment.

Intellectually, morally, politically such an attitude is disastrous since the equation between understanding and condoning is profoundly wrong, and very far from being true. What most Americans find difficult to believe is that in the Middle East and Arab world U.S. actions as a state—unconditional support for Israel, the sanctions against Iraq that have spared Saddam Hussein and condemned hundreds of thousands of innocent Iraqis to death, disease, malnutrition, the bombing of Sudan, the U.S. "green light" for Israel's 1982 invasion of Lebanon (during which almost 20,000 civilians lost their lives, in addition to the massacres of Sabra and Shatila), the use of Saudi Arabia and the Gulf generally as a private U.S. fiefdom, the support of repressive Arab and Islamic regimes—are deeply resented and, not incorrectly, are seen as being done in the name of the American people. There is an enormous gap between what the average American citizen is aware of and the often unjust and heartless policies that, whether or not he/she is conscious of them, are undertaken abroad. Every U.S. veto of a UN Security resolution condemning Israel for settlements, the bombing of civilians, and so forth, may be brushed aside by, say, the residents of Iowa or Nebraska as unimportant events and probably correct, whereas to an Egyptian, Palestinian or Lebanese citizen these things are wounding in the extreme, and remembered very precisely.

In other words, there is a dialectic between specific U.S. actions on the one hand and consequent attitudes towards America on the other hand that has literally very little to do with jealousy or hatred of America's prosperity, freedom, and all-round success in the world. On the contrary, every Arab or Muslim that I have ever spoken to expressed mystification as to why so extraordinarily rich and admirable a place as America (and so likeable a group of individuals as Americans) has behaved internationally with such callous obliviousness of lesser peoples. Surely also, many Arabs and Muslims are aware of the hold on U.S. policy of the pro-Israeli lobby and the dreadful racism and fulminations of pro-Israeli publications like *The New Republic* or *Commentary*, to say nothing of bloodthirsty columnists like Charles Krauthammer, William Safire, George Will, Norman Podhoretz, and A. M. Rosenthal, whose columns regularly express hatred and hostility towards Arabs and Muslims. These are usually to be found in the mainstream media (e.g., the editorial pages of *The Washington Post*) where everyone can read them as such, rather than being buried in the back pages of marginal publications.

So we are living through a period of turbulent, volatile emotion and deep apprehension, with the promise of more violence and terrorism dominating consciousness, especially in New York and Washington, where the terrible atrocities of 11 September are still very much alive in the public awareness. I certainly feel it, as does everyone around me.

But what is nevertheless encouraging, despite the appalling general media performance, is the slow emergence of dissent, petitions for peaceful resolution and action, a gradually spreading, if still very spotty, relatively small demand for alternatives to more bombing and destruction. This kind of thoughtfulness has been very remarkable, in my opinion. First of all, there have been very widely expressed concerns about what may be the erosion of civil liberties and individual privacy as the government demands, and seems to be getting, the powers to wire-tap telephones, to arrest and detain Middle Eastern people on suspicion of terrorism, and generally to induce a state of alarm, suspicion, and mobilization that could amount to paranoia resembling McCarthyism. Depending on how one reads it, the American habit of flying the flag everywhere can seem patriotic of course, but patriotism can also lead to intolerance, hate crimes, and all sorts of unpleasant collective passion. Numerous commentators have warned about this and, as I said earlier, even the president in his speech said that "we" are not at war with Islam or Muslim people. But the danger is there, and has been duly noted by other commentators, I am happy to say.

Second, there have been many calls and meetings to address the whole matter of military action, which according to a recent poll, 92 per cent of the American people seem to want. Because, however, the administration hasn't exactly specified what the aims of this war are ("eradicating terrorism" is more metaphysical than it is actual), nor the means, nor the plan, there is considerable uncertainty as to where we may be going militarily. But generally speaking the rhetoric has become less apocalyptic and religious—the idea of a crusade has disappeared almost completely—and more focused on what might be necessary beyond general words like "sacrifice" and "a long war, unlike any others." In universities, colleges, churches and meeting-houses there are a great many debates on what the country should be doing in response; I have even heard that families of the innocent victims have said in public that they do not believe military revenge is an appropriate response. The point is that there is considerable reflection at large as to what the U.S. should be doing, but I am sorry to report that the time for a critical examination of U.S. policies in the Middle East and Islamic worlds has not yet arrived. I hope that it will.

If only more Americans and others can grasp that the main long-range hope for the world is this community of conscience and understanding, that whether in the protection of constitutional rights, or in reaching out to the innocent victims of American power (as in Iraq), or in relying on understanding and rational analysis "we" can do a great deal better than we have so far done. Of course this won't lead directly to changed policies on Palestine, or a less skewed defense budget, or more enlightened environmental and energy attitudes: but where else but in this sort of decent backtracking is there room for hope? Perhaps this constituency may grow in the United States, but speaking as a Palestinian, I must also hope that a similar constituency should be emerging in the Arab and Muslim world. We must start thinking about ourselves as responsible for the poverty, ignorance, illiteracy, and repression that have come to dominate our societies, evils that we have allowed to grow despite our complaints about Zionism and imperialism. How many of us, for example, have openly and honestly stood up for secular politics and have condemned the use of religion in the Islamic world as roundly and as earnestly as we have denounced the manipulation of Judaism and Christianity in Israel and the West? How many of us have denounced all suicidal missions as immoral and wrong, even though we have suffered the ravages of colonial settlers and inhuman collective punishment? We can no longer hide behind the injustices done to us, anymore than we can passively bewail the American support for our unpopular leaders. A new secular Arab politics must now make itself known, without for a moment condoning or supporting the militancy (it is madness) of people willing to kill indiscriminately. There can be no more ambiguity on that score.

I have been arguing for years that our main weapons as Arabs today are not military but moral, and that one reason why, unlike the struggle against apartheid in South Africa, the Palestinian struggle for self-determination against Israeli oppression has not caught the world's imagination is that we cannot seem to be clear about our goals and our methods, and we have not stated unambiguously enough that our purpose is coexistence and inclusion, not exclusivism and a return to some idyllic and mythical past. The time has come for us to be forthright and to start immediately to examine, re-examine and reflect on our own policies as so many Americans and Europeans are now doing. We should expect no less of ourselves than we should of others. Would that all people took the time to try to see where our leaders seem to be taking us, and for what reason. Skepticism and re-evaluation are necessities, not luxuries.

Judith Butler

Judith Butler was born in 1956. She attended Bennington College, then received her Ph.D. from Yale University in 1984. She now teaches Comparative Literature and Rhetoric at the University of California, Berkeley. She is known for her theoretical work in studies of gender, identity politics, sexuality and power. Her book Gender Trouble *critiques the binary between male and female, suggesting that these roles are highly socially constructed. She is the author of numerous other texts, including* The Psychic Life of Power: Theories in Subjection, and Subjects of Desire: Hegelian Reflections in Twentieth Century France. *In this piece, published in the online journal* Theory and Event *in December of 2001, Butler steps back and evaluates the rhetoric and reactions of the "left" and the "right" four months after the 9.11 attacks. Though the text is highly theoretical, and thus occasionally difficult to understand, it is a very useful work in that it provides on the of first distanced theoretical evaluations of America's reaction to 9.11. For the purposes of this chapter, then, it serves as a critique of the ways in which witness was used by those who interpreted and presented 9.11 to audiences.*

Explanation and Exoneration, or What We Can Hear

1. The left response to the war currently waged in Afghanistan has run into serious problems in part because the *explanations* that the left has provided to the question, "why do they hate us so much?" have been dismissed as so many *exonerations* of the acts of terror themselves. This does not need to be the case. I think we can see, however, how moralistic anti-intellectual trends coupled with a distrust of the left as so many self-flagellating first world elites has produced a situation in which our very capacity to think about the grounds and causes of the current global conflict is considered impermissible. The cry that "there is no excuse for September 11th" has become a means by which to stifle any serious public discussion of how U.S. foreign policy has helped to create a world in which such acts of terror are possible. We see this most dramatically in the suspension of any attempt to offer balanced reporting on the international conflict, the refusal to include important critiques of the U.S. military effort by Arundhati Roy (*The Guardian*,

---

Reprinted from *Theory and Event*, 5:4, (2002), by permission of The Johns Hopkins University Press.

9/29/01) and others within the mainstream U.S. press, the unprecedented suspension of civil liberties for illegal immigrants and suspected terrorists, the use of the flag as an ambiguous sign of solidarity with those lost on September 11th and with the current war, as if the sympathy with the one translates, in a single symbolic stroke, into support for the latter. The raw public mockery of the peace movement, the characterization of anti-war demonstrations as anachronistic or nostalgic, work to produce a consensus of public opinion that profoundly marginalizes anti-war sentiment and analysis, putting into question in a very strong way the very value of dissent as part of contemporary U.S. democratic culture.

2. The articulation of this hegemony takes place in part through producing a consensus on what certain terms will mean, how they can be used, and what lines of solidarity are implicitly drawn through this use. We reserve "acts of terror" for events such as the September 11th attacks on the U.S., distinguishing these acts of violence from those that might be justified through foreign policy decisions or public declarations of war. On the other hand, these terrorist acts are construed as "declarations of war" by the Bush administration, which then positions the military response as a justified act of self-defense. In the meantime, there is ambiguity introduced by the very use of the term "terrorist" which is then exploited by various powers at war with independence movements of various kinds. The term "terrorist" is used, for instance, by the Israeli state to describe any and all Palestinian acts of violence, but none of its own. The term is also used by Putin to describe the Chechen struggle for independence, which then casts its own acts of violence against this province as justified acts of national self-defense. The U.S., by using the term, positions itself exclusively as the sudden and indisputable victim of violence, and there is no doubt that it has suffered violence, terrible violence.

3. The point I would like to underscore here is that a frame for understanding violence emerges in tandem with the experience, and that the frame works both to preclude certain kinds of questions, certain kinds of historical inquiries, and to function as a moral justification for retaliation. It seems crucial to attend to this frame, since it decides, in a forceful way, what we can hear, whether a view will be taken as explanation or as exoneration, whether we can hear the difference, and abide by it.

4. There is as well a narrative dimension to this explanatory framework. In the U.S., we start the story by invoking a first-person narrative point of view, and tell what happened on September 11th. And it is that date, and the unexpected and fully terrible experience of violence that propels the narrative. If someone tries to start the story earlier, there are only a few narrative options. We can narrate, for instance, what Mohammed Atta's family life was like, whether he was teased for looking like a girl, where he congregated in Hamburg, and what led, psychologically, to the moment in which he piloted the plane into the World Trade Center. Or what was bin Laden's break from his family, and why is he so mad? That kind of story is interesting to a degree, because it suggests that there is a personal pathology at work. It works as a plausible and engaging narrative in part because it resituates agency in terms of a subject, something we can understand, something which accords with our idea of personal responsibility, or with the theory of charismatic leadership that was popularized with Mussolini and Hitler in WWII. And this is easier to hear than that a network of individuals dispersed

across the globe conjured and implemented this action in various ways. If there is a network, there must be a leader, a subject who is finally responsible for what others do. Perhaps we can hear, in a limited way, about the way in which the Al-Qaida group makes use of Islamic doctrine, and we want to know, to shore up our liberal framework, that they do not represent the religion of Islam, and that the vast majority of Muslims do not condone them. Al-Qaida can be "the subject," but do we ask where this comes from? Isolating the individuals involved absolves us of the necessity of coming up with a broader explanation for events. Though we are perhaps perplexed by why there is not a greater public repudiation by Muslim leaders (though many organizations have done that), we cannot quite understand why it might be difficult for Muslim leaders to join publicly with the U.S. on this issue even as they condemn quite clearly the acts of violence.

5. Our own acts of violence do not receive graphic coverage in the press, and so they remain acts that are justified in the name of self-defense, but also justified by a noble cause, namely, the rooting out of terrorism. Recently, it is reported that the Northern Alliance may have slaughtered a village: will this be investigated and, if confirmed, prosecuted as a war crime? When a bleeding child or dead body on Afghani soil emerges in the press coverage, it is not framed as part of the horror of war, but only as a critique of the military's capacity to aim its bombs right. We castigate ourselves for not aiming better, but we do not take the sign of destroyed life and decimated peoples as something for which we are responsible, or indeed understand how that decimation works to confirm the U.S. as performing atrocities. Our own acts are not considered terrorist. And there is no history of acts that is relevant to the self-understanding we form in the light of these terrible events. There is no relevant prehistory to the events of September 11th, since to begin to tell the story a different way, to ask how things came to this, is already to complicate the question of agency which, no doubt, leads to the fear of moral equivocation. In order to condemn these acts as inexcusable, absolutely wrong, in order to sustain the affective structure in which we are, on the one hand, victimized and, on the other, engaged in a righteous cause of rooting out terror, we have to start the story with the experience of violence we suffered. We have to shore up the first person point of view, and preclude from the telling accounts that might involve a decentering of the narrative "I" within the international political domain. This decentering is experienced as part of the wound that we have suffered, though, so we cannot inhabit that position. This decentering is precisely what we seek to rectify through a recentering. A narrative form emerges to compensate for the enormous narcissistic wound opened up by the public display of our physical vulnerability. Our response, accordingly, is not to enter into international coalition where we understand ourselves to be working with institutionally established routes of consensus-building. We relegate the United Nations to a second order deliberative body, and insist instead on American unilateralism. And subsequently we ask, Who is with us? Who is against us? As a result, we respond to the exposure of vulnerability with an assertion of U.S. "leadership," showing once again the contempt we have for international coalitions that are not built and led by us. Such coalitions do not conflict with U.S. supremacy, but confirm it, stoke it, insist upon it, with long-term implications for the future shape and possibility of global cooperation.

6. Perhaps the question cannot be heard at all, but I would still like to ask: can we find another meaning, and another possibility, for the decentering of the first person narrative within the global framework? I do not mean that the story of being attacked should not be told. I do not mean that the story that begins with September 11th should not be told. These stories have to be told, and they are being told, despite the enormous trauma that undermines narrative capacity in these instances. But if we are to come to understand ourselves as global actors, and acting within an historically established field, and one that has other actions in play, we will need to emerge from the narrative perspective of U.S. unilateralism and, as it were, its defensive structures, to consider the ways in which our lives are profoundly implicated in the lives of others. My friends on the left joke about having lost their first world complacency. Yes, this is true. But do we now seek to *restore* it as a way of healing from this wound? Or do we allow the challenge to first world complacency to stand and begin to build a different politics on its basis?

7. My sense is that being open to the explanations, poorly circulated as they are in the U.S., that might help us take stock of how the world has come to take this form, will involve us in a different order of responsibility. The ability to narrate ourselves not from the first person alone, but from, say, the position of the third, or to receive an account delivered in the second, can actually work to expand our understanding of the forms that global power has taken. But instead of remaining open to a consequential decentering of first-worldism, we tend to dismiss any effort at explanation, as if to explain these events would accord them rationality, as if to explain these events would involve us in a sympathetic identification with the oppressor, as if to understand these events would involve building a justificatory framework for them. Our fear of understanding a point of view belies a deeper fear that we will be taken up by it, find it is contagious, become infected in a morally perilous way by the thinking of the presumed enemy. But why do we assume this? We claim to have gone to war in order to "root out" the sources of terror, according to Bush, but do we think that finding the individuals responsible for the attacks on the U.S. will constitute having gotten to the root? Do we not imagine that the invasion of a sovereign country with a substantial Muslim population, supporting the military regime in Pakistan that actively and violently suppresses free speech, obliterating lives and villages and homes and hospitals, will not foster more adamant and widely disseminated anti-American sentiment and political organizing? Are we not, strategically speaking, interested in ameliorating this violence? Are we not, ethically speaking, obligated to stop its further dissemination, to consider our role in instigating it, and to foment and cultivate another sense of a culturally and religiously diverse global political culture?

8. Part of the problem the U.S. is up against is that liberals have quietly lined up behind the war effort, and supplied in part the rationale that keeps our own violence from being labeled as terrorist. It is not just the conservative republicans who do not want to hear about "causes." The "Just war" liberal-left has also made plain that it does not want to hear from "excuseniks." This coinage, rehabilitating the cold war rhetoric about Soviet Russia, suggests that those who seek to understand how the global map arrived at this juncture through asking how, in part, the U.S. has contributed to the making of this map, are themselves, through the style of their inquiry, and the shape of their questions, complicitous with an assumed enemy. But

to ask how certain political and social actions come into being, such as the recent terrorist attacks on the U.S., and even to identify a set of causes, is not the same as locating the source of responsibility for these actions or, indeed, paralyzing our capacity to make ethical judgments on what is right or wrong.

9. No doubt there are forms of left analysis which say simply that the U.S. has reaped what it has sown. Or they say that the U.S. has brought this state of events on itself. These are, as closed explanations, simply other ways of asserting U.S. priority, and encoding U.S. omnipotence. These are also explanations that assume that these actions originate in a single subject, that the subject is not what it appears to be, that it is the U.S. who occupies the site of that subject, and that no other subjects exist or, if they exist, their agency is subordinated to our own. In other words, political paranoia of this kind is just another articulation of U.S. supremacy. Paranoia is fed by the fantasy of omnipotence, and we see this evidenced in some of the more extreme explanations of this kind, i.e. the attacks on September 11th were masterminded by the CIA or Mossad, the Israeli secret police. It is clear, though, that bin Laden did apprentice to the CIA and that the U.S. supported the Taliban since the 1990s when it was deemed strategically useful. These links are not precisely causal explanations, but they are part of an explanatory framework. They do not translate into the notion that the U.S. did these acts, but one can see how the connection becomes the occasion for the causal reduction, and a certain paranoia amplifies itself by seizing upon part of a broader explanatory picture.

10. What is generally heard when these opinions are expressed is that the U.S. is the culpable agent, that it is, effectively, the author of these events, and that the U.S. is solely responsible for this global outcome. This kind of reasoning is unacceptable to the press, and to the public in general, because it seems to blame the victim in this instance. But is this the only way to hear this point of view? And is this the only form this point of view takes? It seems that being most precise about this point, and publicizing it where one can, will be crucial for any effort by the left to offer an anti-war viewpoint within contemporary public discourse.

11. If we believe that to think radically about the formation of the current situation is to exculpate those who committed acts of violence, we will freeze our thinking in the name of a questionable morality. But if we paralyze our thinking in this way, we will fail morality in a different way. We will fail to take collective responsibility for a thorough understanding of the history which brings us to this juncture. We will, as a result, deprive ourselves of the very critical and historical resources we need to imagine and practice another future, one which will move beyond the current cycle of revenge.

12. When President Arroyo of the Philippines on October 29th, 2001 remarked that "the best breeding ground [for terrorism] is poverty" or Arundhati Roy claims that bin Laden has been "sculpted from the spare rib of a world laid waste by America's foreign policy," something less than a strictly causal explanation is being offered. A "breeding ground" does not necessarily breed, but it can. And the "spare rib" that is said to emerge from a world laid waste by U.S. foreign policy has, by definition, emerged in a strange and alchemical fashion. It is from waste that this rib is formed, as if the bone belongs to the dead, or is itself the animation of a skeletal remain. This is not God creating Eve from the rib of Adam,

life generating life, but death generating death, and through a means that is figural, not precisely causal. Indeed, both of them make use of figures—grounds and bones—to bespeak a kind of generation that precedes and exceeds a strictly causal frame. Both of them are pointing to conditions, not causes. A condition of terrorism can be necessary or sufficient. If it is necessary, it is a state of affairs without which terrorism cannot take hold, one which terrorism absolutely requires. If it is sufficient, its presence is enough for terrorism to take place. Conditions do not "act" in the way that individual agents do, but no agent acts without them. They are presupposed in what we do, but it would be a mistake to personify them as if they acted in the place of us. Thus, we can say, and ought to, that U.S. imperialism is a necessary condition for the attacks on the U.S., that these attacks would be impossible without the horizon of imperialism within which they occur. But to understand how U.S. imperialism figures here, we have to understand not only how it is experienced by those who understand themselves as its victims, but how it enters into their own formation as acting and deliberating subjects. This is the beginning of another kind of account. And this seems to be, for instance, what Mary Kaldor in *The Nation* (11/5/01, p. 16) points to when she claims that "in many of the areas where war takes place and where extreme networks pick up new recruits, becoming a criminal or joining a paramilitary group is literally the only opportunity for unemployed young men lacking formal education." What effect did the killing of an estimated 200,000 Iraqi citizens, including tens of thousands of children, and the subsequent starvation of Muslim populations, predicted by Concern, a hunger relief organization, to reach the number six million by year's end, have on Muslim views of the U.S.? Is the value of Muslim life as valuable as legibly first-world lives? Are the Palestinians accorded the status of "human" in U.S. policy and press coverage? Will those hundreds of thousands of Muslim lives lost in the last decades of strife ever receive the equivalent to the paragraph-long obituaries in the *New York Times* that seek to humanize—often through nationalist and familial framing devices—those who have been violently killed? Is our global capacity to mourn not foreclosed precisely through the failure to conceive of Muslim and Arab lives as lives?

13. Giuliani's response to Saudi Prince Alwaleed bin Talal's remarks on October 11th in New York raises this question of the acceptability of critical discourse emphatically. The Prince came with a ten million dollar check in hand for the World Trade Center relief effort and expressed at the same time horror and moral condemnation of the attacks on the World Trade Center and asked that "the U.S. take a more balanced stand toward the Palestinian cause." *Forbes.com* (on 10/11/01) reported Giuliani's refusal of the check this way:

> While in New York, Alwaleed said, "Our Palestinian brethren continue to be slaughtered at the hands of Israelis while the world turns the other cheek." At a news conference, Giuliani said, "Not only are those statements wrong, they are part of the problem. There is no moral equivalent to this attack. There is no justification for it," the mayor said. "The people who did it lost any right to ask for justification for it when they slaughtered four or five thousand innocent people, and to suggest that there is any

> justification for it only invites this happening in the future." The Saudi prince, the sixth richest man in the world, did say he condemned terrorism, and he expressed his condolences for the more than 5,000 people killed when hijacked jets slammed into the World Trade Center and the Pentagon.

14. In a television report that same day, Giuliani announced that Alwaleed's views were "absolutely wrong." I would suggest that it was not possible to hear both of these views at the same time because the framework for hearing presumes that the one view nullifies the other, so either the claim of grief or the offer of help are considered disingenuous. Or what is heard is that the failure of the U.S. to offer a balanced approach to the Palestinian cause provides a justification for the attacks. Alwaleed is clear, and was subsequently clear in a *New York Times* editorial, that he did not think that the U.S. policy failure, which he deems true, to honor the Palestinian cause *justifies* the attacks. But he did think that long-term U.S.-Arab relations would be improved were the U.S. to develop a more balanced approach. It makes sense to assume that bettering those relations might well lead to less conducive grounds for Islamic extremism. The Bush administration itself, in its own way, attests to this belief by pursuing the possibility of a Palestinian state. But here the two views could not be heard together, and it has to do with the word "slaughter," the utterability of the word "slaughter" in the context of saying that Israelis have *slaughtered* and do *slaughter* Palestinians, and in large numbers.

15. Like "terrorist," "slaughter" is a word that, within the hegemonic grammar, should be reserved for unjustified acts of violence against first-world nations, if I understand the grammar correctly. Giuliani hears this as a discourse of justification, since he believes that slaughter justifies military self-defense. He calls the statements "absolutely untrue," I presume, not because he disputes that there have been deaths on the Palestinian side, and that the Israelis are responsible for them, but because "slaughter" as the name for those deaths implies an equivalence with the deaths of the World Trade Center victims. It seems, though, that we are not supposed to say that both groups of people have been "slaughtered" since that implies a "moral equivalence," meaning, I suppose, that the slaughtering of one group is as bad as the slaughtering of the next, and that both, according to his framework, would be entitled to self-defense as a result.

16. Although the Prince subsequently undermined his credibility when he betrayed anti-Semitic beliefs, claiming that "Jewish pressure" was behind Giuliani's refusal of the check, he nevertheless initiated an utterance and a formulation that has value on its own. Why is it that these two sets of deaths are not viewed as equally horrible? And to what extent has the very refusal to apprehend Palestinian deaths as "slaughter" produced an immeasurable rage on the part of Arabs who seek some legitimate recognition and resolution for this continuing state of violence? One does not need to enter into the dreary business of quantifying and comparing oppressions to understand what the Prince meant to say, and subsequently said, namely, that the U.S. needs to think about how its own political investments and practices help to create a world of enormous rage and violence. This is not to say that the acts of violence perpetrated on Sept. 11th were the "fault" of the U.S., and it does not exonerate those who committed them. One

way to read what the Prince had to say was that the acts of terror were unequivocally wrong, and that the U.S. might also be able to intervene more productively in global politics to produce conditions in which this response to U.S. imperialism becomes less likely. This is not the same as holding the U.S. exclusively responsible for the violence done within its borders, but it does ask the U.S. to assume a different kind of responsibility for producing more egalitarian global conditions for equality, sovereignty, and the egalitarian redistribution of resources.

17. Similarly, the *New York Times* (11/02/01) describes Arundhati Roy's critique of U.S. imperialism as "anti-U.S.," implying that any position that seeks to reevaluate critically U.S. foreign policy in light of Sept. 11th and the ensuing war is anti-U.S. or, indeed, complicitous with the presumed enemy. This is tantamount to the suppression of dissent, and the nationalist refusal to consider the merits of criticisms developed from other parts of the globe. The treatment is unfair. Her condemnation of bin Laden is clear, but she is willing to ask how he was formed. To condemn the violence and to ask how it came about are surely two separate questions, but they need to be posed in tandem, held in juxtaposition, reconciled within a broader analysis. Under contemporary strictures on public discourse, however, this kind of dual thinking cannot be heard: it is dismissed as contradictory or disingenuous, and Roy herself is treated as a diva or a cult figure, rather than listened to as a political critic with a wide moral compass.

18. So is there a way, in Roy's terms, to understand bin Laden as "born" from the rib of U.S. imperialism (allowing that he is born from several possible historical sources), one of which is, crucially, U.S. imperialism, without claiming that U.S. imperialism is solely responsible for his actions, or those of his ostensible network? To answer this question, we need to distinguish, provisionally, between individual and collective responsibility. But then we need to situate individual responsibility in light of its collective conditions. Those who commit acts of violence are surely responsible for them; they are not dupes or mechanisms of an impersonal social force, but agents with responsibility. On the other hand, these individuals are formed, and we would be making a mistake if we reduced their actions to purely self-generated acts of will or symptoms of individual pathology or "evil." Both the discourse of individualism and of moralism (understood as the moment in which morality exhausts itself in public acts of denunciation) assume that the individual is the first link in a causal chain that forms the meaning of accountability. But to take the self-generated acts of the individual as our point of departure in moral reasoning is precisely to foreclose the possibility of questioning what kind of world gives rise to such individuals. And what is this process of "giving rise"? What social conditions help to form the very ways that choice and deliberation proceed? Where and how can such subject formations be contravened? How is it that radical violence becomes an option, comes to appear as the only viable option for some, under some global conditions? And against what conditions of violation do they respond? And with what resources?

19. To ask these questions is not to say that *the conditions* are at fault rather than the individual. But it is to rethink the relation between conditions and acts. Our acts are not self-generated, but conditioned. But we are acted upon and acting, and our "responsibility" lies in the juncture between the two. What can I do with the conditions that form me? What do they constrain me to do? What can I

do to transform them? Being acted upon is not fully continuous with acting, and in this way the forces that act upon us are not finally responsible for what we do. In a certain way, and paradoxically, our responsibility is heightened once we have been subjected to the violence of others. We are acted upon, violently, and it appears that our capacity to set our own course at such instances is fully undermined. But only once we have suffered that violence are we compelled, ethically, to ask how we will respond to violent injury. What role will we assume in the historical relay of violence, who will we become in the response, and will we be furthering or impeding violence by virtue of the response that we make? To respond to violence with violence may well seem "justified," but is it finally a responsible solution? Similarly, moralistic denunciation provides immediate gratification, and even has the effect of temporarily cleansing the speaker of all proximity to guilt through the act of self-righteous denunciation itself. But is this the same as responsibility, understood as taking stock of our world, and participating in its social transformation in such a way that non-violent, cooperative, egalitarian international relations remain the guiding ideal?

20. We ask these latter questions not to exonerate the individuals who commit violence, but to take a different sort of responsibility for the global conditions of justice. As a result, it makes sense to follow two courses of action at once: it is surely important to find those who planned and implemented the violence, and to hold them accountable according to international war crimes standards and in international courts of law, regardless of our skepticism about such institutions (skepticism can furnish grounds for reform). In pursuing a wayward military solution, the U.S. now perpetrates and displays its own violence, offering a breeding ground for new waves of young Muslims to join terrorist organizations. This is poor thinking, strategically and morally. Ignoring its image as the hated enemy for many in the region, the U.S. has effectively responded to the violence done against it by consolidating its reputation as a militaristic power with no respect for lives outside of the first world. That we now respond with more violence is taken as "further proof" that the U.S. has violent and anti-sovereign designs on the region. To remember the lessons of Aeschylus and refuse this cycle of revenge in the name of justice means not only to seek legal redress for wrongs done, but to take stock of how the world has become formed in this way precisely in order to form it anew, and in the direction of non-violence.

21. Our collective responsibility not merely as a nation, but as part of an international community based on a commitment to equality and non-violent cooperation, requires that we ask how these conditions came about, and to endeavor to recreate social and political conditions on more sustaining grounds. This means, in part, hearing beyond what we are able to hear. And it means as well being open to narration that decenters us from our supremacy, in both its right and left wing forms. Can we hear at once that there were precedents for these events, and to know that it is urgent that we know them, learn from them, alter them, and that the events are not justified by virtue of this history and that the events are not understandable without this history? Only then do we reach the disposition to get to the "root" of violence, and begin to offer another vision of the future than that which perpetuates violence in the name of denying it, offering instead names for things that restrain us from thinking and acting radically and well about global options.

Author Index

Title Index